Lecture Notes in Computer Science 10271

Commenced Publication in 1973
Founding and Former Series Editors:
Gerhard Goos, Juris Hartmanis, and Jan van Leeuwen

More information about this series at http://www.springer.com/series/7409

Masaaki Kurosu (Ed.)

Human–Computer Interaction

User Interface Design, Development and Multimodality

19th International Conference, HCI International 2017
Vancouver, BC, Canada, July 9–14, 2017
Proceedings, Part I

Editor
Masaaki Kurosu
The Open University of Japan
Chiba
Japan

ISSN 0302-9743 ISSN 1611-3349 (electronic)
Lecture Notes in Computer Science
ISBN 978-3-319-58070-8 ISBN 978-3-319-58071-5 (eBook)
DOI 10.1007/978-3-319-58071-5

Library of Congress Control Number: 2017939118

LNCS Sublibrary: SL3 – Information Systems and Applications, incl. Internet/Web, and HCI

Printed on acid-free paper

This Springer imprint is published by Springer Nature
The registered company is Springer International Publishing AG
The registered company address is: Gewerbestrasse 11, 6330 Cham, Switzerland

Foreword

The 19th International Conference on Human–Computer Interaction, HCI International 2017, was held in Vancouver, Canada, during July 9–14, 2017. The event incorporated the 15 conferences/thematic areas listed on the following page.

A total of 4,340 individuals from academia, research institutes, industry, and governmental agencies from 70 countries submitted contributions, and 1,228 papers have been included in the proceedings. These papers address the latest research and development efforts and highlight the human aspects of design and use of computing systems. The papers thoroughly cover the entire field of human–computer interaction, addressing major advances in knowledge and effective use of computers in a variety of application areas. The volumes constituting the full set of the conference proceedings are listed on the following pages.

I would like to thank the program board chairs and the members of the program boards of all thematic areas and affiliated conferences for their contribution to the highest scientific quality and the overall success of the HCI International 2017 conference.

This conference would not have been possible without the continuous and unwavering support and advice of the founder, Conference General Chair Emeritus and Conference Scientific Advisor Prof. Gavriel Salvendy. For his outstanding efforts, I would like to express my appreciation to the communications chair and editor of *HCI International News*, Dr. Abbas Moallem.

April 2017 Constantine Stephanidis

HCI International 2017 Thematic Areas and Affiliated Conferences

Thematic areas:

- Human–Computer Interaction (HCI 2017)
- Human Interface and the Management of Information (HIMI 2017)

Affiliated conferences:

- 17th International Conference on Engineering Psychology and Cognitive Ergonomics (EPCE 2017)
- 11th International Conference on Universal Access in Human–Computer Interaction (UAHCI 2017)
- 9th International Conference on Virtual, Augmented and Mixed Reality (VAMR 2017)
- 9th International Conference on Cross-Cultural Design (CCD 2017)
- 9th International Conference on Social Computing and Social Media (SCSM 2017)
- 11th International Conference on Augmented Cognition (AC 2017)
- 8th International Conference on Digital Human Modeling and Applications in Health, Safety, Ergonomics and Risk Management (DHM 2017)
- 6th International Conference on Design, User Experience and Usability (DUXU 2017)
- 5th International Conference on Distributed, Ambient and Pervasive Interactions (DAPI 2017)
- 5th International Conference on Human Aspects of Information Security, Privacy and Trust (HAS 2017)
- 4th International Conference on HCI in Business, Government and Organizations (HCIBGO 2017)
- 4th International Conference on Learning and Collaboration Technologies (LCT 2017)
- Third International Conference on Human Aspects of IT for the Aged Population (ITAP 2017)

Conference Proceedings Volumes Full List

1. LNCS 10271, Human–Computer Interaction: User Interface Design, Development and Multimodality (Part I), edited by Masaaki Kurosu
2. LNCS 10272 Human–Computer Interaction: Interaction Contexts (Part II), edited by Masaaki Kurosu
3. LNCS 10273, Human Interface and the Management of Information: Information, Knowledge and Interaction Design (Part I), edited by Sakae Yamamoto
4. LNCS 10274, Human Interface and the Management of Information: Supporting Learning, Decision-Making and Collaboration (Part II), edited by Sakae Yamamoto
5. LNAI 10275, Engineering Psychology and Cognitive Ergonomics: Performance, Emotion and Situation Awareness (Part I), edited by Don Harris
6. LNAI 10276, Engineering Psychology and Cognitive Ergonomics: Cognition and Design (Part II), edited by Don Harris
7. LNCS 10277, Universal Access in Human–Computer Interaction: Design and Development Approaches and Methods (Part I), edited by Margherita Antona and Constantine Stephanidis
8. LNCS 10278, Universal Access in Human–Computer Interaction: Designing Novel Interactions (Part II), edited by Margherita Antona and Constantine Stephanidis
9. LNCS 10279, Universal Access in Human–Computer Interaction: Human and Technological Environments (Part III), edited by Margherita Antona and Constantine Stephanidis
10. LNCS 10280, Virtual, Augmented and Mixed Reality, edited by Stephanie Lackey and Jessie Y.C. Chen
11. LNCS 10281, Cross-Cultural Design, edited by Pei-Luen Patrick Rau
12. LNCS 10282, Social Computing and Social Media: Human Behavior (Part I), edited by Gabriele Meiselwitz
13. LNCS 10283, Social Computing and Social Media: Applications and Analytics (Part II), edited by Gabriele Meiselwitz
14. LNAI 10284, Augmented Cognition: Neurocognition and Machine Learning (Part I), edited by Dylan D. Schmorrow and Cali M. Fidopiastis
15. LNAI 10285, Augmented Cognition: Enhancing Cognition and Behavior in Complex Human Environments (Part II), edited by Dylan D. Schmorrow and Cali M. Fidopiastis
16. LNCS 10286, Digital Human Modeling and Applications in Health, Safety, Ergonomics and Risk Management: Ergonomics and Design (Part I), edited by Vincent G. Duffy
17. LNCS 10287, Digital Human Modeling and Applications in Health, Safety, Ergonomics and Risk Management: Health and Safety (Part II), edited by Vincent G. Duffy
18. LNCS 10288, Design, User Experience, and Usability: Theory, Methodology and Management (Part I), edited by Aaron Marcus and Wentao Wang

19. LNCS 10289, Design, User Experience, and Usability: Designing Pleasurable Experiences (Part II), edited by Aaron Marcus and Wentao Wang
20. LNCS 10290, Design, User Experience, and Usability: Understanding Users and Contexts (Part III), edited by Aaron Marcus and Wentao Wang
21. LNCS 10291, Distributed, Ambient and Pervasive Interactions, edited by Norbert Streitz and Panos Markopoulos
22. LNCS 10292, Human Aspects of Information Security, Privacy and Trust, edited by Theo Tryfonas
23. LNCS 10293, HCI in Business, Government and Organizations: Interacting with Information Systems (Part I), edited by Fiona Fui-Hoon Nah and Chuan-Hoo Tan
24. LNCS 10294, HCI in Business, Government and Organizations: Supporting Business (Part II), edited by Fiona Fui-Hoon Nah and Chuan-Hoo Tan
25. LNCS 10295, Learning and Collaboration Technologies: Novel Learning Ecosystems (Part I), edited by Panayiotis Zaphiris and Andri Ioannou
26. LNCS 10296, Learning and Collaboration Technologies: Technology in Education (Part II), edited by Panayiotis Zaphiris and Andri Ioannou
27. LNCS 10297, Human Aspects of IT for the Aged Population: Aging, Design and User Experience (Part I), edited by Jia Zhou and Gavriel Salvendy
28. LNCS 10298, Human Aspects of IT for the Aged Population: Applications, Services and Contexts (Part II), edited by Jia Zhou and Gavriel Salvendy
29. CCIS 713, HCI International 2017 Posters Proceedings (Part I), edited by Constantine Stephanidis
30. CCIS 714, HCI International 2017 Posters Proceedings (Part II), edited by Constantine Stephanidis

Human–Computer Interaction

Program Board Chair(s): **Masaaki Kurosu, Japan**

The full list with the Program Board Chairs and the members of the Program Boards of all thematic areas and affiliated conferences is available online at:

http://www.hci.international/board-members-2017.php

HCI International 2018

The 20th International Conference on Human–Computer Interaction, HCI International 2018, will be held jointly with the affiliated conferences in Las Vegas, NV, USA, at Caesars Palace, July 15–20, 2018. It will cover a broad spectrum of themes related to human–computer interaction, including theoretical issues, methods, tools, processes, and case studies in HCI design, as well as novel interaction techniques, interfaces, and applications. The proceedings will be published by Springer. More information is available on the conference website: http://2018.hci.international/.

General Chair
Prof. Constantine Stephanidis
University of Crete and ICS-FORTH
Heraklion, Crete, Greece
E-mail: general_chair@hcii2018.org

http://2018.hci.international/

Contents – Part I

HCI Theory and Education

HCI, Innovation and Technology Acceptance

Interaction Design and Evaluation Methods

User Interface Development: Methods, Tools and Architectures

Multimodal Interaction

Emotions in HCI

Contents – Part II

HCI, Children and Learning

HCI in Complex Human Environments

HCI Theory and Education

Audiovisual Design and the Convergence Between HCI and Audience Studies

Valdecir Becker[1(✉)], Daniel Gambaro[2], and Thais Saraiva Ramos[3]

[1] Postgraduate Program in Computer Science, Communication and Arts (PPGCCA), Informatics Center, Federal University of Paraiba, João Pessoa, Brazil
valdecir@ci.ufpb.br

[2] Postgraduate Program in Audiovisual Media and Processes, School of Communications and Arts (PPGMPA), University of São Paulo, São Paulo, Brazil
dgambaro@usp.br

[3] Audiovisual Design Research Group, CNPq, São Paulo, Brazil
thaissramos@live.com

Abstract. This essay proposes an analytical methodological process called Audiovisual Design, originated from the intersection between HCI theories and Audience Studies. Resources available from this two academic fields are required in the conception of complex audiovisual products, developed from more precise information about the target audiences, and distributed and brought to fruition through interaction interfaces or software. Methodologically, the flow of information inside the traditional communication models has been changed. The introduction of the actions of interaction, sharing and spread of content modified the audiovisual fruition, previously considered passive. This new dynamic is graphically represented as a workflow of Audiovisual Design. Therefore, it becomes possible to predict and design new interactive products, adapted to the needs of integration and sharing present in the contemporary audiovisual consumption. Moreover, it allows the analysis and identification of inherent issues and equivocated approaches of already concluded products.

Keywords: HCI · Audience studies · Communication models · Audiovisual production

1 Introduction

The conception and the development of audiovisual content, including apps that incorporate video, is changing. The technological convergence is bringing together once distinct areas of knowledge, such as the Human Computer Interaction Studies (HCI, Computer Sciences) and the Audience Studies (Communication Sciences), hence generating a theoretical relation that is not currently contemplated by these fields individually.

The design of interactive computer systems, what was initially focused on the problem, the tasks and the functions, and then has slowly turned to a perspective oriented towards possibilities, significances and emotions, now is considering other human

M. Kurosu (Ed.): HCI 2017, Part I, LNCS 10271, pp. 3–22, 2017.
DOI: 10.1007/978-3-319-58071-5_1

behaviors. As an example, the passive fruition now gains relevance when the final object of the multimedia interactive system is an audiovisual content.

An alike phenomenon can be observed from the perspective of the audiovisual consumption, once the experience of using software interfaces has become as important as the quality of the movie, TV series or online video. A characteristic common to the digital means used for accessing video content is the software-mediated interaction. The digital TV schedule guide, the search for a movie title in an app, the recommendation in a social network, all of them offer the spectator an experience that mixes active attitude (browsing and search for information) and passive fruition (video watching). In other words, the simple act of choosing and watching an audiovisual content can demand each individual to perform different roles, that differ in degrees of greater or minor activity in comparison to the traditional notion of audience of mass media. Hence a review of theories and methods that today support the production of this content, especially in the field of Audience Studies, becomes pertinent.

Bearing this premise in mind, our proposal suggests the emergency of a methodological process that reunites and reformulates some concepts originally from those two fields of study. In summary, we are searching a workflow that allows to: (a) analyze the production conceived upon the utilization of tools both from HCI and Audience Studies; (b) predict and propose applications for such tools, enabled by the technical frame available today. We named this methodological set Audiovisual Design, and its main feature is the planning of audio and video production based on four lines that configure and shape the processes: The Individual, the Motivations, the Experience and the Content.

It must be highlighted that the two words composing the name of this discipline have distinguished connotations in the different knowledge fields. In this paper, the term “Design” is understood in its broader meaning, that is, including the whole process of situation analysis, identification of the problem and the demands, elaboration of the solution forwarding, product synthesis and evaluation of results. Likewise, the word “Audiovisual” contemplates the entire range of products based on audio and video, or that are centrally composed by these two elements.

To illustrated the methodological process of this proposal, we described a graphic workflow to analyze production, interaction and fruition methods in the Audiovisual Design. The workflow meets the analytical requirements for finished works, and offer mechanisms for analyzing and projecting possible and necessary interactions during the conception and development of new products. For that matter, it contemplates five roles an individual can perform: The Audience, the Synthesizer, the Modifier, the Player and the Producer.

Following this introduction, this paper is divided in four other sections. Next Sect. 2 contains a discussion on the communication models and the changes resulting from the use of digital technologies to access and share content. Section 3 describes the proposal of a graphic plan of audiovisual production and fruition workflow, while in Sect. 4 is presented the application of this plan in two examples. Finally, Sect. 5 brings the conclusions of this essay.

2 Communication Models

To understand the communicative acts, the people and the technologies involved in communications, the communicational processes can be organized within models. A communication model is a theoretical scheme to show the main elements, how they relate, and how the information flow is generated. Many books in the literature of communication studies summarize these theories, for example Mattelart and Mattelart [1] and Souza [2]. Traditionally, communication is defined as the transmission of a message or a set of messages from one transmitter (or source) to a receiver. A transmission mean (or channel), connects both.

One of the simplest models is Laswell's, which considers communication as a linear process: *somebody say something to someone, using a given mean, generating an effect*. On this case, "somebody says" represents the transmitter of the message and the beginning of the communicational process; "something" is the message, where the content analyses are made; "given mean" stands for the channel connecting the transmitter and the receiver, and can be differentiated between interpersonal or mass communication; "to someone" represents the people affected by the message, the receiver(s); "an effect" is the impact of the message to the receivers, enabling studies on the perception of the message and their significances [1].

A common critic to this model is it doesn't foresee the return or feedback from the receiver to the transmitter. Thus, there is not a conversation, but a monologue. The Schramm model [2] includes the feedback, enabling an exchange (even if limited) between transmitter and receiver, whose are not anymore completely dissociated. The reaction of the receiver facing the message can add new meanings to the message and, in some cases, start a new communication process. On the edge of this process, the roles of transmitter and receiver are confused and alternate through time.

Other models have been proposed. Mainly, there are small alterations to aggregate other elements as "noise", "multiple reception" by a large amount of people, different feedback forms and "feedback loops", sociocultural or cognitive elements [2]. As we can notice, the audience was generally treated as a group of people, be they an undistinctive mass or a segment of a given population. On the other hand, the newer models of communication allow the study of meanings during the fruition process of a media content. In part, this is due to the recognition of people as a group of individuals and of their individualities[1].

According to Hall [3], what has given support to a coherent identity is losing power since the last decades of the 20th Century and the subjects themselves assume different identities in different moments, trying to re-construct a coherent self that is in accordance

[1] For David Harvey, the emancipation of the individual begins with the *Enlightenment* and is accentuated during in the post-modern era, which comprises the second half of the 20th Century. This era is characterized by the fragmentation of the quotidian life and the ephemerality of material and immaterial goodies. The globalization of the Economy and the mundialization of culture are some causes for a renewed need for individual personality. See Harvey D (2001) A Condição Pós-moderna (The Condition of Postmodernity). Edições Loyola, São Paulo (BR).

to each context the person is acting in. With the growth in quantity of communication technologies in the late 1990s, information became itself fragmented, dispersed, although more available and higher in volume. As a result, the contemporary imaginary outlines it is important for people to consume a variety of cultural products and show that they are eclectic, but this variety must be carefully chosen to communicate something about their individuality. In other words, being universal became a value as important as being diversified [4]. The fragment and the bricolage have become necessary in the formation of an individualized self, and it is better in a market logic that these characteristics are also mutable and ephemeral.

We do not want to condemn or praise this generalized feeling, but to point out that it brings up an infinity of connections people can implement between themselves and the world. In the last decades, more than any time before, individuals use the available media – especially the interactive ones – to define their cultural and personal identities, as pointed by Bolter and Grusin [5]. The way people use and interact with the software that make content available became as important as the content itself in the identity formation, consequently making the Human-Computer Interaction part of the communication process.

In this sense, it is fundamental that the conception of media products and their analysis consider the individualities of those who are called the viewers, the users or the audiences. Thus, new models of communication are important to understand how this impact in the media and in the content creation. Jenkins, Ford and Green [6] proposed three simple models to describe the different scenarios of communication today: the communication from one emitter to multiple receivers as Broadcast; the models of online communication as Stickiness, where individuals take the initiative of seeking content; and Spreadable, where content reaches the audiences through the actions of the individuals themselves, mostly using interactive digital tools. We wish now to discuss these three models.

2.1 The Broadcast Model

The broadcast model of audiovisual communication is the most traditional and the one with larger reach. It stands that a transmitter emits a content and the recipients within the transmission range receive it. Approximately from the 1930s on, radio and television consolidated this model around the globe, and it is still the predominant operation pattern for these two means.

A central feature is the concept of audience, which can be treated in a simplified form as 'the collective term for the "receivers" in the simple sequential model of the mass communication process' [7, p. 1]. In other words, they are the readers of printed media, the radio listeners and the television spectators.

The origins of the word resume to the arts, like theater and musical performances, and to games and other spectacles, where the audience can be measured by counting the number of attendees. In addition, people's presence in a performance allows an immediate and complete comprehension of their reaction [7]. Different perceptions of the audience have been proposed with the advent of mass communication means, through which a transmitter sends the content to an unlimited number of receivers.

The then new media, initially newspapers and later radio and television, were different in scale and in operation. First, the reach of radio and television are larger; second, audience and producers turn out to be significantly apart, changing the way the content is generated, as well as how the relation with the public occurs. If previously the physically-present audience allowed a close contact, it does not occur in mass communication, generating an "asymmetry" between the transmission and the reception [8]. The lack of direct contact between transmitter and receivers results in the first role performed by some few companies, and the receivers being every person with access to the communication mean.

While television helped to consolidate this theory due to its centrality in every market where audience is measured, radio and printed media perform only a secondary role, as well as the internet, which audience started being studied in the second half of the 1990s [7–9]. Actually, the inclusion of internet leads to some questioning in regard to the term "audience" representing the measurement of visits to websites. Bermejo [8] considers the internet a mass media, thus the use of the word is correct. Other academics like McQuail [7], Bailén [10] and Webster et al. [11], however, believe that does not exist audience in systems where networks offer segmented, on-demand content. These authors stand that audience is a terminology of mass communication, thus being restricted to the unidirectional and asymmetric reception of the informational flow. Mosco and Kaye [12] also assert that the audience represents a power relationship, based on the asymmetry and hierarchy between who produces and who receives the content. Therefore, there is not audience in communication environments that are not based on asymmetry.

Hence the audience is an abstract entity, gauged by statistical samples and quantified in percentage terms. Analysis and interpretation of behaviors generate information about people, grouped in profiles, with no possible individualization.

In interactive systems, on the other hand, we can identify patterns of use resulting from the interaction, participation and collaboration of people through and with computational systems, and quantify access and usage duration in an individualized manner. Martino [13] explains that a digital system can be defined as a limited set of interacting elements, offering the possible options of action in face of a technology. 'The functioning of any system depends, in great measure, on the interaction between the parts that must know what to do at any time. The information exchange between elements within a system is the driver from which every attitude is organized' [13, pp. 21–22].

That is, opposed to the mass communication means that distribute content independently of the audience action, the digital interactive systems only allow exchange of information after the user's interaction. Therefore, we can identify different behaviors towards a technology, for instance the passive fruition held while watching television, listening to radio or attending a movie section, and an active attitude in digital systems. For decades, the Communication Theory have attributed a passive role to the listener and the viewer. Nonetheless, with audiovisual communication systems based on digital technologies, this role today interposes with moments of action or interaction. New features were brought by the aggregation of computational elements to the audiovisual reception, such as interaction through television, program scheduling guides, Smart TVs apps, online research, simultaneous access and use of social networks, and second (or companion) screen consumption.

The audiovisual content, previously accessible only through a TV set or online video repository, converged into consumption formats that combine audio, video, software and interaction interfaces. Inside these digital systems, the audiovisual content fruition is now integrated to, and sometimes dependent of, the interaction and the use of interfaces to input and output data. Then the intersection with the field of Human-Computer Interaction Studies becomes natural. This intersection is not comprehended by the models of communication that tries to explain the diffusion of information from one transmitter to many receivers.

2.2 The *Stickiness* Model

In addition to the Broadcast, new models of communication were introduced with the dissemination of technologies and the internet access. Content is made available through websites, internet portals and apps, and the individuals have an active attitude to seek information. The content must attract the audiences, involve them, and generate engagement. In other words, audiences must adhere to these contents, in different levels, so they can be considered "successful". This process is called *"Stickiness"* in allusion to the terminology used by Gladwell [14] to explain how good content is fixed in the audiences' minds and produce engagement. Jenkins, Ford and Green [6] expand the perception to the digital commercial environment, stating that Stickiness refers to the centralization of the audiences' presence in an online place to generate income from advertising and sells. That is, the Stickiness model is based upon the access both to gather audience and to produce some profit, be it financial or not. The moment the content rises the public interest and fixates in people's minds, the desire for sharing also emerge, what can result in the Spreadable model of communication – discussed in the next subsection.

It is important to highlight that the Stickiness model only works when the content can attract people to the place where it is available. In opposition to the Broadcast model, where the content is transmitted regardless of the number of receivers, the Stickiness model requires an active attitude of the receivers who, in a way, start the communicational process. It is also the actions of each receiver which completes the cycle, enabling a more precise feedback to the producer than the Broadcast model (through the mining of navigation data, for instance). If the receiver stays inactive, the message remains available online and the reception process is not completed, compromising the communication.

Furthermore, the aspect of "quality" must also be considered. In Broadcast model, the quality of the message or of the content are independent from the quantity of receivers. For example, in a TV transmission, the image quality shall be the same for 10 or 10 thousand viewers. Instead, in the Stickiness model many requests to access a given content at the same time may clutter the network traffic, creating a fruition bottleneck, e.g., a low-speedy video server can produce a visualization queue in the viewers' end. Then, that is another difference between the Broadcast and the Stickiness models, for in the first there is no concern about the quality or the method of access.

The Stickiness model features a series of intersections, allowing us to look at the cultural production from the point of view of the audience or of the content, as well as from the interaction interfaces. We now want to present, grounded on the HCI field, some points related to the design of the interfaces and the part attributed to the individual/ user during the conception.

Jenkins, Ford and Green [6] say that a network-connected culture is an important tool for disseminating information, because it brings together technological innovations and cultural and social practices, which engage people to interact with the information available. The word "information" is easily connected to communication or knowledge, but to Martino 'in the media studies it has a specific meaning, as it can also be understood as any new data that shows up in the system' [13, p.24]. Every data feeds a system and facilitate the decision-making, be it a human system (brain) or a technological system (associated to computers). Thus, 'information is a fundamental element for the decision-making. It shows the better situation within a set of possible situations. In simple terms, they transform probabilities in certainties. Then, to process information is to understand its content and take decisions from that' [13, pp. 24–25].

The Human-Computer Interaction is a central area for the development of systems inside the Stickiness model. One of the main purposes of the disciplines comprised in this field is to support the analysis of systems and people. The comprehension of how the individuals use digital systems increases the possibilities of creating solutions for more efficient computer-mediated interactions, thus providing a more complete experience.

The HCI studies as known today were settled in the middle 1980s, with the increase of the production and types of personal computers and consequent rise on the number of PC users. During the 1990s, this growth became exponential due to the global networks providing a collaborative workflow supported by computers.

The way we use the digital technologies, especially online, has exponentially advanced during the last years. The user interactions are not restricted only to a computer screen. Almost every electronic object carry a computational system and require some level of interaction (from the fridge to the TV set, going through phones, cameras, wearable devices, etc.). Today, a series of devices, further than presenting us information, can also "feel", that is, can generate responsive interactions that goes beyond the users' consciousness and make the daily life more comfortable. When this feature is connected through an online system, e.g. in applications of the Internet of Things, the use each individual perform help to consolidate the Stickiness model by bringing it to everyday life.

All these changes have impacted in the concerns and methodologies of the HCI. Formerly seen only as tasks, goals and efficiencies, today those methods encompass experiences and sensations of satisfaction to supply the actual needs of the individuals, making usability a key point of HCI. So, a set of methodologies, process and tools are being developed inside the HCI field, to help the creation of software as well as complex communication systems that interconnect a variety of types of messages exchange.

In the academic field, the HCI Studies comprise the interactions of people with technologies and foresee the possible applications in design. To construct and develop interventions in the systems, as much as to comprehend the technologies to be used in the interactive process, 'we have to understand the people whom we are designing, why do they want it and how they'll use' [15]. In consequence, there are some defenders of a subdivision called "Human-Centered Design" (HCD) in opposition to "User-Centered Design" (UCD), capable of broadening the discussion and work within the HCI studies. Elmansy [16] puts HCD in the center of every process as a way to validate the design of products linked to the "real world".

If, at one hand, the studies about interaction and usability helped to consolidate the Stickiness model, by making the digital systems easier to use, on the other hand some elements of interaction are incorporated to the Broadcast model. Although there are some similarities between methods from the HCI and the Audience Studies, e.g. the user surveys, both fields still have as challenge the study of interaction interfaces and the development of audiovisual content integrated to the software (the Audiovisual Design).

2.3 The Spreadable Model

Jenkins, Ford and Green [6] consider the Stickiness model driving Web 2.0 insufficient to explain the distribution of messages in the digital universe. There are missing elements that could explain people's motivation and value generation, leading to an imprecise description of the communicational process regarding content circulation. The authors, then, propose a new model to sum up to the other two: The Spreadable, that is, one in which the media spreads.

In summary, 'Spreadability' refers to the technical resources that make it easier to circulate some kinds of content than others, the economic structures that support or restrict circulation, the attributes of a media text that might appeal to a community's motivation for sharing material, and the social networks that link people through the exchange of meaningful bytes [6, pp. 3–4]. Three characteristics of this model must be highlighted for the purposes of our discussion: the connection between individuals, especially through digital social networks; the dispersed content distribution through a variety of means, resulting in people having different experiences when accessing the content; and the opening of a range of uses by the individuals that were not originally predicted by the producer.

It is noticeable that the spreadable media rely on two complementing poles: the audiences' individual actions of commenting, sharing and modifying the original content (that is, the engagement); and the producer action in identifying their demands by using the correct set of software. Obviously, there is not a simple recipe to explain how some content can spread easily, except that each person takes a bunch of decisions before get involved to the media content. Emotional, economic and social mechanisms are considered at this moment. It becomes clear that each individual, when engaging to a media content to at least share it, effectively want do communicate something about themselves. That's why it is so significant the producer think of the user as a human, and the audiences as a collective of individuals with variable preferences, tastes and repertoires.

The cultural fragmentation and the multiple possibilities the individuals possess to construct their selves have become, as mentioned above, elements of distinction. The physical and symbolic products each person can be offered are very diversified. Thus, they can only plan a strategy aiming their individuation through the choice of the products to wear, the brands to convey, the cultural products (movies, music, TV series, comics) to bring to fruition. Also, how and when they choose to use all these materials are relevant and are part of the communication held with others [5]. Two parallel processes take place, especially related to the sharing of content through digital interfaces. First, individuals fulfill "mutable identities" valid while they are connected in a network, more realistic or less realistic towards their true self. Second, the software can read the set of data people share when using digital tools, even without their notice. This creates a suit of interaction possibilities that can be further developed. Moreover, to promote the user's loyalty to a given system, the answers provided by the system must be relatively coherent with the profiles individuals project about themselves ("relatively" because the technological processes also represent the interests of the corporation collecting the data). Some points must be highlighted. In the first place, the contemporary *zeitgeist* implies a sensation of autonomy, liberty and individuation, reflecting in the choice of physical and symbolic products, as well as behaviors, the individuals appropriate to themselves, even if any of these materials follows a pattern. Second, the institution of the media as a social and cultural structure resulted in a facilitated circulation of information. People then have a myriad of possibilities to use and construct profiles and personal narratives in their social networks. In conclusion, these individuals expect that the technological mechanisms use their data to give in return processes and applications that valorize the experience, thus opening a new economic field.

The logic of participation determines this new field: a person wants and needs to be part of a group or process, that is, the increased individuality also leads to the necessity of composing new community links. In this regard, the recommendation of a group member has more strength and worth than the mechanisms used in Broadcast to reach the audience [6]. Therefore, a new "moral economy" emerges, and the value attributed by people to the product they consume (such as a video to be watched or a CD to be owned) becomes even more significant than the actual paid price.

We must take in consideration that most part of the material shared through the social networks is audiovisual, commonly derived from productions of the Broadcast system. This type of appropriation, authorized or not by the creators, shows a significant convergence point of the Broadcast, the Stickiness and the Spreadable models. The large-scale distribution of the first feeds the circulation inherent to the other two, in a controlled manner in the Stickiness, and spontaneously in the Spreadable. The key point is that each individual re-signifies the content, and this appropriations and meanings must, directly or indirectly, compose the feedback for the producer regarding its production.

Finally, a great part of the content in the Stickiness and Spreadable models depends on the digital interfaces, which are occupying the space of the traditional media and becoming, themselves, new media. The producers more and more must make use of interaction tools and incorporate them as internal elements of the production, thus changing the experience of audiovisual fruition, keeping some control over the product, and promoting at least a minimum engagement of the public. Of course, because much of people will relate to the content only in a basic level, the incorporation of those tools cannot diminish the quality of the Broadcast product to the eyes of a passive audience. Also, the interfaces must be designed considering not anonymous users, but individuals who, at some point, may desire to use that audiovisual content as reference to compose part of their narratives in the social networks. We propose, then, a graphic workflow that can summarize the different elements of the Audiovisual Design.

3 The Audiovisual Design Workflow

From the intersections between disciplines from the Audience Studies and the HCI Studies, we propose a graphic plan (Fig. 1), in the shape of a workflow, that enables the comprehension of the dynamic flow of the Audiovisual Design methods, considering the different scenarios and roles performed by the individuals.

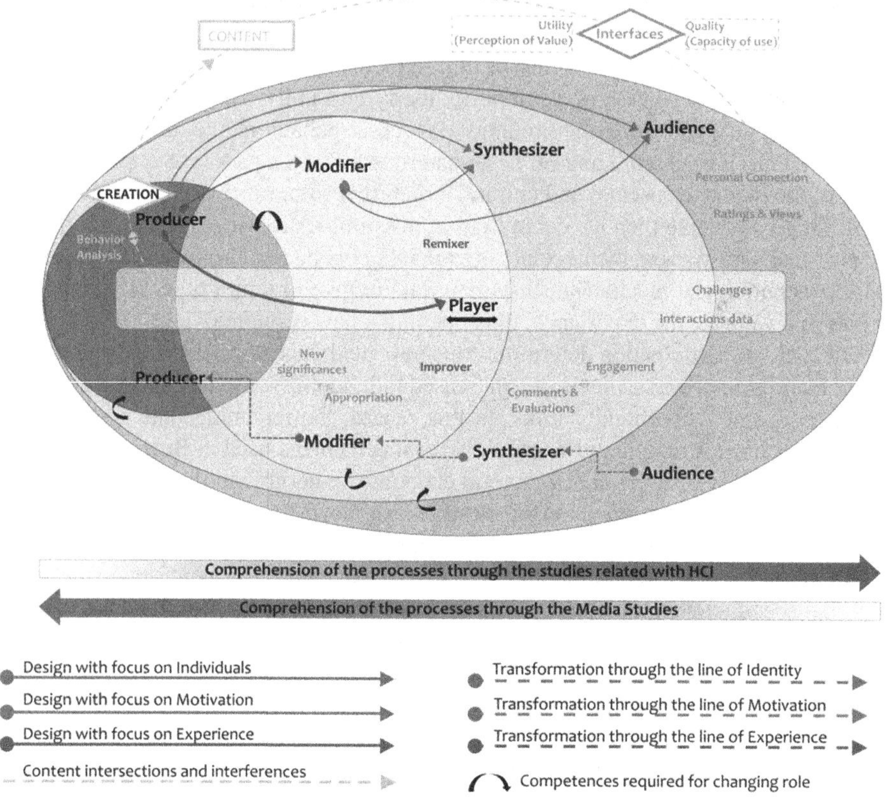

Fig. 1. Processual flow for audiovisual design

First, we must highlight our beliefs that some alterations took place in the hierarchic scales that is normally used to classify producers and audience. The most common graphical representation is a pyramid with producers placed on the top, thus reinforcing the asymmetry of the Broadcast model communication processes. We have used instead the paradigm of "sets", equal to the mathematical sets of numbers, to show the continent and the contained and then represent the continuity amid the roles. We are not defending that a complete end of the asymmetry has been reached, but we indeed understand the positions are more flexible and variating.

Actually, the proposed arrangement of elements shows that each individual can perform different roles at different moments: (passive) Audience, Synthesizer, Modifier,

Player or Producer[2]. The relations intrinsic to these five roles occur through four lines: Identity, Motivation, Experience and Content.

The first role is the most common, thus inherent to everyone involved in the audiovisual process: The *Audience*. This basic role denotates low level or absence of interaction, hence the individual shows a passive behavior towards the content, and the interaction with the digital interfaces are limited to searching and playing videos, the subscription to a channel, etc. Also, on this level the content can provoke intimal feelings to the individual, but these emotions remain "private". Therefore, the relation with the content occurs in the level of personal identification. The audience ratings and the amount of visualizations of the video are what provide some feedback to the Producer, such as data on the Audiences' preferences in relation to the consumed content. As a result, the level of the information does not allow for an individualized identification, but can guarantee some standardization of future content.

The second role is that of the *Synthesizer*, as named by Jenkins, Ford and Green [6]. Here each individual presents the necessary competences to compile the contents that praise them, so they can share, comment, classify and recommend. This behavior is one of the main instrument used for shaping an identity in the network, that is, the impression people have they are creating a controllable online profile that fully represents them. These attitudes change the emotional component from the status of "private" to "public". Nonetheless, this profile is never the pure expression of the individual preferences, it is first a visibility performance in accordance to variable patterns from the social network each person is connected to. The synthesizers' relation with the content is the *engagement*, where certain passion invokes a desire to share with others what is of great value to them. Through the synthesizers' interactions it is possible to measure the level of engagement the audiovisual content incites and, then, to reinforce the aspects that allows the spread of the content.

The third role is the *Modifier*. The competences required for achieving this role include the domain of software applications (such as image and sound editing) to enable the manipulation of the original content in recreations. The relation with the content goes beyond the engagement and becomes *appropriation*: The Modifiers assume they have rights over the content they like and implement their impressions. Yet, it is still an expression of feelings and the creation of a network profile equal to those performed by the Synthesizer. Thus, the set of Modifiers is contained within the Synthesizers'.

We divided this role in two main functions, although there can be more. The Improvers appropriate the content to modify some element that dislikes them, or to emphasize a given characteristic they like (technical, from the script, etc.). The Remixers, on their turn, use the content as base for creating something new, like DJs used to do in Hip Hop battles. This includes internet "memes", videos of commentary about audiovisual content, music videos with movie characters, etc. In consequence, there are a new range of significances attributed to the content that can serve as guidance for the producer in the conception or future audiovisual productions.

---

[2] From this point on, every time the words Audience, Synthesizer, Modifier and Producer are used in this essay to refer to role inside the workflow, it is written with capitalised first letter.

The *Producer*, our fourth role, is represented by those people (or companies) with creative capacity to conceive and design a new product. This production can be inspired in an existing model, but still must be an original creation. This set includes both the creators working for a media corporation and the independent producers, known inside cultural niches or even anonymous. Every Producer is, deliberately, Synthesizer. After all, what is the purpose of producing something and do not share it with others? However, although some people can become Producers by summing up the competences of the Modifiers, this is not a prerogative. Hence the set of Producers and Modifiers are only partially overlapped, as can be seen in Fig. 1. Still, this crossing makes clearer the collaborative production among "common" individuals, and between them and the "official" content producers.

Regarding the content, the producer can use a variety of data from multiple sources, such as audience ratings, fruition models, profiles, modes and strength of engagement, meanings aggregated by people to the modified content, data analysis algorithms, and creation techniques as UCD, HCD and Design Thinking. The acquisition of all this information does not avoid the creative process, since the idea and the production design remain present. Nevertheless, the producers have a possibility to evaluate demands and predict results, directly interfering in the design of the audiovisual product. The set of analyzed information, when added to the creation of content, enables the planning of the content to reach the different roles the individuals can assume. Besides, it is relevant the design takes into account the interfaces to be used by the viewers, regardless of the role they come to assume. Then, it is something common that questions linked to the Utility (perception of value) and Quality (Capacity of use) interfere during the creation process of a content.

About the Audience, for instance, the Producers can base the elaboration upon characteristics of individuals. This spectator that shows little interaction (or interact only with the machines) seeks in the content elements for personal identification, hence the design of the audiovisual product (both the content and the interfaces) must occur on the line of *Identity*. In the relation of the Producers with the Synthesizers, however, the process must run on the line of *Motivation*, since the content circulation does not end with the fruition. On the contrary, the circulation rests upon the action of the individuals that, aiming to communicate something about themselves, spread the content. In this case, the Producers must be concerned about making the viewers leave their passivity to express their feelings about the content. The two processes explained in this paragraph are alike to those concerning the intentions of the Modifier towards the Audiences and the Synthesizers.

Likewise, the intentions of the Producers directed to the Modifiers are processed on the line of Experience. Since the Modifiers have competences that enable them to modify the content, the product must be designed to facilitate this kind of manipulation and involvement. Thus, even if it is not a feature of every work, some content is planned to allow appropriation and use by the Modifiers. When the Producers are responsible for those tools, they can keep to themselves some control over the modifications.

Each one of these roles requires the individuals to incorporate some competences, which can be technical, technological, or social. Subsequently, with access to a defined set of tools, the individuals can be enabled as a Synthesizers, other set turns them into

Modifiers, etc. A more complete analysis, to be held in a future investigation, must help determine which are the minimum required competences for a person to perform a given role.

A remaining point to complete the description of the proposed workflow is the role of the *Player*. This role intersects every other one because it refers to the people who, in each level, use the tools provided by the Producers. To conceive the role of the Players and how they react to the content interaction interfaces results in considerations about the different levels of interaction the designed product can allow. For instance, a Player in the set of Audience can basically perform the programmed functions, like in a video-game where the player only follow the rules. When the Player decides to share the achievements or part of the gaming story they are more engaged, they are operating the role of a Synthesizer much alike to those sharing a TV series' scene.

The role of the Players expects the performance of the totality of activities made available by the Producers during the design, considering inherent limitations. For example, the Player is the one who will better use a tool designed to allow the exploration of an interactive audiovisual content (immersive reality), even if it is offline and the experience remains restricted to the moment of access. Nevertheless, the Player can easily become a Modifier or a Producer, if the Producer who designs the audiovisual content allows the necessary conditions in the product. As consequence, the design towards the Players is also a process on the line of Experience, because these advanced activities will keep them loyal to the content. Players seek challenging contents that make them think of and perform some action, even if isolated from others. Most of the time they can be identified as the "early adopters" or "early users" of a technology, that is, people who assume the risks of using something new and, thus, contribute to its development. By doing so, the Players return the Producers some information about the interactions, which can feed future productions aimed at the other roles.

Finally, the two horizontal arrows composing the workflow indicate the starting points to understand the interaction scenarios, especially within the Spreadable model. HCI Studies offer consistent theories and methods for the Producer or the software developer to design the interaction and the usage. Thus, instruments such as user surveys, formative evaluations of interfaces and usability tests help in the identification of the user demands. The user, although in the center of the software development process, is an abstract individual, commonly identified with archetypes of personas.

On the other hand, the Audience Studies part from the comprehension of behaviors and motivations of the message receivers. The audience analyses, although abstract, generate objective data over actions towards the message. Then, behaviors can be inferred and decision-making processes can be analyzed, even if they are related to a simple change of channel in a TV set during the commercials, or if they are the motivation resulted from the engagement to an online video. The workflow proposed herein contains the intersection of these two fields of study, incorporating elements from the processes of digital systems and interaction interfaces design, as well as analyses over audiovisual content fruition, mixing and alternating the different roles.

4 Examples of Application for the Audiovisual Design Workflow

Per our proposed workflow, the audiovisual design and its economic placement must consider elements such as software development, HCI, data mining in big data environment and the adaptability of the content to a vast array of environments, usage scenarios, screens and markets. To facilitate the comprehension, we present in this essay one real and one projected example about how this workflow is viable in the audiovisual practice.

The real life example is extracted from to the current television and cinematographic productions. Although the movie theater and the broadcast stations remain the 'first paths' followed by the distribution of movies and TV Series (except, of course, for productions in the Netflix's business model), more and more media corporation need to take into account the new reality, that is, the timeshifting, the multiplatform content, and a growing competition with new, different audiovisual producers.

In Brazil, the main TV network (Globo) has been performing tests on this new field, but still in a very limited way. Two digital services gather audiovisual content originally produced by and for the broadcast station, GShow (http://gshow.globo.com) and GloboPlay (https://globoplay.globo.com), operating through websites and mobile apps for Android and iOS. The first is dedicated to expand the company's entertainment content, offering video series exclusive for web, news about the stations' main productions, etc. This portal also delivers edited segments of the television shows (specially the comedy ones), and unaired content. GShow is also present in some social networks, like Facebook, and publishes the content trying to achieve some spread and to engage the Audience, which is mainly formed by youngsters already used to the networks and who normally spend a great amount of time in front of the computer screen. GloboPlay, on its turn, contains a collection of shows on-demand, divided into segments that can be accessed and viewed by anyone after the display of some publicity (similar to YouTube's advertising scheme). Subscribers can watch the integral, ad-free version of the shows, and have access to the live transmission over IP.

The program chosen as an example is a comedy show called "*Tá no Ar: A TV na TV*" (It's On Air: The TV on the TV). Its sketches simulate the television programming and its specific genres and language, such as Newscast, telenovelas, advertising spots, music videos, thus performing an acid critics to the entire television and to the public affairs, including the politics. *Tá no Ar* has short seasons (around 10 episodes) and is on its 4th year. Its increasing popularity is in part due to the actions on the internet. Today, the official Facebook page has around 170 thousand *likes*; segments of the show shared on the page (some exclusive or unaired) reaches around 100 thousand views in two weeks, and the mouth-to-mouth spread contributed to a growing audience rating year after year[3].

It should be stressed that this is a television show planned for a relatively-segmented audience in the Broadcast model (young people that stay awake after 11 pm in

[3] Marcelo Adnet, one of the main comedian of *Tá no Ar*, starred a former show in 2012 that was a public and critics failure, affecting Adnet's image to the point his stay in Globo network was doubted.

weekdays). The criticizing position of the show, however, permitted true humoristic pearls among the sketches, questioning both the political scenario and the population behavior[4]. This type of content facilitates the engagement of people hitherto divided on their political preferences. The show's editing – as if an impatient viewer is changing channel all the time – makes each sketch viable to be reused on the website or Facebook[5]. Consequently, the Audience is easily habilitated as Synthesizers, sharing and commenting the content, and those actions become an important feedback to the editorial line of the show.

During the new season, in 2017, *Tá no Ar* seems to have intensified the tone of the critics and the use of web, distributing memes on social networks (made of extracts from the show) and making available exclusively for GloboPlay subscribers the anticipated launch of the first episodes. On the other hand, the design of the show does not predict tools that could allow a more complete experience of the individual interacting with the production. The broadcaster opted not to use the web tools in their totality. For instance, the content cannot enable people as Modifiers. Most the remixes are made by the Producers, who keep total control over the content itself and over how the content is viewed and enjoyed by the Audience. GShow and GloboPlay's websites and mobile apps miss usability and present a reasonable amount of issues, impeding the users to a smooth experience while watching the videos. It is very difficult, for instance, to search and find a specific part of a show and share it with other people, as a form of expression of the individual self.

Therefore, the return provided by the content is limited to the concepts of Identification, with the due attribution of value to the show by the individuals, and Motivation, by the controlled use of content made available by the Producers. The Audience engagement is also limited to advertising the show on their social networks, just complementing the announcements made by the TV station itself during the commercial breaks. Globo commits a mistake by not allowing the Audience a stronger engagement with *Tá no Ar*, then breaking the logic behind the show's original design of using the internet as support.

GloboPlay's poor web platform does not have an intuitive flow of use. For instance, the suggestions for a next video to be watched not ever exclude the one just viewed. The algorithm suggests random videos disconnected to the individuals' preferences and, when this basic feature is considered, the suggestion returns something that has already been watched. Another issue, the search is limited to the name of the show and the broadcasting date. In the case of *Tá no Ar*, the user have difficulties in searching a sketch using a keyword, since this kind of specific information is not generally added to each piece available. As a result, the search takes more time and, eventually, must be made

---

4 A music video presenting parodies of Chico Buarque's songs reached almost 2.4 million views only in Facebook.

5 The choice for this high fragmentation of the editing, by the way, was present in the show since its beginning, in 2013. It creates more than an accelerate pace in comparison to other, more conventional, TV shows. The editing of the content reshapes the meanings and transforms the contexts of the presented critics, due to phrases and impacting segments of the sketches being chosen to compose the viewer's "zapping", caricaturizing the television.

manually, for the person must open each program tab and look through a long list for the name of the video to share. Even by using a search engine like Google, a crossed search directs the individual back to the GloboPlay portal, and the video platform redirects to the main page, thus having the user go through the longest path to get to the video.

One of the main intentions supporting *Tá no Ar* is to work with the formats and velocity inherent to the web. Therefore, the Audience would be capable of turning into Modifiers and actually appropriate the content, if the broadcaster did not fear to improve their web platform. From this brief analysis, it is possible to point out the methods inherent to the HCI are missing in the show's design – ideally conceived to use web resources. The content was planned considering the Audiences, but not how those people would use it. The user who wants a fragmented, on demand fruition has scarce conditions of appropriation and intervention. Furthermore, apart from data such as number of views and shares, a legacy to the audience analysis from the Broadcast model, the incorporation of complex feedbacks of the individuals in future productions has not been planned in the actual design. In consequence, the attribution of value to the content through web interfaces (utility) and the usage capacity (quality) are absent from the design because they were not included during the development.

To present the possibilities opened under the logic the Audiovisual Design, we present now a projected application of the workflow of Fig. 1. As a start, let's imagine that a company of audiovisual production has decided to offer a web-based, video subscription service. To take a better advantage of the web environment resources and promote this new services, the company wants to offer its subscribers a serial show, in the model of a TV series, but which allows interaction and the construction of the storytelling for and by each subscriber. Nonetheless, the process must not be annoying by demanding too much interactions from the user.

Anyway, the story must allow multiple routes, for example, by emphasizing a given narrative genre as comedy or terror, or a defined character in a plot. In the beginning, the project stays on the common standard for producing audiovisual fictional series, as executed in almost every current TV production: an initial argument is developed into a script, and then into screenplays as the story advances and the audience interacts. Now, let's imagine that the creation team has established a sufficient quantity of routes, broad enough for matching a varied range of demands. This result is achievable by using digital tools that compile and analyze data from other works, like the algorithms capable of generating a coherent literary text from a set of parameters and a broad database. Then, this creation would be a collaborative work between humans and computers, although supervised by humans. It is nothing more than the creation of different scripts inside the same narrative universe. Today, each sequence of the script leads to another sequence, in a linear construction. In this project, each sequence must be planned to present a coherent continuity within different narrative lines, which increases the complexity of the storytelling and demands a very deep creation process, complemented by the computer.

The next step is the shooting of the sequences. The color correction and the music score must be treated as additional procedures and originate separated data, intrinsic to each narrative line, so they can be processed and added to the final video by the system during the viewer's fruition.

Part of the design includes knowing the profiles and preferences of the Audience. So, the platform used to provide access to the subscriber must also collect enough information to allow the recognition of some user's preferences. Just like in Netflix, the users should input data in a form during the first access so the system can add the previous experiences. This questionnaire must be very carefully prepared so the data, when analyzed, can direct the production to a result that each person judges satisfactory. After some time, the reading of each individual's behavior must be enough to feed the database used by the Producers to design the exclusive productions of this service. Besides, it is possible to apply algorithms to read the social network profiles of the subscribers. There are two possible processes: (a) data mining to outline the Audiences profile, which can aid in the creation of a story with enough elements to correspond the expectations of the possible largest number of subscribers; (b) the creation of narratives responsive to the historicity of each user [17], adaptable by software to each person in a relatively individualized manner to correspond to their preferences, through the choice of elements within an available data set.

During this stage of the design it is observable that the Producer (configured as the creation personnel of this company) must reunite a variety of competences, for instance the research and scripting, common to the TV production, and development and use of software to analyze big data, from the field of Computer Sciences. Moreover, this given production demands a specific competence: the ability to create an interface that aggregates value and usability to the user interaction.

When the individuals have their first contact with the series and know the storyline, the system must invite them to choose the narrative genre each one wants to watch (or the character to be emphasized), or even let the algorithm who has read each user profile decides. From the initial information, the software would start to create a story from fragments of scenes previously available in the database. In other words, the system would be designed to be capable of choosing a sequence of scenes to compose a narrative unity – a chapter – and editing them with the necessary elements (music, noises, colors, etc.) to create the atmospheres expected by each separate individual.

Hitherto we were considering the Player on its most basic level, as part of the Audience. The resulting chapter can, them, generate some level of engagement from the users. If they liked it, each one can share their exclusive content on their social networks, preferable from within the platform, supporting the most basic level of synthetization. At the same time, another tool can collect opinions and supply the information database that serve as guidance for the Producers (and the system) during the design. If different Audiences follow the same path, it is possible to sharp both the definitions of the algorithms and the lines of the script.

Another possibility to this phase is to allow the Audience members to interact with and change the story, habilitating them in the third level, as Modifiers. So, the design of the product must anticipate the possible alterations a user may want to make. An Improver may want to add or delete scenes, change soundtracks, re-edit, etc. A Remixer could create memes or other sharable content, such as music videos, or mix different narrative lines into a new storytelling. The handiness of those tools and of the modifiable content can be predicted in the platform, so the system can collect information about the alterations to supply the Producers. From the observation of the Modifiers' works shared with the Producers or with other individuals, another important set of data can be acquired: the significations and resignification of the storytelling. Also, the feedback from Modifiers can even help to improve the tools used in the creation of content.

To the most part of the common seriated audiovisual work, the creation process is never completed when people start to watch the productions. Regarding our example, the Producers would use the continuous flow of information to redesign the interaction route and the storytelling continuities, now supported by the users.

An alternative to this example would be the use of a software-generated animation instead of pre-shot live action sequences. The character's texts and the narrative contexts would be more flexible in a responsive storytelling analyzed and controlled by a computer. Reaching the limit of all these possibilities, it is possible to propose that the machine itself would become the Producer. The analysis of the profile and the actions history of an individual would allow the generation of personalized content, that is, the "generative creation of the storytelling" [17]. The terms "creation" and "authorship" would then be relativized, but this discussion exceeds the scope of this text.

Both examples – the real and the projected – show the recurring need of working the software interfaces the individual will use to access the content, thus being part of the storytelling creation process (even when the audiovisual content produced to the broadcast is transported into the web environment). Likewise, the viewers must be analyzed also as users, altering the way the target audience is defined for an audiovisual product. There is one great difference between the Audience Studies and the HCI Studies during the advent of an audiovisual product. While the first always concerned about the speedy and the instantaneity a content reaches the audience through the Broadcast model, the HCI field, priming for the quality of usage, requires more time of research and development until the definitive application. The projected example showed, however, that this research can be performed concomitantly to the process of realization of the audiovisual work, and to its fruition.

5 Conclusion

This paper proposed a graphic workflow of production, interaction and fruition methods for Audiovisual Design. Different scenarios and roles performed by individuals during the procedures of access, the choice of content, the criterion for sharing, and feedback were considered. The graphic plan is based primarily upon the dynamics inherent to the spread of content, to which there is not anymore a central entity controlling the transmission of messages. The coexistence of this new communication model (the Spreadable) with the Broadcast and the Stickness ones has been contemplated, since different roles inherent to each model can be assumed by one individual during the act of content fruition.

The workflow has two practical applications. First, it offers tools that integrate HCI and Audience Studies to analyze concluded productions. Second, it can be used to predict interactions and propose new products, compatible with the technical and theoretical frames required in modern, attractive content. The set of methodologies used to support this workflow received the name Audiovisual Design, and was assembled around four lines that represent the main concerns a producer should have while designing audiovisual productions: the Individual, the Motivation, the Experience and the Content.

The intersections between the roles of the Audience, the Synthesizer, the Modifier, the Player and the Producer are easily analyzed from the point of view of the technologies and interaction interfaces used by individuals. As a result, usability problems or issues concerning value perception can be identified, generating data for an upgrade of the audiovisual product, from the story script to the interactive software.

The graphical workflow of Audiovisual Design presented in this work was robust enough to analyze two proposed scenarios, one real and one projected. However, more studies must be conducted to identify the key competences required for the individual change from one role to another, and in which contexts they are more relevant. These competences represent a central element to the comprehension of the motivations that lead to moments of passive audience or of an active interaction.

Moreover, the workflow is complex enough to predict applications that use the currently available tools, but it must remain open to incorporate technological changes that can reverse the design flow. Cognitive aspects and reinterpretations on the psychological bases of the HCI and the audience also can impact the flow. This evolution alters mainly the role of the Player, that now partially overlays the other roles. With more interaction tools available and, consequently, more people showing active attitudes towards the audiovisual product, the tendency will be the Player becoming more present and much more relevant during the design.

Finally, the Audiovisual Design as described in this paper will hardly be applied on its full version in the short term, largely due to the production costs and the deficiency of competences among people from every role to use all available tools. To mention some examples, in a country like Brazil a great part of the population still do not use the internet, and the network is important in most of the predictable scenarios. Likewise, the university formation of an audiovisual producer, when incorporates something about the digital systems, barely mentions something other than the basics of the web. Nonetheless, the Audiovisual Design remains a valid methodological set since it allows to think every phase of the design process as an isolated process. Also, it adds elements to the debate about the formation of the professionals who will produce this type of content.

References

1. Mattelart, A., Mattelart, M.: História das Teorias da Comunicação. Edições Loyola, São Paulo (BR), 10th edn. (2007)
2. Souza, J.P.: Elementos de Teoria e Pesquisa da Comunicação e dos Media. Edições Universidade Fernando Pessoa, Porto (PT), 2nd edn. (2006)
3. Hall, S.: A Identidade Cultural na Pós-modernidade. DP&A Editora, Rio de Janeiro (BR), 7th edn. (2003)
4. Ortiz, R.: Universalismo e Diversidade. Boitempo, São Paulo (BR) (2015)
5. Bolter, J.D., Grusin, R.: Remediation: Understanding New Media. MIT Press, Cambridge (2000)

6. Jenkins, H., Ford, S., Green, J.: Spreadable Media: Creating Value and Meaning in a Networked Culture, Kindle edn. New York University Press, London, New York (2013)
7. McQuail, D.: Audience Analysis. Sage Publications, London (1997)
8. Bermejo, F.: The Internet Audience: Constitution & Measurement. Peter Lang, New York (2007)
9. Callejo, J.: Investigar las audiencias: un analisis cualitativo. Paidos Iberica, Barcelona (SP) (2001)
10. Bailén, A.H.: La audiencia investigada. Gedisa, Barcelona (SP) (2002)
11. Webster, J., Phalen, P.F., Lichty, L.W.: Ratings Analysis: The Theory and Practice of Audience Research, 3rd edn. Routledge, London (2006)
12. Mosco V., Kaye, L.: Questioning the concept of the audience. In: Consuming Audience? Production and Reception in Media Research, pp. 31–46. Hampton Press, Sydney (AU) (2000)
13. Martino, L.: Teorias das Mídias Digitais: Linguagens, Ambientes e Redes. Vozes, Petrópolis (BR), 2nd edition (2015)
14. Gladwell, M.: The Tipping Point, Kindle edn. Sextante, Rio de Janeiro (BR) (2000)
15. Dix, A., Finlay, J., Abowd, G., Beale, R.: Human-Computer Interaction, 3rd edn. Pearson Prentice Hall, London (2004)
16. Elmansy, R.: Characteristics of Human Centered Design (2015). http://www.designorate.com/characteristics-of-human-centered-design/
17. Toscano, R.M., Becker, V.: Sistemas audiovisuais inteligentes: um levantamento das práticas que apontam a dinâmica da narrativa responsiva e generativa. In: Proceedings XVIII Communication Sciences Congress of the Brazilian Northest Region (2016). http://www.portalintercom.org.br/anais/nordeste2016/resumos/R52-2327-1.pdf

Human Computer Interaction Research Through the Lens of a Bibliometric Analysis

Konstantinos Koumaditis[1(✉)] and Tajammal Hussain[1,2]

[1] Department of Business Development and Technology, Aarhus University, Aarhus, Denmark
kkoumaditis@btech.au.dk, tajammal@ciitlahore.edu.pk
[2] Department of Statistics, COMSATS Institute of Information Technology, Lahore, Pakistan

Abstract. Human Computing Interaction (HCI) is an expansive research field that covers various disciplines from computer science and engineering to human factors and social science. Navigating in this multidisciplinary field researchers and developers intensively seek to master the capability to understand the dialogue between humans and computers, reflect on the behaviour change caused by this interaction and encapsulate their knowledge to design, develop and maintain systems. Our paper aims to put in context and highlight the research done on the HCI field so far. To do so we choose a method that can provide a well-carved piece of literature and assure legitimacy in the representation of the research, i.e. a bibliometric analysis. Following this research path, we retrieved a data set of 962 publications covering the period from 1969 to early 2017. The analysis revealed a core set of forty-six articles structuring four main factors of HCI. Preliminary analysis highlights HCI design aspects, data management, user interaction, psychology and cognition and more recent trends in HCI in the workplace, sensors and wearables.

Keywords: Human-Computer interaction · Factor analysis · Bibliometric analysis

1 Introduction

Human Computer Interaction (HCI) has expanded rapidly and steadily for more than four decades. From its origins in human factors engineering and cognitive science into an acclaimed discipline, attracting academics and industry professionals into a multi-discipline dialogue integrating diverse methods, theories and practices. Methodology, theory, and practice in the field of HCI all share similar goals of producing interactive artefacts that can be utilised efficiently, effectively, safely, and with additive user-satisfaction.

Nevertheless, since the early years and the emphasis on usability, HCI has been constantly denoted as the discipline where different epistemologies and paradigms can be reconciled and integrated in an innovative and dynamic intellectual project. Examples of HCI projects may include social and organizational computing, artificial intelligence, computer vision, face recognition, motion tracking, accessibility for the

M. Kurosu (Ed.): HCI 2017, Part I, LNCS 10271, pp. 23–37, 2017.
DOI: 10.1007/978-3-319-58071-5_2

elderly as well as the cognitively and physically impaired, and for all people, and for the widest thinkable spectrum of human interactions (Carroll 2013; Sebe et al. 2005). In more detail, HCI quickly extended from early graphical and desktop office applications to include medical and pedagogical applications, gamification of education, business and innovation, sustainability and resilience, emergency planning and response, and systems to support collaboration and community to name a few.

HCI is cross-disciplinary in its conduct and multi-disciplinary in its roots (Hartson 1998). Hence, the vast body of literature that accumulated the last four decades originates from various disciplines and is disseminated in a wide range of outlets. Publications that include myriad research paradigms and methods, frameworks and models, interface design techniques and devices, technologies and digital artefacts, multi-modal interactions, tool support for model-based user interface specification, and a host of emerging ubiquitous, handheld and context-aware and virtual interactions.

Therefore, taking as a point of departure the need to comprehend and analyse the body of HCI literature, the authors proceeded in a systematic literature research and bibliometric coupling analysis to investigate the issue at hand. The actual selection of relevant literature in this case as in any review is a non-trivial task; yet many literature reviews do not offer clarity about how and why they obtained their specific samples of literature or adequately explicitly express the methods of analysis that were used (Wolfswinkel et al. 2013). The bibliographic analysis not only satisfies the aforementioned good literature review ingredients of clarity and rigorousness, but also delivers greater legitimization of the process. The researcher is unbiased and does not intervene in the choice of the representative publications (the ones that form the representative set), s/he only sets the qualitative constraints (e.g. number of citations) (Waltman et al. 2010). We believe that our choice to apply a bibliometric analysis, a well-established methodology but quite new and undiscovered in the HCI research discipline, enhances the value and originality of this paper.

With this Sect. 1 representing the Introduction to the research, Sect. 2 depicts the Methodology utilised and the parameters and constraints used. Next, Sect. 3 analyses the Findings from this process, Sect. 4 contains the discussion and finally Sect. 5 presents the Conclusions.

2 Methodology

This research aims to enhance the readers' understanding of the research published in the HCI field. To do so, initially we proceeded to a literature investigation and analysis by exploring Elsevier' Scopus database and retrieved a dataset with research publications and citation data for a period from 1969 to early 2017. Previous research has shown that Scopus can be used as a sole data source for citation-based research and evaluation in HCI (Meho and Rogers 2008). In our case in order to ensure the credibility of selected documents, the search was restricted to journal and conference publications available in English language only. For the research the keywords "Human Computer Interaction" was utilised, focusing on the "title" and "keywords" fields of the publication. This process revealed 1,843 publications, spanning in a wide range of dissemination outlets and research interests. To this data, we imposed a qualitative measure of at least-one citation and extracted a data set of 962 publications (depicted in Sect. 3). Progressing our investigation with a sophisticated bibliometric method, we retrieved four factors corresponding to an over 80% representation of our data set (depicted in Sect. 4). A brief account of the bibliometric methodology utilised herein is the subject of the next section.

2.1 Bibliographic Coupling Analysis

Recently, bibliometric methods have gained an increased appreciation as a prolific technique to understand the knowledge base of a research field, especially if the research field is vast and complex to analyse (Acedo et al. 2006; Di Stefano et al. 2010; Vogel and Güttel 2013). One may legitimately argue that the recent interest in the bibliometric analysis is realised due to the increasing accessibility of publication databases containing bibliometrics, such as the number of publications, citations, co-citations, bibliographic couplings etc. As in many sectors, technical and computational advancement has made it feasible to conduct analysis on very large and complex bibliometric data; data that previously would have been difficult to address with limited resources (e.g. time and human resources).

The bibliographic coupling (BGC) used herein is a bibliometric method that identifies the clusters of publications and those linked to each other through the same cited publication (Zupic and Čater 2015). In essence, the number of co-coupled documents defines the strength of links and association (Boyack and Klavans 2010). Following this technique, the bibliographic coupling data is analysed through a software computation (BibExcel) to generate a matrix comprised of the BGC frequency (Persson et al. 2009). Next, to gauge the strength of similarities between the publications, Pearson's correlation coefficient matrix is generated from the BGC matrix (van Eck and Waltman 2014). An advanced multivariate statistical technique of factor analysis is then applied to the correlation matrix to produce clusters (e.g. groups, sets) of publications representing distinguished sub-domains of the research field(s). The details and findings from this process are depicted in the following section.

3 Findings

3.1 Findings from Systematic Literature Search

The span of literature identified, covers a period of forty-seven years as depicted in Fig. 1, with a healthy exponential growth of publications each year (later 2017 data that are not covered herein present a normalization of the exponential growth of publications for year 2016).

Findings of main data set reveal that 42% of the publications hold a computer science subject, while 18% of the publications cover an engineering theme. An overview description of the subjects, their account in publications and their representation percentages are illustrated in Fig. 2. (NOTE: Each publication may hold more than one subject).

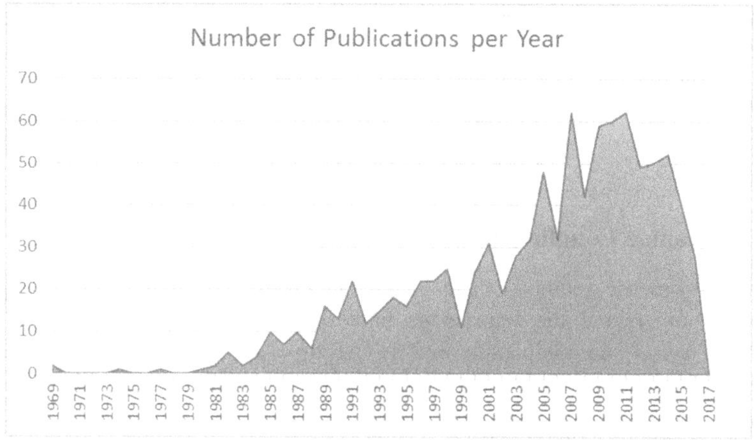

Fig. 1. Number of HCI publications per year

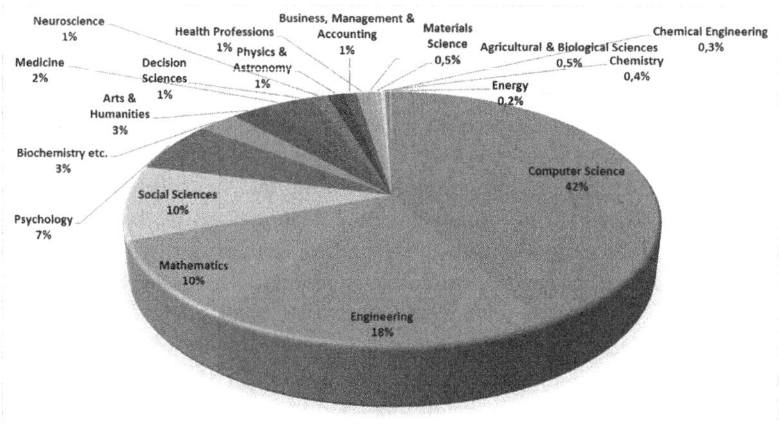

Fig. 2. Main themes

By inspection of the data set with focus on authors with the most publications (regardless of authors order in publication) and narrowing the inspection (for simplicity) to at least four research papers in the field of HCI, a set of twenty-two authors was produced. This is seen in Fig. 3.

Furthermore, the descriptive analysis provided details on the dissemination outlets, as seen in Fig. 4. "*The Lecture Notes Series*" journal and the proceedings from the "*Conference of Human Factors*", both outlets that welcome the technology and human behaviour themes, hold high places among the set of outlets.

To the aforementioned data set (e.g. 962 publications), we ran a series of analytical tests to highlight the authors that inspired the field and ultimately shaped the body of literature with their work. The analysis was based on the use of the 962 publications

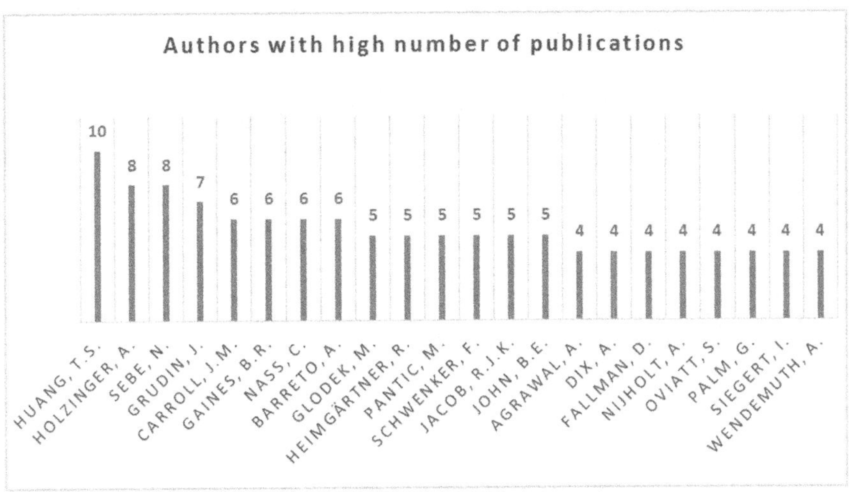

Fig. 3. Researchers with high numbers of publications

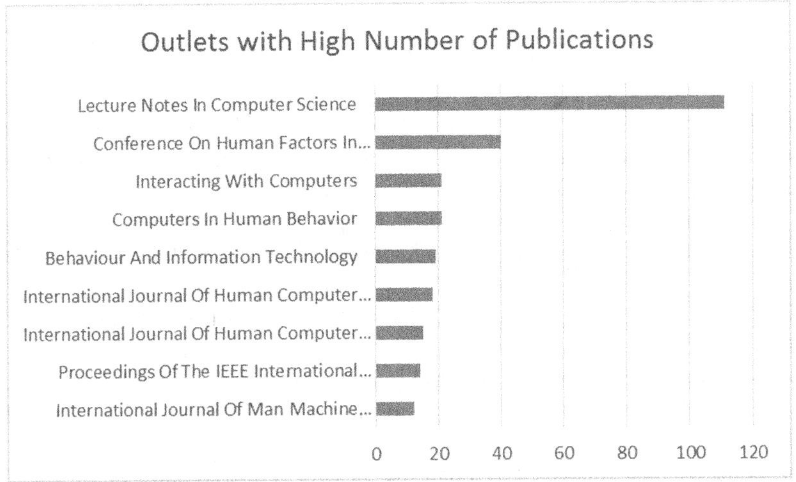

Fig. 4. Source journals of HCI research

(full data in .csv file), the utilisation of VOSviewer software tool and the condition of co-citation of author as a parameter (van Eck and Waltman 2014). The result of this process was a cluster-cloud of the 100 most influential researchers as seen in Fig. 5. In more detail, the figure depicts 100 authors matched in more than twenty clusters (the clustering symbolises authors that are tighter linked in-between them), holding a total number of 1344 links. The relative size of each author's depiction (diameter of cycle symbol) is significant and depicts its linkage strength. For example, Professor Palm

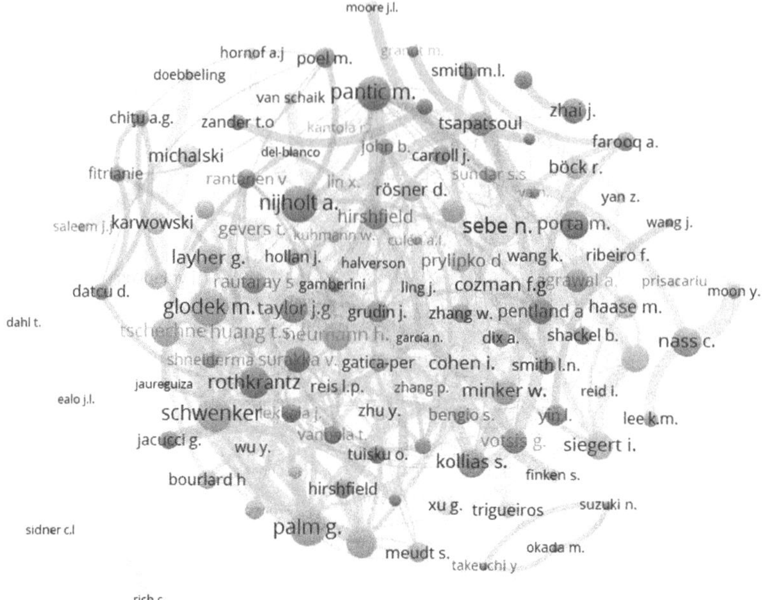

Fig. 5. Top 100 influential researchers of the PT field

from the Institute of Neural Information Processing at Ulm University seen in the bottom right part of the cluster cloud holds a bigger contribution strength compared to his colleague S. Meudt, who is also part of the same cluster.

Observing the results of this analysis, it is apparent that the data set is vast containing many interlinked contributors and intense research clusters that inspired the HCI field.

Additionally, when the focus placed on the co-citation of references (e.g. the references utilised by the authors of the 962 publications) the analysis resulted in a cluster-cloud of one hundred most referred publications, seen in Fig. 6. Moreover, the figure depicts publications matched in seven clusters, holding a total number of 367 links.

The value of this analysis lies not only in observing the impact of well cited publications like Cowie et al. (2001) and MacKenzie (1992) but also in identifying the point of departure for many of these researchers, like well-established reviews like Pavlovic et al. (1997).

Nevertheless, it is evident, that the relative size of the data set and the linkage in-between them, as depicted in the Figs. 5 and 6, provides limited opportunities to understand the HCI field by observation. Thus, in an effort to further explore and investigate this body of literature we proceeded in the use of factor analysis, a method presented in the following sections.

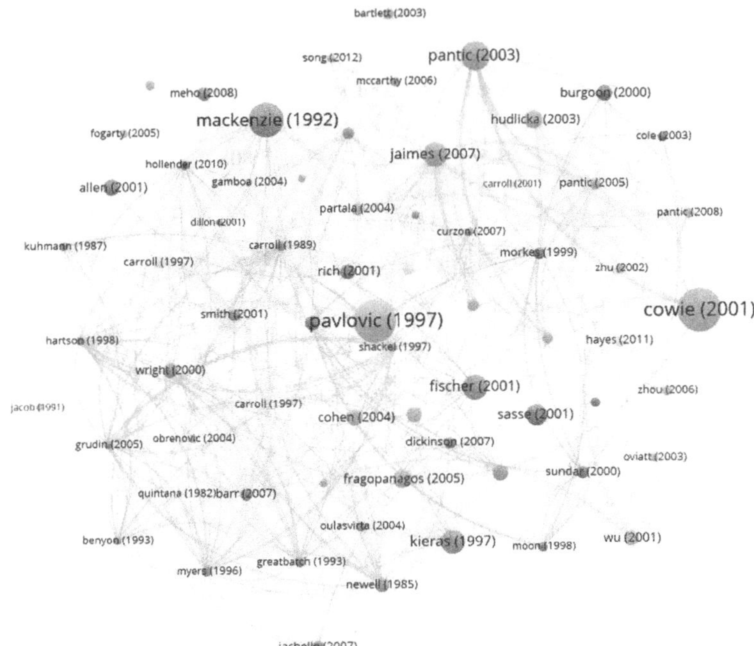

Fig. 6. Frequent *references of the HCI field*

3.2 Findings from the Factor Analysis

An advanced bibliometric coupling matrix was extracted from the Scopus dataset by using Bibexcel software (Persson et al. 2009). The generated coupling matrix comprised of Ri rows and Cj columns where the ricj matrix element shows the frequency of the number of articles cited by both ith and jth publications simultaneously. The bibliographic coupling matrix, was standardized by transforming into correlation bibliographic coupling matrix in order to retrieve coefficients of similarities/dissimilarities between the publications with common research theme and publications with Multivariate Technique (MV) of data reduction, Factor Analysis (FA), was used to extract the distinct aspects of HCI research, and to cluster the correlating articles contributing to a common knowledge base in the field. The correlation bibliographic coupling was analyzed by applying Principal Factor Analysis (PCA) method with Varimax rotation, rotated solutions, and four fixed number of factors, as seen in Table 1 (with the first holding ≈33.5%, the second ≈3.1%, the third ≈2.6% and the fourth ≈2.2% of the total).

The fixed number choice is opted because scree plot suggested a many distributions with each factor after the fourth having a relatively small contribution in explained percentage of variance (<2.0%). Thus, the PCA yielded a set of six factors containing forty-six articles with 81.383% explained variance. As each further incremental factor was explaining an insignificant variance and in order to perform a cohesive analysis, only four factors were retained. Table 2 provides the result core representative set of pattern matrix which is comprised of correlation coefficients associated with each publication.

Table 1. Findings of Factor Analysis (FA) with items and factor loadings

Total variance explained			
Component	Rotation sums of squared loading		
	Total	% of Variance	Cumulative %
1	33,562	65,808	65,808
2	3,103	6,084	71,892
3	2,586	5,071	76,963
4	2,254	4,420	81,383

Table 2. Findings of Factor Analysis (FA) with items and Factor loadings

Authors	Factor loading			
	F1	F2	F3	F4
May et al. (2008)	.994			
Plouznikoff et al. (2006)	.994			
Schwarz et al. (2011)	.994			
McCowan et al. (2003)	.994			
Palacios et al. (2013)	.994			
Carneiro et al. (2016)	.994			
Suzuki et al. (2004)	.993			
Schlick et al. (2010)	.993			
Chavarriaga (2010)	.993			
Yan et al. (2011b)	.993			
Fitrianie et al. (2007)	.993			
Plouznikoff et al. (2005)	.993			
Zhai et al. (2005a)	.993			
Suzuki et al. (2003)	.992			
Yan et al. (2011a)	.992			
Maeda et al. (2006)	.992			
Leiser et al. (1989)	.991			
Zhang et al. (2016b)	.991			
Schwarz et al. (2011)	.991			
Minami et al. (2007)	.990			
Schlick et al. (2003)	.990			
Avons et al. (1989)	.990			
Zhai et al. (2005b)	.990			
Elbahi and Omri (2015)	.990			
Alnuaim et al. (2014)	.990			
Palacios et al. (2013)	.990			
Chathuranga et al. (2010)	.988			
Pimenta et al. (2016)	.988			
Zhang et al. (2016a)	.988			

(continued)

Table 2. *(continued)*

Authors	Factor loading			
	F1	F2	F3	F4
Asare (2010)	.987			
Rantanen et al. (2011)	.986			
Deniz et al. (2004)	.874			
Siegert et al. (2014a)		–.718		
Prylipko et al. (2014)		–.698		
Siegert et al. (2014b)		–.648		
Siegert et al. (2014c)		–.648		
Sebe et al. (2005)			–.686	
Cohen et al. (2004)			–.593	
Sebe et al. (2005)			–.593	
Kächele et al. (2015)			.693	
Scherer et al. (2012)			.670	
Trigueiros et al. (2014)				–.663
Maqueda et al. (2015)				–.663
Schels et al. (2014)				.602
Glodek et al. (2015)				.598
Tang et al. (2015)				–.535

3.3 Factor Analysis

The core representative set of forty-six publications divided in four factors, was explored for common themes and patters. This resulted in four descriptions where each factor is analysed with the representative publications of each group:

F1–HCI Theories, Associations and Interaction with Devices. The first factor (F1) is the largest set with thirty-three publications from as early as 1989 to more recent ones as 2016. This set highlights work that emphasizes on theories, associations and devices. Moreover, the authors propose research models and identify theoretical issues (Yan et al. 2011a,b), discuss HCI in connection with effectiveness in education (Alnuaim et al. 2014) and workers' performance management (Carneiro et al. 2016) and associate HCI with specific theories as ambient intelligence (Maeda et al. 2006; Minami et al. 2007), complexity (Schlick et al. 2003; Schlick et al. 2010) and crisis management (Fitrianie et al. 2007). Furthermore, this set of publications includes research on the link between HCI and devices. For example input devices (Asare 2010) composite devices and systems (Chavarriaga et al. 2010), sensors (Palacios et al. 2013) and wearables (Plouznikoff et al. 2006).

F2–Communication Attributes and HCI. The second factor (F2), constitutes a condense but inspiring literature topic, the research on HCI and human linguistic attributes, or more specifically human speech and its underlining attributes like dialog events, feedback signals and interaction corpora. In more detail, in this four publications' set, published in 2014, the authors address issues of automatically detecting significant dialog events (SDEs) in naturalistic HCI, deducing trait-specific conclusions relevant for the design of spoken dialog systems (Prylipko et al. 2014) and investigate the influence of specific feedback signals, known as discourse particles (DPs), with communication style and psychological characteristics within a naturalistic HCI (Siegert et al. 2014b). In addition, they depict their investigation for emotional annotated interaction corpora and present methods to improve the reliability (Siegert et al. 2014a) and provide design guidelines for future automatic designated "companion" systems (Prylipko et al. 2014).

F3–Data classification and User(s) issues for HCI applications. The publications in the third factor (F3) differentiate in comparison to the previous factors, as the authors place their focus on the aggregation and classification of data. In more detail they discuss training probabilistic classifiers with labelled and unlabelled data for HCI applications and show how the resulting algorithms are successfully employed in facial expression recognition, face detection and recognition and skin detection (Cohen et al. 2004; Sebe et al. 2005; Sebe et al. 2005). In the same lines additional research exposes the issue of evaluation of the results that are computed using statistical classifiers (Kächele et al. 2015). Yet, the authors also propose the use of fuzzy memberships in order to model affective user state and endorse respective fuzzy performance measures (Kächele et al. 2015). This set also includes a generic framework that may minimise difficulties associated with real world user behaviour analysis (i.e. uncertainty about the ground truth of the current state, subject independence, dynamic real-time analysis of multimodal information, and the processing of incomplete or erroneous inputs, e.g. after sensor failure or lack of input) (Scherer et al. 2012).

F4–HCI and Recognition Systems. The fourth factor (F4) includes publications dealing with HCI and hand-gesture recognition systems. Hand gestures are a powerful way for human communication, with lots of potential applications in the area of HCI. In this set of publications, the authors' propose various approaches with significant results. In more detail, one may observe a generic system architecture based on computer vision and machine learning, able to be used with any interface for real-time human-machine interaction (Trigueiros et al. 2014), a robust vision-based hand-gesture recognition system divided into three stages: detection, tracking, and recognition (Maqueda et al. 2015), and a technique for three dimensional non-contact sensing of hand motion through electrostatic field (Tang et al. 2015). In similar lines the information fusion principles (such as perception-level fusion, knowledge-based fusion and application-level fusion) in cognitive technical systems (CTS) architectures for Companion Technologies are illustrated with examples of characteristic algorithms (Glodek et al. 2015)

4 Discussion

Applying the Factor Analysis in the literature segment (e.g. forty-six publications with a 81.3% representation) provides a distinctive analytical lens into the past, current and future dimensions of HCI research. Through our analysis we observed that the majority of authors and cases were resonating in Europe (32/46 publications), following Asia (6/46 publications), USA (5/46 publications) and the rest from Canada and Africa. This finding supports the notion of western and developing countries increased interest in HCI research.

Our analysis did not highlight any novel HCI approach but rather adds emphasis on well-document HCI sub-fields and research interests like gaze-tracking (Rantanen et al. 2011), face-recognition (Sebe et al. 2005) and affective computing (Kächele et al. 2015; Schels et al. 2014) and in more recent studies the utilization of sensors (Palacios et al. 2013) and wearables (Rantanen et al. 2011).

Supplementary to the aforementioned research and supportive to our own experiences with HCI, we identified some emerging trends relating HCI and the workplace. Especially, the utilisation of technology in the professional workspace and investigation of the underlined HCI issues like monitor and improving performance (Carneiro et al. 2016) and mental fatigue and efficient fatigue management initiatives, mainly in the context of desk jobs (Pimenta et al. 2016) seem to be trends that are scaling up on the research agenda.

5 Conclusions

Today, HCI is a vast and multifaceted community, bound by the evolving concept of usability, and the integrating commitment to value human activity and experience as the primary driver in technology.

Over the last decades, the interest in HCI has grown and so has the body of literature. A literature that spawns from and thus links, a variety of disciplines. We observed this dissemination flow in the form of productive discussions, experiments and results in an increasing collection of scientific conferences and journals. In an effort to outline, the multidiscipline body of HCI literature and formulate a deeper, more profound understanding of HCI issues we proceeded in a literature analysis through the lens of a bibliometric investigation. Our analysis started by covering the period from 1969 to 2017. The data was analysed in relation to their publication year (seen in Fig. 1), subject area (seen in Fig. 2), researchers (seen in Fig. 3) and publication outlet (seen in Fig. 4). Additionally, we investigated the body of literature and depicted the most influential authors (seen in Fig. 5) and the origins of HCI in terms of our data set (seen in Fig. 6) thus, providing a clear overview of the topic.

Nevertheless, the novelty of this research derives from the findings of the explorative focused analysis of the representative data set (forty-six publications), which revealed interesting facts about HCI as a developing research field. With factor analysis, we identified four core sets of research from theoretical concepts, design aspects and association to user issues, affective computing and recognition systems and sensors. Thus, one can follow the methodology utilised herein and investigate in depth one or more of the HCI intriguing aspects.

References

Acedo, F.J., Barroso, C., Galan, J.L.: The resource-based theory: dissemination and main trends. Strateg. Manag. J. **27**(7), 621–636 (2006)

Alnuaim, A., Caleb-Solly, P., Perry, C.: Evaluating the effectiveness of a mobile location-based intervention for improving human-computer interaction students' understanding of context for design. Int. J. Mob. Hum. Comput. Interact. **6**(3), 16–31 (2014). doi:10.4018/ijmhci.2014070102

Asare, P.: A sign of the times: a composite input device for human-computer interactions. IEEE Potentials **29**(2), 9–14 (2010). doi:10.1109/MPOT.2010.936235

Avons, S.E., Leiser, R.G., Carr, D.J.: Paralanguage and human-computer interaction. Part 1: identification of recorded vocal segregates. Behav. Inf. Technol. **8**(1), 13–21 (1989). doi:10.1080/01449298908914534

Boyack, K.W., Klavans, R.: Co-citation analysis, bibliographic coupling, and direct citation: Which citation approach represents the research front most accurately? J. Am. Soc. Inform. Sci. Technol. **61**(12), 2389–2404 (2010)

Carneiro, D., Pimenta, A., Gonçalves, S., Neves, J., Novais, P.: Monitoring and improving performance in human-computer interaction. Concurrency Comput. **28**(4), 1291–1309 (2016). doi:10.1002/cpe.3635

Carroll, J.M.: Human Computer Interaction-Brief Intro. The Encyclopedia of Human-Computer Interaction, 2nd edn. (2013)

Chavarriaga, R., Biasiucci, A., Förster, K., Roggen, D., Tröster, G., Del Millán, J.R.: Adaptation of hybrid human-computer interaction systems using EEG error-related potentials. In: Paper Presented at the 2010 Annual International Conference of the IEEE Engineering in Medicine and Biology Society, EMBC 2010 (2010)

Cohen, I., Cozman, F.G., Sebe, N., Cirelo, M.C., Huang, T.S.: Semisupervised learning of classifiers: theory, algorithms, and their application to human-computer interaction. IEEE Trans. Pattern Anal. Mach. Intell. **26**(12), 1553–1567 (2004). doi:10.1109/TPAMI.2004.127

Cowie, R., Douglas-Cowie, E., Tsapatsoulis, N., Votsis, G., Kollias, S., Fellenz, W., Taylor, J.G.: Emotion recognition in human-computer interaction. IEEE Signal Process. Mag. **18**(1), 32–80 (2001). doi:10.1109/79.911197

Deniz, O., Falcon, A., Mendez, J., Castrillon, M.: Useful computer vision techniques for human-robot interaction. In: Campilho, A., Kamel, M. (eds.) ICIAR 2004. LNCS, vol. 3212, pp. 725–732. Springer, Heidelberg (2004). doi:10.1007/978-3-540-30126-4_88

Di Stefano, G., Peteraf, M., Verona, G.: Dynamic capabilities deconstructed: a bibliographic investigation into the origins, development, and future directions of the research domain. Ind. Corp. Change **19**(4), 1187–1204 (2010). doi:10.1093/icc/dtq027

Elbahi, A., Omri, M.N.: Conditional random fields for web user task recognition based on human computer interaction. In: Paper Presented at the 23rd International Conference in Central Europe on Computer Graphics, Visualization and Computer Vision, WSCG 2015–Posters Proceedings (2015)

Fitrianie, S., Poppe, R., Bui, T.H., Chiţu, A.G., Datcu, D., Dor, R., Zwiers, J.: A multimodal human-computer interaction framework for research into crisis management. In: Paper Presented at the Intelligent Human Computer Systems for Crisis Response and Management, ISCRAM 2007 Academic Proceedings Papers (2007)

Glodek, M., Honold, F., Geier, T., Krell, G., Nothdurft, F., Reuter, S., Schwenker, F.: Fusion paradigms in cognitive technical systems for human-computer interaction. Neurocomputing **161**, 17–37 (2015). doi:10.1016/j.neucom.2015.01.076

Hartson, H.R.: Human-computer interaction: Interdisciplinary roots and trends. J. Syst. Softw. **43**(2), 103–118 (1998)

Kasun Chathuranga, S., Samarawickrama, K.C., Chandima, H.M.L., Chathuranga, K.G.T.D., Abeykoon, A.M.H.S.: Hands free interface for human computer interaction. In: Paper Presented at the Proceedings of the 2010 5th International Conference on Information and Automation for Sustainability, ICIAFs 2010 (2010)

Kächele, M. et al.: On annotation and evaluation of multi-modal corpora in affective human-computer interaction. In: Böck, R., Bonin, F., Campbell, N., Poppe, R. (eds.) MA3HMI 2014 Workshop. LNCS, vol 8757, pp. 35–44. Springer, Cham. doi:10.1007/978-3-319-15557-9_4

Leiser, R.G., Avons, S.E., Carr, D.J.: Paralanguage and human-computer interaction. part 2: Comprehension of synthesized vocal segregates. Behav. Inf. Technol. **8**(1), 23–32 (1989). doi:10.1080/01449298908914535

MacKenzie, I.S.: Fitts' law as a research and design tool in human-computer interaction. Hum.-Comput. Interact. **7**(1), 91–139 (1992). doi:10.1207/s15327051hci0701_3

Maeda, E., Minami, Y., Miyoshi, M., Sawaki, M., Sawada, H., Nakamura, A., Higashinaka, R.: The world of mushrooms - a transdisciplinary approach to human-computer interaction with ambient intelligence. NTT Tech. Rev. **4**(12), 17–24 (2006)

Maqueda, A.I., Del-Blanco, C.R., Jaureguizar, F., García, N.: Human-computer interaction based on visual hand-gesture recognition using volumetric spatiograms of local binary patterns. Comput. Vis. Image Underst. **141**, 126–137 (2015). doi:10.1016/j.cviu.2015.07.009

May, M., George, S., Prévôt, P.: A closer look at tracking human and computer interactions in web-based communications. Interact. Technol. Smart Educ. **5**(3), 170–188 (2008). doi:10.1108/17415650810908258

McCowan, I., Gatica-Perez, D., Bengio, S., Moore, D., Bourlard, H.: Towards computer understanding of human interactions. In: Aarts, E., Collier, René W., Loenen, E., Ruyter, B. (eds.) EUSAI 2003. LNCS, vol. 2875, pp. 235–251. Springer, Heidelberg (2003). doi:10.1007/978-3-540-39863-9_18

Meho, L.I., Rogers, Y.: Citation counting, citation ranking, and h-index of human-computer interaction researchers: a comparison of scopus and web of science. J. Am. Soc. Inform. Sci. Technol. **59**(11), 1711–1726 (2008). doi:10.1002/asi.20874

Minami, Y., Sawaki, M., Dohsaka, K., Higashinaka, R., Ishizuka, K., Isozaki, H., Maeda, E.: The world of mushrooms: human-computer interaction prototype systems for ambient intelligence. In: Paper Presented at the Proceedings of the 9th International Conference on Multimodal Interfaces, ICMI 2007 (2007)

Palacios, J.M., Sagués, C., Montijano, E., Llorente, S.: Human-computer interaction based on hand gestures using RGB-D sensors. Sensors (Basel, Switzerland) **13**(9), 11842–11860 (2013). doi:10.3390/s130911842

Pavlovic, V.I., Sharma, R., Huang, T.S.: Visual interpretation of hand gestures for human-computer interaction: a review. IEEE Trans. Pattern Anal. Mach. Intell. **19**(7), 677–695 (1997). doi:10.1109/34.598226

Persson, O., Danell, R., Schneider, J.W.: How to use Bibexcel for various types of bibliometric analysis. In: Celebrating scholarly Communication Studies: A Festschrift for Olle Persson at his 60th Birthday, pp. 9–24 (2009)

Pimenta, A., Carneiro, D., Neves, J., Novais, P.: A neural network to classify fatigue from human-computer interaction. Neurocomputing **172**, 413–426 (2016). doi:10.1016/j.neucom.2015.03.105

Plouznikoff, A., Plouznikoff, N., Robert, J.M., Desmarais, M.: Enhancing human-machine interactions: Virtual interface alteration through wearable computers. In: Paper Presented at the Conference on Human Factors in Computing Systems–Proceedings (2006)

Plouznikoff, N., Plouznikoff, A., Robert, J.M.: Object augmentation through ecological human–wearable computer interactions. In: Paper Presented at the 2005 IEEE International Conference on Wireless and Mobile Computing, Networking and Communications, WiMob 2005 (2005)

Prylipko, D., Rösner, D., Siegert, I., Günther, S., Friesen, R., Haase, M., Wendemuth, A.: Analysis of significant dialog events in realistic human-computer interaction. J. Multimodal User Interfaces **8**(1), 75–86 (2014). doi:10.1007/s12193-013-0144-x

Rantanen, V., Vanhala, T., Tuisku, O., Niemenlehto, P.H., Verho, J., Surakka, V., Lekkala, J.: A wearable, wireless gaze tracker with integrated selection command source for human-computer interaction. IEEE Trans. Inf Technol. Biomed. **15**(5), 795–801 (2011). doi:10.1109/TITB.2011.2158321

Schels, M., Kächele, M., Glodek, M., Hrabal, D., Walter, S., Schwenker, F.: Using unlabeled data to improve classification of emotional states in human computer interaction. J. Multimodal User Interfaces **8**(1), 5–16 (2014). doi:10.1007/s12193-013-0133-0

Scherer, S., Glodek, M., Layher, G., Schels, M., Schmidt, M., Brosch, T., Palm, G.: A generic framework for the inference of user states in human computer interaction: how patterns of low level behavioral cues support complex user states in HCI. J. Multimodal User Interfaces **6**(3–4), 117–141 (2012). doi:10.1007/s12193-012-0093-9

Schlick, C.M., Winkelholz, C., Motz, F., Brütting, M.: Complexity and human-computer interaction. In: Paper Presented at the Proceedings of the IEEE International Conference on Systems, Man and Cybernetics (2003)

Schlick, C.M., Winkelholz, C., Motz, F., Duckwitz, S., Grandt, M.: Complexity assessment of human-computer interaction. Theor. Issues Ergon. Sci. **11**(3), 151–173 (2010). doi:10.1080/14639220802609903

Schwarz, L.A., Bigdelou, A., Navab, N.: Learning gestures for customizable human-computer interaction in the operating room. In: Fichtinger, G., Martel, A., Peters, T. (eds.) MICCAI 2011. LNCS, vol. 6891, pp. 129–136. Springer, Heidelberg (2011). doi:10.1007/978-3-642-23623-5_17

Sebe, N., Cohen, I., Cozman, F.G., Gevers, T., Huang, T.S.: Learning probabilistic classifiers for human-computer interaction applications. Multimedia Syst. **10**(6), 484–498 (2005). doi:10.1007/s00530-005-0177-4

Sebe, N., Cohen, I., Huang, T.S., Gevers, T.: Human-computer interaction: a Bayesian network approach. In: Paper Presented at the ISSCS 2005: International Symposium on Signals, Circuits and Systems–Proceedings (2005)

Siegert, I., Böck, R., Wendemuth, A.: Inter-rater reliability for emotion annotation in human-computer interaction: Comparison and methodological improvements. J. Multimodal User Interfaces **8**(1), 17–28 (2014a). doi:10.1007/s12193-013-0129-9

Siegert, I., Haase, M., Prylipko, D., Wendemuth, A.: Discourse particles and user characteristics in naturalistic human-computer interaction. In: Kurosu, M. (ed.) HCI 2014. LNCS, vol. 8511, pp. 492–501. Springer, Cham (2014b). doi:10.1007/978-3-319-07230-2_47

Siegert, I., Prylipko, D., Hartmann, K., Böck, R., Wendemuth, A.: Investigating the form-function-relation of the discourse particle "hm" in a naturalistic human-computer interaction. In: Smart Innovation, Systems and Technologies, vol. 26, pp. 387–394 (2014c)

Suzuki, N., Kakehi, K., Takeuchi, Y., Okada, M.: Social effects of the speed of hummed sounds on human-computer interaction. Int. J. Hum. Comput. Stud. **60**(4), 455–468 (2004). doi:10.1016/j.ijhcs.2003.09.007

Suzuki, N., Takeuchi, Y., Ishii, K., Okada, M.: Effects of echoic mimicry using hummed sounds on human-computer interaction. Speech Commun. **40**(4), 559–573 (2003). doi:10.1016/S0167-6393(02)00180-2

Tang, K., Chen, X., Zheng, W., Han, Q., Li, P.: A non-contact technique using electrostatics to sense three-dimensional hand motion for human computer interaction. J. Electrostat. **77**, 101–109 (2015). doi:10.1016/j.elstat.2015.07.006

Trigueiros, P., Ribeiro, F., Reis, L.P.: Generic system for human-computer gesture interaction. In: Paper Presented at the 2014 IEEE International Conference on Autonomous Robot Systems and Competitions, ICARSC 2014 (2014)

Eck, N.J., Waltman, L.: Visualizing bibliometric networks. In: Ding, Y., Rousseau, R., Wolfram, D. (eds.) Measuring Scholarly Impact, pp. 285–320. Springer, Cham (2014). doi:10.1007/978-3-319-10377-8_13

Vogel, R., Güttel, W.H.: The dynamic capability view in strategic management: A bibliometric review. Int. J. Manage. Rev. **15**(4), 426–446 (2013)

Waltman, L., van Eck, N.J., Noyons, E.C.: A unified approach to mapping and clustering of bibliometric networks. J. Informetrics **4**(4), 629–635 (2010)

Wolfswinkel, J.F., Furtmueller, E., Wilderom, C.P.: Using grounded theory as a method for rigorously reviewing literature. Eur. J. Inf. Syst. **22**(1), 45–55 (2013)

Yan, Z., Kantola, R., Zhang, P.: A research model for human-computer trust interaction. In: Paper Presented at the Proceedings of the 10th IEEE International Conference on Trust, Security and Privacy in Computing and Communications, TrustCom 2011, 8th IEEE International Conference on Embedded Software and Systems, ICESS 2011, 6th International Conference on FCST 2011 (2011a)

Yan, Z., Kantola, R., Zhang, P.: Theoretical issues in the study of trust in human-computer interaction. In: Paper Presented at the Proceedings of the 10th IEEE International Conference on Trust, Security and Privacy in Computing and Communications, TrustCom 2011, 8th IEEE International Conference on Embedded Software and Systems, ICESS 2011, 6th International Conference on FCST 2011 (2011b)

Zhai, J., Barreto, A.B., Chin, C., Li, C.: Realization of stress detection using psychophysiological signals for improvement of human-computer interactions. In: Paper Presented at the Conference Proceedings–IEEE SOUTHEASTCON (2005a)

Zhai, J., Barreto, A.B., Chin, C., Li, C.: User stress detection in human-computer interactions. Biomed. Sci. Instrum. **41**, 277–282 (2005)

Zhang, W., Smith, M.L., Smith, L.N., Farooq, A.: Eye center localization and gaze gesture recognition for human-computer interaction. J. Opt. Soc. Am. A **33**(3), 314–325 (2016a). doi:10.1364/JOSAA.33.000314

Zhang, W., Smith, M.L., Smith, L.N., Farooq, A.: Gender and gaze gesture recognition for human-computer interaction. Comput. Vis. Image Underst. **149**, 32–50 (2016b). doi:10.1016/j.cviu.2016.03.014

Zupic, I., Čater, T.: Bibliometric methods in management and organization. Organ. Res. Methods **18**(3), 429–472 (2015)

Guidelines for a University Short Course on Human-Computer Interaction

Martin Maguire(✉)

Loughborough Design School, Loughborough University, Leicester LE11 3TU, UK
M.C.Maguire@lboro.ac.uk

Abstract. This paper presents experience in running HCI short course as part of an Ergonomics Masters programme. It comprises of a series of lectures, and practical exercises to develop the skills and knowledge required for undertaking interaction design work and usability and UX evaluation. These cover the psychology underlying human-computer interaction and user experience, user-centred design process (UCD), user research, prototyping, user testing, control of systems, information architecture, persona and scenario based design techniques, user interface design, usability testing, and HCI in certain application areas. The course tries to adopt best practice based on constructivist learning and Bloom's taxonomy where students can relate the teaching to their own experiences and are guided through a UCD process starting with research and creating an application. A SWOT analysis highlights some key areas where the course can improve if it is to keep up with learning techniques and technologies and to become efficient in a world where University courses are becoming more expensive. Opportunities for the future of the course are to learn more technical tools for prototyping, breaking out of the classroom to interact with people in the real world, and better integration of all presentations to create providing a stronger unifying HCI theme. Guidelines are offered for organisers of similar courses in the future.

Keywords: Human-Computer Interaction · Courses · Training · Education · Teaching · Learning

1 Introduction

Loughborough University's Ergonomics Masters programme is based on a style of teaching where each module runs for one week. This model of teaching is regarded as being suited to mature students in work enabling them to take short periods out from their work to attend a single course module and to carry out private study and coursework assignments between modules. One of the course modules is Human-Computer Interaction which provides students with a working knowledge and practical experience of the design and evaluation of human-computer interfaces to interactive products and systems. It provides with the skills to conduct user research, develop representative user personas and scenarios of use, create wireframes to test on paper and create a more realistic software prototype for usability testing.

M. Kurosu (Ed.): HCI 2017, Part I, LNCS 10271, pp. 38–46, 2017.
DOI: 10.1007/978-3-319-58071-5_3

The paper discusses issues relating to HCI teaching and practical sessions that may be useful to organisers of similar short courses.

2 Learning Theory

Constructivism is a theory, proposed by educationalists such as Jean Piaget and Jerome Bruner about how people learn. Drawing on observation and scientific study, it is based on the idea that people are not a blank slate to be filled with content knowledge, but construct their own understanding and knowledge of the world, through experiencing things and reflecting on those experiences. When a student encounters something new, they have to reconcile it with their previous ideas and experiences, possibly revising what they believe, or discarding the new information as irrelevant. People are active creators of their own knowledge. But to do this, they must ask questions, explore, and assess what they know [1].

In the classroom, the constructivist view of learning can point towards a number of different teaching practices. In general, it usually means encouraging students to use active techniques (experiments, real-world problem solving) to create more knowledge and then to reflect on and talk about what they are doing and how their understanding is changing. The teacher tries to comprehend the students' pre-existing conceptions, and guides the activity to address them and then build on them.

Constructivist teachers encourage students to constantly review how classroom exercises are improving their understanding of a subject. By questioning themselves and their strategies, students become experienced learners acquiring the tools to help them keep learning. With a well-planned classroom environment, the students learn how to learn. The approach is summed up by Benjamin Franklin's famous quotation: "Tell me and I forget, teach me and I may remember, involve me and I learn."

The HCI course tries to apply constructivist teaching by (1) presenting examples of principles that students can relate to in daily life, (2) encouraging discussion during presentations, (3) providing principles that are tested in practice, and (4) reflecting on the main lessons learned during the course and in completing the coursework. However it is necessary to take account of the learning styles that students are familiar with before starting the course. International students, for instance, may be used to a more traditional style of teaching that teachers need to extend and challenge to enable them to learn in new ways. The HCI course also includes traditional teaching where the lecturers present ideas to the students to absorb, but the in-class discussions and exercises can help to engage teachers more and enhance their learning. By providing learning materials within a virtual learning environment, this allows students to follow lectures on laptops and tablets without having to write many notes down, thus freeing them to think about and understand the information presented by the teacher better.

Benjamin Bloom's Taxonomy of Educational Objectives [2] is a good basis for thinking through how to develop student competence by stages from three perspectives: cognitive, affective, and psychomotor. On each of these dimensions, a hierarchy of knowledge with associated verbs is offered that can be used in developing learning outcomes. Thus for cognitive learning, the scale points can be thought of as: recalling data, understanding, applying (using), analysing, synthesizing and evaluating.

Thus learning starts from absorbing information and principles (e.g. user interface evaluation heuristics), moving on to understanding them, knowing how to apply them, critiquing them and adapting them for a particular application area (e.g. mobile devices or speech based interfaces).

Figure 1 shows the process of learning that the course tutors generally follow, based upon these learning theories:

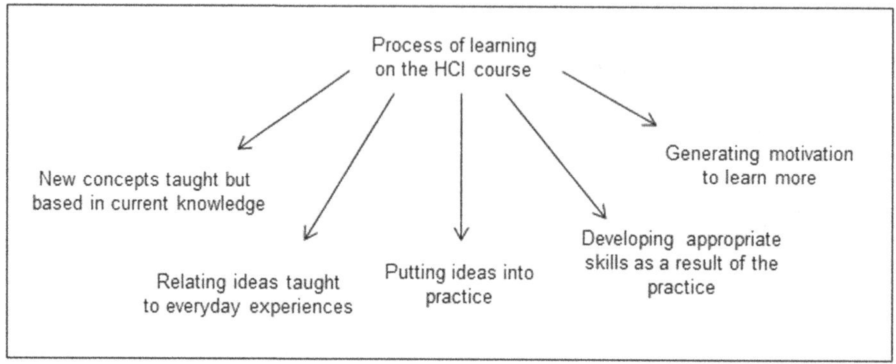

Fig. 1. Process of learning within the HCI course

3 Course Aims and Attendee Needs

The course aims to give students a working knowledge and practical experience in the design and evaluation of interactive applications and systems whatever their role. Some of the students on the Ergonomics programme are physiotherapists, health and safety specialists, care workers, nursing staff and administrators, so may need to evaluate interactive systems provided as part of their professional work. By taking the course they will better understand the principles behind usable systems enabling them to fulfil roles as user representatives within system design or procurement.

Another group of attendees are engineers, technicians, business people and product designers who may be involved in the creation of software systems and for whom a better understanding of HCI principles will assist them when working within the system design process.

A third group are those planning to be practitioners such as usability specialist, interaction designers or user experience designers. The module can give them a better understanding of the principles and practices enabling them to conduct activities such as user research, requirements specification, concept development or rapid prototyping within an HCI-related project.

4 Content and Module Structure

The course covers a range of HCI related topics including:

- Introduction to the history of HCI and design principles
- Psychology of HCI and User Experience design
- Human-centred design process
- User research
- User interface design

Table 1. Course timetable

Course timetable	
Monday morning **Presentation:** Introduction to HCI **Presentation:** Psychology of HCI	**Afternoon** *Coursework 1 introduction – An assignment to develop a simulated application working in groups* *Brainstorm of ideas and identification of questions and locations to conduct user research* Presentation: Information architecture for web
Tuesday morning **Presentation:** Persuasive HCI (gamification) **Presentation:** Ergonomics aspects of the control of systems (overview of systems concepts, the importance of feedback and control, user roles, and user interface design considerations)	**Afternoon** **Presentation:** Briefing prior to user research exercise *User research exercise for insights (outside class) and generation of design concept on A3 sheet* *Expert feedback exercise (round robin sessions with visiting staff)* *Presentations of application concept on flipchart sheet (plenary)*
Wednesday morning **Presentation:** Prototyping and user testing **Presentation:** Smart homes and the Internet of Things **Presentation:** Project management in industry	**Afternoon** *Transformation of concepts into paper prototypes* *User testing of paper prototype*
Thursday morning **Presentation:** HCI in vehicles **Presentation:** Air traffic control and rail signalling	**Afternoon** **Presentation:** Psychology of user experience design *PowerPoint prototype development and project report writing*
Friday morning **Field trip:** Coach trip to visit to local company's Usability lab *Continuation of PowerPoint prototype development and project report writing*	**Afternoon** *Completion of PowerPoint prototype development and project report writing* *Coursework 2 introduction – Individual work to test prototype and report on it* *Presentations of PowerPoint prototypes by each of the student groups (plenary)*

- Information architecture
- Prototyping and user evaluation
- Gamification and persuasiveness in user interaction
- Control of systems and HCI
- Case studies of HCI in rail and air traffic control
- Smart homes and the Internet of Things
- HCI in vehicles
- Project management and system implementation

One of the challenges is to maintain a thread throughout the lecture sessions where each lecturer's material can be seem to fit together, reinforcing key points across the course and forming a coherent whole.

Each day within the teaching week follows a general pattern with lectures in the morning and practical work in the afternoon. This approach has several benefits:

- Lectures in the morning provides a new stimulus each day
- Students can take on board the content offered and apply it later in the day to their practical work
- By holding the practical sessions in the afternoon, students have the flexibility to organize themselves, take their own breaks and either go home, possibly to work there, or continue working as a group into the early evening.

The day runs from 9.00 am–5.30 pm with a one hour lunch break and additional short breaks during the morning and afternoon. This enables students to catch up with email, phone calls, library visits, etc., outside of the course while keeping it tight and focused. An example schedule for the week is shown in Table 1. The items shown in normal text are presentations and those shown in italics represent student practical work.

5 Assignment and Practical Activities

The assessment for the module requires the students to identify and develop and test a concept for a software application. Within the teaching week, the students work in teams to develop a concept, create scenarios of use, develop and test a paper prototype representing it, and produce and a final software simulation together with a report of the process followed. This is based on the ISO 924-210 Human-centred design process [3] and the UK Design Council's 'Double Diamond process' [4]. One of the challenges of the week is to encourage creative thinking to solve problems, employ new technologies, and avoidreplicatingstandard applications that do not stretch the student's design skills. Another pitfall is the natural tendency to createdesigns based on one's own perceptions and needsrather thanbeing led by the user research delivering insights from the user's profiles, context, and problems with current tasks, identified task, usability and experience goals. A third important lesson to convey is not to spend too long on developing and polishing an early prototype application but to create something quickly and obtain feedback or test it with users. This more agile and flexible approach allows teams to generate and test more ideas and to move more quickly towards an effective design solution. This approach is summed up by the following rules for prototyping [5]:

(1) Each prototype should take less than an hour to make.
(2) The first prototype you create for a product should be so simple that anyone can build it.
(3) Build ugly.

Following the teaching week, students are required on an individual basis, plan and run a series of user trials of the software prototype that the team developed and to report on this, offering recommendations for change.

In order to assess the HCI course, a SWOT analysis was conducted of it as shown in Table 2.

Table 2. HCI course SWOT analysis

Strengths	Weaknesses
• Easy to relate HCI to everyday experience • Students generally respond well to questions • Practical activities and group work allows for learning and creativity • Continuous working on project throughout the week • The short period of the course allows focus on a single subject • Motivated by group dynamics • Conference style event encourages networking and team working outside standard hours • Room allocated for whole week • Range of skills and backgrounds can create a stimulating mix • Charismatic guest speakers provide new perspectives on HCI	• Can be tiring with a week of lectures, practicals and exercises and group coursework • Little time to absorb and understand material as between weekly sessions • Challenging to meet the needs of students with different level of interest in pursuing an HCI-related career
Opportunities	**Threats**
• Learning wider range of tools for prototyping • Breaking out of classroom for interaction outside (on campus, in Town) • More focused pre-reading to allow faster start on course • More integration of presentations so that speaker's presentation sessions link together smoothly	• Organizer may be unwell so replacement has to manage whole week of course • Growth of free online courses may be more cost-effective, reducing demand for classroom based courses

One of the main strengths of the HCI course is that a group of highly motivated students from a range of backgrounds, nationalities and professions come together to learn about the area and gain practice in applying it to the design and evaluation of a product concept. As it is an intensive and demanding course, a lot gets done and students are often surprised by the progress they make by the end of the week.

The main weaknesses are that the course demands a high level of commitment and energy and those who commute from a distance can miss out when group work overruns into the early evening. A lot of material is presented which students may not have the time to absorb fully; to appreciate how the different presentations fit together and to make the most use of them when applying it to coursework.

There is a named deputy who can take over in case the main organizer is unable to teach the course, but they will be less familiar with the structure and material and may have other tasks during the same week meaning that they cannot devote themselves to the course full time.

The opportunities include making the coursework more realistic by asking the students to go into the outside world to carry out user research and to use more specialized tools to create prototypes of their designs. However this can be a challenge to learn the tools and apply them during the short period of the course.

6 Guidelines for Development and Running of HCI Short Courses

This section offers general guidelines for running a short course in HCI to provide the students with a positive learning experience:

- In order to allow students to get started quickly on the practical assignment, the specification should be concise and clear.
- In order to enable the students to complete the first coursework that takes place during the week, the practical sessions should be structured around particular activities so that they move on from one activity (e.g. user research, concept development, paper prototyping, etc.) to the next rather than spending too long on a single activity and getting left behind. This approach is quite similar to agile system design [6] where client, UX designers, users and programmers have to work quickly and flexibly to enable and iterative design approach within a limit series of 'sprints'.
- Having a number of speakers is important to give students a variety of speakers and perspectives on HCI. It is helpful if those speakers themselves can set short exercises to reinforce their material and also so that the students are not solely focused on the main assignment and can take time off from it.
- Creating mixed groups is generally a good idea since this allows the organizer to bring together people with different skills and disciplines (e.g. design, psychology, physical ergonomics, engineering, health and safety) together so they can benefit from this in terms of the coursework and, typically. This also provides the chance to meet and work with new people on the course.

- It is a essential to keep interacting with the groups during assignments to help them stay on track, challenge their thinking, ask questions, etc. It also allows formative feedback to be given as they work.
- Encourage group members to share skills and practice new skills, so rather than the most advanced person at sketching doing all the design work, encourage them to oversee others to design and sketch so they can practice and learn new skills.
- When the group develop ideas for an application, keep challenging their ideas by asking questions such as: 'what is original about the application?', 'would a user want to do that with the application?', 'could the task be done more efficiently?' Offer to be a test user of a groups' paper or software prototype and give immediate feedback.
- Try to keep things moving with new activities to stimulate the group e.g. bring in members of staff to move between the groups to provide constructive criticism of each design, send each group out to carry out some user evaluation or 'guerrilla testing' of their paper simulation, encourage them to move on from rough sketches as a basis for discussing concepts to creating a paper prototype which can then be tested to see if the design concept is feasible and the interface is usable.

7 Future Developments

The HCI module has received positive feedback from the students but it is recognized that there always room for improvement to make the course run more smoothly, to enable students to learn more effectively and to keep up with new ideas and technologies within HCI. The following areas are being considered for future development:

- User research could be facilitated further by arranging transport to specific locations in town in order to talk to members of the public or there could an arrangement where members of the public visit the University to discuss with students. There could also be an arrangement whereby students can speak with members of staff on campus in different roles such as security, catering, estates, etc., to give their opinion on an application concept if it has some relevance to them.
- The user research data could be analyzed more formally so that the students develop personas for their target users. This may involve pooling all the facts and stories that have been recorded during the user research and using a technique such as affinity diagrams [7] with post-its laid out on a wall or work-surface to assess and try to identify key characteristics of users within the data that can be formed into personas as described in [8].
- There could be a clearer framework for the specific UX design skills being learned and practical sessions could be organized so that everyone gets the chance to practice each skill such as leading the a discussion or interview with a user, creating simple prototypes and taking an active part within prototyping such as moderating the test session or controlling the prototype.
- Provide clear links between the presentations and the practical coursework. This could be achieved by listing all the main principles to be covered in the course and asking each speaker to identify which they will cover. Alternatively by briefing the

presenters on the structure of the course and nature of the coursework, they provide clearer links from their own sessions to other elements of the course. The design process that the course follows be annotated with the stages of the process that each presentation relates to. Several of the sessions are application specific so the overall process would need to be adapted to include different applications of HCI.

- During the week, the students do not have a lot of time for learning to use prototyping software and so, after paper prototyping, presentation software is normally used to create prototypes. It would however be useful to gain skills in using more specialized tools. This could be achieved by allowing students in the follow-on coursework to develop more interactive prototypes as a result of their individual usability sessions and to create a revised version that in a real design situation could be used for another round of user testing.

Students on the course often feel that the coursework set is a lot to achieve during the period of a single week when a good part of it is attending to presentations as well as practical work creating and testing application for the coursework. However it has been found that once they get started, the students enjoy the challenge and by the end of the week are surprised by how much they have achieved. This inspires some to want to carry out a UX design project for their main course dissertation and to consider a career in HCI. For others, knowledge of interaction design and user experience design gives them an insight into the topics that may apply in their work if they use software applications and are given the chance to influence which ones their organization adopts. For other students, knowledge of HCI helps them to appreciate the benefits of usable software that is enjoyable to use and meets their needs.

References

1. Fry, H., Ketteridge, S., Marsall, S. (eds.): A Handbook for Teaching and Learning in Higher Education, Chap. 5 Student Learning. Routledge, Abingdon (2015)
2. Bloom, B.S., Engelhart, M.D., Furst, E.J., Hill, W.H., Krathwohl, D.R. (eds.): Taxonomy of Educational Objectives, Handbook 1: The Cognitive Domain. David McKay Co Inc., New York (1956)
3. ISO 9241-210 - Human-centred design for interactive systems. Ergonomics of human-system interaction. International Organisation for Standardisation, Geneva (1999)
4. Design Council: A study of thedesign process - Eleven lessons: managing design in eleven global brands. Design Council, 34 Bow Street, London WC2E 7DL (2017). www.designcouncil.org.uk/sites/default/files/asset/document/ElevenLessons_Design_Council%20(2).pdf
5. Spool, J.: Rules for Prototyping, Adapted from: 'So… what do I make? Exploring the world of modern UX design' a virtual seminar with Dan Mall, UIE (User Interface Engineering) All you can learn library (2017)
6. Highsmith, J.: Manifesto for agile software development (2001). www.agilemanifesto.org
7. Beyer, H., Holtzblatt, K.: Contextual Design: Designing Customer-Centred Systems. Morgan Kaufmann Publishers, San Francisco (1998)
8. Cooper, A., Reimann, R.: About Face: The Essentials of Interaction Design, 4th edn. Wiley, New York (2014)

The Interplay Between Human and Machine Agency

J. Brian Pickering, Vegard Engen(✉), and Paul Walland

IT Innovation Centre, University of Southampton, Gamma House, Enterprise Road, Southampton, SO16 7NS, UK
{jbp,ve,pww}@it-innovation.soton.ac.uk

Abstract. Human-machine networks affect many aspects of our lives: from sharing experiences with family and friends, knowledge creation and distance learning, and managing utility bills or providing feedback on retail items, to more specialised networks providing decision support to human operators and the delivery of health care via a network of clinicians, family, friends, and both physical and virtual social robots. Such networks rely on increasingly sophisticated machine algorithms, e.g., to recommend friends or purchases, to track our online activities in order to optimise the services available, and assessing risk to help maintain or even enhance people's health. Users are being offered ever increasing power and reach through these networks by machines which have to support and allow users to be able to achieve goals such as maintaining contact, making better decisions, and monitoring their health. As such, this comes down to a synergy between human and machine agency in which one is dependent in complex ways on the other. With that agency questions arise about trust, risk and regulation, as well as social influence and potential for computer-mediated self-efficacy. In this paper, we explore these constructs and their relationships and present a model based on review of the literature which seeks to identify the various dependencies between them.

Keywords: General: HCI methods and theories · Human-machine networks · Agency · Trust · Modelling · Self-efficacy

1 Introduction

A definition of agency based on the notion of non-deterministic behaviours [1] fails to recognise the increasing variety and complexity of human-machine networks[1] (HMNs) [2], the intention of technology designers [3], and active intervention by bots within social networks [4, 5]. The concept of agency is particularly problematic in human-machine interactions [6]. Machine or material agency may be seen as automation, which originally required some tolerance from human agents [7]. But this is no longer true: technology can actively support human activity [8], and manifests increasingly complex interaction types [9]. Machine and human agency may not be the same and yet equally valid [10]; machine agency may be just "perceived autonomy" [11]; and it certainly enables human agency [12]. Indeed, agency may well be becoming a social and group

[1] In the following we use *human-machine network* and *network* interchangeably.

M. Kurosu (Ed.): HCI 2017, Part I, LNCS 10271, pp. 47–59, 2017.
DOI: 10.1007/978-3-319-58071-5_4

construct where both humans and machines play a part [13, 14]; and used effectively, agency may even lead to innovative review of working practice [15].

The enabling contribution of machine agents within a network may have an effect on self-efficacy. Bandura's original definition of self-efficacy as an individual's belief in their ability to be able to achieve a given objective [16–18] has also been applied to technology [19, 20] and its acceptance [21]. There are, however, constraints on the support and positive contribution of technology to human self-efficacy, not least in terms of anxiety and suspicion around technology use [22, 23]. This may be further exacerbated by increasing machine animism: it may not always be obvious what machines are doing or what information they are collecting on other agents in the network [24, 25]. With this in mind, regulation is seeking to impose safeguards [26], but with only limited success [27]. Any consequent perception of risk can undermine a willingness to engage in some online activities [28]. However, assuming scepticism can be kept low, regulation can reduce the negative effects of risk across a number of contexts, leading to an increased level of trust [29].

Bringing together some of these constructs, this paper proposes updates to a recent model of trust in information technology [30, 31] with a detailed exploration of self-efficacy as it relates to agency [3, 18]. Since human-machine networks can be characterised by independently varying levels of agency [2], either or both may influence self-efficacy [18]. Further, introducing regulation and perceived risk [32], how these influence agency and, in turn, behaviours within an HMN, need consideration [33, 34]. On the other hand, for this exploratory study, we do not consider affect [35] or other motivators such as social identity or task [36] which may mediate behaviour in online networks. Similarly, we discount environmental trust as factors affecting both behaviour and self-efficacy [37].

In the original study by Thatcher et al. [31], the final set of constructs was based on an extensive literature review [30], and its validation via an opportunity sample of students and IT professionals to establish inter-construct dependencies and correlations. The intent to explore technology was seen to be dependent on social norms and computer self-efficacy, while the influence of trust in IT and in support personnel is mediated by the technology acceptance model (TAM) constructs of perceived usefulness and ease of use. The relationship between interpersonal, organisational and technology trust is well motivated in light of theoretical considerations of trust transfer [38], and of trust as an overall organising factor [39]. However, given the various interactions between agents within an HMN, both human-to-human and machine-to-machine, the question remains whether McKnight et al. [30] had captured all relevant constructs. Further, participants were drawn from a narrow field who may show a priori increased propensity to engage and persevere with technology [40]. Revisiting and extending their original model with specific reference to HMNs, therefore, implies careful consideration of those constructs as well as participant selection in validating the resulting research model.

2 Modelling Trust

Interpersonal and person-to-organisation trust is based on the judgement of perceived benevolence, integrity and competence [41, 42]. More recently applied to technology and its acceptance, self-efficacy and agency in HMNs interact with one another as well as influence trust. It is, therefore, appropriate to reconsider a model of trust in online interactions.

2.1 Related Research

In a series of studies McKnight, Thatcher and their colleagues explored different constructs associated with trust in technology [30, 31]. They found that trust in technology and a willingness to explore its use could be predicted from individual propensities to trust. Further, context-specific factors including social context and an individual's computer self-efficacy were found to relate directly to this willingness to explore technology [31].

Other studies, however, highlight a range of different constructs. For example, an extensive literature review suggests personal, organisational as well as cultural factors as instrumental for online trust [43]. Many studies stress the social [44, 45], not least the importance of communication and group adherence [46] and self-efficacy [37]. However, this social dimension is closely connected with agency [47]. Still others explore the interplay of risk, assurances of privacy and security [29, 48]. Drawing all of this together suggests an extension to the Thatcher et al. model to incorporate greater focus on the social on the one hand, but also regulation and risk perception on the other.

2.2 Research Model

The focus of the proposed research model is human behaviour in an HMN. For an HMN to be successful, and both gain and sustain participation, it needs to enable benefits for the human agents within the network. Although there are a number of human participants taking different roles, it may well be that the network benefits one group in a different, or preferential, way to others. This does not alter the fact that the network, and the machine agents within it, are established in order to provide benefit to the human actors in that network.

We are concentrating on human behaviour in the HMN, rather than human actions. This is an important distinction, since, as has been discussed elsewhere [49], human actors exhibit 'conscious intentionality', which is to say that the human actors have certain freedom of choice regarding their actions, whereas the machine agents exhibit 'programmed intentionality' in the sense that they can also influence behaviour, but do so according to their pre-determined programming and rule sets [50]. How a human behaves in a particular network and circumstance will depend upon a number of factors acting upon them, which are reflected in Fig. 1. The main proposition is that a human agent will behave in a manner which is determined by two considerations: their belief that they can achieve what they want in the network (self-efficacy) [16–18] and the level of risk that they perceive in performing those actions (trust) [28, 29]. What other constructs should be included is the purpose of this section.

First, we introduce the effect of regulation on agency, since regulation, whether legislative, standardisation or commercial restriction, will set limits on both machine agency and human agency [32]. Another effect of regulation is to modify the perceived risk involved in performing actions, positively or negatively [26, 32]. We identify perceived risk rather than actual or absolute risk, because it is perceived risk that determines human behaviour, not the actual level of risk, as established in a broad spectrum of research, including inter alia online

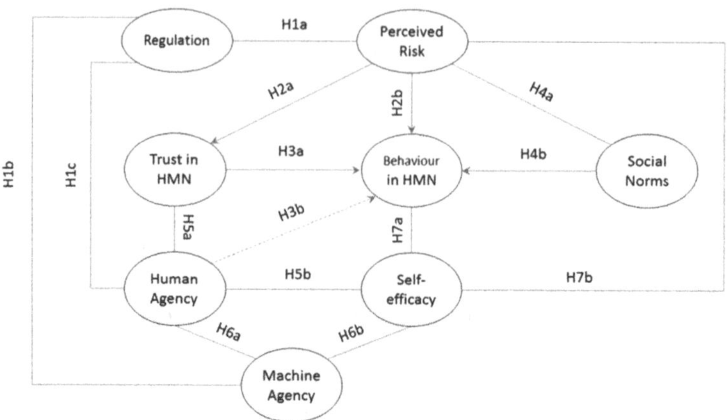

Fig. 1. Research model

consumer behaviour [51, 52], health care [53], and engineering and natural disasters [54]. For example, vanishingly rare events such as the murder of a child affect parents' perception of risk to their child, even though the actual risk is very small, and lower than the risk of injury at home. Thus, anything that modifies perceived risk is important, even if the actual level of risk is unchanged. We can, therefore, also conclude that trust is a reflection of perceived risk, and that behaviour is a reflection of willingness to accept a certain level of risk, both of which are based on belief, not on absolute or measurable parameters [31, 55]. Risk perception, trust and behaviour can all change with time, and can be modified by changes in circumstance, such as external influences (social norms) [56, 57].

Behaviour is also determined by ease of use of the network, expressed as the ability to achieve pre-determined goals (self-efficacy). Machine agency can operate in a supportive role, enabling ease of use and hence supporting self-efficacy [50], leading to more positive or interactive behaviour and better achievement of objectives by the human agent. Limitations to the supportive ability of the machine agent, either through regulatory limitations or functional limitations, may reduce the self-efficacy they can support, leading to more cautious behaviour [31]. This would suggest an association with perceived risk: belief in one's own capabilities and therefore the ability to manage perceived risks.

3 Model Constructs and Research Hypotheses

As the central construct of our model, Human Behaviour in HMN[2] is affected directly or indirectly by all of the remaining constructs. In consequence, we have developed hypotheses for all the remaining constructs in the following sections. These will determine relationships with Behaviour in HMN.

[2] Abbreviated to "Behaviour in HMN" in the remaining discussion.

3.1 Regulation

We include laws (legislations), codes of practice and standards as part of this construct. As discussed above, regulations may constrain agency. It may also have enabling effects, such as technology standards improving on technology interoperability and ensure security and privacy for end-users [58], which are all key to HMNs dealing with personal data. Standardisation efforts, such as HL7 in healthcare[3], may, therefore, have a positive impact on both human and machine, as well as reducing the perceived risk. Miltgen and Smith [32] have already shown that higher levels of perceived regulatory protection is associated with a decrease in the risks that people perceive to their privacy. In this vein, we hypothesise the following.

H1a: Perceived risk is negatively correlated with changes in regulation.

However, regulation may also stifle innovation and constrain what actors are allowed to do, directly reducing both human and machine agency[4]. Reasons for regulations to be constrictive may be to, e.g., address concerns regarding the increasing autonomy of machines [2], raising ethical issues about responsibilities and accountability [59]. Thus, we hypothesise:

H1b: Machine agency is negatively correlated with increasing levels of regulation.

In the discussion above, we can see that the effect on human agency can vary, depending on the increase in regulations. On the one hand, it may increase human agency due to the reduction in the perceived risk (via trust in the HMN, as discussed further below). On the other hand, it may decrease human agency due to the reduction in machine agency, as hypothesised above. Therefore, we simply put forth the following hypothesis:

H1c: Regulation affects human agency.

3.2 Perceived Risk

The perception of risk and uncertainty was considered by Thatcher et al. [31], but was omitted from their proposed model. Here, we focus on the perception of risk as experienced by the human participants in an HMN. However, we do note that this also affects other actors, such as providers and even machines although their response is deterministic. While exploring the different types of risk that could affect trust and the behaviour of participants in an HMN is outside the scope of this paper, this could include any factors of an HMN pertaining to, e.g., monetary loss or loss of privacy, as discussed in [32, 60]. We focus here on the perception of risk experienced when participating in HMNs, which may well differ from actual risk as discussed above; the former affecting behaviour [31, 55], which pertains to the central construct we are interested in here (Behaviour in HMN). Pavlou [60], in proposing extensions to the TAM, found that trust influences perceived risk. Here we focus on how perceived risk affects trust in the HMN, leading to the following hypothesis:

---

[3] HL7 – Health Level Seven. http://www.hl7.org.uk/.

[4] EC H2020 SHiELD Project, 2017, http://cordis.europa.eu/project/rcn/207185_en.html.

H2a: The perception of risk negatively affects trust in an HMN.

While previous work, as discussed above [55, 60, 61], establishes that trust affects the perception of risk, we also hypothesise a direct relationship between Perceived Risk and Behaviour in HMN.

H2b: The perception of risk negatively affects the behaviour in an HMN.

3.3 Trust in HMNs

As a construct, trust pervades almost all interactions between individuals and is traditionally the result of perceived benevolence, competence and integrity [41]. Over time, it may be lost but also rebuilt [42], largely due to context and reassessment of behaviours and intention. If trust is an overall organising principle [39], then it makes sense to attempt to extend the construct to technology [30] and online networked activities [38]. So trust will affect self-efficacy [31, 37] and be associated with social norms [31]. It may well be that interpersonal and technology trust differ in the detail, but collectively influence a willingness to adopt the technology [62]. Once online, traditional behaviours occur: communication is important [46], and social trust will affect willingness to engage [63]. Further, increasing familiarity with the technology may well influence trust and thereby agency [20, 30], though there will be a moderating effect in relation to security risk or privacy exposure [48]. We therefore hypothesise that:

H3a: HMN trust will positively influence the behaviour in an HMN.

further

H3b: HMN trust will mediate the effect of human agency on the behaviour in an HMN.

3.4 Social Norms

A significant research body on social norms in the offline world is gradually being extended into the virtual world, already finding parallels even down to eye gaze and social gestures [64] and group composition [65]. A willingness to engage online involves social pressures from the immediate social group, social identity [66] and trust in other network members [63]. Indeed the desire to be seen online will often motivate the adoption of strategies to mitigate against potential risk [56, 57], or even adapt structures such as reputation and social presence in decisions to engage, for instance in eCommerce [67]. Along with (computer) self-efficacy, social norms may also influence participation in social networks [68], and even encourage emergent and shared agency within the virtual group [13]. Thatcher et al. [31] were clearly right to include social norms in their model, though they did not necessarily explore the full implications of its influence. Specifically, social norms can reduce perceived risk, as well as directly encourage online engagement and behaviours. In consequence, we propose that:

H4a: Social norms will affect the extent to which perceived risk influences the behaviour in an HMN.

and

H4b: Social norms will directly and positively correlate with the behaviour in an HMN.

3.5 Human Agency

A pragmatic definition of Human and Machine Agency in HMNs has been discussed in [3] on the basis of a review of social psychology literature, such as Structuration Theory [61] and Social Cognitive Theory [49]. Adopting the definition of agency from [3] we understand agency "as the capacity to perform activities in a particular environment in line with a set of goals/objectives that influence and shape the extent and nature of their participation". In practice, agency, therefore, indicates what a human actor can actually do in the network, and how this aligns with the objectives they would have for using the network, or their belief in their ability to achieve their goals. This, in turn, influences their behaviour in the network. We hypothesise a direct relationship between human agency and self-efficacy in terms of the behaviour in the HMN, as follows:

H5a: Trust in the HMN is positively correlated with human agency.
H5b: Human agency is related to self-efficacy.

3.6 Machine Agency

As per [3], we can apply the same definition for Human Agency, as discussed above, to Machine Agency. While there are distinctions between the two, such as the lack of intentionality in machines [69, 70], they are increasingly active and visible participants in HMNs, even exhibiting human-like characteristics, capable of exerting influence and enhancing Human Agency [3]. The latter is due to a characteristic that Bandura [49] refers to as proxy agency, in which an agent may increase their own agency by utilising the capabilities of other agents, which could indeed be machines. However, it is far from clear whether machine agency might be perceived as a constraint on human activity itself or in overall processes [15]. Similarly a unidirectional relationship may not hold: human agency may well constrain machine agency if this means that human agents simply do not need the full capabilities of machines. Indeed, Følstad et al. [59] indicate a bi-directional and synergistic relationship, which warrants further exploration. Thus, we pose the following generic hypothesis:

H6a: Machine agency in an HMN is directly related to human agency.

The nature of this relationship may need more careful consideration. A similar issue arises regarding the relationship between Machine Agency and Self-efficacy, confounded by factors such as the age and cultural background of those engaging in the HMN. Whilst increasing machine agency may indeed increase the self-efficacy of certain population groups, it may have the opposite effect on others depending on their appraisal of technology [71].

H6b: Machine agency affects computer self-efficacy.

3.7 Computer Self-efficacy

As stated, self-efficacy is a personal belief in one's ability to achieve [16, 18]; and in terms of technology use, often referred to as computer self-efficacy, it may be understood as internal (a belief that I can do it myself) or external (a belief that I can do it with appropriate support) [19]. It is assumed that younger people are more willing to engage with technology and see what happens, which seems to be the case [22]. Further, since on the one hand people change in their experience and expectations, and on the other technology develops, so we need to be sensitive to such change especially in our metrics [20]. In HMN terms, it turns out that self-efficacy is related to trust and TAM constructs such as usefulness and ease-of-use [30]; and along with trust, it influences network behaviour [37]. Further, it is not self-esteem or extroversion which predict successful online presence, but self-efficacy [72]. Indeed, as well as social pressure (see Social Norms above), self-efficacy affects the willingness to engage in online networks [68]. We therefore hypothesise that:

H7a: Computer self-efficacy is positively correlated with Behaviour in HMN.

On the other hand, it appears that self-efficacy is negatively correlated with anxiety [73], which may be associated with perceived risk [74]. So a second hypothesis obtains:

H7b: Computer self-efficacy is negatively correlated with perceived risk.

4 Research Design

Having established an initial research model and formulated a set of hypotheses (see Table 1, below) based on our review of pertinent literature over the past decade, we are now

Table 1. Hypotheses

H1a	Perceived risk is negatively correlated with changes in regulation
H1b	Machine agency is negatively correlated with increasing levels of regulation
H1c	Regulation affects human agency
H2a	The perception of risk negatively affects trust in an HMN
H2b	The perception of risk negatively affects the behaviour in an HMN
H3a	HMN trust will positively influence the behaviour in an HMN
H3b	HMN trust will mediate the effect of human agency on the behaviour in an HMN
H4a	Social norms will affect the extent to which perceived risk influences behaviour in an HMN
H4b	Social norms will directly and positively correlate with behaviour in an HMN
H5a	Trust in the HMN is positively correlated with human agency
H5b	Human agency is related to self-efficacy
H6a	Machine agency in an HMN is directly related to human agency
H6b	Machine agency affects computer self-efficacy
H7a	Computer self-efficacy is positively correlated with Behaviour in HMN
H7b	Computer self-efficacy is negatively correlated with perceived risk

in the process of organising both qualitative and quantitative investigation of that model. Following a similar qualitative approach to [75], we are starting with a focus group of those familiar with trust as a concept, how it is traditionally thought to relate to human-to-human interactions, and how it may transfer to technology – our expert group – to provide an initial evaluation of our research model. We are targeting six to ten participants for this group. Using the feedback from that group to identify potential refinements, we will then conduct a quantitative survey using a set of questions based on the instruments suggested by researchers in our literature review [30, 31, 37, 48], but extended and updated to reflect experience in the specific environment of HMNs [20, 48]. In an attempt to avoid the demographic constraints in many studies where respondents are confined to undergraduate students or a similar cohort, we are creating a publically available survey to be hosted by the University of Southampton which will run for approximately four weeks. We will combine this with snowball participant sampling if necessary to achieve a target of some 200 valid responses. These will be analysed using a structural-equation modelling analysis in line with work reported in [48]. On this basis, we hope to be in a position to report our results and present a validated research model associated with our hypotheses in the coming months.

5 Conclusions and Future Work

Based on a review of current work on computer self-efficacy, agency and trust, we have developed a model which extends work reported by Thatcher et al. [31] to include a set of constructs known to influence these constructs and behaviour within online networks. Validating this model will increase our understanding of online behaviours which is of interest to those who engage with the networks, but also those who seek either to monitor and understand or regulate online behaviours, as well as those building networks who wish to explore factors which will support the long-term health of that network. More especially, our model seeks to extend our understanding of the interplay between agency and trust on the one hand, but also self-efficacy and indeed social influence on the other. What we have proposed is, therefore, intended to advance our general understanding of interactions between human and machine agency in human-machine networks. In this way, we hope to throw some light on how conscious as well as programmed agency influence one another and affect the willingness to engage online as well as individual self-belief in the capability to achieve personal goals.

Acknowledgements. This work has been conducted as part of the HUMANE project, which has received funding from the European Union's Horizon 2020 research and innovation programme under grant agreement No 645043.

References

1. Applin, S., Fischer, M.: Watching Me, Watching You. (Process surveillance and agency in the workplace). In: 2013 IEEE International Symposium on Technology and Society (ISTAS), Portland, OR, pp. 268–275 (2013)

2. Tsvetkova, M., Yasseri, T., Meyer, E.T., Pickering, J.B., Engen, V., Walland, P., Lüders, M., Følstad, A., Bravos, G.: Understanding Human-Machine Networks: A Cross-Disciplinary Survey. arXiv Prepr. (2015)
3. Engen, V., Pickering, J.Brian, Walland, P.: Machine agency in human-machine networks; impacts and trust implications. In: Kurosu, M. (ed.) HCI 2016. LNCS, vol. 9733, pp. 96–106. Springer, Cham (2016). doi:10.1007/978-3-319-39513-5_9
4. Boshmaf, Y., Muslukhov, I., Beznosov, K., Ripeanu, M.: The socialbot network: when bots socialize for fame and money. In: Proceedings of the 27th Annual Computer Security Applications Conference, pp. 93–102 (2011)
5. Chu, Z., Gianvecchio, S., Wang, H., Jajodia, S.: Who is tweeting on twitter: human, bot, or cyborg? In: Proceedings of the 26th Annual Computer Security Applications Conference, ACSAC 2010, p. 21 (2010)
6. Rose, J., Jones, M.: The double dance of agency: a socio-theoretic account of how machines and humans interact. Syst. Signs Actions **1**, 19–37 (2005)
7. Lee, J.D., Moray, N.: Trust, control strategies and allocation of function in human-machine systems. Ergonomics **35**, 1243–1270 (1992)
8. Norman, D.A.: Living with Complexity. MIT Press, Cambridge (2010)
9. Berberian, B., Sarrazin, J.-C., Le Blaye, P., Haggard, P.: Automation technology and sense of control: a window on human agency. PLoS ONE **7**, e34075 (2012)
10. Rose, J., Jones, M., Truex, D.: Socio-theoretic accounts of IS: The problem of agency. Scand. J. Inf. Syst. **17**, 8 (2005)
11. Rose, J., Truex, D.: Machine agency as perceived autonomy: an action perspective. In: Baskerville, R., Stage, J., DeGross, Janice I. (eds.) Organizational and Social Perspectives on Information Technology. IFIP, vol. 41, pp. 371–388. Springer, Boston (2000). doi: 10.1007/978-0-387-35505-4_22
12. Applin, S., Fischer, M.: Cooperation between humans and robots: applied agency in autonomous processes'. In: 10th ACM/IEEE International Conference on Human/Robot Interaction, The Emerging Policy and Ethics of Human Robot Interaction Workshop, Portland, OR (2015)
13. Jones, C., Healing, G.: Net generation students: agency and choice and the new technologies. J. Comput. Assist. Learn. **26**, 344–356 (2010)
14. Jia, H., Wu, M., Jung, E., Shapiro, A., Sundar, S.S.: Balancing human agency and object agency: an end-user interview study of the internet of things. In: Proceedings of the 2012 ACM Conference on Ubiquitous Computing, pp. 1185–1188. ACM Press, New York (2012)
15. Leonardi, P.M.: When flexible routines meet flexible technologies: affordance, constraint, and the imbrication of human and material agencies. MIS Q. **35**(1), 147–167 (2011)
16. Bandura, A.: Self-efficacy: toward a unifying theory of behavioral change. Psychol. Rev. **84**, 191 (1977)
17. Bandura, A.: Self-efficacy mechanism in human agency. Am. Psychol. **37**, 122 (1982)
18. Bandura, A.: On the functional properties of perceived self-efficacy revisited. J. Manage. **38**, 9–44 (2012)
19. Thatcher, J.B., Zimmer, J.C., Gundlach, M.J., McKnight, D.H.: Internal and external dimensions of computer self-efficacy: An empirical examination. IEEE Trans. Eng. Manag. **55**, 628–644 (2008)
20. Marakas, G.M., Johnson, R.D., Clay, P.F.: The evolving nature of the computer self-efficacy construct: An empirical investigation of measurement construction, validity, reliability and stability over time. J. Assoc. Inf. Syst. **8**, 15 (2007)

21. Mun, Y.Y., Hwang, Y.: Predicting the use of web-based information systems: self-efficacy, enjoyment, learning goal orientation, and the technology acceptance model. Int. J. Hum Comput Stud. **59**, 431–449 (2003)
22. Simsek, A.: The relationship between computer anxiety and computer self-efficacy. Online Submiss. **2**, 177–187 (2011)
23. Shu, Q., Tu, Q., Wang, K.: The impact of computer self-efficacy and technology dependence on computer-related technostress: a social cognitive theory perspective. Int. J. Hum. Comput. Interact. **27**, 923–939 (2011)
24. Hildebrandt, M.: Profile transparency by design?: Re-enabling double contingency. In: Hildebrandt, M., de Vries, K. (eds.) Privacy, Due Process and the Computational Turn: The Philosophy of Law Meets the Philosophy of Technology, pp. 221–246. Routledge, New York (2013)
25. Hildebrandt, M.: Promiscuous Data-Sharing in times of Data-driven Animism (2016)
26. European Commission: Regulation (EU) 2016/679 of the European Parliament and of the Council of 27 April 2016 (2016)
27. Hildebrandt, M.: Smart Technologies and the End of Law: Novel Entanglements of Law and Technology. Edward Elgar Publishing Ltd., Cheltenham (2015)
28. Featherman, M.S., Miyazaki, A.D., Sprott, D.E.: Reducing online privacy risk to facilitate e-service adoption: the influence of perceived ease of use and corporate credibility. J. Serv. Mark. **24**, 219–229 (2010)
29. Poortinga, W., Pidgeon, N.F.: Exploring the dimensionality of trust in risk regulation. Risk Anal. **23**, 961–972 (2003)
30. McKnight, D.H., Carter, M., Thatcher, J.B., Clay, P.F.: Trust in a specific technology. ACM Trans. Manag. Inf. Syst. **2**, 1–25 (2011)
31. Thatcher, J.B., McKnight, D.H., Baker, E.W., Arsal, R.E., Roberts, N.H.: The role of trust in postadoption IT exploration: an empirical examination of knowledge management systems. IEEE Trans. Eng. Manag. **58**, 56–70 (2011)
32. Miltgen, C.L., Smith, H.J.: Exploring information privacy regulation, risks, trust, and behavior. Inf. Manag. **52**, 741–759 (2015)
33. Acquisti, A., Grossklags, J.: Privacy and rationality in individual decision making. IEEE Secur. Priv. **3**, 26–33 (2005)
34. Acquisti, A., Brandimarte, L., Loewenstein, G.: Privacy and human behavior in the age of information. Science **347**(80), 509–514 (2015)
35. Lin, K.-Y., Lu, H.-P.: Why people use social networking sites: An empirical study integrating network externalities and motivation theory. Comput. Human Behav. **27**, 1152–1161 (2011)
36. Kwon, O., Wen, Y.: An empirical study of the factors affecting social network service use. Comput. Human Behav. **26**, 254–263 (2010)
37. Hsu, M.-H., Ju, T.L., Yen, C.-H., Chang, C.-M.: Knowledge sharing behavior in virtual communities: the relationship between trust, self-efficacy, and outcome expectations. Int. J. Hum Comput Stud. **65**, 153–169 (2007)
38. Stewart, K.J.: Trust transfer on the world wide web. Organ. Sci. **14**, 5–17 (2003)
39. McEvily, B., Perrone, V., Zaheer, A.: Trust as an organizing principle. Organ. Sci. **14**, 91–103 (2003)
40. Bennett, S., Maton, K., Kervin, L.: The "digital natives" debate: a critical review of the evidence. Br. J. Educ. Technol. **39**, 775–786 (2008)
41. Mayer, R.C., Davis, J.H., Schoorman, F.D.: An integrative model of organizational trust. Acad. Manag. Rev. **20**, 709–734 (1995)
42. Schoorman, F.D., Mayer, R.C., Davis, J.H.: An integrative model of organizational trust: past, present, and future. Acad. Manag. Rev. **32**, 344–354 (2007)

43. Beldad, A., de Jong, M., Steehouder, M.: How shall I trust the faceless and the intangible? A literature review on the antecedents of online trust. Comput. Human Behav. **26**, 857–869 (2010)
44. Lewis, J.D., Weigert, A.J.: The social dynamics of trust: theoretical and empirical research, 1985–2012. Soc. Forces **91**, 25–31 (2012)
45. Chaouali, W., Ben Yahia, I., Souiden, N.: The interplay of counter-conformity motivation, social influence, and trust in customers' intention to adopt Internet banking services: the case of an emerging country. J. Retail. Consum. Serv. **28**, 209–218 (2016)
46. Sarker, S., Ahuja, M., Sarker, S., Kirkeby, S.: The role of communication and trust in global virtual teams: a social network perspective. J. Manag. Inf. Syst. **28**, 273–310 (2011)
47. Friedman, B., Khan Jr., P.H., Howe, D.C.: Trust online. Commun. ACM **43**, 34–40 (2000)
48. Shin, D.-H.: The effects of trust, security and privacy in social networking: a security-based approach to understand the pattern of adoption. Interact. Comput. **22**, 428–438 (2010)
49. Bandura, A.: Social cognitive theory: an agentic perspective. Annu. Rev. Psychol. **52**, 1–26 (2001)
50. Fogg, B.: Persuasive computers: perspectives and research directions. In: The SIGCHI Conference on Human Factors in Computing, pp. 225–232 (1998)
51. Garbarino, E., Strahilevitz, M.: Gender differences in the perceived risk of buying online and the effects of receiving a site recommendation. J. Bus. Res. **57**, 768–775 (2004)
52. Kim, D.J., Ferrin, D.L., Rao, H.R.: A trust-based consumer decision-making model in electronic commerce: the role of trust, perceived risk, and their antecedents. Decis. Support Syst. **44**, 544–564 (2008)
53. Leventhal, H., Kelly, K., Leventhal, E.A.: Population risk, actual risk, perceived risk, and cancer control: a discussion. J. Natl. Cancer Inst. Monogr. **25**, 81–85 (1999)
54. Covello, V.T.: Actual and perceived risk: a review of the literature. In: Technological Risk Assessment, pp. 225–245 (1984)
55. Brown, H.G., Poole, M.S., Rodgers, T.L.: Interpersonal traits, complementarity, and trust in virtual collaboration. J. Manag. Inf. **20**, 115–137 (2004)
56. Tufekci, Z.: Can you see me now? Audience and disclosure regulation in online social network sites. Bull. Sci. Technol. Soc. **28**, 20–36 (2008)
57. Strater, K., Lipford, H.R.: Strategies and struggles with privacy in an online social networking community. In: Proceedings of the 22nd British HCI Group Annual Conference on People and Computers: Culture, Creativity, Interaction-Volume 1, pp. 111–119. British Computer Society (2008)
58. Saravanakumar, C., Arun, C.: Survey on interoperability, security, trust, privacy standardization of cloud computing. In: 2014 International Conference on Contemporary Computing and Informatics (IC3I), pp. 977–982. IEEE (2014)
59. Følstad, A., Engen, V., Haugstveit, I.M., Pickering, J.B.: Automation in human-machine networks: how increasing machine agency affects human agency. In: International Conference on Man-Machine Interactions (submitted, 2017)
60. Pavlou, P.A.: Consumer acceptance of electronic commerce: Integrating trust and risk with the technology acceptance model. Int. J. Electron. Commer. **7**, 101–134 (2003)
61. Giddens, A.: The Constitution of Society: Outline of the Theory of Structuration (1984)
62. Li, X., Rong, G., Thatcher, J.B.: Does technology trust substitute interpersonal trust? J. Organ. End User Comput. **24**, 18–38 (2012)
63. Chow, W.S., Chan, L.S.: Social network, social trust and shared goals in organizational knowledge sharing. Inf. Manag. **45**, 458–465 (2008)

64. Yee, N., Bailenson, J.N., Urbanek, M., Chang, F., Merget, D.: The unbearable likeness of being digital: The persistence of nonverbal social norms in online virtual environments. CyberPsychol. Behav. **10**, 115–121 (2007)
65. Lowry, P.B., Zhang, D., Zhou, L., Fu, X.: Effects of culture, social presence, and group composition on trust in technology-supported decision-making groups. Inf. Syst. J. **20**, 297–315 (2010)
66. Cheung, C.M.K., Lee, M.K.O.: A theoretical model of intentional social action in online social networks. Decis. Support Syst. **49**, 24–30 (2010)
67. Gefen, D., Straub, D.W.: Consumer trust in B2C e-Commerce and the importance of social presence: experiments in e-Products and e-Services. Omega **32**, 407–424 (2004)
68. Gangadharbatla, H.: Facebook me. J. Interact. Advert. **8**, 5–15 (2008)
69. Rose, J., Jones, M., Truex, D.: The problem of agency: how humans act, how machines act. In: International Workshop on Action in Language, Organisations and Information Systems (ALOIS 2003) (2003)
70. Friedman, B., Kahn, P.H.: Human agency and responsible computing: implications for computer system design. J. Syst. Softw. **17**, 7–14 (1992)
71. Gist, M.E., Mitchell, T.R.: Self-efficacy: a theoretical analysis of its determinants and malleability. Acad. Manag. Rev. **17**, 183–211 (1992)
72. Krämer, N.C., Winter, S.: Impression management 2.0. J. Media Psychol. **20**, 106–116 (2008)
73. İskender, M., Akin, A.: Social self-efficacy, academic locus of control, and internet addiction. Comput. Educ. **54**, 1101–1106 (2010)
74. Kim, Y.H., Kim, D.J., Hwang, Y.: Exploring online transaction self-efficacy in trust building in B2C e-commerce. J. Organ. End User Comput. **21**, 37 (2009)
75. Dickinger, A., Arami, M., Meyer, D.: The role of perceived enjoyment and social norm in the adoption of technology with network externalities. Eur. J. Inf. Syst. **17**, 4–11 (2008)

Software as a Medium for Understanding Human Behavior

Joshua Poore(✉), Emily Vincent, and Laura Mariano

Draper, Cambridge, MA, USA
{jpoore,evincent,lmariano}@draper.com, poorejc@apache.org

Abstract. Our ability to understand users constrains our ability to design, create, and develop for them new ways of interfacing with technology. In turn, our ability to measure and derive insights from user behavior in real-world environments constrains our ability to truly understand them and how they will use the technology we develop for them. The psychological sciences (broadly defined) remain steadfastly locked in a tradition of experimental artifice—they make sense of our observations of humans by artificially constraining the environment (the laboratory) and human experience (experiments). However, the rate at which real-world endeavors are finding analogous virtualized platforms (e.g., entertainment, productivity, and sociality) is dramatically increasing; people are using software for more aspects of their lives than ever. This presents new measurement opportunities because software is a tool, and if we can instrument tools while they are used to perform tasks, then we can understand how humans approach those tasks. In this way, software is a new, virtualized medium for understanding real-human behavior in new compelling ways that bridge the gap between foundational research in the psychological science and applied research in the fields of human computer interaction (HCI). In this review paper, we will describe advances in gathering meaningful data from human in software environments and how it may be used to improve how people interface with their technology, understand cognition, as well as our understanding of people.

Keywords: User event · Logging and analysis

1 Introduction

In this paper, we review literature, methods, and technologies related to capturing high-resolution user activity in order to make inferences about user cognition. Beyond a direct benefit to the Human Computer Interaction (HCI) community, there is much deeper benefit to be had. Namely, bridging gaps in the psychological sciences for understanding human beings in real-world environment (even if they are virtual environments). If those gaps can be bridged, we might see far future advances in how humans can connect to their technology in the near future. A key theme in this paper is that the psychological sciences will not close these gaps alone. In fact, lacking the requisite skill-set and the technology, the psychological sciences will depend on HCI community to understand people in the virtual environments that they live, work and play in. Most importantly, it will be the HCI community that capitalizes on the knowledge we gain about people in real-world (virtual) environments to build new ways of interfacing with technology that everyone will benefit from.

M. Kurosu (Ed.): HCI 2017, Part I, LNCS 10271, pp. 60–73, 2017.
DOI: 10.1007/978-3-319-58071-5_5

2 (Psychological) Science and Technology

Science is a method for generating knowledge. Currently, it's the best one we have. Two things that people forget about science are that (1) Francis Bacon laid the groundwork for scientific principles of falsification, replication, and generalizability in the same source text [1], and (2) he did not necessarily believe in knowledge for its own sake. In fact, Bacon was pretty clear on the added value of science to human kind and the value he saw was in the science's ability to shape the world through technology.

> *"The making of great scientific discoveries seems to have a pride of place among human discoveries... Why? Because the benefits of scientific discoveries can extend to the whole of mankind, and can last for all time... This is nowhere more obvious than ... the arts of printing, gunpowder, and the natural compass... there seems to have been no empire, no philosophical system, no star that has exerted greater power and influence in human affairs than these mechanical discoveries"*
>
> -Francis Bacon, Novum Organum (1620), Aphorism 129

To Bacon, it wasn't enough to generate knowledge, even though he gave us a very good method for doing so (science). It's equally, if not more important to use scientific discoveries to push the human condition forward through technology that exploits those discoveries. This point is built into the scientific method, into what we call today generalizability—that we can't understand the nature of a thing in the thing itself and we must make our scientific inquiries as general as possible to really understand the limits and conditions of the natural principles we discover. This is very difficult in the psychological sciences.

Bacon recognized that to make progress in generating knowledge, our findings need to be replicable—discoveries need to be repeated, and observations need to be made more than once—in order to safeguard that they aren't a fluke. Generalizability falls right out of that—that we can replicate discoveries under different conditions. It's clear that Bacon never saw psychology coming. Psychology is unique in that what we are trying to observation is the mind, but it is not a thing we can point to in the natural world or gauge with a direct sensor. It's this fact that makes replicability and generalizability very difficult for the psychological science; defining measures of the mind is difficult because the mind, per se, has no physical referent. So make sacrifices are made in service of science, but at a disservice to developing useful technology.

The psychological sciences sacrifice generalizability in order to make measurements. We call this compromise "the laboratory", or maybe *experimental control*. In the laboratory, how people experience stimuli and the conditions under which they experience them can be rigidly controlled. The laboratory itself is a test-medium, a metaphorical bath-tub full of water that people can be passed through to understand their qualities. Sometimes studies send people out into the world with technology to provide reports on how they're feeling at random intervals during the day. This is a step closer to generalization. However, it is important to note that even then it's those reports that are observed and neither actual feelings, nor any real behaviors are observed upon which their actual feelings and thoughts could be inferred. It's this inability to measure real-behavior and the control exerted over experience, in service of measurement that constrains generalizable research. In turn, this makes it very difficult to lean on the knowledge created by to psychological sciences to create technology that might better the human condition. New measurement opportunities exist, however, in software environments. With these opportunities the field of HCI will take the lead in facilitating a deeper understanding of human behavior and cognition, and developing new, advanced technology that capitalizes on this understanding.

3 Software Is the New Human Measurement Medium

Alex (Sandy) Pentland at MIT's Human Dynamics Lab did something very ambitious. He and his team led by Nadav Aharony instrumented research participants with mobile devices (e.g., smart phones) that captured how those participants interact with one another—when they were proximal to one another and how much time they spent in that state—and how they interacted with other social and marketing media. They sent these participants back into the "wild" and let them interact with one another and their phones. Ambition is a good thing and through their Friends and Family study, Dr. Pentland and his colleagues were able to track human behavior in the wild and predict things like social contagion (e.g., "meme" spread), buying preferences, and other great things [2]. Almost more important than their findings in the Friends and Family study and other notable investigations [3, 4] was what they were able to accomplish in terms of measuring real people, doing real things in the real-world. It's also worth noting that was first accomplished by a few psychologists working with computer and data scientists and not psychologists alone, even though the same technology (e.g., Bluetooth-enabled phones with SDKs) was available many years earlier.

Dr. Pentland and his colleagues made real progress on the front of how to capture real world human behavior in the real world. His insight to use the technology that people bring with them into the real-world to enable real-world measurement was simple and elegant. This is extremely clever, in fact, because it highlights a thing about humans that is very important and often taken for granted: humans use tools. There are those that effectively argue that humans' ability to be social and to use sociality itself as a tool to further their agendas is the sine qua non of the human condition [5]. This is probably true, but our knack for using and inventing new tools to shape our environment is part of a much older lineage and is likely convoluted with a number of other socio-cognitive feats that humans pride themselves on [6]. Software is a tool that people use to perform myriad tasks in myriad real-world environments and proving the value of exploiting software for the purpose of understanding people well is the very brilliant thing that Dr. Pentland demonstrated so well.

As of 2013, US persons spend an estimated average of 37 h per month using smartphone applications and browsers, another 27 h per month using the internet on personal computers, and 133 h per month watching live television [7]. Each of these environments are now mediated (almost fully) by some software interface. That's nearly 40% of human waking hours plugged into virtual, but real, environments for entertainment, commerce, and productivity. More importantly, that's nearly 40% of human endeavors that we can capture through software environments. So, why haven't the psychological scientists seized on this opportunity?

Since Dr. Pentland's research, some psychologistshave started to capitalize on virtual mediums as ways to understand human behavior in real-world environments. In addition to getting increasingly clever about using mobile devices to administer questionnaire methods, and the like [8–10], they are also trying to understand publically available data in communities like Facebook and Twitter [11–14]. What they aren't doing, however, highlights a missing voice at the table of the psychological sciences and a skill-set that is sorely missing from the field—that of the Human Computer Interface (HCI) researcher. What they aren't doing is two-fold: (1) turning dynamic user activity data into models of human behavior and cognition and (2) using the design of software tools to solicit behavior from humans so that we can learn more from them. The third thing to note is that HCI researchers and practitioners are in the perfect position to make good on a deeper, generalized understanding of humans in ubiquitous software environments by developing technology that exploits this understanding to benefit everyone; they are best positioned to cover these gaps as they live in the bridge between software and humans, and in the bridge between software and the value that humans take from it.

4 Making Software a Sensor for Human Behavior

In the bulk of psychological research studies that have explored human behavior native to software environments, data collection is generally restricted to artifacts of software use, rather than the use itself. The difference is large and important. An artifact of software use might be subscribing to research participants' Twitter, Instagram, or Facebook feed. These are the things that are left behind in software environments, and while they are descriptive of human behavior in these environments, at an aggregate level, they are not themselves behavior. Even in Dr. Pentland's research, mobile devices were "instrumented" in so far as Bluetooth and sensor data (e.g., accelerometer, etc.) were recorded. However, participants purchasing history was collected through credit card statements given over by participants, and social media data was collected by opting into a Facebook "scraping" application [2].

By analogy, capturing artifacts of human behavior in software environments is like an archeological approach to studying to human behavior—we can learn from people by studying the tools, art, and literature they leave behind. However, the real opportunity for understanding the human mind or *cognition* in software environments is, by analogy, watching how the tools, art, and literature are made. This is a key philosophical and methodological gap that very often prevents research in the psychological sciences from meeting criteria for generalizability—artifacts are, by definition, firmly rooted within the context in which they emerge. The skills, processes, and behaviors that create artifacts are, however, portable and repurposed across contexts. Measuring the former, and not the latter is a road map toward generalizable scientific research that could culminate into technology for large-scale consumption and use.

In software environments, every action initiated by users and software (e.g., automation) can be logged and recorded, in real-time. So, rather than restricting data collecting to what people leave behind in software environments, we can collect on *how* users search through other Tweets before they respond or compose new content, or *how* much time they spend editing their profile. The question of how—the process—with which people use tools to perform tasks and how their immediate context shapes that process and informs the artifacts produced is the important one. It is process where information pertaining to learning, memory, attention, perception, reasoning, and decision-making lives; these are the hallmarks of cognition and how the mind works [15]. Can software act as a sensor to capture behavior rich enough to make strong inferences about the cognitive processes underlying that behavior?

A software sensors' output is a software log—of user or system changes. Logging user activities for a variety of use-cases is not a new idea. From keystroke logging, to mouse logging, and click-counting, numerous studies have used this data for purposes ranging from usability analysis to workload monitoring [16–19]. Software development kits (SDKs) and application program interfaces (APIs) are now so commonplace, that virtually anyone with some competency in a relevant programming language can build "hooks" into an application, or "instrument" software, so that user activities can be collected. There are even myriad commercial and open-source approaches for collecting user activity logs. However, each of these approaches fall short of capturing cognition.

There are three reasons why approaches fall short of accurately capturing behavior: (1) specificity, (2) context, (3) labeling. **Specificity** refers to whether user activity logs contain sufficient information to capture behavior as it unfolds over time. By analogy: if user behavior is the signal, and software is the sensor, do the channels through which sensor data is collected have sufficient information to recreate behavior? **Context** refers to other information present at the time user behavior that is useful for isolating various behaviors. Sometimes in order to improve signal-to-noise-ratio (SNR), other information is needed to deconvolute one signal from another. **Labeling** refers to turning machine readable user activity logs into human readable logs. This is a problem of semantics—conceptually mapping user behavior activity to cognitive processes. Without a humanized understanding of the signal, we have no way of comparing different types of behavior and the various conditions under which it is samples. Without that we can't understand humans in our own terms.

We take a signal processing approach to the problems described above. Over the course of nearly 5 years of research and development, we have made some progress in solving them, at least as they pertain to user activity modeling in graphic user interfaces (GUIs) for productivity applications. Our best guidance for aspiring psychological scientists within the field of HCI is to take the simile of software as a sensor very seriously.

1. **Specificity** is fundamentally a discrimination problem. If users are interacting with data analytics application, for example, we need to be able to understand how they interact (and across) different elements of that application in a software logging scheme if we are to replicate their actual behavior. We might think about this in the same terms we think about the sensitivity and discriminatory power of survey question items—whether each item uniquely captures specific information and their redundancy with other items. To illustrate, Google Analytics makes a good "strawman". Google Analytics (and other "tag" management interfaces) doesn't require that all activities are uniquely, or fully specified. If only a subset of application features are reporting user activities, then we lose critical data for interpreting users' choice of activity given the range of choices they have. In this respect, we need to capture all user activities, which includes both user events (e.g., inputs) as well as the elements with which those events are nested—this is the anatomy of an activity.

This is critical for understanding decision-making, attention, which in turn are key for understanding how people experiment and learn [20, 21]. Put differently, if we're to understand how a tool is used to perform a task, then we need to understand the degrees of freedom with which to the tool can be applied. With this information, however, then behavioral data can be used to inform decision science.

A second point about specificity: we need to be able to finely discriminate within elements. Google Analytics has a very simple Category-Action-Label-Value structure in their logging schema [22]. In the application of this schema, developers will apply category inputs that are either too granular (e.g., button label), or too general (e.g., "button"), depending on their needs. In many cases this makes it difficult to discern user activities between elements. This prevents us from being able to make a full and accurate account to collecting rich-enough user activity logs to be able to recreate human behavior in software environments.

We have made progress in addressing this gap as part of the Apache Software as a Sensor project. Our solution for both web and thick-client productivity applications is to simply log every user event, the target GUI element that event targeted, and how that GUI element is nested among others (e.g., Document Object Model). Our logging service—the User Analytic Logging Engine (UserALE)[1] collects all this data, cursor position, as well as key-strokes. This provides a comprehensive open-source data stream for replicating human behavior from logs collected in situ [23].

2. **Context** aids in how to interpret user activity data. Context helps answer the question as to *why* users might have behaved a certain way and can often take the form of other data that can be fused with user activity data. For example, feedback to the user through a GUI can offer context for how users might engage in recursive behavior or how patterns of use might become more systematic overtime through feedback-driven reinforcement learning. Analogously, we might think about context as though they were independent variables or experimental factors, which given context to dependent variable behavior in an experimental design. Context is very difficult to capture in software, but far easier than capturing context in the real world. In order to capture context effectively, we need access other data exposed to the user through the software. While this can be difficult given varied data formats used by applications, a key consideration that can help simplify data fusion is *time*. Like any sensor synchronization effort, developing a software sensor requires that each user activity log is accurately time-stamped so that other sources of data can be co-registered. In this respect, in order to be useful user activity logs need be represented as a time-series. This is relatively commonplace in any logging framework (system or user log frameworks). However, capturing both client-side timing, as well as a logging server clock time, provides a way of reconciling the timing of other data received from other services (e.g., context data) that may be operating on different clocks.

[1] For code, documentation and demonstrated of the Apache Software as a Sensor user activity logging capability, visit http://senssoft.incubator.apache.org.

3. **Labeling**, as noted, is a matter of semantics. How best to apply human-readable labels to user activity logs, is typically proscribed by the use-case for analyzing user activity logs. For example, in previous versions of UserALE, we experimented with labeling each user activity log with a corresponding analytic workflow process label, given that this version was developed for data analytic applications. The important thing to note here is that labels should be fluid—in order to make more generalized inferences from behavior in software behavior, we must be able to relabel data so that data collected from different use-cases can be analyzed together or at least compared (Fig. 1).

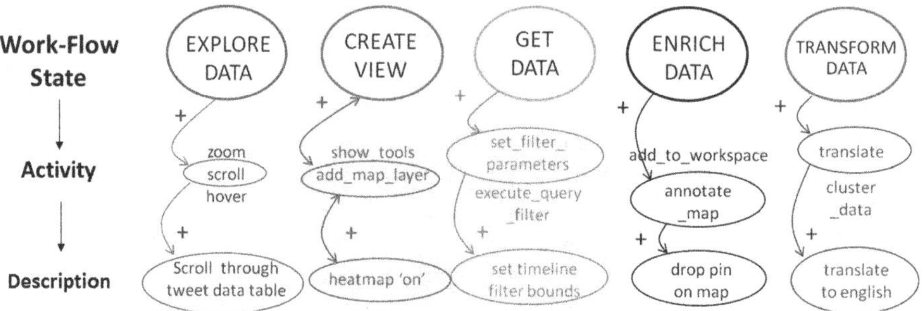

Fig. 1. Semantic labels incorporated into logging schemas fail in implementation and scale

In the early version of the UserALE logging scheme we asked too much of developers: they were to assign mutually exclusive labels to each software event that ascribed semantic meaning relevant to users' analytic workflow to each pair of user activity and the GUI element target. To our chagrin, we found that these labels were applied inconsistently by developers, making those semantic labels useless in analysis—user activity and target element data remained useful, however. Our insight, which we offer here, is that user activity logs should be collected and stored in a raw machine-readable format, which can then be labeled with human-readable logs ex post facto, and relabeled as needed through either manual or automated processes (e.g., Machine Learning). This provides a way to make logging more useful from an informational perspective and provides the ability to scale that real generalizable science requires. There are other advantages to collecting user activity log data in a portable, machine-readable data in formats, which we will discuss in other sections.

Making inferences about the mind-at-work is about capturing a human *process*. Currently, the psychological sciences largely constrain themselves to capturing the outputs of human process—performance metrics, work products, and artifacts left in the wake of process. The information from process is much richer and ripe for modeling behavior in such a way as to make inferences about cognition clearer and a path toward generalization and invention more navigable.

The first step to achieving an understanding of how people use software tools in service of understanding what *how* reveals about cognition is capturing process-level data through software instrumentation. Yes, this is possible. However, standard guidelines and design principles are needed for portable log formats that both meet requisite needs for specific use-cases, and yet at scale can accumulate into a large corpus of data for conducting scientific analyses. Of course, the next step is what to do with process data once you've collected it. Fortunately, there has been some progress made there, too.

5 Modeling and Making Sense of Process

Software logs in service of capturing cognition (at least as proscribed above) contain three different kinds of information—time, space, and opportunity. Formally speaking, software user activity logs are categorically specified, sequential event data, nested within a time-series. **Time** indicates when events took place as well as the distance between one step in a sequence and the next. **Space** indicates where in the GUI users' efforts were allocated, or rather what element of the GUI effort was directed toward. Finally, **opportunity** indicates where users did not go or where they could go next. These are all essential elements of modeling user activities from which inferences about cognition or, more coarsely mental states can be made. There is much work left to do in order to get cognition from behavior. However, below we describe a few approaches that are different in how they use this information to understand people.

One approach we've seen is a frequentist accounting of what humans do. Here we refer to "click-counting" or other aggregations of specific user interactions within GUIs that are expressed as a rate, count, mean or variance [17, 24–28]. These approaches are very often used to infer "cognitive states"[2] such as stress (an arousal/anxiety state), frustration, or cognitive load [29] (the extent to which some task requires mental effort beyond the implicit task demands). The information we are using to compute metrics (e.g., click-rate) that we might use to infer cognitive state can be said to implicate time and space in GUIs. However, the use of time and space information is used strictly for aggregation. What we are really modeling in this way is simply user effort out, not process. Sometimes metrics like these are useful when we need a continuous data stream to correlate with some other measure as it pertains to an evaluation. But, this approach aggregates otherwise rich data into oblivion, sacrificing a true accounting of human behavior in service of performance metrics. We advocate for a different approach—one where you can model human behavior and have your metrics, too.

If software is a sensor for human processes, then models are different perspectives of what that signal looks like, emphasizing different dimensions. Purely aggregative approaches can be said to be models only in so far as we are fitting a simplified (or fused) data stream into a simple distribution of values and describing that distribution with simple measures of central tendency and distributional width. By definition, aggregation reduces the amount information into a single dimension. We advocate that researchers not start with this step, but rather start by building rich models of behavior that account

[2] Cognitive States aren't the same thing as cognition, which is how we process information, decide, select actions, not how we feel at any given time (affect has states) but it's has a lot of domain relevance to HCI.

for space, time and opportunity, then follow by aggregating model features to produce continuous metrics for whatever purpose. Below is an example:

Rather than purely emphasizing the amount of activities users pour into a GUI, we sought to understand how users' effort was distributed across different elements in the GUI, in time, and how these different allocations changed throughout tasks with analytic (productivity) applications. We envisioned these allocations as states of a human-computer system, or different strategies users might take to interacting with the applications, where we could observe those states changing into others: a Markovian process. The trouble with Markov Models is that they are typically one-off—each different user by application pairing represents a different system that needs to be modeled separately. This would result in "apples to oranges" comparisons between users, which means that we wouldn't have sufficient context to understand what those states mean. So, we adapted a Bayesian approach to Hidden Markov Models [30] to suite our needs. The result was a Beta-Process Hidden Markov (BPHMM) modeling approach that is largely unsupervised and allows us to assign each user to states within a global library of states that characterize how an entire ensemble of users allocate effort across the application. The result was pretty interesting (Fig. 2).

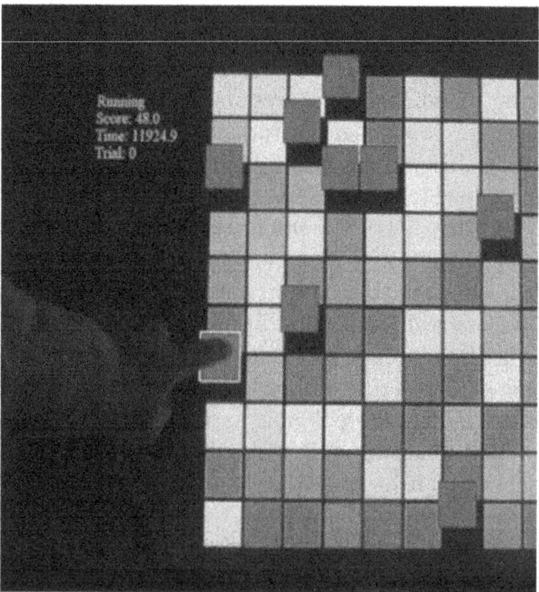

Fig. 2. "Wiggle" game used in BPHMM pilot

In a pilot study, using a rudimentary user activity logging schema applied to a simple video game (something like Bejeweled). Our research participants (users) were told that in the game could acquire points, and their goal was to figure out how to acquire as many points as they could, but we did not tell them how to acquire points. They were tasked to explore how to put together different user activities and elements and learn the rule of the game through trial and error. We then applied this modeling technique to user activity data collected, in situ, during their task.

Our models illustrate how user behavior coalesce into strategies (states), emphasizing different patterns of use of each of the different elements in the game. Strategies can be described in a multinomial plot describing the relative probability of observing each availability, relative to one another. These states are bounded by time, and while the modeling solution produces a single global state-space across users, each users' transition probability between the various state remains unique (Fig. 3).

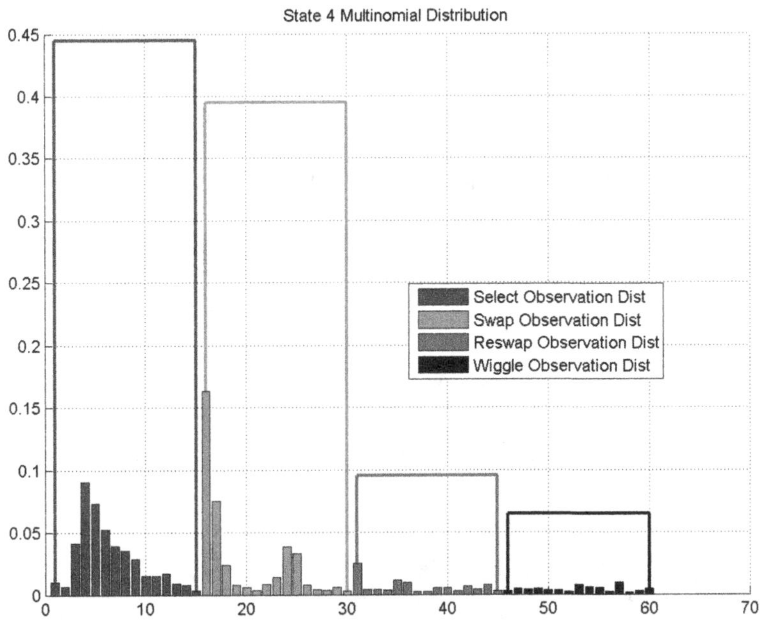

Fig. 3. BPHMM example usage state

This isn't cognition either, but it is a solution for accurately accounting for how users make use of the space in applications, how that usage changes with time, and importantly, what features of GUIs users did *and* didn't use (opportunity). We were able to compute metrics describing the distributional aspects of each the states. We computed a measure of each states' kurtotic qualities—whether effort was distributed across different elements or focused on specific elements. Classifying states in this way, we then tabulated the percentage of time users spent in one type of state or another. For our purposes at the time, we hypothesized that users who spent the most in states emphasizing a single activity (GUI element) didn't really evidence an understanding of how different activities fit together to produce points. Our results indicate that our hypotheses was not false. Almost unequivocally, participants who were incorrect in reporting the rule for getting points they were tasked to discover spent their time in these states [30]. The time users spent in these states was also correlated with their post-task reports of workload and mental effort (cognitive load), and the likelihood that participants transitioned from these states to other states of this kind reported less of a proclivity for exploring complex problem (need for cognition). Finally, we found that the predictive power of this metric over self-reported task difficulty exceeded that of simple activity-rate calculations.

In our current work, we're focusing on a different dimension of user process: sequence. Specifically, we are using extensible graph models and methods derived from genetic subsequence analysis to understand how users individually and en masse chain activities together to complete tasks with data analysis applications. Using graph metrics like betweenness-centrality and others, we are able to show how various features of GUIs are centroids of use, gating the flow of user effort from one part of the application space to others. This modeling approach has been reduced to practice and embedded in the open-source Apache Software as a Sensor project. At present, we're replicating and extending our state- and sequence-based findings in actual data analytic applications that people use [31], as well as finding other applications for the rich data in user activity logs to improve signal to noise ratio in other sensor data (e.g., physiological data) [32] (Fig. 4).

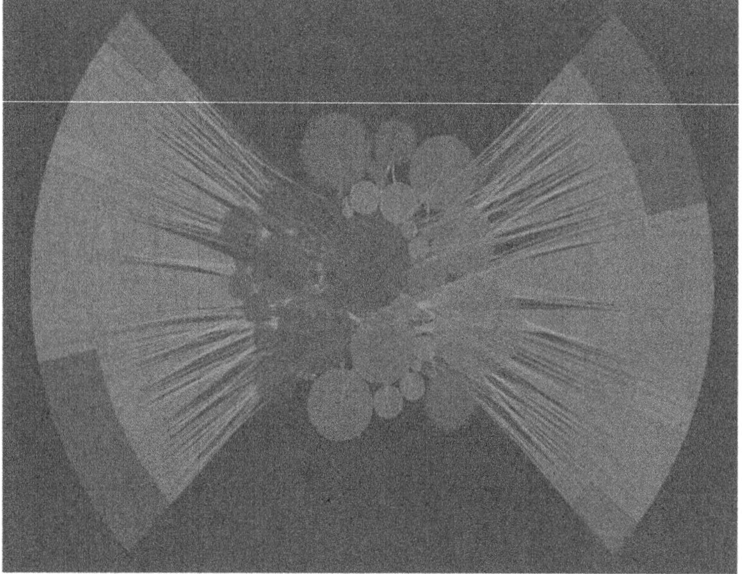

Fig. 4. The "Bowie" plot for visualizing graph workflow metrics

State and sequence are different and powerful modeling approaches for understanding behavior, but they aren't quite cognition either. It's worth asking what will cognition look like? Will we know it when we see it? We believe it will take many forms. The brain is a complex system of many networks composed of the same sub-networks. The overarching network of activity in the brain is constantly adapting with new sensory inputs modifying previous network states and shaping or biasing the basis for future network states [33, 34]. Behavioral models of cognition will likely look similar because job number 1 of the brain is to coordinate behavior.

What is presently missing from our ability to model behavior and make strong inferences about cognition is *context*. Context—information users are exposed to during software use—is the hardest thing to capture in software environments, for both technical reasons and because it's very difficult to label context in order to understand whether it represents, for example, feedback from some other process and whether that feedback was reinforcing or whatever. But with context, we can turn models of user activity into the basis for decision- and learning-science. Context gives use stimulus-response cases for why users change their frequency of use of certain aspects of application space. It gives us change-points within a time-series, and a way of inferring whether a selection between different elements of a GUI represents an opportunity taken or simple habit. That being said, the corpus of signal processing and modeling approaches at our disposal today is probably sufficient for capturing cognition, even while our ability to capture and effectively label context is not.

6 HCI Will Lead Progress Toward Cognitive Modeling

We believe that the psychological sciences will not naturally move to a methodological framework for capturing human behavior process from software environments, even though they are increasingly apt to explore human behavioral artifacts in these environments. Their widespread inclusion of neurotechnologies and mobile devices is evidence of their readiness to adopt new technology [35, 36], but evidence is lacking to suggest that they themselves innovate new technologies in support of scientific inquiry. This is mostly due to the fact that historical trends in the psychological sciences promote training targeted at producing more psychologists that will practice in academic environments. Outside of industry, these psychologists will be reinforced based on a throughput of research studies at small scales to support a steady stream of publications that in turn provide a commodity for advancement, etc. Promising new trends see the psychological sciences selecting new students and post-docs with programming skills in Python, Ruby, and other languages that lend themselves well to building technology that will shape research methods to come. But, they are not there yet.

We believe that HCI researchers will pave the way to fully realize the opportunity for measuring human behavior in ubiquitous software environments, for a number of reasons. First, HCI researchers have motivation to capture human process given a field wide focus on human cognition, how humans digest information in digital environments, and how best to minimize and ameliorate the burdens placed on users by poorly engineered digital technology. Whereas, psychologists may settle for capturing artifacts of human behavior, a distinct focus on the process through which humans efficiently produce work is a hallmark of HCI. Second, HCI researchers have many of the requisite skill sets needed to build upon and improve apparatus for collecting data with the quality needed for high resolution behavioral modeling. Third, HCI researchers have been acquiring new skills related to large scale data analysis owing to growth in commercial tools for user event logging and the resultant blend between HCI and digital marketing enterprises.

Most importantly, HCI is a technology focused field. In addition to innovating new methods and techniques for understanding human in real-world environments, HCI researchers are best positioned to transition understanding into technology for widespread use. With access to users and their needs, HCI is positioned to become the new field of applied psychology. Rather than the clinician/practitioner model that currently occupies the largest segment of applied psychology, HCI would add a much needed segment of *technologists.* As these HCI technologists improve methods to capture and quantify behavioral process in service of developing technology, they will in turn be creating new methodologies and apparatus that improve the quality and generalizability of foundational research in the psychological sciences.

References

1. Bacon, F.: Novum Organum. Clarendon press, Oxford (1878)
2. Aharony, N., et al.: Social fMRI: investigating and shaping social mechanisms in the real world. Pervasive Mob. Comput. **7**(6), 643–659 (2011)
3. Montjoye, Y.-A., Quoidbach, J., Robic, F., Pentland, A.: Predicting personality using novel mobile phone-based metrics. In: Greenberg, A.M., Kennedy, W.G., Bos, N.D. (eds.) SBP 2013. LNCS, vol. 7812, pp. 48–55. Springer, Heidelberg (2013). doi:10.1007/978-3-642-37210-0_6
4. Pentland, A.: Social Physics: How Good Ideas Spread-the Lessons from a New Science. Penguin, New York (2014)
5. Byrne, R., Whiten, A.: Machiavellian intelligence: Social Expertise and the Evolution of Intellect in Monkeys, Apes, and Humans. Oxford Science Publications, Oxford (1989)
6. Matsuzawa, T.: Primate foundations of human intelligence: a view of tool use in nonhuman primates and fossil hominids. In: Matsuzawa, T. (ed.) Primate Origins of Human Cognition and Behavior, pp. 3–25. Springer, Tokyo (2008)
7. Nielsen: The US Digital Consumer Report (2014). http://www.nielsen.com/us/en/insights/reports/2014/the-us-digital-consumer-report.html. Accessed 16 Oct 2015
8. Berkman, E.T., Graham, A.M., Fisher, P.A.: Training self-control: a domain-general translational neuroscience approach. Child. Dev. Perspect. **6**(4), 374–384 (2012)
9. Berkman, E.T., Falk, E.B., Lieberman, M.D.: In the trenches of real-world self-control neural correlates of breaking the link between craving and smoking. Psychol. Sci. **22**(4), 498–506 (2011)
10. Berkman, E.T., Lieberman, M.D.: What's outside the black box?: The status of behavioral outcomes in neuroscience research. Psychol. Inq. **22**(2), 100–107 (2011)
11. Falk, E.B., et al.: Social network structure modulates neural processes involved in successful communication and message propagation. In: 21st Annual Meeting of the Cognitive Neuroscience Society, Boston (2014)
12. Falk, E.B., Way, B.M., Jasinska, A.J.: An imaging genetics approach to understanding social influence. Front. Hum. Neurosci. **6**, 168 (2012)
13. Bayer, J., et al.: Facebook in context(s): measuring emotional responses across time and space. New Media Soc. 1461444816681522 (2016)
14. Schmaelzle, R., et al.: Brain connectivity dynamics during social interaction reflect social network structure. bioRxiv. 096420 (2017)
15. Neisser, U.: Cognition and Reality: Principles and Implications of Cognitive Psychology. WH Freeman/Times Books/Henry Holt & Co., New York (1976)
16. Boi, P., et al.: Reconstructing user's attention on the web through mouse movements and perception-based content identification. ACM Trans. Appl. Percept. (TAP) **13**(3), 15 (2016)

17. Durkee, K.T., et al.: System decision framework for augmenting human performance using real-time workload classifiers. In: 2015 IEEE International Multi-disciplinary Conference on Cognitive Methods in Situation Awareness and Decision. IEEE (2015)
18. Holzinger, A.: Usability engineering methods for software developers. Commun. ACM **48**(1), 71–74 (2005)
19. Preece, J., Rombach, H.D.: A taxonomy for combining software engineering and human-computer interaction measurement approaches: towards a common framework. Int. J. Hum Comput Stud. **41**(4), 553–583 (1994)
20. Rolls, E.T.: Memory systems in the brain. Annu. Rev. Psychol. **51**(1), 599–630 (2000)
21. Glimcher, P.W., Fehr, E.: Neuroeconomics: Decision Making and the Brain. Academic Press, London (2013)
22. Google, I.: Anatomy of events. https://support.google.com/analytics/answer/1033068?hl=en#Anatomy. Accessed 27 Feb 2017
23. Apache, User Analytic Logging Engine (UserALE.js), The Apache Software Foundation
24. Hill, R.G., Sears, L.M., Melanson, S.W.: 4000 clicks: a productivity analysis of electronic medical records in a community hospital ED. Am. J. Emerg. Med. **31**(11), 1591–1594 (2013)
25. Rodrigues, M., Gonçalves, S., Carneiro, D., Novais, P., Fdez-Riverola, F.: Keystrokes and clicks: measuring stress on e-learning students. In: Casillas, J., Martínez-López, F., Vicari, R., De la Prieta, F. (eds.) Management Intelligent Systems. AISC, vol. 220, pp. 119–126. Springer, Heidelberg (2013). doi:10.1007/978-3-319-00569-0_15
26. Xu, K., et al.: Analytic provenance for sensemaking: a research agenda. IEEE Comput. Graph. Appl. **35**(3), 56–64 (2015)
27. Brown, J., et al.: Characterizing mission and user context for proactive decision support. In: Proceedings of the Human Factors and Ergonomics Society Annual Meeting. Sage Publications (2016)
28. Jones, R.M., et al.: Using cognitive workload analysis to predict and mitigate workload for training simulation. Procedia Manuf. **3**, 5777–5784 (2015)
29. Ayres, P., Paas, F.: Cognitive load theory: new directions and challenges. Appl. Cognitive Psychol. **26**(6), 827–832 (2012)
30. Mariano, L.J., et al.: Modeling strategic use of human computer interfaces with novel hidden Markov Models. Front. Psychol. **6** (2015)
31. Poore, J., et al.: Modeling strategic use of human computer interfaces II: addressing critical methodological shortcoming in understanding human behavior in ubiquitous software environments (In Preparation)
32. Poore, J.C., et al.: Operationalizing engagement with multimedia as user coherence with context. IEEE Trans. Affect. Comput. **8**, 95–107 (2016)
33. Buzsaki, G.: Rhythms of the Brain. Oxford University Press, Oxford (2009)
34. Buzsáki, G., Draguhn, A.: Neuronal oscillations in cortical networks. Science **304**(5679), 1926–1929 (2004)
35. Ochsner, K.N., Lieberman, M.D.: The emergence of social cognitive neuroscience. Am. Psychol. **56**(9), 717 (2001)
36. Lieberman, M.D.: A social cognitive neuroscience approach. Soc. Judgm. Implicit Explicit Process. **5**, 44 (2003)

Vocational Training of IT-Professionals

Coping with Future Demands

Henrik Schwarz(✉) and Stephanie Conein(✉)

Federal Institute for Vocational Education and Training (BIBB), Robert-Schuman-Platz 3, 53175 Bonn, Germany
{schwarz,conein}@bibb.de

Abstract. Since their implementation in 1997 the four German training occupations in the field of information and communication technology are writing a success story. Nevertheless they are facing big challenges because of the rapid development of technology and the increasing digitalization of production, service and consumption. The German Federal Institute for Vocational Education and Training (BIBB) has evaluated the existing IT-training occupations. The Results are based on a broad survey conducting interviews in companies with different target groups combined with an online questioning of more than 6,000 participants. Findings suggest that although there is a common contentment among companies, trainers and Trainees, new contents should be included in the training and the training profiles as well as their inner structure should be revised.

Keywords: Information technology · Training occupation · ICT · Training system · Initial training

1 Introduction

Germany's economic success is mainly based on well-trained skilled workers, whose qualification profiles are regularly adapted to new requirements. Within its so-called "Dual System" (see Table 1) annually more than 500,000 school leavers conclude an training contract with a company in currently 327 state recognized occupations.

In the nineties of the last century Germany experienced an intensive debate about the further development of its dual system. The increasing automation and computerization of production coupled with the development of new industries and business models in the service sector necessitated a profound adjustment of the dual training professions. Within the last 20 years, more than 230 training profiles have been modernized and over 60 new training profiles have been developed. Accordingly in 1997 four new IT occupations have been implemented, addressed to suppliers of Information and Communication Technology (ICT) and service as well to companies in other sectors using ICT to run their business and production (see Table 2).

M. Kurosu (Ed.): HCI 2017, Part I, LNCS 10271, pp. 74–85, 2017.
DOI: 10.1007/978-3-319-58071-5_6

Table 1. Characteristics of then German Dual System of initial training

Duality of Training venues	Alternating company- and school-based vocational education and training
Duality of legal jurisdiction	In-Company training is based on federal law (Federal vocational training act) School based training is under federal states law
Duality of funding	Financed by Companies providing training (training allowance, trainers, training workshops, equipment) and (partially) by the government
Shared responsibilities	Common steering and organisation of vocational education and training by the government and the representatives of employer & employee organisations (decisions based on consensus)
Training contracts	Legal relationship between Trainee and Employer (rights and duties for both sides) based on educational laws and labour law
Quality assurance	Occupational standards valid throughout the country, Examination & monitoring standards based on the federal vocational training act

Table 2. IT-Training occupations and main activities

Training occupation	Main activities
IT-Specialist (m/f) with two specializations[a] (a) System integration (b) Application development	(a) Maintenance and administration of IT systems (b) Software development and programming
IT-Systems electronics technician (m/f)	Installation and repair of IT systems
IT-System support specialist (m/f)	Selling hard- and software
IT Officer (m/f)	Buying hard- and software, training of staff

[a]In the German vocational training system, some training occupations have selectable and/or combinable differentiations. If a training occupation has "specializations" it means that one third of the training content & objectives are different. For example: in a three-year training period the third year is split up into different specializations. For more details see Schwarz et al. 2015.

With their introduction in 1997, the IT occupations have embarked on a booming information and communication technology (ICT) sector. Beyond customer and business-process orientation the four IT occupations were developed to fit to rapid technological change and fast-changing market demands. By combining common, broad-based IT core qualifications with profound specialist qualifications, their flexible structure and an audit model oriented to the company's practice, the training occupations met the great needs of the economy.

In the first year of their existence, nearly 5,000 training contracts were concluded, and many new companies could be won for dual training in this area for the first time (see Borch and Schwarz 1999). Now, the number of training contracts signed annually is relatively stable at around 15,000, recently increased up to 16,000. Since their introduction, more than 250,000 skilled IT professionals have been trained in these four occupations (see Fig. 1).

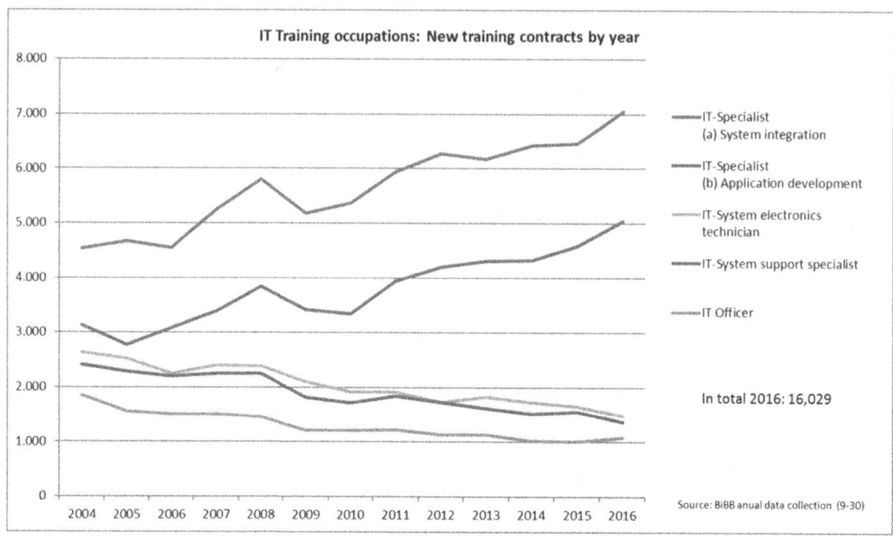

Fig. 1. IT Training occupations: new training contracts by year

The development of the Internet of Things will continue to drive the demand for IT skills in all economic sectors. Since 2008, there are more internet-connected things than humans on Earth. It is assumed that by 2020 the number of internet-capable interacting devices such as smartphones, cars, machine tools, consumer & entertainment devices connected by sensors, software and transmission technology will increase up to more than 200 billion (see Sharma 2014). This requires operating systems, processors, sensors, storage technologies, applications, service and network technology.

"Last year 15% of companies in the business sector hired new employees with IT competences and 15% are planning to do so by the end of 2018. During the same period of time the numbers for the demand for skilled workers in the ICT sector will be 31% and 43% respectively." (BMWi 2016: 14). However, many companies fear that, in particular, the shortage of skilled workers can hinder the advancement of digitalization (BMWi 2016: 69). Estimates on the labor market development are assuming that by 2030 the additional demand for IT professionals will be as much as 3.15 per cent higher per year than without the digitalized industrial production so called as industry 4.0. Beyond that the "additional demand for IT professions will be 37% outside the ICT sector, in the manufacturing sector" (Hall et al. 2016: 6, 18 p.).

The increasing number of networking sensors and actuators in production, software-intensive embedded systems as well as the digitalization of entire business processes will further increase the requirements for stable and safety networks, real-time processing, cyber security and the processing of large amounts of data. Accordingly, topics like software development, cloud computing and big data, as well as IT security as a mega-topic are not fundamentally new, however, complex production & application scenarios lead to new requirements for IT professionals.

These requirements address not only the area of IT skills, but also the personal and social skills. IT professionals are increasingly working in interdisciplinary teams and dealing with complex cross cutting issues along the whole business process chain. For them, the "key qualifications" such as "willingness to learn, teamwork, flexibility, problem analysis and problem-solving abilities, as well as management and project control competences", will become more important (Aichholzer 2016: 31)

From the point of view of vocational training, the described developments raise the question of the extent to which the existing IT occupations, even considering their flexible and thus also adaptive structure, can cover the current and future needs for IT professionals quantitatively and qualitatively.

2 Evaluation of the IT Occupations

The BIBB evaluation of the IT occupations, which was finished at the end of 2016, aimed at identifying current and foreseeable requirements for IT professionals and at developing proposals for the future design of the IT occupations. Central issues have been:

- contents and objectives;
- required profiles, structure and design;
- further education and permeability between VET and the academic system.

The study, commissioned by the Federal Ministry of Economics and Energy and accompanied by a specialist advisory board, followed a three-step design consisting of an exploratory phase, a phase with qualitative and a phase with quantitative surveys (see Conein and Schwarz 2015).

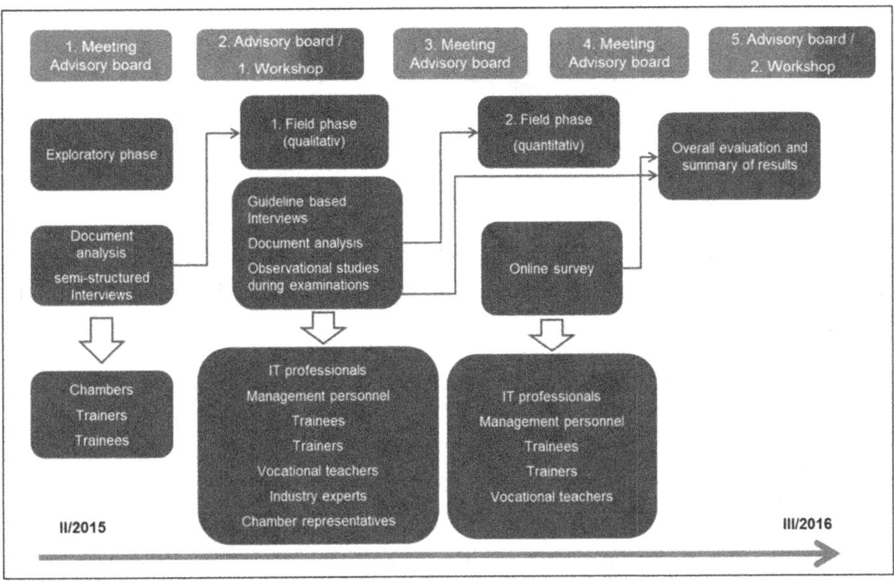

Fig. 2. Research design

The research design (see Fig. 2) allows the triangulation of data and methods. For example: data triangulation is possible because of having asked the same questions to different target groups. Different views on the same topics could be presented in this way. In addition, the same questions were asked both in the qualitative interviews and in the quantitative online survey, whereby a method triangulation was realized.

During the first exploratory phase the field was investigated and the access was prepared. Methods were document analysis and semi-structured, guideline based expert interviews with some target groups (trainees, trainers, representatives from chambers of commerce and industry).

In the second phase, qualitative data were collected. Methods were case studies of ten companies with up to five semi-structured, guideline based expert interviews per company. Nine additional interviews were carried out with industry experts, teachers and representatives from chambers of industry and commerce. In total 54 approx. 60 min interviews were conducted and analyzed by using the qualitative content analysis based on Mayring (2015) (Fig. 3).

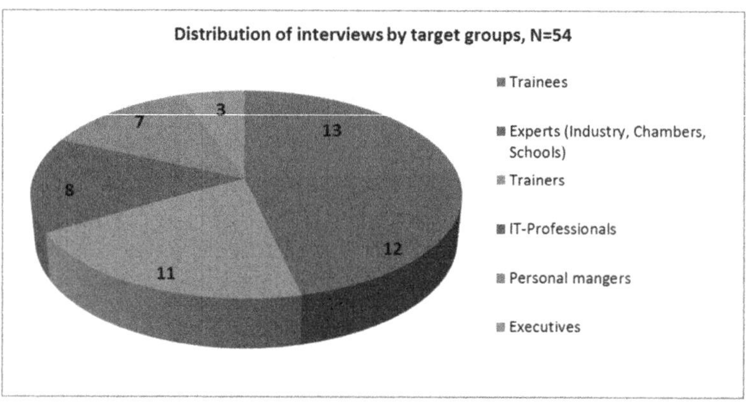

Fig. 3. Interviews by target groups

The results of the qualitative phase served as basis of an online survey which represents the third phase. The online questionnaire was fully answered by more than 6,000 participants (see Table 3).

Table 3. Respondents of the online survey by target group

Target group	N	%
IT-professionals	1,911	31.3%
Traineess	1,767	29.0%
In company Trainers	1,237	20.3%
Management personnel, work council members	748	12.3%
Teachers from vocational schools	438	7.2%
Total	6,101	100.0%

The surveyed IT professionals are working in all economic sectors. They belong for about one-third to the ICT industry, while two-thirds are spread over almost all other economic sectors, including 11% of the manufacturing sector, followed by public administration, other services and financial & insurance services.

In the following, the main focus will be on selected results of the BIBB evaluation study, which refer to the urgent need for change in the current IT training. They concern conceivable changes to the occupational profiles and certain training content (for further results, see the final report at www.bibb.de/voruntersung_itberufe).

3 Findings

3.1 Demarcation of Occupational Profiles

Asked about the relevance of competences in 18 selected fields of occupational requirements, it becomes clear that the various occupational profiles require very different, but in some cases very similar competences. The two specializations of the IT-Specialist (System integration and Application development) are clearly differentiated (see Fig. 2). For example, the areas of software development and databases play an important role for IT-Specialists/Application development. IT-Specialist/System integration mainly require competences in the areas of network engineering, administration & operating systems as well as IT security. The two specializations of the IT-Specialist have proved their worth. From the interviews, there are indications to separate these profiles even more. While 44.4% of the respondents voiced their opinions in favor of maintaining the specializations, 37.8% supported a separation into two independent occupational profiles.

Occupational requirements of the IT-System electronics technician and the IT-Specialist/System integration are overlapping, especially in the fields of network engineering, hardware knowledge, installation and service. Only in the field of electrical engineering/electronics, as a major domain of IT-System electronics technicians, there is a significant demarcation in the requirements. The statement that the two occupations should be put together was supported by 54.2% of the surveyed IT-systems electronics technicians, but only by 22.0% of the IT-Specialists/System integration.

There is even more profile-overlapping between the two business-oriented IT training occupations IT-System support specialist and IT Officer. The occupations only differ in terms of supply & contract management as well as technical marketing, with about 0.4 points (Fig. 4).

Information on whether and how the occupations are differentiated from one another can also be derived from the information about which occupations are trained together in the same company. The data from the online survey result in the following picture: About half of the enterprises (52.9%), who train IT-Specialists/System integration also train IT-Specialists/Application development. From this constellation, it can be deduced that the two IT-Specialists complement each other, because otherwise not so many companies would probably offer both trainings.

IT-System electronics technicians are rarely trained together with IT-Specialists. Just as well IT-System support specialists are rarely trained together with IT Officers

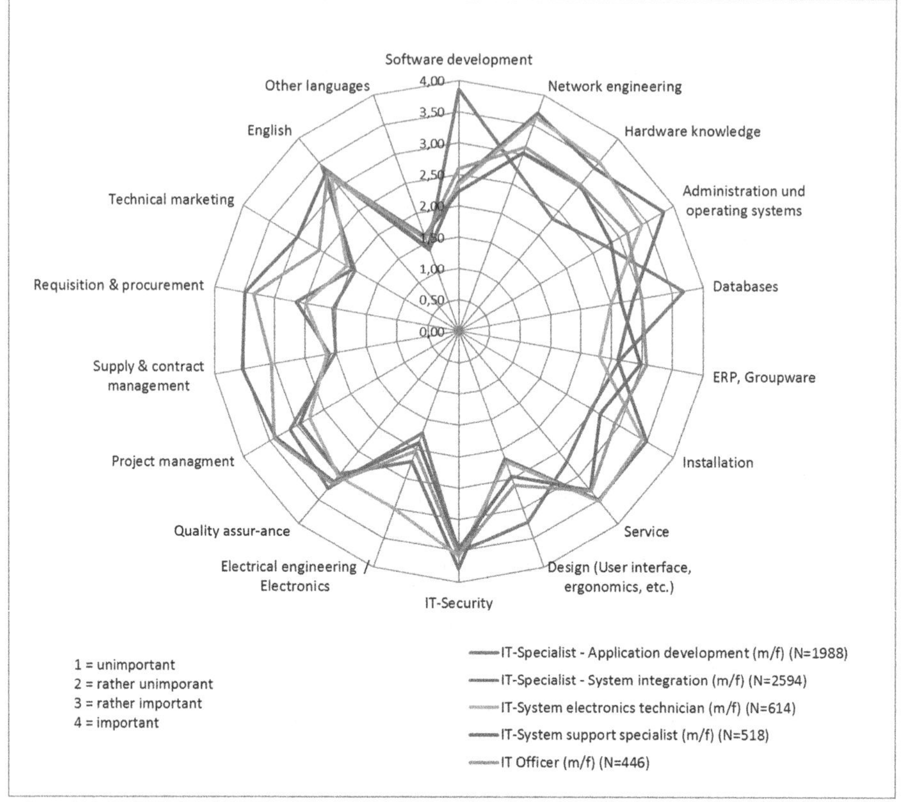

Fig. 4. The Importance of IT competences in some fields of occupational requirements (Based on their own knowledge about the vocational occupations in question (for example by their own training), the respondents in the online survey assessed up to two vocational occupations. An algorithm ensured a distribution of the vocational occupations corresponding to their distribution in the sample. Therefore, the number of cases does not correspond to a person in the present Figure, but to a person's vote for an occupation. Per person, two N could be generated.)

(14.2%), and vice versa (17.6%). This constellation indicates that a company rarely has a need for both business-oriented IT professions.

3.2 Need for Change in Training Contents and Objectives

Overall, there is great satisfaction with the current training content; more than half of all respondents deny the question of missing content. (See Fig. 5).

When missing training content is identified, primarily topics such as virtualization, mobile computing, mobile devices, cloud computing or big data are mentioned. In this respect, there are only marginal differences across all occupations and between different economic sectors.

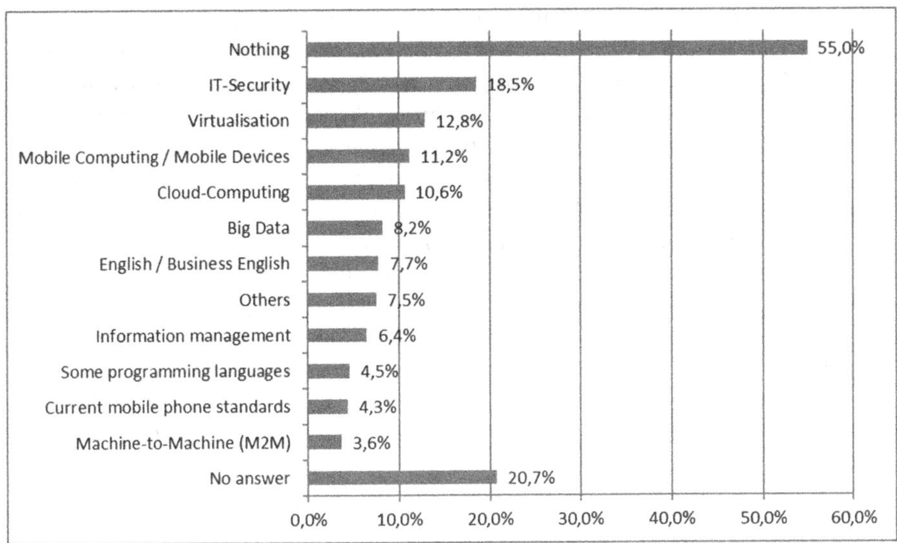

Fig. 5. Which training content are missing? (N = 5,450)

The highest importance regardless of target group, economic sector or company size is attached to IT security. The last finding is underlined by the outcomes of the interviews:

- *"There are, however, topics which are generally not well-established in the market. This includes IT security, since there are already very good experts, but the quality of training is not sufficient"* (Interview 0207_ManagementPersonnel: 55) *["Es gibt aber Themen, die sind generell am Markt noch nicht gut besetzt. Dazu gehört das Thema IT-Sicherheit, da gibt es schon sehr gute Experten, aber die Ausbildungsqualität kommt nicht hinterher."]*[1]
- *"IT security is underestimated"* (0100_ExpertChamber: 114) *["… IT-Sicherheit kommt zur kurz im Moment."]*
- *"The whole topic of cloud computing is, as far as I know, hardly any training content, but is a huge topic for IT operators."* (Interview 0207_ManagementPersonnel: 55) *["Das gesamte Thema Cloud-Computing ist, soweit ich weiß, kaum Ausbildungsinhalt, ist aber ein riesiges Thema für IT-Betreiber."]*
- *"I miss very much mobile device management or generally mobile computing."* (Interview 0307_Trainee: 108) *["Ich vermisse sehr stark Mobile Device Management oder allgemein Mobile Computing."]*

With regard to the topics of industry 4.0 and the internet of things, the interview partners primarily point to the fact that existing specialist's competences and expertise need to be updated continuously and situation-related as the complexity and individualization of the production processes increase.

[1] Translation of interview statements by Schwarz & Conein.

- *"Yes, the requirements have changed, especially in the area of agile software development; (...) the versatility has grown, and has become bigger now. Now I see there also industry 4.0 (...) Before one had learned in a certain programming language, now one learns programming situation-related. I program adequate to the device, which means, I can have both a classic programming language like C, but also a web programming language like PHP, as well as AJAX or Frameworx, there are many frameworx, so there is now a greater variety."* (Interview 08_ExpertIndustry: 65) *["Ja, die Anforderungen haben sich verändert, insbesondere in dem Bereich der agilen Softwareentwicklung, (...) die Vielseitigkeit ist höher, größer geworden inzwischen. Jetzt sehe ich da noch Industrie 4.0 (...) Vorher hatte man in einer Programmiersprache gelernt, inzwischen lernt man programmieren auch situationsbezogen. Also ich programmiere passend fürs Device, ich kann da sowohl eine klassische Programmiersprache wie C haben, dann aber auch eine Web-Programmiersprache wie PHP, wie auch AJAX oder wie Frameworx, es gibt viele Frameworx, die passen müssen, also da ist jetzt eine größere Vielfalt."]*

3.3 Soft Skills Needed

In the online survey the respondents were asked to assess the importance of selected personal and social competences. Almost all competences to be assessed are classified as important or very important by all target groups and across all occupations and regardless of company size or economic sector.

In particular, the competency of learning-readiness is seen as the most important competence with regard to almost all professions. This finding is also supported by the results of the qualitative interviews. Personnel managers and executives who consider further training of IT professionals as important expect learning-readiness from the employees. Being also relevant to all occupations is conscientiousness, self-responsibility and result-oriented action. In addition, the competences for a systematic-methodological approach and problem-solving capacity are considered to be particularly relevant in the two specializations of the IT-Specialist.

The two business-oriented IT occupations emphasize the ability to communicate and the competence for customer & user orientation. As less relevant to all occupations is the ability to resolve conflicts, to make decisions, and, finally, the language.

All of these results are by no means surprising and again support the demand for the provision of personal and social skills, especially in the information technology occupations.

3.4 Implementation of Training in Companies and Vocational Schools

The trainees' appraisal of training in the IT sector is generally positive across all four occupations. Thus, 48.6% of trainees in the online survey rate their training as good, 16.8% even as very good. Differences can be observed with regard to different economic sectors. The IT training in the defense sector is assessed in particular positive, 92% of the trainees designated the training as good or very good. Trainees in companies in the energy sector (78.3%) and financial and insurance services (79.5%) also assess the training very positive. Only in the transport and warehousing sector, less than half of the trainees rate the training very well or well.

Trainees in smaller companies with up to 19 employees are much less likely than in larger companies to grade their current training at least very well or well. Nevertheless, this still amounts to 51.1% or 54.2%. In addition, trainees of older companies are more likely to evaluate their training with good or very good, as trainees of companies that have not existed for so long.

There are great differences in the assessment of the two learning venues, the company and the school. Within the framework of the online survey the trainees were asked the four questions:

- What do you find particularly positive in terms of vocational school training?
- What do you find particularly positive in terms of company training?
- What do you find particularly negative in terms of vocational school training?
- What do you find particularly negative in terms of company training?

Figure 6 shows the frequencies with which the "Nothing" option was selected for all four questions. It is to be noted that with almost the same frequency, with which nothing positive is seen regarding vocational school training, nothing negative is seen in the case of company training, and vice versa. The frequency of "nothing positive" for the company training is comparable to the frequency of "nothing negative" for the vocational school training.

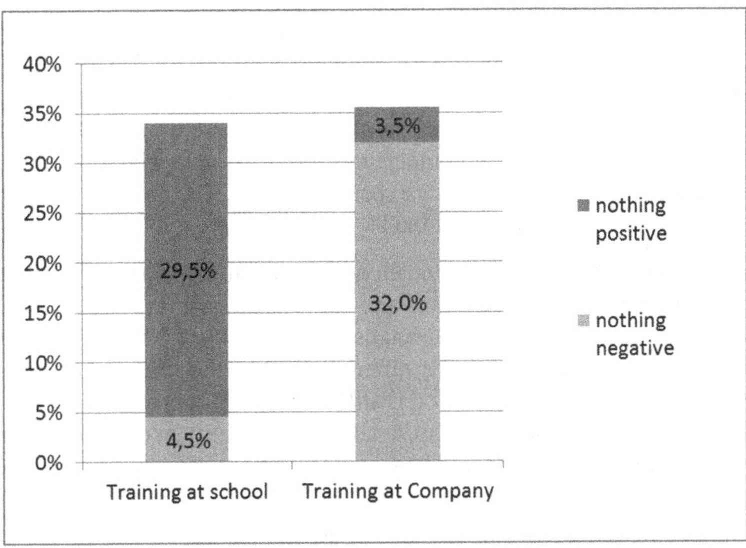

Fig. 6. Distribution of answers to the questions: "What did you see as positive/negative during your training at school/company?" (N = 1703)

Assessment of Company Training

The ability to work independently is the most frequently cited positive aspect of the respondents currently being trained. 82.6% of the trainees represent this view.

Approximately three-quarters (76.5%) of trainees also mention the working atmosphere in their respective training company as a particularly positive aspect. Almost every second trainee (48.2%) has a particularly positive experience with the trainers.

Criticism of the company training mainly refers to the fact that there was not enough guidance (29.9%) and a too company-specific and/or a very one-sided training (27.2%).

Assessment of Vocational School Training

In terms of vocational school training, the good support for the preparation of the examination and the relevant technical content are at the top of the positive aspects. Approx. 30% of the trainees have named these aspects. 28.7% emphasize the commitment of the teachers as a positive aspect.

Especially the non-occupation-related subjects as part of the vocational school curriculum are seen as negative (64.8%). Outdated teaching material is perceived as particularly negative by approximately half of the trainees (50.8%) and outdated teaching methods of 45.3% of the trainees.

4 Conclusions and Recommendations

IT occupations are both, occupations especially related to the manufacturers and suppliers in the ICT sector, as well as occupations for users of ICT services across all economic sectors. In addition, they are interfaces that combine information and communication technology with production technology and business management. The increasing digitalization of all economic sectors will greatly increase the number of networking and interacting systems and thus further increase the complexity of these interface functions. In addition to IT competences, personal and social skills will be even more important in the assessment of the experts surveyed. The present results suggest a substantive and structural revision of the IT professions:

- The two business-oriented IT occupations IT-System support specialist and IT Officer should be merged because main areas of activities are very much overlapping.
- The two specializations of the IT-Specialist should be resolved into separate occupations, since their profiles are clearly different. Beyond that, the numbers of trainees are high and the labor market demand is still increasing for both profiles.
- The issue of IT security (data security, availability, integrity of data and data protection including legal aspects) should be significantly strengthened (e.g. risk analysis, protection of hardware and networks/infrastructure, encryption, authorization, legal requirements, certification, user training, etc.).
- Two-thirds of IT professionals work in sectors outside the ICT industry, including manufacturing. With regard to the topic of industry 4.0, consideration should be given to anchoring contents such as production control, virtualization, and embedded systems in the fields of application development and system administration.
- Within the content of the training, personal competences should be fully taken into account. In particular, it should be reflected in which contexts these training contents can be conveyed as well as be assessed.

- In order to meet the increasing complexity, heterogeneity and speed of change of the requirements, internally differentiation in kind of selectable optional qualifications[2] should be introduced.
- The reorganization of the IT occupations could be a good starting point not only to revise training contents and objectives, but also to improve the cooperation between training companies and vocational schools, e.g. in terms of common training projects and workshops.

With regard to reorganize the IT occupations, these and other proposals are currently under discussion by the stakeholders in the employers 'and employees' associations.

References

Aichholzer, G.: Industrie 4.0: Perspektiven für Arbeit und Beschäftigung. In: TAB-Brief Nr. 47/ Juli 2016, S. 31 (2016). https://www.itas.kit.edu/downloads/tab-brief/tb047_aich16a.pdf Accessed 10 Feb 2017

BMWi - Bundesministerium für Wirtschaft und Energie (Hrsg.): Monitoring-Report, Wirtschaft DIGITAL 2016, Berlin (2016). https://www.bmwi.de/Redaktion/DE/Publikationen/Digitale-Welt/monitoring-report-wirtschaft-digital-2016.pdf?__blob=publicationFile&v=10. Accessed 10 Feb 2017

Borch, H., Schwarz, H.: Zur Konzeption und Entwicklung der neuen IT-Berufe. In: Borch, H., et al. (ed.) Gestaltung der betrieblichen Ausbildung in den neuen IT-Berufen. (S.22). Bertelsmann, Bielefeld (1999)

Conein, S., Schwarz, H.: IT-Berufe auf dem Prüfstand. BWP **2**, 58–59 (2015). ww.bibb.de/bwp-7872. Accessed 10 Feb 2017

Hall, A., et al.: IT-Berufe und IT-Kompetenzen in der Industrie 4.0. BIBB Publikationen (2016). https://www.bibb.de/veroeffentlichungen/de/publication/download/id/7833. Accessed 10 Feb 2017

Mayring, P.: Qualitative Inhaltsanalyse: Grundlagen und Techniken. Beltz, Weinheim (2015)

Schwarz, H., Conein, S., Tutschner, H., u.a.: Voruntersuchung IT-Berufe, Abschlussbericht, Bonn (2017). https://www2.bibb.de/bibbtools/tools/dapro/data/documents/pdf/eb_42497.pdf. Accessed 10 Feb 2017

Schwarz, H., Bretschneider, M., Schröder, J., u.a.: Strukturierung anerkannter Ausbildungsberufe im dualen System: Forschungsprojekt 4.2.381, Bonn, 125 S (2015). https://www2.bibb.de/bibbtools/tools/dapro/data/documents/pdf/eb_42381.pdf. Accessed 10 Feb 2017

Sharma, N.: The Context of Everywhere: The Internet of Things & The Explosion of Data. Pitney Bowes Inc. (Hrsg.) 28 April 2014. http://blogs.pb.com/digital-insights/2014/04/28/internet-things-big-data/. Accessed 10 Feb 2017

[2] For more details about internally differentiations and how to structure the curriculum of training occupations see Schwarz et al. 2015: 67 p.

Human-to-Human Interaction: The Killer Application of Ubiquitous Computing?

Salvatore Sorce[1], Stefano Ruggieri[2], Vito Gentile[1], Antonio Gentile[1], and Alessio Malizia[3](✉)

[1] Dipartimento dell'Innovazione Industriale e Digitale (DIID), Università degli Studi di Palermo, 90128 Palermo, Italy
{salvatore.sorce,vito.gentile, antonio.gentile}@unipa.it

[2] Independent Researcher, Charlottesville, USA
stefanoruggieri@gmail.com

[3] Human Centred Design Institute (HCDI), Brunel University London, Uxbridge, Middlesex UB8 3PH, UK
Alessio.Malizia@brunel.ac.uk

Abstract. Twenty-five years past the Weiser's vision of Ubiquitous Computing, and there is not a clear understanding of what is or is not a pervasive system. Due to the loose boundaries of such paradigm, almost any kind of remotely accessible networked system is classified as a pervasive system. We think that is mainly due to the lack of killer applications that could make this vision clearer. Actually, we think that the most promising killer application is already here, but we are so used to it that we do not see it, as a perfect fitting of the Weiser's vision: the Human-to-Human Interaction mediated by computers.

Keywords: Ubiquitous computing · Social factors · Computer-Mediated communication

1 Introduction

The Weiser's vision of Ubiquitous Computing (UC) [1] is hard to be framed within a clear definition because it is a multi-disciplinary research field, it addresses many facets of our lives, and overall, it is not only about what Weiser wrote.

Often we refer to the UC-derived paradigms to understand the Weiser's comprehensive vision, such as the Pervasive Systems or the Internet of Things. Scientists and researchers, from all around the world and throughout the last twenty-five years, largely discussed psycho-social factors and both software and hardware technologies needed in order to fulfill and implement the original vision of pervasive systems.

Nevertheless, the common perception of this paradigm has loose boundaries, so that almost any system relying on a network of two or more devices, equipped with a bunch of sensors and somehow remotely accessible, is frequently classified as a pervasive system relying on an IoT.

By contrast, according to the actual Weiser's vision, in the Ubiquitous Computing world, common objects are equipped with some additional features, thus becoming 'smart'.

M. Kurosu (Ed.): HCI 2017, Part I, LNCS 10271, pp. 86–93, 2017.
DOI: 10.1007/978-3-319-58071-5_7

They should seamlessly react to changes occurring within the surrounding environment to provide useful and personalized services to their users. Access to ubiquitous systems should become as transparent and natural as wearing eyeglasses.

For example, a table equipped with load sensors should alert when it is near its breaking point; a coffee cup equipped with NFC and sensors should alert its owner when the coffee inside is too cold or when it is almost empty. These examples are what we consider good examples of UC according to the Weiser's vision. However, they are quite distant from what is currently available. Indeed, in most cases sensors are attached to everyday objects, to detect some parameter of the surrounding environment (i.e. something not strictly related to the object nature or purpose). Moreover, "smart things networks" are mainly based on proprietary protocols, with evident limitations in terms of interoperability and proactivity, that is their capability to self-discover, configure and cooperate as a whole.

We think that one of the main reason why there is no clear understanding of what a pervasive system is hitherto, and also perhaps of what a pervasive system is not, consist in the lack of killer applications. The most promising applications (pervasive advertisement and service provision in public places [12]) are strictly related to social factors and behaviors, but they are not as "pervasive" as in the Weiser's vision [2]. This is the main reason why human-to-human interaction, which is more and more mediated by one or more networked devices, seems to be the best candidate to become the application that will bring the pervasive vision at everyone's hands.

2 Social Factors

Many studies have shown the theoretical limits of Human-Computer Interaction (HCI) approaches based on cognitive ergonomics [3], which focuses its attention almost exclusively on the interaction between a single user and a technological system.

Therefore, over the last decade, a relevant number of studies have been aimed at analyzing the role of interaction with other people when it is made through the use of technological tools. The computer and the Web, therefore, represent a tool capable of assisting interaction between individuals through the medium. In this respect, a key role is played by the introduction of models and analysis tools derived from social psychology, which has a long tradition in the study of the interaction between individuals, including interaction that takes place through distributed computer systems.

Alongside the HCI model, there is that of Computer-Mediated Communication (CMC) which originated with a reflection on a specific phenomenon of the Web: the use of the network as a means of interpersonal communication [4]. As regards the communicative aspect, the two paradigms refer to two different models of interaction: interaction "with the medium" and interaction "through the medium".

The basic assumption of the interaction *with the medium* is that it involves a user and an environment; they are located within a common area and interact through an interface having "mediation functions" that establishes a shared code inspired by the logic of the human mind. The interaction is aimed at achieving a goal and it is often possible to assess the effectiveness of the exchange in terms of how close the user comes to achieving that goal. Not surprisingly, to address the issue of the usability of an interface, quantitative criteria tend to be used most, and they are expressed in terms of effective performance. By way of example, we cite a few commonly used indicators like those that measure the time required to complete a task, the number of errors committed or the percentage of sub-goals achieved, or those not achieved or achieved only partially.

In terms of the interaction *through the medium*, the scenario changes because the interaction involves human users located in remote areas, who communicate through an interface and whose task is to define and establish a shared context in which the actions of the participants are intertwined. The interactivity of a virtual space, from this point of view, is defined by the effectiveness with which its users make contributions and interventions consistent with the multiple lines of development of the issue, allowing communicative exchanges and the establishment of relationships between the participants in the interaction.

In contrast to the previous type, communication through the medium invokes a complex and reticular type of communicative exchange in the development of interaction between users of the system. Relationships develop between the users, whose rules are defined within the system that is the mean of communication. Common indicators are the number of communication exchanges or the use of a formal or informal communication, or the satisfaction to interact with others.

3 Interaction with the Medium

Nowadays there are several modalities for using interactive systems. Considering displays, for instance, the new technological advances allow for interacting via keyboards and mice, as well using touch-based interactions or even touchless ones. If we shift the focus on more general media, a plethora of modalities may be considered.

As explained in the previous sections, the naturalness of the interaction is one of the most promising features that can facilitate HCI paradigms to emerge. We can see today a lot of interfaces designed more to amaze people than to make them interact with the system in easy, intuitive ways. Introducing new interaction modalities, such as the use of in-air gestures (easily recognized by wearable devices), should be only due to their naturalness.

The HCI paradigm is strictly related to the need of using some device, wearable or not, that constitute the aforementioned "medium" by mean of which users will interact. With this in mind, gestural interaction seems to be one of the most adequate modality, both for its naturalness and because of the recognition capabilities of the currently available technology [5]. Indeed, in order to recognize gestures via Kinect-like devices [14] (with more "traditional" algorithms), many issues arise due to the need of controlled or semi-controlled environments where the recognition can be performed. Using wearable devices, such problems fade away: accelerometers and gyroscopes can be used as data input for gesture recognition, with no need of using cameras.

A more difficult issue to solve is the cultural dependency and constraints of the gestures. From a mere technical point of view, interacting with a device should be the same in every part of the world, to ease both the implementation and recognition tasks. Actually, several issues related to customs and traditions need to be overcome instead.

For instance, the same swipe gesture explained to two different people, is usually performed in slightly different ways. The difference (which can be easy to understand for a human) may be difficult to be discerned with an algorithm.

The pressing needs of communication, everywhere and every time, regardless of the distance among people, are pushing the boundaries of actual implementations towards the overcoming of such technical and social constraints. This is the reason why we are witnessing the evolution of adaptive interfaces, to take into account variations due to culture and other social factors, physical factors, users' profiles, etc.

4 Interaction Through the Medium

In recent years, there have been many studies that have analyzed the dynamics of social groups that work or interact in various ways online. This came about for two reasons. First, these studies have the merit of having analyzed theories and models of social psychology, but in areas very different from those where they originated. Virtual environments increasingly exist alongside real life, and it is, therefore, necessary to test the ability of psychosocial models to explain how interaction in these new environments works. Secondly, research on computer-mediated groups (CMG) has a strong empirical character, especially for those who design systems for virtual interaction, with the aim of optimizing processes in function of the objectives to be achieved.

The analysis of these studies is essential for all those who design systems for virtual interaction, given that an understanding of the dynamics of the social functioning of groups that collaborate and interact remotely is of fundamental importance. One can thus truly speak of social ergonomics, which together with cognitive ergonomics designs these contexts from a perspective of individual usability, that is, a perspective characterized by rules and guidelines to follow in order to accurately design the communication environments. All this with the aim of optimizing the interactive process in accordance with the goals to be achieved, and in such a way that the CMC can produce the best results in terms of interaction, user satisfaction, performance, efficiency, but also stability and cohesion among the members of the group.

It is precisely the definition of these contexts of use that will pave the way for social ergonomics, by which, in accordance with the theoretical assumptions and the most recent studies of CMC and HCI, we mean the rules, models and guidelines to be followed and implemented in order to accurately design interactive environments (for recreational, educational and professional purposes, among others). All this, with the aim of optimizing the communication process in relation to the objectives of the context in which the individual works, the target audience where the action is directed, the time frame available and the type of task that must be completed.

Thus, an understanding of the dynamics that govern, for example, leadership, status, cohesion in virtual teams and decision-making can assist in making a careful choice of the most appropriate methods and tools for planning and organizing virtual interaction environments. A key role is played by the concept of the environment and the different meanings with which it can be understood. In fact, there are different types of mediated environments that have their own peculiar characteristics and thus are different from those on which many HCI studies focus. Clark and Brennan [13] distinguish certain characteristics of communication environments that characterize the real nature of interactions:

- *co-presence*: group members occupy the same physical location);
- *visibility*: the possibility of seeing each other;
- *audibility:* the ability to hear each other;
- *co-temporality*: communications are received more or less as soon as they are sent;
- *simultaneity*: the members of the group can send and receive messages at the same time;
- *sequentiality*: members of the group usually speak to each other in a sequential manner.

A paradigmatic case is the development of Learning and Content Management Systems (LCMS), which, in just a few years, have reached high levels of standardization. This has created a new profession, the instructional designer, a systems designer for training courses, who operates in online environments and contexts in order to achieve the best combination between the environment and the learning process. The opportunity to program the LCMS allows the instructional designer to create, for each context, the most appropriate tool for the group that will benefit from it. In this sense, the crucial aspect upon which the success of the teaching/training project depends is the ergonomics of the social system created, i.e. the ability of the system implemented to ensure the effective use and the socialization of the knowledge it contains, as well as the ability to create new and innovative knowledge through mutual exchanges. Thus, by analyzing (1) how to enact the dynamics of leadership – i.e. the status, (2) the creation of social ties, (3) group cohesion and decision-making in virtual environments, it will be possible to make a careful choice of the most appropriate methods and tools to be used for specific purposes. For instance, the designer could decide whether to use tools for synchronous communication (chat, video conferencing, etc.), or for asynchronous communication (mailing lists, forums, etc.); or decide whether members of working groups are thoroughly described or identified by a generic alias; or decide whether to adopt a collaborative rather than a competitive approach, to name just a few features that can be systematically analyzed according to the canons of social ergonomics.

It goes without saying that this process cannot be implemented exclusively by using electronic tools, but instead requires careful work: first research, and then design.

4.1 Status in Virtual Interactions

Years of research have shown that the *status* is one of the most salient aspect influencing interactions within groups [6]. In general, individuals with a higher status more frequently assume the position of leader, speak quickly and often with little hesitation, dominate the conversation, tend to centralize resources, exert a decisive influence on decision-making, maintain eye contact during interaction and are also perceived as more competent [16, 17]. In contrast, members of low status exert less influence on the decisions of the group, they tend to let others make the decisions, they care more about being accepted by members of high status and they conform more.

The theme of status within CMGs has produced a wealth of results, particularly related to the principles of democracy and equality, which the Internet has always declared as its watchwords.

Not all research, however, has produced converging results, demonstrating that technological mediation is not always able to reduce the effects of status.

How to explain these contradictory results? To provide an explanation, authors have suggested that the process of technological mediation can interact with the status at least on three different levels. The first, consistent with the average richness theory [10], is represented by the reduced transfer of status-related social cues through electronic media with respect to FTF contexts. Media richness theory is a commonly used theory for explaining how different communication media affect task performance. A rich medium allows for: (1) transmitting multiple verbal and nonverbal cues, (2) using natural language, (3) providing immediate feedback, and (4) conveying personal feelings and emotions. The richest medium is FTF communication, followed by telephone, chat, e-mail, and print communications. Newer technologies, such as video conferencing, are thought to rank above telephone communication, but below FTF communication, in terms of media richness. Technologies that allow the recipient(s) to see physical gestures and facial expressions are thought to increase the richness of the information conveyed, thereby contributing to the greater richness of the video conference, as compared to telephone or text-based media.

A reduced amount of information is an obstacle for the correct identification of the status. Thus, when the identity of the members is made visually evident, status differences persist even in a CMC setting. A second possibility is that the effect of status indicators is different in the two contexts. Visual clues, such as visible exchanges, the free flow of gestures and the tone of voice characterize FTF interaction. Replacements for these indicators, although they may be present in technologically mediated contexts, may not have the same impact. Some studies have shown how gestures can lose some of their meaning if they are produced in the form of visual technological mediation [18]. A third aspect refers to the rules governing the process of status acquisition. When a failure to respect the hierarchy of status occurs within a group, there is generally a reaction against those who committed the violation. Typically, in FTF interactions, we observe an exchange of glances that usually end up in the classic "dirty look". This and other reactions meant to bring those who violate status-imposed standards back into line are significantly weakened in CMC interaction. It is likely that these three levels can actually act together, and thereby give rise to the contradicting results we find in the literature.

One aspect that seems to be decisive in the creation of bonds of status is the temporal context. Typically, in groups of unequal status, the status structure develops rapidly, while in groups whose members share equal status, development is slower, given that it is a function of the contributions made by the members of the group during their interaction. This has important implications for the life of a group. In particular, it was found that in groups that interact over a long period of time, the strong initial impact of status decreases, while the interaction becomes increasingly modeled by the quality of the contributions made by the group's members. The effects of the technological mediation and translation of the observable indicators of status thus become less relevant for team interaction with the passage of time [9].

Those who design devices to support the activities of a work group should consider not only the purely technical aspects but include a priori a way to manage the status in virtual groups. In order to exploit the various effects of this variable, hierarchical user profiles should be designed, while to ensure interaction based on equal status, an environment should be built that masks these differences.

5 Concluding Remarks

The Weiser's vision of UC is a paradigm so wide and so comprehensive, that it is difficult for common people to clearly identify what can be classified as one of its implementations or not. On the other hand, we are experiencing a growing need for interaction among humans at any time and at any place. This need can only be completely fulfilled if computers somehow mediate the interaction.

The design of virtual communication environments is most clearly affected by discoveries achieved in all the involved research fields. The goal is to optimize the interactive process on the basis of the objectives to be achieved so that Computer-Mediated Communication can produce the best results in terms of fluid interaction, user satisfaction, performance, and efficiency, but also in terms of the stability and cohesion of the group's members. All this is to be considered in function of the objectives of the specific context, the target group to which the action is directed, the available time frame, and the type of task to be completed.

The human-to-human interaction mediated by computers is a field that involves all the above-discussed aspects, both from the technological and social points of view. In the next future people will probably interact among them unconsciously by means of an interaction media the same way they wear their eyeglasses to enhance the vision of the surrounding world. One promising way of computer-mediated interaction among humans is the gesture-based one. People are used to interact with the support of body gestures, and in some case, gestures are the only way to convey information, for example in the case of language or physical hindrances. There are several studies in the field of the HCI by means of gestures, and a lot of them are aimed at the intuitiveness of such interaction [15]. This is the needed preliminary step to achieve the goal of a gesture-based HHI mediated by computer.

All these aspects need to be considered by future research with the fundamental goal of giving online groups the benefits of a carefully designed workplace and learning space, as well as the benefits of optimal conditions for communication. Such benefits are based on the principle that certain contexts are more suitable than others for achieving group objectives, given that they follow a logic of affordances determined by the type of interaction used in the operating environment.

The HHI mediated by computers and networks seems the best candidate to become the killer application of Ubiquitous Computing, because it is an actual, pressing and largely shared need, and it must have all the features envisioned by Mark Weiser to be effective. At that point, we should talk about an Internet of Humans, instead of an Internet of Things.

Acknowledgements. This paper is funded on a research grant by the Italian Ministry of University and Research, namely project NEPTIS (Grant no. PON03PE_00214_3).

References

1. Weiser, M.: The computer for the 21st century. Sci. Am. **265**(3), 66–75 (1991)
2. Krumm, J.: Ubiquitous advertising: The killer application for the 21st century. IEEE Pervasive Comput. **10**(1), 66–73 (2011)
3. Norman, D.A.: The Invisible Computer: Why Good Products Can Fail, the Personal Computer is So Complex, and Information Appliances are the Solutions. The MIT Press, Cambridge (1998)
4. Boca, S., Gentile, A., Ruggieri, S., Sorce, S.: An evaluation of HCI and CMC in information systems within highly crowded large events. In: Sixth International Workshop on Intelligent Interfaces for Human-Computer Interaction (IIHCI-2013), pp. 600–604, Asia University, Taichung, Taiwan, 3–5 July 2013. doi:10.1109/CISIS.2013.108
5. Gentile, V., Malizia, A., Sorce, S., Gentile, A.: Designing touchless gestural interactions for public displays in-the-wild. In: Kurosu, M. (ed.) HCI 2015. LNCS, vol. 9170, pp. 24–34. Springer, Cham (2015). doi:10.1007/978-3-319-20916-6_3
6. Brown, R.: Group Processes: Dynamics Within and Between Groups, 2nd edn. Blackwell, Oxford (2000)
7. Levine, J.M., Moreland, R.L.: Progress in small group research. Annu. Rev. Psychol. **41**, 585–634 (1990)
8. Ruggieri, S.: Leadership in virtual teams: A comparison of transformational and transactional leaders. Soc. Behav. Pers. **37**(7), 1017–1022 (2009)
9. Driskell, J.E., Radtke, P.H., Salas, E.: Virtual teams: effects of technological mediation on team performance. Group Dyn. Theor. Res. Pract. **7**, 287–323 (2003)
10. Daft, R.L., Lengel, R.H.: Information richness: A new approach to managerial behavior and organization design. Res. Organ. Behav. **6**, 191–233 (1984)
11. Doherty-Sneddon, G., Anderson, A., O'Malley, C., Langton, S., Garrod, S., Bruce, V.: Face-to-face and video-mediated communication: A comparison of dialogue structure and task performance. J. Exp. Psychol. Appl. **3**, 105–125 (1997)
12. Genco, A., Sorce, S., Reina, G., Santoro, G.: An agent-based service network for personal mobile devices. IEEE Pervasive Comput. **5**(2), 54–61 (2006)
13. Clark, H.H., Brennan, S.E.: Grounding in communication. In: Resnick, L.B., Levine, J.M., Teasley, S.D. (eds.), Perspectives on Socially Shared Cognition, pp. 13–1991. American Psychological Association (1991)
14. Gentile, V., Sorce, S., Gentile, A.: Continuous hand openness detection using a Kinect-like device. In: Proceedings of the Eighth International Conference on Complex, Intelligent and Software Intensive Systems (CISIS), pp. 553–557. IEEE (2014). doi:10.1109/CISIS.2014.80
15. Malizia, A., Bellucci, A.: The artificiality of natural user interfaces. Commun. ACM **55**(3), 36–38 (2012)
16. Zigurs, I.: Leadership in virtual teams: oxymoron or opportunity? Org. Dyn. **31**, 339–351 (2003)
17. Hambey, L.A., O'Neill, T.A., Kline, T.J.B.: Virtual team leadership: The effects of leadership style and communication medium on team interaction style and outcomes. Organ. Behav. Hum. Decis. Process **103**, 1–20 (2007)
18. Heath, C., Luff, P.: Media space and communicative asymmetries: preliminary observations of video-mediated interaction. Hum. Comput. Interact. **7**, 315–346 (1992)

Requirement on Personnel and Organization for Safety and Security Improvement by Accident and Error Model

Hiroshi Ujita(✉)

Institute for Environmental and Safety Studies, 38-7 Takamatsu 2-chome, Tokyo, Toshima-ku 171-0042, Japan
kanan@insess.com

Abstract. As a sequel to the technology systems becoming huge, complex and sophisticated, safety issues are shifted to the problem of organization from human, and further from hardware, such socialization is occurring in every technical field. For this reason, the analytical methods, as well as type and social perceptions of error or accident, are changing with the times also. Human error and Domino accident model had initially appeared, are then has been changing to system error and Swiss cheese accident model, and recently move to safety culture degradation and the organizational accident. Whereas the direction which discusses the safety from the accident analysis, a new trend of analytical methods such as resilience engineering, high reliability organization, or risk literacy research, which analyze the various events by focusing on the good practices, are becoming popular. To further, as the center of the information security field, the social engineering research has just begun as the recent research theme, to consider as the way to induce to a certain behavior of the person, by utilizing the essential weakness with the human, and its measures.

Keywords: Accident model · Human model · Social model · Domino model · Swiss cheese accident model · Resilience engineering · Bounded rationality · Social engineering

1 Introduction

Here, requirement on personnel and organization for safety and security improvement is discussed by using accident model and error model. As a sequel to the technology systems becoming huge, complex and sophisticated, safety issues are shifted to the problem of organization from human, and further from hardware, such socialization is occurring in every technical field. On the other hand, there is no science and technology that does not include risk, but it is also the fact that it has been accepted so far because it has utility beyond risk.

Whereas the direction which discusses the safety from the accident analysis, a new trend of analytical methods such as resilience engineering, high reliability organization, or risk literacy research, which analyze the various events by focusing on the good practices, are becoming popular. To further, as the center of the information security field, the social engineering research has just begun as the recent research theme, to

M. Kurosu (Ed.): HCI 2017, Part I, LNCS 10271, pp. 94–102, 2017.
DOI: 10.1007/978-3-319-58071-5_8

consider as the way to induce to a certain behavior of the person, by utilizing the essential weakness with the human, and its measures.

The relationship between safety issues and security problems is summarized. In security problems, there is a difference from safety that it is necessary to think separately on the standpoint of perpetrators and victims. In the field of engineering such as information systems, attacks called "social engineering" that use psychological weak points of general users are on the rise, and it is difficult to ensure reliability only with technical measures such as information security. Human characteristics on security and its countermeasures are also discussed.

2 History of Accident and Human Error Type

The history of accident and human error type trend is shown in Fig. 1.

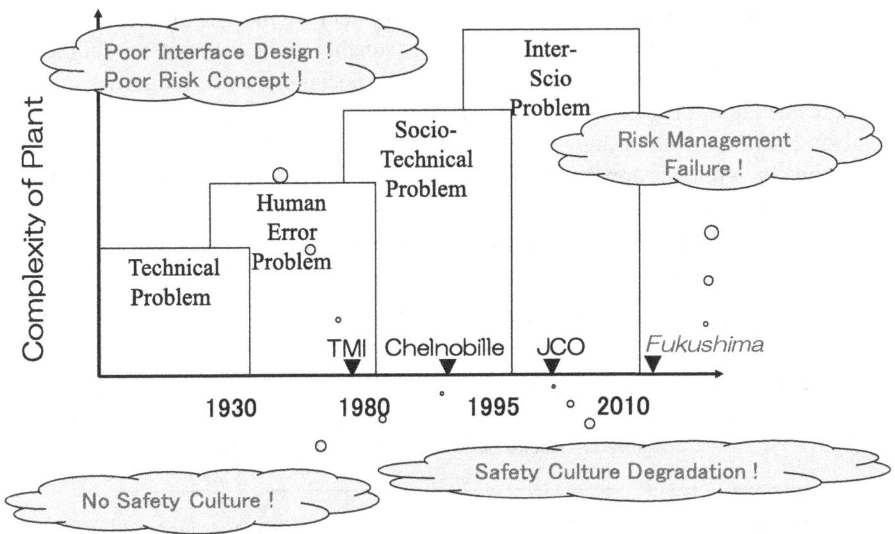

Fig. 1. Safety issue scope (Reason, 1993).

In the era when the plant system was not so complicated as in the present age, it was thought that technical defects are the source of the problem and accidents can be prevented by technical correspondence. As the system became more complex, it came to the limit of human ability to operate it, accidents caused by human error occurred. Its typical accident happened at Three Mile Island (TMI) nuclear power plant in 1979. For this reason, individuals committing errors are considered to be the source of the problem, improvement of personnel capacity by appropriate selection and training of personnel, and proper design of interface design are considered effective for error prevention.

Thereafter, accidents caused by complicated interrelationships of elements such as technology, human, society, management, organization and so on occurred, and then the problem was interaction between society and technology. Furthermore, not only within the plant and enterprises but also accidents where the relationship failure with external stakeholders and organizations is a source of the problem becomes noticeable, and a framework for comprehensive problem solving including inter-organizational relationship has become to be necessary. A recent accident is a so-called organizational accident in which the form of an accident is caused by a complex factor and its influence reaches a social scale [1].

For this reason, the analytical methods, as well as type and social perceptions of error or accident, are changing with the times also. Human error and Domino accident model had initially appeared, are then has been changing to system error and Swiss cheese accident model, and recently move to safety culture degradation and the organizational accident.

3 Bounded Rationality in Context vs. Judge by God

In the field of cognitive science and the cognitive system engineering, the human being is considered as to think and judge something reasonably along the context while there are information and time limitations. Sometimes the decision may be judged as an error by the outside later. It is called "bounded rationality in the context" vs. "judge by God". The absurd action of the organization had been often explained in human illogicality conventionally, while the approach has recently come out to think that the human being rationality was the cause.

There are three approaches proposed from Organizational (Behavioral) Economics as shown in Table 1 [2]:

1. business cost theory (reluctant to do)
2. agency theory (information gap), and
3. proprietary rights theory (selfishness).

Table 1. Accident model and error model.

Accident Model	Error Model	Analysis Method	Management
Domino (failure chain)	Component Failure and human Error	Cause-Consequence Link	Encapsulation, Seek & Destroy
Swiss Cheese (Loss of Diversity)	System Error (Common mode Failure)	Risk Evaluation	Defense & Barrier
Organizational Accident (Fallacy of Defense in Depth)	Safety Culture Degradation	Behavioral Science Safety Culture Check List	Monitor & Control (Organizational Learning)

Design ↕ Management

Business cost theory analyses action of opportunity principles and sunk cost, agency theory, moral hazard and adverse selection (lemon market), and proprietary rights theory, cost externality. The common supposition is ''the bounded rationality and the utility maximization''.

It is necessary to find the social context that the error is easy to occur, in the engineering for human being hereafter. In other words, a way of thinking has changed in the direction to analyzing the social context that is easy to cause an error, from analyzing direct cause of the error. Because this direction is beyond the range of conventional ergonomic treating the contents of the error, it is very difficult. However, we should recognize it now, if we do not analyze an error from the viewpoint of the relationship between safety and security with the environmental element surrounding human being, we can not to lead to measures. The measures should be matched with human rational characteristics.

Countermeasure on Business cost theory is business cost saving system which changes organizational style from group organization, via. centralization of power type organization, and to decentralization of power type organization, agency theory, agency cost reduction system based on mutual exchange of the information, and proprietary rights theory, internalization of the system externality based on proprietary rights distribution.

4 Accident Model and Error Model

As a result, that the technology systems become huge, complex and sophisticated, safety issues are shifted to the problem of organization from human, and further from hardware, such socialization is occurring in every technical field. For this reason, the analytical methods, as well as type and social perceptions of error or accident, are changing with the times also. Table 2 shows trends of the accident model and error model [3]. Human error and Domino accident model had initially appeared, are then changing to system error and Swiss cheese accident model, and recently move to safety culture degradation and the organizational accident.

Table 2. Three approaches by behavioral economics (The organization fails rationally: Kenshu Kikusawa 2009).

	Transaction cost theory (Bothersome)	Agency theory (Information gaps)	Property rights theory (Selfish)
Object	Business relationship	Agency relationship (Principle and Agency)	Ownership relationship
Inefficiency	• Opportunistic behavior • Sunk cost	• Moral Hazard • Adverse Selection (Lemon Market)	Externalities
Institutional resolution	Transaction cost saving system (Organization style change: fellow- centralized-decentralized)	Agency cost reduction (Symmetrical information)	Internalization of externalities (Ownership allocation)
Example	• One-man management - external monitoring	• Work sharing	• Fellow consciousness and organizational concealment

A conventional accident model is the Domino model, in which the causation of trouble and the error is analyzed and measures are taken. In the model, slip, lapse, and mistake are used which are the classification of the unsafe act to occur by on-site work. These are categorized as the basic error type, while violation which is intentional act violating rule has become increased recently and considered as cause of social accident.

Design philosophy of the defense in depths has been established, and the accident to occur recently is caused by the excellence of the error of a variety of systems. The analysis of the organization blunder is necessary for the analysis by the Swiss cheese accident model in addition to conventional error analysis.

An organization accident is a problem inside the organizations, which reaches earth-shaking event for the organization as a result by the accumulation of the best intentions basically. It is an act of the good will, but becomes the error. As for the organization accident, the interdependence inside of the organization or between the organizations is accumulated by fallacy in the defense in depths, and it becomes a problem of the deterioration of the safety culture in its turn. The organizational management based on the organization analyses such as behavioral sciences will be necessary for these measures.

Swiss Cheese Model proposed by Reason, J indicates operational problem other than design problem [1]. Fallacy of the defense in depth has frequently occurred recently because plant system is safe enough as operators becomes easily not to consider system safety. And then safety culture degradation would be happened, whose incident will easily become organizational accident. Such situation requires final barrier that is Crisis Management.

Concept of "Soft Barrier" has been proposed here [3]. There are two types of safety barriers, one is Hard Barrier that is simply represented by Defense in Depth. The other is Soft Barrier, which maintains the hard barrier as expected condition, makes it perform as expected function. Even when the Hard Barrier does not perform its function, human activity to prevent hazardous effect and its support functions, such as manuals, rules, laws, organization, social system, etc. Soft Barrier can be further divided to two measures; one is "Software for design", such as Common mode failure treatment, Safety logic, Usability, etc. The other is "Humanware for operation", such as operator or maintenance personnel actions, Emergency Procedure, organization, management, Safety Culture, etc. Following the safety design principle of "Defense in Depth", three level safety functions should be considered for the hardware. Those are, the usual normal system, usual safety system, and emergency system including external support function. On the other hand, software for design including common mode failure treatment, safety logic, and usability should be improved together with the humanware for operation including personnel actions, emergency procedure, organization, management, and safety culture.

5 The Methodology on Resilience Engineering, High Reliability Organization, and Risk Literacy

Whereas the direction which discusses the safety from the accident analysis, a new trend of analytical methods such as resilience engineering, high reliability organization, or risk literacy research, which analyze the various events by focusing on the good practices, are becoming popular.

The resilience is the intrinsic ability of a system to adjust its functioning prior to, during, or following changes and disturbances, so that it can sustain required operations under both expected and unexpected conditions. A practice of Resilience Engineering / Proactive Safety Management requires that all levels of the organization are able to [4]:

- Monitor
- Learn from past events
- Respond
- Anticipate

Organizational process defined by the High Reliability Organization is listed as follows [5]. There are 5 powers in 2 situations.

- Preparedness for Emergency Situation in Ordinal Time:
  - Carefulness (Confirmation),
  - Honesty (Report),
  - Sensitivity (Observation),
- Emergency Response in Emergency Situation:
  - Alert (Concentration),
  - Flexibility (Response),

Ability of Risk Literacy is also defined by followings, which is largely divided to 3 powers and further classified to 8 sub-powers [6].

- Analysis power
  - Collection power
  - Understanding power
  - Predictive power
- Communication power
  - Network power
  - Influence power
- Practical power
  - Crisis Response Power
  - Radical Measures Power

6 Relationship Between Safety Issues and Security Problems

Table 3 summarizes the relationship between safety issues and security problems.

In security problems, there is a difference from safety that it is necessary to think separately on the standpoint of perpetrators and victims. First of all, in the safety problem, basically the target is an expert, who is expected to be able to make efforts to ensure system safety based on good intention and ability. However, as individuals, safety consciousness deteriorates during the transition of safety activities for many years. Moreover, in the case of an organization, where the safety design based on the idea of defense in depth is sufficiently realized, safety will be sufficiently kept even if it violates

Table 3. Relationship between safety issues and security problems

Safety Issues	Security Problem - Victim	Security Problem - Perpetrator
Expert	Expert+ General User [1]	Outsider+ Insider [2]
Good Faith	Good Faith	Malice
Degradation of safety awareness	Degradation of security awareness 1 Lack of Security Literacy	Greed (Financial Purpose) / Resentment 1 Social Engineering
• Fallacy of Defense in Depth • Degradation of Safety Culture • Organizational Accident Chain	• Fallacy of Defense in Depth • Degradation of Security Culture • Security Incident Chain	• Planned Crime
Regular monitoring of organizational culture	Regular monitoring security culture 1 Security Education	Environmental Criminal Measures 2 Healthy Organization

safely even in operation, so that experts would have the confidence in the safety of the system. As a result, eventually a chain occurs, where a defense in depth error that depends on the inherent safety of the system occurs, gradually deteriorating the safety culture, and that leads to an organizational accident. As a countermeasure against this problem, constant safety monitoring of the safety culture can be considered.

Meanwhile, when thinking about security issues, correspondence between perpetrators and victims is totally different, so consider the issues and countermeasures separately for this position. First of all, looking at the victim, the characteristic of the security problem is the need to think about countermeasures for general people as well as experts. If we consider about expert, the safety problem and aspect are exactly the same, and we can rearrange the problem by replacing safety with security. There are issues similar to general users as well as experts, but in addition to that, the lack of security literacy emerges as an important issue. The measures will be thorough security education.

The most difficult task is how to protect systems and users from perpetrators. The perpetrator can also be divided into an attacker from the outside and an internal criminal. In any case as it goes against the maliciously planned crime, the countermeasure is exhaustively and rationally carried out based on the system thinking is required. For internal criminals, it is often the case that the cause is greed or grudge, so it is important to maintain a common but healthy organization. For external attackers, internal measures such as thorough education cannot be used, so it is important not only to thoroughly build diverse barriers based on defense in depth thought, to counter social engineering technology targeting general users. It is essential to fully recognize the importance of psychological measures such as social psychology and criminal psychology.

7 Human Characteristics on Security and Its Countermeasures

In the field of engineering such as information systems, attacks called "social engineering" that use psychological weak points of general users are on the rise, and it is difficult to ensure reliability only with technical measures such as information security.

The main methods of social engineering are impersonation to gather necessary information by impersonating others, garbage box fishing to acquire the desired information from among the things discarded as garbage, cleaning workers, electric/telephone workers, security impersonate as a member, invades the site into offices, factories, etc., peeping to acquire PC information from the back, and the like.

Social engineering is to induce people to certain actions by using the essential weakness of human beings, but there are also many studies outside the field of information security. One of them is systematization of human weakness in the study of Chardini [7], who gives six tactics as a tactic of guidance induction: "returnability", "commitment and consistency", "social proof", "favor", "authority", "rarity". In social engineering, measures against criminal psychology and others are also being applied, and countermeasures are currently being studied.

In the field of information security in recent years, there is movement to utilize psychology such as game theory and incentive mechanism and economic knowledge. However, due to the problem of subjectivity derived from human beings, difficulty of utilization has been pointed out. From the viewpoint of risk management of the system, it is important not only to reduce the risks derived from psychology and behavior but also to control the change in risk to suppress the fluctuation in the performance of the entire system, such as high resilience system is expected to realize.

8 Conclusion

As a sequel to the technology systems becoming huge, complex and sophisticated, safety issues are shifted to the problem of organization from human, and further from hardware, such socialization is occurring in every technical field. For this reason, the analytical methods, as well as type and social perceptions of error or accident, are changing with the times also.

Human error and Domino accident model had initially appeared, are then has been changing to system error and Swiss cheese accident model, and recently move to safety culture degradation and the organizational accident. Whereas the direction which discusses the safety from the accident analysis, a new trend of analytical methods such as resilience engineering, high reliability organization, or risk literacy research, which analyze the various events by focusing on the good practices, are becoming popular.

To further, as the center of the information security field, the social engineering research has just begun as the recent research theme, to consider as the way to induce to a certain behavior of the person, by utilizing the essential weakness with the human, and its measures.

To achieve safety and security, it is indispensable to consider not only the values and ethics of people, the behavior style (safety culture), but also the social acceptance and the impact on accidents on society and the environment.

On the other hand, there is no science technology that does not include risk, but it is also true that it has been accepted so far because it has utility beyond risk. For that purpose, it is desirable to establish a systematization of safety science that can handle safety issues and security problems in a unified way.

Acknowledgments. This work was supported in part by the member of the committee for survey of risk management based on information security psychology in The Institute of Electrical Engineers of Japan.

References

1. Reason, J.: Managing the Risks of Organizational Accidents. Ashgate, Hampshire (1997)
2. Kikusawa, K.: Absurdity of Organization. DIAMOND, 2000. (in Japanese)
3. Ujita, H., Yuhara, N.: Systems Safety. Kaibundo (2015). (in Japanese)
4. Hollnagel, E.: Safety Culture, Safety Management, and Resilience Engineering, ATEC Aviation Safety Forum, November 2009
5. Weick, K.E., Sutcliffe, K.M.: Managing the Unexpected. Jossey-Bass, San Francisco (2001)
6. Lin, S.: Introduction of Risk Literacy-Lessons Learned from Incidents. NIKKEI-BP, Tokyo (2005). (in Japanese)
7. Chardini, R.B.: Influence: Science and Practice (1991)

Brain-Computer Interfaces: Agency and the Transition from Ethics to Politics

Andreas Wolkenstein(✉)

Institute for Medical Psychology and Behavioural Neurobiology, University of Tübingen, Tübingen, Germany
mail@andreaswolkenstein.com

Abstract. Given the need of normatively assessing new technologies on the one hand, and problems with traditional approaches in ethical and legal scholarship on the other hand, a new approach is proposed. To accomplish this, the paper pursues two guiding questions: (1) how should we understand the ethical questions surrounding the development and use of BCIs in a way that is both technologically adequate and close to the phenomena?; and (2) what means are there to push technology development in the "right" direction, i.e. the direction that reasonable ethical reflection reveals as pressing?

In what follows I will *first* introduce a distinction aimed at helping ethical evaluations of technology to get a grip on the phenomena they deal with (Sect. 2). The result is a better view on the phenomena at hand, enabling a more precise assessment based on a particular distinction between two forms of agency. I will briefly apply it to the ethics of BCIs.

Second, I will broaden the perspective and ask how the ethical consideration can be applied in the real world (Sect. 3). The main emphasis will lie on outlining a philosophical move from ethics to politics. It is proposed that ethical questions are better solved by having the right political institutions, rather than having the right ethical point of view.

Keywords: Brain-computer interfaces · Technology ethics · Technology politics · Agency

1 Introduction

The use of brain-computer interfaces (BCIs) has seen a lot of success during recent years [1–8]. It was mainly in the medical area where BCIs have proven to solve many problems and help many patients lead an increasingly decent life. As assistive technology, BCIs enable people to communicate (e.g. for ALS patients), to move (e.g. neuroprothetics) and to direct external devices such as wheelchairs [9–11]. Questions of feasibility form the cornerstone of BCI research in this domain, and ethical questions have been addressed based both on the current technological status quo and a projection into the future of how BCIs might look like [12–17]. Beyond the medical context, BCIs are currently used for entertainment where issues of enabling better usability and gaming experience form the major line of research [18, 19]. The automotive sector is one further

M. Kurosu (Ed.): HCI 2017, Part I, LNCS 10271, pp. 103–118, 2017.
DOI: 10.1007/978-3-319-58071-5_9

area where BCIs can serve important goals such as supervising and directing a driver's performance, extending beyond the automobile to apply to many more contexts where attention and vigilance is important [20–26]. In addition, the military has also developed BCI technologies that serve, among others, to enable "silent talk" between soldiers in the field [27]. Another area has attracted increased attention is the industrial sector where BCIs can support human workers in enabling them to handle an external device (such as a robot arm or a vehicle) with the help of a BCI [28–30].

Given the rapid development of BCI technology and its impact on individual and social life, a reflective view is thoroughly needed. As is the case with all forms of (technological) progress, it is reasonable to assume that the consequences of an increasing use of BCIs will have both positive and negative aspects. To design technology to make human lives better, normative reflection about these aspects is crucial. Furthermore, technological progress is not determined and unchangeable. Rather, it follows and is dependent on human decisions and agency. Consequently, an ethical view on technology is both needed and feasible.

However, there are some problems with such a view. *First*, reflective views are typically too late since new technologies emerge more rapidly than any normative assessment can do. *Second*, the normative world is characterized by pluralism. That means, no one has ever succeeded in finding the "right ethics" for questions not just surrounding technology, but regarding any aspect of human activity. Whether pluralism as an ethical view is finally correct or not is hotly debated [31, 32], and it might turn out that in fact monism is true, i.e. the view that there exists some single true morality. But we are far from reaching it, and given the complexities of human thinking and judging, is seems reasonable to assume that we must live with pluralism indefinitely. *Third*, not only pluralism, but the complexity of modern societies and technology itself makes it hard or even impossible to identify responsibility for the goods and bads that arise in or out of the use of technology. This problem is intensified by autonomous technology that has the capability to "act" independently of human supervision and action. Artificial intelligence that can and will be found in many everyday applications, that allow us to have driverless cars or workerless factories, for example, shows how hard it is to find those who are responsible for ethical failures, misuse or accidents. This is particularly the case when a problem scales up due to the interconnectedness of these technologies. In technology, as in economics, for example, the systems are often too complex to reliably find knots of responsibility, agents that we can attribute with knowledge, causal impact, intentions and so on, all of which is necessary to hold someone responsible. Consider driverless cars to see how the question of responsibility is at the core of current ethical and political debates [33].

The current practice in the field of technology ethics often proceeds by merely listing the ethical challenges in a broad way, without putting much effort into thinking about how exactly "the good" can be brought about. Also, it is often characterized by a lack of being close to the phenomena. This means, for example, that the various contexts in which BCI technology, for example, are used, are insufficiently taken into account when it comes to assigning responsibility. Moreover, technology that acts at least partly autonomously requires a different evaluation than technology that is not. When an approach is chosen that sees the implementation of values as residing in the process of technology development itself, such as value-by-design, the broader implications of making ethics effective, such as pluralism or regulatory issues, are rarely addressed. Finally, scholars regularly try to find facts about what it means to be responsible, descriptive facts as well as normative ones, and to propose legal regulation to counteract problematic consequences and avoid unwanted implications of new technology.

But, as [34] has shown in another context, this approach faces problems. One of these problems is that the descriptive and normative criteria and facts about responsibility are not simply "there", waiting to be found by a thorough philosophical analysis. Rather, these factors are flexible and open to being assigned after a social process of finding (temporal) agreement. In addition, the traditional way often does not sufficiently address questions of (artificial) agency and the question of who is the agent in what way, when it comes to determining responsibility.

Still, however, finding the right addressees to go to for making technological progress ethical is crucial. We cannot simply list all the ethical issues and either leave the solution up to others, or avoid thinking about how ethical thinking can be made effective, because this would make ethical reasoning rather superfluous. Given the need and feasibility of normatively assessing new technologies on the one hand, and the problems with traditional approaches in ethical and legal scholarship on the other hand, a new approach is proposed. To accomplish this, the paper pursues two guiding questions: (1) how should we understand the ethical questions surrounding the development and use of BCIs in a way that is both technologically adequate and close to the phenomena?; and (2) what means are there to push technology development in the right direction, i.e. the direction that reasonable ethical reflection reveals as pressing?

In what follows I will *first* introduce a distinction aimed at helping ethical evaluations of technology to get a grip on the phenomena they deal with (Sect. 2). The result is a better view on the phenomena at hand, enabling a more precise assessment based on a particular distinction between two forms of agency. I will briefly apply it to the ethics of BCIs.

Second, I will broaden the perspective and ask how the ethical consideration can be applied in the real world (Sect. 3). The main emphasis will lie on outlining a philosophical move from ethics to politics, that is, the proposal that ethical questions are better solved by having the right political institutions, rather than having the right ethical point of view.

2 Establishing an Ethics Matrix to Assess BCIs

2.1 Primary and Secondary Agency

According to almost all philosophical theories, ethics is about agency [35]. An ethical evaluation, proceeding under the fundamental distinction between good and bad, or right and wrong, applies crucially to acts of agents. Only if something can be classified as an action, committed by an agent, can it be reasonably scrutinized. Particularly for questions of responsibility agency is crucial, since we ascribe responsibility primarily to agents. This also holds true for larger questions as they are typically dealt with in political ethics, social ethics and the like, in which case it is particularly important to know (and often not directly picked out as a central issue) who the agent in question is. However, it is also true in the ethics of technology where the question about agency is no less complex than in the case of political or social ethics.

This is so because, *first*, much like in the latter domains where we talk about political communities, the state and other agents, in the development and production of technology we often also find collective agents such as corporations or the scientific community to which we apply our ethical reasoning. However, the actions of these collectives depend on individual actions and their interrelations. Just as it is not the government per se that acts, but individual politicians, judges or public officials, it is a plurality of agents within technology development that are responsible for the results. *Second*, the products of technological progress themselves, i.e. technological devices, exhibit what we might reasonably call agency. What is meant by ascribing agency to technological artefacts is what currently drives, among others, the development of artificial intelligence, the relative autonomy and automatization of technologically-initiated or – mediated processes. For example, if a car can drive without a human driver, it exhibits at least some degree of agency. Similarly, a BCI used as assistive device can also exhibit agency to a certain extent. This is the case, as will be discussed below, when a brain-input is used to automatically direct or set in motion other process, e.g. in a car.

There are many accounts of agency, prominent in disciplines such as philosophy, psychology or cognitive science [36]. According to the received opinion (and one that the proposed concept will be based upon), agency consists of intentional action as a special sort of behavior, i.e. behavior that is accompanied and/or caused by certain mental states: desires, beliefs and intentions. They are followed by carrying out the intention through a physical movement. This includes also non-movements, as in the case where one refrains from doing something, based on a desire, a belief and an intention. Thus understood, an action is distinguished from mere reactive behavior, but it includes habitual and complex actions, where there is not a desire, belief and intention for each part of the action.

There is anything but agreement on many questions surrounding the notion of an action [37]. For example, it is not clear how actions can be individuated, how collective action is feasible, or how exactly basic and more complex actions hang together. Moreover, an action's mental parts that are thought to cause it, or that are at least presupposed when identifying an action, are not unanimously understood. Whether talk of intentions, for example, refers to mental states or rather to reasons for actions, is debated. Finally, whether and how our everyday talk about agency and agents applies to artificial agents and if machines can properly be called agents, beyond the technological feasibility to implement agency-like capabilities, is also up to be debated.

So, both the plurality of agents (and subsequently of the various types of activities that need to be scrutinized ethically) and multiple forms of agency call for a systematic approach in order to get a full view of ethical issues and ways to solve them. The promise of this is that we get a clearer picture of what is at stake and how we need to act to address the ethical issues of technological progress, i.e. whom we need to address and which areas we need to look at in our attempt to develop "good technology". To accomplish this, I propose an alternative view about agency. In it, the major distinction is not between agents and non-agents, or between human and artificial agents, but between *primary* and *secondary agents*. The criterion for distinguishing these two concept is (1) being able to implement and control action, and (2) being able to take over steps of complex actions.

To illustrate the point, consider the following examples:

(Production) *Ed works at RainDrops, a company that produces drip moldings. He assembles moldings of diverse length and robustness into the final products. Because of the physical shape of the raw material, the moldings, Ed's work is very hard. Therefore he uses a robotic arm to support him. This external device is directed through a BCI with which Ed starts a process whereby the robotic arm delivers moldings with a particular length and size to Ed. The robot's activity is pre-programmed, so that Ed simply gives the signal to start the series of actions the robot has to accomplish.*

(Automobile) *Anthony drives in his new car that is equipped with a BCI device. It continually surveilles Anthony's mental states, particularly his affective states. The roads Anthony uses to get to his office are usually very crowded. This causes Anthony to be stressed, he feels annoyed about the other cars' drivers. At one point, he wants to overtake another car and therefore speeds up. However, the BCI prevents Anthony from speeding up and overtaking the other car, because it is programmed to do so when it detects signs of stress in Anthony.*

In both *Production* and *Automobile*, we face what can be called a *primary agent*. Whereas in *Production*, it is clearly Ed who is the agent, using as an assistive device the BCI-controlled robot, in *Automobile* we see that it is the car's BCI that controls the situation. In at least one case, however, we also find a *secondary agent*. Consider Anthony, the driver. Anthony is in possession of the ability and the resources to drive his car, and he is free to do so in a way that pleases him, but only to a certain extent. His mental states are causally efficacious up to the point where he intends to do something potentially harmful. The reduction of intentional efficacy is what makes him a secondary agent, as compared to the BCI in his car.

Both the primary and the secondary agents can, but need not exhibit what action theory holds as essential prerequisites for action, namely beliefs, desires and intentions. However, only the primary agent's mental states or programs are fully efficacious, which means that only Ed and the BCI in *Automobile* can to force courses of action upon others, i.e. fulfull criterion (1) above. So, the reach of a primary agent's mental states is such that they not only cover a specific action, i.e. the one that the agent sets out to do. What adds to this is the ability to be *authoritative in providing constraints or even whole courses of self-chosen actions for others*. The BCI is, in this sense, authoritative in that it allows Anthony to act freely in a more or less clearly demarcated frame. It has "the last word" on what actions can or cannot be taken, even though it is preprogrammed to detect the limits of this frame (i.e. Anthony's mental states that trigger the prohibition of taking over, for example). This is the case even though the process upon which the BCI operates is automatized and does not itself imply freedom of action. Similarly, Ed provides the frame of action for the robot since he authorizes the robot's movements to start or stop.

Moreover, a primary agent is characterized by the ability to independently take over the steps of a (complex) action, that is, it fulfills criterion (2) above. *Production* and *Automobile* both show that the primary agent, as compared to the secondary agent, acts independently from the authority or permission of others. It is true that the BCI remains inactive until it detects stress and Anthony attempts to overtake another car. Therefore, it is dependent on another event or agent. But this is not to say that its action rests on another agent's authorization. It is caused by a trigger, but this is hardly comparable to when Ed authorizes the robot to start its movement. All human action is triggered by something else, at least most of the time, but we would not take this fact to say that humans are not agents who take over steps of a complex action. This, again, shows how, for primary agents, the reach of their mental states is larger than for secondary agents. The former have the capacity to act according to a variety of plans (as a variety of combinations of beliefs, desires and intentions), and they adapt their options to the environment as a reaction to what they perceive, whereas the latter are confined to a specific course of action that is dependent on the permission or inhibition of another (primary) agent.

These examples show that the distinction between primary and secondary agency is not identical with the one between a human (or a full) and an artificial agent. It is not relevant whether the primary agent has freedom of action or is self-aware and has consciousness, for example. What counts is its ability to be authoritative in forcing frames of action upon others and to initiate courses of actions.

Furthermore, it is also compatible with other agents being responsible for the kind of (automated) activity of an artificial agent, even of an artificial primary agent. That is, we can still say that programmers or producers are responsible for a BCI's activity, reliability etc., although the agent is a primary one. Being dependent on another event or agent (as in *Automobile*) does not exclude primary agency, nor does having been pre-programmed (or educated) by another party. This is because what exclusively counts for primary agency is the authority to force frames of possible actions on others. This authority can be caused and supervised by other agents, even pre-programmed, without the primary agency to cease. Consequently, we can assign responsibility to third parties without having to remove primary agency. The pressing ethical question, then, is: when is implementing or installing authority permissible or good. More on this below.

Note also that one and the same entity can be both a primary and secondary agent in various contexts, depending on what role it has. Consider the BCI in *Automobile* where it is the primary agent. But imagine also another scenario where, although it has the same capabilities, the BCI is used as a device to control the entertainment system: here the BCI is a secondary agent. Moreover, both sorts of agencies can exist simultaneously.

What use is there for distinguishing primary and secondary agency? *First*, we can assign responsibility in a much more nuanced way than had we merely one sort of agents. For instance, a self-driving car as a primary agent is certainly more of a primary agent-kind than, say, a car that is only partly automatized. Still, parts of the secondary agent can be, in their specific context, a primary agent as well, and we have seen that primary agency still allows for third-party responsibility. *Second*, and more importantly, distinguishing primary and secondary agents enables us to groups various ethical questions along the idea of agency and thus establish an ethical matrix. This in turn enables us to find the right person, institution or any other entity to which we assign responsibility and where action needs to be taken to account for the ethical questions we pose. To illustrate and explain this point, let us now outline an ethical matrix for the use of BCIs, grouped according to the idea of agency. Before doing that, however, we need to consider modes of acting as part of the matrix.

2.2 Modes of Acting

Human (and for that matter, technological) actions are plural. We carry out a huge number of actions on a daily basis, and it is a philosophical question itself whether a single physical movement represents one action or rather a number of different actions [38]. Still, we can simplify the issue and hold that, broadly speaking, actions fall into one of two categories. The first is the category of *initiate, allow, inhibit*. Under this rubric we can find actions where we think the agent does something to start off an activity and to bring about an effect, or to let something else happen. Here, the agent either refrains from interfering with a process that has already started, or he refrains from refraining, when an agent stops another process. The second category is that of *mediating* between two processes. This takes place when an agent causes some process to go into a desired direction.

The former type of action consists of an agent who has authority to cause a course of action to begin or end. Moreover, there are processes involved that can, but need not, be correlated or hang together in some sense, other than one action being the cause of another one. Consider *Automobile* again: the BCI that allows or prohibits Anthony to overtake another car exemplifies an action of the *initiate, allow, inhibit*-category since the computer's task is to not allow another action (the overtaking) to take place. The actions involved are not correlated other than that the BCI's intervention causes another event (not) to take place.

Actions in the *mediating*-category, on the contrary, relate two other actions with each other in a way that exploits, uses, or establishes a connection between them. Consider the following example:

(Research) *Automobile giant BAW (Bajuwarische Autowerke) is currently working on autonomously and semi-autonomously driving cars. The trend towards automatization does not stop in front of the automobile industry. On the contrary: driving is one of the major fields of research and progress in the automatization process. However, there are many open questions regarding the design of these cars and other features that determine the popularity and acceptance of autonomous cars. To gain knowledge about these questions, BAW uses the whole range of marketing instruments such as surveys and analyses. Another instrument is the use of BCIs to see how people react to different features of a car. Therefore, when subjects test a car, BAW plugs them to a BCI, modifies the car's features and measures the subject's reaction to this in real-time. With the help of a BCI it is possible to automatize the research process and to gain fine-grained and ecologically valid data that help shape the final product.*

What *Research* shows is how an agent – the BCI – can act to mediate between the interests and actions of various agents – the BAW company and (future) customers. It acts in a somewhat autonomous manner. But in its actions, it just measures what happens in the subject's brains, subsequently changes the car's features and thereby collects data about people's preferences regarding the car. The company's and people's actions (producing and consuming) have an internal relation with each other: the production needs to match the preferences so that the company does earn money, and people can happily fulfill their desires.

The same can be said of examples where technology is the primary agent in accomplishing mediating tasks:

(Entertain) *Babette starts her smart TV because she wants to see the latest episode of their favorite series "The Walking Dead". The TV device has a menu with several elements such as Photo Library, Web Browser, and Apps from services such as Amazon and Netflix. A BCI helps her find the right item in the menu with a remote control. She moves the cursor towards the streaming app and clicks through the various items in the menu. Her brain reacts accordingly and when positive signals are detected the TV get the information to continue in the menu. When negative signals are detected, the TV goes one step back in the hierarchy of the menu.*

We might say that in *Research* and *Entertain*, the BCI is used in an instrumental way, and that this use differs from it acting more autonomously in *Production* and *Automobile*. This is true, but only as far as it goes. For, *first*, in *Research* the BCI is also acting autonomously, it adapts to the people's reaction towards the car and modifies the car's features accordingly. *Second*, in *Production* and *Automobile* we might also say that the BCI is used as an instrument by human agents. For example, Anthony, the driver, uses the BCI not directly as an instrument, but indirectly, by buying and using a BCI-controlled car as such, not in every case of driving to the office where it operates autonomously.

It is worth noting the advantages of the approach pursued here: If one speaks of automatization in a general way, and of technology as being instrumental for human interests in a similarly general way, one misses important distinctions between the various uses of technology. It poses a normatively relevant difference if the BCI is used in *Research* or in *Automobile*, although both uses are instrumental and simultaneously exemplifying autonomously acting technology. And different agents must be addressed to solve the ethical issues. So being able to use a better distinction according to which uses of technology is distinguished according to the criteria *primary/secondary agency* and *mode of agency* allows for a more fine-grained ethical analysis of the question at stake. Moreover, this distinction might be helpful in identifying or ascribing responsibility for the ethically relevant implications and consequences.

2.3 Ethical Issues Related to BCIs

From what has been said so far, a matrix of ethical issues emerges. The two dimensions according to which the matrix is organized are the criteria "primary/secondary agency" and "mode of agency":

When BCIs are used as primary agents, as in *Automobile*, the important question relates to issues of autonomy, risk and privacy. Autonomy is addressed through a BCI's capability of implementing and controlling actions. Since primary agents have, by definition, the last word on some decisions, one might question whether they have the right form of authority. In other words, the primary question is whether it is allowed, permissible or good to create the authority represented by the BCI. What are the proper rules guiding this question? And where can we look to find an answer? The ethical matrix not only allows us to answer these question by looking at various proposals in different areas of applied ethics (business ethics, medical ethics), but also to find solutions in political philosophy where the issue of authority has been extensively studied [39]. This stands in contrast to many debates in applied ethics and public policy that merely look at autonomy per se, without considering the processes that lead to accepting forms of authority (Table 1).

Table 1. Ethical matrix

	BCI as primary agent	BCI as secondary agent
Initiate, allow, inhibit	*Automobile* e.g. authority, autonomy, risk, privacy	*Production* e.g. functionality, safety
Mediate	*Entertain* e.g. authority, functionality, safety, privacy	*Research* e.g. research ethics

Other areas of inquiry are not in fact specifically tied to a BCI, but they obtain another status when they are seen under the perspective of authority, particularly authority represented by a technological device. If a BCI reduces my freedom to overtake other cars on my way to the office, I am indeed no longer the one who is in charge. But does this reduce my autonomy? It does not, of course, if I agreed to using it. It does, for example, when BCIs in cars are mandatory. This, however, is another question, namely one about the proper way to regulate risks by reducing freedom of action. Again, the question of political authority emerges, because the question is what the processes are by which we organize the regulatory business. New fields of inquiry can and must be addressed, such as business ethics or political philosophy. Again, traditional approaches, stemming mainly from medical ethics or bioethics, are not the sole locus of inquiry here.

Risk is in fact a very important question, and in the case of *Automobile*, many dimensions of risk are involved. *First*, there is the risk that I might die from a car accident by reckless driving, something the BCI aims at preventing. *Second*, there is the risk of others to die from my reckless driving. In this case, we face the question of how to regulate social risks, apart from paternalistically preventing people from harming themselves as in the first example.

Next, consider privacy. Presumably there will be many data that arise and can get stored when using the BCI. Of what kind are these data? What can one do with them, for instance the car company, the BCI producer or the car insurance company? It is not only the data gathered by the device, but also the driver's behavior generates data that can be used, for example if she turns off the BCI to finally overtake. Or should the possibility of a driver turning off the BCI be prohibited?

In other cases, such as *Entertain*, when BCIs are used as primary agents for an action of the *mediating*-type, questions of functionality and safety emerge. We would certainly not want a BCI to explode while we navigate through our TV. The same holds for BCI as secondary agent, i.e. as agent that strictly executes actions after another agent's initiation. In *Production*, the BCI would not be widely used in factories if it did not do its job, namely to reliably assist the worker.

In *Research*, the major questions do not exactly lie in the use of the BCI device, but in the broader context of research ethics. It can be used for various goals, such as market research or research examining design features of electric seats. Also, it can be used by a totalitarian dictator, trying to find out how he can manipulate his subordinates, or it can be used by a research organization with a high reputation in a working democracy. It can involve participants who gave or did not give their informed consent, and it can be part of a well-designed study or of a fake study, carried out by malicious companies.

Now, given these questions and problems, how are we to find ethical solutions? Can the distinction between primary and secondary agent help in identifying ethical solutions to these questions? They certainly can, at least to a certain extent. As was said before, the proposed agency-distinction can help make people such as programmers and engineers be responsible for the algorithms they program. Also, managers can be made responsible for carrying out this and that kind of research, and developing this and that technological device. Finally, consumers have a choice as well, in form of the reward they give to a company or producer through their consuming choices. Even if a BCI is the primary agent, there are always others who are developing, producing and buying these agents. Unless these decisions will be made by an artificial agent, then, responsibility lies with these agents.

Crucially, however, with the secondary/primary-agent-distinction, we are freed from looking at things from an individual value-perspective and can move on to regard things from a procedural perspective. If agency is understood in these broad ways, we are brought to see different contexts and types of activities that we need to ethically evaluate, both in terms of primary and secondary agencies. Furthermore, we are brought to see that it is not only the individual questions of an agent using a BCI that are at the center of an ethical inquiry, but the ways we (as a community or society) regulate different approaches to different areas of use. What the distinction between primary and secondary agent thus aims at illuminating is the necessary shift from a mere individual ethics approach to questions of technology to a more political and social approach. This one looks at processes by which different areas of technology use are regulated, based on what questions emerge given the agency-distinction discussed above.

3 From Ethics to Politics

These ethical issues are hardly new, but a way to finally solve them is not in sight. Many books and articles have been written about every aspect of the ethical, social, and legal aspects of emerging technology. A Google Scholar search returns over 34.000 entries for the query “ethical issues emerging technology” (between 2016 and 2017). Many base their assessment on future developments and more or less realistic scenarios [13]. And even though the previous pages outlined an alternative view about agency and questions surrounding them in the case of BCI technology, they are of little or no help in finding those who are responsible for when something goes wrong with the technology, or, with a look ahead, who are responsible for getting things right. The reasons have been mentioned before: technology’s more rapid development, compared to ethical analysis; pluralism; and the nature of responsibility. Among these issues, pluralism provides the most challenging factor.

However, we might want to start thinking about whether finding such an agreement is in fact needed. Or at least, whether *thinking ethically* about these questions is adequate to find solutions. It seems as if many people assume that doing ethics of technology as part of the academic world will eventually lead us to the "right answer". This is why there are so many attempts to critically assess existing and new technology, and to examine all the impacts and consequences. But it might turn out that thinking about technology is not the right way to find right answer. Perhaps technology must rather be used, experimented with, and tested. Is this not the proper use of technology, i.e. to actually *use* it and not (only) to think about it?

What is needed, then, is a way to allow experimentation with the development and use of technology such as BCIs. Since we cannot find all answers and not even all problems that might arise, it is crucial that there be ample room for experimentation and testing. Consequently, when it comes to deciding about this or that technology, the decider should not be the ethics community, nor the politicians who draft regulation and who are often seen as *ethics executors*. Rather, the deciders should be the *consumers*, those for whose lives technology has an impact. In other words, technology must prove successful and acceptable through *market mechanisms* that are free from any external regulation and attempts to guide the development of technology in a direction that appears preferred either by politicians, the industry itself or any other powerful agent other than the consumers themselves.

This proposal amounts to shifting the debate about acceptable technology *from ethics to politics*. It might sound surprising since markets are typically thought to be opposed to politics. However, this view overlooks a very important fact: Markets are dependent on a lot of political efforts to uphold them, just as politics is. The picture of markets used here is broader than the one used when markets are brought into opposition to politics. It is based on the view that underlying all institutions that enable and facilitate cooperation in a society are based on a deeper form of cooperation, trust and the effort to uphold these institutions. Here the call for experimentation and what [40] calls "permissionless innovation" shows its radical innovative perspective with the promise to change not only the way we deal with technology, but also with the way we deal with dealing with technology.

Arguing for an experimentation-first approach to technology development therefore means that not only finding technological solutions to current problems must be subject to market-based experimentation, but also the mechanisms to govern these processes. This is where the concept of markets, alluded to above, shows that it is deeper than the traditional one involved in opposing markets to politics. It means, for example, that jurisdictions and, more generally, regulatory institutions (law-making, administrations) need to be open to flexible experimentation. The important distinction is not so much the one between politics and markets, but rather between politics and ethics.

Whereas ethics typically tries to find criteria with which technology can be assessed, and to propose adequate measures to make sure these criteria are met – mostly legal regulation –, the political approach concentrates on other processes by which people find ways to interact with each other, propose social change and try to influence others to accept their ethical views. The important point is that it is not only coercive law-making by which these processes proceed, but by implementing social conventions.

Law-making tries to fix problems by finding facts and proposing ways to deal with these facts, making these ways compulsory for everybody. The political solution, however, conceives of these facts as conventional and malleable, being dependent on interpretation and always open to being amended, redefined and negotiated [34].

It is important to bind both the market-orientation and the political approach together. To do this note, *first*, that "political" does not refer to the institutionalized political process as we know it and that operates under the assumption of political authority. Rather, "political" refers to the "sub-political" (in the first sense of political) processes by which social life is organized (cf. for the following [34]). These processes contain social practices, norms and expectations, in brief, social conventions. These conventions form the basis for interpreting ethical questions such as who is responsible, and the fact upon which we build our ethical assessment of responsibility. Since these social conventions are dependent upon interpretation and differ between individuals, depending on their views, beliefs and norms, they are somewhat free-floating – and malleable. The malleability of norms and ethical views requires, and justifies, a constant endeavor to be socially and politically active in favor of one's preferred view. In brief, the political sphere wherein the regulation of social life and technology takes place, comprises efforts to shape answers to ethical questions surrounding technology by influencing rule-making through public persuasion and working on social conventions. It is not as if there was a factual answer to ground and identify responsibility. Rather, what constitutes these grounds and identifications is an open process.

Second, to enable these processes to take place, i.e. to empower people to be able to follow their preferences and norms, and to assume the work of having social influence, a free market is the best way to accomplish this. Only if interactions are based on the free exchange of ideas and the freedom to express one's preferences through mechanisms of effectively rewarding those who share our preferences can progress be made. So, free markets should be the institution of choice when it comes to addressing the malleable and conventional nature of ethics.

Third, all of this does not rule out law-making or regulation, as should be obvious from the fact that social conventions often do and sometimes need to be codified and implemented in public law. However, here the idea behind letting markets decide about ethics must be applied to the political sphere as well. This means that the institutions of law-making and public regulation need to be chosen in and through market processes, just as the production of goods and services needs to be guided by market-based mechanisms. In other words: To not fall back into a system of coercive law and politics, trying to shape technological progress by ethical reasoning "in the dark", we need to insert flexibility into the political system itself. As a consequence, people must be fully able to enter and exit political communities with law-making authority that transcendent currently existing national borders, and in some cases even physical borders. People must be free to join political units that sometimes do, sometimes do not depend on or cover any physical territory, but that are authorized to make laws and govern the respective communities. This ensures that people have full control over how things need to be regulated, according to their own view. It makes sure people can live in communities that express their points of views, that allow certain technologies and not others. The political approach to ethics pursued here relates back to theories in political philosophy and economy such as in [41, 42], from which important insights into feasible political structures can be derived.

While it might be possible that people form communities with others who share their views, and thus relatively homogeneous communities start to exist, including those with very poor morality, the process does not stop there. Rather, the freedom to leave political units and join others will, over the course of time, lead to an open world, where many goods and services are provided by a free market because this tends to progress much better into an ethical society than when it is directed through ethical reasoning and political implementation. This world will be one that is supported by people's plural ethical views, and it will be stable because rules, institutions and mechanisms will have emerged that tend to enable people to prosper and flourish by giving them the freedom to shape the world according to their views.

4 Conclusion

In this paper, I have proposed a distinction between forms of agency that can be helpful in ascribing responsibility in cases where technology assumes some degree of autonomy. Responsibility is one of the major issues when it comes to assessing and evaluating technological progress. However, this account is not likely to settle questions about responsibility. The reason lies mainly in ethical pluralism. Therefore, I have proposed to shift normative reflections on ethical questions from ethics to politics. This means that to direct technology development in the right direction, it is necessary to have adequate political institutions and to assign processes of interaction and persuasion a more crucial role in finding out what is right and wrong with technology. The political of this approach thus can be found along two dimensions: the politics of social interaction, and the politics of institutional design. With these two dimensions in place, we can have trust in the development of BCIs that work for the benefit of all humans.

Further work needs to be done regarding the proper foundation of such a view, its relation to other works in political philosophy, and about its realization in the real world. Among other things, empirical work about how "permissionless innovation" in both technology and politics can and does work to the benefit of all humans is thoroughly needed. Finally, a more detailed account of how particular technologies can be developed based on this approach is also needed.[1]

References

1. Nicolas-Alonso, L.F., Gomez-Gil, J.: Brain computer interfaces, a review. Sensors **12**, 1211–1279 (2012)
2. Ortiz-Rosario, A., Adeli, H.: Brain-Computer Interface technologies: from signal to action. Rev. Neurosci. **24**, 537–552 (2013)

[1] This work is part of the research project EMOIO (FKZ 16SV7196), funded by the German Ministry of Education and Research (BMBF).

3. Hassanien, A.E., Azar, A.T. (eds.): Brain-Computer Interfaces. ISRL, vol. 74. Springer, Cham (2015). doi:10.1007/978-3-319-10978-7
4. Graimann, B., Allison, B., Pfurtscheller, G. (eds.): Brain-Computer Interfaces. Revolutionizing Human-Computer interaction. Springer, Heidelberg (2010)
5. Allison, B.Z., Dunne, S., Leeb, R., Millán, J.D.R., Nijholt, A. (eds.): Towards Practical Brain-Computer Interfaces. Bridging the Gap from Research to Real-World Applications. Springer, Heidelberg (2012)
6. Clerc, M., Bougrain, L., Lotte, F. (eds.): Brain-Computer Interfaces 1. Foundations and Methods. Wiley, London (2016)
7. Clerc, M., Bougrain, L., Lotte, F. (eds.): Brain-Computer Interfaces 2. Technology and Applications. Wiley, London (2016)
8. Coyle, D. (ed.): Brain-Computer Interfaces: Lab Experiments to Real-World Applications. Elsevier, Amsterdam (2016)
9. Grübler, G., Hildt, E. (eds.): Brain-Computer Interfaces in Their Ethical, Social and Cultural Contexts. TILELT, vol. 12. Springer, Dordrecht (2014). doi:10.1007/978-94-017-8996-7
10. Fawrowicz, M., Marek, T., Karwowski, W., Schmorrow, D. (eds.): Neuroadaptive Systems: Theory and Applications. CRC Press, Boca Raton (2013)
11. Millán, J.D.R., Rupp, R., Müller-Putz, G.R., Murray-Smith, R., Giugliemma, C., Tangermann, M., Vidaurre, C., Cincotti, F., Kübler, A., Leeb, R., Neuper, C., Müller, K.-R., Mattia, D.: Combining Brain-Computer Interfaces and assistive technologies: state-of-the-art and challenges. Front. Neurosci. **4**, 1–15 (2010)
12. Clausen, J.: Bonding brains to machines: ethical implications of electroceuticals for the human brain. Neuroethics **6**, 429–434 (2013)
13. Tamburrini, G.: Brain to computer communication: ethical perspectives on interaction models. Neuroethics **2**, 137–149 (2009)
14. Tamburrini, G.: Philosophical reflections on Brain–Computer Interfaces. In: Grübler, G., Hildt, E. (eds.) Brain-Computer-Interfaces in their ethical, social and cultural contexts. TILELT, vol. 12, pp. 147–162. Springer, Dordrecht (2014). doi: 10.1007/978-94-017-8996-7_13
15. Keebler, J.R., Taylor, G., Philips, E., Ososky, S., Sciarini, L.W.: Neuroethics: considerations for a future embedded with neurotechnology. In: Fafrowicz, M., Marek, T., Karwowski, W., Schmorrow, D. (eds.) Neuroadaptive Systems: Theory and Applications, pp. 333–350. CRC Press, Boca Raton (2013)
16. Jebari, K.: Brain machine interface and human enhancement–an ethical review. Neuroethics **6**, 617–625 (2013)
17. Li, Q., Ding, D., Conti, M.: Brain-Computer Interface applications: security and privacy challenges. In: 2015 IEEE Conference on Communications and Network Security (CNS). IEEE, Florence (2015)
18. Blankertz, B., Tangermann, M., Vidaurre, C., Fazil, S., Sannelli, C., Haufe, S., Maeder, C., Ramsey, L., Sturm, I., Curio, G., Müller, K.-R.: The Berlin Brain-Computer Interface: non-medical uses of BCI technology. Front. Neurosci. **4**, 198 (2010)
19. Blankertz, B., Acqualanga, L., Dähne, S., Haufe, S., Schultze-Kraft, M., Sturm, I., Uscumlic, M., Wenzel, M.A., Curio, G., Müller, K.-R.: The Berlin brain-computer interface: progress beyond communication and control. Front. Neurosci. **10**, 1–24 (2016)
20. Berka, C., Levendowski, D.J., Lumicao, M.N., Yau, A., Davis, G., Zitkovic, V.T., Olmstead, R.E., Tremoulet, P.D., Craven, P.L.: EEG correlates of task engagement and mental workload in vigilance, learning, and memory task. Aviat. Space Environ. Med. **78**, B231–B244 (2007)

21. Dijksterhuis, C., de Waard, D., Brookhuis, K.A., Mulder, B.L.J.M., de Jong, R.: Classifying visuomotor workload in a driving simulator using subject specific spatial brain patterns. Front. Neurosci. **7**, 149 (2013)
22. Haufe, S., Kim, J.-W., Kim, I.-H., Sonnleitner, A., Schrauf, M., Curio, G., Blankertz, B.: Electrophysiology-based detection of emergency braking intention in real-world driving. J. Neural Eng. **11**, 56011 (2014)
23. Papadelis, C., Chen, Z., Kourtidou-Papadeli, C., Bamidis, P.D., Chouvarda, I., Bekiaris, E., Maglaveras, N.: Monitoring sleepiness with on-board electrophysiological recordings for preventing sleep-deprived traffic accidents. Clin. Neurophysiol. **118**, 1906–1922 (2007)
24. Simon, M., Schmidt, E.A., Kincses, W.E., Fritzsche, M., Bruns, A., Aufmuth, C., Bogdan, M., Rosenstiel, W., Schrauf, M.: EEG alpha spindle measures as indicators of driver fatigue under real traffic conditions. Clin. Neurophysiol. **122**, 1168–1178 (2011)
25. Sonnleitner, A., Treder, M.S., Simon, M., Willmann, S., Ewald, A., Buchner, A., Schrauf, M.: EEG alpha spindles and prolonged brake reaction times during auditory distraction in an on-road driving study. Accid. Anal. Prev. **62**, 110–118 (2014)
26. Lin, C.-T., Chen, Y.-C., Huang, T.-Y., Chiu, T.-T., Ko, L.-W., Liang, S.-F., Hsieh, H.-Y., Hsu, S.-H., Duann, J.-R.: Development of wireless brain computer interface with embedded multitask scheduling and its application on real-time driver's drowsiness detection and warning. IEEE Trans. Biomed. Eng. **55**, 1582–1591 (2008)
27. Kotchetkov, I.S., Hwang, B.Y., Appelboom, G., Kellner, C.P., Connolly, E.S.: Brain-Computer Interfaces: Military, neurosurgical, and ethical perspective. Neurosurg. Focus **28**, E25 (2010)
28. Bell, C.J., Shenoy, P., Chalodhorn, R., Rao, R.P.N.: Control of a humanoid robot by a noninvasive Brain-Computer Interface in humans. J. Neural Eng. **5**, 214–220 (2008)
29. Zhang, B., Wang, J.: Fuhlbrigge: a review of the commercial Brain-Computer Interface technology from perspective of industrial robotics. In: IEEE International Conference on Automation and Logistics (ICAL). IEEE, The Chinese University of Hong Kong and University of Macau Shatin, Hong Kong (2010)
30. Bi, L., Teng, T.: Using a head-up display-based steady-state visually evoked potential Brain-Computer Interface to control a simulated vehicle. IEEE Trans. Intell. Transp. Syst. **15**, 959–966 (2014)
31. Mason, E.: Value pluralism. In: Zalta, E.N. (ed.) The Stanford Encyclopedia of Philosophy (2015). https://plato.stanford.edu/archives/sum2015/entries/value-pluralism/
32. Gaus, G.F.: Contemporary Theories of Liberalism. Public Reason as a Post-Enlightenment Project. Sage Publications, London (2003)
33. Lin, P.: Is Tesla Responsible for the Deadly Crash On Auto-Pilot? Maybe. Forbes.com (2016). http://www.forbes.com/sites/patricklin/2016/07/01/is-tesla-responsible-for-the-deadly-crash-on-auto-pilot-maybe/#47bf2ec05bbc
34. Goodhart, M.: Interpreting responsibility politically. J. Polit. Philos. (2017, online first)
35. Birnbacher, D.: Analytische Einführung in die Ethik. Walter de Gruyter, Berlin (2007)
36. Schlosser, M.: Agency. In: Zalta, E.N. (ed.) The Stanford Encyclopedia of Philosophy (2015). https://plato.stanford.edu/archives/fall2015/entries/agency/
37. Kühler, M., Rüther, M. (eds.): Handbuch Handlungstheorie. J.B. Metzler, Stuttgart (2016)
38. Budnik, C.: Handlungsindividuation. In: Kühler, M., Rüther, M. (eds.) Handbuch Handlungstheorie, pp. 60–68. J.B. Metzler, Stuttgart (2016)
39. Christiano, T.: Authority. In: Zalta, E.N. (ed.) The Stanford Encyclopedia of Philosophy, https://plato.stanford.edu/archives/spr2013/entries/authority/ (2013)
40. Thierer, A.: Permissionless Innovation. The Continuing Case for Comprehensive Technological Freedom. Mercatus Center at George Mason University, Arlington (2016)

41. Frey, B., Eichenberger, R.: The New Democratic Federalism for Europe. Functional, Overlapping and Competing Jurisdictions. Edward Elgar Publishing Limited, Cheltenham (1999)
42. Tucker, A., de Bellis, G.P. (eds.): Panarchy. Political Theories of Non-Territorial States. Routledge, New York and London (2016)

HCI, Innovation and Technology Acceptance

The Experiential Utility
How Behavioural Economics Can Help HCI to Define Quality

Stefano Bussolon(✉)

Department of Psychology and Cognitive Science, University of Trento, Trento, Italy
stefano.bussolon@unitn.it

Abstract. Economists define utility as the total satisfaction received from consuming a good or service. Neoclassical economics assume that humans act as perfectly rational agents whose ultimate goal is to maximize their subjective utility. Behavioral economists and psychologists, however, showed that people behave in ways that violate the neoclassical axioms, and follow a number of cognitive heuristics. Nonetheless, the concept of utility is useful, psychologically intuitive, and there is some evidence that some regions of the primates' brain encode a form of "common currency" of the value of a good [21].

I will present an experiential utility model that is psychologically plausible, and the main dimensions of the model will be mapped on an experiential utility space. The practical applicability of the map will be shown in a case study where two types of insurance companies - traditional (broker mediated) and direct (online) companies will be mapped on the dimensions of the experience utility map.

Neoclassical economists assume that people behave and think as perfect rational agents, the so called homo economicus.

If they were right, the hci field would be quite different. Even the concept of quality would be useless, because it would be translated in a form of expected value formula. Behavioral economists and psychologists, however, showed that the human behavior systematically differ from what predicted by the neoclassical school.

The first reason of that difference has been attributed to the bounded rationality: humans lack the computational resources to calculate the expected utility of every choice. A second stream of research showed that humans tend to rely on a number of heuristics instead of basing their decisions on the expected utility theorems.

Those researches proved that humans do not behave as the rationalist model expected. But there are reasons to believe that even for an artificial intelligence would be impossible to become an Olympian Rationality decision maker.

The first reason is grounded in computational theory: the computational complexity of many real world problems exceeds the power of the best computers, and many problems are even undecidable.

M. Kurosu (Ed.): HCI 2017, Part I, LNCS 10271, pp. 121–133, 2017.
DOI: 10.1007/978-3-319-58071-5_10

A second problem is intrinsic to the rational models: to avoid the complexity of the distinction between risk and uncertainty, they assume that the probability estimates of any outcome should be subjective. This choice opens the gates to - well - subjectivity and heuristics. It looks like there can be no intelligence without heuristics.

The distinction between risk and uncertainty has been developed by Knight and Keynes in the twenties [32]. Risk is when probabilities are well-understood, uncertainty when there is insufficient information to form a probability judgment [31]. The subjective utility model is reasonable when the agent needs to handle risks, but becomes inapplicable when probabilities are uncertain, because the Bayesian inference is not rich enough to describe one's degree of confidence in one's assessments. [18]

When the problem is too complex, or the information is insufficient, a less analytical and more heuristic approach becomes mandatory. Indeed, there is increasing evidence that complex judgment tasks do not always need complex cognitive strategies to be solved successfully [28], and in some circumstances simpler rules lead to better performances than complex, rationalist approaches [29].

An evolutionary perspective sees heuristics as adaptations: the assumption is that the ultimate goal of cognition is to increase the reproductive fitness of genes, not to increase the rationality of humans [43]. Within this framework, human performance is assumed as normative.

If we accept the criticism to the rationalist approach, the rational utility theories will loose also their status of normative model. Nonetheless, they would maintain both a practical and a theoretical value. From a practical point of view, whenever applicable, the rational approach remains the best *weapon of choice*. From a theoretical perspective, it still constitutes the most important point of reference: the entire field of behavioral economics bases its research paradigms on the differences from the rational models.

The most important models of rational behavior are the Utility Theory proposed by Morgenstern and von Neumann, the Savage's Subjective Expected Utility Model, the Weighted Sum Model.

Although different, the models are based on two parts, conceptually similar to the map and reduce approach of some functional languages [9]. The map part applies a function to the relevant dimensions of the problem (the outcomes, in the Savage model, the features in the weighted sum model). The reduce function takes the vector provided by the map and generate a smaller vector (often a single value, like the utility value).

The aim of this work is to begin to define a framework - based on the evidences of the behavior economics - to estimate the subjective quality of an experience.

1 The Experiential Utility Model

The framework is based on the same two steps: the definition of the rules of the *reduce* function, and the identification of the dimensions to be mapped on the mapping function. I'm dividing the two steps for three reasons: for a matter of clarity, because it is conceptually similar to the utility models, and because I believe the reduce function can be applied on different mapping functions, and it should be as *universal* as possible, whereas the mapping functions can be adapted on the specific knowledge domains.

The reduce function here proposed assumes that:

- the output value is not cardinal, but ordinal
- it is an estimate based on the affect heuristic
- the positive and the negative values are evaluated separately;
- it is influenced by:
  - the sum of the positive and the negative elements
  - the mean of the positive and of the negative elements
  - the maximum and the minimum (the absolute maximum of the negative elements)
  - the outcome (the end rule) of the experience

The mapping function is assumed to be a weighted vector of the following dimensions of an experience:

- the instrumental, extrinsic, functional value;
- the intrinsic value: its ability to fulfill one or more human basic needs, personal values, or interests;
- the ability to form an habit, or to become part of an existing one;
- the economic costs, in terms of money or the use of other valuable resources;
- the cognitive costs;
- the physical effort;
- the emotional component;
- the psychological time

1.1 The *reduce* Function

The assumption I'm making is that the synthesis humans make from the mapping of the salient dimensions of the choices is far more complex than a simple sum of the positive and negative values.

First, we tend to base our decisions both on cognitive and affective evaluations. Second, negative values are not just subtracted from the positive ones. Third, the gestalt of a past or foreseen experience is remembered (or imagined) and evaluated [17], and some characteristics (the maximum positive and negative aspects, and the outcome) are more salient and play a greater role in the utility evaluation. Forth, there is evidence that often the mean, and not the sum of the values is used in evaluating an option.

The Affect Heuristic. One of the characteristics of the experiential system is its affective basis [42]. Decisions are often based on subjective affective responses to the options, that humans believe is indicative of the options' values [34]. This process is known as *affect heuristic* or *feelings-as-information* [38]: people may integrate - or just simplify - the judgmental task by asking themselves "How do I feel about it?". Slovic et al. [41] define affect as "the specific quality of goodness or badness (a) experienced as a feeling state (with or without consciousness) and (b) demarcating a positive or negative quality of a stimulus".

The affect heuristic is linked with affective forecasting, the prediction of how one will feel in the future. Affective forecasting can be divided into four components: predictions about emotional valence, the specific emotions experienced, their duration, and their intensity [47]. Affective forecasting has also the role to motivate the action of the agent, and feelings can signal the fitness value (and therefore the utility) of future events and choices.

In accordance with the evolutionary paradigm, the affect heuristic is not necessarily seen as a negative bias, because reliance on affect and emotion is a quicker, easier, and more efficient way to navigate in a complex, uncertain, and sometimes dangerous world [42].

1.2 The Gestalt of the Experience

Experiences can be remembered and imagined [7]. Tulving [46] defined the episodic memory as a time travel machine that allow us to mentally travel back to the past and forward to the future. The episodic memory summarizes the past experiences, retaining some important gestalt: the trend of the experience, the most intense moments and, if the experience is extrinsically motivated, it's end [2,22].

1.3 The Mean: More Is Less

List [26] did a field experiment at a sportscards show; the experimental design was an auction: a group of participants had to make a bid for a set of 10 good sportscards; another group had to make a bid for a set of 13 pieces: the same 10 good ones, and 3 poor ones. The mean offers for the set of just 10 cards was higher than the one of the 13 cards.

Kralik [24] showed the same result when testing nonhuman primates: when given a choice between a greater good alone versus the greater good together with a lesser one, the monkeys preferred the greater good alone, contrary to the utility maximization normative model.

In some circumstances, therefore, the mean, and not the sum of the values is used to evaluate different options.

2 The Mapping Function

The subjective utility models are completely abstract and universal: no assumption is made about which aspects an agent takes into account in evaluating the utility of a choice. The assumption I'm making here is that a limited number of experiential dimensions are evaluated, usually unconsciously, by human decision makers.

In this Sect. 1 will analyze some of the dimensions of the experiential utility model.

2.1 Motivation

Human behavior can be intrinsically motivated, extrinsically motivated or the result of habits.

Within the reinforcement learning paradigm, habits are described as a model-free mechanism, whereas goal oriented behavior as model-based [19].

A model-free system learns action values directly, by trial and error, without building an explicit model of the environment, and thus retains no explicit estimate of the probabilities that govern state transitions. In a model-based system, a cognitive map or model of the environment is acquired, which describes how different "states" (or situations) of the world are connected to each other. Action values for different paths through this environment can then be computed by a sort of mental simulation

The model-free mechanism avoids the representation of the structure of the activity and works by reinforcing successful actions. The goal-directed mechanism works by using an "internal model" of the task to evaluate candidate actions and outcomes [8].

Intrinsic motivation refers to doing something because it is inherently interesting or enjoyable; extrinsic motivation refers to doing something because it leads to a separable outcome [36]. Intrinsic motivation is defined as the motivation to perform an activity for its own sake in order to experience the pleasure and satisfaction inherent in the activity. Extrinsic motivation focuses more on the consequences to which the activity leads than on the activity itself [13].

The Self-Determination Theory assumes that activities are intrinsically motivated when they provide satisfaction of basic psychological needs [36].

2.2 Goals

Fishbach and Ferguson [14] define a goal as a cognitive representation of a desired endpoint that impacts evaluations, emotions and behaviors.

Goals are represented in memory, can be activated, can be linked to multiple memories, as a wide array of interconnected memories related to the goal.

Goals contain information about end states, the reference points toward which behavior is directed. They can have different level of abstractness. They include the plans, behaviors and objects that enable one to reach that end state.

End states can be seen as means for higher-order goals, within a hierarchical organization. The end state has to be desirable, and has to be associated with a positive affect. This gives it a motivational force, linked to the value of the end state and it's attainment.

When people are actively pursuing a goal, they want (desire) those things that can help them achieve the goal, and should not want those things that prevent them from reaching the goal.

There is a relationship between goals and values [15]:

- priming a goal increases the value of the end state
- people assign positive value to things that are conducive for goal achievement and negative value to things that are detrimental for goal achievement.

- goals involve emotion and energy mobilization. People feel happy, satisfied, and/or relieved when they achieve a goal; they feel frustrated, tense, and/or depressed when they fail to achieve the goal; and they feel energized, eager, or vigilant in the process of striving toward the goal.
- goals are sensitive to changes in value—they become stronger or weaker if value increases or decreases, respectively.

2.3 Basic Human Needs

Deci and Ryan [11] define needs as innate psychological nutriments that are essential for ongoing psychological growth, integrity, and well-being.

Baumeister and Leary [3] identify some criteria to identify fundamental human needs: they are universal, are activated frequently, influence and correlate with subjective well-being, influence cognition and emotions, affect a broad variety of behaviors and elicit goal-oriented behaviors believed to satisfy them. The *fundamental* needs are not derivative of other needs.

The identification of the list of the human needs is a difficult endeavor: different authors have diverse opinions. The following list is the integration of the work of a number of authors and models:

- health and physical wellness [10];
- safety [30];
- material and economical resources [10,12,30];
- the need of self realization, competence, and mastery [11,20,35,39];
- the need of autonomy [11,20,35,39];
- the need of relatedness [11,20,35,39];
- the need to develop an integrated self identity [5,37];
- the need to experience a meaning in life [16,44];
- the need of a good self esteem [4,27];
- pleasure, stimulation and hedonic needs [40].

An experience is supposed to have an intrinsic value if it satisfy at least one of the fundamental needs.

2.4 Cognitive Costs: The Fluency

When people perceive, process, memorize and recall information, they experience and implicitly evaluate the cognitive difficulty of the tasks, and this experience strongly influences judgments and decisions [33].

For example, people tend to associate fluency with truth and disfluency with untruth, feel greater confidence in their performance when a task is fluent. Fluency increases the likeability of a stimulus, its aesthetic value. Fluency tend to elicit positive affect, facilitate the decisional process and decrease the probability of purchase decision deferral.

Increasing trust, likeability, confidence, positive affect may have a strong positive influence on the user experience, improving the satisfaction and the usability of the product.

But how can fluency be obtained? A number of factors have been shown to influence it, and many of them can be directly addressed in the ux design process [1].

1. Perceptual fluency - the ease of processing the physical features of a stimulus
   - figure / background contrast: contrast increases fluency, and there is a linear correlation between contrast and prettiness judgment, and judgment of truth
   - font legibility: smaller fonts decrease the fluency of the task, whereas highly legible fonts increase it
2. Familiarity (mere exposure effect): things that are familiar - or just previously seen - increase the fluency, and are judged in a more positive light
3. Linguistic fluency
   - lexical fluency: using common instead of uncommon words increases fluency, and the author is judged as more intelligent
   - syntactic fluency: the use of simple syntactic construction of phrases
   - information intensity: there is a reversed-u shaped relationship, where too much information decreases fluency
4. Mnestic, categorical and semantic fluency
   - semantic fluency: elements with a common semantic root are processed more fluently, as are terms primed by semantically related concepts; conceptual analogies make subsequent information easier to process;
   - typicality: prototypical members of a category are judged as more fluent
   - memory availability increases fluency
5. Imaginative fluency: stories that elicit immersive imagination and transportation increase fluency
6. Decisional fluency: help the user to decide increases fluency and decreases purchase decision deferral

2.5 Psychological Time

Time plays an important role in the evaluation of an experience. As with the other dimensions, it is the subjective, phenomenological experience of time that is evaluated.

Time plays a role in different ways to the evaluation of an experience: both time discounting and fatigue constitute costs that can be mapped on the temporal dimension.

Time is seen as a cost when an experience is extrinsically motivated, whereas time spent in an intrinsically pleasurable experience is seen as a value. Furthermore, extrinsically motivated task tend to be perceived as boring or demanding. With extrinsically motivated experiences, time is seen as the delay from the onset (or the present moment) and the attainment of the valued goal.

It has been extensively demonstrated that both humans and animals value immediate reward more than delayed reward [23]. People tend to prefer to gain 70 euros now than 100 in a year, even if the difference represents an interest rate that is really high. People use spatial metaphors to represent time [45], and the values of distant future outcomes are discounted (time is seen as a cost).

Mental fatigue refers to the feeling that people may experience after or during prolonged periods of cognitive activity. They generally involve tiredness or even exhaustion, an aversion to continue with the present activity, and a decrease in the level of commitment to the task at hand [6]. Mental fatigue tend to be observed when the executive functions are recruited for a long time on a task.

Mental fatigue has been associated with impaired cognitive and behavioral performance: tasks that engage executive functions show performance decrements over time [25].

Interestingly, some recent models [25] see mental fatigue as an affective evaluation of the allocation of limited resources (attention and executive functions) over time. Spending time over a task has opportunity costs, and cognitive fatigue is supposed to map the increasing cost in carrying an extrinsically motivated task. This view is consistent with the experiential utility model: time as a resource that becomes a cost if spent in an activity that is not intrinsically interesting.

3 The Experiential Utility Map

The main claim of this work is that the experiential utility of a product or service can influence the intentions of actual and potential users to adopt it. The direct consequence of this hypothesis is that mapping a product on the multidimensional experiential space, and comparing it with the direct competitors, can help designers and stakeholders not only to increase its experiential value, but also to identify a strategic position. Strategic positioning reflects choices a company makes about the kind of value it will create and how that value will be created differently than rivals. We can see the dimensions of experiential utility as the conceptual space where a product or service can find a *profitable market niche*. I will present a case study to exemplify the potential use of the experiential utility map in identifying the different market spaces of two types of insurance companies: the traditional ones, where a broker mediates the relationship between company and clients, and the direct, online companies. We will see that the two types of organizations map on different points of the space, and this can explain the choices of customers with different priorities.

3.1 The Case Study

Last year I was involved in a competitive usability test for an insurance company. Before the test, we interviewed the participants to investigate - among other things - why and how they chose their insurance company. Moreover, we were interested in understanding if they decided to choose a traditional insurance broker or a direct, online insurance. Four different basic motivations emerged from the research, that we synthesized in four personae.

For Ilaria, the first persona, the most important factor is to avoid to waste her time: she is interested in an insurance whose processes are fast and easy. She could accept to spend some more euros if the process can help her to save time.

Marco is price sensitive: he is interested in saving money. He is not very tech-savvy, so he asks her daughter to help him with Internet and the aggregators to find out the less expensive quote.

Alberto is overwhelmed by the complexity of the information required to choose an insurance policy: he is not an expert, and he wants somebody who he can trust and who can guide him with the choice.

Claudio has a brand new car. With the old one, he was price sensitive, mainly interested in saving money. Now, however, he is more interested in the coverage of the policy, and he can accept to spend something more to have better guaranties.

Not surprisingly, Ilaria and Marco opted for a direct insurance, whereas Alberto and Claudio preferred to rely on a broker.

We represented in Fig. 1 the main needs, the influencers, the criteria for the inclusion set, the extension of the research process, the channels used to gather information, the criteria used to make the final choice from the inclusion set, and the channel of subscription (the traditional broker channel vs online).

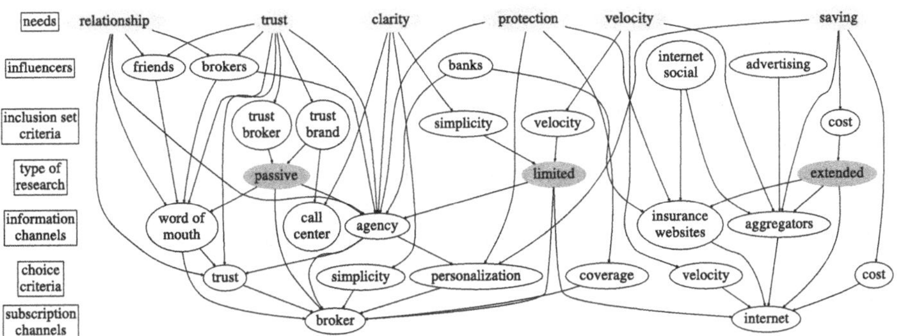

Fig. 1. Motivational graph

Figure 2 represents the positioning of the two kinds of companies on the experience utility map. Direct companies tend to have lower premiums and faster subscription processes. Traditional companies (at least in Italy) have a richer portfolio. Furthermore, people like Alberto appreciate the presence of a broker, who helps him to overcome the complexity of the choice of an insurance product, and who increases him trust in the company. The trust, and the personal relationship with the broker, have been mapped on the intrinsic motivations dimension, and the presence of the broker as a mediator decreases the cognitive costs of the choice.

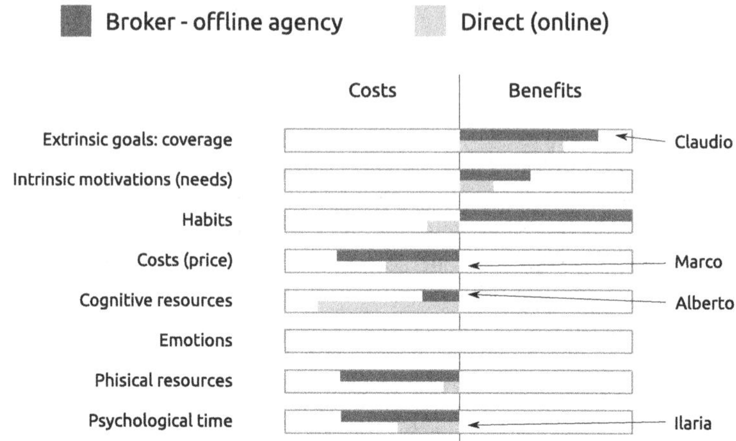

Fig. 2. Experience utility map

4 Conclusions

In this article, I presented a first version of a model of experiential utility. The model is still under development, and some parts need to be refined. Nonetheless, the model defines a multidimensional space that can be used to map the values and costs of a product or service. Positioning a product on the experience utility map can help stakeholders and designers to discover a market niche, identify its strengths and weaknesses and increase its overall quality.

It is often asked if an experience can be designed. The position here held is that ux designers design products and services, not experiences, but they are - at least implicitly - aware that the value of their work is evaluated in experiential terms. The aim of the experiential utility model is to provide a methodological toolkit to design and evaluate the quality of a product or service.

References

1. Alter, A.L., Oppenheimer, D.M.: Uniting the tribes of fluency to form a metacognitive nation. Pers. Soc. Psychol. Rev.: Official J. Soc. Pers. Soc. Psychol., Inc. **13**(3), 219–235 (2009). ISSN: 1088-8683. doi:10.1177/1088868309341564
2. Ariely, D., Carmon, Z.: Gestalt characteristics of experiences: the defining features of summarized events. J. Behav. Decis. Making **13**, 191–201 (2000)
3. Baumeister, R.F., Leary, M.R.: The need to belong: desire for interpersonal attachments as a fundamental human motivation. Psychol. Bull. **117**(3), 497–529 (1995)
4. Baumeister, R.F., et al.: Does high self-esteem cause better performance, interpersonal success, happiness, or healthier lifestyles? Psychol. Sci. Public Interest **4**(1), 1–44 (2003)

5. Berzonsky, M.D., et al.: The how and what of identity formation: associations between identity styles and value orientations. Pers. Individ. Differ. **50**(2), 295–299 (2011)
6. Boksem, M.A.S., Tops, M.: Mental fatigue: costs and benefits. Brain Res. Rev. **59**(1), 125–139 (2008)
7. Bussolon, S.: The X factor. In: Marcus, A. (ed.) DUXU 2016. LNCS, vol. 9746, pp. 15–24. Springer, Cham (2016). doi:10.1007/978-3-319-40409-7_2
8. Daw, N.D., et al.: Model-based in influences on humans' choices and striatal prediction errors. In: Neuron **69**(6), 1204–1215 (2011), ISSN: 1097-4199. doi:10.1016/j.neuron.2011.02.027. http://linkinghub.elsevier.com/retrieve/pii/S0896627311001255%20, http://dx.doi.org/10.1016/j.neuron.2011.02.027/npapers3://publication/doi/10.1016/j.neuron.2011.02.027%20, http://www.ncbi.nlm.nih.gov/pubmed/21435563%20, http://www.pubmedcentral.nih.gov/articlerender
9. Dean, J., Ghemawat, S.: MapReduce: simplified data processing on large clusters. Commun. ACM **51**(1), 107–113 (2008)
10. Deaton, A.: Income, health and wellbeing around the world: evidence from the gallup world poll. J. Econ. Perspect.: J. Am. Econ. Assoc. **22**(2), 53 (2008)
11. Deci, E.L., Ryan, R.M.: The what and why of goal pursuits: human needs and the self-determination of behavior. Psychol. Inq. **11**(4), 227–268 (2000)
12. Diener, E., et al.: Wealth and happiness across the world: material prosperity predicts life evaluation, whereas psychosocial prosperity predicts positive feeling. J. Pers. Soc. Psychol. **99**(1), 52 (2010)
13. Dysvik, A., Kuvaas, B.: Intrinsic and extrinsic motivation as predictors of work effort: the moderating role of achievement goals. Br. J. Soc. Psychol. **52**(3), 412–430 (2013)
14. Fishbach, A., Ferguson, M.J.: The goal construct in social psychology (2007)
15. Förster, J., Liberman, N., Friedman, R.S.: Seven principles of goal activation: a systematic approach to distinguishing goal priming from priming of non-goal constructs. In: Pers. Soc. Psychol. Rev.: Official J. Soc. Pers. Soc. Psychol., Inc. **11**(3), 211 (2007)
16. Frankl, V.E.: Man's Search For Meaning. Simon and Schuster (1985)
17. Gilbert, D.T., Wilson, T.D.: Prospection: experiencing the future. In: Science (New York, N.Y.) **317**(5843), 1351–1354 (2007). doi:10.1126/science.1144161
18. Gilboa, I., Postlewaite, A., Schmeidler, D.: Is it always rational to satisfy savage's axioms? Econ. Philos. **25**(03), 285 (2009). ISSN: 0266-2671. doi:10.1017/S0266267109990241. http://www.journals.cambridge.org/abstract%7B%5C_%7DS0266267109990241
19. Gläscher, J., et al.: States versus Rewards: dissociable neural prediction error signals underlying model-based and model-free reinforcement learning. Neuron **66**(4), 585–595 (2010), ISSN: 08966273. doi:10.1016/j.neuron.2010.04.016. http://linkinghub.elsevier.com/retrieve/pii/S0896627310002874
20. Hagger, M.S., Chatzisarantis, N.L.D., Harris, J.: From psychological need satisfaction to intentional behavior: testing a motivational sequence in two behavioral contexts. Pers. Soc. Psychol. Bull. **32**(2), 131–148 (2006)
21. Kable, J.W., Glimcher, P.W.: The neurobiology of decision: consensus and controversy. Neuron **63**(6), 733–745 (2009). ISSN: 08966273. doi:10.1016/j.neuron.2009.09.003. arXiv: NIHMS150003. http://dx.doi.org/10.1016/j.neuron.2009.09.003
22. Kahneman, D., Wakker, P.P., Sarin, R.: Back to bentham? explorations of experienced utility. Q. J. Econ. **112**(2), 375–406 (1997)
23. Kim, S., Hwang, J., Lee, D.: Prefrontal coding of temporally discounted values during intertemporal choice. Neuron **59**(1), 161–172 (2008)

24. Kralik, J.D., et al.: When less is more: evolutionary origins of the affect heuristic. PLoS ONE **7**(10), e46240 (2012), Addessi, E. (ed.). ISSN: 1932-6203. doi:10.1371/journal.pone.0046240. http://dx.plos.org/10.1371/journal.pone.0046240
25. Kurzban, R., et al.: An opportunity cost model of subjective effort and task performance. Behav. Brain Sci. **36**(06), 661–679 (2013)
26. List, J.A.: Preference reversals of a different kind: the "More is less" phenomenon. Am. Econ. Rev. **92**(5), 1636–1643 (2002)
27. Lyubomirsky, S., Tkach, C., DiMatteo, M.R.: What are the differences between happiness and self-esteem. Soc. Indic. Res. **78**(3), 363–404 (2006)
28. Marewski, J.N., Gaissmaier, W., Gigerenzer, G.: Good judgments do not require complex cognition. Cogn. Process. **11**(2), 103–121 (2010). ISSN: 16124790, doi:10.1007/s10339-009-0337-0
29. Marewski, J.N., Gigerenzer, G.: Heuristic decision making in medicine. Dialogues Clin. Neurosci. **14**(1), 77–89 (2012)
30. Maslow, A.H.: A theory of human motivation. Psychol. Rev. **50**, 370–396 (1943)
31. Al-Najjar, N.I., De Castro, L.: Subjective Probability. Wiley Encyclopedia of Operations Research and Management Science (2010)
32. Nelson, S., Katzenstein, P.J.: Uncertainty, risk, and the financial crisis of 2008. **68**(2), 361–392 (2014), ISBN: 0020818313000, doi:10.1017/S0020818313000416
33. Oppenheimer, D.M.: The secret life of fluency. Trends Cogn. Sci. **12**(6), 237–241 (2008). ISSN: 13646613. doi:10.1016/j.tics.2008.02.014
34. Pham, M.T., Avnet, T.: Contingent reliance on the affect heuristic as a function of regulatory focus. Organ. Behav. Hum. Decis. Process. **108**(2), 267–278 (2009). ISSN: 07495978. doi:10.1016/j.obhdp.2008.10.001. http://dx.doi.org/10.1016/j.obhdp.2008.10.001
35. Reis, H.T., et al.: Daily well-being: the role of autonomy, competence, and relatednes. Pers. Soc. Psychol. Bull. **26**(4), 419–435 (2000)
36. Ryan, R., Deci, E.: Intrinsic and extrinsic motivations: classic definitions and new directions. Contemp. Educ. Psychol. **25**(1), 54–67 (2000). ISSN: 0361-476X, doi:10.1006/ceps.1999.1020. http://www.ncbi.nlm.nih.gov/pubmed/10620381
37. Schwartz, S.J., et al.: Examining the light and dark sides of emerging adults' identity: a study of identity status differences in positive and negative psychosocial functioning. J. Youth Adolesc. **40**(7), 839–859 (2011)
38. Schwarz, N.: Feelings-as-information theory. In: Handbook of Theories of Social Psychology, vol. 1, pp. 289–308, January 2012, ISSN: 0857029606. doi:10.4135/9781446249215.n15. http://sk.sagepub.com/reference/hdbk%7B%5C%7Dsocialpsychtheories1/n15.xml
39. Sheldon, K.M., Filak, V.: Manipulating autonomy, competence, and relatedness support in a game-learning context: new evidence that all three needs matter. Br. J. Soc. Psychol. **47**(2), 267–283 (2008)
40. Sheldon, K.M., et al.: What is satisfying about satisfying events? testing 10 candidate psychological needs. J. Pers. Soc. Psychol. **80**(2), 325 (2001)
41. Slovic, P., et al.: Affect, risk, and decision making. Health Psychol. **24**(4S), S35 (2005)
42. Slovic, P., et al.: The affect heuristic. Eur. J. Oper. Res. **177**(3), 1333–1352 (2007). ISSN: 03772217. doi:10.1016/j.ejor.2005.04.006. arXiv:1011.1669v3
43. Stanovich, K.E.: On the Distinction Between Rationality and Intelligence: Implications for Understanding Individual Differences in Reasoning, pp. 343–365. Oxford University Press, Oxford (2012). ISBN: 9780199968718. doi:10.1093/oxfordhb/9780199734689.013.0022. http://oxfordhandbooks.com/view/10.1093/oxfordhb/9780199734689.001.0001/oxfordhb-9780199734689-e-22

44. Steger, M.F.: Experiencing meaning in life: optimal functioning at the nexus of well-being, psychopathology, and spirituality. In: The Human Quest for Meaning: Theories, Research, and Applications, 2nd edn. (2012)
45. Trope, Y., Liberman, N.: Construal-level theory of psychological distance. Psychol. Rev. **117**(2), 440 (2010)
46. Tulving, E.: Episodic memory: from mind to brain. Annu. Rev. Psychol. 53(1), 1–25 (2002). ISSN: 0066-4308, doi:10.1146/annurev.psych.53.100901.135114. http://www.annualreviews.org/doi/10.1146/annurev.psych.53.100901.135114
47. Wilson, T.D., Gilbert, D.T.: Affective forecasting. Adv. Exp. Soc. Psychol. **35**, 345–411 (2003)

Assessing Organization-System Fit in ERP Selection Procedures – A Literature Review

Marcus Fischer(✉), David Heim, Marion Hösselbarth, and Axel Winkelmann

Chair of Business Information Systems, University of Wuerzburg, Würzburg, Germany
{marcus.fischer, david.heim, marion.hoesselbarth, axel.winkelmann}@uni-wuerzburg.de

Abstract. To remain competitive in a rapidly changing environment, SMEs rely on technologies that provide support for their business operations. Although an increasing number of SMEs use ERP systems, one of the major challenges is the selection of a software that fully meets their business needs. ERP systems generally come as standardized software packages, that fit generic rather than enterprise-specific requirements. Thus, mutual alignments to business and IT are inevitable when implementing a new system into an existing organizational structure. Consequently, ERP implementation projects face major risks, including users avoiding or misusing the system, or adopting it in a way that does not fully capture the project's expected benefits. However, the magnitude of organizational adaptations depends on the initial degree of organization-system fit. Thus, this contribution aims to examine current ERP selection methodologies by performing a literature review. Results reveal that most approaches exhibit two major weaknesses. First, instead of providing decision support, they focus on high-level recommendations, insufficiently addressing the degree of organization-system fit. Second, decision-making remains complex throughout the entire selection process, as methodologies do not provide mechanisms to establish an adequate preselection. Thus, the present paper introduces a innovative approach for selecting ERP software based on measures of business process similarity.

Keywords: Organization-system fit · Business process management · Business process similarity · Enterprise resource planning selection

1 Motivation

To remain competitive in a rapidly changing environment, effective methods for processing, storing and analyzing data are highly relevant for organizations today. Due to the integration of business processes and information, enterprise resource planning (ERP) systems enable enterprises to organize their resources more effectively [1, 2]. Although information systems positively affect the competitiveness of an enterprise, implementation projects often come with tremendous demands on time and financial resources. Limited resources, such as a tight time schedule or a lack of process knowledge and IT skills, as well as the highly differentiated market, can turn the selection of an adequate ERP system into a highly complex task [3]. Since ERP

M. Kurosu (Ed.): HCI 2017, Part I, LNCS 10271, pp. 134–149, 2017.
DOI: 10.1007/978-3-319-58071-5_11

systems generally provide best practice operations for a certain industry, their implementation is frequently linked to the adjustment of organizational structures [4]. While business operations may increase in efficiency and effectiveness, the disruption of established workflows can result in users' resistance towards change, hampering the potential benefits of an ERP project [5]. If the organization is unable to align to the system's structure, efforts on customization and software re-configuration are inevitable. Thus, organizational resources are at stake and non-competitive operations are transferred into an individualized software. From a human-computer-perspective, a suitable, user-oriented, and carefully selected ERP system, can reduce the necessity for adjustments and increase the likelihood of an implementation project's success. While small and medium enterprises (SME) are still subject to activities of business process re-engineering (BPR), aiming to absorb the system's inherent best practices, efforts decrease with the degree of IT-business-conformance.

To address these challenges, the present paper examines current ERP selection approaches. Results reveal that most approaches suffer from two major weaknesses. First, instead of performing an initial examination of the degree of organization-system fit, most approaches only provide high-level recommendations. Second, decision-making remains complex throughout the entire selection process, since methodologies do not provide adequate mechanisms to reduce the highly diversified ERP market to a smaller number of relevant systems. We argue that pitfalls during ERP selection can be adequately addressed by utilizing methods of business process similarity. Our research can be summarized by the following research questions:

(1) How do methodologies for ERP selection address the degree of organization-system fit?
(2) Do methodologies for ERP selection offer mechanisms to narrow down the market for ERP systems?

This contribution is organized as follows: Sect. 2 describes the ERP selection process and introduces relevant dimensions of organization-system fit. In Sect. 3, the methodology underlying this research endeavor is presented and a theoretical framework to structure the results is introduced. Subsequently, identified methodologies are examined in Sect. 4, while Sect. 5 provides an innovative approach to address process fit during ERP selection. Concluding this contribution, Sect. 6 summarizes the main findings and gives an overview of limitations and future research potentials.

2 Theoretical Foundations

2.1 ERP Software Selection

As illustrated in Fig. 1, the process of ERP selection comprises four main stages: objective definition, requirements engineering, market analysis, and preselection as well as final decision-making.

The process is initiated by the phase of objective definition. Based on the formation of an adequate ERP team, objectives are defined and categorized into fundamental and

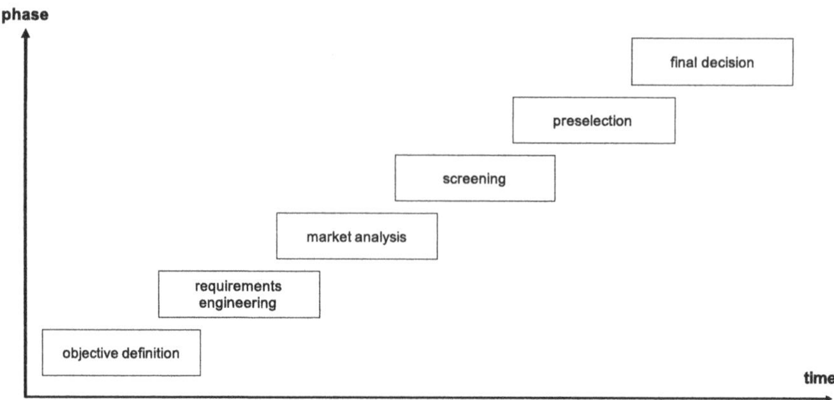

Fig. 1. Process model for ERP selection [6]

mean objectives in order to structure and prioritize corresponding evaluation criteria [6, 7]. Thus, the ERP team should define the project's scope, based on a company's policy, business attributes, the industrial environment, and overall strategic goals [8]. Furthermore, business processes should be analyzed based on customer interviews or company internal investigations. Thus, most relevant processes and organization-system interfaces are identified [9]. Subsequently, requirements engineering starts with the definition of organizational demands regarding technical, process, cultural, and functional needs. Aiming to reduce the likelihood of users' resistance in subsequent phases of an ERP project, requirements definition should take the current organizational structure into account. Thus, activities should be performed top-down as well as bottom-up. To avoid transferring non-competitive processes into a new ERP system, as-is business processes should be transformed into a to-be concept [10]. Based on organizational requirements, enterprises must acquire an adequate comprehension of available systems. Thus, information sources for ERP software, such as magazines, exhibitions, yearbooks, or the Internet, should be screened [7]. However, to gather in-depth information, requests for proposals, information, and cost estimates are sent to potential vendors [7]. Subsequently, the received information should be screened carefully to evaluate the degree, to which a system meets the predefined requirements. Narrowing down the number of potential systems continuously, a preselection of systems is established. Consequently, final decision-making is initiated, e.g., by using an analytical hierarchy process (AHP), evaluating each system regarding organizational objectives and requirements [11].

2.2 Perspectives on Organization-System Fit

Implementing and adopting new information technologies can transform people's work, organizational business processes, or an enterprises performance significantly [5]. Based on the centralization of organization-wide data, cross-functional integration, and the streamlining of processes, ERP systems generally come with potential benefits in terms of an increasing efficiency, quality, and customer satisfaction [12]. Frequently offered as standardized software packages, ERP systems are designed to meet generic rather than specific organizational requirements, most likely resulting in an imperfect fit for any enterprise-specific implementation project. Referring to Markus, only 70% of an average organization's needs are addressed by an ERP system [5]. By contrast, Foster suggests that 80% of a software package should fit the intended structure of an organization before an implementation project is initiated [13].

According to Strong and Volkoff, potential sources of organization-enterprise system misfits can be divided into six categories, which are summarized in Table 1 [4].

Table 1. Types of organization-system misfits [4]

Misfit	Definition
Functionality	Occurs when executing business processes using an ERP system results in less efficiency and/or effectiveness compared to the situation before implementation
Data	Occurs when data stored in or needed by the ERP system result in poor quality in terms of inaccuracy, inconsistency, inaccessibility, lack of timeliness, or inappropriateness for users' contexts
Usability	Occurs when user interactions with the ERP system are obstructive and/or confusing
Role	Occurs when roles in the ERP system do not match the available skills; this creates imbalances in the workload or generates inconsistencies regarding responsibility and authority
Control	Occurs when control mechanisms in the ERP system are too strict and productivity is thereby reduced or minimized, so performance cannot be monitored appropriately
Culture	Occurs when operating the ERP system conflicts with organizational or national norms

In line with that, Markus refers to business processes, culture, and incentives as the most relevant types of organization-system misfits [5]. As each misfit can cause ERP implementation project failure, the present paper argues that an insufficient process fit hampers system adoption and facilitates the development of other misfits. Based on the re-engineering of business processes, workflows and operations can be subject to adaptations, resulting in user resistance and system avoidance. Thus, the probability of data misfits increases, since relevant data are not stored and processed appropriately when users work around the system. Process misfits negatively affect the perceived usability of an ERP system and produce conflicts to the existing organizational structure and corresponding roles. As users avoid the system's functionalities, control mechanisms are ineffective, providing only limited insights into organizational performance measures.

3 Research Design

To answer the predefined research questions, we aim to perform a structured literature review to analyze current methodologies for ERP selection in regards to recommendations for managing organization-system fit. Investigating existing methodologies for literature reviewing, we selected the framework by vom Brocke et al., who highlight the need for documenting the process of literature search and analysis [14]. Recently, literature reviews have been criticized because they lack validity and reliability. Thus, we aim to follow the proposed methodology rigorous and to provide a detailed description of the knowledge creation process. The framework comprises the five phases summarized in Fig. 2.

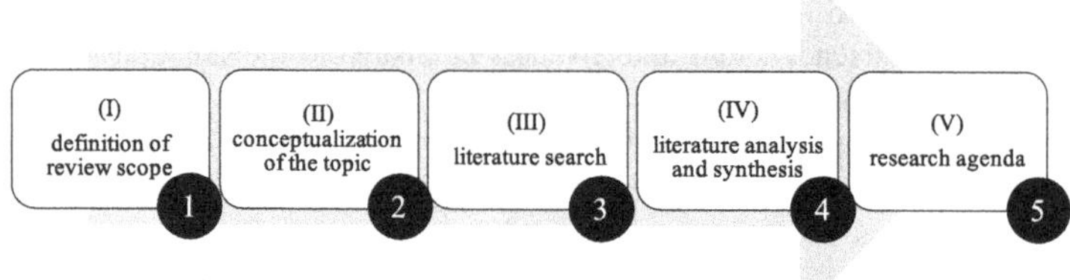

Fig. 2. Framework for literature reviewing [14]

According to vom Brocke et al., one of the major challenges when performing a literature review is to define an adequate reviewing scope [14]. Thus, we utilize the established taxonomy of Cooper (Fig. 3), who specifies the scope using the dimensions of 'focus', 'goal', 'organisation', 'perspective', 'audience' and 'coverage' [15].

As we aim to evaluate the consideration of organization-system fit in current ERP selection methodologies, this literature review focuses on research outcomes and real-world applications. Our goal is to integrate existing approaches to acquire a structured overview of procedures, selection criteria, and decision parameters. In line with that, the organization of our literature review is methodological. The reviewing process is performed from a neutral perspective and is addressed to researchers and practitioners, as findings are relevant for both audiences. However, we do not claim our

	characteristics	categories			
(1)	focus	research outcomes	research methods	theories	applications
(2)	goal	integration	criticism	central issues	
(3)	organisation	historical	conceptual	methodological	
(4)	perspective	neutral representation	espousal of position		
(5)	audience	specialized scholars	general scholars	practitioners/politicians	general public
(6)	coverage	exhaustive	exhaustive and selective	representative	central/pivotal

Fig. 3. Definition of review scope [15]

sample to be exhaustive, but rather a representative selection of high-quality contributions.

In the second phase, a broad conception of what is known about the topic is required to construct a reviewing framework [16]. As suggested by Webster & Watson and Fettke, a literature review framework provides helpful guidance during the reviewing process [17, 18]. To expose and structure the identified methodologies, we integrate the frameworks of Markus and Strong & Volkoff, as introduced in Sect. 2 [4, 5]. The resulting framework of analysis is illustrated in Fig. 4.

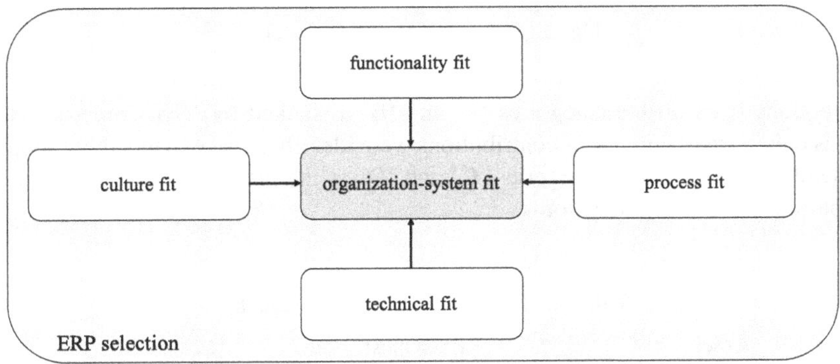

Fig. 4. Framework of analysis [4, 5]

Constructing the framework, we built upon the interpretation of Markus and Cooprider & Henderson, who explicitly distinguish between functionality fit and process fit [5, 19]. However, this appears to be reasonable, as functionality misfits are generally addressed by software customization, while process misfits result in necessary BPR activities. Additionally, potential misfits caused by inadequate incentives, poor usability, or role conflicts are summarized by ‘culture fit’. Finally, ‘technical fit’ includes a system’s capability to store and process data as well as characteristics, such as customizability and performance.

In the third step, the process of literature search is specified [14]. Thus, selected databases and used keywords must be appropriately documented and steps to analyze and structure findings are described. Figure 5 provides an overview of databases and summarizes outcomes of each step of the searching procedure. The decision whether a retrieved article is analyzed in detail was made based on its title and abstract. If the title implicated that a contribution could be relevant within the scope of this review, the abstract was screened subsequently. Relevant contributions were then analyzed performing a keyword and full-text analysis and a final decision was made. To consider relevant papers not detected within the regular searching process, we performed a backward search and forward search.

Aiming to identify relevant contributions from high-quality IS conferences, such as ICIS, ECIS, or AMCIS, we initiated the literature search process by querying the digital libraries of AISel, ScienceDirect, and EBSCOhost. We initially focused on

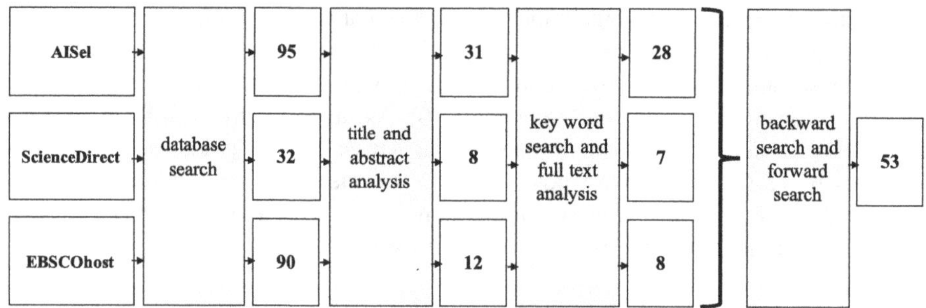

Fig. 5. Process of literature search

contributions listed in the categories 'A' and 'B' as ranked by VHB-Jourqual. However, as only a small number of contributions were identified, we expanded the scope of the literature search to the categories 'C' and 'D' as the research progressed. Table 2 summarizes the selected keywords.

Table 2. Keywords for literature search

	AISeL	EBSCOhost	ScienceDirect
Keywords	('ERP selection' OR 'ERP pre-implementation' OR 'ERP selection model′ OR 'ERP selection' AND 'organization-system fit)	AB ('ERP selection' OR 'ERP pre-implementation' OR 'ERP selection model' OR 'ERP selection' AND 'organization-system fit')	('ERP selection' OR 'ERP pre-implementation' OR 'ERP selection model' OR 'ERP selection' AND 'organization-system fit')

Keywords included the terms 'ERP selection', 'ERP pre-implementation', 'ERP selection methodology', and 'ERP implementation methodology'. Furthermore, the selection was completed by adding a combination of the terms 'ERP selection' and 'organization-system fit' to control for methodologies or theories, that especially address the fit between ERP systems and organizational structures. Finally, 53 articles broaching the topic of ERP selection were identified.

4 Literature Analysis

4.1 Meta-analysis

Subsequently, contributions identified within the literature search process are analyzed regarding their research design, ranking, and year of publication. Results are illustrated in Fig. 6.

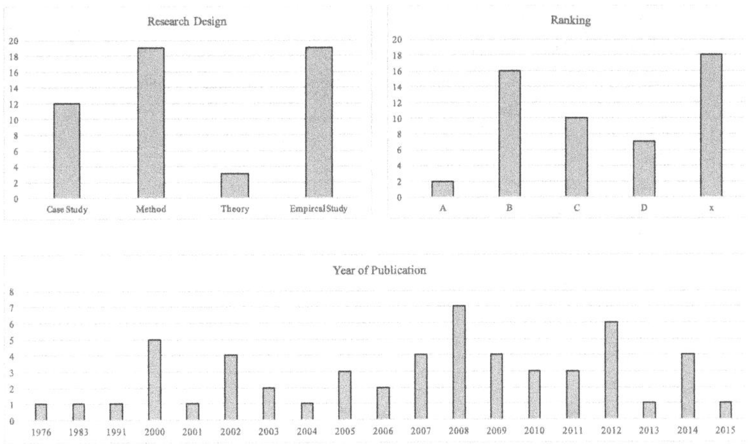

Fig. 6. Meta-analysis of identified contributions

With more than 50% of contributions ranked 'C' or higher, the sample can be regarded as high-qualitative. However, almost 35% of the identified articles are not ranked. Publication dates range from 1976 to 2015, with many articles published in the years of 2000, 2008, and 2009. However, as the number of publications decreased in recent years, a lack of up-to-date research can be observed. Applied research designs include case studies, methodological approaches, theory building, and empirical studies. However, each category exhibits differences regarding goals, scope, and results. While case studies and empirical studies are used to validate assumptions and theoretical implications, they do not provide guidance for the actual process of ERP selection. Thus, the present paper focuses exclusively on methodological and theoretical contributions.

4.2 Literature Analysis and Synthesis

Following the recommendations of Webster & Watson, identified articles are analyzed and categorized using the theoretical framework introduced in Sect. 3 [17]. Table 3 summarizes the consideration of organization-system fit in current ERP selection methodologies.

As many methodological contributions exhibit a similar research design, but differ in terms of goals and scope, we further distinguish between methods that exclusively focus on decision support and methodologies for ERP selection. However, as final decision-making is part of the overall process of ERP selection, corresponding methods are analyzed separately.

Decision-making in ERP selection projects. Decision-making methods are either particularly designed for ERP selection or have been adopted from the selection of information systems in general. They contain techniques and mechanisms to analyze, aggregate, and prioritize selection criteria.

Table 3. Organization-system Fit in ERP selection methodologies

	Functional fit	Process fit	Technical fit	Cultural fit
Adinnour-Helm et al. (2003)	×			×
Alpers et al. (2014)	×		×	
Alsulami et al. (2014)	×			×
Batenburg et al. (2008)			×	
Benlian and Hess (2010)				×
Bernroider and Koch (2000)	×	×	×	
Bernroider et al. (2009)	×		×	×
Birdoğan and Kemal (2005)	×		×	
Bolenta (2011)	×		×	
Brainin (2008)				×
Bueno and Salmeron 2008	×		×	
Buss (1986)	×		×	
Christofi et al. (2009)		×		
Chun-Chin et al. (2005)	×		×	
Cil et al. (2005)	×		×	
Deep et al. (2008)	×	×	×	×
Deltour (2012)			×	
Dey (2002)	×		×	
Everdingen et al. (2000)	×			
Gall et al. (2009)			×	
Ghapanchi et al. (2008)	×			×
Gronau (2001)	×		×	×
Gürbüz et al. (2012)	×		×	
Hakim and Hakim (2010)	×	×	×	×
Hallikainen et al. (2002)	×			
Han (2004)	×		×	×
Hustad and Olsen (2011)	×		×	
Johansson et al. (2013)	×		×	
Keil und Tiwana (2006)	×		×	×
Kilic et al. (2014)			×	×
Kilic et al. (2015)	×		×	×
Kumar et al. (2002)	×			×
Liang (2003)	×		×	
Liao et al. (2007)	×			
Livermoore and Ragowsky (2002)				×
Lucas and Moore (1976)	×		×	
Mitlöhner (2012)	×			
Ng (2006)	×		×	×
Percin (2008)	×		×	×
Pitic et al. (2014)	×			
Poon and Yu (2010)	×		×	×
Ram and Pattinson (2009)	×		×	
Ratkevičius et al. (2012)	×		×	×
Sammon and Adam (2007)		×	×	
Schniederjans and Wilson (1991)	×			
Seethamraju and Seethamraju	×			×
Stefanou (2000)	×	×	×	×
Stewart (2000)				×
Teltumble (2000)	×		×	×
Tsai et al. (2012)	×		×	×
Wei et al. (2005)	×		×	
Wu et al. (2007)	×		×	
Zach and Munkvold (2011)	×		×	
Total	**43**	**6**	**37**	**24**

Relevant approaches range from scoring and ranking methods, to mathematical optimization and multi-criteria decision-making models [20]. While multi-criteria scoring techniques have been introduced by Lucas and Moore, ranking-based selection methods were first mentioned by Buss [21, 22]. Although approaches of this kind are easy to use and understand, they lack an adequate consideration of decision makers' opinions and preferences [20]. Defining the selection-decision as a mathematical optimization problem, Schniederjans and Wilson designed a method that integrates goal programming into the AHP procedure to reduce the task of ERP selection to a multi-alternative resource allocation problem [23]. AHP describes a technique for organizing and analyzing complex decisions, by decomposing a decision problem into a hierarchy of sub-problems that can be analyzed independently. It is designed to support group decision making and helps to understand a decision problem to identify its most suitable solution. Multiple AHP-based methods have been introduced, varying in terms of decision scope, underlying mechanisms, and computation techniques [24]. Exemplary, Wei et al. (2005) define a comprehensive AHP-based decision-making framework, that focuses on comparing an enterprise's overall goals and strategies to objectives linked to an ERP implementation project [11]. Thus, the decision problem is decomposed into several smaller problems that are analyzed independently by a standardized evaluation process. Furthermore, Percin extends traditional approaches by introducing a mechanism for decision-making based on an analytical network process (ANP) [20]. Thus, goals, decision criteria, and alternatives are structured as a network, allowing to perform feedback loops and to integrate a bottom-up perspective [20].

Functional Fit. Numerous contributions refer to an ERP system's functionalities as one of the most important criteria for system selection [25–28]. Gronau suggests that functional requirements of an organization should be carefully documented and weighted by their relative importance. In general, criteria to assess functionality fit include an ERP system's functional range, conformance with existing business needs, cross-module integration, compatibility to other system as well as its adaptability, and modularity [29, 30]. Wei et al. further add security features and functional performance to the catalogue of potential selection criteria [11].

In order to acquire relevant information, Verville & Hallingten emphasize the importance of external and internal information sources [7]. Aiming to avoid overlooking feasible systems, different sources, such as the Internet, professional magazines, or vendor exhibitions, should be screened carefully. Cil et al. further introduce a web-based framework that supports the assessment of organization-system functionality fit [31]. The framework contains two main components. First, mechanisms for group decision making allow different stakeholders to participate in the process of requirements engineering and objective definition. Second, criteria-based techniques are applied to narrow down the ERP market to a smaller number of adequate systems. To support the selection decision, Han distinguishes three levels of functionality [32]. On the first level, basic functionalities account for essential features, such as supporting and executing business routines. Level 2 comprises desired functions that facilitate increases in business process productivity and efficiency. Consequently, the third level includes additional functionalities, enabling BPR to absorb the system's best practices. Utilizing this classification, potential systems can be evaluated and prioritized to generate a short list of vendors that is analyzed in more detail subsequently. To evaluate the predefined selection criteria from different perspectives, Baki and Cakar further suggest to form a cross-functional ERP team [29]. According to Hecht, functionality should not carry more than one-third of the weight in overall decision-making [33]. By contrast, Wei et al. use a relative weighting factor of 0.45 to integrate an ERP systems functional characteristics into AHP procedures [11]. Although several concepts provide criteria and support for assessing the functional fit of an ERP system, most approaches lack a definition of mechanisms to match business needs and system functionalities.

Process Fit. To analyze the measure of process fit, Markus emphasizes that differences in business processes and work routines can result in users' resistance and avoidance of the system [5]. In line with that, Stefanou defines discrepancies in business processes as one of the most important organizational constraints in ERP projects [8]. According to Motwani et al., mutual alignments of business and IT are necessary to enhance organizational performance, quality, costs, flexibility, and responsiveness [34]. Furthermore, process fit has been defined as one of the most relevant critical success factors in numerous contributions [35–38].

While efforts on BPR are traditionally performed during the phase of ERP implementation, Christofi et al. suggest to identify, explore, and improve deficient business processes as a preparatory step before the ERP project is initiated [39]. Thus, potential BPR efforts are reduced and the likelihood of a successful system adoption increases. Although process fit is essential for ERP implementation projects to succeed, existent methodologies do not provide techniques or measures to assess the initial process fit.

Technical Fit. To analyze an ERP system's technical fit, methodologies suggest to investigate system characteristics, such as customizability, integration capacity and its migration ability. Wei et al. further mention adequate technical support as a relevant criterion for assessing technical fit [11]. According to Gall et al., customizability includes all activities that align the system to specific business needs [40]. Potential criteria to evaluate customizability include a clear distinction between different tiers, functionalities to store modifications centrally, and potential impacts on the installation of service packs and new product releases. Furthermore, systems should provide an integrated development environment, predefined interfaces, tools to administer databases, and possibilities to access external data structures [40]. Evaluating integration capacities, a system should be able to integrate an organization's existing software systems. Thus, adequate functionalities to ensure external connectivity must be provided. Corresponding selection criteria cover the availability of application programming interfaces, data integration capabilities supported by the database system, and the range of supported file formats for data exchange. Additionally, systems should provide features to map data and fields dynamically and to monitor the amount of exchanged data [40]. Finally, migration ability describes the necessary time and efforts to migrate the new ERP system from a previous system. Evaluation criteria include the existence of data migration and application tools as well as tools to migrate predefined modifications [40]. Referring to Gronau, technical criteria should be documented and evaluated [6]. Applying the decision framework of Wei et al., technical fit accounts for 65% of ERP vendor characteristics [11]. Gürbüz et al. integrate technical aspects as a major software related selection criterion [41]. In line with that, Kilic et al. define technical criteria as one of the three most important factors that influence the decision-making process [30].

Although methodologies provide a variety of evaluation criteria, only little support is provided for the acquisition of relevant information and for the evaluation of ERP features and organizational needs.

Cultural Fit. To investigate the degree of cultural fit, an ERP system's usability, conformance of required and available skills, and inherent control mechanisms are evaluated. Furthermore, cultural fit includes conflicts with organizational or cultural norms. Usability is defined as the simplicity of training and use [11]. Thus, the system should allow to be used intuitively and without the need for acquiring additional knowledge [26]. Referring to Ratkevičius, IT skills of future users should be considered when selecting an ERP system [42]. Hence, user interfaces of potential ERP systems should be examined by users from different departments. To address cultural conflicts, Brainin offers an overview of cultural differences between countries and their relation to different stages of technology implementation [42]. Thus, guidelines are developed, that define mechanisms to support the implementation of information technology in cross-country-scenarios. Nevertheless, valuable implications can be drawn on achieving cultural fit within an enterprise-specific implementation project. However, identified contributions neither provide detailed evaluation criteria nor an adequate support for decision-making during ERP selection.

5 Assessing Process Fit in ERP Implementation Projects

As revealed by the literature review, most contributions on ERP selection only provide limited support when evaluating organization-system fit. However, misfits can produce users' resistance towards the system and cause ERP projects failure. On the one hand, efforts on BPR are considered as one of the most important critical success factors for ERP implementation projects. However, methodologies for ERP selection do not account for the initial degree of process fit. On the other hand, the highly diversified market for ERP systems turns ERP selection into a highly complex task. Although a few methodologies suggest to determine a preselection of most suitable ERP systems, little guidance in efficiently narrowing down the market is provided. Thus, the present paper introduces an innovative approach for addressing process fit as an extension of traditional ERP selection methodologies. Based on the measure of feature-based similarity, organizational structures are automatically evaluated towards ERP reference processes stored in a process repository. Figure 7 illustrates the suggested process of ERP selection.

The proposed methodology exhibits two major advantages. First, an initial assessment of process fit allows to minimize subsequent BPR efforts. Thus, selected systems comply with the intended to-be process structure, positively influencing the likelihood of system adoption and usage. Second, as measures of business process similarity can be computed automatically, they enable enterprises to examine available system faster and more accurately. Sorting each system by its similarity score, an initial ranking can be established. Thus, the ERP market is narrowed down to a small number of suitable systems and more detailed, but time-consuming investigations, such as on-site system presentations, can be performed.

The approach builds upon the fact, that ERP systems are based on continuously improved process models that hold the best practice for a class of business processes for a certain industrial sector. For example, the SAP reference model comprises over 600 business process models providing a process structure for SAP R/3. Given a repository of different ERP reference processes, enterprise specific business process models can be used as query objects, aiming to identify similar process models. While various approaches to measure business process similarity exist, most techniques require an exact matching and compare process models pairwise. Thus, underlying formalisms are hard to understand and computation time is high. By contrast, feature-based similarity is designed to query large repositories of business processes by analyzing process features instead of full-scale process models. Following Yan et al., features are defined as simple but representative abstractions of process models [43]. As illustrated in Fig. 7, the proposed procedure comprises four sequentially ordered steps. First, adequate features are defined that represent the processes to be compared. Based on those features, the similarity of a query process model and a collection of ERP-specific reference process models are evaluated within the second step. Third, relevant systems are identified according to their feature similarity score. In the fourth step, identified systems are ranked to provide enterprises with a convenient decision support for ERP selection.

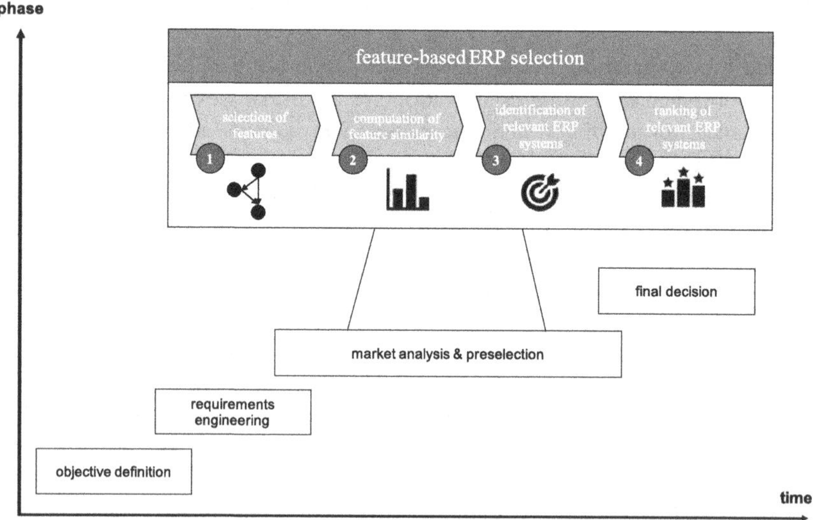

Fig. 7. Methodology for feature-based ERP selection

6 Conclusion

As ERP systems provide an automated support for an enterprise's business operations, their implementation and usage is highly important to remain competitive in a rapidly changing environment. However, many ERP projects fail due to users' resistance towards the system. In fact, adoption and usage of ERP systems significantly depend on the degree of organization-system fit. While adjustments during the implementation phase are costly, time-consuming, and complex, the present paper argues that potential misfits can be addressed within the process of ERP selection. Performing a structured literature review, current methodologies are evaluated in terms of their consideration of organization-system fit. Results reveal that most approaches focus on the assessment of functional and technical fit, while misfits in the dimension of culture and processes are neglected. However, changes in business processes and work routines can trigger users to the avoid the system.

Thus, this contribution introduces an innovative approach for ERP selection that allows to initially assess process fit by utilizing measures of business process similarity. Consequently, enterprises are enabled to analyze process fit before the implementation process is initiated and the large ERP market is narrowed down to a smaller number of relevant systems, increasing the efficiency of selection methodologies.

However, approaches of this kind have a variety of well-known limitations. First, this literature review is based on a representative selection of relevant contributions regarding the examined topic. Thus, articles could have been overlooked and relevant implications were not integrated into this analysis. However, we believe that the identified contributions, the detailed documentation of the literature search procedure, the proposed categorization as well as the suggested selection approach offer valuable insights that can help to improve the addressed field of research. Furthermore, we did not control for other types of misfits, that were identified to be underrepresented in current selection methodologies. More detailed research must be done to account for the degree of functional, technical, and cultural fit during ERP selection. Furthermore, applicability and impacts of the suggested procedure should be evaluated experimentally in future studies.

References

1. Pitic, L., Popescu, S., Pitic, D.: Roadmap for ERP evaluation and selection. Procedia Econ. Financ. **15**, 1374–1382 (2014)
2. Beheshti, H.M., Blaylock, B.K., Henderson, D.A., Lollar, J.G.: Selection and critical success factors in successful ERP implementation. Compet. Rev. **24**, 357–375 (2014)
3. Ali, M., Cullinane, J.: A study to evaluate the effectiveness of simulation based decision support system in ERP implementation in SMEs. Procedia Technol. **16**, 542–552 (2014)
4. Strong, D., Volkoff, O.: Understanding organization-enterprise system fit: a path to theorizing the information technology artifact. MIS Q. **34**, 731–756 (2010)
5. Markus, M.L.: Technochange management: using IT to drive organizational change. J. Inf. Technol. **19**, 4–20 (2004)
6. Gronau, N.: Handbuch der ERP-Auswahl. GTO mbH Verlag, Berlin (2012)

7. Verville, J., Halingten, A.: A six-stage model of the buying process for ERP software. Ind. Mark. Manag. **32**, 585–594 (2003)
8. Stefanou, C.: The selection process of enterprise resource planning (ERP) systems. In: AMCIS 2000 Proceedings, pp. 988–991 (2000)
9. Alpers, S., Becker, C., Eryilmaz, E., Schuster, T.: A systematic approach for evaluation and selection of ERP systems. In: Wrycza, S. (ed.) SIGSAND/PLAIS 2014. LNBIP, vol. 193, pp. 36–48. Springer, Cham (2014). doi:10.1007/978-3-319-11373-9_4
10. Scheer, A., Habermann, F.: Enterprise resource planning: making ERP a success. Commun. ACM **43**, 57–61 (2000)
11. Wei, C.C., Chien, C.F., Wang, M.J.J.: An AHP-based approach to ERP system selection. Int. J. Prod. Econ. **96**, 47–62 (2005)
12. Becker, J., Kugeler, M., Rosemann, M.: Prozessmanagement. Springer, Heidelberg (2012)
13. Foster, S.: Oracle E-Business Suite 11i: Implementing Core Financial Applications. Wiley, New York, USA (2001)
14. von Brocke, J., Simons, A., Niehaves, B., Riemer, K., Plattfaut, R., Cleven, A., Reimer, K.: Reconstructing the giant: on the importance of rigour in documenting the literature search process. In: 17th European Conference on Information System, vol. 9, pp. 2206–2217 (2009)
15. Cooper, H.M.: Organizing knowledge syntheses: a taxonomy of literature reviews. Knowl. Soc. **1**, 104–126 (1988)
16. Torraco, R.J.: Writing integrative literature reviews: guidelines and examples. Hum. Resour. Dev. Rev. **4**, 356–367 (2005)
17. Webster, J., Watson, R.T.: Analyzing the past to prepare for the future: writing a literature review. MIS Q. **26**, 36–43 (2002)
18. Fettke, P.: State-of-the-art des state-of-the-art: eine untersuchung der forschungsmethode "review" innerhalb der wirtschaftsinformatik. Wirtschaftsinformatik. **48**, 257–266 (2006)
19. Cooprider, J.G., Henderson, J.C.: Technology-process fit: perspectives on achieving prototyping effectiveness. In: Proceedings of the Twenty-Third Annual Hawaii International Conference on System Sciences, pp. 623–630 (1990)
20. Perçin, S.: Using the ANP approach in selecting and benchmarking ERP systems. Benchmarking Int. J. **15**, 630–649 (2008)
21. Buss, M.D.: How to rank computer projects. Harv. Bus. Rev. **61**, 118–125 (1983)
22. Lucas, Jr., H.C., Moore Jr., J.R.: A multiple-criterion scoring approach to information system project selection. INFOR **14**, 1–12 (1976)
23. Schniederjans, M.J., Wilson, R.L.: Using the analytic hierarchy process and goal programming for information system project selection. Inf. Manag. **20**, 333–342 (1991)
24. Teltumbde, A.: A framework for evaluating ERP projects. Int. J. Prod. Res. **38**, 4507–4520 (2000)
25. van Everdingen, Y., van Hillegersberg, J., Waarts, E.: Enterprise resource planning: ERP adoption by European midsize companies. Commun. ACM **43**, 27–31 (2000)
26. Keil, M., Tiwana, A.: Relative importance of evaluation criteria for enterprise systems: a conjoint study. Inf. Syst. J. **16**, 237–262 (2006)
27. Kumar, V., Maheshwari, B., Kumar, U.: Enterprise resource planning systems adoption process: a survey of Canadian organizations. Int. J. Prod. Res. **40**, 509–523 (2002)
28. Liao, X., Li, Y., Lu, B.: A model for selecting an ERP system based on linguistic information processing. Inf. Syst. **32**, 1005–1017 (2007)
29. Baki, B., Çakar, K.: Determining the ERP package-selecting criteria. Bus. Process Manag. J. **11**, 75–86 (2005)
30. Kilic, H.S., Zaim, S., Delen, D.: Development of a hybrid methodology for ERP system selection: the case of Turkish airlines. Decis. Support Syst. **66**, 82–92 (2014)

31. Cil, I., Alpturk, O., Yazgan, H.R.: A new collaborative system framework based on a multiple perspective approach: InteliTeam. Decis. Support Syst. **39**, 619–641 (2005)
32. Han, S.W.: ERP – enterprise resource planning: a cost-based business case and implementation assessment. Hum. Factors Ergon. Manuf. **14**, 239–256 (2004)
33. Hecht, B.: Choose the right ERP software. Datamation **43**, 56 (1997)
34. Motwani, J., Mirchandani, D., Madan, M., Gunasekaran, A.: Successful implementation of ERP projects: evidence from two case studies. Int. J. Prod. Econ. **75**, 83–96 (2002)
35. Holland, C.R., Light, B.: A critical success factors model for ERP implementation. IEEE Softw. **16**, 30–36 (1999)
36. Fui-Hoon Nah, F., Lee-Shang Lau, J., Kuang, J.: Critical factors for successful implementation of enterprise systems. J. Bus. Process Manag. J. **7**, 285–296 (2001)
37. Umble, E.J., Haft, R.R., Umble, M.M.: Enterprise resource planning: implementation procedures and critical success factors. Eur. J. Oper. Res. **146**, 241–257 (2003)
38. Finney, S., Corbett, M.: ERP implementation: a compilation and analysis of critical success factors. Bus. Process Manag. J. **13**, 329–347 (2007)
39. Christofi, M., Nunes, J., Peng, G.: Identifying and improving deficient business processes to prepare SMEs for ERP implementation. In: Proceedings of the UK Academy for Information Systems (UKAIS), pp. 1–17 (2009)
40. Gall, M., Sterba, C., Grechenig, T.: Technical criteria for the comparison of modern erp systems for usage in orchestra companies. In: Proceedings of the 3rd European Conference on Information Management and Evaluation (ECIME) (2009)
41. Gürbüz, T., Alptekin, S.E., Işıklar Alptekin, G.: A hybrid MCDM methodology for ERP selection problem with interacting criteria. Decis. Support Syst. **54**, 206–214 (2012)
42. Ratkevicius, D., Ratkevicius, C., Skyrius, R.: ERP selection criteria: theoretical and practical views. Ekonomika **91**, 97–116 (2012)
43. Yan, Z., Dijkman, R., Grefen, P.: Fast business process similarity search with feature-based similarity estimation. In: Meersman, R., Dillon, T., Herrero, P. (eds.) OTM 2010. LNCS, vol. 6426, pp. 60–77. Springer, Heidelberg (2010). doi:10.1007/978-3-642-16934-2_8

Overcoming the Innovator's Dilemma in Disruptive Process Innovation Through Subject Orientation

Albert Fleischmann[1], Werner Schmidt[2(✉)], and Christian Stary[3]

[1] InterAktiv Unternehmensberatung, Pfaffenhofen, Germany
albert.fleischmann@interaktiv.expert
[2] Technische Hochschule Ingolstadt, Ingolstadt, Germany
werner.schmidt@thi.de
[3] Johannes Kepler University, Linz, Austria
christian.stary@jku.at

Abstract. Once digital technologies trigger business process management and change, organizations are challenged to (re)position their products and services. Thereby, creating disruptions could help overcoming the threat of being blindsided by novel developments. We consider Subject-oriented Business Process Management being capable to create socially acceptable organizational disruption through process modelling and explorative execution. S-BPM capabilities adjust changes in customer, product and organizational management through its unifying communication perspective. In this contribution, we report on creating disruptive innovation starting with subject-oriented re-design of work and production processes. The presented case, a large transformation process of an automotive company reveals that this type of disruptiveness enables an integrative perspective on existing work procedure in an aligned, since synchronized way. Hence, we can conclude that a starting point for innovation is grasping the collaborative nature of existing processes rather re-establishing functional positions and procedures.

Keywords: Subject-oriented business process management · Innovation · Disruptive development

1 Introduction

New digital technologies start changing business and production processes substantially. In 'The Innovator's Dilemma' Clayton Christensen [1] has analysed how companies can be blindsided by low-end products from competing organizations. In 'The Innovator's Solution' Christensen et al. [2] reveal how organizations can create disruptions themselves rather than being blindsided by them. Subject-oriented Business Process Management [3] has not only been successfully introduced into various fields [4], including digital production [5], but is rather capable to create socially acceptable organizational disruption through process modelling and explorative execution [6]. The major reason for that are the S-BPM capabilities allowing to adjust changes in customer, product and organizational management through a unifying communication pattern.

M. Kurosu (Ed.): HCI 2017, Part I, LNCS 10271, pp. 150–165, 2017.
DOI: 10.1007/978-3-319-58071-5_12

In line with Christensen, in this contribution, we discuss creating disruptive innovations through subject-oriented re-design of work and production processes. We present a case from automotive industry undergoing a large transformation process. The subject-oriented intervention reveals that this type of disruptiveness enables an integrative perspective on existing work procedure for the first time. The behavior of stakeholders and systems can be aligned through synchronizing their specification, in particular their communication patterns. To achieve such integration, we can conclude, the collaborative nature of existing processes should serve as a starting point for innovation. As such, focusing and finally re-establishing functional positions and procedures should move to the background in the course of organizational interventions.

The contribution is structured as follows. After this introduction, we reflect on the major reasons Christensen identified for enterprises being blindsided by disruptors. The recommendations how to avoid this and how to drive disruptive innovation successfully are also subject of Sect. 2. In Sect. 3 we present Subject-oriented Business Process Management (S-BPM) as an approach for mastering organizational disruption. Section 4 exemplifies a corresponding use case stemming from automotive industry. We conclude the contribution sketching the objective, achievements, and further research.

2 The Innovator's Dilemma and Solution

When analyzing the Innovator's Dilemma Christensen distinguishes between sustaining and disruptive innovation [1]. Sustaining innovation is characterized by performance improvement of existing products along attributes being valued by major customers in the mainstream market.

To profitably satisfy the needs of their customers, enterprises work in a certain value network with channel partners and suppliers. The value network determines the operating processes and the cost structure (indirect, direct cost), with the latter also impacting the need for size, margin and growth.

The value network determines the cost structure (indirect, direct cost), and depending on that, the need for size, margin and growth. It also shapes the organizational capabilities, according to Christensen becoming manifest in the Resources-Processes-Values Framework (RPV). Resources like people, equipment, technology, product designs, brands, information, cash, relationships with partners (customers, suppliers, distributors etc.) are the most tangible, visible and measurable factors. They are quite flexible and can relatively easy be exchanged, transferred across organizational boundaries etc. Processes are patterns of interaction, coordination, communication, and decision-making through which organizations transform inputs into outputs. They can be formal or informal and are always used to perform specific tasks efficiently. Well-performing organization have their processes optimally aligned to the tasks, assuring that employees perform recurrent tasks in a consistent way. Changes are not intended, and if, however, needed, must follow tightly controlled procedures. Hence, the value creation processes tend to be very solid. Values include the criteria managers and employees on every level of the organization use when making prioritization decisions. They usually reflect the cost structure and business model, mainly gross margin and size of a business to be accepted. As resources can be exchanged easier, organizational capabilities primarily reside in processes and values.

Based on these facts, Christensen observed that established competitors are very good in marketing sustaining innovation within their existing value network and with their given cost structure. The market is well known and the customers are well understood and are offered improved products at the high end of the market. This gives the incumbents the opportunity to strive for high margin and high growth. They have well-defined processes in place, optimally adjusted to the tasks to be accomplished.

However, this quite comfortable position makes enterprises prone to be blindsided by newcomers with disruptive innovations. Here the value proposition brought to market is different. With products, which are simpler, smaller, cheaper and more convenient to use disruptors aim for the low end of a market or a completely new market. Surprisingly this is also true in many cases, where established enterprises for example were the first to develop innovative technology. The reasons presented by Christensen are manifold. Rather than finding and shaping a new market, the incumbents try to sell the innovation in the existing market, where customers currently do not show need for the new product or service. They have no practiced processes to handle disruption which comes too fast, and disruption is inconsistent with the existing values. As a consequence, they often try to use the processes which work well for their established business also for marketing the disruptive innovation (one-size-fits-all processes). But capabilities are shaped within value networks and thus very specialized and different for launching sustaining innovation on existing markets and bringing disruptive innovation to new markets.

Taking these observations into account, Christensen and Raynor suggest several principles to solve the Innovator's dilemma [2]. Following them should facilitate incumbents to successfully launch disruptive innovation and not leave space for newcomers to jump in. Selected principles are:

1. Grant autonomy: disruptive business needs the freedom to create a new organization, in particular new processes, and to build a unique cost structure in order to be profitable.
2. Avoid one-process/one-organization-fits-all policy for all types of innovation: disruptive change requires the creation of new resources, new processes and new values.
3. Create new processes and align every critical process and decision to fit the disruptive circumstance: radically different processes are not created by drawing flow charts but by 'heavyweight' teams which are confronted with problems the organization never faced before [7].
4. Follow emergent strategy making approach: particularly in early stages of disruption, where it is not clear, what the right strategy would be, strategy comes up from day-to-day decisions.
5. Develop an understanding of technology, customers and markets: try, fail, learn quickly and try again.
6. Assign managers with the right 'school of experience': a person in charge for a disruptive business should have experience in managing disruptive innovation, no matter if successful or not, as long as he or she went through a learning process.

3 Tackling the Innovator's Dilemma with Subject-Oriented Business Process Management (S-BPM)

In this section, we firstly introduce S-BPM as an approach managing business processes before applying its concept to handle disruptive interventions for innovating the structure of work organizations.

3.1 Subject-Oriented Business Process Management in a Nutshell

S-BPM Fundamentals. Subject-oriented BPM (S-BPM) is a stakeholder- and communication-oriented paradigm [3]. It focuses on subjects as the acting parties in processes (people, systems) who represent abstract behavior descriptions and exchange messages in order to coordinate their mutual work. Activities in a behavior are denoted by predicates and objects are the targets of the activities. Subject representatives can specify their behaviors independently as long as they do not touch the messages (interfaces) or agree upon changes with their communication partners. This behavior encapsulation allows highly flexible self-organization, with the communication structure assuring overall coordination. Subject-orientation has been inspired by various process algebras, the basic structure of nearly all natural languages (Subject, Predicate, Object) [3], and the systemic sociology developed by Luhmann [8]. An easy-to-use graphical notation with only a few symbols allows non-method expert to model the subjects' interaction and behaviors. Figure 1 summarizes the various inspirations, the resulting development phases of S-BPM and enhancements.

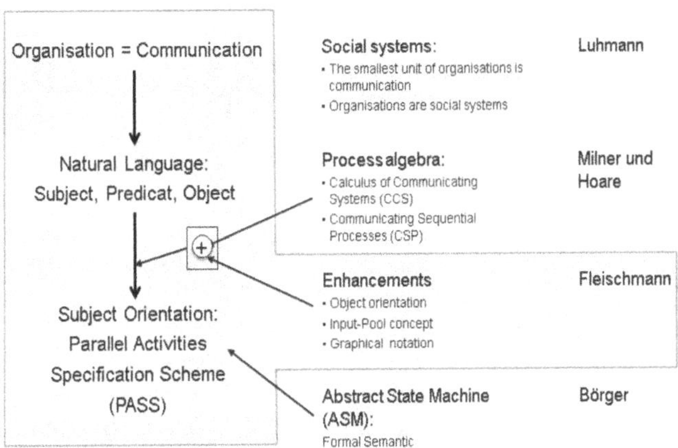

Fig. 1. S-BPM foundation

S-BPM notation. The easy-to-use graphical notation needs only five symbols to build the two diagrams necessary to describe a process. In the so-called subject interaction diagram (SID), the subjects as process-specific roles and their message exchange are documented. Payloads of messages are complex business objects or simple parameters. Figure 2 shows the two language elements needed to model an SID for a simple process,

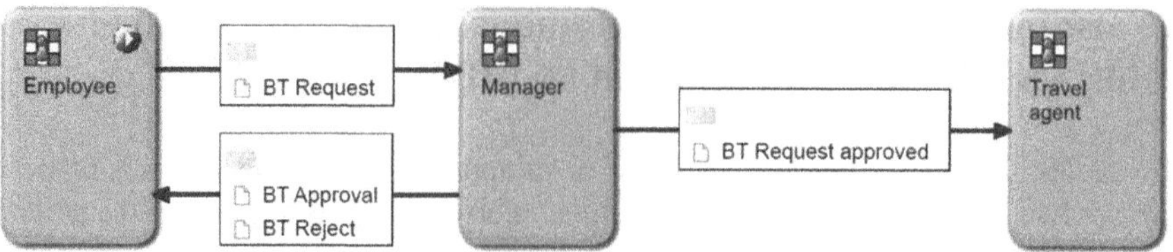

Fig. 2. Subject interaction diagram (BT = Business Trip)

where employees send business trip requests to a manager, who decides on the request, informs the applicant respectively, and, in case of approval, passes the request on to a travel agent for further processing.

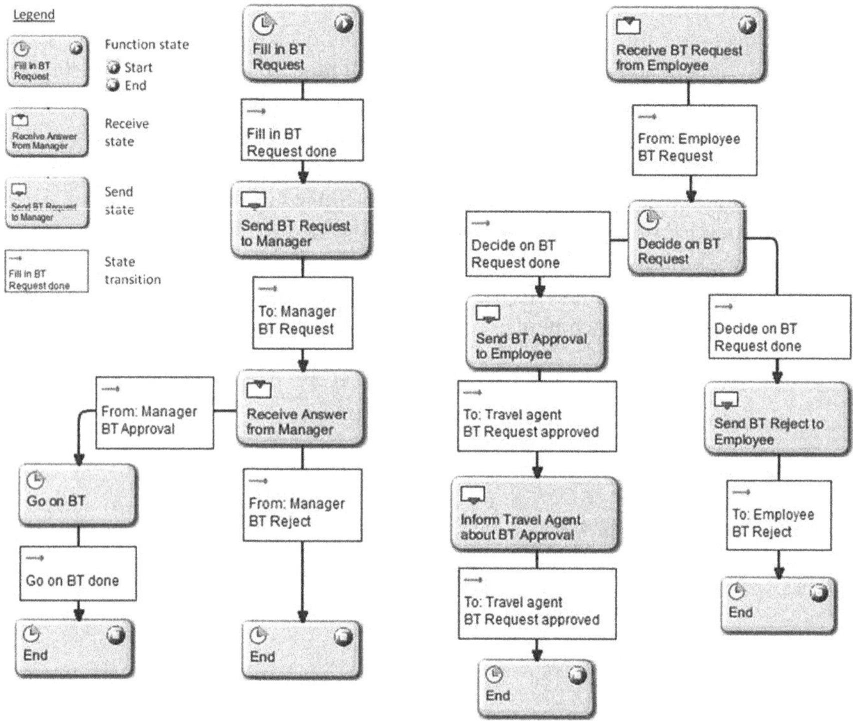

Fig. 3. SBD 'employee' (left) and SBD 'manager' (right)

In a refinement step, the subject behavior diagrams (SBD) are created. Subject representatives as modelers specify the activities and interactions their roles have to perform when executing the process. They also define data structures for business objects to be created, manipulated and exchanged in the subject behavior. Figure 3 depicts the subject behaviors of the employee (left) and the manager (right). With only three different notation elements each diagram shows the sequence of executing internal actions (functions) as well as sending and receiving operations. The state transitions 'To: Manager; BT Request' in the employee behavior and 'From: Employee; BT Request' in the manager behavior are examples for how the subjects synchronize their communication via messages during process execution. The transition 'To: Travel agent; BT Request approved' links to the behavior of the subject travel agent, which in its behavior (not included in the figure) receives the message and processes the data before it comes to an end.

S-BPM roles [14]. S-BPM lifecycle activities are driven and performed by persons acting in certain roles triggering, guiding, implementing and reflecting process management projects: Governors care about the constraints under which BPM activities are performed by focusing on influential factors of change processes. They also set up S-BPM structures by addressing relevant BPM stakeholders. Actors execute business procedures, and interact mutually, to deliver products and services. They are supported by experts and facilitators with respect to S-BPM activities. Experts are IT architects, organizational developers, or specific domain specialists, and support S-BPM activities on demand. Finally, facilitators are required for guiding development processes, as they take care about the social acceptability of change proposals on the organizational level.

S-BPM lifecycle activities [14]. Each of the introduced roles might get involved in each of the following bundles of S-BPM activities:

In the course of analysis models are set up reflecting a situation of an organization 'as it is'. Facilitators, governors, and actors collaborate to scope a certain universe of discourse (Analyzing). While modeling, envisioned processes are specified (Modeling). They need to be validated to ensure their effectiveness (Validating). It is checked whether a process produces expected results. In this bundle of activities mostly the actors and method specialists are involved, as they need to validate communication and functional procedures with respect to the quality of work results. Once a process has been validated, it can be optimized to certain criteria, checking the efficiency of a modeled process (Optimizing).

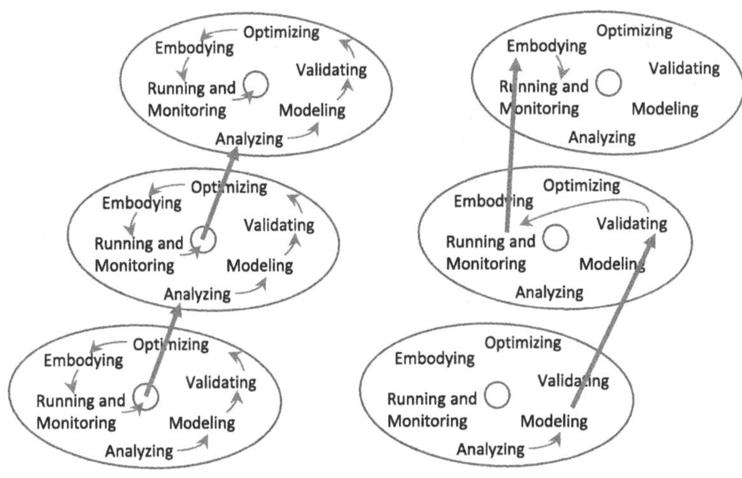

Fig. 4. Flexible S-BPM life cycle

Resource-specific aspects such as time and material consumption are investigated, and might lead to significant changes. To feed the results back to the running business, the process models must become operational on the organizational and technology level (Embodying). Governors and facilitators guide this alignment to existing structures, infrastructure, and strategy of an organization. Once in operation, business processes need to be monitored and analyzed again (Running and Monitoring). The sketched lifecycle activities are in line with existing BPM approaches and can be performed in linear sequence or non-linear order (see Fig. 4).

3.2 S-BPM Featuring Disruptive Innovation

In the following we review the key characteristics of S-BPM in the context of triggering disruptive interventions and guiding constructive exploration of stakeholder and system behavior. We start out with detailing today's intervention scenarios and proceed with structuring the organizational development process along the Innovator's solution principles.

Starting either with low- or high-end disruption, processes and all related (re-) engineering tasks are affected. It is not only the management per se that has become crucial for operating a business [2], but the way of organizing them and the quality that can be achieved by that organization: 'Processes are defined or evolve to address specific tasks, and the efficiency of a given process is determined by how well these tasks are performed. Processes that define capabilities in executing certain tasks concurrently define disabilities in executing others. Consistency is key - processes are not as flexible as resources, and must be applied in a consistent manner, time after time.' ([9], p. 7).

Given the current trend in digitalization, individual stakeholders design business operation, so that changes directly propagate from specification to operation. Adaptation of business processes at an early stage, including introducing automated behaviour through digital systems, seems to be the key [10]. Thereby, customers, network partners, management, and workers are involved, as processes concern all stakeholders. S-BPM involves them not only according to their mutually interacting functional roles or in terms of networked organisational units, but also as designers, and more particularly, engineers. The engineering part is required since ad-hoc dynamics of change are becoming common due to concepts like demand-driven excellence [11].

As such concepts shift organizational change management to the level of business operation, S-BPM actors require a proper support reaching beyond traditional domains skills. Any notation and change management needs to consider collaboration, thus, challenging means of communication rather than domain expertise. With respect to process design and engineering activities, both the notation, and modelling process including stakeholder validation, need to be supported in a human-centred way. Otherwise, stakeholder participation is likely to lead to re-specifying existing patterns and behaviour rather than letting emerge novel designs (cf. [12]).

Setting the stage for disruptive, stakeholder-driven work re-design and process engineering, S-BPM implements all principles of Christensen's solution:

- Utilizing S-BPM modeling and execution capabilities actors can create a completely new organization, and thus system and role behaviors. As parallelism is key, the cost structure for each behavior can be considered separately without lacking general profitability.

- Behavior particularities can be kept as long as communication interfaces between subjects are included in design considerations. Rather than standardized behaviors, a variety of ways to accomplish tasks can be expected.
- Innovation is actively run by concerned actors by means of S-BPM due its simple notation, role concept, and development procedure. Facilitators guide the S-BPM process, whereas governors take care of organizational particularities. Finally, experts could jump into development processes to clarify S-BPM or domain issues.
- Strategy can emerge in a coherent (not on day-to-day basis) from the bottom to the top, since S-BPM needs the operational basis through its models, however representing the entire organization – since each stakeholder or system becomes a subject, their interaction pattern finally represents an organization's behavior (albeit asynchronous behavior encapsulation representing parallelism as in real life).
- S-BPM considers technology, customers, and markets at the same time, and in a dynamic way: Customers and market representatives are modeled as subjects, and thus, their behavior is captured the same way. Once processes are validated they can be implemented technically through model execution. The cycle 'try, fail, learn quickly and try again' is supported for each stakeholder or system represented as subject.
- S-BPM's facilitators and governors are in charge for managing disruptive innovation, both from the domain, and social process perspective. However, they do not interfere in actors' individual behavior modeling.

Consequently, each disruptive innovation through S-BPM is a two-staged procedure, driven by the specifying self-contained operation entities (subjects) and then, executing those specifications to evaluate whether business objectives can be achieved running the operation in the novel way.

Autonomous self-organization. The actor-based, decentral specification of work behavior as a characteristic of S-BPM is a cornerstone of autonomously creating new processes for the disruptive business. The approach and the easy-to-use notation facilitate comprehensive stakeholder inclusion. This allows to form a heavyweight team of people from various functional units, who are involved in the process to be developed. Each member represents a subject, describes the respective behavior and altogether they coordinate their interaction and thus build the process.

Explorative process execution. The graphical notation of the S-BPM modeling language is based on a process algebra with a clear formal semantic allowing automated code generation. This makes subject-oriented processes built by the participant's executable on the fly. It empowers them to instantly validate their work design without having IT specialists involved ('what you model is what you execute'). Issues identified during validation can be changed in the model and the result be tested again right away. Same is valid for weaknesses or other needs of changes which actors observe when they execute implemented processes in daily operation. The S-BPM lifecycle allows for non-linear sequences of BPM activities, depending on the particular situation. Hence, stakeholders can easily and quickly align new and existing processes to disruptive circumstances. Organizational development based on the S-BPM approach facilitates the development and maintenance of adequate business processes for various types of business. It thus helps overcoming the one-process/one-organization-fits-all policy and the disadvantages related to it. This individual, situational fit of processes and the agility with respect to adapting them to changing circumstances form the basis for emergent strategy making and learning as recommended by Christensen and Raynor.

4 Use Case

In this section, we only outline a very complex use case. We show a process system of process systems. This means the complete system consists of several layers of subsystems. These subsystems are connected via messages. According to the subject oriented paradigm these messages are asynchronously exchanged. In this paper, we only show the network hierarchy of the process system. Due to the limited space, we do not show all the message types exchanged between the various systems and components.

4.1 Background and Requirements

Automotive industry will dramatically change during the next couple of years. Digitization will have significant impacts on the physical product car and related services. Services around the automobile "that are sold and delivered digitally are disrupting today's business processes and models and providing entirely new capabilities." [16] From a business point of view the major difference between services and classical products is that producing and delivering a service is the same process. In the business with physical products you have production processes, sales processes and service processes around your product.

Digitization will change the car business manifold. There will be new types of cars with alternative drives and fuels, new marketing and sales methods and new mobility related services e.g., multimodal travel services, commerce services, alternatives to ownership, vehicle health diagnostics.

A car will become something like an internet of things. Sensors and physical actors communicate with software actors. Together they build a complex system called car. Cars itself are connected with other cars and various support systems. Cars are a subsystem in a system of systems. Mobility related service processes are also systems in a system of systems.

Car manufacturers will cooperate with respective partners to offer and to produce these new types of cars and the related services. According to [16], about 75% of executives expect highly intense collaboration with other industries to be a growth driver. However, issues at play in the automotive industry are interrelated. Digitization will be shaped by emerging economies and widespread urbanization. Regulations will continue to compel innovation in automobile technology and related service processes [15].

Services that are sold and delivered digitally are disrupting today's business processes or models and providing entirely new capabilities [16].

The trends outlined above has some significant implications on the design of mobility related products and services. Products and services must be easily adaptable to regulations and preferences of markets. Since these regulations and preferences can change very fast, a mobility system of systems must be adapted to new requirements. These adaptions must be done fast and efficiently. In the best case. this can be done by the related business people.

One system design approach to overcome these problems is reactive programming [17]. Systems built as Reactive Systems are more flexible, loosely-coupled and scalable. Reactive systems are responsive, reactive elastic and message-driven. The S-BPM philosophy meets these requirements. Therefore, this philosophy has been used to design a process system capturing future developments. In addition, reactive process designs can be easily transformed into software systems which support these processes.

4.2 Process Architecture

In this section, we will outline the structure of the aftersales process system. Currently this system covers the subsystem "Accident support" (AS) and "Web service management" (WSM). Basically, these two systems are connected with the messages "Announcement car arrival" and "Confirmation car arrival". Figure 5 shows the top-level structure of the considered process system.

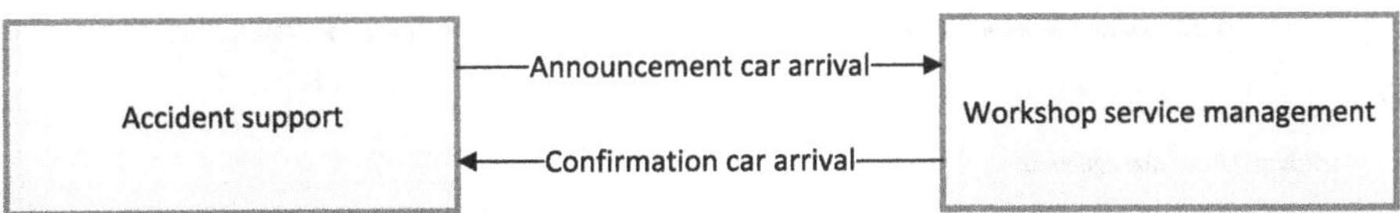

Fig. 5. Process system overview

The messages transport the data required in the receiving system. There is no common data access for these two systems. If a message is sent from one system to the other system, a subject in one system sends the message and another subject in the receiving system accepts its. These subjects are called interface subjects.

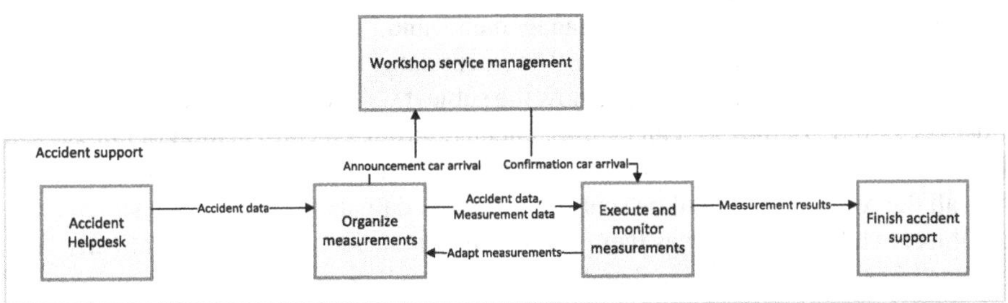

Fig. 6. Details of accident support

Each system can be divided into smaller systems which are also connected with messages. Figure 6 shows the internal structure of the process system "Accident support" This process system consists of four other process systems connected with messages.

In this more detailed description the message "Announcement car arrival" is sent from a subject in the process system "Organize measurement".

Like the process system "Accident support", the process system "Workshop service management" can be subdivided in process systems. Figure 7 shows that the process system ''Workshop service management" is structured by seven process systems. In this structure the message "Announcement car arrival" sent from inside "Accident support" will be received inside the process system "Agree appointment".

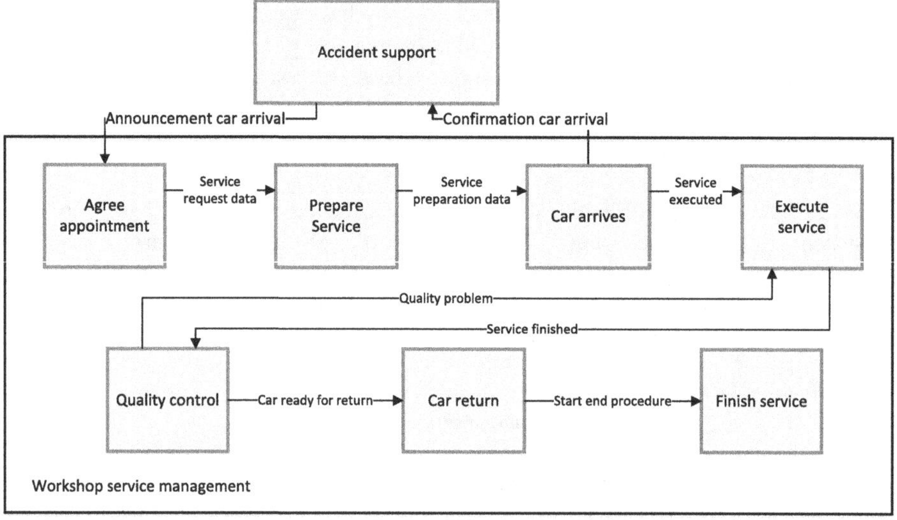

Fig. 7. Details of workshop service management

This hierarchy of networks of process systems can have any number of levels depending on the complexity of the considered process system.

The lowest level ends up in a Subject Interaction Diagram (SID). Figure 8 shows the internal structure of the process system "Accident Helpdesk" which is contained in the system "Accident support". The system "Accident Helpdesk" consists of the subjects "Customer", "Helpdesk", "Car data management" and "Ticket system". In this SID, the subject "Helpdesk" sends the message "Accident data" to the subject "Organize measurement". In the SID, it is not defined how the subject will be implemented. The subjects "Customer" and "Helpdesk" can be implemented through a combination of human and IT or even completely by IT, if a car is equipped with an automatic accident call. In this case, all the required data will be sent like location, damages, car type, owner, etc. The IT-subject "Helpdesk" receives them and creates an accident ticket automatically. The subjects "Car data management" and "Ticket system" represent data systems anyway and will be completely implemented by IT. Hence, independently from the implementation technology, the communication structure need not be changed, and there will be no impact on the other subjects.

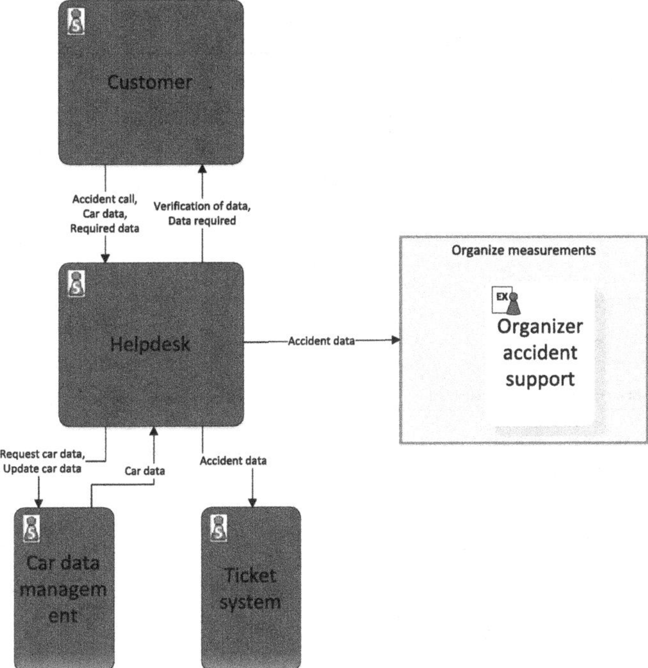

Fig. 8. Details of accident help desk

For each subject the Subject Behavior Diagram (SID) defines the allowed sequences in which messages are received, sent and internal activities are executed. Figure 9 shows part of the behavior diagram of subject "Helpdesk". In the start state the message "Accident call" is expected. Most messages transport data as payload. A copy of these payload is stored in the internal data of a subject. This corresponds to the concept of micro-services. Each micro-service has its own data and do not share data directly also subjects do. Each subject has only its private data, thus, data required by a subject from another subject must be transferred by messages from on subject to the other.

This means additional to the behavior diagram, the specification of a subject also contains its local data, and for each message sent or received the data transported with that data need to be defined. The specification also describes which message parameters are stored in which local data in the case of receiving messages. If a message is sent, then it is defined from which local data the values for the message parameters are copied.

So far, we have outlined the process system "Accident helpdesk" down to the SID-level and a cutout of the SBD of subject "Helpdesk''. The system "Organize measurement" is more complex. It has several more layers and systems because in this system several partners like workshops, towing companies etc. are involved. It does not matter

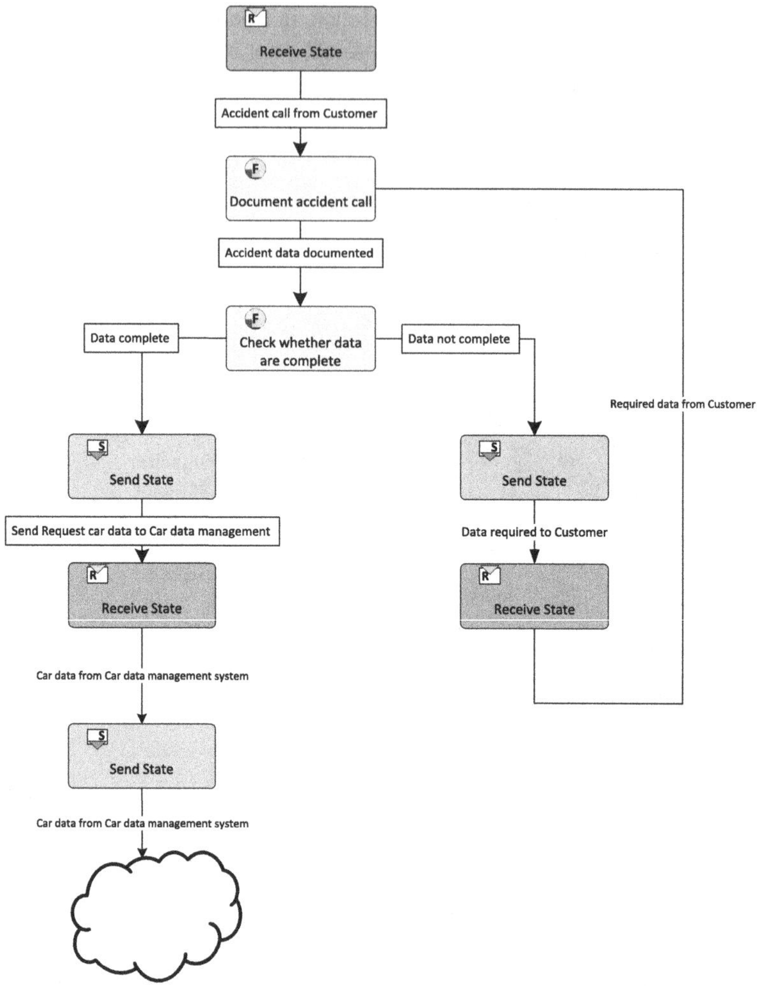

Fig. 9. Behavior of accident help desk

that these are external organizations. They are also represented by corresponding subjects. A subject-oriented process specification is nearly independent from organizational structures. In particular, services delivered by external parties, can easily be attached to existing internal process systems. Messages are a simple way to connect organizations loosely.

4.3 Tools for Describing Processes

For describing the process system for the two aftersales processes the corresponding standards of the company must be applied. According to play the project management, BPMN must be used as model notation and the tool must be ARIS. For specifying process systems according, the subject-oriented paradigm while utilizing BPMN, a corresponding BPMN subset must be defined. We call it S-BPMN [18]. Figure 10 shows a simple process described in S-BPMN.

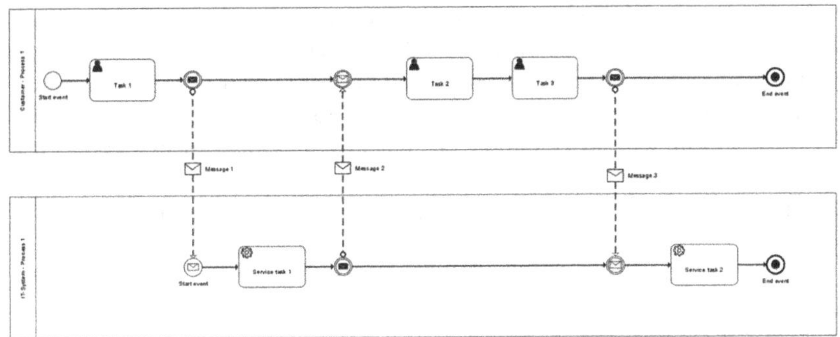

Fig. 10. Behavior in S-BPMN

Subjects are represented by pools, internal activities by tasks, send states by send events and receive messages by receive events. To describe alternative receive messages in BPMN, event-based gateways must be applied and for case distinction the exor gateway is used. To describe the data objects of subjects (pool) and the data payload of messages we use Entity Relationship Diagrams (ERM). BPMN and ERM are supported in ARIS and we connect the various information with each other by links.

For describing the systems hierarchy, we took some other symbols and mechanisms available in ARIS. In general, ARIS was used as a process repository.

ARIS allows exporting BPMN process models in BPMN-XML format. BPMN-XML is a standard for the XML representation of BPMN models. It turns out that ARIS supports event-based gateway symbols, but it does not export it in BPMN-XML. Therefore, we used a normal exor gateway followed by the corresponding receive events.

Data models are not supported by the BPMN-XML export. There is no appropriate direct export available. Here some further investigations are required.

Due to the restricted number of BPMN symbols, we could use the TIBCO (www.tibco.com) workflow engines to execute the process behaviour, however without data. The problem has been that TIBCO does not support BPMN-XML. TIBCO uses XPDL as an internal format. Therefore it was necessary to transform BPMN-XML to XPDL. In the trial, the transformation was done manually. We modelled the test process again by using the TIBCO Studio.

4.4 Experience and Status

The first process-system version has focused on the German market. When propagating into other markets it turns out that it is easy to adapt processes to other markets. Process systems can be removed if they are not required, e.g., as insurance processes are different in the various markets. This shows that the process systems down to subjects can be easily adapted to new situations.

It shows that most business and IT people are not trained in choreography-based BPM approaches like S-BPM. Most people think in control flows. Control flow-oriented BPM concepts like EPC create strongly related activities. Monolithic systems are created which can be changed only with significant effort. There are no building blocks which can be removed, replaced or adapted without impact on other parts of a system. Systems loosely coupled with each other can be easily deployed because a system can be replaced without impact to the other systems if the communication interface is not changed.

One drawback was the migration into a workflow system. Processes should be supported by IT with less programming. To reach best agility process models need to be imported into a workflow engine directly. Our tests showed that this is partially possible, but modelling tools and execution platforms need to be harmonized to that respect.

5 Conclusion

In line with Adam Smith [13] who was looking for a balance of opposing forces, S-BPM provides capabilities of digital process techniques and technologies to recognize and account for human needs when innovating organisations. Striving for a balance means to look beyond 'training the troops' [9] as part of the innovator's solution), since today's innovation can only sustain through actively engaged stakeholders supported by concepts and tools beyond their domain, focusing on reflective engineering for disruptive socio-technical design.

Hard coded processes prevent progress. New products with different complementary services, marketing and sales strategies must be supported by appropriate processes which can be implemented fast and with less effort. Otherwise innovations can be killed by "hard coded" processes.

References

1. Christensen, C.: The Innovator's Dilemma: When New Technologies Cause Great Firms to Fail. Harvard Business Review Press, Brighton (1997)
2. Christensen, C., Raynor, M.: The Innovator's Solution: Creating and Sustaining Successful Growth. Harvard Business Review Press, Boston (2003)
3. Fleischmann, A., Schmidt, W., Stary, C., Obermeier, S., Börger, E.: Subject-oriented Business Process Management. Springer, Heidelberg (2012)
4. Fleischmann, A., Schmidt, W., Stary, C.: S-BPM in the Wild: Practical Value Creation. Springer, New York (2015)
5. Neubauer, M., Stary, C.: S-BPM in the Production Industry: A Stakeholder Approach. Springer, Cham (2017)
6. Fleischmann, A., Schmidt, W., Stary, C.: Subject-Oriented BPM = socially executable BPM. In: Proceedings IEEE 15th Conference on Business Informatics (CBI), pp. 399–407. IEEE (2013)
7. Clark, B., Wheelwright, S.: Organizing and leading heavyweight development teams. Calif. Manag. Rev. **34**, 9–28 (1992)
8. Berghaus, M.: Luhmann leicht gemacht. Böhlau (2011)

9. Christensen, C., Raynor, M.: Creating and sustaining successful growth. The innovator's solution, Soundview Executive Book Summaries, 25(11) Part I, pp. 1–8. Harvard Business Review Press, Boston (2003)
10. Jensen, B., Koch, M.: Mensch und Maschine: Roboter auf dem Vormarsch; Folgen der Automatisierung für den Schweizer Arbeitsmarkt, Deloitte AG, Zurich (2016)
11. Aronow, S., Burkett, M., Nilles, K., Romano, J.: The Gartner Supply Chain Top 25 for 2016. Gartner, Stamford (2016)
12. Allmer, T., Sevignani, S., Prodnik, J.A.: Mapping approaches to user participation and digital labour: a critical perspective. In: Fisher, E., Fuchs, C. (eds.) Reconsidering Value and Labour in the Digital Age. DVWS, pp. 153–171. Palgrave Macmillan UK, London (2015). doi: 10.1057/9781137478573_9
13. Smith, A.: The Theory of Moral Sentiments. Pengiun, New York (2009)
14. Fleischmann, A., Schmidt, W., Stary, C.: A primer to subject-oriented business process modeling. In: Stary, C. (ed.) S-BPM ONE 2012. LNBIP, vol. 104, pp. 218–240. Springer, Heidelberg (2012). doi:10.1007/978-3-642-29133-3_14
15. Gao, P., Hensley, R., Zielke, A.: A road map to the future for the auto industry, McKinsey Report 2014 (2014).http://www.mckinsey.com/industries/automotive-and-assembly/our-insights/a-road-map-to-the-future-for-the-auto-industry. Accessed 2017
16. IBM Center for Applied Insights, Digital disruption and the future of the automotive industry (2017).http://www-935.ibm.com/services/multimedia/IBMCAI-Digital-disruption-in-automotive.pdf. Accessed Jan 2017
17. The Reactive Manifesto,(v1.1), 23 September 2013. http://www.reactivemanifesto.org/#the-need-to-go-reactive. Accessed Jan 2017
18. Fichtenbauer, C., Fleischmann, A.: Three dimensions of process models regarding their execution. In: Proceedings of the 8th International Conference on Subject-oriented Business Process Management, p. 7. ACM (2016)

How to Model Value-Creating Communication

Collaboration Process as an Example

Yuri Hamada[1(✉)] and Hiroko Shoji[2]

[1] Graduate School of Chuo University, Tokyo, Japan
hmd11416@gmail.com
[2] Chuo University, Tokyo, Japan
hiroko@indsys.chuo-u.ac.jp

Abstract. The authors are conducting research on "Value-creating communication". Value-creating communication process is a process that people embody and clarify their own values and form new values through communication. Therefore, we analyze the collaboration process of interior coordination as an example of value-creating communication. First, we took notice of remarks and analyzed collaboration process qualitatively. Then, we revealed the characteristics of the internal value creation. Second, we modeled collaboration process using Bayesian network and examined the validity and usefulness of the constructed model. A feature of the Bayesian network is to predict the likelihood and possibility of occurrence of an uncertain event by expressing the causal structure as a network and then performing probabilistic reasoning. As a result, we found that the point which participants pay attention to is different in respective items. Furthermore, "conception" affected the choice of the item, and it was suggested that the share of "conception" is important to support collaboration process.

Keywords: Communication · Collaboration · Bayesian network

1 Introduction

The authors are conducting study on value-creating communication process. Value-creating communication process is a process that people embody and clarify their own values and form new values through communication. It is defined as value creation including not only creation of new ones but also refinement of ambiguous ones. Here, the value handled in this study refers to internal value.

In modern society, the focus is on how to make a rational decision, however in communication, participants are not necessarily rationally deciding solutions. Fujii points out the limit of optimization method in consensus building [1]. Optimization is to reasonably determine the solution so that the degree of satisfaction of people is high as average. Fujii cited as not having enough consistency for each person's preference as its problem. Kuwako is conducting field communication observations on social consensus formation [2]. In consensus building, not only the opinions of participants but also the history of reasons for opinions are important. And it is important that setting of the place considering Kansei of participants. From this also, participants are thought to

M. Kurosu (Ed.): HCI 2017, Part I, LNCS 10271, pp. 166–176, 2017.
DOI: 10.1007/978-3-319-58071-5_13

have derived solutions that each person can convince, while sharing their opinions and history with each other through communication.

Therefore, in this paper, we analyze cooperative process of interior coordination as an example of value creation communication. First, we extract the characteristics of the process by conversation analysis. Next, we construct a model of value creation communication process using Bayesian network. Then, we investigate the validity and usefulness of the constructed model.

2 Observation and Analysis of Collaboration Process

We introduce the observation and analysis of the collaborative work process we conducted. See [3] for details.

2.1 Observation Method

The theme of collaborative work is "to create a layout of a common living room", and the subjects created a layout using an interior coordinate system [4]. The user can select a furniture such as a chair or desk and place it as many as desired in the space. Subjects were two pairs and observed the collaboration process of the five groups.

2.2 Features of Collaboration Process

In order to clarify the characteristics of the collaboration process, we visualized the process with the remarks of subjects as indicators. Subject's remarks on items were classified according to Table 1. "Conception" is a remark that includes intention and grounds, I think that the conception reflects the values of the members.

As a result of visualizing the process, it seems that the items and emphasis items differ depending on the item. In addition, the conception often appeared with other items. From this, it was suggested that the selection of items will change according to the conception determined.

Table 1. Reason classification table

Conception	Remarks including intention, grounds
Place	Remarks on impression of location and distance
Hotel	Remarks in accommodation type, bathing facilities, amenity
Surrounding Facilities	Remarks on facilities and incidental facilities around the accommodation
Cost	Remarks on accommodation expenses, usage fee of surrounding facilities, food expenses, transportation expenses
Transportation	Remarks on transportation means such as trains, buses, cars
Other	Remarks on conference rooms, services, etc.

2.3 Influence of Conception

Next, we examine the influence of the conception.

In Group II, the table initially agreed to the conception of "place to eat". But while comparing the tables, B said "I want to use this space as a study, not as a dining table." By this remark, the space where the desk is located was decided to study. By becoming a conception of "study space" they chose chairs those that are likely to be in the office, with casters. Regarding the storages as well, saying, "Because it's a study, let's make it a bookshelf," they decided "storage for placing books." In this way, Group II initially agreed on the conception of "place to eat", but as the table was compared, the conception was changed to "study space". And, according to that conception, it was observed that they chose chairs and storages.

3 Analysis and Discussion by Bayesian Network

3.1 Bayesian Network

The feature of the Bayesian network is to predict the likelihood and possibility of occurrence of an uncertain event by expressing the causal structure as a network and then performing probabilistic reasoning [5]. The Bayesian network is a network-like probabilistic model defined by three variables: random variable, conditional dependency between random variables, and conditional probability. According to Motomura [5], the Bayesian network uses random variables as nodes and expresses dependency relationships between variables as effective links. For example, the conditional dependency between random variables is denoted by, and the node (in this case) that comes before the link is called a child node, and the node under the link (in this case) is called the parent node. When there are multiple parent nodes, let be a set of parent nodes of child node. The dependence between and is quantitatively expressed by the following conditional probability.

$$P(X_j|P_a(X_j))$$

Furthermore, considering each of the individual random variables as child nodes in the same way, the joint probability distribution of all the random variables is expressed by the following equation.

$$\mathrm{P}(X_1,\ldots,X_n) = P(X_1|P_a(X_1)) \cdot P(X_2|P_a(X_2))\ldots \cdot P(X_n|P_a(X_n))$$

A probabilistic dependency between these variables can be modeled by a Bayesian network constructed by linking each child node and its parent node (Fig. 1). The probability distribution of all variables is obtained by calculating the previous joint probability distribution.

In this study, we use BAYONET [6] to construct a Bayesian network. BAYONET is a Bayesian network construction support system implemented by Java developed by Motomura et al. [7–9]. In this study, "reason" for "object" is a factor, "evaluation" is the result. We analyze by Bayesian network by expressing the remarks in the consensus building process as a causal structure.

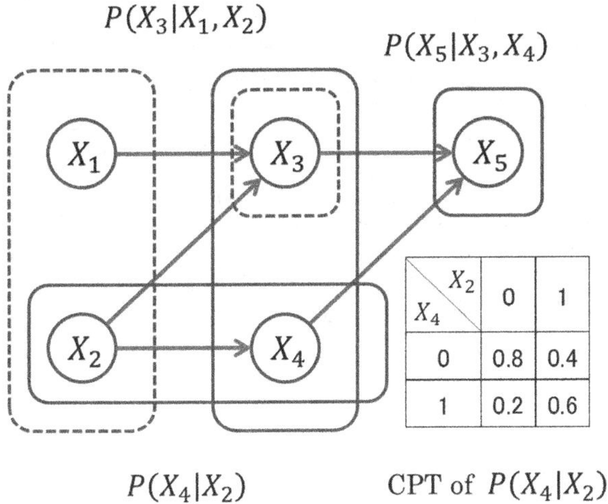

Fig. 1. Bayesian network

3.2 Constructing a Bayesian Network Model

In this section, we construct a Bayesian network model. We construct the network using a node with "conception", "color", "size", "shape/design", "functionality", "material/image", "balance", "quantity/placement", "other" (Fig. 2). The state of "reason" is "A" if it is described for each item, and "None" if it is not stated. The state of "object" is one of "Wall Color", "Floor and Door Color", "Table", "Chair", "Sofa", "Law Table", "TV Lack" and "Storage". "Evaluation" status is "Positive" or "Negative". One sentence is one remark and the item of "reason" necessarily selects "A" or "None." However, since BAYONET has a function to complement missing values using a neural network [7], "choices", "evaluation" does not necessarily need to select a state and there may be a blank.

A part of the data used for the analysis is shown in Table 2. For example, the remark of number 1 in Table 2 is a classification of the remarks that "this low table is not good because legs are black (Color)". Therefore, we set "Object" is "Low Table", "Evaluation" is "Negative", "color" is "A", and other nodes are "None".

3.3 Analysis Focusing on Items that Each Group Places Importance on

Sensitivity analysis was performed using the constructed Bayesian network model. Sensitivity analysis is a method of quantitatively calculating the influence of each factor in a model where an event is generated from a plurality of factors. BAYONET has a sensitivity analysis tool, it can infer with the specified explanatory variable and search for explanatory variable with a large influence on the objective variable. In Sect. 2.2, we stated that items to be emphasized are different when selecting each item in the collaboration process. Therefore, we clarify by sensitivity analysis what "reason" which greatly influences "object". We analyzed the objective variable as "object",

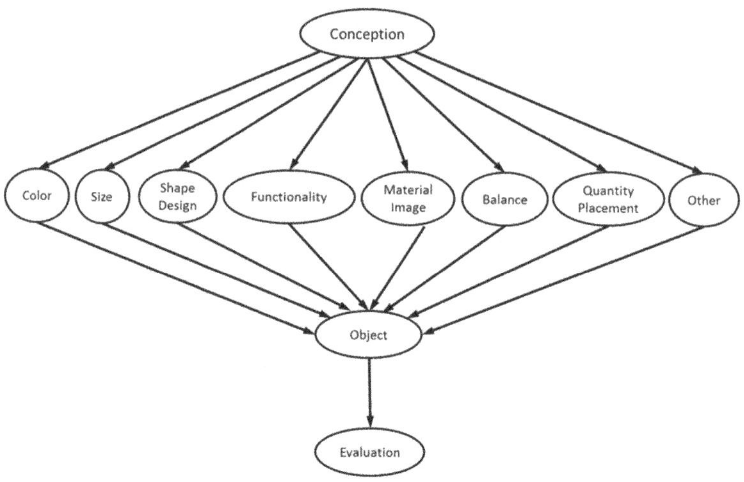

Fig. 2. Bayesian network model constructed

Table 2. Data used for analysis (partial excerpt)

Number	Item	Evaluation	Conception	Color	Size	Shape Design	Functionality	Material Image	Balance	Quantity Placement	Other
1	Low Table	Negative	None	A	None	None	None	None	None	None	None
2	Low Table	Positive	None	None	None	None	None	A	None	None	None
3	Low Table	Negative	None	A	None	None	None	None	None	None	None
4	Low Table	Negative	None	None	None	None	None	None	None	None	None
5	Low Table		None	None	None	A	None	None	None	None	None
6	Low Table	Positive	None	None	None	A	None	None	None	None	None
7	Low Table	Positive	A	None	None	A	None	None	None	None	None
8	Low Table	Positive	None	None	None	None	None	None	A	None	None

explanatory variable as “conception”, “color”, “size”, “shape/design”, “functionality”, “material/image”, “balance”, “quantity/placement”, “others”. In the sensitivity analysis, we make several pairs of values from explanatory variables and input them into the model to infer. Here, it is possible to specify the upper limit of the number of input values to the model, but in this study the maximum number of combinations is set to 2. This is because as can be seen from the remarks of “Because I want to eat (conception), a big desk is good”, not the conception which is an explanatory variable appears alone but the concept often appears together with other items.

For each items, a part of the result of sensitivity analysis is shown in Tables 3, 4. “Probability value” in Tables 3, 4 is the probability value (posterior probability) of the objective variable under the condition that the value of the explanatory variable is input. This indicates the probability that item is selected when a value of a specific explanatory variable is inputted. “Difference in probability” is the difference between the prior probability and the posterior probability for the objective variable. “Lift value” represents the ratio of the probability (certain posterior probability) of occurrence of a certain

Table 3. Sensitivity analysis result (Low Table)

Number	Conception	Color	Size	Shape Design	Functionality	Material Image	Balance	Quantity Placement	Other	Probability Value	Difference in Probability	Lift Value
1	A				A					0.313	0.175	2.257
2					A			None		0.308	0.169	2.219
3		None			A					0.306	0.167	2.200
4					A	None				0.300	0.161	2.157
5			None		A					0.283	0.144	2.037
6				None	A					0.278	0.140	2.004
7					A				None	0.278	0.139	2.000
8					A		None			0.277	0.138	1.996
9					A					0.271	0.133	1.954
10	None				A					0.262	0.123	1.883

Table 4. Sensitivity analysis result (Chair)

Number	Conception	Color	Size	Shape Design	Functionality	Material Image	Balance	Quantity Placement	Other	Probability Value	Difference in Probability	Lift Value
1						A		None		0.288	0.072	1.334
2		None				A				0.277	0.061	1.283
3					None	A				0.263	0.047	1.217
4			None			A				0.263	0.047	1.217
5						A			None	0.260	0.044	1.203
6						A	None			0.259	0.043	1.200
7				None		A				0.259	0.043	1.198
8						A				0.254	0.038	1.176
9	None					A				0.254	0.038	1.176
10	A					A				0.253	0.037	1.171

state when observation is input and the probability (prior probability) of occurrence of that condition irrespective of the condition. That is, the higher the lift value, the greater the influence of the selected "reason" set on "evaluation". The data in Tables 3, 4 are arranged in descending order of the lift value. In addition, the prior probability value of Low Table (Table 3) is 0.139, Chair (Table 4) is 0.216. According to Table 3, since "functionality" is located at the top of Low Table and the combination of "Conception" and "functionality" is also confirmed, it is found that they emphasized on the item "functionality" and considering "Concept". Equally, according to Table 4, in the chair, it is found that they emphasized on the item "material/image" and considering "Concept". From this, it is understood that the items to be emphasized are different according to each item, and the items associated with the "concept" also change.

3.4 Analysis Focused on the Influence of Conception

We analyze the influence of the conception described in Sect. 2.3. In Group II, in the process of choosing Table, the conception of "Let this space be a study" emerged, and this conception seems to influence the choice of Chair and Storage. Therefore, the process is divided before and after the conception "study" appears and we performed analysis by Bayesian network.

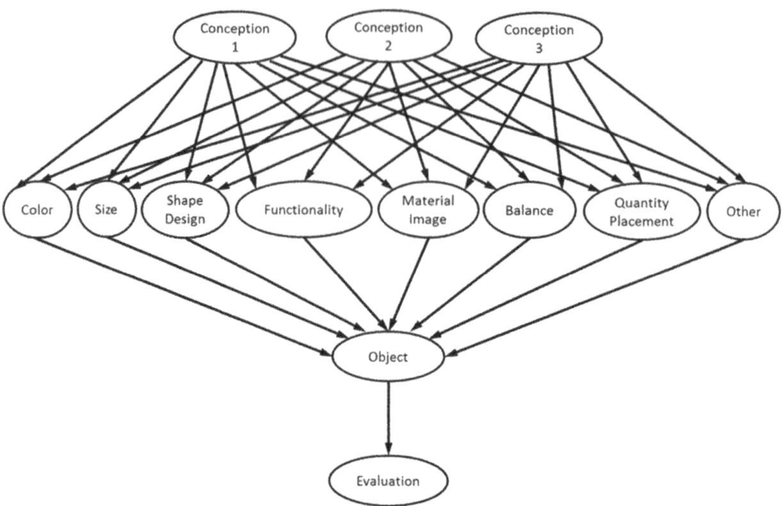

Fig. 3. Bayesian network model constructed (first half)

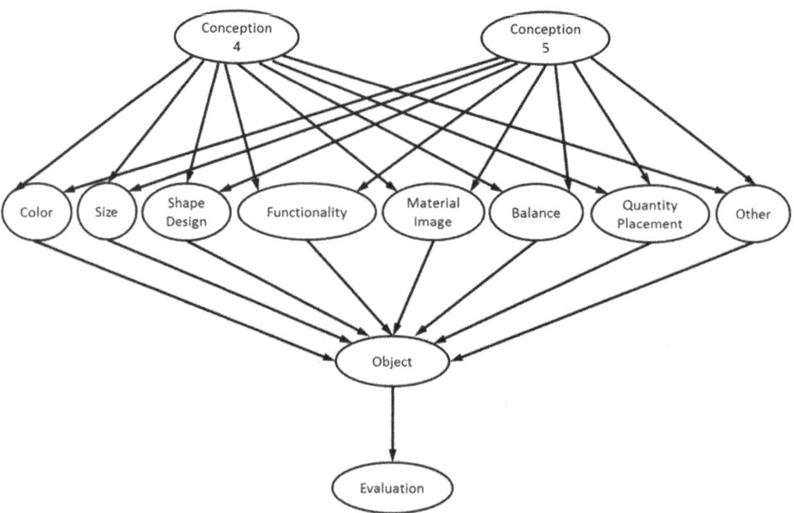

Fig. 4. Bayesian network model constructed (latter half)

The conceptions that appeared in Group II could be classified into five. "Conception 1" means "They want to sleep", "Conception 2" means "They want to put drinks such as tea", "Conception 3" is "Places to eat", "Conception 4" is "Study", "Conception 5" is "They want to place a fancy vase". Conceptions 1, 2, 3 appeared in the first half of the process, and conceptions 4, 5 appeared in the latter half. Also, the items determined in the first half are TV Rack, Sofa, Low Table, and the items determined in the latter half are Table, Chair and Storage. Figures 3 and 4 show the constructed Bayesian network model.

Table 5. Sensitivity analysis result of TV Rack (first half)

	Conception1	Conception2	Conception3	Color	Size	Shape Design	Functionality	Material Image	Balance	Quantity Placement	Other	Probability Value	Difference in Probability	Lift Value
1					None		A					0.359	0.160	1.800
2							A			None		0.320	0.120	1.603
3							A	None				0.306	0.107	1.535
4		A		None			A					0.303	0.103	1.517
5							A		None			0.296	0.096	1.482
6							A				None	0.293	0.093	1.466
7		None					A					0.291	0.091	1.457
8						None	A					0.289	0.089	1.446
9	None						A					0.288	0.089	1.445
10			None				A					0.284	0.084	1.421
11							A					0.281	0.081	1.408
12					None					A		0.257	0.058	1.289
13						A	A					0.250	0.051	1.255
14					A					None		0.240	0.040	1.201
15					A	None						0.239	0.039	1.195
16					A		None					0.235	0.036	1.178
17						None				A		0.234	0.034	1.172
18							None			A		0.232	0.033	1.164
19					A			None				0.232	0.032	1.162
20				None	A							0.230	0.030	1.152

Table 6. Sensitivity analysis result of Sofa (first half)

	Conception1	Conception2	Conception3	Color	Size	Shape Design	Functionality	Material Image	Balance	Quantity Placement	Other	Probability Value	Difference in Probability	Lift Value
1					None		None					0.230	0.044	1.238
2					None					None		0.222	0.037	1.199
3					None	None						0.221	0.035	1.189
4					None				None			0.214	0.029	1.154
5					None						None	0.213	0.027	1.146
6							None			None		0.212	0.027	1.143
7	None				None							0.211	0.025	1.135
8						None	None					0.210	0.025	1.133
9		None			None							0.210	0.025	1.132
10				None	None							0.210	0.024	1.131
11					None			None				0.210	0.024	1.129
12			None		None							0.209	0.023	1.126
13					None							0.209	0.023	1.123
14						None				None		0.205	0.020	1.107
15							None		None			0.205	0.019	1.104
16			A		None							0.204	0.018	1.099
17							None				None	0.203	0.018	1.096
18					None			A				0.202	0.016	1.089
19	None						None					0.202	0.016	1.086
20				None			None					0.202	0.016	1.086

The sensitivity analysis results in the first half are shown in Tables 5, 6 and 7, and the sensitivity analysis results in the second half are shown in Tables 8, 9 and 10. TV Rack, which was decided in the first half, emphasizes "functionality" and "Conception 2" is associated with "functionality", and Sofa seems to have been decided without deciding which items to emphasize. The Low Table emphasizes "shape, design" and "size", and it turns out that "Conception 1" and "Conception 3" are associated with "shape/design". In the second half, they emphasize "size" in table, "color" and "shape/design" in chair, "quantity/ placement" and "functionality" in the storage. Also,

Table 7. Sensitivity analysis result of Low Table (first half)

	Conception1	Conception2	Conception3	Color	Size	Shape Design	Functionality	Material Image	Balance	Quantity Placement	Other	Probability Value	Difference in Probability	LiftValue
1						A	None					0.227	0.076	1.509
2						A				None		0.226	0.076	1.506
3						A		None				0.221	0.071	1.471
4					None	A						0.220	0.070	1.467
5				None		A						0.218	0.068	1.454
6						A					None	0.214	0.064	1.423
7	None					A						0.213	0.062	1.416
8						A			None			0.212	0.062	1.415
9		None				A						0.212	0.062	1.410
10			None			A						0.209	0.059	1.393
11						A						0.208	0.058	1.383
12					A	A						0.186	0.036	1.237
13			A			A						0.183	0.033	1.217
14	A					A						0.174	0.024	1.159
15					A					None		0.170	0.020	1.132
16					A		None					0.169	0.019	1.123
17					A			None				0.168	0.018	1.117
18				None	A							0.167	0.017	1.113
19					A				None			0.167	0.017	1.112
20					A						None	0.166	0.015	1.102

Table 8. Sensitivity analysis result of Table (latter half)

	Conception4	Conception5	Color	Size	Shape Design	Functionality	Material Image	Balance	Quantity Placement	Other	Probability Value	Difference in Probability	LiftValue
1				A					None		0.372	0.113	1.437
2				A		None					0.369	0.110	1.425
3				A	None						0.366	0.107	1.412
4		None		A							0.358	0.099	1.383
5			None	A							0.356	0.097	1.374
6					None				None		0.355	0.096	1.371
7				A			None				0.355	0.096	1.369
8	A					None					0.354	0.095	1.366
9	A			A							0.349	0.090	1.347
10						None			None		0.346	0.087	1.336
11				A				None			0.337	0.078	1.302
12				A						None	0.337	0.078	1.302
13				A							0.337	0.078	1.302
14			None						None		0.328	0.069	1.266
15	A								None		0.327	0.068	1.263
16	A				None						0.321	0.062	1.238
17							None		None		0.321	0.061	1.237
18	None			A							0.317	0.058	1.225
19					None	None					0.315	0.056	1.217
20		None							None		0.313	0.054	1.207

in table, "Size" appeared together with "Conception 4". In chair, "Shape/Design" appeared together with "Conception4". In storage, "Quantity/Location" and "Functionality" appeared together with "Conception 4".

From this, it was possible to select the item at the beginning even if the conception and the items to be emphasized were not clarified. However, the "conception 4" appeared on the way and it affected the item selection. Thus, as the conception emerged, it turned out that items of other furniture were determined according to the conception.

Table 9. Sensitivity analysis result of Chair (latter half)

	Conception4	Conception5	Color	Size	Shape Design	Functionality	Material Image	Balance	Quantity Placement	Other	Probability Value	Difference in Probability	Lift Value
1			A						None		0.482	0.246	2.043
2			A		None						0.458	0.222	1.940
3					A				None		0.444	0.208	1.881
4			A			None					0.432	0.196	1.832
5			A				None				0.424	0.188	1.796
6			A	None							0.419	0.183	1.776
7		None	A								0.410	0.174	1.739
8			None		A						0.406	0.170	1.722
9			A					None			0.403	0.168	1.710
10			A							None	0.403	0.168	1.710
11			A								0.403	0.168	1.710
12	None		A								0.402	0.166	1.705
13					A		None				0.396	0.160	1.679
14					A	None					0.395	0.159	1.673
15				None	A						0.394	0.158	1.669
16		None			A						0.386	0.150	1.636
17					A			None			0.380	0.144	1.613
18					A					None	0.380	0.144	1.613
19					A						0.380	0.144	1.613
20	A				A						0.377	0.141	1.597

Table 10. Sensitivity analysis result of Storage (latter half)

	Conception4	Conception5	Color	Size	Shape Design	Functionality	Material Image	Balance	Quantity Placement	Other	Probability Value	Difference in Probability	Lift Value
1					None				A		0.474	0.181	1.619
2			None						A		0.451	0.158	1.540
3							None		A		0.437	0.145	1.495
4						None			A		0.435	0.143	1.488
5				None					A		0.434	0.142	1.485
6		None							A		0.424	0.132	1.450
7								None	A		0.418	0.125	1.429
8									A	None	0.418	0.125	1.429
9									A		0.418	0.125	1.429
10	None								A		0.414	0.122	1.416
11	A								A		0.406	0.113	1.386
12				None		A					0.388	0.095	1.325
13			None			A					0.384	0.091	1.312
14					None	A					0.382	0.090	1.307
15						A	None				0.381	0.089	1.304
16						A			None		0.381	0.088	1.301
17		None				A					0.377	0.084	1.289
18	A					A					0.373	0.080	1.274
19						A		None			0.366	0.073	1.251
20						A				None	0.366	0.073	1.251

4 Summary

In this paper, as an example of "value-creating communication", collaboration process of interior coordination was taken up and analysis of value creation process by communication was conducted. As a result, it was found that in the collaborative work of interior coordination, the items which are important to each items are different. In addition, it was suggested that "Conception" influences selection of items, and sharing "conception" facilitates collaboration process.

In the future, we also analyze interior coordination of other subjects and clarify the tendency of collaboration process. We also analyze the value-creating communication process for participants who have various attributes and backgrounds, such as when they are in a hierarchical relationship or conflict relationship, or in a dialogue between experts and non-experts.

References

1. Fujii, S.: Examination on the problem of consensus building. Oper. Res. Manag. Sci. Res. **48** (11), 795–801 (2003)
2. Kuwako, T.: Consensus building and Kansei in communications. J. Institute Electr. Inf. Commun. Engineers **92**(11), 967–969 (2009)
3. Hamada, Y., Maruyama, T., Shibata, T., Ogino, A., Shoji, H.: Analysis on collaboration process of interior coordination. In: Life Software & Kansei Workshop Joint Symposium 2016 (2016)
4. Shibata, T., Ogino, A.: Impression modeling using shape and color features of interior coordinate system. In: Proceedings of Spring Meeting of the 12th Annual Meeting of the Japan Society of Kansei Engineering (CD-ROM) (2016)
5. Motomura, Y., Iwasaki, H.: Bayesian network technology-user and customer modeling and inference of uncertainty. Tokyo Denki University Press (2006)
6. NTT DATA Mathematical Systems HP. http://www.msi.co.jp/bayonet/
7. Motomura, Y.: BAYONET: Bayesian network on neural network. In: Foundation of Real-World Intelligence, pp 28–37. CSLI, California (2002)
8. Motomura, Y.: Bayesian network software. J. Japan. Soc. Artif. Intell. **17**(5), 559–565 (2002)
9. Motomura, Y.: Bayesian network software Bayo Net. J. Soc. Instr. Control Eng. **42**(8), 693–694 (2003)

Appeals of Product Pictures on the Product Detail Page - The Effect of Mental Imagery

Chu-Ting Lee(✉) and Man-Ying Wang

Department of Psychology, Soochow University, Taipei, Taiwan
amygm307@gmail.com, mywang@scu.edu.tw

Abstract. Online shoppers are not able to touch and feel products when perusing online stores. Product images on the product detail pages are the main sources of information that users rely on to construct their interactions with a product. This study investigates how the appeal type of product images (attribute-based vs. benefit-based) influences shoppers' attitudes and purchase intention toward a product as well as the mediation of this process by the vividness and elaboration of mental imagery. The results shows that appeals of product images affect shoppers' attitude via vivid and elaborated imagery, but purchase intention is impacted by elaborated imagery only. For shoppers, the effect of attribute-based appeals on imagery elaboration is significantly more prominent for well-known brands than for less-known brands. The implication for product detail page design is to emphasize product attributes over benefits for well-known brands while the reverse is true for less-known brands.

Keywords: Product detail page · Product image · Mental imagery · Purchase intention · Attribute-based appeal · Benefit-based appeal

1 Introduction and Hypothesis Development

While the product detail page of an online store is likened to the merchandise display of a physical store, online shoppers are unable to touch and feel products when shopping over the Internet. Product pictures on the product detail pages are one of the main sources of information for product evaluation, resulting in a strictly visual mode of shopper-product interactions. Product pictures convey important information concerning product attributes (details on looks and functions) and benefits (what the product is good for). Few previous studies, if any, have looked into how these two types of information in product pictures can facilitate purchase decisions. A possible psychological mechanism adopted by shoppers to process product attributes and benefits is mental imagery, which has been consistently found to affect consumer responses [1–3]. This study investigates how product appeals (attribute-based vs. benefits-based) affect shoppers' visual interaction with the product in the form of mental imagery as well as how such experiences may be used to enhance users' product attitudes and purchase decisions. This study also clarify how these different effects could be modulated by brand awareness of the product.

M. Kurosu (Ed.): HCI 2017, Part I, LNCS 10271, pp. 177–187, 2017.
DOI: 10.1007/978-3-319-58071-5_14

1.1 Product Detail Page Design

Most product-related information is generally shown on the product detail page of online stores. From an overview of the situation for China, the product detail page can divided into three parts: product descriptions, customers' reviews, and sellers' commitment; and product descriptions typically use a large amount of pictures to depict the products. Previous research indicated that object interactivity information (e.g., 3D interactive pictures), instead of descriptive text, on the product detail page evokes vivid mental imagery of products and thus increases intentions [3]. Depicting product pictures in different ways affects consumers' product simulating experience as well [4].

An important yet largely unanswered question on product detail page design concerns how marketing messages could be incorporated to facilitate shoppers' purchase decision. Lancaster [5]'s definition of the persuasiveness of message type is adopted here to distinguish between two types of product information depicted by product images. The attribute-based appeal emphasizes physical properties and visual characteristics that are measurable, concrete, and relevant in discerning alternatives attached to the product. By contrast, the benefit-based appeal highlights the results of possessing or using the products in terms of value, happiness, convenience, satisfaction etc. Regarding the persuasiveness of attribute-based and benefit-based appeals, previous studies provide mixed evidences. For example, Graeff [6] indicates that, compared to inferences about concrete attributes and features, inferences about self-relevant product consequences have stronger effects on consumers' brand attitudes. By contrast, Lautman and Percy [7] find that the attribute-based campaign commercials outperform the benefit-based oriented campaigns. However, it seems that these appeal types bring into play on different situations. Hernandez, Wright and Rodrigues [8] conclude that, benefit-based appeals are more persuasive than attribute-based appeals when a purchase is planned for the distant future or when construal levels are high.

1.2 Mental Imagery

Mental imagery is a process by which sensory information is represented and used in much the same way as perceptions of external stimuli, as a form that is "very like picturing and very unlike describing" [9, 10]. When drawing on imagery processing, consumers mentally embody the shopping experience. They may visually imagine a product in use, not only including the product's attribute information, but the benefit that consumers obtain from owning and using the product. Mental imagery processing is at play when one processes affect-rich information in particular [1, 2], and as such it has important roles in persuasion. Strong mental imagery improves attitude, induces intention, and is related to consumption experiences [10–16].

Mental imagery is defined along three dimensions: vividness, quantity, and elaboration [17]. Vividness is the most frequently studied imagery dimension and refers to the intensity and clarity of the imagery that arises. As the intensity of vividness rises, consumers are much more able to imagine the details of the product. Elaboration refers to the extent to which the information stored in long-term memory - that is, information other than that provided by a stimulus - is activated and retrieved to working memory in information processing. It reflects the extent to which information is integrated with prior knowledge. Previous studies indicated that imagery elaboration could induce psychological ownership, or a feeling of "the object is mine" [15, 16]. Quantity refers to the amount of different images generated. As imagery quantity is redundant with the degree of elaboration [15], the current study focuses on imagery vividness and elaboration.

Although mental imagery can be induced by pictures, concrete words, and instructions for imagination, pictures are the most established predictors of imagery [10]. Product pictures on the product detail page are likely to induce mental imagery, varying on the dimension of vividness and elaboration, which in turn affect shoppers' attitude and purchase intention toward the product. Thus, this study presents the first hypothesis.

H_1: Mental imagery is induced by product pictures on the product detail page. The differences in imagery vividness and elaboration are positively related to product attitude and purchase intention. Vividness and elaboration of mental imagery induced by product pictures on the product detail page are positively related to product attitude and purchase intention.

1.3 Brand Awareness

Brand awareness is an important contributing factor to product evaluation and purchase intention. It reflects the extent of marketing commitment by the enterprise or sellers. Consumers are likely to base their choices on brand awareness consideration under low involvement [18, 19]. Research also suggested that improving brand awareness can enhance brand loyalty and thus generate repurchase behavior [20].

Brand awareness is based on one's brand knowledge that can be conceptualized in associative network memory terms. Brand knowledge consists of a set of nodes in the network where brand related information is stored [19]. Relationships between brand attributes are amassed in links that vary in strength. The strength of the associated links between the activated nodes determines the extent to which information spreads through related nodes and the extent of retrieved memory representation [21, 22]. Product or brand-related information may thus serve as the retrieval cue by activating nodes in the brand knowledge network. For example, "running shoes" is strongly associated with the well-known brand node "Nike", which in turn is associated with other brand-related properties. Consumers are likely to think of the well-known brand name Nike when considering purchasing running shoes. Knowledge that is linked to Nike should also come into mind, such as the concrete product features, self-image, and identity that consumers can obtain by owning the product, past usage experience, or a recalled image from recent advertising content.

Shoppers are accordingly more likely to retrieve brand knowledge related to the benefits of product use as the basis for elaborated imagery for high awareness brands (versus low awareness ones) even when merely concrete attributes of the product are presented in the product picture. In other words, shoppers are able to retrieve benefit-related information through a previous experience with a well-known brand based on the attribute-based appeal product picture. This leads to the next hypothesis.

H_2: The effect of attribute appeal from a product picture on imagery elaboration is more prominent on higher awareness brands.

2 Method

2.1 Pre-Test

This study implements a pre-test to determine the level of awareness for the backpack brands used herein. A total of 43 students (11 males and 32 females, $M_{age} = 20.2$ years) at Soochow University took part in the study. Participants completed a paper-and-pencil questionnaire that assessed their brand awareness. Four brands are assessed according to two items: "I can recognize X among other competing brands." and "I am aware of X." (1 = very agree; 7 = very disagree) [23]. Participants completed demographic measures, including age and gender in the end.

A one-way ANOVA reveals different brand awareness between the chosen brands (Adidas, Nike, AspenSport, and MCYS&JPN) ($F(3,168) = 158.88$; $p < .001$). A post hoc test shows that there is no difference respectively between Adidas and Nike, and between AspenSport and MCYS&JPN ($M_{Adidas} = 5.59$, $M_{Nike} = 6.03$, $p = .31$; $M_{AspenSport} = 1.95$, $M_{MCYS\&JPN} = 1.86$, $p = .98$); in addition, students are more aware of Adidas and Nike than they are of AspenSport and MCYS&JPN($M_{Adidas} - M_{AspenSport} = 3.64$, $p < .001$; $M_{Adidas} - M_{MCYS\&JPN} = 3.73$, $p < .001$; $M_{Nike} - M_{AspenSport} = 4.08$, $p < .001$; $M_{Adidas} - M_{MCYS\&JPN} = 4.17$, $p < .001$). Thus, Adidas and Nike are chosen to be used in the high awareness group, while in comparison, AspenSport and MCYS&JPN are chosen to be used in the low awareness group. A follow-up pretest taken by 49 participants was implemented to confirm whether the stimuli of the four brands are different in perceived quality and product attitude. The result presents that neither perceived quality nor product attitude are different in the four brands (product attitude: $t\ (48) = -1.40$, $p = .17$;perceived quality: $t\ (48) = -1.63$, $p = .11$).

2.2 Participants

A total of 117 adults (42 males and 75 females, $M_{age} = 21.7$ years) recruited from the Internet by snowball sampling took part in the study online. Most of them are students.

2.3 Procedure

Pictures of backpack products were first collected from the Internet. Participants browsed six backpack products' detail pages, each one composed of two pictures depicting the backpack and a brief text explaining some product detail including the brand name (see Fig. 1). Among the six backpacks, half are low awareness brands, and the other half are high awareness brands chosen from the pretest. The presentation sequence was counterbalanced. After browsing each product detail page, participants completed a questionnaire that assessed all variables. On average, participants took 15 to 20 min to complete it.

Fig. 1. An example of a product detail page used in this study (from www.tmall.com)

2.4 Materials

All items were assessed under 7-point scales. The assessment order follows the description below.

All pictures of the product depict both the attribute and benefit appeals. For example, a picture depicting a model carrying a backpack not only presents the attribute of the backpack, but also conveys the benefit information, such as the self-image that the user can get by carrying the backpack. Participants are assessed on the attribute and benefit appeals that they were aware of from the product detail page. Attribute and benefit appeals are each assessed by one item based on Lancaster [5] ("I am aware of the concrete characteristics of the backpack via the pictures", and "I am aware of the values or utilities from the possession of the backpack via the pictures".).

This research assesses mental imagery by Babin and Burns [17], capturing all the dimensions. Vividness is measured on a semantic scale comprising eight items ("The product image that occurred was detailed/clear/weak/fuzzy/vague/vivid/sharp/well-defined"; construct α = .93). Elaboration is taken on three items ("I can mentally image the backpack in the ad"; "I imagined what it would be like to use the backpack"; and "I imagined the feel of the backpack"; construct α = .80).

Product attitude is assessed on two items [15] ("All in all, I evaluate the backpack very positively"; and "I really like the backpack"; construct α = .90). Purchase intention is assessed on two items [4, 14] ("I might purchase this backpack"; and "I am willing to find the backpack in the store and purchase it"; construct α = .97).

2.5 Result

This research executes path analysis using the maximum likelihood estimation in AMOS. Two dependent variables, purchase intention and product attitude, are inspected as separate outcome variables. In particular, the study performs multi-group analyses to compare the findings between two levels of brand awareness.

Descriptive Analysis. Table 1 shows the mean scores and standard deviations of all variables. The normality assumption [24] and the offending estimate checks are conducted following the suggestions by [25] (i.e. skewness > 3; kurtosis > 10) and [26] (i.e. standardized estimate < 0.95 and standard errors are not negative; see Table 2). The values of all variables fall well within the permissible ranges for the conduction of further analyses.

Table 1. Mean, standard deviation of all variables

Construct	Overall sample (n = 234)		High awareness brand (n = 117)		Low awareness brand (n = 117)	
	M	SD	M	SD	M	SD
Benefit-basedappeal	4.59	1.11	4.58	1.13	4.60	1.10
Attribute-based appeal	4.75	1.12	4.72	1.07	4.77	1.17
Imagery vividness	4.70	.93	4.68	.94	4.73	.92
Imagery elaboration	4.04	1.10	3.95	1.11	4.12	1.08
Product attitude	3.71	1.12	3.58	1.17	3.83	1.06
Purchase intention	3.00	1.20	2.88	1.22	3.07	1.17

Notes: M = mean; SD = standard deviation.

Path Analysis. Figure 2 illustrates the path model. Table 3 indicates that model fits are good for both product attitude and purchase intention. To verify whether mental imagery mediates the effect of attribute-based and benefit-based appeals on purchase intention and product attitude, the study employs bootstrap estimation with 1000 resamples. The results show that all the indirect effects in the model are significant (see Table 4).

According to the above findings, Hypothesis 1 is partially supported. As expected, attribute-based and benefit-based appeals could improve both imagery vividness and imagery elaboration. Different from the proposed model, imagery vividness does not affect purchase intention significantly. Imagery vividness reflects the intensity and clarity of the image that arises, rather than the interaction between the individual and the product. By contrast, imagery elaboration refers to the information retrieved from long-term memory, and it reflects more information related to the individuals. Thus, imagery elaboration is an important predictor of purchase intention. However, the effect of imagery vividness on product attitude is significant ($p < .05$). Purchase intention reflects the behavior level rather than product attitude; and compared with product attitude, even if the perception of the image is clear and detailed, the influence on purchase intention is limited.

Table 2. Path coefficient of the model across two models

	Overall sample (N = 234)		High awareness (N = 117)		Low awareness (N = 117)		Path difference
	Estimate	S.E.	Estimate	S.E.	Estimate	S.E	*z*
Att → Vivid	.44***(.53)	.05	.44***(.50)	.08	.44***(.55)	.07	−0.01
Att → Ela	.36***(.36)	.07	.50***(.48)	.11	.26**(.28)	.09	−1.78*
Ben → Vivid	.24***(.29)	.05	.26***(.31)	.08	.22**(.26)	.07	−0.40
Ben → Ela	.36***(.36)	.07	.24**(.25)	.10	.45***(.45)	.09	1.47
Ela → PI	.78***(.72)	.05	.79***(.72)	.07	.76***(.70)	.07	−0.32
Ela → PA	.73***(.71)	.05	.78***(.74)	.08	.66***(.68)	.07	−1.11
Vivid → PI	.08(.06)	.07	.34(.03)	.10	.13(.10)	.10	0.68
Vivid → PA	.14**(.12)	.06	.09(.07)	.09	.20**(.17)	.08	0.92

Notes:

1. Att = Attribute-based appeal; Ben = Benefit-based appeal; Vivid = Vividness of imagery; Ela = Elaboration of imagery; PI = Purchase intention; PA = Product attitude.
2. Values in parentheses are standardized estimates.
3. *** $p < 0.01$; ** $p < 0.05$; * $p < 0.10$.
4. *Path difference* refers to the difference in path coefficients between high and low brand awareness groups.

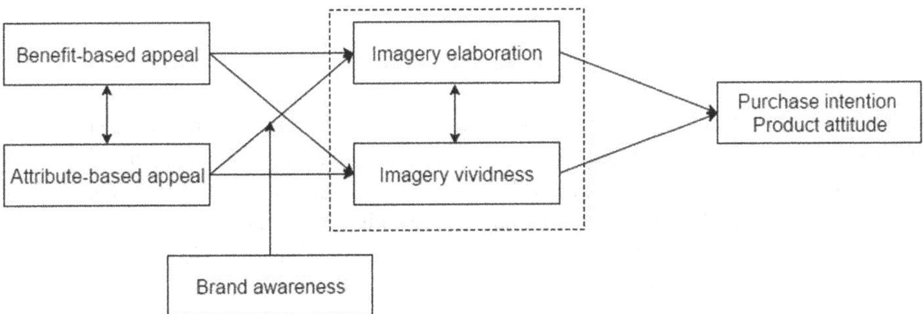

Fig. 2. Illustrated effects of appeal types on mental imagery, product attitude, and purchase intention (see Table 2 for the significance of paths)

Table 3. Model fit indices of overall sample and multi-group sample

	χ^2 (*df*)	*p*	RMR	GFI	NFI	CFI	RMSEA
Overall sample							
Purchase intention	1.116(2)	.943	.004	.100	.100	1.00	.000
Product attitude	1.662(2)	.436	.010	.997	.998	1.00	.000
Multi-group sample							
Purchase intention	3.267(4)	.514	.015	.994	.995	1.00	.000
Product attitude	5.253(4)	.262	.016	.991	.993	.998	.037

Table 4. Bootstrap estimation result

	Attribute appeal	Benefit appeal
Purchase intention	.002 (.177, .374)	.002 (.187, .385)
Product attitude	.002 (.220, .413)	.002 (.207, .391)

Notes: Values in parentheses are 95% confident interval; values outside parentheses are p-value.

Multi-group Analysis. The multiple group moderation analysis was performed to verify the moderation by brand awareness on the effect of attribute appeal on imagery elaboration. The Chi-square difference test is first employed to verify the overall difference in two brand awareness groups, followed by critical ratios used to check the difference of each path in the model. The results indicate that the effect of attribute-based appeals on imagery elaboration is more prominent on higher awareness brands (see Tables 2 and 5). Hypothesis 2 is thus supported.

Table 5. Result of Chi-square difference test across two models

	χ^2_{diff}	df_{diff}	p
Purchase intention	2.885	4	.577
Product attitude	4.124	5	.532

3 Conclusion

This study examines findings from 117 participants, each person browsing six products' detail pages. The resulting model explains how the appeal of product pictures influences purchase intention and product attitude via imagery vividness and elaboration. Imagery elaboration, not imagery vividness, mediates the effects of attribute-based and benefit-based appeals on purchase intention. However, imagery vividness and elaboration both mediate the effect of attribute- and benefit-based appeals on product attitude. An elaborated imagery is characterized by the imagined product interaction with the shopper. Representing the product as such may serve as a significant basis for psychology ownership, i.e., the mental state in which individuals feel that the product is 'theirs' [27]. The connection with "inferred" ownership could explain why imagery elaboration effectively predicts purchase intention in the current study [28]. By contrast, vividness of imagery reflects the clarity of details in product representation and predicts product liking. However, it is less effective in creating a link between the product and the shopper and thus does not affect purchase intention.

Depicting benefit and attribute information in the product picture helps imagery vividness and elaboration to different degrees. Attribute-based appeals appear to more effectively increase imagery vividness, while benefit-based appeals influence imagery elaboration more. Attribute-based appeals highlight the physical properties and visual characteristics of the product that may contribute to the intensity and clarity of the imagery that arises or just the simply vividness of the imagery. By contrast, benefit-based appeals emphasize the values and utilities of owning and using a product to depict the product picture. The self-related information in the product picture helps enhance the generation of elaborated imagery.

The results from multiple group analysis show that the effect from attribute-based appeals on imagery elaboration is more prominent on well-known brands than on less-known brands by the shopper. The brand knowledge activated by products of well-known brands supplements the benefit information of the product when merely product attributes are depicted in the picture. Such information may be used to induce elaborated imagery. For example, it could be relatively easy for a shopper to "feel" like an athlete by imagining wearing the Nike sports shoes while noticing the air cushion and the texture of the Nike product picture. Such a process is unlikely when the product brand is less known. Product pictures of unknown brands should explicitly demonstrate and emphasize the benefits of the sports shoes to support elaborated imagery.

To conclude this discussion, the current study has set out to examine the effect of attribute-based and benefit-based appeals of product pictures. The results provide clear implications for product detail page design by showing that attribute-based appeals are more useful for well-known brands while benefit-based appeals are critical for less-known brands. Product pictures devised as such may facilitate imagery elaboration that positively predicts both purchase intention and product attitude of shoppers.

Limitation and Future Research Opportunities. The high covariance of attribute-based and benefit-based appeals (standardized coefficient = .68) found in the current study may constitute a limiting factors for our results. This covariance may have to with how different types of appeals were measured in the current study. It may also result from the fact that the information participants relied on to rate attribute- and benefit-based appeals is implemented within the same merchandize. The relatedness may not be unexpected.

The second possible limitation has to do with the product category. As the product we used in this study was a backpack, for which users can mentally create interactions and relationships [29] with relative ease, as they interact with such product frequently in daily lives. It awaits future studies to exemplify the extent to which current findings apply to other product categories. It is interesting to investigate similar effects for products that are less likely to establish extensive user-product relationships (e.g. projector).

Sellers often use pictures exhibiting attribute-based and benefit-based appeals together on the product detail page. Thus, examining the proportion and sequence of presentation might be more valuable for practical use. In addition, users' browsing behavior data on the product detail page can be taken into account, which could more accurately reflect real web-browsing behavior.

References

1. Crisp, R.J., Birtel, M.D., Meleady, R.: Mental simulations of social thought and action trivial tasks or tools for transforming social policy? Curr. Dir. Psychol. Sci. **20**(4), 261–264 (2011)
2. Holmes, E.A., Mathews, A., Mackintosh, B., Dalgleish, T.: The causal effect of mental imagery on emotion assessed using picture-word cues. Emotion **8**, 395 (2008)
3. Schlosser, A.E.: Experiencing products in the virtual world: the role of goal and imagery in influencing attitudes versus purchase intentions. J. Consum. Res. **30**, 184–198 (2003)
4. Elder, R.S., Krishna, A.: The "visual depiction effect" in advertising: facilitating embodied mental simulation through product orientation. J. Consum. Res. **38**(6), 988–1003 (2012)
5. Lancaster, K.J.: Consumer demand: A New Approach. Columbia University Press, New York (1971)
6. Graeff, T.R.: Comprehending product attributes and benefits: the role of product knowledge and means-end chain inferences. Psychol. Mark. **14**(2), 163–183 (1997)
7. Lautman, M.R., Percy, L.: Cognitive and affective responses in attribute-based versus end-benefit oriented advertising. NA-Adv. Consum. Res. **11**, 11–17 (1984)
8. Hernandez, J.M.D.C., Wright, S.A., Rodrigues, F.F.: Attributes versus benefits: the role of construal levels and appeal type on the persuasiveness of marketing messages. J. Advertising **44**(3), 243–253 (2015)
9. Fodor, J.A.: Imagistic representation. In: Imagery. MIT Press, Cambridge (1981)
10. MacInnis, D.J., Price, L.L.: The role of imagery in information processing: review and extensions. J. Consum. Res. **13**(4), 473–491 (1987)
11. Burns, A.C., Biswas, A., Babin, L.A.: The operation of visual imagery as a mediator of advertising effects. J. Advertising **22**(2), 71–85 (1993)
12. Babin, L.A., Burns, A.C.: Effects of print ad pictures and copy containing instructions to imagine on mental imagery that mediates attitudes. J. Advertising **26**, 3 (1997)
13. Petrova, P.K., Cialdini, R.B.: Evoking the imagination as a strategy of influence. In: Handbook of Consumer Psychology, pp. 505–524 (2008)
14. Bone, P.F., Ellen, P.S.: The generation and consequences of communication-evoked imagery. J. Consum. Res. **19**, 93–104 (1992)
15. Kamleitner, B., Feuchtl, S.: "As if it were mine": imagery works by inducing psychological ownership. J. Mark. Theory Pract. **23**, 208–223 (2015)
16. Kamleitner, B.: When imagery influences spending decisions. J. Psychol. **219**(4), 231–237 (2011)
17. Babin, L.A., Burns, A.C.: A modified scale for the measurement of communication-evoked mental imagery. Psychol. Mark. **15**, 261–278 (1998)
18. Aaker, D.A.: Managing Brand Equity. Free Press, New York (1991)
19. Keller, K.L.: Conceptualizing, measuring, and managing customer-based brand equity. J. Mark. **5**, 1–22 (1993)
20. Hollis, N.: Ten years of learning on how online advertising builds brands. J. Advertising Res. **45**(2), 255–268 (2005)
21. Collins, A.M., Elizabeth, F.L.: A spreading activation theory of semantic processing. Psychol. Rev. **82**, 407–428 (1975)
22. Raaijmakers, J.G.W., Richard, M.S.: Search of associative memory. Psychol. Rev. **88**, 93–134 (1981)
23. Yoo, B., Donthu, N.: Developing and validating a multidimensional consumer-based brand equity scale. J. Bus. Res. **52**(1), 1–14 (2001)
24. Curran, P.J., West, S.G., Finch, J.F.: The robustness of test statistics to nonnormality and specification error in confirmatory factor analysis. Psychol. Methods **1**(1), 16 (1996)

25. Kline, R.B.: Principle and Practices of Structural Equation Modeling. Guilford, New York (1998)
26. Hair, J.F., Anderson, R.E., Tatham, R.E.T.L., Black, W.C.: Multivariate Data Analysis with Reading. Maxwell MacMillan International, New York (1998)
27. Pierce, J.L., Kostova, T., Dirks, K.T.: Toward a theory of psychological ownership in organizations. Acad. Manage. Rev. **26**, 298–310 (2001)
28. Morewedge, C.K., Giblin, C.E.: Explanations of the endowment effect: an integrative review. Trends Cogn. Sci. **19**(6), 339–348 (2015)
29. Baxter, W.L., Aurisicchio, M., Childs, P.R.N.: A psychological ownership approach to designing object attachment. J. Eng. Des. **26**(4–6), 140–156 (2015)

Change Management of ERP Usage

Zhaopeng Meng[1(✉)] and Fan Zhao[2(✉)]

[1] Procter & Gamble, Cincinnati, USA
meng.ar@pg.com
[2] College of Business, Florida Gulf Coast University, Fort Myers, USA
fzhao@fgcu.edu

Abstract. IS continuance usage is getting more attention recently. For both ERP vendors and organizations adopted ERP systems, intension of continuance usage is critical in change management. The purpose of this paper is to survey the current literatures and summarize the factors influencing ERP users' behaviors. In this study, we propose a research model to predict ERP users' continuance usage behaviors. We believe this framework will help both researchers and practitioners in ERP research, design and development.

Keywords: ERP · Continuance usage · Change management

1 Introduction

ERP software (also known as enterprise systems, among other names) is a large software package designed to provide a single comprehensive database for business activities and integrate business processes across business functions into a single computer system. Through data standardization and process integration, ERP systems have the potential to facilitate communications and co-ordination, enable the centralization of administrative activities, reduce IS maintenance costs and increase the ability to deploy new IS functionality [1]. When they are well implemented, ERP systems are able to bring operational, managerial, strategic, IT infrastructure and operational benefits to their customers [2]. ERP systems have spread rapidly among organizations. According to Forbes [3], ERP market size was $24.5 Billion in 2012 (Fig. 1).

Although ERP systems promise a great deal, there are many aspects of ERP, such as implementation failures and cost of ERP, to be further studied in order to improve the effectiveness and efficiency of ERP features and functions in daily business operations. Statistics show that, before 2005, more than 70% of ERP implementations fail to achieve their corporate goals and the number of horror stories about failed or out-of-control projects is growing [4]. Despite great technical challenges, the biggest problems in ERP implementations are business problems [5] (Fig. 2).

Unlike traditional software packages whose emphasis was on technical aspects, an ERP system's development process shifts from writing software to understanding business processes [6]. Having extensively examined business practices in different industries, vendors of ERP packages write their own versions of best practices for business rules, norms and values into the software. In other words, these software packages have

M. Kurosu (Ed.): HCI 2017, Part I, LNCS 10271, pp. 188–202, 2017.
DOI: 10.1007/978-3-319-58071-5_15

their own inherent business strategy and structure. Moreover, since these systems involve different people from different departments within an organization, they have strategic implications and direct impacts on a company's organization and culture. In this sense, adopting an ERP system is not a matter of changing software systems but a matter of repositioning the organization and transforming its business practices (Fig. 3).

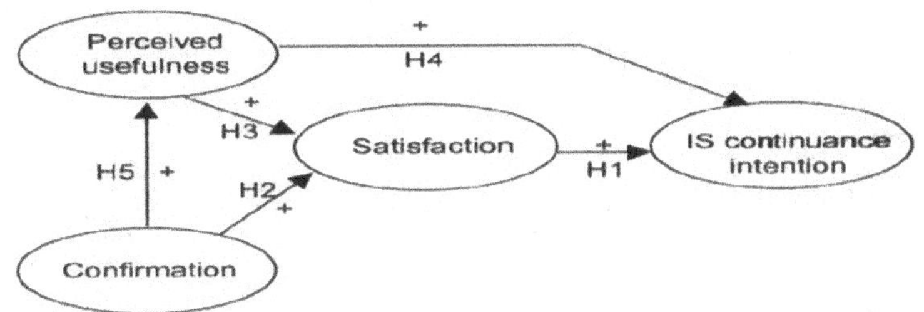

Fig. 1. A post-acceptance model of IS continuance

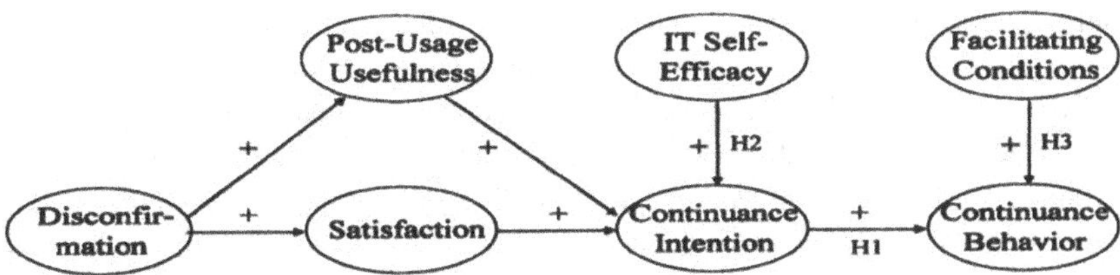

Fig. 2. The extended model of IT continuance #1

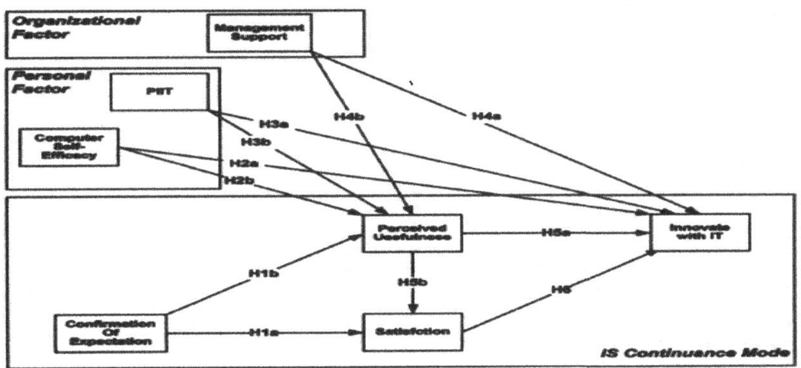

Fig. 3. The extended model of IT continuance #2

Recent literature reviews [7, 8] show that most existing ERP research focuses on package selection, implementation, training and managerial issues of ERP systems, not on ERP's post-implementation issues. With more and more experiences gained from past two decades, organizations and consultant companies are more confident of implementing and running ERP systems successfully. According to Staehr et al. [9], the ultimate impacts of ERP on the organization – once the system has been implemented and has been "shaken down" – are not as thoroughly researched. Therefore, understanding post-implementation of ERP will help organizations succeed longer after the ERP implementation. Recently, post-implementation issues are getting more attention, such as, optimization of ERP [7]. ERP optimization includes usefulness of ERP, achievement of competitive advantage though ERP, issues of ERP users and financial benefits of ERP [8] (Fig. 4).

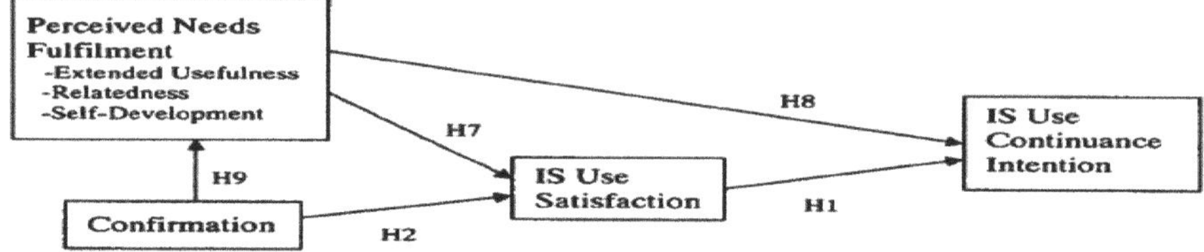

Fig. 4. Predicting continuance intention using perceived needs fulfilment.

User's perspective of ERP systems attracts researchers' attentions in current studies [7]. However, most of the current studies focus on system adoption and user satisfactions of the ERP systems [10]. Limited research reported in the literature are confined to areas such as usefulness of the system from the users' perspective [11, 12], and their conclusions solely rely on users' subjective opinions through survey questionnaires. This is the first study with experimental design to evaluate user activities and perspectives in ERP usage (Fig. 5).

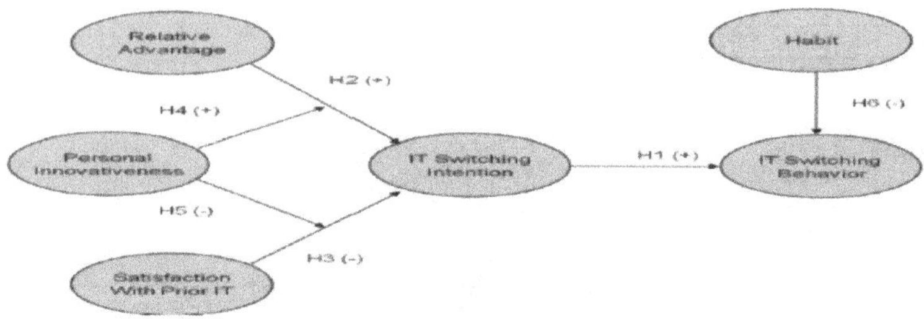

Fig. 5. IT usage switching model

2 Literature Review

There are many studies focus on how to persuade users to use IS or IT devices, such as research on IS acceptance models [13]. Recently, more and more researchers start to switch to post-adoption studies [14], such as how to attract consumers to continually use IS or IT devices, because IS/IT vendors and developer realize that retain their customers to keep using the IS or IT devices is getting more and more important to help them expand their revenue (Fig. 6).

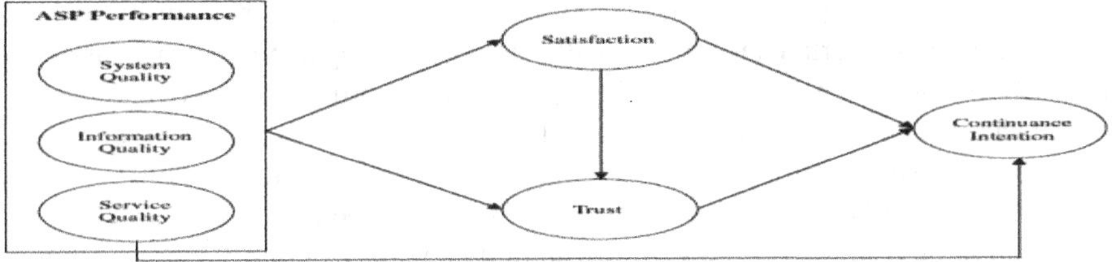

Fig. 6. Antecedents of application service continuance

2.1 Post-Acceptance Model of IS Continuance

The initial IS continuance research model, explaining customer behaviors of their intentions to continually use IS or IT devices, was developed by Bhattacherjee based on expectation-confirmation theory (ECT) [15]. Bhattacherjee [15] argues that Users' extent of Confirmation, which represents the level of a customer's evaluative response regarding his/her expectations of the IS [16], is positively associated with their satisfaction of using the IS and is positively related to perceived usefulness;

Users' perceived usefulness of IS, which is one of the key variables in technology acceptance model (TAM) [13], is positively associated with their satisfaction with IS use and associated with there is continuance intention;

Users' level of satisfaction with initial IS use is positively associated with there is continuance intention (Fig. 7).

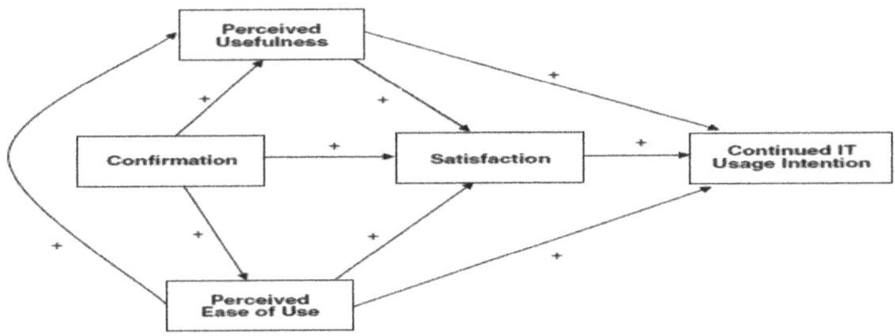

Fig. 7. Extended ECM

The author summarizes that IS continuance more depend on users' first-hand experience with the IS. IS vendors and developer should adopt two different strategies to maximize their return on investments in customers' training: emphasize potential benefits to the new customers while educating continued users on how to use the IS efficiently [15].

2.2 An Extended Model of IT Continuance

Based on the Post-Acceptance Model, Bhattacherjee, et al. [17] extend the model by adding three more variables: IT self-efficacy, facilitating conditions, and continuance behavior. Self-efficacy refers to one's conviction or belief in his/her ability to independently complete a certain task successfully [18]. According to previous research [19, 20], IT self-efficacy is a positive indicator to predict users' utilizations of computers and IS. Bhattacherjee, et al. [17] demonstrate that IT self-efficacy tends to cause users' belief in their ability to successfully utilize the IS right after their initial usage. However, they argue that and self-efficacy will not impact users' decisions/behaviors to continually use IT/IS. Facilitating conditions refer to the availability level of external resources required by IT usage, such as the speed of the Internet when users are playing online games. In the extended model of IT continuance, Bhattacherjee, et al. [17] conclude the following additional relationships:

Users' IT self-efficacy is positively associated with their IT continuance intention;
Users' perception of facilitating conditions is positively associated with their IT continuance behavior;
Users' IT continuance intention is positively associated with their IT continuance behavior.

In addition, by adding both organizational and personal factor groups, Wang et al. [21] propose a more complicated theoretical model. In this research model, one organizational factor, management support, and two personal factors, self-efficacy (CSE) and Personal IT Innovativeness (PIIT), are emphasized. Authors believe that management support includes most of the employee's IT usage expectations in organizational contexts, and CSE and PIIT are the two most recognized predictors of cognitive beliefs and IT usage behavior (Fig. 8).

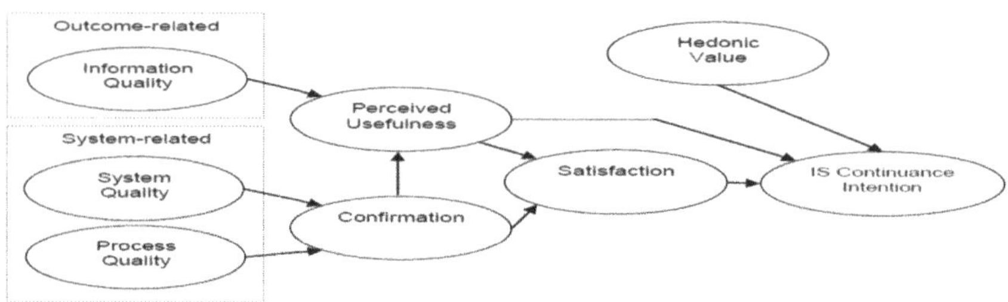

Fig. 8. Extended model of IS continuance for mobile applications

2.3 IS Use Continuance Intention Prediction Using Perceived Needs Fulfilment

Based on theory of human needs [22] and existence, relatedness and growth needs (ERG) theory [23], Yeh and Teng [24] develop a research model to predict users' IS continuance usage from perceived needs fulfillment. They claim that existence need from ERG theory, which refers to users' needs to perform the assigned job duty successfully, can be transferred to extended usefulness with perceived efficiency and perceived effectiveness. Additionally, the authors believe that relatedness need, which refers the individual intentions to communicate with other human beings, can be reflected to perceived relatedness to increase the users' interactions with others while using the IS. Similarly, growth need, which relates to "the urge of an individual to fully develop his/her potential", is transferred as perceived self-development fulfilment to obtain the opportunities to encourage users' learning, growth and self-development. In this research model, Yeh and Teng [24] suggest three new relations:

Users' perceived needs fulfilment of IS use is positively related to their IS use continuance intention;
Users' perceived needs fulfilment of IS use is positively related to their satisfaction with IS use;
Users' extent of confirmation is positively related to their perceived needs fulfilment of IS use.

2.4 IT Usage Switching Model

Prior IT usage studies, researchers in marketing started brand and/or services switching long time ago. Therefore, Bhattacherjee et al. [25] demonstrate a research model in merging of innovation diffusion framework and relationship between satisfaction and consumers' future choice behavior. Additionally, they believe that users' IT usage habits are directly influence IT usage because IT usage habits usually represent automatic and subconscious use with less reasonable intensions (Fig. 9).

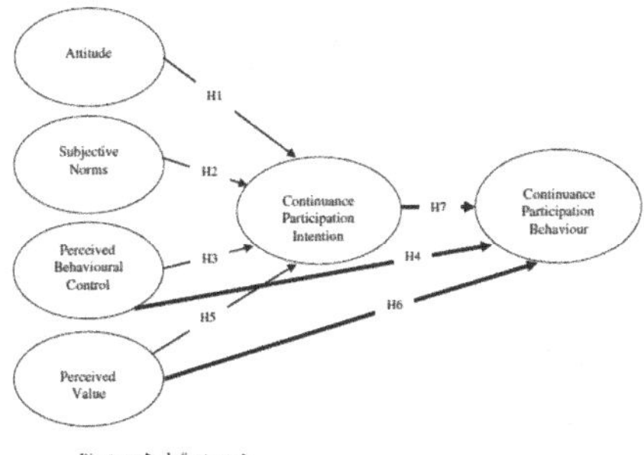

Fig. 9. Research model 1 for social network services

2.5 Research Model from System Perspectives

There are researchers who develop IS usage model from system perspectives instead of user perspectives. Kim et al. [26] believe that three Application Service Provider (ASP) performance constructs will impact users' trust and satisfaction of the IS and further influence users' continuance intension (Fig. 10).

2.6 Applications of Information Systems Continuance Models

Research model adopted to Mobile applications. Hong et al. [27] compared three research models, TAM, expectation-Confirmation Model (ECM) by Bhattacherjee [15], and the proposed Extended ECM by the authors, in mobile Internet. Since this is an early

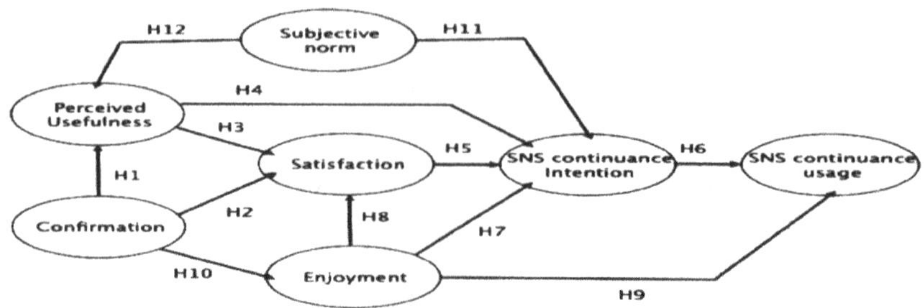

Fig. 10. Research model 2 for social network services

study, authors are kind of misunderstand the three models. They include TAM as one of the continuance research model. According to Bhattacherjee [15], TAM is just an IS acceptance model which focus on the initial usage of IS while as the other two models in Hong et al.'s study are related to continuance usage of IS. One variable that this study added is perceived ease of use, which is adopted from TAM. In the context of mobile Internet, it is a reasonable factor that impacts the satisfaction and IS continuance (Fig. 11).

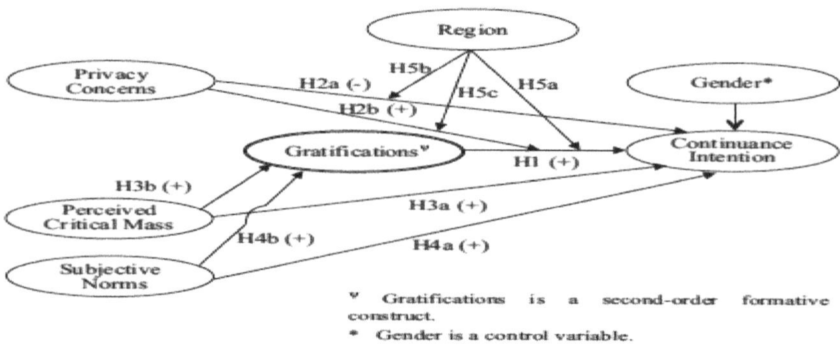

Fig. 11. Research model 3 for social network services

Chen et al. [28] expand the ECM with four more variables: Information Quality, System Quality, Process Quality, and Hedonic Value. Information quality, which refers to the quality of information output by the IS, and system quality, which focuses on the quality of functions/features in the IS, are generated from DeLone & MeLean research [29], whereas hedonic value, which refers to users' enjoyment of using IS, is adopted from Karaiskos et al. study [30] (Fig. 12).

Research model adopted to Social Network. With the development of web 2.0, social network becomes to a popular study area. By analyzing 403 students' data on Facebook, Al-Debei et al. [31] support the proposed model extended from theory of planned behavior (TPB). Perceived behavioral control, which refers to individual's perception of the behavior difficult level of completing certain tasks, and perceived value, which is

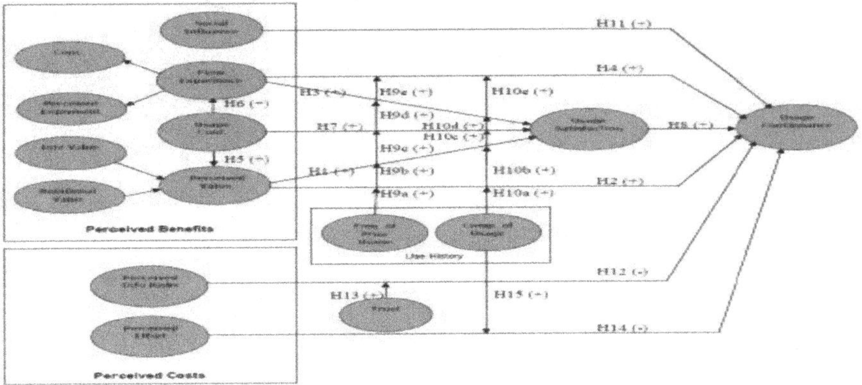

Fig. 12. Research model 4 for social network services

an extended construct of perceived usefulness, are added to the model predicting the continuance participation behaviors of students in Facebook.

Extended from ECM, subjective norm and enjoyment were added to the research model in context of social network [32]. Different from most of the IS, social network focus on communications among users, therefore, subjective norm, which refers to a person's behavioral intentions influenced by people who are important to him/her, is positively related to social network use. Enjoyment is another special factor associated with social network because one of the purposes people use social network is to have fun. Therefore, authors demonstrate that enjoyment is positively related to satisfaction, continuance intention, and continuance usage of social network (Fig. 13).

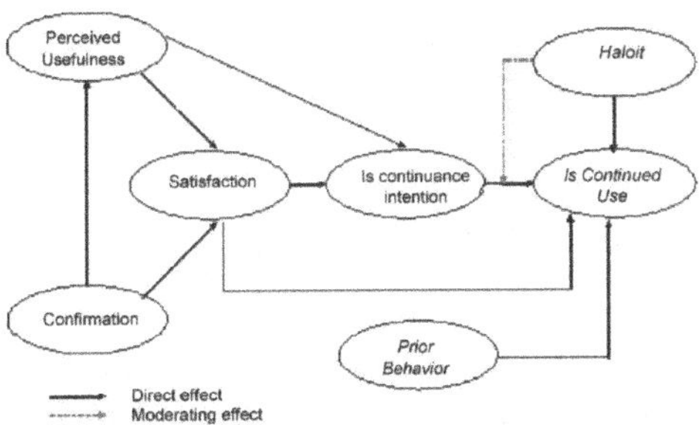

Fig. 13. Research model 1 for online learning

By comparing users in US and Taiwan, Ku et al. [33] propose another research model for social network continuance usage. Besides privacy concerns, region, and gender, which are three special factors in this study, perceived critical mass is a new variable in this model. Critical mass refers to the intention to use the social network when sufficient number of users are using the same system. Gratifications in this research model is the same factor as the previous one named enjoyment (Fig. 14).

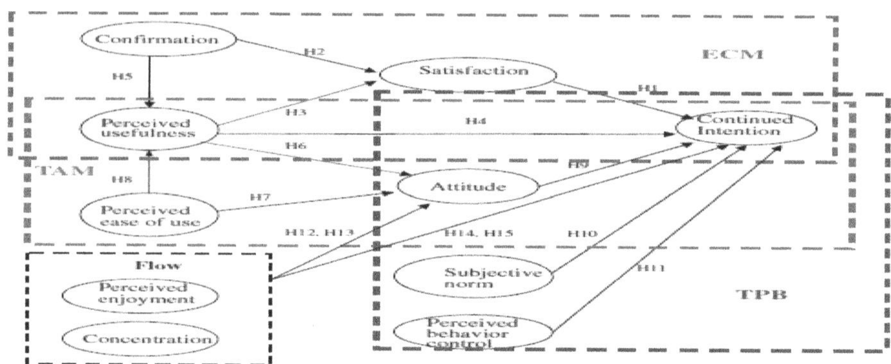

Fig. 14. Research model 2 for online learning

To better understand users' behaviors of continuing usage of social networking services, Hu and Kettinger [34] suggest adding three more constructional sections to the research model of IS Continuance based on social exchange theory, social capital theory, and flow theory. Perceived benefits include social influence, flow experience, usage confirmation, and perceived value. Perceived costs include perceived information risks and perceived effort. Use history includes frequency and comprehensiveness of usage (Fig. 15).

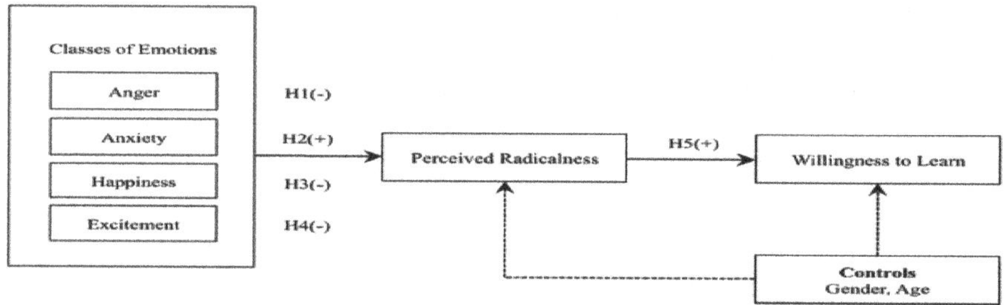

Fig. 15. Research model for IS training

Research model adopted to Online Learning Technology. In the proposed research model, Limayem and Cheung [35] argue that habit of using a technology could cause the continuance use because habit strengthens the continuance activities or decisions without thinking about it or performing further decision making process [36, 37]. Habit is added as a moderator variable impacting on the relationship between continuance intention and continuance usage.

By merging with TAM, Flow, TPB, and ECM research theories, Lee [38] introduces a research model for predicting users' continuance intention toward e-learning. 10 constructs are all suggested by previous research models. The results show a significant support of satisfaction as the predictor of users' continuance intention (Fig. 16).

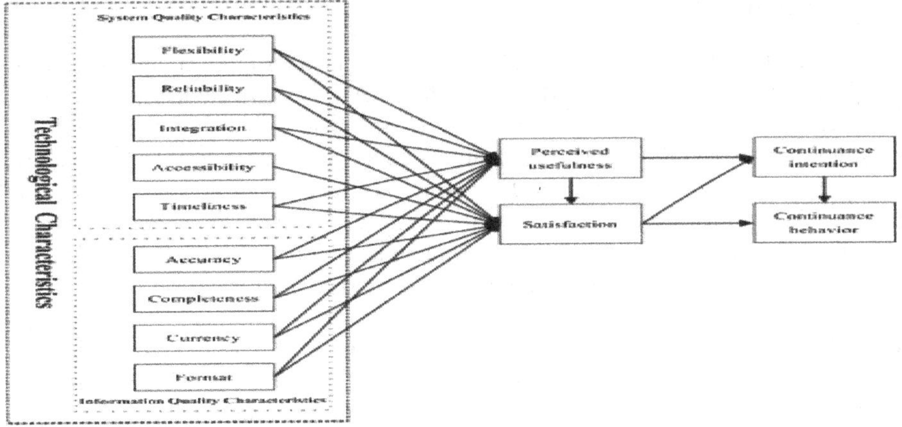

Fig. 16. Impact of ERP technology on user continuance behavior

Research model adopted to technology training. Without adopting any IS continuous theory, a unique study conducted by Darban and Polites [39] focus on users' emotions toward the continuous usage of IS from training perspective. Authors list four classes of emotions IS users may have during their trainings and suggest the emotions influence perceived radicalness and further impact willingness to learn under several control variables, such as gender and age.

3 Research Model

Most of the studies of continuous usage generally applies on any Information Systems. However, ERP is a special system that integrates many large Information Systems each including modules with hundreds of business processes. Therefore, we need to specialize our studies and find unique characteristics of continuous usage toward ERP systems (Fig. 17).

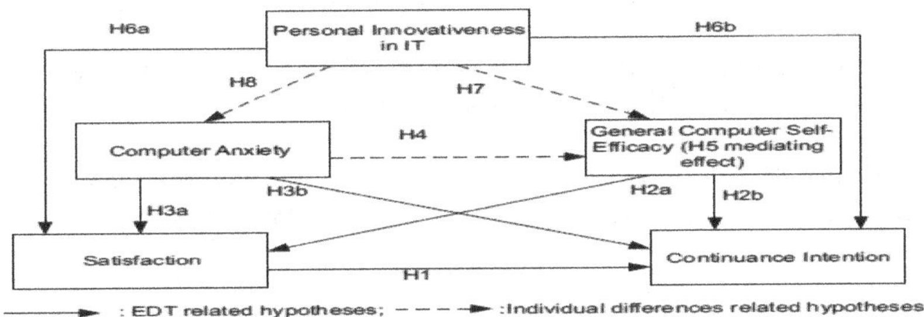

Fig. 17. Research model of continuance intention of ERP usage

3.1 Studies in ERP Usage

First, different with small information systems, ERP includes more complicated technological characteristics. Sun and Mouakket [40] categorize two technical sections from ERP technology perspective. System quality characteristics include flexibility, reliability, integration, and timeliness. Information quality characteristics include accuracy, completeness, currency, and format. However, data analysis results only support the positive relationships from reliability and completeness to both perceived usefulness and satisfaction, and three relationships including flexibility and perceived usefulness, accessibility and satisfaction, and accuracy and perceived usefulness.

Secondly, ERP end users have variety of computer background. Therefore, individual differences will impact users' continuance intention [41]. Based on expectation-confirmation theory (ECT) [42], Chou and Chen [41] proposed a research model of continuance intention of ERP usage and found all three individual differences factors, including general computer self-efficacy, computer anxiety, and personal innovativeness in IT, affect continuance intention either directly or indirectly through satisfaction construct (Fig. 18).

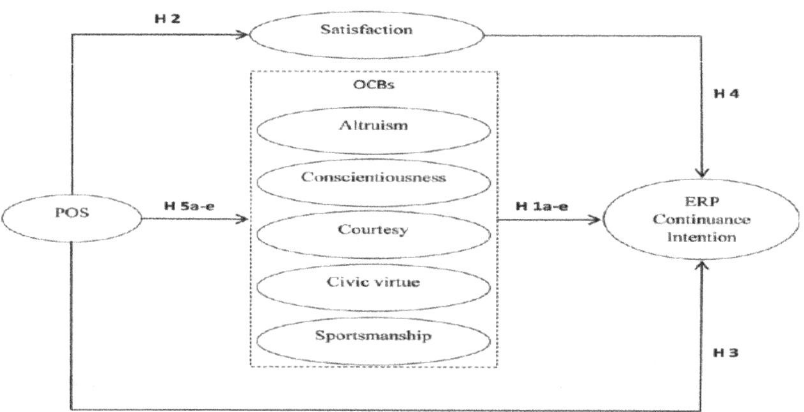

Fig. 18. Research model with OCBs' impact on ERP usage

Lastly, the users have to take various significant impacts from the organization regarding to the usage of ERP [43]. By considering Organizational Citizenship Behaviors (OCBs), and characteristics of perceived organizational support (POS), Soltani et al. [43] propose that OCBs impact users' ERP continuance intention and found conscientiousness, civic virtue, and sportsmanship mediated the relationship between POS and continuance intention.

3.2 Research Model

This study focus on ERP usage behaviors from change management perspective. Every three years, a major ERP upgrade and several small upgrades are typically needed to keep the system running smoothly. Therefore, organizations will spend a significant amount of money on employee training, especially after each major ERP upgrade. ERP projects bring a massive change in an organization's structure and affect the way people work and interact. Therefore the introduction of a new ERP system can cause resistance, confusion, redundancies, and errors. It is estimated that half of ERP projects fail to achieve expected benefits because organizations significantly underestimate the efforts involved in change management [44, 45].

To have a thorough understanding of users' reaction toward new ERP systems, we want to study what factors/constructs and how they may impact end users' continuance usage after switching to the new ERP system.

Based on the previous research models and previous ERP studies, we propose a conceptual ERP continuance model as depicted in Fig. 19. This model integrates the motivational perspective into the extended IS continuance framework and OCBs.

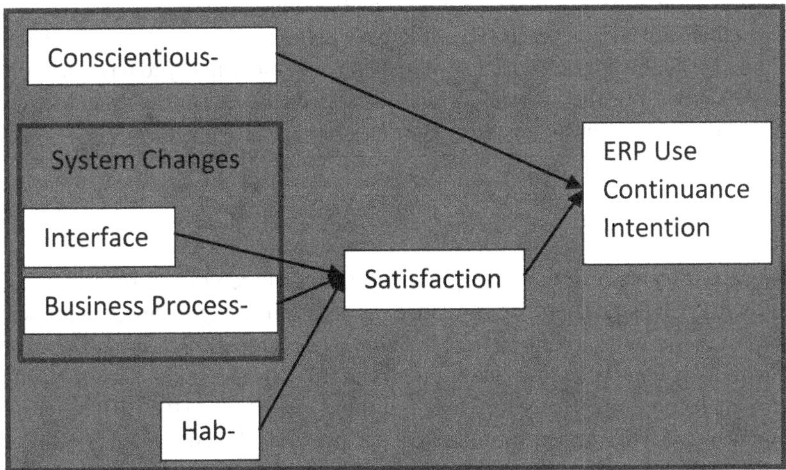

Fig. 19. Proposed Research Model

3.3 Constructs in Research Model

Conscientiousness. Conscientiousness refers to an employee's behavior following company rules and regulations [43]. The daily job for an ERP end user is to apply ERP functions and features to complete certain business processes. Employees are required, pushed, and regulated to be skillful in using ERP systems related to their daily job. Therefore, we believe employees who follows company rules and regulations are more likely to form continuance intention in ERP usage after the upgrade.

System Changes. According to Sun and Mouakket [40], technological characteristics of ERP systems influence end users' continuance intention and continuance behavior. From system upgrade perspective, most of the technological characteristics are similar or better comparing to the system before upgrade, such as reliability, integration, etc. However, after a major upgrade, system interface and some of the business processes will be dramatically updated. Therefore, ERP end users may have trouble with the interface of the new system and some of the new designed best practices upgraded from previous business processes. Hence, we propose that both system interface and business processes changes will impact end users' continuance intention.

Habit. Limayem et al. [46] argue that IT users who have been using a certain technology for some time are predisposed to continually use the system in an automatic and unthinking manner. A user's habit in IS usage becomes to an inertia to drive his/her continuance intention and less likely to switch to another system. This leads us to posit that ERP end users' habits will more likely influence their continuance usage of an upgraded system.

Satisfaction. Lee identifies, through his e-learning study, that satisfaction has the most significant effect on users' continuance intention. Previous studies from past two decades have shown that satisfaction positively influences behavioral intentions [47]. When end users satisfied with the upgraded ERP systems, they are more likely to have the behavior intention to keep using the systems. Thus, we argue that end users' satisfaction will positively impact their continuance usage of an upgraded ERP system.

4 Conclusions

The purpose of this study is to develop a theoretical research model regarding the key factors affecting ERP end users' continuance usage, from change management perspective, based on a literature review. There are studies developed IS continuance research model and models for applications in mobile technology usage, social network adoption, and e-learning technology. However, there is no study focusing on the ERP usage change management area. This paper summarizes the previous IS continuance studies and proposes a complete research model to explain our research question: what factors/ constructs and how they may impact end users' continuance usage after switching to the new ERP system.

References

1. Gattiker, T., Goodhue, D.: Understanding the plant level costs and benefits of ERP: will the ugly duckling always turn into a swan. In: Proceedings of the 33rd Hawaii International Conference on System Science, Hawaii (2000)
2. Shang, S., Seddon, P.B.: A comprehensive framework for classifying the benefits of ERP systems. In: Proceedings of the Americas Conference on Information Systems, Long Beach, CA (2000)
3. Forbes News. http://www.forbes.com/sites/louiscolumbus/2013/05/12/2013-erp-market-share-update-sap-solidifies-market-leadership/
4. Olson, D., Kesharewani, S.: Enterprise Information Systems: Contemporary Trends and Issues. World Scientific, Singapore (2010)
5. Davenport, T.: Putting the enterprise into the enterprise system. Harv. Bus. Rev. **76**, 121–131 (1998)

6. Kelly, S., Holland, C., Light, B.: Enterprise resource planning: a business approach to systems development. In: Proceedings of the Americas Conference on Information Systems, Milwaukee, WI (1999)
7. Schlichter, B., Kraemmergaard, P.: A comprehensive literature review of the ERP research over a decade. J. Enterp. Inf. Manage. **23**(4), 486–520 (2010)
8. Grabski, S., Leech, S., Schmidt, P.: A review of ERP research: a future agenda for accounting information systems. J. Inf. Syst. **25**(1), 37–78 (2011)
9. Staehr, L., Shanks, G., Seddon, P.: Understanding the business benefits of enterprise resource planning systems. In: Proceedings of the 8th Americas Conference on Information Systems, Dallas, TX, pp. 899–905 (2002)
10. Chang, M., Cheung, W., Cheng, C., Yeung, J.: Understanding ERP system adoption from the user's perspective. Int. J. Prod. Econ. **113**, 928–942 (2008)
11. Amoako-Gyampah, K.: Perceived usefulness, user involvement and behavioral intention: an empirical study of ERP implantation. Comput. Hum. Behav. **23**, 1232–1248 (2007)
12. Jones, M., Zound, R.: ERP usage in practice: an empirical investigation. Inf. Resour. Manage. J. **19**(1), 23–42 (2006)
13. Davis, F.D.: Perceived usefulness, perceived ease of use, and user acceptance of information technology. MIS Q. **13**(3), 319–339 (1989)
14. Shaikh, A.A., Karjaluoto, H.: Making the most of information technology & systems usage: a literature review, framework and future research agenda. Comput. Hum. Behav. **49**, 541–566 (2015)
15. Bhattacherjee, A.: Understanding information systems continuance: an expectation-confirmation model. MIS Q. **25**(3), 351–370 (2001)
16. Anderson, E., Sullivan, M.: The antecedents and consequences of customer satisfaction for firms. Market. Sci. **12**(2), 125–143 (1993)
17. Bhattacherjee, A., Perols, J., Sanford, C.: Information technology continuance: a theoretic extension and empirical test. J. Comput. Inf. Syst. **49**(1), 17–26 (2008)
18. Ajzen, I.: Perceived behavioral control, self-efficacy, locus of control, and the theory of planned behavior. J. Appl. Soc. Psychol. **32**(4), 665–683 (2002)
19. Compeau, D., Higgins, C., Huff, S.: Social cognitive theory and individual reactions to computing technology: a longitudinal study. MIS Q. **23**(2), 145–158 (1999)
20. Venkatesh, V., Morris, M., Davis, G., Davis, F.: User acceptance of information technology: toward a unifying view. MIS Q. **27**(3), 425–478 (2003)
21. Wang, W., Butler, J.E., Hsieh, J.P.A., Hsu, S.H.: Innovate with complex information technologies: a theoretical model and empirical examination. J. Comput. Inf. Syst. **49**(1), 27–36 (2008)
22. Maslow, A.: A theory of human motivation. Psychol. Rev. **50**, 370–396 (1943)
23. Alderfer, C.P.: An empirical test of a new theory of human needs. Organ. Behav. Hum. Perform. **4**(2), 142–175 (1969)
24. Yeh, R., Teng, T.: Extended conceptualization of perceived usefulness: empirical test in the context of information system use continuance. Behav. Inf. Technol. **31**(5), 525–540 (2012)
25. Bhattacherjee, A., Limayem, M., Cheung, C.M.: User switching of information technology: a theoretical synthesis and empirical test. Inf. Manage. **49**(7), 327–333 (2012)
26. Kim, J., Hong, S., Min, J., Lee, H.: Antecedents of application service continuance: a synthesis of satisfaction and trust. Expert Syst. Appl. **38**(8), 9530–9542 (2011)
27. Hong, S., Thong, J., Tam, K.: Understanding continued information technology usage behavior: a comparison of three models in the context of mobile internet. Decis. Support Syst. **42**, 1819–1834 (2006)

28. Chen, L., Meservy, T., Gillenson, M.: Understanding information systems continuance for information-oriented mobile applications. Commun. Assoc. Inf. Syst. **30**, 127–146 (2012)
29. DeLone, W., McLean, E.: Information systems success: the quest for the dependent variable. Inf. Syst. Res. **3**(1), 60–95 (1992)
30. Karahanna, E., Straub, D.: The psychological origins of perceived usefulness and ease-of-use. Inf. Manage. **35**(4), 237–250 (1999)
31. Al-Debei, M.M., Al-Lozi, E., Papazafeiropoulou, A.: Why people keep coming back to Facebook: explaining and predicting continuance participation from an extended theory of planned behaviour perspective. Decis. Support Syst. **55**(1), 43–54 (2013)
32. Yoon, C., Rolland, E.: Understanding continuance use in social networking services. J. CIS **55**(2), 1–8 (2015)
33. Ku, Y., Chen, R., Zhang, H.: Why do users continue using social networking sites? an exploratory study of members in the United States and Taiwan. Inf. Manage. **50**, 571–581 (2013)
34. Hu, T., Kettinger, W.J.: Why people continue to use social networking services: developing a comprehensive model. In: ICIS 2008 Proceedings, vol. 89 (2008)
35. Limayem, M., Cheung, C.M.: Understanding information systems continuance: the case of Internet-based learning technologies. Inf. Manage. **45**(4), 227–232 (2008)
36. Aarts, H., Verplanken, B., Van Knippenberg, A.: Predicting behavior from actions in the past: repeated decision making or a matter of habit? J. Appl. Soc. Psychol. **28**(15), 1355–1374 (1998)
37. Mittal, B.: Achieving higher seat-belt usage: the role of habit in bridging the attitude-behavior gap. J. Appl. Soc. Psychol. **18**(12), 993–1016 (1998)
38. Lee, M.C.: Explaining and predicting users' continuance intention toward e-learning: an extension of the expectation–confirmation model. Comput. Educ. **54**(2), 506–516 (2010)
39. Darban, M., Polites, G.L.: Do emotions matter in technology training? exploring their effects on individual perceptions and willingness to learn. Comput. Hum. Behav. **62**, 644–657 (2016)
40. Sun, Y., Mouakket, S.: Assessing the impact of enterprise systems technological characteristics on user continuance behavior: an empirical study in China. Comput. Ind. **70**, 153–167 (2015)
41. Chou, S.W., Chen, P.Y.: The influence of individual differences on continuance intentions of enterprise resource planning (ERP). Int. J. Hum Comput Stud. **67**(6), 484–496 (2009)
42. Oliver, R.L.: Cognitive, affective, and attribute bases of the satisfaction response. J. Consum. Res. **20**(3), 418–430 (1993)
43. Soltani, S., Elkhani, N., Bardsiri, V.K.: The effects of perceived organizational support and organizational citizenship behaviors on continuance intention of enterprise resource planning. Int. J. Enterp. Inf. Syst. (IJEIS) **10**(2), 81–102 (2014)
44. Motwani, J., Subramanian, R., Gopalakrishna, P.: Critical factors for successful ERP implementation: exploratory findings from four case studies. Comput. Ind. **56**, 529–544 (2005)
45. Pawlowski, S., Boudreau, M.: Constraints and flexibility in enterprise systems: a dialectic of system and job. In: Proceedings of the Americans Conference on Information Systems (AMCIS), Milwaukee, pp. 791–793 (1999)
46. Limayem, M., Hirt, S.G., Cheung, C.M.: How habit limits the predictive power of intention: the case of information systems continuance. MIS Q. **31**, 705–737 (2007)
47. Ajzen, I., Fishbein, M.: Understanding attitudes and predicting social behavior. Prentice-Hall, Englewood Cliffs (1980)

Fashion and Technology: Implications for the Social Acceptability of a Wearable Device

Kaitlyn Ouverson[1(✉)], Norene Kelly[2], and Stephen B. Gilbert[1]

[1] Iowa State University, Ames, USA
{kmo, gilbert}@iastate.edu
[2] User Experience Group, San Francisco, USA
norene@uegroup.com

Abstract. Where would you expect to find a smartwatch? Near fitness equipment, in a mobile phone store, or at a fashion accessory counter? The question of to which standards a wearable device should be held is an important one, impacting marketing, development, and research on wearable devices. This paper is an investigation of the relationship of aesthetics considerations, such as fashion, to the social acceptability of wearable devices, items often marketed as fashionable. By following the journey of the aesthetics items used by Kelly (2016) in the creation of the WEAR Scale, it is made clear that social acceptability and fashion are indeed separate constructs.

Keywords: Social cognition · Wearable technology · Social acceptability · Fashion · Aesthetics · Wearable computers · Human-computer interaction

1 Introduction

Wearable technology presents an interesting design problem in that wearables are not clearly defined as either "fashion accessory" or "technological innovation." This ambiguity makes it difficult to predict which factors determine whether a wearable, like FitBit activity trackers or Spectacles by Snap, will be adopted by a broad audience of potential wearers. For her dissertation, author Kelly [8] systematically created and validated the WEAR Scale, a 14-item questionnaire for predicting the social acceptance of a wearable device. As she followed steps for validation outlined by DeVellis [4], she gathered data about wearable acceptance from four studies. While she successfully validated the WEAR Scale, her data from the four studies offered varied results regarding the extent to which fashion and aesthetics affect the adoption of wearable devices. The current paper explores her results with a focus on that particular issue, looking more closely at the aesthetic considerations that have been identified as important in literature, as well as at data by experts on fashion and in the area of wearables, themselves.

Up to this point in the history of wearables, the focus of innovation has been in functionality despite the growing calls for fashion and aesthetic considerations for wearable tech [6, 11, 14, 16]. This push for more fashionable wearable tech has

M. Kurosu (Ed.): HCI 2017, Part I, LNCS 10271, pp. 203–213, 2017.
DOI: 10.1007/978-3-319-58071-5_16

produced worry for some, however. Edwards [3] expressed a fear of the marketing drive for fashion audiences limiting the innovation of the technology. His concern seems to have been realized in the success and failure stories of the wearable tech that have surfaced since Edwards's writing in 2003. Google Glass was briefly released for public beta testing from 2011 to early 2013 [11] and the Glass Explorer program was officially shut down in January of 2015 [2]. As highlighted by Page [11], the public welcomed Glass with incredible enthusiasm, but ultimately the wearable receded from the public eye as a highly unfavorable device. Google's failure with Glass was a multifaceted phenomenon. "Glassholes," as the early Glass adopters came to be called, eventually found little functionality in the device, while some others reported the failure to be largely due to the unattractiveness of Glass[11]. Still others noted that Glass was actually quite attractive in its design, insisting that developers simply needed a lesson in how to move from "attractive" to "fashionable" [16]. Additionally, the computer-enhanced eyewear raised a number of privacy concerns both for potential users in the medical field [17] and for anyone who had to wonder whether they were being recorded without warning [2].

However, the success of other devices, such as the FitBit and JawboneUP activity tracker bracelets and the Apple Watch, is proof that wearables do interest the public. In order to make the full shift from the attention of early adopters and technology-enthusiasts to the general public, however, wearable developers must gain a better understanding of how to market their devices. In her previous work, Kelly [8] defined wearables as computers or electronic devices displayed voluntarily in a manner similar to fashion accessories, like jewelry or sunglasses. For such devices, she noted, social acceptance is imperative because the indulgence in wearable technology is a very public affair.

As noted above, there is a lot of evidence pointing toward the importance of a fashionable, aesthetically pleasing wearable device. As noted by Aspers and Godart [1], fashion persists throughout contemporary life. It is of little surprise, therefore, that wearable devices are also influenced, and often molded by fashion. Besides this more philosophical reflection of the influence of fashion, it is also notable that like fashion accessories which are also worn publically, wearables are a form of nonverbal communication. Wearables establish an identity for those who don them, are expected to communicate positive messages, and display membership to likeable social groups[1, 7]. Fashion items must be consistent with the person's self-image to be acceptable on a personal level[7], and can even elicit dominance and subordinance behavior interaction in dyads, if the dress of one member signifies membership to a higher social class[9].

When author Kelly conducted research on wearables to construct the WEAR Scale [8], she gathered data from multiple sources:

1. Interviews with potential users of wearables ($N = 9$)
2. Survey of experts in the field of wearables ($N = 3$)
3. Survey 1 of potential users of wearables (Study 1, $N = 221$)
4. Survey 2 of potential users of wearables (Study 2, $N = 306$)

To explore the issue of whether fashion aesthetics contributes to a decision to adopt a wearable, it is worth examining findings related to aesthetics in each of these. At each step of the data gathering process, the focus was on determining which items (questions) for the WEAR Scale would be most predictive of social acceptability of a wearable device. While Kelly [8] focused on the construct of social acceptability of a wearable, a factor which she noted would be necessary for broad adoption, is it worth examining the data further to see whether "fashionable" might be an additional construct that is required for adoption.

2 Interviews and Experts

In initial interviews with the WEAR Scale's target population, people aged 18–30, fashion was indeed a consideration for some when assessing the social acceptability of a wearable. Fashion was mentioned as one purpose that a wearable could take on as well as a somewhat-important criterion for choosing a wearable. Interestingly, fashion considerations were not a popular answer among interviewees, as they believed that a "fashionable" wearable would wane in popularity when it is no longer trendy and that fashion isn't important to all the potential users of wearable devices. Thus, overall, despite the trends described above, the interview participants de-emphasized the role of fashion in wearable adoption. This was expected to be an artifact of the small sample size ($N = 9$), initially, but as discussed later in this paper, it is possible that this trend first noted in these interviews is an idea shared by many.

Kelly [8] also vetted the WEAR Scale items with three experts in the field of wearable technology for review. Two scale items, This device is stylish and This device is fashionable, related directly to fashion and were rated as being very relevant to social acceptability of a wearable. The experts rated the question category that these items belonged to, Aesthetics, as being quite relevant overall, averaging 1.60 out of 3, where 1 is very relevant, 2 is somewhat relevant, and 3 is not relevant to social acceptability of a wearable. This rating was among the best, with only the category Others' thoughts being rated as more relevant. Additionally, some of the experts offered comments which emphasized a focus on the aesthetics of the device.

It is worth exploring the trend uncovered in the population interviews further; does fashion matter when talking about the social acceptability of a device? Yang et al. [18] found that both social image and visual attractiveness are important factors in the public perception of wearables. If that is true, they may be part of the same construct, social acceptability. If not, the question of whether fashion or social acceptability is more important for wearable adoption is worth examining. By looking further at the procedural construction of the WEAR Scale, specifically in the journey of the question items which pertain to aesthetics, the authors seek to answer such questions.

3 Study 1

The WEAR Scale initially consisted of 50 question items and was established using the results of a thorough literature review, initial population interviews, and expert item review, all three of which were briefly described previously [see 8]. Not discussed in her previous work are the conclusions about fashion's role in the social acceptability of a wearable which can be pulled from her data. To test the validity of the WEAR Scale, the researcher recruited 221 participants from the Iowa State University student body to take a survey which asked those original 50 WEAR items, as well as demographic questions and questions which captured information on related concepts, such as Usability and Ease of Use and technology adoption preferences. Validation of the WEAR Scale also had implications for the relationships between concepts thought to drive the social acceptability of wearable devices.

3.1 Methods

Participants. All participants were required to be aged 18 to 30, because this is the population for which the WEAR Scale was developed. This population was targeted because young adults are generally considered the largest age demographic for technology adoption[15]. Of the 221 participants whose data was used in analysis, 57.5% were male ($N = 127$), 42.1% were female ($N = 93$), and 1 did not answer. The majority of the sample had some college ($N = 150$, 67.9%), 17 had graduated from high school (7.7%), 18 had graduated from college (8.1%), 21 had some graduate work (9.5%), and 15 held Masters, Ph.D., or other advanced degrees (6.8%).92.3% of participants did not identify as Hispanic or Latino/a ($N = 204$, 1 unanswered), 82.4% of participants identified as White ($N = 182$), 10.9% identified as Asian ($N = 24$), 3.2% identified as Black ($N = 7$), less than 3% identified as Native Hawaiian/Pacific Islander or American Indian/Alaska Native (2.3%, $N = 5$), and 3 participants did not supply their race.

Tasks. After reviewing the informed consent approved by the Institutional Review Board, participants completed the survey online, consisting of the 50 WEAR items as well as demographic and validation items. Participants were presented with two photos of the LG Tone + HBS-730 Wireless Bluetooth Stereo Headset Neckband (Fig. 1), and a description of the functions and purpose of the wearable. The Bluetooth headset was chosen for this study because it was expected to evoke useful variability – the neckband did not resemble a common accessory, but it was an existing product that participants might own themselves, or may have seen on other people.

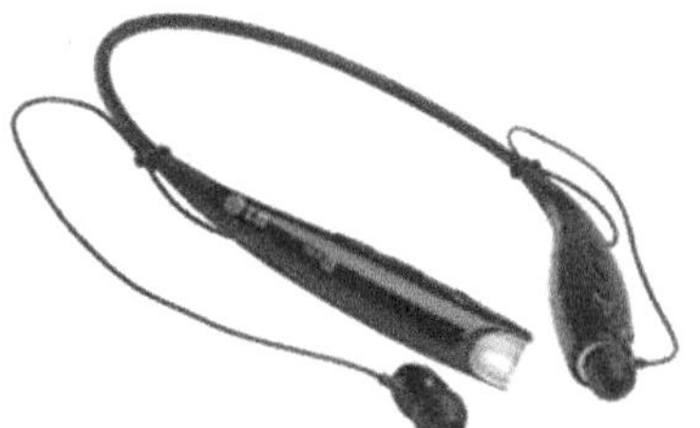

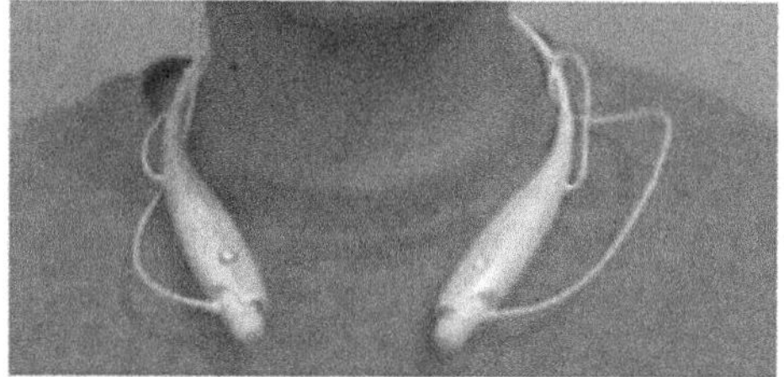

Fig. 1. The pictures shown to participants along with a description of the functions and purpose of the device. Left: vapingunderground.com/threads/lg-tone-hbs-730-wireless-bluetooth-stereo-headset-neckband-style-hbs730.73983/. Right: www.youtube.com/watch?v=ucFnZS8sOww

Dependent Variables. While many different dependent variables, including device WEAR Score and participant optimism, were collected, those of interest in this paper are those WEAR items relating to aesthetic (Table 1). These were originally included because the social acceptability of wearable devices was assumed to be related to theories of dress and fashion, as revealed in the literature review and the expert review. These variables also were used in the second user study, detailed below.

Table 1. The initial WEAR scale's aesthetic items loading values and the component each loaded on, when applicable, based off data collected using the Bluetooth Headset. The first three items loaded significantly onto a single component, while the remaining four did not.

Items	Component	Loading
Included in 31-item WEAR:		
This device is fashionable	2	0.85
This device is stylish	2	0.80
This device is aesthetically pleasing	2	0.78
This device is sleek, not clunky	2	0.56
This device seems to offer options for personalization, so that everyone is not wearing the "same thing"	2	
Not included in 31-item WEAR:		
This device might be considered disfiguring to its wearer*	–	0.34 and 0.33
This device is goofy*	–	0.72 and 0.35

* = Reverse scored

3.2 Initial Results

Of the 302 participants, 221 gave usable data. Of the 50 WEAR items, 31 items were found to significantly load onto one of two components. In this phase of testing, many of the aesthetics items (Table 1) were found to contribute to the understanding of the "social acceptability of a wearable device."

Two components or factors were identified, and items were attributed to a factor if orthogonal (Varimax) rotation resulted in a loading of at least 0.30 on one, but not more than one, factor. When an item loads on more than one factor, it becomes the responsibility of the researcher to assign said item to a factor – a process which adds subjectivity to the structure of the survey. Because a simple structure was desired for WEAR, an item loading on more than one factor was considered complex and was excluded. Before discussing the implications of this result for aesthetics, it is useful to consider Study 2.

4 Study 2

Because the WEAR Scale is intended to be valid for testing the social acceptability of any wearable device, the preceding Bluetooth study needed to be repeated with additional devices, with the intention of arriving at a common solution for all devices tested. As in the Bluetooth study, wearables were sought that would evoke sufficient variability. Therefore, Apple Watch (Fig. 2) and Google Glass (Fig. 3) were selected, with the Watch likely to be considered more acceptable due to its similarity to the common wrist watch, and Glass less acceptable because it is a head-worn device that initially raised some controversy.

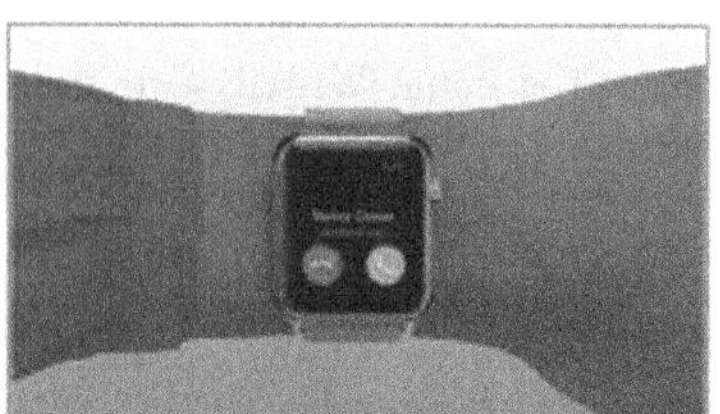
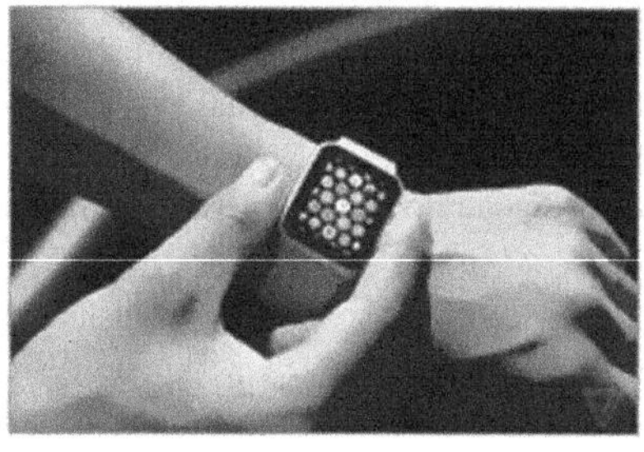

Fig. 2. The image of Apple Watch, shown to participants during the second user evaluation of the WEAR Scale. Left image: www.apple.com/shop/buy-watch/apple-watch-sport. Top right image: www.macworld.co.uk/how-to/apple/guide-phone-calls-on-apple-watch-3607555/. Bottom left image: www.theverge.com/2014/9/9/6124253/apple-watch-hands-on-video-photos.

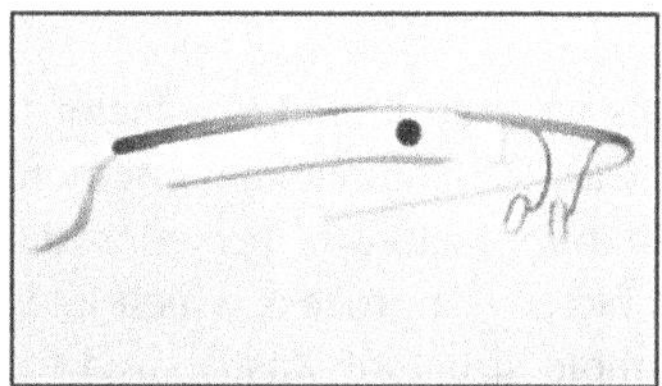
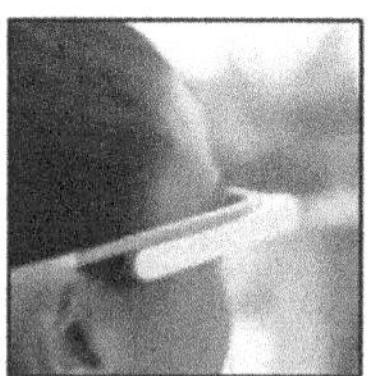
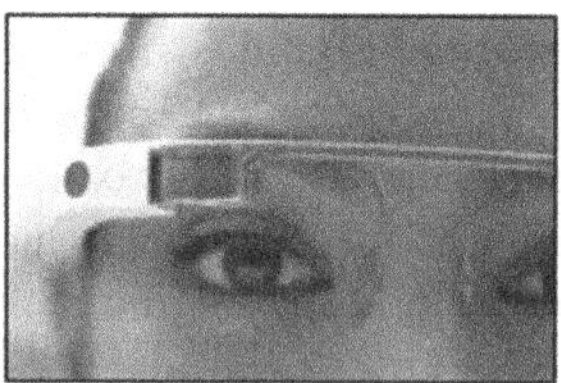

Fig. 3. The image of Google Glass, shown to participants during the second user evaluation of the WEAR Scale. Left image: www.pcadvisor.co.uk/feature/gadget/google-glass-release-date-uk-price-specs-3436249/. Middle and right image: fortune.com/2015/12/28/new-google-glass/.

4.1 Methods

Participants. As with the first study, all students at Iowa State University were invited via email to complete the survey online and were required to be aged 18 to 30 to participate. Of the 306 participants whose data was used in analysis, 56.5% were female (N = 173), 41.5% were male (N = 127), 1.6% didn't identify as male or female (N = 5), and 1 participant didn't answer. Again, the majority of the sample had completed some college (N = 234, 76.5%), followed by having completed some graduate work (N = 29, 9.5%), holding a high school diploma (N = 17, 5.6%), holding a college degree (N = 17, 5.6%), and holding Masters, Ph.D., or other advanced degree (N = 8, 2.6%). One participant did not respond to this question. 94.1% of participants did not identify as Hispanic or Latino/a (N = 288), 88.6% of participants identified as White (N = 271), 7.8% identified as Asian (N = 24), less than 3% identified as Black or American Indian/Alaska Native (1.3%, N = 7), none (N = 0) identified as Native Hawaiian/Pacific Islander, and 4 participants did not supply their race.

Tasks. A description of each device's functions and purpose again accompanied the images of Apple Watch and Google Glass. Because of the length of the survey, participants answered two surveys one week apart: the questions with regard to Watch and the questions with regard to Glass (with the demographic and validation items split between the two administrations). To account for the possibility of order effects, half of the sample saw the Apple Watch survey and accompanying validation items first and the other half saw the Google Glass survey and accompanying validation and demographic items first.

4.2 Initial Results

Again, some data were dropped due to participant age, short survey time, or skipped WEAR items, leaving 306 instances of usable data. Four components or factors were identified and items were attributed to a factor if Oblim in rotation resulted in a loading of at least 0.30 on one, but not more than one, factor. Just as for the first study, researchers desired simple structure for WEAR, so an item loading on more than one factor was considered complex and was excluded.

Of the 50 WEAR items, 34 items were found to significantly load onto one of four components for Apple Watch, and 30 loaded significantly onto one of four components for Google Glass. By examining the number of items loading, alone, one can see that some items needed to be thrown out due to inconsistency. Additionally, by examining Table 2, which details the loadings of the aesthetics items for Apple Watch, and Table 3, which details the same for Google Glass, one can see that there is inconsistency between items across components. Prior to this phase of testing, many of the aesthetics items (Table 1) were found to contribute to the understanding of the "social acceptability of a wearable device." However, the noted inconsistencies in how these items filter onto components speak to the importance of aesthetics in the social acceptability of a wearable device.

Table 2. The initial WEAR scale's aesthetic items loading values and the component each loaded on, when applicable, based off data collected using Apple Watch. The first three items loaded significantly onto a single component, while the remaining four did not.

Items	Component	Loading
Included in 31-item WEAR:		
This device is goofy*	3	−0.45
This device is sleek, not clunky	3	−0.77
This device seems to offer options for personalization, so that everyone is not wearing the "same thing"	3	−0.42
Not included in 31-item WEAR:		
This device is stylish	–	0.32 and −0.63
This device is aesthetically pleasing	–	0.36 and −0.58
This device might be considered disfiguring to its wearer*	–	0.31 and 0.32
This device is fashionable	–	0.30 and −0.57

* = Reverse scored

Table 3. The initial WEAR scale's aesthetic items loading values and the component each loaded on, when applicable, based off data collected using Google Glass. The first two items loaded significantly onto a single component, while the remaining four did not.

Items	Component	Loading
Included in 31-item WEAR:		
This device is sleek, not clunky	4	0.76
This device might be considered disfiguring to its wearer*	4	0.57
Not included in 31-item WEAR:		
This device is fashionable	–	0.54 and 0.39
This device is stylish	–	0.43 and 0.51
This device is aesthetically pleasing	–	0.33 and 0.53
This device seems to offer options for personalization, so that everyone is not wearing the "same thing"	–	<0.30
This device is goofy*	–	0.43 and 0.43

* = Reverse scored

5 Discussion

When comparing aesthetics items across surveys for Apple Watch (Table 2) and Google Glass (Table 3), it is apparent that none of the aesthetic items loaded consistently on a component, which means that any attempts to wrangle the items into a specific component or category is a very subjective choice. When deciding whether a question item belongs with all of the others that currently fit into a component, researchers add their own personal bias to the survey. This isn't to say that surveys in which this method of organization has been used are not valid, but rather that author Kelly did not want to complicate her survey.

Additionally, when comparing between the surveys for all three wearable devices, it is clear that none of the aesthetics items loaded consistently on any one component. It is important that the items load onto the same items when tested in different situations so that a survey continues to measure a construct reliably in different contexts. Kelly, by comparing the results in the two studies described above, determined that a 14-item, two-factor solution was the most appropriate structure for the WEAR Scale. All items included in this solution loaded consistently across surveys, and average Cronbach's alpha for the final solution was 0.84. [8 gives more detail about this process.]

Thus, the WEAR Scale was determined to be composed of the two factors Aspirational Desires and Social Fears. Despite the significance of aesthetics and fashion in the literature and in the initial analysis of the scale, this pattern of the importance of aesthetics in social acceptability of wearable devices was not stably supported in the WEAR Scale. The factor analysis suggested that aesthetics might be a construct completely separate from social acceptability, which, based off the responses of the three experts called upon to give insight to the WEAR scale, is not as clear for those developing wearable devices or researching their impact on and influence by human behavior. Reflecting on the interview data, while it was true that aesthetics did appear in respondents' answers, the responses more often pointed for a need of an absence of aesthetics as a consideration in social acceptability. Indeed, it is telling that participants indicated their belief that the trendiness of a wearable would negatively correlate with the lifespan of the device.

Another important lesson from the WEAR Scale is spelled out in the second factor, Social Fears. Arguably the biggest reason for Google Glass's downfall was the creepiness of the device [12]. Glass had video-capture functionality, and the only indication of whether the camera was active was a tiny light at the corner of the device's frame. Because of the inconspicuousness of Glass's recording function, it was quickly banned from bars due to privacy concerns, and from places like movie theaters and casinos where unauthorized recording is not condoned. Based on research demonstrating a preference for the socially acceptable variety of uniqueness [10], it could be argued that wearables are endeavoring to walk a very narrow path of uniqueness which falls at the edge of socially acceptable uniqueness, such as owning thrifted items, and socially unacceptable uniqueness, such as disregarding others' reactions to a behavior or item.

An alternative explanation of the threat sometimes caused by wearables comes out in a discussion of how fashion can be used. By observing what someone is wearing, it is possible to discern social rank, as shown in work by Kraus and Mendes [9]. Additionally, their research showed that in pairs, when it is clear that one is of a lower social class than his or her partner, the person of lower social standing will experience increased threat vigilance and an alteration of hormone levels, which is to say that knowing someone holds social dominance over oneself causes distress. Regardless of whether the social fears are due to the surreptitious functions of some wearables, or the symbol of power that they instill, it is clear that if a wearable is to survive among consumers, it must sufficiently deal with such social considerations.

6 Conclusion

It was hypothesized that fashion would be a central concept to the social acceptability of a wearable; however, it is apparent that such aesthetic considerations are actually *separate* from, but related to, a wearable device's social acceptance. Perhaps Wasik [16] had greater insight than he'd intended when he noted that wearables should either be hyper-attractive or microscopic. It would appear that subtlety is the most important aesthetic consideration when designing a socially acceptable wearable, as seen in the work done by Toney, Mulley, Thomas, and Piekarski [13] during the development of their e-SUIT.

Regarding the eventual exclusion of the aesthetic items that were originally part of the WEAR item pool, it is clear that there are discrepancies between experts in the field and the data obtained in empirical research. Aesthetics, though related to social acceptability, does not fall under the same construct. Further research should be done to determine exactly how these constructs are related.

Aesthetic appeal cannot outweigh the fears and concerns associated with wearables, which go beyond those noted with regards to Glass. These results suggest that it is important for industry designers to reduce the focus put onto aesthetics of such devices when designing for social acceptability, making sure to heed the potential social fears that such a device could trigger. If a wearable device has the potential to negatively impact the welfare of others or rejects social conventions, such as manners, it will lose favor with the public.

References

1. Aspers, P., Godart, F.: Sociology of fashion: order and change. Ann. Rev. Sociol. **39**(1), 171–192 (2013). doi:10.1146/annurev-soc-071811-145526
2. Bilton, N.: Why Google Glass broke. New York Times (2015). https://www.nytimes.com/2015/02/05/style/why-google-glass-broke.html?rref=collection%2Fcolumn%2Fdisruptions&action=click&contentCollection=style®ion=stream&module=stream_unit&version=latest&contentPlacement=37&pgtype=collection. Accessed 1 Feb 2017
3. DeVellis, R.: Scale Development: Theory and Applications. SAGE Publications, Thousand Oaks (2012)
4. Edwards, C.: Wearable computing struggles for acceptance: technology: the ultimate fashion item? IEE Rev., 24–25 (2003)
5. Gaddis, R.: Wearable technology and fashion: can they merge? Forbes (2014). http://www.forbes.com/sites/forbesstylefile/2014/02/10/wearable-technology-and-fashion-can-they-merge/. Accessed 31 Jan 2017
6. Gibbons, K., Gwynn, T.: A new theory of fashion change: a test of some predictions. Br. J. Soc. Clin. Psychol. **14**, 1–9 (1975). doi:10.1111/j.2044-8260.1975.tb00142.x
7. Johnson, K., Yoo, J., Kim, M., Lennon, S.: Dress and human behavior: a review and critique. Cloth. Tex. Res. J. **26**(1), 3–22 (2008). doi:10.1177/0887302X07303626
8. Kelly, N.: The WEAR scale: development of a measure of the social acceptability of a wearable device. Ph.D. Dissertation, Iowa State University (2016)

9. Kraus, M., Mendes, W.: Sartorial symbols of social class elicit class-consistent behavioral and physiological responses: a dyadic approach. J. Exp. Psychol. Gen. **143**(6), 2330–2340 (2014). doi:10.1037/xge0000023
10. Lynn, M., Harris, J.: The desire for unique consumer products: a new individual differences scale. Psychol. Mark. **14**(6), 601–616 (1997). http://scholarship.sha.cornell.edu/articles/183/. Accessed 9 Feb 2017
11. Page, T.: Barriers to the adoption of wearable technology. i-manager's J. Inf. Technol. **4**(3), 1–14 (2015)
12. Tene, O., Polonetsky, J.: A theory of creepy: technology, privacy and shifting social norms. Yale J. Law Technol. **16**, 59–102 (2013). http://digitalcommons.law.yale.edu/yjolt/vol16/iss1/2. Accessed 10 Feb 2017
13. Toney, A., Mulley, B., Thomas, B., Piekarski, W.: Social weight: designing to minimize the social consequences arising from technology use by the mobile professional. Pers. Ubiquit. Comput. **7**(5), 309–320 (2003). doi:10.1007/s00779-003-0245-8
14. Tzou, R., Lu, H.: Exploring the emotional, aesthetic, and ergonomic facets of innovative product on fashion technology acceptance model. Behav. Inf. Technol. **28**(4), 311–322 (2009). doi:10.1080/01449290701763454
15. Van Hemel, S., Pew, R. (eds.): Technology for Adaptive Aging. National Academies Press, Washington, D.C. (2004)
16. Wasik, B.: Try it on. Wired **22**(01), 90–99 (2014)
17. Wright, R., Keith, L.: Wearable technology: if the tech fits, wear it. J. Electron. Resour. Med. Libr. **11**(4), 204–216 (2014). doi:10.1080/15424065.2014.969051
18. Yang, H., Yu, J., Zo, H., Choi, M.: User acceptance of wearable devices: an extended perspective of perceived value. Telemat. Inform. **33**(2), 256–269 (2016). doi:10.1016/j.tele.2015.08.007

"Human Chef" to "Computer Chef": Culinary Interactions Framework for Understanding HCI in the Food Industry

So Yeon Park(✉), Sohyeong Kim, and Larry Leifer

Center for Design Research, Mechanical Engineering, Stanford University, Stanford, CA, USA
{syjpark, sohkim, larry.leifer}@stanford.edu

Abstract. Food is important and pertinent to everyone in more ways than one with its physical, social, mental, and cultural implications. The significance and interest in food and food-related activities are growing, and along with this movement there is a surge of human-computer interaction technologies in the food industry, also known as human-food interaction (HFI). There is a need to make sense of this burgeoning field, especially in a structured means to comprehend and analyze these technologies. The primary purpose of this paper is to introduce *Culinary Interactions Framework*, which provides a way of positioning and evaluating each HFI product and service in the food subsystem that focuses on the culinary processes, helps understand the HFI technology landscape, and identifies more nuanced points of interactions between human and robot. We also present ideas for future works to develop this framework further, with respect to more sophisticated levels of autonomy, expansion to other food subsystems beyond the culinary processes, and exploration of latent needs around HFI. The framework and further discussions are intended to better articulate, evaluate, and inform design and developments in HFI.

Keywords: Human-food interaction · Human-computer interaction · Human-robot interaction · Autonomy · Food · Food technologies · Cooking · Culinary process · Framework · Levels of robot autonomy · New product development · Ideation · Chef

1 Historical Background and Recent Trends in Human-Food Interaction Development

Computers entered the ecosystem of food production and consumption in the 19th century when vending machines were invented in England. Soon after, the concept of automation came not only to food production, but also to food service. The very first Automat was introduced in Philadelphia in 1902, and the New York-debut in 1912 enabled the Automat to spread out nationwide [1]. Inspired by the modernity and uniformity of automobile factories, as characterized by conveyor belts, buttons, and distributed labors, the Automat became the embodiment of technology at the manufacturing front in a commercial form. This automated service model birthed the rise of

M. Kurosu (Ed.): HCI 2017, Part I, LNCS 10271, pp. 214–233, 2017.
DOI: 10.1007/978-3-319-58071-5_17

fast food restaurants, with A&W Restaurants opening in 1919 and White Castle, McDonald, and Burger King joining its movement [1].

From the early 1950s, automation moved into private American households with inventions such as refrigerators and dishwashers. These sparked the emergence of the home appliance market as early forms of "personal service robots" [2]. Conceptualizations extending the home appliances to the smart age came with the prominence of spaceships in 1960s that brought the imagination of "smart home" to the public [3].

Since the Automaton and smart home appliances, robot development and commercialization in the food domain has been and is currently occurring at an unprecedented pace. All "three kinds of robots" classified by the United Nations (UN) have been on a steady rise, and this is true also for food technologies [2]. Examples of "industrial robotics" and "professional service robotics" in the food domain are as follows:

- Momentum Machines (http://momentummachines.com/) built a machine that autonomously produces 400 customized burgers in an hour without human input,
- Eatsa (https://www.eatsa.com/) takes orders via tablet computers and vends out freshly-prepared quinoa bowls, and
- Starbucks app (https://www.starbucks.com/coffeehouse/mobile-apps) allows you to order the drink you want at the location of choice on personal mobile devices.

From the three, the "highest expected growth rate," as forecasted by UN and currently holds true, is in "personal service robotics" [2]. This trend is also applicable for development of food robotics, and some examples of such are as follows:

- Moley (http://www.moley.com/) takes recipes and cooking methods of celebrity chefs and prepares world-class meals in personal homes with a robotic kitchen setup,
- June Intelligent Oven (https://juneoven.com/) allows users to broil, bake, and cook smart using its computer-based settings,
- Nomiku (https://www.nomiku.com/) automates and enhances part of cooking processes based on a sous-vide approach, and
- Starship Technologies (https://www.starship.xyz/) dispatches food delivery robots door-to-door.

As exemplified from emerging food technologies, computers and robots interpose between creator and end user in multiple ways. The most prevalent dynamics of interaction today seems to be HCHI (human-computer-human interactions). For example, when at Eatsa or when using the Starbucks app, there arises two human-computer interfaces, of one being an interface between the chefs (or baristas) and the orders and another interface between the customers and the devices.

Another popular trend is the conversion of what was originally an HHI (human-human interaction) model into an HCI model. Oftentimes, there is no direct interaction between the customers and chefs. Hence, we are prone to treating the chef as a robot, tastefully producing the food that is served. This dynamic has been heightened with the increasing automation in the production of fast foods, for which robots become the chefs. Such is the case of the automatic burger machine created by Momentum Machines. Taking the analogy further, the chefs are now "computers," the retailers are "interfaces," and the consumers are "humans." This is also the case with

Moley, a fully automated and integrated robot that cooks meals upon selection of the recipe and arrangement of the ingredients. In both instances, machines are not only transferring culinary experiences, but also replacing humans.

2 Problem Statement

Along with the rising trend in food technologies, academics and practitioners have started looking at food with the perspective of HCI since the early 2000s. Most research has been for development of specific applications such as cooking support, 3D fabrication, and nutritional consumption, to name a few [4–6]. Following the growing interest and development in food and HCI, HFI overviews and frameworks have also emerged.

However, in our investigation into food technology products and services, we found a dearth of academic research that covers and makes sense of the current trends in HFI development, despite steady growth in the general HRI research. For example, there have been extensive conceptual papers published in recent years to frame levels of robot autonomy [7] and to review frameworks of computational HRI to offer design guidelines for developing robots by considering social interactions with humans [8]. Yet, we have not found relevant literature that convey the human interactions with robot and computer chefs along with a series of culinary processes. We attribute this to the sudden growth in HFI technologies, for which the development of academic overviews and frameworks in the food domain have not been able to catch up. As there is no framework of HRI that is established for the domain of food itself, we have found a need for revisiting previous frameworks regarding HCI and HRI with a focus on food.

In HRI literature, the subject matter of the robot's levels of autonomy has been explored in depth. However, following the lack of research on HFI, the changes in the role of human with respect to the different degrees of autonomy of robots also have not yet been discussed for HRI of food technologies. With the rapid emergence of automated food products and services, we clearly see the need for developing frameworks that embrace the factors we listed above in order to suggest design guidelines and principles and to evaluate the effectiveness of available products.

In addition to the lack of HFI frameworks, there seems to be no connection made between the food-related activities, from food production to food waste, and the HFI products and services that address one or some of these activities. The food domain is expansive and the number of and kinds of stakeholders (e.g., farmers, chefs, distributors, consumers, etc.) involved in each of the subsystems and activities related to food vary at lengths. A relevant and comprehensive overview that aims to cover the trend of HFI research and interest recognizes that the food system is so large that "what is loosely referred to as 'food practices'—for example, shopping, eating, cooking, growing, and disposal—have grown out of the periphery of HCI research to become a central topic of interest in and of themselves" [6]. Although there are various attempts to define food practices [9, 10], it is difficult to find an overarching framework that embraces the myriad of food-related activities with socio-economic, technological, and environmental perspectives. Such an understanding will enable us to obtain a better sense of the HFI landscape, which includes what HFI products and services look like, how HFI developments occur, and how humans interact with these technologies.

The previous academic works in HFI can be summarized into two main topics, concerning (1) technological and computational challenges, and (2) socio-economic and cultural issues. The metaphor of "Star Trek-esque food scenario" seems to enlarge the opportunities of designing future food by addressing the technological part, yet we should not forget the core values of food as means of supplying nutrition, well-being, pleasure, connectivity, etc. [6]. Echoing this consideration, we also paid attention to research addressing human-centered approaches. For example, Grimes and Harper emphasize the significance of socially positive values of food technologies as "celebratory technologies" [4]. "Celebratory technologies," inspired by the "positive aspects of people's interactions with food," contrast with "corrective technologies" that aim to curb undesired user behavior and problems associated with food [4]. This is an important contribution that encourages addressing aspects other than "problems" around food, but the dyadic framework may be an oversimplification. We have therefore found a need to build a consolidated framework that addresses other sources of inspiration for the development of HFI technologies. This framework will inform and support the creation of guidelines for designers and developers.

3 Culinary Interactions Framework

3.1 Food Systems

We begin with a review of food systems as it is necessary to understand what activities happen in the world of food and what sort of food interactions between stakeholders occur during the activities. There are many different ways to define and display food systems based on varying perspectives of food traditions, food policy, food security, sustainability, regional boundaries, etc. [9, 10]. Among them, we look at food systems from production ("farm") to consumption ("table"), summarizing the primary activities in Table 1 below. Among the broad range of food-related activities, we have decided to focus on the culinary and serving pursuits in order to discern a series of human activities and to investigate the interactions between "human" and "computer/robot" chefs. We have decided to include "serving" in our scope of work, as it is a critical step that connects a chef/cook to a customer, by exchanging feedback in between.

3.2 Culinary Processes and Serving

"Culinary" process defines practices related to kitchen or cookery. Although cooking is one of the oldest human practices, codifying this practice as knowledge and processes has been relatively recent. Auguste Escoffier greatly contributed to the industrialization and modernization of the restaurant kitchen. His book, *Le Guide Culinaire* [11], introduces the culinary processes from ingredient preparation, sanitation, and cooking methods to presentation and services [12]. Horng and Hu [13] claim there are two sides of culinary processes, a survival-based side and a cultural-aesthetic one.

Table 1. Primary food-related activities in the food subsystems. (Table 1 includes both the industrial (B2B) and consumer (B2C) food subsystems and activities.)

Subsystems	Examples of activities
Production	Farming, growing, harvesting
Storage	Packaging, labeling, freezing
Culinary processing	Preparing, cooking
Foodservice	Serving, catering, transporting, wholesale/retailing
Food data management	Communicating, collecting, storing and accessing data (e.g., nutrition, culinary know-how, and knowledge, etc.)
Consumption	Eating, digesting
Waste	Composting, recycling

Whereas the former side of cooking is generally operational, we view the latter part as creative. The aim of this paper is to generate a conceptual framework that displays how a human and/or computer chef creates a new dish/meal and how they cooperate/collaborate for a creation of food. Thus, it was necessary to review the food-related activities mapping with the new product development (NPD) process, often framed in six steps: planning - concept development - system level design - detail design - testing and refinement - production and ramp-up [14].

Drawing parallels between the NPD and food creation/development, we framed the processes for the use of HCI in food into the following six steps: ideation - procurement - preparation - cooking - plating/assembly - serving. The first five steps occur in the back-side of house, which usually take the form of a kitchen, and the serving part takes place in the front-side of house, which could be in the context of a restaurant, takeout/delivery service, or even in the domestic context. We articulate these steps in order to systematically study and analyze the processes in food creation/development. We recognize that these steps may not occur in the order presented and are interchangeable in some cases, but we have chosen to follow this order as they are standard protocol that we follow, and because by establishing this can we then expand upon it further.

Ideation is the stage during which chefs generate a concept of dish/meal by considering multiple factors such as dining ambiances, financial limitations, customer needs, prep/cooking times, etc. A big part of ideation is inspiration, which plays a significant role in bringing creativity and motivation to chefs before and/or during the ideation stage. Inspirations come from seasonality, nutrition and health concerns of customers, socio-economic contexts of consumption, food technologies, globalization/ internationalization of cuisines, special ingredients, etc. Studies about renowned chefs reveal that these inspirations are used as the basis for creative methods of cooking [15]. Once the ideation of a concept of dish/meal is completed, the ingredients, tools, and materials need to be in-hand and available for use. We call this process **procurement**, and this can be achieved by various means such as grocery shopping, retail/distribution, etc. Another means is "foraging," which is carried out by a professional procurement personnel to search and source the raw materials. Oftentimes packaged goods are kept in reserve before their use, thus we include in this step the concept of storage, which considers packaging size, shelf life, and quantity. **Preparation** stage is after all the procurement is completed. Tasks are distributed to the relevant cooks/chefs, usually based on their experiences and expertise. The activities associated with preparation ranges the whole gamut, from washing, rinsing, and plucking, to chopping, slicing, and mashing. Once the preparation of raw ingredients is completed, **cooking** begins. Cooking is a series of activities whereby raw ingredients are transformed generally by a reaction to heat, although there are exceptions such as Japanese sushi and Peruvian ceviche. Cooking methods vary based on food cultures, regions, technologies, traditions, economics, tools, etc. For the last two decades, technology and science have played a significant role in the cooking world by birthing new cooking techniques and tools/appliances. Molecular gastronomy, experimental cuisine, and multi-sensory cooking are such examples. **Plating/Assembly** is the final step at the kitchen before the finished dish/meal is served to the customer. Plating includes choosing an appropriate container to serve; balancing colors, textures, and portions; and finishing the food at the right temperature. As this step usually completes the final products, it requires an aesthetically-pleasing presentation. According to an experiment at Oxford University [16], people perceive better taste and dining experience by an enhanced visual presentation of food. This study argues for the importance of an aesthetic appeal, by claiming that "people eat by eyes first." **Serving** food is the step in between cooking and eating, and this can be manifested in various types from professional individual service (waiter/waitress), take-out service, self-service, group service (i.e., buffet), etc.

So far, we have described the food-making processes based on "human" chefs' activities as the basis for HFI development. These six steps will serve as a conceptual foundation to view the HFI activities from the next section.

3.3 Primitives of Robotics in HFI

The rise in development and popularity of food technology is currently disproportionate with our understanding of HRI and robot autonomy categorized in the food domain. There is also a lack of a comprehensive understanding on how the HRI viewpoint fits into the bigger food system.

As developments in HFI are based on the concepts foundational to HRI, we build upon the established three primitives of robotics: sense, plan, and act (SPA) [17]. Here, we do not distinguish between the three paradigms of the primitives (i.e., hierarchical, reactive, and hybrid deliberative/reactive). Although the dynamics and causalities between the primitives are important, our aim is to bring more clarity to the overall understanding of HFI. Thus, we have constructed a framework that explains SPA primitives for HFI in its relevant context and captured examples of HFI products and services that help illustrate what the change from human to robot entails for these primitives.

As we have previously discussed, we constructed the *Culinary Interactions Framework* for the front-house and back-house culinary processes. In our examination of the primitive of "sense," we have found that breaking it down to who, what, when, where, and how helps paint a more comprehensive picture of the wide range of sensory

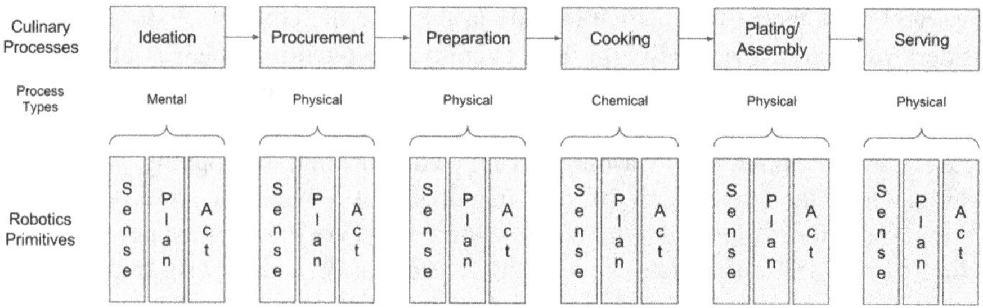

Fig. 1. Robotics primitives within the culinary processes and serving

input that gets translated into the output of sensed information. As for the primitive of "plan," the directives that are derived as output from the sensed information are done so by algorithms. There are many variations in the algorithms—it could be implemented by a human or robot, it could be based on subjective judgment or objective empirical data, it could be static or evolving as it learns, etc. However, one constant goal for the "plan" primitive is to take all the input to derive a directive that leads to "a well-balanced and optimized final decision and action," whether it is in the form of a sequence, method of choice, etc. Lastly, the primitive of "act" is the "actuator commands that stem forth usually from the "how" asked in the primitive of "sense" [17].

Having laid out the primitives of sense, plan, and act—primitives that are developed for robotics but comes from conventional human roles and actions—the tasks that the robot can perform in place of the human becomes very clear. With this clarity of tasks performed by the robot, we are able to articulate the role of the robot, identify the points of human-robot interaction, and further redefine autonomy in the current context of HFI.

3.4 Levels of Autonomy

We have applied the rigor and framework of HRI research to our analysis of HFI, including the concepts of autonomy appropriate for this domain. As stated by Beer et al., "in HRI, there are two schools of thought in conceptualizing autonomy: (1) higher robot autonomy requires less frequent interaction; and (2) higher robot autonomy requires higher levels or more sophisticated forms of interaction" [7].

These two conceptualizations, though important, are not embedded in the definition of autonomy proposed by Beer et al.: "the extent to which a robot can sense its environment, plan based on that environment, and act upon that environment with the intent of reaching some task-specific goal (either given to or created by the robot) without external control" [7]. With HFI in particular, we also find that the word "environment" may limit our understanding with its implication for physical boundaries. Therefore, we propose the following as our definition of autonomy for the clarity of this paper:

The quantitative and/or qualitative extent to which a robot can **sense** its environment, constituents in the environment, and/or relevant sensory signals for a designated goal; **plan** based upon such sensory input to obtains directives; and **act** upon one or a combination of these inputs (sensed information or directives) with the intent of reaching a **defined task-specific goal** without external **stimuli**.

Here, by "quantitative" we mean the number of tasks the robot is capable of performing continuously on its own without human interaction, and by "qualitative" we mean the level of difficulty, sophistication, or complexity of tasks. With the SPA defined for each of the stages within the culinary process, the *Culinary Interactions Framework* helps to better understand autonomy of HFI.

Figure 1 and Table 2 exemplify tasks in the culinary process and these tasks can be completed either by a robot or human. By identifying the tasks that can be carried out by an HFI product or service through the *Culinary Interactions Framework* (Fig. 1 and Table 2), we are able to get a clear picture of the tasks that can be or are carried out by the robot instead of the human, leading to a comprehensive overview of the robot's role. Furthermore, by making connections between the tasks described, we can deduce the number of tasks or processes the robot is able to perform without human interaction. In other words, HFI products and services that have longer chains of tasks can be interpreted as having "higher robot autonomy." With the numeration of continuous task-completions made possible by this framework, we are able to start quantifying "robot autonomy" with regards to required frequency of human interaction.

3.5 Human Roles and Points of Interactions

The second conceptualization of robot autonomy deals with the quality of the interaction. "Sophisticated forms of interaction" can be difficult to define, as they may be subjective. Though difficult, we can begin to address the sophistication level of interaction by further distinguishing the tasks that the robot implements (i.e., answering the "why" question in the completion of task) of either human-supporting or self-implementing, or both.

For example, in the case of the robot implementing an action, often the human's role becomes one that is supervisory. This is a passive role that may or may not lead to sophisticated action-taking. In the event that there is no intervention, the human is on standby, a rudimentary level of interaction. On the other hand, if a technical failure occurs, higher levels of interaction will be necessary: while the robotic system senses, identifies, analyzes, and notifies the human of the issue, the human learns about and tries to fix the issue. Such scenarios will also be applicable for our interactions with HFI as the basic interactions between humans and robots are similar. In addition, we are certain that the level of sophistication will increase, especially in the domain of food, as we often associate food and the practices around it with our emotions and feelings. With a focus on these two core intangible manifestations and increasing development of social robots, higher levels of HFI will be possible and Table 2 will be helpful in identifying the various ways in which "higher levels of interaction" or "sophisticated forms of interaction" can be explored.

We aim to address each of the primitives of robotics and levels of autonomy by exemplifying some of current products/services in Tables 3–6, which supports the identification of the points of HFI through the articulation of:

Table 2. Examples of robotics primitives within the culinary processes and serving.

Culinary Processes	Ideation			Procurement			Preparation		
SPA	Sense	Plan	Act	Sense	Plan	Act	Sense	Plan	Act
Examples of SPA Tasks	**Who:** Who will be eating the food–babies or people with dietary restrictions? **What:** What is in season? What are the nutritional needs of the consumers? What is the context of this meal? What kind of recipes are available? What is the budget for the meal? What kind of emotions or experiences will the meal trigger? **When:** When will the food be served–when it is done, at a specified time, etc.? **Where:** Where will the food be served–at home, at a facility, at a restaurant, etc.? **How:** How will the food be procured, prepared, cooked, and served? How will the food look, feel, smell, and taste? How will the consumers feel about the dish/meal and the ambience?	Decide which of these sensed conditions to consider for a well-balanced and optimized final decision and action for ideation–sequence, method of choice, etc.	Create or decide upon a menu, food concept, etc. and on the compatible or appropriate cooking methods/general guidelines for preparation work.	**Who:** Who is ordering, searching, or delivering? **What:** What ingredients are available and what are missing? What transportation methods are available for delivery to the kitchen? **When:** When will the ingredients be procured–right before the preparation stage, weeks in advance, while cooking, etc.? **Where:** Where will the ingredients be sourced–locally or globally? **How:** How will the ingredients be acquired–delivery by car, plane, etc.? Will it be packed as is in a styrofoam box with dry ice, as frozen, or by a refrigeration unit inside vehicle maintained at its optimal temperature?	Decide which of these sensed conditions to consider for a well-balanced and optimized final decision and action for procurement--sequence, method of choice, etc.	Shop, purchase, and acquire new ingredients or reuse what's in the fridge, inventory, etc.	**Who:** Who will be preparing–washing, chopping, julienning, slicing, etc.? For whom is the preparation necessary–the cook, the consumer, etc.? **What:** What are the ingredients to be prepared? What tools will be used to prepare the ingredients? **When:** When should each of the ingredients start being prepared? **Where:** Where should the ingredients be prepared–at which station, on which chopping board, in which bowl, etc.? **How:** How will the ingredients be prepared–will they be diced or sliced, will they be kept in a particular container or method after the preparation work before the actual cooking, etc.?	Decide which of these sensed conditions to consider for a well-balanced and optimized final decision and action for preparation–sequence, method of choice, etc.	Wash, cut, dice, julienne, smash, roll, scrub, mix, freeze, shred, etc.

(continued)

Table 2. *(continued)*

Culinary Processes	Cooking			Plating/Assembly			Serving		
SPA	Sense	Plan	Act	Sense	Plan	Act	Sense	Plan	Act
Examples of SPA Tasks	**Who:** Who will be cooking–head chef, sous chef, robot, etc.? For whom is the food cooked? **What:** What is going to be cooked? What tools or facilities will be utilized for cooking? **When:** When will the cooking happen–right before or days before serving? **Where:** Where will the cooking occur–in a stove, on the grill, out in the backyard, etc.? **How:** How will the food be cooked (methods)?	Decide which of these sensed conditions to consider for a well-balanced and optimized final decision and action for cooking–sequence, method of choice, etc.	Sautée, pan-fry, bake, fry, broil, etc.	**Who:** Who will assemble and plate the food? Who decides the final display and readiness of the food for serving? **What:** What is the food to be assembled together? What are the tools used to assemble the dish? Which plate or platform will be used to display the food? What rules of plating will be applied? What will be the plating proportions? **When:** When should the assembly and plating occur–after heating up the plate, right after the food has been cooked? Does the dish need to rest before serving? **Where:** Where should the assembly occur–next to the stove, at another station, in front of the consumer, etc.? **How:** How will the food be assembled or plated together–three-dimensionally, by painting, in clockwise direction, or from hot to cold?	Decide which of these sensed conditions to consider for a well-balanced and optimized final decision and action for plating/assembling–sequence, method of choice, etc.	Plate, assemble, mix, pile, drip, etc.	**Who:** Who will be serving–by a server or a robot? Who will be served–for an individual, the group, all the customers, or for takeaway customers or those dining in, etc.? **What:** What will be served–dish, condiments, etc.? **When:** When will the food be served? **Where:** Where will the food be served–at the counter, where the customer is seated, at a buffet setup, for delivery, etc.? **How:** How will the food be served–all at once or at separate intervals, at room temperature or at extreme temperatures, from left to right or vice versa, etc.? How long will the servicing take?	Decide which of these sensed conditions to consider for a well-balanced and optimized final decision and action for serving–sequence, method of choice, etc.	Service à la russe (serve individually over multiple times in a formal dining context), service à la française (serve a group meal), handover (takeaway/to-go meals), deliver, etc.

- Switch in performer of tasks, from human to robot,
- Delineation of robot roles and the respective changes in roles of human,
- Points of interaction between human and robot, and
- Types and forms of interaction between human and robot.

With our framework, listing, visualizing, and understanding the points of interaction between human and robot become easier. This, in turn, allows designers in HFI development to systematically create a variety of interactions between human and robot.

3.6 Interpreting "Celebratory Technologies"

In our framework, we have identified tasks that the robot takes on in lieu of the human. Addressing these task-oriented outcomes with the skew of HRI may easily lead to "corrective technologies" [4]. This is especially true for tasks in the culinary processes, as these technologies aim to prevent, support, or substitute human behaviors/activities. Though an important distinction, the naming and descriptions of corrective and celebratory technologies may convey that the former only solve "problems," eliminating negative emotions without producing positive feelings [4]. Although the motivation for HFI development may be focused on such, the results are not as the model may suggest.

Corrective technologies are not mutually exclusive from celebratory technologies, and they may also engender the positive emotions and benefits that the celebratory technologies aim to fulfill. We find that what is classified as examples of "positive interactions" achieved by celebratory technologies are usually the by-products or higher goals of the products and services developed. HFI that tackle conventional problems of efficiency, productivity, safety, and delegation, may also produce benefits that were not articulated during the design process and/or prior to use.

Looking at our framework, the emphasis of celebratory aspects is especially important at the ideation stage. Through a systematic exploration in the ideation stage of the primitive "sense" with questions such as "what kind of feelings are we trying to imbue with the food" or "what kind of emotions or experiences will the meal trigger," we can develop ways in which we can stimulate positive values including creativity, pleasure, connectedness, and curiosity.

4 Application of Culinary Interactions Framework

We apply relevant examples of HFI products and services to the framework (Fig. 1, Table 2) to result in Tables 3, 4, 5, and 6. By utilizing and garnering insights from the framework, we can identify who does what (i.e., human or robot performing which task and what the change in task implementer entails). This, in turn, equips the designers and developers with a systematic way of distinguishing each of interaction points between the robot and human, and therefore allow them to comprehensively address how these interactions will occur.

We have looked into commercial examples such as Moley, Amazon, and Eatsa in particular to show the variety of specific SPA tasks that covers the range of all the culinary processes (Tables 4, 5, and 6). In doing this, we have also made a simple distinction between human-supporting and self-implementing to address "why" a certain task is carried out by the robot. This is an important distinction that demonstrates the robot's purpose of task and scope of work. It also exemplifies how the framework can be further broken down to capture nuances of information that are crucial for HFI analyses.

4.1 Moley

The Moley has by far the most number of continuous tasks performed without human interaction or intervention (all tasks within the cooking and plating/assembly steps are self-implementing). This reflects its respective higher level of autonomy than any other HFI product or service we are reviewing. As for the qualitative extent of robot autonomy, we have yet to conduct primary user-testing research to make a definitive statement. However, we infer that the level of interaction between human and robot will be more sophisticated than current HFI products and services [18]. Such an inference stems from Moley being able to fulfill both human-supporting and self-implementing roles for the ideation and preparation stages, a combination that allows for multiple types of interactions, which can be indicative of higher forms of interactions. Our inference is also based on the functions that are to be included, such as sensing and analyzing human movements to not only replicate the human chef's culinary processes for the recreation of a meal, but also for future collaborations between the human and robot.

4.2 Amazon

Amazon provides a range of levels of autonomy through various procurement services that it provides. The Amazon Dash Button, for instance, was introduced to deliver a seamless ordering experience by providing a physical button for certain products that customers frequently need to refill depending on when the item was last ordered, how often the customer purchases, etc. In each of the SPA tasks, it is evident that Amazon plays both the human-supporting and self-implementing roles by utilizing its various platform products and services. Furthermore, the extent of self-implementation of the procurement action is prone to change with Amazon's "flying warehouse" or airborne fulfillment center (AFC) and drones that are to be used in conjunction in the future [19].

4.3 Eatsa

Eatsa, offers a waiter-less experience at the front-side of house. When the Eatsa kiosk or app takes an order, it transmits the order to "human" chefs/cooks in the kitchen, and informs the staff which dishes to be placed at which windows once cooking is completed. Although menu offerings are selective, customers are able to customize their meals based on specific needs without verbalizing their order to a server. Moreover, they no longer need to wait in line. As a modern interpretation of the Automat, Eatsa has digitized the ordering and serving systems, and effectively brought forth the illusion of digitized cooking (but actually run by people behind the screens).

Table 3. Application of *Culinary Interactions Framework* with HFI technologies. (▲ = Human-supporting. △ = Self-implementing)

Culinary Processes	Ideation			Procurement			Preparation			Cooking			Plating/Assembly			Serving		
SPA	Sense	Plan	Act	Sense	Plan	Act	Sense	Plan	Act	Sense	Plan	Act	Sense	Plan	Act	Sense	Plan	Act
Moley	▲△		▲				▲ △	▲ △	▲ △	△	△	△	△	△	△			
June										△	△	△						
Foodini	▲△	▲ △	▲							△	△	△	△	△	△			
Momentum Machines							▲ △	▲△	▲△	△	△	△	△	△	△			
Amazon				▲ △	▲ △	▲ △												
Eatsa																▲	△	▲△

Table 4. Application of *Culinary Interactions Framework* with examples of Moley.

Culinary Process	SPA	Description
Ideation	Sense	**Human-supporting**: In the case that the user wants a chicken dish, Moley finds recipes that it can cook with chicken as the main ingredient **Self-implementing**: Moley collects, stores, and brings up recipes in its extensive library of recipes of various celebrity chefs.
	Act	**Human-supporting**: Although the Moley doesn't decide what the consumer ultimately eats, it helps the consumer decide what to eat or order from Moley with all the information included in its library of recipes by food types, celebrity chefs, etc.
Preparation	Sense	**Self-implementing**: Moley senses ingredients that are laid out. **Human-supporting**: Moley notifies the user whether all the necessary ingredients for the dish have been prepared.
	Plan	**Self-implementing**: Moley plans its course of action: which ingredient to start chopping first, which ingredients have multiple steps in the preparation process, where it should place the prepared ingredients into, etc. **Human-supporting**: With the preparation steps laid out by Moley, users are able to time or strategize their part of the preparation accordingly.
	Act	**Self-implementing**: Moley dices, juliennes, slices, etc. to perfection all the ingredients that have been laid out in front. **Human-supporting**: User customization is possible with the preset settings of the ingredients that are ready to be cooked.
Cooking	Sense	**Self-implementing**: Moley senses the pre-cooked, prepared ingredients that are ready to be cooked.
	Plan	**Self-implementing**: An action plan is created with consideration of what to cook first, degree of "cookedness" necessary for each sub-stage of the cooking process, optimal strategy for sequencing, etc.
	Act	**Self-implementing**: Moley cooks according to the plan that it has drawn up, frying or flipping the food with perfect timing.
Plating/Assembly	Sense	**Self-implementing**: Moley senses when the meal is cooked to completion, what the resulting volume of food is (portion), what the finished food temperature is, etc. In addition to the edible product, Moley also gathers information on various plating rules and assembly methods.
	Plan	**Self-implementing**: With the various factors for plating and assembling taken into consideration, Moley plans the sequence of activities.
	Act	**Self-implementing**: Moley plates/assembles the final dish together so that the meal ends up the way that the chef has intended.

Table 5. Application of *Culinary Interactions Framework* with examples of Amazon.

Culinary Process	SPA	Description
Procurement	Sense	**Human-supporting**: Amazon keeps order information. **Self-implementing**: Amazon automatically recognizes when items need to be refilled and alerts its inventory management system when the Dash Button is pressed or subscription settings are activated to restock olive oil, canned tuna, etc.
	Plan	**Human-supporting**: Taking all the input together, Amazon creates plans and algorithms that create the most accurate predictions and recommendations for the user's food purchases. **Self-implementing**: From the various inputs, including the Dash Button and subscription service, Amazon creates an action plan that includes when to get the food items from inventory, pack into boxes, ship for delivery, etc. to perform based on the automatic settings of fulfillment.
	Act	**Human-supporting**: Amazon receives customer's orders, payment, etc. **Self-implementing**: Amazon optimizes the delivery routes and time, and dispatches the delivery personnel.

Table 6. Application of *Culinary Interactions Framework* with examples of Eatsa.

Culinary Process	SPA	Description
Serving	Sense	**Human-supporting**: When chefs/cooks in the kitchen finish cooking and are ready to place the plate behind the vending window, Easta senses who the meal is for, which vending windows are available, etc.
	Plan	**Self-implementing**: Eatsa decides which vending window the final meal is to be placed in to provide a playful, streamlined, and customized experience.
	Act	**Human-supporting**: Easta notifies staff where to place the finished meal. **Self-implementing**: Once the plate is placed in the vending window, Eatsa displays the name of customers on the windows.

5 Conclusions and Future Directions

5.1 Conclusions

With *Culinary Interactions Framework*, we have attempted to address the challenges we have identified in HFI development, as discussed earlier.

First, we bring the sophisticated understanding of HRI to the food domain, including task distinctions and levels of autonomy. We have explored how these make sense within the HFI context. We have also demonstrated a systematic way of identifying all the task-specific goals (both operational and the non-operational, such as the "cultural-aesthetic" side) that the robots can address. We can now quantify "robot autonomy" by counting the number of continuous task-completions possible without human interactions. We also bring up the possibility of a qualitative aspect in which we can begin to understand how to rate the sophistication level of human-robot interactions. We will discuss this further in future works.

Second, we have attempted to bridge the gap between academic research and the sudden growth of HFI technologies in the real world through this investigative paper. We have met our intent to create a conceptual framework that current HFI technologies can be applied to and we consider this the first step in bringing together the theoretical and practical worlds.

Third, our framework allows us to examine every point of HFI, which not only increases our awareness of interaction points, but also can lead to the creation of design guidelines and principles for interaction types, forms, etc. Such guidelines and principles will allow for more user-centered HFI development and concurrently help devise a scheme for evaluation of the effectiveness of available products.

In addition, the framework also provides a structured method of viewing the subsystems of food. Articulating and creating similar frameworks for other subsystems of food will enable streamlining between the subsystems. The consequent clarity and seamlessness will allow designing for an integrated food system with a holistic understanding.

Last but not least, we have built upon the academic research related to HFI and have drawn meaningful conclusions from them. In future works, we will expand on this further by addressing the seeming inefficacy of the distinction between corrective and celebratory technologies through the discussion of latent needs, an important concept in user-centered design.

5.2 Overview of Future Directions

Through the development of our framework, we foresee how academic work in HFI can expand. Future works that we propose can be grouped into the following:

- Refinement of framework with articulation of robotic autonomy,
- Expansion of the framework to other subsystems within the larger food system (e.g., production, foodservice, waste, etc.),
- Further development of the framework with a focus on users' latent needs,
- Research of social impact and repercussions resulting from HFI development.

Greater Articulation of Robotic Autonomy. The framework we have developed thus far provide the fundamentals for a better understanding of the types of HFI that exist today, trend in HFI development, and the larger HFI landscape. We find that expansion upon and adaptation to *Culinary Interactions Framework* will be invaluable as one can further incorporate details and nuances that are not yet captured. For example, the framework shows nodes of tasks that the robot performs, but we have not created the connections between these nodes, such as determining the necessity or directionality of the connections. A clear visualization with this sort of data, along with quantified levels of autonomy, embedded is needed.

We have also started discussion regarding the qualitative extent of robotic autonomy, but this ought to be further explored through more in-depth user studies and analyses of the HFI technologies. One direction we suggest in addressing interactions that require "higher levels or more sophisticated forms" is the application of the hierarchical structure of the kitchen to the inspection of the sophistication levels of autonomy. It is conventional knowledge that the higher up on the hierarchy, the higher your level of decision-making and involvement are. Having a higher placement in the hierarchy may imply not only implementing and being responsible for higher levels of tasks themselves, but it may also entail higher levels or more sophisticated forms of interactions with others, such as morale management, knowledge transfer, team dynamics, collaboration, group learning, etc. Hence, one of the future directions is to translate such existing models into the concept of autonomy in HFI.

Expansion to Other Food Subsystems. With our mapping, we have also kept our scope of the breakdown to the front-house and back-house processes of food (culinary processes and serving), and we are currently validating the framework for current and future HFI technologies. However, there are many subsystems of food as identified in Table 1, each of which have their unique processes that involve different stakeholders in a variety of ways. We hope to continue charting the robot's multitudinous roles in the bigger process beyond the six steps we have identified: ideation - procurement - preparation - cooking - plating/assembly - serving.

As the progress towards *Internet of Food (IoF)* continues, articulating, distinguishing, and mapping the processes of each of the subsystems will allow for a holistic understanding of the all the activities and stakeholders pertaining to food as well as the dynamics of influence. More importantly, it will also allow for seamless development in HFI connections and relationships as the food data from each subsystem would be gathered, analyzed, and utilized through a common data architecture. Furthermore, this seamless connection between the various subsystems will also bring greater efficiency and sustainability in the whole food system.

Exploration of Latent Needs. The current framework that we have developed is task-based, as per the widely-accepted HRI academic literature. Taking such HRI research as the foundation for our framework, we defined autonomy as being SPA implemented with the "intent of reaching a defined task-specific goal without external control." The goals being "task-specific" naturally makes it difficult to include in its scope the deeper, intrinsic needs of the users that are neither easily nor often expressed as "tasks." However, chefs/cooks do not simply perform operational and replicated tasks, but also enhance and innovate new dish, drawing from inspirations such as creativity, emotion, and/or senses. As exemplified in Table 2, questions addressing such are in the "sense" primitive, especially in the ideation stage of the culinary process.

Although we find that the manifestation of HFI technologies are not as mutually exclusive as implied by the corrective and celebratory distinction, we agree that HFI development can also stem from positives [4]. The "six positive aspects of human-food interaction" that Grimes and Harper suggest as starting points for "future possibilities for HCI" are creativity, pleasure and nostalgia, gifting, family connectedness, trend-seeking, and relaxation. These positives are often articulated as higher goals in NPD or are effects that often appear as a by-product from addressing the more explicit needs. Moreover, these are all factors considered by some of the best chefs from celebrity restaurants to our homes, usually in the ideation step of the culinary process.

Taking the design and ethnography approach, we can see that these positives are rather "latent needs and desires": people often have the innate desire and/or need for creativity, pleasure and nostalgia, gifting, family connectedness, trend-seeking, and relaxation [4, 18]. The importance of discovering and addressing "latent needs and desires" is highlighted in design literature, such as *Designing Interactions* [20], which states "when you are trying to understand the latent needs and desires of potential users before a design is created, it is important to learn about their existing habits and context of use—things they are rarely able to tell you about explicitly".

Referring to the examples listed by Grimes and Harper and classifying them as "latent needs," we have started constructing Table 7 below. In Table 7, we expand upon the latent needs whilst creating a distinction between the level or unit of influence these have. These latent needs were discovered from our exploratory pilot study on U.S. college students with a sample of 11 participants. Our preliminary findings demonstrate that there is a potential causality between explicit needs and latent needs. Although the respondents listed "efficiency," "affordability," and "better health outcomes" as benefits from HFI (addressing explicit needs), they also mentioned the individual "pleasure" and "socially connected" influences food technology has had in their lives (addressing latent needs). They also found it, "interesting" and "fun to see and imagine".

We have also classified the latent needs as having influence on the "individual" or "social" level as per the qualitative results garnered. We believe this is a very important categorization especially for designers as this unit of influence will greatly impact the technological development in its form, shape, functionality, etc.

Expanding upon the above latent needs of users is crucial to gain a better understanding of what future users may expect and desire for HFI technologies. As social robotics and other HRI development proceeds, so will that of HFI technologies. Just as HFI has benefited from the expansion of HRI technologies, the reverse of HFI development based upon a better understanding of the latent needs can also be helpful to the larger HRI development. We believe that this is an urgent task and therefore will continue to conduct qualitative research to finalize our conclusions and to develop framework regarding these latent needs.

Uncovering and treating these latent needs as inspirations for HFI development, in addition to conventional explicit needs such as efficiency, productivity, safety, etc., may lead to innovative designs in technologies and interactions. We hope to expand upon other latent needs that exist, observe what kinds of designs stem forth from this new directionality, and evaluate the similarities and differences in technological manifestations that address the same latent needs such as collaboration, sustainability, etc. Such a framework to help identify latent needs users have for food technologies will help designers understand their users at a deeper level and allow for more effective practices and implementations in design.

Table 7. Exploration of latent needs pertaining to food experiences.

Level of influence	Latent needs	Description
Individual	Creativity	The desire for originality, authenticity, novelty, etc. (could be for self-expression, self-fulfillment, etc.)
	Pleasure	Stimulating the senses in a way that brings hedonic experiences
	Nostalgia	Stimulating past memories and contexts associated with experiences
	Curiosity	Interest into trends, types of cuisines, knowledge of cooking, etc.
	Relaxation	The state of feeling free, whether it is obtained through the mental association we have with particular food or through the chemical and physical responses (e.g., anti-stress after a glass of wine)
Social	Collaboration	Enjoyment from working towards a shared goal with others (e.g., cooking, dining, cleaning, etc.)
	Empathy-building	Cultural sharing/understanding
	Sustainability	Consideration of environmental values
	Connectedness	Feeling and affirmation as a social being through family relationships, friendships, etc.
	Gifting	Contentment arising from selfless acts or consideration for others

Social Concerns Regarding Future Food Experiences. Though the speculation of future food seems quite welcoming to a lot of us, we urge to pay attention to potential social concerns, such as an accountability issue. For instance, who is going to be responsible for the food poisoning caused by human-robot cooked meals? Such accountability concerns have been heftily raised in the autonomous vehicle development, and the same analogy would soon apply for the food sector.

Lastly, we would like to bring up the potential issue on the absence of human factors. When cooking altogether becomes "food manufacturing" or "food engineering," where can we find humanized/humane interfaces and elements in this process? Replacing low-wage human labors by robots is yet another large issue with the current projection of ubiquitous food manufacturing. The top 10 low-wage occupations in U.S. include cashiers, food-preparation workers (in fast food contexts), and cooks, and the current movement towards automation makes us concerned about the future of employment [21].

These are but a few of the social concerns that have emerged through our preliminary research, and these matters ought to be captured and considered in HFI development.

References

1. Diehl, L., Hardart, M.: The Automat: The History, Recipes, and Allure of Horn & Hardart's Masterpiece. Clarkson Potter, New York (2002)
2. Thrun, S.: Toward a framework for human-robot interaction. Hum. Comput. Interact. **19**(1–2), 9–24 (2004)
3. Lynch, T.W.: The History of Smart Appliances (2013). http://ovens.reviewed.com/features/the-history-of-smart-appliances
4. Grimes, A., Harper, R.: Celebratory technology: new directions for food research in HCI. In: Proceedings of the SIGCHI Conference on Human Factors in Computing Systems, pp. 467–476. ACM (2008)
5. Svensson, M., Höök, K., Laaksolahti, J., Waern, A.: Social navigation of food recipes. In: Proceedings of the SIGCHI Conference on Human Factors in Computing Systems, pp. 341–348. ACM (2001)
6. Comber, R., Choi, J.H., Hoonhout, J., O'hara, K.: Designing for human–food interaction: an introduction to the special issue on 'food and interaction design'. Int. J. Hum. Comput. Stud. **72**(2), 181–184 (2014)
7. Beer, J., Fisk, A.D., Rogers, W.A.: Toward a framework for levels of robot autonomy in human-robot interaction. J. Hum. Rob. Interact. **3**(2), 74–99 (2014)
8. Thomaz, A., Hoffman, G., Cakmak, M.: Computational human-robot interaction. Found. Trends Robot. **4**(2–3), 105–223 (2016)
9. Vitousek, P.M., Mooney, H.A., Lubchenco, J., Melillo, J.M.: Human domination of earth's ecosystems. Science **277**(5325), 494–499 (1997)
10. Ericksen, P.J.: Conceptualizing food systems for global environmental change research. Glob. Environ. Change **18**(1), 234–245 (2008)
11. Escoffier, A.: Le Guide Culinaire: The First Complete Translation Into English. Mayflower Books (1921)
12. Kim, S.H.: Open Innovation Ecosystem: Chez Panisse Case Study. UC Berkeley Doctoral Dissertation (2013)
13. Horng, J.S., Hu, M.L.: The impact of creative culinary curriculum on creative culinary process and performance. J. Hospitality Leisure Sports Tourism Educ. (Pre-2012) **8**(2), 34 (2009)
14. Eppinger, S., Ulrich, K.: Product design and development. McGraw-Hill Higher Education, New York (2015)
15. Kudrowitz, B., Oxborough, A., Choi, J.H., Stover, E.: The Chef as Designer: Classifying the Techniques that Chefs Use in Creating Innovative Dishes (2014)
16. Michel, C., Velasco, C., Gatti, E., Spence, C.: A taste of Kandinsky: assessing the influence of the artistic visual presentation of food on the dining experience. Flavour **3**(1), 7 (2014)
17. Murphy, R.: Introduction to AI robotics. MIT Press, Cambridge (2000)
18. Burgess, M.: Robot chef that can cook 2,000 meals set to go on sale in 2017 (2017). http://factor-tech.com/robotics/17437-robot-chef-that-can-cook-any-of-2000-meals-at-tap-of-a-button-to-go-on-sale-in-2017/
19. Spieler, G.: Your warehouse in the sky (2017). http://www.huffingtonpost.com/geri-spieler/your-warehouse-in-the-sky_b_14119132.html
20. Moggridge, B., Atkinson, B.: Designing Interactions. MIT Press, Cambridge (2007)
21. Frey, C.B., Osborne, M.A.: The future of employment: how susceptible are jobs to computerisation? Technol. Forecast. Soc. Chang. **114**, 254–280 (2017)

Enough or Too Much in EMR Training and Education?

Joshua Tabner(✉), Fan Zhao, Nick Pavel, Kevin Kincaid, and Connor Murphy

Lutgert College of Business, Florida Gulf Coast University, Fort Myers, USA
{jatabner2109,pnpavel7142,kjkincaid0775,
comurphy}@eagle.fgcu.edu, fzhao@fgcu.edu

Abstract. The healthcare industry is constantly growing and changing to keep up with the rising demand for treatment and technological improvements to treatment. With this growth and new technology comes a similar rise in costs. In order for healthcare systems to stay in the green they must constantly seek new ways to save money and better treat patients in an efficient manner. One of the tools the healthcare industry has chosen to lean on in order to facilitate this need is healthcare ERPs. The challenge of implementing ERP is tremendous. Many critical factors contribute to the success or demise of as a successful implementation. In order for these ERP systems to be effective however, end users must be willing and able to utilize the system as designed in an efficient manner. As such user acceptance is a key component in implementation success and healthcare IT needs to keep this at the forefront of their thoughts throughout the implementation process. User acceptance will increase through adequate training. Through research we have developed the Training Intensiveness Model. We propose this model will benefit other researchers and practitioners alike through its simplicity and ease of use.

Keywords: Critical factors · End user participation · Value usefulness · ERP implementation · Training · Training intensiveness model · Key users · Healthcare

1 Introduction

The healthcare industry has numerous different organizational structures that make up the overall industry. A large healthcare system can be made up of independent physicians, clinician offices, outpatient centers, and hospitals just to name a few. Each of these different business types requires a different level of information and/or functionality when considering an ERP option. Even within one of these practices, whether it is an entire hospital or even an independent physician practice numerous different types of users will need to utilize the system and pull different types of information to fulfill their duties [1]. Making a decision without factoring in this knowledge will put an entire IT project at risk from the onset, making it a critical point in the ERP implementation timeline.

Once an organization has identified the users that will be affected by an ERP implementation other factors more closely associated with user adoption will begin to become apparent. Most healthcare professionals see the benefit of the integrated healthcare solution that an ERP can provide. They appreciate the improved documentation tracking

M. Kurosu (Ed.): HCI 2017, Part I, LNCS 10271, pp. 234–244, 2017.
DOI: 10.1007/978-3-319-58071-5_18

and the increased reliability of said documentation. Paper forms are easily lost and handwriting between individuals can vary greatly in quality, ERP systems standardize this process and greatly improve readability and access to these records [2]. However, in order to reap the benefits of an ERP system, data must be entered into the computer systems by these same employees wishing to reap its benefits; this is where user rejection begins to occur. Healthcare professional's site usability problems as their primary concerns over medical ERPs, these concerns must be worked through in order to have a successful go-live. As health staff encounters usability issues to a process they perceived as being unintuitive, time spent with patient's decreases and time spent within the ERP increases [2]. This can have a significant impact on patient care as discussed later in the Critical Success Factors section of the paper.

Mitigating the effects of poor end user adoption levels should be a primary goal of IT professionals when choosing and developing an ERP system for a healthcare organization. This paper identifies critical success and failure factors discovered from literature review that are linked to user training and propose a training design model for efficiently promoting user adoption levels of an EMR system.

2 Literature Review

Hundreds of previous studies mentioned system education and training is one of the key success factors in Information Systems implementations and operations. Alcivar and Abadclaim that issues with ERP systems are due to poor user training and underestimating the importance of training [3]. ERP systems have a long history of training issues that led to failure. Companies are usually surprised by the knowledge gap between the training provided by the ERP system's vendor and the knowledge required by staff for them to work effectively with a new ERP system. This can be due to training being provided too early, insufficiently or even incorrectly [4]. Users must have a firm understanding on how to use a system or they will make critical errors when attempting to perform basic business functions which result in money and man hours spent fixing the issue when they should have been spent on training. Getting users trained and up to speed as the implementation is performed will help achieve the benefits of the ERP system [5].

In a study on rural health care industries, Trimmer emphasizes Efficiency of Operations in their list of CSFs that are important for a hospital's success [6]. Healthcare costs are an ever rising burden on healthcare systems across the board. Due to these increasing costs, the government and healthcare organizations are always looking for new ways to improve efficient care and documentation methods. According to our research healthcare firms look towards ERP to improve efficiency in much the same way as industrial firms do [7]. By gathering patient data into integrated systems end users can more easily monitor a patient's stay throughout a health system through to discharge? While the technical accumulation of data has clear benefits, concerns have been raised towards working through the social aspects of a hospital system. Understanding that patients are not simply data and that your end users ability to interact with the system and provide care with the collected data is a key concern when developing a healthcare ERP system [8]. More details on the social implications of an ERP system can be found in the following sections concerning CSFs.

In addition to the inherent problems in collecting patient data, hospital staff must become efficient in utilizing an ERP before truly reaping the efficiency benefits the system offers. One such problem affecting the efficiency of staff is their general attitude towards the ERP system. Physicians function at a certain level of autonomy that is allowed by their importance in the healthcare industry and extensive training. In healthcare systems that are only first implementing ERP systems, some physicians see the system as a threat to their professional autonomy and will resist the change [9]. Working with their staff to identify such physicians and utilizing other physicians to champion the software and pressure their peers to accept the system can assist IT leaders in improving adoption during implementation. Additionally, sufficient training can definitely help users change their attitudes towards the EMR [10].

There are other ways to assess ERP success by looking at critical failure factors summarized from previous studies and research. There are total 35 failure factors categorized in seven components proposed in the study. These factors come up regularly in failure cases and there is a lot of research that points back to these factors as having a negative impact on successful IT Adoption in healthcare. While it is impossible to note all existing factors, these are most common. Also, there is not one factor that is more important than others. It truly depends on each unique situation and set of challenges that are faced. Lack of employees' morale and motivation, inadequate employee involvement, high employee's resistance to change, lack of people skilled in the organization's processes, inadequate education and training, and poor key users are the failure factors related to user education and training aspects.

Lack of employee morale and motivation is one of the most common and well documented themes relating to failure of IT Adoption in Healthcare. It takes leadership at every level to boast motivation and improve morale. A true leader will command their role and not demand it. That is why it is so important to have all employees involved and hands on. The challenge with this critical failure factor is that it is qualitative and harder to get a grasp on or measure. End user's really needed to be involved at inception and given the opportunity to take on leadership roles throughout the planning and implementation stages. Healthcare providers that follow this path have shown to be far more successful with faster implementations.

"The reason change initiatives are unsuccessful are the failure to change mindsets, attitudes and culture" [11] Changing mindsets, attitude and culture truly resembles the biggest challenge in a successful ERP implementation. Employees need to understand the value and benefits of new systems. The sooner they can be involved and feel a "part of" the process the better. Overcoming cultural resistance to change can prove to a kiss of death if not addressed early on.

Many healthcare organizations lack people who are skilled in the organization's processes. This is often because employees perform specialized jobs and are very segmented between departments. The lack of process knowledge becomes a critical failure factor as these employees are not engaged during implementation. "Lack of user involvement: IT projects require all users of the system to be involved. Lack of user involvement and stakeholder participation may hamper the success of IT systems.

Hierarchical structures and top-down management practices may often come in the way of user involvement" [12].

In the healthcare industry, many employees will have varying skill sets and education that is in no way related to Information Technology. This isn't an issue of low skills or less education but miss-applied skills and specialties. When you are in the testing stages it would be conducive to get employees and end users with different skill sets involved early. Their feedback will be tremendous when working out bugs and redundancies that may come about later.

Employees with less education and a lower skill level will present challenges during IT adoption. It is nearly certain that training and getting these employees on board will require more training with greater interaction at an early stage. As stated earlier in this paper, less education and low skill is not necessarily a concern within the healthcare industry. Unfortunately, often times the education and skills are so specialized that there may be some barriers involved. For this reason Davis has created an Information technology Acceptance Model. (Figure 1) "ITAM is however interesting as it introduced the notion of fit, explaining that it is not individual attributes which are important, but the quality of fit between e.g. IT complexity and IT knowledge" [13].

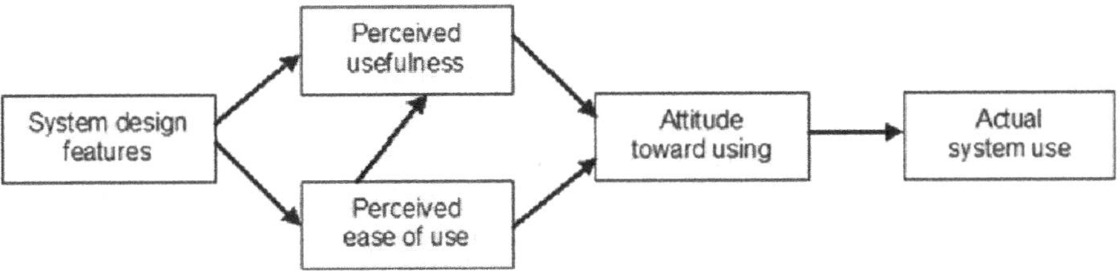

Fig. 1. TAM model

In the ITAM you can see the employees will need to perceive the usefulness and ease of use in an IT adoption before they will develop a positive attitude towards and then begin to actually use the system. This process may take longer for employees who have less education, a lower skill level or specialized skills and education. It may be difficult to get physicians to buy in as they may feel superior to learning something new as they already have a high level of specialized education. This can lead to critical failure quickly if the value usefulness is not communicated early and often. The best way to address this is through leadership at all levels and finding the right agents of change.

When implementing IT, one question should be, do we have the right people and key users? We know that people are the most important asset in business so people should be our first priority. "Modern IT is designed to foster input from individual end users. This increasingly human centered design should promote honest and active feedback" [14] the human centered design is paramount and is ultimately the theme of this paper. If you focus your efforts on empowering your employees and offering them leadership opportunities your results will be tremendous. You will get a better buy in and feedback that will help speed the process of adoption and eliminate potential problems and bugs down the road. Much of this starts with identifying the right people early on.

Potential key users should be tested to see if they possess the leadership qualities needed to become the agents of change that are necessary for a key role.

Providers will need to bring in or train employees so that they have skill level necessary to complete and implement ERP. This will include key users who are aware of organization processes across all function units. There will need to be a clear process in place so that the vision maybe carried out and management will need to employ long term planning to ensure that the implementation is a success before, during and after. This will include evaluation of processes and potentially the further implementation of modules and updates.

3 Research Method and Data Collection

To properly answer both our question regarding users' education and training, we adopted case study method to find hidden facts or themes behind daily operations of EMR systems. We have used a combination of information from the reviewed literature and interview data a large healthcare provider in southwest Florida. Semi-structured, in-depth interviews were adopted for data collection in the case study. The interview process aimed to explore the subjective accounts of people working at the organization with regard to three main phases: the selection and adoption of the EMR system, the implementation process and the post-implementation phase.

As part of the research process, a pair of interviews with technology perspectives were held with the CIO and two of the IT system directors, the System Director for Revenue Cycle Information Technology, and the System Director for Clinical IT. Additionally, four doctors and 6 nurses were interviewed about issues of daily operations and EMR training and education. The healthcare organization has enjoyed a multitude of successful go-lives of various IT implementations including Epic medical records system, their ERP of choice.

The interview with the system director was an exploratory interview of LMHS. Information was gathered concerning some of the systems LMHS uses to track and gather information and why they were chosen. In this discussion, the topic of implementation was discussed and the importance of user involvement was highlighted. The system vendor made it a point to contact operational staff in making their decisions on which systems to implement. This decision falls in line with our research as a good practice, and has been utilized with success in other healthcare organizations [15]. The IT teams in the healthcare organization developed a list of criteria from previous input that the operational staff could utilize to grade vendor presentations. Using this tool, the organization was able to make an informed decision on their new IT projects with end user input. Once a better understanding of their organizational structure was gathered, a more focused interview on user acceptance was scheduled with the system director of IT.

The director has an extensive history in the clinical field, particularly with this healthcare organization. Her 30 years of experience with the organization has been a useful tool in her role as clinical director. She highlighted the importance of focusing on the concept of transformation of care rather than simply implementing new software. Healthcare institutions are well known to resist change [16], and ERP systems in particular completely change how healthcare can be administered. Nursing leaders were brought into monthly transformation meetings which became more frequent as go-live drew nearer. These transformation meetings focused on the difficulties associated with the upcoming go-live. Leaders were given assignments to provide lists of complicated areas of work and to provide information down to their staff in order to better prepare end users for the upcoming change. This placed a higher level of expectation on the end user leadership by making them accountable for pieces of the implementation. The increase in ownership and accountability is believed to have made a large impact on the go-live and post go-live efforts. These practices fall in line with the research, by increasing end user participation and involvement LMHS improved their overall acceptance [17].

The third interview was conducted with the CIO of the organization. This time, user education and training was the main topic. Key factors and issues were identified and discussed from a technology perspective.

A focus group of four doctors and six nurses were interviewed lastly to collect more data from users' perspectives about user training and education of EMR in the organization.

There are two critical systems adopted in the healthcare organization: Epic and 3M including 3M automated coding. Epic is specialized in data aggregation and while it does expand its offerings, it leaves resources intensive tasks to outside vendors. 3M performs some of these resource intensive tasks in their natural language processing software and coding suites. It is believed that in the future, a new feature of 3M software that will provide instantaneous feedback on documentation processes to physicians.

4 Discussion and Research Model

Information System training is known as one of the key success factors influencing the system adoption and usage. [18] Once the Information System has been implemented, the entire system and all of its functions can raise concerns. Being exposed to the full scale and scope of an EMR system can be very daunting to an inexperienced user. These systems can be complicated as there is much for users to learn, this is especially true if their training was lacking. It is difficult for many users to grasp the system once it is fully available to them. After the system is installed, there are still many supports the company may need, and that is where post implementation support comes in. It is a fact that lack of hands-on training will cause issues [19].

Although training programs enable users to gain operation skill and to understand how EMR systems change business processes, the complexity of EMR systems limits the amount of knowledge that users can absorb before they actually use the system [20]. Users have to engage in post-implementation learning to obtain the knowledge and skills required for effective EMR usage [4]. With a system that has a wide array of capabilities it would be difficult for users to learn how to use each of the modules efficiently within the first few weeks or months with the systems.

Employee efficacy is affected by the amount of support a company provides after implementation. The employees, after having the system installed and working, have to use it to complete work just as they did before, however now the new system is their main method of delivering the work they provided before [21]. If the employees have trouble with the system and completing their work, they are going to be stressed, leading to an overall decrease in productivity. The EMR system must have post implementation support to avoid these kind of negative build ups. An EMR system is so complicated that the amount of post implementation support required is vital to the life of the ERP software in an organization.

Most companies use training they provide to users as their form of post implementation support. The idea being that this training is more like preparation for use, so by the time training is complete, the user should be quite familiar with the system [4]. The problem with having training as the only kind of post implementation support is that if the training is not effective, end users will have even more trouble and no way to reach out for help. The healthcare organization had training programs, but they were treated like as part of their post implementation support, as opposed to part of the implementation itself, which is a reason why users are still having trouble with the system six months after implementation.

EMR employee training is without a doubt a necessity. In cases where a company must utilize consultants for the EMR system—whether for training employees or actually operating the EMR system—the company should expect to pay $150–225 per hour for a consultant [22]. Therefore, training employees to perform tasks in order to reduce the need for a consultant is a must [23]. The cost of an EMR consultant per hour shows why many companies take training into their own hands. It is important for the company to take their time with the vendor's representatives seriously and take their advice on what the most efficient methods of training are. Vendor's want their systems to succeed as much as the companies that purchased them because a good success rate with the software makes it easier to sell to future customers.

Training as a whole is expensive to businesses as there is no limit to how much it can cost as employees being trained are not doing their day-to-day job and others are being paid to train. These costs will unfortunately cause organizations to rush the training process to save costs. The reason this training is so expensive is that training may involve 10–20% of the personnel and take about 20% of the budget [5]. In a vain attempt to save money, a company may choose to provide lackluster training or no training at all. EMR system implementation is already so costly; this training cost seems to sneak up on a lot of companies. There any many things affecting these costs, such as personal skill, training packages and the personnel required to train each user.

One thing in particular that drives these costs higher is the competencies of the personnel. If users that plan on using the system are unfamiliar with EMR systems of a similar nature, they are going to have a lot more trouble understanding and navigating the system. Users who do not have a complete understanding of an EMR system can make critical and costly mistakes. These can cost the organization a tremendous amount of time and money to fix. Training cannot be delivered with a "one size fits all" approach; training is more beneficial if it can be tailored to each user's individual skill level in order to better help them understand the new system. Unfortunately, most organizations have training budgets and doing this is not realistic. When a new EMR system is implemented in an organization, training is not something to be taken lightly; poor training can result in errors that would potentially be more costly.

EMR training packages need to be evaluated in order to make sure the training offered is going to be effective. Training packages can come in the form of automated training, such as programs that provide general instruction and user based training, such as bringing in an expert on the system to teach individually. The difference being that automated training tends to be over the internet via prerecorded videos and help systems [24]. Training the users without making sure the program is going to teach them key skills is a waste of time and money. Training should be able to offer an effective knowledge transfer and be cost effective [24]. To make a training package cost effective, it has to give the user the right tools to use the system. The problem with automated training is that you cannot modify the training package to better suit individuals and it can be harder for the trainee to have their specific questions answered. However, automated training is less expensive as you do not have to pay a trainer for multiple hours with different groups or individuals. Another tactic some companies use is to hold a web conference with screen sharing and allow users to comment and ask questions. The host of these conferences can walk users through various processes and answer their questions live. Companies can then save the video conference and have it available for their employees to access at later dates.

According to the literature review and our case study, we believe most of the organizations, during both their EMR implementations and post-implementations, understand the importance of training. However, there are still many studies, including our case, showing that training budget and programs is one of the first parts to be cut off while facing to limited project budget. Most of the current training programs are providing similar trainings to everyone and hope employees could understand the whole system, especially on current module they are using in their daily business operations. However, the results are far from what organizations expected. Some users can easily handle their module while others still have difficulties after the same training, and some of the users actually were trained beyond what they need. The training cost on each user is similar, but the outcome is significantly different. Some training may be wasted on those users who can easily understand the contents while others may be not enough. Therefore, we suggest customizing the training based on several factors we found out from the literature and case study. Additionally, we use a new concept, training intensiveness, in our proposed model to help organizations provide trainings more efficiently with limited budget (Fig. 2).

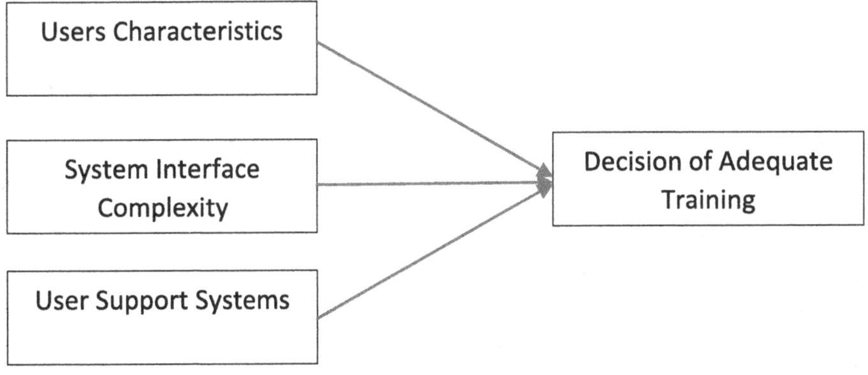

Fig. 2. Proposed training model

User characteristics represent the pre-training individual differences among all the users. Age and Prior Computer Experiences are the two components associated with this variable. We propose that older users with lack of computer experiences will need more intensive training while younger users with more computer usage background will need less training.

System Interface Complexity represents how complicated the EMR system is. The more complicated the system is, the more training may be required and the higher intensive training needed.

User support system includes knowledge support system embedded in the ERM system, help desk, help from consultants, and vendor support. A good knowledge support system will help users easily find correct answers of their questions. Most of the questions may be answered and handled by the system instead of sending requests to help desks, consultants or the system vendor. The most expensive supports are from the consultants and vendor.

Training Intensiveness includes training materials, frequency of training events/classes, percentage of key members in each user group, length of training events/classes, and knowledge of training instructors.

Once we can customize the training based on our proposed model, organizations can identify users in different groups and provide different training programs. Organizations will not only save their training cost, but also provide users with adequate and efficient trainings.

5 Conclusions

The role of end user adoption in a healthcare IT implementation holds great importance towards the success of a project. When it comes down to it, all the money spent on an expensive EMR system integration is practically thrown away if the training provided to the users is not effective. If users can not complete their jobs basic functions or take extremely long to do things that took them moments on the legacy system. This is why it is important for companies to not slack at all when they provide training. [Alcivar and Abad 2016, 3]. All the benefits the new EMR system may provide the organization are lost when the training provided is not effective or not efficient.

In order for training provided by the healthcare organization to be effective, managers need to consider critical success factors needed for EMR when designing the implementation process to ensure success. These critical success factors contribute greatly to a successful implementation of an EMR system. These critical success factors have a better chance of being met if they examined early on in the EMR implementation. It is imperative that employees become acquainted with critical success factors so everyone is working towards the same goals.

To prevent EMR users from becoming frustrated with the documentation and turning to more expensive forms of support such as the helpdesk or other users, the documentation should facilitate learning by explaining the rationale for transformed processes as well as emphasize support for new tasks [Scott 2008, 25]. Just creating step-by-step guides and sending them to schools is not enough to support staff members while implementing a new EMR. Managers must ensure that they are distributing the guides in an efficient manner. Out-of-date information should be avoided by printing only the more static content in manuals and posting the dynamic content online where it is more easily updated. A learning management system would help organize training related content [Scott 2005, 26]. This way if the system is updated which is natural for a new system with any organization, the resources can be adjusted in one place as opposed to recalling all the outdated guides. Documentation can be a very practical and inexpensive way to train but these are point that are important to consider before committing to a distribution structure.

Under the findings of the research presented, we proposed a training model that will help the healthcare industry identify different end users and customize their training programs. The results of our proposed model will benefit other research as it provides a simple template to the decision of adequate training. When making these decisions considering the following components of; User Characteristics, System Interface Complexity and User Support Systems will assist the decision maker. Much of the research was centered on end user participation, training and critical factors. A more customized training derived from the components listed above should provide value usefulness and greater end user participation.

The results of our proposed model will benefit practitioners such as healthcare organizations and hospitals through its simplicity and ease of use. Healthcare organizations often seek to save money to stay within budget. Frequently, training is reduced as a result of budget limitations. Research shows this to be counter-productive as adequate training is the key theme in successful ERP implementations. Knowing this, our model can be utilized to identify the adequate level of training needed for all users. Our Training Intensiveness Model can be used to stay within a limit budget while providing the adequate training necessary employed to set expectations for users, decision makers and implementation teams.

References

1. Zhenbin, Y.: Examining the pre-adoption stages of healthcare IT. Inform. Manage. **52**, 454–467 (2015). Accessed 12 Dec 2015
2. Janols, R., Lind, T., Goransson, B., Sandblad, B.: Evaluation of user adoption during three module deployments of region-wide electronic patient record systems. Int. J. Med. Inform. **83**(6), 438–449 (2014)
3. Alcivar, I., Abad, A.G.: Design and evaluation of a gamified system for ERP training. Comput. Hum. Behav. **58**, 109–118 (2016)
4. Chang, H., Chou, H.: Drivers and effects of enterprise resource planning post-implementation learning. Behav. Inform. Technol. **30**(2), 251–259 (2011)
5. Dorobat, I., Nastase, F.: Training issues in erp implementations. Acc. Manage. Inform. Syst. **11**(4), 621–636 (2012)
6. Trimmer, K.J., Pumphrey, L.D., Wiggins, C.: ERP implementation in rural health care. J. Manage. Med. **16**, 113 (2002)
7. Poba-nzaou, P., Uwizeyemungu, S., Raymond, L., Paré, G.: Motivations underlying the adoption of ERP systems in healthcare organizations: insights from online stories. Inform. Syst. Front. **16**(4), 591–605 (2014)

8. Stapleton, L.: Modes of reasoning in theories of the social impact of advanced technology: a critique of ERP systems in healthcare. Ann. Rev. Control **30**(2), 243–253 (2006)
9. Esmaeilzadeh, P., Sabsivan, M., Kumar, N., Nezakati, H.: Adoption of clinical decision support systems in a developing country: antecedents and outcomes of physician's threat to perceived professional autonomy. Int. J. Med. Inform. **84**(8), 548–560 (2015)
10. Rabbani, F., Hashmani, F., Mukhi, A., Gul, X., Pradhan, N., Hatcher, P., Farag, M., Abbas, F.: Hospital management training for the Eastern Mediterranean Regaion: time for a change? J. Health Organ. Manage. **29**(7), 965–972 (2014)
11. Grenuk, J.: Healthy skepticism. Am. Soc. Qual., 8–9 (2011). Accessed 08 Nov 2015
12. Chowdhury, R.: Healthcare IT project failure. J. Cases Inform. Technol. **9**(4), 1–14 (2007). Accessed 16 Nov 2015
13. Ammenwerth, E.: IT-adoption and the interaction of task, technology and individuals. BMC Med. Inform. Decis. Mak. **6**(3), 1–13 (2006). Accessed 20 Nov 2015
14. Bernstein, M.: Five constants of information technology adoption in healthcare. Hosp. Top. **85**(1), 17–25 (2007). Accessed 06 Nov 2015
15. Abraham, C., Junglas, I.: From cacophony to harmony: A case study about the IS implementation process as an opportunity for organizational transformation at Sentara Healthcare. J. Strateg. Inform. Syst. **20**(2), 177–197 (2011)
16. Phillips, A., Marrill, J.: Innovative use of the integrative review to evaluate evidence of technology transformation in healthcare. J. Biomed. Inform. **58**, 114–121 (2015)
17. Matende, S., Ogao, P.: Enterprise Resource Planning (ERP) system implementation: a case for user participation. Procedia Technol. **9**, 518–526 (2013)
18. Malhotra, R., Temponi, C.: Critical decisions for ERP integration: Small business issues. Int. J. Inform. Manage. **30**, 28 (2010)
19. Sadatsafavi, H., Kim, A.A., Soucek, M.K.: Impact of roles and affiliations on end-users' acceptance of ERP implementation in a large transportation agency. J. Manage. Eng. **32**(6), 016011–016018 (2016)
20. Yi, M.Y., Davis, F.D.: Developing and validating an observational learning model of computer software training and skill acquisition. Inform. Syst. Res. **14**(2), 146–169 (2003)
21. Sykes, T.: Support structures and their impacts on employee outcomes: a longitudinal field study of an enterprise system implementation. MIS Q. **39**(2), 473–511 (2015)
22. Wheatley, M.: ERP training stinks. Cio **13**(16), 86–96 (2000)
23. Dowlatshahi, S.: Strategic success factors in enterprise resource-planning design and implementation: a case-study approach. Int. J. Prod. Res. **43**(18), 3745–3771 (2005)
24. Macris, A.M.: Enhancing enterprise resource planning users' understanding through ontology-based training. Comput. Hum. Behav. **27**(4), 1450–1459 (2011)
25. Scott, J.E.: Technology acceptance and ERP documentation usability. Commun. ACM **51**(11), 121–124 (2008)
26. Scott, J.E.: Post-implementation usability of erp training manuals: The user's perspective. Inform. Syst. Manage. **22**(2), 67–77 (2005)

Changes that Count

Takashi Torizuka[1] and Yushi Fujita[2(✉)]

[1] College of Industrial Technology, Nihon University, Izumi, Narashino, Chiba 275-8575, Japan
toriiduka.takashi@nihon-u.ac.jp

[2] The Ohara Memorial Institute for Science of Labour, Sendagaya 1-1-12, Shibuya Tokyo 151-0051, Japan
yushi1130@gmail.com

Abstract. Continuous improvement is considered vital for maintaining the high safety standard. However, it may have down side. A nuclear criticality accident happened at a nuclear fuel processing factory in Japan illustrates a typical downside. Procedures for manufacturing enriched uranyl nitrate solution had been changed over the years before the accident occurred. The changes were potentially unsafe and must not have been authorized by regulator if applied for permission. A critical change was shared only among the frontline workers as a practice, which caused the accident when workers attempted to manufacture a highly enriched product. It was a typical organizational failure as widely recognized. It can also be seen as a typical example of accidents caused by changes that were invented to satisfy a required quality standard in shorter time. It benefitted the workers in terms of shortening the work time in an adverse work conditions imposed by formal but tedious operating procedures. The traditional view of increasing the productivity for economic reason was not the issue there. How to make the system resilient by stopping such changes, which potentially challenge the defense-in-depth but are made tacitly under the name of continuous improvement, is an important issue.

Keywords: Safety · Resilience engineering · Organizational accident · Nuclear accident · Productivity · Operating procedures · Well-being · Ergonomics · Human factors

1 Introduction

Continuous improvement is considered vital for maintaining the high safety standard. Very few people contend this view. Continuous improvement is believed to be needed for many reasons.

When the Japanese bullet train opened for business in 1964 for the operation between Tokyo and Shin-Osaka, the maximum operating speed was 210 km/hr. It has been increased to 285 km/hr. The interval has been reduced from 15–30 min to 3–10 min. It took 4 h to travel from Tokyo to Shin-Osaka. Now, it takes 2 h and 35 min. The number of cars has been increased from 12 to 16. The maximum operating speed depends on various factors, not on the mechanical performance alone. In fact, the maximum operating speed is set at 300 km/hr. for a different bullet line. The highest speed of the

M. Kurosu (Ed.): HCI 2017, Part I, LNCS 10271, pp. 245–253, 2017.
DOI: 10.1007/978-3-319-58071-5_19

Japanese bullet train recorded in a technical test is reported to be 443 km/hr. What this story implies is that it is the fate of almost any joint systems that people try to maximize the efficiency in a balanced way under given conditions. There are various driving forces such as the corporate responsibility for fulfilling economic demands, the desire to develop new and better technologies.

Continuous change is also an important driving force to maintain the high spirit of people from the viewpoint of human resource management. Even employees sometimes want to improve the efficiency for the benefit of themselves, where the better efficiency does not compete against the better well-being. People are always motivated to change the system under the name of 'improvement.'

However, continuous improvement may have down side. This paper intends to argue that continuous improvement can cause fatal accidents. A nuclear criticality accident happened at a nuclear fuel processing factory in Japan is used as an example.

2 The Accident

The JCO Co Ltd. was involved in the manufacturing of materials used for nuclear fuel. JCO still exists even though they closed the manufacturing. They usually manufactured low-enriched products of 3 to 5% U235 concentration. A few times a year, they were asked to manufacture a high-enriched product of 18.8% U235 concentration which was used for an experimental fast-breeder reactor. The same facility and process were used to manufacture the both low-enriched and high-enriched products. The accident happened on September 30, 1999 when the high-enriched product was manufactured. It was a nuclear accident called 'criticality accident' in which uncontrolled nuclear reactions occurred successively – chain reaction. Two workers lost their lives as a result of exposure to strong neutron flux emitted by the reaction.

2.1 The Original Process

Chemical Process. The nuclear fuel is made by sintering enriched uranium dioxide (UO2). The enriched uranium dioxide is produced typically from uranium concentrate called 'yellow cake' through two major chemical processes – (i) the conversion process to produce uranium hexafluoride (UF6) from yellow cake and (ii) the re-conversion process to produce uranium dioxide. JCO was a unique company which was specialized for the re-conversion process.

The re-conversion process is divided into several stages. On the day of the accident, JCO was involved in the stage of harmonizing the uranium concentration. For the purpose of harmonization, nitric acid (HNO3) was added to enriched uranium powder – triuranium octoxide (U2O8), which yielded uranyl nitrate solution (UO2(NO3)2). Several batches of solution obtained with enriched uranium powder of slightly different concentration were mixed to harmonize the uranium concentration. The criticality accident happened during the mixing process.

Production Process. The basic production process is simple. Nitric acid is added to enriched uranium powder in the dissolution tower to obtain uranyl nitrate solution. Then, the solution is filled in a small container for delivery. Figure 1 presents the authorized production process [1].

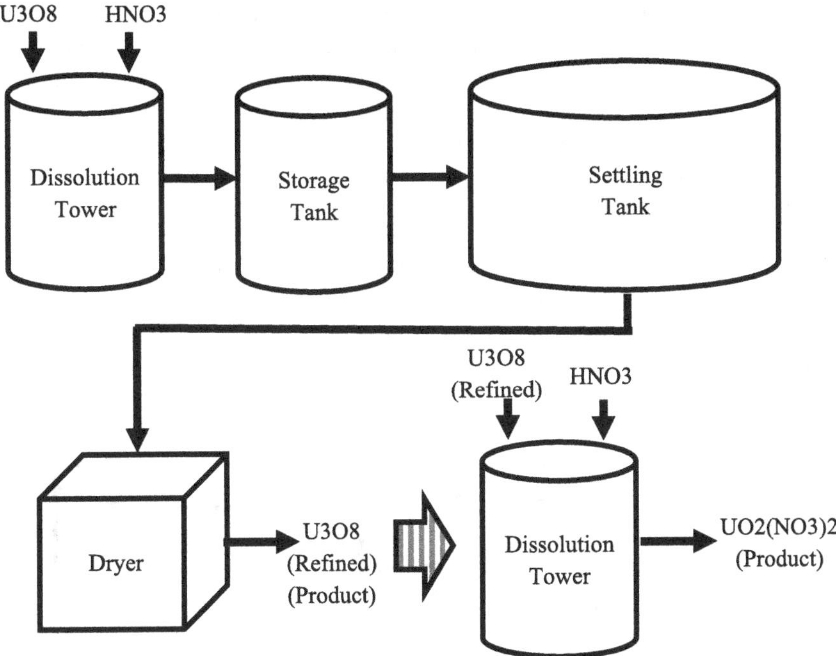

Fig. 1. The authorized iterative production process for producing triuranium octoxide (U2O8) and uranyl nitrate solution (UO2(NO3)2) [1]

For a larger amount of production, this process has to be iterated because the dissolution tower is designed to be small in order to avoid the criticality. The volume of the container for delivery was only 4 L. The uranium concentration of uranyl nitrate solution obtained from different processing is not uniform. The uranium concentration has to be harmonized by a method called 'cross-blending'. Several batches of uranyl nitrate solution were mixed (blended) bit by bit with small containers. Then, the harmonized uranyl nitrate solution is filled in small containers for delivery. This was the authorized production process which was supposed to be followed strictly by the workers of JCO.

2.2 Changes

The authorized production process was successively changed three times [2].

1. For the dissolution of enriched uranium material, the dissolution tower was replaced by a stainless bucket around 1993. The volume of the bucket was 10-L, which was larger that of the dissolution tower. The use of the bucket was authorized by JCO,

and was considered to be part of standard production process. Authorized in-house operating procedures were specified and implemented. This change, which intended to increase the volume of each batch for efficiency, was not applied for permission by the regulatory agency. Therefore, it was an illegal change. The rest of the process was not changed.

2. For the harmonization of uranium concentration of uranyl nitrate solution, the cross blending was replaced by the storage tank around 1995. This additional change, which intended to remove the tedious and technically difficult cross-blending for efficiency and easier production, was not applied for permission by the regulatory agency. Therefore, it was an illegal change. Together with the use of the stainless bucket, this change was specified as part of in-house standard production procedures authorized by JCO.
3. For the harmonization, the storage tank was further replaced by the settling tank. This change, which intended to increase the efficiency of harmonization, was improvisational and shared only among workers. This change is reported to be made a day before the accident and implemented successfully. [3] Fig. 2 presents the illegal process that caused the criticality accident [1].

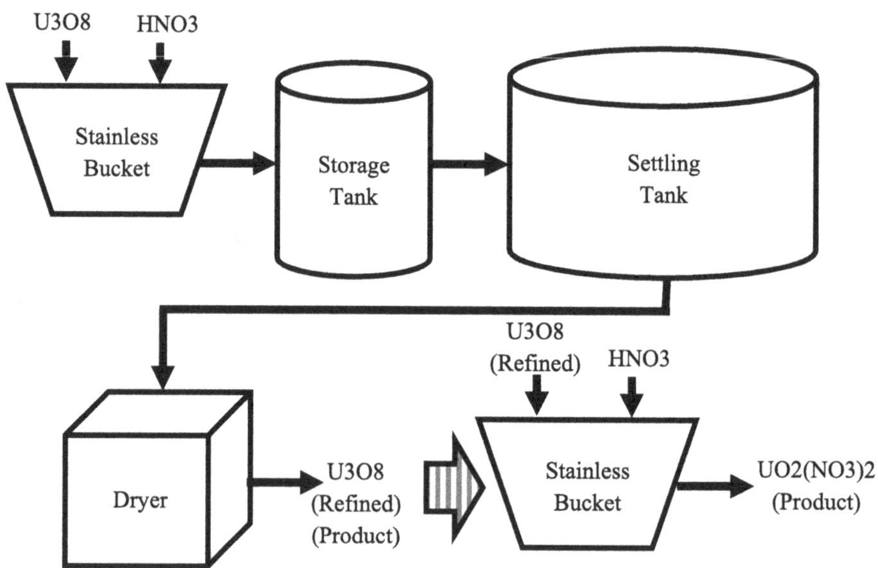

Fig. 2. The illegal process that caused the criticality accident [1]

2.3 The Fatal Operation

On the day of the accident, the workers were involved in the harmonization of high-enriched (18.8% U235) uranyl nitrate solution. The workers took the risk of using the settling tank rather than the storage tank for harmonization – the third and last change mentioned earlier.

It was unfortunate that the settling tank was totally unsuitable for the use of harmonization – See discussion in Clause 3.1. The criticality was triggered when the workers poured a large amount of highly enriched uranyl nitrate solution into the settling tank. The amount exceeded the safety limit.

Table 1 summarizes the development of changes including one that caused the accident – Change 3.

Table 1. Changes of equipment / method made at the JCO enrichment process

Process	Original Authorized procedures (Legal)	Change 1	Change 2	Change 3
		In-house standard procedures (Illegal)		Improvisational (Illegal)
Dissolution	Dissolution Tower	Stainless Bucket	Stainless Bucket	Stainless Bucket
Harmonization	Cross Blending	Cross Blending	Storage Tank	Settling Tank

3 Discussions

3.1 Technical Aspect

The accident occurred when the workers attempted to harmonize the concentration of uranyl nitrate solution using the settling tank. The use of settling tank for the harmonization was totally irrelevant in terms of nuclear safety, and it was a violation of the authorized procedures. [4, 5] The authorized procedures specify the use of the cross-blending technique for the harmonization.

It is not known if the procedures explicitly prohibit the use of the settling tank for the harmonization thought, it was probably beyond the imagination of the system designers and regulators that the settling tank could be used that way.

The settling tank was designed for its own purpose. It has a rounded shape. Because of the rounded shape, more neutrons stay longer inside the tank, increasing the chance of neutrons to react with uranium. The dissolution tower on the other hand was thin and tall, which does not allow neutrons to stay long inside the tower, decreasing the chance of neutrons to react with uranium. In addition, the settling tank was surrounded by a cooling jacket, which was not the case with the dissolution tower. This also causes more neutrons to stay longer inside the tank, increasing the chance of neutrons to react with uranium. Both of these design features are not suitable for handling radioactive materials. They only increase the chance of the criticality. Technically speaking, it was totally prohibitive to use the settling tank for the harmonization.

3.2 Administrative Aspect

Operating procedures are an essential human-system interface. It conveys what engineers want users to do. They often times include remarks for the purpose of maintaining the user safety and the system integrity. But, they seldom mention the underlying engineering considerations.

How to train workers such that they acquire sufficient knowledge about underlying engineering considerations and related principles is generally considered to be an administrative issue. It is also considered to be an administrative issue how to keep the workers complying with the operating procedures which are assumed to be reflecting engineering demands and regulatory requirements correctly. Obviously, these administrative measures were not strictly implemented at all at the JCO fuel processing plant. One of the three workers who survived is reported to have answered to Japanese media [6]:

1. The company did not caution the danger of the criticality.
2. Workers were aware of the illegality of actual operating procedures and they were not proud of it.
3. Workers never thought that accidents could happen with the liquefied uranium.
4. The interviewee concluded that the ignorance was the cause of the accident.

These comments clearly indicate that effective administrative control was virtually non-existent at JCO. The answer #2 is interesting. The answer #3 must sound totally irrational to those who has elementary knowledge of nuclear physics. Both answers vividly illustrate that people can do anything when they are not appropriately trained through administrative control and education.

The authors, however, believe that it was not only the lack of appropriate administrative control and education alone but the 'successful experiences' also played a major role: Nothing wrong happened even though illegal procedures were implemented. Nothing wrong happened even though the understanding of underlying physics was wrong.

3.3 Legal Aspect

The accident investigation reports, as well as media, identified the accident as an organizational accident and accused JCO of their negligent administrative control. JCO and its six employees were sentenced an order of compensation and suspended prison terms three and a half years after the accident.

3.4 Human Factors View

Human Factors/Ergonomics (HFE). HFE is an interdisciplinary engineering, of which foundation is the scientific studies of human characteristics. [7] The scope of HFE has been expanded considerably as joint human-machine systems become much larger and more complicated. Consequently, systemic views are prevailing in recent HFE researches and practices. The contemporary HFE tries to look at as many as possible related elements (e.g., machine systems, users, customers, employees, administrative and regulatory systems, general people and the society) from various viewpoints including cognitive, organizational and sociological viewpoints, and try to find issues and balanced solutions from the eyes of people. One of the critical problems of large-scale, safety-critical systems is that various mismatches existing among the above-mentioned elements tend to cause catastrophic accidents.

Relevant Human Characteristics. One of the authors identified several human characteristics that challenge safety-critical systems. [8] The two characteristics cited below look particularly relevant to the JCO accident.

The nature of changes in systems: Human in systems (e.*g.*, operators, maintenance people) are essentially alike and are, in general, adaptive and proactive. These are admirable qualities, but of limited scope. Adaptive and proactive behaviors can change system continuously, but humans at the front end alone may or may not be able to recognize the potential impact that the changes can have on the system, especially the impact when several changes are put into effect simultaneously. Humans at the back end (e.g., administrators, regulators) tend to have sanguine ideas such as that the system is always operated as planned, and the rules and procedures can fix the system at an optimal state. Mismatches caused by these two tendencies constitute latent hazards, which may cause the system to drift to failures.

Rules and Procedures: Work rules and operating procedures are much less effective than they are normally believed to be. Trying to fix the system at an optimal point for extended time with work rules and procedures may be a feeble idea. "Situated Cognition," a school of sociology, argues that the idea of controlling work with rules and procedures is only an administrative view…

In fact, major changes were made to the operating procedures at least three times at JCO (Table 1). Obviously, the reason for the changes was a desire to improve the tedious works. There is no evidence that the workers were under pressure for higher productivity in normal sense. The formal procedures were just tedious and technically not easy. The use of informal equipment such as stainless bucket and settling tank made the operation so much easier and quicker.

Both the front end workers and the back end administrators at JCO were ignorant of fatal risk associated with the changes. The regulator, who usually assumes that authorized procedures are implemented, was a typical back end people who do not see what is really taking place. There was a huge mismatch between those two groups of people.

It was unfortunate that the sense of violating rules which was recognized among the workers and perhaps among the administrators of JCO as well was suppressed by successful experiences. The changes did not cause anything wrong when the low-enriched products were manufactured.

A Human Factors Argument. Taking all the discussions mentioned earlier into considerations, the authors find it fair to argue that some important discussions are missing.

Obviously, formal conclusions publicly made are based on a belief that the system should be operated safely when formal procedures and any other rules are observed. However, there were accidents, which vividly exemplified that the belief was rooted in a weak ground.

It has been a recent trend to question the final responsibility to the organizations involved in accidents. It is probably because that organizations have been becoming larger and more complicated for the past decades, and many of them are susceptible to administrative deficiencies. But, administrative deficiency is too vague a title to dig into details that underlie critical accidents. In case of the JCO accident, there were some important questions that were not asked.

Firstly, it was totally prohibitive to use the settling tank for the harmonization. However, the discussions made previously in Clause 3.1 are a hindsight that can only be argued by integrating knowledge of nuclear safety engineering after the accident happened. How could workers develop such a professional reasoning? How can we be sure that such a professional reasoning is taught to workers before the accident occurs? It is not fair to criticize the workers and organization based on technical hindsight without evaluating how well the underlying engineering considerations are in effect in reality.

Secondly, how can we be sure that the information provided by engineers (and regulators) are good enough for the end users to learn and operate the given system? There is a strong sense on the side of engineers and regulators that rules are based on the best engineering knowledge and regulatory judgement, and therefore they must be observed. But, how can we be sure that rules do not make the jobs very difficult to implement? There is no evidence that the JCO works and administrators were supported by safety engineers and regulators to make their jobs easier to conduct.

Thirdly, people make changes for many reasons as discussed in Chapter 1. In the JCO's case, procedures were changed three times. The worker who survived mentioned that JCO workers were aware of illegality, but it did not stop them making changes because they were not accused of committing minor violations such as not maintaining a specified spatial separation between small containers filled with uranium nitrite solution. He further explained that he never thought that the use of settling tank for harmonization of liquefied uranium solution could cause accident, because it worked successfully for the production of low-enriched product. [5] A common underlying characteristics is that tendency to make changes can be enforced significantly by experience if nothing wrong happened out of doing something. How can we be sure that administrative and regulatory controls can stop this characteristics? Aren't many of past accidents suggesting that we cannot be?

4 Concluding Remarks

It appeared from the post-accident investigation that the workers of JCO were using illegal procedures. It further appeared that a major change was made three times. The last change which replaced the storage tank with the settling tank for harmonization was potentially fatal because of the technical features of the settling tank. But it worked for manufacturing the low-enriched products. On the day of the accident, the workers were involved in the production of high-enriched uranyl nitrate solution. It was a hindsight that the combination of these caused the process to go beyond the safety limit. It was a typical organizational failure as it is widely acknowledged.

But, it is also seen as a typical example of accidents caused by changes that were invented to satisfy a required quality standard more efficiently. It was also believed to have benefitted the workers in terms of making the job easier in an adverse work condition imposed by the formal but tedious operating procedures. Hazards associated with the changes that happened overtime at JCO became difficult to recognize because of successful experiences. Many other accidents, in which similar mechanisms contributed significantly, can easily be found.

All these accidents clearly show the need to recognize that people are expensing the safety margin from day to day under the name of 'improvement.' It is therefore crucially important to focus on everyday changes that are not causing any problems under normal conditions. But, they may be undermining the resilience soundlessly. It is not relevant to overestimate the administrative control. It is too late to enforce the administrative control after experiencing accidents.

One of the authors points out [8]:

> *Knowing the existence of mismatches between reality and formality is the first step for better remedy. Enforcing rules without understanding the mismatches is not an effective remedy. Appropriate monitoring mechanisms are a prerequisite for knowing the existence of mismatches. So are appropriate evaluation mechanisms for understanding mismatches. These mechanisms should maintain independence from and authority over administrative mechanisms.*

HFE provides various methods for detecting the mismatches. The methods are based largely on systematic observations with the knowledge of human characteristics taken into account. Any detected significant mismatches need to be examined by safety engineers to judge if significant hazards are associated with the mismatches. It is better to let HFE specialists and safety engineers to work together rather than blindly believe that the works will just follow what operating procedures specify.

References

1. Adopted and modified from. http://www.weblio.jp/content/JCO 臨界事故 (in Japanese)
2. Accident Investigation Report: Nuclear Regulation Authority (1999). (in Japanese)
3. Tokaimura nuclear accident: Wikipedia, Modified at 21:13 on 12 January 2017. https://en.wikipedia.org/wiki/Tokaimura_nuclear_accident
4. International Atomic Energy Agency: Report on the Preliminary Fact Finding Mission Following the Accident at the Nuclear Fuel Processing Facility in Tokaimura, Japan (1999). http://www-pub.iaea.org/MTCD/Publications/PDF/TOAC_web.pdf
5. U.S. Nuclear Regulatory Commission: NRC Review of The Tokai-Mura Criticality Accident (2000). https://www.nrc.gov/reading-rm/doc-collections/commission/secys/2000/secy2000-0085/attachment1.pdf
6. The Mainichi - daily newspaper: Posted to Yahoo Blog at 15:16 on 30 September 2005. http://blogs.yahoo.co.jp/fum_0015/12180948.html (in Japanese)
7. International Ergonomics Association: Definition and Domains of Ergonomics/What is Ergonomics?. http://www.iea.cc/whats/index.html
8. Hollnagel, E., Woods, D.E., Leveson, N. (eds.): Resilience Engineering – Concepts and Prospects. Ashgate, Aldershot (2005)

Acceptance of Automated Driving Across Generations: The Role of Risk and Benefit Perception, Knowledge, and Trust

Carley Ward(✉), Martina Raue, Chaiwoo Lee, Lisa D'Ambrosio, and Joseph F. Coughlin

Massachusetts Institute of Technology AgeLab, Cambridge, MA, USA
carleyw@mit.edu

Abstract. The eventual adoption of automated vehicles seems inevitable. With the potential to reduce traffic accidents caused by human error [1], decrease congestion, increase mobility, and yield more efficient use of commuting time, most major automakers as well as several technology companies have invested in their development. Policymakers and manufacturers need to understand people's risk and benefit perceptions around automated vehicles in order to understand their likelihood of adoption, as well as to communicate about vehicles' potential benefits and to address risks effectively. This study draws on data from a survey of 1,765 adults in the United States with an embedded experiment to examine risk and benefit perceptions around automated vehicles across different generations to understand how factors such as people's generational age, knowledge and trust affect attitudes toward acceptance and use. Generations differed in driving behaviors and perceptions of driving-related technologies. Participants' attitudes toward automated vehicles were predicted by age group and gender, but not by experimental condition. Independent of condition, however, exposure to the intervention did have an effect on attitudes: participants' risk perceptions decreased after viewing an informational video, while their benefit perceptions increased. Consistent with earlier research, trust, knowledge, and risk and benefit perceptions are related to acceptance of automated vehicles. Our results also show, however, that informational materials that may enhance positive feelings about the technology can increase people's benefit perceptions. This work provides a basis for further research into the acceptance of automated vehicles and the risks associated with them as they approach consumer markets.

Keywords: Automated driving · Technology acceptance · Risk perception · Traffic safety · Survey research

1 Introduction

For the first time in fifty years, the number of traffic fatalities in the U.S. is increasing, claiming 35,092 victims in 2015 [2]; 94% of these fatalities were caused by driver errors [3]. Automated vehicles, vehicles that perform all aspects of the dynamic driving task under all roadway and environmental conditions that can be managed by a human driver

M. Kurosu (Ed.): HCI 2017, Part I, LNCS 10271, pp. 254–266, 2017.
DOI: 10.1007/978-3-319-58071-5_20

[4], have the potential to reduce traffic accidents caused by human error [1]. They may also decrease congestion, increase mobility, and yield more efficient use of commuting time. Many major automakers as well as several technology companies are currently invested in their development. If the successful adoption of automated vehicles is to occur, policymakers and manufacturers need to understand people's risk and benefit perceptions around automated driving as well as their knowledge about and trust in automated vehicles in order to communicate about their potential benefits and to address risks effectively. Little is known, however, about the interplay of these factors concerning automated driving. Thus, continued efforts are needed to explore people's risk perceptions and attitudes toward the future of driving and automated vehicles. A better understanding of the public's view of automated driving may provide policymakers and automakers with valuable information in developing regulations, technologies, and education to maintain and enhance public safety and to educate consumers about the choices available to them.

2 Literature Review

2.1 The Real Risk of Driving

Motor vehicle crashes are a leading cause of death and harm in the United States. In 2015, there were over 35,000 automobile-related fatalities [2], with traffic accidents the leading cause of death among 15–29 year olds [5]. In addition, in 2014, over 2.3 million people were injured by cars, causing property damage, lost earnings, medical costs, legal costs, and lost quality of life [1]. Despite these sobering statistics, the American Automobile Association (AAA) reports that Americans have become less concerned about hazardous driving behaviors such as drunk, aggressive, and drowsy driving [6].

The primary reason that driving is so dangerous is the drivers themselves. Ninety-four percent of all traffic accidents occur as a result of human driver errors [3]. Most of these were recognition errors such as inattention and inadequate surveillance of surroundings (41%) and decision errors such as driving too fast or too aggressively (34%) [7]. Alcohol impaired drivers were involved in 31% of all fatalities [2].

Despite these data, people tend to overestimate their own driving skills and underestimate the risks, leading many to fail to take adequate precautions (e.g., [8, 9]). By removing human error, it is anticipated that increased automation, and eventually automated driving, will have the potential to reduce traffic accidents and traffic fatalities dramatically. The Insurance Institute for Highway Safety estimates that if all vehicles on the road today had forward collision and lane departure warning systems, blind spot detection, and adaptive headlights, nearly a third of crashes and fatalities could be prevented [10]. However, advanced vehicle technologies and automated driving tend to be viewed as risky. How will factors such as risk and benefit perception, knowledge, and trust affect the acceptance of automated vehicles as they approach consumer markets?

2.2 Factors Involved in Technology Acceptance

Though some research has explored acceptance and use of public transit with automated vehicles [11], there has been minimal exploration into the attitudes and acceptance of privately owned automated vehicles for personal use. Research suggests that risk and benefit perception are important predictors of acceptance of emerging technologies (e.g., [12–14]). When evaluating new technologies, risk and benefit perceptions are often negatively correlated [15–17]. This may occur because people assess hazards as general attitudes and affect, as people experience negative affect with high risks and positive affect with high benefits [15]. Also, people prefer consistency among their beliefs to reduce cognitive dissonance, so they may evaluate risks as fewer and benefits as greater for technologies perceived as favorable [15]. Despite common belief, risks and benefits are often positively correlated.

Perception of risk of technologies and artificial intelligence increases with more novelty [18] and less familiarity [19] of the technology. As such, people accept lower levels of risk around technologies that are unfamiliar, as well as those that evoke a feeling of dread, or are thought to be poorly understood by scientists [20]. For example, the limited research in automated driving indicates that risk perception of automated vehicles systematically varies by subgroups. One study found that men tend to anticipate higher levels of pleasure and lower levels of anxiety using automated vehicles than women do [21]. This suggests that men may view automated vehicles as having more benefits and lower risks while women may view them as having fewer benefits and higher risks. This is consistent with König and Neumayr's [22] findings that older people and women are more concerned about automated driving than younger people or men. The biggest concerns people reported overall were attacks by hackers and the general safety of the automated systems.

In addition, acceptance is often influenced by trust in the manufacturers, software developers, and others involved in the technology's development [23]. For example, in one study, those who trusted the companies and scientists involved in gene technology perceived fewer risks and more benefits associated with it than those who did not trust them [12]. This confidence and trust is particularly important for technologies people do not have much knowledge about [24]. The more knowledge people have about a technology, the more accurately they may be able to evaluate it. Knowledge leads to a more accurate understanding of small risks and large benefits [25]. With the exception of early adopters and technology enthusiasts, however, most people have few resources to obtain up to date information on automated driving, other than the media, which tends to focus more on risks than benefits, for example, by reporting on accidents, legal or ethical issues.

If people view a new technology as highly risky, do not know much about it, and do not trust the company that produces it, they are much less likely to adopt it. However, risk perception, knowledge level, and trust are not included in the Technology Acceptance Model [26], which is used to predict the likelihood of acceptance of new technologies by examining perceived usefulness, perceived ease of use, and behavioral intentions. Therefore, as automated vehicles approach consumer markets, we set out to examine whether these factors play a role in their acceptance and what measures of acceptance may be most appropriate.

2.3 The Present Research

In the midst of a national epidemic of traffic accidents, the rapid development of automated vehicles may offer some relief. However, for the successful integration of these vehicles into mainstream traffic, it is imperative for policymakers and manufacturers to be aware of the public's understanding of the risks and benefits associated with automated driving. This study explores risk and benefit perceptions, knowledge, and trust of automated driving affect attitudes toward acceptance and behavioral intentions. The Massachusetts Institute of Technology AgeLab conducted a national survey to assess factors (risk and benefit perception, knowledge, and trust) that influence acceptance of automated driving. We also included a video experiment that aimed at manipulating participants' feelings towards traditional driving (positive vs. negative).

3 Methods

In this study conducted by the MIT AgeLab, an online survey was fielded with a U.S. national sample of adults.

3.1 Participants

Participants were 1,765 (46.2% female, 52.9% male, and .9% other or did not respond) self-selected adults from all 50 states, recruited from Qualtrics Panels. Participants self-identified as 79.9% White, 8.3% Black, 4.3% Asian American, 3.2% Latino, and 4.0% other or multiracial. Our sample ranged in age from 18 to 91 years old (M = 49.3, SD = 17.9). A breakdown of participants by generation is shown in Table 1. Participants took a median of 26 min to complete the survey. Twenty participants were excluded from analyses because they failed the manipulation check and could not report what the video manipulation was about.

Table 1. Participants by generation

Generation	Year of birth	Percent of sample
Silent Generation	1945 or before	13.7%
Older baby boomers	1946–1954	17.2%
Younger baby boomers	1955–1964	19.3%
Generation X	1965–1980	18.8%
Older millennials	1981–1989	17.4%
Younger millennials	1990–1998	13.7%

3.2 Measures and Procedure

We conducted an online national survey of attitudes and perceptions of automated driving with an embedded experiment to explore predictors of the acceptance of automated vehicles. Participants answered items about trust in general and level of knowledge of automated vehicles (from *no knowledge* (1) to *a great deal of knowledge* (5)). They were then provided with a definition of a self-driving car: "For the purpose of this study, we define self-driving cars as those in which operation of the vehicle occurs without the driver controlling the steering, acceleration, and braking; the driver is not expected to constantly monitor the roadway." They were then asked about their trust in automated vehicles to work reliably, in poor weather, and on old roads in need of repair (from *no trust* (1) to *high trust* (5)), under which conditions they would anticipate using an automated vehicle, how they believe automated driving will affect safety on the roads, how risky and beneficial they perceive automated vehicles to be (on a scale of *not at all* (1) to *very much* (5)), technology adoption habits, current driving behaviors and driving history, and vehicle ownership and transportation alternatives.

Near the end of the survey, participants were introduced to the experiment. Participants then viewed a short (2-min) video about driving safety in general and automated driving. They were randomly assigned to listen to one of two versions of audio that accompanied the video. In one condition, participants heard a description of how driving has become increasingly safer in the past four decades, during the beginning of the video. In the other condition, participants heard that driving is a leading cause of death and the driver is usually to blame for such crashes, during the beginning of their video. All participants listened to the same description of automated driving at the end of the video.

Finally, they were again asked about perceived risks and benefits of automated vehicles, how they believe automated driving will affect safety on the roads, and intentions to use or purchase an automated vehicle automated in the future. Demographic questions were asked at the end of the questionnaire. This questionnaire was run on the Qualtrics platform (http://qualtrics.com).

4 Results

4.1 Knowledge, Trust, and Risk and Benefit Perception

Generations differed in driving behaviors and perceptions of driving-related technologies. Older participants perceived driving as being more risky and perceived more human error while driving ($F(5, 1759) = 3.23, p = .006, \eta^2 = .009$). Younger generations also reported taking more risks when driving (e.g., texting and driving) ($F(5, 1568) = 44.54, p < .001, \eta^2 = .124$) and being stopped more frequently by police ($F\ (5, 1568) = 15.03, p < .001, \eta^2 = .046$). Younger generations, however, felt that safety features in new vehicles were more important than older generations did ($F(5, 1568) = 2.78, p = .017, \eta^2 = .009$), and they reported feeling safer with the latest technologies installed in their vehicle ($F(5, 1568) = 7.62, p < .001, \eta^2 = .024$). They had greater knowledge of automated vehicles ($F(5, 1759) = 37.77, p < .001\ \eta^2 = .097$) (see Fig. 1), which was positively correlated with trust in the technology ($r = .369, p < .01$) and in companies working to produce automated vehicles (e.g., automobile manufacturers such as BMW, Volvo, Toyota, etc., and technology companies such as Google, Apple, etc.) (r = .288, p < .01) In line with this, younger generations trusted the automated vehicles to work ($F(5, 1759) = 28.12, p < .001$, $\eta^2 = .074$), and companies involved in manufacturing them more than older generations ($F(5, 1512) = 16.09, p < .001, \eta^2 = .051$).

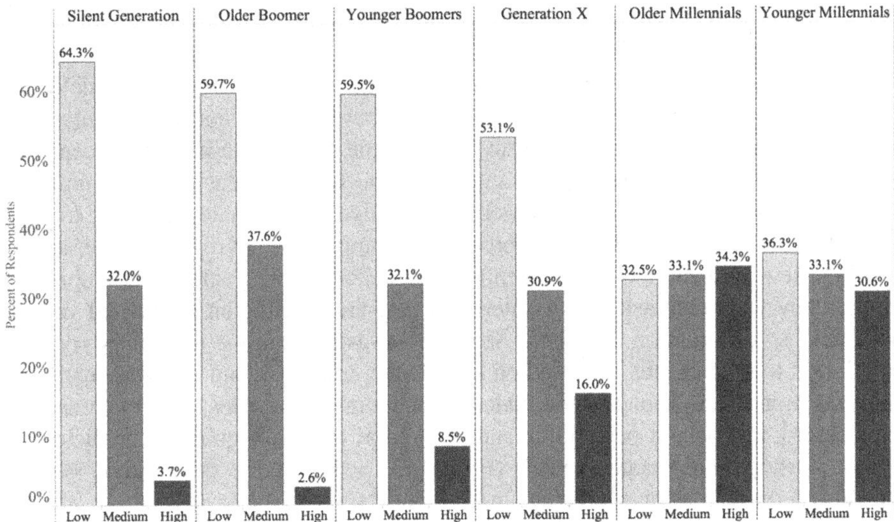

Fig. 1. Level of knowledge by generation

There was general interest to engage in automated driving. Overall, 38% of respondents reported they were quite or very much interested in using an automated car, and 17% indicated they would be quite or very likely to purchase one in the future. Clearly,

Table 2. Most favored benefits of automated vehicles

Benefits	Percent ranked in top three
Impact on safety	63.9%
Ability to do other things while driving	48.8%
Impact on convenience	42.9%
Impact on speed	25.2%
Driver control	24.7%
Impact on mobility	24.3%
Impact on congestion	24%
Impact on environment	17.5%
Impact on costs	11.7%
Liability	10.5%
Impact on data privacy	3.2%

Note: Because participants could choose up to three benefits, percentages do not add up to 100%.

participants saw many of the benefits that automated driving may offer. The three things that people liked most about automated driving across generations were impact on safety (64%), ability to do other things while driving (49%) and impact on convenience (43%) (see Table 2). However, many still harbored concerns, and 23% considered using an automated vehicle quite or very risky.

4.2 Measuring Acceptance of Automated Driving

There are many ways to measure acceptance. However, because automated vehicles are not yet available to consumers and manufacturers have not announced a definite sales model, it is challenging to decisively say which is the best way to measure acceptance of automated driving. This research examines four acceptance measures using ordinary least squares regression. Predictors were: knowledge of automated driving, trust in automated vehicles, risk and benefit perception of automated driving, and generation.

After viewing a short video with information about driving safety and automated driving, they were then asked how interested they are in using an automated vehicle (Measure 1). A regression model for Measure 1 was fitted to the data on N = 1,765 participants to predict interest based on knowledge, trust, risk and benefit perception, and generation. It was found that knowledge of automated vehicles, trust of automated vehicles, risk and benefit perception, and generation were all significant predictors of interest in using an automated vehicle ($F(9, 1755)$, = 17.87, $p < .001$, with $R^2 = .68$). See Table 3 for regression coefficients for all models.

Table 3. Results of fitted multiple regression models predicting automated vehicle acceptance (unstandardized coefficient B)

	Measure 1	Measure 2	Measure 3	Measure 4
Level of knowledge	.032***	.048***	−.008	−.001
Trust	.296***	.310***	.059	.130***
Risk perception	−.017**	−.007	−.090***	−.020***
Benefit perception	.168***	.138***	.092***	.114***
Silent generation	−.179***	−.125***	.044	.059**
Older boomers	−.138***	−.108***	.040	.019
Younger boomers	−.074***	−.066**	.061*	.038*
Generation X	−.054**	−.019	.022	.007
Older millennials	−.022	−.006	−.017	.019
(Intercept)	−.182***	−.271***	.347***	.314***
R^2	.680	.602	.318	.427
Std. error of estimate	.208	.221	.279	.199

Notes: *$p < .05$, ** $p < .01$, *** $p < .001$

Measure 1 examines interest in using an automated vehicle, Measure 2 examines anticipated likelihood to purchase an automated vehicle, Measure 3 examines maximum level of automation comfortable with, and Measure 4 examines features participants want in their next vehicle.

Participants were also asked how likely they would be to purchase an automated vehicle (Measure 2). A regression model for Measure 2 was fitted on N = 1,765 participants to predict anticipated likelihood to purchase based on knowledge, trust, risk and benefit perception, and generation. It was found that knowledge, trust, risk perception, and generation were significant predictors of anticipated likelihood to purchase an automated vehicle if one were made available ($F(9, 1755) = 294.54$, $p < .001$, with $R^2 = .60$). Risk perception was not a significant predictor of purchase intentions.

Another way of exploring acceptance of autonomous driving is to ask participants more concretely what kinds of technology they would want in their vehicles using familiar terminology. Participants were presented with four statements ranging from "the driver is in complete control of the vehicle at all time" to "the car preforms all driving functions and monitors roadway conditions for an entire trip. This includes both occupied and unoccupied vehicles." They were asked to indicate which best describes the maximum level of automation they would be comfortable with in their car (Measure 3). A regression model for Measure 3 was fitted to the data on $N = 1,765$ participants to predict the maximum level of automation they would feel comfortable with based on knowledge, trust, risk and benefit perception, and generation. It was found that risk and benefit perception were significant predictors of level of comfort with automation ($F(9, 1755) = 90.90$, $p < .001$, with $R^2 = .32$). Knowledge, trust, and generation were not significant.

Participants were then asked how much they would want a variety of features in their next vehicle on a scale from "do not want" (1) to "want very much" (5). The features were: those that reduce the potential or severity of a collision, those that help with speed control, those that help with steering, and those that periodically take control of driving. These items were highly correlated and summed into one variable ($\alpha = .862$) (Measure 4). A regression model for Measure 4 was fitted to the data on $N = 1,765$ participants to predict how much participants desire highly automated features in their vehicle based on knowledge, trust, risk and benefit perception, and generation. It was found that risk and benefit perception and trust were significant predictors of desire for highly automated features in their next vehicle ($F(9, 1755) = 145.02$, $p < .001$, with $R^2 = .43$). Knowledge was not a significant predictor.

4.3 Experimental Manipulation

We also examined the effect of the experimental manipulation. We conducted repeated measure ANOVAS with experimental conditions, age group, and gender as between-subject variables to examine how risk and benefit perception as well as automated driving acceptance were affected by the manipulation.

Risk perception decreased ($F(1,1724) = 302.61$, $p < .001$, $\eta^2 = .15$), but neither condition ($p > .05$) nor age group ($p > .08$) had an effect on this decrease (see Fig. 2). Women had higher risk perceptions ($p < .001$) and the decrease was stronger among women than men ($F(1,1724) = 12.70$, $p < .001$, $\eta^2 = .007$). Benefit perception increased ($F(1,1724) = 245.28$, $p < .001$, $\eta^2 = .13$), but there was no interaction with condition ($F < 1$, $p > .99$) (see Fig. 3). However, both age group ($F(5,1724) = 2.48$, $p = .03$, $\eta^2 = .007$) and gender ($F(1,1724) = 11.70$, $p = .001$, $\eta^2 = .007$), affected the increase in benefit perception. While benefit perception increased among all age groups, it was generally lower for older than younger participants ($p < .001$). Men's benefit perceptions were absolutely higher than women's ($p < .001$), but perceived benefits increased more for women than men.

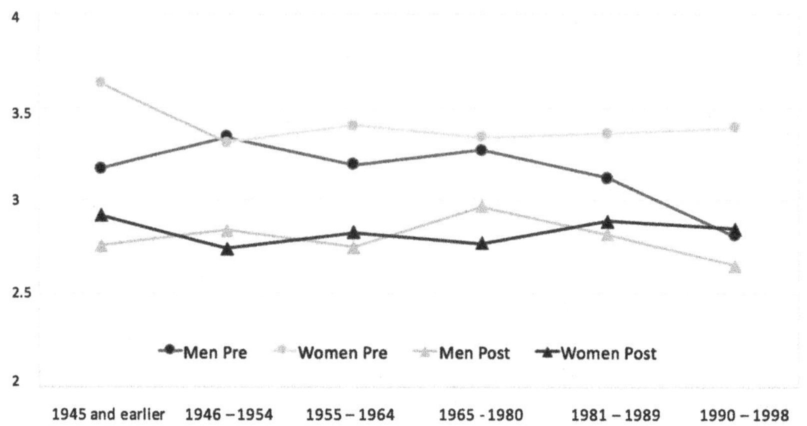

Fig. 2. Pre- and post-manipulation perception of risks of automated driving by gender and generation (asked on a 5-point scale from 1 = not at all risky to 5 = very much)

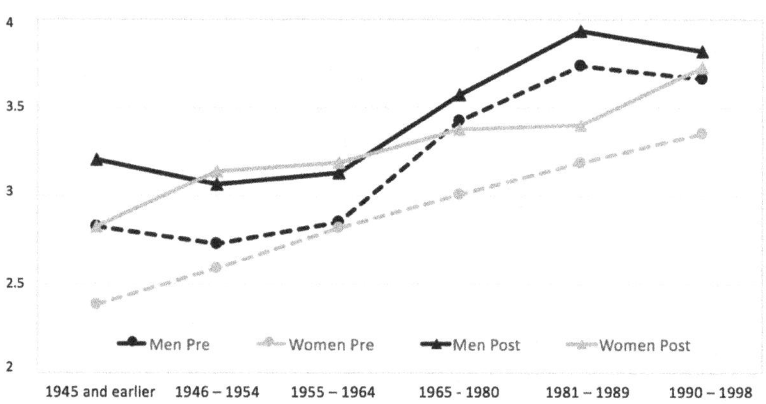

Fig. 3. Pre- and post-manipulation perception of benefits of automated driving by gender and generation (asked on a 5-point scale from 1 = not at all beneficial to 5 = very much)

General interest in use increased ($F(1,1724) = 234.37$, $p < .001$, $\eta^2 = .12$), but this was not affected by condition, age group or gender ($F < 3.68$, $p > .06$). Anticipated likelihood of purchase also increased ($F(1,1724) = 138.45$, $p < .001$, $\eta^2 = .07$); there was no inter-action with condition or age group ($F < 1$, p > .77), but gender affected the increase ($F(1,1724) = 4.76$, $p = .03$, $\eta^2 = .003$). Likelihood of purchase was higher for men than for women ($p < .001$), but increased more for women than men.

The maximum level of automation one would be comfortable with increased ($F(1,1724) = 133.45$, $p < .001$, $\eta^2 = .07$), but there was no interaction with condition, age group, or gender ($F < 3.74$, $p > .05$). Additionally, the amount of highly automated features participants wanted in their next car increased ($F(1,1724) = 103.83$, $p < .001$, $\eta^2 = .06$), but there was no interaction with condition, age group or gender ($F < 2.14$, $p > .06$).

5 Discussion and Conclusion

This research sought to examine the factors that influence the acceptance of automated driving, including knowledge, trust, risk and benefit perception, and generation, by conducting an online national survey and experiment.

5.1 Measuring Acceptance

Consistent with earlier research, knowledge, trust, risk and benefit perceptions, and age were found to be related to acceptance of automated driving. Benefit perception in particular seems to be important as it was a significant predictor across all four measures of acceptance.

All five predictors, knowledge, trust, risk perception, benefit perception, and generation, had a significant impact on interest in using an automated vehicle. However, when examining if participants would want to purchase one, risk perception was no longer significant. It is interesting that trust remained significant when risk was not. It seems that when evaluating automated vehicles for purchase, perceptions of safety may not be as important as the benefits it may bring to one's life. Generation was also a significant predictor for these two acceptance variables.

Interestingly, when asked specifically about the level of automation one would feel comfortable with and the types of features one would want on their next vehicle, knowledge of automated vehicles was not significant. Perhaps this is because the items themselves gave participants specific information in easy to understand terms. Participants did not require any preexisting knowledge of automated vehicle technology to make an informed decision. In addition, in examining the level of automation one would be comfortable with, trust was also not significant. This may be because this measure of acceptance is more abstract: the other measures ask about what respondents would want, this asks what respondents would be comfortable with. Using a different measure of trust may yield different results. The effect of generation was less clear for these acceptance variables. This could be because whereas the acceptance variables in Measures 1 and 2 ask specifically about automated vehicles, those in 3 and 4 ask more generally about advanced vehicle technologies.

5.2 Effects of the Experiment

In the experiment, we did not find a statistically significant difference by condition (where people heard audio describing how driving has become increasingly safer or how driving is very risky). Perhaps the lack of an effect of the manipulation was because the two conditions were too similar. The differences in the audio participants heard may have been too subtle or were not attended to carefully with the more stimulating video footage that accompanied it.

However, exposure to the information on automated vehicles provided in both of the experimental conditions seemed to lead participants to report fewer risks and more benefits of automated driving. Providing participants with more information about automated driving in the second half of the video, which were the same in both conditions, may have informed participants about some of the potential benefits of automated driving. Our findings are consistent with [22], who also found that the more people know about automated driving, the more positive their attitudes toward automated driving tend to be.

Providing interested individuals with accurate, easy to understand information about the expected risks and benefits of automated driving may be key in helping people make informed decisions about automated vehicle acceptance and adoption. These informational appeals may want to specifically target women and older adults who generally have less favorable views of this technology. Older adults especially have the potential to lead consumers in purchasing automated vehicles as they have a great deal of buying power and will be reluctant to give up their independence as they age. Baby boomers, for example, control 70% of all disposable income in the U.S. [27].

In addition, all four of the acceptance measures, interest in using automated vehicles, anticipated intention to purchase an automated vehicle, level of automation respondents would be comfortable with in their next vehicle, and the extent to which participants desired highly automated features in their next vehicle, increased after the manipulation. This may be because risk and benefit perception also increase after the manipulation, and the information in the video may have increased participants' knowledge of automated vehicles. Knowledge, risk perception, and benefit perception were significant predictors in several of the acceptance measures presented.

This work provides a basis for further research into the acceptance of automated driving and the risks associated with them as they approach consumer markets. More research is needed to track how these attitudes and intentions to use highly automated vehicle technology and engage in automated driving evolve as these vehicles approach and eventually enter markets around the world. Policymakers and vehicle manufacturers require up to date consumer information to understand road users' concerns and develop vehicles and policies to effectively meet their needs. If they are successful as we enter this new era of transportation, widespread adoption could lead to a plethora of benefits for society including saving thousands of lives each year by taking human error out of driving.

Acknowledgment. The authors gratefully acknowledge research support from a grant from the United States Department of Transportation's Region One University Transportation Center at MIT.

References

1. Anderson, J.M., Kalra, N., Stanley, K.D., Sorensen, P., Samaras, C., Oluwatola, O.A.: Autonomous vehicle technology: a guide for policymakers (2016). http://www.rand.org/content/dam/rand/pubs/research_reports/RR400/RR443-2/RAND_RR443-2.pdf. Accessed 1 June 2016
2. National Highway Traffic Safety Administration: Traffic safety facts research note. 2015 motor vehicle crashes: overview (2016)
3. National Highway Traffic Safety Administration: Traffic safety facts crash stats. critical reasons for crashes investigated in the national motor vehicle crash causation survey (2015). https://crashstats.nhtsa.dot.gov/Api/Public/ViewPublication/812115. Accessed 1 June 2016
4. Society of Automotive Engineers: Automated driving: levels of driving automation are defined in new SAE international standard J3016 (2016). https://www.sae.org/misc/pdfs/automated_driving.pdf. Accessed 7 Feb 2016
5. World Health Organization: Global status report on road safety 2013: supporting a decade of action (2013). http://www.who.int/violence_injury_prevention/road_safety_status/2013/en/index.html. Accessed 3 Jan 2017
6. American Automobile Association: Americans growing less concerned about dangerous driving behaviors (2013). http://newsroom.aaa.com/2013/08/americans-growing-less-concerned-about-dangerous-driving-behaviors/. Accessed 7 Feb 2017
7. National Highway Traffic Safety Administration: National motor vehicle crash causation survey (2008). https://crashstats.nhtsa.dot.gov/Api/Public/ViewPublication/811059. Accessed 7 Feb 2017
8. Svenson, O.: Are we all less risky and more skillful than our fellow drivers? Acta Psychol. **47**(2), 143–148 (1981)
9. Weinstein, N.D.: Optimistic biases about personal risks. Science **246**(4935), 1232–1233 (1989)
10. Insurance Institute for Highway Safety: New estimates of benefits of crash avoidance features on passenger vehicles (2010). http://www.iihs.org/iihs/sr/statusreport/article/45/5/2. Accessed 7 Feb 2017
11. Madigan, R., Louw, T., Dziennus, M., Graindorge, T., Ortega, E., Grandorge, M., Merat, N.: Acceptance of automated road transportation systems (ARTS): an adaptation of the UTAUT model. Transport. Res. Procedia **14**, 2217–2226 (2016). doi:10.1016/j.trpro.2016.05.237
12. Siegrist, M.: The influence of trust and perceptions of risks and benefits on the acceptance of gene technology. Risk Anal. **20**, 195–203 (2000)
13. Siegrist, M., Cousin, M.E., Kastenholz, H., Wiek, A.: Public acceptance of nanotechnology foods and food packaging: the influence of affect and trust. Appetite **49**(2), 459–466 (2007)
14. Wallquist, L., Visschers, V.H.M., Siegrist, M.: Impact of knowledge and misconceptions on benefit and risk perception of CCS. Environ. Sci. Technol. **44**, 6557–6562 (2010)
15. Alhakami, A.S., Slovic, P.: A psychological study of the inverse relationship between perceived risk and perceived benefit. Risk Anal. **14**(6), 1085–1096 (1994)
16. Frewer, L.J., Howard, C., Shepard, R.: Understanding public attitudes about technology. J. Risk Res. **1**, 221–235 (1998)
17. Gregory, R., Mendelsohn, R.: Perceived risk, dread, and benefits. Risk Anal. **13**, 259–264 (1993)
18. Kleijnen, M., Lee, N., Wetzels, M.: An exploration of consumer resistance to innovation and its antecedents. J. Econ. Psychol. **30**(3), 344–357 (2009)

19. Hengstler, M., Enkel, E., Duelli, S.: Applied artificial intelligence and trust – the case of autonomous vehicles and medical assistance devices. Technol. Forecast. Soc. Chang. **105**, 105–120 (2016)
20. Fischhoff, B.: Acceptable risk: a conceptual proposal. Risk Health Saf. Env. **1**, 1–28 (1994)
21. Kyriakidis, M., Happee, R., De Winter, J.C.F.: Public opinion on automated driving: results of an international questionnaire among 5000 respondents. Transp. Res. Part F Traffic Psychol. Behav. **32**, 127–140 (2015)
22. Konig, M., Neumayr, L.: Users' resistance towards radical innovations: the case of the self-driving car. Transp. Res. Part F **44**, 42–52 (2016)
23. Siegrist, M., Cvetkovich, G.: Perception of hazards: the role of social trust and knowledge. Risk Anal. **20**(5), 713–720 (2000)
24. Siegrist, M., Cvetkovich, G.: Perception of hazards: the role of social trust and knowledge. Risk Anal. **20**(5), 713–720 (1999)
25. Evans, G., Durant, J.: The relationship between knowledge and attitudes in the public understanding of science in Britain. Public Underst. Sci. **4**, 57–74 (1995)
26. Venkatesh, V., Davis, F.D.: A model of the antecedents of perceived ease of use: development and test. Decis. Sci. **27**(3), 451–481 (1996)
27. US News and World Report: Baby boomer report (2015). http://www.usnews.com/pubfiles/USNews_Market_Insights_Boomers2015.pdf. Accessed 1 June 2016

Interaction Design and Evaluation Methods

The Design Process to Healthcare Applications: Guidelines Mapping to Integrate User´s Contexts and Abilities

Janaina Cintra Abib[1(✉)] and Junia Anacleto[2]

[1] Federal Institute of São Paulo, Araraquara, SP, Brazil
janaina.abib@gmail.com, janaina@ifsp.edu.br
[2] Federal University of São Carlos, São Carlos, SP, Brazil
junia.anacleto@gmail.com, junia@dc.ufscar.br

Abstract. In this paper we present a set of guidelines to support the designer's activities during the development process of healthcare applications. The presented guidelines conduct the work of designers in the stages of collection and analysis of requirements and in the construction stage of the design process model, focused on the different contexts of users of these applications and their abilities. The design process is a multidisciplinary activity involving techniques and expertise in human factors, ergonomics, and the context of use. The consideration of these elements in the application design increases effectiveness and use efficiency, improves human labor conditions, and counteracts possible adverse effects of use by professionals in areas of healthcare, security, performance, among others. Adopting a design process model involves not only defining functional aspects and application features, but mainly being aware of the user's needs, knowledge, and abilities, as well as his/her limitations and resources. The motivation for developing this project emerged from the difficulty of finding directions on how to conduct the design process of applications for healthcare professionals and meet the specific characteristics of such professionals, who are nomadic, have long working hours, and blend personal and social activities with professional ones. This mix of activities and contexts increases especially when it comes to healthcare professionals looking after patients who require continuous care, for these professionals, in addition to shared activities with their peers, still need to support daily activities of patients, both personal as therapeutic ones. This lack of guidance for designers, often caused by the characteristics of the healthcare professional's activities, expands itself by the fact that designers are not ready to consider such peculiar characteristics of these users and they are not attentive to the mixing of contexts that happens naturally in their work. These facts make the design process of applications for healthcare professionals more complex and require a new perspective, wider than the one proposed by classical development process models. Thus, our proposal is the creation of guidelines to support the designer´s work in the application of a design process model that considers users' contexts, their needs, and abilities, facilitating the adoption and allowing the appropriation of the developed design solutions. The guidelines that we present were mapped for a design process model of applications for healthcare professionals. Such model allows and encourages the integration of contexts and considers the healthcare professional's abilities through the experience of use of technological resources

M. Kurosu (Ed.): HCI 2017, Part I, LNCS 10271, pp. 269–282, 2017.
DOI: 10.1007/978-3-319-58071-5_21

and exchange of experiences among them, favoring the adoption and the appropriation, and providing the experience of new abilities for the healthcare professional. Following the tendencies of Bring Your Own Device (BYOD) and Bring Your Own Application (BYOA), the presented guidelines conduct and stimulate the use of personal technological resources, like mobile devices, in the professional environment, allowing that the experience of use of such resources is utilized to promote personal, social, and professional integration in the workplace. The guidelines presented here consider the different contexts of healthcare professionals, integrating them in order to facilitate the management and execution of their professional, personal, and social activities and encouraging the use of technological resources to support this integration without harming the workflow of the professionals. Additionally, the guidelines consider the healthcare professional's previous knowledge and abilities to facilitate the search for improvement and the support for the addition of new abilities for these professionals, stimulating the support for the communication and information practices and promoting the formalization and documentation of the practices in the work of the professionals. A case study was conducted to validate the guidelines and map them in the adopted design process model, with the participation of application designers and healthcare professionals in a partner hospital. The purpose of the study was to follow the activities of the stage of collection and analysis requirements and the construction stage of the adopted model, applying the guidelines to propose a design solution, the prototype of an application that meets the wishes and needs of a group of healthcare professionals, so that the solution can be naturally adopted, according to users' knowledge and workflow and not only considering the best practical use of the technological resources. After the validation and analysis of the results obtained in the case study, the guidelines were mapped for the adopted model, conducting the employment of the guidelines in every stage and activity of the model. As a result, we present (1) the conducted case study and the final prototype developed during this study, (2) the healthcare professionals' impressions on the design process, (3) the considerations, obtained through interviews, of designers who participated in this study, related to the use of the guidelines during the development of the design solution, highlighting the positives points perceived by the designers and found problems, and (4) the mapping of guidelines for the steps and activities of the adopted model.

Keywords: Design process · Interaction design · Guidelines to design process · Healthcare professionals

1 Introduction

It is a hard task to follow the evolution and advance of the concepts, methods, and applications related to information and communication technologies, which are always in transformation. Such transformations have happened mainly in the forms of user interaction with computational applications and the professionals, who work with interaction design, according to [1], need continuous update on design models and approaches, mainly for applications that use technologies in the interaction, like technologies by gesture, touch, sound, movement, among others. In order to create good interaction designs – the ones that allow to access characteristics and functionalities in a pleasant way [2] –, and that the process of adoption and appropriation of new technologies is effective and may expand the users' abilities, it is important to think about the process of appropriation of technological innovation. During the process of appropriation the user realizes clearly his/her abilities, the best way of interacting with technologies, how to adapt them to new uses and contexts, and what he/she is capable of doing and which aspects he/she can improve [8, 20–24]. An interaction design model is pertinent to assist and guide designers during the process of conception, development, and validation of applications with natural interaction, since it utilizes the user's personal, social, and professional experiences with technological resources, which he/she already knows and use, to make interactions more natural and close to such experiences, thereby being able to support the professionals' experience of new abilities.

To do so, it is necessary that the design process integrates different contexts in which the user is inserted, personal, social, and professional ones, searching their experiences and abilities through the stimulus of the use of personal devices that the user is already familiarized with. In this paper, we present a set of guidelines mapped in the stages and activities of a design process model with such focus. The Design Process Model for Application in Healthcare: Integrating Contexts and Adding Abilities (ICAH, initials in Portuguese), which is adopted here, emerged departing from the observations and experimentation with collaborative work between designers and users and allowed to create an assistance instrument to the interaction design [3–7]. The model and the guidelines contribute to facilitate the task of the designer during the development of applications with natural interaction that considers the use of new technologies, experience of use, adoption and appropriation to enable the healthcare professional's experience of new abilities, integrating the different contexts of such professional.

2 Design Process Model for Applications in Healthcare Field

The need to create the Design Process Model for Application in Healthcare: Integrating Contexts and Adding Abilities (ICAH) came from the Laboratory of Advanced Interactions (LIA, initials in Portuguese) team's experiments conducted in a partner hospital CAIS Clemente Ferreira situated in Brazil [4, 5, 8–17]. Such need also came from the field study performed with the COLLAB application [6, 7], the data analysis on the design process of applications that integrate contexts and add abilities to users, and the characteristics of interactive applications in the healthcare field. The ICAH model was developed from the identification of the flow of necessary tasks during the design process. Such activity allowed to structure the cycles of the process that groups the tasks in accordance with the techniques and approaches used in each one of them. With the definition of the cycles and the observations and experiments conducted in the partner hospital, we realized that the stages of collection and analysis of requirements of more traditional design process models do not consider, widely and adequately, the users' characteristics necessary to integrate their different contexts, nor they assist in the extension or allow the addition of abilities. Therefore a survey research was

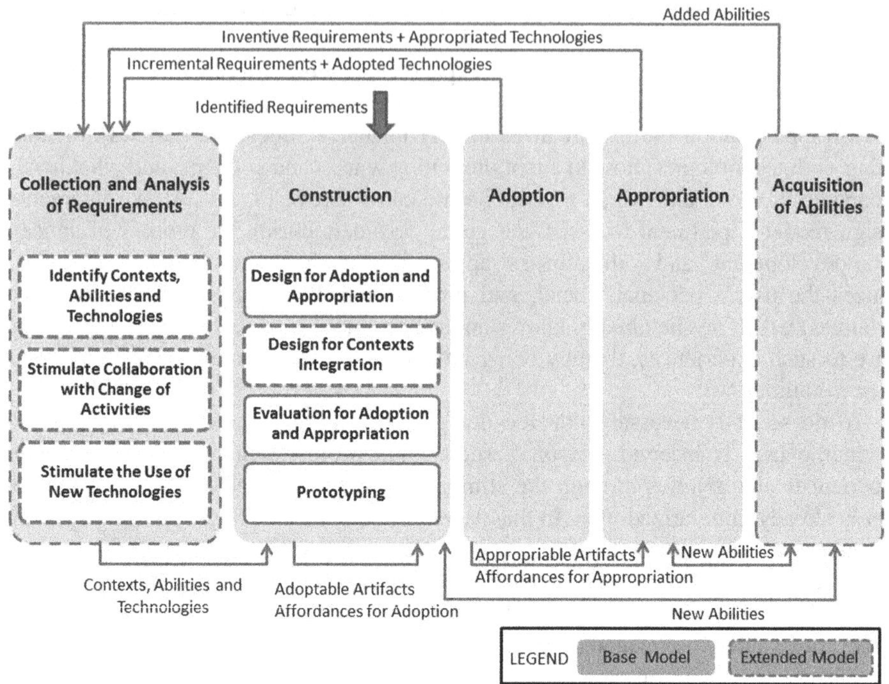

Fig. 1. ICAH model stages and activities

conducted with developers of applications/software in general and also from the healthcare field in order to verify how the stages of collection and analysis of requirements are being performed during the design process. After the analysis of data obtained with the survey research, it was possible to elaborate the process model adopted in this paper and, parallelly, creates a set of guidelines to direct the designers on how to perform the integration of different contexts, in which users are inserted and which they blend, naturally, during their professional activities. Finally, the guidelines and the created process model were validated.

Most recent researches in the interaction design process models and many studies [21–23, 28–30] have demonstrated that appropriation is a concept worth of investigation, particularly in terms of its nature for interactive design and collaborative computing. The ICAH model is an extension of the Model for Appropriation proposed by [8, 18] and Fig. 1 shows the stages and activities of ICAH and the relation among them, highlighting with dotted lines the new stages and activities proposed in ICAH and with continuous lines the original stages and activities of the Model for Appropriation.

Considering that an interaction design process is not a top-down activity, the ICAH Model describes an iterative sequence of stages, in order to guide the application designer during the whole process of development. The model allows the designer to get a global vision of the design process, its stages and activities of each one of the stages, and conduct a structured, systematic, and organized work. The stage of Collection and Analysis of Requirements begins the sequence of stages and the activity Identify Contexts, Abilities, and Technologies is the spotlight of such stage, which is provided with the requirements, technologies, and adopted, appropriated, and added abilities that result from the stages of Adoption, Appropriation, and Acquisition of Abilities.

3 Presentation of the Employed Guidelines for the Design Process Model

To facilitate the employment of the ICAH model, it was elaborated a set of guidelines that assists the integration of the personal and social contexts to the professional one and provides users in the involved contexts the experience of new abilities, allowing that, during the design process, the appropriation of technologies is encouraged and the users' abilities are widened.

The guidelines were created considering two domains to guide the designers: (1) support for the integration of contexts and (2) addition of abilities for the user. Such domains present common objectives to facilitate the appropriation: inasmuch as the integration of contexts happens, users become aware of the use of technologies and applications in different contexts, in addition to the effective adoption of these technologies. Besides that, the extension of the use of such technologies favors the exchange of experiences and expands the abilities of the users involved in the design process. And in this sense, the concepts of BYOD and BYOA [16, 25, 26, 27] gave support to the elaboration of the guidelines.

These domains and the set of 12 guidelines initially created were published and presented in [3, 19]. The guidelines were refined and complemented after validating them and the model, totalizing 18 guidelines, 10 guidelines of the addition of abilities domain and 08 guidelines of the integration of contexts domain (Table 1).

The presented guidelines make the monitoring of the design process activities clearer and facilitate the work of the developers and designers during the process of development of applications.

3.1 Case Study for Validation of the Guidelines

For the validation of the presented guidelines it was elaborated a case study involving application developers in the healthcare field. The purpose of the study was to follow the activities of the stage of collection and analysis of requirements of the ICAH model, employing the design guidelines to propose a solution, the prototype of an application that meets the wishes and needs of a group of healthcare professionals. Seven healthcare professionals and three teams of designers participate in the study, following the ICAH model and employing the guidelines. The study was divided into four moments: (a) presentation meetings and initial collection of requirements at the users' workplace (Fig. 2); (b) meetings and encounters outside the users' workplace for refinement of requirements, creation of personas and scenarios; (c) meeting for

Table 1. Guidelines for the design process model

	#	Title	Guideline
Guidelines to integrate the user's context domain	1	Make clear the purpose of sections design	Before beginning the first session of the interaction design process, it is important to talk with the users group and explain how the design process and their activities will be performed. Before each design session, present the activities that will be performed, the expected objectives and results and the duration of the session
	2	Promote a fast socialization before the design sessions (ice breaking)	Design sessions must be initiated with a socialization activity and each participant must be encouraged to expose what they expect to happen in the end of the session/day/week/month. In case the design process already got results, the participant must comment about the design activities that already happened and the perceptions they had
	3	Identify which e-communication services user participates or knows	Designers must know how the users interact among them, mainly if they user any electronic device to this end, if they do it outside the workplace environment and in which situation
	4	Use group sessions techniques to understand what kind of messages users usually share	It is interesting to know what kinds of messages, annotations, information, and reminders users share among them in workplace environment or outside it and dynamics techniques may facilitate the designers' work
	5	Provide quick breaks/intervals between sessions of design with the user (coffee breaks)	Small breaks during design sessions proportionate relaxing moments between activities and must be used by designers to observe the users' behavior and how it is the interaction among them
	6	Design for appropriation	t is important that the design process is flexible and robust enough to allow the technological resources appropriation
	7	Observe and promote integration among users in professional context and outside it	The integration among users happens naturally in professional activities, but it is important to propitiate integrated cooperation among users in different contexts, mainly social relationship to stimulate the appropriation
	8	Identify the lead user	The lead user is the one that will be able to point out the potential needs and good solution ideas. They direct the validations during the solution development and encourage the use of adopted innovations

(continued)

Table 1. (*continued*)

	#	Title	Guideline
Guidelines to extend the user´s abilities domain	1	Don´t waste the user´s time	Design sessions must be planned with antecedence and there must be a beginning and an end – delays in starting and ending the session must be avoided
	2	Ask user what technological resource he/she knows	It is important to ask which resources the user knows and uses to facilitate in the choice of solutions to be proposed in the design solutions
	3	Ask user which application he/she uses in everyday activities	The user experience with some applications may assist in the acceptance and adoption of new applications that have similar forms of interaction
	4	Encourage communication among users and designers through new technological resources besides of the presence meetings	Designers must encourage and proportionate the use of communication environments and applications that users do not know or are not familiarized with. This is an opportunity for the users to know a new technology and/or communication form
	5	Observe and use language and terms the user knows	Designers must use a vocabulary familiar to the user's environment, synonyms and popular terms and also observe the terms the users employ among them to refer to technological resources and applications. Users may say they do not know some technological resource or application, but it is common they just know such resources or applications by other names
	6	Program design sessions to be performed in the user's workplace environment	Designers must consider the user's workplace environment as an adequate place for design sessions, respecting the timetable and users' workplace rules, without disturbing or interfering in the workplace environment
	7	Program design sessions to be performed outside the user's workplace environment	Design sessions outside the workplace assist in the discovery of the user's abilities and knowledge on hardware and software technological resources that may be incorporated in the design solution. Besides, it proportionates the sharing of experiences, favoring the adoption and appropriation
	8	Stimulate the cooperation and change of activities among users	During tests with the evolutionary prototype, stimulate the change of

(*continued*)

Table 1. (*continued*)

#	Title	Guideline
		activities among users. The designer must monitor how the activities will be performed by the user who was changed and verify if appropriations and new forms of performing the activities occurred
9	Encourage the use of new technologies	It is important to offer new resources and forms of use of performing the tasks which are already consolidated in the professional environment, so that users realize the different ways of using the technological resources and their different purposes
10	Observe the things that users carry	Understand that the user may not be willing to carry one more item or material, or even due to their activities it is impossible, what may restrict the adoption of the chosen design solution

Fig. 2. Meetings at the healthcare professionals' workplace

presentation of initial prototypes and incremental refinements; (d) encounter for presentation of final prototypes and interview with users. After the interviews, users chose a prototype to be developed (Fig. 3).

At the end of the study, designers reported their experiences with the use of the model and the guidelines, and described how and in which stage and phase each one of the guidelines assisted the development process. The designers reported that observations and direct questions to the users helped in the identification of abilities, knowledge, and personal technological resources in use, mainly at the meetings that happened outside the users' workplace. Besides, they said that knowing the users' workplace allowed to verify their real routine and activities, as well as choosing technological resources to be used in the design solution.

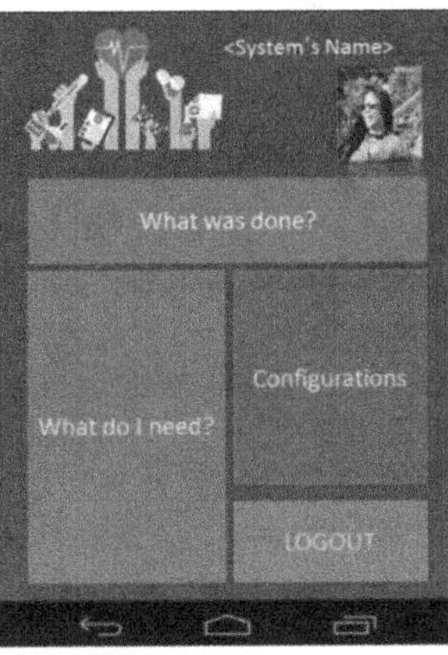

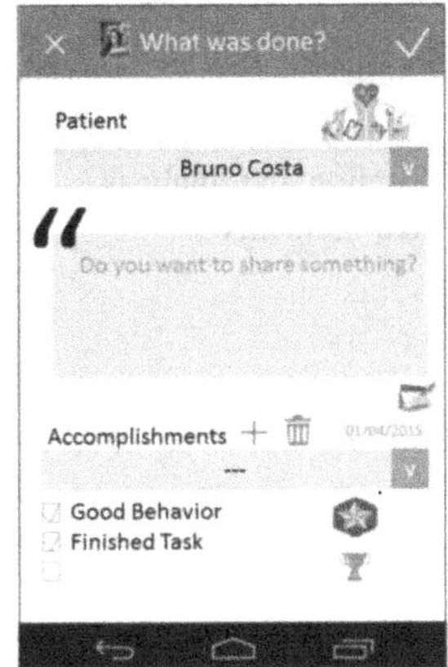

Fig. 3. Final prototype chosen by the healthcare professionals

We monitored the study and observed the employment of the guidelines in order to understand how the designers used them effectively. Such monitoring and the conducted interviews with the designers who took part in the study made possible mapping each one of the guidelines for the stages and activities of the model.

4 Mapping of the Guidelines for the Design Process Model

The guidelines were mapped for the stages and activities of the ICAH model, according to the results obtained in the case study for the validation of the guidelines. Thus, we present the mapping in every stage.

The stage of Collection and Analysis of Requirements is divided into the activities: Identify Contexts, Abilities, and Technologies; Promote the Collaboration with Change of Activities; and Encourage the Use of New Technologies. Such stage aims to identify how the different contexts integrate themselves at the user's workplace, which previous knowledge and abilities the user has, which technological resources are provided at the workplace, and which ones are the user's. And it also tries to identify how, when, and what for the technological resources are used. Therefore, for this stage the following guidelines were mapped:

- Integration of Context Domain: guidelines 1 and 8.
- Addition of Abilities Domain: guidelines 1, 2, 5, 6 and 10.

For the activity "Identify Contexts, Abilities, and Technologies", the guidelines 2, 3, 4, 5 and 7, from the integration of contexts domain, were mapped. For the activity "Promote the Collaboration with Change of Activities", the guideline 8, from the addition of abilities domain, was mapped. And for the activity "Encourage the Use of New Technologies", the guidelines 4 and 9, from the addition of abilities domain, were mapped. Table 2 presents the mapping for such stage.

Table 2. Mapping of the guidelines for the stage collection and analysis of requirements

STAGE	Activity	Integration of context	Addition of abilities
Collection and analysis of requirements		1, 8	1, 2, 5, 6, 10
	Identify contexts, abilities, and technologies	2, 3, 4, 5, 7	3, 7
	Promote the collaboration with change of activities		8
	Encourage the use of new technologies		4, 9

The stage Construction is divided into the following activities: Project for Adoption and Appropriation; Project for Integration of Contexts; Prototype; and Evaluate for Adoption and Appropriation. It is in this stage that the design solutions are elaborated, prototypes are evolutionally created and evaluated after. This stage is iterative, starting with project activities: for adoption and appropriation, and for the integration of contexts, prototyping, and evaluation. Consequently, new abilities can be incorporated in the user's routine and new appropriations can happen. For this stage the following guidelines were mapped:

- Integration of Context Domain: guidelines 6 and 8.
- Addition of Abilities Domain: guidelines 3 and 7.

The stage Acquisition of Abilities happens inasmuch as the design solutions are adopted and appropriated. User's abilities and knowledge are used in other contexts, in other ways and with other technologies. Experiences must be shared between users and designers, and such process allows that new appropriations are observed. Allowing the experience of new abilities assists in the process of adoption of employment and the new abilities acquired and adopted by the users are added to their previous ones. These new abilities will also be able to be used as entrance artifacts in the next collections of requirements for new applications and in the evolution or improvement of solutions already in use. For this stage the following guidelines were mapped:

- Addition of Abilities Domain: guidelines 4 and 9.

The stages of Adoption and Appropriation were incorporated to the ICAH model departing from the model for Appropriation proposed by [8, 18] and guidelines were not mapped for these stages. Figure 4 presents, schematically, the complete mapping of the guidelines for the ICAH model.

For this final mapping, we conducted the case study with developers of applications and healthcare professionals, and the proposed guidelines were utilized during the study for the proposal of an application solution in a hospital. Design sessions and interviews were performed during the employment of the study and design solutions were presented. The healthcare professionals and the developers reported their experiences during the whole process and the latter evaluated the used guidelines.

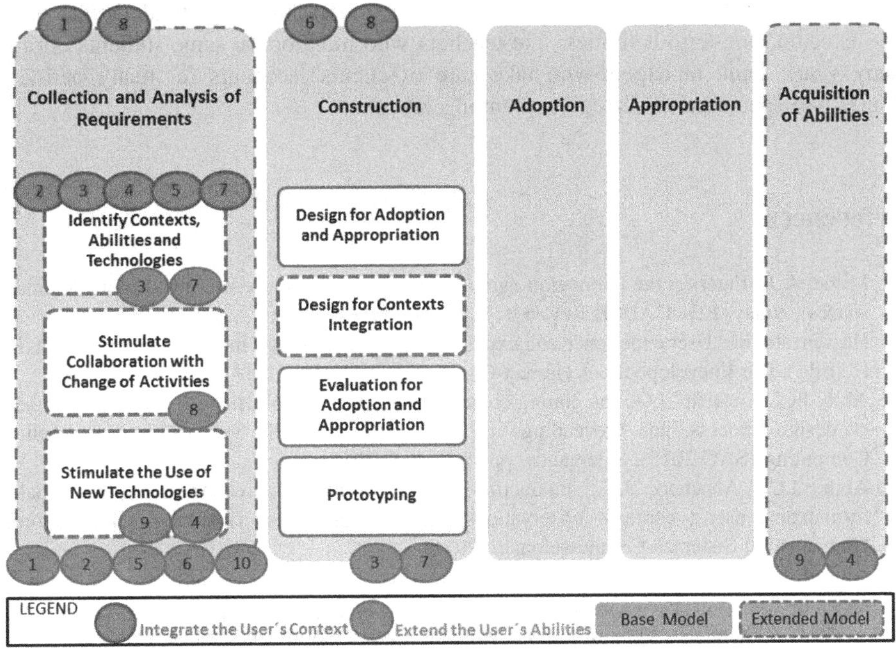

Fig. 4. Mapeamento das Guidelines

Finally, an apparent validation was conducted with specialists in application development to validate the proposed model.

5 Contributions and Future Work

This paper exposes a set of guidelines mapped for the ICAH Process Model of Development for healthcare applications.

The guidelines for Integrate Contexts consider the healthcare professionals' different contexts, integrating them in order to facilitate the management and execution of their professional, personal, and social activities. It also considers the use of technological resources to support this integration of contexts without harming the workflow of the professionals. The guidelines for Add Abilities consider the healthcare professional's previous knowledge and abilities to facilitate the search for improvement and the support for the addition of new abilities for these professionals, stimulating the support for the communication and information practices and promoting the formalization and documentation of the practices in the work of such professionals.

In conclusion, this paper presents a research that contributes and assists designers in the development of interactive applications for healthcare professionals, especially in long-term and constant care, integrating the personal and social contexts to the professional one and supporting the addition of abilities for these professionals through the offered assistance. It still contributes for future researches that may be conducted to refine or extend the proposed solutions for other professionals, particularly the ones who execute long-term activities, like teachers who monitor the same students during many years, bank managers who take care of clients' accounts for many periods, elderly and special needs caregivers, among others.

References

1. Milne, A.J.: Entering the interaction age: implementing a future vision for campus learning spaces…today. EDUCAUSE Rev. **42**(1), 12–31 (2011)
2. Hassenzahl, M.: User experience and experience design, 2nd Edn. In: Soegaard, M., Dam, R. F. (Eds.) The Encyclopedia of Human-Computer Interaction (2013)
3. Abib, J.C., Anacleto, J.C.: Integrating contexts in healthcare: guidelines to help the designers at design process. In: Proceedings of 30th ACM/SIGAPP Symposium on Applied Computing (SAC 2015), Salamanca, pp. 182–184 (2015)
4. Abib, J.C., Anacleto, J.C.: Interaction design process for healthcare professionals: formalizing user's contexts observations. In: XIV Simpósio Brasileiro sobre Fatores Humanos em Sistemas Computacionais (2015)
5. Abib, J.C., Anacleto, J.C.: Modeling a design process to natural user interface and not ICT users. In: The 18th ACM Conference on CSCW: Workshop Doing CSCW Research in Latin America: Differences, Opportunities, Challenges, and Lessons Learned (2015)
6. Abib, J.C., Anacleto, J.C.: Improving communication in healthcare: a case study. In: 2014 IEEE International Conference on Systems, Man and Cybernetics (SMC), 2014, San Diego, pp. 3336–3348 (2014)
7. Abib, J.C., Bueno, A., Anacleto, J.: Understanding and facilitating the communication process among healthcare professionals. In: Duffy, Vincent G. (ed.) DHM 2014. LNCS, vol. 8529, pp. 313–324. Springer, Cham (2014). doi:10.1007/978-3-319-07725-3_31
8. Anacleto, J.C., Fels, S.: Adoption and appropriation: a design process from HCI research at a Brazilian Neurological Hospital. In: Proceedings of the Conference on Human-Computer Interaction (INTERACT 2013), South Africa, vol. 8118, pp. 356–363 (2013)
9. Anacleto, J.C., Silva, M.A.R., Hernandes, E.C.M.: Co-authoring proto-patterns to support on designing systems to be adequate for users′ diversity. In: Proceedings of the 15th International Conference on Enterprise Information Systems, vol. 1, pp. 84–89. SCITE-PRESS Science and Technology Publications, Portugal (2013)
10. Anacleto, J.C., Fels, S., Silvestre, R.: Transforming a paper based process to a natural user interfaces process in a Chronic Care Hospital. Procedia Comput. Sci. J. **14**, 173–180 (2012)
11. Anacleto, J., Fels, S., Silvestre, R., Souza Filho, C.E., Santana, B.: Therapist-centered design of NUI based therapies in a neurological care hospital. In: Proceedings of the IEEE International Conference on System, Man, and Cybernetics, Korea, pp. 2318–2323 (2012)
12. Britto, T., Abib, J.C., Camargo, L.S.A., Anacleto, J.C.: A participatory design approach to use natural user interface for e-Health. In: Proceedings of 5th Workshop on Software and Usability Engineering Cross-Pollination: Patters, Usability and User Experience, pp. 35–42 (2011)
13. Calderon, R., Fels, S., Anacleto, J., Oliveira, J.L.: Towards supporting informal information and communication practices within a Brazilian healthcare environment. In: Proceedings of the ACM CHI Conference on Human Factors in Computing Systems - Extended Abstracts (CHI EA 2013), pp. 517-522, France (2013). ACM 978-1-4503-1952-2/13/04

14. Calderon, R., Fels, S., Oliveira, J.L., Anacleto, J.: Understanding NUI-supported nomadic social places in a Brazilian health care facility. In: Proceedings of the 11th Brazilian Symposium on Human Factors in Computing Systems, Brazil, pp. 76–84 (2012)
15. Oliveira, J.L.: Sistema de Recomendação para Promoção de Redes Homófilas Baseadas em Valores Culturais: observando o impacto das relações hemofílicas na reciprocidade apoiada pela tecnologia. Dissertação de Mestrado, Universidade Federal de São Carlos, p. 76 (2013). In Portuguese
16. Silva, M.A.R., Anacleto, J.C.: Adding semantic relations among design patterns. In: Proceedings of the 15th International Conference on Enterprise Information Systems, vol. 1, pp. 1–11. SCITEPRESS Science and Technology Publications, Portugal (2014)
17. Silva, M.A.R., Anacleto, J.C.: Patterns to support designing of co-authoring web educational systems. In: Proceedings of IADIS WWW/Internet 2013 Conference, Fort Worth, pp. 117–124. International Association for Development of the Information Society (IADIS Press) (2013)
18. Anacleto, J.C., Fels, S.: Lessons from ICT design of a healthcare worker-centered system for a chronic mental care hospital. In: Proceedings of the ACM Conference on Human Factors in Computing Systems (CHI 2014), Canada (2014)
19. Abib, J., Anacleto, J.: Guidelines to integrate professional, personal and social context in interaction design process: studies in healthcare environment. In: Kurosu, M. (ed.) HCI 2015. LNCS, vol. 9169, pp. 119–131. Springer, Cham (2015). doi:10.1007/978-3-319-20901-2_11
20. Lindtner, S., Anderson, K., Dourish, P.: Cultural appropriation: information technologies as sites of transnational imagination. In: Proceedings of the ACM Conference on Computer Supported Cooperative Work (CSCW 2012), pp. 77–86 (2012)
21. Salovaara, A., Höök, K., Cheverst, K., Twidale, M., Chalmers, M., Sas, C.: Appropriation and creative use: linking user studies and design. In: Proceedings of the ACM Conference on Human Factors in Computing Systems (CHI 2011), pp. 37–40, Canada (2011)
22. Salovaara, A.: Studying appropriation of everyday technologies: a cognitive approach. In: Proceedings of the Extended Abstracts on Human Factors in Computing Systems (CHI EA 2009), pp. 3141–3144 (2009)
23. Salovaara, A.: Appropriation of a MMS-based comic creator: from system functionalities to resources for action. In: Proceedings of the SIGCHI Conference on Human Factors in Computing Systems, pp. 1117–1126 (2007)
24. Robinson, M.: Design for unanticipated use.... In: Proceedings of the 3rd European Conference on Computer-Supported Cooperative Work (ECSCW 1993), pp. 187–202 (1993)
25. French, A.M., Guo, C., Shim, J.P.: Current status, issues, and future of Bring Your Own Device (BYOD). Commun. Assoc. Inf. Syst. **35**, 191–197 (2014)
26. Scarfo, A.: New security perspectives around BYOD. In: Proceedings of the 7th International Conference on Broadband, Wireless Computing, Communication and Applications, pp. 446–451 (2012)
27. Earley, S., Harmon, R., Lee, M.R., Mithas, S.: From BYOD to BYOA, Phishing, and Botnets. IT Prof. **16**(5), 16–18 (2014)
28. Salovaara, A., Höök, K., Cheverst, K., Twidale, M., Chalmers, M., Sas, C.: Appropriation and creative use: linking user studies and design. In: Proceedings of the ACM Conference on Human Factors in Computing Systems (CHI 2011), Canada, pp. 37–40 (2011)

29. Dourish, P.: The appropriation of interactive technologies: some lessons from placeless documents. Computer Supported Cooperative Work **12**(4), 465–490 (2003)
30. Wakkary, R., Maestri, L.: The resourcefulness of everyday design. In: Proceedings of the 6th ACM SIGCHI Conference on Creativity \& Cognition (C\&C 2007), pp. 163–172 (2007)

Failures Supporting the Evolutionary Design in the Wild of Interactive Systems for Public Spaces

Vinicius Ferreira(✉), Junia Anacleto, and Andre Bueno

Federal University of São Carlos, São Carlos, Brazil
{vinicius.ferreira,junia,andre.obueno}@dc.ufscar.br

Abstract. In this paper, we describe the lessons learned from an experience of deploying an interactive public installation adopting a methodology that intertwines aspects of in-the-wild study and evolutionary design. This methodology shrinks the cycle of design of a prototype and allows researchers and practitioners continuously design improvements while they learn from evaluating the prototype in the wild. Thereby, multiple settings can be explored, minimizing the need to conduct new experiments that demand time and resources. Considering the metaphor of a wishing well, we designed a public interactive installation, allowing people to make wishes using their personal or a shared device to throw a virtual coin into a real water fountain augmented with a wall-sized screen displaying a "pool of wishes." We deployed this interactive installation in a passageway of building for eight days, collecting data from observations, questionnaires, interviews, photos and video recordings. Based on the failures in our first cycle of design with the prototype, we present our findings and directions to apply our methodology. We claim the need of a pilot study in situ and having a team committed in collecting and analyzing data, discussing the insights and changes. In addition, the system design must support predictable, orderly and managed evolution. Finally, we contribute to the ubicomp field, demonstrating the implications for evaluating evolutionary prototype in the wild.

Keywords: Prototyping methods · In-the-wild · Evolutionary design · Ubicomp

1 Introduction

Interactive technologies are increasingly spreading through the urban environment, moving Human Computer Interaction (HCI) into a new research paradigm. Researchers are shifting from their labs into the real world, developing and deploying pervasive technologies for people [15]. This in-the-wild movement emphasizes performing in situ user studies with new technologies to uncover design probes in real-life context settings [16]. Moreover, this approach differs from previous ethnographic approaches applied to interaction design that propose to observe existing practices to elicit system requirements and general implications for the design [15].

In-the-wild approach focuses on learning from users experimenting and adopting a prototype in situ. From this approach, several insights can emerge that demand modifications on the prototype and require new experiments, which consumes resources and

M. Kurosu (Ed.): HCI 2017, Part I, LNCS 10271, pp. 283–296, 2017.
DOI: 10.1007/978-3-319-58071-5_22

time for planning and execution. To mitigate that, we have included aspects of evolutionary design into the in-the-wild approach. Thus, this new methodology augments the in-the-wild approach by encompassing aspects of evolutionary design, allowing to designer to learn from evaluating the prototype and improving it in situ.

The rise of the support of ubiquitous and pervasive technologies to the Online Social Networks is modifying the way we interact with others. People have more opportunities to socialize in the virtual world and to be context aware. This expansion of our social world supported by technologies allows people to have their social needs attended, even though it is clearly not enough to attend our human needs for contact [12]. With such understanding, we want to explore the process of iterating in-the-wild with a public interactive installation that aims at support and promote the sharing of personal content in public. This public sharing would be the chance for people to know their own community, in a process of socialization.

In this paper, we present our lessons learned from a case study with a situated public interactive installation, indicating how evolutionary design of interactive systems for public spaces can accommodate and support in-the-wild studies.

2 Related Work

The demand for novel technologies that can improve people's lives is leading to the growing interest in in-the-wild studies. The in-the-wild approach shifts the design thinking model of designing a solution, exploring new possibilities that can change and even disrupt human behavior. This fact differs from previous ethnography methods that focus on producing a solution according to the established practices [16].

Using the in-the-wild approach to evaluate novel technologies is valuable to capture people's reactions when first experiencing these solutions. This evaluation process encompasses observing and recording people's behavior while interacting with a prototype. From the outcomes of in-the-wild studies, researchers can better understand how people use and appropriate solutions of technology on their own terms and for their own situated purposes [16]. According to Rogers et al. [15], lab studies may fail in capturing the complexities of the situations in which ubiquitous applications will pass when launched in the real world. Another difference in this kind of study is the absence of a facilitator explaining the purposes and functionalities of the application to the participants. This fact can make users behave more naturally, increasing the ecological validity of the outcomes and findings. On the other hand, ethical, legislation and privacy concerns are crucial in this approach to not expose the participant to risks [13].

During a deployment in the wild, several insights can emerge as researchers learn from observing the participants. However, to test these insights in the wild, the prototype must be robust and flexible enough to enable modifications on the design as the research evaluation is carrying. Providing this flexibility for interactive systems is one of the main goals of the evolutionary design, which focuses on continuous improvement of a solution [18].

For Dittrich et al. [6], with technologies evolving at a rapid pace, new applications should provide forms of maintenance, tailoring, adaptation and further development.

They propose a model, called "design-during-use", in which a system is updated to a new version according to explicit requests from end-users or changes in the system. This practice is related to the participatory design, in which all stakeholders are involved in the design process.

Botero and Hyssalo [3] used the co-design to extend the evolutionary design as they learn and engage users to collaborate on evolving the prototype. Once their users were elderly people with no expertise in design and few skills in technology, they outline their lessons learned from a study case and provide a set of guideline to help designers to engage co-designers.

Carter and Mankoff [4] present their findings on how to evaluate ubiquitous applications from a case study with three applications, using non-interactive and interactive prototypes. From the non-interactive prototypes, they valued as useful for rapid iteration and for getting early, but limited, feedback on the situated use. On the other hand, interactive prototypes provide more helpful and invaluable feedback about the use and for the co-evolution of the application. However, interactive prototypes are difficult and time consuming to deploy.

Crabtree et al. [5] outline key challenges in applying in-the-wild studies. In this kind of approach, using video recording can be difficult to identify and extract of useful information as well as to synchronize different sources of video and log system. They claim the need for a tool to support the analysis of the footage. In contrast, Hazlewood et al. [10] describe the evaluation issues in using observation approach, which can be limited, affected by the lack control of context, and hard to avoid contamination of the researchers. Besides that, opinions and behaviors reported in the interviews cannot match with the data captured using the sensors or system logs.

Summarizing, the in-the-wild approach involves performing studies by deploying novel technologies in real-world conditions to observe and understand how people use and appropriate them [16]. On the other hand, evolutionary design approach provides a model for incrementally creating and modifying an application, over the system lifetime [18]. This evolution is characterized by adaptability of the system, enabling to adapt rapidly to changes in the environment, including user needs and wants, and other externalities.

Based on the previous lessons learned from evolutionary design and in-the-wild studies, in this paper, we explore a model that allows to evaluate different settings and scenarios as we learn from observing users interacting with the system. This prototyping approach differs from others [3, 4, 5, 7, 10, 13, 15] by providing a model for planning, deploying, evaluating, gathering requirements, and modifying the prototype to enhance the design in situ.

3 Iterating a Prototype in-the-Wild

Deploying prototypes in the real-world conditions such as public spaces can be very challenging for researchers [7]. Many aspects not envisioned in the design process can emerge during the experiment. To address that, we present a prototyping approach that intertwines aspects of in-the-wild study and evolutionary design, enabling the designer to modify the software characteristics to evaluate them in real-world settings.

Considering that interactive technologies are becoming part of urban and everyday experience and that the urban space is dynamic and complex, systems for these conditions should support predictable, orderly and managed evolution. This evolution and changes on the design depends on certain design qualities. For the code, the system should avoid duplications of code; keep the code simple, clear, cohesive and decoupled; isolate third-party code [18]. Scenarios can be used to foresee possible changes on the prototype and make them easily deployable. However, system should also allow the designer to implement unforeseen changes in those scenarios. Furthermore, changes in the prototype are not limited to the code and include changes in the components of the prototype and in the context in which the prototype is deployed.

Considering an evolutive public interactive installation, the prototype should be robust, flexible and highly parameterized, allowing to make and test changes in the prototype efficiently and incrementally. Test-Driven Design and automated tests can be used to ensure quality and stability in the system. The prototype must provide useful information, once the lack of feedback is recognized as the main issue to evolve interactive systems [17]. Changes in the prototype should ensure reliability, availability, and safety of the system, providing an efficient evolution without impacting the system's service to its users. To support these requirements, the code can use a modular architecture using reusable components and services-oriented system. In addition, the prototype must be user piloted to certify that there are no functionality issues before the real deployment.

4 Case Study

Aiming at exploring our methodology, intertwining aspects of the evolutionary design and in-the-wild approach, we created an interactive installation called WishBoard. WishBoard is a digital art project that promotes a collaborative expression of the wishes of its participants, aiming at promoting a sense of community. With their personal mobile devices, such as smartphones, people can interact with the technological installation contributing to the collective construction of the artwork. The installation aims to provoke a reflection about the future, celebrating local culture and promoting contemplation. People can share their wishes and dreams, anonymously, using their mobile devices and accessing to the installation website and filling out a sentence.

For this project, we have been using different metaphors to embody it, as shown in Fig. 1. Taking our previous experiences with other WishBoard installations [9], we used a new metaphor aiming at transforming a socially abandoned space into a more social and interactive place. This space is the old Student Union Building at the University of British Columbia.

Fig. 1. WishBoard installations exploring multiple screens and projections.

4.1 The Old Student Union Building at the Campus

Since a new Student Union Building (SUB) was introduced in the campus of the University of British Columbia (UBC), a process of replacing the old building was established among the students. The old Student Union Building, referred here as "the old SUB", was built in 1968 and for more than 50 years has been considered the heart of student life at the UBC's Vancouver campus. For a long time, students used the place to study, eat, shop and socialize. The space functioned as the third place for the students, offering restaurants, bars, stores, meeting rooms, a movie theater, and leisure area. However, with the growth of the campus student population over the time, the space has become ineffective. Thus, people began gradually to avoid the old SUB and to gather in other spaces in a decentralized manner, causing a community fragmentation and affecting the social experience of the campus [1].

Third places comprise a generic description for a variety of public places (e.g. bars, cafes, barbershops and beauty salons), where people voluntarily and regularly attend for casual encounters and social interaction, enjoying each other's company. These places are crucial to the maintenance of community life, promoting intimate personal ties among individuals beyond the realms of home (first place) and workplace (second place). In addition, having a harmonious balance between the domestic, productive, and sociable realms of everyday life is necessary to maintain a good quality of life [14].

After a process of seven years, the new SUB, formally named as the AMS Student Nest, was established from the scratch, focusing on the needs and desires of the students on campus. Aiming at ensuring a student-centered hub of activity, the place creates a welcoming environment for all students, introducing new sustainability practices and goals. With the release of the new SUB at UBC, the old SUB has become increasingly a deposit, since the remaining restaurants struggle to keep their patrons. In addition, the space lost attributes of an inviting place, such as, cleaning, attractiveness and accommodation. This lack of maintaining can lead to an urban disorder, vandalism and antisocial behavior, according to the broken windows theory [19]. As people start to avoid staying there, the space becomes more abandoned. However, people still use the main hallway of old SUB to transit between the bus stop and the new SUB. Figure 2 shows the difference between the old and new SUB.

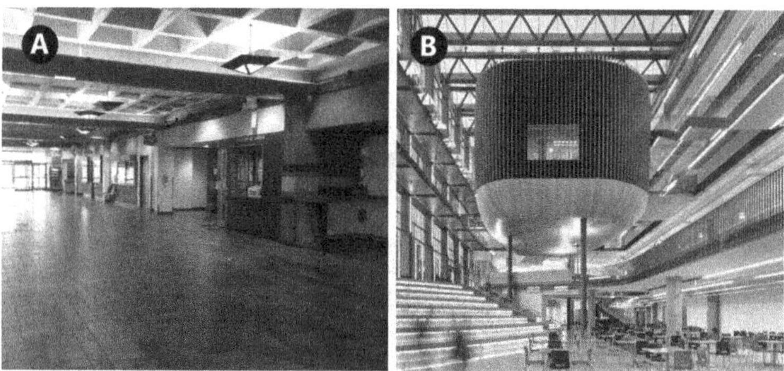

Fig. 2. (a) Old SUB versus (b) AMS Student Nest building. Photo credit: Ema Peter/Vancouver Sun. 2007. Retrieved from: http://www.vancouversun.com/story.html?id=12729426

In partnership with the student society of UBC (Alma Mater Society) and aiming at making people pay attention to the old SUB, we propose to create an interactive installation using the concept of the WishBoard. By promoting the sharing of wishes in public spaces, WishBoard purposes to make people aware about the existence of a greater community around the space. Thus, the installation could bring social life to the abandoned space, which has been once considered the third place on the campus.

4.2 Designing the Public Installation

We started our design collecting some requirements, such as, spaces available and which spaces are still in use. After that, we performed brainstorming sessions to refine the requirements and elicit metaphors for sharing wishes. Our goal was to create a technological installation, rethinking how people make wishes and considering cultural issues. To refine the ideas, we performed some brainstorming sessions with the support of the sketching technic to assist the visual thinking.

Having collected ideas of metaphors, we chose the idea of a wishing well in which people throw coins into a water fountain. This metaphor represents our thoughts on how technology can metaphorically be the "new fountain" on public spaces, attracting people and augmenting public spaces.

Fountains were people aggregators for centuries. Originally, they were purely functional, providing water for drinking, bathing and washing to the residents of cities, towns and villages. Therefore, fountains were used for decoration and to celebrate their builders, glorifying their power over nature. Water is vital for sustaining human life, for ancients having drinking water was a gift from the heavens. Since indoor plumbing became popular by the end of 19th century, urban fountains have become purely ornamental. Nowadays, they are used to decorate parks and squares, promoting contemplation and charming place. Fountains are also used for recreation and for entertainment [11]. The tradition of throwing coins into fountains came from an ancient practice of presenting gifts to gods aiming to appease angry gods or offering payment for a request. In modern times, people still practice this tradition, usually making a wish as we can observe at Trevi Fountain in Fig. 3. Eventually, the tradition has evolved and other ideas were introduced, such as, throwing two coins into the fountain will make easier to find the soul mate. This tradition is widely spread that thousands of coins are thrown daily in the Trevi Fountain, which are swept out and donated to the local charities [2].

Fig. 3. Person making a wish by throwing a coin into the Trevi Fountain.

In order to promote a temporary appropriation of a space in a process of replacement, an approach is to promote self-expression. This kind of expression is a powerful sign of freedom, in which, individuals project their thoughts, feelings, opinions, and identity into the world [12]. Using urban interactive installations to foster self-expression can help to strengthen the sense of community and interconnection among people in a community. People may feel connected to the community once they share similar goals, preferences, beliefs or values.

Using the principles of interactive aesthetics, we designed an instance of the WishBoard project. According to Fels [8], people build relationships with external objects to their own self depending on how deeply embodied the person is into an object or an object is into the person. He suggests four relationships: response, control, contemplation, and belonging. These types of relationships occur during the interactive experience and may overlap, increasing the intimacy relation between a person and an object. The interaction began in an exploratory way, aiming at understanding the installation. After that, the user feels able to interact with the installation and then people can begin a reflection on the installation. At the end, people can actually participate of the installation contributing with their message and becoming part of the installation. Furthermore, messages and the quantity of messages can induce contemplation, making people spend more time on the installation. Together, all four interactive aesthetic components were included in the design of WishBoard.

WishBoard prototype reinterprets the metaphor of making wishes in a wishing well. As shown in Fig. 4, the installation is composed of a water fountain and a wall-sized projection screen behind. The water fountain represents a "wish catcher" – in reference to the "dream catcher" from Native American culture – that receives and selects the wishes, filling the "pool of wishes" represented by the large screen. People can watch the shared wishes projected coming from the water fountain to the large screen, floating on a virtual "pool of wishes" as if they were leaves. To encourage people to share their wish, every time a new wish is thrown into the fountain, the system presents the wish in a magical and captivating way by making it appear as if it was streaming out with the water stream of the real fountain and making a splash sound, giving feedback to the newcomer that their wish was received. After that, the wish joins the collective wishes floating as a leaf in the projected water motif. With this collaborative expression, the installation provides the sense of belonging to the community and place attachment, as if a part of themselves was "rooted" in that place.

Fig. 4. WishBoard installation at the old SUB at the UBC.

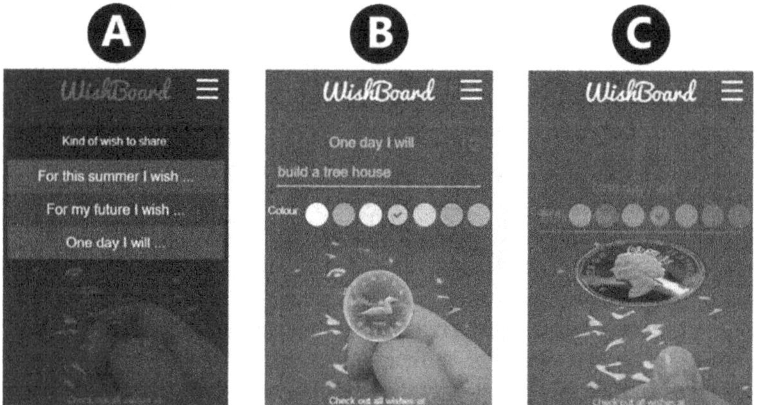

Fig. 5. Sharing a wish with WishBoard using a mobile device

To share a wish on WishBoard, users use should access the installation website and complete one of the template wish statements, e.g., "One day I will ___", as shown in Fig. 5. They can also choose the font color of their wish. After filling out the wish, users can virtually throw the coin into the fountain by swiping the coin towards the top of the device. When the installation registers the wish arriving, a splash sound is played and the wish streams out of the water fountain. By using this approach, this project explores the interaction with contextualized situated public displays using personal and shared mobile phones, to build promote the development of intimacy and embodiment between people and people, and people and the dynamic art-system. Thus, WishBoard (Fig. 6) offers a space for self-reflection and contemplation, creating a rich aesthetic interactive experience on the behavioral, visceral, and reflective levels.

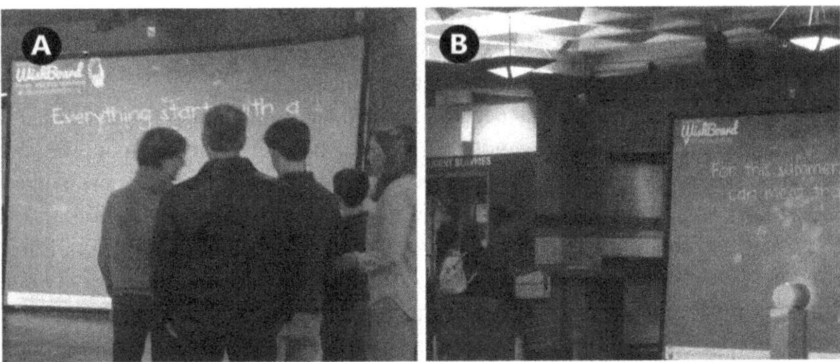

Fig. 6. People making wishes on WishBoard using (a) their own mobile devices and (b) a public ready-to-use device.

4.3 Study Design

Using a simpler version of the WishBoard prototype, we planned our experiment to collect data, in eight days, from interviews, questionnaires, photos, video recordings, and system logs. Researchers were present in strategic spaces, taking field notes without disturbing the normal characteristics of the space. We applied questionnaires and interviews to understand how people perceived the installation and collect feedbacks for improvements. To deal with ethical issues, users were presented to the consent form after sharing a wish inviting to collaborate with the study. In addition, we had approval from the UBC Research Ethics Board to run this study. We de-identified all data that can identify participants or that might embarrass them and we did not collect personal contact data (e.g. name and e-mail).

4.4 Results

In this section, we describe how we applied our methodology with the WishBoard, describing the design decisions, defining the metrics and the evaluation methods. Following these steps, our goal was to test the successes and failures in our design decisions for the first version of the WishBoard and, consequently, elicit requirements for the next iterations.

To share a wish on WishBoard, the users need to access the installation website through a mobile device (e.g. smartphones) and fill out a sentence, as shown in Fig. 5. Once the interaction with public displays using personal mobile devices is not common around the campus, we wanted to collect people's feedback about this form of interaction without prejudicing the aesthetics of the installation. Consequently, to invite people to interact with the installation we decided to display "Please, make your wish at shareyourwishes.ca." near to the WishBoard logo in the upper left corner of the projection screen. We designed the url in order to be inviting and ease to recall. Once the installation should be self-explanatory and provide discoverability, we avoid to use additional supportive materials, such as banners, posters and folders. With this design, we expected that people would understand how to interact with the installation by sharing and visualizing their wishes on the installation. We defined as a success metric having at least 20% of people who stopped at the installation sharing a wish. However, after 4 h of experiment, it was evident that people did not understand they could interact with the installation using their smartphones. We found evidence of that, observing most of people that deeply explored the installation left it without sharing a wish. Although there was a large amount of people crossing the installation, we counted only seven people posting wishes. In the interviews, people said that they saw something different at the passageway, but most of them thought that was a presentation or a static video, and some of them asked if it was necessary to pay to use the installation. Based on those findings, we concluded that the installation should provide more interactivity clues.

Aiming at investigating how to address the lack of interactivity clues, we interviewed more three people who stopped by but did not share wishes, asking them the following questions: "What do you think this installation is about?", "Do you find out how to put your wish in there?", "Do you see any clue on the installation on how to do that?", "Do you know that you can use your phone to access that website on the installation?." In the answers, most of people mentioned that the installation was quite interesting due to the water fountain and sound. The funny wishes on the screen called their attention. Regarding to the url on the screen, two people said that they noticed a website url, however, they thought that they should use a computer to access that. Thus, we decided that the installation need to provide signifiers for interaction with smartphones. To address that, we believe that using a visual representation (icon) can support the inviting message in the interface.

In order to improve the attractiveness of the installation, we combined a big screen and a water fountain. We used sounds, animations, projection-based augmented reality, and other metaphors associated to the theme "wish." This would create a more sensorial and cozy environment for exploration, which could make people spend more time in the installation, unwinding, contemplating, and socializing with others. We established as success metrics having at least 10% of passersby stopping at the installation and sharing a wish and 20% of those people staying there for more than 60 s. Based on our previous measurements, the average time to make a wish on WishBoard is approximately 35 s. Although it is difficult to accurately measure how long each person remained in the installation, after 14 h of experiment, it was clear that most people who stopped were staying less than 20 s. In despite of people were being attracted by the installation turning their heads at the installation when they were crossing the installation, few people deeply explored the installation. We could count more than 300 people crossing the installation, but only 24 people engaged in a deeper exploration of the installation sharing a wish and 19 of these stayed in there for more than a minute. We counted more 7 people exploring the installation for more than a minute, however, they just read the wishes and 2 people took a picture of the installation. In the interviews, we asked to 6 participants what would make them stay more in the installation. In the answers, they pointed out that the installation was a great addition to the space to the building, however, it should provide more comfort to make people stay there for a long period.

To increase the inviting appeal of the installation, we decided to use a physical object – a small water fountain – to compose the installation. We believe that the relationship between the physical and the virtual object would complement the playfulness of the installation and could be an invitation to explore and then interact. We stated as a success metric, 20% of people commenting aloud, looking at or pointing at the water fountain. After 14 h of experiment, we noticed that the water fountain was more attractive than the screen behind. People were attracted to the fountain and water sound, and we counted 10 people touching the water in the fountain and we heard people saying: "Is that real water?", "Oh, my gosh! It's water", and "Can I touch it?." Although including water fountain was successful, some people were not engaging to explore the screen behind. Furthermore, as the people approach to the water fountain, reading what is on the screen becomes difficult due to the projection resolution. For the next iteration, we should explore better the water fountain area to make people want to fully explore the installation.

In order to display the shared wishes, we used a projection screen and explored projection-based augmented reality. By presenting randomly the shared wishes, we expected to make people stay around the installation reading the shared wishes, motivating people to discuss about the wishes, promoting socialization and making people return to the space. Due to the infrastructure limitations, we had to use front projection, consequently, in the first 4 h, we noticed more than 20 people avoiding crossing between the projector and the projected screen. Furthermore, we noticed people saying to others to avoid crossing in front the projector, people making a late stop when they noticed the presence of the projector and then crossing in front quickly or avoiding crossing in front the projector, and it was evident to hear people apologizing. In the interviews, people pointed out that they were avoiding crossing in front the projector to not disturb someone's presentation. Interestingly, we noticed 3 people being attracted by the brightness coming from the projector and starting to play with shadows, without interacting with the installation. We believe that the brightness, clarity and resolution of the projection were not enough to the context where the installation was set. In addition, until the end of the study, we did not notice same people returning to the installation on the same day or on different days. However, this fact can demonstrate how difficult is to identify people in the crowd through observation. For the next iteration, we need to explore means to make people more comfortable crossing in front of the projector, such as covering or hiding the hardware, once using front or rear projection was not viable. Based on those findings, we conclude that running a short pilot in that space before the real test could be enough to refine and improve some installation characteristics and other context related features such as the lighting.

Regarding to the advertising strategy, we planned to use videos and animations, in order to invite people to come to the old SUB and make a wish. However, we waited to evaluate if the installation was self-sufficient in attracting people. As we noticed that the number of people were decreasing in consequence of the beginning of the summer vacations, we started to announce the installation in the digital signage around the campus using videos. We thought that would attract more people to use the installation. However, we failed in our strategies to advertise the installation due to the attractiveness of the advertisements and late advertising. We noticed that people were not aware in advance of the installation. In the interviews and questionnaires, people discovered the installation only when they were walking through the installation. Only a person said that decided come to the installation because a friend has commented on it.

Aiming at extending the engagement with/within the installation, we had a profile on twitter where people could comment and share the wishes shared on the installation. This online presence would allow people to interact with other participants. However, we had no follower on our profile. We failed because we only advertised the twitter account on our website. For next experiments, we must use a better strategy to improve the visibility of our profile and. For example, previously announcing online our profile at the main twitter accounts and mailing list of the campus.

In order to test a new scenario, we introduced a public shared device – a tablet – in the installation, allowing people to have a ready-to-use device. After doing that, we noticed an expressive increase in the number of users from 37 to 160. Nevertheless, we observed one person leaving the tablet without sending the typed wish. This fact occurred in virtue of a disengagement of user, giving up sharing the wish and that could affect the next user with a non-fresh state of the system. To address this problem, we introduced a timer that refreshes the system if there is no user interacting with the interface for longer than 45 s. In the system logs, we counted that 70% of the wishes were shared through the public device.

Overall, successes and failures are part of the process of experimentation and learning. Learning as much as possible from failures is important to improve designs and make better design decisions. In the questionnaires applied to people that shared wishes at the installation, 91% of people felt that the process of interacting with WishBoard was straightforward. However, only 18% said that they could share a wish accessing through their own phones. On the other hand, 95% said that they could use the public shared device to share a wish. In addition, they said that WishBoard brought fun to the space and one of them commented that sharing wishes on WishBoard was "quick and fun!." In the interviews, people said they rather use the tablet with the application ready to use due to being faster and more convenient. From that evidence of weak commitment to interact with that kind of "not ready to use" interface, we suggest that public installations need to grab audience attention directly to present its purpose and mechanisms of interaction.

5 Implications for Evolutionary Prototypes in the Wild

With our case study, we learned that evaluating prototypes in the wild is difficult, especially in relation to ensure the accuracy of the data. Assessing the metrics in a public space by manually counting requires focus and agility. Researchers should have some expertise on in-the-wild studies to elicit situations that are worth to count or take notes. Although it is necessary, it is hard to predict which data will be useful to gain a deeper insight. Furthermore, the more data is collected, the more the researchers will spend time, resources and skills to analyze them. However, when systems for monitoring human behavior and physiological responses become more refined and reliable, capturing and classifying data will be more automatized providing richer analysis and new interpretation opportunities.

In in-the-wild studies, several unexpected bugs and needs can arise due to lack control of context. For studies carried out in public spaces, some bugs can emerge early in the beginning of the study. Therefore, we highly encourage researchers to run a pilot in the space before the experiment. In order to make easier to modify the prototype and test different settings, we strongly suggest to use modularization and parameterization, and to create a control panel, allowing to make adjustments and tuning of the system.

To make evaluating and iterating feasible, a team-based research approach is required. The researchers must discuss the insights emerge from the successes or failures on their design decisions. They also should be open to test the different solutions, and have the commitment in evaluating and continuously improving the design in the face of time pressure. However, researchers need to minimize as much as possible their impact to avoid compromising the ecological validity of the outcomes and findings.

6 Conclusion

In-the-wild studies provide invaluable feedback on the use of interactive prototypes, enabling to improve the design. However, performing several in-the-wild studies consumes time and resources. In order to shrink the cycle of design of a prototype, we included aspects of evolutionary design into the in-the-wild approach. To make that possible, we used a team-based research approach and a prototype ready to evolve. Considering that successes and failures are important to understand how to build better solutions, learning as much as possible from field-based studies is essential. In addition, learning from failures is important to refine and improve methods and techniques.

Based on our analysis from 199 people making 273 wishes, we describe a set of lessons learned. In public installations, provide clues of interactivity and the necessary affordances for people to effectively understand how to interact with the installation. Keep in mind that people are in public spaces with a goal and an expectation. Then, do not expect too much concentration during the process of exploring the installation. Breaking the barriers in the interaction, such as using a public ready to use input device can be more efficient than asking people to use their own devices. For greater thirdplaceness experience, provide a cozy and comfortable space for people to hang out around. Make a plan to advertise the installation to create a buzz and invite people to use the installation. Physical affordances can attract people attention, encouraging exploration of the installation. Providing anonymity is key to leverage public expression, enabling also introvert people to have the opportunity to express. The personal circumstances of passersby highly influence the interaction potential. Using certain kind of approaches such as direct inductive approach can be very intimidating, making people uncomfortable in using the installation. Overall, designing for playfulness have a key role in attracting people.

With our prototype, we bring significant contributions to the understanding on how to conduct an experiment with an evolutionary situated prototype. Future work will involve refining this approach and designing tools to support ethnographers and researchers to study ubiquitous computing.

Acknowledgments. We thank all the participants, the fellows from the Advanced Interaction Lab (LIA at UFSCar) and Human Communication Technologies Lab (HTC Lab at UBC), and our sponsors Peter Wall Institute for Advanced Studies (PWIAS/UBC), Boeing, FAPESP, and CAPES.

References

1. AMS of UBC: Building the student nest (2015). https://youtu.be/xaExo_vpydo
2. BBC - Trevi coins to fund food for poor (2006). http://news.bbc.co.uk/2/hi/6188052.stm
3. Botero, A., Hyysalo, S.: Ageing together: steps towards evolutionary co-design in everyday practices. CoDesign **9**(1), 37–54 (2013). doi:10.1080/15710882.2012.760608
4. Carter, S., Mankoff, J.: Prototypes in the wild lessons from three ubicomp systems. IEEE Pervasive Comput. **4**(4), 51–57 (2005). doi:10.1109/MPRV.2005.84
5. Crabtree, A., Benford, S., Greenhalgh, C., Tennent, P., Chalmers, M., Brown, B.: Supporting ethnographic studies of ubiquitous computing in the wild. In: Proceedings of the 6th conference on Designing Interactive systems (DIS 2006), pp. 60–69. ACM, New York (2006). doi: 10.1145/1142405.1142417
6. Darlow, A., Goldin, G., Sloman, S.: Causal interactions. In: Proceedings of the SIGCHI Conference on Human Factors in Computing Systems (CHI 2014), pp. 1655–1664. ACM, New York (2014). doi:10.1145/2556288.2557216
7. Dittrich, Y., Eriksén, S., Hansson, C.: PD in the wild: evolving practices of design in use. In: Participatory Design Conference. Malmö, Sweden (2002)
8. Fels, S.: Designing intimate experiences. In: Proceedings of the 9th International Conference on Intelligent User Interfaces, pp. 2–3. ACM, New York (2004). doi:10.1145/964442.964443
9. Ferreira, V., Anacleto, J., Bueno, A.: Sharing wishes on public displays: using technology to create social places. In: Abascal, J., Barbosa, S., Fetter, M., Gross, T., Palanque, P., Winckler, M. (eds.) INTERACT 2015. LNCS, vol. 9298, pp. 578–595. Springer, Cham (2015). doi: 10.1007/978-3-319-22698-9_40
10. Hazlewood, W., Stolterman, E., Connelly, K.: Issues in evaluating ambient displays in the wild: two case studies. In: Proceedings of the SIGCHI Conference on Human Factors in Computing Systems (CHI 2011), pp 877–886. ACM, New York (2011). doi:10.1145/1978942.1979071
11. Juuti, P., Antoniou, G., Dragoni, W., El-Gohary, F., Feo, G., Katko, T., Rajala, R., Zheng, X., Drusiani, R., Angelakis, A.: Short global history of fountains. Water **7**(5), 2314–2348 (2015). doi: 10.3390/w7052314
12. Kim, H., Sherman, D.: "Express yourself": culture and the effect of self-expression on choice. J. Pers. Soc. Psychol. **92**(1), 1–11 (2007). doi:10.1037/0022-3514.92.1.1
13. Marshall, P., Morris, R., Rogers, Y., Kreitmayer, S., Davies, M.: Rethinking 'multi-user': an in-the-wild study of how groups approach a walk-up-and-use tabletop interface. In: Proceedings of the SIGCHI Conference on Human Factors in Computing Systems (CHI 2011), pp. 3033–3042. ACM, New York (2011). doi:10.1145/1978942.1979392
14. Oldenburg, R.: The Great Good Place: Cafés, Coffee Shops, Bookstores, Bars, Hair Salons, and Other Hangouts at the Heart of a Community. Marlowe (1999)
15. Rogers, Y., Connelly, K., Tedesco, L., Hazlewood, W., Kurtz, A., Hall, R.E., Hursey, J., Toscos, T.: Why it's worth the hassle: the value of in-situ studies when designing Ubicomp. In: Krumm, J., Abowd, Gregory D., Seneviratne, A., Strang, T. (eds.) UbiComp 2007. LNCS, vol. 4717, pp. 336–353. Springer, Heidelberg (2007). doi:10.1007/978-3-540-74853-3_20
16. Rogers, Y.: Interaction design gone wild: striving for wild theory. Interactions **18**(4), 58–62 (2011). doi:10.1145/1978822.1978834
17. Salasin, J., Shrobe, H.: Evolutionary design of complex software (EDCS). In: SIGSOFT Software Engineering 1995. Notes 20, 5 December 1995
18. Shore, J.: Continuous design. IEEE Softw. **21**, 20–22 (2004). doi:10.1109/MS.2004.1259183
19. Wilson, J., Kelling, G.: Broken windows. Critical issues in policing: Contemporary readings (1982)

Methods for Evaluation of Tooltips

Helene Isaksen[1(✉)], Mari Iversen[1], Jens Kaasbøll[1], and Chipo Kanjo[2]

[1] University of Oslo, Oslo, Norway
{helenis,mariive,jensj}@ifi.uio.no
[2] University of Malawi, Zomba, Malawi
chipo.kanjo@gmail.com

Abstract. Tooltips are context-sensitive help aimed at improving learnability of a system. Evaluation of tooltips would therefore be a part of evaluation of documentation, which is a subcategory of evaluation of software learnability. Previous research only includes two evaluations of tooltips, both gauging learning outcome after initial training, while the purpose of tooltips is helping users whenever in doubt when using systems after training. The previous evaluations are therefore of a low content validity. This paper concerns data field tooltips aimed at improving correctness of data entry. It present studies a scale of content validities. On the low level is a questionnaire on users' opinion, which is a cheap evaluation. The medium type of evaluation was an adapted question-suggestion test measuring learning outcome. The high content validity evaluation method was a field experiment over two weeks, which demonstrated improved performance caused by tooltips. If the cheap questionnaire came out with the same preferences as the costly experiment, doing the questionnaire could have replaced experiments. However, the experiment did not confirm the results from the questionnaire.

Keywords: Research methods · Usability evaluation · Learnability · Context-sensitive help · Content validity · Explanatory power · Predictive power

1 Introduction

The case triggering this research is a patient information system for nurses in developing countries, which is also used by health personnel below the nursing level due to scarcity of nurses. It was observed that the lower level personnel struggled with entering medical data. The practical objective of this research is to bring the lower level health personnel up to the nurses' level at entering health data. Due to other means of training being too costly and other interface design too inefficient, tooltips were deemed the most feasible way to improve the health workers' performance. Due to lack of knowledge on contents and expression in tooltips, the research aimed at finding design criteria for these two aspects.

The main purpose of a tooltip is to provide additional help to the users who are unsure about what to do, such that they are more likely to complete their tasks successfully. Tooltips are therefore aimed at improving software learnability and should be evaluated accordingly.

M. Kurosu (Ed.): HCI 2017, Part I, LNCS 10271, pp. 297–312, 2017.
DOI: 10.1007/978-3-319-58071-5_23

Grossman et al. [6] suggested a taxonomy of learnability definitions, including the user's competence level, their ability to improve performance and the time period over which improvement is going to take place. This study concerns the ability to improve performance over specific intervals for users whose domain knowledge is below optimal. Two different time intervals are included; one hour and two weeks.

Tooltips are parts of user documentation, hence their evaluation belongs in the metrics based on documentation usage in Grossman et al.'s [6] categories of learnability metrics.

The case concerns the lower level cadres' ability to perform at the nursing level after some practice. An evaluation of their work sometime after initial learning would constitute an appropriate measure of what the tooltip intervention aimed at, and we will call such appropriateness of the measurement method high content validity. However, field tests in real life settings are in general costly. Thus, a simple method for zooming in on the more useful types of tooltips before embarking on the most expensive evaluation would be advantageous.

A sequence of usability evaluations from cheap and theoretical to cumbersome and realistic could be:

- Heuristic expert evaluation according to guidelines for design.
- Lab experiment with users, e.g., thinking aloud.
- Field evaluation of actual use.

Since no guidelines for tooltip contents seem to exist, a heuristic evaluation was impossible. A questionnaire to the target user group on their preference was chosen as a low cost alternative. The questionnaire did not measure the health workers' learning, hence being of low content validity.

Lazar et al.'s [14] textbook on HCI research methods brings up the validity of methods in the sense of applying well documented procedures. Surveys with questionnaires can be carried out with rigor, but that does not improve their content validity in our case.

Content validity and cost are important qualities when selecting evaluation method. Since no assessment of learnability evaluation methods with respect to these qualities seem to exist, this paper aims at filling these knowledge gaps. In addition, the power of research findings to explain or predict is a consequence of choice of method and will therefore also be considered.

The next session introduce tooltips. Thereafter the theoretical background for content validity and power of output are presented, and these qualities will be used for characterizing previous tooltip evaluations. The evaluation methods applied in this research will be presented and assessed on these qualities. The methods will be compared and a taxonomy of evaluation methods will be built. In the conclusion, evaluation of tooltips for domain data will be compared to tooltips for IT functionality and to other inline help.

2 Tooltips

In this paper, we stick to an understanding of tooltips as a small window with help, which appears besides a button or data field on mouse-over or by tapping particular places on a touch screen. The tooltip disappears when the button is tapped or when the user starts or completes entering data in the field. This definition excludes in-line help, which stays on the screen until removed by the user. It also excludes alerts which pop up after a particular user operation or seemingly by itself, as for instance the Office97 Clippy [18].

When designing the tooltip, an important aspect is to not to overload the screen with extraneous information [9]. Earlier research has shown that too much help information may confuse the user, and prevent them from gathering the information needed to do the task [1]. Therefore, it is important to allow the user to stay focused by excluding unnecessary information. Both the need for keeping the task visible on the screen and making help minimal imply that tooltips should be short. Thus, the main challenge is to identify the necessary information for the tooltip and the right delivery mechanism for the information.

3 Aspects of Research Methods

This section will present literature on research methods relevant to our purpose.

3.1 Content Validity

The term validity has been used for several qualities of research methods. The validity type of particular interest for assessment of methods in this study, is whether the method measures what it aims at. Measure will be taken in a broad sense to include qualitative as well as quantitative data.

Since this paper deals with learnability, validity concepts from educational science are adopted. In educational science, the quality of "measuring what it aims at" is called content validity [15] and this term will thus be used in this paper.

We assume that tooltips and any other interventions to improve learning amongst users aim at long term impacts like improved efficiency, effectiveness (including fewer mistakes), safety, satisfaction, etc. Methods for evaluating tooltips should therefore measure such impacts in order to reach the highest content validity. Impact evaluations would require evaluation of the possible impacts (for instance, fewer mistakes) some time after the introduction of the tooltips, and attribution of the impacts to the introduction of the tooltips. Randomized controlled trials with a control group receiving placebo tooltips would be the method of choice, but these studies are normally very expensive and ethically questionable, since they require surveillance and the control group may receive a less desirable outcome.

Kirkpatrick [12, 13] developed a four level model for evaluation of in-service training, where impact is the highest level and the lower levels have lower content validity and also normally lower costs:

- Reaction. Reaction is the participant's' opinion of the training. The reaction can, e.g., be found through a questionnaire asking their opinion of the training material and teaching.
- Learning. This is an assessment of what the user has learnt from the training. A pre-test before and a post-test after training will gauge the learning outcome.

- Behavioral change. An investigation of people's use of their new competence when back in business. For example, ask the users about to what extent they use some IT functionality being taught in the training or observe their use.
- Impact. This is a measurement of changes in organizational performance, for example the number of mistakes being made.

Both in-service training and tooltips are interventions for improving performance at work, and there is nothing inherent in the overall description of Kirkpatrick's model above which prevents it from also being used for other interventions than training.

Evaluations at any of these levels can illuminate tooltips. The extent to which a user opens tooltips would be a Level 3 measurement which could be found by observing or logging use. A multiple-choice test of users before and after being exposed to a series of tooltips explaining domain concepts (Level 2) could unveil whether they improved their conceptual understanding. A questionnaire concerning alternative ways of presenting tooltips would be a Level 1 evaluation.

While a Level 4 evaluation would have the highest content validity, combining it with evaluation at Level 1 or 2 can also bring insight into why certain impacts are reached.

3.2 Power of Methods

Gregor [5] characterizes four different outcomes of information systems research;

1. Analysis and description of constructs. Relationships and generalizability, but no causality. E.g., "all novel users open tooltips" would be a description with no bearing on learning.

2a. Explanation of why things happened, causality. E.g., the user tells that she opened the tooltip because she wanted to know what the data field was about.

2b. Prediction of what will happen in the future if conditions are fulfilled. Predictions could be based on statistical correlation between a before and an after situation without being able to explain the mechanism behind the change.

3. Prescription, like a recipe which will bring about the wanted result. This could be a set of all necessary predictions to bring about the result. A sequence of instructions for carrying out a task could be a prescription of what individual users do. However, many users refrain from [19] or are not capable of [8] following such prescriptions, hence no results can be guaranteed.

We would say that this list constitutes an increasing power of the results of the research. Since Power 3 seems unattainable for tooltip evaluations, powers 2a and b are desirable.

4 Previous Evaluations of Tooltips

After extensive search, we have only come across two scientific papers evaluating tooltips. The evaluation methods in these papers are presented below and characterized according to content validity, power and cost.

4.1 Questioning Users on Preferences for Tooltip Expressions

A study by Petrie et al., [17] identified four ways of expressing tooltips for deaf and hearing impaired users: Sign Language, Human Mouth, Digital Lips and Picture tooltips. The 15 informants used the tooltips (randomly ordered) in two tasks. Thereafter they were asked to rate understandability, satisfaction, order of preference and provide other comments. Results were statistically significant with a non-parametric test.

Petrie et al., [17] asked the participants on their opinion of the tooltips, hence their method was at Kirkpatrick level 1. We therefore do not know whether the preferred tooltips will have a higher impact than those disliked by the informants. To get up to level 3 or 4 in content validity, the research should have included a test at a later stage than the introduction, where use of tooltips should have been correlated with the outcome of the task tested.

The significant preference implies that the results are predictive in the sense that other people in the target group will respond similarly. The open questions yielded qualitative data on why the Human Mouth and the Digital Lips were inappropriate, hence the power is at level 2a and b.

Nothing is stated concerning the cost of this study. A lot of investment has probably been made in setting up the tooltips and the system used. An additional test to improve content validity could therefore have been a worthwhile extension of the study.

4.2 Pre- and Post-test and Interviews

Dai et al. [3] developed a tooltip software extending Google Chrome and tested it with seniors.

Five seniors were questioned concerning their understanding of five functions, yielding a total of 3 correct answers. Then they were shown the tooltips for these functions. Afterwards, the same questions were given as a post-test; now with a total score of 24 for all participants. The evaluation was at the level 2 on content validity. No statistics were shown, thus the test has no predictive power. One participant said in an open interview that the tooltips were instrumental for him being able to search the internet, hence 2a explanatory power was demonstrated. Again, the authors seem to have invested a lot in the tool without carrying out the test which could have provided content validity at levels 3 or 4.

Some of the help provided by their software consisted of step-by-step instructions for carrying out tasks. Since tooltips disappear after one operation, they are unsuitable for displaying sequences of instructions. We therefore interpret Dai et al.'s [3] series of instructions as in-line help which falls outside the tooltip concept.

In summary, no evaluation of tooltips at content validity levels 3 or 4 seem to exist. Our recent studies target also these levels, and our methods and experiences will be presented in the sequel.

5 Evaluations Carried Out

The tooltips in our research concern data fields for Antenatal Care (ANC) for health workers in African countries. Tooltips explaining data fields are of particular importance in low income countries where nursing work is often carried out by health staff with lower qualifications. Our user evaluations were carried out in Ethiopia (low income), Malawi (low) and South Africa (middle income country).

As indicated in the Introduction, we opted for evaluations at several levels.

5.1 Expert Evaluation

Heuristic review based on design [14] constituted our initial consideration. The only design criterion, as mentioned above, is that tooltips should be short, and we saw no need for an external usability expert to measure the length of the tooltips. The way of triggering the tooltips in the software was given and outside of our control. Hence, heuristic evaluation in the HCI sense was deemed useless.

The authors are IT experts, while the tooltips concern medical data for users being health personnel. Therefore, we had the contents of the tooltips checked by two nurses and one medical doctor. They responded with three comments leading to some changes in the tooltips.

Kirkpatrick's level 1 Reaction is the participants' opinion of the training. Extending the concept of the participant to include external evaluators of the training material, an expert evaluation can be considered at the lowest level of content validity. It has explanatory (2a) power but not predictive, and it has the obvious advantage of low cost.

5.2 Questionnaire with Subsequent Interview

We aimed at finding out the preferred contents and expression format for tooltips for data fields; the study is presented in (Isaksen et al., submitted for publication). For these objectives, we followed the approach from Petrie et al. [17], asking our users to rank different tooltips according to preference, and followed up with conversations/interviews based on their answers to the questionnaire.

We first interviewed researchers familiar with ANC systems in African countries, which lead to the following suggested tooltip content types:

- The formal medical definition, e.g., Fundal height is the distance from pubic bone to the top of the uterus.
- Normal values for the medical term, e.g., Normal fundal height measurement: 20 weeks = 17–20 cm, 28 weeks = 25, 5–28, 5 cm, 36 weeks = 33–35 cm, 40 weeks = 36–38 cm
- Treatment following danger signs, e.g., If measurement is abnormal, please refer the patient to a specialist.
  These types were included in the questionnaire. After 28 responses, a fourth content type was also identified;
- procedures in order to find values.

Since this type came up late, we decided to keep the questionnaire with the three first content types.

Several delivery mechanisms or expression formats were also identified; text, illustration, videos and table. However, due to limitations we were not able to use video as expression format in the questionnaire. The tooltips in the questionnaire included the five combinations illustrated in Fig. 1.

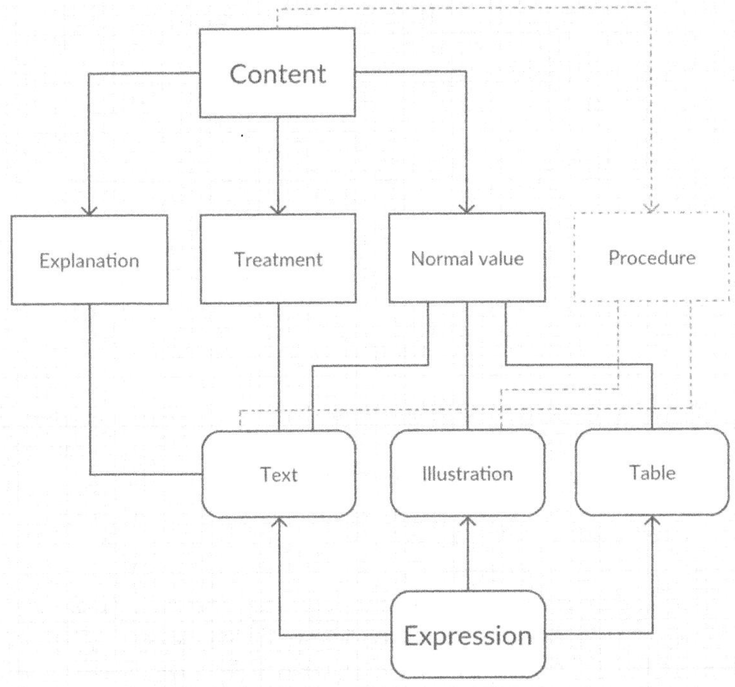

Fig. 1. Combinations of content and expression types in questionnaire

The questionnaire consisted of three cases where the informants were supposed to rank the different options on a scale of 1 to 4, were 1 was the most preferred one. Figure 2 shows an example. The labels next to the boxes in the lower right corners were not included in the questionnaire but added here for clarification.

Statistically significant differences were found from 58 respondents, see Isaksen et al. [10].

After the informants had filled the questionnaire, we asked them to elaborate on why they answered the way they did, or if they had any further comments or suggestions. Some referred to the textbooks they were familiar with as the cause of their preference, since the tooltip resembled the explanation in their textbook.

Corresponding to Petrie et al. [17], our method was at Kirkpatrick level 1, meaning we don't know the possible outcomes of using the tooltips. Also like Petrie et al. (2004), the qualitative interviews provided some explanations, such that the power is at level 2a and b.

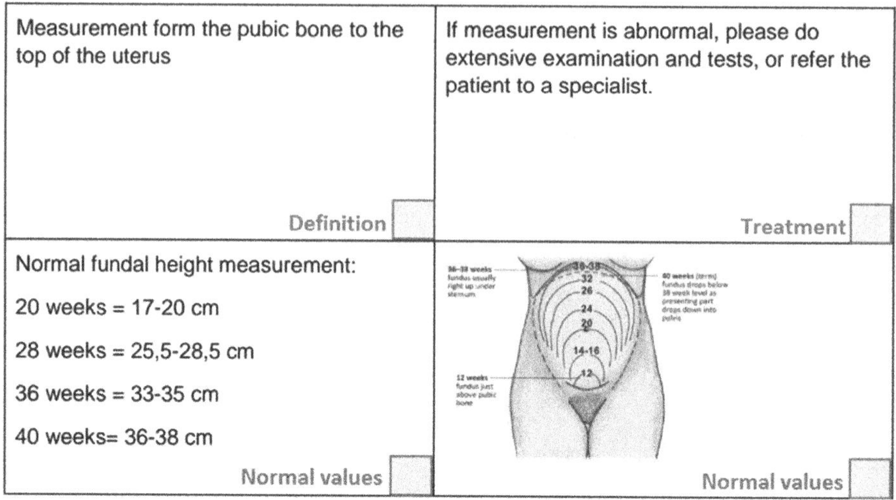

Fundal Height
Measurement form the pubic bone to the top of the uterus
Definition
If measurement is abnormal, please do extensive examination and tests, or refer the patient to a specialist.
Treatment
Normal fundal height measurement:
20 weeks = 17-20 cm
28 weeks = 25,5-28,5 cm
36 weeks = 33-35 cm
40 weeks= 36-38 cm
Normal values
Normal values

Fig. 2. An example from the questionnaire

Some of the informants were not fluent English speakers, even if they used English for patient recording. One of the researchers translated into local language. This observation concerned also the two evaluations following below.

One unexpected lesson early in the study, was that presenting the questionnaire before the informants had actually seen or used the tooltips, left them in limbo as to what tooltips were.

Hence, after five informants, we changed the order, doing the Adapted Question Suggestion (below) before the questionnaire. This provided the participants with some experience while filling the questionnaire, and increased their understanding of the task.

5.3 Adapted Question Suggestion

This evaluation aimed at finding out how users managed to open and understand the tooltips in an application. Thus we were aiming for more than Kirkpatrick level 1 and needed users to test the tooltips in our ANC system.

The applications were built within the District Health Information System [4], using its Tracker Capture app for Android devices. The informants were 17 health workers with different level of knowledge and experience in both domain and technology, and 11 students, a total of 28 informants in Ethiopia and Malawi. The informants were recruited either by showing up at their respective clinics and asking for their time, or by calling shortly ahead, asking for permission to visit them. This was a convenience sample, and all informants were recruited through local contacts, who also contributed with translations when needed.

Two testing programs were created, one for informants in Ethiopia and one for the informants in Malawi. The application used in Ethiopia was based on the Ethiopian community health information system program form for ANC, while the program for Malawi consisted of a selection of data elements in the Malawian health passport for pregnant women.

To structure the testing sessions, we developed cases, where the aim was to make the informants to go through the testing program and use the provided tooltips. We wanted to observe whether they were able to enter the information without any problems or issues and whether they opened the tooltips.

Our initial thought was to develop two cases of various difficulties, aiming to see how the different informants would cope. The first version used the same expressions in the case as in the data field title, aiming for an easy start. The second type of case challenged the informants by not using the same expression as the data field title, but rather using the terms which appeared in the tooltip. However, after trying out the cases on our first group of informants, we figured that one case was enough due to time constraints, so the simple case was abandoned.

A sentence from the case is:

During Manjula's first pregnancy, she lost her female child in the 36th week of pregnancy, before the onset of labour.

The correct data entry based on this sentence would be to tick the data field

Antepartum Stillbirth

Users who were unsure about where to tick could open the tooltip for Antepartum Stillbirth and find:

Birth of a fetus that shows no evidence of life. Occurring before the onset of labour.

The tooltip has expressions which match the case, hence the user could infer that this is the correct choice.

Evaluating the use of tooltips could be carried out in several ways.

Time to complete a case is a metric for learnability [6], but requiring that the user looks up tooltips on the way may be counterproductive, since tooltips should be accessed only when in doubt. In our study, correct data entry is more important than speed. One way of comparing the effects of tooltips would be to set up groups of users with the same system and cases but different tooltip contents. This might have been achievable in a lab session lasting a couple of hours. However, at the time of setting up the test, we did not have the questionnaire response, and we were not able to gather a sufficient number of informants for testing five different type of tooltips and compare the outcome. Hence, we used the medical definitions, since this seems to be the common way of providing explanations.

Methods for evaluation of software usability have not targeted inline help, like tooltips. Grossman et al. [6] developed the question suggestion (QS) procedure which targets software learnability specifically. Since we would evaluate learnability, we took QS as a starting point. QS builds on the Thinking-Aloud protocol. It requires an expert sitting alongside the learner suggesting alternative ways of working, and this has unveiled 2–3 times as many learnability issues as thinking-aloud [6].

Our aim was not testing learnability of the software, but of the tooltips in the software. Distinct from Thinking-Aloud, QS could take our users past possible difficulties they may encounter with the system, and allow focusing on the actual use of tooltips, rather than the learnability or the natural use of the system. Without this adaptation, QS has the disadvantage of only making the user access some tooltips, otherwise tooltip suggestions may constitute obstacles for the learner.

We also switched QS from lab to field, since this cater for more reliable results [4]. This implied that we had to cater for the available group of informants, and could not assign one expert to one informant. With up to five informants, it was difficult for two expert to follow up all. At times, some of the informants held the tablet in front of them, disabling observation. Figure 3 shows a session in a health facility.

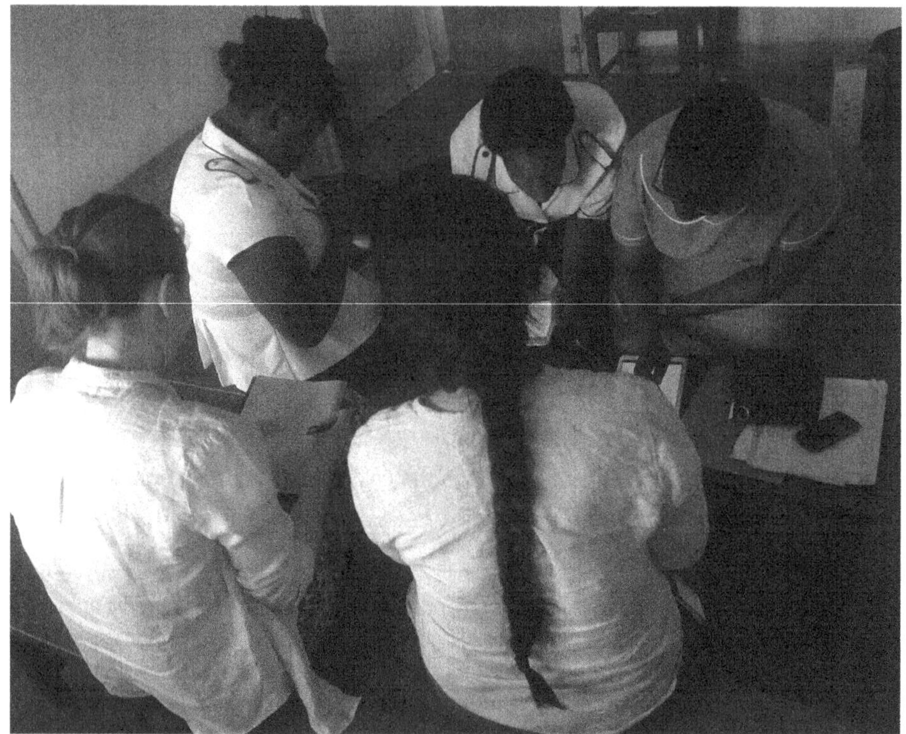

Fig. 3. Adapted QS in the patients' waiting area. The back of two of the researchers.

The QS session started out with a short introduction and asking the informants some basic questions about their technological experience. We then proceeded to going through the case with the users, helping them if we saw them struggling with anything. We always ensured the users that asking questions was okay. We introduced them to tooltips by showing where to tap and explaining the purpose of the tooltips. We also asked them questions along the way and reminded them of the option of accessing the tooltip button if we saw them answering wrongly.

We tried to install software in the tablets to log use, but the software failed. We therefore only observed and noted what the informants did. As stated above, this was impossible at times.

In summary, the observations showed that nurses and midwives often knew which data to enter. However, informants with less education were often unsure about the match between the case information and the data fields, and were encouraged to look up the tooltips to answer correctly. In some cases, it helped them understand the titles, but many of them still answered wrongly. These results are at Kirkpatrick level 2, showing the learning outcome of the tooltips. No statistical data was collected, but the difference between health workers with and without nursing degrees was clear from the qualitative and partly quantitative observations, hence providing a modest predictive power.

Two nursing students in years 3–4 were actively using the tooltips and mostly entering correct data. They explained that the tooltips were used just to verify their own input to the system. This answer was surprising and provided a new insight into the learning effects of tooltips, as verification is a positive reinforcement of learning [16]. Second, it points to that learning effects of tooltips cannot be measured only by looking for users who look up tooltips before entering data. Third, it provided some explanatory power to the results, such that the experiment had some power at level 2a and b.

Similar to the studies of Petrie et al. [17] and Dai et al. [3], the cost of this experiment was relatively high without bringing about a higher content validity.

Since the questionnaire had come out with normal values as preferred tooltips with medical definitions significantly lower ranked, and since the investment of setting up the test could be reused in a test with higher validity, we decided to also carry out a test at Kirkpatrick level 3 or 4. This test is described in the next section.

5.4 Logging Use

Evaluations of in-service training at level 3 and 4 concern users' application of what they have learnt during training in their work. This is called transfer of training to work and is, counter to intuitive beliefs, normally unsuccessful [7].

Kirkpatrick level 3 evaluates behavioral change. In an experiment [10] tooltips were introduced in a training session similar to the adapted QS. We thus interpret behavioral change as users opening tooltips also for a prolonged time after the introduction. Level 4 concerns improvement of performance, and this would in our case be an increased percentage of correct data entered. To ensure a time distance from the introduction to use of the system and the tooltips, we let the users use the system for two weeks.

Transfer should be to work. Being a system under development, we had to substitute work with work-like, fake data. We developed a booklet consisting of 22 cases, where our informants had to, each day during a period of 11 days, use the cases and fill information into the app. The booklet also included open ended questions for the day. We followed the same style in the cases as we did during the adapted QS. In order to measure the learnability of the tooltips, during a period of time, similar cases appeared at different days. The aim was to see whether or not the tooltips provided were understandable.

Based on the results from the questionnaire, we chose to compare explanations and normal values as content type for tooltips. By using the existing testing program from Malawi, with a few minor changes, we created a copy of the program and changed most of the tooltips to normal values. Both programs were installed on 30 tablets, and given to 20 participants in Malawi and 10 in South-Africa.

The participants were again recruited by convenience, although we tried to avoid those who did the Adapted QS. All participants were given one tablet (including a SIM card and airtime), locked for all other use than the test program. In order to track the informants' progress we implemented the screen recording program "UXcam" on each tablet. UXcam enabled us to record and watch every touch points and gestures the informants made and analyze the outcome. Thus, we were able to see whether the informants opened the tooltips and whether they filled in the correct information and used the correct data element. We emphasized to our participants that they should have internet connectivity whenever they use the program. We informed the participants that the screens were recorded and that they should never enter real patient data in the system, only the cases we provided.

In order to motivate all participants to fulfill the test, we told them that they could keep the tablet after the test and that we would open it for any use. Since we had no other plans for the tablets after the experiment and since paying cash to participants in foreign countries out of a university account is a bureaucratic process which has previously failed, we went for the gift option. The value of the tablet could correspond to half a month's salary for the health workers in Malawi, and we hoped that this would lead to all the participants to completing the experiment.

We handed out 22 cases of pregnant women to each participant and gave them the same open ended questions to fill daily. Over a period of about 2 weeks, they entered information from two cases a day in the system and answered the questions of the day. The two first authors watched the videos and entered data for opening of tooltips and correct data in Google sheets and also carried out all statistical analysis there.

After two weeks, we returned to the participants, and interviewed them on why they did as they did, and what they think of the experiment now that it's done.

At the deadline of paper submission, 15 of the participants had completed the experiment. Due to internet issues, only 2/3 of the videos were recorded.

Figure 4 shows the trend in opening tooltips less frequently over the cases. This gauges the behavioral change at Kirkpatrick Level 3.

A successful tooltip is when the user has opened the tooltip for the data field and entered correct data. Due to that some users opened the tooltip to verify data entered, we do not distinguish between opening the tooltip before entering data or vice versa.

In order to analyze differences over time, we compared the first third of the cases with the last third. The average number of successful tooltips during the first seven cases was 1.52, and in the last seven cases 0.62, which is a significant difference (T-test, two sided, paired, Google sheets, $p = 0.02$). Thus the log has a predictive power (2a) concerning tooltip use.

The reason given by the participants in the interview was that after some time, they knew and didn't have to look it up more times. Thus explanatory power (2b) was added in the interviews. The booklets assisted the participants during the post-interviews, and

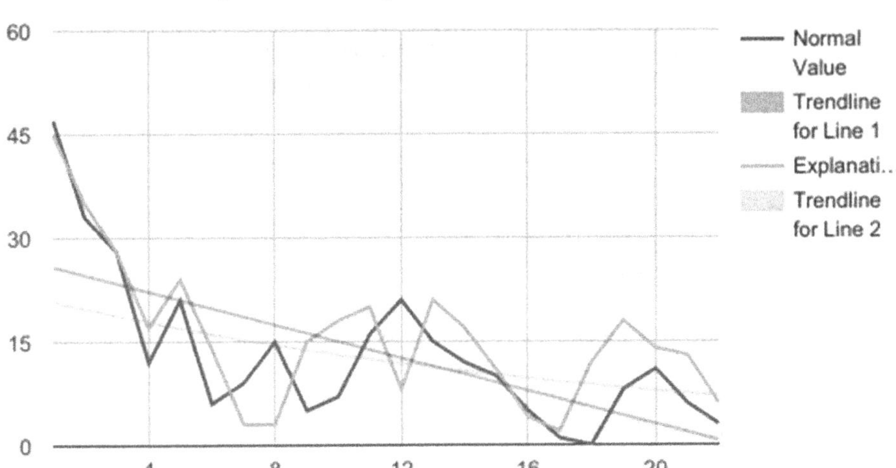

Fig. 4. Number of opened tooltips throughout the cases.

they referred to it when they, for example, explained what they found confusing in the cases. It also contributed to further discussions, as we were able to ask them about things they might not have memorized.

Table 1 summarizes results from the 15 participants on changes in performance. Due to videos not being recorded, only 13 users had traceable results both during the first and last seven cases. Pairwise statistically significant differences are marked in grey.

Table 1. Results on correct data entry from logging use

	Average % correct first 7	Average % correct last 7
Normal values (n = 7)	76	87
Explanations (n = 6)	83	85
All participants	79	86

Significant improvements and significant difference between the normal value and explanation group and interview results, made Isaksen et al. [11] to conclude that tooltips caused impact on correctness, (Kirkpatrick level 4) with predictive (2a) power without being able to state the size of the improvement in correct data entry.

5.5 Summary of the Evaluations

The evaluations carried out by the authors are summarized according to the content validity levels as defined through Kirkpatrick's [12] model, see Table 2.

Table 2. Outcome of evaluation methods according to Kirkpatrick's four level model for evaluation of training

	Opening tooltip	Tooltip content and expression
1 - Reaction	Interviews (2b)	Questionnaire + interviews (2a + b)
2 - Learning	Adapted QS (2a + b)	
3 - Behavioral change	Logging use + interviews (2a + b)	
4 - Impact	Logging use + interviews (2a + b)	Logging use (2a)

A weakness in the logging at levels 3 and 4 was that the participants did not use the system as part of their job, but as a side activity for which they were rewarded.

The series of evaluations required about two years of work for the researchers. The 30 tablets cost USD 10 000, and travel costs are additional.

6 Discussion and Conclusion

Grossman et al. [6] categorized learnability metrics concerning use of IT. They identified documentation usage area as one out of seven categories, and the assessment methods in this paper concerns tooltips, which is within the documentation category.

Previous evaluations of tooltips [3, 17] gauged users' opinion and learning outcome of the tooltips. The three first studies carried out by the authors of this paper, expert evaluation, questionnaire and adapted QS, also measured opinion and learning outcome. All of these studies required a considerable amount of work for setting up the systems and creating the tooltips. The purpose of tooltips is to assist users learning about the system during use. Yet, all of these studies were only able to find users' opinion of tooltip contents or gauge the learning outcome at the end training, hence the studies did not measure precisely what they were supposed to. This is characterized as low content validity.

A model for evaluation of training [12] has come up with four levels of content validity, where the learners' opinion and their learning outcome are the two lowest levels. With heavy investments already done, in our case, 15 months, it was a pity not to follow up with a study at higher content validity level, where the informants used the system for some period for its normal purpose in a real or close to real setting. Our approach was to give the informants tablet PCs and cases to enter over a two weeks period where they worked on their own but could also consult colleagues. Their activities were logged. This last experiment consumed around 9 months of work.

The experiment was able to demonstrate that users opened tooltips after the initial training, and that their usage dropped because they learnt more of the system by means of the tooltips. Their opening of the tooltips is a behavioral change resulting from the training. Behavioral change is at level 3 of content validity in the training evaluation model [12], being more valid than the user opinions and learning outcomes.

Finally, the experiment also demonstrated that the tooltips worked as intended, in the sense that users entered more correct data as a consequence of opening tooltips. These findings explained what happened in addition to being able to predict that tooltips will help users enter more correct data. With no placebo tooltips included, it is impossible to conclude about the proportion of improvement caused by the tooltips.

A research question in the questionnaires and in the experiment was which type of contents of the tooltips that were superior. In the questionnaire, normal values for a variable was preferred over a medical explanation. If normal values also led to more correct data entry than the explanations in the experiment, this would have been an indication that future tooltip designers could do with a cheap questionnaire instead of setting up a costly experiment. Unfortunately, the explanations provided more correct already from the start, while the normal value group reached the same or a better level after having entered 17 cases in the system. Based on these findings, we cannot conclude that questionnaires can replace experiments.

This study consumed approximately two years of work, plus 30 tablet computers. Such an investment could not be justified for a system with a small user group. The point-of-care system studied could potentially have tens of thousands of users. For such a user base, improved tooltips could replace parts of costly training and possibly also reduce errors; the latter being crucial in health services.

This study also aimed at the more general research objective of finding out the better type of contents in tooltips. The explanation type yielded quicker improvement in performance, hence this type of tooltip could also be used for information systems in other domains until other research demonstrates otherwise. Also the study showed that tooltips help, meaning that other system developers should include the small effort of making the tooltips, even if they don't evaluate them.

Acknowledgement. This research has been supported by QU Horizon 2020 "mHealth4Afrika - Community-based ICT for Maternal Healthcare in Africa" (project 668015, topic ICT-39-2015), Norwegian Centre for International Cooperation in Education "Scholarly Health Informatics Learning" (UTF-2016-longterm/10032) and Norwegian Agency for Development Cooperation "Support to the Health Informations Systsem Project - HISP" (QZA-14/0337).

References

1. Carroll, J.M.: The Nurnberg Funnel: Designing Minimalist Instruction for Practical Computer Skill. MIT Press, Cambridge (1990)
2. Dai, Y., Karalis, G., Kawas, S., Olsen, C.: Tipper: contextual tooltips that provide seniors with clear, reliable help for web tasks. In: CHI 2015 Extended Abstracts, pp. 1773–1778 (2015)
3. DHIS2 (2017). https://www.dhis2.org/
4. Duh, H.B.L., Tan, G.B.C., Chen, V.H.H.: Usability evaluation for mobile device: a comparison of laboratory and field tests. In: Proceedings of the 8th Conference on Human-Computer Interaction with Mobile Devices and Services, Helsinki, Finland, pp. 181–186 (2006)
5. Gregor, S.: The nature of theory in information systems. MIS Q. **30**(3), 611–642 (2006)

6. Grossman, T., Fitzmaurice, G., Attar, R.: A survey of software learnability: metrics, methodologies and guidelines. In: Proceedings of the SIGCHI Conference on Human Factors in Computing Systems, Boston, MA, USA, pp. 649–658 (2009)
7. Grossman, R., Salas, E.: The transfer of training: what really matters. Int. J. Train. Dev. **15**, 103–120 (2011)
8. Hadjerrouit, S.: Using a learner-centered approach to teach ICT in secondary schools: an exploratory study. Issues Informing Sci. Inf. Technol. **5**, 233–259 (2008)
9. Instone, K.: Heuristics for the Web. http://instone.org/heuristics
10. Isaksen, H., Iversen, M., Kaasbøll, J., Kanjo, C.: Design of Tooltips for Health Data. In: Proceeding of IST/Africa (2017)
11. Isaksen, H., Iversen, M., Kaasbøll, J., Kanjo, C.: Design of tooltips for data fields: a field experiment of logging use of tooltips and data correctness. In: HCI International (2017)
12. Kirkpatrick, D.L.: Techniques for evaluating training programs. J. Am. Soc. Train. Directors **13**, 21–26 (1959)
13. Kirkpatrick, D.L., Kirkpatrick, J.D.: Evaluating Training Programs: The Four Levels. Berrett-Koehler, San Francisco (2006)
14. Lazar, J., Feng, J.H., Hochheiser, H.: Research Methods in Human-Computer Interaction, vol. 295. Wiley, West Sussex (2010)
15. Messick, S.: Standards of validity and the validity of standards in performance assessment. Educ. Meas. Issues Pract. **14**(4), 5–8 (1995). doi:10.1111/j.1745-3992.1995.tb00881.x
16. Ormrod, J.E.: Human Learning. Merrill, Englewood Cliffs (2012)
17. Petrie, H., Fisher, W., Weimann, K., Weber, G.: Augmenting icons for deaf computer users. In: CHI 2004 Extended Abstracts on Human Factors in Computing Systems, Vienna, Austria, pp. 1131–1134 (2004)
18. Shroyer, R.: Actual readers versus implied readers: role conflicts in office 97. Tech. Commun. **47**(2), 238–240 (2000)
19. Smart, K.L., Whiting, M.E., Detienne, K.B.: Assessing the need for printed and online documentation: a study of customer preference and use. J. Bus. Commun. **38**, 285–314 (2001)

An Analysis of CAD Modeling Procedure Data Collection Using Synchronous and Retrospective Think Aloud Techniques

Michael D. Johnson(✉) and Karl Ye

Texas A&M University, College Station, Texas, 77843, USA
mdjohnson@tamu.edu, Kaiba545@yahoo.com

Abstract. CAD is a critical tool for engineers in the 21st century. To improve CAD usage and education, methods for assessing and evaluating modeling procedures and decision making are necessary. To this end, two common verbal data collection methods are assessed for analyzing CAD modeling procedures. Stimulated recall and concurrent think aloud are compared to each other and screen capture video data. While the concurrent think aloud method seems to increase the necessary modeling time, the think aloud requirement does not affect the proportion of time spent on particular activities. A novel method of using Cohens Kappa with time usage data was implemented to compare the audio methods to screen capture video data. Neither audio method showed significant agreement with the video data when corrected for chance agreement. It is likely that both video and audio data are required to observe significant insights with respect to CAD modeling procedures and decisions. Drawbacks and benefits associated with alternative methods are also highlighted.

Keywords: Design: analysis and design methods · UX and usability: evaluation methods and techniques · Stimulated recall · Think aloud

1 Introduction

Computer-aided design (CAD) tools are at the nexus of the product commercialization process. This makes CAD modeling a critical skill for the modern engineer. Understanding how engineers model components can inform the design process as well as design education. CAD education is often viewed as lacking by practitioners who complain that engineers are entering the workforce unable to adequately translate design ideas into digital artifacts. This is often blamed on the focus of most CAD education on "cookbook" button pushing (declarative knowledge) as opposed to strategic design thinking (procedural knowledge) [1, 2]. What is needed is a way to capture the CAD modeling activities and the intent of those activities. Verbal data allows for these to be captured during CAD modeling; verbal data allows for significantly more content to be captured [3].

Verbal data can be a rich source of information for determining the processes associated with an activity; these data can either be concurrent (or synchronous) or

M. Kurosu (Ed.): HCI 2017, Part I, LNCS 10271, pp. 313–324, 2017.
DOI: 10.1007/978-3-319-58071-5_24

retrospective [3]. The concurrent data collection process is often termed *think-aloud* or *concurrent think aloud*. In this type of data collection process, participants provide a running commentary of their activities and thought processes. The retrospective data collection method is usually in the form of a *stimulated recall*. In stimulated recall, some form of media (i.e., photos, audio recordings, videos) is used to stimulate the participant's memory of their activity and inform their commentary on their thoughts and procedures. While both methods have been used to capture verbal data for a variety of activities, they have drawbacks. Think-aloud techniques may not work when participants are engaged in an activity that requires a "heavy cognitive load", they may stop talking; retrospective or stimulated recall techniques may be too general and lack the desired details [3].

Concurrent think aloud has been used in a wide array of situations to collect verbal data. This has included educational research examining student problem solving in Sudoku [4] as well as spatial ability problems [5]. The ability to capture this qualitative data improves the understanding of how people are solving problems. One aspect that is a concern in concurrent think aloud is the effect of the data collection on the activity in question. As noted above, when significant cognitive effort is needed, this method may not be effective [3]. One study examining the use of a disk utility tool found that those participants using think aloud actually performed better (faster and with less errors) [6]. One area where concurrent think aloud is widely used to collect thought processes is in design. Tolbert and Cardella [7] use video, screen capture, and audio data to examine how students think about a design process. Srinivasan and Chakrabarti [8] also use think aloud to capture the design process, and note that the verbal data collected allows them to assess a design's novelty. Mentzer, Becker and Sutton [9] use think aloud to compare the processes of students and experts in designing a playground. Kelley, Capobianco and Kaluf [10] use think aloud and coded data to examine how much time students spend on particular design activities. Think aloud has also been used to examine the effect that CAD tools have on the design process [11].

Retrospective data collection, or specifically stimulated recall, has also been widely used across numerous areas of study. Stimulated recall provides the ability to capture declarative knowledge while providing limited capabilities for procedural knowledge [12]. Ryan [12] notes that in the case of retrospective data collection, a stimulus should be used and that the time between the activity and the data collection should be limited to prevent "memory decay". Artzt and Armour-Thomas [13] use stimulated recall to capture declarative knowledge related to the solving of math problems; students are shown videos of themselves and asked to examine their metacognitive processes. Stimulated recall has also been used to assess students thoughts and feelings when solving physics problems [14]. Surgeons have been shown videos of themselves operating and asked to explain their decision making processes [15]. Video informed stimulated recall has also been used to evaluate the decision and actions of teachers [16] and counselors [17]. Stimulated recall can also be informed by photographs [18]; however, trying to use non-video stimulated recall has its limitations [19].

While both concurrent and retrospective data collection have their strengths, multiple methods are needed to provide richer data [4]. Trevors, Feyzi-Behnagh, Azevedo and Bouchet [20] use a combination of eye tracking data, concurrent, and retrospective data verbal data collection to examine the understanding of science concepts. Bruun and Stage [21] examined alternative methods to assess usability; they found that coaching (or engaging the participant in conversation) performed better than silent observation. Kuate, Soh Fotsing and Kenmeugne [22] use both concurrent and retrospective methods examining CAD modeling; they find less stated information regarding design intent in the retrospective case. This contrasts the expected result of retrospective methods providing more information regarding declarative knowledge which would include design intent. The current study also examines CAD modeling procedure; both concurrent and retrospective methods are used.

2 Methods

The data presented in this work was collected during a junior-level computer aided design course. Near the end of the semester, after most significant instruction in the CAD program (Creo Parametric 2.0) had been completed, students were assigned one of three alternative modeling situations. These included modeling a component from a drawing of that component, modeling the same component from a physical representation of the component, or modeling a component of the student's choosing that they had brought from home (Fig. 1). These alternative modeling tasks were part of a broader research project, but for the purposes of this work were useful in providing variability in the tasks being assessed.

2.1 Video Capture and Modeling Procedure Analysis

All CAD modeling activity was recorded with the screen capture software Camtasia. This usage data was examined using a continuous time log to assess what the participant was doing in increments of seconds. The modeling time was divided into five categories [23]: doing, searching, thinking, trial and error, and waiting. Doing was defined as the actual modeling of the component (i.e., using tools and features to create geometry). Thinking was any time there was a lack of cursor movement or panning and rotating without a clear purpose. Searching was defined as looking for particular items by clicking on menu items or icons. Trial and Error was the creation of geometry and then its complete deletion at a later time. Waiting (or regeneration) time was the user waiting for the completion of graphical rendering or some other computational process.

2.2 Concurrent Think Aloud Data Capture and Analysis

Concurrent think aloud data was captured for a subset of the overall modeling group.

This included 8 participants: 3 modeling using the drawing, 3 with the physical model, and 2 with items from home. Students were given up to 75 min to finish their modeling activities. Each participant was told that they would be providing a running commentary of their modeling activities. They were all primed with a simple task of putting together a 9-piece puzzle. They were asked to talk about what they were doing and how they were solving the puzzle. After they completed the puzzle task both the

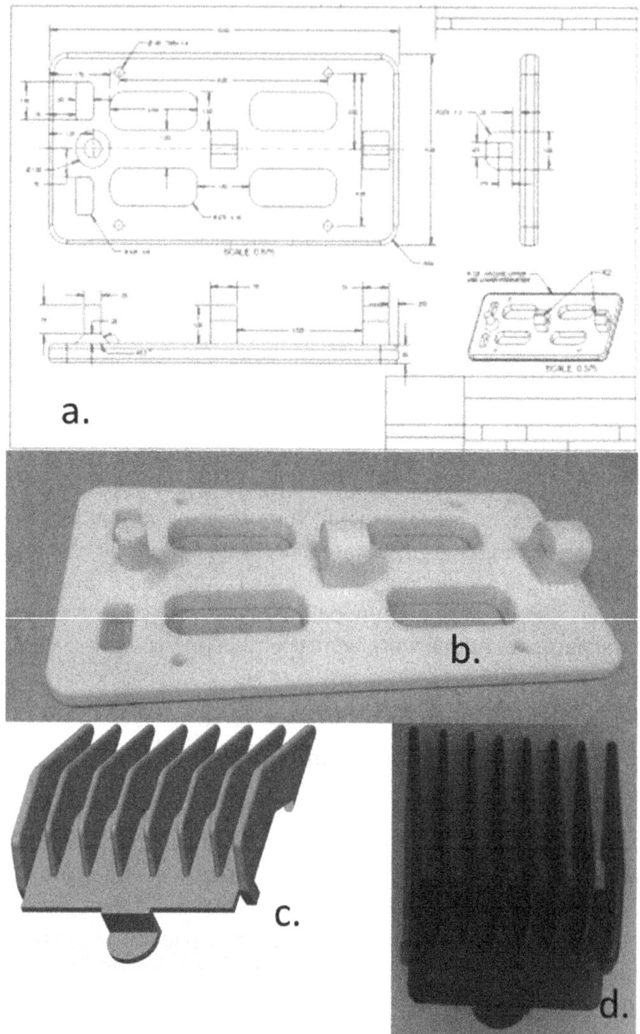

Fig. 1. Drawing of standard component (a), physical model (b), student selected component CAD model rendering (c), and photo of student selected component (d)

audio recording and the Camtasia screen capture program were started. The screen capture run time was noted on the audio recording to allow for the synchronization of the two data collection methods. The participants were prodded with the phrase "what are you doing now" whenever there was a period of silence. When the participant announced that they felt they were done, both the audio and screen capture recording were stopped.

The analysis of the audio data was similar to that of the screen capture data described above. However, given the inability to verbally differentiate between productive modeling (Doing) and modeling that was later deleted (and would therefore be coded as Trial and Error), Trial and Error was combined into doing. An additional category of indeterminate was also added capture audio data that could not be appropriately categorized. The time for each activity was noted in a running log in increments of seconds.

2.3 Stimulated Recall Data Capture and Analysis

Again, the stimulated recall data was collected from a subset of the overall modeling group. This included 9 participants: 4 modeling using the drawing, 2 with the physical model, and 3 with items from home. Again, students were given up to 75 min to complete their modeling activities. In the case of the stimulated recall data collection, screen capture data was collected without any interaction with the participant. Once the modeling was complete, participants were asked to watch the captured video of their modeling activities and comment on what they were doing at that point in the video. This discussion of their activity was audio recorded. Participants were prompted with the phrase "what are you doing now". Similar to the concurrent think aloud data these data were tabulated into the same categories as above (including an indeterminate one).

2.4 Comparison of Audio and Video Data

Cohen's [24] Kappa (κ) was used to determine the agreement between audio data and the screen capture video data (with combined Trial and Error and Doing). Indeterminate data was not included in the comparison of video and audio analysis since it has no video analog. Cohen's Kappa is often used to assess inter-rater agreement and takes into account chance agreement. In the case of this work, it is used to see if either the synchronous or asynchronous audio data provided better agreement with the video data. The amount of overlap in time for each category was tabulated. The agreement among the categories was corrected for chance to determine Cohen's Kappa. Readers interested in a more detailed description of this process are referred to Gwet [25]. Cohen's Kappa was also used to assess the agreement between two raters that analyzed the audio data. Two of the concurrent think aloud audio recordings were assessed and had an average κ value of 0.711. This represents substantial agreement [26]. An additional two audio recordings of the stimulated recall data were compared between two raters. These had an average κ value of 0.775.

3 Results

The goal of this work was to compare alternative audio data collection techniques for CAD modeling procedure analysis. The basis for the comparison is video data collected from the screen capture of the modeling activity. It should be noted that the audio data analysis and the screen capture data analysis were not done concurrently (i.e., the raters would not have recognized the audio of a video that they had previously viewed). Two raters were used; they were also not involved in the initial data collection process. While inter-rater agreement data is often reported for rating nominal data (e.g., a medical condition), this stringent condition is of use for methodological data as well. Often general agreement among raters or methods is reported; however this data does not take into account chance agreement. The use of Cohen's Kappa (κ) corrects for this chance agreement [24]. This allows for a quantitative basis to be used along with qualitative observations to evaluate the positive and negative aspects of the alternative audio data collection methods.

An example of the agreement between audio and video time usage data is shown in Table 1. In the case of the audio data, a doing proportion of 56.6% is reported; for the video data, it is 43.9%. When comparing the time logs for each of the data sources, an overlap of 39.2% total modeling time for doing was found. For the overall modeling activities, an overall percent agreement (P_0) of 71.5% was found. Given the alternative data sources, this would likely be seen as a high level of agreement. However, when correction for the chance agreement percentage (P_C) of 44.4% is taken into account, it is less impressive. This results in a Kappa (κ) of 0.488 from a maximum Kappa (κ_M) of 0.646. κ_M corrects for the disagreement of off diagonal results (i.e. the original distribution of time usage for each method).

Table 1. Video and audio data comparison analysis example

		Video				
		Doing	**Searching**	**Thinking**	**Waiting**	
Audio	**Doing**	39.2%				56.5%
	Searching		0.0%			5.7%
	Thinking			32.2%		35.4%
	Waiting				0.1%	0.5%
		43.9%	0.8%	55.1%	0.2%	

To examine if the data collection method (namely the think aloud requirement) had an effect on the modeling procedure the modeling times for each category and the overall modeling times were compared. These are shown in Table 2. All modeling time categories, along with the overall modeling time, were greater for the concurrent think aloud protocol. This could be due to the person having to provide a verbal commentary on what they are doing; this could slow them down or increase the cognitive load associated with their modeling activity. It should be noted that while the differences in the Doing and overall time categories are large (over 500 and 700 s, respectively), these differences are not statistically significant at the a = 0.05 level. There is also a chance that the small data set could result in individuals that are less skilled modelers taking longer and skewing the results. The composition of the modeling activities is such that the stimulated recall group should have an equal or greater time requirement; based on the authors' experience and observations, the individual items brought from home require the longest modeling time. There is a larger percentage of those items in the stimulate recall data set.

Table 2. Comparison of absolute time usage audio data for alternative methods

	Concurrent Think Aloud		Stimulated Recall			
	Mean	*SD*	Mean	*SD*	*t*	*p*
Doing (s)	2176.6	403.2	1672.3	571.5	2.075	0.056
Searching (s)	222.9	139.7	214.0	146.6	0.127	0.900
Thinking (s)	703.1	518.0	474.9	233.6	1.147	0.280
Waiting (s)	23.5	32.0	17.4	14.6	0.513	0.616
Total (s)	3148.3	851.8	2378.7	722.5	2.016	0.062

To correct for the effect of the think aloud requirement on the overall time required for the modeling activities, the percentages associated with each of the time usage categories were also compared. These are shown in Table 3. In this case, the results are comparable. Both the think aloud and the stimulated recall groups use approximately 70% of their modeling time for productive geometry creation in the Doing category. The next largest category of time usage was Thinking; it was approximately 20% in both cases. These results show that while the think aloud method may have extended the time, it did not alter the distribution of time that the participants used to complete certain tasks.

Table 3. Comparison of time usage audio percentage data for alternative methods

	Concurrent Think Aloud		Stimulated Recall			
	Mean	*SD*	Mean	*SD*	*t*	*p*
Doing (%)	71.3%	12.9%	69.9%	6.3%	0.276	0.788
Searching (%)	6.7%	2.6%	8.8%	5.3%	-1.002	0.332
Thinking (%)	20.5%	12.3%	20.4%	9.7%	0.023	0.982
Waiting (%)	0.7%	1.1%	0.8%	0.8%	-0.187	0.854

To compare the agreement between audio and video data for the two alternative audio data collection methods, their nominal agreement (P_0) along with their corrected Cohen's Kappa (κ) agreement were compared. The effect of collection method on chance agreement (P_C) maximum Kappa (κ_M) are also shown in Table 4. While the Kappa for stimulated recall is slightly higher than that of the think aloud method, this difference is not statistically significant. According to Landis and Koch [26] this agreement is deemed "slight" bordering on "fair". As noted above, the use of Cohen's Kappa is a stringent condition for this type of data. These results are less disappointing when examining the maximum Kappa (κ_M) data. Given the general disagreement between the audio and visual data sets, the best possible results would be deemed Moderate [26]. Even the nominal agreement (P_0) between the audio and visual data is only slightly greater than 50%. Overall there was no statistically significant difference between the agreement variables for the two audio data collection methods. The lack of significant agreement also does not allow one to say that either method would be preferable based on its agreement with the video data. The lack of agreement also does not allow for audio data to be a substitute for the video data analysis. The analysis of the screen capture videos typically required 3 to 4 times the modeling time for analysis (i.e., it required 4 h to analyze a 1 h video). The analysis time requirements for the audio data were closer to 2 times. As Vandevelde, Van Keer, Schellings and Van Hout-Wolters [4] pointed out, there is often a need for multiple methods.

Table 4. Comparison of audio and video agreement variables for alternative methods

	Concurrent Think Aloud		**Stimulated Recall**			
	Mean	***SD***	**Mean**	***SD***	***t***	***p***
k	0.178	0.171	0.201	0.125	-0.321	0.752
k_M	0.462	0.183	0.535	0.094	-1.016	0.333
P_0	56.2%	10.4%	55.2%	3.9%	0.254	0.805
P_C	46.7%	5.1%	43.2%	6.5%	1.244	0.233

The last aspect that was investigated was the relationship between Kappa and the various time usage categories. The percentages of the overall time usage was used for comparison given that it is not affected by the audio data collection method. These comparisons are shown in Table 5. Among the time usage variables, the percentage Doing time is negatively correlated with both the Searching time and the Waiting time. This negative correlations are statistically significant. This is an expected result; Searching is not productive use of time (like Thinking) and just adds to the overall modeling time. The same is true of Waiting. Kappa is negatively correlated with both Doing percentage and Thinking percentage; results are not statistically significant. Kappa is significantly positively correlated with the percentage Searching time Waiting time. This is an expected result as these two categories have less coding ambiguity with respect to video analysis. As the percentages of Searching and Waiting time increase, the ability to find agreement between the audio and video data increases. Overall, the results show that audio data collection is probably not a viable substitute for screen capture data analysis and that multiple methods are likely needed.

Table 5. Comparison of Cohen Kappa and activity categorization percentages

	2	3	4	5
1. Video – Percentage Doing	-0.632** (0.007)	0.057 (0.829)	-.690** (0.002)	-0.378 (0.134)
2. Video – Percentage Searching		-0.779** (0.000)	0.943** (0.000)	0.537* (0.026)
3. Video – Percentage Thinking			-0.752** (0.000)	-0.414 (0.099)
4. Video – Percentage Waiting				0.539* (0.026)
5. Kappa (k)				

Note: Significance shown in parentheses below correlation; *Correlation is significant at the 0.05 level (2-tailed); **Correlation is significant at the 0.01 level (2-tailed)

4 Discussion

Verbal or audio data is often collected to help understand thought processes and decision making. The two main methods for this data collection include a synchronous, concurrent think aloud, method as well as an asynchronous, stimulated recall, method. Both of these methods have been used to collect data around design processes and design decision making in general [8–10] and computer-aided design (CAD) in particular [11, 22]. This work compared these two verbal data collection methods to examine how participants used their time modeling various components in CAD. The time usage was tabulated into four main categories: Doing, Searching, Thinking, and Waiting. The tabulations for time usage from the audio data was compared to that collected from screen capture videos of the modeling process. Unique to this work, these comparisons used agreement between audio and video data based on running time logs and corrected for chance agreement using Cohen's Kappa [24].

Screen capture data analysis, concurrent think aloud, and stimulated recall all have their associated benefits and drawbacks. In the case of video analysis, the intent and activities of the participant must be inferred by the analyst without input from the participant. This is also a time consuming process that often involves pausing, rewinding and re-watching the video. Concurrent think aloud requires that the participant actively detail what they are doing while they engaged in the activity. If the activity is cognitively demanding, this may slow their verbal response or their progress in the activity. The concurrent think aloud data in this work was quicker to analyze than the screen capture video data and provided firsthand knowledge of what activities were being done. Concurrent think aloud methods may provide better results when procedural knowledge is sought. Stimulated recall requires that some stimulus be used to elicit a response for the activities under investigation; there are limits to the effectiveness of this method when a stimulus such as video is not available [19]. Stimulated recall has the ability to better capture declarative knowledge, but may not excel at capturing procedural knowledge [12]. Stimulated recall also puts an additional burden on the participant; they must engage in the activity and then relive the activity to provide the audio data. To assess these alternative methods, CAD modeling procedure data were collected using all three methodologies.

A comparison of the absolute time durations for the various activity categories showed that the concurrent think aloud modeling procedure took a longer time overall as well as for the various time usage categories than stimulated recall. This was an expected result; the requirement to verbally detail the procedures as well as carry them out added to the overall time. However, when comparing the proportional time usage tabulations, the two methods had very similar proportions for the various categories.

Unique to this work, a method for comparing the various time usage data sets and correcting for chance agreement was implemented. This allowed for the audio data collection methods to be compared to the video screen capture data. While often used for nominal comparisons between raters, Cohen's Kappa [24] was used to compare the time used for various modeling activities. While this is likely a more rigorous test of agreement than necessary for time usage data, it does provide for the necessary correction to account for chance agreement among the data. A comparison of the agreement variables did not show any significant differences for the two audio data collection methods when compared for agreement with the screen capture video data. The corrected agreement κ was also somewhat low for both methods; with κ averages of 0.178 for concurrent think aloud and 0.201 for stimulated recall, this agreement would be deemed slight or fair [26]. The correlations of κ with the various modeling proportions showed that agreement was significantly positively correlated with both Searching time and Waiting time. This is to be expected as these categories have less coding ambiguity with respect to agreement between audio and video analysis; increases in proportion of time spent doing these activities would increase agreement. Given the overall lack of agreement between the audio and video data, both are likely needed to provide quality insights into design processes and procedures.

4.1 Conclusions

CAD modeling procedure data for two verbal data collection methods, stimulated recall and concurrent think aloud were compared to each other and screen capture video data. While the concurrent think aloud method seemed to increase the necessary modeling time, it did not affect the proportion of time spent on particular activities. A novel method of using Cohens Kappa with time usage data was used to compare the audio methods to screen capture video data. Neither audio method showed significant agreement with the video data when corrected for chance agreement. Given this, a combination of both audio and video data are likely necessary to collect significant insights into modeling procedures and design decision making. Depending on the focus of the analysis either stimulated recall (for declarative knowledge focused work) or concurrent think aloud (for procedural knowledge focused work) can be used.

4.2 Limitations

The above conclusions should be viewed in light of the limitations associated with this work. First, the limited sample size of 8 for the concurrent think aloud method and 9 for the stimulated recall method limit its broad applicability. Also, it should be noted that the participants were all students. This may increase the variability of their modeling performance and affect the overall data set. Future work will attempt to increase the sample size and enlist professional CAD users to provide data.

Acknowledgements. This material is supported by the National Science Foundation under EEC Grant Number 1129403. Any opinions, findings, conclusions, or recommendations presented are those of the authors and do not necessarily reflect the views of the National Science Foundation.

References

1. Hamade, R.F., Artail, H.A., Jaber, M.Y.: Evaluating the learning process of mechanical CAD students. Comput. Educ. **49**, 640–661 (2007)
2. Lang, G.T., Eberts, R.E., Gabel, M.G., Barash, M.M.: Extracting and using procedural knowledge in a CAD task. IEEE Trans. Eng. Manag. **38**, 257–268 (1991)

3. Ericsson, K.A., Simon, H.A.: Verbal reports as data. Psychol. Rev. **87**, 215–251 (1980)
4. Vandevelde, S., Van Keer, H., Schellings, G., Van Hout-Wolters, B.: Using think-aloud protocol analysis to gain in-depth insights into upper primary school children's self-regulated learning. Learn. Individ. Differ. **43**, 11–30 (2015)
5. Mohler, J.L.: Examining the spatial ability phenomenon from the student's perspective. Eng. Des. Graph. J. **72**, 1–15 (2008)
6. Wright, R.B., Converse, S.A.: Method bias and concurrent verbal protocol in software usability testing. Proc. Hum. Factors Ergon. Soc. Annu. Meet. **36**, 1220–1224 (1992)
7. Tolbert, D., Cardella, M.E.: CAREER: mathematics as a gatekeeper to engineering: the interplay between mathematical thinking and design thinking - using video data. In: ASEE Annual Conference and Exposition, Conference Proceedings
8. Srinivasan, V., Chakrabarti, A.: Investigating novelty-outcome relationships in engineering design. Artif. Intell. Eng. Des. Anal. Manuf. AIEDAM **24**, 161–178 (2010)
9. Mentzer, N., Becker, K., Sutton, M.: Engineering design thinking: high school students' performance and knowledge. J. Eng. Educ. **104**, 417–432 (2015)
10. Kelley, T.R., Capobianco, B.M., Kaluf, K.J.: Concurrent think-aloud protocols to assess elementary design students. Int. J. Technol. Des. Educ. **25**, 521–540 (2015)
11. Salman, H.S., Laing, R., Conniff, A.: The impact of computer aided architectural design programs on conceptual design in an educational context. Des. Stud. **35**, 412–439 (2014)
12. Ryan, J.: Stimulated recall. In: Researching Language Teacher Cognition and Practice, pp. 144–161 (2012)
13. Artzt, A.F., Armour-Thomas, E.: Mathematical problem solving in small groups: exploring the interplay of students' metacognitive behaviors, perceptions, and ability levels. J. Math. Behav. **16**, 63–74 (1997)
14. Appleton, K.: Problem solving in science lessons: how students explore the problem space. Rese. Sci. Educ. **25**, 383–393 (1995)
15. Chen, X., Williams, R.G., Smink, D.S.: Dissecting attending surgeons' operating room guidance: factors that affect guidance decision making. J. Surg. Educ. **72**(6), e137–e144 (2015)
16. Hubber, P., Tytler, R., Haslam, F.: Teaching and learning about force with a representational focus: pedagogy and teacher change. Res. Sci. Educ. **40**, 5–28 (2010)
17. Stockton, R., Morran, D.K., Clark, M.B.: An investigation of group leaders' intentions. Group Dyn. **8**, 196–206 (2004)
18. Fox-Turnbull, W.H.: The nature of primary students' conversation in technology education. Int. J. Technol. Des. Educ. **26**(1), 21–41 (2015)
19. de Smet, M., van Keer, H., de Wever, B., Valcke, M.: Studying thought processes of online peer tutors through stimulated-recall interviews. High. Educ. **59**, 645–661 (2010)
20. Trevors, G., Feyzi-Behnagh, R., Azevedo, R., Bouchet, F.: Self-regulated learning processes vary as a function of epistemic beliefs and contexts: mixed method evidence from eye tracking and concurrent and retrospective reports. Learn. Instr. **42**, 31–46 (2016)
21. Bruun, A., Stage, J.: An empirical study of the effects of three think-aloud protocols on identification of usability problems. In: Abascal, J., Barbosa, S., Fetter, M., Gross, T., Palanque, P., Winckler, M. (eds.) INTERACT 2015. LNCS, vol. 9297, pp. 159–176. Springer, Cham (2015). doi:10.1007/978-3-319-22668-2_14
22. Kuate, G., Soh Fotsing, B.D., Kenmeugne, B.: Restitution of design intents by computer aided design models. Int. J. Appl. Eng. Res. **7**, 277–291 (2012)

23. Johnson, M.D., Ozturk, E., Yalvac, B., Valverde, L., Peng, X., Liu, K.: A methodology for examining the role of adaptive expertise on CAD modeling. In: ASME 2015 International Mechanical Engineering Congress & Exposition, IMECE2015-50296. ASME, Houston (2015)
24. Cohen, J.: A coefficient of agreement for nominal scales. Educ. Psychol. Meas. **20**, 37–46 (1960)
25. Gwet, K.L.: Handbook of inter-rater reliability: the definitive guide to measuring the extent of agreement among raters, 3rd edn. Advanced Analytics, LLC, Gaithersburg (2012)
26. Landis, J.R., Koch, G.G.: The measurement of observer agreement for categorical data. Biometrics **33**, 159–174 (1977)

Adoption of the Focus Groups Technique in the Open Source Software Development Process

Lucrecia Llerena[1(✉)], Nancy Rodríguez[1], John W. Castro[2], and Silvia T. Acuña[1]

[1] Departamento de Ingeniería Informática, Universidad Autónoma de Madrid, Madrid, Spain
{llerena,nrodriguez}@uteq.edu.ec, silvia.acunna@uam.es

[2] Departamento de Ingeniería Informática y Ciencias de la Computación, Universidad de Atacama, Copiapó, Chile
john.castro@uda.cl

Abstract. The growth in the number of non-developer open source software (OSS) application users has drawn attention to usability in the OSS community. OSS communities do not generally know how to apply usability techniques and are unclear about which techniques to use in each activity of the development process. The aim of our research is to determine the feasibility of applying the focus groups technique in the OSS ERMaster project. To do this, we participated as project volunteers. We used the case study research method to investigate technique application and OSS community participation. As a result, we identified adverse conditions that were an obstacle to the application of the original technique. We then adapted the technique to make it applicable in an OSS project. We can conclude that was not easy to recruit OSS users and developers to participate in technique application.

Keywords: Open source software · Usability techniques · Requirements engineering · Product concept development · Focus groups

1 Introduction

Open source software (OSS) has spread so swiftly that it now rivals commercial software systems [1]. OSS communities do not as yet enact standard processes capable of ensuring, bearing in mind the characteristics of the OSS community as a whole, that the products that they develop have the attributes of good software [2]. An inadequate definition of processes, activities, tasks and techniques within OSS development has led researchers from several areas to gravitate towards this field of research with the aim of correcting this situation [3–5]. The growth in the number of non-developer open source software (OSS) application users and the escalating use of these applications have created a need for and interest in developing usable OSS [6–10].

Usability is one of the key quality attributes in software development [11]. In recent years, OSS has come to be an important part of computing [12–15]. However, several authors have acknowledged that the usability of OSS is poor [6, 16, 17]. In this respect, the empirical study conducted by Raza et al. [7] reports that 60 per cent of respondents (non-developer users) stated that poor usability is the main obstacle to be overcome by

M. Kurosu (Ed.): HCI 2017, Part I, LNCS 10271, pp. 325–340, 2017.
DOI: 10.1007/978-3-319-58071-5_25

OSS applications if users are to migrate away from commercial software. On this ground, OSS projects must tackle their level of usability and usability-related problems more conscientiously [17].

On one hand, the human-computer interaction (HCI) field offers usability techniques whose key aim is to build usable software. However, they are applied as part of HCI methods and not within the OSS development process. On the other hand, the OSS development process focuses on source code and thus on feature development. The OSS development process has a number of characteristics (for example, developers and users are usually the same person). This prevents many of the HCI usability techniques from being adopted directly [18].

Even so, the OSS community has now started to adopt some usability techniques. Most of the techniques that the OSS community has taken on board are for evaluating usability [18]. Some usability techniques have been adapted ad hoc for adoption in OSS development projects [18]. This paper addresses the research problem of how to adopt the focus groups usability technique for requirements engineering activities as part of the development process of a real OSS project known as ERMaster[1]. To do this, we first identified and analysed which obstacles had to be overcome in order to apply focus groups in OSS projects.

Ferré [19] compiled a list of usability techniques recognized by HCI. He determined the most representative HCI process activities: use context specification, usability specifications, product concept development, prototyping, interaction design and usability evaluation. He then mapped these activities (and each of their associated techniques) to software engineering (SE) development stages: requirements engineering, design and evaluation.

Our research spans two areas: SE and HCI. We use usability techniques as a bridge to communicate these two areas, where our aim is to deploy HCI knowledge in the SE field and especially in the OSS development process. If adapted, usability techniques can be adopted in the OSS development process [18]. Therefore, this paper has two goals. Firstly, we intend to adapt the focus groups usability technique [20] for adoption in the OSS development process. Secondly, we aim to determine the feasibility of adopting this usability technique in a real OSS project.

Requirements engineering activities play a very important role in the success or failure of an OSS project. However, they are sometimes extremely hard to perform because there is no definition of OSS user segments before the software is developed. Also, it is far from straightforward to address all the requirements analysis activities due to the particular characteristics of OSS development groups (for example, global geographic distribution of user sites or code-focused world view). On this ground, this paper considers just the product concept development activity. Additionally, OSS projects have not adopted many usability techniques related to the requirements engineering and product concept development activities [18]. The next step after selecting the activity is to pick a related usability technique for adoption in the OSS development process.

[1] https://sourceforge.net/projects/ermaster/?source=updater.

The main reasons for the generally poor usability of OSS developments are: OSS developers have tended to develop software for themselves [4, 10] and the developer community is very much in the dark about who its users are [9, 16]. The aim of the focus groups technique is to gather information related to user opinions, problems and concerns at meetings scheduled for this purpose [18–20]. This technique helps to focus product concept design on its hypothetical functionality [20]. The focus groups technique requires a small research sample for the purposes of product evaluation. Consequently, the participation of just a few users is sufficient to represent the product concept model, that is, developers use this technique to discover a user's mental model of the product. On this ground, we selected the focus groups technique for adoption in an OSS project.

This paper makes a significant contribution to the field of SE and particularly to OSS development projects because we have not been able to identify papers reporting the use of the focus groups technique and detailing how it has been applied in OSS development projects [21, 22].

There are several OSS project repositories. One of the most popular is SourceForge.net [23]. This repository classifies OSS projects by categories. Since this technique is related to requirements engineering for product concept development, we looked at projects with a low level of coding (that is, projects where key features were still being added) that were not overly ambitious and were at the very early development stages (alpha version) in order to select a suitable OSS project in which to adopt the selected usability technique. Considering the above, we selected the ERMaster OSS project. Thanks to the characteristics of this project, we can adopt a usability technique related to a requirements activity (product concept development). Therefore, the benefits of applying the technique will have a bigger impact on the development process and software system usability. We have adapted the technique based on the integration framework proposed by Castro [18].

We used a case study as the research method to test the feasibility of our proposal for adopting usability techniques in OSS projects [24]. Consequently, we had to volunteer for the selected OSS project and join the community.

This paper is organized as follows. Section 2 describes the characteristics of the OSS projects. Section 3 illustrates the research method followed to apply the usability technique in an OSS project. Section 4 outlines the state of the art. Section 5 reports the proposed solution. Section 6 discusses the results. Finally, Sect. 7 outlines the conclusions and future research.

2 OSS Project Characteristics

OSS applications are typically built by a group of independent developers and volunteers distributed all over the world [18]. The OSS community uses different web artefacts to communicate and synchronize its development practices (for example, email lists, Internet Relay Chat (IRC), source code repositories and bug reporting systems). Text is the OSS community's primary means of communication, as well as the main object of interest (specifically, source code). Developers mainly contribute to OSS communities by developing new features and fixing bugs reported by users [25].

At the beginning of the OSS movement, application developers and users were one and the same people. As the years have gone by and the popularity of OSS has grown, the user profile has changed. Today, there are basically two groups of OSS users. On one hand, we have users that are computer literate, experienced software users or are very interested in anything technology related. This is the group of users that are more often in contact with the principal developers and provide the best feedback. On the other hand, we have users in the strict sense. This group of users have switched over to and use these applications at their workplace [18].

Even though OSS community developers and users are geographically distributed, there are meeting points, like conferences or workshops, which are generally sponsored by companies. These events are organized with the aim of officially releasing new versions of the applications and offering tutorials and workshops where developers and users can exchange opinions. For example, developers and users participated in a meeting held in Madrid (Spain) in June 2013 to present BonitaSoft 6.0 (a business process management application).

A few OSS projects are sponsored by companies, and thus have the resources that they need to apply usability techniques as prescribed by HCI (for example, usability experts and usability laboratories). For example, the usability specifications technique [16, 26] has been adopted in some OSS projects that could bank on the participation of usability experts. These are, however, exceptions because most OSS projects are run by volunteers working to small budgets and cannot afford external experts (like graphic designers or usability experts) [4, 9, 16].

3 Research Method

We used a case study as the research method to validate our research [27]. From a case study, we learn about the experiences of applying usability techniques adapted to OSS projects. This research method is used when the phenomenon under investigation (in this case, the adoption of an adapted usability technique) is studied within its real setting (in this case, an OSS project). OSS projects are the perfect setting for the case study reported here because OSS communities are generally uninformed about usability techniques, do not have the resources to test usability and cannot usually count on usability expert involvement [4, 9, 16].

The case study addresses the following research question (RQ): Is it possible to determine whether, if adapted, the focus groups usability technique can be used in requirements engineering activities within an OSS project?

ERMaster, a graphical editing tool for entity-relation diagrams (ERD), was selected as the OSS project in which to adopt the focus groups technique [28].

In this research, we first identified the obstacles to applying the focus groups technique in the ERMaster project. We then decided how to deal with the obstacles. Finally, we proposed the adaptations necessary to adopt the focus groups technique in this project.

We created web artefacts to improve communication with OSS community members and efficiently synchronize the necessary activities to apply the focus groups usability technique. The web artefact used to test the feasibility of the proposed technique was a forum. Forums are used in the focus groups technique to gather information and compile sketches related to the application user interface. Thanks to this web artefact, we were able to set up a virtual meeting point with OSS users who are geographically distributed all over the world. Using such web artefacts, we aimed to record user opinions about the selected OSS project user interface.

4 State of the Art

In recent years, the worldwide OSS community has adopted just over 50% of the HCI techniques related to evaluation. However, only about 20% of the usability techniques related to requirements engineering and design activities have been adopted [18]. Therefore, more research is required to support the adoption of techniques related to requirements engineering in OSS developments.

In view of the importance of HCI and SE, it is only logical to study the user-centred software development activities in OSS projects. This is especially true of the requirements engineering stage, because the discovery of user requirements during the early development activities is useful for putting right any defects in software detected later on [26].

The HCI vision of software development is somewhat different to the usual SE approach. Despite being based on the same development processes and activities, HCI focuses primarily on the user as the hinge of the system. Coutaze claims that HCI and SE intersect [27], whereas Ferré defines a scheme categorizing HCI activities and their relationship to SE [19].

There are a wide variety of techniques in HCI. The same technique may be referred to differently by different authors, and there may be different variants of the same technique. Fortunately, SE authors have already put together a catalogue of HCI techniques [19]. We referred to the catalogue of techniques compiled by Ferré [19]. The activities reported in this catalogue tie in with the early software development activities corresponding to requirements engineering, whose aim is to model users and determine their mental model [19]. This is a tricky issue owing to the types of development environments and user participation in the field of OSS.

In this paper, we adapt the focus groups technique used in the product concept development activity. According to Preece et al. [27], product concept development relies on the creation of a mental model based on psychological theories related to HCI. Ferré explains that this activity covers issues regarding how users envisage the system [19]. Therefore, this activity aims to provide a picture of the product before defining the features that the system should offer.

Usability technique definition and integration into OSS projects is a complicated process, about which there are few papers [6, 26, 29, 30]. These papers suggest that usability techniques should be reconceptualized, but they do not explain how the OSS community should go about adaptation. Nichols and Twidale [4] are the only authors to put forward some general ideas for improving usability. However, the issues to be taken into account to adopt such techniques in OSS developments are unclear.

On the other hand, Castro [18] proposes a framework for integrating usability techniques into OSS developments. This framework is composed of a number of adaptations in response to the adverse conditions for adopting usability techniques in OSS development projects. In order to adopt usability techniques in OSS development projects, it is, according to Castro [18], necessary to: (i) study the adverse conditions preventing the use of HCI techniques, and (ii) analyse what types of and which adaptations are necessary if these techniques are to be used in OSS projects.

Although research examining usability in OSS has been published [9, 26, 31, 32], there is no standardized procedure for determining how to adopt usability in OSS development. The first step in our research is to study how the OSS community uses usability techniques in their development projects. Castro's is the only published research to study usability problems and techniques occasionally adopted in OSS projects in an integrated manner and to report the current state of usability in the OSS community [18].

It appears to be less straightforward to integrate usability into the OSS development process than into commercial development projects due to some of the characteristics of the OSS community, like: (i) feature-centred development, (ii) worldwide geographical distribution, (iii) limited resources, and (iv) a culture that may be alien to interaction designers. Consequently, usability technique adoption is a demanding task because most HCI techniques are not designed for the type of environment in which OSS is developed [18].

In the wake of the literature review, we can say that only one of the research papers reports a general and systematic proposal for integrating usability techniques into the OSS development process [18]. To do this, it considers the particular characteristics, philosophy and idiosyncrasy of the OSS development process, without forfeiting the essence of usability techniques. Two systematic mapping studies (SMS) related to usability in OSS were conducted in advance of our research. A SMS reviews the literature on a particular field of interest [32]. The first SMS was conducted by Castro [18] reviewing papers published up until 30 July 2013. The second SMS was conducted with a search range from 1 August 2013 to 30 April 2015 [33].

Castro's research [18] was validated on only two OSS projects (OpenOffice Writer and FreeMind) and for three usability techniques (user profiles, direct observation and post-test observation). Therefore, Castro's proposal [18] requires further validation by adapting new usability techniques and participating in more OSS projects.

5 Proposed Solution

In this section, we describe the focus groups usability technique applied in an OSS project. Firstly, we describe the case study design. Secondly, we specify the characteristics of the selected OSS project (ERMaster). Thirdly, we describe the selected usability technique (focus groups) as prescribed by HCI. We then introduce the adaptations made to the focus groups technique for application in an OSS project. Finally, we report the results of applying the focus groups usability technique.

5.1 Case Study Design

Case studies are one of the most popular forms of qualitative empirical research [34]. A case study investigates the phenomenon of interest in its real-world context. The phenomenon of interest for this research is the adoption of usability techniques with adaptations, whereas the real-world context is OSS projects. It is not easy to run controlled experiments in the field of OSS because the characteristics of OSS communities (for example, age, availability, expertise, experience, etc.) are unmanageable. Since not all OSS project team members have the same characteristics, it is impossible to minimize the effects of external factors (for example, geographic distribution and time differences). This rules out evaluation by means of an experiment. On this ground, we selected the case study methodology to validate the feasibility of our proposal for adopting a usability technique in an OSS project.

We describe the case study following the guidelines set out by Runeson and Host [24]. According to these guidelines, we divide our research into two parts: an exploratory part and a descriptive part. We start by looking at what happens in a real-world scenario and then we describe what happens when we apply the adapted techniques to improve application usability [24].

5.2 ERMaster OSS Project Characteristics

We selected ERMaster [28] as the OSS project in which to adopt the focus groups technique. ERMaster is an Eclipse plug-in and is very useful for novice or expert database (DB) designers. The reported number of downloads from its website is 1200 per week [28].

5.3 Focus Groups Usability Technique Description

The focus groups technique is a useful tool for evaluating user needs and feelings about a product expressed at group sessions [35]. More formalized definitions in the field of HCI describe the focus groups technique as a qualitative technique whose aim is to gather information about user opinions, problems and concerns at meetings planned for the purpose [18–20].

According to the literature, several authors [18, 19, 36] neither consider the planning required before and after applying the focus groups technique nor propose definite steps for applying the technique either. By contrast, Mayhew proposes a number of specific steps for applying this technique [20]. According to Mayhew [20], the focus groups technique is composed of the five steps described below.

Step 1 (Design the focus groups format) involves designing a script for the purpose of implementing a planned sequence of activities to be performed before, during and after conducting the focus group in order to achieve the goals set out in this study. Step 2 (Design data collection forms) involves designing a data input form (for example, to note down the opinions, problems and comments raised by focus group participants). Additionally, a list of specific questions (related, for example, to the user interface and the work environment) has to be compiled and addressed and discussed by the focus group. Step 3 (Conduct the focus group) should take about one to two hours. According to Mayhew, a good-sized focus group would have between six and eight members. Additionally, she believes that the moderator and note-taker play a very important role with respect to the key information stated by participants [20]. Steps 4 and 5 of the focus groups technique (Analyse data and Draw/document conclusions) address the transcription, analysis and summary of the results to draw and document the focus group conclusions.

5.4 Adaptations of the Focus Groups Usability Technique

The focus groups usability technique cannot be applied directly in the OSS development process because this community has features that do not conform to the HCI world, like, for example: the worldwide geographical distribution of its members, a code-centred world view, a shortage of resources and a culture that can be somewhat alien to interaction developers. Even though usability techniques demand conditions that, as a rule, OSS projects cannot meet, the techniques can be adapted to bring them into line with the idiosyncrasy of the OSS world. In the following, we describe the adaptations of the focus groups usability technique for application in OSS projects.

A usability expert is indispensable for applying Step 1 (Design focus group format) of the technique [20]. This expert is needed to structure the scripted objectives, topics and questions to be analysed when the focus group is conducted. We propose to substitute this expert with the principal developer, an experienced OSS project user or a HCI student under the supervision of a mentor to guide the focus groups format development. With regard to Step 2 (Design a data collection form), we found that the topics to be dealt with in the focus group cannot be physically handed out to participants because they are distributed all over the world. On this ground, we suggest that remote participation in the OSS community should be logged (online forum). Additionally, the outline of the topics should be posted on the same online forum so that users can recall their experiences with the software system interface under study.

In Step 3 (Conduct focus groups), we found that users are required to meet face to face to participate in technique application. Additionally, we found that a moderator and a note-taker had to be there in person to guide discussions and take notes during focus group application, respectively. This condition cannot be met due to the characteristics of OSS projects. On this ground, we suggest the following adaptations: (i) users will participate remotely in virtual meetings via the online forum; (ii) the moderator will be replaced by the principal developer, an expert OSS project user or a HCI student under the supervision of a mentor, (iii) there will be no note-taker during the conduct of the focus group because the online forum will be logged automatically.

In Step 4 (Analyse data), the information should be organized and then grouped by characteristics (such as age range, gender, occupation, etc.) before analysis. This simplifies the process of data analysis for the purpose of comparing and correctly interpreting the information gathered in the focus group [37]. Finally, Step 5 (Draw/document conclusions) draws the conclusions with respect to the opinions expressed by users. We did not identify any adverse conditions for the last two steps, and therefore no adaptations had to be made. Table 1 summarizes the steps, identified adverse conditions and suggested adaptations for the focus groups technique [20]. There are mainly two adaptations. First, users participate online via a forum. Secondly, the usability expert is replaced by a developer, expert user or a HCI student under the supervision of a mentor. In this particular case, a HCI student under the supervision of a mentor substituted the expert.

Table 1. Steps, adverse conditions and proposed adaptations for the focus groups technique

Focus group technique steps		Adverse conditions	Proposed adaptations
1	Design the focus group format.	•A usability expert is required to participate in the project.	•The expert may be a developer, an expert user or a HCI student (under the supervision of a mentor).
2	Design the data collection form.	•The list of topics to be discussed in the focus groups cannot be handed out as printed matter because the users do not attend in person. •No printed matter to help users recall their experiences with the user interface can be handed out.	•The users will participate remotely via forums. •The guides and the list of topics to be discussed are published on the online forum. •Each community member's log will be recorded in the online forum.
3	Conduct the focus group.	•Users are required to participate in person to apply this technique. •A moderator, which could be the principal developer or an experienced user, and a note-taker are required to attend in person. •Focus groups are hard to video and audio record. •The number of participants is limited (from 6 to 9). •The duration of the focus group is limited (from 1 to 2 h).	•Users will participate remotely via the online forum. •The moderator may be an expert OSS project user or a HCI student (under the supervision of a mentor). •The online forum log will serve as the minutes of the meeting. •The number of participants in the online forum is unlimited. •The time available for submitting opinions to the online forum will depend on each participant.
4	Analyse data.	•No adverse conditions were identified.	•As no adverse conditions were identified, no adaptations are required in this step.
5	Draw/ document conclusions.	•The adaptation is the result of the OSS community work method and is not a response to an adverse condition.	•The conclusions and recommendations of the focus group will be reported via the online forum.

According to HCI prescriptions, design tips for a new application feature output by the focus groups technique are appraised by a usability expert [19]. In the adapted focus groups technique, the end users submitted their designs and opinions via web artefacts (like forums and emails) and not at face-to-face meetings due to the characteristics of the OSS communities.

In sum, two main adaptations were taken into account for the adoption of the focus groups technique in OSS projects. Firstly, the focus groups usability technique requires a usability expert for application, as a result of which we recommend that the expert be replaced by a HCI student (under the supervision of a mentor). Secondly, as this technique is reliant on user participation, we propose that OSS users participate remotely via chats, forums, blogs and wikis.

5.5 Case Study Results

We applied the focus groups technique in the ERMaster project. This is a DB data management application that works with several DB engines. We had trouble recruiting real users because it took a long time to get permission from the principal developer. We had to contact the principal developer by means of several media (email and personal wiki) before he gave us his consent. Six ERMaster users participated in the focus groups technique application.

After designing the focus group format taking into account the stated topics and objectives, we proceeded to phrase the questions in order to apply the focus groups technique. Table 2 shows the (unstructured) format design. The questions should be aligned with the objectives addressed in the focus groups and are related to the ERMaster application work environment. The focus groups questions are designed to evaluate usability issues such as ease of learning, efficiency of use, memorability, errors and satisfaction [36]. By studying these factors, we focus on user-centred design, an issue neglected in OSS development projects. We sent the questions and an invitation to participate in the focus groups technique to a mailing list of active ERMaster community users. This list was supplied by the ERMaster principal developer. The questions that were sent to the users by electronic mail are listed on the web site[2]. We expected a higher rate of participation from the ERMaster community. Since it took a long time to get the principal developer's permission and users did not show much interest in participating in our research, we only managed to recruit six participants.

The focus group was moderated by the principal developer. However, he did not comment on the opinions of the users posted on the online forum. We believe that the principal developer did not get involved in the open online forum because he was not unduly concerned about improving the usability of the OSS application. The presence of a note-taker was unnecessary in order to conduct the focus group, as, on one hand, the comments posted on the open online forum were logged automatically and, on the other, the researchers kept all the emails that they received.

The principal developer sent an introduction and formal invitation to the ERMaster project community to participate in the open online forum. For many application users, however, their forum registration is the only record available as they did not post any opinions. Some users answered the questions and submitted their responses by email instead of publishing them on the forum. Other users eventually responded to one or two questions related to their major field of interest but failed complete the entire questionnaire. A few other users stated that they were happy with the tool and did not answer

[2] https://goo.gl/uRmVYn.

any of the questions. We then screened all the feedback, and selected the contributors who answered all or most of the questions. As a result of this screening, we got a sample of six users for our research.

Table 2. Focus groups technique format

Activities	Scenarios	Actors
1. Determine the focus groups objectives.	•Emails	•Principal developer, expert user belonging to the ERMaster community or a HCI student (under the supervision of a mentor). •I2-TIC master student
2. Encourage the OSS community to participate in the forum, considering its importance.	•SourceForge web site online forum	•ERMaster principal developer •I2-TIC master student
3. Briefly explain the aim and benefits of applying the technique in the OSS project	•SourceForge web site online forum	•ERMaster principal developer •I2-TIC master student
4. Determine the topics to be addressed (with regard to the user interface and work environment).	•Focus group format	•ERMaster principal developer •I2-TIC master student
5. Design the questions in line with the focus group topics.	•Question format design	•I2-TIC master student
6. Conduct the online forum.	SourceForge forum	•OSS community (ERMaster)
7. Review the focus group participant responses (forum/ email). Email was an easy option for users due to time constraints. The responses to the questions were sent to one of the researchers.	•Emails and SourceForge forum	•I2-TIC master student
8. Compile the data and enter in data collection form (using an Excel spreadsheet designed for the purpose).	•Focus groups application data collection form (Excel)	•I2-TIC master student
9. Analyse and interpret the collected data.	•Results reporting	•I2-TIC master student
10. Submit a report with the conclusions.	•Report containing the conclusions and recommendations of the focus groups data analysis	•ERMaster principal developer •I2-TIC master student

The noteworthy results of the application of the focus groups technique considering the data gathered include: (i) novice users had problems with installation (because it is an Eclipse plug-in), (ii) expert users regard ERMaster is being a tool that is easy to learn, easy to use and easy to understand and had no trouble remembering how to use it, (iii) ERMaster is designed ergonomically using menus, action bars and easy access icons, but some users requested the addition of options of interest (for example, export DBs to Excel), and (iv) users consider the ERMaster work environment to be adequate, as there are Help and Query tools.

6 Discussion of Results

After applying the focus groups technique to the ERMaster project, we were able to confirm that it is very hard to get a representative set of users. We believe that the main reason for this is that users are unmotivated. We had to be persistent and use different communication mechanisms (for example, personal wikis and electronic mails) to get the consent of the principal developers (only one out of five principal developers responded). The biggest problem with applying the focus groups technique was user availability: most users are volunteers and had very little spare time. In fact, the participants did not have the time to enter their comments in the online forum and ended up emailing their opinions to one of the researchers. Since the focus groups participants had a medium level of experience with respect to both the ERMaster tool and the field of computing, they did not pinpoint any major problems which novice users may have had.

Table 3. Summary of the case study for the adapted focus groups technique

Case study:	ERMaster
HCI technique	Focus Groups
Strategy:	Forum, emails
Application type:	ERD graphical editor
User participation:	Low
Developer participation:	Low
Number of participant users:	6
User type:	Students, professionals
Number of contacted developers:	6
Number of developers that responded:	1
Strengths of applying the technique	The use of web artefacts (like forums) create opportunities for discussions as part of virtual meetings and improved communication with the user community
Weaknesses of applying the technique:	It was hard to communicate with developers. User participation was low
Adoption	Reliable

Table 3 summarizes the results of the analysis of the characteristics of the case study. Note that the bottom row is shaded grey, denoting, for the purposes of this research, that the adoption of the adapted focus groups technique was acceptable as this technique requires a small number of participants to get reliable results. With regard to our proposal of substituting a developer, expert user or HCI student under the supervision of a mentor for the usability expert, the expert was replaced in this case by a HCI student supervised by a mentor. Note that this student was in his final year of the Master of Information and Communication Technologies Research and Innovation at the Autonomous University of Madrid and was taking two HCI courses. Additionally, the student was supervised by two usability experts. On this ground, there is no risk of the proposed adaptation for the selected technique having a negative impact on the quality of the software.

Note that the problem stated and the solution proposed in this research are of interest and importance not only to OSS development communities but also to the field of global software development (GSD), since GSD business and industrial settings share a number of the characteristics of OSS communities. GSD is now a major issue in SE research and practice [38]. Some noteworthy negative factors that GSD has to tackle are neglect by project managers, member participation and allocated resources influencing organizational success [39]. Against this backdrop, the results of our research can be extrapolated in order to deal with the above negative factors within the GSD field.

We can conclude that the results of the adoption of the focus groups usability technique were not what we expected. Firstly, we banked on the participation of a large number of users based on the statistics provided on the application web site. Secondly, it was hard to contact and recruit users to participate in the research. Note that OSS community members are all volunteers, and they participate in their spare time. Despite all these problems, however, the adaptation of the focus groups technique was reliable for adoption in the ERMaster project, as it does not take many users to get a reliable result.

7 Conclusions and Future Research

The goal of this research was to evaluate the feasibility of adopting HCI usability techniques in OSS projects. We adapted the focus groups technique for adoption. Through adaptation, we were able to account for some OSS development characteristics that pose an obstacle to the application of the technique as per HCI recommendations (for example, OSS developers and users are geographically distributed). In particular, we adapted the focus groups usability technique for application in the ERMaster OSS project.

It is not easy to recruit volunteer users to participate in OSS usability projects. As already mentioned, users often do not have much time, and it is hard to get them to take part without an incentive. With the focus groups technique, although we did not get much collaboration from users or even the principal developers, we did manage to apply the technique because it requires only a small number of participants to get a reliable result [19, 20, 35–37]. Author opinions differ as to the number of users to be taken into account for the focus groups technique to be successful [19, 20, 35–37]. Most of these authors agree that a focus group should include from six to nine users if it is to work. Fewer than six participants would not generate enough ideas for discussion. In this research, however, any users that are willing to collaborate are allowed to, that is, there is no limit on the number of users because this would go against the working philosophy of the OSS community where anyone who wants to is welcome to participate. In sum, our proposed adaptation does not place any constraints on the number of technique participants. This adaptation is a response to the OSS community working philosophy rather than to an adverse condition posing an obstacle to technique application.

The focus groups technique is useful for gathering opinions and suggestions from participant users for the product concept development activity and its results are descriptive. After analysing and applying the focus groups usability technique in requirements engineering activities in OSS developments, we found that there are adverse conditions that are an obstacle to its application like, for example, the shortage of OSS users interested in applying the technique, community geographical and temporal distribution and OSS community motivation.

We believe that, in order to improve the integration of usability techniques in OSS projects, the OSS community has to start attaching importance to and raising awareness about the repercussions that the issues addressed by the HCI field have on software development. Additionally, as HCI techniques need to be adapted to overcome the adverse conditions for adoption in OSS development projects, the OSS community also has to broaden its view of software development in order to consider usability and not focus exclusively on feature development. In the future, we aim to conduct further case studies to adapt and apply other usability techniques in OSS projects. We will analyse other web artefacts that can be adapted to improve communication in OSS communities (for example, social networks) and gradually raise the awareness of OSS developers about the benefits of applying HCI usability techniques.

Acknowledgments. This research was funded by the Secretariat of Higher Education, Science, Technology and Innovation (SENESCYT) of the Government of Ecuador as part of academic scholarship granted for postgraduate training, and Quevedo State Technical University through doctoral scholarships for higher education professors. Also this research was funded by the Spanish Ministry of Education, Culture and Sports FLEXOR (TIN2014-52129-R) and TIN2014-60490-P projects and the eMadrid-CM project (S2013/ICE-2715).

References

1. Schryen, G., Kadura, R.: Open source vs. closed source software. In: 2009 ACM Symposium on Applied Computing - SAC 2009. ACM, pp. 2016–2023 (2009)
2. Noll, J., Liu, W.-M.: Requirements elicitation in open source software development: a case study. In: 3rd International Working on Emerging. Trends Free. Source Software Research Development - FLOSS 2010, pp. 35–40. ACM (2010)
3. Madey, G., Freeh, V., Tynan, R.: The open source software development phenomenon: an analysis based on social network theory. In: Proceedings of Eighth Americas Conference on Information Systems, pp. 1806–1813 (2002)
4. Nichols, D.M., Twidale, M.B.: The usability of open source software. First Monday **8**, 21 (2003)
5. Raza, A., Capretz, L.F., Ahmed, F.: Maintenance support in open source software projects. In: Eighth International Conference on Digital Information Management (ICDIM 2013), pp. 391–395. IEEE (2013)

6. Çetin, G., Gokturk, M.: A measurement based framework for assessment of usability-centricness of open source software projects. In: 4th International Conference on Signal-Image Technology & Internet-Based Systems – SITIS 2008, pp. 585–592. IEEE (2008)
7. Raza, A., Capretz, L.F., Ahmed, F.: An empirical study of open source software usability: the industrial perspective. Int. J. Open Source Softw. Process. **3**, 1–16 (2011). doi:10.4018/jossp.2011010101
8. Smith, S., Engen, D., Mankoski, A., et al.: GNOME Usability Study Report. Technical Report, Sun Microsystems (2001)
9. Nichols, D.M., Twidale, M.B.: Usability processes in open source projects. Softw. Process. Improv. Pract. **11**, 149–162 (2006). doi:10.1002/spip.256
10. Raza, A., Capretz, L.F., Ahmed, F.: An open source usability maturity model (OS-UMM). J. Comput. Hum. Behav. **28**, 1109–1121 (2012)
11. Ferré, X., Juristo, N., Windl, H., Constantine, L.: Usability engineering-usability basics for software developers. IEEE Softw. **18**, 22–29 (2001)
12. Hars, A., Ou, S.: Working for free? – Motivations of participating in open source projects. In: 34th Hawaii International Conference on System Science, pp. 1–9. IEEE (2001)
13. Mockus, A., Fielding, R.T., Herbsleb, J.D.: Two case studies of open source software development: apache and mozilla. ACM Trans. Softw. Eng. Methodol. **11**, 309–346 (2002)
14. O'Mahony, S.: Guarding the commons: how community managed software projects protect their work. Res. Policy **32**, 1179–1198 (2003)
15. Scacchi, W.: Understanding requirements for open source software. In: Lyytinen, K., Loucopoulos, P., Mylopoulos, J., Robinson, B. (eds.) Design Requirements Engineering: A Ten-Year Perspective. LNBIP, vol. 14, pp. 467–494. Springer, Heidelberg (2009). doi:10.1007/978-3-540-92966-6_27
16. Benson, C., Müller-Prove, M., Mzourek, J.: Professional usability in open source projects: GNOME, OpenOffice.org, NetBeans. In: CHI 2004 External Abstract Human Factors in Computin System - CHI EA 2004, pp. 1083–1084. ACM (2004)
17. Raza, A., Capretz, L.F., Ahmed, F.: Users' perception of open source usability: an empirical study. Eng. Comput. **28**, 109–121 (2012). doi:10.1007/s00366-011-0222-1
18. Castro, J.W.: Incorporación de la Usabilidad en el Proceso de Desarrollo Open Source Software. Tesis Doctoral. Departamento de Ingeniería Informática. Escuela Politécnica Superior. Universidad Autónoma de Madrid (2014)
19. Ferré, X.: Marco de Integración de la Usabilidad en el Proceso de Desarrollo Software. Tesis Doctoral. Facultad de Informática. Universidad Politécnica de Madrid (2005)
20. Mayhew, D.J.: The Usability Engineering Lifecycle: A Practitioner's Handbook for User Interface Design. Morgan Kaufmann, San Francisco (1999)
21. Beckert, B., Grebing, S., Böhl, F.: A usability evaluation of interactive theorem provers using focus groups. In: Canal, C., Idani, A. (eds.) SEFM 2014. LNCS, vol. 8938, pp. 3–19. Springer, Cham (2015). doi:10.1007/978-3-319-15201-1_1
22. Olembo, M.M., Volkamer, M.: E-Voting System Usability: Lessons for Interface Design, User Studies, and Usability Criteria. In: Proceedings of Human-Centered System Design For Electronic Governance, pp. 172–201 (1999)
23. SourceForge (1999). https://sourceforge.net/
24. Runeson, P., Host, M., Rainer, A., Regnell, B.: Case Study Research in Software Engineering: Guidelines and Examples. John Wiley & Sons, Hoboken (2012)
25. Raymond, E.S.: The Cathedral and the Bazaar: Musings on Linux and Open Source by an Accidental Revolutionary. O'Reilly & Associates, Sebastopol (2001)

26. Terry, M., Kay, M., Lafreniere, B.: Perceptions and practices of usability in the free/open source software (FOSS) community. In: Proceedings of the 28th International Conference on Human Factors Computer System CHI 2010, pp. 999–1008. ACM (2010)
27. Coutaz, J.: Evaluation techniques: exploring the intersection of HCI and software engineering. In: Taylor, Richard N., Coutaz, J. (eds.) SE-HCI 1994. LNCS, vol. 896, pp. 35–48. Springer, Heidelberg (1995). doi:10.1007/BFb0035806
28. ERMaster (2015). https://sourceforge.net/projects/ermaster/?source=updater
29. Çetin, G., Verzulli, D., Frings, S.: An analysis of involvement of HCI experts in distributed software development: practical issues. In: Schuler, D. (ed.) OCSC 2007. LNCS, vol. 4564, pp. 32–40. Springer, Heidelberg (2007). doi:10.1007/978-3-540-73257-0_4
30. Hedberg, H., Iivari, N., Rajanen, M., Harjumaa, L.: Assuring quality and usability in open soruce software development. In: Proceedings of the First International Work Emerging Trends FLOSS Research Development – FLOSS 2007, pp. 1–5. IEEE (2007)
31. Paul, C.L.: A survey of usability practices in free/libre/open source software. In: Boldyreff, C., Crowston, K., Lundell, B., Wasserman, Anthony I. (eds.) OSS 2009. IAICT, vol. 299, pp. 264–273. Springer, Heidelberg (2009). doi:10.1007/978-3-642-02032-2_23
32. Kitchenham, B., Budgen, D., Pearl Brereton, O.: Using mapping studies as the basis for further research-a participant-observer case study. Inf. Softw. Technol. **53**, 638–651 (2011)
33. Llerena, L.: Transformación de Técnicas de Usabilidad Relacionadas con las Actividades de Ingeniería de Requisitos para su Incorporación en el Proceso de Desarrollo Open Source Software. Trabajo de Fin de Master. Departamento de Ingeniería Informática. Universidad Autónoma de Madrid (2015)
34. Runeson, P., Höst, M.: Guidelines for conducting and reporting case study research in software engineering. J. Empir. Softw. Eng. **14**, 131–164 (2009). doi:10.1007/s10664-008-9102-8
35. Hernández, P., Cortés, C., Balboa, A., et al.: Métodos Cualitativos para Estudiar a los Usuarios de la Información. Universidad Nacional Autónoma de México (2008)
36. Nielsen, J.: Usability Engineering. Morgan Kaufmann, San Francisco (1993)
37. Hernandez Sampieri, R., Fernandez Collado, C., Baptista Lucio, P.: Libro Metodología de la investigación. Hill, McGraw (2014)
38. Vizcaíno, A., García, F., Piattinil, M.: Visión general del desarrollo global de software. Int. J. Inf. Syst. Softw. Eng. Big. Co. **1**, 8–22 (2014)
39. Khan, A.A., Keung, J.: Systematic review of success factors and barriers for software process improvement in global software development. IET Softw 1–11 (2016). doi:10.1049/iet-sen. 2015.0038

Game for Heuristic Evaluation (G4H): A Serious Game for Collaborative Evaluation of Systems

Paulyne Matthews Jucá(✉), Ingrid Teixeira Monteiro, and José Cezar de Souza Filho

Universidade Federal do Ceará, Quixadá, CE, Brazil
paulynejuca@gmail.com, ingrid@ufc.br, cezarbx@gmail.com

Abstract. Many initiatives have promoted Collaborative Heuristic Evaluation in order to avoid discrepancies between evaluator's ratings. This paper presents a gamification called G4H (Game for Heuristic Evaluation), a card game proposed to increase the engagement of different evaluators in an evaluation process based on Heuristic Evaluation. This paper presents all the rules, cards, game loop and the results of a preliminary study made to validate the game. The G4H can be used as complementary material in HCI courses. The preliminary study demonstrated an increase in satisfaction in participating of system evaluation using the G4H.

Keywords: Heuristic evaluation · Gamification · Card game

1 Introduction

Heuristic Evaluation (HE) is a usability inspection method, in which some evaluators inspect a system interface searching for violations of one or more usability heuristics [1], which are general principles for interaction design. One of the steps of HE is rating the violations in order to prioritize the fixing efforts. Despite being a very popular evaluation method, HE faces serious criticisms of its validity and reliability [2]. One of these criticisms are the large discrepancies between the individual severity ratings of evaluators, indicating challenges with the rating process [3]. Some initiatives have been proposed to increase the number of evaluators in order to promote collaboration and enable sharing the "challenge and frustration of the evaluation process" [2]. Other authors have been investing in turn HE easier, for instance, [4] that proposes a guide for expert evaluation and [5] that proposes UX Check, a tool to support HE. In addition, Collaborative Heuristic Evaluation (CHE) [2], which is not new, represents a possible improvement in the evaluation results. This paper presents a gamification called G4H (Game for Heuristic Evaluation) based on competitive mechanics in order to increase the engagement of different evaluators in an evaluation process based on HE.

2 Related Work

There are two main types of related work to this paper: collaborative evaluation and gamification used for HCI. The first group contains papers like [1–5] that debate the challenges and advantages on using collaborative methods to achieve better evaluations.

M. Kurosu (Ed.): HCI 2017, Part I, LNCS 10271, pp. 341–352, 2017.
DOI: 10.1007/978-3-319-58071-5_26

They are related to this paper because they have the goal to promote collaboration, but the main difference with this paper is that they don't use game mechanics to promote engaging. This paper intends to use game elements to increase, promote and engage user (especially non-specialists and end-users in heuristic evaluation).

The second group is composed by works that already promoted the use of gamification with HCI. In [4], the authors propose a gamification that should be used for specialists. That itself represent a significant difference for the proposition presented by this paper. In [7], the author intends to indicate how the gamification is being used in HCI area. It comments that the majority of the work that combines gamification and HCI intends to understand how different players and the system personalization influences on interaction. This paper intends to present a gamification that uses Nielsen heuristics to promote collaborative evaluation that can be used by non-specialists and end-users. G4H was initially tested using undergraduate students. It is expected that an improved version of this gamification can be used by HCI teachers during their lectures as a side class exercise.

3 Gamification

Gamification [6] is the use of game elements and mechanics on non-game problems in order to provide fun to increase engagement. "In HCI, the study of gamification has been often part of the sub-domains of Player-Computer Interaction (PCI) and Player Experience (PX), which study the experience of players interacting with games" [7]. This paper presents a gamification focused on Heuristic Evaluation.

The gamification framework proposed by Kevin Werbach and Dan Hunter [8] was used to create the gamification in this paper. The main objective is to engage non-expert and/or end users in collaborative heuristic evaluation. To achieve this goal, the gamification focus on the extrinsic motivation of been recognized by the pair as a good evaluator and the intrinsic motivation of doing accurate evaluation and violation identification. The competitive character of the gamification is presented on the possibility of buy a new reevaluation phase if the player is not the winner of the level. The competition is designed to increase debate on the evaluation and it increases the quality of the final evaluation. The proposed gamification was based on the 10 heuristics of Nielsen, but it can be adapted for other heuristic frameworks. The Game for Heuristic Evaluation (G4H) will be presented in the next section.

4 Game for Heuristic Evaluation (G4H)

The gamification has a simple game loop in four steps: initial heuristic violation classification, initial severity classification, negotiation phase and reevaluation. In G4H, each heuristic is a level in the game. In each level, the player has to decide if the system in evaluation violates that heuristic (or not) and gives a grade according to the gravity of the fault. It is expected that different evaluators have different grades, especially if the evaluator has different experience in HCI and heuristics usage.

The game enables negotiations where players have to convince each other about the found violations and about the given grades. After negotiation, all players vote for violations that must be kept, changed or removed and also for a new grade for each heuristic violation based on their arguments. The player that grade correctly (most voted) wins the level and earn a point. At any level, the player can trade two points for the possibility of a new negotiation phase (with new votes replacing the previous votes). It increases the player's chance of convincing others on his/her arguments and win the level. The player who has more points will win the game.

The G4H will be presented in details in next sections.

4.1 G4H Setup

The setup represents all the necessary things that is supposed to be available before the game starts. All items that need to be available before the game are listed below:

- Heuristic violation cards (one set per player): each card represents one of the 10 heuristics.
- Severity cards (one set per player): each card represents one of the five severity levels of each violation found.
- Point cards: represent the rewards granted to player for evaluating the severity in the right way. The player with the greater amount of point at the end of the list of problems previously found wins the game.
- Tasks to be performed during the previous evaluation of the system. Each player individually performs the system inspection in order to find problems. The list of problems found will be used during the game, but the evaluation itself is out of the game context. Each problem identified will represent a round in the game.
- Access to the system under evaluation.
- A support card with a brief description of each heuristic. It can be used by the players to remember what each heuristic is about.
- List of problems found by each player.
- At least 3 players

4.2 G4H Cards

G4H has 3 types of cards: heuristics, severities and points. Table 1 shows the prototyped version of heuristics cards.

Each player receives a set of these 11 cards representing the 10 violation types and 1 card to represent that the player believes that the problem presented is not a violation. A problem found previously (see G4H setup) on the system can represent one or more violations.

Table 1. Heuristics cards

VISIBILIDADE DO STATUS DO SISTEMA Visibility of system status	MAPEAMENTO ENTRE O SISTEMA E O MUNDO REAL Match between system and the real world	CONTROLE E LIBERDADE DO USUÁRIO User control and freedom	USO DE PADRÕES E CONSISTÊNCIA Consistency and standards
PREVENÇÃO DE ERROS Error prevention	RECONHECIMENTO AO INVÉS DE MEMORIZAÇÃO Recognition rather than recall	Ctrl C EFICIÊNCIA DE USO E FLEXIBILIDADE Flexibility and efficiency of use	ON ESTÉTICA E DESIGN MINIMALISTA Aesthetic and minimalist design
RECONHECIMENTO, DIAGNÓSTICO, E RECUPERAÇÃO DE ERROS Help users recognize, diagnose, and recover from errors	AJUDA E DOCUMENTAÇÃO Help and documentation	NÃO É VIOLAÇÃO It is not a violation	

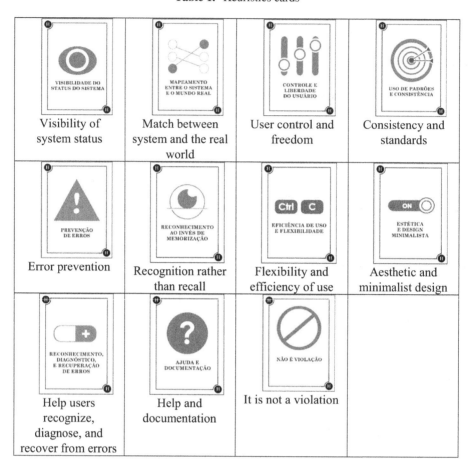

Table 2 presents the severity cards used by the players to grade the violation's level of gravity.

Table 2. Severity cards

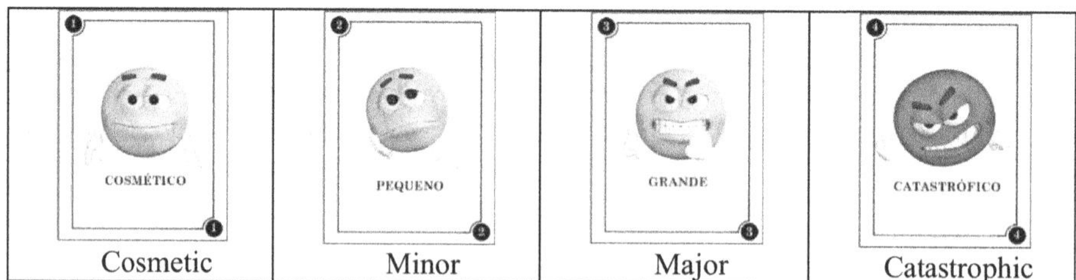

COSMÉTICO Cosmetic	PEQUENO Minor	GRANDE Major	CATASTRÓFICO Catastrophic

Regarding the point cards, the players receive one of the cards presented in Table 3 when they win a round. They can use these cards to buy reevaluation rounds.

Players win one point when the result of the evaluation is unanimous. Otherwise, the players that win the round receive two points.

Table 3. Point cards

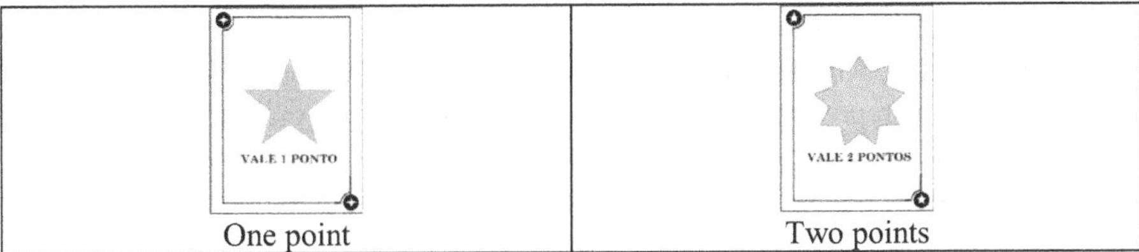

One point	Two points

4.3 G4H Gameloop Rules

The gamification has a simple game loop in four basic steps: initial evaluation of the heuristic violation, first evaluation of the severity, negotiation phase and reevaluation. The G4H full gameloop steps are:

1. The first player chooses one of the problems found previously by him/her. This will be the problem of the round. Repeated problems shouldn't be reevaluated unless that it represents a different violation. The player of the round may describe the problem found to the others. The players discuss the problem and make comments and questions to the player that found the problem at the system. The players can also access the system to demonstrate the problem by executing again the task that has the problem.
2. Heuristic Evaluation: the players choose one or more cards of heuristic (Table 1) to indicate the violation for the problem found. These cards should be hidden at first in order to not influence other player's evaluation. When all the players have ended their evaluations, they all turn their cards at the same time.
3. Debate about the heuristic selection. The players, one at a turn, debate how and why they have selected the violations cards.
4. Final selection of heuristic violation. The players vote again on which violations they consider right. The violated heuristic chosen by the greater number of players is the one considered to the next steps. One exception is when the majority of players decide that it is not a violation and the game returns to step 1.
5. Severity classification. Since a heuristic violation is confirmed, the players need to classify the severity of this violation. Again, each player chooses a severity card (Table 2) and maintains it hidden until all the players finish selecting a card in order to avoid cross player influence. The players show their cards at the same time. If all the players agree with the same classification, each player receives 1 point (Table 3) and the round ends here. If there is some divergence on the severity classification, the game continues to renegotiation step. It is important to remember the selection of each player in order to define the winner of the round after the renegotiation.

6. Negotiation. In this step the players need to explain the reasons that lead them to choose their severity classification (step 5). G4H doesn't define a fixed amount of time for negotiation, but it is recommended that each player talks at least one time. It can be a conversation and the player may make questions and debate. When the player decides that they have enough information to make a new classification, the game proceeds to next step.
7. Reclassification. All players select a severity card (that can be the same of the step 3 or a new one representing a change on his/her opinion). Again the selected card is maintained hidden until all players select their cards. The classification that is most selected is the severity chosen. Next step consists in defining the winner(s) of the round
8. Distributing points. The game awards the players that better guessed the final severity level (defined at the end of round 7) at first chance (step 5). The distribution of points for the players is made as follows: the player that has more selections of severity in final selection similar of their severity selection in step 3 receives 2 points. For instance: imagine one scenario where there are 3 players A, B and C. If during step 3 player A chooses "major", and player B and C chooses "minor" and after negotiation (step 7) the majority of player chooses "major", only player A wins 2 points. But if after renegotiation the majority of players chooses "minor", players B and C each receives 2 points. The last possibility is for the majority select a different severity classification, for instance "catastrophic". In this case, the player that is closer to the final classification wins 1 point. In the example, player A (that chosen "major" in step 5) wins 1 point. This can sounds difficult to understand, but the players in experiment had no difficult to use these rules.
9. Buying new negotiations. After negotiation, players can buy the chance of a renegotiation. It is interesting when the decision is almost even and a player wants another chance to win the round. In order to do this, the player gives 3 points away. These 3 points are lost independently of the results of the new negotiation. The points of the last step are returned and steps 6, 7 and 8 are replayed. There is only one renegotiation for round.
10. Game continues with the player at left. If this player doesn't have new problems anymore in his/her list, the game continues with the player at left until all problems previously found be evaluated.

4.4 Frequent Suggestions About the Rules

The game has been informally tested many times before the first experiment with users. The interesting part is that some beta testers and others HCI researchers that had access to the game have made questions in order to change the rules, specially about giving points to heuristic violation classification. The questions and suggestions were so common that they need to be also presented in here.

Balancing a game may be difficult and it is necessary to imagine how the solutions provided could be misused by the players. The gamification designers need to prevent misuse because it can lead into results much different from the previously desired. Some of the most common suggestions are listed below.

Reward the player that found a problem in the system
The number of problems found is not the same for each player. The main goal of the game is not award the better inspector or specialist but it is to promote the collaboration. This is the motive why heuristics violation identification in step 1 does not result in points. If it does, the game would need to make the concurrency just by limiting the number of rounds by the minimum number found by each player.

Reward renegotiate heuristic violation classification
Both the heuristic violation classification and severity classification are part of one round. The rewards are from the round. Putting more points on the table could make the renegotiation cost too cheap and not valuable to the players.

Reward player according their guess after negotiation and not the severity level chosen before negotiation
There is also a reason to not reward the person that changed the opinion. By doing so, some players could during the renegotiation chose a classification that is not correct just to win points. In this way, the players that understood that their first classification were incorrect tend to reevaluate the classification in better way since it doesn't alter their point rewards.

5 Using G4H

In order to investigate the reception of the initial version of the game, we performed a preliminary study with participants evaluating an academic system.

The study was made with 5 undergraduate students of the Federal University of Ceará. All the students have concluded at least one course on HCI and had previous basic knowledge on Nielsen Heuristics and System Evaluation. It was the main criteria for participating of the study since the player had to prepare a list of problems found in the system to start the game.

The system under test was a system to search and compare prices of different products and find products with better prices. This system is very popular in Brazil[1].

All the students previously received the necessary information do evaluate the system (and a set of tasks to perform on the system) and were instructed on the G4H gamification rules.

The names of the students were changed in order to respect their privacy. A term of consent was also signed by all the participants.

To guarantee that all the players understood the rules of the game, a demonstration round was performed.

The players had 30 min to evaluate the system individually in order to create the list of problems found. During the study, each player used 1 problem (5 in total) because of time limitations (the game last around 50 min). The number of problems found (within the 30 min provided) by each player was:

---

[1] The system was Mercado Livre ("free market"): http://www.mercadolivre.com.br/.

- Natalia: 5 problems;
- Igor: 3 problems;
- Marcos: 4 problems;
- Davi: 4 problems;
- Alice: 2 problems.

5.1 Demonstration Round

In this demonstration round the problem found in the system was the difficulty on finding a product category because they are located at the bottom of the page and the user has to roll the full page in order to see the information.

The players debated about the violations, and after the card selection the most chosen violated heuristic were: Consistency and standards and Flexibility and efficiency of use.

After the selection of the heuristic, the researcher instructed the players that they need to select the severity level of the violation and highlighted that this was an important evaluation since that it is the part of the game that will be considerated in the distribution of points. At first, 2 players selected "major" for severity level and 3 selected "minor" for severity level.

The player of the round (the same that identified the problem) justified that he has chosen "major" imagining that his mother wouldn't use this system since she couldn't find the tags at the bottom at the page. This was one of the arguments in this discussion.

After negotiation, all players selected the severity level "minor" and 3 players won 2 points each.

During this round, some players made some interesting comments about the game and the cards. They are listed as follows:

- Alice commented that the cards were difficult to use. It happened because it was a prototype of the game cards, the cards were small (around 5 cm × 3 cm) and impressed in standard A4 paper.
- Alice had doubts if she could use the guide with the heuristic descriptions during the game and commented that the usage could made the game last too long.
- Some players asked if they could select more than one heuristic violation.
- One player asked if the severity level was applied to each heuristic or to the problem.
- Some players have shown surprise ("Eita!" and "Vixe!" expressions that are similar to "Wow!" in English language) with the heuristic selected by other players.

5.2 Effective Rounds

The effective rounds were performed without the help of the researchers. The researchers acted only as observers of the study.

Problem 1

Description: The system doesn't allow the user to increase the number of products on the order and doesn't inform max available number of the product in stock as an error message.

After debate the players selected Visibility of system status as the violated heuristic.

During the first severity level rating, 4 players selected "major" and 1 player selected "cosmetic". After negotiation, all players agreed on "major" severity rating.

The researchers reminded the players of the possibility of buying renegotiations, but they decided that it was not worth it.

The most interesting comments of the round were:

- The player that has chosen "cosmetic" started the discussion reflecting on if the severity level should be selected considering only the user described on the task scenario or if they could evaluate based on the problem itself and considering other users. The research informed that the task is a guide, but the evaluation should be over the system and its usage.
- Alice asked "Nobody else has chosen more than one heuristic?" and "You have chosen only that?". Davi answered "Accept it!". And Alice responded "I do not." and then laugh. Alice said "I don't know. There isn't any other violation?". At the end she said "Ok, I accept it.".
- During the heuristic violation debate, Marcos said "And what's next?" and "Does anybody want to say anything more?". Alice answered "No, all we need to do is to go".
- During the negotiation of severity level, the players again have shown surprise about the cards selected. Davi said "Only me have chosen cosmetic?" and 2 other players asked "Why cosmetic?"
- Alice said to Davi "Now you are going to lose 2 points. That's what is going to happen". But Marcos asked Davi "What else you have to say about that?"
- After the new severity card selection Alice said "He has been convinced" and everybody laughed.

Problem 2

Description: It isn't clear if the medal symbol that represents the best sellers refers to the seller of the product listed. To know for sure, it is necessary to click at the symbol and then the system selects a filter for best sellers. The page doesn't order the products for better qualified sellers.

At first, only one player selected 2 types of heuristic violation. But after the debate, the majority of players decided to select 2 violations: Visibility of system status and Consistency and standards.

During the selection of severity level, all the players agreed at first with "minor" and all won 1 point each.

The most interesting comments of the round were:

- Davi said "I think that is Consistency and standards" and Marcos answered "Ok, but only this?" and Igor said "No, I think that there is more than one in here."
- Natalia had trouble classifying the problem and joked "I think I will put all of them". And other player answered "I think that it will worth 4 points to whom get it right" making others players to laugh.
- When they all got the same severity level selection, Alice said "We only like when make fun of others, isn't it?"

Problem 3

Description: The system doesn't allow selecting more than one brand on the search filters.

At first the majority of the players select the two heuristics that remain until the final selection: Consistency and standards and Flexibility and efficiency of use. Just on player had chosen just one violation at first.

The main discordance occurred during the severity rating when at first 3 players selected "minor", 1 player selected "major" and 1 player selected "cosmetic". The final rating was "minor".

The most interesting comments of the round were:

- Just after Davi presented the problem found, Alice said "I already know the answer" and laugh. And Natalia said "She knows because I said to her" and Davi said "What? That's persuasion" and they laugh again.
- But during the selection she already had second thoughts and said "Wait!", "It is not that", "Ah… it is also part of the answer" and "Done".
- After first selection of heuristic violation only Igor had selected just one violation and Davi said "We only have to convince Igor" and Alice agreed and Natalia said "We don't need to, because it is the majority that decides" and Alice said "Sorry, Igor"
- After the first selection of severity rating the players have shown surprise. They said things like "ops, ops" and "easy, easy"
- During the reclassification Marcos said "Hold on, I'm analyzing case by case" and all players laugh. Then Davi said "the grandma, the great grandmother…" and Marcos agreed saying "I'm also thinking since grandmother…"
- Alice said "With this error, I would lose my patience and quit buying anything"

Problem 4

Description: It is not possible to inform the Zip code to calculate the shipping tax and the page rolls to the end when user tries to write comments to the seller.

When the problem is presented, Davi discuss that the problem doesn't occur with every product, just with some specific type of transactions. Because of this, Alice asked whether this is a case of non-violation, but after some debate they decide that it is a violation and identify not just one, but 3 of them: Help and documentation; Visibility of system status and Consistency and standards.

All players but Igor decided for "major" as severity level.

The most interesting comments of the round were:

- When classifying the heuristic for the first time, Marcos said "Eita (equivalent to Wow)" and Davi said "Lots of questions"
- Alice said "This was easier than the others"
- When she saw that her heuristic violation was similar to the majority, she said "Ehh" (wining sound) and "Everybody but Igor won 2 points, isn't it?"

After this round, the researchers decided to stop the study for 2 reasons: it already lasted 50 min (plus 30 for pre-evaluation of the system) and each player had run a round. But some players asked if this was the last round and have shown interest on continuing to play. After asked if they found interesting to apply this gamification during heuristic evaluation they all agreed that would be interesting and would like to participate. They also said that in this way, they could debate more about the classification than when they have done the evaluation alone.

The final points were:

- Natalia: 7 points;
- Igor: 7 points;
- Marcos: 7 points;
- Davi: 7 points;
- Alice: 4 points.

6 Risks

If some player has significant superior level of convincement or even power or hierarchic position upon the others players it can unbalance the evaluation levels during negotiation phase.

Too competitive persons, like Alice can create a tension that can prevent other players to make comments. In this study, it wasn't a problem, because the students were colleagues and they understood her comments as jokes. But this problem would occur in every collaborative method and not only with this game.

7 Conclusions

This paper has proposed a gamification system to increase collaboration during heuristic evaluation. In order to investigate the reception of the initial version of the game, we performed a preliminary study with participants of different profiles evaluating a system for compare prices and sell products. During the application of the game, the volunteers demonstrated an increase in satisfaction in participating of system evaluation. The result is interesting especially when involving non-specialists and end-users working in the evaluation of the same system. Participants, in general, provide positive feedback and suggested some improvements that will be addressed in next versions of the game.

References

1. Nielsen, J., Molich, R.: Heuristic evaluation of user interfaces. In: Chew, J.C., Whiteside, J. (eds.) Proceedings of the SIGCHI Conference on Human Factors in Computing Systems (CHI 1990), pp. 249–256. ACM, New York (1990). doi:http://dx.doi.org/10.1145/97243.97281
2. Petrie, H., Buykx, L.: Collaborative heuristic evaluation: improving the effectiveness of heuristic. In: Proceedings of the UPA Conference, Muniche (UPA 2010) (2010)
3. Herr, S., Baumgartner, N., Gross, T.: Evaluating severity rating scales for heuristic evaluation. In: Proceedings of the 2016 CHI Conference Extended Abstracts on Human Factors in Computing Systems (CHI EA 2016), pp. 3069–3075. ACM, New York (2016). doi:http://dx.doi.org/10.1145/2851581.2892454

4. Lucero, A., Holopainen, J., Ollila, E., Suomela, R., Karapanos, E.: The playful experiences (PLEX) framework as a guide for expert evaluation. In: Proceedings of the 6th International Conference on Designing Pleasurable Products and Interfaces (DPPI 2013), pp. 221–230. ACM, New York (2013). doi:http://dx.doi.org/10.1145/2513506.2513530
5. Gallello, C.: Low cost usability testing Or...why I built UX Check. https://medium.com/@cgallello/low-cost-usability-testing-61b5f8a2a1be#.xvgurmt7e
6. Deterding, S., Dixon, D., Khaled, R., Nacke, L.: From game design elements to gamefulness: defining "gamification". In: Proceedings of the 15th International Academic MindTrek Conference: Envisioning Future Media Environments (MindTrek 2011), pp. 9–15. ACM, New York (2011). doi:http://dx.doi.org/10.1145/2181037.2181040aa
7. Tondello, G.: An introduction to gamification in human-computer interaction. In: Crossroads: The ACM Magazine for Students. http://xrds.acm.org/blog/2016/04/introduction-gamification-human-computer-interaction/
8. Werbach, K., Hunter, D.: For the Win: How Game Thinking Can Revolutionize Your Business. Wharton Digital Press, Philadelphia (2012)

Using Spatio-Temporal Saliency to Predict Subjective Video Quality: A New High-Speed Objective Assessment Metric

Maria Laura Mele[1,2,3(✉)], Damon Millar[3], and Christiaan Erik Rijnders[3]

[1] Department of Philosophy, Social and Human Sciences and Education, University of Perugia, Perugia, Italy
marialaura.mele@gmail.com

[2] ECONA, Interuniversity Centre for Research on Cognitive Processing in Natural and Artificial Systems, Sapienza University of Rome, Rome, Italy

[3] COGISEN Engineering Company, Rome, Italy
{marialaura,damon,chris}@cogisen.com

Abstract. We describe a new Objective Video Quality Assessment (VQA) metric, consisting of a method based on spatio-temporal saliency to model human visual perception of quality. Accurate measurement of video quality is an important step in many video-based applications. Algorithms that are able to significantly predict human perception of video quality are still needed to evaluate video processing models, in order to overcome the high cost and time requirement for large-scale subjective evaluations. Objective quality assessment methods are used for several applications, such as monitoring video quality in quality control systems, benchmarking video compression algorithms, and optimizing video processing and transmission systems. Objective Video Quality Assessment (VQA) methods attempt to predict an average of human perception of video quality. Therefore subjective tests are used as a benchmark for evaluating the performance of objective models. This paper presents a new VQA metric, called Sencogi Spatio-Temporal Saliency Metric (Sencogi-STSM). This metric generates subjective quality scores of video compression in terms of prediction efficacy and accuracy than the most used objective VQA models. The paper describes the spatio-temporal model behind the proposed metric, the evaluation of its performance at predicting subjective scores, and the comparison with the most used objective VQA metrics.

Keywords: Objective video quality assessment · Video compression models · Spatio-temporal saliency · Video quality assessment metrics

1 Introduction

Humans are the end-users of most multimedia applications. Since objective models are unable to perfectly model human vision, the most accurate methodology of video quality assessment is still through subjective perception [1].

M. Kurosu (Ed.): HCI 2017, Part I, LNCS 10271, pp. 353–368, 2017.
DOI: 10.1007/978-3-319-58071-5_27

Predicting subjective quality ratings in a reliable way is one of the main issues facing objective video quality assessment (VQA) models, because subjective tests require high cost and time effort. Moreover, the State of the Art on subjective VQA shows a wide range of evaluation methods. At the moment, the most used methods follow the ITU-R Recommendation BT.500 [2], which proposes standardized presentation formats to measure human participants' mean opinion scores of video quality. The main issue of subjective VQA measurement is that it is often time-consuming and requires the recruitment of a high number of participants to be statistically reliable, thus incurring high costs.

To avoid the cost and delay of subjective VQA, objective VQA is often used. The current objective VQA methods can be classified in three categories: full-reference VQA, reduced-reference VQA, and no-reference VQA. In full-reference VQA methods, an undistorted quality reference video is fully available for comparisons with distorted videos. In reduced-reference VQA methods, only some features of the undistorted quality reference video is used to evaluate the quality of distorted videos. In no-reference VQA methods, the reference video is not available at all [3]. This paper focuses on full-reference methods.

The first section of this paper describes the most commonly used full-reference objective VQA methods i.e., Peak Signal to-Noise Ratio, which is a simple and easy to calculate algorithm but it does not highly correlate with perceived quality subjective evaluations, and the more accurate Structural Similarity Index (for a review on all the existing objective VQA methods see [3]). Neither of these objective VQA metrics are able to calculate whether the relationships among pixels is perceptually salient, so they cannot be applied to evaluate saliency-based compression algorithms. The second section of the paper describes a new metrics, called Sencogi Spatio-Temporal Saliency Metric (Sencogi-STSM), designed by an engineering company called Cogisen (www.cogisen.com). The metric is based on a model using spatio-temporal saliency to account for human visual perception. Sencogi-STSM is compared to the performance of both PSNR and SSIM, taking as a benchmark the subjective evaluation of compressed videos.

2 Quality Assessment Methods

This section describes two quantitative VQA methodologies: the most used objective quality assessment methods and metrics, and the VQA methods and metrics based on saliency models.

2.1 Objective Quality Assessment Methods

Objective VQA methods provide video quality scores without the involvement of participants. Since there is no delay for human testing, objective VQA scores allow practitioners to quickly develop video codecs. Many types of objective VQA methods (e.g. Video Quality Metric (VQM); Visual Information Fidelity (VIF), see [3]), have been proposed in the literature but there is no objective measurement which is able to predict subjective quality scores in all experimental testing conditions, as the research results of the Video Quality Experts Group (VQEG) show [4].

Two existing objective methods will be described: Peak Signal to Noise Ratio (PSNR) [5] and Structural Similarity index (SSIM) [6]. The selected methods –which are widely cited in the literature and provide the most used measures by practitioners– belong to Image Quality Metrics (IQMs). IQMs attempt to measure the quality of a single static image, and can also be used to measure video quality by treating the video stream as a collection of images, and calculating an aggregate score.

PSNR is a full reference QA method able to measure the ratio between the maximum power of a signal and the power of corrupting noise, by performing a pixel-by-pixel comparison of a video-frame before and after it is processed [5]. As a first step, PSNR calculates the Mean Square Error (MSE) of each bit, so that the maximum possible pixel value is squared and divided by MSE, and a logarithm taken of it to give the related PSNR index. PSNR is widely used because it provides a simple measure of the distortion and noise in a processed video-frame, even though it is not able to model human perception in a significant way—all pixels are treated as being of equal importance. Due to its inability to model human vision, PSNR is becoming less useful as modern video codecs increasingly apply human perception rules to eliminate the information that falls beyond the visual perception threshold.

Another QA method used is SSIM, which models human perception by calculating an index of "structural similarity" that aims to emulate how the human visual system perceives quality. In SSIM, video-frame degradation is considered as a change in structural information. The model behind SSIM considers pixels as having strong interdependencies, especially when they are spatially close. Pixel interdependencies are therefore able to convey important information about the structure of visual scene. SSIM calculates three visual components of a frame –luminance, contrast and structure– according to the following weighted combination:

- *Luminance.* High values of luminance are weighed more. The luminance of each pixel is twice the product of average x and y over the sum of the square of average.
- *Contrast.* Locally unique pixel values of contrast are weighed more. The contrast of each point is twice the product of variance x and y over the sum of the square of average.
- *Structure.* The more pixel values change together with their neighbours, the more they are weighed. The structure of each point is the covariance of x and y over the product of the variance x and y.

Variants of SSIM have been proposed [7], such as the Multi-Scale SSIM index (MSSIM), which is a measure based on the multi-scale processing of the early vision system. Both SSIM and MSSIM have shown to be highly predictive of human quality scores, but they are more complex to calculate than PSNR, and they have been both been originally designed for static images, thus they do not properly measure visual distortion among the frames in a video. Moreover, although SSIM/MSSIM is able to measure structural relationships among pixels, they are still unable to measure whether those relationships are perceptually salient. This issue affects the evaluation score especially when salient information is selectively compressed following saliency based compression algorithms (Saliency-based video compression models use saliency to provide better quality in salient areas by keeping the average distortion levels unvaried). Subjective scores report higher values of video quality compared to saliency-based bit distribution, even though MSSIM does not report any improvement. New objective QA models are still needed that are able to calculate the salient parts of video information.

2.2 Saliency-Based Quality Assessment Methods

Saliency is an attention process that helps humans to focus their cognitive resources on the most pertinent subgroup of data, since our visual system can only process partial amounts of information from the wide stream of information that surrounds us [8]. This selection process functions as a filter regulating the access of salient visual information to high level processing systems in the brain, allowing only salient information to reach our awareness.

Since the human visual system (HVS) is the ultimate assessor of image quality, the effectiveness of an Image Quality Metrics (IQM) is generally quantified by to what extent its quality prediction is in agreement with human judgments [9]. The relationship between salience and quality perception has led to a number of approaches that try to integrate salience into IQA metrics to improve their prediction performance [10]. Saliency-weighted IQAs have successfully improved SSIM and PSNR performance [11].

Most saliency algorithms use spatial properties of an image to predict visual salience. There are more than ten spatial saliency algorithms [12]. One reason that there are so many salience algorithms is that the quality of the salience algorithm is important - Zhang et al. found that the difference in predicting human fixations between saliency models is sufficient to yield a significant difference in performance gain when adding these saliency models to IQMs [12].

Some saliency algorithms use frequency domain properties of the image to determine salient areas [13–18]. Frequency domain saliency algorithms respond to patterns in the image, and are typically modelled on the biological properties of the visual cortex of the human eye. Salience maps generated by frequency domain algorithms can solve many problems typically seen in spatial salience calculation methods [19]. Spatial domain algorithms typically produce low-resolution salience maps, have ill-defined object boundaries from severe downsizing of the input image, and fail to uniformly map the entire salient region.

Most saliency-based perception models described in the literature follow two theoretical approaches to obtain saliency: the bottom-up and the top-down approach. The bottom-up approach follows the visual saliency hypothesis [16], which explains the selection of a fixation site as a feature-guided process, and considers visual attention as a data-driven reaction to visual features. The top-down approach is based on the cognitive control hypothesis [16, 20], according to which visual attention is guided in a top-down way according to the task-related needs of the cognitive system. Visual stimuli are relevant (as they are for the bottom-up theory), but this relevance is determined by cognitive information rather than inherent visual saliency [8]. Bottom-up video compression models predict visual saliency from visual patterns, for example using pixel-level contrast or colour differences from the average video-frame colour [16, 21].

However, perceptual sensitivity may not be able to completely explain human visual attention, because it does not consider other variables related to context or cognition. In order to solve this problem, top-down video compression models aim to predict visual saliency starting from representations of viewers' goals and tasks [22]. A problem with top-down saliency models is that they are meant to calculate the saliency on a visual scene, ignoring what is salient or may become salient due to compression artefacts, e.g. ringing, contouring or aliasing. Zhang at el. found that image quality degradation could give rise to changes in images' salience maps [10].

Objective Video Quality Metrics (VQMs) differ from IQMs because human perception of static images is different than moving images. VQMs also differ from IQMs in

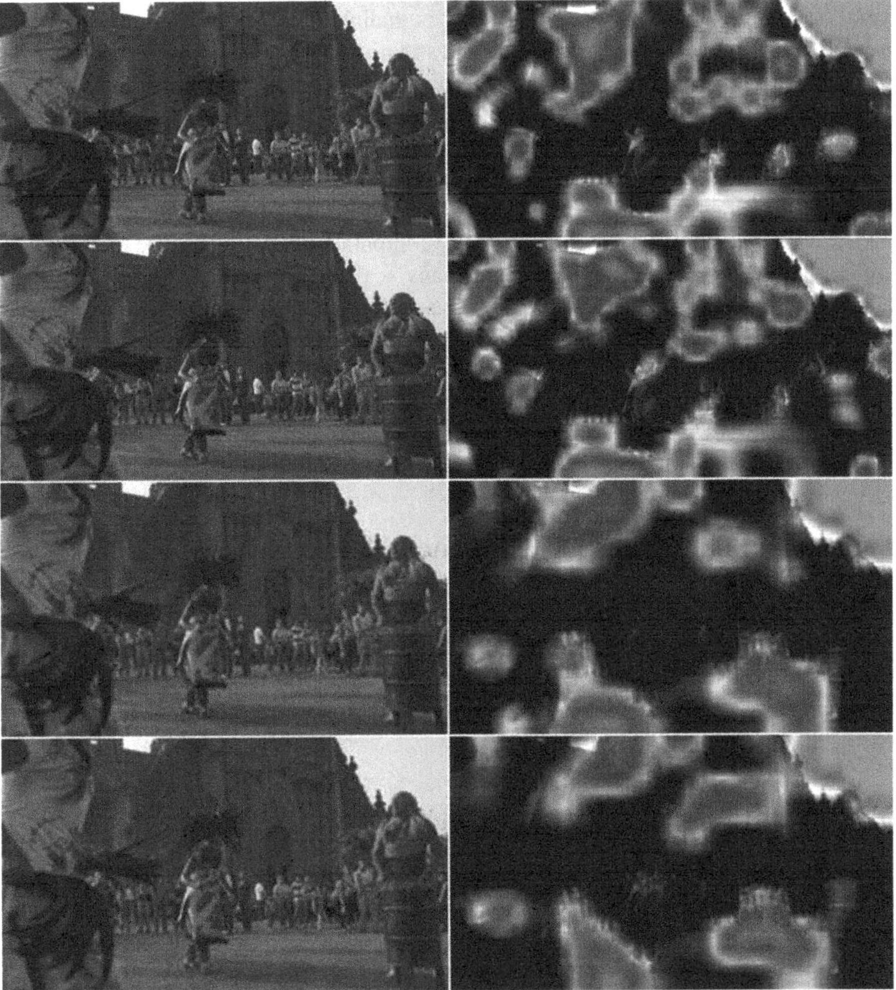

Fig. 1. Video frame at progressively lower resolutions and quality, and the spatial salience map of the frame. The salience map has readily visible changes in response to quality.

that there is a timeliness requirement - processing video can be resource-intensive. The saliency analysis of videos is more complicated than that of still images because there is a spatio-temporal correlation between regions of consecutive frames. The motion of objects changes their importance in a scene and leads to a different saliency map [23]. To address the changing salience of video, some VQMs attempt to incorporate spatio-temporal measures of salience. VQMs that incorporate a measure of salience, perform significantly better than traditional IQAs at predicting subjective image quality [10].

Video compression often produces distortions turning non-salient parts of a visual scene into salient areas. Both bottom-up and top-down video compression models only consider within-frame visual saliency (called "spatial saliency"), thus not properly calculating between-frames spatio-temporal saliency, also called "spatio-temporal saliency".

In the literature, less attention is given on spatio-temporal saliency compared to spatial saliency. Spatio-temporal saliency is mainly studied in cognitive science research, which aims to model perceptual and attentional processes [24–26], and spectral analysis research, which aims to extend frequency domain use of phase data [27, 28]. Applying spatio-temporal saliency to compression may be complicated because of noise produced by camera sensor or compression codec, which can be difficult to discriminate from salient motion. Most of the compression models based on spatio-temporal saliency use global search methods based on a single phenomenon such as motion, optical flow, flicker, or interest points. They impose heavy computational costs because they need to combine many such search algorithms at many scales. Measures of the salience map deformation are a good basis for VQA, because: (1) changes in quality are more visible in salience maps than in video images (Fig. 1); (2) changes in salience can cause a scene to be regarded differently by a viewer (e.g. regarding a different part of a scene) affecting subjective quality; (3) if video has been encoded using a salience-aware codec, that more heavily compresses parts of the frame it predicts as non-salient, then deformations in the salience map may cause the viewer to attend to heavily compressed areas.

3 Sencogi Spatio-Temporal Saliency Metric (Sencogi-STSM)

A new saliency-aware VQA metric called Sencogi-STSM has been developed by Cogisen. The metric is able to predict subjective evaluation of quality for compression models without using cohorts of human viewers. Unlike most objective VQA models, Sencogi-STSM is able to evaluate the quality of videos compressed by saliency-based codecs.

3.1 Cogisen's Video Compression Algorithm

The VQA metric is based on saliency algorithms that Cogisen developed for video compression. Cogisen's video compression algorithms were designed for low bandwidth video applications, such as mobile, that have low video resolution/quality. At low resolutions, it can be challenging for video encoders to calculate saliency, because there are not enough pixels to calculate edges and contrasts. Although low-resolution is difficult to compress, low bandwidth is particularly important for devices that have limited processing capacity and data bandwidth, such as smartphones. Smartphones are becoming the dominant device used for video recording and playing [29]. Smartphone video is also frequently used for live video streaming, such as video chat communication, where latency and delays are easily apparent, so suitable video compression algorithms should meet tight speed and low bandwidth targets.

Cogisen's salience-enabled video compression algorithms were developed for real-time live video, where each frame is compressed in the time between subsequent frames, which requires very fast saliency calculations. Four different types of saliency algorithms are simultaneously run on a real-time video stream and combined to drive the codec's variable macro-block compression. Cogisen's saliency is used in a different way than other salience-based video compression algorithms: many algorithms use saliency to variably drive compression level, to find an acceptable quality trade-off, where videos can have a lower subjective quality in non-salient parts in order to obtain extra compression gains. In Cogisen's implementation, the saliency algorithms are tuned for threshold rather than trade-off. Using a saliency threshold ensures there is no visible loss anywhere in a video. The use of four salience drivers ensures that information removal in one domain does not introduce salient artefacts in another domain.

3.2 A New Saliency-Aware Video Quality Assessment

The salience algorithms from Cogisen's video compression were used to create Sencogi-STSM, a new saliency-aware VQA. The four types of salience computed are:

- *Pixel Noise Detection*, which discerns between pixel noise and motion. Camera sensors produce noise, which appears as random bit changes in the frame. In some situations where a small part of the sensor's dynamic range is used (e.g. low light conditions) pixel noise can be the majority of the change between frames. Pixel noise is the first type of saliency to be calculated, because spatio-temporal algorithms cannot discern genuine scene motion from sensor pixel noise.
- *Static Saliency,* which is saliency within a video frame.
- *Spatio-Temporal Saliency*, which is saliency of the motion between frames. Some types of motion are more salient than others. Once the pixel noise has been identified, the spatio-temporal saliency gives an indication of how strong the video compression can be in different parts of the frame. Spatio-temporal saliency, in particular the prediction of spatio-temporal saliency artifacts, was found to be the most influential factor in subjective image quality, especially in low bandwidth implementations. In low quality videos, any reduction in quality or resolution may result in distortions such as blurry edges due to ringing artifacts or shadowing effects behind the motion. At even lower resolutions and quality levels, a moving object may not even be recognizable but it will be a blob. Cogisen's spatio-temporal saliency algorithm is able to detect those parts that might become salient due to new pixel noise artifacts, by calculating the correlation between the original high quality saliency map and the saliency map of the compressed video.
- *Delta-Quality Saliency*, which calculates whether a quality change is noticeable subjectively by a user, affecting the natural scene salience [30]. If part of a video

becomes better or worse quality, it can attract attention, depending on the amount of quality change. We term this induced saliency "Delta-Quality Saliency". It is a separate saliency calculation for each macro-block that is correlated to the amount of compression change that would lead to the video quality being perceived as changed.

The salience maps are weighted by tunable thresholds, then added to form an overall salience map (Fig. 2). A video quality score is obtained by comparing the overall salience maps of the compressed and reference videos (see Fig. 3) using SSIM.

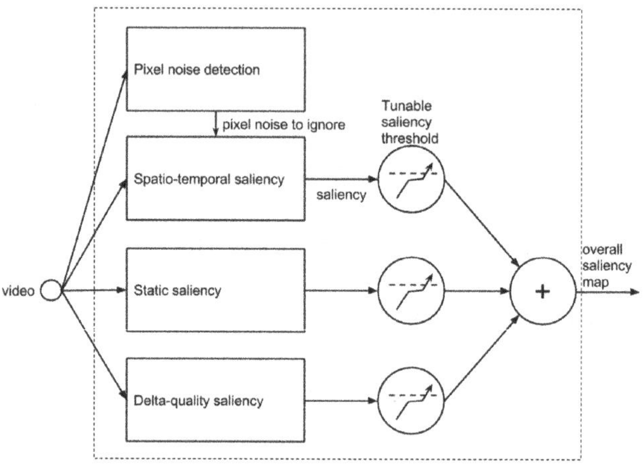

Fig. 2. Figure shows how the different saliency types are combined.

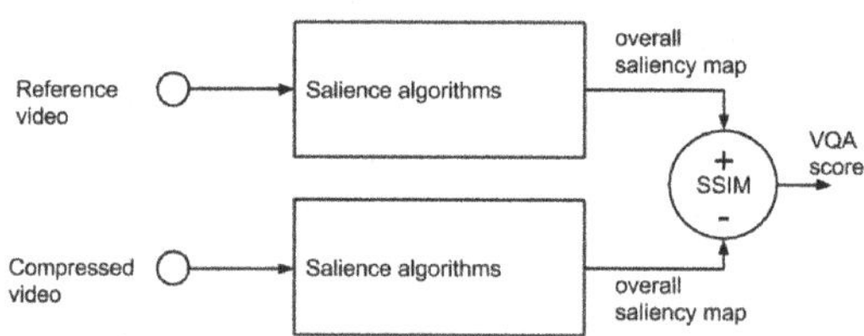

Fig. 3. Figure shows how video quality is measured as a change in saliency map.

4 Performance Evaluation of the Sencogi Spatio-Temporal Saliency Metric

4.1 Methodology

The evaluation of the performance of the Sencogi-STSM followed three phases. In Phase 1, a subjective model was followed to create a benchmark database. In Phase 2, objective VQA scores were calculated by applying both the most used objective

VQA metrics (PSNR, and SSIM), and Sencogi-STSM. In Phase 3, we compared the subjective quality scores obtained in Phase 1, to the objective score obtained in Phase 2.

4.2 Phase 1. Subjective Video Quality Assessment Database

In order to create a subjective video quality database for benchmarking the evaluation of the Sencogi-STSM, the subjective opinion scores were calculated of videos compressed at different Constant Rate Factor (CRF) values, and by two different compression methods. Constant Rate Factor is a setting that instructs the encoder to attempt to achieve a certain output quality by reducing the bitrate. The range of the quantizer scale is 0–51: where 0 is lossless, 23 is default, and 51 is worst possible. A lower value is a higher quality and a normal range is 18–28. CRF 18 is considered to be visually lossless [31]. Reference videos were compressed by two video compression models: ×264 (which does not include a salience model) and the ×264 codec with compression weighted by a salience model that was previously proven to increase compression without affecting subjective scores. The saliency-based video compression model has been recently validated and evaluated [32, 33]. Video compression was performed at two compression levels: Constant Rate Factors (CRF) 21 and CRF 27. The experimental design was 5 (reference videos) × 2 (compression methods) × 2 (compression levels). Subjective opinion scores assigned to each compression level were collected to create a VQA database.

4.2.1 Materials

Five benchmark videos (called "Big Bucks Bunny", "Bouncing balls", "Netflix ritual dance", "Crowd run" and "Tears of steel") with high technical complexity related to the current compression methods were selected. The selected videos lasted less than 10 s and were in the uncompressed YUV4MPEG 4:2:0 format. Only one video was in the MP4 format ("Bouncing Balls") because it was unavailable in an uncompressed format. All videos were 426 × 224 landscape resolution. The raw source of each file was encoded into the MPEG4 format. Reference videos were compressed with a visually lossless CRF value of 10. CRF 10 reference videos were then compressed using both the standard H264 compression and the saliency based model, each video was compressed to two levels: CRF 21 and CRF 27.

4.2.2 Procedure

The Single Stimulus Continuous Quality Scale (SSCQS) method with hidden reference removal was used [2]. The SSCQS method presents one video at a time to the viewer. An example of a high quality video is presented only once at the beginning of the test. Reference high quality videos are randomly shown during the test as a control condition, and participants are not aware of that. The sequence presentations are randomized to ensure that the same video is not presented twice in succession (the randomization is performed when the survey is developed – every user receives the same randomized sequence). As the presentation of each trial ends, observers evaluate the quality of each video using a grading scale of integers in the range 1–100. The scale was marked numerically and divided into five equal portions, which were labelled with adjectives: “Bad”, “Poor”, “Fair”, “Good”, and “Excellent”. The position of the slider is automatically reset after each evaluation. The survey was created and administered using a web-based survey software tool called SurveyGizmo (www.surveygizmo.com), following an online-based methodology, whose validity was previously assessed by the authors [32].

4.2.3 Subjects

Thirty-nine participants (mean age 31.6 years old, 70.9% male, 17.9% expert viewers, 58.9% indoor with artificial lights, 41.1% indoor with natural lights) completed the subjective test in a single session on November 4, 2016. The pre-screening of the subjective test scores consisted of determining if the participants met the preliminary requirements (no vision impairments, only personal computers, no smartphone or tablets, maximum brightness on, bandwidth speed higher than 40 megabits/seconds). Six outliers were removed.

4.2.4 Results of Subjective Video Quality Assessment

The Mean Opinion Scores assigned to the reference videos were used to calculate the Difference Mean Opinion Scores (DMOS) between each compressed video and the relating reference using the following formula:

$$d_{ij} = r_{iref(j)} - r_{ij}$$

where r_{ij} is the raw score for the i-th subject and j-th image, and $r_{iref(j)}$ denotes the raw quality score assigned by the i-th subject to the reference image corresponding to the j-th distorted video [35].

Scale assessment. Internal consistency was supported by Cronbach’s alpha (alpha = 0.969), Spearman Brown split-half value (rho = 0.932) (Cronbach’s Alpha = 0.951 for the first half and alpha = 0.931 for the second half), meaning that all the items of the scale measured the same dimension.

Opinion Scores. The mean opinion scores (MOS) were calculated for each subject. The Difference Mean Opinion Scores (DMOS) were obtained by calculating the difference between the MOS of reference videos and the MOS of the related processed videos (H264 DMOS TOT = 15.46; saliency based compression DMOS TOT = 14.52; H264 DMOS CRF 21 = 2.90; saliency based compression DMOS CRF 21 = 0.06; H264 DMOS CRF 27 = 12.5; saliency based compression DMOS CRF 27 = 14.16).

4.3 Phase 2. Objective Video Quality Assessment

The quality of each reference and compressed videos (used in Phase 1 to assess the subjective perception of quality) was measured by the following VQA metrics: (1) PSNR; (2) SSIM; (3) Sencogi-STSM.

4.3.1 Results of Objective Video Quality Assessment

Table 1 shows the total results for each objective metric (Means: PSNR = 35.898, SSIM = 0,951, Sencogi-STSM = 3.19).

Table 1. Objective VQA metrics for compressed video

	"Big bucks bunny" video		"Tears of steel" video		"Neflix ritual dance" video		"Crowd run" video		"Bouncing balls" video	
	H264	Saliency-based com-pression	H264	Saliency-based com-pression	H264	Saliency-based com-pression	H264	Saliency-based com-pression	H264	Saliency-based com-pression
PSNR	42.80	42	36.917	36.740	35.484	35.084	32.17 6	32.102	33.048	32.614
SSIM	0.983	0.981	0.964	0.963	0.933	0.931	0.934	0.935	0.945	0.941
Sencogi-STSM	3.325	3.218	3.167	3.177	2.877	2.888	3.313	3.339	3.305	3.288

4.4 Phase 3. Prediction Performance of Objective Models

Phase 3 consisted of four comparative analyses between the objective metrics calculated in Phase 2 and the subjective scores calculated in Phase 1 (Fig. 4). This phase followed the methodology recommended by the ITU Telecommunication Standardization Sector [33].

4.4.1 Procedure

The performance of all objective models was tested by using the following metrics:

- The *Spearman Rank Order Correlation Coefficient* (SROC) measures the prediction monotonicity of an objective metric, that is to say, the index in which objective scores are able to predict subjective scores.
- The *Pearson Linear Correlation Coefficient* (PLCC) measures prediction accuracy, that is to say the capability to predict the subjective scores with low error. The Pearson linear correlation it is usually calculated after applying a nonlinear regression with a logistic function as recommended by the ITU Telecommunication Standardization Sector.
- The *Outlier Ratio* (OR) is defined as the percentage of the predictions number that falls outside 2 times the standard deviation of subjective DMOS.
- The *Root Mean Square Error* (RMSE) measures prediction accuracy like the Pearson linear correlation [39].

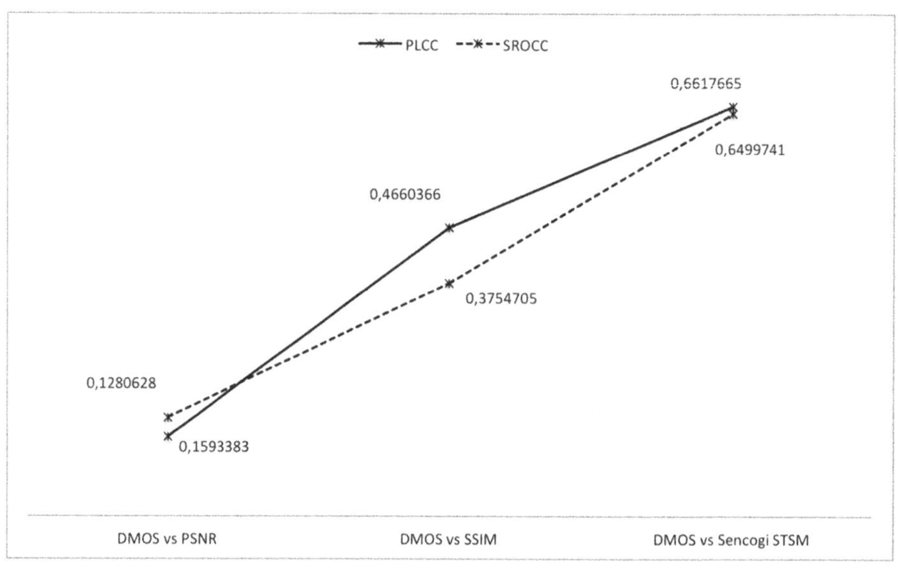

Fig. 4. Comparison among correlations between DMOS and objective metrics

4.4.2 Results of Objective Video Quality Assessment

- *Spearman Rank Order Correlation* (SROC). Results on both CRF 21 and 27 show a significant positive correlation between Sencogi-STSM values and DMOS values (rho = 0.650, $p < 0.01$). No significant correlation between both PSNR (rho = 0.159, $p > 0.05$) and SSIM (rho = 0.375, $p > 0.05$) values and DMOS values was found.

- *Pearson Linear Correlation Coefficient* (PLCC). Results on both CRF 21 and 27 show a significant positive correlation between objective measures and DMOS subjective scores for both Sencogi-STSM ($r = 0.662$, $p < 0.01$) and SSSIM ($r = 0.466$, $p < 0.05$). No significant correlation between PSNR and DMOS was found ($r = 0.128$, $p > 0.05$). Comparison of both Spearman's (SROC) and Pearson's (PLCC) correlation among PSNR, SSSIM and Sencogi-STSM and DMOS values.
- *Outlier Ratio* (OR). Only 7% of the values predicted by both SSIM (OR = 0.65) and Sencogi-SMST (OR = 0.70) fall outside ± 2 of the standard deviation of subjective DMOS, whereas all PSNR values (OR = 1) fall outside ± 2 of the SD of subjective DMOS.
- *The Root Mean Square Error* (RMSE). Paired t test showed that SSIM scores ($t(10) = 10.32$, $p = 0.000$) and Sencogi-STSM scores ($t(10) = 12.66$, $p = 0.000$) are more statistically significant than PSNR scores. Moreover, Compared to PSNR and SSIM, Sencogi-STSM prediction scores have significantly lower RMSE than SSIM scores ($t(10 = 2.29$, $p = 0.048$) with Sencogi-STSM RMSE = 9.045; PSNR RMSE = 29.898, SSIM RMSE = 10.201.

5 Discussion

Based on the analyses presented in this work, the new Sencogi-STSM metric is an effective metric for predicting the subjective quality scores of videos. A significant positive Spearman's correlation uniquely between the Cogisen's metric scores and DMOS scores highlights that Sencogi-STSM is the only metric that was able to show an increase of prediction associated with an increase of subjective DMOS in a statistically relevant way, compared to PNSR and SSIM performance. Both Sencogi-STSM and SSIM were able to predict estimates of the subjective scores with a minimum average error, but Sencogi-STSM had a prediction accuracy that was significantly better than both SSIM and PSNR. The improvements in prediction performance found with Sencogi-STSM over the classic SSIM and PSNR metrics, is likely because the method is weighted on perceptual quality, so that the most salient parts of each video-frame affect the VQA metric more than the less salient ones.

6 Conclusion

A new Video Quality Assessment (VQA) metric was developed, called Sencogi Spatio-Temporal Saliency Metric (Sencogi-STSM). Sencogi-STSM is based on a spatio-temporal saliency model that is able to better predict subjective perception scores of video compared to the most used objective VQA metrics, because it uses a saliency model of human visual perception. Sencogi-STSM combines noise detection, the saliency within a video-frame, the saliency of the motion between video-frames, and the delta-quality saliency indicating where a quality change man be noticed by a human viewer. We have assessed the performance of Sencogi-STSM at predicting subjective scores, and compared that performance with the most used VQA metrics, i.e. PSNR and

SSIM. We found that Sencogi-STSM more accurately predicts subjective scores than the most used objective VQA models. The difference between Sencogi-STSM and the most used VQA models (such as PSNR and SSIM) is that Sencogi-STSM uses salience to decide how important each part of a frame is, in terms of quality perception. Future works could be focused on improving the saliency model by combining bottom-up spatio-temporal saliency to top-down saliency, accordingly to task-centred and contextual factors.

References

1. Pedram, M., Abbas, E.-M., Shahram, S.: Subjective and objective quality assessment of image: a survey. CoRR abs/1406.7799 (2014)
2. BT.500: Methodology for the subjective assessment of the quality of television pictures (n.d.). https://www.itu.int/rec/R-REC-BT.500-7-199510-S/en. Accessed 30 Jan 2017
3. Chikkerur, S., Sundaram, V., Reisslein, M., Karam, L.J.: Objective video quality assessment methods: a classification, review, and performance comparison. IEEE Trans. Broadcast. **57**, 165–182 (2011)
4. Brunnstrom, K., Hands, D., Speranza, F., Webster, A.: VQeg validation and ITU standardization of objective perceptual video quality metrics [Standards in a Nutshell]. IEEE Sign. Process. Mag. **26**, 96–101 (2009)
5. Zhang, X., Zhang, X., Silverstein, D.A., Farrell, J.E., Wandell, B.A.: Color image quality metric S-CIELAB and its application on halftone texture visibility. In: Proceedings of IEEE COMPCON 1997. Digest of Papers (n.d.). doi:10.1109/cmpcon.1997.584669
6. Wang, Z., Bovik, A.C., Sheikh, H.R., Simoncelli, E.P.: Image quality assessment: from error visibility to structural similarity. IEEE Trans. Image Process. **13**, 600–612 (2004)
7. Wang, Z., Simoncelli, E.P., Bovik, A.C.: Multiscale structural similarity for image quality assessment. In: The Thrity-Seventh Asilomar Conference on Signals, Systems and Computers (2003). doi:10.1109/acssc.2003.1292216
8. Duchowski, A.: Eye Tracking Methodology, Theory and Practice, vol. 373. Springer Science & Business Media, New York (2007)
9. Wang, Z., Bovik, A.C.: Modern image quality assessment. In: Synthesis Lectures on Image, Video, and Multimedia Processing, vol. 2, pp. 1–156 (2006)
10. Zhang, L., Shen, Y., Li, H.: VSI: a visual saliency-induced index for perceptual image quality assessment. IEEE Trans. Image Process. **23**, 4270–4281 (2014)
11. Larson, E.C., Chandler, D.M.: Unveiling relationships between regions of interest and image fidelity metrics. In: Visual Communications and Image Processing 2008 (2008). doi: 10.1117/12.769248
12. Zhang, W., Borji, A., Wang, Z., Le Callet, P., Liu, H.: The application of visual saliency models in objective image quality assessment: a statistical evaluation. IEEE Trans. Neural Netw. Learn. Syst. **27**, 1266–1278 (2016)
13. Achanta, R., Estrada, F., Wils, P., Süsstrunk, S.: Salient region detection and segmentation. In: Gasteratos, A., Vincze, M., Tsotsos, John K. (eds.) ICVS 2008. LNCS, vol. 5008, pp. 66–75. Springer, Heidelberg (2008). doi:10.1007/978-3-540-79547-6_7

14. Hou, X., Zhang, L.: Saliency detection: a spectral residual approach. In: 2007 IEEE Conference on Computer Vision and Pattern Recognition (2007). doi:10.1109/cvpr.2007.383267
15. Harel, J., Koch, C., Perona, P.: Graph-based visual saliency. In: Advances in Neural Information Processing Systems, pp. 545–552 (2007)
16. Itti, L., Koch, C.: A saliency-based search mechanism for overt and covert shifts of visual attention. Vision Res. **40**, 1489–1506 (2000)
17. Li, J., Levine, M., An, X., He, H.: Saliency detection based on frequency and spatial domain analyses. In: Proceedings of the British Machine Vision Conference 2011 (2011). doi:10.5244/c.25.86
18. Ma, Y.-F., Zhang, H.-J.: Contrast-based image attention analysis by using fuzzy growing. In: Proceedings of the Eleventh ACM International Conference on Multimedia, MULTIMEDIA 2003 (2003). doi:10.1145/957092.957094
19. Achanta, R., Hemami, S., Estrada, F., Susstrunk, S.: Frequency-tuned salient region detection. In: 2009 IEEE Conference on Computer Vision and Pattern Recognition (2009)
20. Wolfe, J.M.: Visual search in continuous, naturalistic stimuli. Vision Res. **34**, 1187–1195 (1994)
21. Mishra, A.K., Aloimonos, Y., Cheong, L.-F., Kassim, A.A.: Active visual segmentation. IEEE Trans. Pattern Anal. Mach. Intell. **34**, 639–653 (2012)
22. Judd, T., Ehinger, K., Durand, F., Torralba, A.: Learning to predict where humans look. In: 2009 IEEE 12th International Conference on Computer Vision (2009). doi:10.1109/iccv.2009.5459462
23. Yubing, T., Cheikh, F.A., Guraya, F.F.E., Konik, H., Trémeau, A.: A spatiotemporal saliency model for video surveillance. Cogn. Comput. **3**, 241–263 (2011)
24. Muddamsetty, S.M., Sidibe, D., Tremeau, A., Meriaudeau, F.: Spatio-temporal saliency detection in dynamic scenes using local binary patterns. In: 2014 22nd International Conference on Pattern Recognition (2014). doi:10.1109/icpr.2014.408
25. Bruce, N.D.B.: Saliency based on information maximization. In: Advances in Neural Information Processing Systems, p. 155 (2006)
26. Mahadevan, V., Vasconcelos, N.: Spatiotemporal saliency in dynamic scenes. IEEE Trans. Pattern Anal. Mach. Intell. **32**, 171–177 (2010)
27. He, X., Gao, X., Zhang, Y., Zhou, Z.-H., Liu, Z.-Y., Fu, B., Hu, F., Zhang, Z.: Intelligence Science and Big Data Engineering. In: 5th International Conference on Image and Video Data Engineering, IScIDE 2015, Suzhou, China, 14–16 June 2015, Revised Selected Papers. Springer, Heidelberg (2015)
28. Bian, P., Zhang, L.: Biological plausibility of spectral domain approach for spatiotemporal visual saliency. In: Köppen, M., Kasabov, N., Coghill, G. (eds.) ICONIP 2008. LNCS, vol. 5506, pp. 251–258. Springer, Heidelberg (2009). doi:10.1007/978-3-642-02490-0_31
29. Cisco: Cisco VNI mobile forecast (2015–2020). Cisco (2016). http://www.cisco.com/c/en/us/solutions/collateral/service-provider/visual-networking-index-vni/mobile-white-paper-c11-520862.html. Accessed 31 Jan 2017
30. Redi, J., Liu, H., Zunino, R., Heynderickx, I.: Interactions of visual attention and quality perception. In: Human Vision and Electronic Imaging XVI (2011). doi:10.1117/12.876712
31. FFMPEG: https://trac.ffmpeg.org/wiki/Encode/H.264. Accessed 13 Feb 2017
32. Mele, M.L., Millar, D., Rijnders, C.E.: The web-based subjective quality assessment of an adaptive image compression plug-in. In: 1st International Conference on Human Computer Interaction Theory and Applications, HUCAPP, Porto, Portugal (2017)

33. Mele, M.L., Millar, D., Rijnders, C.E.: Validating a quality perception model for image compression: the subjective evaluation of the Cogisen's image compression plug-in. In: Kurosu, M. (ed.) HCI 2016. LNCS, vol. 9731, pp. 350–359. Springer, Cham (2016). doi: 10.1007/978-3-319-39510-4_33
34. ITU-T Study Group 12: Contribution COM 12. Evaluation of new methods for objective testing of video quality: objective test plan 1998

An Exploratory Study on the Predictive Capacity of Heuristic Evaluation in Visualization Applications

Beatriz Sousa Santos[1,2(✉)], Samuel Silva[2], Beatriz Quintino Ferreira[2], and Paulo Dias[1,2]

[1] Department of Electronics Telecommunications and Informatics, University of Aveiro, Aveiro, Portugal
bss@ua.pt

[2] Institute of Electronics Engineering and Informatics of Aveiro/IEETA, Aveiro, Portugal
{sss,mbeatriz,paulo.dias}@ua.pt

Abstract. Heuristic evaluation is generally considered as an adequate method to perform formative usability evaluation as it helps identify potential problems from early stages of development and may provide useful results even with a relatively low investment. In particular, the method has been adapted and used to evaluate visualization applications. This paper presents an exploratory study aimed at better understanding the capacity of heuristic evaluation to predict the issues experienced by users when using a visualization application and how to assess it. The main usability potential problems pointed out in a visualization application by 20 evaluators using heuristic evaluation are compared with the problems reported for the same application by 44 users.

Keywords: Information visualization · Heuristic evaluation · User study

1 Introduction

Heuristic evaluation is a well-known discount usability inspection method that has been widely used by Human-Computer Interaction practitioners for years [1]. It is considered adequate to perform formative evaluation as it helps identify potential problems and improve the application before giving it to users. It is applicable throughout the whole development cycle and is considered as generally providing useful results with a relatively low investment, albeit often finding too specific and low-priority usability problems. This evaluation method has been adapted to evaluate visualization applications [2], namely by developing visualization-specific sets of heuristics (e.g. [3–7]). However, the capacity of heuristic evaluation to predict the issues later experienced by users, when using a visualization application, is yet to be assessed. In our previous work [8], we also suggest that heuristic evaluation is useful to evaluate Visualization applications, since it fosters a more systematic inspection of the relevant aspects of the application's user interface. Following on those results, we now aim to assess the predictive capacity of the method, by checking if the potential problems identified through heuristic evaluation, for a visualization application, match those experienced by its users. This paper presents

M. Kurosu (Ed.): HCI 2017, Part I, LNCS 10271, pp. 369–383, 2017.
DOI: 10.1007/978-3-319-58071-5_28

a user study performed to compare the potential usability issues identified through heuristic evaluation with the difficulties felt by users while using a specific visualization application. In the context of our research, this worked as a first instantiation of a method that, we argue, might be used to compare different sets of heuristics in specific contexts.

The remainder of the paper is organized as follows: Sect. 2 addresses the usage of heuristic evaluation in visualization. The materials and methods used in the study are presented in Sect. 3, namely its design, the visualization application used, the main potential usability issues found using heuristic evaluation, the tasks performed by the participants and the questionnaire developed. Section 4 presents and discusses the main results obtained from the answers of 44 participants compared with the potential problems pointed out by 20 evaluators through heuristic evaluation. Finally, in Sect. 5 some conclusions and potential avenues for future work are drawn.

2 Heuristic Evaluation in Visualization

Several authors have emphasized the relevance of using heuristic evaluation in Information Visualization evaluation, either in research or along the development of visualization applications. Tory and Möller [9, 10] consider using heuristic evaluation a valuable means to evaluate visualization techniques during exploratory phases of research when goals are not yet clear and formal laboratory user studies may be premature. Moreover, these formal studies may have too high a cost for early phases of the development cycle [12, 13] and in this case heuristic evaluation may be more suitable. According to Munzner [13, 14], heuristic evaluation is an adequate evaluation method to be used at the visual encoding/ interaction design level of her model for the visualization design and validation process. This author considers heuristic evaluation as a way to systematically assess that specific guidelines are not violated by the design, as well as to help fixing usability problems, ensuring that the design effectively communicates the desired abstraction to the user. Sedlmair et al. [15] have used heuristic evaluation during the development of information visualization tools in the context of large companies, and report that it helped sparing experts' time. Lam et al. [16] propose seven evaluation scenarios to help visualization researchers and practitioners decide upon evaluation approaches, with heuristic evaluation being included in the list of methods that can be used in Collaborative Data Analysis. Nonetheless, we argue that its applicability should not be restricted to such a specific scenario. In an early work, Freitas et al. [17] used two sets of criteria to evaluate 'visual representations' and 'interaction mechanisms' to find potential usability problems. Later on, several visualization-specific heuristics sets have been proposed to be used in the scope of heuristic evaluation of Visualization techniques and applications (e.g. [4, 6, 7]). In a more recent work, Freitas et al. [18] address the evolution of visualization techniques evaluation, review main contributions in this area, identify problems and propose a set of guidelines for user-centered evaluation of information visualization techniques. One of these guidelines is "Guideline#4: Evaluating early" and, according to the authors, expert-based evaluation methods, as well as other analytic methods, are useful to identify and help fixing basic usability issues before entailing a more complex evaluation phase, namely involving users.

On the use of inspection evaluation methods and empirical methods, Hollingsed and Novick [19], based on an overview of usability evaluation methods, suggest that empirical and inspection methods should, somehow, be unified, by combining their multiple perspectives. This requires an understanding on how different methods relate in their ability to detect usability issues. Naturally, different methods will provide different (possibly overlapping) ranges of results, at different costs, and one important goal is to determine the boundaries of such overlap. Based on those findings, we can more precisely define what to expect from each method or redesign less expensive methods, such as heuristic evaluation, to provide the best possible approximation to more complex methods such as user studies. Additionally, in the long run, it might also help us to establish what kind and optimal amount of each evaluation method should be considered at each phase, properly balancing cost and maximizing results.

Therefore, the reviewed literature elicits the proposal of a systematic approach that fosters additional insight over: (1) the advantages of using heuristic evaluation in Information Visualization contexts; (2) the predictive value of heuristic evaluation in the context of Information Visualization, when compared with empirical evaluation; and, to address the previous point, (3) how to establish a relation between the outcomes of inspection and empirical methods. Motivated by these aspects, our previous work [8] discussed the advantages of heuristic evaluation in Information Visualization and in the present work we consider the predictive value of a heuristic evaluation by assessing if its outcomes actually translate into problems felt during a user study in a specific setting.

In this context, we should highlight the work by Hearst et al. [20] discussing the subject of evaluating the relation between the outcomes of heuristic evaluations and the problems felt by users in the context of Information Visualization.

Their work shares several aspects with our own, in terms of general methodology, by also comparing the outcomes of a heuristic evaluation with those gathered through a questionnaire. However, we do not only aim at developing a framework for teaching and assessing visualizations, but we also seek to develop a method that might be used to compare different sets of heuristics regarding their performance and adequacy to different situations (e.g. web or mobile visualization, or different audiences).

3 The Study: Materials and Methods

In summary, our goal was to establish how to collect user data that would be useful to assess the relevance of the heuristic evaluation outcomes. In what follows, we describe the most important aspects of the study, namely the overall design, the visualization application used, the main potential issues found using heuristic evaluation, the tasks performed by the users, the questionnaire they answered, the participants profile and number, as well as the registered data.

3.1 Study Design

Figure 1 shows the overall organization of the study: an application was evaluated using heuristic evaluation by 20 evaluators having some experience in evaluating visualization applications using this method; the ten most often reported potential usability issues were identified; a set of tasks and a questionnaire addressing these aspects were developed and 44 participants used the application to perform the tasks and answer the questionnaire. Finally, the results obtained from the participants' answers to the questionnaire were compared with those obtained by the evaluators.

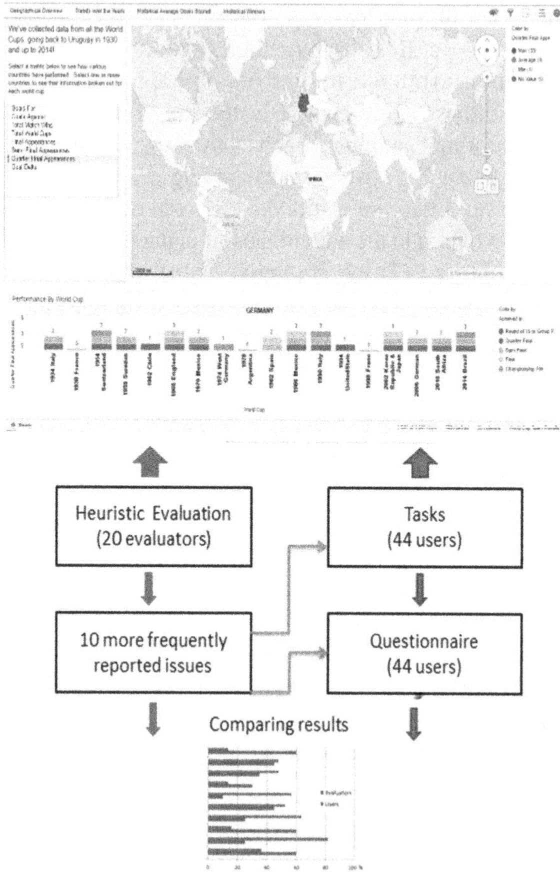

Fig. 1. Overall organization of the study: 20 evaluators use heuristic evaluation to analyze an application; 44 users perform tasks and answer a questionnaire, results are compared.

3.2 Application Evaluated

The evaluated application was a simple example from the Spotfire demo gallery (http://spotfire.tibco.com/demos/spotfire-soccer-2014) providing interactive visualizations of data from the soccer world cups going back to Uruguai 1930 until Brasil 2014. Figure 2 shows the main aspects of the Geographical overview tab of the application. This tab allows visualizing on a map data corresponding to the selected country concerning a specific "metric" (goals for, goals against, total match wins, total world cups, final, semi-final and quarter-final appearances, and goal delta); beneath the map a bar chart displays data corresponding to the performance of the selected country by world cup. Figure 3 shows the type of information provided by a tooltip when the user selects a country.

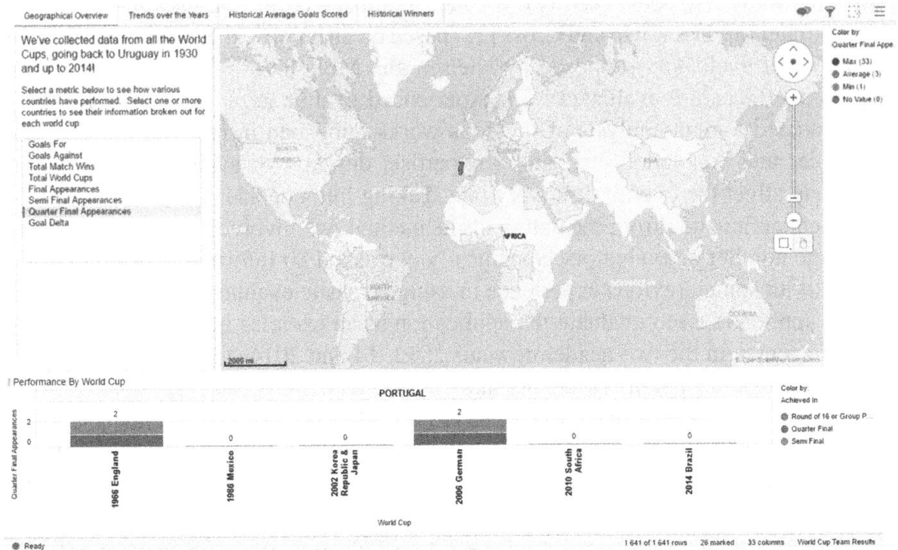

Fig. 2. World cup soccer analysis (spotfire demo gallery) – general aspect of the geographical overview tab of the application.

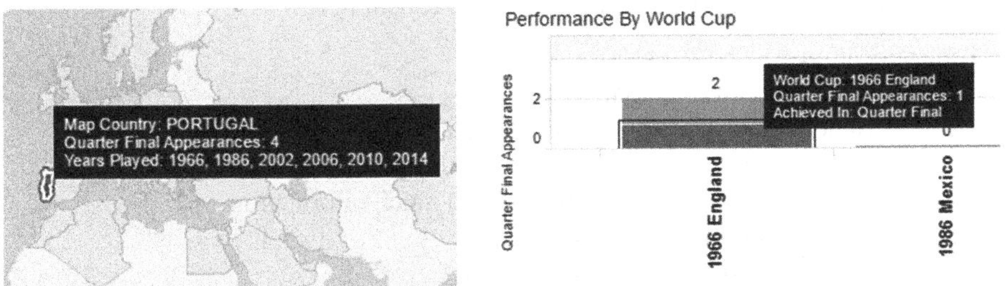

Fig. 3. World cup soccer analysis (spotfire demo gallery) – tooltips providing data concerning a specific metric for a country selected on the map (left), and on the bar chart beneath the map (right).

This application was chosen due to the concrete and easy to understand data set visualized. Moreover, we considered the topic would be motivating for most students who were going to perform the heuristic evaluation, promoting the discovery of a higher number of problems.

3.3 Potential Problems Identified Using Heuristic Evaluation

The number of evaluators using heuristic evaluation needed to find a significant percentage of the potential usability problems has been subject to debate. Nielsen and Molich [21] initially reported that five evaluators found about 2/3 of usability problems in a specific study, and consequently the "magic number five rule" has been widely used. However, later on, Slavkovic and Cross [22] based on an empirical study, suggested that the number of evaluators proposed by Nielsen and Molich does not generalize when complex interfaces are evaluated by inexperienced evaluators. Hwang and Salvendy [23] conducted a meta-analysis of previous works published in relevant journals and conferences and concluded evaluator's expertise, duration of evaluation, and report format may affect the overall discovery rate. Taking into consideration these findings, which seem anticipated from the nature of the method, we involved in the study a relatively large number of evaluators. Specifically, we asked 20 Information Visualization students (with some previous experience in using heuristic evaluation to evaluate visualization applications) to evaluate the application as an exercise in a lab session at the end of the course in the two academic years 2013–14 and 2014–15. The students were first informed that the results of their evaluation would be used in a study about heuristic evaluation in Visualization and were asked to find at least 6 potential problems, register them in a paper form and submit immediately after completing it. To close the session, the students were involved in a general discussion on the method, the heuristics used, and the specific application evaluated. The evaluation was performed on a voluntary basis, with no grading; however, students were asked to sign the forms in order to foster effort in finding the problems. These 20 evaluators found and described a total of 140 problems. The descriptions were analyzed to classify the issues into different categories and recognize repetitions. This allowed identifying the following potential problems more often pointed out by the evaluators (most frequent first):

- The application may be too slow
- Colors may be difficult to discriminate
- Meaning of colors may be difficult to understand
- Zoom and Scroll may be difficult to use
- Some aspects of the application may have too much information
- Help and documentation may be insufficient
- The lack of Undo may have a negative impact
- Multiple country selection may be difficult to find
- Small items may be difficult to select
- Charts at the bottom may not be visible (depending on the screen size)

3.4 Questionnaire

The questionnaire was an important part of the work and some care has been put in its development. Since our goal was to assess if the outcomes of the heuristic evaluation translated into actual problems, detected by users, we considered the problems identified by the evaluators to guide the design of the tasks. Each selected task required the use of one or more potentially problematic features. Then, we devised a set of questions that would elicit the envisaged tasks. An on-line questionnaire was developed including these questions, all implying performing data analysis tasks with the application. By accounting for the potential problems, when designing the tasks to be performed by the users, we aimed at: (1) ensuring that they were faced with the potential problems; and (2) easing the a posteriori match between the outcomes of both evaluation methods, a potentially challenging task [24]. The questionnaire is composed of three parts: six questions forcing the participants to use several aspects of the application, a set of questions concerning personal and platform data, and a final set of questions to obtain participants' opinion of the application. The questionnaire was implemented based on an on-line questionnaire platform used at our University, which allowed retrieving the time taken to answer each question.

Part I: Task Related Questions – At the beginning of the questionnaire, the participants were asked to become familiarized with the application by freely exploring it for at least five minutes. After this, they were presented with the questions, designed with different degrees of difficulty, involving performing tasks that would force them to use the functionality and user interface aspects where potential problems had been identified. All these questions had a quantitative answer so that task correctness was easily assessed (Table 1). Also, the task difficulty, as perceived by the participant, was assessed through a Likert-type scale immediately after answering each question (Fig. 4). Times were logged during the participants' activity.

Table 1. Questions to be answered by the participants that imply using the application to perform tasks

#	Question
1	How many goals has Portugal scored in all championships?
2	How many goals has Portugal scored in semi-finals?
3	In how many championships did Portugal score as much goals as Spain?
4	Where and when did that happen?
5	How many games did Germany win in the 1954 championship, in Switzerland?
6	How many games did Germany win in the "Round of 16", at that same championship?

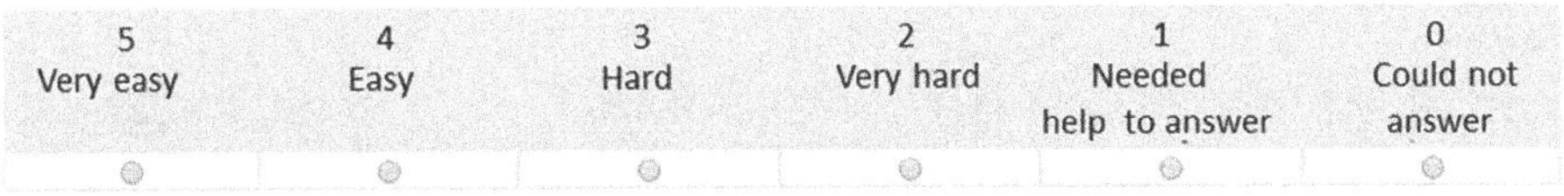

Fig. 4. Likert-type scale used to obtain difficulty perceived by the participants to answer the questions in Table 1

Part II: User and Platform Characterization – After concluding the tasks and answering the corresponding questions, data was collected regarding: (1) demographics (gender, age); (2) color perception, through a partial Ishihara color test to identify possible color perception difficulties; and (3) platform characterization (screen size, input device, browser, etc.).

Part III: Detailed Application Experience – Participants were also asked about their experience with the application through closed-ended questions addressing specific aspects and the overall usability of the application (Fig. 5), as well as an open-ended question to express their general opinion and any comments. These questions were meant to assess if the participants had noticed or had been able to easily use functionality/aspects that had been considered potentially problematic by the evaluators. Additionally, and to avoid leading participants to think that all questions were about severe usability issues, some questions addressed aspects that were not among the most often reported issues. To make the questions more understandable, some of them were illustrated with an example from the application (Fig. 5).

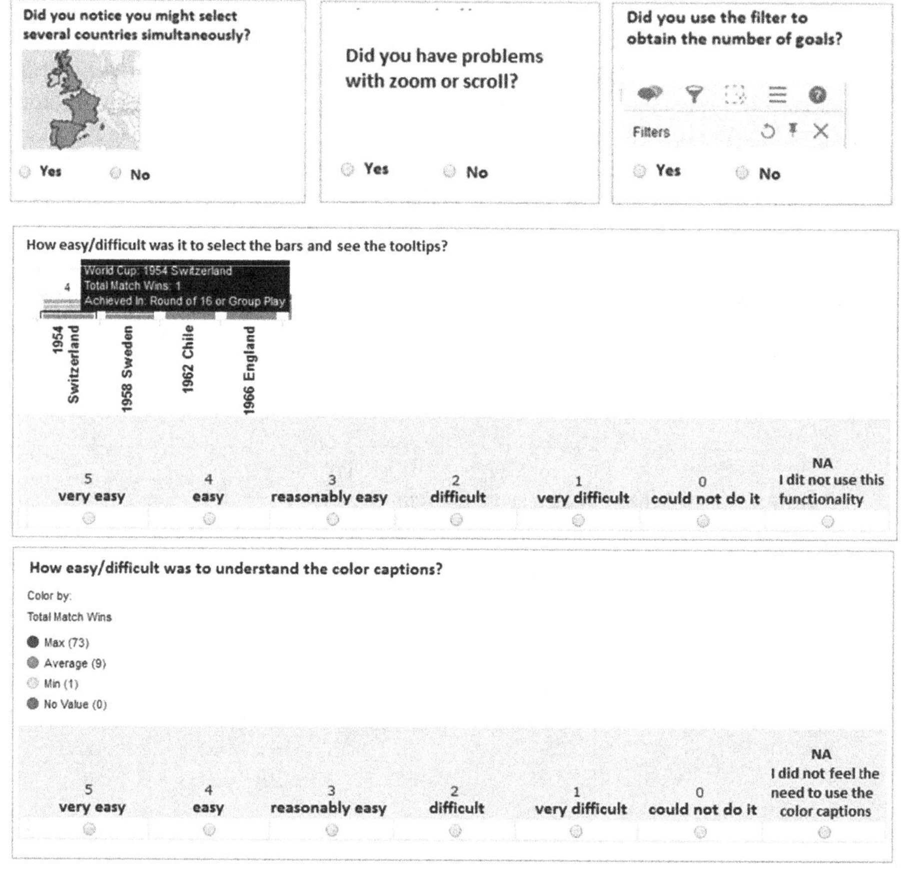

Fig. 5. Closed-ended questions addressing specific aspects of the application (translated from the original questionnaire in Portuguese)

Finally, participants were asked about the overall usability of the application (also using a Likert-type scale: 5-very good, 4-good, 3-reasonable, 2-bad, 1-very bad) and to select from a list of possible undesirable characteristics the ones that, in their opinion, had a more negative impact on the application usability and user experience. This list was organized alphabetically and this was stated in the questionnaire so that participants would not infer any order of importance. After reaching this part, it was not possible to go back in the questionnaire and change the answers given to the previous questions.

3.5 Participants

The participants were 44 students (9 females and 35 males, aged 19 to 31) attending a course on Human-Computer Interaction (BSc level) or on Information Visualization (MSc level) at our Department. They did not know the application a priori, but all had some knowledge concerning usability and had already analyzed the usability of interactive applications. The questionnaire was answered during a laboratory class as an exercise.

4 Main Results and Discussion

In what follows, we first present and discuss the main results from the user study. We go through the data gathered from the questions that implied using the application to find a quantitative answer, as well as from the questions about specific aspects of the application. Finally, we bring back the data from the heuristic evaluation and compare it with this novel data in order to assess the extent to which the problems detected by evaluators actually materialized in problems felt by users.

4.1 Questions Implying Using the Application to Perform Tasks

All participants were able to answer correctly most questions concerned with the data. This suggests that they were engaged in performing the tasks needed to find the answers, and adds value to their answers concerning the experience of using the application, as well as to their opinion on the overall usability and of specific aspects of the application. Nevertheless, some users were not able to answer the questions that were more complex by design, such as questions 3 and 4 (Table 2), and implied using features pointed out by the evaluators as potentially problematic.

Table 2. Answers to the questions that imply using the application (Table 1)

Question #	# of right answers	# of wrong answers	# of no answer	Median (easy-difficult)	Average time (s)
1	38	6	0	4	74
2	31	5	8	3	93
3	28	4	12	3	137
4	30	0	14	3	36
5	38	5	1	4	92
6	37	3	4	4	43

Figure 6 shows the difficulty stated by participants for each of the questions in Table 1 using a Likert-type scale (5-very easy, 4-easy, 3-difficult, 2- very difficult, 1-needed help, 0-could not do it). Tasks 3 (In how many championships did Portugal score as much as Spain?) and 4 (Where and when?) appear as the most difficult tasks with a relatively high percentage of the participants not being able to complete them (27% and 32%, respectively) and a median difficulty value of 3 (difficult). Task 3 has a higher inherent complexity and this is probably reflected on the higher average time participants took to answer the corresponding question. These tasks are related and several participants mentioned in their comments that the small size of the bars made them difficult to perform. This issue had been pointed out by evaluators as one of the potential usability issues, and confirmed in the second part of the questionnaire as a problem felt by many participants.

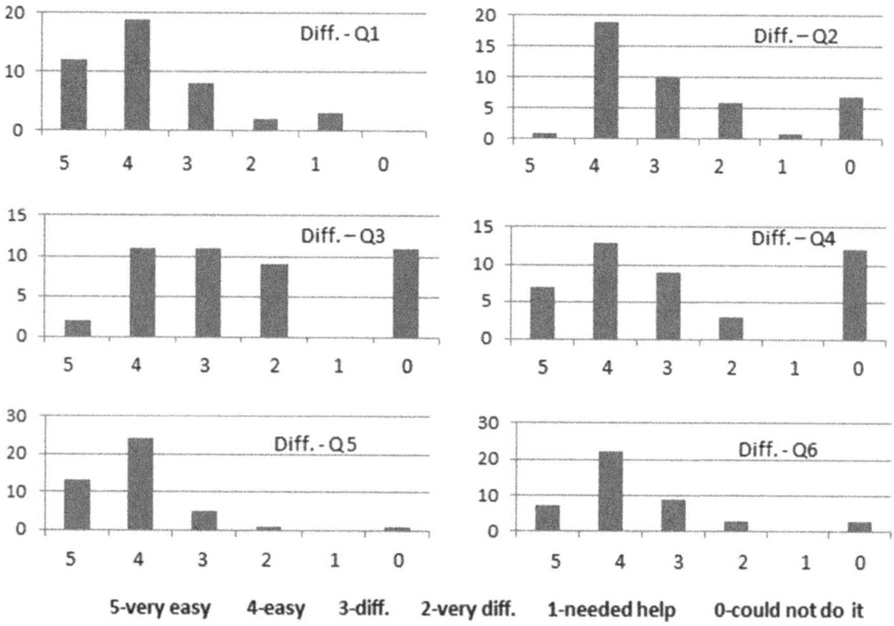

Fig. 6. Difficulty perceived by the participants to answer the questions that imply using the application (Table 1)

Figure 7 shows the boxplots of the times to answer these questions. Participants took in average longer to perform task 3, which confirms that this task was more complex.

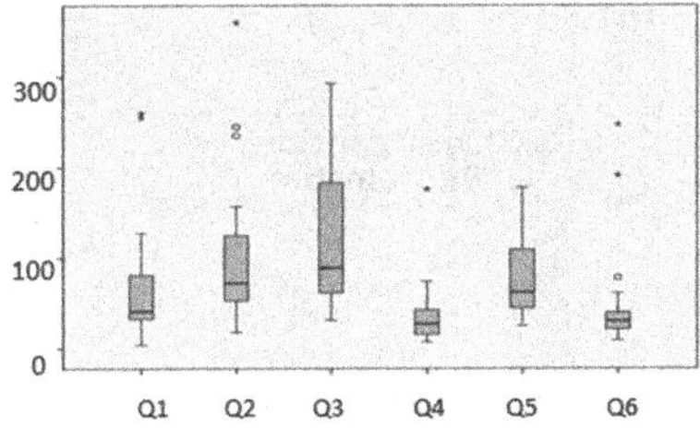

Fig. 7. Boxplots corresponding to the times (s) to answer the questions that imply using the application (Table 1)

4.2 Questions Addressing Specific Aspects of the Application

Tables 3, 4, and Fig. 8a show the results to the closed-end questions addressing specific aspects of the application. These results suggest that zoom and scroll may be difficult to use and the possibility of selecting multiple countries may be difficult to notice; both aspects were pointed out as possible usability issues by the evaluators. On the other hand, these answers suggest that filters, while available, may not be noticeable, in spite of not being one of the issues most mentioned by the evaluators.

Table 3. Number of answers to the closed-end (yes/no) questions (in Fig. 5) addressing specific aspects of the application

Question (Yes/No)	Yes	No
Did you have problems with zoom or scroll?	29	15
Did you notice you might select several countries simultaneously?	18	26
Did you use the filter to obtain the number of goals?	3	41

Table 4. Number of answers to the closed-end multiple choice questions (in Fig. 5) addressing specific aspects of the application

Question (multiple choice)	5	4	3	2	1	0	NA
How easy/difficult was to select the bars?	5	8	10	14	5	2	0
How easy/diff. to understand color captions?	6	11	22	4	0	0	1

Figure 8b shows the participants' answers regarding the usability of the application. Twenty participants rated it as 3-reasonable; however, nineteen participants rated it as 2-bad or 1-very bad. These results are in line with the overall opinion of the evaluators collected informally in the general discussion to close the evaluation sessions with the Information Visualization students.

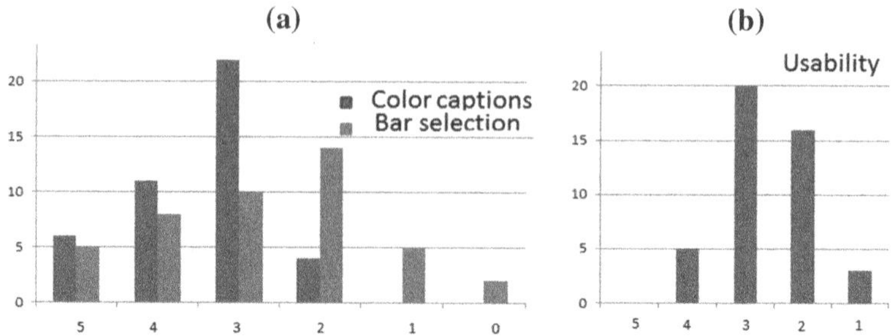

Fig. 8. (a) Answers to the questions addressing two specific aspects of the application in a Likert-type scale (5-very easy;…, 1-very difficult; 0-couldn't do it) (b) Usability of the application according to the participants (5-very good, 4-good, 3-reasonable, 2-bad, 1-very bad)

4.3 Heuristic Evaluation *Vs.* User Study

Figure 9 allows comparing the percentage of participants that considered as an undesirable characteristic each of the ten potential problems more often found by heuristic evaluation with the percentage of evaluators that found it. It is noticeable that all identified potential problems were experienced by participants; yet, the issue most reported by participants ("multiple selections difficult") was not the potential problem identified by most evaluators, and the problems identified by most evaluators (concerning response time, and color related problems) were not among the most reported by participants.

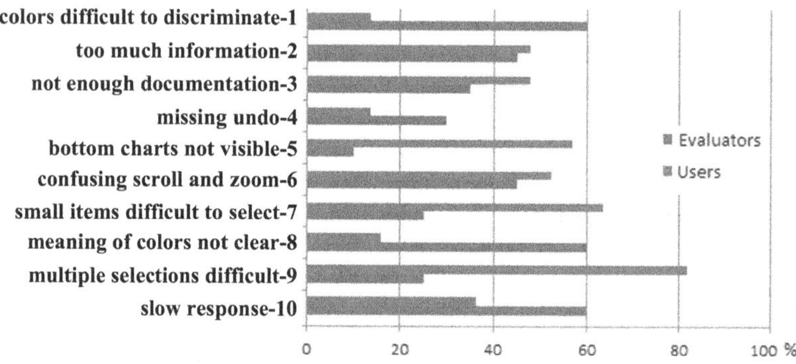

Fig. 9. Main application issues identified by the participants (users) and evaluators. The bars represent the percentage of people identifying the issue, for each method

The results obtained confirm the relevance of heuristic evaluation to predict usability problems with a real impact in using the application, even though the relative importance given to the diverse issues was different, which is possibly due to the dissimilar mindsets of the participants when compared with the evaluators. On a closer look, there are five items for which the difference between users and evaluators is larger. On one hand, items 1 and 8 have been strongly mentioned by evaluators and far less by users. Curiously, these two refer to the use and interpretation of color; their greater importance, to the evaluators, might indicate a stronger evaluators' awareness for the issues arising from incorrect color usage possibly due to specific heuristics, something that users might not easily detect, unless they suffer from any type of color vision deficiency. On the other hand, items 5, 7 and 9, have been widely detected by users and considerably less by evaluators. These items concern visibility and selection, two aspects interfering with tasks the users had to accomplish. Since the participants actually had to fight against the issues to complete a task, this potentially increased the negative impact and visibility of these problems.

5 Conclusions and Future Work

This paper presents an exploratory study aimed at better understanding the capacity of heuristic evaluation to predict the issues experienced by users when using a visualization application. The study had several limitations concerning the number and relative inexperience of the evaluators, the narrow profile of the participants that acted as users, the short length of the questionnaire addressing only a few aspects of the application, and the specific nature of the application; yet, results do show a relation between the potential problems identified by evaluators and the problems participants found while performing the tasks. Specifically, potential problems detected through heuristic evaluation seem to carry over to usability issues during user experimentation (all potential problems identified by evaluators are also identified by application users). Therefore, we argue our study helped develop and illustrate a method that might be used to compare several sets of heuristics for specific contexts (as Visualization applications).

Naturally, the fact that the heuristic evaluation was successful in pointing out issues that had an impact on the application's usability, as experienced by users, does not mean that these are the only issues present. The assessment of that aspect would require a much more complex user study and a more elaborate method for matching outcomes between both evaluation methods. This is left for a future study.

To enable the comparison among heuristics sets, the proposed method should be used in the scope of a controlled experience, for instance asking different groups of evaluators to use different sets of heuristics. This would have to be carefully counterbalanced as to avoid possible differences of evaluators' experience, requiring an even more careful characterization of their profile, namely specifying their experience in using heuristic evaluation and their understanding about each heuristic set. A more systematic and quantitative registration of each of the problems detected, and its severity, should also be implemented. The questionnaire used for the heuristic evaluation could be adapted to collect even further details concerning the evaluators profile and detected issues. Additionally, and to ensure a similar level of familiarity with the heuristics and their use, specific procedures might be considered, such as preliminary training. Regarding the user study, and also to further enable the comparison among different heuristics sets, the tasks and the questions about the application, given to a more diverse group of users, should be extended in order to address more aspects of the application. Finally, statistical (including multivariate) and visualization methods should be used to analyze all the data collected from evaluators and users. The match between both sets of data is, as previously observed, one of the inherent challenges.

All considered, this seems a daunting task, given the complexity and range of resources required, to which we also look from the point of view of graduate education in the fields of HCI and Visualization. In fact, we consider that the research questions we address should also be a part of the inquiring mind of any one learning and applying inspection and empirical methods for usability evaluation. At our Department, we offer, every year, a course on Information Visualization, where students are trained to analyze visualization applications, a course on Human-Computer Interaction, were students evaluate interactive applications, and participate in evaluations organized by others. These audiences, we argue, should be exposed to such questions and are natural candidates to participate in these studies as part of in-class exercises that also introduce them to the issues of using the experimental method, while contributing to a better understanding of the different methods.

Acknowledgments. The authors are grateful to the Information Visualization students who performed the heuristic evaluations, as well as to the participants who used the application and answered the questionnaire.

This work was partially funded by National Funds through the Portuguese FCT - Foundation for Science and Technology, in the context of the project UID/CEC/00127/2013. Samuel Silva acknowledges funding from FCT, grant SFRH/BPD/108151/2015.

References

1. Nielsen, J.: Usability Engineering. Morgan Kaufmann Publishers, San Francisco (1993)
2. Carpendale, S.: Evaluating information visualizations. In: Kerren, A., Stasko, J., Fekete, J.D., North, C. (eds.) Information Visualization: Human-Centered Issues and Perspectives, pp. 19–45. Springer, Heidelberg (2008)
3. Amar, R., Stasko, J.: A knowledge task-based framework for design and evaluation of information visualizations. In: Proceedings of IEEE Symposium on Information Visualization, pp. 143–150. IEEE (2004)
4. Forsell, C., Johanson, J.: An heuristic set for evaluation in information visualization. In: Proceedings of AVI 2010, pp. 199–206. ACM, New York (2010)
5. Scholtz, J.: Developing qualitative metrics for visual analytic environments. In: BELIV 2010, pp. 1–7. ACM (2010)
6. Zuk, T., Schlesier, L., Neumann, P., Hancock, M. S., Carpendale, S.: Heuristics for information visualization evaluation. In: BELIV 2006, pp. 1–6. ACM, New York (2006)
7. Zuk, T., Carpendale, S.: Theoretical analysis of uncertainty visualizations. In: Proceedings of SPIE & IS&T Conference on Electronic Imaging, Vol. 6060: Visualization and Data Analysis 2006, p. 606007. SPIE (2006)
8. Santos, B.S., Ferreira, B.Q., Dias, P.: Heuristic evaluation in information visualization using three sets of heuristics: an exploratory study. In: Kurosu, M. (ed.) HCI 2015. LNCS, vol. 9169, pp. 259–270. Springer, Cham (2015). doi:10.1007/978-3-319-20901-2_24
9. Tory, M., Möller, T.: Human factors in visualization research. IEEE Trans. Vis. Comput. Graph. **10**(1), 72–84 (2004). IEEE
10. Tory, M., Möller, T.: Evaluating visualizations: do expert reviews work? IEEE Comput. Graph. Appl. **25**(5), 8–11 (2005). IEEE

11. Freitas, C., Pimenta, M.S., Scapin, D.: User-centered evaluation of information visualization techniques: issues and perspectives. In: Anais do Colóquio em Informática: Brasil/INRIA, Cooperações, Avanços e Desafios, pp. 2603–2606 (2009)
12. Isenberg, P., Zuk, T., Collins, C., Carpendale, S.: Grounded evaluation of information visualizations. In: BELIV 2008, pp. 1–8. ACM, New York (2008)
13. Munzner, T.: A nested process model for visualization design and validation. IEEE Trans. Vis. Comput. Graph. **15**(6), 921–928 (2009). IEEE
14. Munzner, T.: Visualization Analysis and Design. AK Peters. CRC Press, Boca Raton (2014)
15. Sedlmair, M., Isemberg, P., Baur, D., Butz, A.: Information visualization evaluation in large companies: challenges, experiences and recommendations. Inf. Vis. J. **10**(3), 248–266 (2011). SAGE Publications
16. Lam, H., Bertini, E., Isenberg, P., Plaisant, C., Carpendale, S.: Empirical studies in information visualization: seven scenarios. IEEE Trans. Vis. Comput. Graph. **18**(9), 1520–1536 (2012). IEEE
17. Freitas, C., Luzzardi, P., Cava, R., Winckler, M., Pimenta, M.S., Nedel, L.: Evaluating usability of information visualization techniques. In: Proceedings of the 5th Symposium on Human Factors in Computer Systems, IHC 2002, pp. 40–51 (2002)
18. Freitas, C., Pimenta, M.S., Scapin, D., Maria, C., Sasso, D., Pimenta, M.S.: User-centered evaluation of information visualization techniques: making the HCI- InfoVis connection explicit. In: Huang, W. (ed.) Handbook of Human Centric Visualization, pp. 315–336. Springer, New York (2014)
19. Hollingsed, T., Novick, D. G.: Usability inspection methods after 15 years of research and practice. In: Proceedings of the 25th Annual ACM International Conference on Design of Communication - SIGDOC 2007, pp. 249–255. ACM (2007)
20. Hearst, M.A., Laskowski, P., Silva, L.: Evaluating information visualization via the interplay of heuristic evaluation and question-based scoring. In: Proceedings of the 2016 CHI Conference on Human Factors in Computing Systems, pp. 5028–5033. ACM (2016)
21. Nielsen, J., Molich, R.: Heuristic evaluation of user interface. In: CHI 1990 Conference Proceedings, pp. 249–256. ACM (1990)
22. Slavkovic, A., Cross, K.: Novice HEs of a complex interface. In: CHI 1999 Extended Abstracts on Human Factors in Computing Systems, pp. 304–305. ACM (1999)
23. Hwang, W., Salvendy, G.: Number of people required for usability evaluation: the 10 ± 2 rule. Commun. ACM **3**(5), 130–133 (2010). ACM
24. Hornbæk, K., Frøkjær, E.: Comparison of techniques for matching of usability problem descriptions. Interact. Comput. **20**(6), 505–514 (2008). Elsevier

Usability Matters

User Experiences of Visually Impaired Older Adults

Miroslav Sili(✉), Matthias Gira, and Christopher Mayer

Center for Health and Bioresources, AIT Austrian Institute of Technology GmbH, Vienna, Austria
miroslav.sili@ait.ac.at

Abstract. Many applications and services are not accessible for all people. Especially visually impaired and blind people are often excluded or severely limited in their use. This is even more severe, when we consider the Active and Assisted Living (AAL) domain and its primary target group of older adults, additionally suffering from other age related physical and cognitive impairments, and with limited technological experience. In this paper we present the user centered design process of reaching an in- and outdoor navigation solution, suitable for this target group, mitigating shortcomings of conventional applications. In total we conducted six user involvement and User Experience (UX) evaluation actions with different approaches and engaging different stakeholders. The paper describes the gradual realization of such an application prototype, accessible to visually impaired and blind people, highlighting the impact of the user centered design approach at all stages.

Keywords: User experience · Usability · Visually impaired people · Assistive system · Navigation · Localization · Indoor · Outdoor · Modality conversion · MMI

1 Introduction

Nowadays we are used to interact with various mobile applications in our daily lives. Our smartphones are available almost all the time and we use them in many situations and in different places. Furthermore, we use them as an information source (e.g., mobile internet) and for orientation purposes. We use them for social inclusion, for communication and for entertainment purposes. These examples illustrate the variety of use cases for mobile applications and other digital services behind.

However, these applications and services are not accessible for all people in the same manner. Visually impaired or blind people are very often excluded, or at least limited in their use. Although offered accessibility features such as screen readers are specially designed to overcome (or at least to reduce) these barriers, their helpfulness depends on various factors, ranging from environmental conditions, over the complexity of the content in need of conversion, up to the user her or himself and her or his physical and cognitive conditions (similar to the context of use as described in [7]).

Especially the last aspect, the physical and cognitive condition of the user, limits the use of accessibility or screen reader tools very often. This becomes more obvious, when we consider the Active and Assisted Living (AAL) domain and its primary target group of older

M. Kurosu (Ed.): HCI 2017, Part I, LNCS 10271, pp. 384–394, 2017.
DOI: 10.1007/978-3-319-58071-5_29

adults. Additionally to visual impairments, older adults suffer very often from other age-related physical or/and cognitive impairments. The majority of older adults represent the so-called "digital novices", i.e., they have little experience with technology, digital services and novel interaction patterns and gestures. Designing systems, meeting the requirements of visually impaired or blind users, digital novices and users, who have potentially also other age-related diseases, is a highly challenging task.

The project *Indoor and Outdoor Navigation for Increasing Independence* (ION4II) addresses these challenges and aims to develop an **assistive system** for visually impaired or blind older adults. By using a dedicated care and residential facility as the target setting, the project focuses on the increase of the quality of assistive interaction techniques, on the development of a seamless in- and outdoor navigation service, and on the development of various personalized information exchange and security services, like personalized meal plan, personalized walking/travel times and orientation services.

This work-in-progress paper provides an overview of the developed assistive system and the user involvement within the design and development process. We will present the used methodology and the successive elaborated results, including their influence, in form of improvements to our final prototype.

2 Background and Motivation

The project was started by key partners from different research areas such as experts in localization and navigation, researchers and developers in the Human Computer Interaction (HCI) and Assistive Technology (AT) field and a professional end user organization, specialized on assisted living. For this special target group, we relied on an end user organization experienced in operating a residential and care facility for visually impaired and blind seniors (*Haus Waldpension*, Lower Austria). The facility offers accommodation and services for short-term vacationers and for permanent residents. Thus, *Haus Waldpension* provided a great setting for the User Centered Design (UCD) [1] approach applied in the development phase.

The user requirements elaboration was subdivided into two phases. The first phase involved caregivers and facility staff members. We focused on the elaboration of use cases and scenarios, which potentially help end users to become or remain informed, independent and self-confident in the dedicated residential and care facility. This phase capitalized on the empirical data, regarding wishes and residential needs, provided by experienced staff members. The second phase mainly involved primary end users. The focus was on the evaluation of their current physical conditions. The following section will discuss the elaborated results which were used as basis for the design and development of the assistive system prototype.

2.1 Use Cases and Scenarios

Use cases and scenarios are based on a list of well-known problems, provided by caregivers and facility staff members. It was reduced to the following five use cases for the assistive system:

- Welcome tour: A guided tour through the facilities essential areas, including explanations; Targeted at new residents.
- Indoor navigation, including explanations of near-by areas.
- Information about the weekly meal plan, and reminding of the users' choice.
- Personalized appointments and notifications based on walking time estimations.
- Guided outdoor navigation through the adjacent park including a seamless indoor-outdoor transition.

The list of use cases emphasizes that the solution addresses two main areas, namely the increase of autonomy and the management of time and place related information.

2.2 Users' Physical Conditions

The evaluation of users' physical condition helped us to identify supplementary and complimentary input/output modalities, and to evaluate their usefulness for the target group. The evaluation followed the human senses: (a) hearing, (b) the tactile perception and (c) the visual perception. Figure 1 illustrates the applied test setting: a hearing test, a tactile perception test and a visual perception test (from left to right).

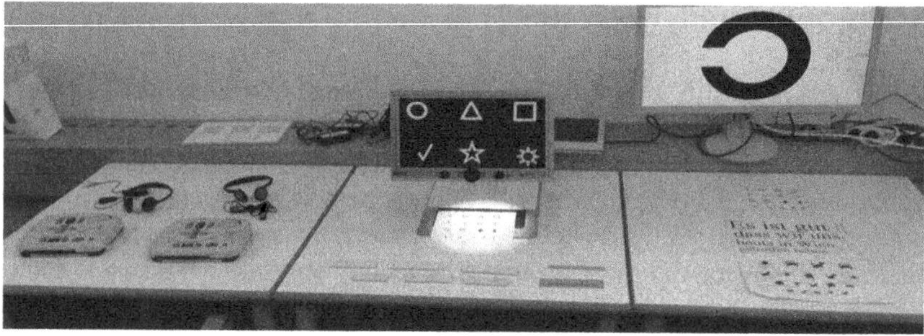

Fig. 1. Test setting for the evaluation of users' physical condition. Hearing test, tactile perception test and visual perception test (from left to right).

Table 1. Physical conditions evaluation results of nine participants

	Test	Description
Hearing	Mean voice output speed	136 words per minute
	Mean pitch	69 dB (at 50 cm distance)
	Preferred voice	Female (5 female, 3 male, 2 both ėqual)
Tactile	Braille comprehensibility	0 out of 9 participants
	Tactile perception	Rounded pin >= 2 mm
	Recognition of shapes	Circle 100%, two dots 100%, line 100%, square 78%
Visual	Visual acuity[a]	0.0125, 0.4, 0.016, 0.025
	Contrast threshold[a]	63%, 3%, 40%, 25%
	Best contrast	Negative contrast (black background, white foreground)

[a]Results for 4 out of 9 participants with measureable visual function

Nine participants (N = 9; 5 female/4 male) with an age range from 45 to 92 and a mean age of 80.78 (15.74 SD) years were involved in the tests. Five participants (n = 5) were blind (visual function not measureable) and four participants (n = 4) were severely visual impaired according to the International Classification of Diseases ICD-10 [2]. Table 1 summarizes the evaluated results.

Summary and Conclusions

- Hearing: As already expected, users of this target group suffer from age-related hearing loss. The vocal output modality is feasible but the volume of the output should be adjustable up to 85 dB. Users preferred a female voice with an average speed of 136 words per minute.
- Tactile Perception: Users are able to distinguish different shapes using their touch sense with a minimum high difference of 2 mm. None of the participants was capable to use the Braille lettering. Thus, an automatic conversion of visual letters into corresponding Braille letters is not applicable.
- Visual perception: Five of nine users had no measureable visual function. The remaining four users were classified as severely visually impaired. Thus, a purely visual modality, such as a conventional Graphical User Interface (GUI) is not applicable. However, a simplified, high contrasted GUI may still be useable for some users.

3 Architecture Design

The architecture design was guided by two main aspects: Firstly, by the main application themes (increase of autonomy and information exchange) and secondly, by the target group's accessibility challenges. The findings of the user involvement were used as a basis for the technical specification, incorporating the following requirements:

(a) Mobile solution, with smart phone like form factor
(b) Support of real-time indoor and outdoor localization and navigation
(c) Support for remote manageable and personalized data (e.g., personal schedule)
(d) Support of multimodality and adaptivity according users' needs and wishes

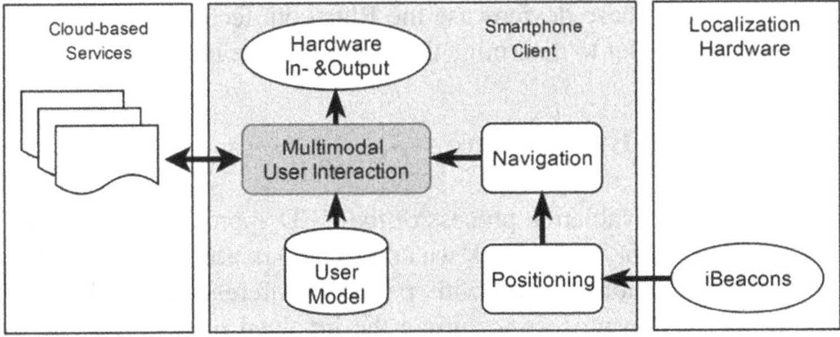

Fig. 2. Architecture of the assistive system

Figure 2 sketches the architecture of the assistive system. It shows three main parts, namely (a) the cloud-based repository for personalized data, (b) the smartphone client for the localization, navigation and multimodal user interaction at the center, and finally (c) the localization hardware deployed in the care facility.

Cloud-Based Services. One of the requirements of the assistive system is the support of remotely manageable data. Most of the user's appointments and the personal meal plan are managed by facility staff members. Thus, an easy to use and centrally manageable information and scheduling system was the appropriate solution. We decided to use existing web-based services such as ownCloud [4] and Google Calendar [5] for this purpose. These systems provide an appropriate user (data) management, which on the one hand can be accessed remotely and on the other hand integrated easily.

Smartphone Client. The smartphone client represents the core module of the assistive system solution. It orchestrates the cloud-based services and the localization and navigation functionality. The smartphone client is also handling the personalized user interaction. This dictates that it holds an up-to-date user model and the functionality for an automatic User Interface (UI) adaptation.

One of the main goals was the design of a software solution that is easy to use and accessible for the target group. The solution should be useful for visual impaired and blind people, but nevertheless usable for people with normal vision. Thus, the multimodality and modality conversion, e.g., visual textual to the corresponding audio representation, was of outermost importance. In order to reach this goal, we decided to utilize the Multimodal Interaction Activity (MMI) Architecture. The architecture was first published as a Recommendation of the W3C Multimodal Interaction Working Group. "The MMI Architecture provides a loosely coupled architecture for multimodal user interfaces, which allows for co-resident and distributed implementations, and focuses on the use of well-defined interfaces between its constituents [3]."

Localization Hardware. The project has high requirements regarding the accuracy of the user localization. It is well known, that conventional solutions, like the built-in position detection of smartphones or tablet devices, provide unreliable results. Considering the special target group, it becomes obvious, that the aimed assistive system requires additional hardware in order to provide an accurate user position. We used state-of-the-art indoor position technology and equipped the entire facility with small, iBeacon-compatible [6] devices. These devices use the Bluetooth technology to communicate with mobile devices in order to determine their approximate location.

4 User Experience Evaluation

The iterative design and evaluation process of the UCD approach helped us to build a stable and accessible prototype. In total, we conducted six user involvement and User Experience (UX) evaluation actions with partially different stakeholders. Table 2 summarizes the evaluation process including the involved participants and the main objectives of the investigation.

Table 2. Summary of the user experience evaluation process during the project

Test type	Duration/Date(s)	Participants	Object(s) of investigation
Mockup tests	1 Day, 30.09.2015	5 end users (2 female/3 male)	System usability
Expert tests I	1 Day, 29.02.2016	2 experts (1 UI/1 localization)	Position accuracy, navigation instruction usability
Expert tests II	1 Day, 11.04.2016	2 experts (1 UI/1 localization)	Position and navigation accuracy and timing
Friendly user trials	1 Day, 22.04.2016	2 friendly users (2 male)	Overall User Experience
Expert tests III	3 Days, 17.08.2016–19.08.2016	4 experts (2 UI, 1 localization, 1 navigation)	Navigation accuracy and timing
Short-term field trials	2 Days, 23.11.2016–24.11.2016	12 (5 female/7 male)	Overall UX
Long-term field trials	8 Weeks, 01.03.2017–26.04.2017	-	Information services, orientation service, overall UX

4.1 Mockup Tests

The user experience evaluation started with a mockup test in September 2015. For this purpose, we developed a functional, interactive, smartphone-based mockup, following the recommendations of the user requirements phase (see Sect. 2). Figure 3 depicts two screenshots of the GUI that were presented to the end users on two mobile devices (Samsung Galaxy Tab4 [9] and Samsung Galaxy S4 [10]). Next to the graphical representation and touchable input we also used the audio output modality. The audio channel was rendered on the built-in speakers of the used mobile devices and on a bone conduction headphone (Aftershokz, Bluez 2 [8]). This early mockup neither provided actual localization nor navigation functionality. The mockup was controlled by an additional device, to pre-test the navigation features, by manually triggering concrete navigation instructions on the user's device remotely.

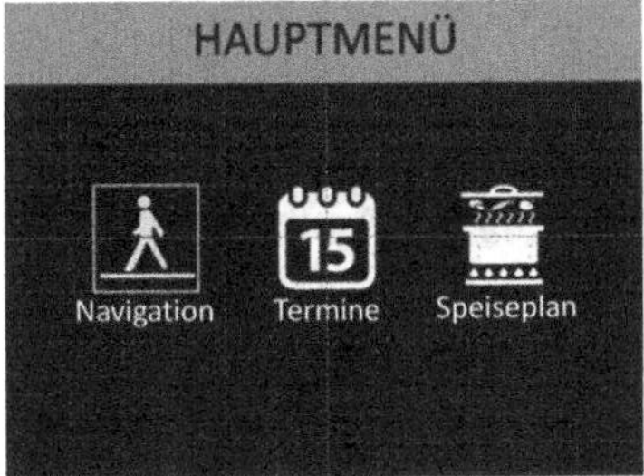

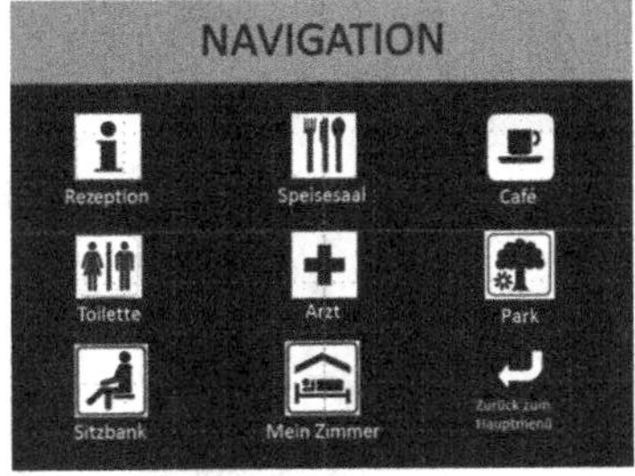

Fig. 3. Screenshots of the GUI presented to end users during the first mockup tests.

Five participants (N = 5; 2 female/3 male) with an age range from 46 to 90 and a mean age of 74.4 (18.64 SD) years were involved in the tests. Four participants (n = 4)

were blind (visual function not measureable) and one participant (n = 1) was severely visual impaired. Only one participant (n = 1) used his smartphone on a regular basis. The remaining others (n = 4) owned a smartphone, but used it just for incoming calls.

Mockup Test Evaluation Results. As expected, none of the participants was able to read the presented text nor to clearly to identify any of the presented pictograms. Only the navigation pictogram was partly recognized by the participant with measureable visual function. The audio output modality was only conditionally suitable for the participants. The implemented functionality (read aloud by touch) was not practicable because participant experienced difficulties to orient themselves on the multi-line GUI. Even the participant familiar with smartphone screen readers was unable to operate the mockup. The person had troubles to estimate and identify the location of the pictograms and of the interactive elements.

Implications for Further Developments

- Plain GUI-based interaction methods are not applicable for the target group. The prototype may support a GUI, but it must also be operable without clear knowledge of pictogram positions.
- Conventional screen reader functionality, reading aloud the textual content of GUI elements, is not applicable for the target group. Although audio output represents the main output modality for the majority, a plain GUI-to-audio conversion is insufficient and does not provide the required accessibility.

4.2 Expert Tests (I, II and III)

Since our solution is targeting people with normal vision as well as visually impaired people, we considered also other users as potential experts regarding the user experience evaluation. This was especially true for users who were confronted with the prototypes unsupervised and for the first time. Thus, we involved also this target group into our evaluation and we had in total three phases of expert tests. All tests were conducted at the real setting at *Haus Waldpension* and under real conditions (excluding potential long-term aspects).

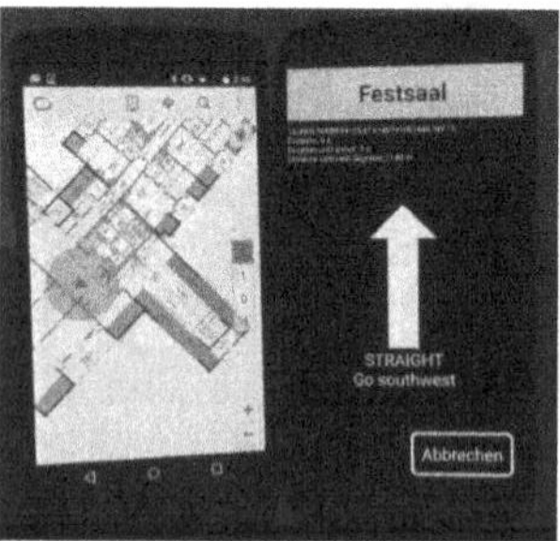

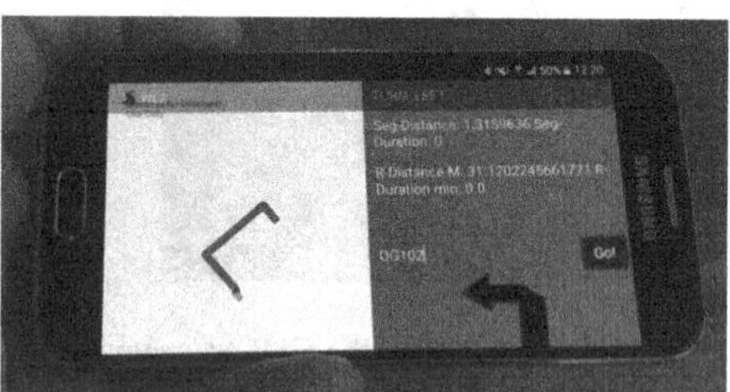

Fig. 4. Test situation for expert test I (left side) and the expert test II (right side).

Figure 4 illustrates the test situations during the expert test I (left side) and the expert test II (right side). The focus was mainly on the evaluation of the indoor position and navigation accuracy, but the tests contributed also towards usability improvements. Users were asked to follow the presented instructions and to interact with the system. In doing so, we evaluated aspects like instruction timing and latency, possibilities to repeat instructions, volume, pitch and voice of the audio output and the sentence style and syntax regarding the understandability of the resulting Text To Speech (TTS) output.

Five experts (N = 5) were involved in the tests, the group was composed of two UI and architecture developers (n = 2), two indoor position experts (n = 2) and one navigation and routing expert (n = 1). All experts were members of the ION4II consortium. Expert test I and II were run as one-day tests whereas the expert test III was run as a workshop-like improvement and evaluation test lasting for three days.

Expert Tests Evaluation Results. Although the focus of the expert tests was mainly on the evaluation of the accuracy of the indoor localization and navigation, we observed additionally several usability issues. For instance, it turned out that compass-based direction instructions (e.g., turn south-west) and distance indications in meters were hard to interpret. Also, there is a need for continuous position updates and repeated output of the current position in order to confirm that the user is still following the right path. Additionally, we had also several timing problems causing a delay of navigation instructions.

Implications for Further Developments

- Navigation instructions should support distance estimations in step-units rather than in meters. Also a compass-card-based direction instruction should be replaced by simple directions like left, right, straight ahead etc.
- Implementation of periodic audio output functionality and the possibility to repeat the last instruction via one click.

4.3 Friendly User Test

Results gained from the expert tests helped us to improve and to optimize the prototype towards general usability. However, to enhance the accessibility for the primary target group, we relied on concrete interaction experiences from visually impaired people. For this reason we invited two (N = 2) so-called "friendly users", to evaluate our early prototype in the field. The visually impaired participants where outside the AAL target group (both participants were under 50 years old and were technologically skilled). Both participants tested the menu guidance, the calendar and the indoor navigation feature in *Haus Waldpension*.

Figure 5 Screenshots of the prototypes visualizing three direct clickable elements (left) and one direct clickable element and two menu navigation areas (right) visualizes the prototypes used during the friendly user tests. The left image illustrates a version with three direct clickable interactive elements and the right image illustrates a version with one clickable interactive element (middle area) and two menu navigation areas (top and bottom area of the threefold image).

Fig. 5. Screenshots of the prototypes visualizing three direct clickable elements (left) and one direct clickable element and two menu navigation areas (right)

Friendly User Test Evaluation Results. We identified several shortcomings of the indoor navigation use case. The problems ranged from instruction language mix (e.g., "turn sharp-left" instruction read aloud by the German TTS), over distance estimations with three digits after the decimal point, to contradictory navigation instructions. We identified several problems from the usability perspective.

In contrast to blind participants, people with minimal visual perception would appreciate graphical representation of interactive elements, e.g., colored areas for menu navigation areas. Also, there is a need for audio-based self-explanations of interactive elements triggered e.g., by the first touch. Next, friendly users emphasized that every change on the GUI had to be explained by the audio output modality precisely. As an example, the visualization of an empty set of user appointments requires a corresponding audio representation, e.g., in form of an audio output "you do not have any appointments scheduled for today".

Implications for Further Developments. The friendly user tests emphasized that there was still a need for a visual feedback for people with minimal visual perception.

However, the "friendly user" test was performed before the last Expert Test III (see also Table 2). At this point we were confident to eliminate all indoor navigation problems before the start of the short-term trials. Unfortunately, the following Expert Test III clarified that the aimed indoor navigation could not reach the necessary stability within the remained project period. In order to maximize the project outcome for the end users we decided to offer an indoor orientation service instead of a full turn-by-turn indoor navigation service.

The improvements on the indoor position localization (accuracy $\leq$ 2 m) facilitated a precise real-time estimation of the users' positions. Thus, we annotated navigation zones with additional semantic information that could be directly delivered to the end user. Doing so, we enabled users to orient themselves within the facility by querying their current position and the nearby point of interests.

4.4 Short-Term Field Trials

Short-term field trials were performed in November 2016 with the main scope on the evaluation of the overall user experience of the pre-final prototype. Figure 6 illustrates two screenshots of the prototype presented to the end users. The left image illustrates a version with three interactive elements (menu backward on the top, menu item in the middle and menu forward on the bottom) and the right image illustrates a version with two interactive elements (menu item on the top and menu forward on the bottom). Besides these differences, both versions worked in the same manner. A single click on any interactive area causes the TTS output, explaining the current selected menu item in the middle. The prototype provided also two different menu item activation styles. In one version, the selected item was activated by a two taps and in the other version by a single tap followed by holding for one second.

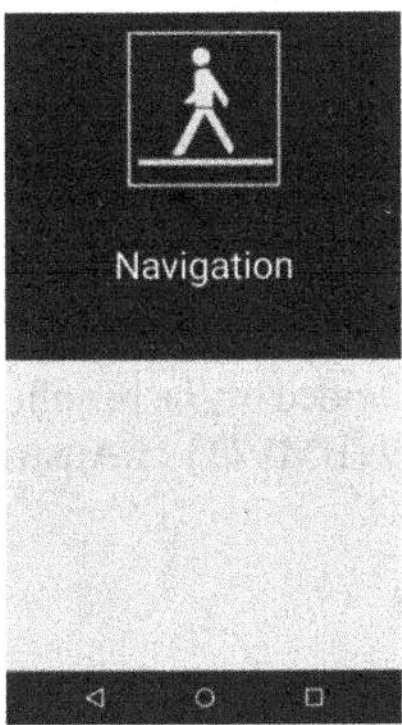

Fig. 6. Screenshots of the GUI presented to end users during the short-term field trials.

Twelve participants (N = 12; 5 female/7 male) with an age range from 47 to 88 and a mean age of 68.67 (12.11 SD) years were involved in the tests. Three participants (n = 3) were blind (visual function not measureable) and nine participants (n = 9) were severe visually impaired. Three participants (n = 3) did not use any digital devices. Seven participants (n = 7) used a smartphone on regular basis and the remaining two participants (n = 2) used the PC at least once a week.

Short-Term Field Trials Evaluation Results. One third of the participants could independently use the application within a few seconds. The second third required one or two explanations and the last third had comprehension problems even after few explanation rounds. It turned out that participants with minimal visual perceptions were able to use the application very well, whereas blind participants required tactile feedback in order to be able to identify interactive elements on the smartphone screen. Regarding the two different interaction methods, participants preferred the version with two interactive areas. This was mainly because of the reduction of elements and the increase of touchable areas for the remaining two interaction elements. Regarding the activation style and audio output, participants preferred two taps for the activation of the selected menu item. The TTS output was clearly understandable for all participants.

5 Conclusions and Outlook

The short-term field trials highlighted that at least two thirds of the participants were able to interact with the application independently. However, in order to make the application accessible to all users, the final prototype requires additional tactile feedback that supports users to distinguish between different interactive areas. We will implement a haptic barrier on the phone screen in the final prototype and by doing so, we hope to provide additional support, especially for blind users.

We are planning to invite at least fifteen (N = 15) participants into the long-term field trials and to test the prototype over a period of 8 weeks. We will conduct a pre-interview in the beginning of the trial, two interviews during the trial (scheduled for the week 2 and the week 5) and a final workshop including all participants at the end of the trial phase. The pre-interview aims to inquire users' expectations regarding the assistive system. The following two interviews aim to inquire users' experiences during the trial and to support users in case of any obscurities. And the final workshop aims to recapitulate experiences, to work out positive and negative aspects and to generate ideas for further developments and application possibilities.

Acknowledgements. The project Indoor and Outdoor Navigation for Increasing Independence (ION4II) is co-funded by the benefit programme of the Federal Ministry for Transport, Innovation and Technology (BMVIT) of Austria.

References

1. Abras, C., Maloney-Krichmar, D., Preece, J.: User-centered design. In: Bainbridge, W. (ed.) Encyclopedia of Human-Computer Interaction, vol. 37, no. 4, pp. 445–456. Sage Publications, Thousand Oaks (2004)
2. WHO|Visual impairment and blindness (2014). http://www.who.int/mediacentre/factsheets/fs282/en/. Accessed 23 Feb 2017
3. W3C Multimodal Interaction Working Group (2012). https://www.w3.org/2002/mmi/spec_notes.html#mmi-arch. Accessed 23 Feb 2017
4. ownCloud.org (2017). https://owncloud.org/. Accessed 23 Feb 2017
5. Google Kalendar (2017). http://calendar.google.com. Accessed 23 Feb 2017
6. Kontakt.io-Beacons & Beyond – Kontakt.io (2017). https://kontakt.io/. Accessed 23 Feb 2017
7. Mayer, C., Zimmermann, G., Grguric, A., Alexandersson, J., Sili, M., Strobbe, C.: A comparative study of systems for the design of flexible user interfaces. J. Ambient Intell. Smart Environ. **8**, 125–148 (2016)
8. Bluez 2S – AfterShokz. https://aftershokz.com/products/bluez-2s. Accessed 23 Feb 2017
9. Galaxy Tab 4 (7.0, Wi-Fi) – Tablet|Samsung. http://www.samsung.com/de/consumer/mobile-devices/tablets/others/SM-T230NYKADBT/. Accessed 23 Feb 2017
10. Galaxy S4|Samsung Österreich. http://www.samsung.com/at/consumer/mobile-devices/smartphones/galaxy-s/GT-I9505ZKAATO/. Accessed 23 Feb 2017

User Interface Development: Methods, Tools and Architectures

Practical Aspects of Pattern-Supported Model-Driven User Interface Generation

Jürgen Engel[1,2(✉)], Christian Märtin[1], and Peter Forbrig[2]

[1] Faculty of Computer Science, Augsburg University of Applied Sciences, An der Hochschule 1, 86161 Augsburg, Germany
{Juergen.Engel,Christian.Maertin}@hs-augsburg.de

[2] Institute of Computer Science, University of Rostock, Albert-Einstein-Straße 21, 18059 Rostock, Germany
{Juergen.Engel,Peter.Forbrig}@uni-rostock.de

Abstract. Today, highly interactive software has become a crucial ingredient of the daily life. Rapidly evolving technologies and simultaneously increasing user demands make human-computer interaction (HCI) more and more a major criterion for the judgement on success or non-success of software and electronic devices. Contemporary users expect that software products run on a variety of heterogeneous devices with a consistent look and feel, invariable high usability, and a high degree of appealing user experience. In addition, people tend to be impatient and like to have their applications contemporaneously available on their different devices. In order to meet these requirements we have combined a model-driven user interface development process with pattern-based methods in order to realize the best possible reuse when constructing models which subsequently serve as basis for at least semi-automatic user interface generation. This hybrid development approach is the fundament of the PaMGIS framework which is explicated in theory and primarily in practice within the following sections.

Keywords: Model-based user interface development · Pattern-based development · User interface modeling · User interface generation · HCI patterns

1 Introduction

Prior to the design of the current version of the combined model-driven and pattern-based PaMGIS framework a total of 18 model-based user interface development environments (MBUIDE) have been analyzed and evaluated. A résumé of the related results is provided in [5]. In addition, eight user interface description languages (UIDL) have been examined. An overview of the achievements is recapitulated in [4]. The findings of these assessments served as groundwork for the model-driven part of the PaMGIS framework which was designed in the style of the CAMELEON Reference Framework (CRF) [1]. In particular, the ontological domain and context-of-use models are used as proposed by the CRF. However, we decided to split the CRF platform model into a device model and a UI toolkit model. While the former

M. Kurosu (Ed.): HCI 2017, Part I, LNCS 10271, pp. 397–414, 2017.
DOI: 10.1007/978-3-319-58071-5_30

comprises all relevant characteristics of the respective end-user device, the latter holds information about the user interface (UI) elements that are available on the respective underlying software development platform. This avoids redundancies especially in cases where the same software basis supports significantly different devices, e.g. Android on smartphones and tablet computers. A dialog model comprises the dynamic aspects of the future user interface. On the basis of the domain and dialog models an abstract user interface model is derived which is subsequently transformed into a concrete and lastly into a final user interface model. The various user interface model transformations are affected by the information which is deposited within the context of use model. An overview of the PaMGIS models is given inside the dotted box in the upper part of Fig. 1.

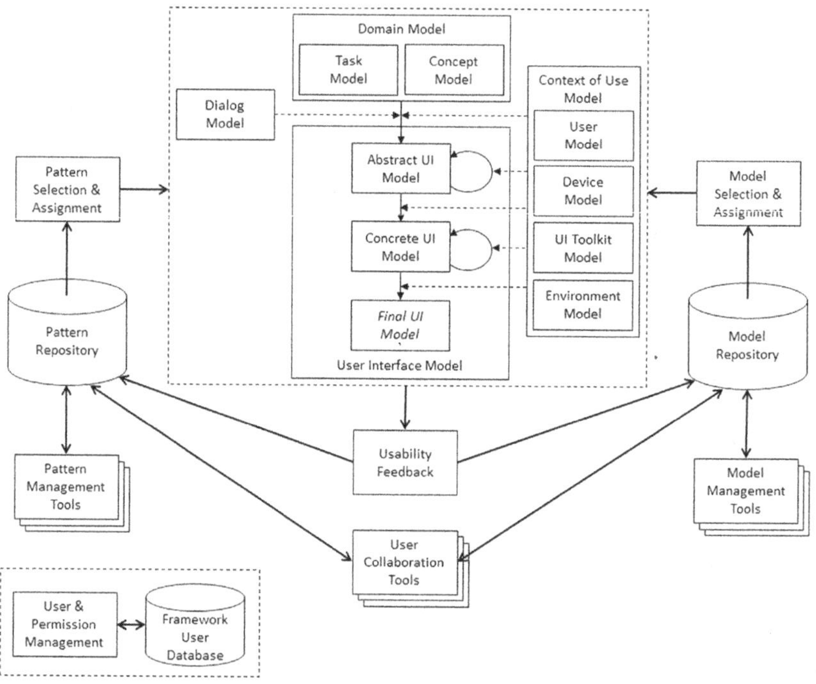

Fig. 1. Logical overview of the PaMGIS framework architecture

In order to alleviate the sometimes complex construction of the models required for user interface generation, the model-driven approach is supported by pattern-based development techniques. For this purpose, we have developed the XML-compliant PaMGIS Pattern Specification Language (PPSL) which was designed to meet two major goals. On the one hand, it shall be possible to easily transform already existing patterns from popular and well-accepted pattern collections, such as *Designing Interfaces* of Jenifer Tidwell [11], *Patterns in Interaction Design* of Martijn van Welie [12], and *Design of Sites* of Douglas van Duyne [2] into the PPSL formalism. On the other hand, the patterns shall be augmented with any kind of information required for supporting the model-driven user interface generation with PaMGIS.

Regarding the former target, we explored six existing pattern description languages, including PLML 1.1 [8]. Results concerning this matter can be retraced in [6, 7]. Further, five pattern collections were analyzed. An excerpt of the related conclusions is outlined in [6]. We already have demonstrated in [5] that patterns from [2, 11, 12] can be mapped to PLML 1.1 at least in a semi-automatic manner. In [7] it is demonstrated that patterns being specified by means of PLML 1.1 can be translated to PPSL without loss of information.

The basic idea in terms of the latter goal is to equip patterns with pre-assembled model fragments which can be used as building blocks for the construction of the domain and UI models. In addition, certain patterns could also provide valuable input for the various model transformation steps. The complete specification of PPSL is presented in [7].

In preparation of the specification of the tool set required for pattern authoring and management a total of fourteen pattern tools have been analyzed and evaluated. The related results are documented in [3]. The tools for both the pattern-based and model-driven part of PaMGIS are indicated in Fig. 1.

2 The Hybrid Development Process of the PaMGIS Framework

The hybrid development process follows a model-driven methodology which is extended by pattern-based techniques, i.e. patterns are equipped with task, concept, and dialog model fragments which serve as building blocks during the construction of the related models. As soon as a pattern is selected and applied, the fragments are integrated into the overall models. An overview of the development process is provided in Fig. 2. It encompasses nine major steps. Gray-shaded arrows indicate that the associated efforts can generally be supported by the use of patterns.

The domain model constitutes the starting point of the user interface modeling and generation process. Hence, it is to be specified in the very first step. It comprises of two sub-models, i.e. a task and a concept model. The formalism for describing task models is based on the *ConcurTaskTrees* notation [10] which we have extended according to our needs. Subsequently or in parallel, a concept-of-use model is either to be defined or selected from the PaMGIS model repository. This model includes four sub-models for the intended end user device, the software development toolkit, user, and environment. Then, the dynamic aspects of the user interface are determined in a dialog model. The dialogs and their sequence are specified by means of dialog graphs [9]. The next step is to derive the abstract user interface (AUI) from the domain and dialog models. In consideration of the UI toolkit model, the abstract UI elements are to be transformed into concrete ones and context-specific adaptations are carried out, if necessary. Finally, the CUI is to be translated into the final user interface, i.e. coded in the target programming language. Optionally, the resulting source code must be compiled before the user interface can be executed.

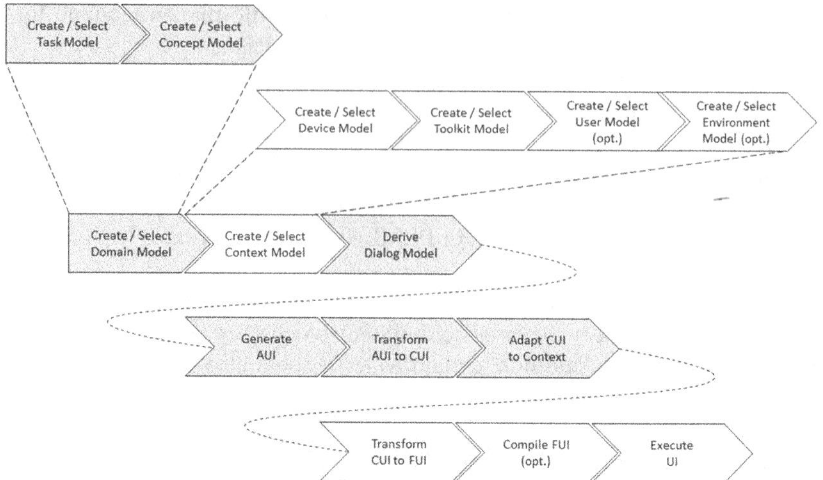

Fig. 2. Development process of the hybrid model-driven and pattern-based approach

In the following sections we describe practical details of (1) how to develop and formalize the various model fragments as integral part of a pattern and (2) how these fragments can be used during the hybrid UI development process.

3 Practical Application of the Hybrid Development Approach

The practical work with the PaMGIS framework is demonstrated using the example of the *Poll* pattern which is part of the pattern collection *Patterns in Interaction Design* [12]. The intention of this pattern is to prompt users' opinions in terms of a specific aspect of the current web site. The original pattern specification is outlined in Table 1.

Before we translated the pattern into the PPSL format we generalized it in a way that it can be used to query users' attitudes towards any matter of fact, not solely toward a particular topic of a web site. Ex ante, we do not decide the concrete appearance of user interface elements, i.e. radio buttons, but employ an abstract user interface (AUI) element which will be replaced by a concrete widget when iteratively transforming the entire AUI model into a concrete user interface (CUI) model. Additionally, we decided to change the implied course of action and enable access to the overall result values not until the vote has been accomplished.

In summary, the UI must display a question to the user and offer a set of possible answers to this question from which the user can choose the one that fits best in his view. Further, three different interaction elements must be provided to confirm the choice, to request the overall results, and to finally quit the poll procedure.

In order to benefit from the pattern within the hybrid development approach it must be analyzed in detail and inherent task, concept, and dialog model portions have to be extracted, formally described, and accommodated in the <Deployment> <PaMGIS> <ModelFragments> section of PPSL.

Table 1. Excerpt of the Poll pattern specification according to [12]

Element	Description
Problem	Users want to state their opinion about a certain statement that is relevant to the site's content
Solution	List the statements as exclusive options and present the results directly after voting
Use when	You are designing a site where interaction with the users is desired. Typically this will be a News Site or Community Site where visitors are to be encouraged to share their opinions and improve interactivity
How	The poll consists of two steps. First the list of options is presented, usually using radiobuttons, together with a 'vote' button. After clicking the vote button, the results are displayed. The results include both a percentage and an absolute number
Why	A poll is a very simple and direct page element that invites users to interact with the site. Users can even do it anonymously so there is no barrier at all to participate. Polls are often linked to content on the site such as articles or products, and the results of a poll can be linked to a discussion in a Forum

3.1 Task Model Fragment

Within this subsection it is shown how the task model fragment (TMF) of the *Poll* pattern is implemented by means of PPSL.

As illustrated in Fig. 3, the root element of the task model is an abstract task named *poll* which consists of the three subtasks *vote*, *retrieve results*, and *terminate*. Here, the *retrieve results* task is defined to be optional and therefore is not necessarily executed by the user.

The *vote* subtask consists, in turn, of subordinated application tasks for displaying the question and the possible answers, user tasks for reading the system output and picking the best fitting answer, interaction tasks to confirm that answer and submit the choice, and an additional application task to send the data from the user interface to the instance representing the business logic of the system. The *retrieve results* task incorporates an interaction task to request the poll results and three application tasks to

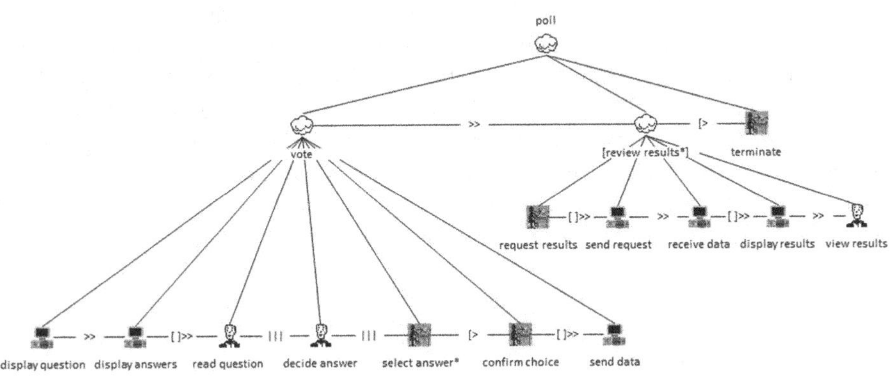

Fig. 3. Entire task model fragment of the *Poll* pattern

send out that request, to receive the related result data, and to display the values on the screen. Finally, the purpose of the *terminate* interaction task is to abandon the poll procedure.

In the following steps this fundamental task model fragment is reduced in order to incorporate solely the information that is relevant for user interface generation. Amongst others, the user tasks indicate the required cognitive workload of the user and provide information to evaluate whether he/she has been provided with all data necessary to correctly complete the next process step. Apart from that, they do not considerably contribute to the UI specification and are therefore not required for our purposes as illustrated in Fig. 4.

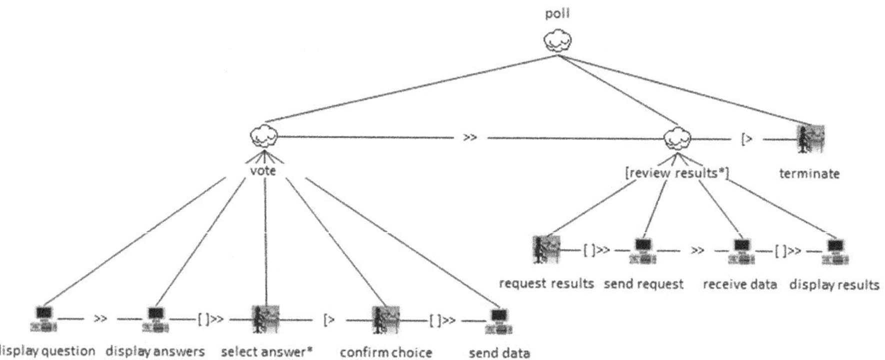

Fig. 4. Task model fragment of the *Poll* pattern reduced by user tasks

Some of the remaining subordinated tasks possess temporal dependencies which are indicated by the temporal operator *enabling with information passing* ([]≫). In this case both adjacent tasks deal with the selfsame data element respectively the selfsame set of data. Therefore, in these cases we can eliminate the respective application tasks without losing significant information required for the user interface generation process. In the given example, these application tasks are *display answers*, *send data*, *send request*, and *receive data*. The remaining TMF is depicted in Fig. 5.

In order to increase the flexibility of the patterns, we introduced a new task type. Besides the standard abstract, user, application, and interaction types of CTT, PaMGIS supports dummy tasks. Please note that such tasks may only appear in task model fragments, but not in task models. Dummy tasks act as templates for variable parts of a TMF and are to be replaced before the pattern is used. If a user selects a pattern by means of the *Pattern Selection & Assignment* function and tries to apply it, the tool will automatically open a dialog and ask whether and how the dummy tasks should be adopted. Here, the predetermined texture of the dummy tasks serves as construction plan, i.e. the resulting task type, the position inside the TMF and the temporal dependencies to sibling tasks. The TMF of the *Poll* pattern including related amendments is shown in Fig. 6.

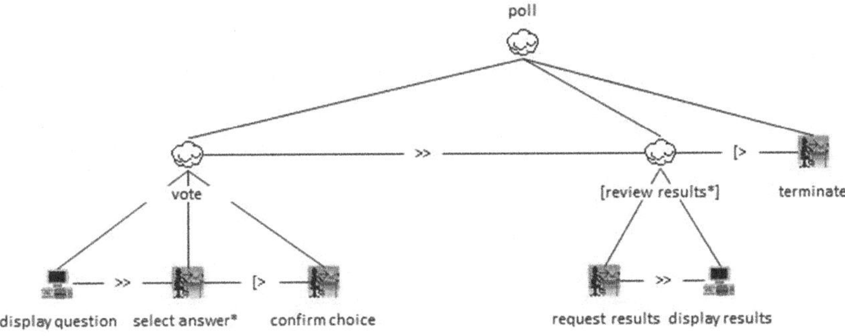

Fig. 5. Task model fragment of the *Poll* pattern further reduced by redundant application tasks

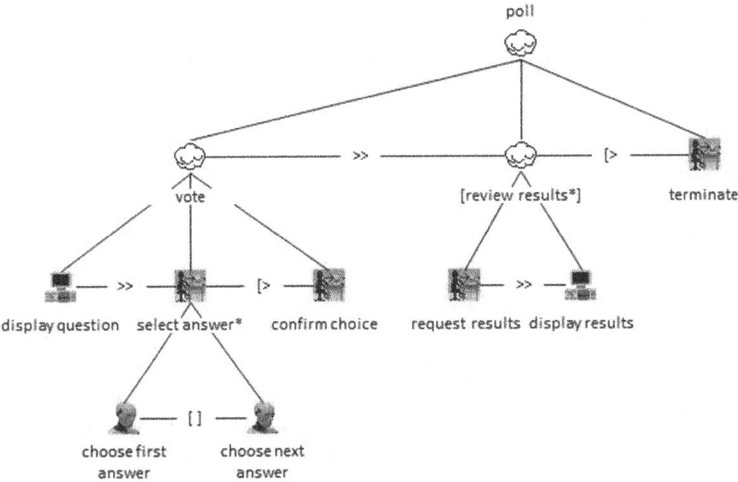

Fig. 6. Task model fragment of the *Poll* pattern supplemented by dummy tasks

The PaMGIS user may change the name of the task interactively within the mentioned dialog and can decide on how often the dummy mechanism is to be repeated. Please note that the concept model fragment of the pattern also contains related dummy concepts which have to be adapted where necessary, too.

In our example the *choose first answer* dummy task is renamed to *choose "excellent"* and *choose next answer* to *choose "fair"*. Further the right dummy task is applied a second time and renamed to *choose "poor"*. The resulting task model fragment is illustrated in Fig. 7. If the user decides not to use the pre-designed dummy tasks, the tool will remove them automatically.

The task model fragment is coded in PPSL format and stored with the pattern. Basically, the same syntax rules apply as for task models. The beginning of this XML compliant representation is provided in Fig. 8. Please note that line numbers have been included for better orientation.

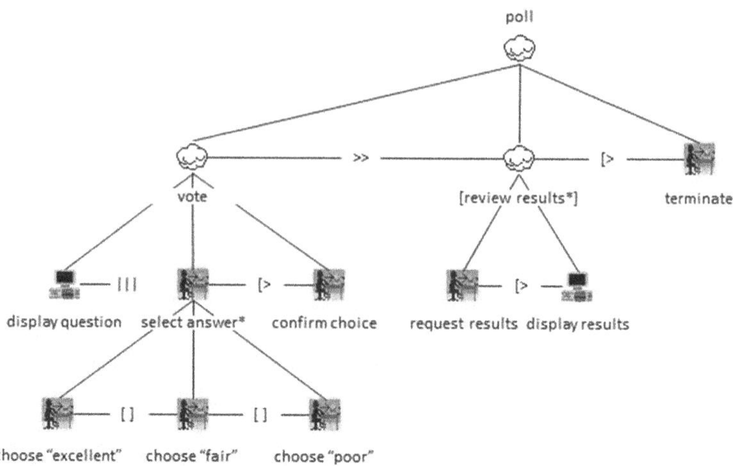

Fig. 7. Resulting task model fragment of the *Poll* pattern after dummy task resolving

When the pattern is applied the task model fragment has to be integrated into the overall task model the user is working on. This can be achieved by simply interlinking the root task of the TMF with the desired sibling tasks and the new parent task inside the task model. The specification of the TMF root element starts at line 10 in Fig. 8.

Once the user has specified the position inside the overall task model where the pattern shall reside this can be performed automatically. In a first step, the entire content of the <TMF_Content> element is copied into the overall task model specification. Subsequently, the identifier and name of the new parent task have to be set accordingly in the <Parent> section of the TMF root element (see lines 25 and 26). If applicable, this must also be done in analogous manner for the left and right siblings (refer to line 29 and 30 resp. 33 and 34). Further, the identifier and name of the pattern's root task (see lines 11 and 12) must be copied into the <RightSibling> section of the preceding and the <LeftSibling> section of the successive task. The temporal relation between the TMF root element and its right sibling is defined straight forward by means of the <TemporalOperator> element (see line 37). A proposed value for the temporal relation between the left sibling and the TMF root element is included in the <TMF_ProposedTempOp> element (see line 08). Here, the user can decide whether to accept or override this suggestion. As a last step, this value must be registered within the <TemporalOperator> element of the left sibling. An exemplary illustration of the resulting task model can be viewed in Fig. 9. Here, the names of the tasks which are not shipped with the TMF are marked with in bold.

3.2 Concept Model Fragment

This subsection shows how the concept model fragment (CMF) of the *Poll* pattern is constructed and formalized using PPSL.

```
<ModelFragment>
<MDFR_Type>Task</MDFR_Type>
<MDFR_FragmentID>"__TMF_0001_01"</MDFR_FragmentID>
<MDFR_Label>"Poll"</MDFR_Label>
<MDFR_Diagram>"see Fig. 7"</MDFR_Diagram>
<MDFR_Fragment>
<TMF_IncludesDummy>True</IncludesDummy>
<TMF_ProposedTempOp>Interleaving</TMF_ProposedTempOp>
<TMF_Content>
<Subtask>
<TaskID>"__TSK_0001_01_0001"</TaskID>
<TaskName>"poll"</TaskName>
<TaskDescription>""</TaskDescription>
<TaskType>Abstraction</TaskType>
    <TaskOrigin>
<TaskOriginPatternID>"PPT_0100_0001"</TaskOriginPatternID>
<TaskOriginPatternName>"Poll"</TaskOriginPatternName>
<TaskOriginPatternVersion>"0001"</TaskOriginPatternVersion>
<TaskOriginPatternRevision>"0000"</TaskOriginPatternRevision>
</TaskOrigin>
<Optional>False</Optional>
<Iterative>False</Iterative>
<Position>
<Parent>
<ParentID>""</ParentID>
<ParentName>""</ParentName>
</Parent>
<SiblingLeft>
<SiblingLeftID>""</SiblingLeftID>
<SiblingLeftName>""</SiblingLeftName>
</SiblingLeft>
<SiblingRight>
<SiblingRightID>""<SiblingRightID>
<SiblingRightName>""</SiblingRightName>
</SiblingRight>
</Position>
<TemporalOperator>Interleaving</TemporalOperator>
<UIConcepts></UIConcepts>
<Subtasks>
<Subtask>
<TaskID>"__TSK_0001_01_0002"</TaskID>
<TaskName>"vote"</TaskName>
......
```

Fig. 8. Excerpt of the XML representation of the TMF of the *Poll* pattern

A concept model comprises high-level specifications of all data elements and interaction objects elements that are relevant for the user interface. Hence, all concepts required by the *Poll* pattern have to be identified. In addition, we have to define the abstract type of the concepts. The most common types are listed in Table 2.

When having a look at the TMF of the *Poll* pattern eight required concepts can be identified.

As illustrated in Fig. 10 these are: (1) a <DataOutput> element for the *display question* task, (2) <SingleChoice> for *select answer*, (3) <ChoiceItem> for the first dummy, (4) another <ChoiceItem> for the second dummy, (5) <Activator> for *confirm choice*, (6) <Activator> for *request results*, (7) <DataOutput> for *display results*, and (8) a <Navigator> element for the *terminate* task in order to abandon the poll procedure.

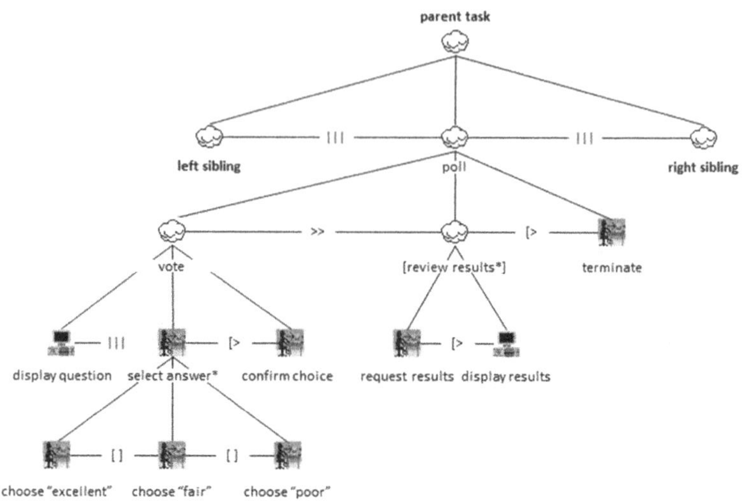

Fig. 9. Task model fragment of the *Poll* pattern integrated in the overall task model

Table 2. Most common concept types

Type	Purpose
DataOutput	Making information perceptible for the user, e.g. displaying it on screen or replaying an audio stream
DataInput	Request input from the user
Activator	Activate a user interface element or call a function
Navigator	Navigate to a different window, screen or dialog
SingleChoice	Select exactly one of several options
MultiChoice	Select none, one, or more of several options
ChoiceItem	A single item that can be chosen by SingleChoice or MultiChoice
UserFeedback	Providing feedback to the user, e.g. about the current system state
Alarm	Providing urgent feedback to the user, e.g. in case of system error or emergency
Cluster	Construct consisting of several components of any type

All required concepts are listed within the concept model fragment of the pattern as presented in Fig. 11. Each concept specification includes links to the tasks that use the concept (see lines 28 and 28 in Fig. 11).

Vice versa, the task specifications contain references to the concepts which are required for their completion (please refer to lines 31 and 32 in Fig. 12).

When the pattern is applied, the user is prompted by the PaMGIS *Pattern Selection & Assignment* function whether the concepts being listed within the CMF should be adopted. If this is the case, the concepts of the pattern will simply be copied into the list of the overall concept model.

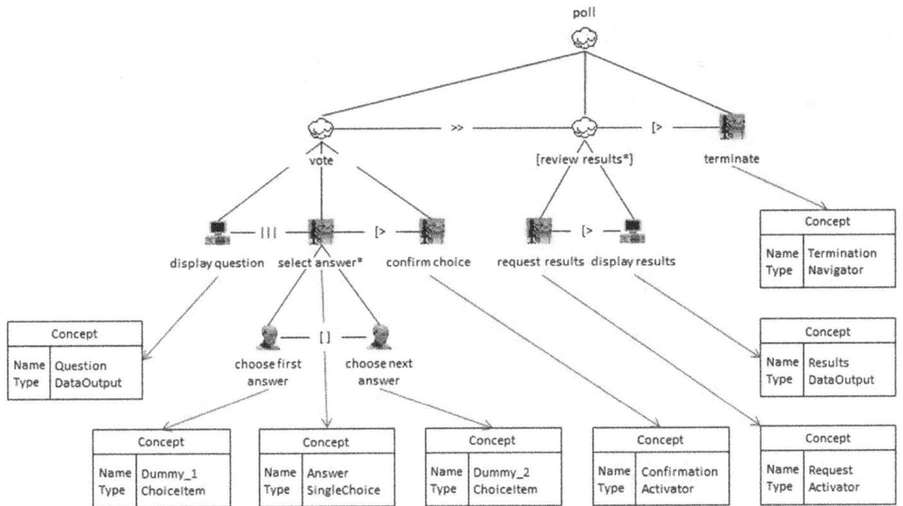

Fig. 10. Deducing required concept from the task model fragment of the *Poll* pattern

3.3 Dialog Model Fragments

While patterns can possess at most one TMF and one CMF they may comprise multiple dialog model fragments (DMF). The task model serves as basis for the specification of dialog models. In consideration of the intended context of use, e.g. the capabilities of the target end user device, it is divided into different sets of closely related tasks, i.e. the dialogs. In addition, the transitions between these dialogs have to be defined. Valuable indications for this work are the hierarchical structure of the task model, i.e. the various sub-trees and the temporal relationships between the tasks.

In the context of PaMGIS dialog models and DMF are specified by means of dialog graphs [9]. Dialogs are represented as boxes containing the name of the dialog as well as the different task that are covered by the dialog. The flow between the various dialogs is specified by arrows, whereupon the arrowheads indicate the direction.

Figure 13 illustrates a possible dialog graph regarding the application of the *Poll* pattern for desktop computers with a large screen. All tasks involved in the poll (see Fig. 7) are combined into one single dialog.

The PPSL representation of this DMF is shown in Fig. 14. The actual dialog specification starts at line 10. The <Position> section (see lines 16 to 39) incorporates information regarding potential predecessor and successor dialogs. The related description elements have to be specified when the pattern is applied. Especially the concepts that trigger the transitions forth and back between the dialogs must be specified, where applicable. This work cannot be accomplished in a fully automated way. Hence, the user must decide how to integrate the DMF into the overall dialog model and which triggers shall be used. However, the PaMGIS *Pattern Selection & Assignment* function offers support regarding this procedure. The tasks being included within the dialog are specified in the <DLG_Tasks> section (see lines 40 to 56). Not necessarily every single task has to be listed here. With the <DLG_TaskProcessing>

```
<ModelFragment>
 <MDFR_Type>Concept</MDFR_Type>
 <MDFR_FragmentID>"__CMF_0001_01"</MDFR_FragmentID>
 <MDFR_Label>"Concepts for poll pattern"</MDFR_Label>
 <MDFR_Fragment>
  <CMF_Content>
   <Concept>
    <CCPT_ConceptID>"__CPT_0001_01_0001"</CCPT_ConceptID>
    <CCPT_ConceptName>"Question"</CCPT_ConceptName>
    <CCPT_Description>"Question to be displayed"</CCPT_Description>
    <CCPT_Label>""</CCPT_Label>
    <CCPT_Perceptible>True</CCPT_Perceptible>
    <CCPT_Enabled>True</CCPT_Enabled>
    <CCPT_Required>False</CCPT_Required>
    <CCPT_ConceptType>DataOutput</CCPT_ConceptType>
    <CCPT_DataType>"String"</CCPT_DataType>
    <CCPT_ConceptOrigin>
     <CCPT_OriginPatternID>"PPT_0100_0001"</CCPT_OriginPatternID>
     <CCPT_OriginPatternName>"Poll"</CCPT_OriginPatternName>
     <CCPT_OriginPatternVersion>"0001"</CCPT_OriginPatternVersion>
     <CCPT_OriginPatternRevision>"0000"</CCPT_OriginPatternRevision>
    </CCPT_ConceptOrigin>
    <CCPT_Preconditions></CCPT_Preconditions>
    <CCPT_Postconditions><CCPT_Postconditions>
    <CCPT_DataLink></CCPT_DataLink>
    <CCPT_TaskLinks>
     <CCPT_TaskLink>
      <CCPT_TaskID>"__TSK_0001_01_0005"</CCPT_TaskID>
      <CCPT_TaskName>"display question"<CCPT_TaskName>
     </CCPT_TaskLink>
    </CCPT_TaskLinks>
   </Concept>
   <Concept>
    <CCPT_ConceptID>"__CPT_0001_01_0002"</CCPT_ConceptID>
    <CCPT_ConceptName>"Answer"</CCPT_ConceptName>
......
```

Fig. 11. Excerpt of the XML representation of the CMF of the *Poll* pattern

element (refer to lines 44, 49, and 54) it can be indicated whether solely the related sub-task itself (*Exclusive*) or also all defined subtasks shall also be included in the dialog specification (*Recursive*).

A second scenario for another DMF for the *Poll* pattern is the implementation on mobile devices with limited screen space, such as a cell phones or smart phones. Due to the display size limits it is not possible or reasonable to display all interaction elements simultaneously. Therefore, we opt for the definition of two different dialogs with a transition between them as illustrated in Fig. 15.

The question which tasks to include in which dialog can be answered when having a look at the task model structure. Very often, it is a promising approach to combine the task elements included in the selfsame sub-tree because they are closely related to each other. All of them have to be completed in order to achieve the superordinate goal related to the top element of the task sub-tree. In the present case we decided to assign the sub-tree starting at the *vote* task to the first (named *Vote*) and likewise the sub-tree beginning at the *review results* task to the second dialog (named *Results*). Since it makes no sense to treat the remaining single interaction task *terminate* separately,

```
<Subtask>
 <TaskID>"__TSK_0001_01_0005"</TaskID>
 <TaskName>"display question"</TaskName>
 <TaskDescription>""</TaskDescription>
 <TaskType>Application</TaskType>
 <TaskOrigin>
  <TaskOriginPatternID>"PPT_0100_0001"</TaskOriginPatternID>
  <TaskOriginPatternName>"Poll"</TaskOriginPatternName>
  <TaskOriginPatternVersion>"0001"</TaskOriginPatternVersion>
  <TaskOriginPatternRevision>"0000"</TaskOriginPatternRevision>
 </TaskOrigin>
 <Optional>False</Optional>
 <Iterative>False</Iterative>
 <Position>
......
 </Position>
 <TemporalOperator>Interleaving</TemporalOperator>
 <UIConcepts>
  <UIConcept>
   <UIConceptID>"__CPT_0001_01_0001"</UIConceptID>
   <UIConceptName>"Question"</UIConceptName>
  </UIConcept
 </UIConcepts>
</Subtask>
......
```

Fig. 12. Excerpt of the XML representation of the *display question* subtask

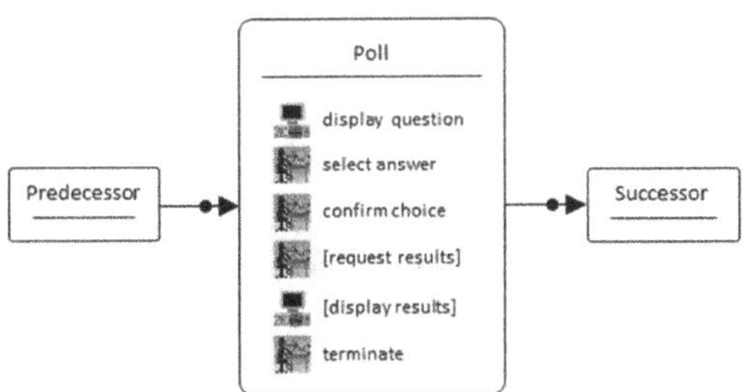

Fig. 13. Dialog model fragment of the *Poll* pattern for desktop computers (large screen)

we added it to the *Results* dialog. The transition from the *Vote* to the *Results* dialog is triggered as soon as the *confirm choice* task is completed. The integration of the DMF into the overall dialog model as soon as the pattern is applied is carried out under the same conditions as described before.

Due to lack of space we abstained from including the PPSL specification of this second dialog model fragment into the document at hand. But its derivation is straight forward and similar to the previous example (see Fig. 14).

```
<ModelFragment>
<MDFR_Type>Dialog</MDFR_Type>
<MDFR_FragmentID>"__DMF_0100_01"</MDFR_FragmentID>
<MDFR_Label>"Poll"</MDFR_Label>
<MDFR_Purpose>"DMF for large screens"</MDFR_Purpose>
<MDFR_Diagram>"see Fig. 13"</MDFR_Diagram>
<MDFR_Fragment>
<DMF_ContextModelReferences></DMF_ContextModelReferences>
<DMF_Content>
<Dialog>
<DialogID>"__DLG_0100_01_01"</DialogID>
<DialogName>"Poll"</DialogName>
<DialogDescription>"Poll for large screens"</DialogDescription>
<DialogLabel>"Poll"</DialogLabel>
<DialogType>Modal</DialogType>
<Position>
<Predecessors>
<Predecessor>
<PRED_DialogID>""</PRED_DialogID>
<PRED_DialogName>""</PRED_DialogName>
<PRED_TransitionType>Sequential</SUCC_TransitionType>
<PRED_Trigger>
<PRED_TaskID>""</SUCC_TaskID>
<PRED_TaskName>""<SUCC_TaskName>
<PRED_Trigger>
</Predecessor>
<Predecessors>
<Successors>
       <Successor>
 <SUCC_DialogID>""</SUCC_DialogID>
<SUCC_DialogName>""</SUCC_DialogName>
<SUCC_TransitionType>Sequential</SUCC_TransitionType>
<SUCC_Trigger>
<SUCC_TaskID>"__TSK_0001_01_0004"</SUCC_TaskID>
<SUCC_TaskName>"terminate"<SUCC_TaskName>
<SUCC_Trigger>
       </Successor>
</Successors>
</Position>
<DLG_Tasks>
<DLG_Task>
<DLG_TaskID>"__TSK_0100_01_0002"</DLG_TaskID>
<DLG_TaskName>"vote"</DLG_TaskName>
<DLG_TaskProcessing>Recursive</DLG_TaskProcessing>
<DLG_Task>
<DLG_Task>
<DLG_TaskID>"__TSK_0100_01_0003"</DLG_TaskID>
<DLG_TaskName>"review results"</DLG_TaskName>
<DLG_TaskProcessing>Recursive</DLG_TaskProcessing>
<DLG_Task>
<DLG_Task>
<DLG_TaskID>"__TSK_0100_01_0004"</DLG_TaskID>
 <DLG_TaskName>"terminate"</DLG_TaskName>
<DLG_TaskProcessing>Exclusive</DLG_TaskProcessing>
</DLF_Task>
</DLG_Tasks>
</Dialog>
</DMF_Content>
</MDFR_Fragment>
</ModelFragment>
```

Fig. 14. XML representation of DMF of the *Poll* pattern for desktop computers (large screen)

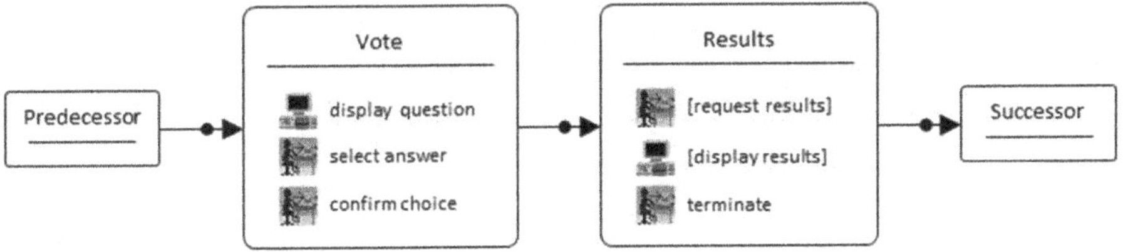

Fig. 15. Dialog model fragment of the *Poll* pattern for mobile devices (small screen)

3.4 Derivation of the User Interface

In an initial step, the structure of the abstract user interface (AUI) must be built up. Here, the dialog model delivers fundamental input. The tasks which are combined within the dialogs include links to the particular concepts being required to complete these tasks. As illustrated in Fig. 16 for the DMF of the *Poll* pattern for mobile devices, these concepts are mapped to corresponding AUI elements. The dialogs themselves are treated as <Cluster> elements. In the example at hand, the *display question* task is linked to a concept of the type *DataOutput*. It is intended to hold a string variable specifying the question for the poll. The *select answer* task and its sub-tasks provide the information regarding the selection of the best fitting answer. Hence, it is a matter of a <SingleChoice> AUI element with related <ChoiceItem> elements. The *confirm choice* and *request results* tasks contribute <Activator> elements while *display results* relates to a <DataOutput> element for displaying an image and *terminate* to a <Navigator> element allowing to abandon the poll process and effect the transition to the subsequent dialog.

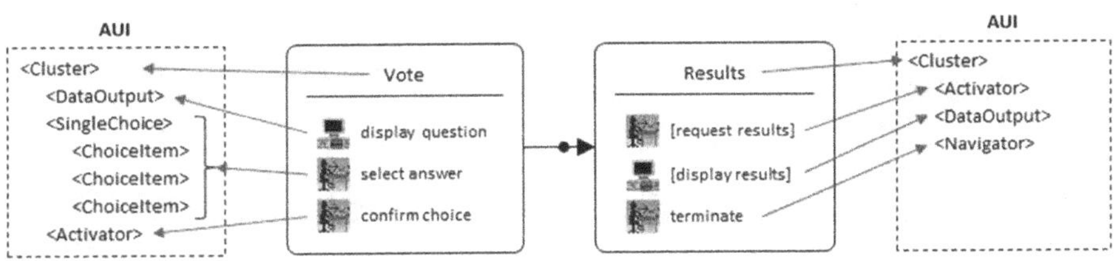

Fig. 16. Deriving the AUI from the DMF of the *Poll* pattern for mobile devices (small screen)

The XML representation of the related AUI excerpt is sketched in Fig. 17. Here, the *Vote* dialog is covered by the first <Cluster> element (see lines 01 to 30), the *Results* dialog by the second one (see lines 31 to 46).

In the next process step, the AUI specification is to be translated into a concrete user interface (CUI) description. In the example we want to arrive at a final user interface (FUI) coded in Hypertext Markup Language (HTML). In this regard, the <Cluster> AUI elements are mapped to <Form> CUI elements as illustrated in Fig. 18. The <DataOutput> element for the poll question is represented as a <TextField> and the <SingleChoice> element together with its associated <ChoiceItem> elements is

```
<Cluster>
  <ClusterID=>"__GRP_01"</ClusterID>
  <ClusterName>"Vote"</ClusterName>
<DataOutput>
<ConceptID>"__CPT_0001_01_0001"</ConceptID>
<ConceptName>"Question"</ConceptName>
</DataOutput>
<SingleChoice>
   <ConceptID>"__CPT_0001_01_0002"</ConceptID>
   <ConceptName>"Answer"</ConceptName>
   <ChoiceItems>
    <ChoiceItem>
     <ConceptID>"__CPT_0001_01_0007"</ConceptID>
     <ConceptName>"Answer1"</ConceptName>
    </ChoiceItem>
<ChoiceItem>
<ConceptID>"__CPT_0001_01_0008"</ConceptID>
<ConceptName>"Answer2"</ConceptName>
</ChoiceItem>
<ChoiceItem>
<ConceptID>"__CPT_0001_01_0009"</ConceptID>
<ConceptName>"Answer3"</ConceptName>
</ChoiceItem>
</ChoiceItems>
</SingleChoice>
</Activator>
<ConceptID>"__CPT_0001_01_0003"</ConceptID>
<ConceptName>"Confirmation"</ConceptName>
  </Activator>
</Cluster>
<Cluster>
<ClusterID>"__GRP_02"</ClusterID>
<ClusterName>"Results"</ClusterName>
<Activator>
<ConceptID>"__CPT_0001_01_0004"</ConceptID>
<ConceptName>"Request"</ConceptName>
  </Activator>
<DataOutput>
<ConceptID>"__CPT_0001_01_0005"</ConceptID>
<ConceptName>"Results"</ConceptName>
</DataOutput>
<Navigator>
<ConceptID>"__CPT_0001_01_0006"</ConceptID>
<ConceptName>"Termination"</ConceptName>
</Navigator>
</Cluster>
```

Fig. 17. XML representation the AUI of *Poll* pattern for mobile devices (small screen)

translated into <Radiobuttons> on the CUI level. The <Activator> and <Navigator> elements are transformed into <Button> elements and the remaining <DataOutput> element into a <Picture> CUI element.

Finally, the CUI specification must be transformed into the final user interface, i.e. HTML source code. The <Form> elements are both replaced by <form target="_blank"> constructs that each incorporate the required UI elements of the original *Vote* resp. the *Results* dialogs. The <TextField> element is realized by a <p> HTML tag while the three radio buttons appear as <input type="radio"> and the <Button> elements as <button type="submit"> tags. Finally, the <Picture> CUI element is translated into a <img> tag. Figure 19 shows screenshots of the resulting HTML FUI. The red arrow indicates the transition from the *Vote* to the *Results* dialog when the confirm button is pressed.

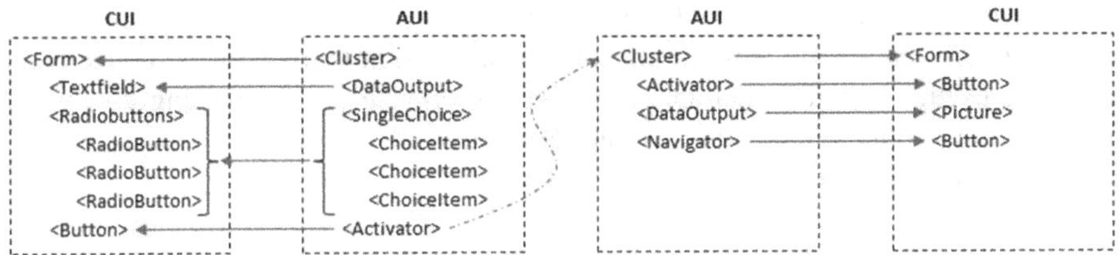

Fig. 18. Deriving the CUI from the AUI of the *Poll* pattern for mobile devices (small screen)

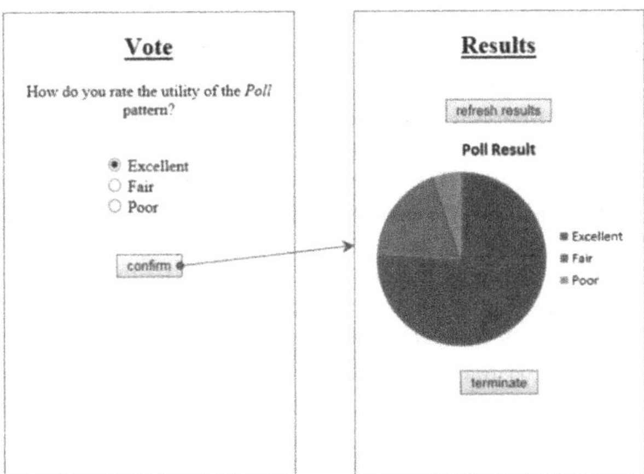

Fig. 19. Realization of the dialog model for mobile devices (small screen) (Color figure online)

4 Conclusion

The PaMGIS framework combines a model-driven user interface development approach and pattern-based development techniques. It allows for the creation of abstract user interface models (AUI) on the basis of fundamental information stored in task, concept, and dialog models. In consideration of context-of-use characteristics held in user, device, UI toolkit, and environment models, the AUI is iteratively transformed into a concrete UI representation which, in turn, is used to generate respective user interface source code for the intended context.

In the current paper, we emphasized on practical aspects of the work with the PaMGIS framework. Using the example of the *Poll* pattern which we have adopted from Martijn van Welie's pattern collection *Patterns in Interaction Design* [12] and translated into PPSL, we have demonstrated how task, concept, and dialog model fragments can be derived from the pattern description. In addition, we delivered insight into the formal description of these model fragments and showed how they can be used as building blocks during the construction of the respective constitutive PaMGIS models when a pattern is applied.

We believe that the hybrid UI development process can accelerate the model-driven design process, feature the reuse of already existing design know-how, and effectively contribute to high usability and appealing user experience of the resulting user interfaces. Amongst others, our plans for future research include various studies to substantiate these presumptions and render related facts more precisely.

References

1. Calvary, G., et al.: The CAMELEON Reference Framework. Document D1.1 of the CAMELEON R&D Project IST-2000-30104 (2002)
2. van Duyne, D., et al.: The Design of Sites: Patterns for Creating Winning Websites, 2nd edn. Prentice Hall International (2006). ISBN 0-13-134555-9
3. Engel, J., Herdin, C., Märtin, C.: A review of HCI pattern tools. In: Proceedings of IHCI 2015, Las Palmas de Gran Canaria, Spain, 22–24 July 2015, pp. 51–58. IADIS Press (2015)
4. Engel, J., Herdin, C., Märtin, C.: A review of user interface description languages. In: Proceedings of the 6. Forum Medientechnik, St. Pölten, Austria – Next Generation, New Ideas, vwh, pp. 183–198 (2014)
5. Engel, J., Herdin, C., Märtin, C.: Evaluation of model-based user interface development approaches. In: Kurosu, M. (ed.) HCI 2014. LNCS, vol. 8510, pp. 295–307. Springer, Cham (2014). doi:10.1007/978-3-319-07233-3_28
6. Engel, J., Herdin, C., Märtin, C.: Exploiting HCI pattern collections for user interface generation. In: Proceedings of PATTERNS 2012, Nice, France, IARIA 2012, pp. 34–44 (2012)
7. Engel, J., Märtin, C., Forbrig, P.: A unified pattern specification formalism to support user interface generation. In: Kurosu, M. (ed.) HCI 2016. LNCS, vol. 9731, pp. 445–456. Springer, Cham (2016). doi:10.1007/978-3-319-39510-4_41
8. Fincher, S., et al.: Perspectives on HCI patterns: concepts and tools (introducing PLML). In: CHI 2003 Workshop Report (2003)
9. Forbrig, P., Reichart, D.: Spezifikation von "Multiple User Interfaces" mit Dialoggraphen. In: Processdings of INFORMATIK 2007: Informatik trifft Logistik. Beiträge der 37. Jahrestagung der Gesellschaft für Informatik e.V. (GI). Bremen (2007)
10. Paternò, F.: ConcurTaskTrees: an engineered approach to model-based design of interactive systems, ISTI-C.N.R., Pisa (2001)
11. Tidwell, J.: Designing Interfaces: Patterns for Effective Interaction Design, 2nd edn. O'Reilly Media Inc. (2011). ISBN 978-1-449-37970-4
12. van Welie, M.: Patterns in interaction design. http://www.welie.com. Accessed 6 Jan 2016

How Cloud Computing Is Addressed for Software Development in Computer Science Education

Dahai Guo(✉) and Anna Koufakou

Department of Software Engineering, Florida Gulf Coast University, Fort Myers, USA
{dguo,akoufakou}@fgcu.edu

Abstract. Cloud computing is bringing a paradigm shift in the field of software development. It has changed how software is developed and accessed. The numerous Software as a Service (SaaS), Platform as a Service (PaaS), and Infrastructure as a Service (IaaS) products in the cloud have provided software developers with not only "unlimited" computing resources, but also a great variety of development tools which may increase their productivity. Compared with the popularity in the industry, the coverage of cloud computing in higher education appears to have fallen behind. While a number of documented courses have been developed to introduce cloud computing to students, their coverage appears to be insufficient, compared with the wide-spread impact of cloud computing in the industry. This is understandable, especially considering cloud computing has matured for only about ten years. This paper surveys a number of documented courses on cloud computing in a computer science or related curriculum. It also presents a list of key topics which should be addressed in a comprehensive cloud computing course, based on related literature, and discusses the coverage of these topics in the surveyed courses.

Keywords: Cloud computing · Computer science education

1 Background of Cloud Computing and Its Impacts in the Industry

According to the National Institute of Standards and Technology (NIST), "cloud computing is a model for enabling ubiquitous, convenient, on-demand network access to a shared pool of configurable computing resources (e.g., networks, servers, storage, applications and services) that can be rapidly provisioned and released with minimal management effort or service provider interaction" [1]. In the past decade, cloud computing has brought a paradigm shift to the field of computing. According to a study conducted in November 2012 [2], "half of enterprises worldwide felt 'cloud computing' was a high IT priority" and "almost two-thirds of enterprises are planning, implementing, or using cloud computing in some fashion". In a report published by McKinsey & Company in January 2015 [3], "recent growth in cloud-based software as a service (SaaS) is expected to continue at 20% each year through 2018, when the global market could reach nearly $85 billion." Many software services have been hosted in the cloud. For example, Netflix, an online streaming service provider hosts a majority of its software systems in the cloud [4]. Siemens Healthcare Diagnostics performs nine billion

M. Kurosu (Ed.): HCI 2017, Part I, LNCS 10271, pp. 415–426, 2017.
DOI: 10.1007/978-3-319-58071-5_31

diagnostics tests annually, utilizing computing resources in the cloud [5]. Zillow, an online real estate company hosts 100 TB of data in the cloud, including 300 million images and more than 1 billion objects [6]. In addition, cloud providers have been continuously adding and improving their cloud services to meet users' needs. For example, Amazon Web Services (AWS) [7], the front runner in the cloud computing is currently providing 55 different services. Microsoft Azure, another major cloud provider has 59 difference services available for their users [8]. Apparently, both cloud providers and cloud users are working towards expanding the functionality and usage of cloud computing.

As stated in [9], "Cloud computing environments offer three major types of services: Infrastructure as a Service (IaaS), Platform as a Service (PaaS), and Software as a Service (SaaS)." The capability provided to the consumer is to use the provider's applications running on a cloud infrastructure. [1] The PaaS and IaaS models offer services to benefit the software development process. Within the IaaS model, software developers are able to provision computing resources, such as computing power and storage space, in an off-premise way often via the Internet [1]. Software developers can provision and terminate the resources at any time. The developers can also use programs to manage the amount of resources dynamically based on the demand to avoid service degradation or unnecessary spending. This feature in the cloud is called auto-scaling. The IaaS model does not require any capital expenditure ahead of time and can greatly improve resource utilization, therefore saving the cost of running the software. In addition to IaaS, cloud computing also offers many software platforms to enable software developers to focus on their application development, instead of software installation, software maintenance, security configuration, etc. For example, many cloud providers, such as AWS and Azure offer container services, message queue services, and database services. When using these services, developers are freed of resource allocation/termination, load balancing, some security configuration, runtime environments, data replication, etc. These software platforms are referred to as Platform as a Service (PaaS) [1]. In a survey to 1358 cloud users in 2014 [10], 41% of the respondents have adopted PaaS products in the cloud which represents nearly six-fold increase in just four years.

2 Brief Overview of the Coverage of Cloud Computing at the Undergraduate Level

The higher education world has responded to the popularity of cloud computing by developing a number of courses, such as [11–21, 25, 26]. Some courses [11–20] utilize the cloud as a pool of virtualized resources, such as computing power, memory, and storage. As explained previously, cloud's off-premise way of resource provisioning appears to be a cheaper alternative than maintaining a cluster of computers on campus. In other words, these courses mainly use the cloud as a virtual computing infrastructure or an IaaS provider. In Sect. 3, the courses that mainly use cloud's IaaS aspect are discussed.

In contrast, other courses [21, 25, 26] provide a broader introduction to students about cloud computing, not only introducing the IaaS aspect of the cloud, but also introducing a variety of the PaaS tools for software development to students. These courses may be more effective in educating students to be proficient users of the cloud since many of them become a software developer when they graduate. A challenge in teaching students PaaS development tools is that numerous such tools exist, dealing with databases, message queues, event-driven programming, MapReduce, machine learning, etc. It is impossible to teach students all these tools in a linear way. The courses which cover PaaS development tools choose to teach a small subset of the PaaS tools available in their selected cloud vendor. In Sect. 4, these courses are discussed in detail. In Sect. 5, we discuss what students should learn in a course on cloud computing so that they can proficiently use the cloud in the software development process.

It is notable that this survey does not concern the cloud as an IT infrastructure in general. The survey [27] is very comprehensive about using the cloud in education in general, instead of a survey specifically on the cloud as a software development environment.

3 Courses that Use Cloud Computing as a Resource Pool

Many educators have realized that cloud provides a much cheaper alternative to maintaining a cluster of computers on campus. They have chosen cloud as a pool for hardware resources, such as computing power and storage space, supporting their teaching agenda. A common characteristic in their courses is that the main subject of the course is not cloud computing. Instead, the cloud mainly acts as resource provider. In this section, a number of such courses are summarized. They are also grouped based on the main subject in the class.

Big data analytics may require a great deal of computing resources. The "unlimited" computing power in the cloud provides a great way for students to write programs to practice algorithms for big data analytics. In the related courses [11–13], MapReduce is often used as a programming model for big data analytics. In [11], an upper-level High-Performance Computing (HPC) course using the cloud is reported. Students used Amazon's Elastic MapReduce (EMR) cloud, a service in AWS. In the process, students first got familiar with some of Amazon's primary services, such as (i) Elastic Compute Cloud (EC2) and (ii) Simple Storage Service (S3). For assignments with MapReduce, students initially used a single-node Hadoop server, hosted in their college and then developed MapReduce applications on Amazon's EMR. Students were also introduced other technologies such as OpenMP and MPI. Based on their observations, message-passing computing with MPI was the least attractive for students –for example, this was the least selected for a term project. On the other hand, students were interested, motivated, and involved in the study of EMR and chose it the most for their projects. Another course [12] is a data-intensive computing course, based on which a certificate program is also offered. Among other technologies, the course introduced cloud computing infrastructures such as Google App Engine (GAE) and Amazon Elastic Compute Cloud (EC2). The topics in [12] included machine learning and probability and statistics. A similar course is discussed in [13], where students were provided with scripts to launch a Hadoop MapReduce cluster on Amazon's Elastic Compute Cloud (EC2) and run MapReduce programs on it. In student projects, as large as about 20 GB of textual data were input to students' MapReduce programs. In these data analytics-related courses, the cloud provides an accessible resource pool for the students to practice related algorithms with possibly a large amount of data.

We also found the teaching of computer networks, especially cybersecurity has been supported by the computing resources in the cloud. As stated in [14], the students could easily launch multiple virtual machines in the cloud to develop networking programs in a real network. This helps avoid physically maintaining a networking lab. In [15], a cloud-based framework, called EDURange framework, is discussed. It hosts on-demand interactive cybersecurity scenarios. Each EDURange exercise is specified by a YAML file, which is similar to XML but more concise. As described in the [15], this framework can be deployed on the AWS and be accessed by students and faculty anywhere. They administered surveys and interviewed participants at several events, such as two hackathons and workshops for faculty at SIGCSE. Their findings showed that faculty was interested in using EDURange to stimulate interest when introducing a topic and towards assessment. Also, that students agreed that the exercises contributed to their learning, as long as the game was at the appropriate level for the audience. Another course is a one-semester course on cybersecurity [16], also using Amazon Web Services (AWS). They briefly described several cloud-based cybersecurity hands-on exercises that were assigned to senior students as part of an introductory course on network security. The topics in [16] covered included Packet Sniffing, Network Footprinting and Port Scanning. The authors of [16] also found that not all of the cybersecurity lab exercises are amenable to be carried out using the cloud, for example, exercises involving disk or smart phone forensics. Another limitation is that configuring and managing the student accounts is not straightforward.

Finally, the cloud has also been used in teaching programming. In [17], a web-based programming environment for Python programming (Pythy) is implemented to help novice programmers by eliminating issues such as installing an IDE or the Python runtime. Pythy also provides cloud storage of student work, so they have access to their code from anywhere without worrying about file organization. They used Pythy in January 2013 in a new service course at Virginia Tech for non-CS majors taking a programming course (Computational Problem Solving in Python). They compared this course experiences with a CS1 course where students learn Python using JES, the Jython Environment for Students. Based on surveys they gave to both classes, students who used Pythy agreed more strongly that it was easier to start using, that it provided more assignment support, that it made it easier to consult examples, and that it helped them figure out when their programs did not behave as required by the assignment. It appears that this cloud-based Pythy did provide students with a user-friendly environment to learn programming. Similar ideas are discussed in [18–20]. Another cloud-backed programming IDE is called Cloud9 IDE and a workshop on it was hosted at SIGCSE in 2016 [18]. The article [19] discusses an environment based on Google App Engine (GAE) which allows students to collaborate. The course in [20] also used GAE in teaching students web-based programming with servlets and JSP.

4 Courses that Focus on Cloud-Based Software Development

While cloud is recognized by many educators as a resource pool, the impact of cloud computing well exceeds that. As discussed previously in Sect. 1, cloud computing has changed how software is developed. There exist a large variety of PaaS tools, dealing with databases, data analytics, containers, batch processing, MapReduce, etc. These tools largely free software developers from installing, maintaining, and configuring development environments. Compare with the number of documented courses that use cloud computing as a type of resource supporting teaching (Sect. 3), we only found three documented studies which significantly address software development in the cloud. They are summarized in this section.

In [21], a course titled "Cloud Computing and Architecture" was offered to 130 graduate students. The discussion in [21] focuses on the student project which evolved from a simple application (Skycave) to a cloud-based, highly available, fault tolerant, and scalable massive multi-user system. The application (Skycave) is a kind of social media web application. The 130 students were split to 60 groups for the project. The students received a set of fully functional programs and asked to improve and deploy the application in the cloud so that it could handle more than 10,000 users concurrently. The development of the project follows the DevOps [22] approach in which students' work included not only their programs, but also scripts that defined the runtime environment. In detail, the students used the Docker containers [23] to define light-weight virtual machines, containing students' programs. These containers were saved in a centralized repository, called Docker Hub [23]. In order to make the application highly available, MongoDB with replicas were used. RabbitMQ [24] was mentioned to address the area of scalability, using a queuing system. The students were asked to deploy the final result of the project in a commercial cloud. It was mentioned in [21] that some evaluation of the student work was performed by manual code review because of the overwhelming complexity in setting up the testing environment. It is noteworthy that the software tools (MongoDB, RabbitMQ, and Docker containers) were all "developer-controlled". This may explain the complexity of setting up the testing environment. Meanwhile, these three technologies, containers, message queues, and NoSQL database have all been offered in form of PaaS services by cloud vendors, such as AWS and Azure. Since these PaaS services are fully managed, the complexity of the runtime configuration would have been much less if these PaaS tools had been used instead of the "developer-controlled" tools.

Compared with [21], the course in [25] covered PaaS services in the cloud much more significantly. This article discusses the authors' experience in teaching an introductory course on cloud computing three times from 2013 to 2015. This course was developed for juniors, seniors, or graduate students. The prerequisite was an introductory computer systems course. Students in this course used AWS for projects. The topics covered included (1) introduction, (2) data centers, (3) resource sharing and virtualization, (4) cloud storage, (5) programming models, and (6) analytics engines. The first three topics focus on either the basics of cloud or IaaS aspect of the cloud. The next three topics significantly deal with the software development process in the cloud. The discussion of "cloud storage" concerns not only the virtualized file systems, such as virtual block services, but also a number of database solutions, mainly NoSQL solutions. The programming models covered classical programming models, such as shared-memory, message passing, synchronous, and asynchronous communication. The MapReduce programming model was discussed, regarding to analytics engine. From the selection of the topics, this course [25] successfully addressed the cloud as not only a distributed system with enormous amount of resource, but also a set of PaaS tools which exploit the capacity of the cloud. In this course, students were supposed to complete five projects, summarized in Table 1. Clearly, the students were greatly exposed to the software development process in the cloud, often using its PaaS solutions.

Table 1. Description of the projects in [25]

Project number	Description	Cloud features addressed
1	Provisioning computing instances in the AWS cloud to implement an algorithm for text analytics	Off-premise resource provisioning
2	Developing an auto-scaled and load-balanced web service	Elasticity
3	Benchmarking two NoSQL solutions, based on AWS DynamoDB and Apache HBase	Managed database solution
4	Developing a MapReduce application for input text predictor	Elastic MapReduce
5	Implementing a scalable Extraction-Transformation-Loading (ETL) process in the cloud based on social media data	Scalability

Another article [26] discusses a much more comprehensive approach to cover cloud computing. Instead of teaching cloud computing in just one course, it was taught in seven courses ranging from data management and analysis, high performance computing to scientific computing and visualization according to [26]. As explained in the article, "a cloud module in our case serves as a small module for existing courses, typically for a week or two. Therefore, the goal is to provide students with hands-on cloud experiences as a useful problem-solving tool in the field covered by the course, rather than an in-depth introduction to the computing model itself or one of its related technologies." [26] The seven courses involved are listed as follows:

1. Advanced Database Systems
2. Web Information Systems
3. Service-Oriented Architectures
4. High-Performance Computing
5. Visualization, Computer Graphics and Data Analytics
6. Scientific Computing: Advanced Techniques and Applications
7. Applications of Scientific Computing

As stated in [26], these seven courses are related to large-scale data processing, analysis and visualization. The cloud related technologies used in these courses were

AWS EC2 and Azure Cloud Service for hosting web services, and Hadoop and its related tools for parallel computing. It was not clear whether the Hadoop environment was the managed cloud services or configured by the instructors. Figure 1 is from [26], describing the mapping between cloud technologies and the seven courses, listed previously. The cloud services were not used only as a set of virtual hardware, but also a development environment for big data applications. Apparently, the integration of cloud computing is very impactful, as described in [26]. Such large-scale integration of a certain subject into a curriculum may require lots of work and coordination while it only addressed a few services out of many other services in the cloud.

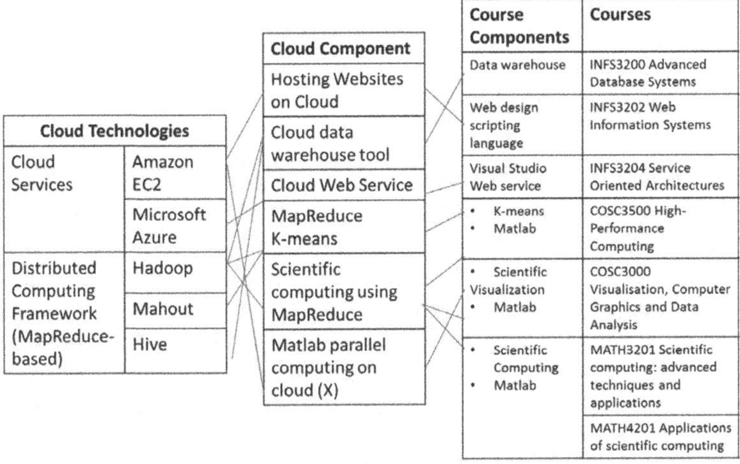

Fig. 1. Mapping of courses and cloud technologies (adopted from [26])

5 Discussion

While the maturity of cloud computing has only about a 10-year history, it has significantly changed the field of computing. The higher education world has responded to this paradigm change. The off-premise and on-demand resource provisioning in the cloud make it an efficient pool of resource in some courses [11–21, 25, 26]. However, the cloud's impact on the software development process has not been addressed sufficiently in higher education. We only found three articles that discuss the cloud as a platform for software development in the higher education world. Given the vast popularity of cloud computing in software development, it is expected that many graduates from a Computer Science or related program need to develop software in the cloud. In this section, we discuss the question: "what topics should a comprehensive course on cloud computing cover?" Two articles, [28] by Sommerville and [29] by Border, were found to address this question, instead of discussing a specific course. The first article [28] by Sommerville discusses the key concepts and principles that might be covered in a Software Engineering course on cloud computing as follows:

1. The MapReduce paradigm
2. Schema-free (NoSQL) databases
3. Service-oriented computing
4. Multi-tenancy architecture
5. Security and compliance
6. Design for resilience

The second article [29] by Border also identified six technologies that enable the cloud after teaching a cloud computing seminar three times.

1. Segregation of services and multi-systems architecture
2. Workload characterization
3. Identify federation
4. Load balancing
5. Content distribution networks
6. Big data analytics

The subjects in both lists require students to understand the cloud much deeper than just knowing how to provision resources from the cloud in an off-premise way. These two lists overlap to a certain extent. Sommerville's list [28] seems to come from the software developers' perspective while Border's [29] emphasizes the computing infrastructure. The topics identified by [28, 29] may effectively provide a guideline for educators when preparing a comprehensive course on cloud computing. Table 2 repeats both lists and aligns the topics based on similar subjects. For instance, "MapReduce" in Sommerville's list [28] is aligned with "Big data analytics" in Border's [29]. If one topic is in just one list, it is shaded gray and marked "Not Included" in the other list. If a pair of similar topics that appears on both lists, they are combined in the "Combined List". The name in the combined list is chosen to be the more general one, using our judgement. For example, a pair of similar topics have "service-oriented computing" in Sommerville's list [28] and "Segregation of services" in Border's [29]. As to our judgement,

Table 2. Suggested topics to cover in a course on cloud computing

Sommerville [28]	Border [29]	Combined List
MapReduce	Big data analytics	Big data analytics
Schema-free databases	*Not Included*	Schema-free databases
Service-oriented Computing	Segregation of services	Service-oriented computing
Multi-tenancy	Multi-systems architecture	Multi-tenancy architecture
Security and compliance	Identify federation	Security and compliance
Design for resilience	*Not Included*	Design for resilience
Not Included	Load balancing	Elasticity
Not Included	Workload characterization	
Not Included	Content distribution networks	Content distribution networks

"Service-oriented computing" seems to be more general. In addition, two topics "load balancing" and "workload characterization" that only show in Border's list [29] appear to both contribute to the elasticity of the cloud so they are combined to "Elasticity" in the combined list.

According to the combined list, the courses discussed in Sect. 3 cannot be said to be comprehensive as they mostly used cloud as a resource alternative. Some courses [11–13] did cover MapReduce, while missing other items on the combined list. The courses in Sect. 4 appear to address more items on the combined list. Table 3 evaluates the courses discussed previously with respects to the combined list. A mark 'X' indicates that a specific topic is covered in that course.

Table 3. Summary of key topic coverage in surveyed courses

Reference	Big data analytics	Schema-free databases	Service-oriented computing	Multi-tenancy architecture	Security and compliance	Design for resilience	Elasticity	Content distribution networks
[11]	X							
[12]	X							
[13]	X							
[14]					X			
[15]					X			
[16]					X			
[17–20]								
[21]		X				X		
[25]	X	X	X				X	
[26]	X	X						

One issue in developing Table 3 was that we could only decide if a topic was covered in a course based on the related paper. Below are the criteria, using which we decided the coverage:

- Big data analytics: its coverage is easy to decide because of the dominance of MapReduce in the field of big data analytics. Any course that introduces MapReduce in the cloud is considered to have covered big data analytics.
- Schema-free databases: this coverage is also easy to identify because specific NoSQL databases/technologies would be named. For instance, Hive is mentioned in [26], DynamoDB is used in [25], and [21] let students use MongoDB.
- Service-oriented computing: this topic is more difficult to identify. In theory, all resources in the cloud are provided to the users in form of services. But service-oriented computing also emphasizes on that a distributed system is loosely coupled. Therefore, we consider that a course covered service-oriented computing if the students were expected to develop software, involving multiple services working together in the cloud. For example, the third project, discussed in [25] involved multiple services, including load balancing, auto-scaling, and NoSQL databases.
- Multi-tenancy architecture is about designing a software architecture which lets multiple groups of users access a single instances of software for better resource utilization [30]. Unfortunately, we did not find any surveyed courses that have covered this topic.

- Security and compliance: the courses discussed in [14–16] discuss security as the main subject. We did not identify the covering of security in other courses.
- Design for resilience: [21] explicitly discussed deploying redundant NoSQL databases for better availability. No discussion in other surveyed courses was found.
- Elasticity: [25] lets students use auto-scaling and load balancer in AWS to address the changes in demand. Again, no discussion of this topic was found in other surveyed course.
- Content distribution networks: we did not see this topic be discussed in any surveyed course.

Despite the previously mentioned courses on cloud computing, no course in our survey was found to comprehensively cover this subject according to the recommended topics in [28, 29]. Moreover, cloud computing is only suggested as an elective in the area Information Assurance and Security (IAS) in the "Computer Science Curricula 2013" jointly published by IEEE and ACM [31]. In the "Software Engineering Body of Knowledge" [32], cloud computing is minimally mentioned under "Network Communication Basics". In summary, it appears that cloud computing has not been sufficiently and comprehensively addressed in higher-education.

6 Conclusion

In this article, we surveyed thirteen documented courses in a computing related curriculum which addressed cloud computing. Some courses used cloud computing as an alternative computing resource. A few courses introduced cloud to students as a platform for software development. The variety of services in the cloud makes it challenging to cover cloud computing in a comprehensive way. Two lists of topics found by [28, 29] are discussed and combined in this paper to propose recommended topics for educators.

From our survey and our own observations as instructors, it is clear that the coverage of cloud computing has fallen behind compared to how widely it has been adopted in the industry, especially in the area of cloud-based software development. It is expected that many students will be developing software in the cloud after their graduation. Therefore, it is imperative for the educators to identify efficient ways to introduce cloud computing to students so that they can be proficient users of cloud when they enter the professional world.

References

1. Mell, P., Grance, T.: The NIST definition of cloud computing. Special Publication 800-145, National Institute of Standards and Technology, U.S. Department of Commerce, September 2011
2. Anderson, C., Gantz, J.F.: Climate Change: Cloud's Impact on IT Organizations and Staffing, Whitepaper, Microsoft, November 2012
3. Comella-Dorda, S., Gnanasambandam, C., Shah, B., Strain, T.: From box to cloud: an approach for software development executives. McKinsey & Company, January 2015

4. Izrailevsky, Y.: Completing the Netflix Cloud Migration. 11 February 2016. https://media.netflix.com/en/company-blog/completing-the-netflix-cloud-migration. Accessed 22 Sep 2016
5. Heid, A.: AWS Case Study: Siemens. https://aws.amazon.com/solutions/case-studies/siemens. Accessed 22 Sep 2016
6. Zillow, AWS Case Study: Zillow. https://aws.amazon.com/solutions/case-studies/zillow/. Accessed 22 Sep 2016
7. Amazon Web Services. https://aws.amazon.com/. Accessed 22 Sep 2016
8. Microsoft Azure. https://azure.microsoft.com/en-us/. Accessed 22 Sep 2016
9. Wei, Y., Blake, M.B.: Service-oriented computing and cloud computing. IEEE Internet Comput. **14**(6), 72–75 (2010)
10. The Future of Cloud Computing: The 4th Annual Survey 2014. North Bridge Venture Partners. http://www.northbridge.com/industry-largest-cloud-computing-survey-reveals-5x-adoption-saas. Accessed 26 May 2016
11. Radenski, A.: Integrating data-intensive cloud computing with multicores and clusters in an HPC course. In: ITiCSE 2012, Haifa, Israel, 3–5 July 2012
12. Ramamurthy, B.: A practical and sustainable model for learning and teaching data science. In: ACM SIGCSE 2016, Memphis, TN, 2–5 March 2016
13. Rabkin, A., Reiss, C, Katz, R., Patterson, D.: Experiences teaching MapReduce in the cloud. In: SIGCSE 2012, Raleigh, North Carolina, 29 February–3 March 2012
14. Zhu, W.: Hands-on network programming projects in the cloud. In: SIGCSE 2015, Kansas City, MO, 4–7 March 2015
15. Weiss, R., Boesen, S., Sullivan, J., Mache, J.: Teaching cybersecurity analysis skills in the cloud. In: SIGCSE 2015, Kansas City, MO, 4–7 March 2015
16. Salah, K.: Harnessing the cloud for teaching cybersecurity. In: SIGCSE 2014, Atlanta, Georgia, 5–8 March 2014
17. Edwards, S.H., Tilden, D.S., Allevato, A.: Pythy: improving the introductory python programming experience. In: SIGCSE 2014, Atlanta, GA, 5–8 March 2014
18. Ortiz, A.: Programming web services on the cloud with Node.js. In: SIGCSE 2016, Memphis, TN, 2–5 March 2016
19. Bhattacharya, P., Guo, M., Tao, L., Wu, B., Qian, K., Palmer, E.K.: A Cloud-based cyberlearning environment for introductory computing programming education. In: 11th IEEE International Conference on Advanced Learning Technologies, Athens, GA, 6–8 July 2011
20. Hollingsworth, J., Powell, D.: Teaching web programming using the Google cloud. In: ACM SE 2010 Proceedings of the 48th Annual Southeast Regional Conference, Oxford, Mississippi, 15–17 April 2010
21. Christensen, H.B.: Teaching DevOps and cloud computing using a cognitive apprenticeship and story-telling approach. In: ITiCSE 2016, Arequipa, Peru, 9–13 July 2016
22. Loukides, M.: What is DevOps. Oreilly Media, Sebastopol (2012)
23. Docker. www.docker.com. Accessed 24 Feb 2017
24. RabbitMQ. www.rabbitmq.com. Accessed 24 Feb 2017
25. Rehman, M.S., Boles, J., Hammoud, M., Sakr, M.: A cloud computing course: from systems to services. In: SIGCSE 2015, Kansas City, MO, 4–7 March 2015
26. Chen, L., Liu, Y., Gallagher, M., Pailtthorpe, B., Sadiq, S., Shen, H.T., Li, X.: Introducing cloud computing topics in curricula. J. Inf. Syst. Educ. **23**(3), 315–324 (2012). Fall
27. Gonzalez-Martinez, J.A., Bote-Lorenzo, M.L., Gomez-Sanchez, E.: Cloud computing and education: a state-of-the-art survey. Comput. Educ. **80**, 132–151 (2015)

28. Sommerville, I.: Teaching cloud computing: a software engineering perspective. J. Syst. Softw. **86**, 2330–2332 (2013)
29. Border, C.: Cloud computing in the curriculum: fundamental and enabling technologies. In: SIGCSE 2013, Denver, Colorado, 6–9 March 2013
30. Chong, F., Carraro, G., Wolter, R.: Multi-tenant data architecture. Microsoft Developer Network, June 2006. https://msdn.microsoft.com/en-us/library/aa479086.aspx. Accessed 24 Feb 2017
31. Computer Science Curricula 2013, The Joint Task Force on Computing Curricula by Association for Computing Machinery (ACM) and IEEE Computer Society, 20 December 2013
32. Bourque, P., Fairley, R.E.: Guide to the Software Engineering Body of Knowledge. IEEE Computer Society, Washington (2014)

Generalized Reference

Referring with and Without Language by Matching, Pointer, or Address

Roland Hausser(✉)

Universität Erlangen-Nürnberg (em.), Erlangen, Germany
rrh@linguistik.uni-erlangen.de

Abstract. Medieval logic defined reference as a relation between language and objects in the world. Recently, however, the term "representational token" has been used instead of language (Reimer and Michaelson 2014). This allows for reference with and without language. In a similar vein, Database Semantics (DBS) has implemented concept-based reference as a matching between two contents. If a content is attached to a language surface it is called the literal meaning$_1$ of the surface.

Referring with a content (as a representational token), regardless of whether or not it is attached to a surface, leads to a generalized notion of reference (Sect. 6.3). An example of reference without language is identifying a current nonlanguage recognition with something seen before. Another example is identifying a nonlanguage recognition with an earlier language content, e.g. something read (for example, in a guide book) or heard about.

In addition to the concept-based reference mechanism of (i) symbols (We follow the terminology used by Peirce (CP 2.228, 2.229, 5.473) for his theory of signs.) (Sect. 6), natural language uses the reference mechanisms of (ii) indexicals (Sect. 7) based on pointers, and of (iii) names (Sect. 8) based on acts of generalized baptism and coreference by address. This paper systematically reconstructs the mechanisms of reference as they function with and without language in an agent-based computational framework.

Keywords: Agent-based · Matching, pointing, address · Hear mode, speak mode · Time-linear derivation order · Declarative specification · Talking robot

1 Agent-Based Ontology

When two agents communicate with each other by means of a natural language, the speaker uses its external action interface to produce a sequence of language surfaces while the hearer uses its external recognition interface to identify the elements of the sequence. The sequence is time-linear in the sense that it is linear like time and in the direction of time. In accordance with the Western writing convention, the progression of time is shown in the direction from left to right.

M. Kurosu (Ed.): HCI 2017, Part I, LNCS 10271, pp. 427–446, 2017.
DOI: 10.1007/978-3-319-58071-5_32

1.1 Physical Framework of Communication

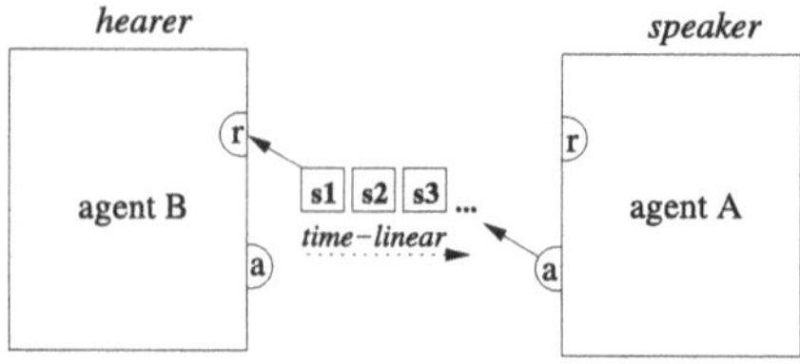

The recognition and action interfaces of the agents are indicated by half circles marked with r and a. The language surfaces are represented by boxes containing s1, s2, s3, ... As agent-external modality-dependent sound waves (speech), dots on paper (writing), or gestures (signing), the surfaces may be measured and described with the methods of the natural sciences, but have no meaning and no grammatical properties whatsoever.

The first surface leaving the speaker is the first to reach the hearer. The last surface leaving the speaker is the last to reach the hearer.[1] All other aspects of language communication are agent-internal, modality[2]-independent, and cognitive.

Modality-independence may be illustrated by the basic operations of arithmetic, i.e., addition, subtraction, multiplication, and division. They exist at a level of abstraction which may be realized equivalently as the operations (i) of a human, (ii) a mechanical calculator, or (iii) an electronic computer.[3]

With autonomous robots still absent in today's computational linguistics, the external framework Sect. 1.1 may be simulated, using the keyboard and the screen of standard computers as primitive recognition and action components. This, however, works only for the transfer of surfaces. It does not work for nonlanguage recognition and action, which are required for a cognitive reconstruction of reference. For example, the agent's ability to refer to agent-external items is needed for fulfilling a request like *Pick up the blue square!* or to report how many blue squares there are in the agent's current task environment.

2 Elementary Concepts

The minimum in reconstructing higher-level cognition is (i) an agent-internal memory, (ii) a central control embedded into and interacting with memory, (iii) a mapping from the recognition interface to central control, and (iv) a mapping from central control to the action interface. The mappings between modality-dependent raw data and modality-independent concepts are formally

[1] In Sects. 1.1, 4.2, and 5.2 this is expressed graphically by placing the hearer to the left and the speaker to the right. If the order is reversed, the progression of time would have to be shown from right to left.

[2] The term *modality* is being used in several different fields of science. As employed here, modality is known as *sensory* modality (Chen 2006, Sect. 6.13.1).

[3] According to Wiener (1961, p. 132): "Information is information, and not matter or energy.".

based on the type-token distinction, familiar from philosophy.[4] The type of a concept describes the *necessary* properties, while an associated token is an instantiation with certain additional *accidental*[5] properties. As an example consider the recognition of colors (Hausser 1989, p. 296 ff). In physics, they are defined as intervals on the one-dimensional scales of electromagnetic wave length and frequency. Accordingly, the type and a token of the color blue may shown as follows.

2.1 Type and Token of the Color Called blue

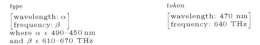

The type specifies the wavelength and the frequency of the color *blue* by means of variables which are restricted to the corresponding intervals provided by physics. The token uses constants which lie within these intervals.

In the recognition of colors, the type provided by memory and the raw input data provided by a sensor interact as follows, resulting in a classified token.

2.2 Concept Type and Token in Color Recognition

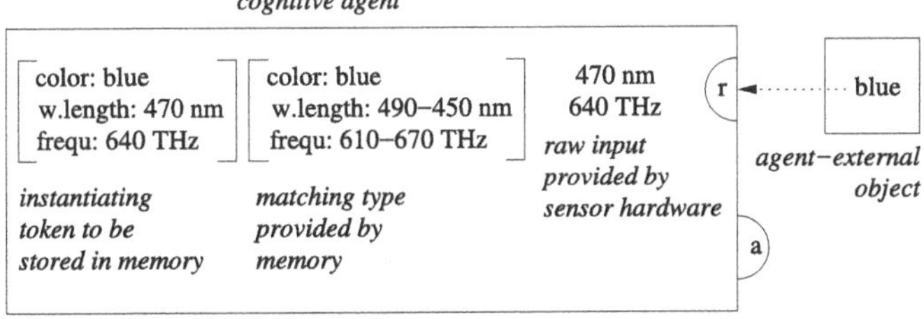

A sensor measures the wavelength 470 nm and frequency 640 THz in an agent-external object. These values lie within the intervals 490–450 nm and 610–6700 THz of the color blue and thus match the type. In the instantiating token, the wavelength and frequency intervals of the type are replaced by the measured values. The feature structures representing types and tokens may be extended as needed, for example, with an additional attribute for color intensity.

Next consider the type and the token of a two-dimensional geometric object.

[4] The type-token distinction was introduced by Peirce (CP 4: 537).

[5] The term accidental is used here in the philosophical tradition of Aristotle, who distinguishes in his Metaphysics, Books ζ and η, between the necessary and the accidental (incidental or coincidental – kata sumbebêkos) properties of an object in nature.

2.3 Concept Type and Token of the Concept square

type	*token*
edge 1: αcm	edge 1: 2 cm
angle 1/2: 90°	angle 1/2: 90°
edge 2: α cm	edge 2: 2 cm
angle 2/3: 90°	angle 2/3: 90°
edge 3: α cm	edge 3: 2 cm
angle 3/4: 90°	angle 3/4: 90°
edge 4: α cm	edge 4: 2 cm
angle 4/1: 90°	angle 4/1: 90°

where α is a length

Here, the type and the token share attributes which specify (i) the number of equally long edges and (ii) the angle of their intersections. The type and the token differ only in their edge lengths. The latter is accidental in that the type matches an infinite number of square tokens with different edge lengths.[6]

In analogy to Sect. 2.2, recognition of a square may be shown as follows.

2.4 Type and Token in Recognizing a Square

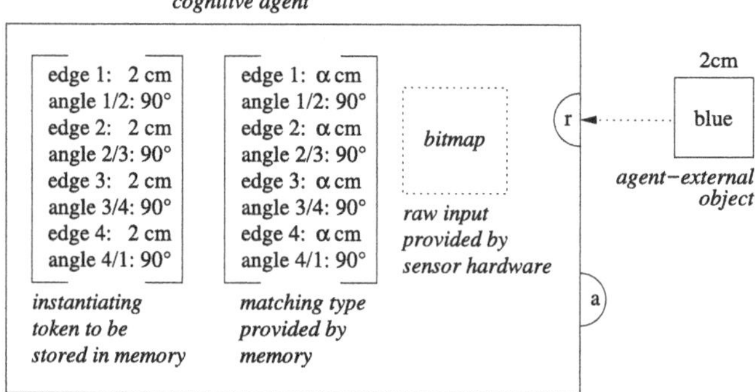

The type matches the outline of all kinds of different squares, whereby its variables are instantiated in the resulting tokens.

Today, there exist pattern recognition programs which are already quite good at recognizing geometric objects.[7] They differ from our approach in that they are based almost completely on statistics. However, even if the terms of the type and the token may not be found in their theoretical descriptions, the type-token distinction is nevertheless implicit in any pattern recognition processing. Furthermore, the rule-based, incremental procedures[8] of pattern recognition presented in Hausser (2005) are well-suited to be combined with statistical methods.[9]

[6] In an artificial agent, the type may be implemented as a pattern-matching software which recognizes tokens by approximating raw bitmap outlines Hausser (1999, 3.2.1).

[7] As shown by the work of Steels (1999), suitable algorithms may evolve new types automatically from similar data by abstracting from what they take to be accidental.

[8] They are based on an incremental, memory-based procedure of pattern recognition using geons (Biederman 1987).

[9] For building a talking robot, the automatic evolution of types has to result in concepts which correspond to those of the intended language community. This may be achieved by presenting the artificial agent with properly selected data in combination with human guidance (guided patterns method, Hausser 2011, Sect. 6.2).

The elementary concepts of nonlanguage recognition are complemented by those of action. For example, the concept *take* is defined as the type of a gripping action which is instantiated as a token to be realized as raw data. The token differs from the type in that it is adapted to a specific gripping occasion. It holds in general for recognition that raw data are classified by a type and instantiated as a token, while in action a type is specialized into a token which is passed to a suitable action component for realization as raw data (Hausser 1999, 3.3.5).

The interaction between the agent's external interfaces, the types, the tokens, and the memory must be hand in glove. For example, if the agent has no sensor for measuring electromagnetic wavelength/frequency, colors cannot be recognized – even if the proper types were available from memory. Conversely, without the types the raw data provided by a suitable sensor cannot be classified and instantiated as tokens. Also, without a memory the types cannot be provided for recognition and action, and the tokens cannot be stored.

3 Data Structure and Database Schema

The concepts defined in Sects. 2.1 and 2.3 constitute elementary cognitive contents, but they do not provide any means for being connected, as in blue_square. For this, DBS lexically embeds the concepts as *core values* into nonrecursive[10] feature structures with ordered attributes, called *proplets* (because they are the elementary building blocks of propositions, in analogy to droplet). A feature structure is built from features. In computer science, a feature is defined as an attribute-value pair (avp), e.g. [noun: square], with noun: as the attribute and square as the value.

The embedding of core values into proplets allows their concatenation by means of value copying. For example, the proplets *blue* and *square* may be connected into the content of blue_square as follows.[11]

[10] A feature structure is nonrecursive if there is no recursive embedding of feature structures as values. Recursive feature structures are unsuitable for (i) contents with a coordination structure, (ii) the pattern matching needed for (a) modeling reference and (b) applying operation patterns to input, and (iii) storage and retrieval in a database. Unordered attributes are inefficient for computers and humans alike. Recursive feature structures with unordered attributes are not used in DBS.

[11] The algorithm used for connecting (hear mode) and activating (think mode) proplets is time-linear Left-Associative Grammar (Hausser 1992). The sur attribute takes the language dependent surface as value. For a detailed description of the attributes and values used in proplets for describing English see Hausser (2006) Appendix A3.

3.1 Concatenation by Cross-Copying

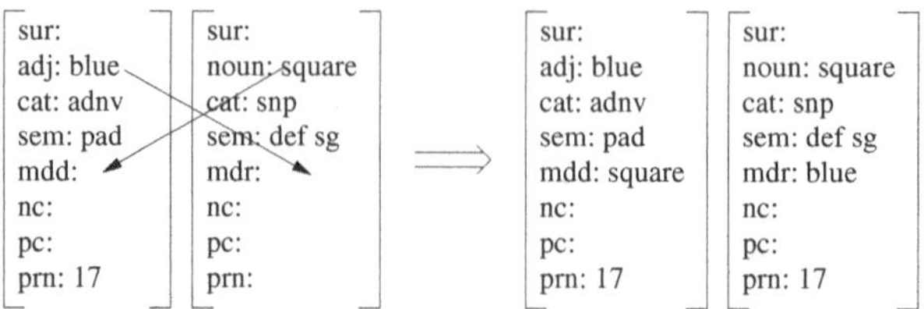

The nature of the semantic relation between *blue* and *square* is characterized by the attributes mdr (modifier) and mdd (modified). The relation is implemented by copying the core value of *square* into the mdd slot of *blue* and the core value of *blue* into the mdr slot *square*. In addition, the prn value of *blue*, here 17, is copied into the prn slot of the next word proplet *square*.

Next consider extending Sect. 3.1 to an intrapropositional coordination.

3.2 Coordination in *big blue square*

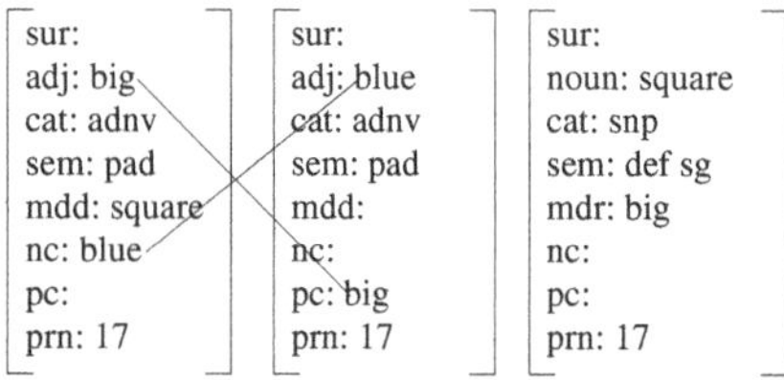

The relation of intrapropositional coordination is coded by the nc (next conjunct) and pc (previous conjunct) attributes of the conjoined adjectives.

The diagonal lines in Sect. 3.2 are intended as optical support for the reader. Technically, however, they are redundant and may be omitted. The real method of establishing semantic relations in DBS is by addresses coded declaratively as values and implemented procedurally as pointers. This method makes the proplets forming a complex content order-free, allowing the database to store them independently of the semantic relations between them.

For example, no matter where the storage mechanism of the database puts the adnominal *big*, its modified may be found via the primary key consisting of the mdd value square and the prn value 17. Similarly, no matter where the noun *square* is stored, its modifier may be found via the mdr value big and the prn value 17. And accordingly for the intrapropositional coordination in Sect. 3.2.

As another example consider the content of Julia knows John., represented as the following set of connected proplets.

3.3 Content of Julia Knows John. As a Set of Proplets

```
[sur: Julia  ] [sur: knows          ] [sur: John  ]
[noun: Julia ] [verb: know          ] [noun: John ]
[cat: snp    ] [cat: #s3' #a' decl  ] [cat: snp   ]
[fnc: know   ] [arg: Julia John     ] [fnc: know  ]
[prn: 625    ] [prn: 625            ] [prn: 625   ]
```

The simplified proplets are held together by a common prn value, here 625. The functor-argument is coded solely in terms of attribute values. For example, the *Julia* and *John* proplets specify their functor as know, while the *know* proplet specifies Julia and John as its arguments. Because of their nonempty sur(face) slots, the proplets are language proplets, in contradistinction to the proplets in Sects. 3.1 and 3.2, which are context proplets.

For storage and retrieval, a proplet is specified uniquely[12] by its core and prn values (primary key). This suggests a two-dimensional database schema, as in a classic network database (Elmasri and Navathe 2010). However, instead of using member and owner records, DBS uses member proplets and owner values.

The result is called a word bank. Its database schema consists of a column of owner values in their alphabetical order (vertical). Each owner value is preceded by an empty slot, called the now front, and a list of member proplets (horizontal); together they constitute a *token line.*[13]

As an example, consider storing a nonlanguage content.

3.4 Storing the Proplets of Sect. 3.3 in a Word Bank

```
                 member proplets      now front    owner values
          [noun: John ]
      ... [cat: snp   ]                            John
          [fnc: know  ]
          [prn: 625   ]
          [noun: Julia]
      ... [cat: snp   ]                            Julia
          [fnc: know  ]
          [prn: 625   ]
[verb: know            ]
[cat: #n-s3'#a'decl    ]
... [arg: Julia John   ]                           know
[prn: 625              ]
```

The proplets in a token line all have the same core value and are in the temporal order of arrival, reflected by their prn values (Hausser 2006, Sects. 11.2, 11.3).

In contrast to the task of designing a practical schema for arranging the books in a private library, the sorting of proplets into a word bank is simple and mechanical. The letter sequence of a proplet's core value completely determines

[12] Propositions containing two or more proplets with the same values, as in Suzy loves Suzy, require extra attention. They constitute a special case which (i) rarely occurs and (ii) is disregarded here because it may be easily handled by the software.

[13] The token line of a core value is found with a trie structure (Briandais 1959). The search for a proplet within a token line may use the prn value of the address in relation to the linear increasing prn values. As pointed out by J. Handl, this may be based on binary search, in time O(log(n)) (Cormen et al. 2009), or interpolation, in time O(log(log(n))) (Weiss 2005), where n is the length of the token line.

its token line for storage: the storage location for any new arrival is the penultimate position (now front) in the corresponding token line. When this slot is filled, the now front is reopened by moving the owner value one slot to the right (or, equivalently, pushing the member proplets one slot to the left, as in a push-down automaton).

By storing content like *sediment*, the stored data are never modified and any need for checking consistency is obviated. Changes of fact are written to the now front, like diary entries recording changes of temperature. Current data which refer to old ones use addresses as core values, implemented as pointers.

4 Cycle of Natural Language Communication

The transfer mechanism of content from the speaker to the hearer is based on external surfaces which have neither a meaning nor any grammatical properties (Sect. 1.1). They must, however, belong to a language which the speaker and the hearer have each learned.

The learning enables the hearer to (i) recognize surfaces, (ii) use the recognized but otherwise unanalyzed surfaces for looking up lexical entries which provide the meaning and the grammatical properties, and (iii) connect them with the semantic relations of functor-argument and coordination. The learning enables the speaker to (i) navigate along the semantic relations between proplets, (ii) produce language-dependent word form surfaces from the core values of proplets traversed, and (iii) handle function word[14] precipitation, micro word order, and agreement.

4.1 Definition of Successful Communication

> Natural language communication is successful if the content, mapped by the speaker into a sequence of external word form surfaces, is reconstructed and stored equivalently by the hearer.

The transfer of information from the speaker to the hearer, based solely (i) on unanalyzed external surfaces, (ii) the data structure of proplets, (iii) the database schema of a word bank, and (iv) the content Sect. 3.4, may be shown schematically as follows.

[14] Examples of function words in English are determiners like a(n), the, some, every, all, prepositions like in, on, above, below, auxiliaries like be, have, do, coordinating conjunctions like and, or, and subordinating conjunctions like that, who, which, when, because.

4.2 Natural Language Transfer Mechanism

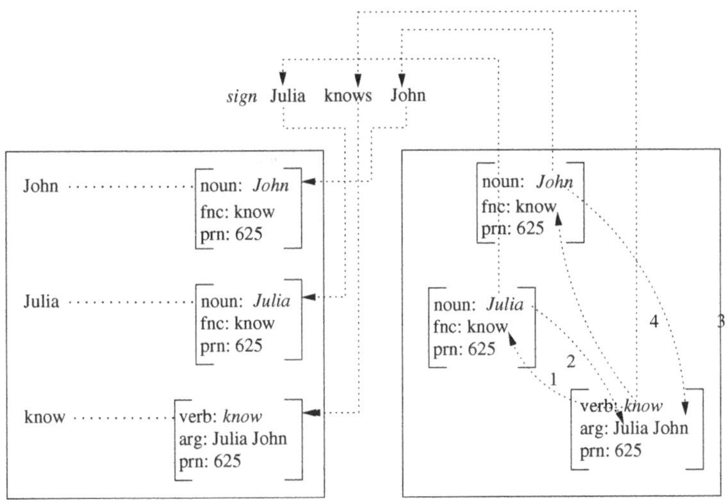

The speaker's navigation through a set of connected proplets serves as the conceptualization (*what to say*) and as the basic serialization (*how to say it*) of natural language production (McKeown 1985; Kass and Finin 1988). The hearer's interpretation consists in deriving a corresponding set of proplets, based on automatic word form recognition and syntactic-semantic parsing. The time-linear order of the sign induced by the speaker's navigation is eliminated in the hear mode, allowing storage of the proplets in accordance with the database schema of the content-addressable[15] word bank. When the agent switches into the speak mode, order is reintroduced by navigating along the semantic relations between the proplets.

5 Conceptual Reconstruction of Reference

In DBS, a cognitive content is defined as a set of proplets connected by address. Proplets with a non-empty sur(face) slot (Sect. 3.3) represent a language content. Proplets with an empty sur slot (Sect. 3.1) represent a context content. Otherwise, language and context proplets are alike. This holds specifically for their storage and retrieval in a word bank, which is based solely on their core value and order of arrival.

Conceptually, however, reference may be modeled by (i) separating the levels of language and context, (ii) introducing the place of pragmatics as an interaction between the two levels, and (iii) distinguishing peripheral and central cognition.

---

[15] As a database, a word bank is content-addressable because it does not use an index (inverted file), in contrast to the widely used coordinate-addressable databases (RDBMS). See Chisvin and Duckworth (1992) for an overview.

5.1 Conceptual View of Interfaces and Components

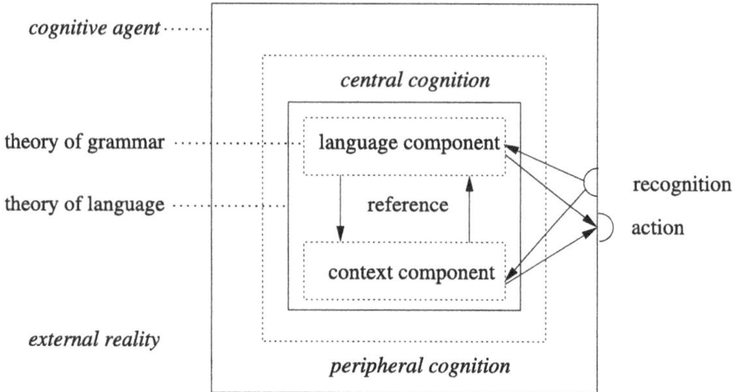

Externally, the agent's interfaces for language and nonlanguage recognition are the same, as are those for language and nonlanguage action.[16] Internally, however, raw input data are separated by peripheral cognition into language and nonlanguage content (diagonal input arrows). Conversely in action, which realizes a content as raw output data regardless of whether it originated at the language or at the context level (diagonal output arrows).

For example, as a sound pattern the surface blue square will have a meaningful interpretation at the language level by someone who has learned English, but be treated as an uninterpreted noise at the context level by someone who has not. Conversely, even though the action of denying entrance may be realized by telling to go away (originating at the language level) or by slamming the door (originating at the context level), both result in raw output data.

The distinction between the language and the context component provides a cognitive treatment of reference. Reference to an object in the agent's current environment is called *immediate* reference, while reference to cognitive content existing only in the agents' memory, for example, J.S. Bach, is called *mediated* reference. For mediated reference, the agent-based ontology of DBS (Sect. 1) is essential.

As an example of immediate reference consider a speaker and a hearer in a common task environment (Newell and Simon 1972) and looking at a blue square. If the speaker says Take the blue square, the noun phrase refers to the object in question. Similarly for the hearer, for whom fulfilling the request requires reference to the same object.

[16] A differentiation into the sensory modalities (vision, audition, locomotion, manipulation) is omitted – not only for simplicity, but also because the meaning of a word or expression is independent of the modality of its external surface. For example, the meaning of the word square (Sect. 2.3) is the same regardless of whether its surface is realized in speech, writing, or signing. A nonlanguage concept like the shape, color, taste, etc., of a blueberry may also be assumed to be independent from the modalities of its recognition (Hausser 2011, Sects. 2.2–2.4).

Postulating an external relation between a surface and its referent would be a reification fallacy. Instead we reconstruct immediate reference cognitively.

5.2 Immediate Reference as a Purely Cognitive Procedure

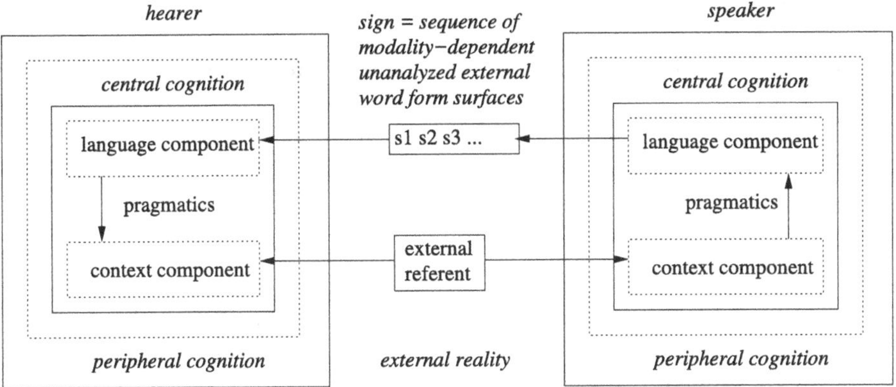

Immediate reference relies on the agents' action and recognition interfaces for language (upper level) and the recognition of nonlanguage content (lower level). Mediated reference, in contrast, relies on language action and recognition (upper level) and the existence of corresponding content in the agent's memory. While immediate reference may be regarded as prototypical for the origin of language, it is a special case of mediated reference in that it has the additional requirement of context recognition (Hausser 2006, Sect. 2.5).

Terminological Remark

Computer Science uses the term "reference" differently from philosophy and linguistics. A computational reference is an address in a storage location. This may be coded as (i) a symbolic address (declarative) or as (ii) a pointer to a physical storage location in the memory hardware (procedural). The term "generalized reference" is used in image reconstruction (computer vision).

In DBS, the term "reference" is used in the sense of philosophy and linguistics. However, the term is generalized insofar as no agent-external "representational token" is required (Sect. 6.3, constellations 1 and 3). Recanati (1997), Pelczar and Rainsbury (1998), and others use "generalized reference" for an analysis of the sign kind name which allows the surface Mary, for example, to refer to several individuals, in contradistinction to Russell's (1905) definite description analysis of "proper" names, which requires a unique referent.

The DBS analysis of names also allows different referents (Sect. 8.4). However, while the "generalized reference" of Recanati, Pelczar et al., and others is based on assimilating names to indexicals, the DBS analysis is based on an act of baptism which is generalized in that it may occur implicitly as well as explicitly. Moreover, generalized reference in DBS is not limited to names, but includes reference by means of matching concepts (symbol) and pointing (indexical).

6 Reference by Matching (Symbol)

The reference mechanism based on matching uses the type-token relation (Sects. 2.1, 2.3) and is associated with the sign kind *symbol*. For example, the terms a blue square and blue squares in the sentence sequence John saw a blue square. ... Blue squares are rare. are related as follows.

6.1 Reference with Language Proplets in Token Lines

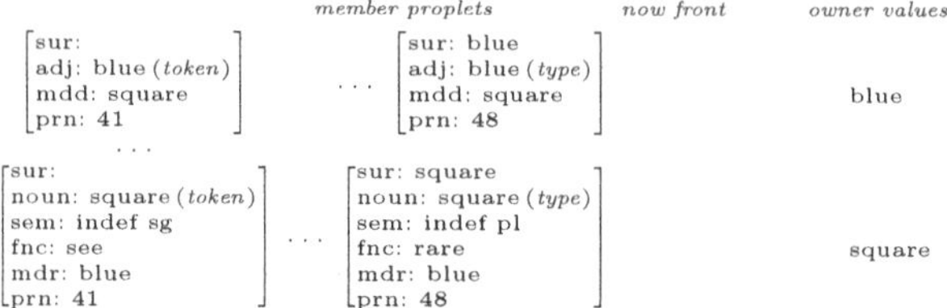

The vertical relation between the language and the context component shown in Sect. 5.1 reappears as a horizontal relation between proplets within token lines. The language proplets with the prn value 48 have non-empty sur slots, while sur slots of the context with the prn value 41 are empty. Reference by matching holds between the two *blue* proplets with the prn values 41 and 48 and similarly between the two square proplets. The distinction between the type and the token, here indicated after the core values, is usually left implicit.

The combination of the proplets *blue* and *square* by means of a functor-argument relation is coded by the features [mdd: square] and [mdr: blue], respectively. The noun proplet with the feature [sem: indef sg] is an indefinite singular, that with the feature [sem: indef pl] is an indefinite plural.

Next consider the same reference relation without language.

6.2 Reference by Matching Without Language

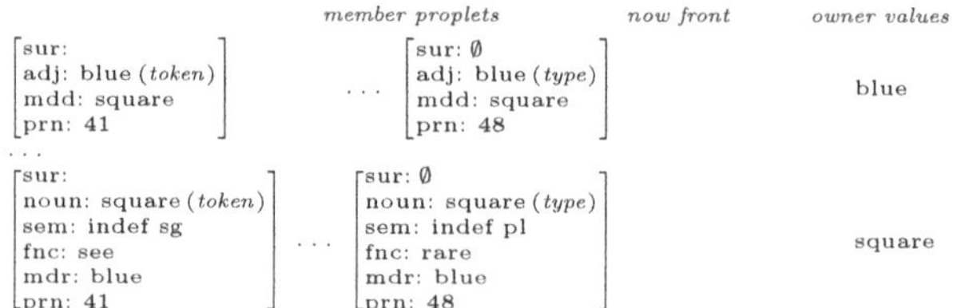

Here the reference relation holds between two nonlanguage contents – and not between a language content (meaning$_1$) and a nonlanguage content, as in Sect. 6.1.

Even though the reference relation is established between two individual proplet pairs in the same token lines, the combination into the complex content corresponding to blue square is accommodated as well[17]: in order to match, the two *blue* proplets must not only have the same[18] core value, but also the same

[17] Apparently, Aristotle struggled to reconcile reference with content combination (Modrak 2001).

[18] Disregarding the type-token distinction.

mdd continuation value, here square, and correspondingly for the mdr values of the two *square* proplets. Their fnc and prn values, however, are different.

Generalizing reference by matching to include referring with nonlanguage content results in the following constellations.

6.3 Constellations of Generalized Reference

1. *Nonlanguage content referring to nonlanguage content*
   Example: Agent identifies something seen with something seen before.
2. *Language content referring to nonlanguage content*
   Example: Agent describes a landscape in speak mode.
3. *Nonlanguage content referring to language content*
   Example: Agent identifies a current nonlanguage recognition with something it has read (for example, in a guide book) or heard about before.
4. *Language content referring to language content*
   Example: Agent describes what it has heard or read.

Cognitive agents without language are capable of reference constellation 1 only, while agents with language may use all four.

7 Reference by Pointing (Indexical)

The second reference mechanism of cognition is based on pointing. In natural language, it is illustrated by the indexical signs, such as the pronouns. The first step toward a computational implementation is the linguistic observation that the indexicals point at only five different parameters, namely (1) first person, (2) second person, (3) third person, (4) place, and (5) time.

In English, the pronouns I, me, mine, we, and us point at the parameter for first person, you points at the parameter for second person, and he, him, his, she, her, it, they, them point at the parameter for third person. The indexical adjs here and there point at the parameter for place. The indexical adjs now, yesterday, and tomorrow point at the parameter for time.

The indexical nouns pointing at the parameters of first, second, and third person are varied by grammatical distinctions. Consider the following examples illustrating grammatical variation in 1st person pronouns of English.

7.1 1st Person Pronouns Distinctions

sur: I	sur: me	sur: we	sur: us
noun: pro1	noun: pro1	noun: pro1	noun: pro1
cat: s1	cat: obq	cat: p1	cat: obq
sem: sg	sem: sg	sem: pl	sem: pl
fnc:	fnc:	fnc:	mdr:
mdr:	mdr:	mdr:	fnc:
nc:	nc:	nc:	nc:
pc:	pc:	pc:	pc:
prn:	prn:	prn:	prn:

The proplets all share the indexical pointer pro1 as their core value. The different cat values s1 (first person singular), p1 (first person plural), and obq (oblique) control verb agreement, preventing, for example, *Me saw a tree or *Peter saw we. *I sees a tree and *he see a tree are prevented by using the different cat values s1 (singular 1st person) and s3 (singular 3rd person).

Indexical nouns combine in the same way into propositions as proplets of the sign kind symbol or name. Consider the DBS analysis of English I heard you..

7.2 Representing I heard you. As a Language Content

sur: I	sur: heard	sur: you
noun: pro1	verb: hear	noun: pro2
cat: s1	cat: #n′ #a′ decl	cat: sp2
sem: sg	sem: past	sem:
fnc: hear	arg: pro1 pro2	fnc: hear
mdr:	mdr:	mdr:
nc:	nc:	nc:
pc:	pc:	pc:
prn: 71	prn: 71	prn: 71

The question raised by this example is how the indexical pointers pro1 and pro2 are to be interpreted pragmatically relative to a context of use.

This leads to the second step of modeling the indexical reference mechanism. It is based on combining a propositional content with a cluster of parameter values of the agent's current STAR (Hausser 1999 Sect. 5.3). The STAR is an acronym for (i) location (Space), (ii) time (Time), (iii) self-identity (Agent), and (iv) intended addressee (Recipient).

The STAR has two functions: (a) keeping track of the agent's current situation (orientation) and (b) providing referents for indexicals occurring in contents.[19] A STAR is coded as a proplet, with the A value serving as the core value and as the owner. In a word bank, a temporal sequence of STARs records the output of the agent's on-board orientation system and is listed as a token line.[20]

7.3 Token Line Example of STARs Defined as Proplets

member proplets				*now front*	*owner value*
S: kitchen	S: kitchen	S: living room	S: garden		
T: $t_1 - t_2$	T: $t_{2+1} - t_3$	T: $t_{3+1} - t_4$	T: $t_{4+1} - t_5$		
A: Sylvester	A: Sylvester	A: Sylvester	A: Sylvester		Sylvester
R: Speedy	R: Speedy	R: Tweety	R: Hector		
3rd:	3rd:	3rd: Speedy	3rd:		
prn: 63–70	prn: 71–78	prn: 79–82	prn: 83–87		

In addition to attributes represented by the letters of the STAR, there is a fifth, called 3rd, for third person indexicals. Though not required for the agent's

[19] Integrating the interpretation of indexicals into the agent's on-board STAR orientation may be seen as an enhancement of Montague (1973), who's sign-oriented approach uses arbitrary parameter values, i.e. i ϵ I for a moment of time and j ϵ J for a possible world (space, location), superscripted at the end of a lambda expression. Introducing additional parameters for 1st, 2nd, and 3rd person, as has been suggested, has been made light of by Cresswell's (1972, p. 4) joking proposal of a "next drink parameter." The parameter approach has resurfaced as "Variablism," i.e. the view that names and pronouns should be treated semantically as variables (Cumming 2008).

[20] Instead of the names John, Mary, etc., usually employed in linguistic examples, Sect. 7.3 uses the animation characters of Sylvester the cat, Speedy Gonzales the mouse, Tweety the bird, and Hector the dog, familiar from TV, as an aid to distinguish the individuals pointed at by indexicals.

basic orientation, 3rd is needed to provide the referent for items which are neither 1st nor 2nd person.[21] As indicated by the prn values, e.g. [prn: 63–70], several consecutive propositions may share the same STAR.

In communication, three perspectives on content must be distinguished (Hausser 2011, Chaps. 10, 11). The STAR-0 is the agent's perspective onto its current environment; it need not involve language. The STAR-1 is the agent's speak mode perspective onto stored content as required for language production; if ongoing events are reported directly, the STAR-1 equals the STAR-0. The STAR-2 is the agent's hear mode perspective onto language content as needed for the correct interpretation of indexicals. As an example of a STAR-0 perspective, consider the non-language content corresponding to I hear you.

7.4 Anchoring a Content to a STAR-0

```
[sur:        ] [sur:              ] [sur:        ]
[noun: pro1  ] [verb: hear        ] [noun: pro2  ] [S: kitchen     ]
[cat: s1     ] [cat: #n′ #a′ decl ] [cat: sp2    ] [T: 2013-09...  ]
[sem: sg     ] [sem: pres         ] [sem:        ] [A: Sylvester   ]
[fnc: hear   ] [arg: pro1 pro2    ] [fnc: hear   ] [R: Speedy      ]
[mdr:        ] [mdr:              ] [mdr:        ] [3rd:           ]
[nc:         ] [nc:               ] [nc:         ] [prn: 63        ]
[pc:         ] [pc:               ] [pc:         ]
[prn: 63     ] [prn: 63           ] [prn: 63     ]
```

This content differs from Sect. 7.2 because (i) it is nonlanguage (no sur values), (ii) the sem value of the verb is pres (present tense) rather than past, and (iii) a STAR is attached by having the same prn value as the content, here 63.

The STAR-0 shows the perspective of the agent Sylvester on his current environment. The S value specifies the location as the kitchen, the pres value of the verb points at the T value, the indexical pro1 points at the A value Sylvester the cat, and pro2 points at the R value Speedy the mouse.

Next Sylvester realizes the content in language by saying to Speedy I heard you. As time has moved, the language content Sect. 7.2 is anchored to a second, later STAR-0 with the prn value 71 (Sect. 7.3). From these two STAR-0, the agent computes the following STAR-1 perspective for the language content Sect. 7.2.

7.5 Speak Mode Anchoring to a STAR-1

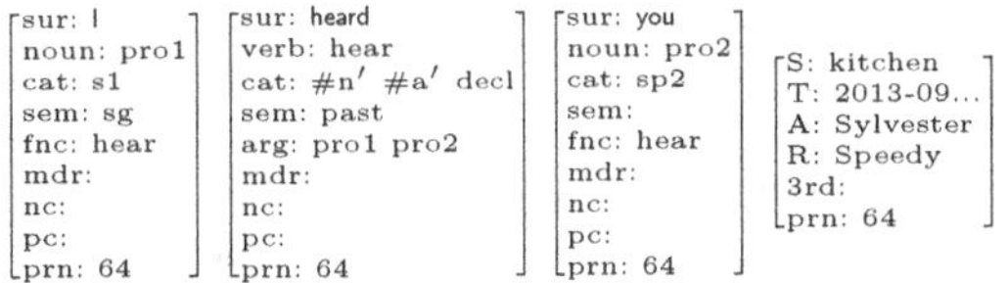

[21] According to King (2014), a context consists of time, location, agent, and world. In a STAR, the S corresponds to King's location, T to time, and A to agent. The counterpart to King's world are R (intended recipient, you) and 3rd (everyone and everything that is neither A nor R). However, DBS distinguishes between the STAR parameters as the agent's on-board orientation system and basis for interpreting indexicals, on the one hand, and the context as a selectively activated content in memory, on the other.

The agent's perspective is looking from his present situation back on the stored content Sect. 7.4 and encoding it in language. The content is connected to the agent's current STAR via the common prn value 64. The content differs from that of Sect. 7.4 in (i) the sem value past (rather than pres) of the verb proplet and (ii) the language-dependent sur values of the content proplets.

When the language content I heard you is interpreted by the addressee (recipient), Speedy the mouse uses the content of the language sign and its current STAR-0 to derive the STAR-2 perspective. The result is as follows.

7.6 STAR-2 Perspective in Hear Mode

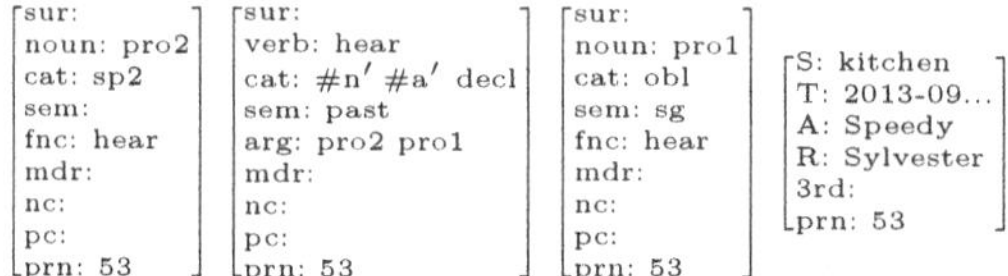

Speedy as the hearer uses his personal prn value and a different STAR: compared to the STAR of Sylvester, the A and R values are reversed and Sylvester's I heard you is reinterpreted by Speedy's STAR-2 perspective as you heard me.

8 Reference by Generalized Baptism (Name)

In DBS, the reference mechanism of the sign kind name is also implemented as a cognitive operation. It consists of (i) establishing *object permanence*[22] and (ii) generalized *baptism* based on cross-copying between a name and its referent.

Object permanence is implemented as identity by address. It is coded by using an address as the core value of the non-initial proplets, pointing at the proplet representing the initial appearance of the referent.

8.1 Object Permanence by Using Address

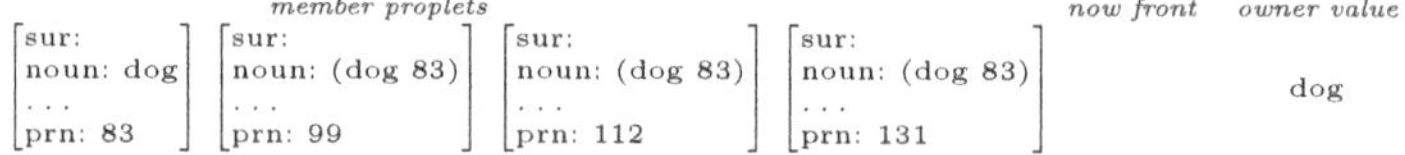

The different prn values indicate that each member proplet is part of a different proposition, allowing different continuation values. The core values (dog 83) of the non-initial member proplets point at the initial proplet, which is the referent and formally recognizable by its *non-address* core value.

A token line like Sect. 8.1 may contain several initial dog referents, each referring to another individual. They are distinguished by their different prn values and the address numbers of the associated coreferent proplets. This is

[22] This notion originated in cognitive psychology (Piaget 1954). It may be regarded as a non-truthconditional, non-modal counterpart to "rigid designators" (Kripke 1972).

sufficient for the agent to properly discriminate between different dog referents in cognition and between their sets of coreferent proplets, all in the same token line.

It is not sufficient, however, for language communication. This is because the prn values of referents are not synchronized between agent. What is needed is a name surface and an interagent consensus on which item(s) the name refers to. The consensus is simply achieved: the not yet initiated agent follows the practice observed because communication would break down otherwise.

The DBS implementation is based on (i) a lexical name proplet which has a sur(face) value but no core value and (ii) a referent proplet which has a core value but no sur value. The two proplets are supplemented by an event of generalized baptism which cross-copies the sur value of the name into the sur slot of the referent and the core value of the referent into core slot of the name.

8.2 Baptism as Cross-Copying

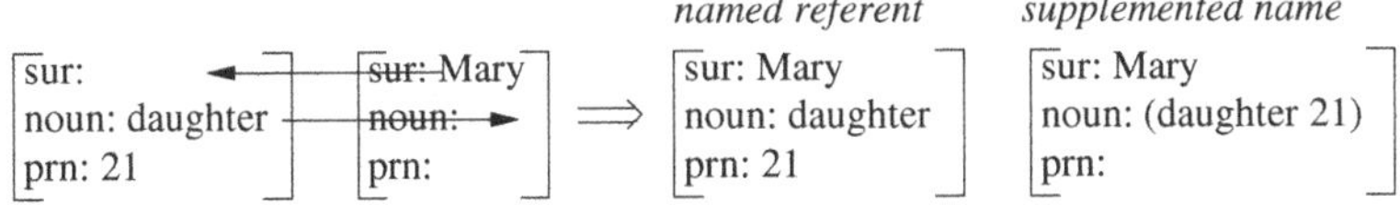

The named referent proplet is stored in the token line of the core value and used in the speak mode. The supplemented name proplet is stored in the token line of the surface and used in the hear mode.

The baptizing event is formalized as the following DBS inference.

8.3 Applying the Formal Baptizing Inference

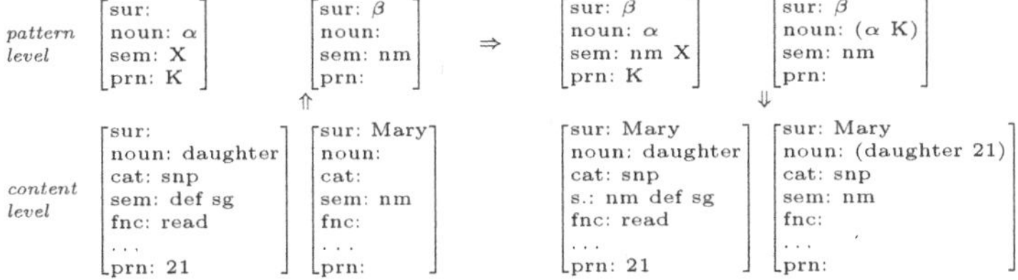

The third content proplet is the named referent, the fourth the supplemented name.

Consider the following word bank containing three referents named Mary, referring to the grandmother, the mother, and the daughter in a family. The token lines are in the alphabetical order *daughter, grandmother, Mary, mother.*

8.4 Name Referring with Multiple Referents

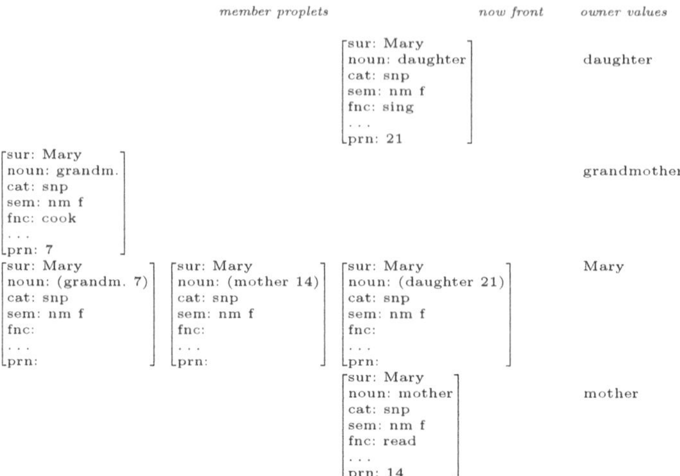

The member proplets show the result of three baptism inferences like Sect. 8.3. In the token line of *Mary*, each supplemented name proplet occurs only once.

Supplemented names are not written into the lexicon because a core value like (daughter 21) is not a convention of the natural language at hand. Instead it is the result of a *generalized* baptism: for applying the inference Sect. 8.3,[23] it is sufficient for the uninitiated agent to witness the use of a name. The supplemented name proplets in the *Mary* token line have a lexical quality insofar, however, as they have neither continuation nor prn values – like the lexical proplets resulting from automatic word form recognition.[24]

When the hearer interprets a sentence containing a name, the name activates the corresponding token line, here that of Mary. The choice between different referents, here the grandmother, the mother, and the daughter, may have one of the following results: (i) the chosen referent equals the one intended by the speaker (correct choice), (ii) does not equal the one intended by the speaker (incorrect choice), or (iii) no referent is chosen (inconclusive result). The choice between multiple potential name referents is usually not at random, however. Instead, the referent most suitable to the utterance situation will usually be the correct one. If uncertainty remains, the hearer may ask for clarification.

For an agent in the speak mode, there is no ambiguity.[25] Instead, the speaker selects the intended referent, e.g. (daughter 21). If the agent acquired

[23] As an agent-based approach, DBS does not use causal chains (Kripke 1972).

[24] Our computational reconstruction of reference with the sign kind of names, based on object permanence and generalized baptism, differs from other theories of naming such as the descriptive theory of proper names (Russell 1905) and the rigid designator analysis (Kripke 1972), which are based on a sign-based ontology (FoCL Sect. 20.4). The formal DBS treatment of name-based reference (Sect. 8.2) provides a simple, efficient procedural implementation suitable for building a talking robot.

[25] Even an ambiguity deliberately created in the speak mode ("diplomatic ambiguity," Pehar 2001) arises only for the hearer.

the appropriate name in the hear mode (Sect. 8.3), it is preserved in the word bank and may be used in the speak mode. If the agent is in the position to select and bestow a name, it is also available for realization.

9 Reference by Address (Coreference)

Coreference by address occurs with all three sign kinds. In name-based reference it is the only mechanism for relating the supplemented name to the named referent (Sect. 8.2). In reference by matching (symbol) and by pointing (indexical), in contrast, it is an additional method.

References

Biederman, I.: Recognition-by-components: a theory of human image understanding. Psychol. Rev. **94**, 115–147 (1987)

de la Briandais, R.: File searching using variable length keys. In: Proceedings of Western Joint Computer Conference, vol. 15, pp. 295–298 (1959)

Burgess, A.: Metalinguistic descriptivism for Millians. Australas. J. Philos. **91**, 443–457 (2012)

Chen, F.: Human factors in speech interface design. In: Designing Human Interface in Speech Technology, pp. 167–224. Springer, New York (2006)

Chisvin, L., Duckworth, R.J.: Content-addressable, associative memory. In: Yovits, M.C., (ed.) Advances in Computer Science, 2nd edn, pp. 159–235. Academic Press (1992)

Cormen, T.H., Leiserson, C.E., Rivest, R.L., Stein, C.: Introduction to Algorithms, 3rd edn. MIT Press, Cambridge (2009)

Cresswell, M.: The world is everything that is the case. Australas. J. Philos. **50**, 1–13 (1972)

Cumming, S.: Variabilism. Philos. Rev. **117**(4), 525–554 (2008)

Elmasri, R., Navathe, S.B.: Fundamentals of Database Systems, 6th edn. Benjamin-Cummings, Redwood City (2010)

Frege, G.: Über Sinn und Bedeutung. Zeitschrift für Philosophie und philosophische Kritik. **100**, 25–50 (1892)

Handl, J.: Entwurf und Implementierung einer abstrakten Maschine für die oberflächenkompositionale inkrementelle Analyse natürlicher Sprache, Diplom thesis, Department of Computer Science, University of Erlangen Nürnberg (2008)

Handl, J.: Inkrementelle Oberflächenkompositionale Analyse und Generierung Natürlicher Sprache. Inaugural dissertation, CLUE, Univ. Erlangen Nbg (2012). http://opus4.kobv.de/opus4-fau/frontdoor/index/index/docId/3933

Hausser, R.: Computation of Language, An Essay on Syntax, Semantics, and Pragmatics in Natural Man-Machine Communication. Artificial Intelligence Symbolic Computation. Springer, Heidelberg (1989)

Hausser, R.: Complexity in left-associative grammar. Theor. Comput. Sci. **106**(2), 283–308 (1992)

Hausser, R.: Foundations of Computational Linguistics. Human-Computer Communication in Natural Language. Springer, Heidelberg (1999). (3rd edn, 2014)

Hausser, R.: Memory-based pattern completion in database semantics. Lang. Inf. **9**(1), 69–92 (2005)

Hausser, R.: A Computational Model of Natural Language Commmunication: Interpretation, Inference, and Production in DBS. Springer, Heidelberg (2006)

Hausser, R.: Computational Linguistics and Talking Robots: Processing Content in DBS. Springer, Heidelberg (2011)

Kass, R., Finin, T.: Modeling the user in natural language systems. Comput. Linguist. **14**, 5–22 (1988)

King, J.: Speaker intentions in context. Noûs **48**(2), 219–237 (2014)

Kripke, S.: Naming and necessity. In: Davidson, D., Harmann, G. (eds.) Semantics of Natural Language, pp. 253–355. D. Reidel, Dordrecht (1972)

McKeown, K.: Discourse strategies for generating natural-language text. Artif. Intell. **27**, 1–41 (1985)

Modrak, D.: Aristotle's Theory of Language and Meaning. Cambridge University Press, New York (2001)

Montague, R.: The proper treatment of quantification in ordinary English. In: Hintikka, J., Moravcsik, J., Suppes, P. (eds.) Approaches to Natural Language, pp. 221–242. D. Reidel, Dordrecht (1973)

Newell, A., Simon, H.A.: Human Problem Solving. Prentice-Hall, Englewood Cliffs (1972)

Peirce, C.S.: Collected papers. In: Hartshorne, C., Weiss, P. (eds.). Harvard University Press, Cambridge (1931–1935)

Pehar, D.: Language and Diplomacy. Lambert, Saarbrücken (2001)

Pelczar, M., Rainsbury, J.: The indexical character of names. Synthese **114**, 293–317 (1998)

Piaget, J.: The Construction of Reality in the Child. Basic Books, New York (1954)

Quine, W.V.O.: Word, Object. MIT Press, Cambridge (1960)

Recanati, F.: Direct Reference: From Language to Thought. Blackwell, Oxford (1997)

Reimer, M., Michaelson, E.: Reference. In: Zalta, E. (ed.) The Stanford Encyclopedia of Philosophy, Winter 2014 edn. http://plato.stanford.edu/entries/reference/

Russell, B.: On denoting. Mind **14**, 479–493 (1905)

Steels, L.: The Talking Heads Experiment, limited Pre-edition for the Laboratorium Exhibition, Antwerpp (1999)

Weiss, M.A.: Data Structures and Problem Solving Using Java, 3rd edn. Pearson Addison-Wesley, Upper Saddle River (2005)

Wiener, N.: Cybernetics, or Control and Communication in Animal and Machine, 2nd edn. MIT press, Cambridge (1961)

SitAdapt: An Architecture for Situation-Aware Runtime Adaptation of Interactive Systems

Christian Herdin[1(✉)], Christian Märtin[2(✉)], and Peter Forbrig[1(✉)]

[1] Department of Computer Science, University of Rostock, Albert-Einstein-Str. 22, 18059 Rostock, Germany
{Christian.Herdin,Peter.Forbrig}@uni-rostock.de
[2] Faculty of Computer Science, Augsburg University of Applied Sciences, An der Hochschule 1, 86161 Augsburg, Germany
Christian.Maertin@hs-augsburg.de

Abstract. New technologies for monitoring biological and visual user data can be exploited to determine the current and changing emotional user states in HCI. This paper discusses SitAdapt, a flexible software architecture for situation analytics that evaluates various visual and biological signals and synchronizes them with eye-tracking and application meta-data in order to arrive at sound decisions for runtime adaptation of the interactive system in use. The SitAdapt system accesses the tools and resource repositories of the model- and pattern-based PaMGIS development framework.

Keywords: Model-based development · Pattern-based development · HCI-patterns · Situation analytics · Eye-tracking · Facial analysis · Emotion-tracking · Adaptive user interface

1 Introduction and Related Work

The use of wearable devices and visual methods for monitoring relevant physiological parameters in health, sport and fitness applications leads to the emergence of new opportunities for recognizing the emotional state, the mood and the stress level of users and for optimizing user experience by individual software adaptation in various other fields, e.g. e-business, human-machine-interaction, and gaming.

Architectures for real-time situation-adaptive HCI systems have to organize the observation and real-time-analysis of data signals gathered from mobile and stationary devices, simultaneously evaluate the task-related and emotional user state, measure the cognitive load and at the same time allow exploiting additional contextual and ambient data. Such architectures have the goal to adapt and tailor both, the user interface and the content, to individual users, interactive devices, and changing work contexts.

1.1 Emotion-Recognition in HCI

In contrast to the experimental and clinical acquisition and analysis of bio-signals for patient-monitoring mobile interactive application environments require unobtrusive

M. Kurosu (Ed.): HCI 2017, Part I, LNCS 10271, pp. 447–455, 2017.
DOI: 10.1007/978-3-319-58071-5_33

measurement and tracking methods with little interference into the freedom of action of the user. However, initial field studies in the forefront of major development projects in the domain of media-rich interactive systems, may permit the laboratory scale acquisition of signal types that up until now were reserved for medical purposes.

The automated evaluation and subsequent use of emotions by intelligent systems is in the focus of the field of Affective Computing, founded by Rosalind Picard. In [15] several research projects for recognizing stress, emotional engagement, and positive emotions are presented. Many of these approaches are based on visual recognition methods.

In [18] methods for measuring non-visual bio-signals are discussed. With the advent of wearable devices, such signals can also be used for emotion analysis. Such data sources include the analysis of psycho-physiological data for heart (ECG), muscle (EMG), eye (EOG) und dermal activity (EDG) [16].

In the field of usability engineering visual methods, like eye- and gaze-tracking, have been applied successfully for many years [20]. However, mature software systems for facial analysis in a very reliable way provide the grades and temporal changes of the base emotions of one or several users in real-time. The research in this area was initiated by Ekman [4] and in the meantime perfected in commercial systems, e.g. [14]. Such methods recognize the 44 typical facial muscle movements, the so-called action units (AUs), which happen in the eyebrow, eye, and mouth area. Combinations of AUs lead to the six human base emotions joy, fear, disgust, surprise, sadness and anger. Based on AU analysis new recognition methods arise steadily.

In [17, 19] new and even more precise emotion classifiers based on the analysis and combinations of facial micro-expressions (< ½ s) and macro-expressions (½ s to 4 s) are presented and discussed. They were derived from having intelligent recognition systems learn from the human assessment of emotion states of persons watched in video clips.

Visual methods can also be useful for measuring the user's stress level. In [12] a contact-free camera-based method is discussed that compares the facial expression to images acquired during vein-based measurements of the cognitive stress-level of test persons.

An example for a non-visual method for the reliable recognition of the major base emotions is the integration of embedded wearable devices into clothes, to detect short-term variations of the pulse rate [8]. For similar purposes also commercially available devices like the Empatica E4 wristband [6] can be used.

An advanced non-invasive method for emotion recognition based on visualization of the human brain activities is presented in [16]. The system that is tested in real human-machine interaction environments uses a head-mounted hood and applies fNIRS (functional Near Infrared Spectroscopy). The achievable results are comparable in quality to magnetic resonance measurements in clinical environments.

The effects of combining several measuring modalities for recognizing emotion levels are discussed in [9].

1.2 Situation Analytics as a Software-Engineering Approach for Adaptive HCI-Systems

The design of practical approaches for using dynamic situation-specific data acquired at runtime in order to build software adaptation mechanisms that react to changing user behavior is a challenge for software engineering.

In [3] the foundations for a strongly user- and situation-aware software engineering are formulated. Chang calls this new software engineering discipline situation analytics. Situation-aware systems observe the dynamic changes of the emotional and cognitive user behavior during the use of interactive software systems.

It is the goal of this innovative software engineering discipline to devise system architectures and tools for analyzing the cognitive and emotional behavior of users within their individual context and to apply intelligent methods and technologies for a steadily running process-accompanying situation analysis. Such practical systems must be able to synchronize, evaluate and exploit the various acquired data at runtime and select and perform the appropriate dynamic adaptations. Thus, varying user requirements and preferences can be recognized and reacted upon, while users cope with their interactive tasks. Chang introduces the *Situ* framework that offers comprehensive modeling and runtime support for situation-adaptive software systems. In [13] the functional language *Situ*^{f} is used to demonstrate, how typical situations can be captured in software development environments and how situation-specific software structures and behavior can be re-used.

In our previous work [10, 11] a prototypical system was introduced that observes users through visual and biophysical channels in order to recognize their detailed emotional reactions while interacting with a prototypical dynamic web application and to exploit the changing user mood for runtime adaptation of the application.

Recently, we have expanded the original system into a development environment for situation-aware adaptive systems. The SitAdapt system and its architecture will be presented in Sect. 2. The architecture enables the system to cooperate with the model- and pattern-based user interface development framework PaMGIS [7]. In addition, SitAdapt uses a runtime-component for intelligent evaluation of the emotion-tracking data and pattern-triggering for dynamic user interface adaptation.

1.3 Adaptive Systems in HCI

Adaptivity and adaptability in HCI systems can be viewed from different angles. With the introduction of systems that exploit individual emotions, cognitive loads and experiential preferences of the user within its dynamically changing ambient environment for software adaptations, the psychological and cognitive aspects can be addressed.

However, the more technical aspects also have to be considered, when system architectures and sustainable development approaches for contemporary interactive system environments are designed and implemented. As the use of interactive software in the everyday life of users is increasing steadily, also the number of devices and their different user interfaces is growing. The programming and the design of user interfaces for interactive applications that are able to migrate between different devices and device types is a challenging problem, because so many different contexts of use (user, platform, and environment) have to be supported [2]. The development of these multiple-adaptive migratory user interfaces (MAMUIs) confronts developers with complex requirements such as task continuity and adaptability to context changes [21].

The PaMGIS framework that is used by the SitAdapt system offers the development and runtime support for such multiple-adaptive migratory user interfaces and can react on context changes in the user's environment in real-time.

In general, three different types of adaption can be distinguished in the field of user interfaces [1, 21]:

- Adaptable user interfaces. The user customizes the user interface to his or her personal preferences.
- Semi-automated adaptive user interfaces. The user interface provides recommendations for adaptions. The user has to decide, whether he or she wants to accept the recommendation or not.
- Automated adaptive user interfaces. The user interface automatically reacts to changes in the context-of-use.

SitAdapt in co-operation with the PaMGIS framework covers semi-automated as well as automated user interface adaptation. In order to arrive at really situation-aware systems, however, SitAdapt in addition to interacting with purely user interface modeling aspects also has to take into account the more content-related static and dynamic system aspects that are typically covered by domain or business models of interactive applications.

2 SitAdapt: A Model-Based Adaptive Architecture with Pattern Triggering

In this chapter, we discuss the *SitAdapt* system that implements an architecture for runtime-support of model-based interactive applications with dynamic adaptation in real-time.

For this purpose, the *PaMGIS (Pattern-Based Modeling and Generation of Interactive Systems)* development framework [7] was extended with runtime access functions. SitAdapt accesses the PaMGIS framework, which is based on the CAMELEON-Reference framework (CRF) [2]. The CRF serves as the de-facto reference architecture for the model-based and model-driven development of user interfaces. The CRF proposes the workflow for the developer on how to transform an abstract user interface over intermediate model artifacts into a final user interface [2]. The PaMGIS structure with the incorporated CRF models is shown in Fig. 1.

The abstract user interface model (AUI) is generated from the information contained in the domain model of the application that includes both, a task model and a concept model. The AUI mainly includes the specifications of the abstract user interface objects. In the domain model and the originally rendered AUI the user interface is still independent of the usage context. After the completion of AUI modeling, the AUI model can be transformed into a concrete user interface model (CUI). The information of the context model and the structure of the dialog model are exploited by this process.

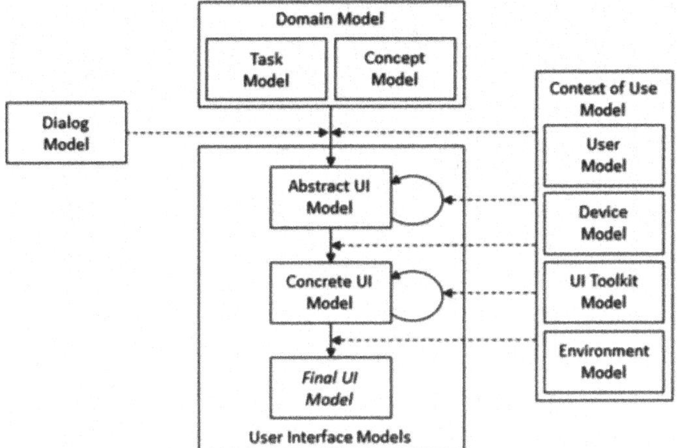

Fig. 1. Overview of the PaMGIS models and their interrelations

For defining the dynamic aspects of the user interface, PaMGIS uses a dialog model. The dialog model is based on dialog graphs that were originally introduced by the TADEUS system [5].

In the next step the final user interface model (FUI) is generated automatically from the CUI model. Depending on the target implementation language, the FUI must either be compiled, or can be executed directly by an interpreter (Execute UI). The specification of the models is done in conformity with the Extensible Markup Language (XML) [2].

PaMGIS serves as the development and implementation environment for SitAdapt applications and as their initial launch platform. It is also used for context and device-specific adaptations whenever the application is started from or migrated to a new target platform.

2.1 SitAdapt Runtime Environment

SitAdapt uses the models and HCI-patterns, accumulated during the development of the interactive system in use and/or residing in the resource repositories as the resulting artifacts of earlier interactive system developments. The SitAdapt process allows for contextual adaptation of the applications at runtime. Thus, user experience, work quality and efficiency can be optimized.

Our earlier work on situation analytics has led to the construction of a prototypical interactive application development environment including situation-aware software adaptation [10, 11]. The SitAdapt runtime architecture, see Fig. 2, discussed in this paper, in addition provides a sound architectural basis for structuring the situation-aware adaptation process, accessing the model and pattern resources, and selecting the chain of necessary parameters changing dynamically over the runtime of the application.

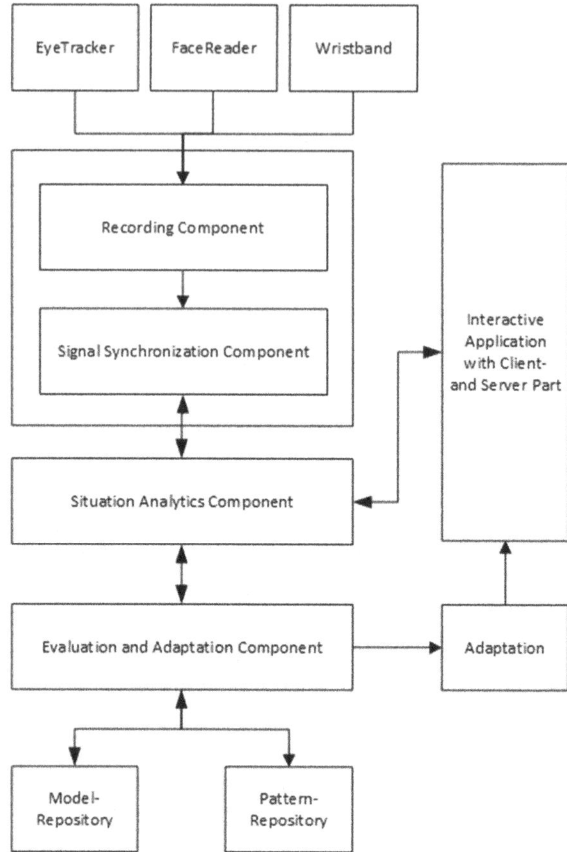

Fig. 2. SitAdapt architecture

The recording component contains the following technologies for data recording:

- Eye- and gaze-tracking of the users and assignment to the interaction objects and design elements of the user interface with the Tobii eye-tracking system [20].
- Emotional video facial expression recognition analysis with the FaceReader software from Noldus [14], which supports six basic facial expressions (happy, sad, scared, disgusted, surprised, and angry). The system also recognizes the gender and an age interval for a user.
- Empatica E4 wristband for heart-beat and stress-level analysis [6].

SitAdapt currently implements an architecture for runtime-support of model-based interactive applications with dynamic adaptation in real-time (Fig. 2) with the adaptation applied at the final user interface (FUI) modeling-level.

All available data from the eye-tracking system, Facereader and the wristband are communicated to the SitAdapt framework over an application programming interface (API). The eye- and gaze-tracking data are synchronized in real-time with the signals for the six basic emotions, the gender and age range of the user, the wristband data (electro-dermal activity sensor, photo-plethysmography sensor) by the signal synchronization component. The situation analytics component recognizes the current situation. This component evaluates the data provided by the various sensors and the metadata and state information provided by the interactive application in order to analyze the situation at a given moment.

Depending on the respective situation and emotional state of the user, the evaluation and adaptation component makes a rule based decision with the help of the data from the situation analytics component about whether and in which way the user interface of the interactive application is dynamically adapted. To configure the adaptation, the component also has access to the domain model, i.e. the task and concept model, of the target application.

For configuring the adaptation, the evaluation component supplies a set of situation patterns, pattern subcomponents and/or templates from the PaMGIS pattern repository, which is used both for modifying the client- and the server part of the target application, depending on the adaptation requirement.

2.2 Example for SitAdapt Operation

SitAdapt is currently used mainly for testing prototypes from the e-business domain. The situation analytics component steadily evaluates the current system of the user and the target application. It can therefore quickly react with individual adaptations to problems encountered by the user during interaction with the application or to new user requirements triggered by a previous adaptation of the user interface.

A typical scenario that can be handled by SitAdapt is the following:

1. The situation analytics component recognizes a change in the application context: the user has finished his or her shopping tour, has put several items into the shopping cart and has entered the checkout counter of the e-shop.
2. The emotion level for happy is high, however a significant level of sadness is also present.
3. The pulse rate is higher than 15 s earlier and the gaze of the user moves steadily from the shopping cart with the selected items to the total price of the purchase indicated at the checkout counter. The mouse button is near the buy button, but the user still hesitates to press the button.
4. A situation pattern is activated that recognizes that the total price is above a certain level. The pattern triggers the display of a beautifully styled voucher with a text indicating that the voucher is valid only, if the user finalizes the purchase within the next ten minutes.

2.3 SitAdapt Implementation

The current SitAdapt test system and evaluation environment, was created with the ASP.NET MVC Web Application framework developed by Microsoft. The example applications implemented for this paper use the open source JavaScript framework

Angular JS and can access the tools and repositories of the pattern- and model-based development framework [11].

All the necessary modifications for supporting the runtime adaptation had to be integrated into the PaMGIS framework components. For building the task models and designing the situation patterns needed for the current e-business example applications, the modeling tools and the PPSL (PaMGIS pattern specification language) could be used.

3 Conclusion and Future Work

New technologies for capturing and observing bio-physical and visual user data make it easier to determine the current and changing emotional and cognitive user status in human-technology interaction. Examples of this are visual emotion detection in the face [17, 19] as well as the evaluation of cardio, brain, muscle, and eye signals [16, 18]. Frequently, features or visual micro- and macro-expressions composed of consecutive single signals are formed, which facilitate the reliable assignment of emotional states.

These newly acquired measurement data can be used to improve information and suggestions for the dynamic adaptation of the interactive software. Currently we are integrating these new measurement data into the SitAdapt system.

In this paper we have discussed the present implementation of the SitAdapt system that uses a well-structured architecture for communicating with the PaMGIS MB-UIDE. In order to allow for real-time adaptation functionality, we had to modify several components of the framework.

The quality of the adaptation process and the rules will be enhanced over time by a deep-learning-based optimization component that evaluates the selected adaptation choices for different applications and users. This component is currently under development and will be a part of future releases of the SitAdapt architecture.

References

1. Akiki, P.A., et al.: Integrating adaptive user interface capabilities in enterprise applications. In: Proceedings of the 36th International Conference on Software Engineering (ICSE 2014), pp. 712–723. ACM (2014)
2. Calvary, G., Coutaz, J., Bouillon, L., et al.: The CAMELEON Reference Framework (2002). http://giove.isti.cnr.it/projects/cameleon/pdf/CAMELEON%20D1.1RefFramework.pdf. Accessed 25 Aug 2016
3. Chang, C.K.: Situation analytics: a foundation for a new software engineering paradigm. Computer **49**, 24–33 (2016)
4. Ekman, P., Friesen, M.V.: The Facial Action Coding System: A Technique for The Measurement of Facial Movement. Consulting Psychologist, Palo Alto (1978)
5. Elwert, T., Schlungbaum, E.: Modelling and generation of graphical user interfaces in the TADEUS approach. In: Proceedings of the Eurographics Workshop in Toulouse, France, 7–9 June, pp. 193–208 (1995)
6. Empatica Website. https://www.empatica.com/e4-wristband. Accessed 10 Jan 2017

7. Engel, J., Märtin, C., Forbrig, P.: A concerted model-driven and pattern-based framework for developing user interfaces of interactive ubiquitous applications. In: Proceedings of the First International Workshop on Large-scale and Model-Based Interactive Systems, Duisburg, pp. 35–41 (2015)
8. Guo, H.W., et al.: Short-term analysis of heart rate variability for emotion recognition via a wearable ECG device. In: Proceedings of the ICIIBMS 2015, Okinawa, Japan, pp. 262–265. IEEE (2015)
9. Lingenfelser, F., Wagner, J., Andre, E.: A Systematic discussion of fusion techniques for multi-modal affect recognition tasks. In: Proceedings of the ICMI 2011, Alicante, Spain, 14–18 November, pp. 19–25 (2011)
10. Märtin, C., Herdin, C., Rashid, S.: Situationsbewusste, patternbasierte Adaption interaktiver Anwendungen durch Auswertung von Emotions- und Biosignal-Daten. In: Mayr, H.C., Pinzger, M. (eds.): INFORMATIK 2016, LNI, Gesellschaft für Informatik, Bonn (2016)
11. Märtin, C., Rashid, S., Herdin, C.: Designing responsive interactive applications by emotion-tracking and pattern-based dynamic user interface adaptation. In: Kurosu, M. (ed.) HCI 2016, Part III. LNCS, vol. 9733, pp. 28–36. Springer, Cham (2016). doi:10.1007/978-3-319-39513-5_3
12. McDuff, D.J., et al.: COGCAM: contact-free measurement of cognitive stress during computer tasks with a digital camera. In: Proceedings of the CHI 2016, San Jose, USA, 7–12 May 2016
13. Ming, H., Chang, C.K.: Can situations help with reusability of software? In: Kurosu, M. (ed.) HCI 2016, Part I. LNCS, vol. 9731, pp. 598–609. Springer, Cham (2016). doi:10.1007/978-3-319-39510-4_55
14. Noldus Inc. FaceReader 6 Application Programming Interface, Technical Note
15. Picard, R.: Recognizing stress, engagement, and positive emotions. In: Proceedings of the IUI 2015, March 29 – April 1, Atlanta, USA, pp. 3–4 (2015)
16. Pollmann, K., Vukelić, M., Birbaumer, N., Peissner, M., Bauer, W., Kim, S.: fNIRS as a method to capture the emotional user experience: a feasibility study. In: Kurosu, M. (ed.) HCI 2016, Part III. LNCS, vol. 9733, pp. 37–47. Springer, Cham (2016). doi:10.1007/978-3-319-39513-5_4
17. Qu, F., Wang, S.-J., Yan, W.-J., Fu, X.: CAS(ME)^2: a database of spontaneous macro-expressions and micro-expressions. In: Kurosu, M. (ed.) HCI 2016, Part III. LNCS, vol. 9733, pp. 48–59. Springer, Cham (2016). doi:10.1007/978-3-319-39513-5_5
18. Schmidt, A.: Biosignals in human-computer interaction. In: Proceedings of the Interactions, pp. 76–79, January-February 2016
19. Sumi, K., Ueda, T.: Micro-expression recognition for detecting human emotional changes. In: Kurosu, M. (ed.) HCI 2016, Part III. LNCS, vol. 9733, pp. 60–70. Springer, Cham (2016). doi:10.1007/978-3-319-39513-5_6
20. Tobii. Tobii Studio SDK. Developer Guide, 8 May 2013
21. Yigitbas, E., Sauer, S., Engels, G.: A model-based framework for multi-adaptive migratory user interfaces. In: Kurosu, M. (ed.) HCI 2015, Part II. LNCS, vol. 9170, pp. 563–572. Springer, Cham (2015). doi:10.1007/978-3-319-20916-6_52

Adapting User Interface Models by Transformations Based on UI Patterns

Mathias Kühn(✉) and Peter Forbrig

University of Rostock, Albert-Einstein-Str. 22, 18051 Rostock, Germany
{mathias.kuehn,peter.forbrig}@uni-rostock.de

Abstract. Models used for software designs are artifacts of today's development culture. Generators and interpreters for models reduce the implementation effort and open a broader range of applications. This also is true for user interface models in any context of use (The Context of Use: http://www.w3.org/2005/Incubator/model-based-ui/XGR-mbui/#the-context-of-use.). UI models that are designed independently of end users together with varying platforms in alternating environments can be used in many contexts. Of course, derived transformations can be complex and are not as simple as needed. Applying reusable solutions to model-based user interface specifications implies transformations that could be performed automatically and adapt user interfaces to specific contexts of use. UIs can benefit from proven structures that are commonly used in cross-domain software. Applying patterns to model-based UI specifications is the focus of the paper. An example shows how UIs can be adapted by transformations based on patterns that are part of relevant specifications.

Keywords: Model-based user interfaces · UI patterns · Context-specific transformations

1 Introduction

Designing software for a broad range of applications is a challenging task. Different contexts of use force to adapt implemented designs accordingly. These adaptations can be based on transformations that could be performed at runtime by interpreters that are used in specific contexts. Design specifications based on models often are used to reduce the implementation effort. This also is true for models that describe the end users interface to the implemented functions. User interfaces (UIs) enable to access software by any user on any platform in any environment [12]. Designs that allow transforming model-based UI specifications to every context of use would further reduce the effort. In order to achieve this goal, UI specifications also need to be adapted.

Transformations for design adaptations can be based on general reusable solutions for commonly recurring problems. Design patterns [5] have an impact on object-oriented designs that also can be structures for interactive systems. Of course, UI designs can benefit from structures that are proven in cross-domain software [15]. Nevertheless, UI model transformations need to be specified for adaptations. Extending UI specifications with notations for pattern applications can reduce the effort for specifying corresponding

M. Kurosu (Ed.): HCI 2017, Part I, LNCS 10271, pp. 456–466, 2017.
DOI: 10.1007/978-3-319-58071-5_34

transformations. Additionally, transformations at runtime depend on specific contexts that adapt solutions to users, platforms, and environments.

The paper is structured as follows: the next section considers model-based UIs together with the CAMELEON Reference Framework [2] that presents an approach for transformations of UIs to any context of use. Additionally, patterns for interactive systems and user interfaces are considered that can be used more explicitly with model-based languages. The following section considers an example that illustrates the idea as implementation of the model-based language UsiXML [10]. Also a pattern-based extension for this language is proposed for the reason of applicability. Section 4 highlights the approach in detail. Benefits and drawbacks are considered that focus on potentials and limitations of the proposed approach. The last section summarizes the paper and gives an outlook on tools that could be improved by the approach.

2 Related Work

Model-based UIs are essential artifacts for operating various interactive devices together with different surfaces. UIs can be specified with model-based languages that are independent of specific contexts. Additionally, UI patterns can implicitly be part of these specifications. Work in the area of model-based UIs together with patterns mostly considers design-time specifications [4, 6, 8, 14]. Pattern specification together with runtime interpretation of corresponding UI models [9, 16] need to be considered more extensively. Transformations based on patterns can be performed within given contexts that adapt UIs accordingly.

Patterns for object-oriented designs [5] were introduced in 1994 and describe structures that have been proven in various software systems from then until now. Applying these patterns to specific contexts helps to get solutions for problems on structures, behaviors, and creations of object-oriented implementations. Patterns for interaction [17, 18] were identified for designs that either focuses the development (based on evolutions of UIs) or the user (based on changes of requirements) of interactive systems. Of course, these patterns target the design of user interfaces directly.

One of the problems that pattern application can solve relates to the navigation within UIs. UI patterns like stepwise, hub-and-spoke, and pyramid (see Fig. 1) can be applied that describe different ways of navigating in the system. Other UI patterns can for instance specify layouts, complex data visualizations, and beautifications.

Navigational patterns allow specifying dialog structures that can later be generated to source code automatically. Applying patterns allows adapting generated UIs to different contexts of use.

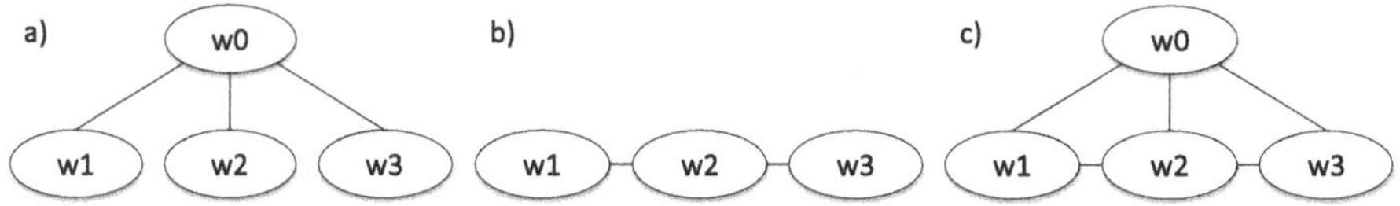

Fig. 1. Visualization of UI pattern applications for (a) hub & spoke, (b) stepwise, and (c) pyramid represented by navigation structures for windows w0, w1, w2, and w3

User interfaces can be specified with model-based languages like MARIA [13] and UsiXML [10, 11] that allow specifying UIs on different levels of abstraction. Both languages allow specifications of models for tasks and abstract & concrete UIs that are grounded on the CAMELEON Reference Framework (CRF). The CRF [2] targets the transformation of UI models from as well as into different contexts. UsiXML additionally allows model-based specifications of contexts, mappings, and transformations. Unfortunately, both languages do not allow specifying UIs together with pattern applications. However, patterns need to be applied within specifications that are based on those languages for adapting UIs by corresponding transformations.

Approaches like Role-Based User Interface Simplification (RBUIS) [1] and Multi-Adaptive Migratory User Interfaces (MAMUI) [20] also are grounded on the CRF and consider adaptations of UIs. In RBUIS UIs are adapted by minimizing features-sets and optimizing layouts for increasing usability. In MAMUI UIs are adapted by an Adaptation Manager that adapts models for task features, navigations, and layouts for improving user experience. However, approaches like those do not consider UI patterns for deriving transformations that could adapt UIs.

Another problem in the area of pattern specification is that formal languages are missing. The Pattern Language Markup Language (PLML[1]) was introduced in 2003 and is used in approaches like [19], but it lacks in formality what makes it problematic for deriving transformations. In contrast to this, DelTa [3] is a visual language that allows describing patterns more formally. However, in our approach we decided to extend UsiXML for applying patterns explicitly as part of specifications. This allows deriving transformations that affect reifications and abstractions of the CRF. These transformations can for instance be made with ATL [7] which is based on QVT[2] and allows describing model-to-model transformations that are needed in the context of CRF.

3 Questionnaire Survey Application

The following section considers an example that illustrates the idea of the proposed approach. Both instances focus the specification of patterns together with UI specifications that later are used for context-dependent transformations. Additionally, screenshots give an impression of resulting instances. An extension of the model-based language UsiXML is used for the reason of applicability.

[1] PLML: http://www.cs.kent.ac.uk/~saf/patterns/CHI2003WorkshopReport.doc.
[2] QVT: http://www.omg.org/spec/QVT/.

3.1 Simple Example

Let's consider a small example that illustrates the idea of the proposed approach. The model-based language UsiXML is used for specifying structures of user interfaces. The language additionally is extended for specifying patterns that are interpreted within specific contexts later. Patterns can be specified by enveloping targeted component specifications with a special XML element. This element is used for applying patterns by performing pattern-related transformations. If necessary, roles within the patterns can be introduced as XML attributes as well.

```
<uimodel>
    <cuimodel>
        <pattern name="stepwise">
            <window name="w0"/>
            <window name="w1"/>
            <window name="w2"/>
        </pattern>
    </cuimodel>
</uimodel>
```

Fig. 2. UI pattern stepwise applied to extended UI model specification

Figure 2 shows an application of the navigational UI pattern stepwise within a concrete user interface model specification that contains three windows. The pattern is applied to components that directly are enveloped by this XML element what are the three windows. These windows can later be extended by elements that are related to the specified pattern. For instance, they could be extended by trigger components (e.g. buttons) that allow users to navigate between them.

Additionally, the dialog structure can also be created for reified windows that refer the behavior of corresponding UIs. However, this could be implemented in different ways for users that interact via speech gestures. Such pattern-related transformations can be performed within given contexts at runtime and for any context at design time. Patterns also can be replaced by others what would lead to other transformations. This has to be done by designers that specify corresponding model-based UIs. Later tools automatically take changes into account.

3.2 Extended Example

Let's consider another more complex example. Someone is conducting a customer survey and is planning to use questionnaires for gathering data. Such questionnaires can be specified as interactive forms that are used within data collection applications later. Additionally, each question of the questionnaire is specified as a single form that contains the question (e.g. label) as well answers (e.g. radio button, check box), for instance with choice questions. Participants are asked about personal information (gender, age group, etc.) and about information on a certain product (satisfaction, etc.).

Figure 3 shows an abbreviated specification of UIs that later are used as interactive forms. The forms contain four questions of the questionnaire. Some of the widgets that can be used together with CUI model specifications are labels and radio buttons. These are parts the following instance.

```
<uimodel>
    <cuimodel>
        <pattern name="stepwise" direction="forward">
            <window name="w0">
                <label>What is your gender?</label>
                <!-- choice -->
            </window>
            <window name="w1">
                <label>How old are you?</label>
                <!-- choice -->
            </window>
            <pattern name="stepwise">
                <window name="w2">
                    <label>How often do you use the product?</label>
                    <!-- choice -->
                </window>
                <window name="w3">
                    <label>How well do the product meet your needs?</label>
                    <!-- choice -->
                </window>
                <!-- more questions -->
            </pattern>
        </pattern>
    </cuimodel>
</uimodel>
```

Fig. 3. Extended UI model specification with UI patterns combined

Figure 3 shows a part of the extended UI model specification for interactive forms of a questionnaire. Two patterns are combined into each other that provide a certain navigation structure within the final user interface. At first, participants will answer questions on personal information. According to the UI specification, they are not allowed to go back when they have finished entering individual information. This is specified by the attribute direction of the pattern element. The value forward is used for parameters of the UI pattern stepwise.

After entering personal information, participants are asked about information on the product itself. They are allowed to go back when they have finished entering any information. This is specified by the enveloping pattern element. No value is specified for the direction attribute what will be interpreted as unspecified and allows to navigate forward as well as backward by default. It is easy to change the navigation structure just by exchanging applied patterns. For instance, exchanging the topmost UI pattern stepwise with pyramid would lead to adding links to each form that refer to an extra form. This extra form is generated automatically and holds links to the specified forms as well.

Regarding the UsiXML extension, UI patterns in general should be specified by XML elements (tags) that directly refer to patterns by their attribute. Of course, patterns also can be applied for beautifications and other purposes. However, the referred user interface elements are enveloped by the XML element for patterns. The corresponding attribute refers to the semantics of the corresponding pattern instance.

The specification of Fig. 3 can be used for generating UIs to different context of use. Patterns are implemented to the reified windows of the final UI specification. Additionally, the pattern-specific dialog structure is implemented for navigating users of FUI instances. Following this, specifications of these transformations do not need to be designed. Figure 4 show examples of some generated UIs.

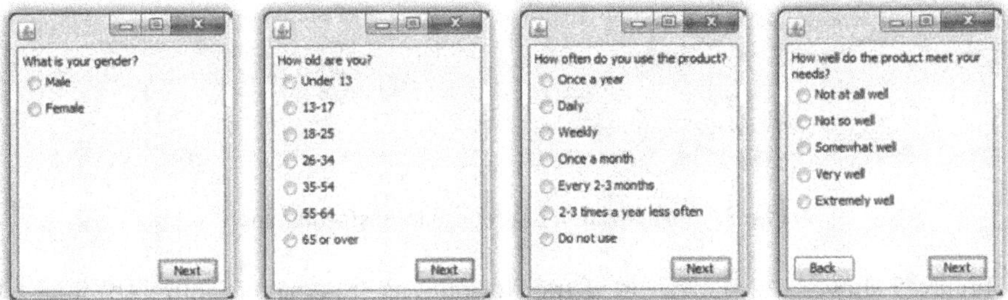

Fig. 4. Screenshots of some generated UIs

Figure 4 shows some screenshots of the generated UIs for the specification in Fig. 3. The windows are adapted to users with Desktop PCs that can use buttons for navigating as it is intended by the patterns. The buttons as well as the dialog structure are generated automatically. Adaptations for users that use vocal interfaces would imply speech gestures instead of buttons together with an equal dialog model. However, UI patterns are applied within given contexts by transforming UI model specifications to final UI instances that depend on pattern-specific dialog models.

4 Approach

The following section discusses the proposed approach in a more abstract way using the discussed example of a transformation. A visualization illustrates modifications that are made while performing adaptations. It also is described how the CRF is applied to achieve mentioned transformations. The approach as well as the corresponding tool support is discussed afterwards. All visualizations are relating to model-based languages in general. Following this, UsiXML is one candidate for applications (compare Fig. 3 with 5a and Fig. 4 with 5b).

FUI model instances are not covered by model-based languages for UIs. Code generators or interpreters can be used for transforming CUI to FUI model instances. According to this, windows of CUI model specifications can for instance be transformed to JFrame implementations in Java programming language. However, an example of a reification transformation is presented in the following figure.

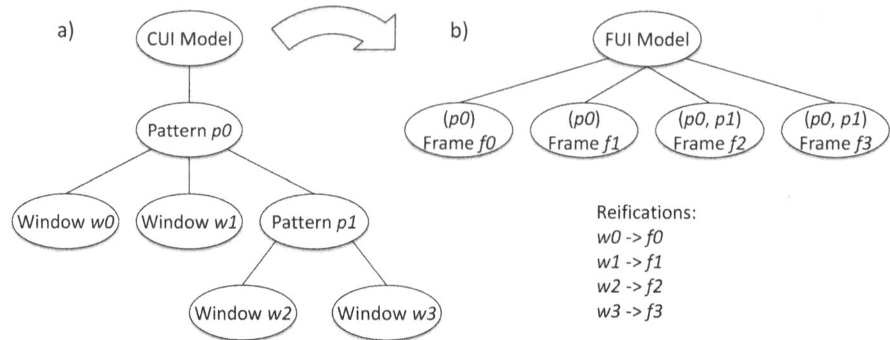

Fig. 5. Visualization of proposed transformations

Figure 5 shows a visualization of transforming an (a) concrete into a (b) final UI model specification. The CUI model specification considers four windows (w0, w1, w2, w3) that are referenced by different patterns (p0, p1). These patterns are part of the CUI model specification and are used for generating pattern-specific structures within the final UI. When performing context-dependent transformations of the CUI model specification, the final UI model can for instance be extended by triggers that allow navigating through windows as specified by the corresponding pattern.

Transformations that result in FUI model specifications are based on CRF. The CRF considers needed reifications for gaining UI instances on specific platforms. These reifications also target applied patterns that need to be implemented accordingly. The following figure shows the relation between patterns and transformations that is implicitly be shown in the figure above.

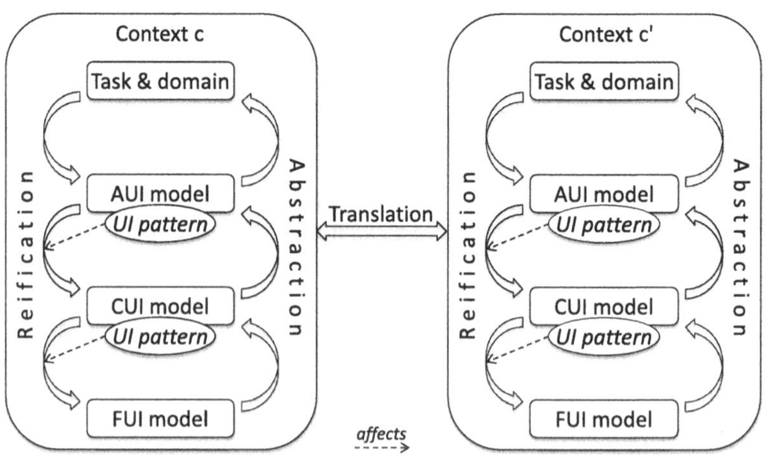

Fig. 6. CAMELEON Reference Framework adapted to the approach

Figure 6 shows the CRF adapted to the proposed approach containing models that can be transformed into each other. The main transformation types are abstraction (concrete to abstract models), reification (abstract to concrete models) and translation (models from one context to another on the same level of abstraction). Abstractions and reifications are considered for a single context only. This is needed to adapt UIs for instance by interpreters at runtime. UIs in general are considered to be on different levels of abstraction (abstract, concrete, final UI).

The level of task & domain would target patterns for user activities and object-oriented structures that rather implicitly is focus of the paper. However, UI patterns can be part of AUI/CUI model specifications and explicitly have an impact on the reification transformations to the underlying model levels. These transformations depend on contexts of use and adapt UI models to runtime use. On abstraction, UI patterns used in CUI models can be moved to AUI models. Applied UI patterns are substituted by their context-dependent implementations on reification.

Any specific UI pattern can be applied either in AUI or in CUI models. Additionally, reified models can be extended with other UI patterns that are more context-specific and meet the end-users needs more. The resulting transformations are based on applied UI patterns that adapt models accordingly. An example of such a transformation is given in Fig. 8 that implements a rule for transforming stepwise pattern instances from AUI to CUI model specifications for graphical UIs.

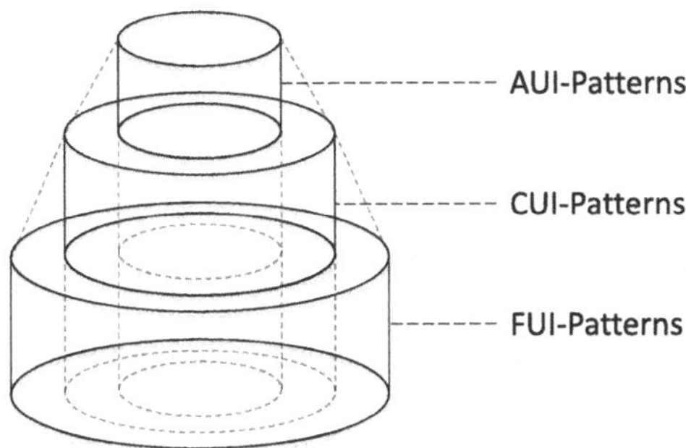

Fig. 7. Visualization of relations between UI pattern applications

Figure 7 shows a visualization of relations between UI patterns that are applied to different UI model specifications. UI patterns that are applied to AUI models remain in CUI models and can be extended with more context-specific patterns. Additionally, UI patterns that are applied to CUI models remain in FUI models and also can be extended with other patterns. However, most patterns can be applied to FUI model specifications that is relating to the CRF. Instances of individual pattern-based solutions depend on any context that they are applied to what is the effect of pattern applications in general.

The approach proposed in the paper considers explicit specifications of UI pattern applications. These specifications allow more context-specific transformations and adapt UIs accordingly. Tools can support designers in specifying pattern applications. According to UsiXML, this can simply be made with XML-Editors that also can be

Text-Editors. Tools that interpret specifications at runtime need to transform instances when contexts of use change. Data that need to be collected for this can be gained by sensors that have to be available for specific platforms.

Transformations can be complex and need to be specified for performing them. Applying patterns explicitly can help to reduce the effort for specifying these transformations. Figure 8 gives an example of such a transformation in ATL. OCL[3] is used for specifying transformations of model instances.

Patterns and components are of type element. Elements can have child nodes that are of type element as well. Components can for instance be transformed to windows of CUI model specifications. However, applications of UI pattern stepwise for AUI model specifications are transformed to CUI model instances. Pattern applications are implemented to sequences of windows. Sequence is an OCL type for collections of ordered elements. These elements can be patterns or components of AUI model instances, respectively.

```
rule StepwiseToCuiModel extends PatternToCuiModel {
    from
        stepwise : IN!stepwise
    to
        windows  : Sequence(OUT!window)
    do {
        for (e in stepwise.elements) {
            if (e.oclIsKindOf(IN!component)) {
                windows <- windows.append(thisModule.ComponentToWindow(e, stepwise.direction));
            }
            if (e.oclIsKindOf(IN!pattern)) {
                windows <- windows.union(thisModule.PatternToCuiModel(e));
            }
        }
    }
}
```

Fig. 8. Example of a transformation specification in ATL

Figure 8 shows an ATL rule for transforming applied stepwise UI patterns from AUI to CUI model specifications within the context of graphical UIs. This transformation rule represents a way of performing model-to-model transformations that are based on patterns. Tools for runtime interpretation of CUI/AUI model specifications need to perform more context-depended transformations like this. Context model specifications can only be gained within specific contexts of use that those tools have to interpret.

The example above demonstrates two kinds of transformations for implementing UI patterns within one rule. One step is to transform instances from abstract to concrete models that are parts of reifications. The other step is to apply patterns to any transformed instance. Someone can imagine that both steps can be performed in any order, but the final results need to be equal. Tools can apply patterns to present instances first and reify them afterwards or they perform reifications first and apply patterns to reified instances then. However, both steps are made with one rule in the example above.

Transforming abstract specifications together with applied patterns to their reified instances is a general assumption for generating adapted UIs within the approach.

---

[3] OCL: http://www.omg.org/spec/OCL/.

Patterns are implemented within concrete specifications. Of course, other patterns can be applied again to reified models, but patterns of abstract specifications are already implemented within concrete instances. Another idea for pattern applications can be to implement UI patterns only on transforming CUI models to FUI models. This can prevent reapplications of patterns and make implementations more comprehensible.

In the end, pattern applications could be commented within source codes. However, replacing applied patterns by more context-specific patterns would also be easier if their specifications explicitly remain in reified instances. Pattern implementations would only be part of code generators then.

5 Conclusion and Future Work

The paper introduces an approach for specifying UI patterns together with UI models on different levels of abstraction. These pattern-related specifications target the transformation of corresponding models that can be used for adapting UIs to specific contexts of use. UI patterns together with UI specifications reduce the effort for specifying transformations that are needed for adapting UIs. Additionally, adaptations can increase usability and improve user experience of resulting generated UIs.

Specifications and transformations can be made with different languages and different tools that allow adapting UIs. The proposed approach suggests a UsiXML extension for specifying UI models together with UI patterns. It is assumed that patterns can be specified on different levels of abstraction and can be extended with more context-specific patterns in reified models. Comparing to [4, 6], the approach does not consider pattern replacements for adapting UIs to specific contexts. Instead of this, it is assumed that transformations implement patterns to their reified instances. An example of a transformation rule is given in ATL (see Fig. 8) and refers to needed tool support.

Further investigations need to be done on giving adequate tool support for applying UI patterns into UI model specifications. An option can be that designers are aware of any pattern that could be applied into specifications. This implies that they also need to be aware of abstraction levels for pattern applications. Another option can be that designers are supported with a common UI design tool that allows applying patterns to UIs for instance with wizards. However, made specifications need to be interpreted on any platform later. This leads to generating UIs which are adapted to a given context.

There might be the problem that patterns could not be adapted to a given context. For instance, UI patterns that are related to graphical UIs cannot be implemented to vocal UIs. This can be a problem if designers specify patterns that only can be applied to graphical UIs. According to this, replacing patterns can be a solution for making UIs more context-dependent. However, tool support needs to be fine-grained relating to this problem what makes it more difficult for designers again.

References

1. Akiki, P.A., Bandara, A.K., Yu, Y.: Engineering adaptive model-driven user interfaces. IEEE Trans. Softw. Eng. **42**(12), 1118–1147 (2016)
2. Calvary, G., Coutaz, J., Thevenin, D., Limbourg, Q., Bouillon, L., Vanderdonckt, J.: A unifying reference framework for multi-target user interfaces. Interact. Comput. **15**, 289–308 (2003)
3. Ergin, H., Syriani, E., Gray, J.: Design pattern oriented development of model transformations. Comput. Lang. Syst. Struct. **46**, 106–139 (2016)
4. Forbrig, P., Saurin, M.: Supporting the HCI aspect of agile software development by tool support for UI-pattern transformations. In: Bogdan, C., Gulliksen, J., Sauer, S., Forbrig, P., Winckler, M., Johnson, C., Palanque, P., Bernhaupt, R., Kis, F. (eds.) HCSE/HESSD -2016. LNCS, vol. 9856, pp. 17–29. Springer, Cham (2016). doi:10.1007/978-3-319-44902-9_2
5. Gamma, E., Helm, R., Johnson, R., Vlissides, J.: Design Patterns: Elements of Reusable Object-Oriented Software, 1st edn. Prentice Hall, Upper Saddle River (1994)
6. Javahery, H., Seffah, A., Engelberg, D., Sinnig, D.: Migrating user interfaces across platforms using HCI patterns. In: Multiple User Interfaces: Cross-Platform Applications and Context-Aware Interfaces, pp. 241–259. Wiley (2004)
7. Jouault, F., Allilaire, F., Bézivin, J., Kurtev, I., Valduriez, P.: ATL: a QVT-like transformation language. In: Proceedings of OOPSLA, pp. 719–720 (2006)
8. Kühn, M.: Applying Patterns when generating code: a model-based design approach. In: Proceedings of MIDI (2015)
9. Kühn, M., Forbrig, P.: Applying UI patterns for modeling dialogs. In: Proceedings of 2nd PAME/VOLT@MODELS Workshop, pp. 13–17 (2016)
10. Limbourg, Q., Vanderdonckt, J., Michotte, B., Bouillon, L., López-Jaquero, V.: USIXML: a language supporting multi-path development of user interfaces. In: Bastide, R., Palanque, P., Roth, J. (eds.) DSV-IS 2004. LNCS, vol. 3425, pp. 200–220. Springer, Heidelberg (2005). doi:10.1007/11431879_12
11. Limbourg, Q., Vanderdonckt, J., Michotte, B., Bouillon, L., Florins, M., Trevisan, D.: USIXML: a user interface description language for context-sensitive user interfaces. In: Proceedings of AVI Workshop, pp. 55–62 (2004)
12. Paterno, F., Santoro, C.: One model, many interfaces. In: Kolski, C., Vanderdonckt, J. (eds.) Proceedings of CADUI, pp. 143–154. Springer, Dordrecht (2002)
13. Paterno, F., Santoro, C., Spano, L.D.: MARIA: a universal, declarative, multiple abstraction-level language for service-oriented applications in ubiquitous environments. ACM Trans. Comput. Hum. Interact. **16**(4), 1–30 (2009)
14. Seffah, A., Gaffar, A.: Model-based user interface engineering with design patterns. J. Syst. Softw. **80**(8), 1408–1422 (2007)
15. Sinnig, D., Gaffar, A., Reichart, D., Forbrig, P., Seffah, A.: Patterns in model-based engineering. In: Proceedings of CADUI, pp. 197–210 (2004)
16. Taleb, M., Seffah, A., Abran, A.: A UsiXML proposal for a pattern-oriented and model-driven architecture for interactive systems. In: Proceedings of ADVCOMP, pp. 24–29 (2013)
17. Tidwell, J.: Designing Interfaces, 2nd edn. O'Reilly Media, Sebastopol (2010)
18. Van Welie, M.: Interaction Design Pattern Library. http://www.welie.com/patterns/
19. Vanderdonckt, J., Simarro, F.M.: Generative pattern-based design of user interfaces. In: Proceedings of PEICS, pp. 12–19 (2010)
20. Yigitbas, E., Sauer, S., Engels, G.: A model-based framework for multi-adaptive migratory user interfaces. In: Kurosu, M. (ed.) HCI 2015. LNCS, vol. 9170, pp. 563–572. Springer, Cham (2015). doi:10.1007/978-3-319-20916-6_52

A POMDP Design Framework for Decision Making in Assistive Robots

Ioannis Kostavelis(✉), Dimitrios Giakoumis, Sotiris Malassiotis, and Dimitrios Tzovaras

Centre for Research and Technology Hellas, Information Technologies Institute, 6th Km Charilaou-Thermi Road, 57001 Thermi, Thessaloniki, Greece
{gkostave,dgiakoum,malasiot,tzovaras}@iti.gr

Abstract. This paper proposes a theoretical framework that determines the high-level cognitive functions for multipurpose assistive service robots, required to autonomously complete their tasks. It encompasses a probabilistic POMDP based decision-making strategy that provides constant situation awareness about the human and the environment by associating the robot awareness about the user with specific clusters of robotic actions. To achieve this, a method for designing POMDP models is presented herein ample to define decision making policies suitable to resolve assistive tasks through a series of robotic actions. The proposed POMDP design methodology compensates the partial and noisy sensor input acquired from the robot sensors by foreseen mitigation strategies on the robot's decisions when a software component fails. The theoretical work presented herein is assessed over well defined robotic tasks and proved capable to operate in realistic assistive robotic scenarios.

Keywords: Decision making · Assistive robots · POMDP · Partial observability · Robot situation awareness

1 Introduction

The autonomy of the contemporary assistive robots relies on their capacity to decide on their own actions based on their cognitive functionalities and realize these actions using their robotic planning mechanisms [1]. However, robot autonomy is not an end in itself in the field of Human Robot Interaction (HRI) but rather a way to support bidirectional interaction using robot actuator movements, communication and representational schemas [2]. Based on this statement, the modelling procedure of the robot cognitive functions, which will eventually determine the decision making mechanism, should take into consideration that the realization of an inferred robotic action will alter the status of the environment and the interaction schema with the user, making thus the robot an active participant in the human-robot cohabitation rather than a passive observer. Following this notion, Markov Decision Processes (MPDs) constitute an efficient solution for decision making and have beeb proved adequate to solve

M. Kurosu (Ed.): HCI 2017, Part I, LNCS 10271, pp. 467–479, 2017.
DOI: 10.1007/978-3-319-58071-5_35

simplified problems with diminished uncertainty [3]. However, it is typical for humans in real life scenarios to make decisions under uncertainty since not all the facts are measurable and not all the required observations are constantly available. When it comes to robotic application development, complete situation awareness is not feasible since the environment should be modeled with limited robot sensors and the acquired sensor observations are noisy; in such applications, the robot belief uncertainty about the current state of the human, the environment and the robot itself is broadened. Partially Observable Markov Decision Processes (POMDPs) are able to model the uncertainties stemming from realistic situations better than the MPDs, while their main difference is that the world's state in the POMDP is not known to the robot; instead, a probabilistic observation corresponding to the state is received from the environment after performing each action [4].

The paper at hand aims to model the high-level cognitive functions of an assistive social robot by formulating a decision making mechanism based on POMDP models. Specifically, an explicit methodology for designing POMDP models is presented herein, comprising a generalized theory in the domain of robot intervention in assistive tasks. This method capitalizes on robot's various perception modalities, yet partially available, to infer an action plan considering clustered type of robotic actions. Contrary to the existing POMDP applications where the designed POMDP models are constrained to resolve specific tasks by selecting optimal robotic actions, the proposed solution tackles the problem from an alternative view point, where the selection of the robotic actions is tightly related to the robot's awareness about the human condition, which is reflected into robot's alert levels. Subsequently, the task to be resolved is the propagation of the robot's states to a lower level of alert.

2 Related Work

2.1 POMDPs as Prompting Systems

A profusion of laborious research has been conducted in the filed of health technology by introducing systems for elderly, possibly with cognitive or physical disabilities, who want to continue living independently in their own homes [5]. Under this scope POMDPs have been either utilized as prompting systems assisting people in their daily life by verbally motivating them to successfully complete specific activities [6], or integrated in robotic agents modelling their action planning mechanism to fulfill their assistive task. The design of prompting systems that react on time while exploit sensing and modelling mechanisms is a laborious work. One exemplar application is the COACH system [7] which uses computer vision to monitor the progress of a person with dementia washing her/his hands and prompts only when necessary by employing a POMDP acting as a temporal probabilistic model based on the sensed observations. However, the COACH system is tailored to specific tasks and requires great amount of expert knowledge for re-designing the POMDP model in order to be useful for different tasks with generalization capacities. The authors in [8] tried to introduce a more generalized framework for building prompting systems using POMDP models by incorporating psychologically justified expert background knowledge. Specifically this method incorporated Interaction Units [9] which is a psychologically justified description of the task and the particular environment where this task is to be carried out that can be generated from empirical data. This is then combined with a specification of the available sensors to build a working prompting system based on POMDPs. However, the automation of this procedure for the production of context aware POMDP models is also limited and still requires the expertise of a psychologist. As an attempt to diverge from the phycological modeling the authors in [10] proposed a probabilistic relational model encoded in a relational database allowing non experts in POMDP design to fill in the necessary details of a task using a simple and intuitive procedure. Although this method proved capable to automatically produce POMDP models for assistive applications, yet the probabilistic database framework was limited to the scale of the problem that could be modeled, also deteriorating the prompting capacities to specific tasks that require well restricted operational environment.

2.2 POMDPs in Robotic Applications

In the service robots domain, the POMDPs have been widely utilized to increase the robot autonomy in human populated environments. This has been achieved in multiple applications levels, concerning examples such as navigation and manipulation. The first attempt for using POMDPs in robotic tasks is the work discussed in [11], where action space was simplified in basic and discretized moves of the robot while the received observations were abstract representations of the environment. The authors in [12] solved a more complicated aspect of the navigation problem using POMDPs, where a point robot was considered by diminishing the state and action space accordingly. The authors proved that a simplified action space during the POMDP design can closely resemble the efficacy of a model with greater resolution in the action space, while also the policy computation time was discussed. In a more sophisticated work, the authors in [13] utilized a hierarchical POMDP framework for robot navigation in the context of which the localization, the local planning and obstacle avoidance was tackled. In this work the occupancy grid map comprised the state space of the robot, while the actions space consisted of a hierarchical discrimination of robot rotational and translation capabilities. In [14], a POMDP model has been developed to determine an objective function that considers both probability of collision and uncertainty at the goal position, providing an alternative path planning decision policy. Moreover, a proof of the usage of POMDPs in a great variety of robotic applications is the work described in [15]. In this application, the authors utilized a POMDP model as a prompting system in a probabilistic planning of a bimanual robot that was targeted to unfold clothes. At this stage, it can be inferred that although the aforementioned methodologies were addressing their targeted functionalities competently, they were limited to their specific task. This can be partially explained by the fact that the computational complexity of solving a POMDP problem instance grows exponentially with the size of the state and action space and thus it is difficult to concurrently model precisely the state and the action space for the human, the robot and the environment. Therefore, specific works tackle the issue from a different view point where the POMDPs are utilized as robot control mechanisms that orchestrate the robots behaviour in a variety of application tasks. In the work introduced in [4], the authors developed hierarchical POMDP models focusing in the abstraction of the action space linking the hierarchy levels with actions tightly related with folded subordinate POMDP models. In this way the authors achieved to design easily manageable smaller POMDP models dedicated to specific robotic actions instead of modeling a global model which is hardly to be solved by the existing POMDP solvers [16]. This way, multiple tasks can be modeled using the POMDP theory. In a more contemporary work [17], the authors introduced a decision making and control supervision system suitable to operate on multi-modal service robots. This bridges the gap of abstraction between designed POMDP models and the physical world concerning actions, while multi-modal perception is processed to extract measurements uncertainty. Complementary to the aforementioned works, a method that determines the human robot interaction with assistive robots through POMDPS is the one described in [18]. The authors designed a POMDP model where the human satisfaction from the collaboration with the robot is the key factor to model the interaction, while the status of the user in terms of awareness and stress determines the human's participation in the execution of the task. However, during the design of the POMDP model, the target task should be explicitly analysed in the expected states of both the human and the robot, comprising an efficient yet hard to be modeled solution.

Considering the existing solutions, the added value of the proposed work is the determination of a theoretical framework that describes an explicit POMDP design methodology. The formulated POMDP models are human-centric and drive the cognitive functions of multipurpose social assistive robots. This statement is based on the principal that the robot should be always on alert and aware about the human cohabitant, while the decided actions should reflect the level of robot's alert. Through this procedure, the robotic actions are tightly related to the amount of assistance that is required to offer to the cohabitant. Specifically, when the robot's level of alert about the human is increased, the planned robot actions should be more intensive and interventional in order the robot to become complacent about the human, while in intermediate levels of robot alert more discreet actions should be planned.

3 Proposed Method for Decision Making Design

3.1 Robotic-Wise POMDP Formulation

For the proposed problem formulation, it is essential to interpret the generic POMDP design theory [19] in a robotic-wise manner, considering the explicit assistive robot scenarios where the problem domain comprises the environment, the human and the robot. Towards, this direction, the discrete POMDP is designed as a tuple $P = \{S, A, \Omega, R\ O, T, b_0\}$ where:

- $S = \{s_1, s_2, ..., s_n\}$ denotes the **States** space that determines the condition of the environment, the human and the robot at each time t.
- $A = \{a_1, a_2, ..., a_n\}$ denotes the **Actions** space that encloses all the actions that the robot is able to perform so as to interact with the human and the environment.
- $\Omega = \{\omega_1, \omega_2, ..., \omega_n\}$ denotes the **Observations** space that comprises the robot perception input from the human and the environment, yet under the assumption that an observation ω partially describes the state of the previous entities.
- $R = (A, S)$ comprises a **Reward** function that determines the restrictions imposed by penalizing or endorsing specific robotic actions (A) during the interaction with the human and the environment (S).

The challenging part during the design of POMDPs is the determination of the probability distributions of the initial state (b_0), the states transitions (T) and the observations (O), something that makes the POMDP designers to frequently rely on phycologists to empirically quantify these values under assumptions that are difficult to be assessed.

- The probability distribution of the *initial state* comprises the likelihood about the environment, the human and the robot to be in specific state s at the time $t = 0$ such as:
$$b_0(s) = P(s_0 = s) \tag{1}$$
- The probability distribution of the *state transition* comprises the probability of propagating to state s' given that the domain is in state s and the robot selects an action a and the its respective expression is provided as:
$$T(s, a, s') = P(s_t = s'|s_{t-1} = s, a_{t-1} = a) \tag{2}$$
- The probability distribution of the *observations* comprises the uncertainty for the perception of an observation ω considering that the environment and the human are in state s and the robot has performed the action a, also expressed as:
$$O(s, a, \omega) = P(\omega_t = \omega|s_{t-1} = s, a_{t-1} = a) \tag{3}$$
- The probability distribution about the *current state* of the environment, the human and the robot assuming to be in s, being partially observable through observation ω. Since it is not possible to define the current state with complete certainty a belief distribution is maintained to express the history of the robotic actions and state transitions of the domain such as at time t, the robot, the human and the environment are at state s considering the sequence of past combination of actions and observations as follows:
$$b_t(s) = P(s_t = s|\omega_t, a_{t-1}, \omega_{t-1}, ..., a_0, b_0) \tag{4}$$

The explicit definition of the aforementioned probabilities indicate the design of a well-formed POMDP model, the solution of which can be achieved through the existing solvers [16]. The outcome of this solution is an action selection policy π that maximizes the sum of the expected future reward up to specific time. This policy comprises a mapping from the current state belief probability to the action space A. Given the computed policy, the robot can select an optimal action by computing its belief state based on the following update rule:

$$b'(s') = \frac{O(s', a, \omega) \sum_{s \in S} T(s, a, s') b(s)}{P(\omega | a, b)} \tag{5}$$

where b' is the updated belief, b is the given belief at the previous time step and (a, ω) is the latest combination of robot action and observation.

3.2 Design Methodology of POMDP Models

Following the aforementioned theory it is revealed that the precise algorithms required for the computation of optimal policies are defined by an exponential computational growth. A single step of value iteration to compute the next selected action is on the order of $|C_t| = O(|A||C_{t-1}|^{|\Omega|})$, where $|C_{t-1}|$ corresponds to the number of components required to represent the next selected action at iteration $t-1$, while the computational burden is estimated by taking into consideration the number of iterations in each step for the $O(|S|^2 A||C_{t-1}|^{|\Omega|})$. This exponential growth for the computation of the optimal policy constrains the experts to design POMDP models limited to solve specific robotic tasks, since the number of states and actions grows drastically when trying to model real life applications scenarios by considering an abundance of environment, human and robot states, and many robotic actions that needs to be determined.

In this scope, the proposed work aims to introduce a POMDP designing methodology suitable for the decision making of multipurpose, social assistive service robots, that will be capable of resolving multiple assistive tasks, as derived in our specific case from computer vision based human activity monitoring.

This is achieved by abstracting the state and action space given the awareness of the robot for the user. Specifically, since the state space is partially observable, it can only be conceptually grouped by defining scalable blocks of states that correspond to distinct levels of robot alert $\overline{S} = \{S_H, S_M, S_L\}$. Herein, the state space is conceptually partitioned in three levels of robot alert namely *High*, *Medium* and *Low*. The states that may belong to the S_H level of robot alert group correspond to phases in the assistive task that the human requires drastic assistance from the robot. The S_M levels of robot alert define the group of states within the task, in which the robot has already been engaged in an assistive task and the levels of awareness about the human have been moderated. Last, the S_L levels of robot alert outlines these states where the assistive scenario has been resolved, the required intervention is diminished and the robot is complacent about the status of the human.

The additive value of the conceptual partitioning of the state space is that it indirectly defines groups of robotic actions, the context of which is related to the type of robot intervention required for the scenario denouement, given the current robot awareness about the human. Towards this direction, the action space is partitioned as follows $\overline{A} = \{A_T, A_C, A_M\}$. The A_T set corresponds to highly interventional robotic actions necessitated when the environment and the human is at the S_H; the A_C set reflects more discreet robotic actions when the status of the domain is assessed to be at S_M and the A_M consists of rather passive robotic actions, in essence applied when the levels of robot alert about the human are diminished, i.e. S_L. More precisely, the A_T set involves all the robotic actions required to fulfil a robot engagement to resolve a specific task i.e. navigation, manipulation, grasping, hand over, which is orchestrated by a task-specific planner. The A_C set of actions is less invasive than the A_T set and comprises the bidirectional communication planning required for the communication with the user supporting modalities such as dialogues, user interface displays, gestures and even notification with augmented reality. The A_M set of actions corresponds to the monitoring components of the robot triggering functionalities suitable for assessment of the current status of the human and the environment, such as human detection and tracking, human cognitive and physical abilities assessment, activities interpretation and objects detection and recognition. It is revealed that this set of actions is passive, since the robot monitors the human and the environment, while the observations acquired from these actions is expected to alter the state of the domain. Although it is evident that complete situation awareness is not feasible since the environment and the human should be modeled and monitored with limited robot sensors and the acquired sensor observations are noisy, the designed POMDP model aims to propagate the system to the S_L set of states by selecting the corresponding set of actions. This feature is regulated in the proposed design methodology by carefully assigning the values at the reward function, endorsing thus the system respectively. In particular, a positive reward value is passed to the model when the selected action transits the system from higher to lower level of robot alert state, while a negative reward value is passed to the model when the selected action tends to bring the system to a higher level of robot alert. A uniform distribution is applied in the rewards function when the system passes from medium to medium levels of robot alert states. Through this methodology, the POMDP model is designed in a human-centric manner, where the partial observable set of states correspond to the status of the human and the environment, while the set of actions are solely robotic related resulting thus, in a prompting system aiming to draw decisions about the robot intervention in order to reduce the awareness of the robot about the human and thus, solve the assisting scenario.

The principal behind the design of such a POMDP model is outlined in Fig. 1, where a conceptual representation of the levels of robot alert along with the actions space and the observations space is graphically illustrated. Specifically, the figure represents all possible triplets (s, a, ω) of actions, states, and observations with respect to their probability of occurrence. The actions space

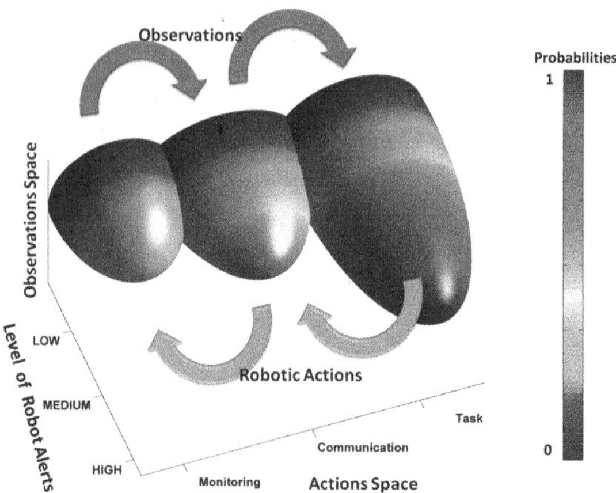

Fig. 1. The conceptual representation of the design methodology. The observations incline to transit the system to higher level of robot alerts while the decided robotic actions tend to switch the system to lower level of robot alert.

is divided into three major categories which subsequently effect the conceptual clustering of the states of the domain in terms of robot alert levels. On the contrary, observations remain the free parameter that dictates the probability of simultaneous occurrence for each triplet. Additionally, the observations probabilities of occurrence are graphically illustrated in terms of a color map in Fig. 1. To this end, the immanent trend of the observations is to increase the robot's alert level i.e. transition to a state that belongs to high level of alert, while the system through actions attempts to stabilize the system in states that belong to a group of lower level of robot alert.

4 An Exemplified Case Study

At this point, it should be stressed that the work presented herein aims at defining a POMDP model-design framework, suitable for decision making in assistive service robotic applications, while the exact solver used for the policy π is out the scope of this work, as we assume that any solver is adequate to converge in a solution given a well structured POMDP model [16]. Since, to the best of our knowledge no similar work that focuses on the design methodology of POMDP models for robotic applications exists and the current applications recall the superior knowledge of the experts for such a design, a direct comparison of our method is not feasible. However, we append herein a realistic modelling of an assistive scenario utilizing our POMDP design methodology, while the validity of the derived decision making policy has been assessed with simulation and proved adequate to resolve the scenario successfully.

A challenging objective for the contemporary service robots living with elderly is to monitor their daily activities, interpret hazardous situations and to notify a relevant or ask for external help. More specifically, we consider the scenario of robot assisting elderly people during cooking activities where it is common phenomenon to forget electric appliances turned on. Specifically, during cooking activity the robot observes the human gathering the products required to prepare a specific meal. The robot monitors this activity and in case that some objects-materials are missing it asks the human if it should fetch those objects and if in cast that it receive an affirmative response it acts accordingly. In the normal situations where all objects have been successfully fetched the robot proactively examines the state of their storage place i.e. fridge, cupboards and identifies their state. The robot once again communicates with the human to notify him/her about the situation and if it is necessary it is engaged in a robotic action to close a forgotten appliance. In hazardous situations the robot assesses the risk, and decides whether external help is required utilizing an external communication channel. It is apparent that the aforementioned scenario is very complex and requires advanced decision making from the robot in order to decide when and how to intervene in order to assist the human.

The flow of this scenario can be ideally described by a state diagram that conjugates the states of the domain with the robot actions as exhibited in Fig. 2,

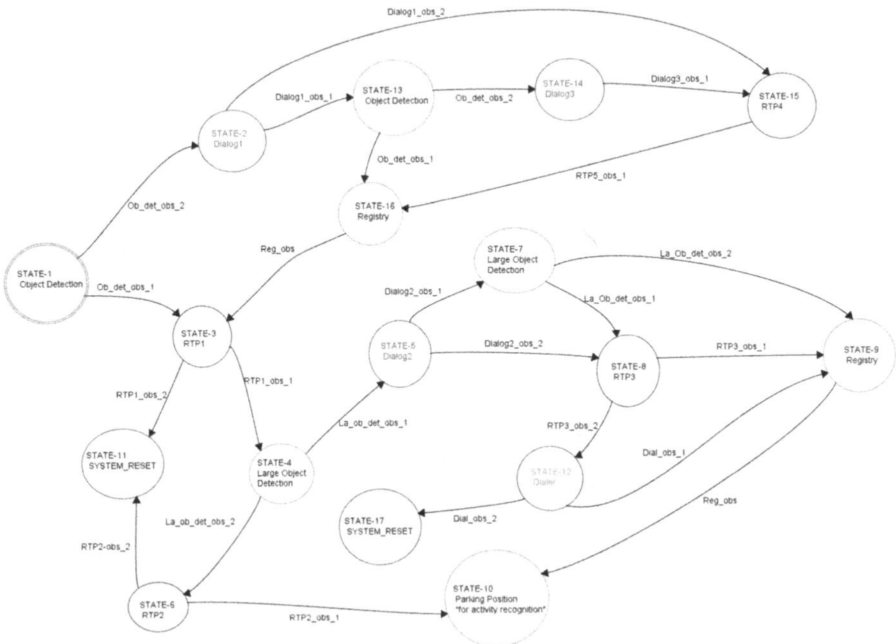

Fig. 2. An indicative state diagram that supports the robot decision making for assisting elderly during daily cooking activities. In this diagram, the task related robotic actions are highlighted with blue, the communication with the humans related actions are highlighted with magenta and the human and environment monitoring robotic actions are highlighted with green. (Color figure online)

the aim of which is to identify all the required robot actions need to be modeled. In this figure, the task related robotic actions are highlighted with blue and retain the abbreviation "$RTP\#$". The robotic actions related to the direct communication with the human are highlighted with magenta and retain the

Table 1. Mapping from state diagram to POMDP interpretation using Level of Robot Alerts (LoRA) and Actions. Note that $State-11$ and $State-17$ are considered to be control states and when the system prompts a respective action the robot is switched to the monitoring state while the scenario could be re-initialized.

Levels of robot alert			Actions		
High	Medium	Low	Task	Communication	Monitoring
State-3	State-2	State-1	**RTP1:** Robot navigates to the parking position suitable to monitor the state of appliance	**Dialog1:** Robot communicates with human about some missing objects and asks if it should fetch them	**Object-Detection:** The SW component suitable to detect and recognize small objects
State-6	State-5	State-4	**RTP2:** Robot navigates to the parking position suitable to monitor the cooking activity	**Dialog2:** Robot communicates with human about forgetting to turn off an appliance and asks if it should close it	**Large object detection:** The SW component suitable to recognize the state of large articulated objects
State-8	State-12	State-7	**RTP3:** Robot plans the actions for navigation and manipulation of appliance	**Dialog3:** Robot informs the human that it will go manipulate the appliance	**Registry:** The SW component suitable to register the incidents
State-15	State-14	State-9	**RTP4:** The robot fetches the missing objects	**Dialer:** The robot failed to turn off the appliance and notifies for external help	**Parking Position:** The SW component suitable to switch the robot in monitoring state where the human and environment are observed
—	—	State-10	—	—	—
—	—	State-13	—	—	—
—	—	State-16	—	—	—

abbreviations "*Dialog#*" and "*Dialer#*", while the monitoring robotic actions connected with the detection of the human and environment state are highlighted with green. A summary of the explicit interpretation of these robotic actions is provided in Table 1. Moreover, following the designed methodology described in Sect. 3.2, the identified robot actions and the domain state space are grouped accordingly. By carefully examining the diagram in Fig. 2 it is revealed that the observations acquired from the actions that belong in the set of actions A_M, tend to transit the system to higher level of alert while the observations gathered from actions linked to A_T and A_C sets, propagate the system to a lower level of robot alert. The aforementioned remark is also justified by the fact that the scenario starts and finalizes from a state that belongs to the S_L conceptual set of domain states. The arrows that link the states are functional operators and correspond to specific observations expected to be returned after the execution of the corresponding action, which are strictly declared within the POMDP model passing increased observation probabilities to the respective (s, a, ω) triplets. During the design phase of the POMDP, such diagrams can be considered as maps that constraint the produced policy π by defining the transition probabilities among the linked states with increased probability values using the expression described in Eq. 2. At the same time, the probabilities stemming from observations among linked robotic actions are also explicitly declared during the design of the POMDP passing increased values to the Eq. 3, while the rest of the observations are modeled within the POMDP as described in [19]. An important role during the design phase is play the definition of the rewards; where a very positive reward is passed to system when it transits from a state of high a state to lower level of alert, while a very negative reward in passed in the opposite situation. Finally, by using the belief state update as described in Eq. 5 the system can start from any state in the derived policy graph π, and is able to reach to a monitoring related state (S_M) due to the descending designed method of the POMDP model in terms of levels of robot alert.

5 Conclusions and Future Work

In this work, a theoretical framework for designing POMDP models suitable for multipurpose robotic applications has been introduced. Specifically, the limitation in the POMDP design due to the great amount states and robot actions that need to be modeled in real life scenarios is tackled herein with a human-centric design method where the robotic actions are decided based on the awareness of the robot about its cohabitant. The POMDP theory has been interpreted in a robotic-wise manner and the methodology presented herein is based on the conceptual abstraction of the state space using level of robot alerts, which are conjugated with respective groups of robotic actions. Through this procedure the context of the robot actions are connected to the type of assistance that is required to offer and it has been proved that intense robotic actions such as navigation and manipulation tend to transit the system at lower level of robot alerts making the robot complacent about the human. The proposed theoretic framework has been applied in a challenging scenario suitable for assistive robots by analyzing the foreseen robotic sub-tasks in a step-wise manner. Through this procedure, designing details about the parameterization of a POMDP model has been provided offering to the respective community a paradigm to design similar decision making models. Through this procedure, a native decision making system has been designed based on prompting system discharging the POMDP model from the burden to handle low-level robotic actions. In our future work we plan to extend our method by connecting the robotic high-level actions with task and communication planners with the aim to introduce a complete decision-and-act system suitable to operate on multipurpose assisting robots.

Acknowledgments. This work has been supported by the EU Horizon 2020 funded project namely: "Robotic Assistant for MCI Patients at home (RAMCIP)" under the grant agreement with no: 643433.

References

1. Bradshaw, J.M., Feltovich, P.J., Jung, H., Kulkarni, S., Taysom, W., Uszok, A.: Dimensions of adjustable autonomy and mixed-initiative interaction. In: Nickles, M., Rovatsos, M., Weiss, G. (eds.) AUTONOMY 2003. LNCS (LNAI), vol. 2969, pp. 17–39. Springer, Heidelberg (2004). doi:10.1007/978-3-540-25928-2_3
2. Goodrich, M.A., Schultz, A.C.: Human-robot interaction: a survey. Found. Trends Hum. Comput. Interact. **1**(3), 203–275 (2007)
3. White, D.J.: A survey of applications of Markov decision processes. J. Oper. Res. Soc. **44**, 1073–1096 (1993)
4. Pineau, J., Thrun, S.: High-level robot behavior control using POMDPs. In: AAAI 2002 Workshop on Cognitive Robotics, vol. 107 (2002)
5. Mihailidis, A., Fernie, G.R.: Context-aware assistive devices for older adults with dementia. Gerontechnology **2**(2), 173–188 (2002)
6. Hoey, J., Poupart, P., Boutilier, C., Mihailidis, A.: POMDP models for assistive technology. In: Proceedings of AAAI Fall Symposium on Caring Machines: AI in Eldercare (2005)
7. Mihailidis, A., Boger, J.N., Craig, T., Hoey, J.: The coach prompting system to assist older adults with dementia through handwashing: an efficacy study. BMC Geriatr **8**(1), 1 (2008)
8. Hoey, J., Plötz, T., Jackson, D., Monk, A., Pham, C., Olivier, P.: Rapid specification and automated generation of prompting systems to assist people with dementia. Pervasive Mob. Comput. **7**(3), 299–318 (2011)
9. Ryu, H., Monk, A.: Interaction unit analysis: a new interaction design framework. Hum. Comput. Interact. **24**(4), 367–407 (2009)
10. Grześ, M., Hoey, J., Khan, S.S., Mihailidis, A., Czarnuch, S., Jackson, D., Monk, A.: Relational approach to knowledge engineering for POMDP-based assistance systems as a translation of a psychological model. Int. J. Approximate Reasoning **55**(1), 36–58 (2014)
11. Cassandra, A.R., Kaelbling, L.P., Kurien, J.A.: Acting under uncertainty: Discrete Bayesian models for mobile-robot navigation. In: Proceedings of the 1996 IEEE/RSJ International Conference on Intelligent Robots and Systems 1996, IROS 1996, vol. 2, pp. 963–972. IEEE (1996)

12. Grady, D., Moll, M., Kavraki, L.E.: Automated model approximation for robotic navigation with POMDPs. In: 2013 IEEE International Conference on Robotics and Automation (ICRA), pp. 78–84. IEEE (2013)
13. Foka, A., Trahanias, P.: Real-time hierarchical POMDPs for autonomous robot navigation. Robot. Auton. Syst. **55**(7), 561–571 (2007)
14. Candido, S., Hutchinson, S.: Minimum uncertainty robot navigation using information-guided POMDP planning. In: 2011 IEEE International Conference on Robotics and Automation (ICRA), pp. 6102–6108. IEEE (2011)
15. Doumanoglou, A., Kargakos, A., Kim, T.K., Malassiotis, S.: Autonomous active recognition and unfolding of clothes using random decision forests and probabilistic planning. In: 2014 IEEE International Conference on Robotics and Automation (ICRA), pp. 987–993. IEEE (2014)
16. Shani, G., Pineau, J., Kaplow, R.: A survey of point-based POMDP solvers. Auton. Agents Multi-Agent Syst. **27**(1), 1–51 (2013)
17. Schmidt-Rohr, S.R., Knoop, S., Lösch, M., Dillmann, R.: Bridging the gap of abstraction for probabilistic decision making on a multi-modal service robot. In: Robotics: Science and Systems (2008)
18. Taha, T., Miró, J.V., Dissanayake, G.: A POMDP framework for modelling human interaction with assistive robots. In: 2011 IEEE International Conference on Robotics and Automation (ICRA), pp. 544–549. IEEE (2011)
19. Littman, M.L.: A tutorial on partially observable Markov decision processes. J. Math. Psychol. **53**(3), 119–125 (2009)

Integration of a Template System into Model-Based User Interface Development Workflows

Christopher Martin(✉) and Annerose Braune

Institute of Automation, Technische Universität Dresden, Dresden, Germany
{christopher.martin,annerose.braune}@tu-dresden.de

Abstract. In order to reduce the work effort necessary for the creation of user interfaces (UIs), Model-Based UI Development workflows have been introduced. They allow the automatic generation of UIs by means of model transformations. Transformation rules define how to query data from the source model and convert it into elements of the target model. By describing rules for the creation of the target model, it also defines the design of the resulting UI. A separation of these two types of information enables an easier adaptation of the resulting design, e.g. to satisfy design guidelines, without having to reprogram complex transformation rules.

We therefore introduce a generic model-based template system that can be integrated into model-based workflows to separate the design from the data query rules. A case study demonstrates the integration of our template system into a workflow that automatically generates Human-Machine Interfaces from engineering data of manufacturing plants.

Keywords: Human-Machine Interfaces · Template systems · Model-Based User Interface Development · Model-based workflows

1 Introduction

Human-Machine Interfaces (HMIs) are used for supervision and control of complex automation processes and systems. Their creation requires a major part of the plant engineering work effort (cf. [1]). As most of the plant engineering is done using computer-aided engineering software, the engineering data is usually digitally available. However, the creation of HMIs is still mostly done manually. First approaches to change this fact and allow for an integrated HMI development process have been developed only recently (e.g. [2,3]). These workflows make use of the *Model-Based User Interface Development* (MBUID) approach that uses models to describe User Interfaces (UIs) at different degrees of abstraction. Model transformations are used to change the level of abstraction, e.g., by converting engineering information of manufacturing plants into the navigation structure, layout, and panel setup of the HMI (cf. [2]). Furthermore, model elements representing UI widgets are created during this concretization process that

M. Kurosu (Ed.): HCI 2017, Part I, LNCS 10271, pp. 480–495, 2017.
DOI: 10.1007/978-3-319-58071-5_36

also have to be parameterized by the model transformation, e.g., the position or size of an UI element has to be defined.

A model transformation aggregates transformation rules that define how elements of a source model can be converted into elements of a target model (cf. [4]). For this, the model transformation rules have to define how to get (resp. query) data from the source model and how it should be displayed in the target model. Hence, in a MBUID workflow the design of a generated user interface is defined by model transformation rules. The final design of a user interface reflects the design decisions that are made by an expert based on domain knowledge, design guidelines, and information about the application's context of use, e.g., about the screen size of the target platform. So far, in MBUID workflows these decisions have to be hard-coded into model transformation rules. In order to enhance the reusability of this expert knowledge, the design decisions have to be formalized and separated from the transformation logic.

In software engineering, template systems merge selected data (usually queried from a database) and templates (representing the design) to create documents (cf. [5]). Thus, they allow a separation of the data and the design of a document. In this paper, we therefore introduce an approach to incorporate such a template system into a Model-Based UI Development workflow, i.e., especially into the transformations used in such workflows. As templates can be formulated in regular UI description languages, the user is also enabled to design the resulting HMI with the help of the respective editors that he is already used to rather than having to rewrite complex model transformation rules. Furthermore, the final design can be previewed and tested more easily as templates may be created as regular UI models rather than a mere set of rules.

After a short introduction of the MBUID concepts in Sect. 2, requirements for the realization of a template system for MBUID workflows will be deduced in Sect. 3. Based on those, a generic model-based template system is introduced in Sect. 4 and demonstrated by means of a case study in Sect. 5. Related work is then discussed in Sect. 6. Finally, in Sect. 7 we will draw conclusions about the applicability of a template system in MBUID workflows and discuss future works.

2 Model-Based User Interface Development

With the increasing number of available hardware platforms, such as smartphones, tablets, or even smartwatches, the work effort required for the creation of user interfaces has also increased in recent years as an UI has to be created specifically for each platform. In an effort to overcome this problem, the concept of Model-Based UI Development has been introduced. It uses formal models to describe UIs at different degrees of abstraction. In order to provide a systematic workflow in MBUID, the *CAMELEON Reference Framework* [6] (CRF) has been introduced. As shown in Fig. 1, it defines a workflow that comprises four levels of abstraction.

The Task and Concept (T&C) level describes the tasks that an user wants to perform with the objects (concepts) of the user interface and the order in which

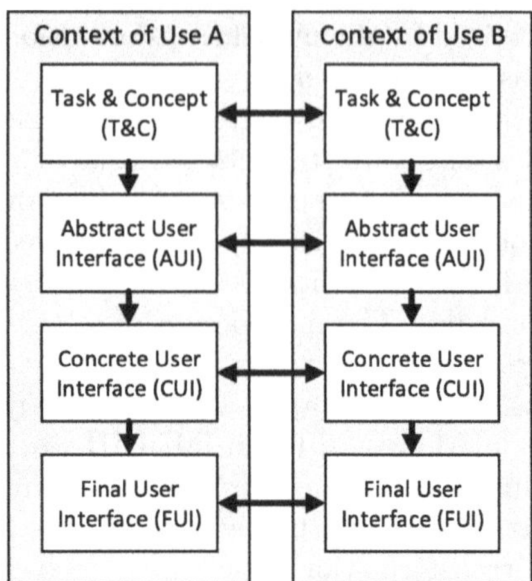

Fig. 1. Simplified representation of the CAMELEON reference framework (cf. [6])

the task are performed. The next level — the Abstract User Interface (AUI) — specifies the structure and elements of the UI in a platform- and modality-independent way. For example, it may define that a multiple choice selection is part of the UI but not if this selection should be represented by a checkbox or a vocal selection. The Concrete UI (CUI) adds information about the modality but not yet about the runtime platform. A CUI model may, e.g., describe a graphical user interface that has a panel which includes the checkbox mentioned before. Lastly, in the Final UI (FUI) the runtime platform is defined, i.e., it represents the actual executable user interface.

A change of the level of abstraction is usually realized by means of model transformations. In order to create a target model, a model transformation has to obtain information from the source model, the context of use, and about elements that have already been created (e.g., if a reference to an already existing element has to be created). Transformation rules specify how both the static and flexible elements of a target model are created. While the static parts are created without the need of data from the source model, the concrete realization of the flexible elements is determined based on data from the source model. Therefore, transformation rules have to define how this data can be queried from the source model and how to translate it into elements of the target model.

In order to convert an abstract UI model into a more concrete description of the UI, additional information has to be added that is not defined by the source model, e.g. about the kind of UI elements and their positioning when transforming an AUI to a CUI. This information is hard-coded into the transformation rules. Thus, different transformation rules are required to change the context of use (cf. Fig. 1), e.g., to create a vocal instead of a graphical user interface. However, this approach requires only one set of transformations that may be reused for every application with the same context of use, i.e., a CUI-to-FUI transformation that creates an executable UI for a certain target technology can be reused for the generation of every UI with the same target technology.

UI models are created by means of UI modeling languages. Various UI modeling languages — such as MARIA [7], UsiXML [8] or Movisa [9] — have been established that allow the definition of UI models at different levels of the CRF. Although efforts for a standardization of a common UI modeling language have been expressed by a W3C working group [10], no modeling language has yet established itself as the standard above the others.

3 Requirements for Model-Based Template Systems

Template systems create documents by merging selected data with the predefined design of templates. To achieve this, a template engine has to query data — e.g., from a database or in case of a MBUID workflow from a source model — as defined by data query rules that are usually written in a normal programming language such as Java [11] or PHP [12]. This data is then used by the template engine to substitute placeholders (also called *template variables*) that have been specified in the templates. A template consists of static parts that do not change based on any data and flexible parts represented by template variables that require the querying of further data to determine their actual value. Thus, the combination of a template including template variables and a set of data query rules is comparable to a transformation rule as both specify rules for the generation of documents. Therefore, template systems can be used to replace regular rule-based model transformations in MBUID workflows.

A resulting workflow for the utilization of a template system in a MBUID workflow is depicted in Fig. 2. In order to allow the generation of a target model, the user first has to define his templates that resembles the desired design of the UI that shall be generated. By assigning template variables as placeholders, the user can declare the flexible elements of the template which shall usually be substituted by source model information or possibly even other sources of information. Once all templates are finished, the data query rules have to be defined, which describe how the data necessary for replacing the template variables can be obtained. In this paper, we will focus on the acquisition of such data only from a source model. While the data query rules should be created by a MBUID expert (as deep knowledge of the source model and the querying language is needed), the templates could be created by a design expert as only knowledge about the target UI modeling language is needed. Finally, the template engine (cf. TE in Fig. 2) replaces the template variables with data from the source model as defined by the data query rules and thus generates the target model.

Templates may be created using the same technology as the document that should be generated. For example, if a website should be created based on a database, a normal template engine such as [11] might allow the specification of the data query rules using Java and the templates could be defined using HTML. As the templates are normal HTML pages — except for the template variables — a designer may create it using his standard web development workflow.

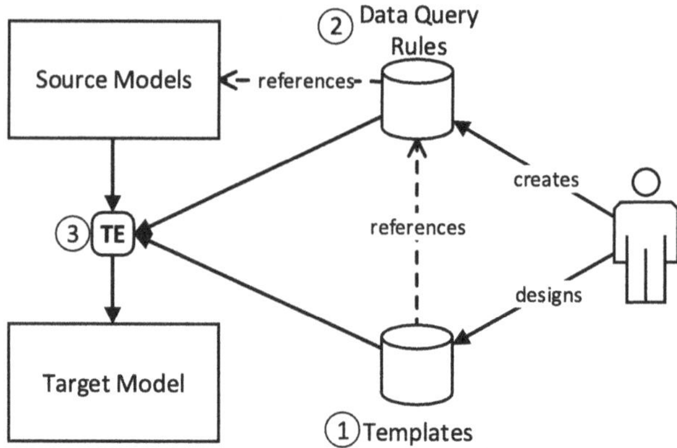

Fig. 2. The workflow for the application of a template system in a MBUID workflow

However, the placeholders have to be specified using a specific syntax to allow the template engine to link the acquired data to its respective template variable. In order to keep this beneficial characteristic of a template system intact when integrating it into a MBUID workflow, templates have to be definable in a regular UI modeling language.

Usually each step of a MBUID workflow is realized using a modeling language that is specific to the level of abstraction of the respective step. The set of modeling languages used in a MBUID workflow can vary widely between different workflows. As described in Sect. 2, no modeling language has established itself as a standard thus far. Hence, if a template system is to be used in a MBUID workflow, it has to be generic in respect to the potential modeling languages of the workflow, i.e., the template system must not be created for a specific UI modeling language but allow the use of any language.

As the creation of model transformations require a large part of the work effort necessary for the creation of a workflow, model transformation languages have been developed — e.g., *ATL* [13] or *Epsilon* [14] — that extend standard programming languages by offering functionalities specific to model editing such as an easier referencing of model objects and values. Hence, when integrating a template system into a MBUID workflow, transformation languages should be used for data querying rather than standard programming languages.

In summary, three components have to be realized in order to integrate a template system into a MBUID workflow. These can be seen in the workflow shown in Fig. 2: ① templates including template variables, ② data query rules required to acquire data from a source model that shall be used for replacing the template variable values, and ③ a template engine that scans the templates, substitutes the template variables based on the data query rules, and thus creates the target model. As also discussed in this section, the definition of all information should be realized generically in order to not restrict the user in his choice of UI modeling or model transformation languages.

4 Generic Model-Based Template System

As defined in the last section, templates should be created as normal UI models using any UI modeling language. The structure of a modeling language is defined by its meta-model. Using the elements that are offered by the meta-model of an UI modeling language, the static part of a template can easily be described. As these meta-models normally do not include elements that allow the specification of template variables, the declaration of the flexible part must be done externally in order to not require any changes to their existing meta-models. Therefore, a new meta-model for the generic annotation of template variables to elements of an UI model has to be created. This can be done using different technologies, as modeling languages can be represented in multiple ways, such as XML or as part of the *Eclipse Modeling Framework*[1] (EMF). While models that are described in XML are based on meta-models that are defined using the *XML Schema Definition* (XSD), meta-models in EMF are created based on the *Ecore meta-model.* However, EMF is also able to load XSD-based models and thus also allows the processing of modeling language that are represented in XML. Furthermore, it provides a large number of tooling for the convenient processing of models such as multiple model transformation languages and generic editors. Consequently, we decided to base our approach on EMF as it offers the most flexibility when working with varying UI modeling languages.

In EMF, a model consists of a hierarchy of objects (*EObject*) that are linked to each other via references (*EReference*). In contrast to XSD-based models, values are only stored in attributes (*EAttribute*) and not as content of an object. Hence, usually only attribute values should be replaced by a template engine as the object structure is already statically defined in the template, i.e., template variables may only be annotated to attributes.

However, certain situations can also require a change of the object hierarchy, e.g., if based on data from a source model an alternative UI widget should be used or if a widget needs to be used repeatedly, because the corresponding source model element has a cardinality greater than one. Thus, an annotation of objects is also necessary but in a different context: the repeating resp. the omitting of an object structure or the selection of alternative model objects is required rather than the substitution of a value. To allow for the specification of this, the template meta-model has to support the annotation of repeatable and optional model objects as well as the definition of the rules that describe how often an object should be instantiated or when an object should be displayed or omitted.

A simplified version of the resulting meta-model is shown in Fig. 3. It does not include any actual UI description elements as the template should be defined as a regular stand-alone UI model. Therefore, only a path to the template is given in the *TemplateModel.* It allows the annotation of template variables by allowing to reference any EAttribute of a template and the assignment of an unique *identifier* which is used for referencing of specific template variables.

[1] http://eclipse.org/modeling/emf/.

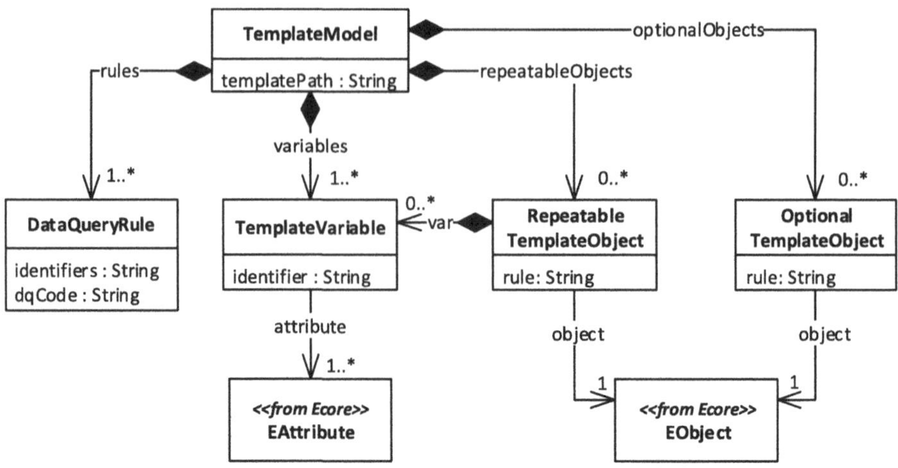

Fig. 3. Simplified subset of the template system meta-model

This enables the linking of a variable to a data query rule. By defining the link using identifier rather than references, a loose coupling of the data query rule and the template variable is achieved which allows for an easy change of the template (and hence the template variables) without the need of recreating any references to data query rules.

Furthermore, template objects can be annotated to allow for the definition of repeatable and optional elements. By allowing the reference of any EObject in a template, the root object of an UI widget can be tagged. The tagging then also applies to all child elements as they are part of the widget that shall be repeated or not displayed. While template variables are occurring in both optional and repeatable objects, only in case of a repeatable object the association of the template variable with the object is relevant as information about the cardinality of the object may be required, e.g., to calculate the size and position of UI elements if aligned in a list. If an object must be repeated, it will be initialized multiple times and its template variables will be reprocessed for every new object. The resulting object can then be added to the containment tree of the target model.

With the template annotations done, data query rules have to be defined. These rules are described as model transformation rule fragments in a transformation language of choice and stored in the *rule* resp. *dqCode* attributes. These fragments have to be called by the template engine when a template variable is applied. However, as the rules can be written in different transformation languages, a transformation language adapter has to be created specifically for each transformation language that should be supported by the template engine. The adapter realizes the calling of the fragments, the handover of parameters such as the source model that shall be queried, and the handling of the return value. When starting the processing of a template, the template engine creates a copy of the template as the new target model. It then iterates the template and processes the template variables and objects when found. The creation of the final model can thus be viewed as an in-place model transformation that works on a copy of the template.

5 Case Study: Template System for AutoProBe

In order to demonstrate our approach, we present a case study that shows the application of the template system in a workflow that allows the (semi-) automatic generation of Human-Machine Interfaces as introduced in the project *AutoProBe* [2]. The workflow used in AutoProBe consists of multiple steps that are depicted in Fig. 4a. Based on a plant model that aggregates data from the engineering process of a manufacturing plant, the plant hierarchy is used to generate a navigation structure (step ①). Next the basic panel setup (step ②) is performed during which most of the UI elements are created and placeholders for the plant-specific elements are placed on the different panels. The positioning is done based on the plant geometry and a predefined fixed layout that can be seen in Fig. 5. The placeholders are then replaced by parametrized library elements (cf. [15]) to create the concrete HMI model (step ③). Information about the actual components and sub-stations are used for the library item initialization. In a last step, code for an executable HMI in HTML/JavaScript is generated. However, an export to industrial HMI tools, such as *SIMATIC WinCC*[2] by Siemens, is also possible if appropriate import interface are offered by the tool.

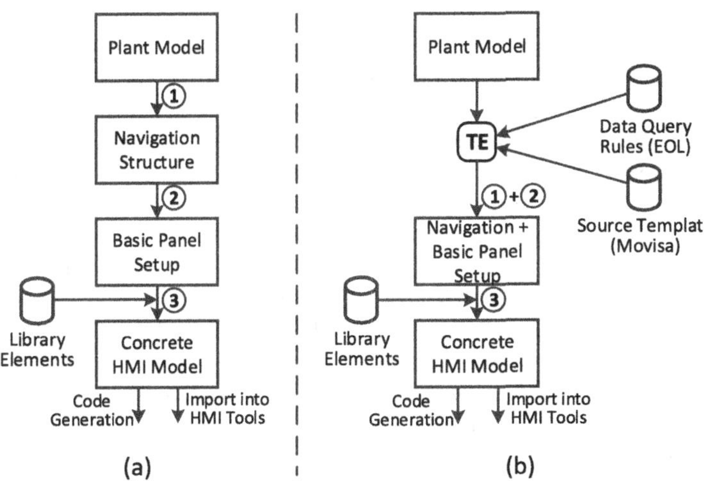

Fig. 4. (a) The AutoProBe workflow as introduced in [2] and (b) the new workflow after integration of a template system

2 http://w3.siemens.com/mcms/human-machine-interface/en/visualization-software/scada/simatic-wincc/Pages/default.aspx.

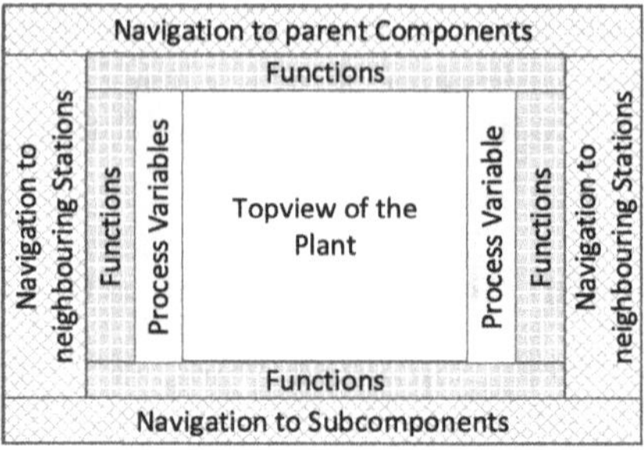

Fig. 5. Default layout used for UI generation in the AutoProBe workflow (cf. [2])

As illustrated in Fig. 4b, we have integrated the template system into the first and second step of the workflow. Those two steps can be merged as a separate transformation step is not necessary anymore, because the creation of the navigation structure can be handled with the help of repeating template objects and the positioning, initializing, and parameterizing of UI elements can now be done in the same step by using template variables. Therefore, in the new workflow steps ① and ② have been merged. The capability to initialize concrete library entries — as normally done during step ③ — has not yet been integrated into the template engine but might also be added to it in the future, i.e., all three intermediary steps could then be processed by the template system. Some of the library elements could in the future even be realized as part of the template and would thus not be needed in the library anymore.

In AutoProbe, the UI modeling language Movisa [9] was used for the definition of the intermediary models, i.e., for all models except for the plant model. Movisa was created to allow the definition of HMIs specifically for the domain of industrial automation and is situated at the CUI level of the CRF. It was also used for our case study and thus the templates have been defined in Movisa. As the transformations in AutoProBe have been implemented using the *Epsilon Object Language* (EOL) [14], the data query rules are also defined in this language. To allow for this, an EOL data query adapter has been implemented for our template engine. It can call EOL operations that query data from a given source model and return a value that is used for the template variable substitution. In order to support the user, an interactive wizard was implemented that allows the annotation of *TemplateVariables* and *TemplateObjects* from the regular Movisa editor. It allows the assigning of identifier and if a *DataQueryRule* element is created, an EOL operation stub for the data query rule is also created automatically. Furthermore, an attribute was introduced that allows the value of template variables that are part of a repeatable object to be made unique upon initialization. As Movisa requires every element to have an unique ID, this avoids redundant data query rules that only checks if an ID is unique and if not appends an unique number to the original value of an attribute.

For our case study, we created two templates that realize two different layouts: the default layout as shown in Fig. 5 and a layout for smaller screens as illustrated in Fig. 6 that uses the *Off Canvas* UI pattern for the navigation menu. It is a very common UI pattern in mobile design (e.g., as recommended by Google [16]) and displays content in a panel that is not shown on screen by default but slides in from the side when activated by hitting the menu button in the top left corner of the UI. Furthermore, functions and process variables are displayed in a scrollable list. The topview of the plant is replaced by a scrollable list of the plant's components.

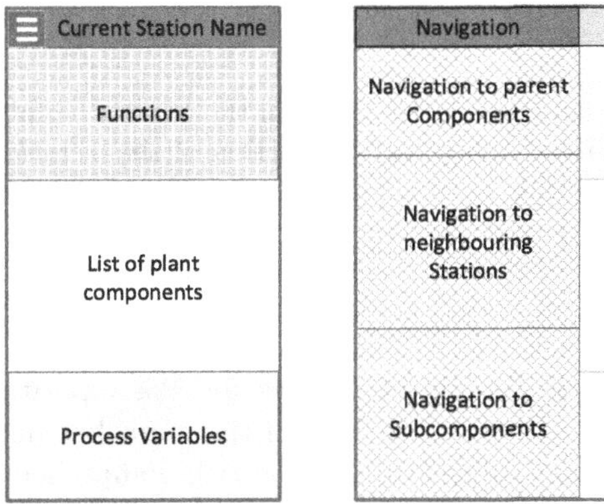

Fig. 6. Alternative layout for mobile devices with hidden (left) and activated (right) Off Canvas navigation menu

An example of the Movisa template can be seen in Fig. 7 which shows the section of the template that is used to generate the top navigation bar in the default layout (cf. Fig. 5). It consists of only a single *Button* that shall be repeated for every available navigation target of a higher level in the hierarchy of the plant. By annotating the element as a *RepeatableTemplateObject* a rule can be defined that specifies for which elements of the source model a new navigation button has to be created. The IDs of all elements are marked to be made unique, because they may be initialized multiple times as they are part of an object that may be repeated. The Button is placed on the screen by defining the x-position (*XScaledProperty*) and y-position (*YScaledProperty*). While the latter is fixed, the x-position depends on the number of buttons in the navigation bar. Therefore, a *TemplateVariable* and a *DataQueryRule* are defined that realize the calculation of the x-position. This way, the buttons are equally spread and center-aligned horizontally in the top navigation bar. For reasons of clarity only this template variable and data query rule as well as only the button's position are displayed in Fig. 7. Similar rules are used for the other navigation bars, functions, and process variables. The topview is positioned on both axes based on a topview of the plant as defined by the plant topology in the plant model.

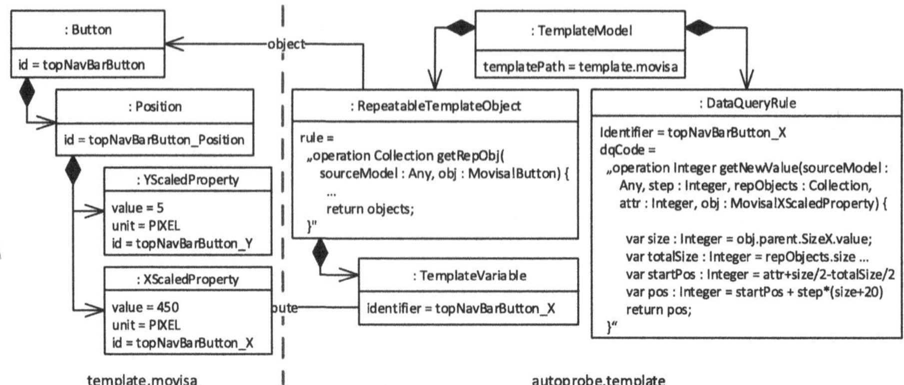

Fig. 7. Simplified representation of the subset of the Movisa template that defines the top navigation bar (left) and the respective section of the *TemplateModel* (right) for the default AutoProBe layout

The Off Canvas layout uses a comparable principal by aligning elements vertically instead of horizontally. Thus, the resulting TemplateModel is quite similar as it also defines TemplateVariables for the y-position of the various RepeatableObjects. However, the topview of the plant has been altered for this design as it becomes too sophisticated to be still comprehensible on the small screen of a mobile device. Therefore, the elements are also aligned vertically in a scrollable list.

Since templates are defined as regular Movisa models, executable code can be generated from them without the need of already having template variables and data query rules specified. This allows the early testing of the template's function already during design phase. Figure 8 shows the generated FUI for the Off Canvas template. The function of the menu activation can already be tested even though the template has not yet been annotated with template variables and data query rules. Furthermore, it enables the designer to get a first impression of the resulting design of the final application at an early phase of the workflow creation process.

Examples of the resulting executable UIs are shown in Figs. 9 and 10 that show the detail page of a quality testing station's PLC and list important process variables of that station. The station and its process variables were described in a plant model that was the input for the workflow. By using a template system, we enable the user to switch the final design of the generated user interface by just switching the template. A change in the static parts of the final user interface — e.g. the background colors or a header logo — does not require reprogramming of transformation rules anymore, but can be realized using the regular Movisa editors. However, if changes to attributes are required that have been defined by a template variable, the respective data query rule has to be reprogrammed as well.

Furthermore, we were able to define templates for the navigation structure, the basic panel setup, and some elements of the concrete HMI model.

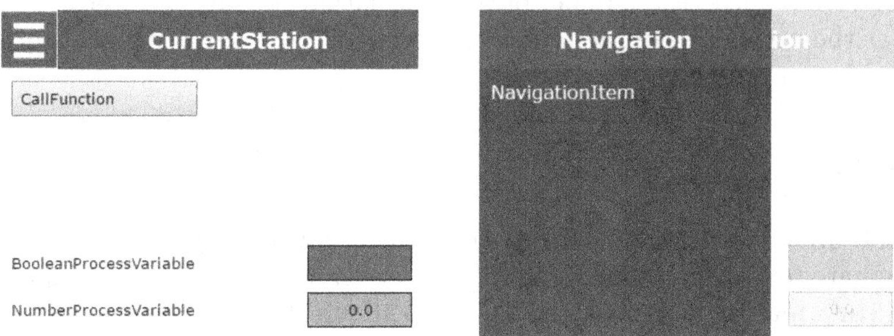

Fig. 8. Generated HTML/JavaScript version of the Movisa template for the Off Canvas layout as introduced in Fig. 6 (empty bottom half was cropped)

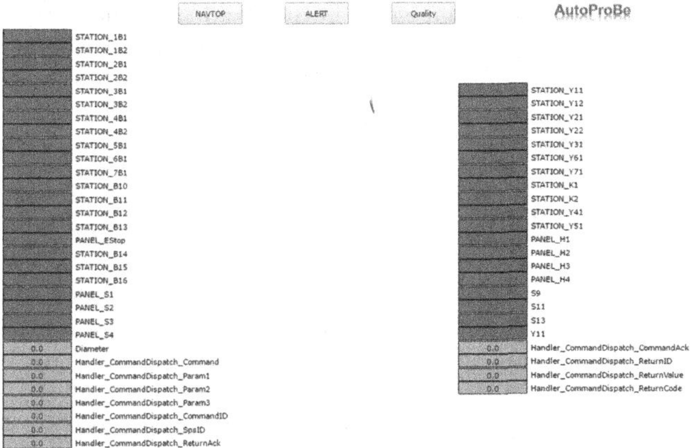

Fig. 9. FUI generated by the AutoProBe workflow for the detail view of a quality testing station using the default AutoProBe layout template

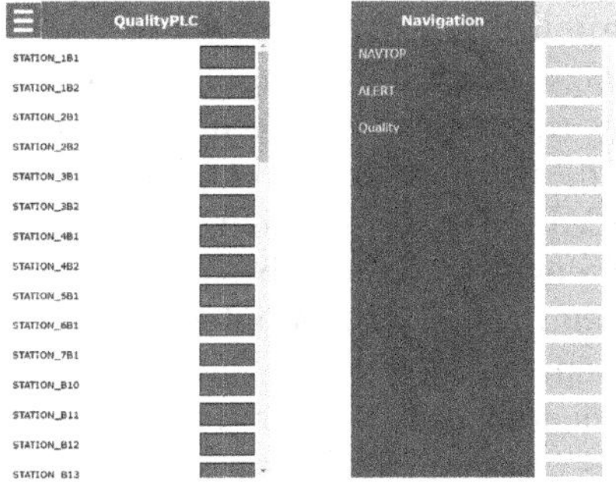

Fig. 10. Detail view of a quality testing station (cf. Fig. 9) generated using the Off Canvas layout template (cf. Fig. 8)

Therefore, we reduced the number of transformations by merging steps ① and ② as well as the number of library elements necessary by integrating some of them into the Movisa template.

6 Related Work

Templates are often used in model-to-text transformations, i.e., transformations that generate text from a source model. One example for this is the standardized XML transformation language *XSLT* [17]. It allows the specification of template rules for XML nodes. If such node is found in the source XML document, the template rule is executed and the results are inserted into the final document. Such rule-based template definition is very common in MBUID workflows as most model-to-text transformations follow the same template-based principle. For example, the *Epsilon Generation Language* (EGL) [18] allows the definition of text snippets as templates that shall be inserted into the target model if a certain element is found in the source model. Model-to-model transformations (e.g. ATL [13]) follow a similar principle by defining transformation rules for source model elements that create target model elements. However, when using these transformation languages, it is still necessary to define rules for the creation of static contents by means of a specific rule definition syntax. Therefore, the design of the generated UI can only be changed by reprogramming complex transformation rules. By default it is not possible to reference templates that are defined in a regular UI modeling language as it is allowed by our approach.

In the domain of web-based user interfaces, template systems are already very common. Content management system, such as *Joomla*[3] or *WordPress*[4], use templates to define the design of the site independent of the actual contents. These templates are usually created as HTML or PHP pages that contain predefined placeholders which are then replaced at runtime by contents from a database. The data query rules used by the template engine are hard-coded into the system though. The principle of this approach is comparable to our solution as it allows the definition of the templates in the target technology. However, as the data query rules are integrated into the system and rely on data from a database, it cannot be applied to MBUID workflows.

Various general purpose template engines exist that allow the definition of templates and data query rules in multiple technologies. Some of them — such as [11,19] — also support the specification of templates in regular XML, i.e., every template is still valid XML. As most modeling languages are defined in XML or XMI, these template engines can also be used to create templates in most UI modeling languages and could thus be integrated into a MBUID workflow. While this enables the separation of the design from the data query rules, the rules have to be implemented in a regular programming language specific to each template engine. As no template engine supports a model transformation language by default yet, it is not possible to use the model accessing and editing

[3] https://www.joomla.org/.
[4] https://wordpress.org/.

capabilities of common model transformation languages for the data query rule definition. In the future, we will continue to analyze more template engines in regard to their applicability to MBUID workflows and in regard to the features offered by the systems in order to further enhance our template system.

In the domain of MBUID, Sinnig et al. [20] describe an approach that uses the template engine *Velocity* for the instantiation of UI pattern in an UI model. The pattern are saved as UI model snippets including template variables that are replaced during initialization. As this solution was created specifically for the XUL modeling language, it is limited to this UI modeling language and thus lacks the required flexibility. In contrast to our approach that uses a template engine for the transformation of a source model to a target model (cf. Sect. 3), the Velocity engine is only used to manually add elements into a preexisting UI model. Thus, it does not allow the specification of data query rules as the template variables are resolved manually.

Aquino et al. [21] present *Transformation Templates* that separate the specification of the structure, layout, and style of UI elements from the model transformation rules by providing them as *Parameters* for the model transformation. However, the definition of such Parameters is done on the meta-model level, i.e., the Parameter is applied for every element of the specified type. This may be limited by use of selectors, but the changes are only applied after the element has been created in the target model. The creation of the target model is not part of this approach and has to be performed separately. Thus, the transformation templates can be seen as a library of target creation rules that describe how the layout of the target model should look like or how an element should be styled. It does not allow the definition of data query rules and can therefore only be used in conjunction with a dedicated model transformation. Furthermore, the definition of the Parameters has to be done in a specific modeling language, i.e., the template may not be created in a regular UI modeling language.

7 Conclusions and Future Work

In this paper, we have presented an approach for the separation of the design from the model transformation rules of MBUID workflows by integration of a template system. To meet the requirements of a template system in a MBUID workflow, we created a generic *TemplateModel* that allows the definition of data query rules and the formal annotation of template variables independent of the UI modeling language. The model transformation language used for data querying may also be changed by implementing a data query rule adapter for the template engine. While this still requires a lot of work, the implementation is only necessary once per model transformation language and can then be used for all template models. Our proposed template system is able to create a target model based on source model data, templates, and the template model.

We have demonstrated the applicability of this approach by means of a case study that showed that a template system promotes the separation of the design and data querying in MBUID workflows. As templates are created as regular UI models, the resulting UI of a workflow can be designed using the regular tools associated with the UI modeling language rather than integrating the design into transformation rules. Furthermore, as templates are valid UI models, they can already be transformed into FUI without the need to execute the whole workflow. This enables the testing of the UI design and some of its mechanics (e.g., the expanding and collapsing of an off canvas panel) at a very early stage of the design process.

Furthermore, we have shown that a change of the design of a generated UI can be realized by just switching the template if only static content should be changed. If attribute values should be changed that were defined by a template variable, the respective data query rule might also need to be changed. As the definition of these rules is still a very complex task, we will examine how to improve this task in future works. One possible solution could be the creation of an explicit model querying language, e.g., based on the source section definition as introduced by *PAMTraM* [22].

As already shown in our case study, UI pattern support the user in the development of user interfaces by offering proven solutions to reoccurring design problems. By providing the user a library of UI pattern, the work effort necessary for the creation of templates can be reduced. In future work, we therefore want to integrate the possibility to store and reuse UI pattern as template fragments.

Additionally, our approach has to be evaluated by means of further case studies. We are currently considering the application of the template system in the context of plug-and-produce scenarios as introduces by the *Industry 4.0* initiative that proposes reconfigurable process and manufacturing plants. At the moment, there is a lack of concepts on how to adapt the HMI to a change in the plant configuration. A template system could eventually be used to overcome this challenge.

Acknowledgments. The IGF proposal 16606 BG of the research association "Gesellschaft zur Förderung angewandter Informatik e.V." (GFaI) is funded via the AiF within the scope of the "Program for the promotion of industrial cooperational research" (IGF) by the German Federal Ministry of Economics and Technology (BMWi) according to a resolution of the German Bundestag.

We gratefully acknowledge funding of the project "KonTrans" – BR4107/2-1 by the "Deutsche Forschungsgemeinschaft" (DFG).

References

1. Myers, B.A., Rosson, M.B.: Survey on user interface programming. In: Proceedings of the SIGCHI Conference on Human Factors in Computing Systems, CHI 1992, pp. 195–202. ACM, New York (1992)
2. Martin, C., Freund, M., Braune, A., Ebert, R.E., Pleßow, M., Severin, S., Stern, O.: Integrated design of human-machine interfaces for production plants. In: Proceedings of 20th IEEE International Conference on Emerging Technologies and Factory Automation (ETFA 2015), pp. 1–6. IEEE, September 2015
3. Schleipen, M., Okon, M., Enzmann, T., Wei, J.: IDA - Interoperable, semantische Datenfusion zur automatisierten Bereitstellung von sichtenbasierten Prozessführungsbildern. In: VDI-Berichte, vol. 2143, pp. 83–86. VDI-Verlag, Düsseldorf (2011)

4. Gruhn, V., Pieper, D., Röttgers, C.: MDA - Effektives Software Engineering Mit UML2 Und Eclipse. Springer, Heidelberg (2006)
5. Niemeyer, P., Knudsen, J.: Learning Java, 3rd edn. O'Reilly, Sebastopol (2005)
6. Calvary, G., Coutaz, J., Thevenin, D., Limbourg, Q., Bouillon, L., Vanderdonckt, J.: A unifying reference framework for multi-target user interfaces. Interacting with Computers **15**(3), 289–308 (2003)
7. Paternò, F., Santoro, C., Spano, L.D.: MARIA: a universal, declarative, multiple abstraction-level language for service-oriented applications in ubiquitous environments. ACM Trans. Comput. Hum. Interact. **16**(4), 1–30 (2009)
8. Limbourg, Q., Vanderdonckt, J., Michotte, B., Bouillon, L., López-Jaquero, V.: USIXML: a language supporting multi-path development of user interfaces. In: Bastide, R., Palanque, P., Roth, J. (eds.) DSV-IS 2004. LNCS, vol. 3425, pp. 200–220. Springer, Heidelberg (2005). doi:10.1007/11431879_12
9. Hennig, S.: Design of Sustainable Solutions for Process Visualization in Industrial Automation with Model-Driven Software Development, 1st edn. Jörg Vogt Verlag, Dresden (2012)
10. Fonseca, J.M.C., Calleros, J.M.G., Meixner, G., Paternò, F., Pullmann, J., Raggett, D., Schwabe, D., Vanderdonckt, J.: Model-based UI XG final report. Technical report, W3C (May 2010)
11. The Thymeleaf Team: Thymeleaf (2017). http://www.thymeleaf.org/
12. New Digital Group, Inc.: PHP Template Engine—Smarty (2016). http://www.smarty.net/
13. Eclipse: ATL - a model transformation technology (2016). http://www.eclipse.org/atl/
14. Kolovos, D.S., Paige, R.F., Polack, F.A.C.: The epsilon object language (EOL). In: Rensink, A., Warmer, J. (eds.) ECMDA-FA 2006. LNCS, vol. 4066, pp. 128–142. Springer, Heidelberg (2006). doi:10.1007/11787044_11
15. Freund, M., Martin, C., Braune, A.: A library system to support model-based user interface development in industrial automation. In: Kurosu, M. (ed.) HCI 2016. LNCS, vol. 9731, pp. 476–487. Springer, Cham (2016). doi:10.1007/978-3-319-39510-4_44
16. Pete LePage: Responsive Web Design Patterns—Web (2017). https://developers.google.com/web/fundamentals/design-and-ui/responsive/patterns
17. W3C: XSL Transformations (XSLT), November 1999. https://www.w3.org/TR/xslt
18. Rose, L.M., Paige, R.F., Kolovos, D.S., Polack, F.A.C.: The epsilon generation language. In: Schieferdecker, I., Hartman, A. (eds.) ECMDA-FA 2008. LNCS, vol. 5095, pp. 1–16. Springer, Heidelberg (2008). doi:10.1007/978-3-540-69100-6_1
19. Wanstrath, C.: Mustache(5) - Logic-less templates (2009). http://mustache.github.io/mustache.5.html
20. Sinnig, D., Gaffar, A., Reichart, D., Forbrig, P., Seffah, A.: Patterns in model-based engineering. In: Jacob, R.J.K., Limbourg, Q., Vanderdonckt, J. (eds.) Computer-Aided Design of User Interfaces IV: Proceedings of CADUI 2004, pp. 197–210. Springer, Dordrecht (2005)
21. Aquino, N., Vanderdonckt, J., Pastor, O.: Transformation templates: adding flexibility to model-driven engineering of user interfaces. In: Proceedings of the 2010 ACM Symposium on Applied Computing, pp. 1195–1202. ACM, New York (2010)
22. Freund, M., Braune, A.: A generic transformation algorithm to simplify the development of mapping models. In: Proceedings of the ACM/IEEE 19th International Conference on Model Driven Engineering Languages and Systems, MODELS 2016, pp. 284–294. ACM, New York (2016)

A Study on Extracting Attractive Regions from One-Point Perspective Paintings

Ryoma Matsuo[1(✉)], Haruka Sugimoto[2], Mamiko Sakata[2], and Michiya Yamamoto[3]

[1] Graduate School of Science and Technologies, Kwansei Gakuin University, Sanda, Japan
matsuo.r@kwansei.ac.jp

[2] Faculty of Culture and Information Science, Doshisha University, Kyotanabe, Japan

[3] School of Science and Technologies, Kwansei Gakuin University, Sanda, Japan

Abstract. According to Takashina's research on art history, Ukiyo-e (Japanese woodblock prints) painters began to use the vanishing point as a *mechanism* to attract viewer's point of view. They did this by setting the main motif on the vanishing point. In this study, we attempted to clarify experimentally the effect created by a composition in which a painter draws the main motif on the vanishing point of a one-point perspective. For this purpose, we performed an experiment to measure gaze points in viewing paintings. In the experiment, we presented six paintings: two paintings with main motifs on the vanishing points, two edited paintings in which the main motifs on the vanishing points were deleted, and two paintings with main motifs not at the vanishing points. For each painting, we measured the gaze for 30 s. The number of participants analyzed was 18. We observed that viewers looked more at main motifs on vanishing points than at other regions. The same result was demonstrated even when the main motifs were deleted. We also observed that viewers looked more at the vanishing point than at the main motif, which is not on the vanishing point. This suggests that viewers enjoy the main motif by seeing it within peripheral visual field. In addition, viewers looked more at the vanishing point than at other regions even when there was no main motif originally. These results demonstrate the powerful effect of vanishing points.

Keywords: One-point perspective · Vanishing point · Gaze analysis

1 Introduction

According to Takashina's research on art history, one-point perspective was originally proposed as a method to draw 3D space on a 2D canvas in Europe [1]. She also pointed out that the vanishing point was a *tentative point*, which we cannot see and which is set experientially. However, after the introduction of the one-point perspective in Japan in the Yedo era, Ukiyo-e (Japanese woodblock prints) painters began to use the vanishing point as a *mechanism* to attract viewer's gaze points by setting the main motifs of their works on the vanishing point. Though we can find few works with such compositions among Western-style paintings, there are many such works in Japan Ukiyo-e in the Yedo and Meiji eras. These can also be found in Western-style oil paintings in the Meiji era in which main motifs were placed on the vanishing points.

M. Kurosu (Ed.): HCI 2017, Part I, LNCS 10271, pp. 496–505, 2017.
DOI: 10.1007/978-3-319-58071-5_37

In this study, we clarify experimentally the effect of composition in which a painter draws the main motif on the vanishing point of a one-point perspective. For this purpose, we measured gaze points in viewing paintings. For successfully accomplishing this, we used eye-tracking, which has been known to be an effective tool for a long time [2].

We selected four typical paintings as shown in Fig. 1(a) "View of Yamagata City", an oil painting by Takahashi Yuichi with its main motif on the vanishing point; (b) "Nihonbashi in Edo", a Ukiyo-e from "Thirty-six Views of Mount Fuji" by Hokusai with its main motif near the vanishing point; (c) "The Bell which Resounds for Ten Thousand Leagues in the Dutch Port of Frankai", a Ukiyo-e by Utagawa Toyoharu in which we can see influence of the Western one-point perspective; and (d) "Nakanocho in the Yoshiwara, n.d.", a Ukiyo-e in the formative era by Masanobu Okumura, which he drew with his original perspective inspired from Chinese paintings. In the paintings in Fig. 1(c) and (d), there were originally no main motifs on the vanishing points.

(a) View of Yamagata City

(b) Nihonbashi in Edo

(c) The Bell which Resounds for Ten Thousand Leagues in the Dutch Port of Frankai

(d) Nakanocho in the Yoshiwara, n.d.

Fig. 1. Four typical paintings related to compositions.

2 Experimental Setup

We measured gaze points by using our original eye-tracker as shown in Fig. 2, in which we introduced an aspherical model of the eye [3]. The accuracy of the system was about 0.71° and this can be realized by one point calibration.

Fig. 2. Experimental setup using an eye-tracker.

In the experiment, we measured in viewing four paintings shown in Fig. 1. In addition, we prepared two paintings—Fig. 3(a)′ View of Yamagata City and Fig. 3(b)′ Nihonbashi in Edo—by deleting the main motifs on their vanishing points. By using graphic editor, we removed the Yamagata prefectural office in Fig. 3(a)′ and the Edo Castle in Fig. 3(b)′ at (near) the vanishing points.

(a)′ View of Yamagata City (without Yamagata prefectural office)

(b)′ Nihonbashi in Edo (without Edo Castle)

Fig. 3. Two edited paintings without main motifs.

We presented these six paintings as stimuli and measured the gaze points in viewing them. First, we calibrated the eye-tracker and presented Fig. 1(a) or Fig. 3(a)′ on display for 30 s. Next, we presented a cross shape as a target at the center of the display for 5 s to serve as an interval between the stimuli. When changing images, we displayed a black screen for 2 s. Further, we moved to Fig. 1(b) or and Fig. 3(b)′ and the cross-shape interval. Subsequently, we moved to Fig. 1(c), Fig. 1(d), Fig. 1(a) or Fig. 3(a)′, and Fig. 1(b) or and Fig. 3(b)′. We counterbalanced the order of presentation of the edited paintings to avoid order effects. While presenting the paintings, we let the participants view the images freely. We asked participants to look at the cross shape during the interval. We used a 15.6 in. 1920 × 1080 monitor as a stimulus. The distance between the participants and the display was 500 mm. The framerate of the eye-tracker was 15.4 fps. The participants were 41 university or graduate students (average 20.85 in age, SD = 1.25).

Before the analysis, we selected and corrected the data. We used the first and fifth cross shape for data correction. In the following sections, we clarify the procedure used for data selection:

(1) Choosing a participant

i. Removal of outliers

We removed coordinates out of monitor resolution from tracking data as errors. Then, we removed coordinates that were more or less than 1.5 times the distance from the median to the first quartile or third quartile. This is shown in Fig. 4. We defined the remaining data as tracked points.

Fig. 4. Removal of outliers.

ii. Calculation of median

We calculated the median of both x and y coordinates. We defined the coordinates as the center of measured data obtained during looking at the cross shape. This meant that the measured data included calibration error as bias, and it could be corrected by calculating the difference as shown in Fig. 5.

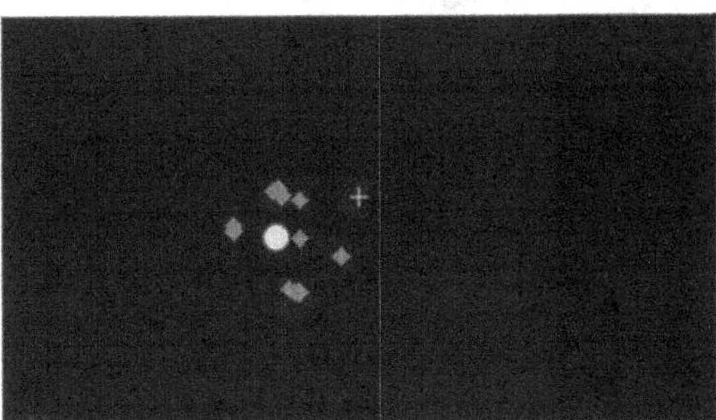

Fig. 5. Calculation of median.

iii. Removal of participant

We calculated distances between each tracked point obtained in step i and the center of measured data obtained in step ii. When the distance was over 125 px (2.5° field of view), we considered the tracked points as errors. If the number of errors exceeded 20% in both cross shapes, we removed the participant from the analysis. For this procedure, we used the data obtained from 18 participants (average 21.67 in age, SD = 1.25) (Fig. 6).

Fig. 6. Selection of data obtained from participants.

(2) Data correction
We calibrated the data measured by using the difference between the calculated median and the coordinates of the center of the cross shape. Further, we calibrated all the measured data during viewing paintings and used this after-correction data for analysis (Fig. 7).

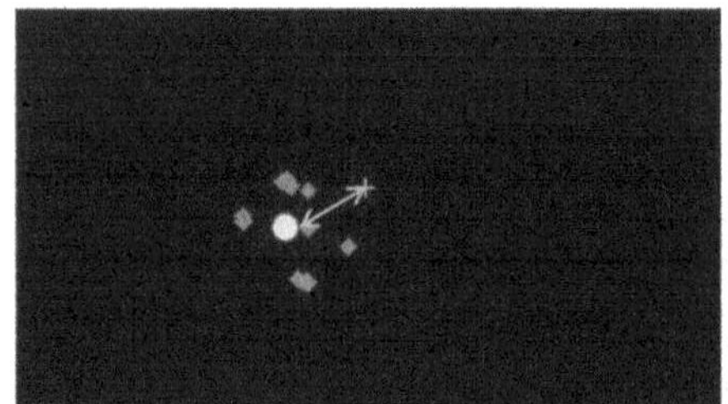

Fig. 7. Data correction.

3 Vanishing Region

To confirm the difference among the compositions of the main motifs and their effects on attraction to viewer's point of view, we determined a *vanishing region*, which is the internal region of a rectangle located around the vanishing point. For example, in Fig. 1(a) View of Yamagata City, we set a rectangle just around the Yamagata prefectural office, its main motif. Next, we compared the number of gaze points inside and outside the vanishing region. For a quantitative comparison, we divided these numbers by the area (Fig. 8).

Fig. 8. Determined vanishing region in View of Yamagata City.

4 Results

Using a two-way analysis of variance, we examined the influence of two independent variables—with or without the main motif, and inside or outside the vanishing region—on the number of gaze points as a dependent variable. Figure 9 shows the results of Figs. 1(a) and 3(a)′ View of Yamagata City and of Figs. 1(b) and 3(b)′ Nihonbashi in Edo. The results show that viewers look around the vanishing point with or without the main motif. We can see the main effects only inside or outside the vanishing region: (a) $F\,(1{,}17) = 17.35, p = .001, \eta_p^2 = .51$, (b) $F\,(1{,}17) = 8.30, p = .01, \eta_p^2 = .33$).

Figure 10 shows the results of Fig. 1(c) The Bell which Resounds for Ten Thousand Leagues in the Dutch Port of Frankai and Fig. 1(d) Nakanocho in the Yoshiwara, n.d. The results indicate that the viewers looked more inside the vanishing point than outside. Again, we can see the main effects only inside or outside the vanishing region: $\mathrm{F}\,(1{,}17) = 15.51$, $\mathrm{p} = .001, \eta_p^2 = .48$.

Next, we divided the paintings into small regions: 9 horizontal regions and 16 vertical regions. Each region is 120 × 120 px. Subsequently, we colored each small region by treating the total number of gaze points of all 18 participants as heat maps. Figures 11, 12 and 13 show the results. The number in each small region indicates the rate gaze points where participants looked. The results were similar to those of the two-way analysis of variance and demonstrated that the vanishing regions were attractive.

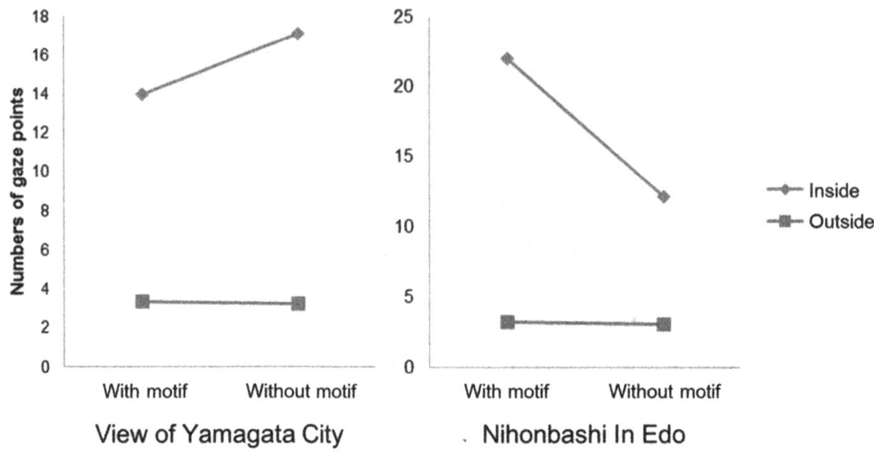

Fig. 9. Numbers of gaze points in viewing paintings with main motif on the vanishing point.

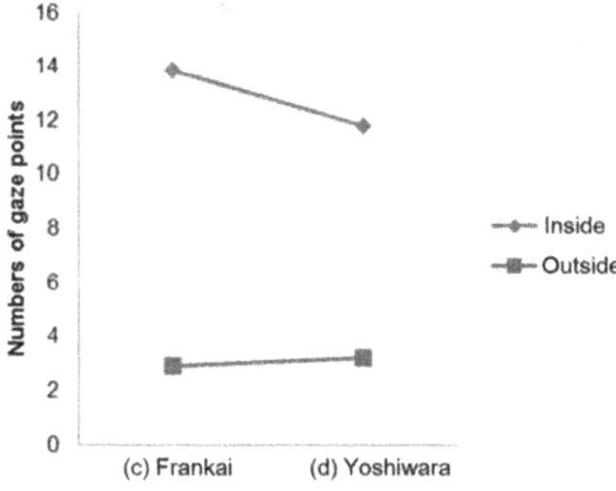

Fig. 10. Numbers of gaze points in viewing paintings without main motifs on the vanishing points.

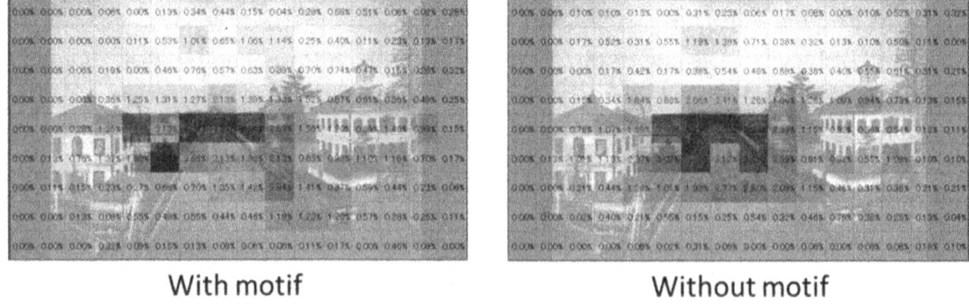

Fig. 11. Rate of numbers of gaze points in Figs. 1(a) and 3(a)′ View of Yamagata City.

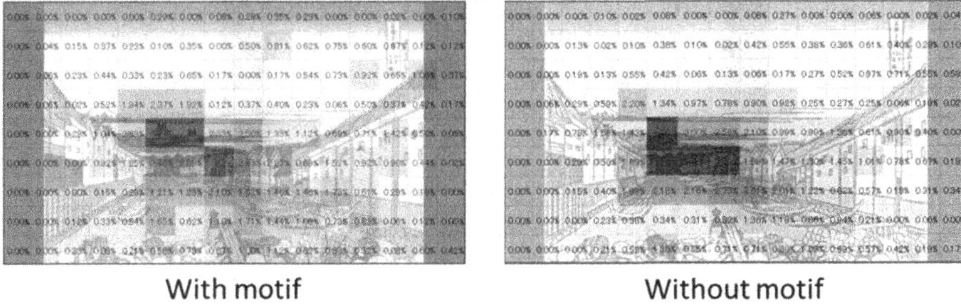

Fig. 12. Rate of numbers of gaze points in Figs. 1(b) and 3(b)′Nihonbashi in Edo.

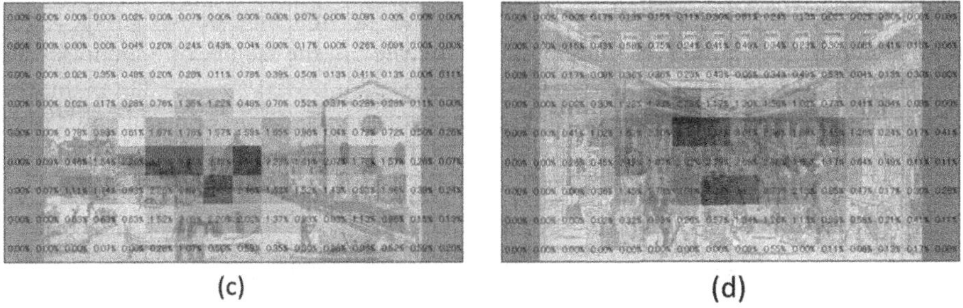

Fig. 13. Rate of numbers of gaze points in (c) and (d).

5 Discussion

As a result of the experiment, we clarified four effects caused by the composition in which painters draw their main motifs on vanishing points.

First, we showed that viewers looked more at the main motif on a vanishing point than at other regions as shown in Figs. 9, 11 and 12. The original idea was proposed by Takashina, but we proved it experimentally. As shown in Fig. 14, this effect is remarkable in case of the painting in Fig. 1(b) Nihonbashi in Edo. According to Takashina, the Edo Castle was arranged just on the vanishing point, and it attracted attention. We can explain this with our experimental results—Mount Fuji, which is the main motif, was arranged within the peripheral visual field of the Edo Castle.

Second, we demonstrated that viewers looked more at the vanishing point than other regions even when we deleted the main motif on the vanishing point as shown in Figs. 9, 11 and 12. As Takashina pointed out, the vanishing point is not a tentative point, but a mechanism to attract viewer's gaze. Originally, this idea was proposed as a composition in the Yedo era, but it can be concluded that we can see this effect even when there is no main motif.

According to Molnar, a viewer looks more at the center of the picture [4]. However, as shown in Fig. 14, the effect of the vanishing point was stronger than that of the center of the picture. This result shows that the vanishing point comprises the figure of figure-ground.

Fig. 14. An example of gaze points in viewing Nihonbashi in Edo.

Third, it was shown that viewers looked more at the vanishing point than the main motif, which is not on the vanishing point, as revealed in the results of Nihonbashi in Edo. Viewers looked more at the Edo Castle than Mt. Fuji. We can see other paintings that use this effect as shown in Fig. 15. We can see the challenge of constructing a new expression when the Western idea of perspective was introduced in the Yedo era in Japan.

Fig. 15. Enoshima in Sagami Province—an example in which Mt. Fuji was drawn separately from the vanishing point, and it could be enjoyed by seeing it within the peripheral visual field, which is just the same as the way we see Mt. Fuji.

Forth, viewers looked more at the vanishing point than other regions even when originally there was no main motif as shown in Figs. 10 and 13. This result is a more clear evidence of the second result, because the painters had no idea of how to lead viewer's gaze point while painting their works. This also should be discussed related to the center effect.

In the future work, we would consider the relationship highlighted by many researchers between gaze, fixation, attention, and what we see, look, and appreciate [5] and would clarify these findings, especially for the analysis of the peripheral visual field.

6 Conclusion

In this study, we clarified experimentally the effect of the compositions in which painters draw their main motifs on the vanishing point in a one-point perspective. For this purpose, we performed an experiment to measure different gaze points in viewing paintings. In the experiment, we presented six paintings: two paintings with main motifs on the vanishing points, two edited paintings in which the main motifs on the vanishing points were deleted, and two paintings with main motifs not at the vanishing points. We measured the gaze for 30 s for each painting. The participant to be analyzed was eighteen. As a result, we clarified that viewers looked more at the main motif on the vanishing point than other regions. They also looked more at the vanishing point when the main motif was deleted. We also clarified that viewers looked more at the vanishing point than the main motif, which is not on the vanishing point. This suggests that viewers enjoy the main motif by seeing it within the peripheral visual field. In addition, viewers looked more at the vanishing point than other regions even when there was no motif originally. These results demonstrate the strong influence of vanishing points.

Acknowledgement. This research was partially supported by JSPS KAKENHI 16H03225, 16H02860, etc.

References

1. Takashina, E.: Takahashi Yuichi's view of Yamagata City and the famous views of Yedo. Zinbun Gakuhō J. Humanit. **101**, 19–35 (2011). (in Japanese)
2. Yarbus, A.L.: Eye Movements and Vision. Prenum Press, New York (1967)
3. Yamamoto, M., Nagamatsu, T., Watanabe, T.: Development of eye-tracking pen display based on stereo bright pupil technique. In: Proceedings of the 2010 Symposium on Eye-Tracking Research & Applications, pp. 165–168 (2000)
4. Molnar, F.: About the role of visual exploration in aesthetics. In: Advances in Intrinsic Motivation and Aesthetics, pp. 385–413 (1981)
5. Wooding, D.S.: Fixation maps: quantifiying eye-movement traces. In: Proceedings of ETRA 2002, pp. 31–36 (2002)

Posture Analysis and Evaluation for Modeling in Elderly Adults

Yumiko Muto[1], Makoto Sugou[2], Kaede Tsumurai[3], Honami Ito[3], Yuichiro Hosono[3], and Takeshi Muto[3(✉)]

[1] Department of Information Processing, Interdisciplinary Graduate School of Science and Engineering, Tokyo Institute of Technology, 4259 G2-1, Nagatsuta, Midoriku, Yokohama, Kanagawa 226-8503, Japan
muto@u.ip.titech.ac.jp

[2] TeleBusiness Inc., 2-12-24, Yaei, Sagamihara, Kanagawa 229-0029, Japan
sugou@tele.jp

[3] Faculty of Information and Communications, Bunkyo University, 1100, Namegaya, Chigasaki, Kanagawa 253-8550, Japan
{b3p31095,b3p31021,b3p31140,muto}@shonan.bunkyo.ac.jp

Abstract. In this study, from the viewpoints of enhancing communication of elderly people, we suggest a model to estimate the distortion value of the human body caused by aging as a new index of aging, which is "distortion age," measured using the robotic "DOCTOR'S EYE", which is equipped with Kinect. As a result, we found a more significant difference of the distortion in the front–back direction of elderly participants between standing and walking than in the distortion of young participants. We also determined the necessity of measuring the difference for a precise evaluation of the distortion and the effectiveness of the easy measurement method of distortion during walking, such as Kinect. In addition, as the results of the analysis of the relationship between the aging and the distortion, we found the two kinds of positive correlations between age of the elderly participants and the horizontal distance between the positions of the head and shoulder, and between age and the value of differences between the horizontal distances of standing and walking. Finally, based on these two correlations, we proposed the model to estimate the distortion age of elderly people for engineering applications, such as installment of the DOCTOR'S EYE.

Keywords: Aging · Gait motion · Posture · Kinect · Elderly

1 Introduction

Body distortion caused by aging is generally known to worsen an individual's posture, as well as cause headache, organ disease, and traffic accidents. In particular, falls in elderly adults cause bone fractures and brain disorders, and falls have been indicated to pose a risk of an individual becoming bedridden [1]. It is one of the major social issues that need to be resolved, from the viewpoints of preventing their social isolation and enhancing their communication.

M. Kurosu (Ed.): HCI 2017, Part I, LNCS 10271, pp. 506–521, 2017.
DOI: 10.1007/978-3-319-58071-5_38

Conventionally, measurement methods used to evaluate body distortion include methods that use motion capture equipment. For example, optical motion capture is highly accurate and reliable; hence, it is widely used to measure various body movements. However, the disadvantages of this method include the necessity of placing markers on the body, creating a substantial burden on the subject, and the high cost involved in introducing this method. Conversely, Kinect (Microsoft Corporation, USA) is non-contact, low cost, and easy-to handle interface. However, there are concerns regarding the accuracy of Kinect measurements; hence, a number of research and clinical facilities in Japan have avoided using Kinect.

Recently, in basic research aiming for clinical application overseas, adequately accurate measurements have been reported to be assured by limiting the measurement methods and targets. For example, when Kinect and optical motion capture were compared when measuring a healthy individual's gait, the report showed that the accuracy of Kinect was slightly lower for the leg swing time and step time, but the accuracy could be sufficiently assured for walking speed, stride, and step distance [2]. In addition, when comparisons were made using a pressure sensor mat, the report indicated that walking speed, stance, step length, and step time could be measured with an equivalent degree of accuracy [3]. A higher degree of accuracy has been reported to be assured by walking slowly and obtaining the measurements from the front, facing the Kinect [3]. Furthermore, based on the advantage that the Kinect can obtain measurements without coming into contact with the patient, other reports [4] have already demonstrated improved effect by using this device in the rehabilitation of patients with stroke-induced hemiplegia [4] and Parkinson disease [5].

Based on the above information, this research focused on the possibility that the user-friendly Kinect may be useful for maintaining the health of elderly people by devising measurement targets and methods. We will also measure and analyze body distortion caused by aging, using the robot DOCTOR'S EYE equipped with Kinect, with the aim of building interface technology to quantitatively evaluate body distortion to maintain the health of elderly people. The posture of elderly adults and younger adults will be particularly measured when they are upright and stationary, while walking, and while walking after standing up from a chair, and parameters for evaluating body distortion will be extracted from coordinate information of the head, shoulders, and hips in relation to the spine. Based on these results, the relationship between the amount of body distortion and the age of the elderly adult will be analyzed, and we will propose a new model to estimate the age index (distortion age) based on body distortion.

2 Method

2.1 Participants

There were a total of 36 participants. The 20 elderly adults were aged 70 to 83 years (mean, 75.55 years), and consisted of 10 men and 10 women. The younger adults were 16 university students aged 19 to 21 years (mean, 20.8 years) (12 men and 4 women). The participants joined the study after receiving sufficient explanation and providing informed consent.

2.2 DOCTOR'S EYE

The robot "DOCTOR'S EYE" ((Inc.) TeleBusiness) used in this experiment is shown in Fig. 1. Kinect V2 for Windows (Microsoft) was loaded into the camera of this robot, whereas a tablet PC (Surface Pro 3, Microsoft) equipped with software to measure posture developed by TeleBusiness was loaded into the monitor. In addition, the Kinect sensor installed in the DOCTOR'S EYE simultaneously collects and records the three-dimensional space coordinates for 25 joints using the same software, and enables reproduction of the imaging information from the front, left, and right sides, and from above. Research in the development of this system and use of the technology in rehabilitation practice have been reported [6–9]. Also former studies reports that the Kinect V2 is accurate enough to measure these clinical parameters in healthy subjects [10, 11]. In this study, we conducted the experiment with the robot in a fixed location, but movement is also possible when controlled by an application developed by TeleBusiness, with a mobile robot (Roomba 500 series, Research and Development Kit, iRobot Corporation, USA) mounted at the bottom of the DOCTOR'S EYE.

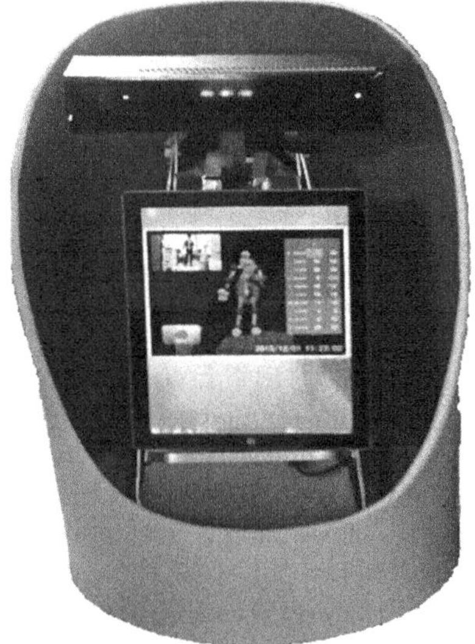

Fig. 1. DOCTOR'S EYE

2.3 Experiment Procedures

To measure the posture of the experiment participants, the DOCTOR'S EYE was set up in a fixed position facing the participant at a distance of 4 m to enable sufficient measurement accuracy. The experiment was conducted under two conditions: walking upright (condition 1), and walking immediately after sitting (condition 2). In condition 1, the participants were required to walk straight toward the robot from an upright and stationary position 4 m from the robot. This was repeated thrice by each participant. Conversely, in condition 2, the participant was required to sit on a chair located 4 m away from the robot, and then to stand and walk straight towards the robot, similar to condition 1. This was repeated twice by each participant. The participants were requested in advance to walk naturally and at their own pace (at their normal speed) while walking for each condition.

2.4 Analysis

The data obtained from the Kinect sensor was collected at a 30-Hz sampling rate as the time-series data for 25 joint (Fig. 2) position coordinates (*x*, *y*, and *z*). In this study from these 25 joints, we focused on joints relating to the head, shoulders, and hips, and the relationship of these joints with the spine, to evaluate posture. The *z* coordinates of these joints were used for analysis. Each *z* coordinate shows the horizontal distance between the Kinect and each of the participant's joints. For example, the head *z* coordinate shows the horizontal distance between the participant's head and Kinect; the right shoulder {Shoulder(R)} *z* coordinate shows the horizontal distance between the Kinect and center of the participant's shoulder (Fig. 3); and the hip center {Hip(C)} shows the horizontal distance between the Kinect and center of the participant's hip. Furthermore, the difference between the hip and head *z* coordinates {Hip(C) - Head} and the difference between the shoulder head *z* coordinates {Shoulder(R) - Head} were calculated to evaluate the distortion of the shoulders and hips using the head position (*z* coordinate) as the criteria. Adopting this method enables quantitative determination of how much horizontal distance is kept in position by the head, shoulders, and hips against the plane of the vertical direction, with the *z* axis as the normal plane. In other words, provisionally, this would mean that if {Hip(C) - Head} = {Shoulder(R) - Head} = 0, then the head, shoulders, and hips are all positioned in one plane of the vertical direction, with the *z* axis as the normal plane. In addition, when {Hip(C) - Head} > 0 and {Shoulder(R) - Head} > 0, the head would be projecting ahead of the hips and shoulders, hence, in other words, quantitatively demonstrating that the participant was stooping would be possible.

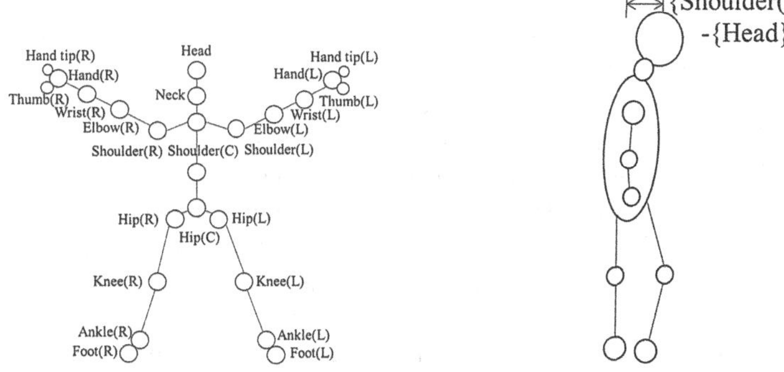

Fig. 2. Skelton model with 25 joints by Kinect

Fig. 3. {Shoulder(R)-Head}

3 Results

3.1 Posture When Upright and Stationary

Comparison of younger and elderly adults. We compared the posture in an upright and stationary position before starting to walk in younger and elderly adults based on data obtained in condition 1. Figure 4 shows the relationship between two types of posture distortions when they were upright and stationary for the 36 participants for three trials. The vertical axis is the difference between the Kinect and right shoulder horizontal distance, and the difference between the Kinect and head horizontal distance. In other words, it shows the horizontal distance between the right shoulder and head {Shoulder(R) - Head} (Fig. 3). The horizontal axis similarly shows the horizontal distance between the hips and head {Hip(C) - Head}.

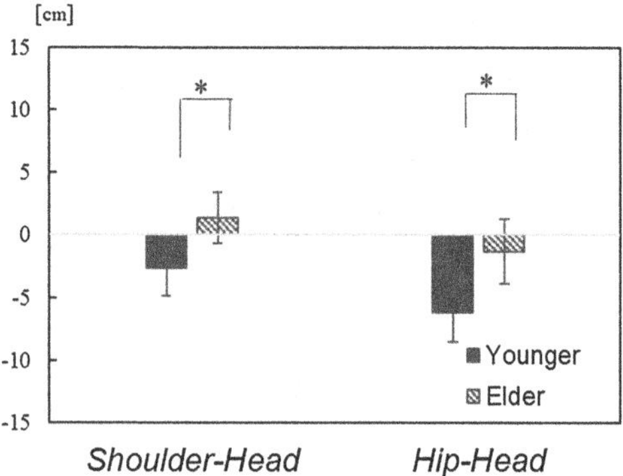

Fig. 4. Comparison between younger and elderly participants in standing condition 4

The mean values for the elderly adults were {Hip(C) - Head} = 1.29 cm (SD = 2.61) and {Shoulder(R) - Head} = 1.35 cm (SD = 2.07), whereas the mean values for the younger adults were {Hip(C) - Head} = −6.16 cm (SD = 2.40) and {Shoulder(R)-Head} = −2.57 cm (SD = 2.26). Furthermore, the younger adults' mean value $\mu \pm 2\sigma$ range is shown in the green frame in the figure, and 95% of the younger adult data are contained within this green frame. From this figure, the comparatively younger adults are determined to be distributed densely around the center of the third quadrant, whereas the elderly adults are more widely distributed mainly in the first and second quadrants. From this information, we determined that the elderly adults showed a positive value in the horizontal distance between the shoulders and head compared with that of the younger adults, and the position of the head had the tendency to project in front of the shoulder position. Furthermore, based on the results of comparing the mean value of elderly adults and younger adults when standing upright and stationary, we determined that a significant difference was found between the elderly and younger adults for the horizontal distance between the shoulders and head and the horizontal distance between the hips and head (Welch t test, $t = -20.60$, $p < 0.001$).

In contrast, when we examined the elderly adult data in detail, we noticed that 25.4% of the elderly adults who participated in this experiment were within the green frame in Fig. 5 (younger adult mean value $\mu \pm 2\sigma$ range). In addition, all the elderly adults who fell within this range were 74 years or younger. These data mean that approximately 25% of the elderly adults aged 74 or younger were able to maintain almost the same posture as the younger adults.

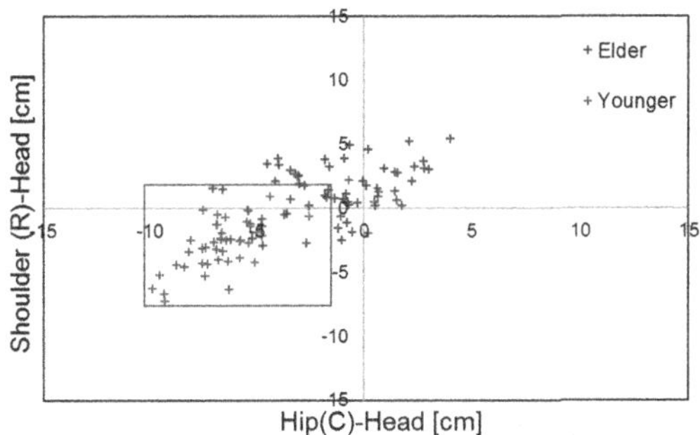

Fig. 5. Scatter plot showing the relationship between each participant's posture in standing condition

Changes in posture with aging. We analyzed the relationship between the age of each participant and the horizontal distance between the right shoulder and the head {Shoulder(R) - Head}, and the horizontal distance between the hips and the head {Hip(C) - Head} when the elderly adult participants were standing upright and stationary, to investigate the changes in posture associated with aging. Figure 6 shows the relationship between the age of the elderly adult and the horizontal distance between the right shoulder and head {Shoulder(R) - Head}. Figure 7 shows the relationship between the age of the elderly adult and horizontal distance between the hips and head {Hip(C) - Head}.

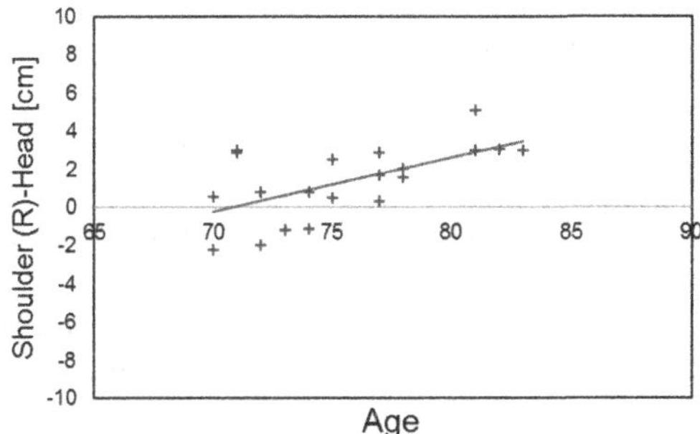

Fig. 6. Relationship between age and {Shoulder(R) - Head} in standing condition

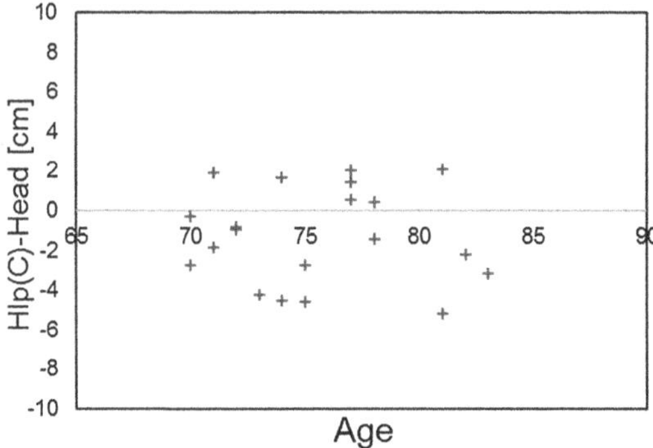

Fig. 7. Relationship between age and {Hip(C) - Head}in standing condition

The results of Investigation of the correlation coefficient for each scatter plot shows that a positive correlation value of $r = 0.64$ between the age of the elderly adult and horizontal distance between the right shoulder and head {Shoulder(R) - Head} when the person was upright and stationary. However, almost no correlation was seen between the age of the elderly adult and horizontal distance between the hips and head {Hip(C) - Head} ($r = -0.18$). Based on these results, we determined that the horizontal distance between the right shoulder and head when the elderly adult was upright and stationary increased with advanced age, and a tendency for body distortion presents in the form where the head projects ahead of the shoulder position.

3.2 Posture When Walking Upright

Comparison of younger and elderly adults. In condition 1, the horizontal distance between the hips and head {Hip(C) - Head} is shown in Fig. 8 to compare the posture in younger and elderly adults. The mean value of younger adults was −5.80 cm (SD = 5.83 cm), whereas the mean value for elderly adults was 2.90 cm (SD = 2.98 cm); hence, a significant difference was found between elderly and younger adults *(Welch t test,* $t = -10.07$, $p < 0.001$). Based on these results, the horizontal distance between the hips and head {Hip(C) - Head} in elderly adults was a positive value, whereas this was a negative value in younger adults. These data indicate that the elderly adult head position was in a more forward position than the hips, whereas the younger adult head position was positioned further back than the hip position. In addition, accurately measuring the horizontal distance between the right shoulder and head {Shoulder(R) - Head} is considered to be difficult, while the participants were walking, due to the movement of the feet and coordinated movement of the arms, despite using this measurement as an index for evaluating posture when the participants were upright and stationary. Hence, for this reason, we conducted an analysis focusing on the hip position only during walking upright based on this measurement method.

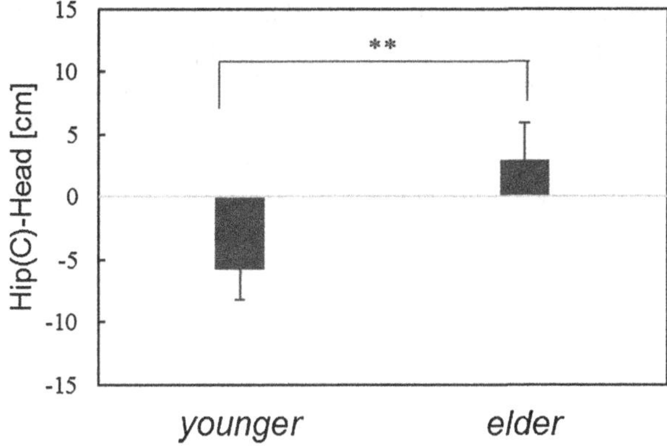

Fig. 8. Comparison between younger and elderly posture in walking condition

Changes in posture with aging. We analyzed the relationship between the age of the elderly adult participant and horizontal distance between the hips and head {Hip(C) - Head} when walking upright to investigate changes in posture with aging (Fig. 9). As a result of investigating the correlation coefficient for both, we obtained a low positive correlation of $r = 0.38$.

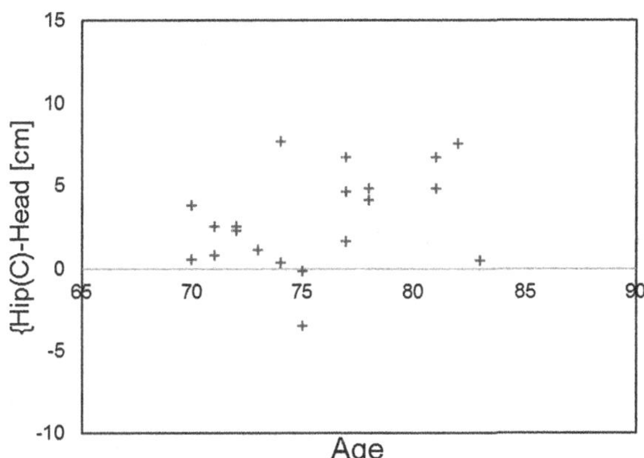

Fig. 9. Relationship between age and {Hip(C) - Head} in walking condition

3.3 Comparison of Posture When Upright and Stationary and When Walking Upright

Comparison of younger and elderly adults. The results of comparing the horizontal distance between the hips and head {Hip(C)} - {Head} when upright and stationary and when walking upright in younger and elderly adults are shown in Fig. 10. No significant difference was found in younger adults between when they were upright and stationary and when they were walking upright ($p = 0.35$), but a significant difference was found in elderly adults (Welch's t test, $t = 2.63$, $p < 0.01$). Furthermore, the horizontal distance between the hips and head {Hip(C) - Head} showed a positive value in elderly adults when walking upright, and they have a tendency to have a more forward leaning posture than when they were upright and stationary. Based on these results, the characteristics of elderly adults were a prominent change in the posture between when they were upright and stationary and when they were walking upright. The elderly adults tended to have a more notable forward leaning posture when they walked upright. Conversely, these changes were not observed in younger adults; thus, this tendency was absent in younger adults.

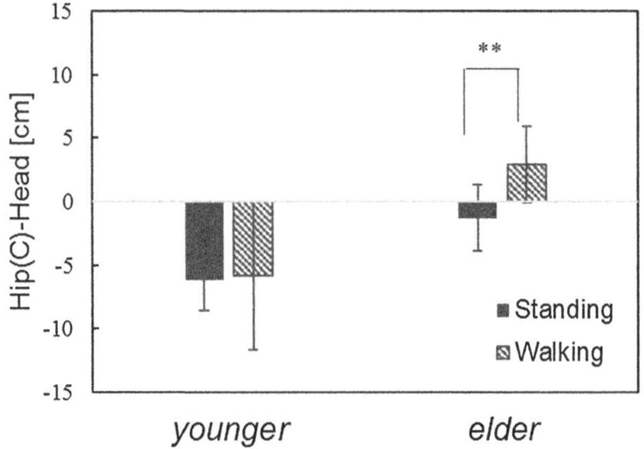

Fig. 10. Comparison between postures during standing and walking

Changes in posture with aging. Based on the results described in Section (Comparison of younger and elderly adults), we calculated the difference (amount of change) in the horizontal distance between the hips and head {Hip(C) - Head} when the elderly adult

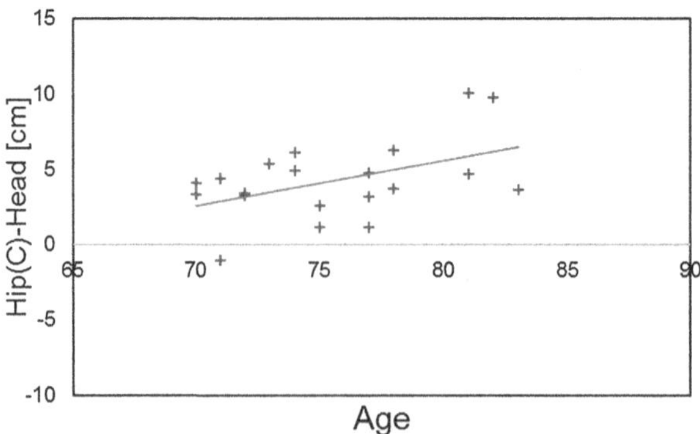

Fig. 11. Relationship between age and {Hip(C) - Head} difference in standing and walking conditions

was walking upright, and the horizontal distance between the hips and head {Hip(C) - Head} when standing upright and stationary. The relationship between the values and ages of the participants is shown in Fig. 11. Furthermore, we detected a significant positive correlation of $r = 0.48$ when we analyzed the correlation coefficient. This was even larger than the value found in Section (Changes in posture with aging) for standing upright and stationary ($r = -0.18$), and the correlation value obtained for walking upright ($r = 0.38$) as a result of the investigation in Section (Changes in posture with aging). Based on this result, we found a higher correlation between the age of the elderly adult and the difference (amount of change) between walking upright and standing upright and stationary in relation to the horizontal distance between the hips and head than the difference between standing upright and stationary and walking upright.

3.4 Posture When Walking Immediately After Sitting

Comparison of younger and elderly adults. The results of comparing the horizontal distance between the hips and head {Hip(C) - Head} in younger and elderly adults when walking immediately after sitting (condition 2) are shown in Fig. 12. The mean value of younger and elderly adults was −3.38 cm (SD = 2.53 cm) and 4.21 cm (SD = 4.11 cm), respectively, indicating that a significant difference was also found between elderly and younger adults in condition 2 (Welch t test, $t = -4.30$, $p < 0.001$).

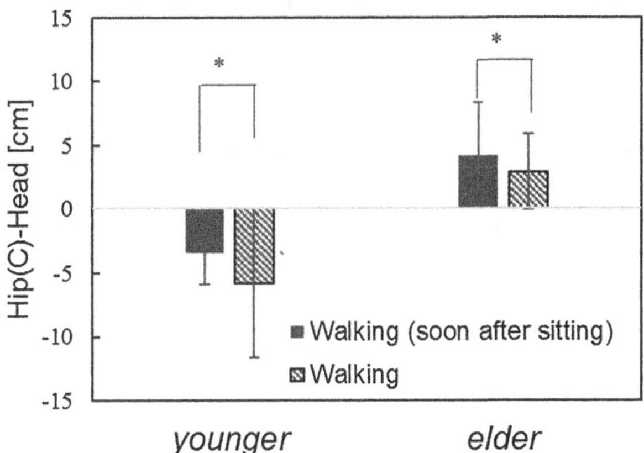

Fig. 12. Comparison between postures during walking immediately after sitting and just walking conditions

Comparison of walking immediately after sitting and walking upright. The results of comparing the horizontal distance between the hips and head {Hip(C) - Head} when walking upright (condition 1) and when walking immediately after sitting (condition 2) are shown in Fig. 13. These results show a significant difference between the horizontal distance between the hips and head {Hip(C) - Head} in both younger and elderly adults when walking upright and walking immediately after sitting (Welch t test, younger adult: $t = -2.50, p < 0.05$; elderly adult: $t = -1.73, p < 0.05$). Based on these data, both younger and elderly adults have a tendency to adopt a more forward-leaning posture when walking immediately after sitting compared with walking upright; hence, we cannot conclude this to be a tendency peculiar to elderly adults.

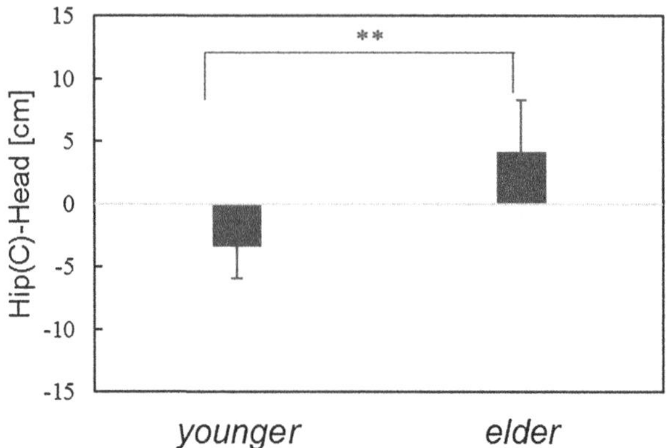

Fig. 13. Comparison between younger and elderly posture in walking immediately after sitting condition

4 Proposal of an Elderly Adult Body Distortion Age Estimation Model

Based on the above results, we proposed in this study body distortion age as a new age index based on elderly adult body distortion, and we are proposing a model to estimate that age.

First, we observed a significant positive correlation of $r = 0.64$ between the age of the elderly adult and horizontal distance between the right shoulder and head {Shoulder(R) - Head} when standing upright and stationary based on the analysis of the relationship between body distortion and age of the elderly adult. However, we did not observe an adequate correlation between the horizontal distance between the hips and head {Hip(C) - Head} ($r = -0.18$).

Although a low positive correlation of $r = 0.38$ was found in the correlation between the age of the elderly adult and horizontal distance between the hips and head {Hip(C) - Head} when walking upright, we detected a more positive correlation of $r = 0.48$ between the age of the elderly adult and change in the horizontal distance between the hips and head {Hip(C) - Head} when walking upright and when standing upright and stationary. Based on these results, we conducted a multiple regression analysis to estimate the age of elderly adult body distortion, setting x_1 as the index relating to the shoulder for the horizontal distance between the right shoulder and head {Shoulder(R) - Head} when standing upright and stationary, and x_2 as the index relating to the hips in the amount of change in the horizontal distance between the hips and head {Hip(C) - Head} when walking upright and the horizontal distance between the hips and head {Hip(C) - Head} when standing upright and stationary, and these were set as objective variables. The proposed model formula is shown in Eq. (1). In addition, x_1 and x_2 are both uncorrelated ($r = 0.03$), and no multicollinearity was observed.

$$y = 1.069x_1 + 0.583x_2 + 71.69 \tag{1}$$

The multiple regression Eq. (1) coefficient of determination was $R^2 = 0.49$. The p value was 1% or less than the significance level, and x_1 and x_2 showed that these variables had a high explanatory power level.

5 Discussion

5.1 Characteristics of Elderly Adult Posture Distortion

The results of comparing younger and elderly adult posture showed prominent differences in body distortion in younger and elderly adults under all the conditions of standing upright and stationary, walking upright, and walking immediately after sitting. The elderly adults particularly tended to have a slouching stooped posture given that the position of the elderly adult head was further forward in the direction of travel than the shoulders and hips.

However, as mentioned in Section (Comparison of younger and elderly adults), we found that 25.4% of the elderly adults who participated in the study maintained almost the same posture as the younger adults when standing upright and stationary. This suggested that factors other than age may be involved in the extent of posture distortion. These 25.4% of the elderly adults were all 74 years old or younger, and this group did not include any participants aged 75 years or older. Therefore, these results suggest that quantitatively demonstrating the extent of body distortion may be beneficial for maintaining the health of elderly adults in line with their age.

In addition, the slouching posture observed in elderly adults may visually narrow the range of attention due to the downward-facing position of the head, which in turn lowers the line of sight, and this is known to increase the risk of falls [12]. Based on this information, quantifying the extent of the forward-leaning posture would be effective in estimating the risk of falls based on the forward-leaning posture of elderly adults.

5.2 Amount of Change in Body Distortion When Walking Upright and Standing Upright and Stationary

Conventionally, assessment of body distortion generally targets the upright and stationary position. However, as a result of comparing postures when upright and stationary and when walking upright, no significant difference was seen between the two in younger adults, but a significant difference was seen in elderly adults. Based on this information, the characteristic of elderly adult body distortion is speculated to be related to the amount of change in posture distortion when walking upright and when standing upright and stationary. Hence, when we observed postures both when standing upright and stationary and when walking upright, we feel that a method to quantitatively evaluate the difference in posture distortion at these times would be effective. However, determining the posture distortion when walking upright and when standing upright and stationary is difficult with qualitative visual evaluation only; hence, using a device able to measure the posture during walking with sufficient accuracy is essential, such as the device used in this study, to evaluate elderly adult body distortion.

5.3 Body Distortion When Walking Immediately After Sitting

The results of comparing body distortion when walking upright and when walking immediately after sitting showed a significant difference in both younger and elderly adults, and we determined that both groups walked with a forward slouch when walking immediately after sitting. We presumed that this was because a forward-leaning posture was adopted to maintain the body balance when standing up after sitting. In other words, these were considered to be changes in posture common to both younger and elderly adults.

5.4 Technological Application of the Elderly Adult Body Distortion Age Estimation Model

The results of investigating the correlation between the age of the elderly adult and body distortion showed a significant positive correlation in the age of the elderly adult and the horizontal distance between the right shoulder and head {Shoulder(R)-Head} when standing upright and stationary, and the amount of change in the horizontal distance between the hips and head {Hip(C) - Head} when walking upright and when standing upright and stationary.

Based on these results, we proposed a model to estimate the age of elderly adult body distortion using multiple regression analysis (Eq. (1)), with x_1 as the index relating to the shoulder for the horizontal distance between the right shoulder and head {Shoulder(R) - Head} when standing upright and stationary, and x_2 as the index relating to the hips for the amount of change in the horizontal distance between the hips and head {Hip(C) - Head} when walking upright and the horizontal distance between the hips and head {Hip(C) - Head} when standing upright and stationary, and these were used as objective variables.

The characteristic of this model formula is that the coefficient of x_1, which is the objective variable in this model formula, is 1.069, whereas the x_2 coefficient is 0.583, hence, the influence of the x_1 value is stronger. In other words, this formula shows that when estimating body distortion age, the influence of the value of x_1 relating to the shoulder position when standing upright and stationary is approximately 1.83 times stronger than x_2 relating to the hip position.

Generally, in measurements of joint positions with Kinect, measurement errors are considered to be generated relating to locations where clothing tends to bulge, such as the hips and chest, and joint locations associated with large movements, such as the upper arm joints, where tracking tends to be lost. In fact, in this study, completely ruling out the effect of the participant's clothing as a reason for the low correlation is impossible ($r = -0.18$) between the age of the elderly adult and the horizontal distance between the hips and head {Hip(C) - Head} when standing upright and stationary. In addition, this may be similarly applicable to the correlation between the age of the elderly adult and the horizontal distance between the hips and head {Hip(C) - Head} when walking upright.

However, the calculations of x_1 relating to the head and shoulder are not easily influenced by bulging of clothing, and these are locations that do not generate comparatively large movements; hence, these errors would be relatively small for these locations. Therefore, the objective variable x_1 could be used even on the premise that Kinect was used for the measurements.

In addition, data on hip coordinates were used to calculate the objective variable x_2, but the value offsets the displacement caused by clothing when standing upright and stationary and when walking upright; hence, it is calculated as the difference between the horizontal distance between the hips and head {Hip(C) - Head} when walking upright and the horizontal distance between the hips and head {Hip(C) - Head} when standing upright and stationary. Therefore, clothing has little influence on the values, and similar to the objective variable x_1, objective variable x_2 could be used even on the premise that Kinect was used for the measurements.

Based on these points, the proposed model for estimating the age of elderly adult body distortion is suitable for measurements using Kinect, which suggests that it would be possible to mount this in the DOCTOR'S EYE, and operate it as a system to estimate the age of elderly adult body distortion.

6 Conclusion

In this study, we quantitatively analyzed body distortion caused by aging using Kinect mounted on DOCTOR'S EYE, and bearing in mind engineering applications, we proposed a model that estimates a new age index (distortion age) based on body distortion.

Specifically, profound differences were found in the size of body distortion in elderly adults when standing upright and stationary and when walking upright compared with that of younger adults. The results demonstrated focusing on these differences is essential when evaluating body distortion. In addition, evaluation of these differences need not be determined visually as is generally the case, or conducted using measurement methods that are a burden for elderly adults, including optical motion capture, rather, significant advantages in achieving these measurements are observed by using routine measurement methods that are inexpensive and have no physical burden. Therefore, evaluation using methods that utilize equipment that can easily measure posture during movement, such as walking, such as the method used in this study, is considered to be more effective for estimating distortion age.

In addition, as a result of investigating the relationship between aging and body distortion, we determined that a significant positive correlation was found in the age of the elderly adult and the horizontal distance between the right shoulder and head when standing upright and stationary, and the difference between horizontal distance between the hips and head when walking upright and when standing upright and stationary. These results are also considered beneficial from the perspective of research relating to decreased exercise capacity associated with aging in the elderly adult. Furthermore, we proposed a model for estimating elderly adult body distortion age based on these two correlations. This model is designed taking into consideration the reliability of Kinect, and we anticipate technological applications, including mounting it on the DOCTOR'S EYE.

To date, there has generally a low expectation of the reliability for the accuracy of Kinect, and while this device is able to measure human body movement easily and at low cost, clinicians in Japan in the fields of medicine and health maintenance has been previously reported to avoid using this device. However, Kinect will be expected to be used in the future as an interface technology that can be used in rehabilitation and to support maintaining health in elderly adults by proactively sharing knowledge on the accuracy of Kinect and by devising methods to the use of the device.

In addition, through technological application of the elderly adult body distortion age estimation model proposed in this study, directly communicating to elderly adults that their posture has become slouched may be possible. Forward-leaning posture narrows the field of vision, which is generally known to increase the risk of falls [12]. Based on this information, the proposed model may be used as a device to prevent falls by directly communicating the risk of falls caused by a forward-leaning posture in an easy-to-understand manner to elderly adults.

Previous measures to prevent falls include local activities aiming to improve motor function through exercise [13] Step+ [15], which was developed based on the effect of cognitive function (dual task ability [14])), and MTST (Multi-Target Step test) [16], however, thus far no one has proposed interface technology from the perspective of evaluating elderly adult posture in everyday life from a scientific perspective to encourage people to improve their posture. In addition, falls in elderly adults are listed as risk factors for a person becoming bedridden; thus, fall prevention is known to be extremely important for maintaining the health of elderly adults. Thus, we hope that it will be possible to enable more effective fall prevention measures by combining the proposed method with conventional fall prevention measures.

References

1. Izumi, K., Makimoto, K., Kato, M., Hiramatsu, T.: Prospective study of fall risk assessment among institutionalized elderly in Japan. Nurs. Health Sci. **4**(4), 141–147 (2002). doi:10.1046/j.1442-2018.2002.00119.x
2. Clark, R.A., Bower, K.J., Mentiplay, B.F., Paterson, K., Pua, Y.H.: Concurrent validity of the Microsoft Kinect for assessment of spatiotemporal gait variables. J. Biomech. **45**(15), 2722–2725 (2013). doi:10.1016/j.jbiomech.2013.08.011
3. Dolatabadi, E., Taati, B., Mihailidis, A.: Concurrent validity of the Microsoft Kinect for Windows v2 for measuring spatiotemporal gait parameters. Med. Eng. Phys. **38**(9), 952–958 (2016). doi:10.1016/j.medengphy.2016.06.015
4. Clark, R.A., Vernon, S., Mentiplay, B.F., Miller, K.J., McGinley, J.L., Pua, Y.H., Paterson, K., Bower, K.J.: Instrumenting gait assessment using the Kinect in people living with stroke: reliability and association with balance tests. J. Neuroeng. Rehabil. **12**, 12–15 (2015). doi:10.1186/s12984-015-0006-8

5. Galna, B., Barry, G., Jackson, D., Mhiripiri, D., Olivier, P., Rochester, L.: Accuracy of the Microsoft Kinect sensor for measuring movement in people with Parkinson's disease. Gait Posture **39**(4), 1062–1068 (2014). doi:10.1016/j.gaitpost.2014.01.008
6. Kitsunezaki, N., Adachi, E., Masuda, T., Mizusawa, J.: KINECT applications for the physical rehabilitation. In: Proceedings of Medical Measurements and Applications (MeMeA 2013), 6 p. (2013). doi:10.1109/MeMeA.2013.6549755
7. Adachi, H., Nakayama, E., Sugo, M., Mizusawa, J.: Real time measurement of large joints from 3D co-ordinates using KINECT. IEICE technical report, MBE2014-32, pp. 25–29 (2014)
8. Adachi, H., Nakayama, E., Sugo, M., Mizusawa, J.: Walking data acquisition using KINECT mounting robot. IEICE technical report, MICT2014-50, pp. 25–30 (2014)
9. Adachi, H., Adachi, E.: Using KINECT to measure joint movement for standing up and sitting down. In: Proceedings of the 9th International Symposium on Medical Information and Communication Technology (ISMICT 2015), 5 p. (2015). doi:10.1109/ISMICT.2015.7107500
10. Otte, K., Kayser, B., Mansow-Model, S., Verrel, J., Paul, F., Brandt, A.U., Schmitz-Hübsch, T.: Accuracy and reliability of the Kinect Version 2 for clinical measurement of motor function. PLoS ONE **11**(11), 17 (2016). doi:10.1371/journal.pone.0166532
11. Mentiplay, B.F., Perraton, L.G., Bower, K.J., Pua, Y.H., McGaw, R., Heywood, S., Clark, R.A.: Gait assessment using the Microsoft Xbox One Kinect: concurrent validity and inter-day reliability of spatiotemporal and kinematic variables. J. Biomech. **48**(10), 2166–2170 (2015). doi:10.1016/j.jbiomech.2015.05.021
12. Paulus, W.M., Straube, A., Brandt, T.: Visual stabilization of posture. Physiological stimulus characteristics and clinical aspects. Brain **107**(4), 1143–1163 (1984). doi:10.1093/brain/107.4.1143
13. Kakuda, W., Abo, M.: Preventing falls: current status of falls and the preparedness action plan. Jikeikai Med. J. **123**, 347–371 (2008)
14. Hauer, K., Marburger, C., Oster, P.: Motor performance deteriorates with simultaneously performed cognitive tasks in geriatric patients. Arch. Phys. Med. Rehabil. **83**(212), 217–223 (2002). doi:10.1053/apmr.2002.29613
15. Yamada, M., Tanaka, B., Nagai, K., Aoyama, T., Ichihashi, N.: Rhythmic stepping exercise under cognitive conditions improves fall risk factors in community-dwelling older adults: preliminary results of a cluster-randomized controlled trial. Aging Mental Health **15**(5), 647–653 (2011). doi:10.1080/13607863.2010.551341
16. Yamada, M., Higuchi, T., Tanaka, B., Nagai, K., Uemura, K., Aoyama, T., Ichihashi, N.: Measurements of stepping accuracy in a multitarget stepping task as a potential indicator of fall risk in elderly adults. J. Gerontol. Biol. Sci. Med. Sci. **66**(9), 994–1000 (2011). doi:10.1093/gerona/glr073

Usability Evaluation of Domain-Specific Languages: A Systematic Literature Review

Ildevana Poltronieri Rodrigues(✉), Márcia de Borba Campos, and Avelino F. Zorzo

PUCRS - Pontifical Catholic University of Rio Grande do Sul, Porto Alegre, Brazil
ildevana.rodrigues@acad.pucrs.br,
{marcia.campos,avelino.zorzo}@pucrs.br

Abstract. Software developers have always been concerned with the quality of the products they produce. Although software engineers use new methods to evaluate the quality of their software, there are still some concerns in several of the methods they use when developing software, for example, when using Domain-Specific Languages (DSLs). One of the main goals of DSLs is to ease the work of developers in different areas. However, to achieve this goal it is necessary to provide an evaluation of the usability of such languages. Although it is possible to find some experiments to evaluate such languages, usually this experiments are subjective and do not use techniques from the Human-Computer Interaction (HCI) area. Therefore, this paper presents a Systematic Literature Review (SLR) in which a discussion on the usability of DSLs is presented. This paper also presents a mapping to show how usability has been assessed by researchers in their work.

Keywords: Human-Computer Interaction · Domain-Specific Languages · Systematic Literature Review · Usability evaluation

1 Introduction

The use of Domain Specific Languages (DSLs) eases software development through the appropriate abstractions and notations [4, 12, 16]. Some studies [4, 5, 12, 15] show the importance of DSLs for increasing productivity when developing a system and also for information exchange among experts from a domain [20]. Furthermore, the use of DSLs may facilitate the understanding of programming code, write it faster, and make it less prone to include faults [13]. There are DSLs for several different domains, for example, robotics [9, 23], software architectures anomalies [1], games [11, 14, 29, 32] or performance testing [6–8].

Although their advantages, some studies [7, 18] show that DSLs usage is not widespread. Among the problems that may prevent their use is the lack of systematic approaches to validate DSLs, mainly regarding their quality of use, such as efficiency, efficacy and usage satisfaction [3]. Furthermore, it is difficult to identify or quantify usability problems in DSLs [13].

M. Kurosu (Ed.): HCI 2017, Part I, LNCS 10271, pp. 522–534, 2017.
DOI: 10.1007/978-3-319-58071-5_39

Therefore, this paper presents a Systematic Literature Review (SLR) to understand the main concerns when designing and using DSLs. This SLR allowed identifying primary studies in Human-Computer Interaction (HCI) and Software Engineering (SE) that performed some form of usability evaluation of DSLs. From those studies, several different used terms were mapped to a taxonomy in usability evaluation of DSLs.

This paper is organized as follows. Section 2 briefly describes the background on DSL and HCI. Section 3 presents the SLR protocol and discusses the main findings of this work. Section 4 describes, briefly, the main structure of a framework for usability evaluation of DSLs. Section 5 presents the final remarks of this work.

2 Background

This section presents the main related areas of this paper, *i.e.*, Domain-Specific Languages and Human-Computer Interaction.

2.1 Domain-Specific Languages

Domain Specific Languages (DSL), also called application-oriented, special purpose or specialized languages, are languages that provide concepts and notations tailored for a particular domain [7, 13]. They differ from a General Purpose Language (GPL), such as Java, C or Python, for example, since they are designed from the problem domain and not from the solution domain. When designing a DSL, it is important to analyze the domain, in order to identify and document features of that domain.

There are several tools that help to create and maintain DSLs. These tools are know as Language Workbench (LW), for example, Microsoft Visual Visualization Studio and Modeling SDK, Generic Modeling Environment (GME), Eclipse Modeling Framework (EMF) or MetaEdit+. Those tools are not restricted to analysis and code generation, but provide also a better experience to DSL developers, since they allow creating DSL editors that are very similar to modern Integrated Development Environments (IDEs) [13].

Similar to other programming languages, a DSL also has a well-defined syntax and semantic. Its syntax describes its structure, while its semantic defines the meaning of each construct. The DSL syntax usually contains: an abstract definition, which is normally specified in a meta model in which the language constructs, properties and relationships are defined; and a concrete definition, in which the elements of the DSL are represented, *e.g.* using tables, text, figures, or matrices [21].

The elements representation must meet the domain concepts that are being modeled. The goal is to meet the representation fidelity [17, 33], in which there is a clear mapping between each representation form to its domain concept. Furthermore, all concepts must be represented in the DSL. As an example, Fig. 1 shows a meta model scenario for a Performance Testing DSL [6–8]. In the figure, there are three types of system users: Browsing, Shopping and Ordering. Each type of user has a different probability of executing an action, *e.g.* the Browsing user has only 25% of chance of performing the Shop action and only 15% of chance of executing the Order action.

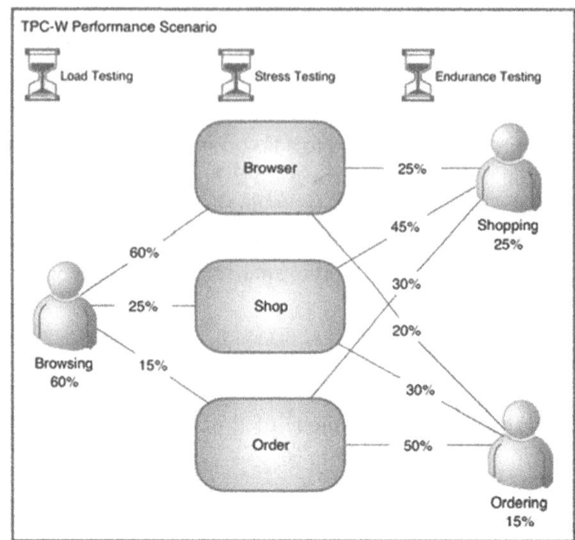

Fig. 1. Meta model scenario for stress testing

Figure 1 also shows that three different types of tests are possible: Load Test, Stress and Resistance [19].

A DSL should be easy to use and its use should be more, or at least as, efficient and efficacious as a GPL. However, experience and literature [10] show that developers consider that the learning curve may be too expensive when comparing the use of known GPLs. Hence more studies are necessary to evaluate the usability of DSLs.

2.2 Human-Computer Interaction

Human-Computer Interaction (HCI) is concerned with the quality of the use of interactive systems and with the impact of their daily use for users [26]. One of the goals of HCI is to obtain practical results related to user interfaces in systems projects [28]. To achieve this goal, researchers try to understand and to acquire methods and techniques that use different quality criteria for interactive systems. This work main focus is on the usability criteria. According to Rogers *et al.* [26], usability criteria includes to be efficient, efficacious, safe, useful, easy to learn and easy to remember how to use.

The design process of an interactive system contains the requirements, design alternatives, prototypes and evaluation. These are all activities that are complementary in an interactive cycle. The evaluation phase is responsible for guaranteeing that the system is adequate to its purpose to the final users [24]. Thus, the evaluation of the quality of use carried out during the process of developing an interactive system and not only in the final phase allows to identify (potential) problems that can affect the use of the system [30].

The evaluation process of an interactive system encompasses to know why, what, where, when and whom evaluates the system. There are different methods and techniques to evaluate system usability. Regarding DSLs, the evaluators could be domain users, analysts, developers, testers or HCI specialists, for example.

3 Systematic Literature Review

This section presents a systematic literature review (SLR) [18], in which the main focus was to identify and to analyze the evaluation process of DSLs. The period in which the SLR was executed was from March to June 2016. This study allowed us to identify primary studies in both Human-Computer Interaction (HCI) and Software Engineering (SE) areas.

3.1 SLR Planning

During this phase, the research goal, research questions, search strategy, and the inclusion and exclusion criteria are defined.

Research goals: based on preliminary studies on the subject, the following goals were established for this SLR: *(i)* whether HCI aspects were considered or not during the development of a DSL; *(ii)* to know the techniques and approaches used to evaluate DSLs; *(iii)* whether there were problems and limitations regarding DSL evaluation when HCI techniques were applied.

Research questions: based on the research goals, the following questions were asked: RQ1: Was the importance of usability considered during the DSL development? RQ2: What were the evaluation techniques that were applied in the context of DSLs? RQ3: What were the problems and limitations identified during the DSL usage?

Search strategy: *the* following digital libraries were used: ACM (http://portal.acm.org/); IEEE (http://ieeexplore.ieee.org/); ScienceDirect (http://www.sciencedirect.com/); and, Scopus (https://www.scopus.com/).

Selection criteria: the following inclusion (IC) and exclusion (EC) criteria were used: IC1 - the study must contain at least one of the terms related to HCI evaluation in DSLs in the title or abstract; IC2 - the study must present some type of DSL evaluation; EC1 – the study is about evaluation but not DSLs; and, EC2 - the study is not written in English;

3.2 SLR Execution

During this phase, the search string construction, studies selection, quality evaluation, data extraction and synthesis were performed.

Search string construction: the search string was build based on terms from DSL and HCI, from usage evaluation and usability, and their synonyms (see Table 1). Table 2 presents the search string.

Table 1. Terms used to build the search string

Terms	Synonyms
Domain Specific Language	DSL, DSM, DSML, Domain Specific Modeling, Domain Specific Modeling Language
Human Computer-Interaction	HCI
Evaluation	Validation, Evaluating, Experiment

Table 2. Search string

(TITLE-ABS-KEY("Domain Specific Language", OR, dsl, OR, dsm, OR, "Domain Specific Modeling", OR, "Domain Specific Modeling Language"), AND, TITLE-ABS-KEY(evaluation, OR, evaluating, OR, experiment), AND, TITLE-ABS-KEY (usability, OR, "User Centered Design", OR, "User Experience", OR, hci, OR, "human computer interaction"))

Quality questions: Each quality question could have the following answers: yes, partially and no. Each answer would be graded as follows: 1 for yes, 0.5 for partially, and 0 for no. After answering the 5 quality questions, only studies that were marked with 2.5 to 5 were considered for further analysis. Table 3 shows only the papers that were considered to be read. The quality questions were: QQ1: Did the paper present any contribution to HCI?; QQ2: Did the paper present any usability evaluation technique?; QQ3: Did the paper present the results analysis?; QQ4: Did the paper describe the evaluated DSL?; and, QQ5: Did the paper describe the found usability problems?

Primary studies selection: the performed search, based on the search string (adapted for each database), returned the number of studies presented in Fig. 2.

Table 3. Quality assessment

Studies				QQ					Quality	
ID	Reference		Year	1	2	3	4	5	Sc	Desc
01	[29]	Sinhá	2006	Y	Y	Y	Y	Y	5	E
02	[4]	Barisic	2011	Y	Y	Y	Y	Y	5	E
03	[2]	Barisic	2012	Y	P	Y	Y	P	3,5	VG
04	[5]	Barisic	2012	Y	Y	Y	Y	P	4,5	E
05	[27]	Rouly	2014	Y	Y	Y	Y	P	4,5	E
06	[12]	Ewais	2014	Y	Y	Y	Y	Y	5	E
07	[3]	Barisic	2014	Y	Y	P	Y	Y	4,5	E
08	[15]	Gibbs	2014	Y	Y	Y	Y	P	4,5	E
09	[31]	Teruel	2015	Y	Y	Y	Y	P	4,5	E
10	[16]	Kabac	2015	Y	Y	Y	Y	P	4,5	E
11	[10]	Cueca	2015	Y	Y	Y	Y	Y	5	E
12	[1]	Albuquerque	2015	Y	Y	Y	Y	Y	5	E

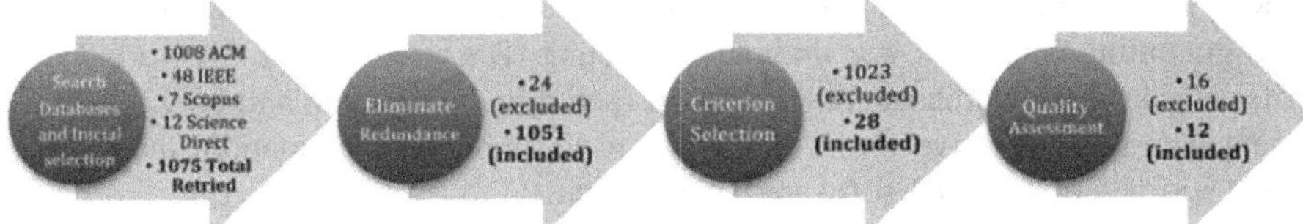

Fig. 2. Selection studies process

In the first phase of the SLR, 1008 papers returned from ACM, 48 from IEEE, 7 from Scopus and 12 from ScienceDirect, resulting in 1075 papers. After applying the inclusion, exclusion and quality criteria, 12 papers were thoroughly read. Figure 2 shows the papers that were selected after each phase.

3.3 Results Analysis

- RQ1 - Was the importance of usability considered during the DSL development?

Barisic *et al.* [2] introduce a methodology that considers usage quality criteria since the beginning of DSL language development to meet the user's expectations. Besides, their study considers usability criteria during the whole development of the DSL and also during the modeling of a system that was developed using the DSL. Their main conclusions were that it is necessary to have a clear definition on the quality criteria that will be used to evaluate the DSL; and, that it is important to integrate the IDE used for the development of the DSL.

Barisic *et al.* [3] propose systematic approaches based on experimental validation with real users. Their study main goal was to assess the DSL impact on domain specialists' productivity when using the DSL. One of the conclusions of their study is that there is a lack of systematic approaches to experimental evaluation of efficiency and efficacy of DSLs.

In order to reflect the user needs, Barisic *et al.* [5] included a usability engineer in the DSL development. The usability engineer participated in all phases of the DSL development, and also during the DSL assessment in an actual context. Their study presents four experiments whose main goals were to evaluate the DSL usability. The experiments were classified using the following attributes: type of evaluation (DSL x GPL, Visual DSL x Textual DSL) and quality (flexibility, productivity, usability, learnability, understanding, user satisfaction, language evolution, effectiveness, efficiency, perceived complexity).

Regarding usability concepts during the modeling process, Sinhá *et al.* [29] describe the use of a set of measures to evaluate DSL usability. This study presents the usability criteria during the functional testing of systems. The usability criteria are based on the ten Nielsen heuristics [22]. They applied the following four heuristics: learnability, effectiveness, efficiency and usage satisfaction. Those criteria were translated to a set of metrics to obtain quantitative data.

Rouly [27] performed a survey to evaluate 25 IDEs used for domains not focused on programming languages, *e.g.* diagrams modeling. The main goal of this work was to verify which functionalities were required in each different domain and how they were presented to the respective user's domain, *e.g.* 3D modeling, animation, music, prototyping, simulation, visual software development.

Similarly to Rouly [27], which was concerned with user-centered development, Gibbs *et al.* [15] propose a methodology and an architecture to separate front-end user interface and back-end coding. Their objective was to increase development environment flexibility, reduce development time and to improve development productivity. Basically the authors propose the use of DSL to describe the user interface, therefore separating the user interface from the rest of the system.

Albuquerque *et al.* [1] proposed the Cognitive Dimension Notation (CDN) to detect usability aspects for tasks maintaining in DSLs. Their study is based on four DSL aspects, *i.e.* expressiveness, conciseness, integration, and performance. For example, expressiveness is related to the fact that DSL artifacts reflects the domain they represent, while conciseness is used to verify whether fewer terms can be used to understand the meaning of the artifacts.

Teruel *et al.* [31] conducted an experiment to assess the usability of DSL for system requirements modeling. The experiment was executed by 38 students, which performed several different modeling tasks, to assess effectiveness, efficiency, and user's satisfaction. Effectiveness was assessed through task finishing rate and help required. Efficiency was measured by expended time and user's productivity when executing a task. Satisfaction was evaluated through questionnaires.

Some of the other selected papers [10, 12, 16], although discuss several aspects related to usability and DSL, do not focus directly on the usability criteria when developing the respective DSL.

Based on the analyzed papers, although few papers were found, all of them described some kind of concern regarding usability when developing DSLs. Some of the studies also were concerned with the easiness for developing DSLs, and, therefore, developed some mechanisms to allow that.

- RQ2 - What were the evaluation techniques that were applied in the context of DSLs?

Albuquerque *et al.* [1] suggested the use of quantitative and qualitative methods. In their study, they present an evaluation method called Cognitive Dimensions (CD) that contains 14 dimensions: viscosity, visibility, compromise, hidden dependencies, expressiveness role, error tendency, abstraction, secondary browsing, mapping proximity, consistency, diffusion, hard mental operations, provisional, and progressive evaluation. The authors presented their method and also applied Goals Question Metric (GQM) to corroborate the qualitative evaluation they performed. In their work, they present two metrics to evaluate DSLs: DSL expressiveness, which refers to in what extend the DSL represents the domain, and DSL conciseness, which refers to what terms can be deleted without compromising the domain artifact representativeness. These two metrics were also divided in other metrics, *i.e.*, expressiveness is composed of hidden dependencies, abstractions, mapping proximity; while conciseness is composed of viscosity, visibility, diffusion and hard mental operations.

Barisic *et al.* [3] suggested that for usability evaluation it is important to first define the usability requirements. Each requirement is assessed by a set of quantitative metrics using GQM. Regarding cognitive aspects, Barisic *et al.* [4] defined a cognitive model to languages based on user scenarios. The cognitive activities in the language are: syntax and semantic learning, syntax composition needed to fulfill a role, syntax understanding, syntax debugging, and changing a function that was written by any developer. In order to evaluate their method, they performed a controlled experiment with six participants. They used a DSL called PHysicist's EAsy Analysis Tool (Pheasant) and a baseline developed using a GPL, *i.e.* C++. At the end, the participants answered a questionnaire to verify whether the use of the DSL was intuitive, adequate and efficient.

Although Ewais *et al.* [12] did not explicitly describe an evaluation method, they used a strategy to evaluate the usability of a language before it would be implemented. To perform this evaluation, fourteen subjects (4 PhD students and 10 instructors) participated in the experiment. The evaluation was divided into 3 steps. In the first step the subjects were exposed to different notations, sample models created using languages, types of relationships, among others aspects. In the second step, the subjects had to construct and adapted 3D Virtual Learning Environment (VLE) using three languages. To realize that task, the subjects had to use paper and pen, since the goal was to assess the level of expressiveness of the language visual notations, and also the effort to create an adaptive 3D VLE using graphical language. In the third step, the subjects answered an online questionnaire.

As mentioned before, Sinha *et al.* [29] based their evaluation on four heuristics proposed by Nielsen, and for each heuristic there was a set of metrics. On one hand, learnability was measured through the number of errors a subject committed, divided by effort; while efficiency was measured by the size of the test set divided by effort. On the other hand, satisfaction was measured in four levels: frustrating, unpleasant, pleasant, and pleasurable. Therefore, it was possible to have a quantitative evaluation of a DSL when analyzing its usability.

Gibbs *et al.* [15] proposed an architecture that considers User Experience (UX) aspects with Model Driven Engineering (MDE). Three premises were used to illustrate the proposed architecture: role specialization to increase productivity and success; the communication gap that may cause confusion and inefficiency; and, communication gap between user interface architecture and code separation.

Cuenca *et al.* [10] described an empirical study to compare efficiency from a DSL to a GPL. Evaluation was performed through observations and interviews conducted with a pre-defined questionnaire. From these instruments conclusion rate, conclusion time, effort and difficulty were measured. These data were collected during programming tasks and usability evaluation during the programming tool usage.

Different from other studies, Barisic *et al.* [5] presented the analysis of four controlled experiments. The authors mentioned that the usability evaluation performed in each experiment was based on users interviews, open questionnaires, testing using tools support and multiple-choice questionnaires.

Barisic *et al.* [2] used a recommendation-based methodology that considers user-centered techniques. Therefore, some activities had to be applied to each phase of the DSL development. The main activities that their methodologies describe are:

domain analysis, language design, controlled experiment as testing, deployment and maintaining.

- RQ3 - What were the problems identified during the DSL usage?

Several studies performed some type of evaluation with users, and most of them did not find any kind of problem that would avoid the use of DSL. For example, Ewais *et al.* [12], Gibbs *et al.* [15] and Kabac *et al.* [16] performed experiments with end users, and analyzed their opinion. Basically, Ewais *et al.* [12] reported that whether the users were able to execute the tasks they were given; whether the users needs were achieved; or, whether the DSL was useful and easy to use.

Rouly *et al.* [27] mentioned that, although the interface design would have a good impact in efficiency, there were some problems regarding the interface of the modeling tool.

Albuquerque *et al.* [1] applied the same DSL to two different systems, *i.e.* HealthWatcher and MobileMedia, and did not present problems, but raised some limitation on their experiments. They applied their experiment considering a set of stable rules, which were not reusable, and they had a very small set of rules to build the systems.

Regarding the evaluation of modeling and developing tools, Barisic *et al.* [4] mentioned that there was a big error rate when inexperienced users used the proposed language. One of the conclusions, from the authors, was that this might have been caused by the lack of feedback that the tool provides for users. Therefore, users did not have the necessary feedback before the authors evaluated the experiment. If they had a feedback, they might have corrected the errors before submitting their results.

Teruel *et al.* [31], different from the other studies, report several problems regarding the representativeness of the used DSL. Based on their experiment, they proposed several modifications in the DSL, for example, change several elements that did not represent the domain.

As mentioned above, most of the studies did not report big problems when using a DSL. Actually, they even present several advantages of using DSL when compared to a GPL used as baseline. However, most of the authors that evaluate their own languages did not report problems in the use of the DSL, since they would use them in domains in which they had already found problems when using a GPL, hence they built a DSL to avoid those problems. Nonetheless, the advantages that were presented indicate that DSLs can provide great advantage in several aspects, for example, increase in productivity, representatives, less effort, and so on.

3.4 Taxonomy for DSL Evaluation

Based on the selected studies and the research questions in Sect. 3.3, this section presents a taxonomy of terms used during the evaluation of DSLs. This taxonomy was structured as a conceptual mapping and is shown in Fig. 3. The taxonomy is structured based on the terms that were mentioned in the studies selected in this SLR. Figure 3 shows the main groups of categories represented as the external rectangles: profile user, data type, usability evaluation methods, empirical methods, metrics, and collection

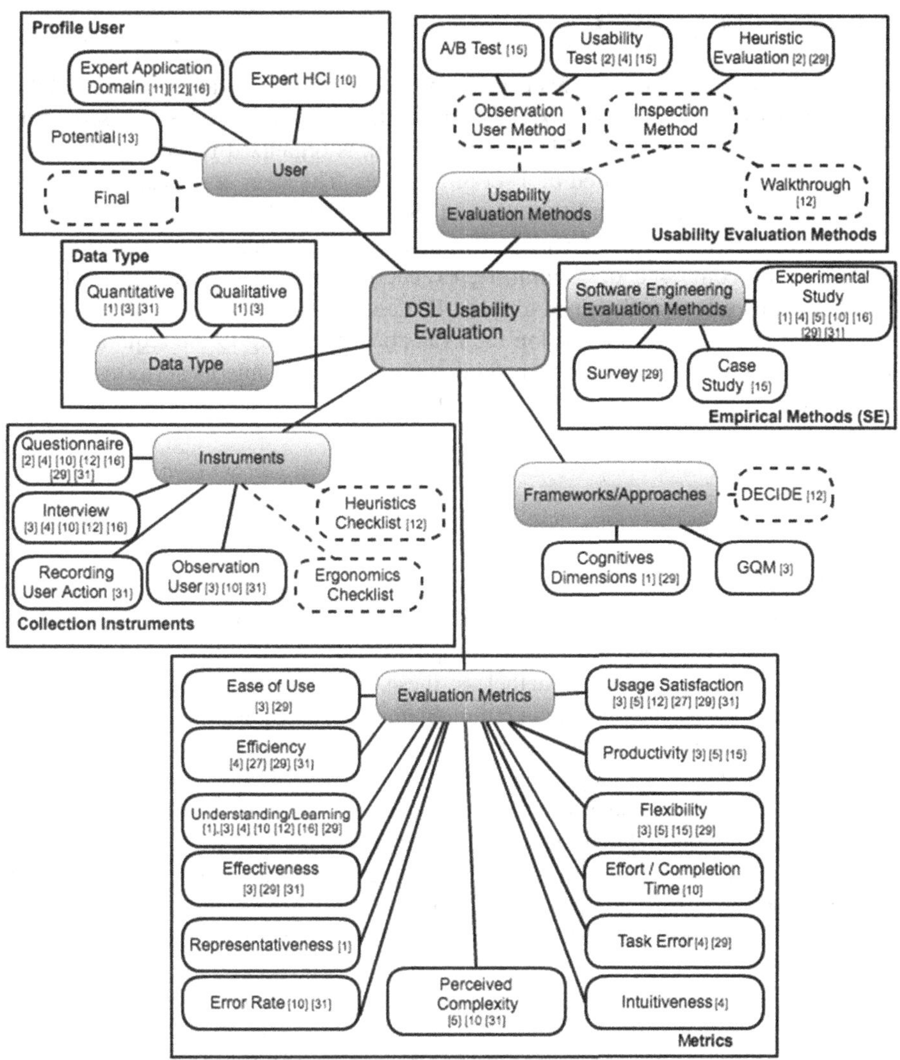

Fig. 3. DSL usability evaluation taxonomy

instruments. Inside each of these rectangles, there is also a rounded rectangle that represents that group. In each of these groups, there is a set of categories, for example, user profile can have the following categories: HCI expert, DSL expert, potential user, final user. Notice that in the figure some of the categories are represented by dashed rounded rectangles. These categories are not directly mentioned in the studies presented in this SLR, but are important in the development of a framework to assess DSLs.

4 *Framework* Usa-DSL

Based on the SLR presented in this paper, a new framework to evaluate DSL usability has been proposed. This framework is called Usa-DSL and its structure is based on the project development life cycle [25]. The framework is organized in steps divided into phases. Each phase is composed of a set of activities. The steps are: Evaluator Profile, Ethical and Legal Responsibilities, Data Types, Empirical Experimental Methods, Evaluation Method, Metrics, Training, Evaluation, Data Packing, Evaluation Reporting. Phases are composed of: Definition, Execution, Analysis and Results. All steps from the framework were designed to meet the needs of each evaluation; therefore, the evaluator has the freedom to develop the evaluation according to the requirements of each language that is being assessed. Furthermore, it is possible to perform the evaluation in an interactive manner. The whole framework is not the subject of this paper and will be presented elsewhere.

5 Conclusion

Although most software is developed using general-purpose languages (GPLs), there are some software that may be developed using domain specific-languages (DSLs). These DSLs provide several advantages compared to GPLs, since they are designed for a specific application domain. Nonetheless, these languages have also to be tested in order to know whether they fulfill the requirements they try to meet. One of such test is regarding whether the languages meet the users needs and expectations. Hence it is important to evaluate the languages efficiency, efficacy, easiness of use, and user satisfaction. Some researchers also try to understand the cognitive effort or learning time users take to comprehend the language they are using.

Considering that, this paper presented a systematic literature review (SLR) to verify if the language designers take into consideration usability aspects when building a new DSL. The Kitchenhan protocol [18] was used to plan, execute and collect data for this SLR.

After applying the SLR protocol, only twelve papers were selected to be analysed. Those papers were used to answer three research questions, basically to understand how usability was considered in the design of DLS, to verify what techniques or approaches were used to evaluate their usability, and to identify what type of problems were raised when the DSL usability was assessed. These results helped to build a taxonomy that may aid researchers either to design new DSLs or, mainly, to evaluate DSLs usability. Furthermore, the results of this SLR helped to identify problems and resources to the proposal of a framework to evaluate DSL usability. This framework, called Usa-DSL, was briefly presented in Sect. 4 and will help new DSL designers to have a strategy to assess their final product in a systematic way. Currently, as this SLR showed, most researchers evaluate their DSL in an *ad hoc* way. This framework will use HCI and DSL knowledge; therefore it is expected to help in the design of better DSLs.

Acknowledgments. Study developed by the Research Group of the PDTI 001/2016, financed by Dell Computers with resources of Law 8.248/91.

References

1. Albuquerque, D., Cafeo, B., Garcia, A., Barbosa, S., Abrahão, S., Ribeiro, A.: Quantifying usability of domain-specific languages: An empirical study on software maintenance. J. Syst. Softw. **101**, 245–259 (2015)
2. Barisic, A., Amaral, V., Goulão, M.: Usability evaluation of domain-specific languages. In: Quality of Information and Communications Technology, pp. 342–347 (2012)
3. Barisic, A., Amaral, V., Goulão, M., Aguiar, A.: Introducing usability concerns early in the DSL development cycle: Flowsl experience report. In: MODELS, pp. 8–17 (2014)
4. Barisic, A., Amaral, V., Goulão, M., Barroca, B.: Quality in use of domain-specific languages: a case study. In: 3rd ACM SIGPLAN Workshop on Evaluation and Usability of Programming Languages and Tools, pp. 65–72 (2011)
5. Barisic, A., Amaral, V., Goulão, M., Barroca, B.: Evaluating the usability of domain specific languages. In: Formal and Practical Aspects of Domain-Specific Languages: Recent Developments (2012)
6. Bernardino, M., Rodrigues, E., Zorzo, A.F.: Performance testing modeling: an empirical evaluation of DSL and UML-based approaches. In: 31st ACM Symposium on Applied Computing, pp. 1–6 (2016)
7. Bernardino, M., Zorzo, A.F., Rodrigues, E.: Canopus: a domain-specific language for modeling performance testing. In: 9th International Conference on Software Testing, Verification and Validation, pp. 1–8 (2016)
8. Bernardino, M., Zorzo, A.F., Rodrigues, E., de Oliveira, F.M., Saad, R.: A domain specific language for modeling performance testing: requirements analysis and design decisions. In: 9th International Conference on Software Engineering Advances, pp. 609–614 (2014)
9. Conrado, D.B.F.: Abordagem para criação de linguagem específica de domínio para robótica móvel. Dissertação de Mestrado – Universidade Federal de São Carlos (2012)
10. Cuenca, F., Bergh, J.V.D., Luyten, K., Coninx, K.: A user study for comparing the programming efficiency of modifying executable multimodal interaction descriptions: a domain-specific language versus equivalent event-callback code. In: 6th Workshop on Evaluation and Usability of Programming Languages and Tools, pp. 31–38 (2015)
11. Dobbe, J.: A domain-specific language for computer games. Master thesis - Delft University of Technology, Netherlands (2007)
12. Ewais, A.B., De Troyer, O.: A usability evaluation of graphical modelling languages for authoring adaptive 3d virtual learning environments. In: 6th International Conference on Computer Supported Education (CSEDU), pp. 459–466 (2014)
13. Fowler, M.: Domain Specific Languages. Addison-Wesley Professional, Boston (2010)
14. Furtado, A.W.B., Santos, A.L.M.: Using domain-specific modeling towards computer games development industrialization. In: 6th OOPSLA Workshop on Domain-specific Modeling (DSM) (2006)
15. Gibbs, I., Dascalu, S., Harris, F.C.: A separation-based UI architecture with a DSL for role specialization. J. Syst. Softw. **101**, 69–85 (2015)
16. Kabac, M., Volanschi, N., Consel, C.: An evaluation of the DiaSuite toolset by professional developers: Learning cost and usability. In: 6th Workshop on Evaluation and Usability of Programming Languages and Tools, pp. 9–16 (2015)
17. Kelly, S., Tolvanen, J.-P.: Domain-Specific Modeling: Enabling Full Code Generation. Wiley-Interscience: IEEE Computer Society, Hoboken (2008)
18. Kitchenham, B., Charters, S.: Guidelines for performing systematic literature reviews in software engineering, ver. 2.3. Technical report, Evidence-Based Software Engineering (EBSE) (2007)

19. Meier, J.: Performance Testing Guidance for Web Applications: Patterns & Practices. Microsoft Press, Redmond (2007)
20. Mernik, M., Heering, J., Sloane, A.M.: When and how to develop domain-specific languages. ACM Comput. Surv. **37–4**, 316–344 (2005)
21. Mernik, M., Porubän, J., Kollár, J., Sabo, M.: Abstraction of computer language patterns: the inference of textual notation for a DSL. In: Formal and Practical Aspects of Domain-Specific Languages: Recent Developments. Information Science Reference (2012)
22. Nielsen, J., Molich, R.: Heuristic evaluation of user interfaces. In: SIGCHI Conference on Human Factors in Computing Systems, pp. 249–256 (1990)
23. Nordmann, A., Hochgeschwender, N., Wrede, S.: A survey on domain-specific languages in robotics. In: International Conference on Simulation, Modeling, and Programming for Autonomous Robots, pp. 195–206 (2014)
24. Prates, R.O., Barbosa, S.D.J.: Avaliação de interfaces de usuário–conceitos e métodos. Jornada de Atualização em Informática do Congresso da Sociedade Brasileira de Computação, Capítulo, vol. 6 (2003)
25. Pressman, R.: Software Engineering: A Practitioner's Approach, vol. 7. Palgrave Macmillan, New York (2005). Capítulo 1–2
26. Rogers, Y., Sharp, H., Preece, J.: Interaction Design. Wiley, New York (2002)
27. Rouly, J.M., Orbeck, J.D., Syriani, E.: Usability and suitability survey of features in visual ides for non-programmers. In: 5th Workshop on Evaluation and Usability of Programming Languages and Tools, pp. 31–42 (2014)
28. Hewett, T.T., Baecker, R., Card, S., Carey, T., Gasen, J., Mantei, M., Perlman, G., Strong, G., Verplank, W.: ACM SIGCHI Curricula for Human-Computer Interaction. Technical report. ACM (1992)
29. Sinha, A.C., Smidts, C.: An experimental evaluation of a higher-ordered typed-functional specification-based test-generation technique. Empirical Softw. Eng. **11–2**, 173–202 (2006)
30. Shneiderman, B.: Designing the User Interface: Strategies for Effective Human-Computer Interaction. Addison-Wesley Longman Publishing Co., Boston (1997)
31. Teruel, M.A., Navarro, E., López-Jaquero, V., Montero, F., González, P.: A CSCW requirements engineering case tool: development and usability evaluation. Inf. Softw. Technol. **56–8**, 922–949 (2014)
32. Walter, R., Masuch, M.: How to integrate domain-specific languages into the game development process. In: 8th International Conference on Advances in Computer Entertainment Technology, pp. 1–8 (2011). Article No. 42
33. Weber, R., Zhang, Y.: An analytical evaluation of Niam's grammar for conceptual schema diagrams. Inf. Syst. J. **6–2**, 147–170 (1996)

Endpoint Fusing Method for Axonometric Drawing of Online Freehand Sketched Polyhedrons

Shuxia Wang(✉), Qian Zhang, Shouxia Wang, Mantun Gao, Xiaoke Jing, and Xiaoming Hui

School of Mechanical Engineering, Northwestern Polytechnical University, Xi'an, People's Republic of China
2008wangshuxia@163.com

Abstract. Endpoint fusing is a highly crucial part in the process of sketch beautification, in which sketch is tackled into tidier one with a certain rule. This paper proposes a new method of endpoint fusing based on angular histogram for axonometric drawing of online freehand sketched polyhedrons, which is an improvement over the existing fusing approaches and lays a solid foundation for further 3D reconstruction. The approach consists of four main steps: Firstly, grouping and paralleling gestures that are the results of recognizing and fitting inputting strokes, and producing correction drawing according to the angular histogram of gestures. Then, clustering endpoints by using adaptive tolerance zone, which refers to grouping adjacent endpoints when both fall within each other's tolerance circles. After that, determining "coordinate system-weight criteria" and getting the order of endpoints fusing. Finally, connecting session is performed under the premise of keeping parallel producing for a neat drawing with perfect connections at the strokes intersection. The method here has been tested with a sketch regularization prototype system called FSR_EF, and experimental results on various freehand axonometric sketches show that it provides a good solution to improve these limitations occurring in most existing sketching systems which only simply conduct pinching without considering context of the sketches. And the test results largely reserve the user's initial intentions and proves that the method achieves an acceptable outcome.

Keywords: Endpoint fusing · Online freehand sketching · Polyhedrons · Axonometric projection · Parallel processing · Sketch regularization

1 Introduction

As the early phase of the design process, conceptual design aimed at obtaining the basic form of product and rapidly express their creative thought with a visual and vivid way for further detailed design [1]. An excellent designer requires good creativities and the capability to present them fluently in a certain way. Freehand sketch is such a representation that can convert and perceive designers' ideas. It also is the most natural and direct means of expressing design innovation and capturing memory. In addition, it's also help to show designers' design thinking and creative activity. Freehand sketch

M. Kurosu (Ed.): HCI 2017, Part I, LNCS 10271, pp. 535–545, 2017.
DOI: 10.1007/978-3-319-58071-5_40

draws fast and produces graceful and natural lines, which impresses people with a strong artistic appeal. Our surveys continued to show that traditional mechanical designer had been accustomed to carry on conceptual design with paper and pencil not computers. Almost 100% drawings from conceptual design are preserved in the form of freehand sketch. However, drawings are always confusing and difficult to correct after several modifications in the process of freehand sketching. Moreover, it's impossible to save the whole design process, and all retained drawings cannot compose a comprehensive design due to the lacking of effectively interactive characteristic. With the rapidly developing of computer technology, online sketches recognition overcomes the shortages of traditional design method and people could interact effectively with work. Such patterned drawing software tools as Visio, Microsoft Office in addition to many CAD systems, finish sketches with overly relying on precise digital information and frequent menu items [2], hence their interface is so typically cumbersome to use and hamper design's creative flow [3] that it's not sufficiently suitable for the fuzzy freehand conceptual design.

In order to well support the freehand sketching design, an efficient and robust sketch interface [4] is necessary, where users can draw sketches on a tablet with a digital pen. The sketch interface is designed to bridge the gap between freehand sketches and computer-based modeling programs, combining some of the features of pencil-and-paper sketching and some of the characteristic of CAD systems to provide a natural, convenient interface to approximate sketch modeling [5]. As early as 1963, Sutherland [6] presented the first interactive sketch system, Sketchpad, which inputted graphs over the screen surface with a light pen. It didn't achieved a desired result due to limitations in performance of the machine and capability of the recognition, but provided a very promising technology. SKETCH [5] allowed users to draw simple geometric figures using a set of predefined gestures. Meyer [7] described a tool called EtchaPad for sketching widgets in the Pad++ system, including many layout operations. Igarashi [8] explained an original sketch into a diagram that looks like a carefully drafted drawing. Zou [9] showed such system that allows users to make an initial sketch by drawing strokes using a pen, reconstruct it, and subsequently add new strokes. After inputting the freehand sketch, computer needs to collect, analyze feature information of sketch, and quickly conduct recognition, interpretation for producing the 2D line drawing of 3D object.

As a symbol of directly recording human consciousness, freehand sketch possesses a variety of features, such as diverse styles, abstraction, imprecision, etc. It's particularly difficult for computer to perfectly interpret the user's design intention by the sketch [4]. Although there has been so many sketch systems described above, producing more sophisticated systems that can improve the shortcomings before for further 3D reconstruction of polyhedral models are necessary. As a very prospective technology without complicated commands, computer sketch interface has been highly focused over recent years. A lot of works has been gone on to research sketch regularization in sketching systems, but there are still great difficulties in systems and even restriction on it's development. In addition, it's a burdensome task presently to design a perfect sketching systems overcoming these inevitable factors. Sketching interpretation is closely related to specific application fields, such as electrical diagrams [10], structure charts of chemical molecules, cartoon animation [11] or architectural drawing [12] etc.

This paper primarily is concerned about the regularization of axonometric drawing of online freehand sketched polyhedrons. Usually a comprehensive projection of 3D object result always requires perfect connection at the strokes intersection, but it is difficult for the user to complete a completely closed sketch, the sketchy line is always not closed or forms a cross near its endpoints. As a consequence, the process of connecting endpoint of strokes correctly, namely endpoint fusing, is a very crucial link during the process of sketch regularization. In the mean time, most of the current systems of freehand sketch complete this module without considering context of sketches, which makes system more liable to make mistakes in interpreting the user's original intentions. Therefore, It remains a issue deserving of further study in online sketch regularization, and specifically addressing the open challenge in this paper.

This paper does an exploratory study about axonometric drawing of online freehand sketched polyhedrons, specifically, endpoints fusing in the process of sketch regularization. Axonometric drawing of freehand sketched polyhedrons consists of a set of line segments whose parallelism is inconsistent and junctions are not neat. And these improper endpoints are great barriers for both correct shape recognition and well regularization. There are considerable researches dedicating to endpoint fusing of freehand sketch, and most of existing approaches are based on tolerance zones of strokes each other. Pavlidis and van Wyk [13] proposed a clustering scheme based on statistical analysis to chose a tolerance zone. Durgun [14] took a percentage of the associated line length as the result of threshold value. And Sun [15] put forward that endpoint of edges should be adjacent to each other if the length of the extension is less than a certain threshold after the shorter strokes extending to intersect with another. Obviously, the methods above cannot be used to obtain the most reliable results. A simple method of connecting endpoints that are purely closer than a minimal threshold distance is far from sufficient. And adopting a relatively fixed threshold value to judge the clustering between strokes, too large one may neglects fine details and lead to fusing overly, too small one may leave endpoints that are supposed to be connected unlinked. The size of the tolerance zone should be determined by the sensibility to the detail in the close vicinity of the endpoint. Lipson [16] proposed a method based on the average distance from each original endpoint to entities in the sketch, which includes the distance from a endpoint to its own entity, namely, half the entity. The smallest average distance is regarded as the size of tolerance circle. The next step involves grouping endpoints falling within each other's tolerance circles, and the procedure is repeated as more and more endpoints are clustered. Finally, each cluster is replaced by one vertex that is the center of each group endpoints. Wang [17] brought up a novel endpoint fusing approach builded on adaptive tolerance zone to improve Lipson's and make the threshold zone more adaptable. However, both of them simply fused endpoints and viewed each entity in isolation without considering the relationship of relative position between all strokes in the final stage of the endpoint integration. It to a certain extent undermines the interrelation between various entities and mistakes user's initial rendering intention. Ku [18] presented a method mainly focusing on the interpretation of online multi-stroke, which translates into five processing phases: stroke classification, strokes grouping and fitting, endpoint clustering, parallelism correction, and in-context interpretation. The shortcomings of this approach include some aspects as follows. First, the method largely lost the initial position information of strokes on account of proceeding parallelism correction after endpoint clustering. Second, the method directly conduct endpoint fusing of gestures with errors and may lead to irregular distortion of projection drawings. Thirdly, the implement algorithm of this method is relatively complicated. Overall, the different fusion methods above on various studies have a certain rationality. Meanwhile, obtaining an excessive fixed tolerance value by experimental statistical analysis or a percentage of the associated line length will lead to an unreliable result. And the method based on adaptive tolerance zone [19] finally cracks the problem, but still exists some deficiencies in fusion manner.

In this paper, we propose a novel endpoint fusing method for axonometric drawing of online freehand sketched polyhedrons, based on our previous research [17], to effectively tidy-up sketches. Firstly, parallelism correction is used to dispose gestures, the result of recognizing and fitting inputting strokes, according to the angular histogram of strokes. Secondly, clustering endpoints using adaptive tolerance zone and obtaining the order of endpoints fusing with "coordinate system-weight criteria". At last, endpoints fusing is carried out in order under the premise of a certain error. This approach adopted a more reasonable method to beautify axonometric drawings of online freehand sketched polyhedrons. In addition, it overcomes the limitation of simple joining gestures without considering in-context information of sketches, and avoids larger shape error of drawings. In addition, a sketching interactive system named FSR-EF that can address the limitations discussed above is proposed. The work perfects the previous methods as well as form the foundation upon further 3D reconstruction of polyhedral models.

2 New Methods

2.1 Overview of Connecting Endpoints

We are going to exploit a system that intends to beautify the freehand axonometric drawing of freehand sketched polyhedron and converts the drawing into a neat line drawing, especially, in terms of endpoints fusing. First of all, as the input of the algorithms in this paper, gestures from recognizing and fitting strokes can be represented by a sequence of line segments $\{L_i;\ 0 \le i < N\}$, and each angle $\{\theta_i;\ 0 \le i < N,\ \ 0 \le \theta_i < 180\}$ is the included angle between x-axis and every line segment, where N is the number of gestures in gesture drawing. The approach here consists of four main steps that are as follows: (1) paralleling gestures under angular histogram and the angle-thresh $\Delta\delta$, with producing a correction drawing; (2) clustering endpoints by using adaptive tolerance zone; (3) sorting order for the "coordinate systems" $\{C_i;\ 0 \le i < H\}$ in accordance with weighting rule; (4) specific part of endpoints fusing is carried out in order. The concrete flowchart of the method in this paper is shown in Fig. 1.

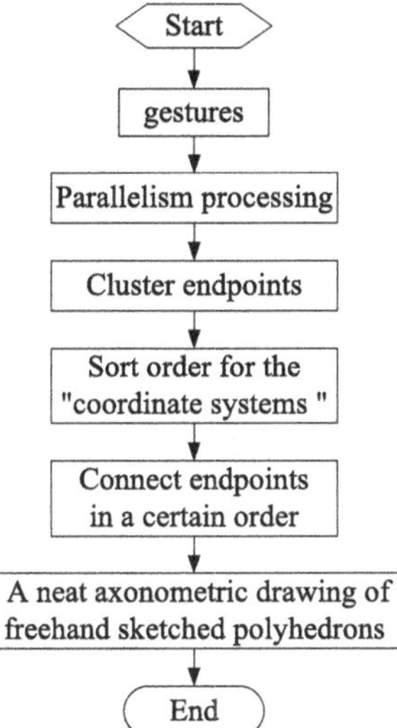

Fig. 1. Process of endpoints fusing for axonometric drawing of online freehand sketched polyhedrons

2.2 Fusion Algorithm

The endpoints usually don't strictly intersect at nodes with existing lots of messy junction, hence we need to connect them tidily. In addition, this section aims to complete concrete operations of endpoint fusing algorithm.

Parallelism processing. Before endpoints joining, we would perform the parallelism processing to calibrate the linearity of gestures in a freehand axonometric drawing with hoping for further improving the reasonableness and accuracy for sketch regularization. we need to extract the in-context information of gesture, then infer structural meaning of sketch from which and adjust messy gestures by imposing linearity constraints and end up with a correction drawing. Generally, we hypothesize that gestures whose angle difference is within angle-thresh $\Delta\delta$ are supposed to be regarded as parallelism in this paper, specially gestures with angles close to the directions along axis in axonometric projection.

Figure 2 shows the major contents for parallelism correction, and the process is summarized by the following steps:

Step1: Extract the endpoints and angle of each gesture $\{L_i;\ 0 \leq i < 18\}$, where L_i represents the gestures whose sequence number is i, and $\theta_i (0 \leq \theta_i \leq 180)$ symbolizes the angle value of L_i.
Step2: Make angular histogram according to the values of i and angle value θ_i. An example shown in Fig. 3.
Step3: Divide gestures in Fig. 3 into groups Q_s by angle-thresh $\Delta\delta$: $Q_1 = \{L_i;\ i = 1, 4, 10, 14, 17\}; Q_2 = \{L_i;\ i = 2, 3, 9, 13, 18\}; Q_3 = \{L_i;\ i = 5, 8\}; Q_4 = \{L_i;\ i = 6, 7, 11, 12, 15, 16\}$.

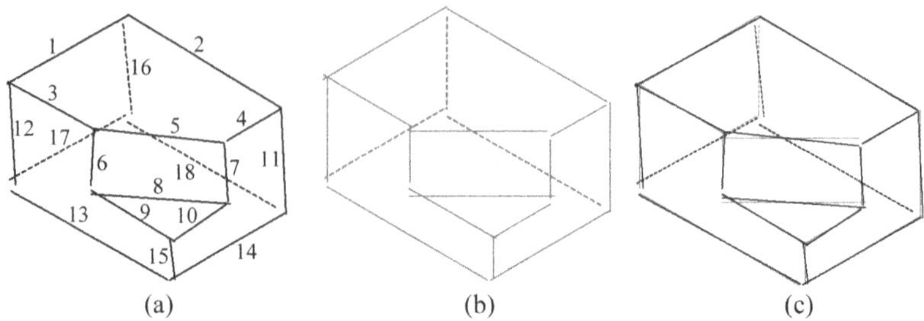

Fig. 2. Parallelism correction (a) gesture drawing. (b) correction drawing. (c) comparison of (a) and (b).

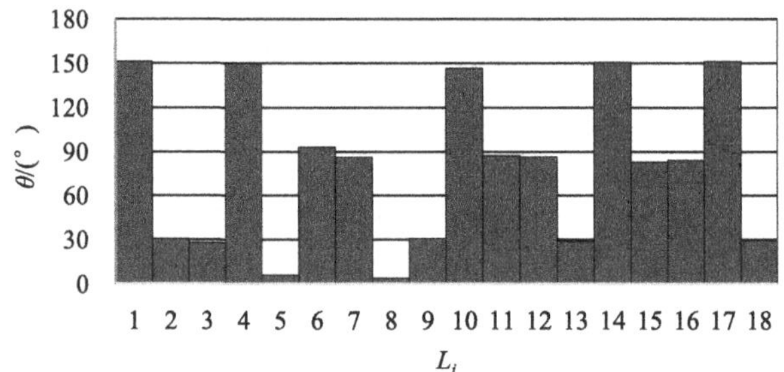

Fig. 3. Angular histogram of gesture drawing in Fig. 2

Step4: Take average angle value $\{\bar{\theta}_s;\ s = 1,\ 2,\ 3,\ 4\}$ for each set of gestures, and respectively correct them by it.

The procedure ends up with a correction drawing, as shown in Fig. 2(b). Figure 2 (c) describes the comparison between two drawings before and after treatment, where the dark one expresses gesture drawing, the light one is correction drawing.

Clustering Endpoints. There are a lot of unconnected endpoints in correction drawing, it's necessary to categorize, store them in one correction drawing and conducive to reasonable connecting. In this paper, we call the potential connection points quasi-fusing endpoints and adopt the method of tolerance zone with variable coefficients to achieve endpoints clustering. The size of tolerance circle here will vary with the whole-text information of sketch. Quasi-fusing endpoints could be grouped into a cluster if they fall within each other's tolerance circle, next repeating the procedure until more and more endpoints are grouped. Each cluster will finally be replaced by one vertex that is explained in more detail below. Moreover, if the number of quasi-fusing endpoints in one cluster greater than 3 or less than 2, it also can be adjusted by appropriately broaden or narrow the tolerance circle. Figure 4 shows the endpoints clustering results.

Sort Order for the "coordinate system". Polyhedron, the planar body with trihedral vertices, is the primary studying object in this paper. And the algorithm here can be

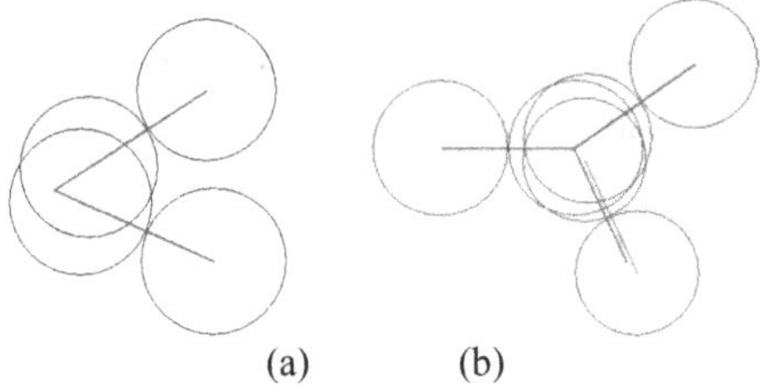

Fig. 4. Determination of clustering endpoints

easily generalized to curved surface objects. For projection drawing of freehand sketched polyhedrons, we assume that there exists one coordinate system at each node including three quasi-fusing endpoints respectively in three different line segments. And directions of the three line segments also individually represent the 3 directions of the coordinate system, each coordinate system consists of a few quasi-fusing endpoints.

Above all, coordinate systems are classified into several groups by determining whether they are consistent in the orientations, and the groups of coordinate systems whose weight is biggest are called level 1 coordinate system G_1, by that analogy, the second most are called level 2 coordinate system G_2, the third most are called level 3 coordinate system G_3, and so on. Because of the level 1 coordinate system G_1 makes up the biggest overweight, it's most rational to first tackle the quasi-fusing endpoints in G_1 and others in turn, we call the rule "coordinate system-weight criteria". There are 12 nodes $\{d_i;\ 0 \le i < 12\}$ in the correction drawing as shown in Fig. 5, correspondingly existing 12 coordinate systems $\{C_i;\ 0 \le i < 12\}$ here. According to "coordinate system-weight criteria", the coordinate systems can be divided into 3 groups: $G_1 = \{C_i;\ i = 1, 2, 3, 8, 9, 10, 11, 12\}$, $G_2 = \{\{C_i;\ i = 4, 6\}, \{C_i;\ i = 5, 7\}\}$. It a priority to tidy-up and connect quasi-fusing endpoints in G_1, and quasi-fusing endpoints in G_2, G_3 one by one.

Connecting Endpoint. In freehand sketched projection drawing, there are three cases after clustering quasi-fusing endpoints: one points clustering, two points clustering and three points clustering ($K = 2,\ 3$). To keep consistent with description above, line segments in correction drawing can be expressed as $\{l_i;\ 0 \le i < N\}$, endpoints of each line segment is $\{d_{ij};\ 0 \le i < N, j = 0, 1\}$, and the tolerance of each quasi-fusing endpoints is $\{R_{ij};\ 0 \le i < N, j = 0, 1\}$. The sequence of line segments consisting of cluster

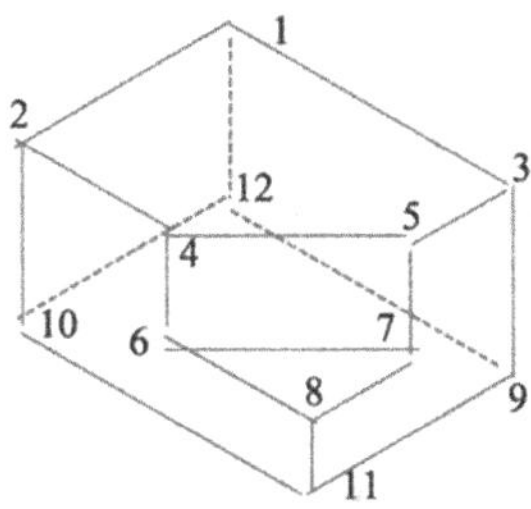

Fig. 5. Correction drawing

points in one group is $\{l_u,\ l_v,\ l_w;\ 0 \le u,\ v,\ w < N\}$, the coordinate systems is $\{C_z;\ 0 \le z < H\}$, and the numbers of line segments that have been involved in the process of endpoints fusing is M $(M = 0, 1, 2, 3)$, where H is the total number of nodes in correction drawing.

Example is shown in Fig. 6, specific steps of algorithm in this paper are as follows:

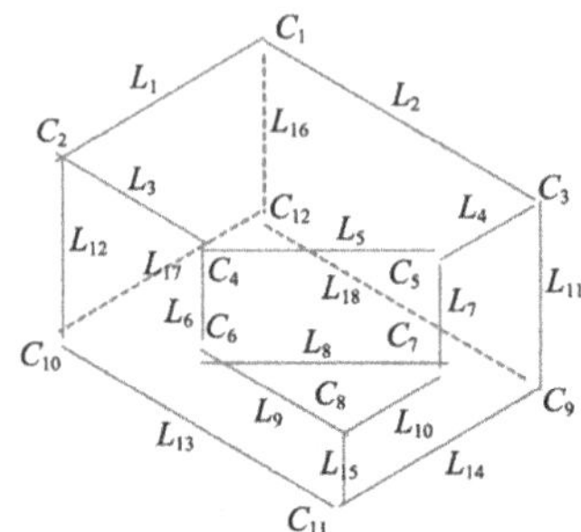

Fig. 6. An example for endpoints fusing

Step1: Cluster quasi-fusing endpoints $\{d_{ij};\ 0 \le i < N, j = 0, 1\}$ in correction drawing into H group by tolerance circle of each endpoint R_{ij}, subsequently with H $(H = 12)$ nodes and H coordinate systems $\{C_z;\ 0 \le z < H\}$. (see Fig. 7);
Step2: Group coordinate systems $\{C_z;\ 0 \le z < H\}$, and sequentially obtain several set of coordinate systems G_1, G_2, G_3: $G_1 = \{C_1\{l_1, l_2, l_{16}\}, C_2\{l_1, l_3, l_{12}\}, C_3\{l_2, l_4, l_{11}\}, C_8\{l_9, l_{10}, l_{15}\}, C_9\{l_{11}, l_{14}, l_{18}\}, C_{10}\{l_{12}, l_{13}, l_{17}\}, C_{11}\{l_{13}, l_{14}, l_{15}\}, C_{12}\{l_{16}, l_{17}, l_{18}\}\}$; $G_2 = \{C_4\{l_3, l_5, l_6\}, C_6\{l_6, l_8, l_9\}, C_5\{l_4, l_5, l_7\}, C_7\{l_7, l_8, l_{10}\}\}$;
Step3: Determine the value of M in each C_z, and respectively collate the sequence of line segments $\{l_u,\ l_v,\ l_w;\ 0 \le u,\ v,\ w < N\}$ in the same coordinate system C_z. Store l_u preferentially if it has already been connected;
Step4: When $M = 3$, $K = 3$, l_u and l_v intersect at P by extending the two line segments. Keep the endpoint that has been addressed in l_w still, and another endpoint in l_w is made into point P. In this case, because all the line segments in one coordinate system has participated in endpoints joining, it's inevitable that there will be fusion errors. For example, we implement connection in $C_{11}\{l_{13}, l_{14}, l_{15}\}$. Because l_{13}, l_{14} and l_{15} have been already tackled, first node 11 is created by intersection of l_{13} and l_{14}, then make l_{15} coincident with node 11, and cause l_{15} rotating in the meantime with certain errors;
Step5: When $M = 0, 1, 2$, $K = 2$, l_u and l_v intersect at P by extending the two line segments;
Step6: When $M = 0, 1, 2$, $K = 3$, first l_u and l_v intersect at P by extending the two line segments. Then translate l_w until one endpoint of it is equal to P and keep it's angle constant. Using $C_6\{l_6,\ l_8,\ l_9\}$ as an example, first node 6 is created by intersection of l_6 and l_9. Then translate l_8 and make it's one endpoint equal to node 6, with the angle constant of l_8.

The process of endpoints fusing in this paper can be classified into two stages: the phase of error-free regularization and the part with errors. At the beginning of endpoints fusing, almost all of line segments in the first few coordinate systems are in unprocessed state. There are only three forms of translation, extension and intersection in this stage with $M = 0,\ 1,\ 2$. Therefore, the stage goes on with zero error. For the latter, all of line segments have involved the endpoints joining and would be carried out the operation of rotating, resulting in the change of angles and accumulation of errors to last level coordinate systems. The most important factors in the process of sketch regularization is to collect drawing intentions of users. however, it is difficult for the user to draw a perfectly sketch, the sketchy line is usually not neat, not absolutely straight, and not entirely parallel between two ones, etc. The method in this paper solves the problems that occurred in user's drawing. We propose a criteria, the angle difference between before and after fusion, is regarded as the assessment for the excellent performance of the method to endpoints fusing.

3 Implementation

Online freehand sketch recognition system FSR is independently researched and developed on Windows 7 using Visual C++ by the team which the author belongs to. The input device is a mouse, and it will interpret the freehand sketch into a neat and clear 2D line drawing. we asked artists to manually draw projection drawing of online freehand sketched polyhedrons, the regularization process and results are summarized in Fig. 7. In addition, the test results largely ensure the output sketch meaningful and show that the approach can support conceptual design based on axonometric drawing of online freehand sketched polyhedrons while achieving a satisfactory interpretation.

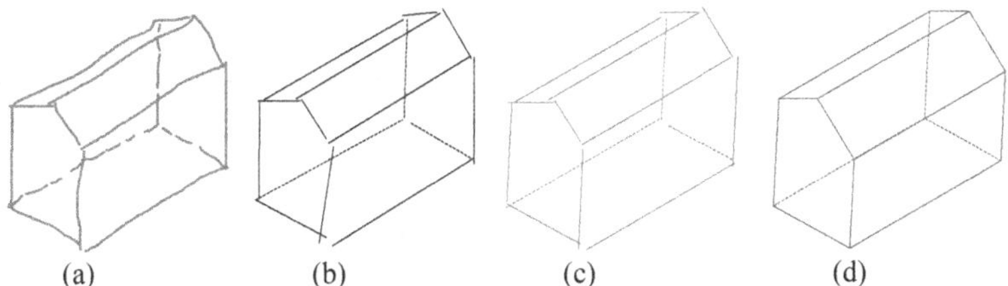

Fig. 7. (a) sketch. (b) gesture drawing. (c) correction drawing. (d) final result.

4 Conclusion

This paper have described a novel method for endpoint fusing of online freehand polyhedrons projection in the prototype FSR_EF system. It improves the existing endpoint fusing methods for online freehand sketched projection. And the test results turns out the better result from the method in this paper by being compared with existing other methods. The study here can improve the accuracy of the sketch regularization and possesses some reference value for the new generation of human computer interaction system supporting conceptual design. Meanwhile, the method here has some limitations. During regularizing some more complicated freehand sketched polyhedrons, there always are larger errors due to the lack of consideration of line-plane relation. The work presented here is only the part of our final sketched based 3D modeling system, and only studies online freehand sketched polyhedrons consisting of single stroke lines, not involving freehand sketched projection including multi-strokes and curves. And further research about how to process the problems above needs to be improved.

Acknowledgements. This work is partly supported by National Natural Science Foundation of China (Grant No. 51105310), Natural Science Basic Research Plan in Shaanxi Province of China (Grant No. 2016JM6054),the Programme of Introducing Talents of Discipline to Universities (111 Project)of China (Grant No. B13044), the Open Project Program of the State Key Lab of CAD&CG (Grant No. A1615) of Zhejiang University.

References

1. Song, B.H.: Research on computer supported intelligent sketching technology for product conceptual design. Northwestern Polytechnical University, D Xi'an (2003). doi:10.7666/d.y568835. (in Chinese) (宋保华. 面向产品概念设计的智能草图研究.D 西安: 西北工业大学)
2. Liu, W.: On-line graphics recognition: state-of-the-art. In: Lladós, J., Kwon, Y.-B. (eds.) GREC 2003. LNCS, vol. 3088, pp. 291–304. Springer, Heidelberg (2004). doi:10.1007/978-3-540-25977-0_27
3. Masry, M., Kang, D., Lipson, H.: A freehand sketching interface for progressive construction of 3D objects. J. Comput. Graph. **29**, 563–575 (2005). doi:10.1145/1281500.1281541
4. Li, B., Lu, Y., Godil, A., et al.: A comparison of methods for sketch-based 3D shape retrieval. J. Comput. Vis. Image Underst. **119**, 57–80 (2014). doi:10.1016/j.cviu.2013.11.008
5. Zeleznik, R.C., Herndon, K.P., Hughes, J.F.: SKETCH: an interface for sketching 3D scenes. In: Conference on Computer Graphics & Interactive Techniques, pp. 163–170 (2007). doi:10.1145/237170.237238
6. Sutherland, I.E.: Sketchpad: a man-machine graphical communication system (1963)
7. Meyer, J.: EtchaPad—disposable sketch based interfaces. In: Conference Companion on Human Factors in Computing Systems, pp. 195–196 (1996). doi:10.1145/257089.257258
8. Igarashi, T., Matsuoka, S., Kawachiya, S., et al.: Interactive beautification: a technique for rapid geometric design. In: 10th annual ACM symposium on User Interface Software and Technology, pp. 105–114 (1997). doi:10.1145/1281500.1281529
9. Zou, H., Lee, Y.: Constraint-based beautification and dimensioning of 3D polyhedral models reconstructed from 2D sketches. J. Comput. Aided Des. **39**, 1025–1036 (2007). doi:10.1016/j.cad.2007.08.002
10. Jun-Wen, X.U., Liao, D.X., Wang, S.X., et al.: Recognition of on-line sketched electrical diagrams. J. Sci. Technol. Eng. **6**, 034 (2007)
11. Zhang, S.H., Chen, T., Zhang, Y.F., et al.: Vectorizing cartoon animations. IEEE Trans. J. Visual. Comput. Graph. **15**, 618–629 (2009). doi:10.1109/TVCG.2009.9
12. Ching, F.D.: Architecture: Form, Space, and Order. Wiley, New York (2014)
13. Pavlidis, T., Van Wyk, C.J.: An automatic beautifier for drawings and illustrations. In: ACM SIGGRAPH Computer Graphics, pp. 225–234 (1985). doi:10.1145/325165.325240

14. Durgun, F.B., Zgüç, B.: Architectural sketch recognition. J. Architectural Sci. Rev. **33**, 3–16 (1990)
15. Sun, J.Y., Jin, X.Y., Peng, B.B., et al.: A method of fast on-line graphics recognition and regularization. J. Comput. Sci. **30**, 172–176 (2003). (in Chinese) (孙建勇, 金翔宇, 彭彬彬, 等(2003) 一种快速在线图形识别与规整化方法. J 计算机科学. 30: 172-176)
16. Shpitalni, M., Lipson, H.: Classification of sketch strokes and corner detection using conic sections and adaptive clustering. J. Mech. Des. **119**, 131–135 (1997). doi:10.1115/1.2828775
17. Wang, S.X., Yu, S.H.: Endpoint fusing of freehand 3D object sketch with Hidden-part-draw. In: 10th International Conference on Computer-Aided Industrial Design & Conceptual Design. IEEE Press, pp. 586–590 (2009). doi:10.1109/CAIDCD.2009.5375407
18. Ku, D.C., Qin, S.-F., Wright, D.K.: Interpretation of overtracing freehand sketching for geometric shapes. In: 14-th International Conference in Central Europe on Computer Graphics, Visualization and Computer Vision, pp. 263–270 (2006)
19. Wang, S.X., Gao, M.T., Qi, L.H.: Endpoint fusing of hand-drawing 3D projection sketches. J. Comput. Aided Des. Comput. Graph. **21**, 81–87 (2009). (in Chinese) (王淑侠, 高满屯, 齐乐华 (2009). 在线手绘投影线图的端点融合. J 计算机辅助设计与图形学学报. 21: 81-87.)

Multimodal Interaction

Implementing a Platform for Complex Information Processing from Written and Spoken Journalistic Data

Christina Alexandris[1(✉)], Konstantinos Mylonakis[1], Stefanos Tassis[1], Mario Nottas[2], and George Cambourakis[3]

[1] National and Kapodistrian University of Athens, Athens, Greece
calexandris@gs.uoa.gr, {kmylo,stassel}@di.uoa.gr

[2] Danube University Krems – National Technical University of Athens, Athens, Greece
manottas@ilsp.gr

[3] National Technical University of Athens, Athens, Greece
gcamb@cs.ntua.gr

Abstract. The implemented platform targets to assist in information processing and decision-making processes concerning online written and transcribed spoken political and journalistic texts. Two separate functions are linked, one evaluating the degree of implied information and connotative features and one allowing access and comparison to related content such as explanatory information and cause-result relations in historic (ancient) "journalistic" texts.

Keywords: Databases · Spoken texts · Connotative features · Ontologies

1 Interaction and Design

The present platform is intended to assist in information processing and decision-making processes concerning online written and transcribed spoken political and journalistic texts such as interviews, live conversations in the Media and discussions in Parliament. The platform links two separate functions with the possibility to (A) provide the User-Journalist with the largest possible percentage of the points in the texts signalizing information with implied information and connotative features (Function A - "TextTone") [2, 12] and to (B) allow access and comparison to related content such as explanatory information and cause-result relations in historic (ancient) "journalistic" texts (Function B - "Echo") [1, 12].

The platform makes use of existing online tools and applications, such as Google Translate, and includes the activation of two databases for each separate function. Implementation is in JAVA [12]. The design and implementation is based on data and observations provided by professional journalists, Program M.A in Quality Journalism and Digital Technologies, Danube University at Krems Austria, Athena - Research and Innovation Center in Information, Communication and Knowledge Technologies, Athens - Institution of Promotion of Journalism Ath.Vas. Botsi, Athens.

M. Kurosu (Ed.): HCI 2017, Part I, LNCS 10271, pp. 549–558, 2017.
DOI: 10.1007/978-3-319-58071-5_41

The browsed and viewed journalistic texts can be subjected to an automatic evaluation of the percentage of non-neutral content and can be directly linked to related information from sources typically constituting reference material that cannot be easily accessed, such as ancient and historical texts. In other words, the current journalistic or political texts can be evaluated in the light of the degree and percentage of non-neutral content and in relation to similar- not identical- situations and lessons learnt from the Past.

From the main menu of the platform, the User selects the type of function to be activated. Function A (TextTone) requests an input of an online journalistic text or transcribed spoken text and generates all elements constituting "marked" information with implied information and connotative features. The TextTone function is a fully automatic process. Function B (Echo), a user-interactive process, operates with an input of selected keywords from current journalistic texts generating passages from the historic texts explaining chronological and "cause-result" relations in politics and diplomacy from the Past, allowing a comparison with events from the Present.

2 Evaluating Degree of (Non) Neutral Tone in Online Journalistic Texts: The "TextTone" Function

The "TextTone" function concerns the signalization of all "connotatively marked" words and expressions in written and transcribed spoken journalistic texts. The function is based on the flouting of Grice's Cooperativity Principle (Grice 1989, Hatim 1997) in Pragmatics theory, especially in regard to the violation of the Maxims of Quality and Quantity [2, 6, 7], since the procedure involves the differentiation between "superfluous" and "necessary" elements in a journalistic text, beyond the absolutely necessary "Who/What-When-Where-(How)" framework expressed by the "necessary" elements [2]. The "TextTone" function operates on a database and generates the percentage of words related to non-neutral content.

2.1 The "TextTone" Function Database

"Connotatively marked" words and expressions whose semantic content is related to connotatively emotionally and socio-culturally "marked" elements may be grouped into a finite set based on word type, word stems or suffix type, namely at word level or at the morphological level [2, 12]. Signalization of word-classes such as adjectives and adverbials is implemented with the Stanford Log-Linear Part-of-Speech Tagger [15]. Additionally, recognition on a word-stem or a suffix basis involves the detection of types of verbs, related to specific semantic features (also accessible with Wordnets and/or Selectional Restrictions [2]).

The word groups concerned are the grammatical categories of (1) adjectives and (2) adverbials, containing semantic features related to (i) descriptive features (ii) mode (iii) malignant/benign action or (iv) emotional/ethical gravity [2, 12]. Word groups with Implied Connotative Features involve specific categories of (3) verbs (or nominializations of verbs) containing semantic features (including implied connotations in

Table 1. Text with high score in "non-neutral" content, signalized marked features as output.

http://edition.cnn.com/2016/04/04/opinions/wisconsin-humble-political-celebrities-opinion-borsuk/index.html	52 matches
humble/JJ big/JJ big/JJ little/JJ humility/NN surprising/JJ loaded/VBN big/JJ like/VBP pretty/RB bit/NN humility/NN humiliation/NN remarkable/JJ best/JJS big/JJ much/JJ likely/JJ just/RB wondered/VBD bit/NN soundly/RB just/RB much/JJ interesting/JJ much/RB much/RB humbling/JJ humiliating/JJ sharply/RB just/RB bluntly/RB much/JJ imagine/VB big/JJ dicey/JJ think/VB great/JJ splintering/VBG just/RB bad/JJ humility/NN humbled/VBN big/JJ best/JJS seems/VBZ bit/NN humble/JJ humility/NN amazing/JJ big/JJ big/JJ	19% Adjectives: 8% Adverbs: 6% Other: 5%
soundly/RB sharply/RB frequently/RB bluntly/RB Literally/RB originally/RB lately/RB belatedly/RB necessarily/RB only/RB	
have/VB: 3 Donald/NNP: 2 Trump/NNP: 2 I/PRP: 2 was/VBD: 2 he/PRP: 2 he/PRP: 3 Hillary/NNP: 2 Clinton/NNP: 2 Sanders/NNP: 2 Sanders/NNP: 2 Clinton/NNP: 2 done/VBN: 2 better/JJR: 2 has/VBZ: 2 much/RB: 2 race/NN: 2 him/PRP: 2 Republican/JJ: 2 would/MD: 2 his/PRP$: 2 would/MD: 2 you/PRP: 2 've/VBP: 2 that/WDT: 2	Word repetitions in same sentence

language use) related to (i) mode (ii) malignant/benign action or (iii) emotional/ethical gravity, as well as (4) nouns with suffixes producing diminutives, derivational suffixes resulting to a (ii) verbalization, (iii) an adjectivization or (iii) an additional nominalization of proper nouns [2, 12]. For journalistic texts, percentages over 18% (Table 1) in "connotatively marked" words signalize a high score of "non-neutral" content. A low score in "non-neutral" content is below 10%. (Table 2).

Table 2. Text with medium to high score in "non-neutral" content, signalized marked features as output.

http://www.bbc.com/news/election-us-2016-35962179	38 matches
much/JJ sharp/JJ sick/JJ quickly/RB fine/JJ disappointing/JJ just/RB decimated/VBN heartily/RB booed/VBN proud/JJ think/VBP important/JJ think/VBP nervous/JJ think/VBP think/VBP sick/JJ negative/JJ surprisingly/RB pessimistic/JJ flaring/VBG pretty/RB relentless/JJ unfortunately/RB worse/JJR think/VBP glad/JJ stumping/VBG harsh/JJ negative/JJ flaring/VBG calm/VB deep/JJ calm/JJ good/JJ just/RB much/RB disastrous/JJ	15% Adjectives: 7% Adverbs: 5% Other: 3%
New/NNP: 2 contests/NNS: 2 he/PRP: 2 her/PRP$: 2 campaign/NN: 2 manufacturing/VBG: 2 her/PRP$: 2 who/WP: 2 Democratic/JJ: 2 people/NNS: 2 vote/NN: 2 we/PRP: 2 he/PRP: 2 state/NN: 2 their/PRP$: 2 as/RB: 4 far/RB: 2 support/NN: 2 I/PRP: 5 can/MD: 2 talk/VB: 2 I/PRP: 2 their/PRP$: 3 are/VBP: 3 he/PRP: 2 Sanders/NNP: 2 campaign/NN: 2 back/RB: 2	Word repetitions in same sentence

3 Current Journalistic Texts and "Echoes" of the Past

Current journalistic and political texts with a high percentage of non-neutral content often concern topics of high importance. These topic types may be registered and compared with similar topics linked to phenomena and situations of the Past for assisting decision-making, for example, in order to avoid conflict, subjection or war. However, information from the Past is often limited to experts and scholars, especially if a different language is concerned. Experts and professionals in the domain of political and journalistic texts compare and contrast events, policies and behavior of the Past to the state-of affairs in the Present.

3.1 User Requirements

Questionnaire–based User Requirements confirm that information from the Past can be relevant to the understanding of the current-state-of affairs, with the following topics consisting typical examples: In particular, Users strongly agreed with the following factors playing a crucial role in understanding cause-result relations in current affairs, directly related to geopolitical and diplomatic information from the "Peloponnesian War" of Thucydides: "Pressure from Allies is always a major factor" (1a), "Casus-Belli is characterized by an evident Cause-Result relation" (1b), "In geopolitical maps some features change, others remain the same" (1c).

Users believed that the following applied in most cases (2): "Citizens' emotions are an unpredictable factor in decision-making" (2a), "Personality of leader is crucial in success of strategy" (2b), "Geopolitics is connected both to the Past and to long-term plans for the future" (2c), "Today, war is not very different: there are other means, plus the factor of globalization" (2d), "Even today, war may be lost due to bad advisors" (2e).

Users believed that the following applied in some cases (3): "Events may be explained by seemly irrelevant incidents" (3a), "Unpredictable behavior of Allies may be due to factors related to domestic politics" (3b).

As an example of ancient texts of World History, the "Peloponnesian War" of Thucydides (Ancient Greek) is taught in military academies, such as West Point (USA). The present application concerns Ancient Greek historic texts, specifically, the "Peloponnesian War" of Thucydides, however, the general modelling approach used can be a starting point for possible adaptations to the specifications of other (ancient) texts, also in other languages.

For professionals, details in historic texts are a must and a generalized type of comparability with information from the Past is often not sufficient: Precision and correctness are of crucial importance in information searched in ancient and historical texts (Requirement A), as a resource of expert knowledge from lessons learnt from the Past. If the information from these resources is to be compared with the current spoken journalistic and political texts, especially for decision-making, quick access to the requested content is a desired feature (Requirement B). Additionally, User requirements regarding the content of the information to be extracted were formulated with the aid of a questionnaire made available to prospective users, especially journalists and military personnel. In accordance to the practices of professionals to be simulated by the present application, the nature and complexity of the information to be extracted requires the integration and formalization of expert knowledge as a starting point of analysis and investigation (Requirement C).

3.2 Combining Online Journalistic Texts with "Echoes" of the Past

The basic functions of the application are to allow direct access to information not easily extracted and to connect spoken texts from the live stream of current events to their "echoes" of related information in the resources concerned, in the present case, the resources from the ancient Past. The sublanguage-based formalization of ontologies in the vocabulary and sentence structure allows the use of keywords, a feature typical of Dialog Systems, where speed is of crucial importance. A database containing keywords related to the domain of Diplomacy and Politics relates topics from the current-state-of-affairs to related passages from the ancient Past.

These keywords are related to predefined ontologies [2] to assist the User's query (Interface Message: Use only nouns, verbs and adjectives), to facilitate search and to extract the requested information. The keyword ontology assisting the User's query can be extended and upgraded (Interface Menu: Save Query). The platform integrates additional user-input, upgrading and updating existing ontologies generated from the interaction.

The sublanguage-specific ontology used to assist the User's query and to refine the User's search is based on keywords clustered around basic concepts related to the sublanguage of "Diplomacy": (1) topic, (2) state, (3) action and (4) result, as an extension from previous studies [2, 5].

The concept of "state" (Category "state") contains singular words or expressions such as "neutrality" or "disadvantage". The concept of "actions" (Category "actions") contains expressions such as "response" - "reaction" - "answer" or "accept" and "rejection". The concept of "result" (Category "result") contains expressions such as "gain" - "benefit" - "profit" or "loss". The sublanguage-specific ontology may be referred to as the "Query Ontology". Furthermore, the Query Ontology (Q-Ontology) contains an additional small set of words with sublanguage-specific tags, such as "Athenians-[Superpower]", to assist Users queries.

For accessing information from ancient texts, keywords are subjected to Machine Translation (MT) prior to any further processing by the "Echo" function. Machine Translation may involve available online MT applications, such as Google Translate or special MT systems and databases, such as the Universal Networking Language (UNL) originally created for processing UN documents in languages as diverse as English, Hindi and Chinese [14].

4 Direct Access to Related Information from Ancient Texts: The "Echo" Function

The second function ("Echo") concerning the processing of complex information in ancient texts intends to address queries regarding diplomatic and political problems, their resolution, correct or bad decisions, mistakes and socio-cultural phenomena related to politics. Although the ancient texts concerned are the texts of Thucydides "Peloponnesian War", these texts may be regarded as a starting-point for further adaptations and upgrading for processing ancient historical texts of other languages, with the integration of expert knowledge, as described in the following strategy, which re-introduces traditional ontology-based approaches and Controlled Languages.

4.1 Strategy

The employed strategy is based on the link of the above presented sublanguage-related ontology with resources of expert knowledge. The ontology enables direct access to the translated ancient texts, an approach that does not employ standard Information Extraction techniques. In particular, the strategy avoids the process of adapting requested information – which is, in the present case, related to mentality, intentions, beliefs, emotions and socio-cultural factors- to practices based on the universal or text-dependent (syntax) logical relations between entities/facts categorized in sublanguage-independent detectable and extractable entity groups and patterns of sequences of words/entities [4, 8, 11]. On the other hand, to conform to the requirements of precision and correctness (Requirement A) but also to achieve speed for accessing requested information also from spoken texts (Requirement B), the strategy integrates practices typical in Controlled Languages [9, 10], by utilizing information contained in vocabulary as well as text and sentence structure. Specifically, a restricted set of words and predefined types of sentence structure related to respective types of content are processed. In the present case, texts facilitating such types of processing are translations very close to the original Ancient Greek text, explicitly presenting most of the information implied by pronouns and other forms of anaphora and context-dependent expressions in the original Ancient Greek text. In these texts, a large number of causal relations is visible with pointers [3] such as "due", which might not be available in other translations [2].

The translations concerned are in formal Modern Greek or "Katharevousa", a "compromise" between Ancient Greek and the Modern Greek, in particular, the translations by prominent Greek statesman and political leader Eleftherios Venizelos (1864–1936), published in 1940 in the University of Oxford, after his death, also provided online (Centre for the Greek language: Portal for the Greek Language: www.greeklanguage.gr, E. Venizelos Translation [1940] 1960) [13]. These translations combining both linguistic proximity to the original text and expert knowledge function as an Assistive-"Buffer" translation, connecting the User's queries with keywords translated from English (or another language) to Greek and presenting respective passages from English translations (or in another language). Therefore, expert knowledge is integrated in the present strategy (Requirement C), often with additional features and information not always visible in translations in other languages, mainly due to linguistic parameters [1]. The example in Table 3 related to the keyword query "allies" and "change sides" illustrates the additional information (in brackets) from the Assistive Translation, as well as its similarity to the original ancient text (We note that the Athenians and Lacedaemonians (Spartans) were the superpowers of the time).

Table 3. Example of query keywords ("allies", "change sides") and sample of related passages.

Query: "allies", "change sides"
English translation (for Queries) (MIT Classics Archive): The Mantineans and their allies were the first to come over [become allies with] through fear of the Lacedaemonians. [Because] Having taken advantage of the war against Athens to reduce a large part of Arcadia into subjection, they thought that Lacedaemon would not leave them undisturbed in their conquests, now that she had leisure to interfere, and consequently gladly turned to a powerful city like Argos, the historical enemy of the Lacedaemonians, and a sister democracy
Assistive Translation (for Search and Extraction): [5.29.1] Πρώτοι οι Μαντινείς και οι σύμμαχοί των προσεχώρησαν εις την συμμαχίαν ταύτην, εκ φόβου των Λακεδαιμονίων. Διότι, διαρκούντος ακόμη του προς τους Αθηναίους πολέμου, οι Μαντινείς είχαν υποτάξει μέρος της Αρκαδίας, και ενόμιζαν, ότι οι Λακεδαιμόνιοι δεν θα τους επέτρεπαν να διατηρήσουν την επ' αυτού κυριαρχίαν, ήδη οπότε αι χείρες των ήσαν ελεύθεραι. Ώστε προθύμως εστράφησαν προς το Άργος θεωρούντες αυτό πόλιν ισχυράν, και ανέκαθεν αντίπαλον των Λακεδαιμονίων, και επί πλέον δημοκρατουμένην, όπως και αυτοί
Original Ancient Text: [5.29.1] Μαντινῆς δ' αὐτοῖς καὶ οἱ ξύμμαχοι αὐτῶν πρῶτοι προσεχώρησαν, δεδιότες τοὺς Λακεδαιμονίους. τοῖς γὰρ Μαντινεῦσι μέρος τι τῆς Ἀρκαδίας κατέστραπτο ὑπήκοον ἔτι τοῦ πρὸς Ἀθηναίους πολέμου ὄντος, καὶ ἐνόμιζον οὐ περιόψεσθαι σφᾶς τοὺς Λακεδαιμονίους ἄρχειν, ἐπειδὴ καὶ σχολὴν ἦγον·ὥστε ἄσμενοι πρὸς τοὺς Ἀργείους ἐτράποντο, πόλιν τε μεγάλην νομίζοντες καὶ Λακεδαιμονίοις αἰεὶ διάφορον, δημοκρατουμένην τε ὥσπερ καὶ αὐτοί

4.2 The "Echo" Function Database

The extraction of requested information from passages in the "Assistive" translation is based on (1) the recognition of a defined set of conjunctions (CONJ) and (2) the recognition of a set of words concerning intention and behavior, annotated as "Intention-Behavior" - IB words (verbs and participles).

The word groups in the "Echo" Function Database may be referred to as the "Search Ontology". One or multiple IB words contained in passages extracted can be related to a singular query containing keywords from the above-mentioned keyword Query Ontology (Q- Keyword):

Query: [Q- Keyword(s)] IB <CONJ> IB [Q- Keyword(s)] [12].

The IB words occur "before" and "after" the conjunction (CONJ). The text containing the IB word(s) before the conjunction CONJ expresses the "Result (Outcome)" relation and the text containing the IB word(s) after the conjunction CONJ expresses the "Cause (Source)" relation. However, for some types of conjunctions, the reverse order applies. The order and type of "Cause (Source)" and "Result (Outcome)" is dependent on the type of conjunction concerned. This type of order is defined according to the information structure in the Assistive Translation, which allows a strict formalization of information content based on syntactic structure similar to formalizations for creating Controlled Languages. This is the basis on which the Cause-Result relations are extracted, outlining the content of the relations.

The group of specified conjunctions describing causal relations contains expressions such as "because" and "due to" ("διότι", "επειδή", "άλλωστε", "δια το", "δηλαδή", "ένεκα", "ένεκεν", "ώστε").

Table 4. Query (Q-keywords: "allies", "revolt") IB words and other Q-keywords in match.

SPOKEN TEXT [Current Journalistic/Political Text] "allies, "revolt" User QUERY: [Q- Keyword(s)] IB <CONJ> IB [Q- Keyword(s)]
[subjects (of superpowers), revolt (Q)] (IB-Int: showed desire) <CONJ:because> (IB-Sp: admit) [carried away (Q), passion (Q)]

Relations between topics may concern IB verbs: (I) of "Feeling-Intention-Attitude" type, what was believed, what was felt, what was intended, what attitude prevailed (Int-Intention), (II) of "Speech-Behavior" type (Sp-Speech), what was said and (III) of "Benign-Malignant Behavior" type, actual behavior (Bh-Behavior). The types of IB verbs are tagged (Int, Sp, Bh) for possible use in other applications.

Examples of the "Feeling-Intention-Attitude" type (Int) are verbs such as "were intended to" ("διατεθειμένοι"), "ignored", "were ignorant about" ("ηγνόουν"), "expected", "calculated", "took into account" ("υπελόγιζαν"). Typical examples of the "Speech-Behavior" type (Sp) are the verbs "asked", "demanded" ("εζήτουν"), "convinced" ("πείσουν"), "supported", "backed" ("υπεστήριζε"). An example of the "Benign-Malignant Behavior" type (Bh) is "secured" (in context of negotiation) ("εξασφαλίσας").

In the following example (implementation in JAVA) [12], the passages contain Cause-Result relations related to the keywords "subjects (of superpowers)","revolt" and "carried away" from the Query Ontology (Q).

A query concerning the possibility of a revolution by people controlled by a superpower ("subjects (of superpowers)" "revolt") is refined and assisted with the aid of keywords from the Query Ontology. Search and extraction is performed by the Search Ontology (IB verbs and CONJ), extracting one or multiple passages containing the keywords from the Query Ontology: (Table 4).

The extracted passages are presented to the User (The Eighth Book, Chapter XXI, Nineteenth and Twentieth Years of the War - Revolt of Ionia - Intervention of Persia - The War in Ionia). The additional information from the Assistive Translation (Katharevousa Greek text) is depicted in square brackets [12]: (Table 5).

Table 5. Example of an extracted passage for Q-keywords: "allies", "revolt".

http://www.mikrosapoplous.gr/thucy/vivlia/vivlio8.htm
English Translation: But above all, the subjects of the Athenians showed a readiness to revolt [against rule] even beyond their ability, [because] judging the circumstances with [carried away by] [revolutionary] passion, and refusing even to hear of the Athenians being able to last out the coming summer
Assistive Translation: Before: CONJ ("διότι")-IB: "εκτιμώμεναι":{Αλλ' οι, υπήκοοι προ πάντων των Αθηναίων εδείκνυαν μεγάλην επιθυμίαν όπως αποτινάξουν την κυριαρχίαν των και αν ακόμη αι δυνάμεις των ορθώς εκτιμώμεναι δεν ήσαν επαρκείς εις τούτο}
After: IB: "παραδεχθούν": {διότι εις τας κρίσεις των παρεσύροντο από τον επαναστατικόν οργασμόν, και δεν ήθελαν να παραδεχθούν καν ότι οι Αθηναίοι ήτο ενδεχόμενον να ανθέξουν κατά το προσεχές θέρος}

5 Conclusions and Further Research

In the constant development of media, access to information expands "horizontally", across various user groups, but gaining an in-depth insight with precision often remains a challenge. In addition, implied information and connotative features as well as benefits of past knowledge, which may be described as a "vertical", in-depth dimension of information, are seldom exploited.

The present platform targets to facilitate the access to "vertical", in-depth information for a broader user group. This type of information may be characterized as complex information, concerning mentality, intentions, beliefs, emotions and socio-cultural factors. Processing of complex information in online written and transcribed spoken journalistic and political texts, involves signalizing implied information and connotative features by the TextTone function, as well as accessing and comparing related content and explanatory information in historic texts by the Echo function. Both functions target to assist in information processing and decision-making processes. In the Echo function, the nature and complexity of the information processed calls for the re-introduction and employment of traditional ontology-based strategies.

Both functions constitute a basis for upgrading and possible adaption to texts of other languages, if applicable. For the TextTone function, this depends on whether implied and connotative features are retrievable in the morphosyntactic or lexical level of linguistic analysis. For the Echo function, the extraction of the type of complex information concerned also depends on text structure and style of the ancient author. Further adaptation and implementation of both functions will provide an insight to possible additional parameters in the strategies presented.

References

1. Alexandris, C.: Accessing Cause-Result relation and diplomatic information in ancient "Journalistic" texts with universal words. In: Kurosu, M. (ed.) HCI 2014. LNCS, vol. 8511, pp. 351–361. Springer, Cham (2014). doi:10.1007/978-3-319-07230-2_34
2. Alexandris, C.: English, German and the international "Semi-professional" translator, a morphological approach to implied connotative features. J. Lang. Translation **11**(2), 7–46 (2010). Sejong University, Korea
3. Carlson, L., Marcu, D., Okurowski, M.E.: Building a discourse-tagged corpus in the framework of rhetorical structure theory. In: Proceedings of the 2nd SIGDIAL Workshop on Discourse and Dialogue, Eurospeech 2001, Denmark, September 2001
4. Angeli, G., Premkumar, M.J., Manning, C.: Leveraging linguistic structure for open domain information extraction. In: Proceedings of the 53rd Annual Meeting of the Association for Computational Linguistics and the 7th International Joint Conference on Natural Language Processing, Association for Computational Linguistics, pp. 344–354, Beijing, China, 26–31 July 2015
5. Crawley, R.: Thucydides' Peloponnesian War. J.M. Dent and Co., London (1903). Translated by Richard Crawley
6. Grice, H.P.: Logic and conversation. In: Cole, P., Morgan, J. (eds.) Syntax and Semantics, vol. 3. Academic Press, New York (1975)

7. Hatim, B.: Communication Across Cultures: Translation Theory and Contrastive Text Linguistics. University of Exeter, Exeter (1997)
8. Jurafsky, D., Martin, J.: Speech and Language Processing, an Introduction to Natural Language Processing, Computational Linguistics and Speech Recognition. Prentice Hall Series in Artificial Intelligence, 2nd edn. Pearson Education, Upper Saddle River (2008)
9. Kuhn, T.: A survey and classification of controlled natural languages. Comput. Linguist. **40**(1), 121–170 (2014)
10. Lehrndorfer, A.: Kontrolliertes Deutsch: Linguistische und Sprachpsychologische Leitlinien für eine (maschniell) kontrollierte Sprache in der technischen Dokumentation. Narr, Tübingen (1996)
11. Mausam, N.V., Schmitz, M., Bart, R., Soderland, S., Etzioni, O.: Open language learning for information extraction. In: Proceedings of EMNLP-CoNLL 2012 -Joint Conference on Empirical Methods in Natural Language Processing and Computational Natural Language Learning, Proceedings of the Conference, Association for Computational Linguistics, pp. 523–534 (2012)
12. Mylonakis, C.: Processing and extracting complex information in written and spoken journalistic data and historic (ancient) texts. Masters thesis, Department of Informatics and Telecommunications, National University of Athens, Greece (2016)
13. Venizelos, E.: Thoukudidou Istoriai: Kata Metaphrasin Eleutheriou Benizelou. [Thucydides' History: Translated by Eleftherios Venizelos], Caclamanos, D. (ed.), vol. 2. Oxford University Press, Oxford (1940)
14. Uchida, H., Zhu, M., Della Senta, T.: Universal Networking Language. The UNDL Foundation, Tokyo (2005)
15. The Stanford Log-linear Part-Of-Speech Tagger. http://nlp.stanford.edu/software/tagger.shtml

MagicPad HD: The Spatial User Interface

Leith K.Y. Chan(✉) and Henry Y.K. Lau

Department of Industrial and Manufacturing Systems Engineering, The University of Hong Kong, Pok Fu Lam, Hong Kong
{lkychan,hyklau}@hku.hk

Abstract. This paper presents the research of inventing a novel and natural spatial human-system interface – MagicPad HD that is to be used in a fully immersive virtual environment. With the advance in Virtual Reality (VR) technology, modern computer systems are capable of immersing users into a synthetic environment. Based on the previous innovations of MagicPad Light and MagicPad AR, MagicPad HD is designed and implemented. It uses a high resolution tablet and capacitive pen to bring the best of both designs. The high resolution tablet compensates the limited resolution of projected images normally found in most VR systems and the capacitive pen provides a flexible tool for writing on the tablet and interacting with 3D virtual objects simultaneously. User study suggests that MagicPad HD user interface is highly effective and intuitive. It also provides strong evidence to the effectiveness of use familiar objects as the tangible devices as the 3D User Interface in an immersive virtual reality system.

Keywords: Virtual reality · Spatial user interface · Human factors

1 Introduction

In a Virtual Reality system, users are immersed in a synthetic environment and surrounded by virtual objects. Traditional human computer interfaces such as mouse and keyboard are no longer useful. Researchers have been actively investigating new ways of interaction and communication between man and machine. Tangible User Interface, which allows users to interface with the virtual world using physical objects in order to bridge the gap between real and virtual world, shows great potential in this area.

This paper presents the research of inventing a novel and natural spatial human-system interface – MagicPad HD that is to be used in a fully immersive virtual environment. In order to realize the overall design and study the concept of the spatial human-system interface, an immersive Virtual Reality system imseCAVE [1], which serves as the test bed of the MagicPad user interface is used. MagicPad HD is designed and implemented on top of the previous innovations of MagicPad interfaces, which are MagicPad Light [2] and MagicPad AR [3]. MagicPad Light creates the magic of projecting images on a piece of paper and it is the first attempt to realize the idea of using "pen and paper" metaphor as a 3D user interface tool. Lightness and the interaction with the infra-red pen are its major advantages but the limited resolution constraints its application. MagicPad AR, being a handheld window to the virtual world, has successfully demonstrated its intuitiveness and capability to thousands of

M. Kurosu (Ed.): HCI 2017, Part I, LNCS 10271, pp. 559–572, 2017.
DOI: 10.1007/978-3-319-58071-5_42

users in different exhibitions [4]. By combining the MagicPad Light and MagicPad AR, MagicPad HD uses a high resolution tablet and capacitive pen to bring the best of both designs. The high resolution tablet compensates the limited resolution of projected images normally found in most VR systems using projectors and the capacitive pen provides a flexible tool for writing on the tablet and interacting with 3D virtual objects simultaneously. User study indicates that MagicPad HD user interface is highly effective and intuitive. It also provides strong evidence to the effectiveness of use familiar objects as the tangible devices as the 3D User Interface in an immersive virtual reality system.

2 Background

2.1 Virtual Reality System

The Cave Automatic Virtual Environment (CAVE) is one of the most famous VR systems and is originally developed by the Electronic Visualization Laboratory (EVL) at the University of Illinois at Chicago. It produces 3-dimensional stereo effect by displaying in alternating succession the left and right eye views of the scene as rendered from the viewer's perspective [5]. These views are then seen by the viewers through a pair of LCD shutter glasses whose lenses open and close at high frequency in synchronization with the left and right eye views that are projected via cathode-ray projectors onto the translucent walls and floor acted as screens. In addition to 3D stereoscopic vision, motion parallax, the apparent displacement of objects when you move, e.g., objects closer to your eyes move faster than objects that are far away, is another very important cue to perceive objects in 3D space. In the immersive virtual reality system, it is at least, if not more, important than stereoscopic vision, especially for the 3D objects closed to the user. For example, if a user looks at a piece of virtual furniture in a CAVE, the user should be able to move around and examine the furniture from different angles. This system should be able to produce the image from the correct perspective corresponding to the relative position of the user and the virtual furniture. Because of this motion parallax cue, the user has the faked perception that the furniture exists at the same 3D space as the user. In order to achieve this motion parallax cue, the system has to know the position and orientation of the user's head in real time and this information has to be provided by a motion tracking system. As a result, the system allows the user to be immersed into the virtual environment and interact with the virtual entities realistically.

Since the CAVE system provides a highly versatile platform for 3-D visualizing complex concepts and systems, it has been deployed to explore new statistical graphics applications [6], simulate complex molecular dynamics and interactions between atomic particles [7], virtual exploration and analysis of archaeological site [8], perform assembly planning [9], and for collaborative product design and development [10].

2.2 MagicPad User Interface

Virtual Reality opens a new door for us to explore the world of imagination. However, unlike the real world, we cannot touch virtual objects with our hands. Even with the latest haptic technology, it is nothing compared to, for instance, the tactile feeling of holding an apple in our hands. In order to interact with the virtual world, we need to develop a set of devices and methodology as user interfaces to the VR systems. The interface is called 3D or Spatial User Interface.

Inspired by the pen and paper, which are something that we use every day, the MagicPad spatial user interface has been designed, implemented and evaluated in this research. In fact, the original innovation of the MagicPad is aimed to provide the similar experience of using a pen and paper. With this familiar interface tools, we target to allow a layman user, even without prior experience in using VR interfaces, to be able to use the MagicPad right away without much training. As a result, two generations of MagicPad User Interface have been developed, each with their own unique design and characteristic. They are MagicPad Light [2, 11–13] and MagicPad AR [3].

2.2.1 MagicPad Light

The MagicPad Light interface mainly consists of one or more flat surfaces, which can be a white cardboard or sketch book pages. The white surface (MagicPad) acts as a display to receive the image from the ceiling mounted projector (Fig. 1). The spatial location (position and orientation) of the MagicPad are tracked by an optical tracking system. When the MagicPad moves, the image projected by the projector will be updated to match the location and motion of the MagicPad. This results in the illusion that the image is glued onto the MagicPad's surface. In addition, the user can use an infrared pen, where position is also being

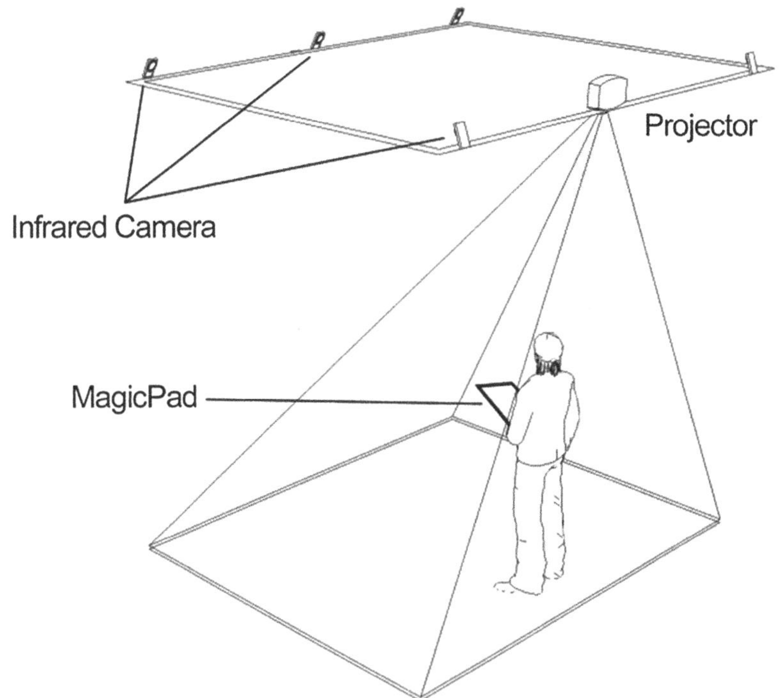

Fig. 1. The design concept and hardware configuration of the MagicPad Light Interface

tracked, to interact with the MagicPad. Since the MagicPad and the infrared pen are very light-weight devices, the user can easily hold them with his/her hands and perform series of 3D interactions with the virtual environment.

As the image projected on the MagicPad is generated in real time, the use of the MagaicPad can be very diverse. For example, it can be used as a 3D painting tool to paint freely in a 3D space, or it can be used as a tangible tool that exists in both the virtual and real world to interact or examine the 3D virtual environment. However, the image quality of the MagicPad Light is limited by the resolution and brightness of projector. In additional, the workable area is constrained by the coverage of projection image.

2.2.2 MagicPad AR

Given the limitation of MagicPad Light, the design of MagicPad AR focuses on the image quantity and the coverage. Similar to MagicPad Light, the MagicPad is tracked by an optical tracking system with a number of infrared cameras. Unlike MagicPad Light, the infrared pen is removed and the paper pad is replaced by a tablet device. By using the tablet instead of the projector, the image quantity in terms of resolution, brightness and contrast, is significantly improved. Figure 2 shows a typical setting of MagicPad AR, the tablet acts as a window to the virtual world and the user is free to walk inside an area and explore the virtual world through the tablet.

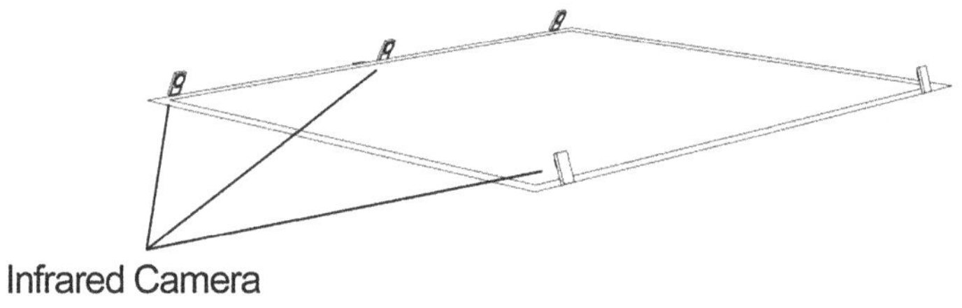

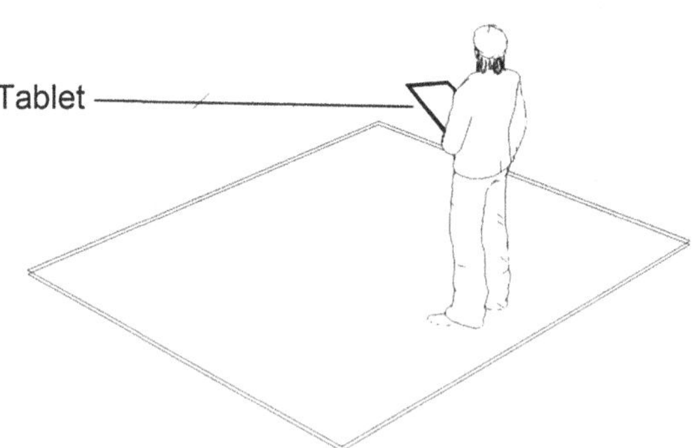

Fig. 2. The design concept of the MagicPad AR

3 MagicPad HD

Upon the successful implementation and positive response of MagicPad AR, the idea of a further enhanced version has been proposed. In fact, the overall concept of MagicPad is to use familiar tools (pen and paper) as the tangible user interface in order to shorten the learning curve of new users, and at the same time, it provides an effective medium to interact with virtual objects in a VR system.

3.1 Design Concept

Although MagicPad AR is proved to be an intuitive user interface, the lack of a pen-like interface limits its ability to interact with users as compared to the MagicPad Light. The design of the MagicPad HD interface combines the best of the MagicPad Light and MagicPad AR. It uses a high resolution tablet as the MagicPad and a custom made pen like device as the MagicPen. The MagicPen can write on both the tablet and in the 3D space. According the experiment of MagicPad Light, bigger MagicPad size provides more usable area and bigger window to the virtual world. However, a bigger size tablet comes with increased weight and we need to get a balance between size and weight.

3.2 System Implementation

MagicPad HD is built on top of the imseCAVE and therefore it also shares the benefit of the effective tracking system and immersive virtual environment. Figure 3 shows the design of MagicPad HD. A SONY Xperia™ Tablet Z is chosen to be the MagicPad. The tablet weights only 495 g and it is one of the lightest tablets available in the market. The size of the screen is 10.1 in. with HD resolution (1920 × 1200). Three retro-reflective markers are

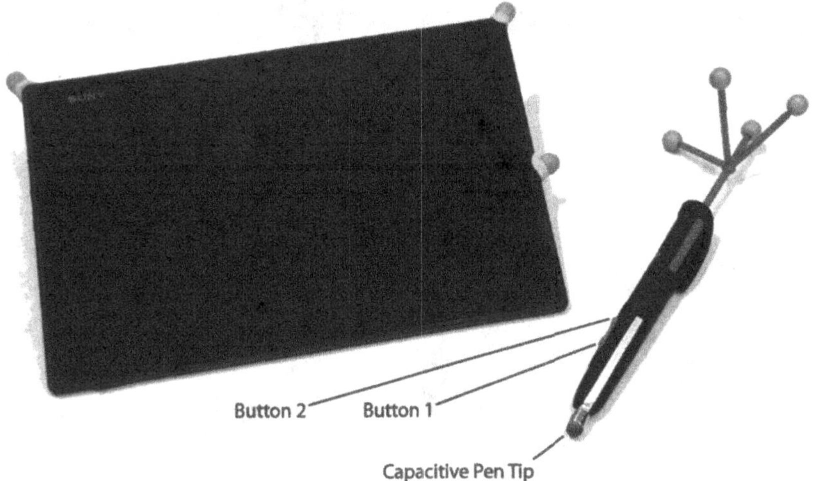

Fig. 3. MagicPad and MagicPen in MagicPad HD interface (Color figure online)

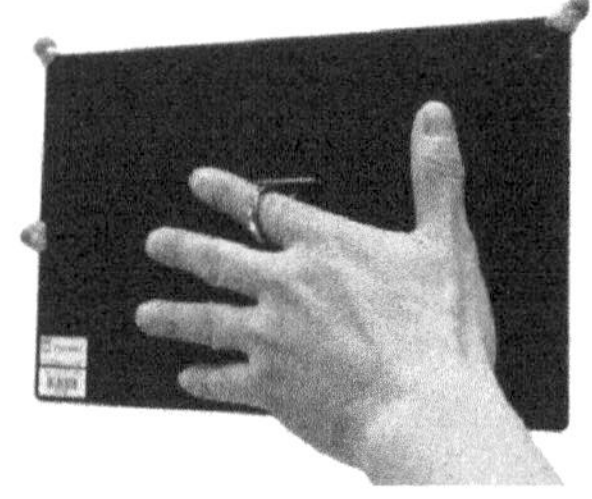

Fig. 4. Holding the MagicPad with one hand with the aid of the ring

attached at the corners for motion tracking. As the user can only use one hand to hold the MagicPad, a metal ring is installed at the back of the tablet and it helps the user to grasp it firmly, as shown in Fig. 4. For the MagicPen, it has a capacitive pen tip so that it can be used to write on the tablet with capacitive touchscreen directly. The thin strip of aluminum foil on the pen tube is used to conduct electric current from the user's finger to the tip of the MagicPen. A custom made tracker with 4 retro-reflective markers is extended from the pen tube and is used for tracking the MagicPen's position and orientation. The MagicPen is wirelessly connected to the system by a USB wireless receiver which plugged in the main computer so that the user can trigger different functions by pressing the two middle red buttons.

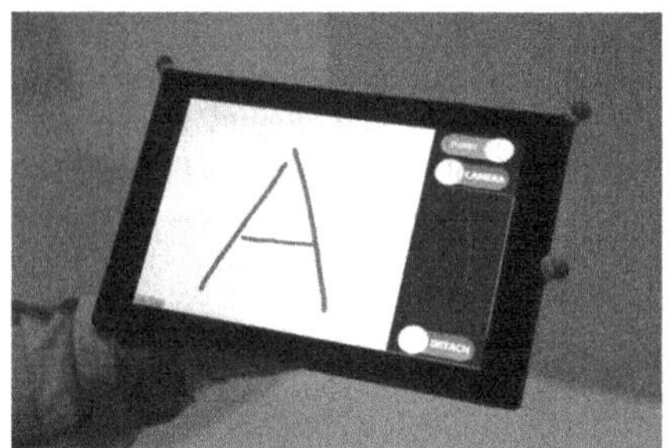

Fig. 5. Paint mode (left) and Camera mode (right) of the MagicPad HD

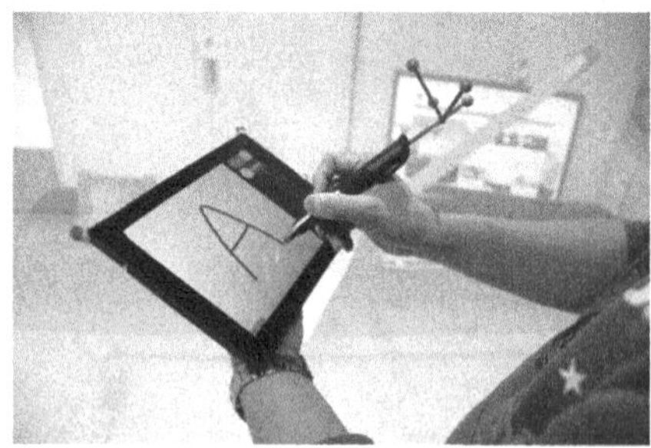

Fig. 6. Paint mode: the user writes on MagicPad and detaches a virtual paper

Similar to MagicPad AR, the processing capability of the tablet is not powerful enough to render the virtual scene efficiently. Therefore, the images displayed on the MagicPad are generated by an additional workstation and streamed to the tablet wirelessly.

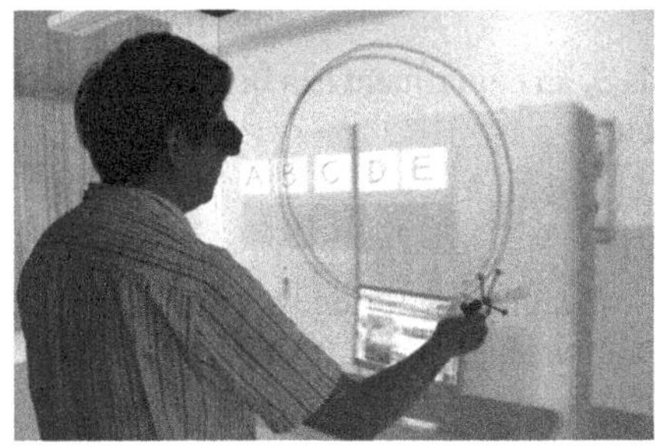

Fig. 7. Paint mode: the user draws freely in 3D space (Color figure online)

Fig. 8. Camera mode: higher resolution image displayed on the MagicPad

In actual operation, the MagicPad HD has two modes: Paint mode and Camera mode (Fig. 5). In the Paint mode, the user can use the MagicPen to write on the MagicPad, as shown in Fig. 6. After writing, the user can swipe the lower right "Detach" button and the system will create a virtual paper with the drawing. The screen of MagicPad will then be cleared out for another drawing. As the virtual paper is floating in the air, the user can use the MagicPen to grab and relocate the virtual paper. This is done by pressing the Button 1 (Fig. 3) and intercepting the virtual paper with the MagicPen simultaneously. In addition, the MagicPen can be used for painting freely in 3D space by pressing the second red button, as shown in Fig. 7. In the "Camera" mode, the MagicPad acts as a window to the virtual world. It displays the same content in the virtual environment from the user's perspective but with much higher resolution than the image from projectors of the VR system, as shown in Fig. 8. This is a very useful compensation to the limited resolution of projected image, especially in some applications that require close examination of virtual objects. Similar to detaching a drawing, the user can also swipe the lower right "Capture" button to create a virtual photo.

3.3 User Study

In order to test the usability of the MagicPad HD, an experiment has been designed and a corresponding user study has been carried out.

3.3.1 Participants

82 participants were recruited via referral by colleagues and friends. Most of them are university students and some outsiders with various age groups. All of them have the experience of using computer.

3.3.2 Experimental Procedures

There are two experiments: Real and Virtual Task Comparison Test, and Virtual Task Test. Real and Virtual Task Comparison Test consist of performing similar tasks in both real and virtual environment. The Virtual Task Test consists of tasks being performed only in the imseCAVE environment. The environment settings for both virtual and real tasks are similar, as illustrated in Fig. 9.

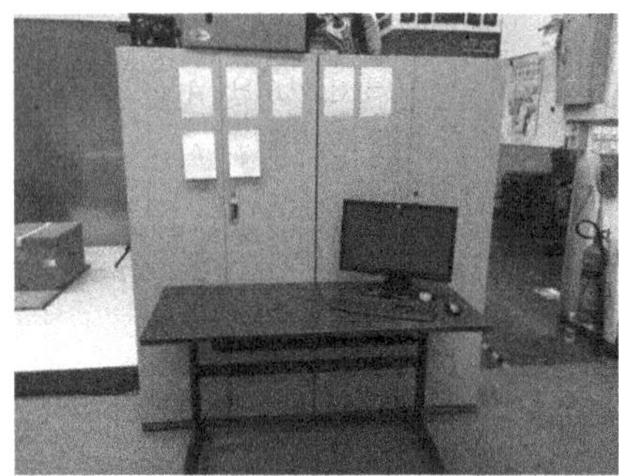

Fig. 9. Environment setting for real (left) and virtual (right) tasks

In the Real and Virtual Task Comparison Test (Fig. 10), the participant has to perform a task in both the real and virtual environments. In the real environment, the participant writes a letter on a memo pad and sticks it on the specific position on the doors of the cabinet. Similarly, the participant is then requested to perform a similar task in the virtual environment with the MagicPad HD interface. In order to get the participant accustomed to the virtual environment, the user is requested to spend a couple of minutes walking around the virtual environment before performing the virtual task. The time taken for both real and virtual tasks is recorded.

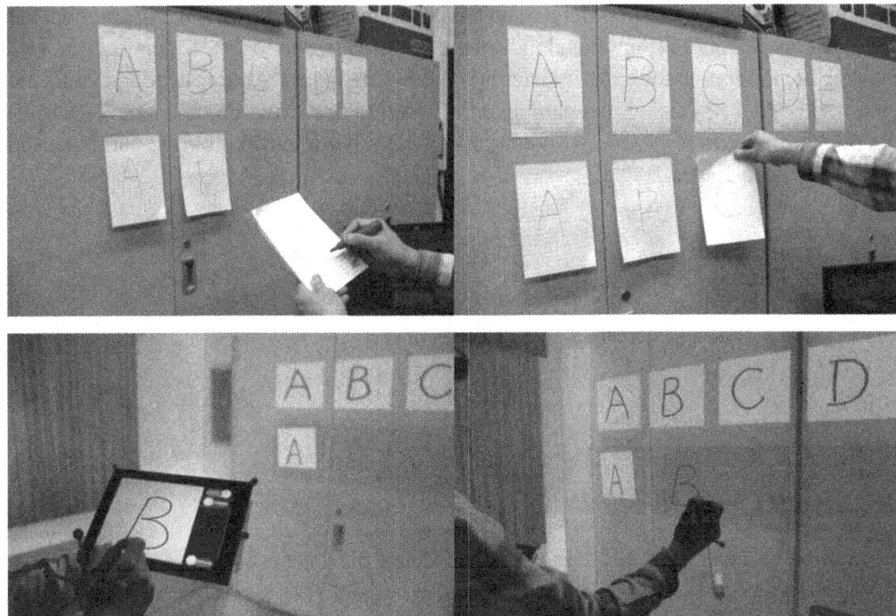

Fig. 10. Performing letter writing task in both real (top images) and virtual environment (bottom images)

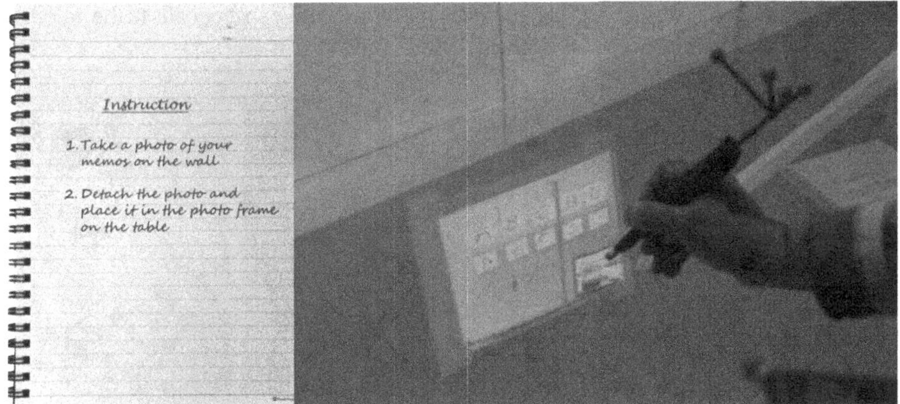

Fig. 11. Instruction for the Camera Tool task and participant placing the virtual photo on the photo frame

In the Virtual Task Test, the participant has to perform three different virtual tasks. They are Camera Tool, 3D Paint and Physics Game. In the Camera Tool task, the participant is first briefed about the usage of the Camera Tool, and the participant is then asked to read and follow the instruction (Fig. 11) in the virtual notepad on the table. As the prints on the virtual notepad are relatively small, the participant will need to take advantage of the higher resolution of the MagicPad in order to read the instruction. By following the instruction, the participant takes a photo (Fig. 8) and moves the virtual photo to the photo frame.

In the 3D Paint task, the experimenter briefs the participant the usage of MagicPad's 3D Paint mode. After practicing, the participant is asked to draw five specific letters (A to E) onto 5 semi-transparent boxes, as shown in Fig. 12. The time taken by the participant in completing the task is recorded.

Fig. 12. Participant performing 3D Paint task

Finally, in the Physics Game task (Fig. 13), the experimenter triggers a series of virtual soccer balls drop from the ceiling. The participant is asked to create virtual papers and arrange the papers into a virtual track for guiding the virtual soccer balls that are dropped from the ceiling to fall into a virtual wooden bin. These soccer balls are automatically generated by the computer in the virtual environment and the experiment records the time taken for a participants to successfully guide the two consecutive soccer balls to the wooden bin from the starting time of the experiment.

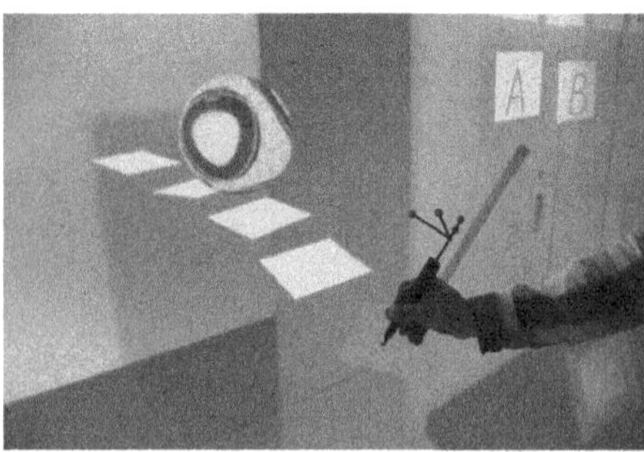

Fig. 13. Physics Game task

4 Discussion and Conclusion

4.1 Evaluation

The results are summarized in Tables 1, 2 and Fig. 14.

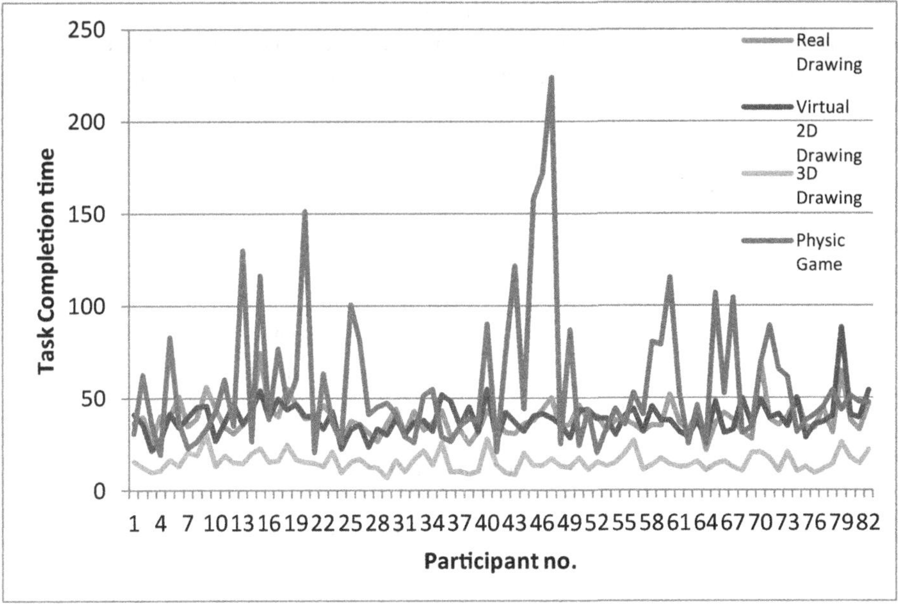

Fig. 14. Line chart of task completion time vs participants for different task

Table 1. Result of average completion time for different tasks of 82 participants

Task	Average completion time (s)	Standard deviation (s)
Real drawing	38.78	9.05
Virtual 2D drawing	38.82	9.23
3D drawing	15.36	4.81
Physics game	57.50	37.77

In Table 1, the average completion time of the Real Drawing and the Virtual 2D Drawing are almost the same (38.78 s vs 38.83 s) and the difference is not statistically significant as revealed in the ANOVA analysis of variances ($F_{1,81}$ = 0.002 ns), which reflects the Virtual 2D Drawing is as effective as the Real Drawing. In fact, participants use even less time to complete the 3D Drawing task. For the comparison between 3D Drawing and Real Drawing, the mean completion time of 3D Drawing task is 19.6 s and the difference is statistically significant as revealed in an ANOVA analysis of variance ($F_{1,81} = 754.263$, $p < .05$). This is mainly due to the fact that drawing directly in 3D space is more effective than 2D drawing because 3D drawing eliminates the need of paper repositioning. This is also part of the reason that participants consider MagicPad user interface provides additional capability of performing tasks than in real world environment (Question 2f in Table 2). In contrast, the result of Physics Game is more diverse, with average completion time of 57.5 s and a much larger standard deviation of 37.8 s. The participants also report that Physics Game task is relatively harder to complete than other tasks (Question 2c in Table 2). It is because this task is more complex and requires different techniques such as problem solving skill, visual spatial skill and hand-eye coordination. All these factors vary a lot between participants and cause the large differences in performance.

Table 2. Results of questionnaire showing the average scores of all participants

Experiment	Question		Score (1–5)	Standard deviation
Experiment 1: 2D drawing	1a	You have performed the drawing task in both real and virtual environment. Do you find these two experiences similar? (1–5)	3.6	1
	1b	Do you find the real task easy to finish?	4.6	0.7
	1c	Do you find the virtual task easy to finish?	4.0	0.8
Experiment 2: Camera tool, 3D draw & Physics game	2a	Do you find the virtual task (Camera Tool) easy to finish?	4.3	0.7
	2b	Do you find the virtual task (3D Draw) easy to finish?	4.6	0.6
	2c	Do you find the virtual task (Physics Game) easy to finish?	3.8	0.8
	2d	Do you agree that the high resolution image of MagicPad (tablet) can compensate the limited resolution of surrounding image projected on the wall?	4.3	0.8
	2e	Do you agree that it is effective to perform the task in virtual environment?	4.0	0.8
	2f	Do you agree that the MagicPad user interface provides additional capability of performing tasks than in real world environment?	4.3	0.8
Overall	3a	Do you find that it is interesting/fun to perform tasks in the virtual environment?	4.8	0.4
	3b	Do you find that using familiar objects (in this case, pen and writing pad) as tools helps you to learn the new interaction in the virtual world more effectively?	4.3	0.7
	3c	Do you find that it is comfortable to perform task in the virtual environment?	3.8	0.7

Remark: Score rating (1 = very negative, 2 = negative, 3 = neutral, 4 = positive, 5 = very positive)

In Table 2, the lowest score (3.5, question 1a) we got in the questionnaire is about the similarity of the Real and Virtual Task Comparison Test. Although the procedure of the both tasks are similar, the participants do not consider these experiences are very alike. At this stage, it is clear that Virtual reality technology still cannot replicate the reality experience completely, especially in the area that requires the sense of touching such as the feeling of writing on a paper and sticking a piece of paper on the cabinet. For the Camera Tool, participants agree that high resolution of the tablet (MagicPad) can compensate the limited resolution of the projected images (Question 2a). This is particularly important if the virtual scene contains lots of detail information. For example, a training system requires the users to examine the detail structure of a machine. With limited resolution, the only way to make the close examination possible is to enlarge the object. However, it is not intuitive and does not reflect the real world situation. With high resolution of the MagicPad, the user has a very effective tool for exploration and investigation in a virtual environment. Moreover, the Camera Tool task is the easiest virtual task (Question 2a), which is aligned with the comments from the users for the MagicPad AR. As a matter of fact, Camera tool is essentially the same as the MagicPad AR discussed in the previous section. Overall speaking, participants have lot of fun in performing the tasks in the virtual environment (Question 3a). They feel great and excited in being able to interact with virtual objects in a synthetic environment when performing the task of Physics Game. Virtual Reality is an effective tool to arouse the interest of users. In addition, the participants agree that it is effective using familiar objects (in this case, pen and writing pad) as user interface tools to learn the new means of interactions (Question3b). This finding supports the original hypothesis of the MagicPad user interface. The Question 3c asked whether the participants feel comfortable to perform task in the virtual environment. The result (3.8, between normal (3) to comfortable) is actually better than expected. The major complaints are the feeling of dazzling and the weight of the tablet.

4.2 Conclusion

One idea, three implementations – the motivation of creating intuitive spatial user interface for immersive virtual environment resulted in three innovations of MagicPad user interfaces: MagicPad Light, MagicPad AR and the latest MagicPad HD. MagicPad Light creates the magic of projecting images on a piece of paper and it is the first attempt to realize the idea of using "pen and paper" metaphor as a 3D user interface tool. Lightness and the interaction with the infra-red pen are its major advantages but the limited resolution constraints its application. MagicPad AR, being a handheld window to the virtual world, has successfully demonstrated its intuitiveness and capability to thousands of users in different exhibitions. By combining the MagicPad Light and MagicPad AR, MagicPad HD uses a high resolution tablet and capacitive pen to bring the best of both designs. The high resolution tablet compensates the limited resolution of projected images normally found in most VR systems and the capacitive pen provides a flexible tool for writing on the tablet and interacting with 3D virtual objects simultaneously. User study proves that this 3D user interface is highly effective and intuitive.

This paper has documented the journey of the successful invention of the MagicPad spatial user interface. In the future, this research can go into two directions. The first direction is to further study the performance of the MagicPad interface in different application domains and different VR systems such as head mounted display system. The second direction is to further improve the performance of the MagicPad, such as the incorporation of new flexible display materials in order to make a lighter yet bigger or even foldable screen. Moreover, a realistic haptic feedback for the MagicPen will be incredibly useful, especially when it is used to interact with virtual objects. However, high fidelity haptic systems often come with a set of bulky mechanical or maglev system. Incorporating a useful haptic in a pen size scale remains a research challenge.

References

1. Lau, H.Y.K., Chan, L.K.Y.: Interactive visualization of express cargo handling with the imseCAVE. In: Proceedings of the Virtual Concept 2005 (2005)
2. Chan, L.K.Y., Lau, H.Y.K.: MagicPad: the projection based 3D user interface. Int. J. Interact. Des. Manuf. **6**(2), 75–81 (2012)
3. Chan, L.K.Y., Kenderdine, S., Shaw, J.: Spatial user interface for experiencing Mogao caves. In: Proceedings of the 1st symposium on Spatial user interaction, pp. 21–24. ACM (2013)
4. Kenderdine, S., Chan, L.K.Y., Shaw, J.: Pure land: futures for embodied museography. J. Comput. Cult. Herit. **7**(2), 1–15 (2014)
5. Cruz-Neira, C., Sandin, D.J., DeFanti, T.A., Kenyon, R.V., Hart, J.C.: The CAVE: audio visual experience automatic virtual environment. Commun. ACM **35**(6), 64–72 (1992)
6. Jürgen, S., Dianne, C., Bradley, D.K., Carolina, C.-N.: Dynamic Statistical Graphics in the CAVE Virtual Reality Environment. City (1996)
7. Disz, T., Papka, M., Pellegrino, M., Stevens, R., Taylor, V.: Virtual reality visualization of parallel molecular dynamics simulation. In: Proceedings of the 1995 Simulation Multiconference Symposium, pp. 483–487 (1995)
8. Vlahakis, V., Ioannidis, N., Karigiannis, J., Tsotros, M., Gounaris, M., Stricker, D., Gleue, T., Daehne, P., Almeida, L.: Archeoguide: an augmented reality guide for archaeological sites. IEEE Comput. Graph. Appl. **22**(5), 52–60 (2002)
9. Ye, N., Banerjee, P., Banerjee, A., Dech, F.: A comparative study of assembly planning in traditional and virtual environments. IEEE Trans. Syst. Man Cybern. Part C Appl. Rev. **29**(4), 546–555 (1999)
10. Bochenek, G.M., Ragusa, J.M.: Virtual collaborative design environments: a review, issues, some research, and the future. In: Portland International Conference on Proceedings of Management of Engineering and Technology, PICMET 2001, vol. 722, pp. 726–735 (2001)
11. Chan, L.K.Y., Lau, H.Y.K.: The magicpad: a spatial augmented reality based user interface. In: Proceedings of the Virtual Concept (2010)
12. Chan, L.K.Y., Lau, H.Y.K.: MagicPad: a projection based 3D user interface. In: Proceedings of the Workshop on Mobile and Personal Projection, ACM CHI 2011 (2011)
13. Chan, L.K.Y., Lau, H.Y.K.: A tangible user interface using spatial augmented reality. In: Proceedings of the IEEE Symposium on 3D User Interfaces, pp. 137–138. IEEE Computer Society (2010)

Controlling Interaction in Multilingual Conversation Revisited: A Perspective for Services and Interviews in Mandarin Chinese

Jiali Du[1,3](✉), Christina Alexandris[1,2], Dimitrios Mourouzidis[2], Vasilios Floros[2], and Antonios Iliakis[2]

[1] Guangdong University of Foreign Studies, Guangzhou, China
dujiali68@126.com
[2] National and Kapodistrian University of Athens, Athens, Greece
calexandris@gs.uoa.gr, {dmour,florbas,antiliak}@di.uoa.gr
[3] Nanjing University, Nanjing, China

Abstract. The present approach targets to provide a framework for facilitating multilingual interaction in online business meetings with an agenda as well as in similar applications in the service sector where there is a less task-oriented form of interaction. A basic problem to be addressed is the control of the topics covered during the interaction and the expression of opinion. In the proposed template-based approach, the System acts as a mediator to control the dialog flow, within the modeled framework of the sublanguage-specific design.

Keywords: Templates · Speech Acts · Skype · Subtitles · Editors

1 Introduction: Assisting Skype Communication

The System involves the strategies employed for the integration of Spoken Mandarin Chinese in a Human-Computer Interaction framework for multilingual applications in routine business meetings as well as in short interviews via Skype. Based on previous approaches, the application concerns Skype communication with subtitles in the foreign language and the possibility of Machine Translation of subtitles and spoken text. The System designed in previous approaches concerns a Speech Act based template and agenda where all interaction is registered and controlled by the System, acting as a mediator between the communicating parties via Skype.

The application processes conversations of a standard and controlled nature, namely routine business meetings via Skype with an agenda as well as short interviews with fixed topics and agenda. Both types of communication are of a less task-oriented type which may include statement of sentiment or opinion. It should be stressed that business meetings or interviews whose main purpose is to persuade or to exercise pressure to obtain information are not handled by the present System.

Face-to-face interaction via Skype allows access to prosodic and paralinguistic information and feed-back from elements such as gestures, facial expression and tone of voice [1].

M. Kurosu (Ed.): HCI 2017, Part I, LNCS 10271, pp. 573–583, 2017.
DOI: 10.1007/978-3-319-58071-5_43

As presented in previous research [1], the application concerned, intended to be adaptable and reusable for various languages, involves a Speech Act based template and agenda, with interaction occurring within a Directed Dialog [2, 15, 16] connected to a respective Speech Act [1], however, with a Mixed Initiative [2, 4]. The Users communicate with each other with the assistance of the System-mediator. Interaction and turn-taking may be considered "push-to-talk conversations" [13].

Interaction is controlled by the mediating Speech Act based template and agenda of the System containing the topics covered during the interaction and checking the flow of the conversation by intervening messages appearing in the screen of the interface (Table 1). In this Mixed Initiative type of interaction, if a topic is not covered, the Users are alerted by the System [1]. The Speech Act based template and agenda contains a predefined set of sublanguage-specific questions/answers and statements and answers incorporated in the template-agenda by the User before the interaction and/or Skype meeting [1]. These (written) utterances may already be subjected to Machine Translation by online and/or commercial Machine Translation tools. Additional free input from the User's utterances is processed by Speech Recognition (ASR) and subsequently by a Machine Translation System after the interaction [1].

Table 1. Overview of system framework.

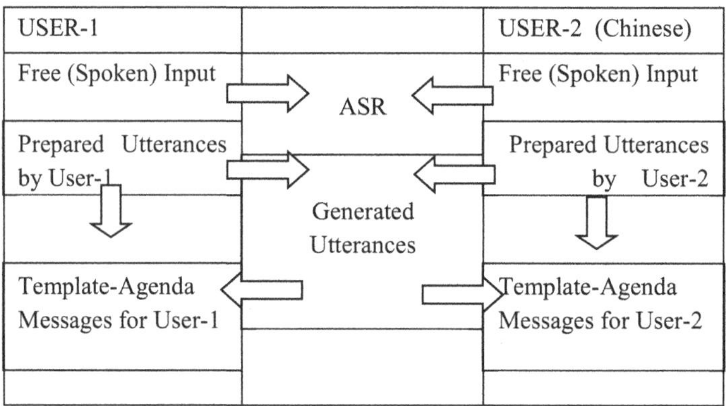

The System is adapted to handle typical problems encountered in Spoken Mandarin Chinese in a Human-Computer Interaction framework with an English-speaking International Public.

Typical problems concern the tendency for native Mandarin Chinese speakers to express themselves implicitly and economically (1, Implicit statements), also with limited syntactic information, including the omission of syntactic elements in Chinese language (2, Omission) as well as the management of lexical ambiguity (3, Ambiguity). Silence, as an effective way of showing modest behavior (4, Silence) as well as a tendency to seldom take the role of the dialog pace-setter and to play a more passive role (5, Passive role in Dialog), constitutes additional problems in international communication with native speakers of Mandarin Chinese.

2 Mandarin Chinese - Design Parameters and Challenges

English and Chinese share some linguistic similarities. For example, both belong to the analytic language branch, which is contrary to inflected and agglutinative one; both linguistic systems work properly on a basis of word order and functional words, etc. However, the difference of syntactic form and semantic expression between English and Chinese makes international communication difficult to remain efficient and effective.

2.1 Implicit Statements

English is considered a low-context language in which nearly all the information has to be shown clearly and openly, especially for the syntactic elements. English has distinctive morphological changes and verbal conjugations as tense, aspect or voice markers. English is more like a subject-verb language for the fully syntactic structure can help readers grasp the grammatical framework easily.

Chinese is regarded as a high-context language in which some of syntactic elements can be omitted without influencing the semantic expression in oral or written practice. It is common for Chinese people to express themselves implicitly and economically. Chinese people tend to mean more than what they say. Principle of Least Effort can be well applied to the Chinese performance in which less words can mean more sense. Sometimes, even the Chinese functional words are omitted without altering the meaning. Chinese has few inflectional phenomenon, and even a Chinese character can yield its full meaning. Characters can convey more information than English words do, and limited Chinese characters can be applied to encapsulate the same meaning conveyed by more English words. In short, Chinese is more like a topic-focused language, and you have to guess the potential meaning by the limited syntactic information.

2.2 Omission

Anaphora is an important means of Chinese discourse cohesion. Zero anaphora in Chinese is sometimes considered to be Chinese empty category (ec). The omission of syntactic elements in Chinese language may greatly influence the quality of bilingual MT. English systems have to be familiar with this kind of Chinese omission and try to make the slots filled with appropriate elements. The cultural context, context of situation, and linguistic context are helpful for regaining the omitted forms [3].

Chinese people are used to omitting the subject, especially the animate subject; Chinese antecedent is usually considered to be the subject of a sentence, and the omitted anaphora phenomenon often appears here and there. Therefore, international English speakers who have access to SKYPE, if possible, have to regain the omitted forms in real-time situation to make the communication clear.

2.3 Ambiguity

If good communication is expected, performers have to pay attention to the ambiguity which may lead to misunderstanding or confusion. Both the lexical and syntactic ambiguity can be resolved by real-time paraphrase.

The application of paraphrase is helpful for ambiguity-free. For example, in the domain of lexical ambiguity, many Chinese speakers can be confused by the expression of "biweekly", which means appearing or happening both "every two weeks" and "twice a week", in the sentence of "the engines in a safe and good working condition should be taken out of service for maintenance work biweekly at least." To avoid the confusion, speakers have to paraphrase "biweekly" clearly, namely, to paraphrase it into every two weeks or twice a week. In the domain of syntactic ambiguity, "the horse raced past the barn fell" is a local ambiguous sentence. In order to alleviate the cognitive suffering, you have to paraphrase the sentence. Both "the horse that was raced past the barn fell" and "the horse drawn past the barn fell" are syntactic ambiguity-free sentences. With the development of translation technology, successful disambiguation is feasible and practical even though the application of SKYPE is now facing the challenge in China: "Meet the challenge and make the change".

2.4 Silence and Passive Role in Dialog

Silence is an effective way to show the modest behavior. Based on Confucianism, the modesty can be shown by keeping silence, and speaking aloud can obviously betray your weakness. Chinese speakers even believe that sometimes the outstanding usually bear the brunt of attack, and that common assumed knowledge is seldom to blame. This is one of the reasons why sometimes Chinese people seldom take the role of dialogue pace-setter in the international communication via SKYPE. According to the statistical data, Chinese scholars find that most Chinese speakers are shame in communicating with foreigners, and seldom lead the conversation in SKYPE-based international communication [19]. Besides focusing on cultural influence on language and behavior, many linguists highlight the ontology of Chinese (e.g. zero anaphora and omission) and try to pave the way for MT across languages.

2.5 Design Parameters

The foreign speakers who have access to SKYPE system have to respect both the cultural difference and linguistic difference between English and Chinese. Meanwhile, they can improve the performance by the suggestions shown as follows:

Providing options is an effective method. During the international communication, misunderstanding and embarrassment may occur here and there. The foreigners who have limited Chinese cultural and linguistic knowledge are suggested to write down the questions and alternative answers in advance before talking. Thus, the alternatives make Chinese speakers have to give a definite reply without considering the cultural and linguistic influence. However, the questions and answers prepared in advance should be logical and unambiguous. Besides that, Chinese people are familiar with the hierarchical and numeral outline. If possible, international speakers are suggested to show the addressees the list of key points of conversation and the questions they expect to be answered.

Bilingual translation systems are helpful for improving the communication skill levels. In China, both SYSTRAN (http://www.systran-software.cn) and GOOGLE (http://translate.google.cn) translation systems are available. Many Chinese speakers try to use the systems to help them deal with some linguistic problems in real-time communication. By analyzing the translation results for 90 English business-related sentences, Chinese scholar [8] finds the fact that SMT (statistical MT) is better than RBMT (rule-based MT) when lexical ambiguity occurs (such as homograph, polysemy, as well as lexical transfer problems), while the effectiveness of two systems is the same when structural ambiguity happens.

3 Interaction and Design for Chinese Users for Services

Preparation before interaction and control of input and output to the Users-Participants are key features of previously designed approaches which are presently adapted to the requirements of Mandarin Chinese native speakers. Specifically, Users determine the types of information contained in the interaction, in the form of a list of prepared questions and possible types of responses and statements [1]. This preparation occurs before the actual interaction and is assisted by pre-determined topic and sublanguage-specific questions, statements and answers. The topics and overall sublanguage-specific framework are determined by the Users, according to the content and agenda of the meeting.

During interaction, the translated message appears on the screen of the User-Receiver in the target language. The topics covered during interaction are registered by the template-agenda. If a topic is not addressed, the template-agenda generates a reminder-message [1].

The construction of the present System with the above-described interaction is based on implemented applications for Spoken Dialog Systems in the Service Sector (Call Centers for mobile telephones) [2], with Directed Dialogs and registration of the path of the interaction with the respective Speech Acts, keywords and free input [2]. The implemented modules of the Dialog System applications [2] are adapted to the needs of Business Meetings (I) and Interviews (II).

3.1 Avoiding Implicit Statements, Omission and Ambiguity

The preparation of utterances to be activated is assisted by an editor controlling the (1) length of the utterances (sentences with a maximum of 30 words to facilitate Machine Translation), confirming the User's choice of topic (TOPIC) and selected Speech Act type (SPEECH-ACT) (2), as well as 1–3 words selected to be highlighted as "keywords" (3) and related to recognizable utterances and acceptable answers.

The defined topics, selected Speech Act types (2) and keywords to be highlighted (3) are the types of pre-determined sublanguage-specific information handled during interaction and are contained in templates filled in by the Users before interaction.

The series of topics and respective templates constitute the template-agenda, activated by the Users during the time of the actual online interaction. Templates related to Speech-Acts constituting questions are designed to contain the phrases such as "Please answer with Yes or No" or "Please reply with X, Y or Z" (X, Y and Z constituting keywords).

Each response and/or message is activated by the User in the appropriate step in the dialog. The activated response or message may be previously translated by an online conventional Text-to-Text Machine Translation System [1].

In particular, the Speaker's input is limited to the topic of the activated prepared messages and a positive or negative answer or a keyword-specific answer, restricting the possibilities of Ambiguity, Implicit Statements and Omission. Additionally, in the case of complications during interaction, a form of "stepping stone" [7] strategy is employed where activated Speech Acts requesting clarification may remind the User to answer in the form of keywords, resembling a typical type of interaction within a strict Directed Dialog and/or traditional Interlingua (ILT) framework [6, 12], targeting to bypass the phenomena of Ambiguity, Implicit Statements and Omission. In other words, the functions of traditional ILTs are performed during the preparation process of the templates with the assistance of the editor. Also, unlike traditional ILTs, the sublanguage of the interaction is not limited to one specialized field but the sublanguage-related subject area and topics can be determined each time by the Users of the System prior to interaction.

The present model of User interaction with the System and Directed Dialog framework [15, 16] on which the previously designed approaches are based [1], aims to prevent an uncontrolled number of possible forms and variations [8] in (a) the expression in the language concerned and in (b) User behavior due to cultural and social factors. For spoken Mandarin Chinese, the above-described restrictions and specifications also contribute to the limitation of phonologically similar keywords but with a different tone.

3.2 Handling Silence and Passive Role in Dialog

Targeting to user-friendliness [14], explanatory repetitions as an alternative version of the so-called "stepping stones" [7] assist the User during interaction [2, 7] as additional Task-related and Non-task related Speech Acts integrated in dialog structure. These Non-Task-related Speech Acts [1], whose determination was based on data from European Union Projects [9], are used for tasks such as "Offer", "Reminder" or "Manage-Waiting-Time" [9], mostly in messages generated by the System.

In the present Mixed-Initiative type of interaction, the activated Non-Task-related Speech Acts (NTRs) may extend the length of the dialog; however, they encourage the participation of the Speakers and contribute to the management of deliberate silence of the Speakers, as in the case of spoken Mandarin Chinese and the native speakers of the language. In the application concerned, NTRs are activated by the User; however, if there is no response or if there is another type of complication during communication, the System's template-agenda reminds the Users to activate an NTR- Speech Act selected from the set of prepared utterances (Table 2).

Table 2. Prepared utterances and Topics (from 1 to X), activated non-task related Speech Acts and template-agenda for interviews.

Prepared Utterances by USER:	SYSTEM: Alert-Messages
TOPIC -1 [A] SPEECH ACT [inform]: □ Utterance 1 □ Utterance 2	
IF: NO-INPUT: NTR- SPEECH ACT Offer-Explain	ALERT: SYSTEM MESSAGE: NO ANSWER OR UNPROCESSABLE INPUT
TOPIC -1 [A] [question]: □ Utterance 1 □ Utterance 2	
IF: NO-INPUT: NTR- SPEECH ACT Reminder-Explain	ALERT: SYSTEM MESSAGE: NO ANSWER OR UNPROCESSABLE INPUT
[….] TOPIC -X [W] SPEECH ACT [[proposal]: □ Utterance 1 □ Utterance 2 TOPIC -X [W] [question]: □ Utterance 1 □ Utterance 2	
[END –OF- INTERACTION] SYSTEM: Template-Agenda	
TOPIC -1: CHECKED ∅ ANSWERED: YES ∅ NO ∅ Confirmed-Silence ∅ [….] TOPIC -X: CHECKED ∅ ANSWERED: YES ∅ NO ∅ Confirmed-Silence ∅	

For spoken Mandarin Chinese, the Non-Task-related Speech Acts (NTRs) are in pre-existing templates prepared by the User and are designed to already contain phrases with explanatory content, in addition to any modifications the User wishes to make. For example, the activated NTR-Speech Act "Offer-Explain" in System output is related to phrases such a "Would you like me to proceed with the next thing you want to tell me?" or the activated NTR-Speech Act "Reminder-Explain" in output is related to phrases such as "I have no information from you about {X}. You must tell me if you want {X}". The "Offer-Explain" NTR-Speech Act is activated in the case of an unanswered question and/or unaddressed TOPIC, after a second attempt of receiving an answer, giving the impression that interaction is "moving forward", according practices in spoken Dialog Systems [7]. The "Reminder-Explain" NTR-Speech Act is activated at the end of a part of the interaction or at the end of the entire interaction, as an additional attempt to receive an answer and/or to address a TOPIC. Both the "Offer-Explain" and the "Reminder-Explain" Non-Task-related Speech Act can be activated before Speech Acts managing silences.

The use of Non-Task-related Speech Acts also allows the insertion and integration of Chinese [10, 17, 18, 20] pragmatically-related politeness forms, without affecting the basic form and content of the original dialog structure. This possibility may also be adapted to languages such as Arabic [11] and Hindi [5] for handling pragmatically-related politeness in the inserted Non-Task-related Speech Acts not containing standardized and cross-linguistic dialog content.

Additional Task-related Speech Acts are introduced such as "Manage-Silence" with System output such as "Please confirm that you have not answered this question by pressing OK", where the System by-passes a situation causing the native speaker of Mandarin Chinese to feel uncomfortable, while at the same time allows the signalization of a deliberate silence as a response from the native speaker of Mandarin Chinese. In contrast to previous approaches [1], unaddressed TOPICs saved in the agenda of the template can either be marked as "Confirmed-Silence" or the default option, "Unaddressed". TOPICs marked with "Confirmed-Silence" are evaluated by the participants.

4 Interaction and Design for Interviews

A similar Mixed-Initiative type of interaction is employed on the case of interviews (Interviews, II) with native speakers of Mandarin Chinese, provided that the interviews are short and contain a specific agenda. In this case, there is the additional possibility of the ad hoc generation of not previously prepared short messages (Table 3). These messages are subjected to online Machine Translation and appear at the bottom of the screen, along with the prepared questions and answers from both parties.

Table 3. Overview of system framework for interviews.

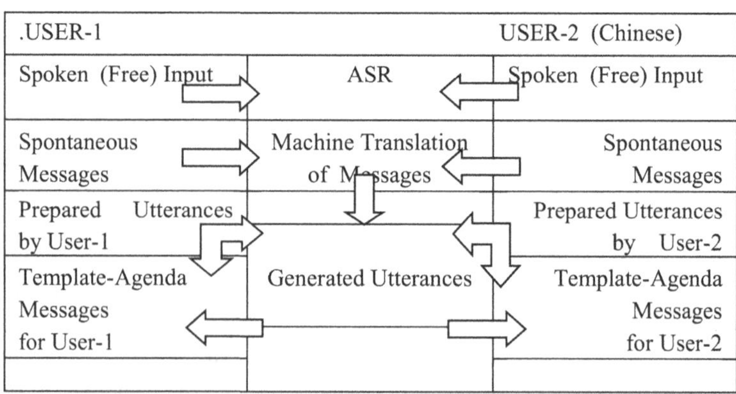

.USER-1		USER-2 (Chinese)
Spoken (Free) Input	ASR	Spoken (Free) Input
Spontaneous Messages	Machine Translation of Messages	Spontaneous Messages
Prepared Utterances by User-1		Prepared Utterances by User-2
Template-Agenda Messages for User-1	Generated Utterances	Template-Agenda Messages for User-2

For short interviews with a specific agenda, the above-presented "stepping stone" option [7], activating Speech Acts requests the User to answer in the form of the determined keywords or with an answer corresponding to a "Yes" or a "No". In other words, the User is directed to a list of possible or acceptable answers, targeting to by-pass the possibilities of Ambiguity, Implicit Statements and Omission. Task-related and Non-Task-related Speech Acts are activated if the content of the produced utterances is unclear or ambiguous, if there is a deliberate silence (Silence) from the Speaker or if the passive role of the Speaker creates complications in the interaction (Passive Role).

Furthermore, in Interviews (II) the content of the Non-Task-related Speech Acts may differ from that of Business Meetings (I). For example, the activated NTR-Speech Act "Offer-Explain" in System output is related to phrases such a "Would you like me to proceed with the next TOPIC?" or the activated NTR-Speech Act "Reminder-Explain" in output is related to phrases such as "TOPIC {X} has not been discussed yet. We must talk about this TOPIC {X}".

As applied in Business Meetings (I), in Interviews (II) the "Offer-Explain" Non-Task-related Speech Act is activated in the case of an unanswered question and/or unaddressed TOPIC, after a second or even a third attempt of receiving an answer, and the "Reminder-Explain" Non-Task-related Speech Act is activated at the end of a part of the interaction or at the end of the entire interaction, as an additional attempt of receiving an answer or resolving an issue concerning a defined TOPIC.

Also, as applied in Business Meetings (I), these Non-Task-related Speech Acts can be activated before the "Manage-Silence" Speech Act. In particular, in the case of Interviews (II), the "Manage-Silence" Speech Act may activate the generation of messages such as "Please confirm that you wish this question to remain unanswered by pressing No-answer", or, if opinions are requested "No opinion". The template-agenda marks the respective choices corresponding to the Speaker's response.

5 Conclusions and Further Research

The presented System concerns Skype communication with Machine Translation of subtitles and generated spoken text with parameters involving spoken Mandarin Chinese. Based on previous approaches, the System contains a Speech Act based template and agenda registering and controlling all interaction and acting as a mediator between the communicating parties. Features of spoken Mandarin Chinese may create complications in communications with the international public, especially speakers of the Western culture, even if conversations of a standard and controlled nature are processed. The applications in the presented framework concern routine business meetings and short interviews with an agenda. Based on standard and Directed Dialog based practices of Spoken Dialog Systems, interaction of the Users with the System is targeted to bypass typical problems in communication related to linguistic and cultural issues. At the same time, the System allows the Users to determine the type of topics and agenda prior to the meeting or the interview, without excluding the processing of free-input.

The limitations of the framework presented is the necessity to prepare utterances with the aid of the System prior to the interaction and to process and evaluate free input after the interaction. In addition, all or most of the topics to be addressed should be defined by both communicating parties. This process may be time-consuming, but on the other hand, it allows the possibility of determining different topics and sublanguage by the Users of the System each time the System is used. Especially in the case of interviews with an agenda, Users are also allowed to determine the content and appropriate style of the activated Speech Acts and messages, including the Non-Task-related Speech Acts assisting interaction. Furthermore, use of already-existing tools in Machine Translation and the adaptation of modules from implemented applications for Spoken Dialog Systems in the Service Sector (Call Centers for mobile telephones) reduce the cost and time involved in building the application.

The designed applications are to be evaluated by a larger user-group to be determined. The envisioned further development includes the design and implementation of an improved user-friendly interface and possible adaptions to other languages.

References

1. Alexandris, C.: Controlling interaction in multilingual conversation. In: Kurosu, M. (ed.) HCI 2013. LNCS, vol. 8007, pp. 3–12. Springer, Heidelberg (2013). doi:10.1007/978-3-642-39330-3_1
2. Floros, V., Mourouzidis, D.: Multiple Task Management in a Dialog System for Call Centers. Masters thesis, Department of Informatics and Telecommunications, National University of Athens, Greece (2016)
3. Hou, M., Sun, J.J.: Zero anaphora in Chinese and how to process it in Chinese-English MT. J. Chin. Inf. Process. **1**, 14–20 (2005)
4. Jurafsky, D., Martin, J.: Speech and Language Processing, an Introduction to Natural Language Processing, Computational Linguistics and Speech Recognition. Prentice Hall series in Artificial Intelligence, 2nd edn. Pearson Education, Upper Saddle River (2008)
5. Kumar, R.: A politeness recognition tool for Hindi, with special emphasis on online texts. In: Proceedings of the WWW Ph.D. Symposium, March 28–April 1, Hyderabad, India (2011)
6. Levin, L., Gates, D., Lavie, A., Pianesi, F., Wallace, D., Watanabe, T., Woszczyna, M.: Evaluation of a practical interlingua for task-oriented dialog. In: Proceedings of ANLP/NAACL-2000 Workshop on Applied Interlinguas, April 2000, Seattle, WA USA (2000)
7. Lewis, J.R.: Introduction to Practical Speech User Interface Design for Interactive Voice Response Applications. IBM Software Group, USA, Tutorial T 2009 presented at HCI 2009 San Diego, CA, USA (2009)
8. Ma, J.: A comparative analysis of the ambiguity resolution of two English-Chinese MT approaches: RBMT and SMT. Dalian Univ. Technol. J. **31**(3), 114–119 (2010)
9. Nottas, M., Alexandris, C., Tsopanoglou, A., Bakamidis, S.: A hybrid approach to dialog input in the citzenshield dialog system for consumer complaints. In: Proceedings of HCI 2007, Beijing, Peoples Republic of China (2007)
10. Pan, Y.: Politeness in Chinese Face-to-Face Interaction. Advances in Discourse Processes series, vol. 67. Ablex Publishing Corporation, Stamford (2000)
11. Shammas, N.A.: Lingua-pragmatic politeness and translatability. Damascus Univ. J. **21**(3+4), 23–56 (2005)
12. Schultz, T., Alexander, D., Black, A., Peterson, K., Suebvisai, S., Waibel, A.: A Thai speech translation system for medical dialogs. In: Proceedings of the conference on Human Language Technologies (HLT-NAACL), Boston, MA, USA (2004)

13. Taboada, M.: Spontaneous and non-spontaneous turn-taking. Pragmatics **16**(2–3), 329–360 (2006)
14. Wiegers, K.E.: Software Requirements. Microsoft Press, Redmond (2005)
15. Williams, J.D., Witt, S.M.: A comparison of dialog strategies for call routing. Int. J. Speech Technol. **7**(1), 9–24 (2004)
16. Williams, J.D., Poupart, P., Young. S.: Partially observable markov decision processes with continuous observations for dialog management. In: Proceedings of the 6th SigDial Workshop on Discourse and Dialog, September, Lisbon (2005)
17. Yin, L.: Cultural differences of politeness in English and Chinese. Asian Soc. Sci. **5**(6), 154–156 (2009)
18. Yu, Z., Yu, Z., Aoyama, H., Ozeki, M., Nakamura, Y.: Capture, recognition, and visualization of human semantic interactions in meetings. In: Proceedings of PerCom, Mannheim, Germany (2010)
19. Zhao, C.R., Liu, R.Q.: An exploration on distance English oral test- an empirical study on English oral test through web phone Skype. Mod. Educ. Technol. **22**(2), 95–98 (2012)
20. Zhu, H., Wei, L., Yuan, Q.: The sequential organization of gift offering and acceptance in Chinese. J. Pragmatics **32**, 81–103 (2000)

Design of Hand Gestures for Manipulating Objects in Virtual Reality

Wanhong Lin[1,2(✉)], Lear Du[3], Carisa Harris-Adamson[3], Alan Barr[3], and David Rempel[3]

[1] China Astronaut Research and Training Center, Beijing, 100094, China
acclwh@hotmail.com
[2] National Key Laboratory of Human Factors Engineering, China Astronaut Research and Training Center, Beijing, 100094, China
[3] Department of Bioengineering, University of California, Berkeley, USA
lxd20@berkeley.edu,
{Carisa.Harris-Adamson,Alan.Barr,david.rempel}@ucsf.edu

Abstract. Virtual reality requires high levels of interaction with the user, a type of human computer interaction. Interactions that match the way humans usually interact with their surroundings should improve training effectiveness. A 3D hand gesture based interface allows users to control the position and orientation of 3D objects by simply moving their hands, thereby, creating a more naturalistic interaction process. The design of hand gestures should be evaluated to determine design features that are the most effective and comfortable for the user. The purpose of this study was to evaluate parameters for the design of 3D hand gestures for object manipulation in virtual reality to optimize productivity and usability. Twenty participants completed object manipulation tasks while wearing an Oculus Rift headset with a mounted Leap Motion depth sensor camera to capture hand gestures. Independent variables were distance from hand to object, hand posture threshold for grab and release, and grab locations on object. The dependent variables were time for task completion and subjective measures of control, fatigue, motion sickness, and preference. The preferred gesture design parameter was related to better control and reduced time to complete the tasks. In conclusion, this study identified important gesture design features that can be optimized to improve usability and throughput for an object manipulation task in Virtual Reality.

Keywords: 3D hand gestures · Human-computer interaction · Hand postures

1 Introduction

With the rapid development of computer technology, Augmented and Virtual Reality (VR) environments have become an integral part of professional training. Since training systems based on virtual reality technology demand more attention and interaction from the user, a type of human computer interaction (HCI) that adopts the way humans usually interact with their real surroundings may be an important component to an effective system. Future training systems will utilize new technologies that require input devices

M. Kurosu (Ed.): HCI 2017, Part I, LNCS 10271, pp. 584–592, 2017.
DOI: 10.1007/978-3-319-58071-5_44

to be easily accessible and instantly available. Such technologies pose several challenges to the GUI (Graphical User Interface) paradigm designed for desktop interaction, particularly with current input devices such as keyboard and mouse [1–4].

An effective system requires control with high degrees of freedom; thus, direct manipulation of a 3D object with a user's hands may provide an improved experience compared to using a mouse or keyboard [3–5]. With this approach, the user can control the position and orientation of a 3D object with their hands similar to how they manipulate objects in the real world. For training VR, this approach more closely approximates the tasks that users will ultimately be performing.

Although wearable gloves can track hand postures, a computer vision based gesture recognition system is a more natural alternative since it is part of the environment and operates remotely. A gesture based interface eliminates the need for pointing devices, saving equipment, time and effort. The purpose of this study was to evaluate various parameters for the design of 3D hand gestures for object manipulation in virtual reality to optimize productivity and usability. Building on prior research [2], we propose using a new technique for estimating the 3D gesture based on the 3D pose of a user's hand detected by a depth camera in real-time. In addition, because performing precision hand gestures in VR for long periods of time may be physically strenuous the study also evaluated the effect of design parameters on user comfort.

2 Gestures Lexicon and Action States Transition

In terms of hand pose, the user controls a virtual hand provided by the Leap Motion hand sensing device to manipulate a virtual object just as humans would do in the real world. There are numerous hand gesture poses that are recognized by the Leap Motion system. The virtual system captures, identifies and associates hand poses with specific gesture commands used to control virtual objects or menus.

One technique to implementing hand based interaction with virtual objects is to model real world physics using physical collision detection. In this study, the collision detection process is simplified by assuming that all objects are intangible. That is, the virtual hand does not manipulate the object from its surface; instead, the hand can pass through the object and attach to the object at various points on the inside or surface of the object. In terms of object manipulation, there are several kinds of actions that need to be carried out by virtual training systems leading to the commands generated by hand pose and gestures. These commands include Grab, Rotate, Move and Release.

Hand motions are continuous and different hand pose commands need to be distinguished by constantly tracking hand pose and movement in real time. This paper proposed two non-contact action determining rules and an action state transition method based on finite state machine (FSM). Finite state machine (FSM) [6, 7] is an effective tool for managing a series of hand action events. The interactive model of FSM for virtual hand action is shown in Fig. 1, where S represents the state, and C represents the states transition conditions.

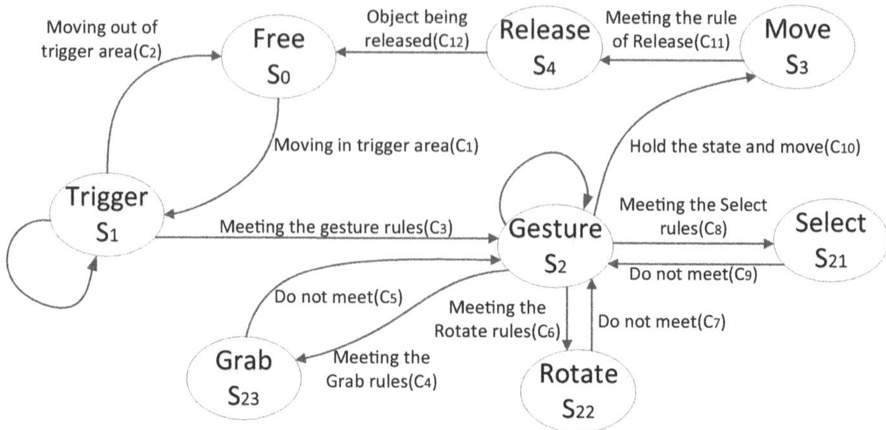

Fig. 1. The finite state machine of action

Rule One: The distance between the object and the virtual hand must be less than a certain critical value.

Rule Two: The feature value of the hand gesture must be less than a certain critical value, which is called the object action trigger threshold.

It was determined that an action was successful only if the virtual hand and the object met the condition of both rules at the same time. After a successful action (i.e. both rules simultaneously satisfied), the object would latch onto the virtual hand and move with it in virtual space. The object was released when the virtual hand did not satisfy rule two (i.e. the object action trigger critical value was exceeded).

According to the principle of FSM, the constituent elements of FSM are defined as: states (S), input events (X), output (Y), states transition function (f) and output function (g).

States (*S*): There are five action states of virtual hand: Free State, Trigger State, Gesture State, Move State and Release State. Each state has its own set of rules that govern how the virtual hand interacts with its surrounding environment.

Input events (*X*): These events correspond to the five states shown in figure one. There are six conditions which are the virtual hand moving into the object action trigger area, the virtual hand moving out of the object action trigger area, the virtual hand meeting the rules of gesture, the virtual hand meeting the rules of move, the virtual hand meeting the conditions of release.

Output (*Y*): This renders the results displayed to the operator.

States transition function (*f*): This function determines the state transition from the current state to the next one. Equation (1) shows its relationship with the states and time, where $X(t) \in X, S(t) \in S$.

$$S(t+1) = f(X(t), S(t)) \tag{1}$$

Output function (g)**:** This function maps the relationship between the current state and the output. Equation (2) shows its relationship with the states, where $Y(t) \in Y$.

$$Y(t) = g(X(t), S(t)) \tag{2}$$

As an example, consider the user transition from the trigger state to the gesture state. The state transition function f determined the state of the hand in the next time frame. If the input event at the current time frame, $X(t)$, met the rules of the grab gesture as defined by rule one and two, and the current state, $S(t)$, was the trigger state, S_1, then the next state $S(t+1)$ would be the gesture state S_2. The output function g rendered the interface displayed to the user based on the input event and the current state. Again, if the user transitioned from the trigger state to the gesture state, the output $Y(t)$ would be an audio sound that let the user know that he or she successfully grabbed the object. Here the states are explained in more detail:

Free State (S_0): The virtual hand did not touch any object. In this condition, the virtual hand moved freely and the finger joints bend freely

Trigger State (S_1): The virtual hand moved into the object action trigger area, but did not meet the action determining rules

Gesture State (S_2): The virtual hand manipulated the object stably by following the gesture determining rules. The object latched onto the virtual hand in the gesture state

Move State (S_3): The virtual hand manipulated the object stably by following the two determining rules. The object rotated and translated with the virtual hand

Release State (S_4): The virtual hand transitioned to the release state when it did not satisfy Rule Two of the action determining rules after manipulating the object. In this state, the virtual hand released the object and then transitioned to the free state

3 Task and Experimental Setup

There are many devices that provide hand pose data such as Intel RealSense, Leap Motion, Kinect etc. Due to the accuracy of Leap Motion and its compatibility with the Oculus Rift [8], we chose the pose data provided by the Leap Motion for gesture recognition. The system set-up is shown in Fig. 2 and the objects that the user sees are indicated in the box.

A Leap Motion hand tracking device was mounted on an Oculus Rift VR headset using a custom mount that oriented the Leap Motion device to point 13° below a line perpendicular to the headset surface. The task involved manipulating a virtual hand to grab a virtual dice from a starting location, move the dice to a precise target location and orientation, and release it. The study was approved by the university Committee on Human Research.

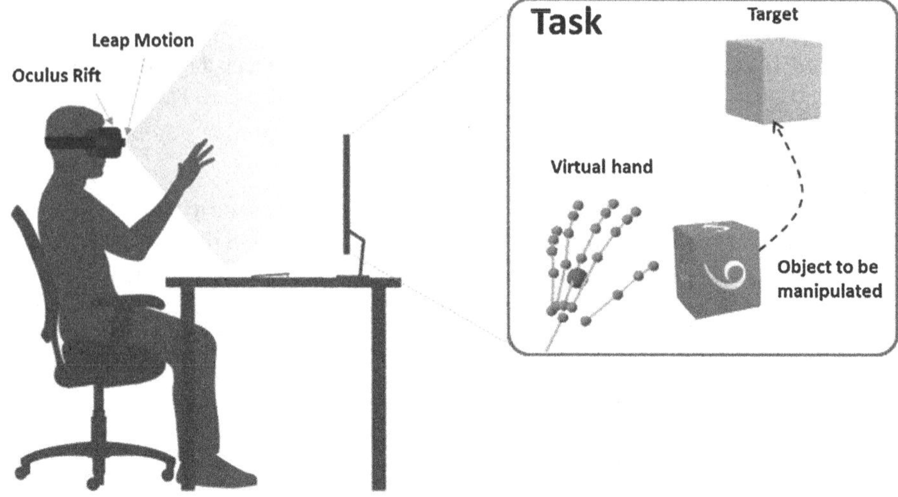

Fig. 2. The manipulation system

As shown in Fig. 3, the virtual skeletal hand model mimics the posture and movements of the user's real right hand based on hand detection by the Leap Motion sensor. Following the FSM model explained in Sect. 2, subjects manipulated the virtual hand to capture, move, rotate, and release the red dice (100×100×100 mm) until the red dice fit precisely inside the blue-green target box. The two requirements were:

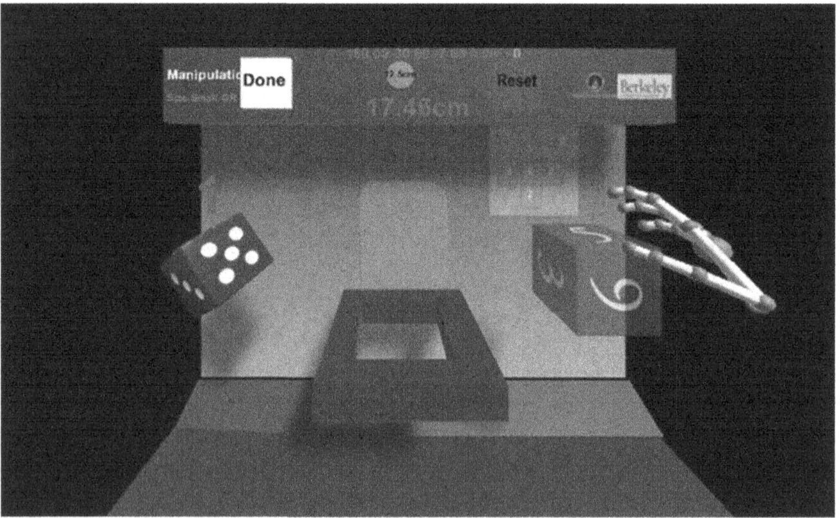

Fig. 3. The manipulation scene (Color figure online)

Position: The center of the red dice had to be within 2 mm of the center of the target box.

Orientation: The dice must be correctly orientated so that the number facing the subject matched the number on the smaller dark blue dice and was upright. The orientation of the red dice had to be within 3° of the target box orientation.

The subject then virtually pressed the DONE button on the upper left corner with their left hand to complete the task. The dice dropped down through the grey hole and appeared back at the original position. The task was repeated with the next number appearing on the front of the blue dice. The task was repeated 6 times (once for each number on the dice) for each parameter-level. The final scene is as Fig. 3.

The gesture commands for object manipulation included: push, grab, rotate, move, and release. The grab gesture modeled a pinch posture, in which the user brought the fingertips together. The threshold for the grab command (G_T) was based on the distance between fingertips and was the length of the subject's thumb metacarpal bone (m; extracted from the Leap Motion data) multiplied by a grab threshold constant, α.

$$G_T = \alpha \cdot m \tag{3}$$

Hence, the grab threshold value was different for each user and was based on their hand size. The release threshold (R_T) determined when the hand pose transitioned out of the grab state and was similar to the grab threshold, except $\beta \geq \alpha$.

$$R_T = \beta \cdot m \tag{4}$$

The release threshold could be set greater than the grab threshold to reduce the chance that the user might accidently transition out of the grab state and unintentionally release the dice.

4 Experiments

Twenty subjects participated in the study; eight were male. The mean age was 22. Only two had familiarity with virtual reality devices.

Four different experiments evaluated 4 parameters on usability, performance and comfort. The parameters were grab distance (distance from palm to object before it can be captured), grab release difference (difference between grab threshold and release threshold: $R_T - G_T$), grab size (difference in α) and grab location (center of dice vs corners of dice). Each parameter was tested at 2 or 3 levels. e.g., Grab Distance was evaluated at 3 levels: short, middle, and large. The parameters and their tested levels are summarized in Table 1. For each parameter, the test order of levels was randomized. For each level, the task was repeated 6 times.

With the Grab Distance experiment, the dice could be grabbed and manipulated from different distances. When the palm pointed to an object and the object was within the proscribed grab distance: short (25–40 cm), middle (40–55 cm), large (55–70 cm), it would change color and could then be captured (grabbed) and moved and rotated. The dice rotated around the center of the palm, instead of around itself, so at the large distance, a small change in hand orientation would magnify the movement of the dice.

Table 1. Parameters tested in the 4 experiments

Parameter	Levels	Values	Concept Model
Grab Distance	Short	25 – 40	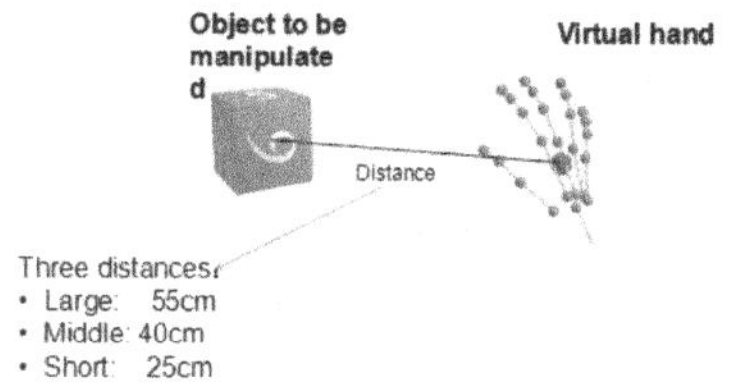
	Middle	40 – 55	
	Large	55 – 70	
Grab Release Difference	Small	0.8 Grab 0.8 Release	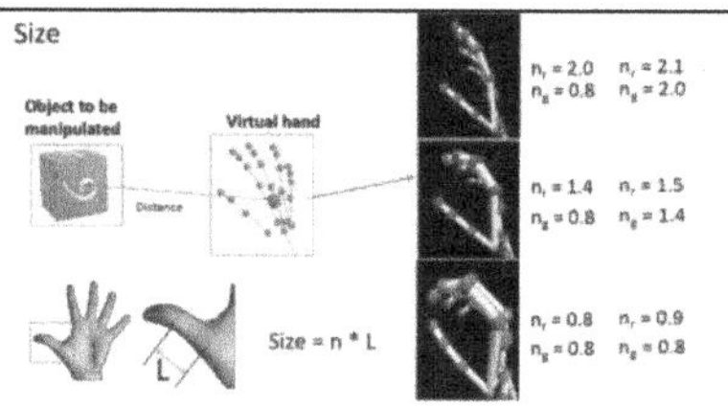
	Middle	0.8 Grab 1.4 Release	
	Large	0.8 Grab 2.0 Release	
Grab Size	Small	0.8 Grab 0.9 Release	
	Middle	1.4 Grab 1.5 Release	
	Large	2.0 Grab 2.1 Release	
Grab Location	Center	Center	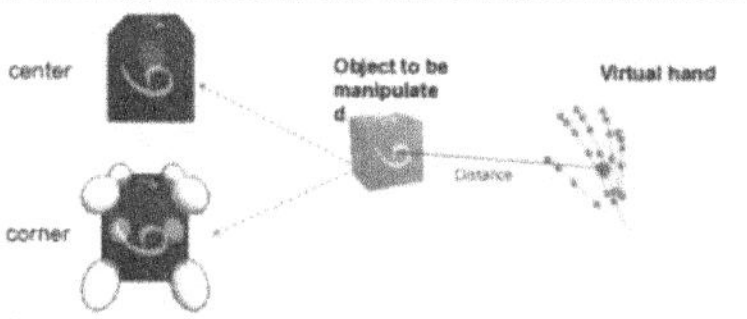
	Corner	Corner	

This is an application of Rule One from section three, in which the center of the palm had to be within a certain range from the center of the dice before it could be captured.

In the Grab Release Difference experiment, the distance for the grab threshold, α, was held constant at 0.8, but the distance threshold for the release, β, was tested at small (0.8), middle (1.4), and large (2.0). The 0.8 release threshold was the same as the grab threshold but the 2.0 release threshold was 2.5 times larger than the grab threshold of 0.8. In theory, a release threshold larger than the grab threshold might prevent the dice from being accidently released. This is an application of Rule Two, in which the spread between grab and release thresholds were different. For this experiment, applying Rule One, the palm center had to be within 12 cm of the dice center before the dice could be grabbed. Rotation was around the center of the dice not around the palm.

In the Grab Size experiment, the grab threshold, α, was varied between small (0.8), middle (1.4), and large (2.0) while difference with the release threshold was held constant ($\beta = \alpha + 0.1$). The purpose was to determine if grab size influenced usability or throughput. Again, for this experiment, the palm center had to be within 12 cm of the dice center before the dice could be grabbed and rotation was around the center of the dice.

The Grab Location experiment evaluated the difference between grabbing the dice at its center compared to grabbing the dice at any one of its 8 corners. The dice rotated around the center if the dice was grabbed at the center or around the corner if was grabbed at the corner. To capture the dice, the palm center had to be within 6 cm from any of the corners of the dice for the corner test, and within 12 cm from the center of the dice for the center test.

After each of the 4 experiments, subjects completed a survey evaluating subjective usability and comfort for each of the levels tested. The survey presented three statements and subjects rated each statement on a five-point Likert scale (1 was strongly disagree and 5 was strongly agree). The statements were (1) I had excellent control, (2) I had no shoulder fatigue, and (3) I feel motion sickness. Subjects also ranked the levels tested on overall preference, 1 being the most favorite and 3 being the least favorite.

Throughput for each level was calculated as the time to complete the 6 dice placement tasks.

Differences between subjective ratings were evaluated with the non-parametric Skillings-Mack test ($p < 0.05$) and differences in time to complete tasks were evaluated with repeated-measures ANOVA.

5 Result and Discussion

For each of the 4 experiments, differences between levels of a parameter had a significant effect on subjective usability, preference and time to complete tasks. For example, grabbing and manipulating an object at its center, as compared to its corners, improved the time to complete the task and the subjective usability rating of "control". Subjects reported greater rotation control with the center than the corner locations. The result is shown in Table 2.

Table 2. Grab location test results; mean (SD) subjective ratings, ranking, and time to complete task. (Likert scale: 1 = strongly disagree, 5 = strongly agree).

	Grab location		p-value
	Center	Corner	
Excellent control	4.3 (0.8)	3.2 (1.1)	0.007
No shoulder fatigue	3.7 (1.3)	3.6 (1.3)	0.65
Motion sickness	1.4 (0.7)	1.4 (0.7)	1.00
Preference (1 = favorite)	1.1 (0.3)	1.9 (0.3)	0.0008
Time (s)	14.5 (8.6)	34.2 (23.5)	< 0.0001

For the other parameters studied, there was significantly better performance and usability for the short grab distance (e.g., 25 to 40 cm), the middle grab release difference ($R_T - G_T = 0.6$) and the largest grab size ($G_T = 2.0$).

Subjects generally reported lower levels of shoulder fatigue for settings that were easier to control. However, significant difference in shoulder fatigue occurred with grab distance ($p = .046$). Participants reported little motion sickness during the experiments (mean rating 1.31 on 1–5 scale). The tasks required relatively little head rotation.

Overall, preference for a gesture design parameter was related to better control and reduced time to complete the tasks.

Some study limitations should be noted. The task was designed to be a relatively high precision task requiring placing the dice to within 2 mm and 3° of the target. In addition, the distance the dice was moved was relatively short. Other tasks will require higher or lower precision and larger movements of virtual objects. These differences in task demands may influence optimal gesture design. The gesture evaluated for object capture was based on distance between finger tips. Other gestures for object capture could be evaluated.

In conclusion, this study identified important gesture design features that can be optimized to improve usability and throughput for an object manipulation task in VR. Further refinement of this optimization may be useful. For example, the interaction between grab size and grab release difference should be explored. In addition, other hand gestures should be compared to the ones used in this study on usability and throughput. Overall, if properly designed and evaluated, 3D hand gestures have the potential to provide very functional human-computer interaction in VR.

Acknowledgments. This work was supported by the Ergonomics Lab at Berkeley, the Office Ergonomics Research Committee, and the China Astronaut Research and Training Center within the following research programs: Advanced Space Medico-Engineering Research Project of China (2013SY54A1303, 9140c770204150c77318, 060601).

References

1. Sen, F., Diaz, L., Horttana, T.: A novel gesture-based interface for a VR simulation: re-discovering Vrouw Maria. In: 2012 18th International Conference on Virtual Systems and Multimedia (VSMM), pp. 323–330 (2012). http://ieeexplore.ieee.org/xpl/mostRecentIssue.jsp?reload=true&punumber=6341172
2. Sato, Y., Saito, M., Koike, H.: Real-time input of 3D pose and gestures of a user's hand and its applications for HCI. In: Proceedings of the Virtual Reality 2001, pp. 79–86. IEEE (2001). http://ieeexplore.ieee.org/xpl/mostRecentIssue.jsp?punumber=7269
3. Lee, C.-S., Oh, K.-M., Park, C.-J.: Virtual environment interaction based on gesture recognition and hand cursor. Electron. Resour. (2008)
4. Dardas, N.H., Alhaj, M.: Hand gesture interaction with a 3D virtual environment. Res. Bull. Jordan ACM **2**(3), 186–193 (2011)
5. Ming, A., Yuqing, L., Bohe, Z., Fuchao, H.: Study on real-time interactive simulation of rotating top in weightlessness. Manned Spaceflight, March 2014. http://zw.yakjfw.org.cn:8081/kns55/loginid.aspx?uid=VlFpZ3Ivb2VqVno5&p=Navi/Bridge.aspx?LinkType=BaseLink&DBCode=cjfd&TableName=CJFDbaseinfo&Field=BaseID&Value=ZRHT
6. Chen, Y., Lin, F.: Safety control of discrete event systems using finite state machines with parameters. In: Proceedings of the American Control Conference, pp. 975–980. American Auotmatic Control Council, Arlington (2001)
7. Feng, Z., Yan, B., Xu, T., et al.: 3D direct human-computer interface paradigm based on free hand tracking. Chin. J. Comput. **37**(6), 1309–1323 (2014)
8. Weichert, F., Bachmann, D., Rudak, B., Fisseler, D.: Analysis of the accuracy and robustness of the leap motion controller. Sensors **13**(5), 6380–6393 (2013)

A Widely Applicable Real-Time Mono/Binocular Eye Tracking System Using a High Frame-Rate Digital Camera

Keiji Matsuda[1(✉)], Takeshi Nagami[1], Yasuko Sugase[1], Aya Takemura[1], and Kenji Kawano[2]

[1] National Institute of Advanced Industrial Science and Technology (AIST), Tsukuba, Japan
k.matsuda@aist.go.jp
[2] Kyoto University, Kyoto, Japan

Abstract. We have developed a new mono/binocular eye tracking system by using an IEEE1394b or USB-3.0 digital camera that provides high sensitivity, high resolution, high frame-rate and no rolling shutter distortion. Our goal is to provide a system that is friendly to researchers who conduct experiments. The system is non-invasive and inexpensive and can be used for mice, marmosets, monkeys, and humans. It has adopted infrared light to illuminate an eye (eyes). The reflected image of the infrared light on the cornea and the black image of the pupil are captured by the camera. The center of the pupil and the center of the corneal reflection are calculated and tracked over time. The movement of the head is compensated by the reflection. Since the high resolution camera has a 2048 horizontal pixels resolution, we can capture the images of both eyes simultaneously and calculate the parameters of the two eyes at each frame. The gaze position data can be read out on-line via computer network and/or DAC (digital analog converter). The adoption of the Windows 10 as the operation system makes this eye tracking system user-friendly. Because of the high frame-rate of the digital camera, the sampling rate of the system can be as high as 700 Hz and the latency less than 4 ms.

Keywords: Eye tracking · Image processing · Oculomotor system · High frame-rate digital camera

1 Introduction

The eye tracking system has been used for various purposes: in psychological studies, understanding visual information processing, analyzing consumers' interests, etc [1,2]. Recently, the eye movement information has also attracted a great deal of attention, because of its applicability in the Human-Computer-Interaction. However, as for the eye tracking system on the market, the hardware and software are incorporated as one manufactured product. As a result,

M. Kurosu (Ed.): HCI 2017, Part I, LNCS 10271, pp. 593–608, 2017.
DOI: 10.1007/978-3-319-58071-5_45

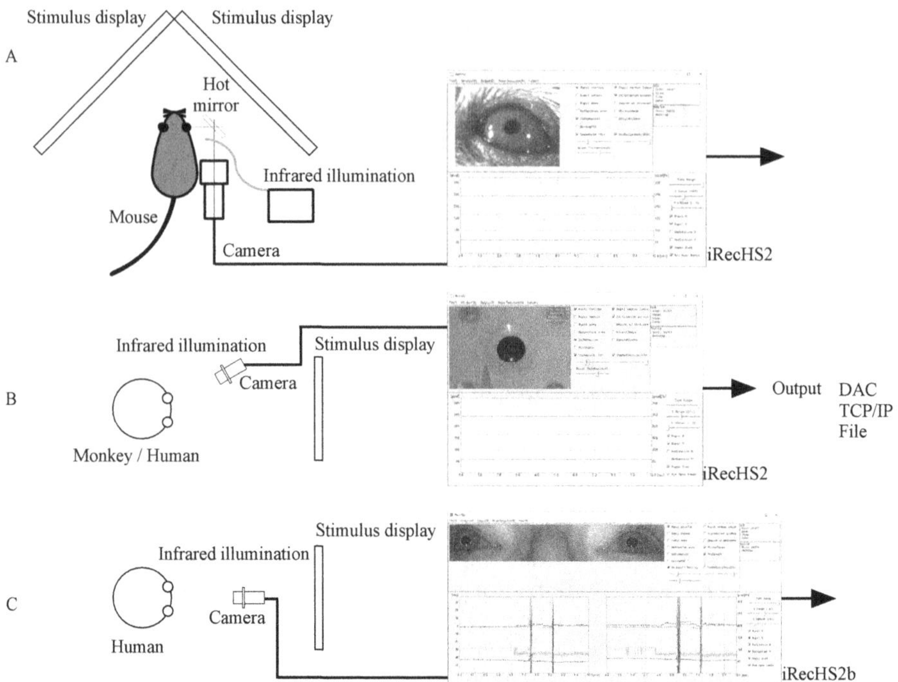

Fig. 1. Eye tracking system outline. In the monocular system (A) (B), the camera can be located at any position within the range where the pupil can be captured. In the binocular eye tracking system (C), the camera should be arranged at the same distance from each eye to be in focus.

the users (researchers) have to select or build up their experimental protocols to fit the eye tracking system that they own, which could limit their experiments. We report here a new user (experimenters) friendly, non-invasive and inexpensive eye tracking system, whose hardware can be selected to suit various experimental protocols. As shown in Fig. 1, there are two sets of software, iRecHS2 for monocular and iRecHS2b for binocular, both of which can be run on Windows 10. The basic requirement of the system's hardware is a digital camera (FLIR Integrated Imaging Solutions, Inc.), which can receive infrared ray and has a global shutter. Other required hardware (infrared light-source, lens, PC, etc.) can be selected according to its application and the system can be used for mice, marmoset, monkeys, and humans, thus, expanding the applicability of the eye movement information over a variety of fields.

2 General Methods

Various types of eye tracking technologies are currently available [1,2]. In the present study, we selected a digital video-based combined pupil and corneal reflection method by using a 3-D (3-Dimension) eyeball model, because it allows for passive calibration on untrained subjects (animals). By real-time image processing, the gaze angle, pupil size, blink (eye openness) and gaze-target position in 3-D space (binocular system) are estimated and the data can be read out on-line via TCP/IP and/or by a DAC (digital analog converter), and also be stored for offline analysis.

2.1 Apparatus

The system consists of the following devices. (1) infrared illumination, (2) visible light cut filter, (3) lens, (4) high frame-rate and global shutter digital camera, (5) Windows 10 personal computer, (6) DAC for output data and DIO (digital I/O) for synchronizing with other devices, (7) cables, camera support member, etc. The device configuration of (1)–(5) can be altered depending on the measurement subject and/or distance between the camera and subject. Details are summarized in Table 1.

Table 1. Equipments' list.

	Mice	Monkey, human
Illumination	LA-100IR halogen lamp	IR LED array
Filter	62S PRO1D R-27 kenko	R-72 M30.5X0.5 Edmund optics
Lens	AIAF MicroNikkor 60 mm f/2.8D Nikon C mount Adapter kenko extender 2x	M7528-MP2 75 mm M3514-MP 35 mm CBC
Camera	GS3-U3-32S4M-C	
	GS3-U3-41C6NIR-C	
	FL3-U3-13Y3M-C (monocular only, not recommend)	
	GRAS-03K2M-C (monocular only, not recommend)	
	FLIR Integrated Imaging Solutions, Inc.	
PC	Windows 10 64 bit	
	Memory 16 GByte	
	Network interface	
	PCI Express x1 for DAC and DIO	
DAC with DIO	AO-1604L-LPE (4 ch DAC, 4 ch DIO for monocular)	
	AO-1608L-LPE (8 ch DAC, 4 ch DIO for binocular)	
	Cable PCB50PS-1.5P	
	Crimp relay terminal block EPD-50A	
	CONTEC	

2.2 3-D Eyeball Model for Gaze Detection

In order to obtain the gaze vector towards the camera, an eyeball model (Fig. 2) was adopted. In this model, the extension of the normal vector (C_x, C_y, C_z) of the pupil plane, passing through the center of the pupil, passes through the corneal curvature center and the eyeball rotation center. The vector (C_x, C_y, C_z) also represents the gaze vector in camera coordinates. We approximate the outline of the pupil in the captured image as an ellipse. We define the pupil center as (X_p, Y_p), the length of the minor axis as S, the major axis as L, and the slope of the minor axis as a. Since the cornea is also a part of a sphere, we refer to the center of the sphere as the cornea curvature center (X_c, Y_c). If the distance between the light/camera and the eyes is sufficiently longer than the head movement, the relationship between the center of the reflection and the cornea curvature center is constant. Thus, when the reflection point is (X_r, Y_r), the cornea curvature center (X_c, Y_c) can be described as $(X_c, Y_c) = (X_r - Offset_x, Y_r - Offset_y)$. We defined the eyeball rotation center in a captured image as (X_o, X_o), length between the pupil center and eyeball rotation center in 3-D space as R and length between the pupil center and the corneal curvature center in 3-D space as R_{pc}. Using these parameters, we can express the gaze vector in two ways.

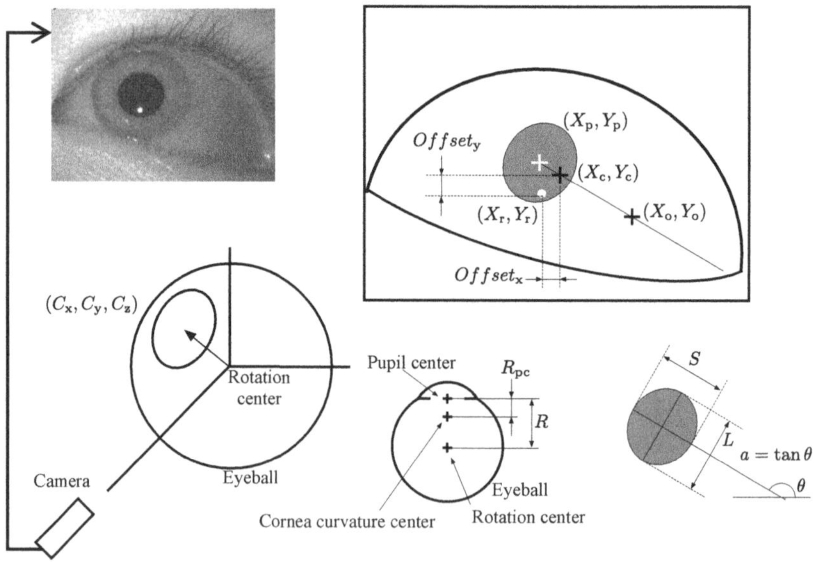

Fig. 2. 3-D eyeball model for gaze detection.

Head-fixed-method. Assess the gaze vector from the vector connecting the pupil center and eyeball rotation center (Eq. (1)). The gaze vector (C_x, C_y, C_z) can be calculated by using Eq. (1) after measuring the pupil center (X_p, Y_p) in the captured image of the eye. However, when the head moves, the eyeball rotation center (X_o, X_o) has to be calculated again. Thus, this method is applicable for the animal whose head is firmly fixed.

$$(C_x, C_y, C_z) = \left(\frac{X_p - X_o}{R}, \frac{Y_p - Y_o}{R}, \frac{\sqrt{R^2 - (X_p - X_o)^2 - (Y_p - Y_o)^2}}{R} \right) \quad (1)$$

Head-free-method. Assess the gaze vector from the vector connecting the pupil center and corneal curvature center (Eq. (2)). The gaze vector (C_x, C_y, C_z) can be calculated by using Eq. (2) after measuring the pupil center (X_p, Y_p), and the gravity-center of the reflection in the captured image of the eye (X_r, Y_r). By this method, the gaze vector can be calculated when the head moves in the picture frame. However, when the distance between the eye and camera changes, the image of the eye would be out of focus. Thus, using a chin-rest to keep the distance between them is preferable. Since the measurement can be taken only when the reflection light is on the cornea, the range of the measurable eye position is narrower than the head-fixed-method. The noise of the measurement might increase because the images of the pupil and reflection are used.

$$\begin{cases} X_c = X_r - Offset_x \\ Y_c = Y_r - Offset_y \\ (C_x, C_y, C_z) = \left(\dfrac{X_p - X_c}{R_{pc}}, \dfrac{Y_p - Y_c}{R_{pc}}, \dfrac{\sqrt{R_{pc}^2 - (X_p - X_c)^2 - (Y_p - Y_c)^2}}{R_{pc}} \right) \end{cases} \quad (2)$$

2.3 Pupil Detecting Method

In this system, an infrared illuminates the eye of the subject. By using a high frame-rate digital camera, the image of the subject's pupil is captured and approximated by an ellipse. To detect the pupil within limited time, we adopted the following procedure:

1. Capture an image from camera.
2. Create a reduced image of the captured image.
3. Create a binary image of the reduced image.
4. Label and measure the objects in the binary image. Detect the largest object as pupil.
5. Approximate the reduced image of the pupil by an ellipse.
6. Fit the ellipse on the original picture and detect the edge of the pupil.
7. Remove reflection of irrelevant objects on the pupil edge (Fig. 3).
8. Approximate the outline of the pupil to an ellipse by least square method.
9. Compare between the vertical height of the ellipse and the distance between the top and bottom of the pupil image to detect eye openness.
10. Create a binary image of the reduced image by using the threshold of the reflection.

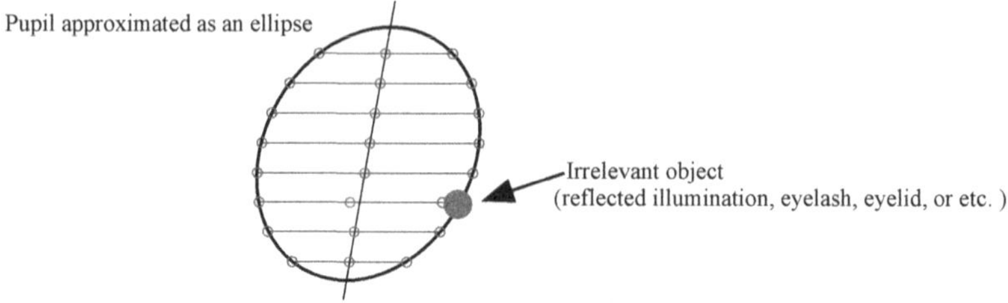

Fig. 3. Removal method for irrelevant reflected objects. Blue circles indicate detected pupil edges. Red circles indicate center of horizontal line segments. The points out of the straight line are omitted for the further calculation. (Color figure online)

11. The reflected image of the light source nearest to the pupil center is used to calculate the gravity-center.

The process between (2)–(5) can be skipped because of the small shift of the pupil during the high frame-rate sampling.

2.4 Passive Calibration

By applying the value of the captured images of the freely moving eye, the pupil rotation center (X_o, Y_o) and pupil rotation radius R are calculated using the head-fixed-method, and the offset between reflection and the corner curvature center ($Offset_x$, $Offset_y$), and the length between the pupil center and corner curvature center R_{pc} are calculated using the head-free-method. When the slope of minor axis of the ellipse is defined as a, (X_o, Y_o) is expressed by Eq. (3). As shown in Fig. 4, the intersections of the minor axes of the pupil-ellipses in multiple picture-frames are located on (X_o, Y_o). $Offset_x$ and $Offset_y$ are calculated by Eq. (4) using data taken from two or more picture-frames (least square method). R is calculated by Eq. (5) with (X_o, Y_o) and (X_{pi}, Y_{pi}). R_{pc} is calculated by Eq. (6) with $Offset_x$, $Offset_y$, (X_{pi}, Y_{pi}), (X_{ri}, Y_{ri}). The calculation-process for R, R_{pc} from the major axis L and minor axis S of the pupil is shown in Fig. 5. By acquiring these parameters, the gaze vector directing to the camera can be calculated. This method is used for the subject who cannot perform the active calibration, for example mouse.

$$\begin{cases} a_i(X_o - X_{pi}) = Y_o - Y_{pi} \\ i = 0 \dots n \end{cases} \tag{3}$$

$$\begin{cases} a_i(X_{ri} - Offset_x - X_{pi}) = Y_{ri} - Offset_y - Y_{pi} \\ i = 0 \dots n \end{cases} \tag{4}$$

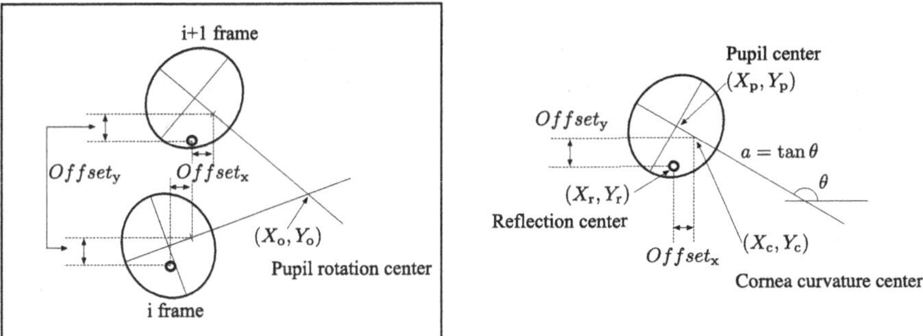

Fig. 4. A schematic representation of the method to calculate (X_o, Y_o), $Offset_x$, $Offset_y$

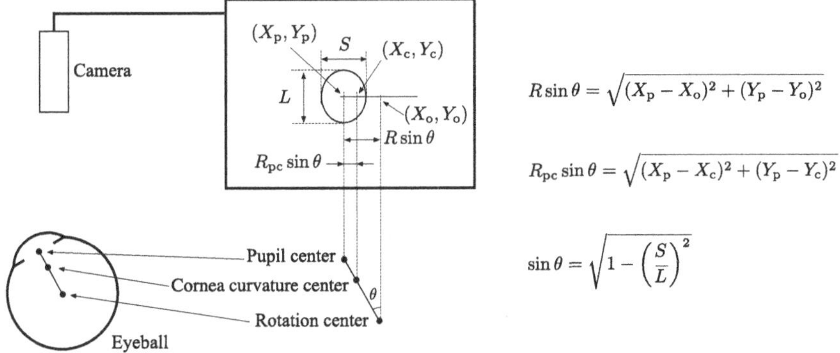

Fig. 5. A schematic representation of the method to calculate R, R_{pc}.

$$\begin{cases} R = \sqrt{\dfrac{(X_{pi} - X_o)^2 + (Y_{pi} - Y_o)^2}{1 - \left(\dfrac{S_i}{L_i}\right)^2}} \\ i = 0 \dots n \end{cases} \tag{5}$$

$$\begin{cases} R_{pc} = \sqrt{\dfrac{(X_{pi} - X_{ri} + Offset_x)^2 + (Y_{pi} - Y_{ri} + Offset_y)^2}{1 - \left(\dfrac{S_i}{L_i}\right)^2}} \\ i = 0 \dots n \end{cases} \tag{6}$$

2.5 Active Calibration, Transformation into Object Coordinates

We calculate a gaze axis vector (C_x, C_y, C_z) in camera coordinates from Eqs. (1), (2). and obtain a gaze axis vector (T_x, T_y, T_z) in object coordinates from target positions. The subject is instructed to fixate small targets, located at 5 (more than 3) positions on the stimulus display to obtain $Offset_{\mathrm{x}}, Offset_{\mathrm{y}}, Rpc$, and a 3×3 matrix M for coordinates transformation (Eq. (7)). Then we can calculate a gaze vector $(O_{\mathrm{x}}, O_{\mathrm{y}}, O_{\mathrm{z}})$ in object coordinates from Eq. (8).

$$M = \begin{pmatrix} \sum_{i=1}^{n} C_{\mathrm{x}i}^2 & \sum_{i=1}^{n} C_{\mathrm{x}i}C_{\mathrm{y}i} & \sum_{i=1}^{n} C_{\mathrm{z}i}C_{\mathrm{x}i} \\ \sum_{i=1}^{n} C_{\mathrm{x}i}C_{\mathrm{y}i} & \sum_{i=1}^{n} C_{\mathrm{y}i}^2 & \sum_{i=1}^{n} C_{\mathrm{y}i}C_{\mathrm{z}i} \\ \sum_{i=1}^{n} C_{\mathrm{z}i}C_{\mathrm{x}i} & \sum_{i=1}^{n} C_{\mathrm{y}i}C_{\mathrm{z}i} & \sum_{i=1}^{n} C_{\mathrm{z}i}^2 \end{pmatrix}^{-1} \begin{pmatrix} \sum_{i=1}^{n} C_{\mathrm{x}i}T_{\mathrm{x}i} & \sum_{i=1}^{n} C_{\mathrm{x}i}T_{\mathrm{y}i} & \sum_{i=1}^{n} C_{\mathrm{x}i}T_{\mathrm{z}i} \\ \sum_{i=1}^{n} C_{\mathrm{y}i}T_{\mathrm{x}i} & \sum_{i=1}^{n} C_{\mathrm{y}i}T_{\mathrm{y}i} & \sum_{i=1}^{n} C_{\mathrm{y}i}T_{\mathrm{z}i} \\ \sum_{i=1}^{n} C_{\mathrm{z}i}T_{\mathrm{x}i} & \sum_{i=1}^{n} C_{\mathrm{z}i}T_{\mathrm{y}i} & \sum_{i=1}^{n} C_{\mathrm{z}i}T_{\mathrm{z}i} \end{pmatrix} \tag{7}$$

$$\begin{pmatrix} O_{\mathrm{x}} \\ O_{\mathrm{y}} \\ O_{\mathrm{z}} \end{pmatrix} = M \begin{pmatrix} C_{\mathrm{x}} \\ C_{\mathrm{y}} \\ C_{\mathrm{z}} \end{pmatrix} \tag{8}$$

2.6 Case of Binocular Vision

We calculate gaze-target positions (x, y, z) in 3-D space from the vectors in object coordinates of two eyes (left $(LO_{\mathrm{x}}, LO_{\mathrm{y}}, LO_{\mathrm{z}})$, right $(RO_{\mathrm{x}}, RO_{\mathrm{y}}, RO_{\mathrm{z}})$) and inter-pupillary distance (IPD) (Eq. (9)).

$$\begin{cases} \dfrac{x + \dfrac{IPC}{2}}{LO_{\mathrm{x}}} = \dfrac{y}{LO_{\mathrm{y}}} = \dfrac{z}{LO_{\mathrm{z}}} \\ \dfrac{x - \dfrac{IPC}{2}}{RO_{\mathrm{x}}} = \dfrac{y}{RO_{\mathrm{y}}} = \dfrac{z}{RO_{\mathrm{z}}} \end{cases} \tag{9}$$

3 Evaluation of the System's Accuracy

3.1 Evaluation of the System's Accuracy of Gaze Angle

We evaluated the system's accuracy by using an apparatus of synthetic eyes. (Fig. 6).

Method. We measured the accuracy of the system in representing monocular gaze angles. First, we calibrated the system while the synthetic eye gazing at 8 points angle of $(horizontal, vertical) = (-10, 10)$, $(0, 10)$, $(10, 10)$, $(-10, 0)$, $(0, 0)$, $(10, 0)$, $(-10, -10)$, $(10, -10)$ degrees. Then, under the head fix method, $(X_{\mathrm{o}}, Y_{\mathrm{o}})$, R, and translation matrix M_{fixed} were calculated, and under the head-free-method, $Offset_{\mathrm{x}}$, $Offset_{\mathrm{y}}$, R_{pc}, and translation matrix M_{free} were calculated. We set the synthetic eye gazing at 25 points, horizontal angle -10 to $+10°$ and vertical angle -10 to $10°$ at intervals of $5°$, and measured the eye's gaze angle for 1 s at each setting. The camera was GS3-U3-41C6NIR-C, and the captured image size was 320×240 pixels.

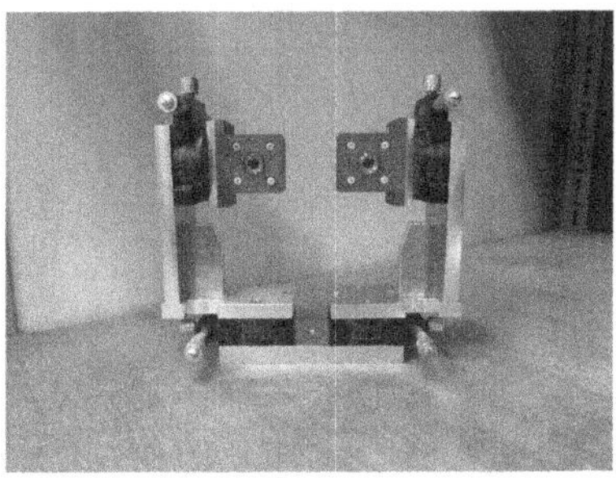

Fig. 6. A pair of synthetic eyes. The cornea was acrylic. The diameter of the pupil: 5 mm. The radius of cornea curvature: 7.7 mm. The radius of rotation of the pupil center: 9 mm. The distance between two eyes: 60 mm. The axis of rotation (both X, Y-axis): high-grade transmission type rotary stage (CHUO PRECISION INDUSTRIAL CO., LTD. RS-4012-R, vernier reading 10 min of arc).

Result. Figures 7, 8 show the distribution of the gaze angles in the head-fixed-method (Fig. 7) and head-free-method (Fig. 8). The gaze angles are plotted in camera coordinates (A) and in object coordinates (B), and superimposed in both coordinates (C). The distribution of the gaze positions in camera coordinates shrank a little from those in object coordinates (C). The means and standard deviations of the errors at 25 points (in object coordinates) are summarized in Table 2. Figure 9 shows the data at the center in a larger scale (A, B) and those after a median filter. The scatter of the errors by using the head-free-method was larger than that by the head-fixed-method.

Discussion. As shown in Figs. 7C and 8C, the distribution of the gaze positions in camera coordinates shrank a little from those in object coordinates. It is because of the shift of the pupil center due to the cornea-refraction. It is

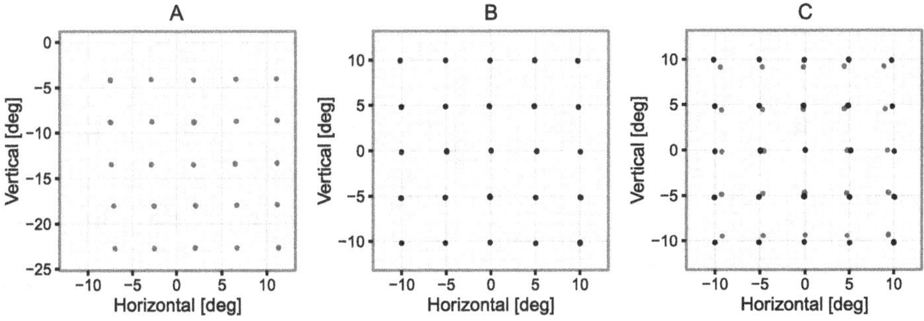

Fig. 7. Head-fix-method. A: After passive calibration, gaze angle in camera coordinates. B: After active calibration, gaze angle in object coordinates. C: The data in A and B are superimpose after parallel shift.

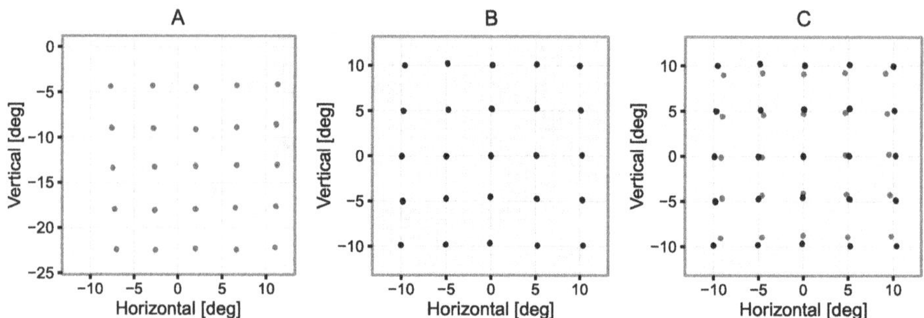

Fig. 8. Head-free-method. A: After passive calibration, gaze angle in camera coordinates. B: After active calibration, gaze angle in object coordinates. C: The data in A and B are superimpose after parallel shift.

Table 2. System's accuracy of gaze angle.

	Head-fixed-method [mean(sd)]	Head-free-method [mean(sd)]
Horizontal	0.028 (0.098) degree	−0.042 (0.138) degree
Vertical	0.096 (0.071) degree	0.047 (0.139) degree

necessary to consider the shift when the subject (such as a mouse) cannot perform active calibration. On the other hand, there is no practical issue for the subject, who can perform the active calibration, because the transformation matrix created by the active calibration compensates the shift. The larger scattering of the errors in the head-free-method (Fig. 9A, B) is due to the measurement error of the gravity-center of the reflection in addition to the measurement error of the pupil center. When the head is fixed perfectly, the head-fixed-method provides higher-accuracy and wider-range measurement. Practically, the researchers can get stable measurements, by applying a median filter or moving average filter (Fig. 9C, D).

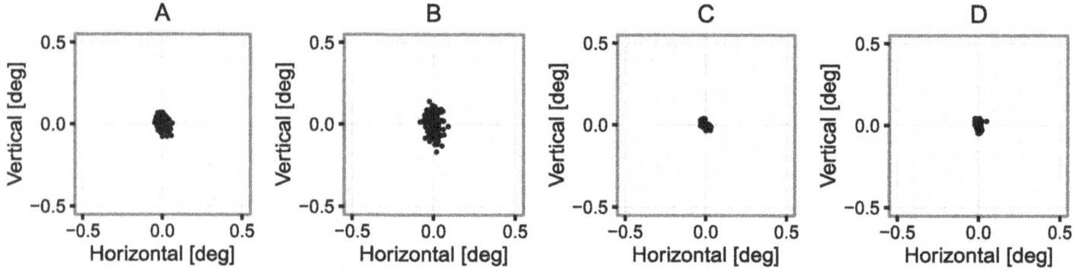

Fig. 9. Distribution of eye position data at the center of fixation point $(0, 0)$. The X- and Y-axis scale are expanded. A: Superimposed eye position data taken by the head-fixed-method. B: Taken by the head-free-method. C: By the head-fixed-method after applying a median filter. D: By the head-free-method after applying a median filter.

3.2 Evaluation of the System's Accuracy of Gaze Position

Method. We estimated the accuracy of the system in representing binocular gaze angles by using a pair of synthetic eyes. First, we calibrated the system while the synthetic eyes gazing at 8 points horizontal angles of $(righteye, lefteye) = (1, -1)$, $(1.5, -1.5)$, $(2.0, -2.0)$, $(2.5, -2.5)$, $(3.0, -3.0)$, $(3.5, -3.5)$, $(4.0, -4.0)$, $(5.0, -5.0)$, $(6.0, -6.0)$, $(8.0, -8.0)$, $(10.0, 10.0)$ degrees, and vertical angle of $0°$. The horizontal position at $(1, -1)$ indicates that the gaze is on the center of the visual field at distance of 1719 mm, and that at $(10, -10)$ indicates at distance of 170 mm. We measured the left and right eyes' gaze angles and calculated the 3-D position of the intersection for 1 s at each setting.

Result. Figure 10 shows the distribution of eye position errors (A, B) and 3-D intersections (C) measured by head-free-method, by using a 10-points moving average filter.

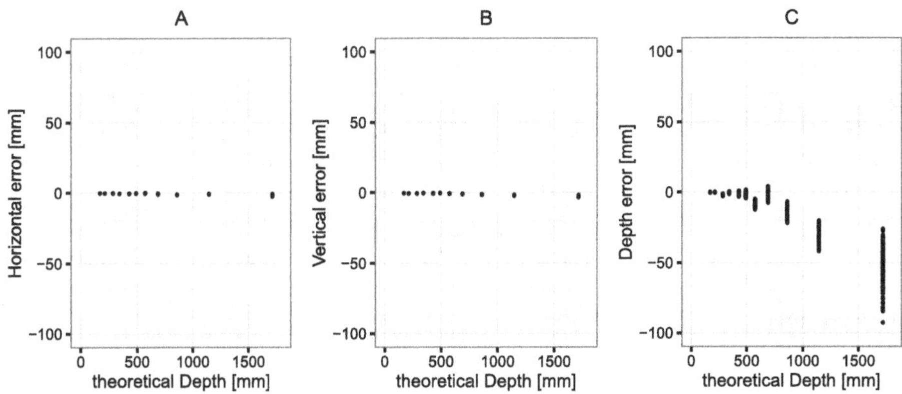

Fig. 10. Distribution of error of position (A, B) and 3-D intersection. A: horizontal B: vertical C: depth.

Discussion. As shown in Fig. 10, when the distance between the subject and the target is larger, the distribution of the measurement errors of the intersection scattered. It is important to notice this characteristic of the 3-D measurement.

4 Evaluation of the System's Latency

We evaluated the system's latency by using an apparatus of synthetic eye (Fig. 11).

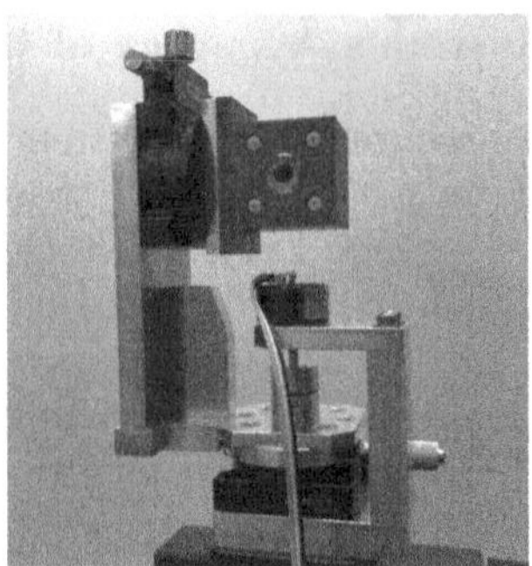

Fig. 11. A potentiometer (Midori Precision CP-2F(b), linearity ±1%) was attached to the synthetic eye. The rotation angle can be measured by applying voltage to its edges.

4.1 Methods

By using the synthetic eye, the system was calibrated. The voltage output from the potentiometer and eye tracking system was sampled at 10 kHz. The synthetic eye was rotated by a hand and the output voltage were recorded and translated into rotation angle and horizontal eye movements (Fig. 12). As shown by the enlarged view in Fig. 12B, D, the time-delay of the system can be observed. The latency of the system is calculated by the following Eq. (10), by using the rotation angle output of potentiometer as $p(t)$ and the output of the eye tracking system as $h(t)$. The latency was obtained when the Error RMS (root mean square) was the minimum. We measured latencies with different sampling frequencies of the picture-frame.

$$Error\ RMS = \sqrt{\frac{1}{n}\sum_{i=0}^{n}\{p(t_i) - h(t_i + latency)\}^2} \tag{10}$$

4.2 Results

The data calculated by using Eq. (10) are shown in Fig. 13A at seven sampling frequencies of the camera-frame. Figure 13B shows the relationship between the minimum value and sampling frequency, suggesting that the system's latency depended on the sampling frequency (= 1/period). The approximated line in Fig. 13B indicates that the latency is represented as the sum of the sampling duration and processing time. The latency was less than 4 ms at 500 Hz sampling rate.

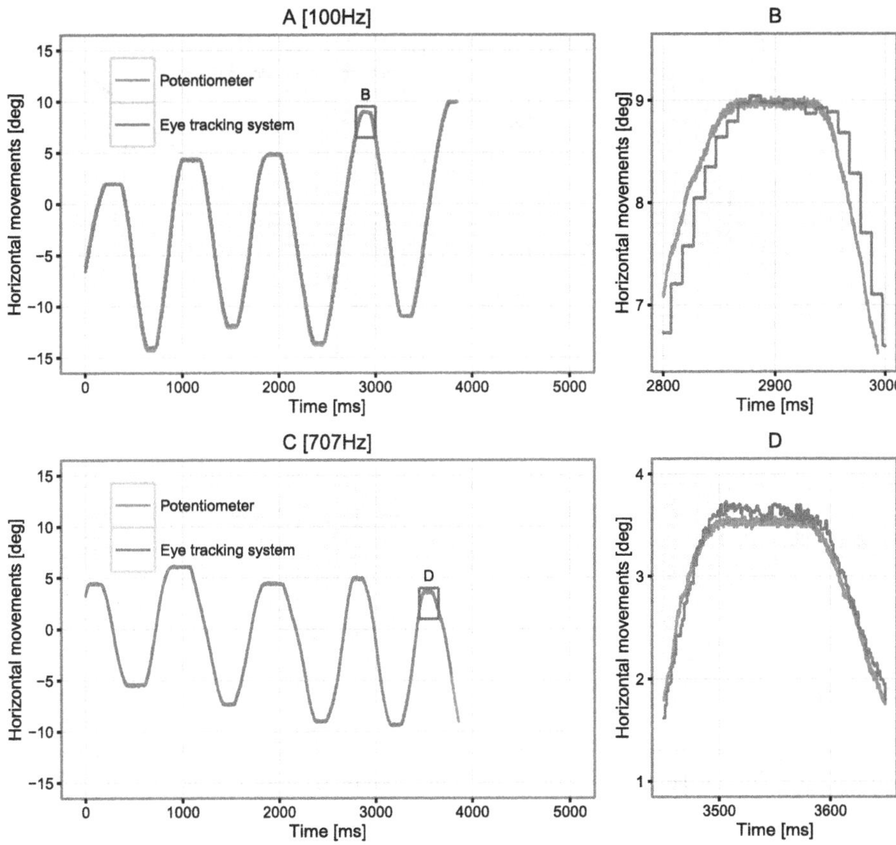

Fig. 12. An example record by using a GS3-U3-41C6NIR-C with two sampling frequencies of the picture-frame (A, B at 100 Hz, and C, D at 707 Hz). Green line indicate potentiometer rotation angle and magenta line the system's output (horizontal eye position). (Color figure online)

4.3 Discussion

The reliable measurement of the system's latency is one of the advantages of this eye tracking system. To get stable measurement, we have suggested application of a median filter or moving average filter. Since a 9-points median filter causes a 4.5-points time delay, the time-delay at the sampling frequency of 500 Hz is estimated as 13 ms. Thus, it is possible to calculate the gaze angle during the period of one frame and to display a new picture on the next-frame of a 60 Hz video display (real-time eye-position feedback experiment).

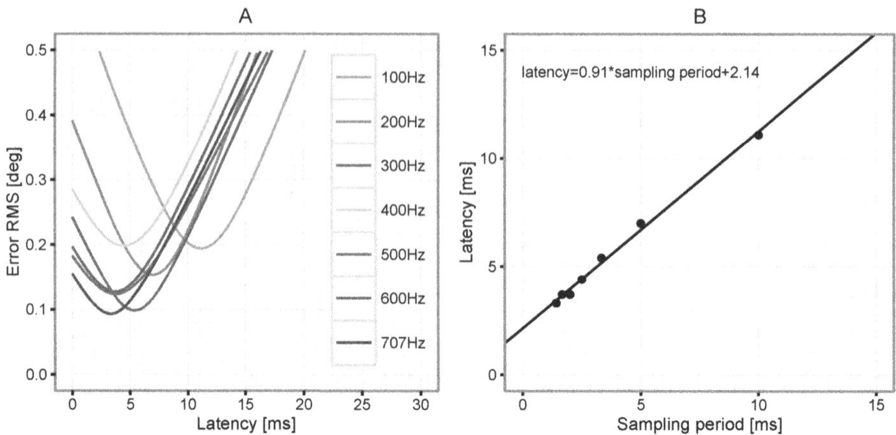

Fig. 13. A: The data calculated from by using Eq. (10). B: The relationship between the minimum value and sampling period. The sampling frequency are 707, 600, 500, 400, 300, 200, 100 Hz.

5 Measuring of Human Gaze Traces in 3-D Space

5.1 Methods

The subject was an adult male wearing glasses. The subject's head was fixed by a chin rest. The system was calibrated by measuring eye positions during the subject fixed targets on the display. After the calibration, the subject transferred his gaze in 5 ways, between the center position (near) to one of the 5 positions (far) (Fig. 14). The sampling frequency was 500 Hz.

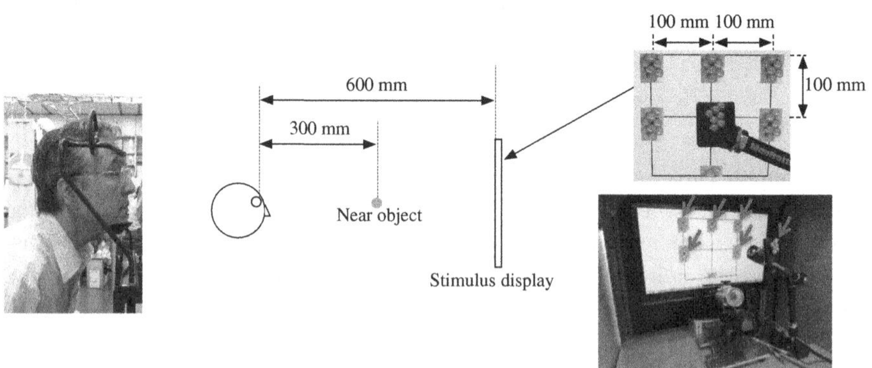

Fig. 14. Schematic representation of the human experiment and visual stimuli in 3-D space. Red arrows indicate one near (at 300 mm) and 5 far (at 600 mm) targets. (Color figure online)

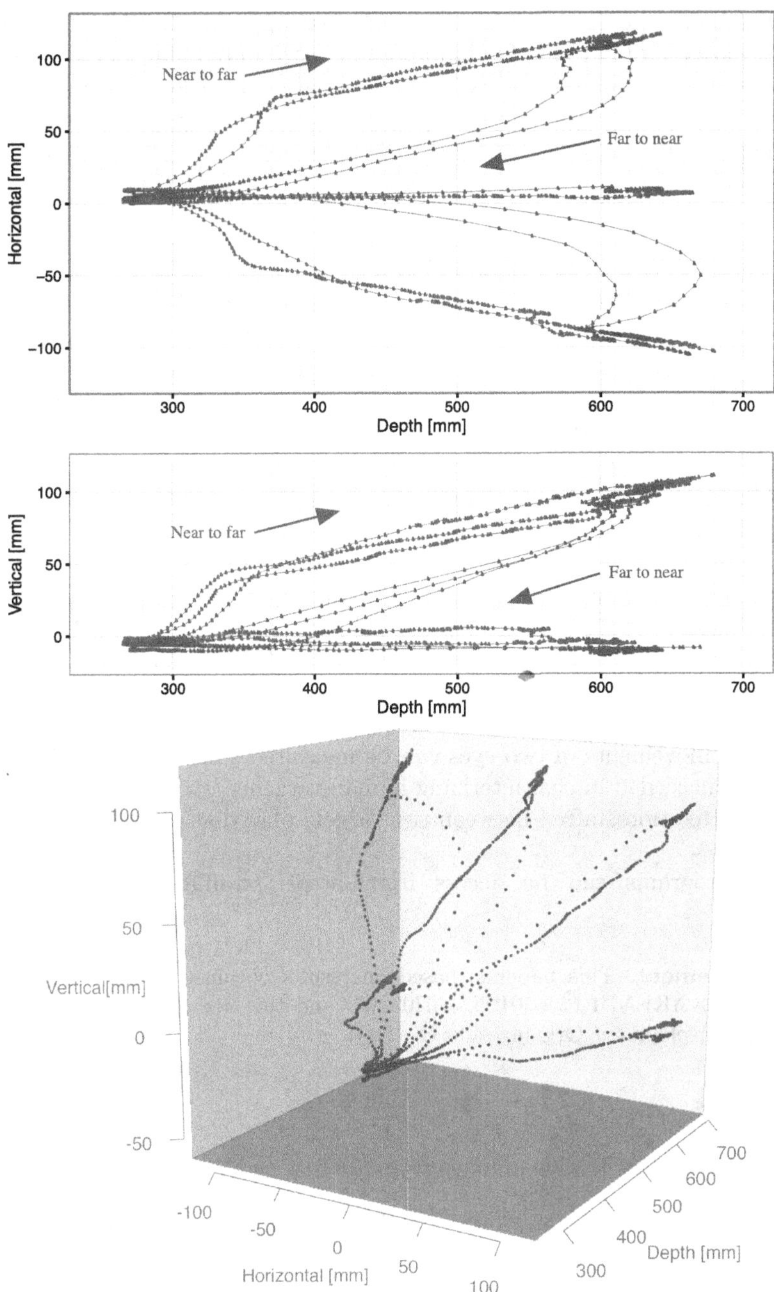

Fig. 15. The gaze transfer traces. (Color figure online)

5.2 Results

Figure 15 shows the gaze transfer traces after applying a 10-points (20 ms) moving-average-filter. It clearly shows that the eye movement traces from near to far (divergence, red trace in Fig. 15) and from far to near (convergence, blue trace) are different in 3-D space. In both cases, the vergence eye movements (convergence and divergence) started earlier than saccade and terminated after the saccades.

5.3 Discussion

The gaze transfers between the near to far positions consisted of combination of saccades and vergence eye movements. The subject transferred his gaze from the near to far (red dots) point and from the far to near (blue dots) point in different ways. In both cases, the vergence eye movements started earlier than saccades. The results are consisted with classical reports by Yarbus (1957) [3] and Enright (1984) [4].

6 Conclusion and General Discussion

We developed a new widely applicable eye tracking system. By using synthetic eyes, we found that the system can measure eye movements with better than 0.2° accuracy and latency was less than 4 ms at 500 Hz. By using this system, eye movements can be measured even when the subject (such as a mouse) cannot perform the active calibration. Since this system takes the images of two eyes by one camera, movements of two eyes can be measured simultaneously. With this system, we succeeded in characterizing human vergence/saccade eye movements when ocular fixation shifted between two targets placed at different distances in 3-D space.

These programs can be access from https://staff.aist.go.jp/k.matsuda/iRecHS2/.

Acknowledgement. This paper is based on results obtained from a project commissioned by KAKENHI (24650105, 16H03297) and the New Energy and Industrial Technology Development Organization (NEDO).

References

1. Duchowski, A.: Eye Tracking Methodology: Theory and Practice. Springer, London (2007)
2. Holmqvist, K., Nystrom, M., Andersson, R., Dewhurst, R., Jarodzka, H., Tracking, E.: A Comprehensive Guide to Methods and Measures. Oxford University Press, USA (2011)
3. Yarbus, A.L.: Eye movements during changes of the stationary points of fixation. Biophysics **2**, 679–683 (1957)
4. Enright, J.T.: Changes in vergence mediated by saccades. J. Physiol. **350**, 9–31 (1984)

Bigger (Gesture) Isn't Always Better

David Novick(✉), Ivan Gris, Adriana Camacho, Alex Rayon, and Timothy Gonzalez

Department of Computer Science, The University of Texas at El Paso, 500 West University Avenue, El Paso, TX 79968-0518, USA
novick@utep.edu, ivangris4@gmail.com, caro4874@gmail.com, {amrayon2,trgonzalez}@miners.utep.edu

Abstract. The literature suggests that familiarity and rapport are enhanced by larger, more extraverted gestures. However, the sizes of the increases in amplitude have not been reported. We sought to determine whether this relationship holds true for interaction between humans and embodied conversational agents. To this end, we conducted an experiment in which we increased gesture amplitude, with quantification of the gesture sizes. We hypothesized that rapport would be increased in the larger-gesture condition. However, our results were exactly the opposite: Rapport fell significantly in the larger-gesture condition. This means that larger may not always be better for building human-agent rapport. Our unexpected results may be because our agent's gestures were simply too big, odd, awkward, or strange, or because of a statistical anomaly.

Keywords: Embodied conversational agent · Gesture amplitude · Rapport

1 Introduction

The development of embodied conversational agents (ECAs) [7] holds the promise of providing important support for their human partners in fields ranging from education to care-giving (see, e.g., [3, 11]). The creation and maintenance of human-agent rapport [12, 13, 21] will be a correspondingly important factor for agents serving in these critical roles. Humans typically signal increased familiarity by, among other things, increasing the amplitude of gestures [6, 19]. However, the reported research on the effects of increased gesture amplitude on human-agent rapport is thin and unsettled. In the work reported here, we test the claim that increasing an agent's gesture amplitude will lead humans to report greater rapport with the agent, and we do so with quantification of the agent's gesture amplitudes. Although our hypotheses in initiating this research were that the larger-amplitude gestures associated with extraversion would produce greater feelings of rapport, our results suggest that this is not true, at least for the gestures and amplitudes that our agent used.

In this paper, then, we briefly review the literature relating gesture amplitude with rapport, describe a 55-subject empirical study of this relationship, report the study's results, and discuss the implications of these results.

M. Kurosu (Ed.): HCI 2017, Part I, LNCS 10271, pp. 609–619, 2017.
DOI: 10.1007/978-3-319-58071-5_46

2 Background

An ECA is a form of human-computer interaction that involves an intelligent virtual character that can communicate by using speech, facial expressions, and gestures [7]. ECAs can vary graphically in appearance depending on the desired virtual environment the ECA lives in and the role assigned to them. A help-desk ECA may only have its upper body visible, while a museum's tour-guide ECA may need a full body to convey more lifelike gestures and behavior [22]. ECAs that appear more human-like are easier for humans to interact with and develop rapport [9]. Their combination of gesture, speech, and facial expressions factor not only into believability and rapport but also into the perceived personality of the agent [20]. ECAs are designed to be used in conversational settings. They should be able to handle the discourse within a conversation and respond in humanlike ways to input [4]. ECAs that do not behave in the same humanlike manner that is expected from them may ultimately lose respect and rapport from the user.

To meet the high expectations of users, several features must be considered when designing an ECA, based on its application. Extraversion, agreeableness, and other Big Five personality traits are important to an ECA's design [8]. Extraversion is being talkative, outgoing, and enjoying social interactions [18]. Users show higher levels of rapport when interacting with extraverted agents even if the users themselves are not extraverted [5, 6]. This may be because extraverts can be perceived as seeking the company of others, and exhibit positive emotions in their behavior [16, 17]. Introverts are characterized by the opposite: they like keeping to themselves, making decisions by reflecting on internal conversations, and avoiding social interactions. These personality traits can be expressed not just through an agent's speech, but also in conjunction with non-verbal behavior [19, 20]).

Because humans use larger gestures to signal increased familiarity, it seems plausible that an agent's use of larger gestures would lead their human conversational partners to perceive greater rapport in their interaction. Neff et al. [19] extensively reviewed the relationship of gesture and extraversion. They summarized the relevant literature, in part, as finding that people express extraversion through gestures that are broad and wide rather than narrow. In their study of human perception of agents' verbal and nonverbal behaviors, they parameterized the relative amplitudes of introverted and extraverted gestures, for the x, y, and z axes of motion respectively, as x*.5, y*.6, z*.8 (introverted) and x*1.4, y*1.2, z*1.1 (extraverted). Their results indicated that, as expected, subjects perceived the larger-amplitude gestures as extraverted.

A subsequent study conducted by Clausen-Bruun, Ek, and Haake [9] examined the effect of gesture amplitude on subjects' uptake of a short narrative but did not provide details on the relative sizes of the lower- and higher-amplitude gestures. The authors created the high-amplitude gestures by manually extending and fine-tuning the low-amplitude gestures on a case-by-case basis. They found that increased amplitude led to significantly improved comprehension. They also asked subjects to provide a scaled answer to the prompt "I like the character" but did not report results relating amplitude to this emotional preference.

Hu et al. [15] found that users notice if an agent is extraverted, based on the amplitude of its gesture. This study used a storytelling scenario between two agents to see if users perceived the personality of each agent. One agent would gesture with large amplitude while the other used gestures that were the same but smaller in size. Users noticed the difference between the two agents and correctly perceived that the larger amplitude agent was the extraverted agent.

Novick and Gris [21] looked explicitly at the relationship between gesture amplitude and human's perception of rapport. However, this study had only 20 subjects, and its results were only weakly suggestive of a positive relationship between gesture amplitude and rapport.

The research to date suggests that agents who perform gestures with high amplitude and frequency do appear extraverted to users. Many of these studies, though, the lack a scale to define the amplitude of the gestures and omit clear full-body measurements of the agent in relation to its gestures. The gestures themselves are given a range between extraverted and introverted on a 3D plane, but there is no measurement of the initial point and apex of a gesture. There could be a limit: if a gesture is too large then it may seem unnatural. The same logic applies to gestures that are too small in amplitude. Also the type of gestures used by extraverts may greatly differ than those used by introverts. If that is the case, then agents who are designed to be extraverted should use these specific gestures more frequently than introverted ones. Introverts tend to perform gestures that are closer to their bodies [2], but in most studies done with ECAs an introverted gesture is the same gesture used by the extrovert, just smaller. We are aware of no study that has looked for a diversity of gestures between these personality traits. So it is possible that users may classify an agent as introverted not only on the size of its gesture but on the different types of gesture it uses.

Accordingly, in the present study we wanted to determine whether there is, in fact, a positive relationship between gesture amplitude and rapport. Moreover, in our study we were able to quantify the gesture sizes absolutely. We hypothesized that rapport would be increased in the larger-gesture condition.

3 Methodology

We studied the relationship of quantified gesture to rapport using the ECA application of Gris et al. [14], "Escape from the Castle of the Vampire King." This is an adventure game, inspired by text-based games such as Zork [1] and Colossal Cave [10], where the user tries to escape from the castle of an evil vampire king. The game had a graphical interface with a full-sized ECA that served as the game's narrator, and the player controlled the game through speech commands. The game comprised 26 different rooms, each with its own secret passages, exits, items and clues. The game included 3D scenery, recorded speech, agent movement based on motion-capture, and the quick-reference commands and incremental map display. Players' interactions occurred in 30-minute sessions on two different days, for a total of approximately 60 min per participant. Figure 1 shows a user interacting in a typical scene in the game, with the narrator agent, one of the rooms in the castle, and a map of the castle's rooms explored to that point in the adventure.

Fig. 1. User interacting in typical scene in "Escape from the Castle of the Vampire King" adventure. The tripod for a video camera, partially hidden in an artificial tree, for recording the user's interaction is visible at the lower left of the image.

The game dialogs spoken by the agent were scripted in such a way so that, even with limited commands, users could answer with natural language constrained by the specific context. Table 1 presents an excerpt of a player's interaction, showing the agent's scripted utterance and the player's verbal production.

Table 1. An interaction transcript from the first session of the "Vampire King" game.

Agent	You enter the courtyard. A fountain rests in the room's center. A chapel lies in the distant west and the lobby to the south
Player	Examine the fountain
Agent	The water is green with algae and unsafe to drink. You notice a sign that reads: No magic allowed
Player	Use the magic potion
Agent	You dump the magic potion into the overgrown fountain. The vines within the fountain begin to smoke and hiss, finally burning away until you can see a dirty red gem lying over the drain in the fountain's base
Player	Pick up the red gem
Agent	You pick up a dirty red gem that looks like an eye
Player	Go to the chapel

The experiment used a between-subjects design. In both the experimental and control conditions, subjects played the first half of the adventure in a 30-minute session with the agent using gestures with introverted amplitude. The subjects then returned a day or two later to play the second half of the adventure, again in a 30-minute session. In the second session, subjects in the control condition continued with the agent using gestures with introverted amplitude, and subjects in the experimental condition continued with the agent using gestures with extraverted amplitude. The sessions were completed by 30 subjects in the control condition and by 25 subjects in the experimental condition.

The agent's gestures were generated via motion capture. Five separate sets of six gestures each were recorded for the high-amplitude and low-amplitude conditions, in an effort to avoid the problems of simple mechanical amplification described by Clausen-Bruun, Ek, and Haake [9]. The gestures were separated into five categories. Three of the categories (A, B, C) were gestures captured from human-human conversation that increased in amplitude. The other two categories (I, E) acted as a control group. The control-group gestures were animated from a previous experiment, with the E animations acting as modified versions of the I gestures but with a larger amplitude. In total there were 30 animations, six from each category. An example of a gesture from each category can be seen in Fig. 2.

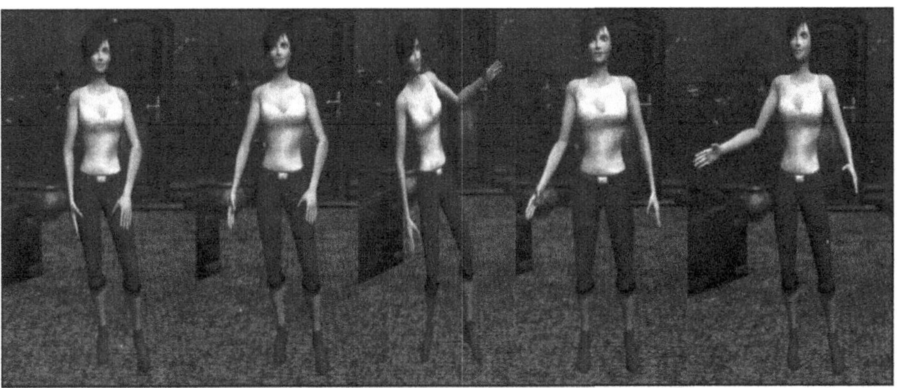

Fig. 2. Gesture from each category from left to right: A, B, C, I, and E. A has the smallest amplitude and E and C have the largest.

Figure 3 presents sequences of agent poses that illustrate of one of the extraverted and one of the introverted gestures. The animation gestures were a variation of hand gestures where the agent appears to be explaining or simply speaking. The first sequence of images represents an extraverted animation gesture where the agent lifts her hands and moves the right hand in circles. The second series of images represent the equivalent introverted animation gestures of the first image sequence. As can be noted from the images, the introverted animation does not have the hands lifted as high as the extroverted one.

We measured the absolute displacements for the six gestures from both versions of the "Vampire King" agent. To do so, we projected the agent in its actual experimental setting and physically measured the x, y, and z displacements of the agent's right and left hands. (We measured the displacements in the actual physical space of the experiment so that the results would be more accurate than if we measured from, say, a desktop display). For each hand, we calculated the hand's displacement vector (in inches) and summed the right and left displacement vectors to produce an overall measure of gesture size. Figure 4 shows one of the authors preparing to measure the x and y displacements for one of the agent's gestures.

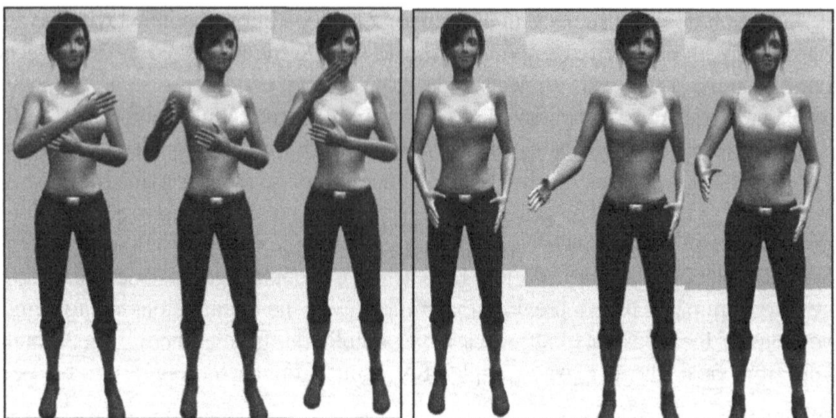

Fig. 3. Image sequences of introverted gesture (left) and extraverted gesture (right). In addition to the hands being higher in the extraverted version than the introverted, the length of time between each image is longer for the introverted animation movements than for the extraverted movements.

Table 2 reports the absolute displacements of representative high- and low-amplitude gestures, Table 3 reports the maximum, minimum, mean, and standard deviation for the gestures, and Fig. 5 compares the mean amplitudes of the stimuli gestures. Overall the gesture stimuli ranged in amplitude from the A gestures as the smallest, through the B, I, and C gestures, to the E gestures, which were the largest.

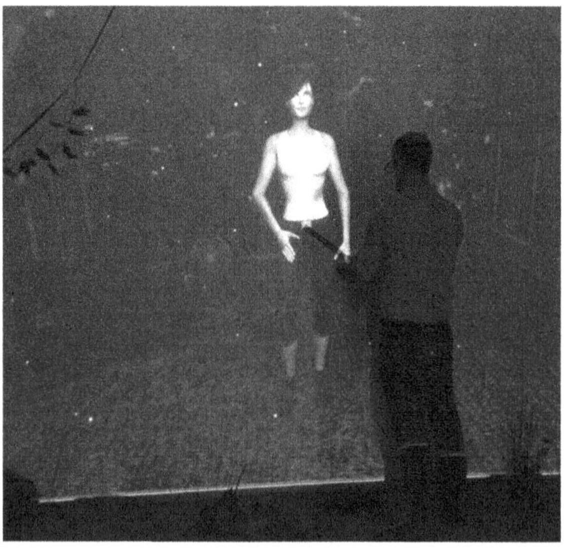

Fig. 4. One of the authors prepares to measure the x and y displacements of one of the agent's gestures.

Table 2. Absolute displacements of representative high- and low-amplitude gestures

Gesture	R vector	L vector	Sum vectors
High amplitude ("Extraverted")			
E1	37.01	4.12	41.14
E2	31.19	31.10	62.29
E3	39.48	38.27	77.75
E4	21.37	31.95	53.32
E5	30.48	28.72	59.21
E6	36.12	6.08	42.21
Low amplitude ("Introverted")			
I1	25.42	4.03	29.45
I2	16.58	18.97	35.56
I3	16.36	19.29	35.65
I4	10.11	11.92	22.03
I5	16.07	13.67	29.74
I6	32.41	5.00	37.41

Table 3. Maximum, minimum, mean, and standard deviation for the gestures

Amplitude	Mean	StDev	Maximum	Minimum
High	55.98	12.52	77.75	41.14
Low	31.64	5.25	37.41	22.03

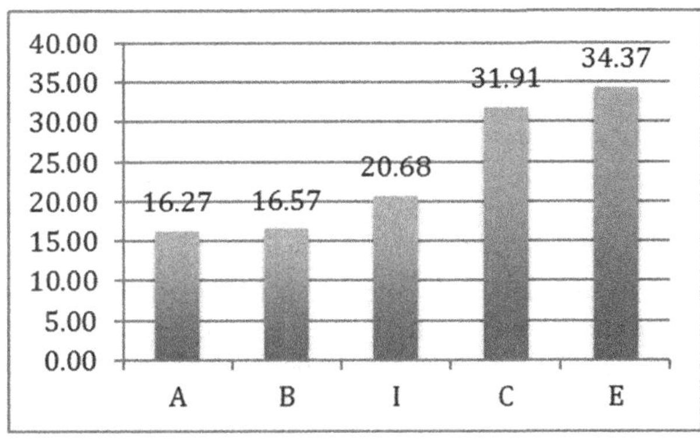

Fig. 5. Mean amplitudes (in inches) of the gestures used in the perception study. Each gesture amplitude was calculated as the maximum of the right-arm and left-arm vectors.

At the conclusion of each session, the subjects completed a twelve-item Likert-scale questionnaire that assessed the three components of rapport proposed in the Paralinguistic Rapport Model [21]: sense of emotional connection, sense of mutual understanding, and sense of physical connection. The questions in each component were balanced with respect to positive and negative responses.

We expected, comparing results in the subjects' second interaction sessions, that subjects in the experimental condition would interpret the agent's larger gestures as indicating increased familiarity on the part of the agent. We expected that subjects in the control condition, where the agent used gestures of similar amplitude in both sessions, would not sense an increase in familiarity on the part of the agent. Accordingly, we hypothesized that:

1. Subjects in the experimental condition would report higher levels of overall rapport than subjects in the control condition.
2. Subjects in the experimental condition would report higher levels of rapport for the component of emotional connection than subjects in the control condition.
3. Subjects in the experimental condition would report higher levels of rapport for the component of mutual understanding than subjects in the control condition.
4. Subjects in the experimental condition would report higher levels of rapport for the component of physical connection than subjects in the control condition.

4 Results

Despite our expectations of a positive relationship between gesture amplitude and rapport, the results of the experiment did not confirm the hypotheses. As reported in Table 4, the subjects' mean ratings for rapport ran consistently in the opposite direction than expected.

Table 4. Mean rapport scores (1–6) for subjects in high- and low-amplitude conditions

Rapport component	Amplitude	
	High	Low
Understanding*	3.42	3.73
Emotional	3.54	3.78
Physical	3.07	3.05
Overall	3.34	3.52

While t-tests for the differences in rapport for the emotional and physical rapport components were not significant ($p = 0.11$ and $p = 0.95$, respectively, two-tailed test), the t-test for the difference in rapport for the understanding component was significant ($p = 0.042$, two-tailed test), and the t-test for the difference in overall rapport approached significance ($p = 0.052$, two-tailed test). Most striking, the difference in across the high- and low-gesture conditions across understanding and emotional rapport components was highly significant ($p < 0.01$, two-tailed test). In sum, not only was our main claim disconfirmed, but the evidence indicates, at least for conditions of this study, that the relationship runs in the opposite direction: the larger gestures here led to lower perceptions of rapport.

5 Conclusion

We hypothesized that rapport would be increased in the larger-gesture condition. However, our results were exactly the opposite: Rapport fell significantly in the larger-gesture condition. This means that larger gestures are not always better. There are several possible reasons for the study's results being the opposite of what we expected. These reasons include:

- The point of the study was to compare the rapport effects of high- and low-amplitude gestures. But it is possible that the high-amplitude gestures we created were simply *too* big. This factor might be clarified by running perception studies of the gestures from this study, plus additional sets of gestures with other amplitudes. In these studies, subjects would rate the gestures for naturalness, thus providing an empirical basis for characterizing agents' gestures as appropriately low- and high-amplitude.
- The agent's gestures were generated through motion-capture. Some of the gestures, especially the agent's full-body movement, seemed exaggerated. It may, in fact, be the case that the particular gestures we used for the agent, especially in the high-amplitude condition, were simply odd, awkward, or strange. While it is true, cf. [19], that extraverted gestures differ from introverted gestures in more ways than just amplitude, for the purposes of basic research into the impact of gestures on rapport it might be better to use the same gestures in both high- and low-amplitude conditions, with only amplitude adjustments.
- The study by Novick and Gris [21] suggested that the difference in gesture amplitude would produce a difference in the subjects' feelings of physical rapport, while the current study produced essentially no difference at all in the subjects' feelings of physical rapport. That study indicated that the difference in gesture amplitude would not produce a difference the subjects' feelings of understanding and emotional rapport, while the current study produced significant differences—in the unexpected direction. This suggests the possibility that the current results can be attributed to statistical anomaly.

The study we report here was subject to several limitations, and the study's results should be interpreted in light of these limitations, which include:

- While the "Vampire King" application produced high levels of user engagement [21], the user-agent dialog and the sets of gestures were limited and repetitive. The possibly higher salience for the high-amplitude gestures may have made these limitations more apparent or salient for the high-amplitude condition.
- The agent's repertoire of six gestures in each condition meant that the results were vulnerable to the presence of even one, or possibly more, unnatural or otherwise uncharacteristic gestures. If the repertoire had been much larger, then the effect of the inclusion of an odd or awkward gesture would have been diminished.
- Cronbach's alpha for the entire survey, combining all three rapport components, was 0.76, which indicates reasonable but not strong consistency among the survey elements. The alpha values for each of the three components was under 0.70. While this may be due simply to having only four questions for each of the components, it may also reflect on the meaningfulness of the survey.

Acknowledgments. The authors thank Jonathan Daggerhart for permission to adapt his original text- based adventure game into "Escape from the Castle of the Vampire King," and Diego A. Rivera, Mario Gutierrez Baltazar Santaella, Juan Vicario, Joel Quintana and Anuar Jauregui for their help in developing the game.

References

1. Anderson, T., Galley, S.: The history of Zork. The New Zork Times **4**(1–3) (1985)
2. Argyle, M.: Bodily Communication. Taylor & Francis, Milton Park (1988)
3. Bickmore, T.W., et al.: Maintaining reality: relational agents for antipsychotic medication adherence. Interact. Comput. **22**(4), 276–288 (2010)
4. Bickmore, T., Cassell, J.: Relational agents: a model and implementation of building user trust. In: Proceedings of the SIGCHI Conference on Human Factors in Computing Systems, pp. 396–403. ACM (2001)
5. Brixey, J.E.: Virtual rapport with extraverted agents. Master's thesis, The University of Texas at El Paso (2015)
6. Cafaro, A., Vilhjálmsson, H.H., Bickmore, T., Heylen, D., Jóhannsdóttir, K.R., Valgarðsson, G.S.: First Impressions: Users' Judgments of Virtual Agents' Personality and Interpersonal Attitude in First Encounters. In: Nakano, Y., Neff, M., Paiva, A., Walker, M. (eds.) IVA 2012. LNCS (LNAI), vol. 7502, pp. 67–80. Springer, Heidelberg (2012). doi: 10.1007/978-3-642-33197-8_7
7. Cassell, J. (ed.): Embodied conversational agents. The MIT Press, Cambridge (2000)
8. Cerekovic, A., Aran, O., Gatica-Perez, D.: How do you like your virtual agent? Human-agent interaction experience through nonverbal features and personality traits. In: Park, H.S., Salah, A.A., Lee, Y.J., Morency, L.-P., Sheikh, Y., Cucchiara, R. (eds.) HBU 2014. LNCS, vol. 8749, pp. 1–15. Springer, Cham (2014). doi:10.1007/978-3-319-11839-0_1
9. Clausen-Bruun, M., Ek, T., Haake, M.: Size certainly matters–at least if You are a gesticulating digital character: the impact of gesture amplitude on addressees' in-formation uptake. In: A, R., Krenn, B., Pelachaud, C., Shimodaira, H. (eds.) IVA 2013. LNCS (LNAI), vol. 8108, p. 446. Springer, Heidelberg (2013)
10. Crowther, W., Woods, D., Black, K.: Colossal cave adventure. Computer Game (1976)
11. DeVault, D., et al.: Verbal indicators of psychological distress in interactive dialogue with a virtual human. In: Proceedings of SIGDIAL, August 2013
12. Gratch, J., Okhmatovskaia, A., Lamothe, F., Marsella, S., Morales, M., Werf, R.J., Morency, L.-P.: Virtual rapport. In: Gratch, J., Young, M., Aylett, R., Ballin, D., Olivier, P. (eds.) IVA 2006. LNCS (LNAI), vol. 4133, pp. 14–27. Springer, Heidelberg (2006). doi: 10.1007/11821830_2
13. Gratch, J., Wang, N., Gerten, J., Fast, E., Duffy, R.: Creating rapport with virtual agents. In: Pelachaud, C., Martin, J.-C., André, E., Chollet, G., Karpouzis, K., Pelé, D. (eds.) IVA 2007. LNCS (LNAI), vol. 4722, pp. 125–138. Springer, Heidelberg (2007). doi: 10.1007/978-3-540-74997-4_12
14. Gris, I., Novick, D., Camacho, A., Rivera, D.A., Gutierrez, M., Rayon, A.: Recorded speech, virtual environments, and the effectiveness of embodied conversational agents. In: Intelligent Virtual Agents 2014, Boston, MA, August 2014, pp. 182–185 (2014)
15. Hu, C., Walker, M.A., Neff, M., Tree, J.E.F.: Storytelling agents with personality and adaptivity. In: International Conference on Intelligent Virtual Agents, pp. 181–193 (2015)
16. Ivanov, A.V., Riccardi, G., Sporka, A.J., Franc, J.: Recognition of personality traits from human spoken conversations. In: INTERSPEECH, pp. 1549–1552 (2011)

17. McCrae, R.R., Costa Jr., P.T.: Personality trait structure as a human universal. Am. Psychol. **52**(5), 509 (1997)
18. Mehrabian, A., Ferris, S.R.: Inference of attitude from non-verbal communication in two channels. J. Couns. Psychol. **31**, 248–252 (1967)
19. Neff, M., Wang, Y., Abbott, R., Walker, M.: Evaluating the effect of gesture and language on personality perception in conversational agents. In: Allbeck, J., Badler, N., Bickmore, T., Pelachaud, C., Safonova, A. (eds.) IVA 2010. LNCS (LNAI), vol. 6356, pp. 222–235. Springer, Heidelberg (2010). doi:10.1007/978-3-642-15892-6_24
20. Neff, M., Kipp, M., Albrecht, I., Seidel, H.P.: Gesture modeling and animation based on a probabilistic re-creation of speaker style. ACM Trans. Graph. (TOG) **27**(1), 5 (2008)
21. Novick, D., Gris, I.: Building rapport between human and ECA: a pilot study. In: Kurosu, M. (ed.) HCI 2014. LNCS, vol. 8511, pp. 472–480. Springer, Cham (2014). doi: 10.1007/978-3-319-07230-2_45
22. Swartout, W., et al.: Ada and grace: toward realistic and engaging virtual museum guides. In: Allbeck, J., Badler, N., Bickmore, T., Pelachaud, C., Safonova, A. (eds.) IVA 2010. LNCS (LNAI), vol. 6356, pp. 286–300. Springer, Heidelberg (2010). doi:10.1007/978-3-642-15892-6_30

Gesture-Based Interactions in Video Games with the Leap Motion Controller

Johanna Pirker[1(✉)], Mathias Pojer[1], Andreas Holzinger[1,2], and Christian Gütl[1,3]

[1] Graz University of Technology, Graz, Austria
{jpirker,cguetl}@iicm.edu, matthias.pojer@student.tugraz.at
[2] Medical University Graz, Graz, Austria
a.holzinger@tugraz.at
[3] Curtin University, Bentley, WA, Australia

Abstract. This paper explores the Leap Motion controller as gesture-controlled input device for computer games. We integrate gesture-based interactions into two different game setups to explore the suitability of this input device for interactive entertainment with focus on usability, user engagement, and personal motion control sensitivity, and compare it with traditional keyboard controls. In a first user study with 15 participants we evaluate the experience with the Leap Motion controller in the two different game setups. We also investigate differences between gamers and non-gamers. The results indicate the potential in terms of user engagement and training efforts for short-time experiences. However, the study results also indicate usability issues. The experiences with gesture-based controls are rated as exhausting after about 20 min. While the suitability for traditional video games is thus described as limited, users see potential in gesture-based controls as training and rehabilitation tools.

Keywords: Game input · Input devices · Hand tracking · Natural input

1 Introduction

The concept of gamification is of increasing interest for the international research community due to the fact that games involve cognitive strategies that developed evolutionary over millions of years [11]. This form of *play* has potential to immerse and engage users in different contexts including non-gaming fields [8,15]. An essential part of every game is the human-game interaction and in recent years, the range of input and interaction devices has advanced with various technologies to control computer-based systems. Whilst previously the focus was on device based interaction [10], recently more innovative and promising ways to interact with computers are provided by controllers with free-hand inputs. While previous research has focused on gesture-based interactions with Microsoft Kinect devices, which captures interactions of the entire body, only a few studies

M. Kurosu (Ed.): HCI 2017, Part I, LNCS 10271, pp. 620–633, 2017.
DOI: 10.1007/978-3-319-58071-5_47

have covered the interaction with the Leap Motion controller, which allows control with hand and finger gestures. Such free-hand interactions controllers show promising potential in entertainment, medical applications, rehabilitation, training, and education [12,13,16]. However, many of these devices were designed for tech enthusiasts and often fail to support the practicability of the technologies for everyday users. In this paper, we want to evaluate the Leap Motion controller as promising free-hand technology [4,21] with focus on investigating differences in the usability and perception between experienced users and non-experienced users. In the study we concentrate on the interactions in the context of video gaming.

In a first study we evaluated the technology of gesture-based interaction with the Leap Motion controller for video games. We integrated gesture controls in two different game setups: (1) a platform game and (2) a local two-player shooter game. We recruited 15 participants to play the two games and assessed the experience based on usability, engagement, personal motion control sensitivity, and compared it with standard keyboard/mouse controls. Both, gamers and non-gamers are represented almost equally among the participant group. First results indicate the potential in terms of engagement and training effect of such devices for short-time experiences, however, they also reveal issues in terms of usability and comfort. Participants would use this control method for short-term experiences (e.g. training), but tend to prefer the keyboard for long-term experiences. They also tend to use different setups for gesture controls, sensitivity behavior and dead zones for different application scenarios. This data could be used to automatically identify gesture types, and allow dynamic and automatic settings and mappings to optimize setups.

With this work we aim to discuss the potential and issues of the Leap Motion controller as gesture-based input device for video games and other application scenarios through the following major contributions:

1. Integration of gesture-based controls in two different video games (a platform game and a local two-player shooter)
2. A user study with 15 participants (gamers and non-gamers) evaluating the two gaming experiences with focus on engagement, usability, and discussion of different application scenarios

The following section addresses background and related work on the Leap Motion controller in different application scenarios. After that we describe the two games used for the study. In Sect. 4 the user study is presented and discussed.

2 Background and Related Work

Introduced in 2013, the Leap Motion is a small device that is meant to be placed facing upwards next to your keyboard or laptop. It features two infrared cameras that capture up to 200 frames per second [2]. Compared to Microsoft's Kinect [3] it has a higher motion resolution, but a smaller observation area, which covers roughly one meter in a hemispherical shape. The controller is primarily marketed as a productivity device and was integrated into laptops, and other devices by HP and other manufacturers. In 2016 the company behind the Leap Motion expanded their strategy and released a new version of the software, named Orion, which focuses exclusively on VR. For this mode, the Leap Motion is mounted onto an Oculus Rift and enhances the virtual world with accurate motion detection [17]. The controller is connected to the PC via USB and requires the installation of a software suite, which contains different playground apps and mini games with simple interactions, such as picking flower leaves and positioning cubes.

There are numerous apps on the store that either integrate the Leap Motion controller into conventional programs, or new software tailored to the motion controls. The Leap Motion has also been used during surgeries as a means to control live medical imaging data. This has been found to reduce the risk of infections in operating rooms, while being very cost-efficient and practical [13]. All those studies show the potential of motion control technology, where the Leap Motion might not be its glorious final iteration, but a necessary and useful playground for generating ideas. As with all motion control systems, the added strain of keeping your hands in the air seems to make the Leap Motion more suitable for shorter infrequent gestures than heavy usage and a full keyboard and mouse replacement.

Several authors have used this device for evaluating various application areas, which require hand-based communication. In [20], the authors present an implementation to use the Leap Motion controller as a tool to recognize characters and words written in the air by hand. One promising research area and possible use case for the controller is sign language recognition. In [16] the authors present a first implementation of using the Leap Motion controller to recognize Australian sign language. While the authors describe the potential of the device for recognizing finger movements, they also describe issues with accuracy in their current implementation. They found that the Leap Motion is capable of recognizing basic signs, however, it fails to accurately detect most movements where the fingers are aligned perpendicular to the cameras. Moreover, complex signs that require simultaneous facial expressions were found to not work at all. The average accuracy of the device has been measured in a 2013 study as 0.7 mm [21], which according to the authors trumps the Kinect and other competitors in this price range. A point which is even more valid today, since the Leap Motion's price dropped to 60$. However, in another study [9] with focus on measuring precision and reliability of the sensors, the authors show limited sensor space and inconsistent sampling frequency, which limits its use as a professional tracking system.

While several evaluations show the potential of the Leap Motion controller for various application scenarios in the fields of communication or recognition tools, there are only a few studies on the potential of the Leap Motion controller as a tool for video gaming. There is an increasing interest in new and innovative input devices to control games and virtual reality experiences, to create more immersive and engaging gaming experiences, and to overcome the limitations of keyboard and mouse input with more natural interactions [6,19]. In the following section we introduce two video games, which are used as a design basis to create and evaluate gaming experience using the Leap Motion controller as interaction device.

3 Leap Motion Game Design

The goal of the first prototype is to evaluate the thesis, that motion controls are more suited for infrequent edge gestures, than for using them as a primary input method. Therefore we aimed to incorporate the controller into conventional games that demand higher reaction speeds and a generally increased rate of interactions. To focus more on the integration than actual game development, we chose to expand open well-designed games. Another important point was that the games' mechanics had to be easy enough for non-gamers to get into, in order to compare their motion control impressions with people who play regularly. Figure 1 illustrated the use of the Leap Motion controller as input device. The controller is placed on the bottom of the monitor.

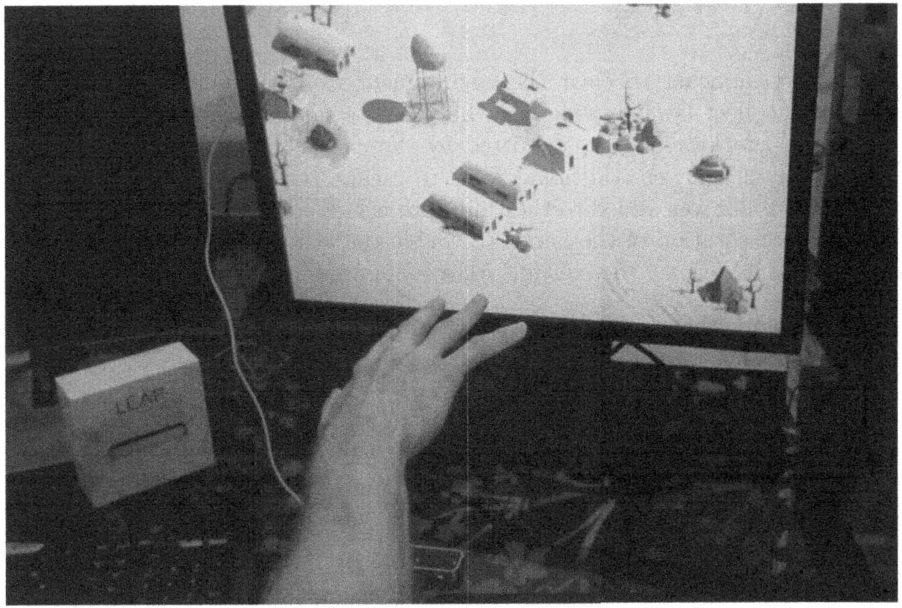

Fig. 1. The Leap Motion controller is used to control the game with hand gestures

3.1 Alien Invasion

Unity's Alien Invasion [1] is a simple 2D platform game where one has to defend a city from aliens (see Fig. 2). The player controls a character that is able to

Fig. 2. Gameplay of Alien Invasion using the Leap Motion controller and visualizing the current position of the hands (at the bottom).

fire a rocket launcher to clear the environment from the enemies. Moreover, players can collect bombs, which can be placed strategically. Building on that we added a shockwave that is emitted by the character and bounces enemies back to give the player additional tools to escape tense situations. The Leap Motion controller was added to the Unity project. We decided to always display a visual representation of the hands to enable the visualization of the tracking. After several iterations, the controls were configured in the following way:

- Left/right movement by rolling the left hand; the direction of the back of the hand determines the direction the character moves
- Jumping by swiping the left hand upwards
- Firing missiles by making a fist with the right hand
- Laying bombs by swiping the right hand upwards or downwards, or any vertical movement with higher velocity
- Emitting a shockwave by swiping the right hand left and right, or any horizontal movement with higher velocity

The gestures are detected by observing the hand models the Leap software maintains and tracks over time. This enables the differentiation between the left and the right hand. However, there is only a very limited amount of gestures detected by the controller natively. In effect, it identifies a circle movement, a swipe as well as forward and downward taps. For the implementation, only the pre-built swipe-gesture was used. Other movements were determined by the angle of the hand, with a dead zone to allow the player to stand still. The fist gesture is detected by calculating the sum of the angles of the finger joints.

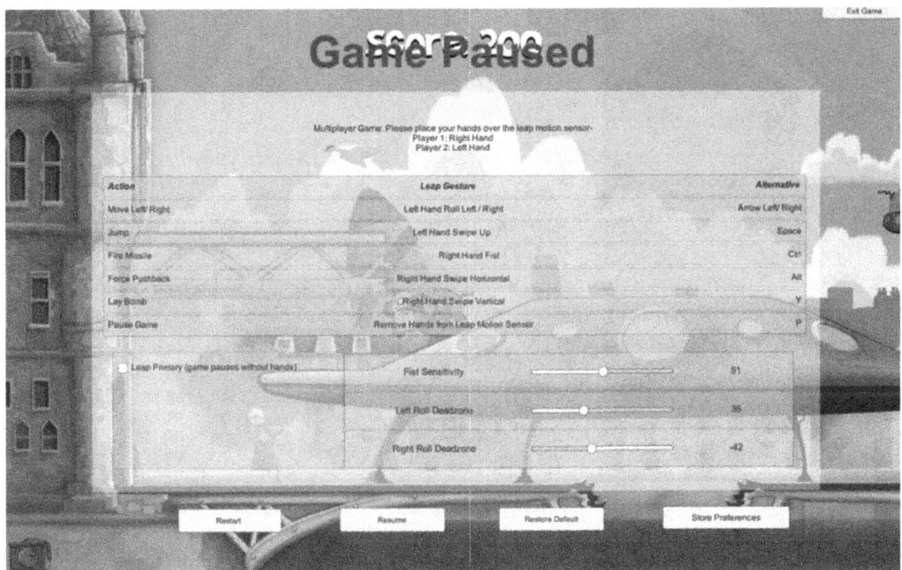

Fig. 3. Settings menu of Alien Invasion.

If they are curved over a threshold, a fist is detected. A pause menu with included sensitivity sliders was added to allow players to adjust the size of the roll dead zone and the fist sensitivity according to their preferences. Furthermore, features to export the chosen settings in order to statistically evaluate them were added. Tailored towards use as a demonstrator, the game now includes a "Leap Primary" mode that pauses the game automatically once no hands are detected, to enable changing the sensitivities without a keyboard (see Fig. 3).

3.2 Tanks!

Aiming to test the controller in a 3D environment the Unity Tanks! multi-player demo [5] was used and extended. The game is a multi-player game, hence the Leap Motion controller as a multi-player input method can be evaluated. The goal of the game is to defeat the enemy tank (see Fig. 4). Therefore, the player can move forwards and backwards, as well as turn left and right. The cannon of the tank is the only weapon and can be charged up to change the distance of the shot. Since the Leap Motion can only distinguish and assign two hands over time, separating the left and right hand, all functionality had to be controlled via gestures of one hand. This means the player who uses the left hand, controls the blue tank, and the player using the right hand controls the red tank. Controlling the game works as follows:

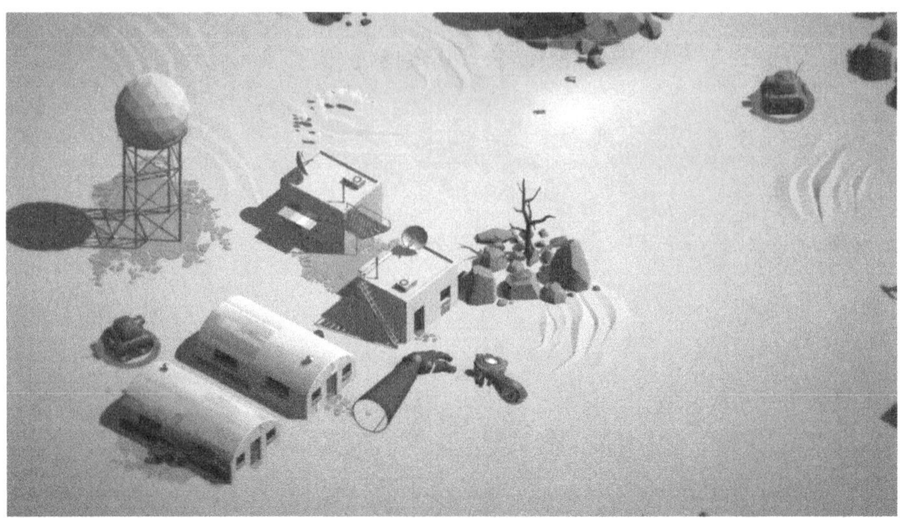

Fig. 4. Gameplay of Tanks! using the Leap Motion controller - different colors represent the two different player hands.

- Left/right turning by rolling the hand; the direction of the back of the hand determines the direction the character moves
- Forwards/backwards movement by pitching the hand; the direction of the back of the hand determines the direction the character moves
- Firing the cannon by making a fist, the shot is charged for as long the hand is closed and the shot discharged once the fist is released

As before, the gestures are detected by observing the hand models. The pitch is detected the same way as the roll movement, just by analyzing a different axis. Due to the higher load of simultaneous gestures per hand, the dead zone is increased in comparison to the first game, Alien Invasion. Since it is difficult to keep the hand angled correctly while loading the shot, there are two additional settings to lock both movement and turning while charging the shot. Resulting from its 3D environment, the difficulty and emphasis of eye-hand coordination is enhanced. Thus a 'Simple Input' mode is also available, whereby a player can only move or turn, effectively only applying the stronger motion vector - a setting aimed at inexperienced players. In addition to the 'Leap Primary' mode of the previous game, there are colored indicators on the sides of the screen that light up in the color of the player when the Leap Motion loses track of the player's hand (see Fig. 5).

In our research, these two games provide the frame conditions for our research to evaluate user interaction and experience of gamers and non-gamers with the different game formats.

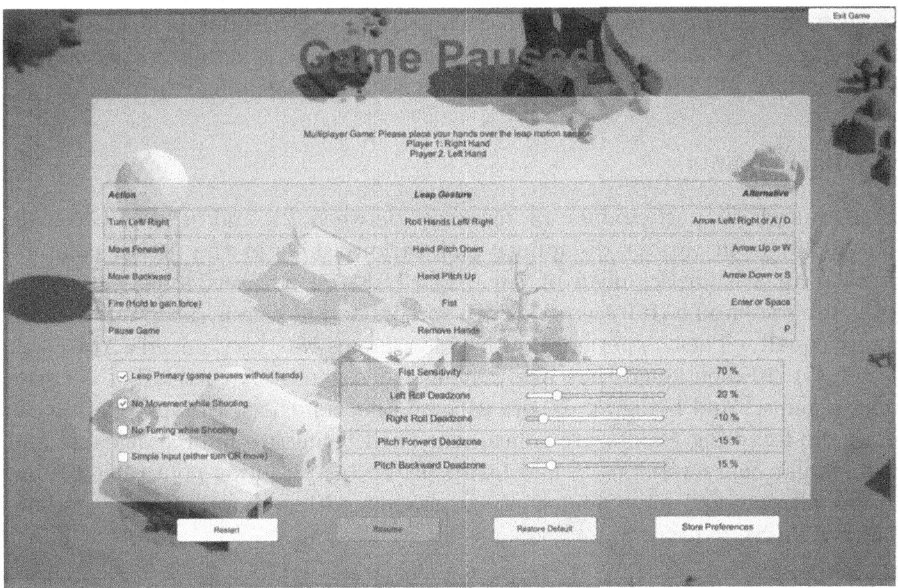

Fig. 5. Settings menu of Tanks!

4 Evaluation

In a first study, we focus on identifying variance in user preferences regarding the motion control settings, usability issues, and engagement and try to compare the experience to the keyboard input. Comparing the Leap Motion input with traditional keyboard interactions input is difficult as they offer a more habitual form of computer interaction. Participants were asked to play both game setups with keyboard and Leap Motion controls. Because of the strong differences in experience with the input device, a detailed analysis does not generate significant results, however, it gives a first impression of the potential of gesture-based devices and discusses application scenarios, which are mentioned by participants as interesting future experiences for this kind of input.

4.1 Material and Setup

For the experiment the two pilot game setup prototypes based on existing games as described above in detail were used: (1) a 2D platform game, Unity's "Alien Invasion", which requires the player to control the character (left/right movement, jumping), collect and fire rockets and bombs. (2) an extension of Unity's "Tanks!" demo, a multi-player game, which requires the user to control a tank (left/right turning, forwards/backwards movement, and firing the cannon). The controls were provided by (a) keyboard and (b) by the described gestures for the Leap Motion controller such as hand rolling, hand movement, or making a fist with the left or right hand. Both chosen games were designed as conventional games that demand higher reaction speeds and a generally increased rate of interactions but are also suitable for user with little gaming experiences.

4.2 Participants

We recruited 15 participants (5 females) between 21 and 67 (AVG = 29.8; SD = 10.58) from various disciplines and various skills in the use of computers with an arithmetic mean of 3.6 (SD = 1.18) on a Likert scale between 1 (fully disagree) and 5 (fully agree). Both gamers and non-gamers are represented almost equally. Their experience with video games was very mixed (AM = 2.4; SD = 1.35). 10 mentioned they like playing video games. A correlation between being a gamer, and being an expert with computers exists. Because of that, as far as the following results are concerned, both terms are interchangeable and yield similar characteristics. 5 had heard of the Leap Motion controller before. Almost all noted to have almost no experience with gesture-based controllers (AM = 1.73; SD = 1.03).

4.3 Methodology and Procedure

In order to rule out the influence of the order in which the different input devices are tried, A/B testing was performed. The testers were put into two groups where group A started with the Leap Motion, and group B started with the keyboard version of the game. Additionally, if there is a difference in perception, this setup aims to reveal it. The survey is performed using LimeSurvey. After filling out a small demographic questionnaire, the participants have to rate both their experience using computers, and their exposure to and skill with motion controls. Following that they play Alien Invasion and are asked to provide written feedback of their experience. Next a SUS - System Usability Scale - is used to rate their subjective experience of the system. This scale developed by Brooke is a tool to quickly assign a global scale to that perspective and has been widely adopted over the years [7]. After playing the game with the other controls, the test moves on to "Tanks!". This survey is shorter than the Alien Invasion part. The participants are asked to play the game at their own pace with both control methods. At the end of the test, they have to select with which device they had more fun, what they would choose for longer gaming sessions, and which mode they prefer overall. Lastly they select gestures that were easy to perform for them, as well as the duration they could possibly play with motion controls.

5 Results

Next, the key elements of the post-questionnaires are discussed and framed with participants' quotes. Summarizing, users experienced the gesture-based controls as more interesting and engaging because of the novelty of the experience. Also the game itself was noted as more interesting with the novel input method, compared to traditional keyboard controls. The multi-player mode was experienced as more challenging, because of the two hands interfering with each other. The gesture-based controls were noted as valuable pedagogical and training tool to e.g. help people - especially children - with gross motor skills/fine motor skills to train in a playful way. However, the experience was also mentioned to be more stressful and less user-friendly compared to keyboard input. Overall, only 3 users would prefer controls with Leap Motion, but 10 rated this form of user input also as the funnier experience. 11 would rather use the keyboard when playing for a longer time.

SUS of keyboard controls is on average 20 points higher than of Leap Motion controls. On average the SUS of keyboard controls is 75 compared to the SUS of 55 with the Leap Motion controls, which is quite a significant difference. According to the SUS rating methodology, the average score is 68, which means the Leap Motion provided a below average experience. Most testers claimed accuracy issues and stated that they could not trust the device to detect the intended gesture. Especially non-gamers tended to stress out and resort to hasty waving in hectic situations: *"It was challenging to get used to the controls. It felt stressful."*; *"The game controls much easier with the keyboard. The controls behave more exact in comparison to the fluid controls the other version provides."*. *"The control was definitely easier on the keyboard - this is most likely also because of the own experience/practice."*

Gamers and experts rate both methods of input higher than inexperienced persons. This result is not really unexpected, since regular gamers are more familiar with both types of games. Therefore they are not as overwhelmed with the game itself, and can concentrate more on mastering the motion controls. However, gamers sometimes picked at the simplicity of the game, especially when using the keyboard.

There is a higher increase in the score of the keyboard, if it was played after the Leap Motion version. It seems that players value the increased accuracy of keyboard controls more after playing with motion controls first. With that subset, the keyboard controls even achieved a score of 83. The increase is more pronounced with gamers. This shows that A/B testing is important to limit the influence of the order on a testing result.

There is a higher spread of score difference of gamers between the two control modes. Having developed a higher standard towards the feel and accuracy of controls, gamers seem to be put off more by the drawbacks of motion controls than non-gamers. On the other hand, this could also mean that having a lot of experience with conventional control schemes reduces the acceptance of new input methods. More investigation into that topic could prove insightful.

Generally people chose a larger left than right dead zone. When tasked with holding their hands straight in front of them, most persons naturally seem to keep their hands slightly curved away from their thumbs. This means that the perceived neutral position of the left hand is slightly rotated counterclockwise in the coordinate system of the leap motion. Another result of this fact is that when both hands are required to perform rolling movements, it is important to provide separate settings for both hands. Otherwise fitting one hand worsens the recognition sensitivities of the other one.

Higher dead zones chosen for "Tanks!". Another attribute of the data set is that the same persons tend to choose higher dead zones for this game. This seems to be a result of having more gestures mapped to one hand. The increased allocation leads to more motion bleeding, whereupon performing a gesture inadvertently influences another gesture. In this particular case, users found it very difficult to perform a fist gesture without altering the angle of their hand in a way that also led to a direction change. Nearly every person locked their movement while channeling a shot. More non-gamers elected to also use the lock of turning motion than their gamer counterparts. This expresses the impulse of gamers to perform minor last minute adjustments. Taken even further, this finding concurs with the thesis that motion controls are unsuitable for fast paced games which require exact timing. By our very nature it is likely to overdo a movement, which can cause mis-detections. More importantly, mixing continuous tracking with concrete gestures is error prone. In our case, we use the angle of the hand in multiple directions as an input parameter. Therefore we cannot use this hand in conjunction with most other gestures, because they alter the directions of the hand. When asked for the maximum amount of gestures that should be loaded onto one hand, the average answer is 3.4 gestures.

Motion controls are experienced as exhausting. Most participants give verbal feedback that they find the Leap Motion controls quite exhausting. On average the duration they could comfortably use it was rated at 23 min. They even stated that this tiring effect would stop them from trying to get familiar with the new control scheme. In that sense, the strenuous nature is counterproductive to the learning motivation. *"A bit tiring for the hands"*; *"The concept is pretty good, but might be a bit exhaustive after a while. This works for short sessions, but I wouldn't play it for much longer."*

Leap Motion mode is rated more fun to use. For 66% of users the motion controls were more interesting and fun than the conventional scheme. However, when asked whether they would prefer this mode overall or for longer playing sessions, the majority chose the keyboard. Further research is needed on how long that feeling lasts, and how it fares with more complex games: *"Harder to control but strangely more fun. But I think that fun is going to wear off soon."*; *"[I liked it] very much. interesting."*

Application scenarios for Leap Motion controls. Users listed mainly short party and sports games as entertaining application scenarios for the gesture-based controller. Additionally, the device was discussed as potential tool to enhance pedagogical and training scenarios such as training of gross motor skills/fine motor skills in a playful way, or hands-free interactions as necessary in surgeries.

6 Discussion and Conclusion

Conducting the study has provided some valuable insight into the perception of motion controls. While the engagement was high and the experience with the Leap Motion controller was noted as interesting and innovative, in many cases keyboard and mouse are still rated as preferred interaction device for games. There are niche cases where they perform exceptionally well, but on average they lack usability mostly because of the aforementioned accuracy issues. Especially accuracy issues like the limited tracking area and visual overlap need to be resolved. None of the participants felt more confident with the motion controls. Playing a game for more than 20 min was rated as exhausting and not a good use case for this input. However, participants noted several application fields where they see promising use cases for the device. This definitely includes gamified training tasks (e.g. therapeutical tasks, rehabilitation). Limitations in our study are given due to the small number of participants and the setup of the A/B study. The results indicate the potential of gesture-based controls to boost the users' engagement and interest in the experience, and show the potential for training and short-time entertainment experiences. We found several issues but also potential in this form of user input. Despite limitations based on accuracy and usability, the Leap Motion controller has been shown as interesting and engaging tool to offer basic hand input for small and short games and applications, which do not require a high accuracy.

For future work, an important step is to research how to enhance usability. One way to enhance usability and learnability of such devices could be the use of machine learning methods. Users tend to play differently and can be automatically categorized into different player types based on their interaction with the game [14]. In this study, it was shown that users often tend to use very different setups for gesture controls regarding sensitivity behavior and dead zones. In a large-scale study, data could be collected and used to automatically identify player types based on their gesture interaction behavior, and allow dynamic and automatic settings and mappings to optimize setups. This would allow the generation and mapping of gesture-based user types to speed up learning of interaction with the device easier. For future work we will also focus on additional engagement elements, such as immersion, which becomes more and more important to create interesting playful entertainment experiences [18]. Thus, the value of the Leap Motion as a VR peripheral needs to be determined in further studies.

References

1. 2d platformer - asset store. https://www.assetstore.unity3d.com/en/#!/content/11228. Accessed 2 June 2017
2. Frames leap motion javascript sdk v3.2 documentation. https://developer.leapmotion.com/documentation/javascript/devguide/Leap_Frames.html. Accessed 2 June 2017
3. Kinect - windows app development. https://developer.microsoft.com/en-us/windows/kinect. Accessed 3 June 2017
4. Leap motion developer. https://developer.leapmotion.com/. Accessed 2 June 2017
5. Tanks! tutorial - asset store. https://www.assetstore.unity3d.com/en/#!/content/46209. Accessed 3 June 2017
6. Blake, J., Gurocak, H.B.: Haptic glove with MR brakes for virtual reality. IEEE/ASME Trans. Mechatron. **14**(5), 606–615 (2009)
7. Brooke, J., et al.: Sus-a quick and dirty usability scale. Usability Eval. Ind. **189**(194), 4–7 (1996)
8. Deterding, S., Dixon, D., Khaled, R., Nacke, L.: From game design elements to gamefulness: defining gamification. In: Proceedings of the 15th International Academic MindTrek Conference: Envisioning Future Media Environments, pp. 9–15. ACM (2011)
9. Guna, J., Jakus, G., Pogačnik, M., Tomažič, S., Sodnik, J.: An analysis of the precision and reliability of the leap motion sensor and its suitability for static and dynamic tracking. Sensors **14**(2), 3702–3720 (2014)
10. Holzinger, A., Softic, S., Stickel, C., Ebner, M., Debevc, M., Hu, B.: Nintendo wii remote controller in higher education: development and evaluation of a demonstrator kit for e-teaching. Comput. Inf. Comput. Artif. Intell. **29**(4), 1001–1015 (2010)
11. Holzinger, A., Plass, M., Kickmeier-Rust, M.D.: Interactive machine learning (IML): a challenge for game-based approaches. In: Guyon, I., Viegas, E., Escalera, S., Hamner, B., Kegl, B. (eds.) Challenges in Machine Learning: Gaming and Education. NIPS Workshops (2016)
12. Khademi, M., Mousavi Hondori, H., McKenzie, A., Dodakian, L., Lopes, C.V., Cramer, S.C.: Free-hand interaction with leap motion controller for stroke rehabilitation. In: Proceedings of the Extended Abstracts of the 32nd Annual ACM Conference on Human Factors in Computing Systems, pp. 1663–1668. ACM (2014)
13. Nicola Bizzotto, M., Alessandro Costanzo, M., Leonardo Bizzotto, M.: Leap motion gesture control with osirix in the operating room to control imaging: first experiences during live surgery. Surg. Innovation **1**, 2 (2014)
14. Pirker, J., Griesmayr, S., Drachen, A., Sifa, R.: How playstyles evolve: progression analysis and profiling in *Just Cause 2*. In: Wallner, G., Kriglstein, S., Hlavacs, H., Malaka, R., Lugmayr, A., Yang, H.-S. (eds.) ICEC 2016. LNCS, vol. 9926, pp. 90–101. Springer, Cham (2016). doi:10.1007/978-3-319-46100-7_8
15. Pirker, J., Riffnaller-Schiefer, M., Gütl, C.: Motivational active learning: engaging university students in computer science education. In: Proceedings of the 2014 Conference on Innovation & Technology in Computer Science Education, pp. 297–302. ACM (2014)
16. Potter, L.E., Araullo, J., Carter, L.: The leap motion controller: a view on sign language. In: Proceedings of the 25th Australian Computer-Human Interaction Conference: Augmentation, Application, Innovation, Collaboration, pp. 175–178. ACM (2013)

17. Robertson, A.: Leap motion's revamped hand tracking is getting built straight into vr headsets - the verge. http://www.theverge.com/2016/2/17/11021214/leap-motion-hand-tracker-virtual-reality-orion-mobile-vr. Accessed 2 June 2017
18. Settgast, V., Pirker, J., Lontschar, S., Maggale, S., Gütl, C.: Evaluating experiences in different virtual reality setups. In: Wallner, G., Kriglstein, S., Hlavacs, H., Malaka, R., Lugmayr, A., Yang, H.-S. (eds.) ICEC 2016. LNCS, vol. 9926, pp. 115–125. Springer, Cham (2016). doi:10.1007/978-3-319-46100-7_10
19. Sturman, D.J., Zeltzer, D.: A survey of glove-based input. IEEE Comput. Graph. Appl. **14**(1), 30–39 (1994)
20. Vikram, S., Li, L., Russell, S.: Handwriting and gestures in the air, recognizing on the fly. In: Proceedings of the CHI, vol. 13, pp. 1179–1184 (2013)
21. Weichert, F., Bachmann, D., Rudak, B., Fisseler, D.: Analysis of the accuracy and robustness of the leap motion controller. Sensors **13**(5), 6380–6393 (2013)

Crafting Concrete as a Material for Enhancing Meaningful Interactions

Yanan Wang[1], Shijian Luo[1(✉)], Shuai Liu[1], Yujia Lu[1], and Preben Hansen[2]

[1] College of Computer Science and Technology, Zhejiang University, No. 38 Zheda Rd, Hangzhou, China
{wangyanan1120,sjluo,shuaidesign,luyujia}@zju.edu.cn
[2] Department of Computer and Systems Sciences, Stockholm University, Borgarfjordsgatan 12, Kista, Stockholm, Sweden
preben@dsv.su.se

Abstract. Concrete is a composite material mostly used for the buildings and road surfaces ever since early human history, and which also can be used in contemporary product design as its unique aesthetic properties. In this paper, we present a series of small-scale explorations of concrete crafted as a central material, first utilizing its hygroscopicity interacting as an ephemeral and dynamic display; and secondly eliciting tactile interaction for its unique surface textures. Through hands-on engagement to unveil concrete potential when fabricated with digital technologies, we discuss how this large-scale and ubiquitous material could bring particular and intriguing experiences in our everyday lives, most importantly how can the potential of concrete be framed and described and enhance meaningful concrete reflections within HCI community.

Keywords: Concrete · Craft practice · Digital technologies · Material properties · Material experience · Material-centered interaction design · Human-Computer Interaction

1 Introduction

Concrete is a composite material composed of sand, gravels and water mixed by cement, which hardens over time [21], thus mostly used for the building and road surfaces, which used as an ubiquitous material for a quite long period of time throughout human history. Materialists investigate concrete for a better performance, for example, stronger hygroscopicity and self-repairing capability through material science perspective. Additionally, as its particular aesthetic (e.g., grey color, unique textures, coldness) and craft properties, designers also use concrete to conduct product design concepts [1, 14] and artistic artifacts. Another corpus of designers attempted to mix concrete with extra materials (e.g., silicon, resin, fiber optic) to change its existing properties for various behaviors.

As the robustness and rigidness, concrete is always used for large-scale installations. In architectural space, Wastiels provided "touching material visually" to assess concrete through its visual aspects as a building material [19]; the recent development of materials

M. Kurosu (Ed.): HCI 2017, Part I, LNCS 10271, pp. 634–644, 2017.
DOI: 10.1007/978-3-319-58071-5_48

also promote designers and architecture researchers to define changeable and responsive properties of this materials. Chronos Chromos Concrete fabricated thermodynamic ink with computational technologies as a dynamic display through color change, holding the properties of ordinary state [16]. Marin Philippe presents an experiment based on the design and fabrication of an interactive concrete surface as a smart material [7]. However, for being such a ubiquitous material in our environment, how to utilize its intrinsic properties and characteristics for new form of interaction design is poorly addressed to date. Through a cross-discipline perspective, concrete is still largely unexplored in the domain of HCI community and interaction design.

In the field of HCI, An increasing number of HCI researchers and scholars have to give a further definition of the material at hand, and also need to explore how they can shape new expressions, experiences, characters and functions of design through their unique properties. By blending digital and physical properties into a composite material, future interactions may benefit from materials-centric modes of development and analysis.

2 Craft in Design and HCI

Craft practice has played a considerable role in practice-led design research for the last two decades, especially as the subject and the media for theoretical inquiry [8]. And considerably, craft practice has already recognized as a logic thinking [2] and a dynamic process of learning and understanding through material experience by hands-on engagement in interaction design research.

A corpus of scholars and researchers in HCI have similarly conducted different types of experiments and exploratory design process by using interactive electronics fabricated with materials such as paper [10, 12], wood [15], some other types of textiles [3, 9, 18], and even crafting code as a digital material [4] and plant as a living material [13]. Vasiliki also presents a series of explorations around leather for providing new types of interactive design by blending traditional craft method with contemporary fabrication [17]. Another relevant orientations within this field tend to articulate a perspective of crafting artifacts could reveal particular 'hidden' qualities of the material [11].

With the concrete material as an entry point, several questions need to be further explored, the most important perhaps what roles will concrete play and how concrete gains new values in designing interactive system. We shed light on two strands of problems for further understanding of concrete, exploring its future possibilities within HCI.

- What are the special properties of concrete? How might we describe this material in terms of material character [20]? How can the potential of this material be framed and described?
- By applying craft practice into our design process when fabricated with digital technologies, what kind of interactions will be elicited, and to what extent the interactions will be extended to a broader areas within HCI community?

In this paper, we tend to articulate how concrete will enhance meaningful interactions and what experiences it will bring through its properties when fabricated with digital technologies, how to "allow material properties to guide our design" [22], and what roles it will play in the future interaction design and HCI domains.

3 Prototypes

We built these two prototypes to illustrate how utilizing concrete properties can shape new meaningful interactions. And each prototype demonstrated a different concrete-based interaction design. There is a detailed explanation of what the properties are, how this property can be associated with people's everyday life, what the prototype does, and how it was crafted. Each prototype is developed as open-ended to encourage more and further exploration.

3.1 Water Shadow

As we know concrete will change its color naturally when meeting with water, and the parts that meet water will change to a darker color than the peripheral parts immediately, which makes it appear various images without any other external components. Especially, the temporary image will disappear following the evaporation of water.

What are we inspired from the 'ephemeral shadow'? What if this properties encounter with human behaviors such as Hand Shadow Games, which is playing when exposure to a strong light environment? And what if people can still play this game without a limiting environment? What kind of different experiences it will bring into everyday lives? If so, what are the differences between the Hand Shadow Games and the Water Shadow? On the other hand, besides the game itself, what it will bring when focusing on the certain material concrete, what kind of new definition or meaning can be framed around concrete in our daily life within HCI community?

Fabrication Process
We conducted a Water Shadow system, which could display a dynamic but ephemeral image according to the hand shadows. We used PO 42.5 cement, which is easy and cheap to achieve from online shops, and then crafted the concrete according to the normal cement-water proportion (3.5:1) within laboratory level. We made a 17 * 25 * 0.8 cm container for crafting the concrete slab. And we would achieve an ideal slab with 5–8 h setting time and the 20 °C room temperature (Fig. 1).

To achieve a better hydrophil effect, we drilled holes into an array at the back of the slab, from where for guiding the water. Then, fixing the transparent pipes onto each hole.

Hygroscopicity Test
With repeating experiments to test concrete hygroscopicity and permeability, we solved the problems around water amount and the needed appearing or vanishing time, and finally found an ideal way to display water traces you needed. Through test, the time for appearing is only 1.5–3 s, the vanishing time will be 1 min–2 min because of the limitation of temperature and ventilation.

Fig. 1. Water Shadow: craft a concrete slab (top left); drill holes on the back of the concrete slab (top right); guide the water through pipes (bottom left); conduct an hygroscopicity test on a small concrete slab (bottom right)

Water Shadow (Fig. 2) contained no extra coloring matter, which is different with Chronos Chromos Concrete [16], but can also make dynamic changes through on or off the water.

Fig. 2. Water Shadow

Technical Design

As the system described (Fig. 3), water goes down through pipes from the water tank on the top to the holes back the concrete slab, and stops when the steering engines cut the current by straining the ropes tying on the pipes, and on the contrary, loose the ropes to keep water flow.

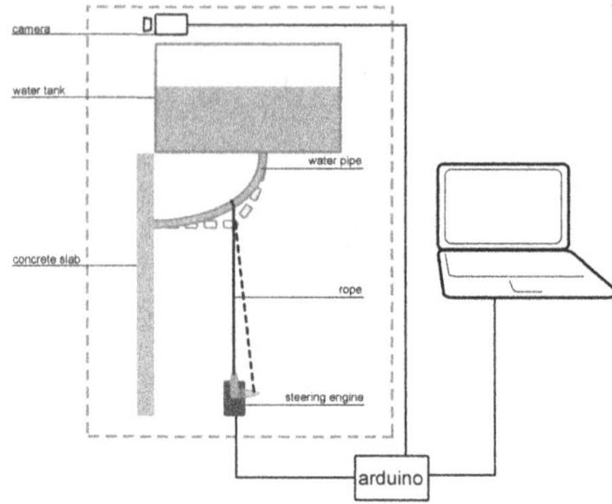

Fig. 3. Technical structure of Water Shadow system

The camera was used for capturing the image of human hands. PC would process the image to a pixel image and then transport the data to the micro controller to actuate the corresponding location of water shadow system. The effects would show within 5 s.

3.2 Live Cube

Concrete is a composite material composed of sand, gravels and water mixed by cement, which leading to unique surface textures. What would happen if we touch the different textures? What if these textures can make a sound, or make different frequencies of vibration? If we give the unique personality to such a material as

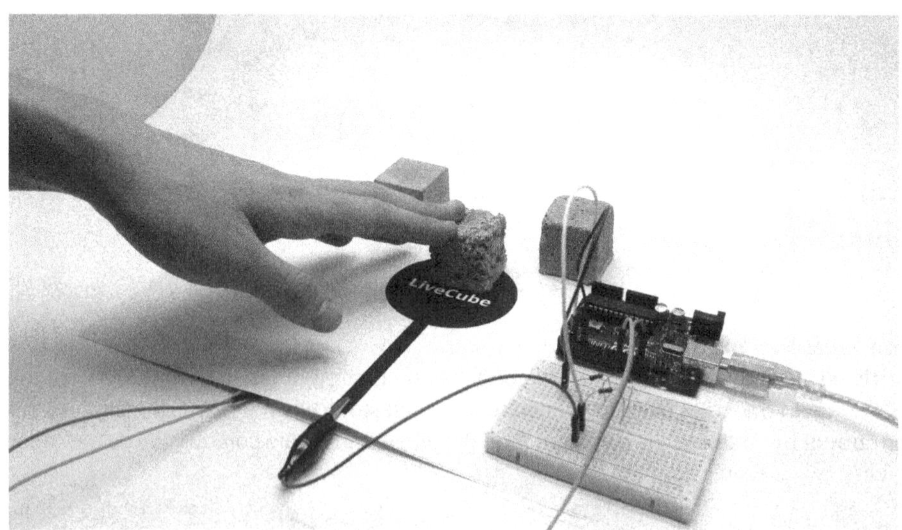

Fig. 4. Live Cube elicits dynamic vibration and tone through 'touching' behaviors, controlled by an Arduino platform

concrete, what will it bring to people's emotion or experiences? How can concrete character be framed in this prototype? (Fig. 4).

We used PO 42.5 cement to craft three samples through three different ingredient's proportion in silicon mould. To underline the surface textures, we crafted concrete into simple cubic shape with sample #1 only with cement and water; sample #2 with cement, water and fine yellow sand; and sample #3 with cement, water, rough gravels, yellow sand, and black sand stones (Fig. 5).

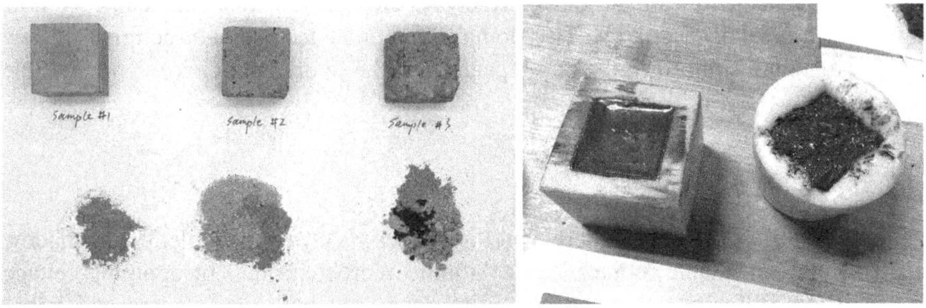

Fig. 5. Three samples with three different ingredient's proportion; craft the concrete in silicon mould

In this system, a camera is conducted to catch each different surface textures, and processing the picture to a black-and-white image (Fig. 6). By embedding with the vibration sensor and buzzer, three different concrete cube could shape three different personality once been touched.

Fig. 6. Live Cube: three samples

Live Cube will give the correspondingly tone and vibration feed back when being touched, through which way makes them like a living human. The smooth one will vibrate strongly and make a smooth but high tone as its unique feedback; on the contrary, the roughest one will act with a weakly vibration and a low, deep tone.

4 User Study

In order to evaluate how are these two prototypes eliciting concrete characters and how they can be framed or described in HCI domain, we conducted a semi-structure interview sessions to gain insight form the participants, also the future applications and possible areas.

4.1 Apparatus

We showed the two different concrete prototypes separately on the table. Water shadow acted as a concrete display controlled by Arduino microcontrollers by applying voltage 220 V. Three different concrete cube were connected with one camera and micro controller and with a PC.

4.2 Participants

The study consisted of 11 participants (4 females) with age range from 21 up to 38 years. The occupation backgrounds ranged from interactive designers, students and animation. In general, 9 participants did not have special experience with concrete before. 3 designers had knowledge of craft method and interactive technologies. The average time spent performing the study was approximately 35 min.

4.3 Procedure

We began each participant with the introduction of a natural concrete sample and its gradients (e.g. cement, sand, gravel) instead of the direct performing and demonstrations of Water Shadow and Live Cube, with questions like: (1) *What are the particular properties of this material in your mind?* (2) *How do you feel this material, physically and emotionally.* In this session, participants were allowed to tinker with this material [5] (e.g. touch, smell, knock). We would like to gain the intrinsic insights in general around the concrete as a material.

Next, we would show the two prototypes separately to the participants, and introduced how the concrete slab display the watermark and how the cubic concrete elicited the personality. Participants were allowed to experience, touch and feel Water Shadow and Live Cube. During this session, we encouraged the participants to talk at length about the aspects of the two prototypes they found interesting and uninteresting, gaining insights into initial interactions and reactions. To extend the usability of these two concepts, we also allowed the participants to describe the potential content design domains, and the ideas for the future applications.

All sessions were video recorded and later transcribed for analysis. Then we analyzed the recorded video and transcripts by using a grounded theory approach [6] in order to reveal how can the potential of concrete be framed and described within HCI community.

5 Findings

5.1 General User Perceptions

In general, most participants consider concrete with the key words like, "*cold*", "*rough*", "*industrialization*", "*large- scale*", "*crack*", "*ambient*", "*lifelessness*". However, during the study participants showed the curiosity, enjoyment and delight to the Water Shadow and Live Cube. P6 stated that the appearance and disappearance of the watermark made him fixate on the concrete slab intently. P2 felt the cubic concrete "*like a cute tiny robot*" which attracted him to touch it more than once. The majority of participants suggested a larger scale system and various forms of information display of Water Shadow, and also more personality and interaction styles for the Live Cube.

5.2 Water Shadow

Different patterns of water traces show on the concrete slab within 1–2 s, and disappear in 1–2 min naturally, high temperature or fast wind blowing will accelerate the evaporation of water to promote this process, controlling the time in 2–3 s. P3 said that "*I can't help fixating on the concrete slab tracing the watermarks, it looks so natural.*" As the specialness of concrete hygroscopicity, we regard this process as a slow motion, which will increase the focus on the water traces from showing to disappearing not limiting the game itself, which is functioned differently than smart phones and Led-based displays, and the aesthetic properties of concrete could be also reflected through this way. On the other hand, as all the controlling system processed mechanically back off the concrete slab, it will result in increased curiosity, examination and repeating play.

Throughout the study participants were encouraged to envision the possible areas and future applications for the display. A range of possible areas domain emerged: artistic installation; dynamic game playing; architectural environment; weather information; display complex information such as breath and heartbeat.

5.3 Live Cube

Through Live Cube, people could touch concrete's surface, feel their unique textures and various vibration frequencies, and listen their different 'voices'. In this design, each cubic concrete were given a personal identifier, and elicited a particular and joyful emotional experience to the users, which enticed users to touch their surface more than once.

In this prototype, we asked questions like: *If the object were a person, what kind of person would it be? And would it have any personality?* As P4 said: "*the smooth one looks like one beautiful lady with a fine voice*", "*the roughest one seems like a man with ruggedface*" (P3). And we also found participants tended to touch the surface repeatedly to feel the different roughness of each concrete sample without seeing them.

With the discussion around Live Cube, we summarized the possible areas and future applications: toy product design such as 3D cubic puzzle according the surface; intelligent tiny robot.

6 Discussion

6.1 Crafting Concrete as a Material

We crafted concrete through a diversity range of ways to explore and understand what is concrete, what is it made of, and what kinds of particular properties does concrete have. By applying craft practice into our design progress, we succeed to give a new definition through its properties and character, and find a great potential of concrete within HCI community. Meanwhile, the exploration of concrete also makes a significant contribution into craft community.

6.2 Concrete Character

Through the study of two prototypes, participants successfully experienced concrete in a different way, most of them would like to redefine concrete properties and gave a novel definition through the concrete character. Also, they have their personal interests. P4 stated that Water Shadow could express its own information by the hydrophillic properties, which could be connected with the *weather*, or *time*; P10 considered that each cubic concrete of Live Cube had their own personality like a real person, which was so different with his previous concept around concrete, and they could be used as some interactive toys. Concrete crafted as a center material elicits different characters through merging with digital technologies, stimulating impression making and emotional attachment.

6.3 Limitations and Future Work

We conducted a small-scale exploration of concrete within a lab level, one 17 * 25 * 0.8 cm concrete slab and three 4 * 4 * 4 cm cubic concrete, participants could experience this material and also give an evaluation around the concrete characters, also several future applications. However, such interactive prototypes would need more improved; adapting to a larger scale system and high-resolution display for Water Shadow, more different forms for Live Cube. As a future work, various ways of crafting of concrete are pursued, more properties and concrete characters hidden inside concrete need to be explored, as well as different kinds of live dynamic data displays and some other meaningful and intriguing interactions for a diverse range of application areas through these two concrete prototypes.

7 Conclusion

Through exploring these two prototypes, we tend to demonstrate that applying craft practice into our studies is quite useful and appropriate, especially when enhancing concrete interactions within HCI community and interaction design field. In this paper, we articulate concrete crafted as a material, merging with computational technologies, can provide a great potential for providing new types of interactions, and most importantly enhancing meaningful user experiences and reflections. Each prototype illustrates the detailed techniques and methods applied, and find exploring new ways to think and tinker with this ubiquitous medium bring new possibilities into future research. Concrete is, after all, as a massive and ubiquitous material in our environment deserves to have been paid more attention, not limited in its present domain, and also deserves to be explored through various ways within HCI in this digital age.

Acknowledgement. This research was supported by the National Natural Science Foundation of China (No. 51675476 and No. 51175458).

References

1. 22TM. http://www.22designstudio.com.tw/
2. Bardzell, S., Rosner, D., Bardzell, J.: The craft of designing for quality: integrity, creativity, and public sensibility. In: Proceedings of DIS 2012, pp. 11–20. ACM Press (2012)
3. Devendorf, L., Lo, J., Howell, N., et al.: "I don't Want to Wear a Screen": probing perceptions of and possibilities for dynamic displays on clothing. In: CHI Conference (2016)
4. Hansen, N.B., Halskov, K.: Crafting code at the demo-scene. In: DIS 2014, pp. 35–38. ACM Press (2014)
5. Jacobsson, M.: Tinkering with interactive materials: studies, concepts and prototypes. Kth School of Computer Science & Communication (2013)
6. Charmaz, K.: Constructing Grounded Theory: A Practical Guide Through Qualitative Analysis. Pine Forge Press, Thousand Oaks (2006)
7. Marin, P., Philippe, L., Blanchi, Y.: Interactive concrete surface an exploration of smart materials. In: Architecture and Civil Engineering, Singapore (2014)
8. Nimkulrat, N.: Hands-on intellect: integrating craft practice into design research. Int. J. Design **6**(3), 1–14 (2012)
9. Persson, A.: Exploring textiles as materials for interaction design (2013). http://bada.hb.se:80/handle/2320/12221.6
10. Qi, J., Buechley, L.: Sketching in circuits: designing and building electronics on paper. In: Proceedings of CHI 2014, pp. 1713–1722. ACM Press (2014)
11. Rosner, D.K., Taylor, A.S.: Antiquarian answers: book restoration as a resource for design. In: CHI 2011, pp. 2665–2668. ACM Press (2011)
12. Shorter, M., Rogers, J., McGhee, J.: Enhancing everyday paper interactions with paper circuits. In: Proceedings of DIS 2014, pp. 39–42. ACM Press (2014)
13. Steer, C., Robinson, S., Jones, M.: Growth, change and decay: plants and interaction possibilities. In: CHI EA 2015, pp. 2037–2042. ACM Press (2015)
14. UBIKUBI Lamp. http://ubikubi.ro/product/lamp/Interactive/
15. Vallgårda, A.: PLANKS: a computational composite. In: NordiCHI 2008, pp. 569–574. ACM Press (2008)

16. Vallgårda, A., Redström, J.: Computational composites. In: SIGCHI Conference on Human Factors in Computing Systems, pp. 513–522 (2007)
17. Tsaknaki, V., Fernaeus, Y., Schaub, M.: Leather as a material for crafting interactive and physical artifacts. In: DIS 2014, pp. 5–14. ACM Press (2014)
18. Wang, Y.S., Hsu, Y.Y., Chen, W.L., Chen, H., Liang, R.H.: Craft consciousness: the powerlessness of traditional embroidery. In: CHI EA 2015, pp. 2259–2264. ACM Press (2015)
19. Wastiels, L., Schifferstein, H.N.J., Wouters, I., et al.: Touching materials visually: about the dominance of vision in building material assessment. Int. J. Design **7**(2), 31–41 (2013)
20. Wiberg, M.: Methodology for materiality: interaction design research through a material lens. Pers. Ubiquitous Comput. **18**(3), 625–636 (2014)
21. Wikipedia: Concrete. https://en.wikipedia.org/wiki/Concrete/
22. Fernaeus, Y., Sundström, P.: The material move how materials matter in interaction design research. In: Proceedings of the Designing Interactive Systems Conference, pp. 486–495. ACM (2012). http://doi.org/10.1145/2317956.2318029

Haptic User Experience Based on User Preference

Hoon Sik Yoo[1(✉)], So Yon Jeong[2], and Da Young Ju[2]

[1] Techno and Design Research Center, Yonsei University, Incheon, South Korea
yoohs@yonsei.ac.kr
[2] Yonsei Institute of Convergence Technology, Yonsei University, Incheon, South Korea
{sjeong3206,dyju}@yonsei.ac.kr

Abstract. As the mobile device and touch screen market grows continuously, the development of Haptic Technology is expected to give a boost to the touch screen market. The inertia based tactile reproduction technology applied to current device is contributing to the expansion of market. The purpose of this study is to analyze what kind of service and material is preferred for the tactile reproduction technology to be applied to mobile device. To carry out the research, 100 surveys were performed and priority based on the surveyed contents was analyzed as well as additional analysis for gender and age to subdivide the demand of the users. The user preference on which haptic technology should be applied first is on movie, reflecting the desire to sensual experience various contents provided by the movies. Users also preferred soft materials such as silk. They also preferred materials which are encountered in daily life such as hanji, plastic, or cotton. For the development of the study, further research on what situation and through what method should be applied for application of higher service is necessary.

Keywords: Haptic technology · Touch display · User experience · User research · User-centered design

1 Research Background and Purpose

As the mobile device and touch screen market grows continuously, the development of Haptic Technology is expected to give a boost to the touch screen market. The inertia based tactile reproduction technology applied to current device is contributing to the expansion of market. Global mobile device companies such as SSE, Apple, and HTC are releasing products with next generation high-precision haptic technology. As can be seen in Fig. 1 according to Lux Research Inc., the global haptic market is expected to grow up to 13.8 billion dollars by 2025.

Up to now, major cases with application of haptic technology provide vibration experience using Actuator. After the commercialization of touch screen, various studies to graft tactile production were in process and studies and cases about haptic technology to feel texture on surface of touch screen has been appearing for few years. Although technological research for the release of product is in progress, Killer

M. Kurosu (Ed.): HCI 2017, Part I, LNCS 10271, pp. 645–655, 2017.
DOI: 10.1007/978-3-319-58071-5_49

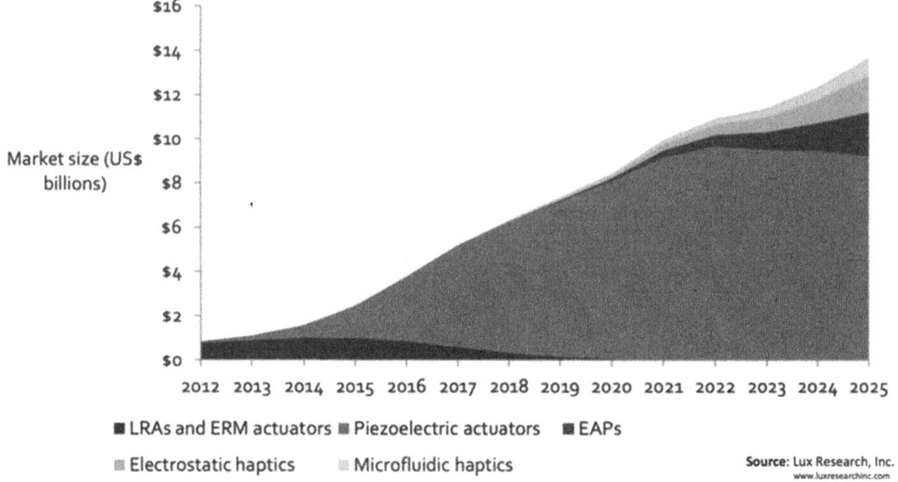

Fig. 1. Expected market size of haptic technology according to types of actuator

application which is applied from the perspective of user with the experience of Haptic is lacking. This is the time when the UX/UI study based on tactile reproduction technology is necessary.

The purpose of this study is to analyze what kind of service and material is preferred for the tactile reproduction technology to be applied to mobile device. If the preferred service is analyzed, the priority of what kinds of application that haptic technology should be applied to can be analyzed. Also, if the material preferred by the user is analyzed, what kind of tactile experience should be embodied first can be analyzed. To carry out the research, 100 surveys were performed and priority based on the surveyed contents was analyzed as well as additional analysis for gender and age to subdivide the demand of the users.

2 Related Work

2.1 Haptic Technology

Various next generation actuator technologies to provide detailed textile feedback from mobile device are in progress. The most representative technology is Electro Active Polymer (EAP). This is a technology that utilizes a polymer which changes its bonding structure based on the electric field; it uses the technique of producing vibration through contract-relax of the mass. It has advantages of good durability and free structure, and the response speed is 5 ms which is relatively fast. Figure 2 shows the structure of the polymer which is a EAP Actuator based Vivi Touch technology developed by the AMI (Artificial Muscle Inc.).

Pacinian Inc. of Fig. 3(left) developed Actuator to embody realistic sense of touch through vibration based on the initial attraction and repulsion produced using two glass

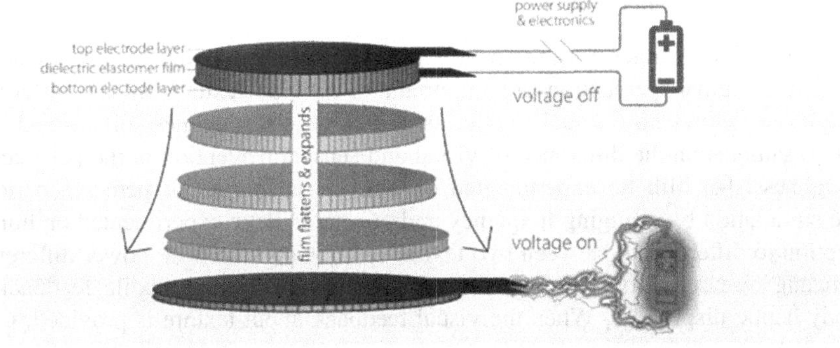

Fig. 2. Vivi touch of AMI

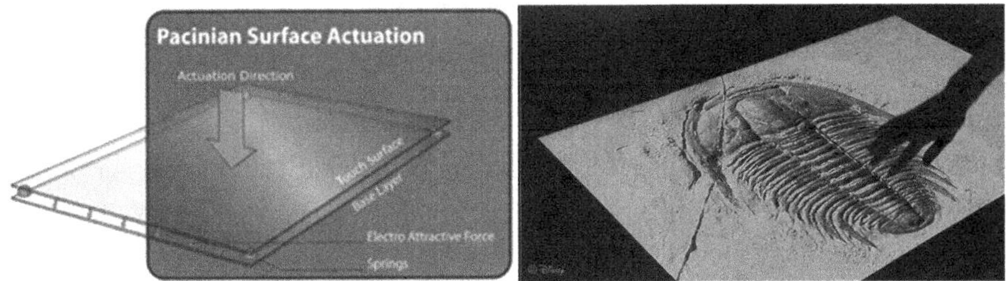

Fig. 3. Vivi touch of AMI

surface charged with different charges. Disney Research of Fig. 3(right) developed Tesla Touch composed of one glass board and insulation board to express the sense of friction through electrostatic force between finger and transparent electrode. [3] Toshiba developed Sensag through similar principles.

RWTH Aachen technical university developed Mudpad which can provide localized haptic feedback to the multi touch screen using Magnetorheological (MR) fluid. Mudpad changed parameters such as Magnet signal and research to provide tactile pattern was also executed; based on this tactile pattern, the User interface which gives impression of touching physical buttons on the touch screen was applied [5] (Fig. 4).

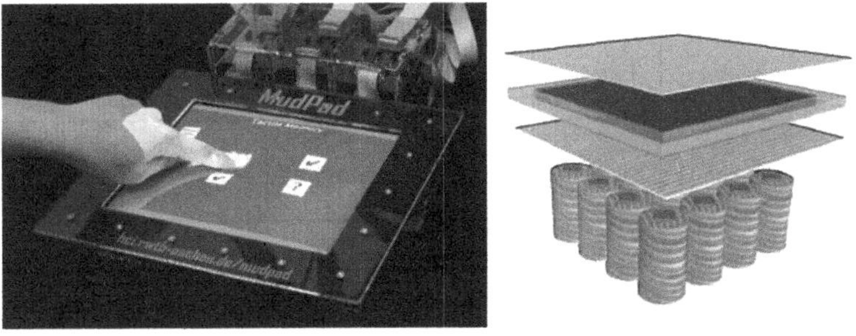

Fig. 4. MudPad's prototype and exploded view of system

2.2 Haptic Experience Study

There are various studies related to haptic; among those, studies related to actual subjects and human perception are important to provide texture on the surface of display. Tiest shows how actual roughness and perceived roughness differs and analyzed 96 samples on the difference of visual and sensual perception in the perspective of roughness. [4] Millette experimented on human capabilities to perceive periodic haptic stimulation by changing frequency and power. Millette experimented on human perception to differentiate between two textile stimulation with 30% power difference. [2] Hwang researched on the influence visual feedback has on textile feedback to embody haptic display. [1] When the visual feedback about texture is provided, users tend to exhibit positive response.

Existing studies focused on the perception and technological perspective. In this study, unlike previous ones, the preferred service and material to apply haptic technology is studies in the perspective of user experience.

3 Research

For this study, surveys targeting 100 users were performed. The information of participants is shown in Table 1.

Table 1. Profile

Item	Contents
Participated people	100 (Male 55/Female 45)
Average age (20s–6s)	Average of 42
Number of smart device owned	Average of 2.9

Through the survey, two following questions were proposed to analyze preference of users related to haptic UX.

Question 1. What is the content that can be utilized the most when texture is provided in display?

Game	Movies	Finance	Education	Weather	Navigation	News	Books
Photo/ video	Shopping	Medicine	Food	Traveling	Music	Health	Video call

Question 2. From the texture provided below, what are the ones that are expected to give positive feeling?

Sand	A4 paper	Photographic paper	Hanji	Sandpaper	Bubble wrap	Brush
Stockings	Natural leather	Artificial Leather	Cotton	Silk	Wool	Morning bread
Rice	Plastic	Wood	Leaves	Rubber	Skin	

4 Results

4.1 Preferred Contents

The user preference on which haptic technology should be applied first is shown in Table 2. Preference on movie is the highest, reflecting the desire to sensual experience various contents provided by the movies. It also showed high preference on shopping service; this is determined to experience the texture of the product prior to purchase. For the navigation, the driver must focus on the front. When the texture feedback is provided, it will be useful.

When the difference between male and female regarding contents preference was compared, both group preferred movie as top priority. For male, the second priority

Table 2. Preferred contents for the application of haptic technology

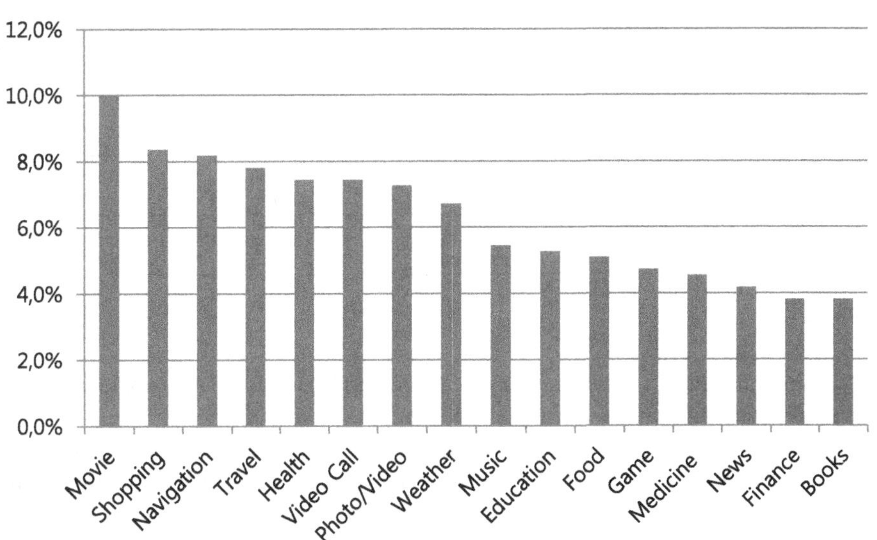

Table 3. Comparison between male and female on contents of haptic technology application

Gender	Male Frequency	Male (%)	Female Frequency	Female (%)
Game	18	5.9	8	3.3
Movie	31	10.2	24	9.8
Finance	9	3	12	4.9
Education	15	4.9	14	5.7
Weather	23	7.5	14	5.7
Navigation	25	8.2	20	8.1
News	11	3.6	12	4.9
Books	10	3.3	11	4.5
Photo/video	23	7.5	17	6.9
Shopping	23	7.5	23	9.3
Medicine	12	3.9	13	5.3
Food	15	4.9	13	5.3
Travel	27	8.9	16	6.5
Music	17	5.6	13	5.3
Health	23	7.5	18	7.3
Video Call	23	7.5	18	7.3
Total	305	100	246	100

was navigation while it was shopping for female. This reflects that male has great interest in automobile while female has in shopping (Table 3).

When the difference between age was compared, young people at the age of 20–40s focused on application on entertainment area such as movie, photo and shopping while older people preferred such technology to be applied to necessary information such as health, news, and navigation (Tables 4 and 5).

Table 4. Comparison between ages on contents of haptic technology application

Age	20s	20s (%)	30s	30s (%)	40s	40s (%)	50s	50s (%)	60s	60s (%)
Gender	3	6.4	9	5.2	11	4.9	3	3.5	0	0
Game	4	8.5	17	9.8	23	10.2	8	9.4	3	15
Movie	2	4.3	4	2.3	9	4	4	4.7	2	10
Finance	2	4.3	12	6.9	10	4.4	4	4.7	1	5
Education	4	8.5	11	6.4	15	6.6	7	8.2	0	0
Weather	3	6.4	13	7.5	18	8	9	10.6	2	10
Navigation	1	2.1	6	3.5	10	4.4	3	3.5	3	15
News	1	2.1	9	5.2	8	3.5	3	3.5	0	0
Books	5	10.6	15	8.7	13	5.8	6	7.1	1	5
Photo /video	5	10.6	15	8.7	21	9.3	5	5.9	0	0
Shopping	1	2.1	8	4.6	12	5.3	3	3.5	1	5
Medicine	3	6.4	9	5.2	12	5.3	3	3.5	1	5
Food	3	6.4	13	7.5	19	8.4	6	7.1	2	10
Travel	3	6.4	6	3.5	15	6.6	6	7.1	0	0
Music	4	8.5	11	6.4	14	6.2	10	11.8	2	10
Health	3	6.4	15	8.7	16	7.1	5	5.9	2	10
Total	47	100	173	100	226	100	85	100	20	100

Table 5. Comparison between male and female on preferred material

Gender	Male Frequency	Male (%)	Female Frequency	Female (%)
Sand	3	1.4	1	0.6
A4 Paper	6	2.8	4	2.3
Photographic paper	2	0.9	6	3.4
Hanji	20	9.4	14	8
Sand Paper	0	0	1	0.6
Bubble Wrap	10	4.7	4	2.3
Brush	2	0.9	6	3.4
Stocking	9	4.2	5	2.9
Nature Leather	30	14.2	24	13.8
Artificial Leather	3	1.4	10	5.7
Cotton	11	5.2	9	5.2
Silk	34	16	28	16.1
Wool	7	3.3	9	5.2
Morning Bread	9	4.2	7	4
Rice	0	0	1	0.6
Plastic	16	7.5	13	7.5
Wood	10	4.7	6	3.4
Leaves	5	2.4	1	0.6
Rubber	11	5.2	8	4.6
Skin	24	11.3	17	9.8
Total	212	100	174	100

Table 6. Comparison between ages on preferred materials

Age	20s	20s (%)	30s	30s (%)	40s	40s (%)	50s	50s (%)	60s	60s (%)
Sand	0	0	2	1.5	1	0.7	1	1.6	0	0
A4 Paper	0	0	3	2.3	3	2	4	6.6	0	0
Photographic paper	1	2.9	3	2.3	4	2.7	0	0	0	0
Hanji	3	8.8	8	6.1	14	9.5	7	11.5	2	15.4
Sand Paper	0	0	0	0	0	0	0	0	1	7.7
Bubble Wrap	3	8.8	4	3.1	6	4.1	1	1.6	0	0
Brush	2	5.9	3	2.3	1	0.7	2	3.3	0	0
Stocking	2	5.9	6	4.6	3	2	2	3.3	1	7.7
Nature Leather	4	11.8	21	16	21	14.3	7	11.5	1	7.7
Artificial Leather	1	2.9	3	2.3	6	4.1	1	1.6	2	15.4
Cotton	1	2.9	8	6.1	6	4.1	5	8.2	0	0
Silk	4	11.8	25	19.1	20	13.6	10	16.4	3	23.1
Wool	3	8.8	8	6.1	2	1.4	2	3.3	1	7.7
Morning Bread	2	5.9	5	3.8	6	4.1	3	4.9	0	0
Rice	0	0	0	0	0	0	1	1.6	0	0
Plastic	2	5.9	8	6.1	15	10.2	4	6.6	0	0
Wood	0	0	5	3.8	9	6.1	2	3.3	0	0
Leaves	0	0	2	1.5	4	2.7	0	0	0	0
Rubber	3	8.8	5	3.8	8	5.4	2	3.3	1	7.7
Skin	3	8.8	12	9.2	18	12.2	7	11.5	1	7.7
Total	34	100	131	100	147	100	61	100	13	100

Table 7. Priority of material preferred by user

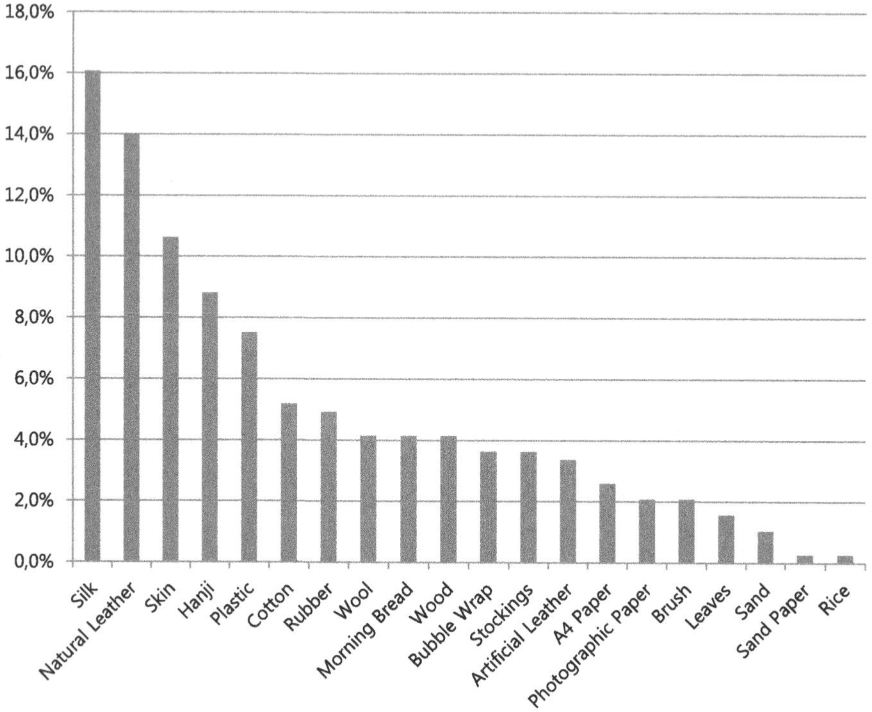

4.2 Preferred Materials

The priority of preferred material is shown in Table 7. Users preferred soft materials such as silk. They also preferred materials which are encountered in daily life such as hanji, plastic, or cotton. Rough materials such as sand or sandpaper or those related to food such as rice aren't preferred.

There weren't any difference between genders regarding preferred material. 1st–3rd of priority were identical and showed similar trend of avoiding rough materials.

There weren't also any difference between ages regarding preferred materials. Overall ranking was similar with high preference toward silk, natural leather, and skin (Table 6).

5 Conclusion and Future Work

This study analyzed the preference of the contents and materials of the users when the haptic technology is applied to the touch display to discover applicable user experience. As a result, uses wanted it to be applied to contents such as movies or shopping and it differs from gender to age. For material, soft materials such as silk, natural leather or skin is preferred and did not show specific difference from gender to age. Based on the results of this study, factors related to the service and materials that must be applied to future haptic display could be defined. For the development of the study, further research on what situation and through what method should be applied for application of higher service is necessary.

Acknowledgments. This research was supported by the MSIP (Ministry of Science, ICT and Future Planning), Korea, under the "ICT Consilience Creative Program" (IITP-R0346-16-1008) supervised by the IITP (Institute for Information and communications Technology Promotion).

References

1. Hwang, H.J., Ju, D.Y.: Finding favorable textures for haptic display. In: Antona, M., Stephanidis, C. (eds.) UAHCI 2015. LNCS, vol. 9176, pp. 94–102. Springer, Cham (2015). doi:10.1007/978-3-319-20681-3_9
2. Millette, C.G.: The Human Perception of Haptic Vibrations. University of Calgary, Calgary (2012)
3. Bau, O., Poupyrev, I., Israr, A., Harrison. C.: TeslaTouch: electrovibration for touch surfaces. In: Proceedings of the 23rd Annual ACM Symposium on User Interface Software and Technology (UIST 2010), pp. 283–292. ACM, New York (2010)
4. Bergmann, W.M., Kappers, A.M.L.: Haptic and visual perception of roughness. Acta Physiol. (Oxf) **124**(2), 177–189 (2007)
5. Jansen, Y., Karrer, T., Borchers, J.: MudPad: tactile feedback for touch surfaces. In: CHI 2011 Extended Abstracts on Human Factors in Computing Systems (CHI EA 2011), pp. 323–328. ACM, New York (2011)

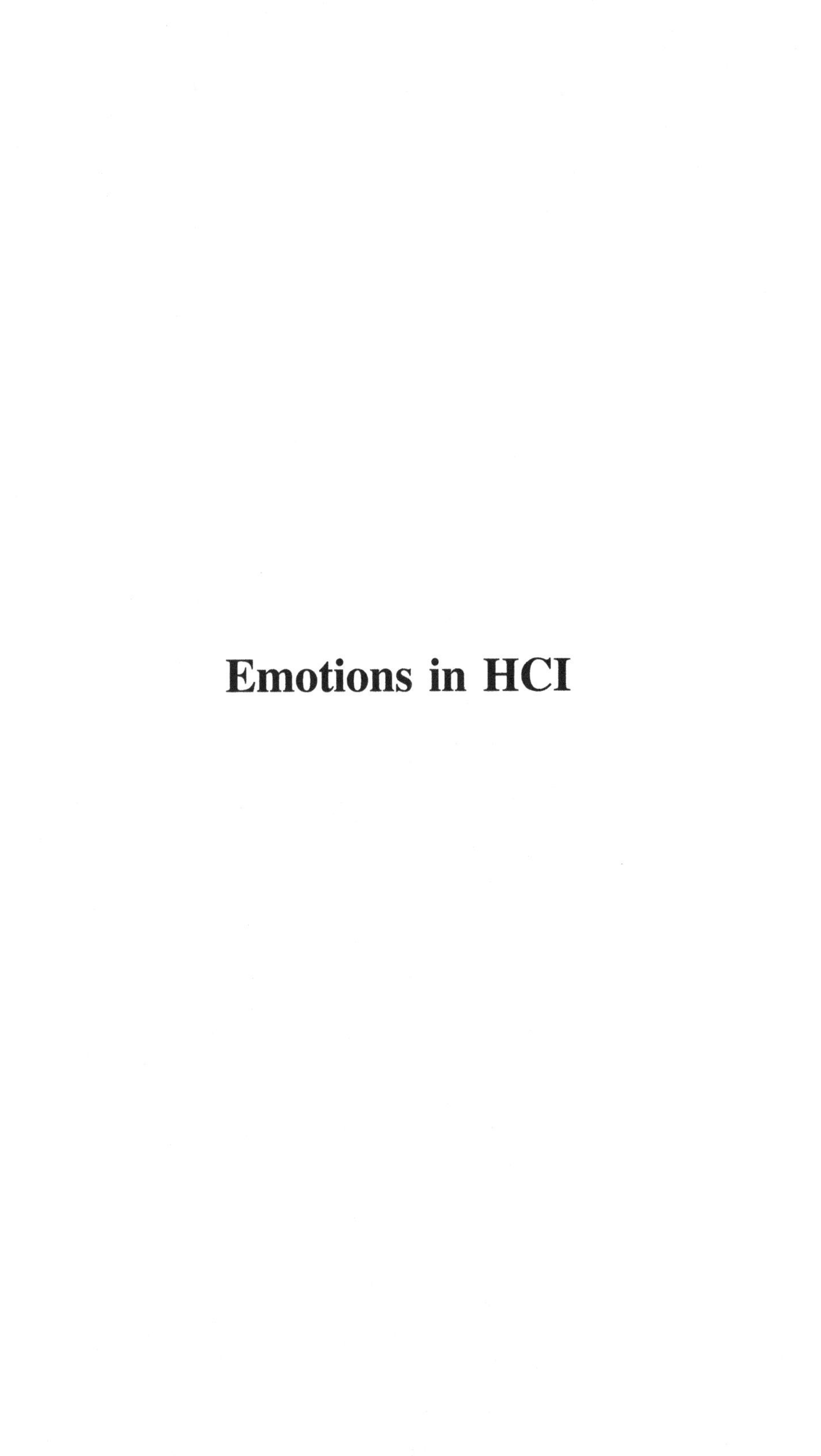

Emotions in HCI

Persuasive Argumentation and Emotions: An Empirical Evaluation with Users

Mohamed S. Benlamine[1(✉)], Serena Villata[2], Ramla Ghali[1], Claude Frasson[1], Fabien Gandon[2], and Elena Cabrio[2]

[1] Heron Laboratory, University of Montreal, Montreal, Canada
ms.benlamine@umontreal.ca
[2] Université Côte d'Azur, CNRS, Inria, I3S, Nice, France

Abstract. In everyday life discussion, people try to persuade each other about the goodness of their viewpoint regarding a certain topic. This persuasion process is usually affected by several elements, like the ability of the speaker in formulating logical arguments, her confidence with respect to the discussed topic, and the emotional solicitation that certain arguments may cause in the audience. In this study, we compare the effect of using one of the three well-known persuasion strategies (Logos, Ethos and Pathos) in the argumentation process. These strategies are used by a moderator who influences the participants during the debates. We study which persuasion strategy is the most effective, and how they vary according to two mental metrics extracted from electroencephalograms: Engagement and workload. Results show that the right hemisphere has the highest engagement when Logos arguments are proposed to participants with Neutral opinion during the debate. We show also that the Logos strategy solicits the highest mental Workload, and the Pathos strategy is the most effective to use in argumentation and to convince the participants.

Keywords: Persuasion · Argumentation · Engagement · Workload · EEG · BCI

1 Introduction

In everyday life, arguments are "reasons to believe and reasons to act". Argumentation is the process by which arguments are constructed and handled. Thus argumentation means that arguments are compared, evaluated in some respect and judged in order to establish whether any of them are warranted. Argumentation is the process by which arguments are constructed and handled in a debate. As explained by Mercier and Sperber [1], the function of reasoning is argumentative. It is to devise and evaluate arguments intended to persuade. A key feature of argumentation is that of being rational and grounded on logical inferences so that it can support *critical thinking*. However, in recent years, some approaches [4–8] have highlighted that argumentation is not a purely rational process but it involves past experience and emotions [9]. Despite the number of contributions studying either the link between emotions and persuasive argumentation from the theoretical point of view (e.g., [2]) or the reasoning attitude evolution when persuasive arguments are presented to users from an empirical point of view (e.g., [3]), none of these approaches tackles the problem of studying the

M. Kurosu (Ed.): HCI 2017, Part I, LNCS 10271, pp. 659–671, 2017.
DOI: 10.1007/978-3-319-58071-5_50

link between persuasive argumentation and emotions in an empirical setting. In this paper, we address this issue through the study of the correspondences between arguments, the adopted persuasion strategy, and the emotions measured using Electroencephalograms (EEG). We designed an experiment where 5 participants interact with each other by debating about a certain topic provided by a moderator. One of these participants, called the persuader (PP), plays a specific persuasion strategy (Ethos, Logos, Pathos) in order to convince the others about the goodness of her point of view.

The remainder of the paper is organized as follows. In Sect. 2, we describe the experimental setting in which our empirical evaluation took place, and the three hypotheses we formulated. Section 3 discusses the obtained results with respect to the three hypotheses. Conclusions end the paper.

2 Experimental Settings

The experiment was distributed over 5 sessions of 4 participants: 20 participants (7 women, 13 men, all right handed and students from the University of Montreal) plus PP, a fictive participant in charge of triggering the persuasion strategy. Participants argue in plain English proposing arguments, which are in favor or against the arguments proposed by the other participants. During these debates, participants are equipped with emotions recognition tools, recording their emotions.

2.1 Persuasion Strategies

During the debate, participant PP adopted one of the following three persuasion strategies [12]:

- *Logos*: logic and rationality are highly valued, and this type of persuasion strategy relies on the use of rational arguments following from logical inferences.
- *Ethos*: if we believe that a speaker has good sense, good moral character, and goodwill, we are inclined to believe what that speaker says, and this type of persuasion strategy underlines that the speaker has the appropriate expertise or authority to speak knowledgeably about the discussed topic.
- *Pathos*: emotions such as anger, pity, fear, and their opposites, powerfully influence humans' rational judgments, and this type of persuasion strategy is directed toward moving the emotions of the debaters.

2.2 Argumentation Model

In order to model the textual debates we collected during the experiment and study them from the argumentation point of view, we rely on abstract bipolar argumentation [10, 11] where we do not distinguish the internal structure of the arguments (i.e., premises, conclusion), but we consider each argument proposed by the participants in the debate as a unique element, then analyzing the relation it has with the other pieces of information put forward in the debate. In particular, in bipolar argumentation two kinds of relations among arguments are considered: the support relation, i.e., a positive relation between arguments, and the attack relation, i.e., a negative relation between arguments.

2.3 Emotion Detection Tools

Each participant was equipped with the following sensors:

- 1 Camera to detect facial expressions.
- 1 EEG headset (associated to engagement/workload indexes detection system).
- 1 EDA bracelet to assess stress.
- 1 Eye-tracker to collect gaze data.

2.4 Cognitive Measures

In this study, we have used two cognitive measures based on EEG physiological data:

- Engagement Index: refers to the level of attention and alertness during a task [13]. The engagement index [14–17] is computed from three EEG frequency bands: α(8–12 Hz), β(12–22 Hz) and θ(4–8 Hz): Engagement = $\beta/(\alpha + \theta)$. This index is computed each second from the EEG signal. To get Left and right engagement indexes, we calculated two averages for each frequency band (α, β and θ) one from the seven sensors located on the left side of the Emotiv headset and the other from the right side.
- Workload Index: refers to a measurable quantity of information processing effort performed by a person on a task. The mental workload is generally related to the level of information loading in the working memory during a task. The EEG workload index was based on pre-trained predictive model [18]. This model was trained using a set of EEG data collected from a training phase during which a group of seventeen participants performed a set of brain training exercises and were asked to report their workload level using the subjective scale of NASA Task load index [19]. The evaluation of this model showed a correlation with the participants' subjective scores NASA TLX reaching 82%.

2.5 Protocol

- *Phase 0*: Pre-selection phase where the participants fill in an online form about their initial opinion on all the topics, then for each debate two participants pro and two con were selected;
- *Phase 1*: Receiving the participants in the experimental room and installing the sensors on them;
- *Phase 2*: Two 15 min debates session in which:
  - An animator introduces the topic to be discussed and asks opinions;
  - Each participant exposes his/her opinion, and comments on the others' opinions;

- PP plays a persuasion strategy, and posts arguments trying to bring participants with opposite viewpoints to the targeted position;

– *Phase 3*: Opinion change self-report.

2.6 Hypotheses

(H1) Logos arguments solicit one side of the brain, while pathos and ethos arguments solicit different brain sides.
(H2) The most effective persuasion strategy is Pathos, even if the participants do not completely reverse their opinion about the debated topic.
(H3) Logos arguments induce higher workload in the debates, while pathos and ethos arguments induce higher engagement.

3 Results

In order to verify the three hypotheses detailed above, we have analyzed the collected data by dividing the debate into three phases: the introduction (*Introduction*), the argumentation (*Argumentation*) and the conclusion (*Conclusion*). In the Introduction phase, participant PP takes a position with regard to the topic of the debate justified with a general statement to support his point of view. In the Argumentation phase, participant PP tries to convince the other participants of the relevance of his opinion by adopting one of the three persuasion strategies (*Logos*, *Ethos* or *Pathos*) to formulate his arguments. In the Conclusion phase, PP point out his final position with an invitation to the other participants to support him. As we are interested in the impact of PP's arguments, we considered the participants' physiological reactions during the 10 s after each PP intervention in the debates. A repeated-measures design for each debate phases was used where average engagement and workload indexes were evaluated for each participant.

To verify these hypotheses, we have computed workload and engagement indexes for each participant. We have run repeated-measure analysis of variance (repeated measure ANOVA) using IBM SPSS statistic software V24 for computing the differences of mean engagement for each brain side for 10 s after PP's intervention.

To verify H1 and H2, we have run the repeated measure ANOVA to evaluate the effect of PP's arguments on the engagement index of each brain hemisphere with regards to the participant final position with respect to participant PP's one (Neutral, Opponent or Supporter). *So, for this analysis, the within-subject factor is Debate_phases (Introduction, Argumentation and Conclusion) and the between-subjects factors are: PP_strategy (Logos, Ethos and Pathos), Brain_sides (Left and Right) and Final_Position (Neutral, Opponent or Supporter).*

3.1 Hypothesis H1

The engagement means of the Left and Right brain hemispheres with regard to the final position of the participant are presented in the descriptive statistics table below (Table 1). The persuasion strategies' mean of engagement in each brain hemisphere are compared for each debate phase depending on the final position to the PP's opinion.

Table 1. Descriptive statistics of engagement index in the brain Hemispheres by debate phases and PP strategies (Data are presented as mean ± SD)

Debate phase	Brain side	Final position	Ethos (N = 16)	Logos (N = 40)	Pathos (N = 24)
Introduction	Left	Neutral	0.59 ± 0.00	1.38 ± 0.00	.
		Opponent	0.73 ± 0.19	0.67 ± 0.22	0.60 ± 0.03
		Supporter	1.14 ± 0.44	0.66 ± 0.27	0.58 ± 0.21
	Right	Neutral	0.59 ± 0.00	2.21 ± 0.00	.
		Opponent	0.95 ± 0.26	0.88 ± 0.34	0.83 ± 0.22
		Supporter	1.81 ± 1.15	0.71 ± 0.29	0.75 ± 0.34
Argumentation	Left	Neutral	0.55 ± 0.00	1.54 ± 0.00	.
		Opponent	0.73 ± 0.26	0.76 ± 0.40	0.86 ± 0.20
		Supporter	1.01 ± 0.40	0.67 ± 0.20	0.59 ± 0.21
	Right	Neutral	0.57 ± 0.00	3.42 ± 0.00	.
		Opponent	0.89 ± 0.26	0.95 ± 0.42	0.90 ± 0.15
		Supporter	1.35 ± 0.60	0.72 ± 0.20	0.76 ± 0.30
Conclusion	Left	Neutral	0.49 ± 0.00	2.10 ± 0.00	.
		Opponent	0.76 ± 0.26	0.62 ± 0.26	0.99 ± 0.61
		Supporter	1.08 ± 0.64	0.64 ± 0.13	0.82 ± 0.91
	Right	Neutral	0.55 ± 0.00	3.75 ± 0.00	.
		Opponent	0.90 ± 0.24	0.91 ± 0.35	1.25 ± 0.28
		Supporter	1.37 ± 0.72	0.74 ± 0.15	1.01 ± 1.03

To validate the repeated-measures of ANOVA, we used a Mauchly's test for sphericity on the dependent variable "debate phases" (sig = .000). According to this test, we assess the significance of the corresponding F with Greenhouse-Geisser correction. So, for the within-subject effect test by applying Greenhouse-Geisser correction, we have a significant effect of debate phases on engagement with $F(1.146,73.346) = 3.425$ and $p = 0.036$. We have similarly significant interaction of Debate_Phases*PP_Strategy with $F(2.292, 73.346) = 3.179$ and $p = 0.041$ that means significant effect on engagement.

By checking Levene's test[1] for homogeneity of variance, we found that variances are homogeneous for the Conclusion phase ($F(15,64) = 1.328$ and $p = 0.213$) and not for the Introduction and Argumentation ones (respectively, $F(15,64) = 2.753$, $p = 0.003$ for

[1] Levene's test is used to assess the equality of variances for a variable calculated for two or more groups.

Introduction and F(15,64) = 2.028, p = 0.027 for Argumentation). The between-subject effects results show that there is significant main effects of the factor Brain_Sides on engagement, F(2,64) = 8.792, p = 0.004, also for the factor Final_Position on engagement, F(2,64) = 5.452, p = 0.007 and then PP_strategy on Engagement, F (2,64) = 5.116, p = 0.009. There is also significant main effect of the factors interaction PP_Strategy*Final_Position on engagement, F(3,64) = 5.452, p = 0.000. However, for the three factors interaction Brain_sides*PP_strategy*Final_Position shows no significant main effect with a good F value (F(3,64) = 2.098, p = 0.109) which means that there is an influence of these 3 factors on engagement but it is not statistically significant.

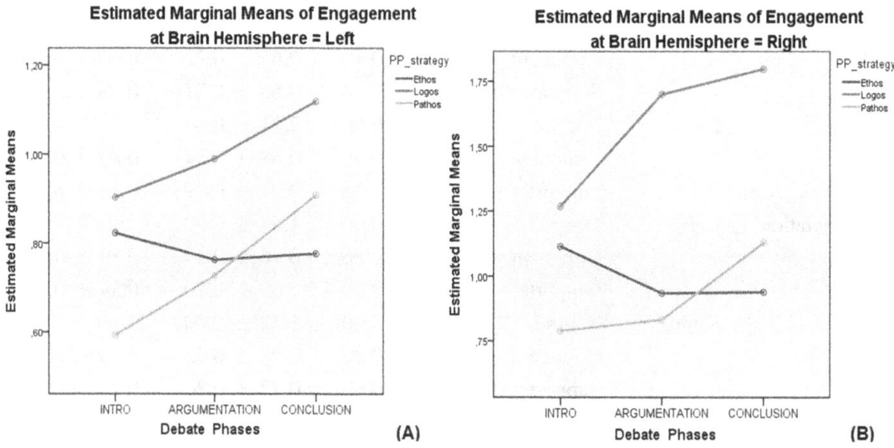

Fig. 1. Means of engagement in brain hemispheres by debate phases for the different persuasion strategies

Figure 1 shows the means of engagement in the brain hemispheres by debate phases for the different persuasion strategies used by PP participant. In order to better understand what's going on in the debates, we focused on the participants' **Final position** towards participant PP targeted opinion (Fig. 2). In fact, the participants who stayed Neutral all over the debates had the highest engagement in both brain sides, but those who tacked position as opponents or supporters of PP's opinion had lower engagements in both brain sides. So participants who have not decided about the PP's opinion were more engaged in looking for the reasons about why that opinion could be right or not. As we can see in Fig. 2, the right hemisphere has generally higher engagement scores. So participants were more relaying on their intuition, imagination and feelings to evaluate PP's arguments.

Comparing Figs. 1 and 2, we can see that the Right Hemisphere (Fig. 1-B) shows high engagement when dealing with Logos arguments, similarly to participants who have Neutral position during the debate (Fig. 2-B).

For those participants who have taken a decision (Opponents or Supporters, Fig. 2), we may note that the mean engagement is almost the same between the three debates'

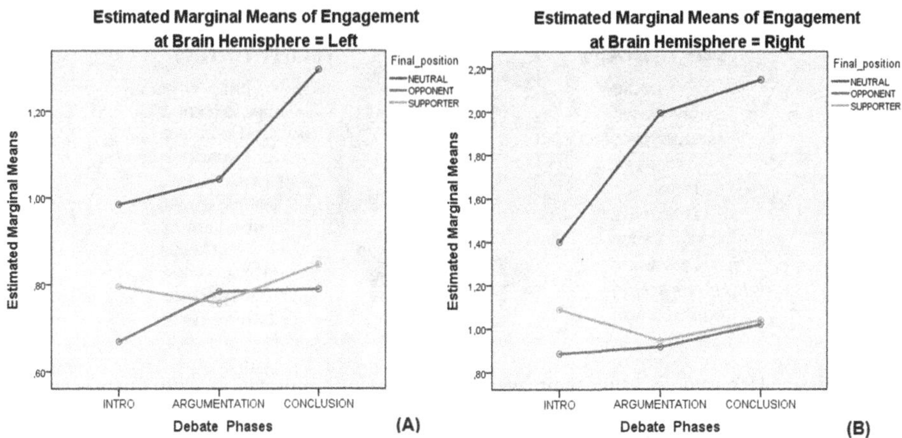

Fig. 2. Means of engagement in brain hemispheres by debate phases for the different Final positions toward the PP participant's opinion

phases (between 0.85 and 1.15 for the Right brain side, and between 0.60 and 0.85 for the Left brain Side), whereas in Fig. 1 for the Pathos strategy the mean engagement is the lowest. Logos Engagement is significantly higher in the Argumentation phase compared to the Introduction phase in the Right brain. Participants are using their intuition to evaluate the Logos arguments of PP but they cannot decide so they stay in the Neutral position. Logos arguments need to be treated analytically to lead to some kind of decision making. Engagement for Ethos and Pathos arguments are more similar to the engagement of the participants that have taken a decision (Supporter or Opponent) with respect to PP's arguments.

For the participants who were Neutral, Fig. 2 shows that the mean engagement is always higher than 1.15 for the Right Side, and 0.85 for the Left Side. However, we may note that for the Ethos strategy, the Right engagement is high in the Introduction phase and falls down in the Argumentation phase. While for the Logos and Pathos strategies, the engagement is lower in the Introduction and goes up in the Argumentation and Conclusion phases, for Right Hemisphere the engagement goes significantly higher.

This result is justified by the simple effect analysis showing a significant mean difference of Right Engagement between Argumentation and Introduction phases with Ethos strategy (Mean difference = −.180, p = .024) and also Logos Strategy (Mean difference = .432, p = .000) but there is near significant difference for the Pathos strategy in the Left engagement (Mean difference = .134, p = .067).

The significant link to the right brain is pretty clear. The specialized characteristics of the right hemisphere make it the seat of curiosity, synergy, experimentation, global thinking, flexibility and feelings. Every one of these characteristics is capable of enhancing an individual's thinking to find a counter example or to make inferences and decisions. For example, an intuitive idea that pops into a person's mind, just after a Logos argument, can lead to accept or refute the others' opinion. That's the right hemisphere part. Now, taking a decision about the opinion requires different specialized mental processes, and these are located in the left hemisphere. Diagnosing the

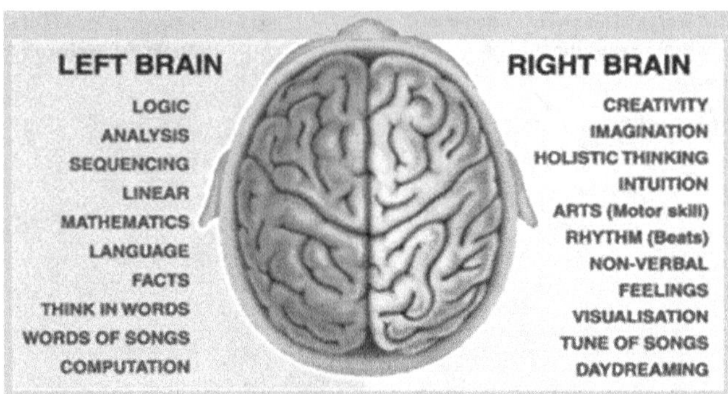

Fig. 3. Brain Hemispheres and their way of processing information (http://ucmas.ca/our-programs/whole-brain-development/left-brain-vs-right-brain/)

proposed argument to decide whether we support it or not, makes use of our rational processes of analysis and logic (Fig. 3).

Since the right hemisphere and the left hemisphere are interconnected through the corpus callosum, it is then possible to iterate back and forth between these modes to arrive to make a decision. The left brain helps keeping the right brain on track during the debate.

3.2 Hypothesis H2

To verify the second hypothesis, about the effectiveness of persuasion strategies to get more supporters, we have run simple effects analysis comparing the three factors interaction: Debate_Phase*PP_strategy*Final_Position with the factor Debate_Phase. To get this supplementary analysis, we have added this instruction in the SPSS script:

```
/EMMEANS = TABLES(DebatePhase*PP_strategy*Final_position)
COMPARE (DebatePhase)
```

Looking at Fig. 4, we get an idea about the different persuasion strategies mean engagement throughout the debate phases classed by final positions as Supporter, Opponent or Neutral with respect to PP's opinion.

For the Supporters, Fig. 4-C shows that the global engagement is higher for Ethos compared to the other strategies. In fact, there is a decrease of engagement (from 1.5 to 1.2) between the Introduction and Argumentation phases for the supporters, with Ethos strategy. For the other strategies, the supporters have almost the same engagement ($\simeq$0.7) during the debate phases except for Pathos it increases to 0.9 in the Conclusion phase. By looking at the simple effect comparison, we also found that the significant mean differences of engagement are between the Introduction and Argumentation phases for Ethos strategy (Mean difference = .293, p = .000) and of Engagement between Argumentation and Conclusion phases for Pathos strategy (Mean difference = .238, p = 0.056). This decreasing and low engagement shows that there is low resistance to PP's arguments from the Supporters.

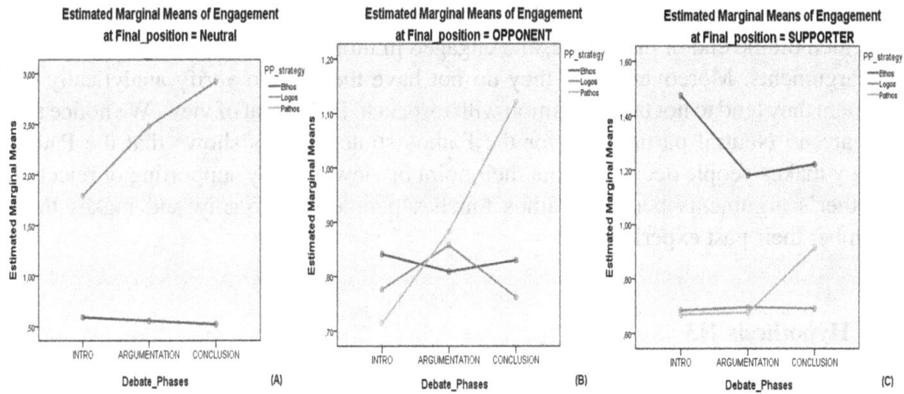

Fig. 4. Means of engagement of PP Strategies by debate phases for the different Final positions

For the Opponents, Fig. 4-B shows that for Ethos strategy the engagement is lower compared to what we have seen for the Supporters in the Ethos strategy. We notice that the opponents' engagement is almost the same (0.85) during the debate and it goes a little bit lower in the Argumentation phase. This means that the opponent rejects PP's argument from the beginning of the debate and does not believe him during the debate as an expert or scientific (or does not have confidence in the provided scientific results). For Logos strategy, the Opponent's Engagement starts from 0.77 and increases a little bit in the Argumentation phase (0.86) but it goes down again till 0.76. This engagement increase may be due to the mental effort in evaluating the arguments and their logical consequences. At the end the engagement goes down because the participant was not convinced with the logical reasons presented by PP. For the Pathos strategy, the Opponent's engagement is still increasing from 0.72 at the Introduction phase, to 0.90 at Argumentation phase, and reaches 1.15 in the Conclusion. Here we have near significant difference for the Pathos strategy between Introduction and Argumentation (Mean difference = .169, p = .072). We note that the engagement of the Opponents remains increasing for Pathos unlike the other strategies where it was relatively low and stable due the rejection from the beginning for the Ethos arguments or the logical weakness of the arguments for Logos during the Argumentation phase. This increasing Engagement shows us the mental resistance to change form Opponent to Supporter. This proves that the Pathos strategy is the most difficult to reject because it connects with people's emotional side.

For the Neutral Participants, Fig. 4-A shows that for Ethos the engagement is the lowest (0.5) compared to the other strategies and also with respect to the other final positions. Ethos may make people indifferent and disengaged in taking a position towards PP's point of view. For the Logos strategy the participant's engagement is the highest compared to the other strategies and also to the other final positions and remains increasing from 1.5 at the Introduction phase to 2.50 at the Argumentation phase and reaches 3.0 in the Conclusion. In the simple effect comparison, we also found a significant mean difference of engagement between the Introduction and Argumentation phases (Mean difference = −.685, p = .000) and between Argumentation and Conclusion

(Mean difference = −.441, p = .010) for the Logos strategy. Logos may make people undecided till the end of the debate, and engaged in intuitively evaluating the validity of PP's arguments. Moreover, since they do not have the time to verify analytically the argument they tend to not take a position with respect to PP's point of view. We notice that there are no Neutral participants for the Pathos strategy. This shows that the Pathos strategy makes people decisive about their point of view even by supporting or rejecting the other's arguments because Pathos touches people emotionally and makes them remember their past experiences.

3.3 Hypothesis H3

For the third hypothesis, we studied the tendencies of the participants' workload and engagement with respect to PP's argumentation strategy. We have extracted the engagement and the workload indexes for the 10 s after PP intervention to verify their evolution through the debate phases and get an idea about which strategy elicits more workload and engagement.

To verify this Hypothesis, we have run the repeated measure ANOVA to measure the effect of PP's arguments on the engagement and workload indexes with regards to the participant's final position with respect to participant PP (Neutral, Opponent or Supporter). So for this analysis, the within-subject factor is debate phases (Introduction, Argumentation and Conclusion) and the between-subjects factors are: PP_strategy (Logos, Ethos and Pathos), Measures (Engagement and Workload) and Final_Position (Neutral, Opponent or Supporter).

For the within-subject effect test by applying Greenhouse-Geisser correction, we did not find significant effects. We found a good factors interaction of: Debate_Phase*Measure*PP_strategy with $p = 0.280$ and $F(2.447, 78.294) = 1.300$ (Mauchly's test for sphericity on the dependent variable "debatePhase": sig = .000). By checking Levene's test for homogeneity of variance, we found that variances are homogeneous for the Argumentation ($p = 0.139$, $F(15,64) = 1.483$) and Conclusion phase ($p = 0.061$, $F(15,64) = 1.762$) except for the Introduction ($p = 0.012$, $F(15,64) = 2.274$). The between-subject effects results show that there are significant main effects in the interaction Measure*Final_position*PP_strategy, $F(3,64) = 5.415$, $p = 0.002$.

Looking at Fig. 5, we get an idea about the different persuasion strategies' mean Engagement and Workload throughout the debate phases. In order to better understand what was going on in the debates, we focused on the participants' final position towards participant PP targeted opinion (Fig. 6).

In fact, the Neutral participants (Fig. 6-A) have Workload and Engagement similar to what we have in the Logos strategy (Fig. 5-B) where the Engagement decreases (from 0.9 to 0.8) in the Argumentation, and goes up to 0.87 in the Conclusion. Also the Workload is about 0.6 between Introduction and Argumentation phases and goes up to 0.67 in the Conclusion phase. The Ethos strategy induces more engagement at the Argumentation phase, and during the Conclusion phase the workload increases reflecting the fact that people's memory is overloaded and they cannot handle such amount of information to make decisions. This leads at the end to Neutral state.

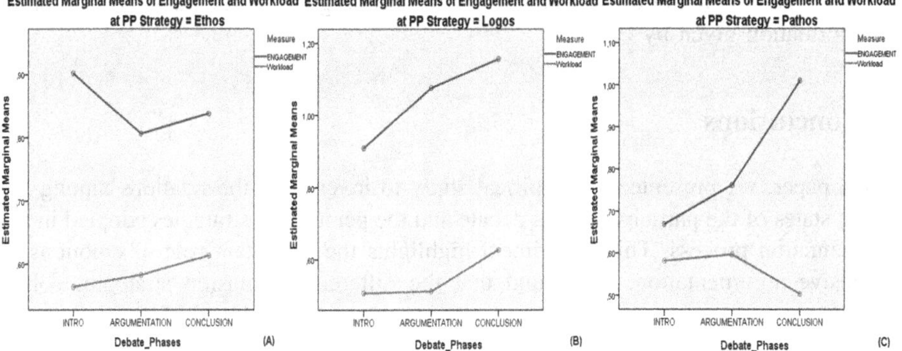

Fig. 5. The Means of engagement and workload by PP strategy through debate phases

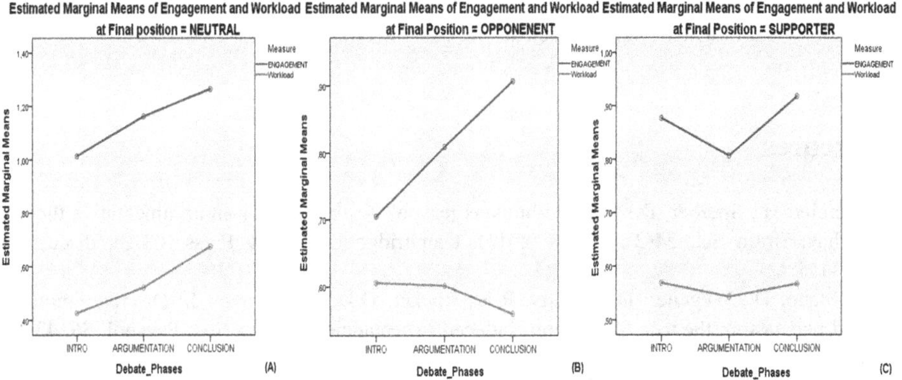

Fig. 6. The means of engagement and Workload by Final Position through debate phases

The workload and engagement of the Opponents (Fig. 6-B) are more similar to what we have in Pathos Strategy (Fig. 5-C) where the engagement increases (from 0.67 to 0.8) in the Argumentation phase and continue to increase till 1.05 in the Conclusion. For the workload in Pathos, it is about 0.6 between Introduction and Argumentation phases and decreases to 0.5 in the Conclusion. So Pathos makes more access to the memory in the Argumentation phase due to the emotional elicitation of the arguments and it decreases in the Conclusion while the engagement increases to take a position with respect to PP's opinion which is more often as Opponent but it can be a supporter too.

Also for the Supporters (Fig. 6-C) their workload and engagement are very similar to what we have in the Ethos strategy (Fig. 5-A) where the engagement decreases (from 0.92 to 0.8) at Argumentation and goes up again to 0.88 at the Conclusion. Furthermore, the workload goes up from 0.55 at the Introduction to 0.59 in the Argumentation phase and increases to 0.62 in the Conclusion. So as PP presents himself as an expert or scientist leading less resistance to his arguments that is manifested as a decrease of the engagement index in the Argumentation phase but the workload index is going up all over the debate meaning that participants are accepting the information given by PP.

4 Conclusions

In this paper, we presented an empirical study to investigate the relations among the mental states of the participants in a debate and the persuasion strategies adopted in the argumentation process. This experiment highlights the important role of emotions in persuasive argumentation. We found that the different persuasion strategies solicit different sides of the brain. Logos arguments involve more workload of the participants while Pathos and Ethos strategies induce more engagement. Finally, Pathos resulted to be the most efficient strategy for convincing the participants to change their opinions.

Acknowledgments. The authors acknowledge the supports from the SEEMPAD associate team project (http://project.inria.fr/seempad/), the FRQNT (Fonds de recherche Québec nature et technologie) and NSERC (National Science and Engineering Research Council).

References

1. Mercier, H., Sperber, D.: Why do humans reason? Arguments for an argumentative theory. Behav. Brain Sci. **34**(2), 57–74 (2011). Cambridge University Press (CUP), discussion 74–111
2. DeSteno, D., Wegener, D.T., Petty, R.E., Rucker, D.D., Braverman, J.: Discrete emotions and persuasion: the role of emotion- induced expectancies. J. Pers. Soc. Psychol. **86**, 43–56 (2004)
3. Cacioppo, J.T., Petty, R.E.: Effects of message repetition and position on cognitive response, recall, and persuasion. J. Pers. Soc. Psychol. **37**(1), 97–109 (1979)
4. Benlamine, S., Chaouachi, M., Villata, S., Cabrio, E., Frasson, C., Gandon, F.: Emotions in argumentation: an empirical evaluation. In: IJCAI 2015, pp. 156–163 (2015)
5. Rahwan, I., Madakkatel, M.I., Bonnefon, J.-F., Naz Awan, R., Abdallah, S.: Behavioral experiments for assessing the abstract argumentation semantics of reinstatement. Cogn. Sci. **34**(8), 1483–1502 (2010)
6. Dalibon, S.E.F., Martinez, D.C., Simari, G.R.: Emotion-directed argument awareness for autonomous agent reasoning. Inteligencia Artificial. Revista Iberoamericana de Inteligencia Artificial **15**(50), 30–45 (2012)
7. Nawwab, F.S., Dunne, P.E., Bench-Capon, T.J.M.: Exploring the role of emotions in rational decision making. In: Computational Models of Argument: Proceedings of COMMA 2010, pp. 367–378 (2010)
8. Lloyd-Kelly, M., Wyner, A.: Arguing about emotion. In: Advances in User Modeling - UMAP 2011 Workshops, pp. 355–367 (2011)
9. Ortony, A., Clore, G., Collins, A.: The Cognitive Structure of Emotions. Cambridge University Press, Cambridge (1988)
10. Dung, P.M.: On the acceptability of arguments and its fundamental role in nonmonotonic reasoning, logic programming and n-person games. Artif. Intell. **77**(2), 321–358 (1995)

11. Cayrol, C., Lagasquie-Schiex, M.-C.: Bipolarity in argumentation graphs: towards a better understanding. Int. J. Approx. Reasoning **54**(7), 876–899 (2013)
12. Berlanga, I., et al.: Ethos, Pathos and Logos in Facebook. User networking: new «Rhetor» of the 21st century/Ethos, pathos y logos en Facebook. El usuario de redes: nuevo «rétor» del siglo XXI. Comunicar **21**(41), 127 (2013)
13. Berka, C., Levendowski, D.J., Ramsey, C.K., Davis, G., Lumicao, M.N., Stanney, K., Stibler, K.: Evaluation of an EEG workload model in an Aegis simulation environment. In: Defense and Security, pp. 90–99. International Society for Optics and Photonics (2005)
14. Chaouachi, M., Chalfoun, P., Jraidi, I., Frasson, C.: Affect and mental engagement: towards adaptability for intelligent systems. In: Paper Presented at the Proceedings of the 23rd International FLAIRS Conference, Daytona Beach (2010). http://citeseerx.ist.psu.edu/viewdoc/download
15. Chaouachi, M., Frasson, C.: Mental workload, engagement and emotions: an exploratory study for intelligent tutoring systems. In: Paper Presented at the Intelligent Tutoring Systems (2012)
16. Chaouachi, M., Jraidi, I., Frasson, C.: MENTOR: a physiologically controlled tutoring system. In: Ricci, F., Bontcheva, K., Conlan, O., Lawless, S. (eds.) UMAP 2015. LNCS, vol. 9146, pp. 56–67. Springer, Cham (2015). doi:10.1007/978-3-319-20267-9_5
17. Pope, A.T., Bogart, E.H., Bartolome, D.S.: Biocybernetic system evaluates indices of operator engagement in automated task. Biol. Psychol. **40**(1), 187–195 (1995)
18. Chaouachi, M., Jraidi, I., Frasson, C.: Modeling mental workload using EEG features for intelligent systems. In: Konstan, J.A., Conejo, R., Marzo, J.L., Oliver, N. (eds.) User Modeling, Adaption and Personalization. LNCS, vol. 6787, pp. 50–61. Springer, Heidelberg (2011)
19. Hart, S.G., Stavenland, L.E.: Development of NASA-TLX (Task Load Index): results of empirical and theoretical research. In: Hancock, P.A., Meshkati, N. (eds.) Human Mental Workload, pp. 139–183. Elsevier (1988). http://ntrs.nasa.gov/archive/nasa/casi.ntrs.nasa.gov/20000004342_1999205624.pdf

Human vs. Computer Performance in Voice-Based Recognition of Interpersonal Stance

Daniel Formolo and Tibor Bosse(✉)

Department of Computer Science, Vrije Universiteit Amsterdam,
De Boelelaan 1081a, 1081 HV Amsterdam, The Netherlands
{d.formolo,t.bosse}@vu.nl

Abstract. This paper presents an algorithm to automatically detect interpersonal stance in vocal signals. The focus is on two stances (referred to as 'Dominant' and 'Empathic') that play a crucial role in aggression de-escalation. To develop the algorithm, first a database was created with more than 1000 samples from 8 speakers from different countries. In addition to creating the algorithm, a detailed analysis of the samples was performed, in an attempt to relate interpersonal stance to emotional state. Finally, by means of an experiment via Mechanical Turk, the performance of the algorithm was compared with the performance of human beings. The resulting algorithm provides a useful basis to develop computer-based support for interpersonal skills training.

Keywords: Emotion recognition · Voice · Interpersonal stance · Experiments

1 Introduction

Conversation is an important way to transmit information between individuals. However, the content of what is said only determines one-third of the information that is communicated. The rest involves prosody, gestures, facial expressions, and others signals [1], which convey much information of speaker`s emotions [2]. In situations where physical presence is not required, prosody is an important source to make the partners aware of the emotional state of the speaker, what is crucial to follow social conventions and to coordinate the interaction [1].

So, for human beings, prosody can be a useful cue to infer information about the socio-emotional state of others. But also for computers, the ability to recognise this in (human) conversation partners is a useful feature, because systems with this ability may reduce user frustration, facilitate more natural communication, resulting in more effective applications [3]. Examples of applications that may benefit from the ability to recognise emotion in the user's behaviour are learning environments for social skills training, therapeutic applications for autistic patients, and entertainment games.

This research described in this paper was triggered by a larger research endeavour that aims to develop a simulation-based training system for professionals that are often confronted with aggressive behavior, with an emphasis on public transport employees [4]. For such a system, being able to recognise socio-emotional cues in the user's voice is very

M. Kurosu (Ed.): HCI 2017, Part I, LNCS 10271, pp. 672–686, 2017.
DOI: 10.1007/978-3-319-58071-5_51

important, as the tone of voice is an important factor in successful aggression de-escalation [5].

Specifically, when it comes to aggression de-escalation, the notion of *interpersonal stance* plays an important role. Interpersonal stance can be seen as the relative position speakers take in relation to the ongoing conversation [6]. To successful de-escalate aggressive behaviour, the stance of the de-escalator should depend on the type of aggression shown by the aggressor. Here, the difference between reactive and proactive aggression is very important: if the interlocutor shows reactive aggression (i.e. aggression caused by frustration of the person's own goals), the best solution is to show an *empathic* response. Instead, if the interlocutor shows proactive aggression (i.e., aggression used as a means to satisfy one's own goals), the best solution is to show a more *dominant* response [5]. Hence, for an effective training tool, it is important if the system is able to distinguish empathic from dominant features in the user's behaviour.

In the current paper, this is realised by developing an algorithm that detects empathy and dominance in vocal signals, based on the OpenSmile toolkit [7]. This was done by creating a database with 1383 samples from 8 speakers from different countries. In addition to creating the recognition algorithm for interpersonal stance, these samples are analysed in more detail, to gain more insight into the nature of empathic and dominant speech (and in particular, in their relation to emotion). Finally, by means of an experiment via Amazon's Mechanical Turk, the performance of the algorithm is compared with the performance of human beings.

The remainder of this article is structured as follows. Section 2 discusses some background information about aggression de-escalation as well as the concepts 'empathy' and 'dominance'. Section 3 describes the algorithm to detect interpersonal stance in vocal signals, as well as an analysis of its performance. Section 4 presents the experiment that was conducted to compare the performance of the algorithm with the performance of human beings. Section 5 presents a conclusion of the research.

2 Background

2.1 Aggression De-escalation

Aggressive behaviour may be caused by a variety of factors. Hence, in order to de-escalate aggression, it is important to recognize the type of aggression that the interlocutor is showing, and subsequently, to show the appropriate communication style (or interpersonal stance) in your own behaviour.

With respect to the type of aggression, two main categories are distinguished in the literature: aggression can be either *reactive* (or *emotional*) or *proactive* (or *instrumental*) [8]. In case of reactive aggression, the aggressive behaviour is typically a response to a negative event that frustrates a person's desires [9]. Such a person is likely to become angry with respect to whatever stopped him or her from achieving his goal. For example, a client may become very aggressive against a desk employee who tells him that their product is sold out, even if this employee cannot do anything about this.

In contrast, proactive aggression refers to aggressive behaviour that is used 'instrumentally', i.e., to achieve a certain goal. Such behaviour is not a direct response to a negative event and is less strongly related to heavy emotions. Instead, it typically is a more planned and calculated type of aggression, often in the form of intimidation. For example, a child may start bullying his classmates because he wants to have power over them.

Based on observations in animals, it has been proposed that reactive aggression is 'hot-blooded', and that proactive aggression is 'cold-blooded'. As a result, the difference between both types of aggression can be recognized (besides looking at the context) by closely observing the non-verbal behaviour of the aggressive individual. The reason for this is that reactive aggression is usually paired with a lot of physiological and behavioural arousal indicating negative affect (such as a flushed face, gestures, and fast speech). Instead, proactive aggression comes with fewer signs of anxiety, but with cues like a dominant posture, slower speech, and sometimes even a smile [8].

Because of the different nature of both types of aggression, it takes a very different approach to deal with each of them. When dealing with an emotional aggressor, supportive behaviour from the de-escalator is required, in order to reduce the aggressor's level of arousal. This can be achieved for instance by ignoring the conflict-seeking behaviour, calmly making contact with the aggressor, actively listening to what he has to say, showing empathy, and suggesting solutions to his problems (see [5]).

Instead, to de-escalate instrumental aggression, showing too much empathy will only make the situation worse, as the aggressor will be reinforced in his belief that his deviant behaviour pays off. In such a case, a directive response is assumed to be more effective. This means that it is necessary to show the aggressor that there is a limit to how far he can pursue his aggressive behaviour and to make him aware of its consequences [10].

A summary of the differences between reactive and proactive aggression is shown in Table 1. Although there is some debate in the literature about whether these two types are really disjoint, in practice, it is often useful to treat them as such because it gives clear guidelines on how to act in confrontations with aggressive individuals[1].

Table 1. Reactive versus proactive aggression.

	Reactive aggression	Proactive aggression
Synonym	Emotional aggression ('hot-blooded')	Instrumental aggression ('cold-blooded')
Underlying mechanism	Behaviour influenced by an emotional state, resulting from the frustration of own goals	Planned, learned behaviour, using intimidation as a means to achieve own goals
How to recognize?	Context, flushed face, gestures, fast speech, …	Context, dominant posture, slower speech, smiling, …
How to de-escalate?	Ignore conflict-seeking behaviour, show empathy, help solve problem	Draw a line, confront aggressor with behaviour, point out consequences

[1] For instance, discussions with domain experts in public transport pointed out that the ability to distinguish between reactive and proactive aggression is a key element in their training program.

2.2 Interpersonal Stance

As mentioned earlier, our long term goal is to develop a simulation-based training system for professionals that are often confronted with aggressive behaviour. Inspired by the literature discussed in the previous section, this system is centred around two main learning goals, namely (1) recognizing the type of aggression of the conversation partner (i.e., reactive or proactive), and (2) selecting the appropriate interpersonal stance towards the conversation partner. Regarding this interpersonal stance, guidelines for how to act are summarized in the last row of Table 1. In the remainder of this paper, we will use the terms *Empathic* and *Dominant* to refer to the appropriate styles to deal with reactive and proactive behaviour, respectively.

We envision a training tool that is able to analyse the behaviour of the trainee, and automatically distinguishes Empathic cues from Dominant cues, in particular with respect to the vocal signals of the trainee's speech. This allows the system to provide feedback on the extent to which the trainee shows the appropriate interpersonal stance to de-escalate a particular aggressive situation. As a first step towards this system, the current paper aims to develop an algorithm that detects Empathy and Dominance in a user's voice. The algorithm will make use of the OpenSmile toolkit [7]. To obtain training data, a number of speakers from different countries will be asked to speak sentences by using either an Empathic or a Dominant interpersonal stance.

To define the concepts of Empathic and Dominant in an unambiguous way, they are related to specific points in circumplex [11]. This theory, also known as Leary's Rose, is often used in training interpersonal skills, and assumes that interpersonal behaviour can be represented as a point in a two-dimensional space determined by the dimensions affiliation (positive versus hostile, or 'together versus opposed') and power (dominant versus submissive, or 'above versus below'); see Fig. 1. Based on discussion with experts in aggression de-escalation training, we define the communicative style called *Empathic* as the border of the categories 'Helping' and 'Cooperative', and the style called *Dominant* as the border of the categories 'Competitive' and 'Leading'.

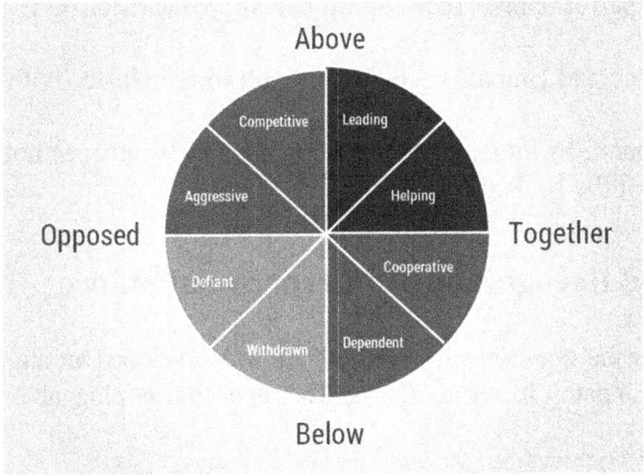

Fig. 1. Leary's Rose.

In addition to developing the recognition algorithm, we aim to gain more insight in the very nature of 'Empathic' and 'Dominant' behaviour, respectively. Even though the distinction seems to be evident based on the explanation above, it may be the case that different individuals interpret these terms rather differently, and show large differences in behaviour when they are asked to produce Empathic and Dominant speech. So, another goal we have is to investigate whether we can identify some common features in people's speech when they are asked to produce Empathic and Dominant behaviour, respectively. To this end, we will relate the Empathic and Dominant samples to the Arousal-Valence circumplex of affect[2] [12], which is an accepted theory in the literature on emotion. This theory views emotions as states that can be represented as points within a continuous space defined by two dimensions, namely valence (i.e., the level of pleasure) and arousal (i.e., a general degree of intensity).

Next, we are interested in the performance of the interpersonal stance recognition algorithm compared to the performance of humans: are computers better in distinguishing Empathic from Dominant behaviour in vocal signals than human beings are? And related to this, is Empathic behaviour more difficult to recognize than Dominant behaviour? To this end, an experiment via Amazon's Mechanical Turk will be set up, in which users are asked to listen to the same samples as used to train the recognition algorithm and classify them as either Empathic or Dominant.

Finally, recognizing the style (the 'how') of an utterance may interfere with processing the content (the 'what') of what is said, which may or may not be consistent with the style. Therefore, an interesting question is whether it makes a difference if people understand what is being said. To this end, we also investigate if people's performance correlates with whether or not the spoken fragments are in a language that they understand.

To summarize, this paper aims to address the following main questions:

1. Can we develop an algorithm that automatically distinguishes Empathy and Dominance in a user's vocal signals?
2. Is it possible to relate the concepts of 'Empathic' and 'Dominant' to specific positions in the Arousal-Valence circumplex?
3. How does the performance of the algorithm compare with the performance of human listeners?
4. Are Dominance and Empathy equally difficult to recognize (both for humans and computers)?
5. Is the performance by human listeners influenced by whether or not they understand the language of the spoken fragments?

3 Automated Recognition of Interpersonal Stance

In order to answer the questions described above, we developed an algorithm to identify Dominance and Empathy in vocal signals. The algorithm is pluggable into a variety of

---

[2] Note that there is an important difference between the interpersonal circumplex and the arousal-valence circumplex: the former is assumed to address interpersonal stance, whereas the latter addresses individual emotions (independent of stance).

human-computer interaction applications, enabling a system to classify the user's voice in real time. In the following sub-sections, the approach to develop the algorithm is explained, as well as its results. In Sect. 4, its performance is compared with that of humans.

3.1 Training and Test Dataset

The data to train and test the algorithm were collected from 8 different people, in 2 different languages. Four of the participants (2 male and 2 female) are native Dutch speakers from The Netherlands, and the other four (2 male and 2 female) are native Portuguese speakers from Brazil. One Dutch male and one Dutch female were professional trainers from the public transport company in Amsterdam, and had expertise in aggression de-escalation. Because the languages Dutch and Portuguese origin from different roots, they have different prosody characteristics, as described in [13]. This was done to prevent the algorithm from overfitting to one single style of prosody, and to check if there are differences between languages in terms of how people produce Dominant and Empathic speech.

For each participant, at least 50 Dominant voice samples and 50 Empathic voice samples were recorded. The first participants recorded 100 samples of each type, and after a preliminary validation, it was noted that the algorithm is able to learn the required patterns with less than 50 samples. Hence, it was decided to record 50 samples for the rest of the participants. All voices were recorded using the same microphone, following the same procedure. Before the start, our interpretation of the terms Empathy and Dominance was explained to all participants (i.e., their positions in Leary's Rose as explained in Sect. 2), and examples of sentences were provided. These sentences addressed situations in public transport in which either an Empathic or Dominant stance could be used (e.g., 'You are not allowed to bring hot coffee in this tram'). All participants started recording the sentences with an Empathic style, after which they recorded the same sentences with a Dominant style.

Table 2 shows an overview of the samples that were recorded. Some people recorded more samples than others and some samples were discarded because they lasted less than 3 s, which makes it difficult to extract features from the voice. This dataset was used to train and test the recognition algorithm, but also in a follow-up experiment to test the performance of human listeners (as explained in Sect. 4).

Table 2. List of vocal samples recorded.

Nationality/Language	Genre	Type	Person 1	Person 2
The Netherlands/Dutch	Male	Empathic	114	100
		Dominant	124	100
	Female	Empathic	96	59
		Dominant	100	59
Brazil/Portuguese	Male	Empathic	111	49
		Dominant	98	50
	Female	Empathic	89	59
		Dominant	101	59

3.2 Recognition Algorithm

The functioning of the recognition algorithm is divided into a training part and a classification part. They run in cycles one after another, starting with the training part. As shown in Fig. 2, the OpenSmile toolkit [7] was used to extract a total of 6552 features from each sample. The extracted features are based on the INTERSPEECH 2010 Paralinguistic Challenge feature set [7]. After that, the non-significant features were removed using the InfoGainAttributeEval algorithm [14]. All features with no information gain were removed, reducing the features to a total of 4959. After that, a Support Vector Machine (SVM) algorithm was trained and a SVM model was generated (through the method described in [15]) to be used for the classification part.

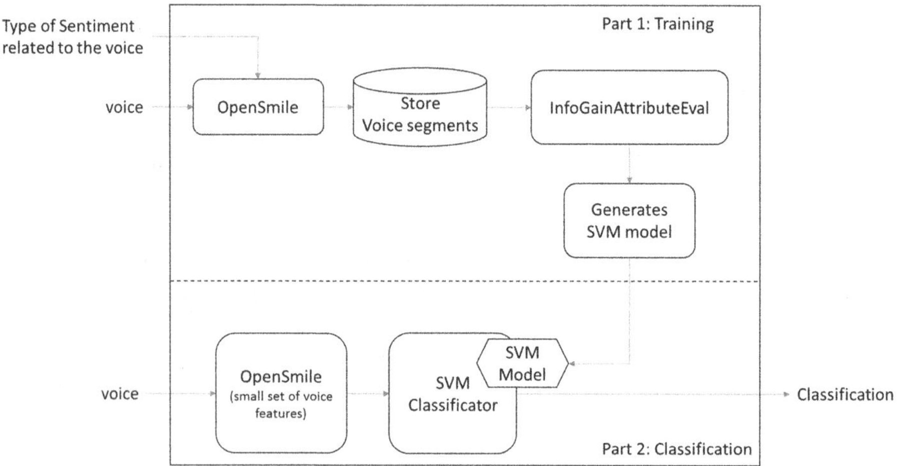

Fig. 2. Block Diagram of the algorithm.

Many algorithms were tested for the task of classifying samples as Empathic or Dominant. Of these algorithms, SVM was selected because it resulted in the best performance. Moreover, it is one of the most frequently used algorithms when it comes to emotion recognition in vocal signals, see for instance [16–18]. The classification part of the algorithm runs for a fixed period of time, classifying and storing the new samples. After that, it returns to training part, in order to train the algorithm again using the old and the new samples and to update the SVM model for a new classification round.

3.3 Performance of the Algorithm

The algorithm was validated with 10-fold cross validation and reached an overall accuracy of 94.58%, with root mean squared error of 0.23. Table 3 shows the results of this evaluation. In addition to the overall accuracy, the accuracy is shown for classifying only the Dominant, Empathic, Dutch, and Portuguese samples. As can be seen, the Empathic samples appeared a bit easier to classify than the Dominant samples. Similarly, the Dutch samples were a bit easier to classify than the Portuguese samples.

Table 3. Computer performance accuracy.

		All samples	Empathic samples	Dominant samples	Dutch samples	Portuguese samples
Algorithm	#samples	1383	823	560	755	628
	Accuracy	94.58%	96.80%	91.60%	96.82%	92.04%

In addition to the above, Table 4 shows a confusion matrix based on the 10-fold cross validation.

Table 4. Confusion Matrix for 10-fold cross validation.

Actual	Predicted		
	Dominant	Empathic	Total
Dominant	**534**	**49**	583
Empathic	**26**	**774**	800
Total	560	823	1383

Finally, the performance of the algorithm was tested by gradually increasing the size of the training set. Figure 3 illustrates how the accuracy increases with a larger number of samples. Notably, there is a substantial increase in accuracy until about 40 samples (reaching 94%), after which the accuracy stabilizes between approximately 96% and 98%.

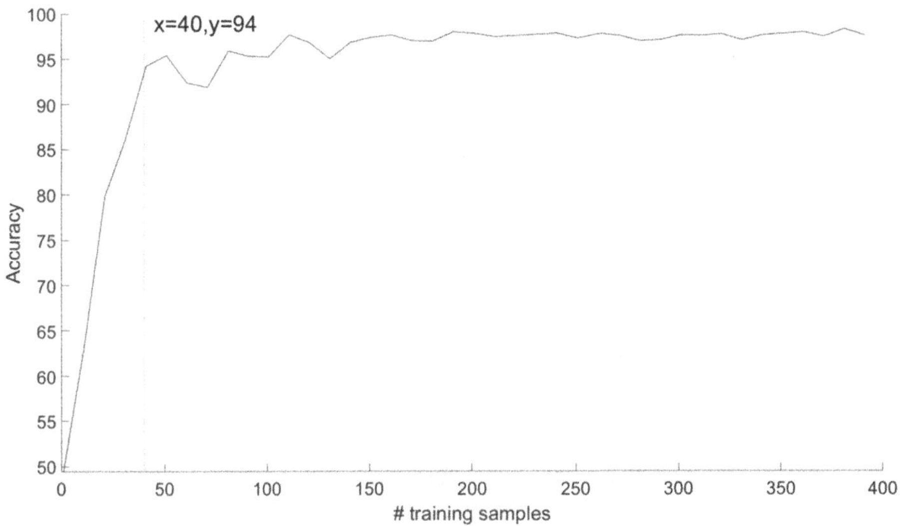

Fig. 3. Performance of the algorithm related to the number of training samples.

Overall, these results are good, which allows us to give an affirmative answer to our ***first research question*** put forward in Sect. 2.

3.4 Relation to the Arousal-Valence Space

To be able to answer our ***second research question***, we changed the SVM model to measure Arousal and Valence. According to many papers [12, 17, 19] it is possible to relate samples of human speech to emotional states, represented as points in the Arousal-Valence space. The question answered in this section is whether there is a pattern when projecting our Empathic and Dominant samples in this A-V space. Figures 4 and 5 show these results for the 8 volunteers that we used to create the dataset. As can be seen, in most cases a clear separation is visible between the Dominant and the Empathic samples, which confirms our finding that it is possible to distinguish between both stances. However, interestingly, the exact pattern differs per individual. For example, the pattern for participant B1 is completely different from the pattern for participant D2. On average, Dominance seems to be correlated with a slightly higher arousal than Empathy, whereas the correlation with Valence seems to depend on the individual.

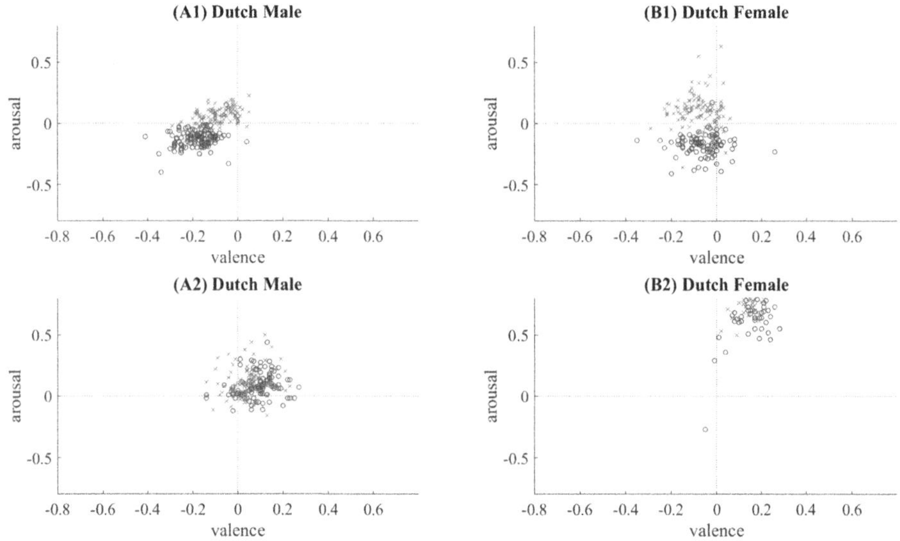

Fig. 4. Arousal and Valence distribution of Dutch samples. Dominant samples are indicated by a cross, whereas Empathic samples are indicated by a circle.

Studying the values of Figs. 4 and 5 in detail, another interesting observation is that the Dutch samples are generally closer to each other, while the Portuguese samples are more spread over the entire spectrum. Possibly, this could be linked to cultural aspects, since all Dutch speakers are from The Netherlands and all Portuguese speakers are from Brazil. Another possible explanation would be that the Portuguese language in itself covers a wider spectrum of prosodic characteristics.

In any case, it is clear from these pictures that there is no direct mapping between the Dominant-Empathic dichotomy and the A-V space. This is interesting, because the algorithm nevertheless showed a good performance in classifying the samples as Dominant or

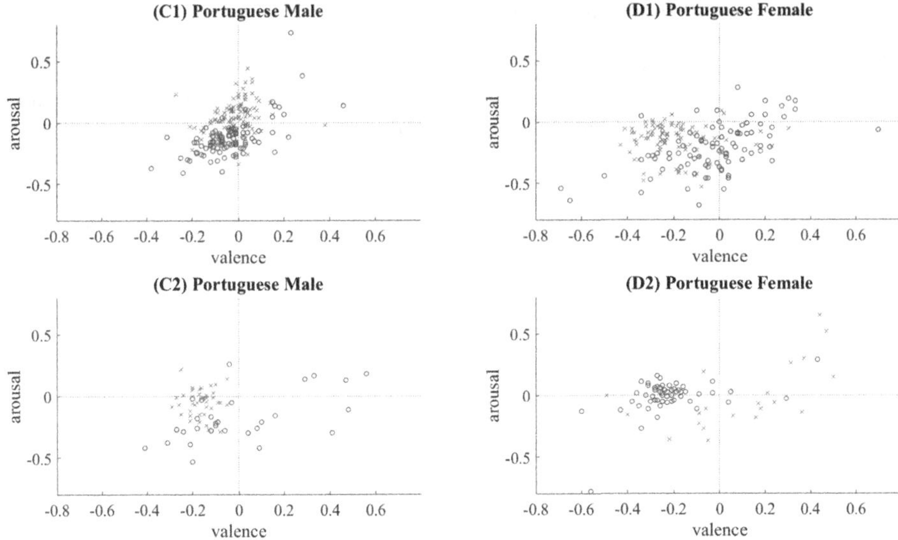

Fig. 5. Arousal and Valence distribution of Portuguese samples. Dominant samples are indicated by a cross, whereas Empathic samples are indicated by a circle.

Empathic, and this algorithm applied the same model to all 8 speakers. So, apparently, it makes use of more low level features that cannot be directly related to the A-V space.

4 Human Recognition of Interpersonal Stance

To be able to compare the performance of the algorithm with the performance of human beings, an experiment via Amazon's Mechanical Turk was set up. The experiment and the results are described in this section.

4.1 Participants and Design

Via Amazon's Mechanical Turk, 88 participants from 3 different countries were recruited: 32 Portuguese speakers that are not able to understand Dutch, 26 Dutch speakers that are not able to understand Portuguese and 30 people from the Philippines that do not understand Portuguese nor Dutch.

Each participant performed the experiment on-line, using the following procedure. They were offered 32 samples which they could hear by clicking a button, and for each of them they were asked to classify them as either Empathic or Dominant. The 32 samples were taken randomly from the database described in Table 2, with the restriction that they included 4 samples from each {language X gender X stance} combination. That is, they were offered 4 samples that were Dutch, Male, and Dominant, and so on.

4.2 Performance of the Human Participants

Table 5 shows the performance of each group, highlighting in bold their overall accuracy. As shown in this table, the overall performance of the human participants is substantially lower than the performance of the algorithm. This provides an answer to our ***third research question*** put forward in Sect. 2.

Table 5. Human performance results in Empathy and Dominance Recognition.

		All samples	Empathic samples	Dominant samples	Dutch samples	Portuguese samples
Dutch Speakers	Accuracy	**69.71%**	73.79%	65.62%	73.31%	66.10%
	Average	18.12	19.18	17.06	19.06	17.18
	σ	3.57	3.00	3.78	2.96	3.87
Port. Speakers	Accuracy	**71.67%**	81.64%	61.71%	76.36%	66.99%
	Average	22.93	26.12	19.75	24.43	21.43
	σ	5.71	3.05	5.96	3.60	6.90
No Dutch and Port. Speakers	Accuracy	**70.52%**	73.95%	67.08%	73.12%	67.91%
	Average	21.15	22.18	20.12	21.93	20.37
	σ	4.28	3.77	4.51	3.78	4.60

Additionally, the differences in performance between the groups seems to be small, which indicates that none of the groups performed significantly better in the classification task. This was confirmed by executing paired t-tests between the groups. Only for classifying the Empathic samples, the Portuguese participants turned out to perform significantly better, with 81.64% accuracy, than the Dutch participants, with 73.97% accuracy ($p < 0.01$) and the participants from the Philippines, with 73.95% accuracy ($p < 0.01$).

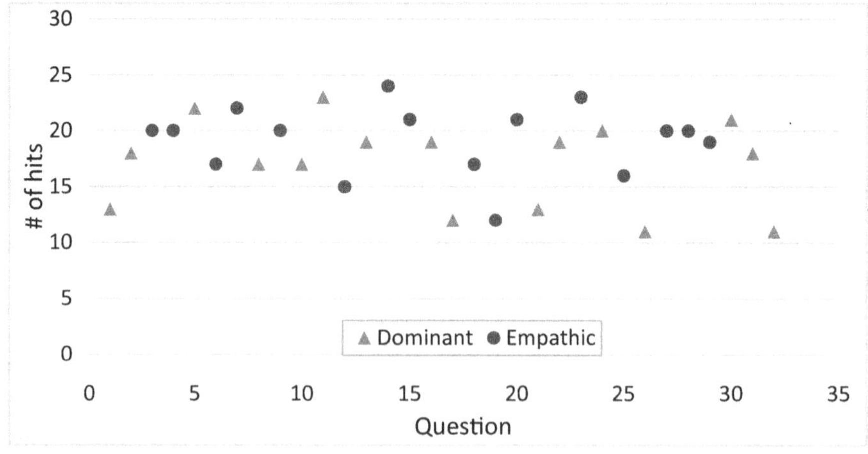

Fig. 6. Number of hits of Dutch participants for each question of the experiment.

We also tested whether the performance of the participants increased over time (i.e., during the experiment). Results about this are shown in Figs. 6, 7 and 8. The question numbers are on the horizontal axis, whereas the number of participants that gave a correct answer is on the vertical axis. These numbers are absolute numbers, which explains why they are highest for the Portuguese group (which was the largest group). The main observation is that in all of these graphs, there are no increasing (or decreasing) trends, what means that the participants did not improve throughout the experiment. This is a fundamental difference with the computer algorithm, which showed a strong improvement in performance until 40 samples and after that remained constant (Fig. 3).

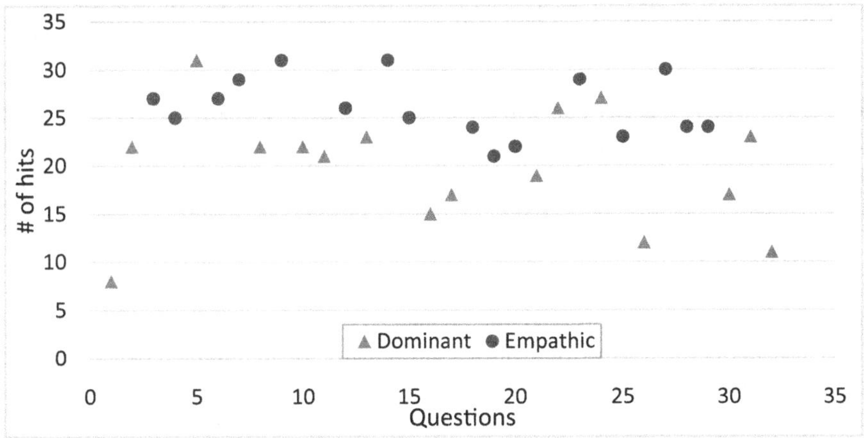

Fig. 7. Number of hits of Portuguese participants for each question of the experiment.

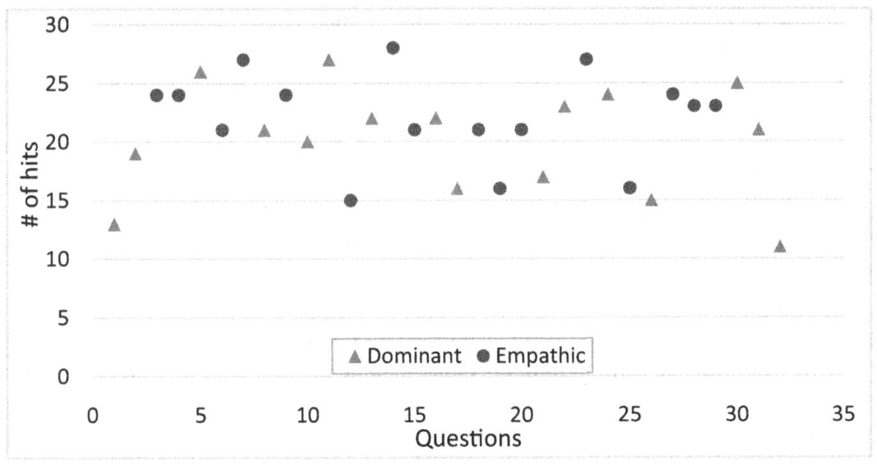

Fig. 8. Number of hits of Philippine participants for each question of the experiment.

More importantly, we tested for the total set of human participants whether they found Dominance and Empathy equally difficult to recognize. As shown in Table 5, it turned out that the Empathic samples (76.46%) were recognized more easily than the Dominant samples (64.80%). An unpaired t-test confirmed that this difference was significant ($p < 0.001$). This result is similar to the results for the automated algorithm, which also had a bit more difficulty with recognizing the Dominant samples. This gives answers to our ***fourth research question***.

Finally, our ***fifth research question*** was whether the performance of human listeners is influenced by whether or not they understand the language of the spoken fragments. To investigate this, we compared the average performance over all samples classified by a listener that understood the language (i.e., all Dutch samples classified by Dutch participants plus all Portuguese samples classified by Brazilian participants) with the average performance over all other samples. And unpaired t-test confirmed that the difference between these two performances was not significant ($p = 0.50$). Hence, in our experiment, being able to understand *what* was said did not help (or hinder) participants in recognizing *how* it was said.

5 Conclusion

This paper presented an algorithm to automatically detect interpersonal stance in vocal signals, especially related to Dominance and Empathy. In addition, an experiment was performed in which we investigated how well human beings performed in the same task. Five research questions were addressed, which yielded the following results.

First, the results of the algorithm points out good perspectives related to the capacity of computers to identify Dominance and Empathy. The average accuracy is 94.58%. Considering the results and the fact that the classification is real-time, it seems promising to apply the algorithm in serious games or other human-computer interaction applications in order to enrich the user's experience. In particular, in follow-up research we aim to use the algorithm for an aggression de-escalation training system for public transport employees.

Second, it was explored whether the concepts of Empathic and Dominant could be related to specific positions in the Arousal-Valence circumplex. In our experiments, we observed that Dominance and Empathy are generally well distinguishable when mapped into this space. However, the way in which both stances are distinguished seems to differ per individual.

Third, it was found that the algorithm substantially outperformed human listeners, which on average reached a performance of 70.64% in the recognition task. The relatively low performance of human beings may also be explained by the fact that in real life, humans use much more than only vocal signals to classify emotions. For instance, they typically combine facial expression, speech content, background knowledge about culture, context situation, and so on. On the other hand, as suggested in [20], computers can also make use of such information to improve their performance.

Fourth, both for human and computer, there turned out to be a slight difference in the capability to recognize Dominance and Empathy. The algorithm performs 5.2%

better in classifying Empathy (96.8%) than Dominance (91.6%). The same trend was found for the 3 groups of participants, where the Empathic samples (76.46%) were recognized more easily than the Dominant samples (64.80%).

Finally, we found that the performance of the human participants was not influenced by whether or not the listener understands the language of the spoken fragments. Hence, being able to understand *what* was said did not help (or hinder) participants in recognizing *how* it was said.

The outcome of this research is two-fold: on the one hand, it resulted in an algorithm that can be useful for the development of human-computer interaction applications (in particular in the domain of aggression de-escalation training). On the other hand, it sheds more light on how human beings recognize interpersonal stance based on vocal signals, and how they differ in this task from computer algorithms.

Acknowledgments. This research was supported by the Brazilian scholarship program Science without Borders - CNPq {scholarship reference: 233883/2014-2}.

References

1. Hogan, K., Stubbs, R.: Can't Get Through: 8 Barriers to Communication. Pelican Publishing Company, Gretna (2003)
2. Patterson, A.E., Berg, M.: Exploring nonverbal communication through service learning. J. Civic Commitment, **21** (2014)
3. Picard, RW.: Affective computing for HCI. In: Proceedings of HCI 1999, Munich, Germany (1999)
4. Bosse, T., Gerritsen, C., de Man, J.: An intelligent system for aggression de-escalation training. In: Proceedings of the 22nd European Conference on Artificial Intelligence, ECAI 2016. IOS Press (2016)
5. Anderson, L.N., Clarke, J.T.: De-escalating verbal aggression in primary care settings. Nurse Pract. **21**(10), 95, 98, 101, 102 (1996)
6. Du Bois, J.W.: The stance triangle. In: Englebretson, R. (ed.) Stancetaking in Discourse: Subjectivity, Evaluation, Interaction, pp. 139–182. John Benjamins Publishing Company (2007)
7. Eyben, F., Weninger, F., Gross, F., Schuller, B.: Recent developments in openSMILE, the Munich open-source multimedia feature extractor. In: Proceedings of ACM Multimedia (MM), Barcelona, Spain, pp. 835-838. ACM, October 2013. ISBN 978-1-4503-2404-5, doi: 10.1145/2502081.2502224
8. Dodge, K.A.: The structure and function of reactive and proactive aggression. In: Pepler, D., Rubin, H. (eds.) The development and treatment of childhood aggression, pp. 201–218. Erlbaum, Hillsdale (1990)
9. Berkowitz, L.: Whatever happened to the frustration-aggression hypothesis? Am. Behav. Sci. **21**, 691–708 (1978)
10. Bosse, T., Provoost, S.: Towards aggression de-escalation training with virtual agents: a computational model. In: Zaphiris, P., Ioannou, A. (eds.) LCT 2014. LNCS, vol. 8524, pp. 375–387. Springer, Cham (2014). doi:10.1007/978-3-319-07485-6_37
11. Leary, T.: Interpersonal Diagnosis of Personality: Functional Theory and Methodology for Personality Evaluation. Ronald Press, New York (1957)
12. Russel, J.A.: A circumplex model of affect. J. Pers. Soc. Psychol. **39**, 1161–1178 (1980)

13. Hirst, D., Di Cristi, A.: A survey of intonation systems. In: Hirst, D., Di Cristo, A. (eds.) Intonation Systems: A Survey of Twenty Languages, pp. 1–44. Cambridge University Press, Cambridge (1998)
14. Mark Hall, M., Frank, E., Holmes, G., Pfahringer, B., Reutemann, P., Witten, I.H.: The WEKA data mining software: an update. SIGKDD Explor. **11**(1), 10–18 (2009)
15. Hsu, C., Chang, C., Lin, C.: A practical guide to support vector classification (2010)
16. Rybka, J., Janicki, A.: Comparison of speaker dependent and speaker independent emotion recognition. Int. J. Appl. Math. Comput. Sci. **23**(4), 797–808 (2013). doi:10.2478/amcs-2013-0060
17. ElAyadi, M., Kamel, M.S., Karray, F.: Survey on speech emotion recognition: features, classification schemes, and databases. Pattern Recogn. J. **44**, 572–587 (2011). doi:10.1016/j.patcog.2010.09.020
18. Lin, C., Liao, W., Hsieh, W., Liao, W., Wang, J.: Emotion identification using extremely low frequency components of speech feature contours. Sci. World J. **2014** (2014). Article id. 757121, Hindawi Publishing Corporation. doi:10.1155/2014/757121
19. Yik, M., Russel, J., Steiger, J.: A 12-point circumplex structure of core affect. Emotion **11**(4), 705–731 (2011)
20. Formolo, D., Bosse, T.: Human vs. Computer performance in voice-based emotion recognition. In: Proceedings of the 19th International Conference on Human-Computer Interaction, HCI 2017. LNCS, pp 285–291. Springer, Heidelberg (2017)

A Proposal of Model of Kawaii Feelings for Spoon Designs

Tipporn Laohakangvalvit[1(✉)], Tiranee Achalakul[2], and Michiko Ohkura[3]

[1] Graduate School of Engineering and Science, Shibaura Institute of Technology, Tokyo, Japan
nb15505@shibaura-it.ac.jp

[2] Department of Computer Engineering, King Mongkut's University of Technology Thonburi, Bangkok, Thailand
tiranee.ach@mail.kmutt.ac.th

[3] College of Engineering, Shibaura Institute of Technology, Tokyo, Japan
ohkura@sic.shibaura-it.ac.jp

Abstract. Affective values are important factors in manufacturing. Kawaii, which is a positive adjective that denotes such positive connotations as cute, lovable, and charming, becomes even more important as an affective value. It plays an important role in the success of many products, such as Hello Kitty and Pokemon. Based on this success, we believe that kawaii will be a key factor for future product design. In our previous study, we performed a comparison of 39 spoon designs based on kawaiiness for Japanese and Thai. As a result, we clarify the similarities and differences of kawaii preferences between Thai and Japanese. From this result, we suggested the design ideas of kawaii spoons to spoon manufacturers. However, the results might not be applicable to evaluate kawaii spoon designs in general. In this study, we proposed models of kawaii feelings for spoon designs which can be used to evaluate the kawaiiness of spoon designs in general. We also clarified useful attributes for kawaii spoon designs. The results suggested the list of attributes to be considered in the design of kawaii spoons.

Keywords: Kansei engineering · Affective value · Kawaii · Spoon designs

1 Introduction

For more than twenty years, affective engineering, which is a consumer-oriented methodology for product development, has been recognized as an important part in a broad range of manufacturing fields. When added to industrial products, affective values can increase economic worth. Based on their benefits, in 2007 the Japanese Ministry of Economy, Trade and Industry (METI) proposed affective values as a new value axis, becoming the fourth most critical characteristic of industrial products after function, credibility, and cost [1]. Examples of affective values that have been widely applied to products include enjoyment, coolness, and user friendliness. Kawaii is also considered an affective value that has such positive connotations as cute, lovable, and

M. Kurosu (Ed.): HCI 2017, Part I, LNCS 10271, pp. 687–699, 2017.
DOI: 10.1007/978-3-319-58071-5_52

charming. It plays an important role in the worldwide success of many products, such as Hello Kitty [2] and Pokemon [3]. Based on this success, we believe that kawaii will be a key factor in future product design.

In our previous study, we experimentally observed kawaii feelings toward spoon designs [4]. We employed 39 kawaii spoon designs and compared them based on their kawaiiness by Japanese and Thai participants. The experimental results clarified the similarities and the differences of kawaii preferences for spoon designs between genders and nationalities. Based on the results, we suggested the design ideas of kawaii spoons to spoon manufacturers for Japanese and Thai consumers. However, the suggestion has limitation to apply because it only showed the examples of spoon designs but could not extend to further detailed analysis such as the suggestion for attributes for kawaii spoon designs. Therefore, the results might not be applicable to evaluate kawaii spoon designs in general.

In this study, we proposed models of kawaii feelings for spoon designs which can be used to suggest the design of kawaii spoons in general. This study has two goals: (1) to clarify useful attributes for kawaii spoon designs, and (2) to propose the model of kawaii feelings for spoon designs. We employed the comparison results of 39 spoon designs and their scores by both Japanese and Thai participants obtained from our previous study. A set of spoon attributes were extracted from these spoon designs. Then we employed machine learning algorithm to construct models. As a result, we proposed the models of kawaii feelings and clarified useful attributes for kawaii spoon designs for males and females.

2 Literature Survey

2.1 Affective Engineering and Kawaii Researches

Affective engineering is defined as "technology that translates a consumer's feeling and image for a product into physical design elements" [5]. By making products to which affective values are added, products can provide greater emotional fulfillment and make a larger impact on first impressions, which is a key to motivate consumer purchases. In our research, we focus on kawaii feelings as affective values. Based on the success of many products that have kawaii as a key factor, we believe that kawaii will be important affective value for future product design.

In our previous research [6], we studied various aspects of kawaii feelings. It explored the idea of designing kawaii products by examining kawaii attributes for shape, color, size, texture, and tactile sensation. However, this research only explored the relationship between kawaii feelings and the attribute one by one. The relationship between kawaii feelings and the combination of attributes has not been explored yet. Therefore, we proposed to study the relationship between them by constructing the model of kawaii feelings.

2.2 Feature Extraction Techniques

Feature extraction is a method to create features or attributes that make the machine learning algorithm work. In this study, we used the spoon designs which were represented as images. Therefore, we needed to use some techniques to extract the attributes from these images in order to learn about the important attributes for kawaii feelings by machine learning algorithm.

In researches related to affective engineering, various of them used shape and color as a basis to deal with the extraction of useful information from the images [7, 8]. Therefore, we considered that shape and color were the key components that can be used to extract the attributes from our images of spoon designs.

There are various techniques for feature extraction. Traditional method extracts the attributes manually which often require expensive human labor because it needs to an observation by human. However, if the problem is not complicated, this method is better for reducing learning time and cost. The other method makes use of the image processing techniques to transform the images into attributes represented in numerical forms. Since color is one of the most important information of images and has been successfully used in various applications [9], we employed some color spaces, such as RGB and HSV, to extract the attributes from our images of spoon designs.

2.3 Machine Learning Techniques

Machine learning algorithms are widely used in many applications to learn and make predictions on data. In this research, we used supervised learning to perform classification in which the computer is presented with inputs and desired outputs, and the goal is to learn a general rule that maps inputs to outputs.

There are various approaches for machine learning algorithms for classification, for example, an artificial neural network (ANN), support vector machine (SVM), Bayesion netowrks, decision tree, etc. In this section, we discussed only SVM algorithms as they have been successfully used in many researches related to image-based classification [10, 11].

SVM classifier is effective in high dimentional feature spaces, especially when the training dataset is small [12]. It can efficiently perform linear or non-linear classification using the different kernels, for example, linear, polynomial, radial basis function (RBF), and sigmoid kernels. Usually, linear and RBF kernels are commonly used as they yield good results. A research [13] showed that the linear kernel is a degenerated version of RBF kernel. Therefore, in many cases, the RBF kernel is chosen.

3 Experiment of Comparison of Spoon Designs Based on Kawaiiness

3.1 Method

This experiment was performed in our previous study to observe kawaii feelings toward spoon designs [4]. We employed the spoon designs from 182 designs by drawn by female students at Tokyo Woman's Christian University (Fig. 1). The 39 spoon designs were selected based on the majority of shape on the designs. They were divided into three groups: the flower group (13 designs), the heart group (13 designs), and the smiley group (13 designs).

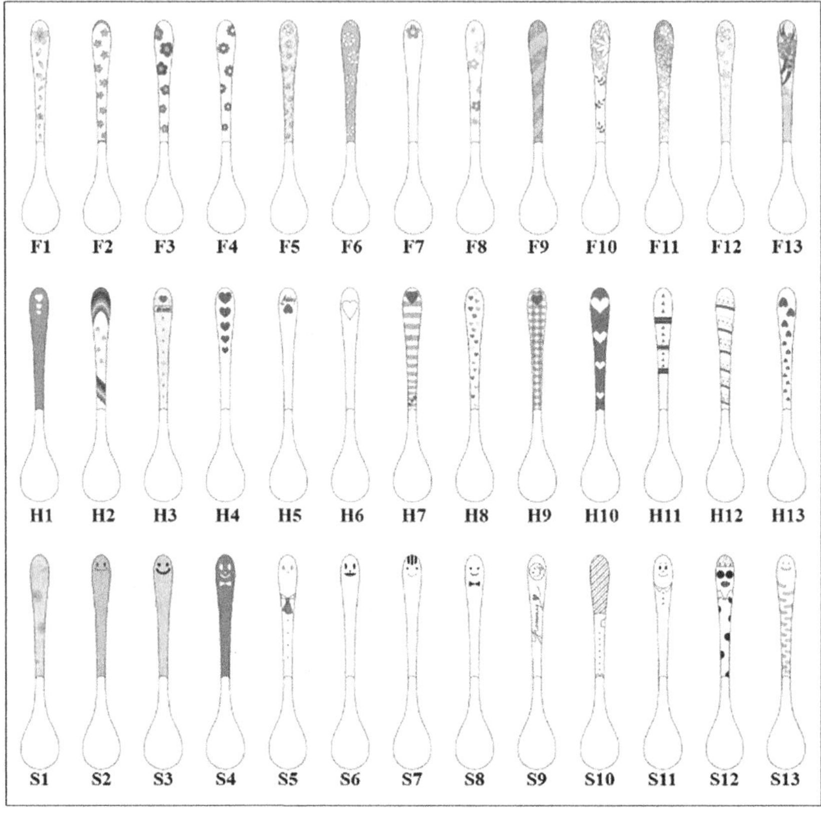

Fig. 1. 39 Spoon designs used for experiment. Numbers below each spoon design denote its ID.

We used a spoon comparison system to collect the comparison results of spoon designs from the participants. The comparison method used in the system was a quicksort algorithm. The spoon designs were displayed in pairs on a PC monitor (Fig. 2). The participants compared the spoon designs and used keyboard's arrow keys to select more kawaii spoon designs (left or right) or equally kawaii.

3.2 Results and Discussion

We recruited 40 participants, who were university students in their 20's, including ten Thai males, ten Thai females, ten Japanese males, and ten Japanese females. From the comparison results of each participant, we sorted all 39 spoon designs and ranked them.

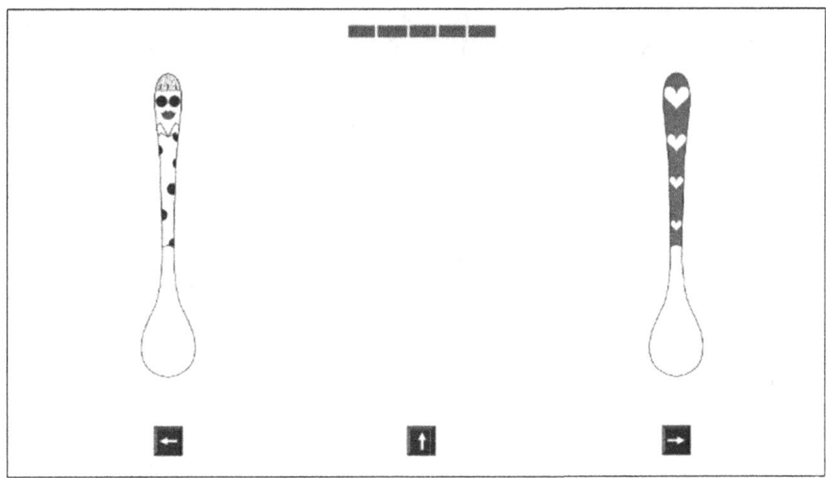

Fig. 2. Screenshot of spoon comparison system displaying two spoon designs

From the rankings, we calculated the scores of all the spoon designs. The score of the 1st rank was 39. If the rank was worse, the score was lowered. We used the scores to analyze the comparisons of the spoon designs. The analyzed results, which were described in a paper [4], are summarized as follows:

- The spoon designs in the heart group were considered as the lowest among the three groups, indicating that they had the least preference for kawaii spoon designs among all of the participants. However, males tended to prefer flower designs, and females tended to prefer smiley designs.
- The correlation between Thai males and Japanese males was the highest indicating that they had similar preferences for kawaii spoon designs. The correlation between Japanese males and females was very low, indicating that they have very different preference tendencies for kawaii spoon designs.
- The results of top and bottom three spoon designs showed the most and least preferences of kawaii spoon designs. In general, the top-three kawaii spoon designs were S4, S5, and F12. The bottom spoon designs were H1, H5 and H12. This result can be suggested to the spoon manufacturers to produce kawaii spoon designs or avoid producing non-kawaii spoon designs.

4 Construction of Model of Kawaii Feelings for Spoon Designs

From the results of the above experiment, we proposed the design ideas of kawaii spoons to spoon manufacturers. However, the suggestion has limitation to apply because it only showed the examples of spoon designs but could not extend to further detailed analysis such as the suggestion for attributes for kawaii spoon designs.

Therefore, the results might not be applicable to evaluate kawaii spoon designs in general. Therefore, we further used the results of previous experiment to construct models of kawaii feelings for spoon designs that can suggest kawaii spoon designs in general. The model construction consists of two processes as follows:

4.1 Feature Extraction

Before constructing the model, we needed to perform feature extraction to create the attributes of spoon designs. This process transformed the input from raw data (i.e. images of spoon designs) into the numerical forms which were necessary as input for constructing the model by machine learning algorithms. We employed two approaches to derive the attributes as described below.

Manual Approach. This method manually observed the appearance of spoon designs. By observing various types of appearance, we obtained 10 attributes based on shape and color. List of these attributes and their categories were shown in Table 1.

Table 1. List of attributes using feature extraction based on manual approach

Attribute	Category
Shape-based attributes	
Shape	Flower/Heart/Smiley
Shape is repeated?	Yes/No
Number of shapes	(Integer)
Shape other than those in Attribute 1 exist?	Yes/No
Background pattern	None/Plain color/Patterned
Color-based attributes	
Shape has color?	Yes/No
Shape has color gradient?	Yes/No
Background has color?	Yes/No
Background has color gradient?	Yes/No
Total number of colors	(Integer)

Image Processing Approach. Applying only the attributes from manual approach might not be efficient. Thus we also employed image processing approach to extract the attributes related to both shape and color from the pixels in the images of spoon designs. For shape-based attributes, we computed the ratio of area that contained such objects of interest as shape, background, etc. For color-based attributes, we employed two color spaces, which were RGB (Red, Green, Blue) and HSV (Hue, Saturation, Value/Brightness), to obtain the average values in the areas of interest. The average values were computed from the values of all pixels in the image. There were three areas of interest: shape, background, and total area in the image.

For example, the spoon shown in Fig. 3(a) has smiley shapes. To obtain the values in shape area, we considered only the areas highlighted in black color shown in Fig. 3(b). Similarly, for background area, we considered the highlighted area shown in Fig. 3(c). The total area was the combination of shape and background areas.

From this approach, we obtained 23 attributes as shown in Table 2.

Table 2. List of attributes using feature extraction based on image processing approach

Attribute	Category
Shape-based attributes	
Ratio of shape area to total area	(Integer, Range = 0 ~ 100)
Ratio of background area to total area	(Integer, Range = 0 ~ 100)
Ratio of colored area to total area (※White color was disregarded.)	(Integer, Range = 0 ~ 100)
Ratio of shape area to colored area	(Integer, Range = 0 ~ 1)
Ratio of background area to colored area	(Integer, Range = 0 ~ 1)
Color-based attributes	
Average R in total area	(Integer, Range = 0 ~ 255)
Average G in total area	(Integer, Range = 0 ~ 255)
Average B in total area	(Integer, Range = 0 ~ 255)
Average H in total area	(Integer, Range = 0 ~ 360)
Average S in total area	(Integer, Range = 0 ~ 100)
Average V in total area	(Integer, Range = 0 ~ 100)
Average R in shape area	(Integer, Range = 0 ~ 255)
Average G in shape area	(Integer, Range = 0 ~ 255)
Average B in shape area	(Integer, Range = 0 ~ 255)
Average H in shape area	(Integer, Range = 0 ~ 360)
Average S in shape area	(Integer, Range = 0 ~ 100)
Average V in shape area	(Integer, Range = 0 ~ 100)
Average R in background area	(Integer, Range = 0 ~ 255)
Average G in background area	(Integer, Range = 0 ~ 255)
Average B in background area	(Integer, Range = 0 ~ 255)
Average H in background area	(Integer, Range = 0 ~ 360)
Average S in background area	(Integer, Range = 0 ~ 100)
Average V in background area	(Integer, Range = 0 ~ 100)

From both approaches, we obtained the total of 33 attributes of spoon designs. The attributes with values as integers could be used directly for the next process. However, the attributes in categorical values needed to be encoded into numerical format, for example, "shape" attribute contained the values 1, 2, and 3 that denoted flower, heart, and smiley respectively.

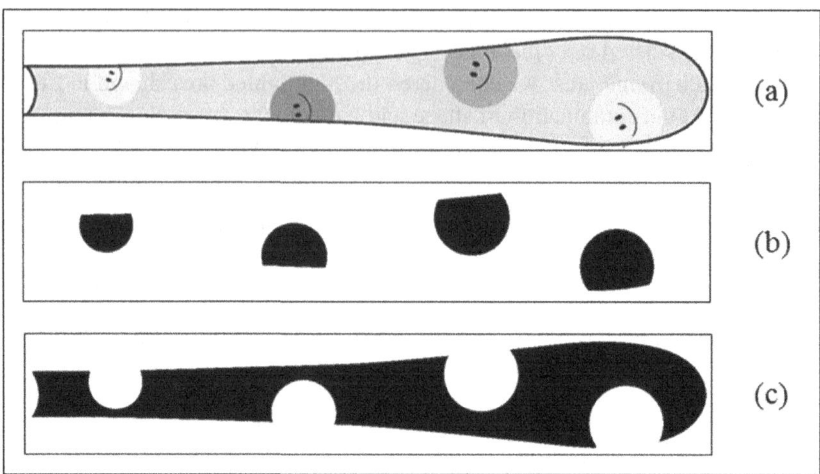

Fig. 3. (a) Original spoon design (b) Highlighted spoon design for shape area (c) Highlighted spoon design for background area

4.2 Model Construction

This process performed model construction by using machine learning. It consisted of two parts: data preparation part and classification. The details are described in the following sections.

Data preparation. First, we prepared the data for the input and the target for model construction. For the input, we used 33 attributes of spoon designs obtained from the previous process. For the output, we employed the scores obtained from the comparison of previous experiment explained in Sect. 3.

As we aimed at performing classification task instead of regression task, the scores as integers were transformed into groups using the process shown in Fig. 4. It was performed to identify top and last 13 spoon designs. Top 13 spoon designs were grouped as high-score group. Last 13 designs were grouped as low-score group. Other 13 spoon

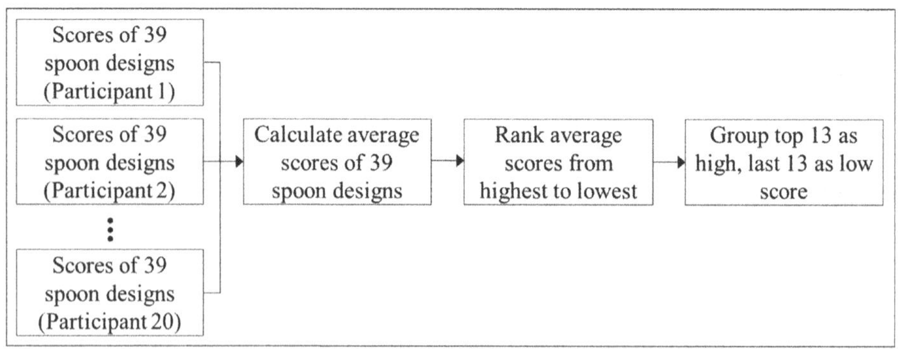

Fig. 4. Process to group the scores of spoon designs into high and low score groups

designs with moderate scores were omitted from the analysis. This method was repeatedly performed to group the spoon designs for all participants, male participants, and female participants, by using their average scores. Finally, we obtained three sets of 26 spoon designs divided into high- and low-score groups for these groups of participants.

Classification. We used SVM (RBF) to perform classification as it has been successfully used in many researches related to image-based classification. It learned the input of 26 spoon designs (each of them contained 33 attributes) to predict the output as high- or low-score group as shown in Fig. 5.

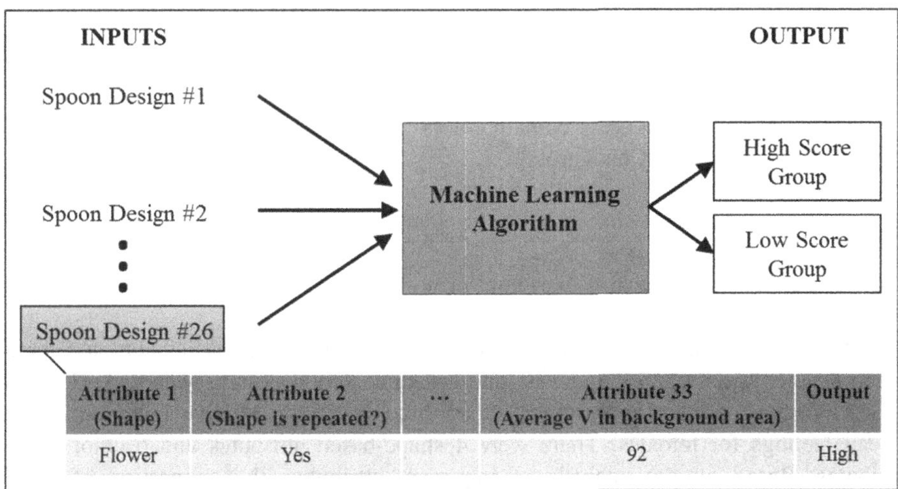

Fig. 5. Structure of classification in training phase using machine learning algorithm

5 Results

5.1 Classification Results

Based on the classification results, we computed the classification accuracy of all, male and female participants (Table 3). The data was splited into 70% training and 30% testing samples. We considered the results between all participants and male/female participants. It showed that dividing the data by genders before constructing the model yielded better accuracy than using the data of all participants.

Table 3. Classification accuracy based on SVM (RBF) algorithm

All participants	Male	Female
100.00%	100.00%	100.00%

5.2 Results of Importance of Attributes

We considered the relative importance of attributes from classification result. The relative importance indicated the attributes that mattered most to the model construction.

Male group. From the ranking of average scores of male participants, top three spoon designs were F9, F12, and F8, and last three spoon designs were S12, H12, and H7. Table 4 shows ten most important attributes and their relative importances for kawaii feelings for males. There were 3 shape-based attributes and 7 color-based attributes. Based on the analysis of important attributes, the suggestion of some characteristics of kawaii and non-kawaii spoon designs for males are as follows:

- Kawaii designs:
  - Designs with flower and smiley shapes with repetition and bright color
  - Most of the design areas contain colors
  - Reddish and bright background
- Non-kawaii designs:
  - Designs with heart shapes in bright color
  - Non-colorful designs
  - Dark and non-reddish background or no background

Female group. From the ranking of average scores of female participants, top three spoon designs were S5, S8, and S10, and last three spoon designs were H4, H3, and F13. Table 5 shows ten most important attributes and their relative importances for kawaii feelings for females. There were 4 shape-based attributes and 6 color-based attributes. Based on the analysis of important attributes, the suggestion of some characteristics of kawaii and non-kawaii spoon designs for females are as follows:

- Kawaii designs:
  - Designs with flower and smiley shapes in small size and light color
  - Non-colorful overall designs
- Non-kawaii designs:
  - Designs with heart shapes in reddish, bright, and no color gradient

Table 4. Ten most important attributes based on the relative importance for male group

Attribute	Relative importance
Average V in shape area	0.0941970
Total number of colors	0.0449730
Shape	0.0432379
Ratio of colored area to total area	0.0354155
Ratio of background area to total area	0.0343211
Shape is repeated?	0.0324299
Background pattern	0.0311283
Average R in background area	0.0309987
Average V in background area	0.0303977
Background has color?	0.0300543

Table 5. Ten most important attributes based on the relative importance for female group

Attribute	Relative importance
Shape	0.0691969
Background has color gradient?	0.0461997
Total number of colors	0.0458560
Ratio of shape area to total area	0.0408475
Average R in shape area	0.0382922
Ratio of shape area to colored area	0.0366352
Ratio of background area to colored area	0.0366352
Average S in shape area	0.0347751
Average V in shape area	0.0346304
Shape has color gradient?	0.0305687

6 Discussion

We compared the classification results between all participants and male and female participants. Using the input divided into male and female participants yielded higher accuracies which showed that male and female participants had different preferences for kawaii spoon designs. Therefore, we suggest that the data should be divided by gender and treated separately in order to obtain good results for the study on kawaii feelings.

From the results of the importance of attributes, we clarified important attributes to construct models of kawaii feelings for spoon designs. From the comparison of ten most important attributes between male and female groups, there were three attributes in common: shape, total number of colors, and average V in shape area. These three attributes were important to kawaii feelings for spoon designs for both genders.

From the construction of models for both male and female groups, we obtained the attributes that had high importance to the kawaii feelings. The results can be used to suggest spoon manufacturers about the attributes that should be taken into account to design kawaii spoons. Considering shape attribute, it was divided into flower, heart, and smiley group based on the majority of designs by female students in previous research. Therefore, the spoon designs with these three shapes have highest possibility to be kawaii spoons.

7 Conclusion and Future Work

In this study, we extended our analysis from our previous study that collected the results of comparison of spoon designs based on kawaiiness. This study aims to propose models of kawaii feelings for spoon designs. The results as the scores of the spoon designs from previous study were used as the target of models in this study. We extracted 33 attributes of spoon designs based on shape and color. The scores and 33 attributes were used to construct the models. We SVM algorithm to classify the data of spoon designs. As a result, we succeeded to construct the models.

Since the performance of classification using the data divided by genders was better than the data of all participants, we proposed the models for male and female groups separately. This indicates the differences in preference for kawaii spoon designs between genders.

Moreover, we clarified the importance of attributes in designing kawaii spoons. By using the list of important attributes and their corresponding relative importance, we can suggest the design idea of kawaii spoons to the spoon manufacturers. If the suggested attributes were adjusted, the spoons are likely to be more kawaii. Spoons with more kawaiiness are more likely to be preferred by customers, which will obviously motivate purchasing habits.

In this research, we began to construct the models of kawaii feelings. Even though we successfully constructed the models for spoon designs, the robustness of the models has not been confirmed yet. For future work, we will confirm it by employing various model structure, for example, ratio of training/testing data, kernel functions, etc.

Acknowledgements. Part of this work was supported by Grant-in-Aid Scientific Research Number 26280104. We thank the students of the Tokyo Woman's Christian University, King Mongkut's University of Technology Thonburi, and the Shibaura Institute of Technology for their participation.

References

1. Ministry of Economy, Trade and Industry; KANSEI Initiative: Suggestion of the fourth value axis (2007). http://www.meti.go.jp/english/information/downloadfiles/PressRelease/080620KANSEI.pdf
2. Kovarovic, S.: Hello kitty: a brand made of cuteness. J. Cult. Retail Image **4**(1), 1–8 (2011)
3. Allison, A.: Portable monsters and commodity cuteness: pokemon as Japan's new global power. Postcolonial Stud. **6**(3), 381–395 (2003)
4. Laohakangvalvit, T., Ohkura, M.: Comparison of spoon designs based on kawaiiness between genders and nationalities. In: International Symposium on Affective Science and Engineering, Tokyo (in press, 2017)
5. Nagamachi, M.: Kansei engineering: a new ergonomic consumer-oriented technology for product development. Int. J. Ind. Ergon. **15**(1), 3–11 (1995)
6. Ohkura, M., Komatsu, T., Aoto, T.: Kawaii rules: increasing affective value of industrial products. In: Watada, J., Shiizuka, H., Lee, K.-P., Otani, T., Lim, C.-P. (eds.) Industrial Applications of Affective Engineering, pp. 97–110. Springer, Cham (2014). doi:10.1007/978-3-319-04798-0_8
7. Chen, Y., Sobue, S., Huang, X.: KANSEI based clothing fabric image retrieval. In: Second International Workshop on Computational Color Imaging, Suzhou, pp. 71–80 (2009)
8. Isomoto, Y., Yoshine, K., Yamasaki, H., Ishii, N.: Color, shape and impression keyword as attributes of paintings for information retrieval. In: IEEE International Conference on Systems, Man, and Cybernetics, Tokyo, pp. 257–262 (1999)
9. Acharya, T., Ray, A.K.: Image Processing: Principles and Applications. Wiley-Interscience Publication, Hoboken (2005)

10. Bejarano, A.M., Calvo, A.F., Henao, C.A.: Supervised learning models for control quality by using color descriptors: a study case. In: XXI Symposium on Signal Processing, Images and Artificial Vision, Bucaramanga, pp. 1–7 (2016)
11. Wong, W., Hsu, S.: Application of SVM and ANN for image retrieval. Eur. J. Oper. Res. **173**(3), 938–950 (2006)
12. Vapnik, V.: The Nature of Statistical Learning Theory. Information Science and Statistics. Springer, New York (2000)
13. Keerthi, S.S., Lin, C.: Asymtotic behaviors of support vector machine with gaussian kernel. Neural Comput. **15**(7), 1667–1689 (2003)

Affective Smile and Interaction

Smile is a Function of Interaction

Hisao Shiizuka(✉)

SKEL Shiizuka Kansei Engineering Laboratory,
Fuzzy Logic Systems Institute, Fukuoka, Tokyo, Japan
shiizuka@flsi.or.jp, shiizuka@skelabo.org

Abstract. It is well known that laughing is good for the health. However, there are many parts that have not been clarified about the manner of laughter. In this paper, we discuss the relationship between facial expressions and affective smile. The face to be handled here uses a line drawing expressed by an illustration. The lines of "eyes" and "mouth" for drawing an affective smile use a logarithmic spiral obtained from the golden ratio. Here we show the relationship between laughter and happiness. People can feel happiness by applying the fact that the brain feels happiness and being deceived by laughing, smiling. The central idea in this paper is that affective smile gives people a feeling of happiness. Also it is shown the hypothesis that affective smile exists in three overlapping intersections "fun", "interesting" and "comfortable". As a result, the following hypothesis is also shown that affective smile is a function of interaction.

Keywords: Affective smile · Golden ratio · Logarithmic spiral · Interaction · UX

1 Introduction

It goes without saying that a smile is very important. Also it will not be an overstatement to say that there is nothing more important than a smile. Because people can communicate with each other anywhere at any time if people can contact with a smile [1]. "I am smiling" when it is open to you (others). It shows a sign of "I do not need to worry" if you are smiling. Therefore, a grumpy face indicates that your heart is closed to other person. In this way, "laughing" is extremely important for human beings, but it has not seen much research on laughter (smile) that caught from a so-called affective point of view.

In this paper, we define the condition of "affective smile" and propose one hypothesis for realizing the affective smile. The "affective smile" proposed in this paper is based on the concept of user experience (UX). Recently, when designing products and services we are always considering UX. We also propose that "affective smile (or emotional smile)" can be one new indicator to evaluate UX.

M. Kurosu (Ed.): HCI 2017, Part I, LNCS 10271, pp. 700–710, 2017.
DOI: 10.1007/978-3-319-58071-5_53

2 Components Consisting of Affective Smile

Here we first propose hypotheses that should be affective smiles. It applies the concept of user experience (UX) to the affective smiles. Originally, the concept of UX is defined as "the whole of the experience gained when actually using a certain product or service and consuming it." More specifically, UX is an experience that people perceive through the use, consumption and possession of products and services. And, it focuses on the process of using products and services, focusing on which users can do "fun", "interesting" and "comfortable" what they really want to do. It also means the concept of thinking as "offer value" different from ease of use [2]. Therefore, as the experience of positive emotions such as pleasure and comfort increases, the value increases. Figure 1 shows the image of UX. Here, we show one hypothesis about the sensitivity smile in this paper.

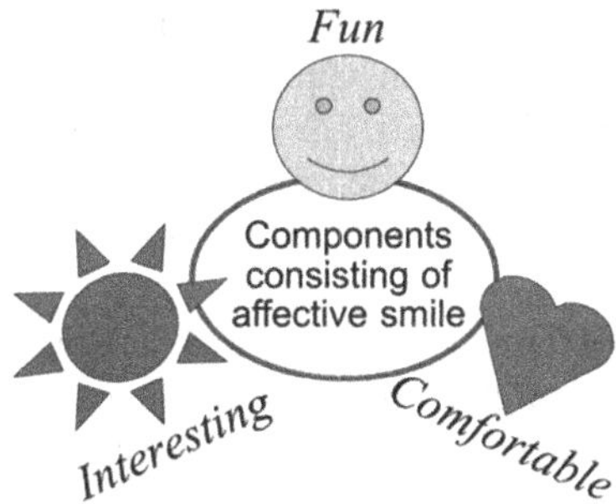

Fig. 1. Components consisting of affective smile

Hypothesis: Affective smile exists in three overlapping intersections "fun", "interesting" and "comfortable".

In addition, as shown in Fig. 2, it can be seen that the region to which this hypothesis is applied is not a crisp region but a fuzzy region. In that sense, this affective smile contains qualitative elements quite a bit.

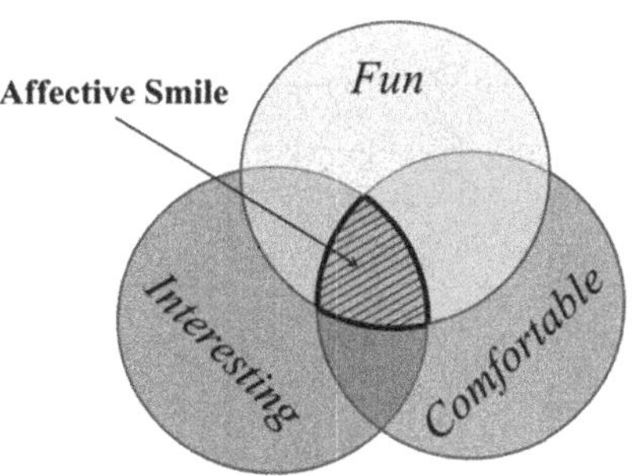

Fig. 2. What region is affective smile?

3 The Uneven Curve Produces an Affective Smile

The golden ratio (1:1.618) is known not only in mathematics but also in art and the like. For example, it is used for the aspect ratio of a postcard, the vanishing point of a masterpiece and the position of a horizontal line, a regular pentagon, a pentagram star or the like. It is also used for buildings such as the Parthenon temple in Greece and the pyramids, and it is a split ratio which is said to be beautiful, such as the arrangement of sunflower seeds and spirals of the Nautilus. Of course, there are no theoretical grounds for these, but there is no doubt that it is a design that stimulates human sensibility.

It is proved that division of diagonals of a regular pentagon is mathematically a golden ratio. Alternatively, when a square is cut out from a rectangle, when the remaining small rectangle is similar to the original rectangle, the ratio of the two sides of the rectangle still forms the golden ratio.

It can easily be proved mathematically that the "limit value" of the ratio of two adjacent terms of the Fibonacci sequence {1, 1, 2, 3, 5, 8, 13, 21, 34,…}. In other words, the proportion of adjacent numbers in this sequence approaches the golden ratio steadily. For example, 1/1 = 1, 2/1 = 2, 3/2 = 1.5, 5/3 = 1.666, 8/5 = 1.6, 13/8 = 1.625,…..).

In this way, it converges to the golden ratio (1.6180339887…) while oscillating. This golden ratio is often used as the most stable beautiful ratio. It has been told that there are many in nature.

We have various ratios of human body, how to attach branches and leaves of plants, and its turning angle is golden angle. It is surprising how sunflower's "flower head" and how "seeds of season" are attached. It seems that it is just turning according to the golden angle, but if it numbers it in that order, it becomes Fibonacci sequence. In this way, it is not the golden ratio that exists in nature a lot, and in fact it notices that there are many Fibonacci sequences. This is a natural result, because the Fibonacci sequence is a permutation of "evolutionary prosperity", it can be interpreted that there are many "evolutionary footprints" in the natural world. It also seems that the shape that makes me feel beautiful is liked by the permutation of evolutionary prosperity engraved on DNA of all of us (by all creatures). In other words, I think that it is not surprising to think that "beautiful" is a shape that can be liked by environmental, cultural and species boundaries (both human and animal).

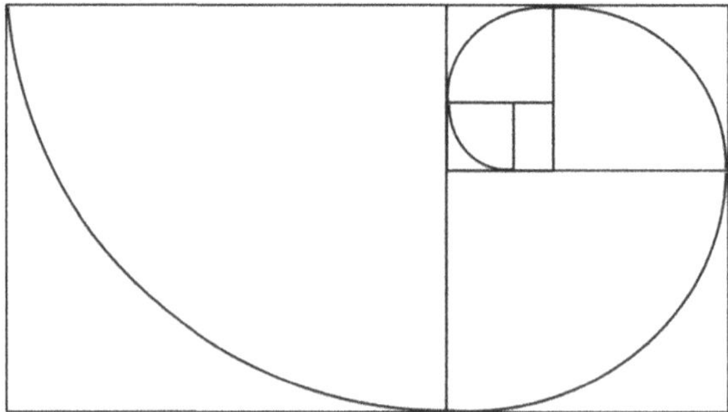

Fig. 3. Logarithmic spiral curve drawn in golden ratio.

"Beautiful" is never a favorite item, it can be said that the footprints of all the lives are marked.

As shown in Fig. 3, it can draw a golden ratio spiral by repeating Kepler's triangle drawing method.

The "mouth" and "eyes" of the affective smile treated in this paper can be realized by using this logarithmic spiral curve. In other words, it can create a smiley smile by using the logarithmic spiral curve drawn in golden ratio. In general, the logarithmic helix is given by:

$$r = a\exp^{b\theta}$$

In the above equation, "a" and "b" are parameters of the spiral curve.

4 Composition of Basic Form of Affective Smile

As shown in Fig. 4, the curves obtained from the logarithmic spiral of golden ratio are used for the shapes of "eye" and "mouth" used in this paper. For creating an affective smile, it can use any part of the spiral curve for "mouth" and "eyes". Of course, it can use the whole.

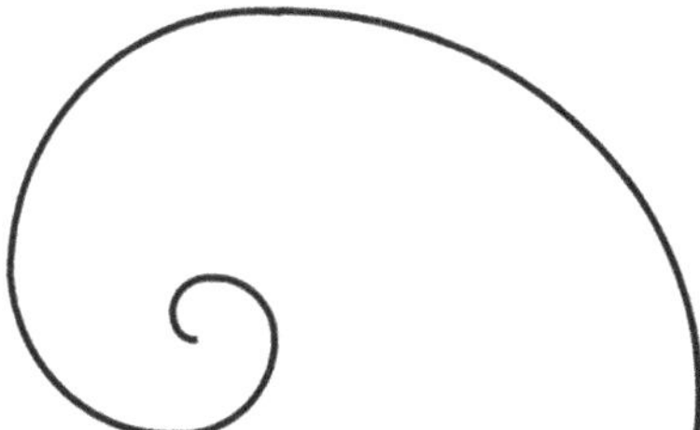

Fig. 4. The spiral from the golden ratio provides the elements that make up the affective smile

Actually, an example of drawing a face using this spiral curve is shown in Fig. 5. There are individual differences, but in this figure (b) would be the smile that is closest to the affective smile. The role of the concavo-convex curve of "eyes" and "mouth" against the smiling face is opposite. In other words, "convex curve" produces a smiling face in "eyes", and "mouth" shows that concave curve leads a smiling face.

Fig. 5. Draw your own portrait and demonstrate it.

Further, as shown in Fig. 6, "comic smile" can be given by making "eyes" comical. These things will be explained from the following:

Logarithmic spiral (uneven curve) → smile → interaction → affiliation feeling

Fig. 6. Comical eyes invite you to laugh.

In this way, by changing the radius of curvature of the logarithmic helix as a parameter, it is possible to create a basic form of affective smile.

Here as shown in Fig. 7, we can show useful hypotheses as follows: "*Affective smile is a function of interaction.*" The meaning of this hypothesis indicates that if there is a sensual smile it will lead to interaction. In addition, this hypothesis offers a new topic in the field of UX. As is known [3], it is argued that "kawaii" is a function of interaction. Therefore, the affective smile is an extension of it, so future development is expected.

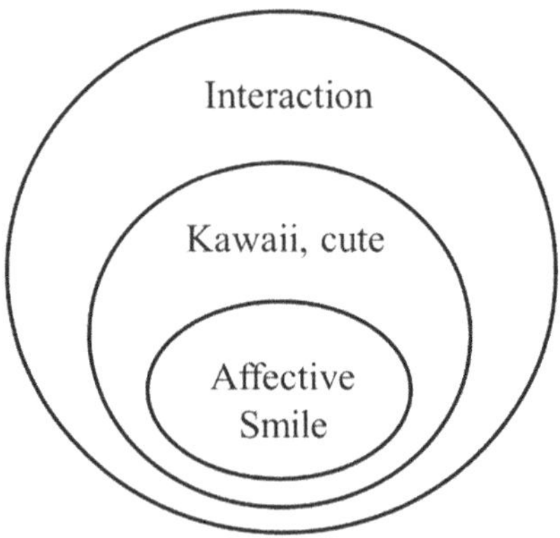

Fig. 7. Affective smile is a function of interaction

Well, the interesting problem here is how to find the boundary point of the affective smile. In other words, it is necessary to have an algorithm to judge the area of affective smile. The area of affective smile will be determined with fuzzy sets.

In general, however, the criterion will be difficult. The reason is that a good method has not been found for judging criteria for "affective evaluation method". For example, as shown in Fig. 8, it is extremely difficult to determine which face gives comfort and which face does not give comfort. On the other hand, as shown in Fig. 9, it is easy to convert from an actual face to a comical face by using a logarithmic spiral curve based on the golden ratio.

Fig. 8. The area of affective smile is ambiguous.

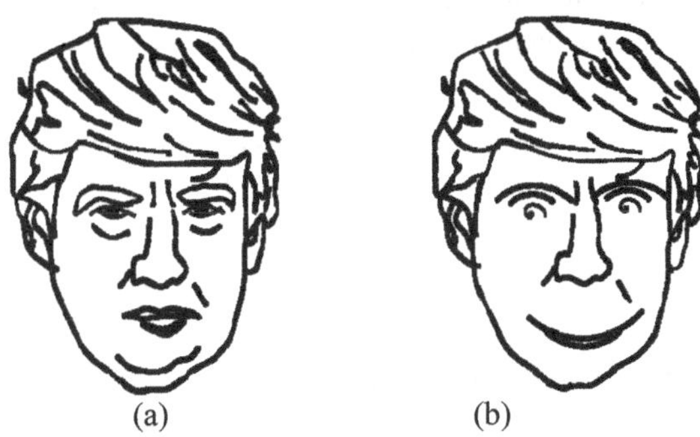

Fig. 9. From real face to comical face by using the spiral curve of golden ratio.

5 Laughter Saves the Earth – Smile and Health

Recently, various studies have revealed that "laughter" relieves stress and keeps diseases away. "Laugh" is very useful for prevention of lifestyle diseases. The rescue play in the San Jose mining slump accident in Chile that occurred in 2010 will still remain in the memory of people all over the world as an impressive event. Thirty-three mining workers were trapped in evacuation centers of 700 m underground and the contact was discontinued for 17 days, after which it was confirmed that they were safe and all were rescued 69 days after the accident. At a later date, the team leader of the worker answered "It was hopeless, continued to be optimistic, and did not forget the humor" about the reason why the worker survived. This tells us how humor and "laughter" are closely related to "the power of human life". Laughter is known to lead to long life and health by making immunity.

Babies grow up mimicking the adult's "laugh". However, when we "bite" the baby, if we do not touch or praise with a smile, that baby will grow up as a child not to laugh. The baby learns smile and "laugh" by being able to admire a smile on adults. When baby become an adult, stress increases with age, the baby would not smile. For generations, "smile often" is 65% in their 30 s, 50% in their 40 s and 45% in their 50 s.

It seems that younger age still laugh often. According to a survey report, elementary school students laugh on average 300 times a day, but in their 70 s they laugh only about twice a day. Why will not you laugh as you age? About this, the stress theory is said to be influential. It means that stress increases with age and it could not make smile.

However, in the previous survey, thirties and forties are the most stressful things in life. On the other hand, there are also views that the factors other than stress are also large because the number of "laughter" is smaller in the 60 s and 70 s. That is, the brain function may be closely related to "laugh". It is thought that this will lead to blurring. "Laughter" 100 times a day is said to be equivalent to a 15 min aero bike.

The act of saying laughter is a feature of a basic human being, and from laughing it can also get along with people. The difference between monkeys and human beings is emotion and pleasure. Especially since we got laughter, it seems that it became human beings.

Let's think about the difference between "smile" and "smiling face".

The difference between them is very subtle. We think that it can say with the following conviction.

- A smile is not to ask for reward simply by throwing it to the opponent.
- We have a consciousness to give a smile to the other party because we want others to return a smile.

The characteristic of both is that "smile" does not show teeth, but "smile" is considered to show teeth.

For example, as shown in Fig. 10, there may be a desire to have people bring their upper teeth and lower teeth at the first meeting and come closer with a smiling face to return something. Then we have the followings.

Smile is smiling face, which is a noun. He greeted me with a smile. Smile is the verb to smile. She smiled at me.

6 Difference Between "Smiling Face" and "Smile"

Let's think about the difference between "smile" and "smiling face". The difference between them is very subtle. We think that it can say with the following conviction.

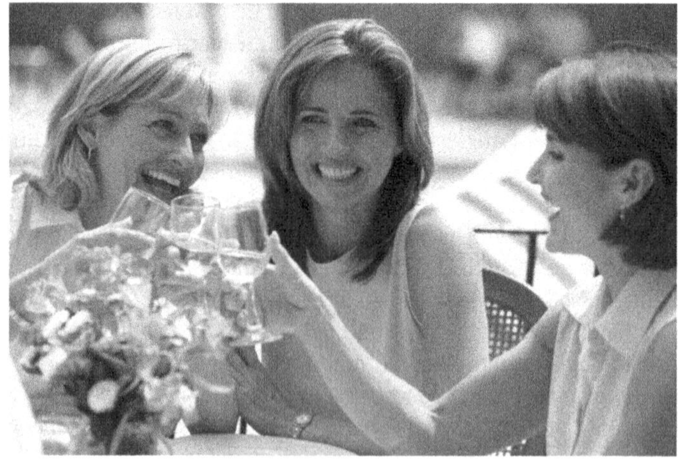

Fig. 10. Laughter brings about health, the meaning of emotional research lurks in the space between laughter and smile.

- A smile is not to ask for reward simply by throwing it to the opponent.
- We have a consciousness to give a smile to the other party because we want others to return a smile.

The characteristic of both is that "smile" does not show teeth, but "smiling face" is considered to show teeth. For example, as shown in Fig. 10, there may be a desire to have people bring their upper teeth and lower teeth at the first meeting and come closer with a smiling face to return something. Then we have the followings.

Smile is smiling face, which is a noun. He greeted me with a smile. Smile is the verb to smile. She smiled at me.

7 Interactivity and Kawaii-ness

What is the relationship between interactivity and kawaii-ness? I'd like to discuss this question using "Homo Ludens," a book written by Johan Huizinga [3]. In his work, Huizinga points out that we find play present everywhere. He defines play as "a free activity conducted within its own proper boundaries of time and space according to fixed rules." He also discusses various concepts of play observed in different human activities. In particular, he provides a very thought-provoking suggestion about the universality of play that "we find play present everywhere."

In fact, this play has a very important relation with interactivity. The relation with kawaii-ness" will be clarified, with play serving as an intermediary.

Huizinga notes that the ancient Greeks differentiated play into two forms: agon and paidia. Agon is play as a competitive activity, a deadly serious pursuit within certain constraining rules, whereas paidia is play as a joyful activity. A track and field event at the Olympic Games is agon, while children playing ball is paidia. There is nothing in common between them. Agon and paidia sharing nothing in common means that track and field athletes cannot play together with children. They cannot coexist simultaneously. Interactivity may be regarded as a catalyst that puts these two very different things together. Let's think about a disagreement in intentions among adults. If the adults fully share the same opinion, their intentions run in parallel. If their opinions are far apart, their intentions collide head-on [3]. There is an intermediate situation somewhere between them. When the intentions of the two parties are the same and run in parallel, there is no wonder, and nothing to learn. They just nod and agree with each other. In other words, nothing is created from a shared identical status. The ground for interaction is produced in a situation where people feel some disagreement in intentions. That is, no interaction will be created if everything is already known [3]. It is also reasonable to assume that interaction occurs where there is high entropy.

Here is one familiar example of interaction. A child deliberately fakes a disagreement in intentions to start an interaction with his parents. That is, the child sometimes plays a little trick to draw their attention. This is a typical example of interaction that occurs when there is a disagreement of intentions between two people. Another example is a Japanese TV program, Shoten, produced by Nippon TV. Members constantly play little tricks on each other, which always create laughter among the audience: there is always interaction among Shoten members [3].

The origin of the feeling of kawaii crucially needs an element of discommunication. The feeling of kawaii holds a fragile balance between the feeling of childishness that is totally devoid of the property of being empathized with, and a sense of eeriness. To engage in interaction with a character, a disagreement in intentions is necessary that can correspond to discommunication. I mentioned earlier that Sanrio characters are metonymic (animal-like) because of their inability to be emphasized with.

Japanese characters are established as extremely distinct signs. They are overwhelmingly emotionless, as you can see from the faces of Rilakkuma, Banao, or Capybara-san. What you sense from them is a childish feeling, devoid of the property of being empathized with, which is considered to create the kawaii property. Based on the relational chains of kawaii, "lack of sympathism," "disagreement in intentions," and "interaction," the kawaii property may be taken as a function of interaction. Hence, we have

$$\text{Degree of kawaii property} = f(\text{interaction})$$

It is speculated that when people find a subject kawaii, they want interact with it and reinforce that interaction. What is called the "creation of kawaii-ness" or constituting the "function of kawaii-ness (function *f*)" needs to be analyzed from the viewpoint of the kawaii system." An approach from the engineering aspect should be useful for specific system configuration. For instance, if you find bread that is shaped like a certain character kawaii, you may feel an unavoidable urge to pick it up and eat it. On the other hand, you may want to keep it without eating it. This is an example of the urge to engage in interaction.

8 The Spiral Curve Represents a "Smile" and "Kawaii-ness"

The smile of Mona Lisa has a very delicate one. It is a work drawn by genius painter Leonardo da Vinci, but he has sharp sensibility. The evidence is how to draw eye curves

Fig. 11. It is worthy of a faint smile of Mona Lisa.

and mouth curves. As shown in Fig. 11, this is the spiral curve of the golden ratio proposed in this paper. On the other hand, it turns out that cute artifacts also have a golden ratio spiral curve. Figure 12 shows a model of "beans".

This example shows that it can be drawn using a spiral curve to express "Kawaii-ness" of "beans".

Fig. 12. Kawaii things have a spiral curve.

In addition, Fig. 13 shows the image at the boundary between the Affective Smile and the Non-Affective Smile. Although it is very interesting to clarify this boundary condition, at the same time, it is also necessary to consider the boundary between laughter and smile. Actually, it seems that there is an important hint at the boundary to clarify the essence of laughter and smile. Currently in the super aged society, we will have to further advance research on laughter and smile to keep health.

Fig. 13. The boundary between a smile and a nonsmile is ambiguous.

9 Concluding Remarks

In this paper, we proposed a basic method to create the affective smile. It showed that by using the spiral curve obtained from the Golden Ratio, it is possible to create various affective and emotional smiles. Also, we proposed one hypothesis that should be the affective smile.

In other words, in order to become the affective smile, we suggested that three of "fun things", "interested things" and "comfortable things" are necessary. This is the same as the concept of user experience (UX). Therefore, with UX's superior product, the user will become the affective smile. As for this, further examination is necessary in the future. It would be provided an interesting result in the field of UX.

Figure 14 shows the elderly dolls, but you can see that every elderly person is represented with a smile. This indicates that a smile is a source of health. It seems that research on smiles needs to be actively made more and more in the future.

Fig. 14. The importance of a smile in an aged society.

Therefore, an important issue to be left for the future is to clarify the hypotheses shown in Fig. 7. It will be appeared in the near future.

Acknowledgement. This work was supported by JSPS KAKENHI Grant Number JP16K00346.

References

1. Fujimoto, K.: Philosophy to Live - To Smile Communication. Hokuju Shuppan (2011) (in Japanese)
2. Shiizuka, H.: Kansei Engineering Hand Book. Asakura Shoten (2013) (in Japanese)
3. Shiizuka, H.: The feeling of kawaii is a function of interaction. In: Kurosu, M. (ed.) HCI 2013. LNCS, vol. 8004, pp. 601–610. Springer, Heidelberg (2013). doi:10.1007/978-3-642-39232-0_65

Inducing Fear: Cardboard Virtual Reality and 2D Video

C. Natalie van der Wal(✉), Annabella Hermans, and Tibor Bosse

Department of Computer Science, Vrije Universiteit, Amsterdam, Netherlands
c.n.vander.wal@vu.nl

Abstract. A Virtual Reality based training can be an interesting method to teach crowd managers and emergency responders how to act in emergency situations under pressure. Compared to watching Two-Dimensional Video, Virtual Reality is assumed to induce stronger emotions and a more real-life experience of the emergency situation. To test this assumption, sixty participants were tested on whether there is a difference in inducing fear between cardboard Virtual Reality glasses and watching a 2D video. Subjective (PANAS) and objective (heart rate, blood pressure) ratings of their mood were measured before, during and after watching a horror movie. Results show that both VR and 2D induced fear significantly in all subjective and objective measures, but that there was no significant difference between these video screen conditions. Based on inducing fear alone, a video based training could be as effective as a cardboard VR training. More research is needed to investigate this further.

Keywords: Mood induction · Fear · Virtual reality · Virtual training · Experiment · Heart rate

1 Introduction

In this work, we are interested in how to design a training for professionals to learn how to act in crisis situations. These professionals could be emergency responders and crisis managers. In real-life crisis situations, people experience fear or anxiety. Therefore, it would be effective if these professionals would experience such anxiety in training, otherwise the transfer of training would be less. For example, Nieuwenhuys and Oudejans [8] determined that training with anxiety has more short- and long-term transfer of training than training without anxiety. In existing paper-based training for emergency situations, trainees do not experience much anxiety. Therefore, it is useful to investigate the possibilities and effectiveness of a virtual training for crisis situations. Another reason for investigating virtual training is the cost-effectiveness. Real-life practice drills of emergency situations, such as an evacuation due to a fire, have the goal to save lives, but cost a lot of time and money to arrange. Therefore, virtual training can also be a cost-effective method to teach these professionals how to act in emergency situations while experiencing anxiety and fear.

Two possibilities for a virtual training will be tested here, cardboard Virtual Reality (VR) versus 2D video. Cardboard VR was chosen because it was easily accessible to the researchers and the differences between inducing fear with cardboard VR or a

M. Kurosu (Ed.): HCI 2017, Part I, LNCS 10271, pp. 711–720, 2017.
DOI: 10.1007/978-3-319-58071-5_54

traditional head mounted display VR seem to be small [1]. 2D video was chosen as the comparison condition, because this could be a good alternative option for a VR based training. It would be less expensive to develop a video based training then a VR based training.

The main research question is: which video screen (cardboard VR or 2D video) induces fear the strongest? An experiment was set up in which participants view a short horror movie. To measure the induction of fear, ratings of fear were made with: (1) subjective ratings: PANAS questionnaire; (2) objective ratings: heart rate and blood pressure. The PANAS was used, because it is a more reliable and valid mood scale, compared to other mood scales [10]. Although more recent research determined that other mood scales are comparable in measuring anxiety [9]. Heart rate and blood pressure were chosen because it is assumed that watching a horror movie will increase fear or anxiety and therefore the heart rate and blood pressure [2]. For heart rate, it is expected that watching the video will increase heart rate significantly. For blood pressure, it is expected that fear increases systolic blood pressure more than diastolic blood pressure. This is based on earlier findings where fear seems to be mainly a sympathetic nervous system reaction, compared to an emotion such as anger which seems to be both a parasympathetic as well as a sympathetic nervous system reaction [2]. Although in previous research not always an effect of anxiety induction by video on heart rate is found [4]. Personality characteristics and gender were measured to answer a secondary research question: does gender or personality have influence on the mood induction? It could be that males or females are more easily induced with fear or that the personality characteristics have an influence on the mood induction. For example, in a review from McLean and Anderson [7], it was determined that females seem to report greater fear and are more likely to develop anxiety disorders than men.

The rest of the article is organized as follows. Next, the method of the experiment is explained in Sect. 2, followed by the results in Sect. 3. The article is summarized and discussed in Sect. 4.

2 Method

Participants. Sixty participants (30 males, mean age 25,4 years) were randomly assigned with a random number generator to one of two conditions: VR or 2D video screen. Participants were recruited on campus and through social networks. They received 5 euro for participation.

Procedure. The participant gave their informed consent, followed by the PANAS questionnaire [10] and a short version of the Big Five questionnaire [5]. Then, the heart rate and blood pressure were measured, followed by inducing the participant's mood by showing a horror video of 3 min. Participants watched either on a 2D smartphone screen (in 360° mode) or through cardboard VR glasses in which you can place a smartphone. During and after watching this movie, the heart rate and blood pressure were measured again. Finally, the participant filled in the PANAS again and a last form with 4 personal questions (age, gender, nationality and education level) and two questions concerning the movie and the induced mood (1. Which emotion did the watching the movie provoke?; 2. How scary did you find the movie?). To make sure the participant left the experiment with a positive mood, he/she would play a video or song that induces a positive mood.

Material. The video was shown on a smartphone with a 5-inch screen size. The horror video that was used can be found here (reference). Cardboard VR glasses were used with a strap around the head, in which the smartphone was placed. In the 2D condition, the participant held the smartphone in his/her hands. In both conditions, the participant sat in a rotatable desk chair, which allowed the participants to move freely. Turning around with the smartphone (2D) or VR glasses made the participant explore the environment in the video (left and right, up and down). Heart rate and blood pressure were measured with a digital OMRON M6 blood pressure meter.

3 Results

3.1 Homogeneity and Manipulation Check

One participant was excluded from the data analysis, because of using antidepressants which influences the mood induction. Fifty-nine participants were included in all data-analyses (29 males, mean age: 25,4 years, range: 19–56 years). See Table 1. Homogeneity tests were performed to test if the variances in both groups were equally distributed and therefore there were no differences in the convenience sample with random assignment. Variances in gender were equal in both groups, $\chi^2(1) = 0.18$, *n.s.* Age was not equally distributed in both video screen conditions, $F(1, 57) = 9{,}445, p < 0.05$. This can be expected in a convenience sample, therefore the medians and the 25th and 75th percentiles are shown as well in Table 1. Education level was equally distributed in both groups, $\chi^2(4) = 2.552$, *n.s.*

Table 1. Group characteristics of participants included in the data-analyses

	Condition 1: VR	Condition 2: 2D	Statistical analysis homogeneity
Gender	15 males, 15 females	14 males, 15 females	n.s
Age	Mean age: 23,97 years, SD = 4,82 years (N = 30) Median = 22 years 25th Percentile = 21 years 75th Percentile = 25 years	Mean age: 26,90 years, SD = 8,62 years (N = 29) Median = 23 25th Percentile = 21 years 75th Percentile = 33 years	* $p < .005$
Education level	High school 14 Professional qualifications 2 Bachelor's degree 8 Master's degree 6 Doctoral degree 0	High school 15 Professional qualifications 3 Bachelor's degree 4 Master's degree 6 Doctoral degree 1	n.s

Next, it was tested if the horror video induced fear in the participants. First, normality was tested with the Kolmogorov-Smirnov test and visual inspection of the Q-Q plots. Both samples for PANAS items 'scared' or 'afraid' were not normally distributed. See

Table 2 for the average scores ± standard deviation and the medians. To test whether the mood induction was successful, the two PANAS items were tested with the Wilcoxon sum-rank test. The scores on both items increased significantly: scared, $W = 764{,}5$, $z = 4{,}47$, $p < .001$, $r = 0{,}58$; afraid, $W = 397{,}5$, $z = 4{,}54$, $p < .001$, $r = 0{,}59$. Moreover, the answers to the two questions at the end of the experiment were analyzed. See Table 3. All answers to question 1 were categorized by two independent reviewers in two categories: fearful/scary emotions versus non-fearful/scary emotions. Examples of answers are: 'fear', 'anxiety', 'sensation', 'neutral', 'tension', 'anticipating'. The agreement between the two raters was 80%. After resolving disagreement, the outcome was 46 fearful/scary emotions versus 14 non-fearful/scary emotions. Therefore 78% of the participants rated the video as provoking a fearful/scary emotion. The average answer to question 2 was 2,75 and the median was: 3. The Likert-scale for the answer was 1 = not scary at all to 5 = very scary. Overall, the participants did find the movie scary and the mood induction was successful.

Table 2. Mean ± standard deviations and medians on PANAS items 'scared' and 'afraid'.

PANAS item	Before video	After video	Statistical analysis
'scared'	Mean = 1,73 ± 1,10, Median = 1	Mean = 2,86 ± 2,00, Median = 1	$^{**}p < .001$
'afraid'	Mean = 1,44 ± 1,00, Median = 2	Mean = 2,34 ± 1,75, Median = 2	$^{**}p < .001$

Table 3. Answers to questions about the provoked emotion

Question	Answers
Which emotion did the movie provoke?	46 fearful emotions (78%) were reported versus 13 non-fearful (as categorized by two independent reviewers)
How scary did you find the movie? (5-point Likert scale; 1 = not scary, 5 = very scary)	Mean = 2,75 Median = 3

3.2 Fixed and Random Effects of Video Screen, Gender and Personality

Normality and homogeneity of variances. First, the data was checked on normality by combining the Kolmogorov-Smirnov test with inspecting the data visually with histograms, P-P and Q-Q plots and also calculating the skewness and kurtosis. The results from the Kolmogorov-Smirnov test corresponded with the visual inspection: most data was not normally distributed. Positive Affect (PA) was not normally distributed at time point 2 (after the video) for both video screen conditions, $D(30) = .169$, $p < 0.05$, $D(28) = .192$, $p < .05$. Negative affect (NA) was not normally distributed before the video for the VR condition, $D(30) = .162$, $p < 0–.05$, and after the video for both conditions, $D(30) = .168$, $p < 0.05$, D(28) = .183, $p < 0.05$. The data for systolic blood pressure and heart rate were normally distributed, but not the diastolic blood pressure data. At time point 1 (before the video) it was normally distributed, but during the video it was not normally distributed for both video screen conditions, $D(30) = 0.33$, $p < 0.001$, $D(28) = 2.57$, $p < 0.01$. And after the video it was not normally distributed in the 2D condition, $D(28) = .195$, $p < 0.01$. The data was checked for homogeneity of variances with Levene's test. For all dependent variables and for both video screen conditions, the variances were equal. When transforming all data in log10 or with square root, the same results showed. Based on these tests, heart rate and systolic blood pressure were analyzed with parametric tests, diastolic blood pressure was rank transformed to allow a parametric test and PA and NA with non-parametric tests.

Fixed Effects of Video Screen and Time on Affect. Table 4 gives an overview of all mean ± standard deviation scores on all dependent variables, sorted by condition (VR or 2D video screen). Before watching the video or after watching the video, PA did not significantly differ between video screen conditions, $U(438)$, $z = .046$, *n.s.*, $r = .006$, U(457), $z = .334$, *n.s.*, $r = .043$. For both VR and 2D conditions, there were no significant differences between PA before and after the video, $W = 235$, $z = .379$, *n.s.*, $r = .049$, $W = 204{,}5$, $z = .373$, *n.s.*, $r = .049$. NA did not significantly differ between video screen conditions at time point 1 (before watching the horror video), but did significantly differ at time point 2 (after watching the horror video), showing a higher score for the VR condition, U = 349,5, z = −1,3, *n.s.*, r = −0.17, U = 301, z = −2,034, p < 0.05, r = −0,26. Looking within each condition, NA did not significantly increase in the VR condition, $W = 248{,}5$, z = 1,039, *n.s.*, $r = 0{,}14$, but did significantly increase in the 2D condition, $W = 210{,}5$, z = 2,208, $p < 0.05$, $r = 0.29$. For both video screen conditions 'scared' and 'afraid' increased significantly. Scared x VR: $W = 276{,}5$, $z = 3{,}213$, $p < .01$, $r = 0{,}42$, Scared x 2D: $W = 127$, $z = 3{,}096$, $p < .01$, $r = 0{,}40$, Afraid x VR: $W = 146{,}5$, $z = 3{,}458$, $p < .01$, $r = 0{,}45$, afraidx2D, $W = 66$, $z = 2{,}965$, $p < .01$, $r = 0{,}39$. Even though the NA increases in the VR condition, it is not significant, like in the 2D condition. The large

Table 4. Mean scores ± standard deviations for all dependent variables

		Before video	During video	After video	*p*-values
PA - PANAS	VR	58,13 ± 13,3	–	57,40 ± 13,94	*n.s.*
	2D	58,13 ± 14,64	–	58,79 ± 14,24	*n.s.*
NA - PANAS	VR	22,27 ± 11,91	–	25,10 ± 11,92	*n.s.*
	2D	17,55 ± 7,721	–	20,76 ± 14,27	**p* < .01
'afraid' item PANAS	VR	1,83 ± 1,21	–	2,87 ± 1,66	**p* < .01
	2D	1,38 ± 1,08	–	2,31 ± 1,93	**p* < .01
'scared' item PANAS	VR	1,50 ± 0,94	–	2,37 ± 1,59	**p* < .01
	2D	1,62 ± 0,98	–	2,90 ± 2,34	**p* < .01
Heart rate	VR	68,30 ± 10,22	78,00 ± 12,17	71,06 ± 11,61	**p* < .001
	2D	75,82 ± 13,21	81,04 ± 14,07	79,18 ± 15,19	
Diastolic blood pressure	VR	74,12 ± 8,08	81,07 ± 22,29	75,87 ± 10,44	*n.s.*
	2D	78,89 ± 7,00	83,79 ± 15,06	83,68 ± 16,69	
Systolic blood pressure	VR	119, 27 ± 14,15	123,07 ± 14,06	117,10 ± 18,26	**p* < .001
	2D	123,11 ± 12,48	126,54 ± 16,40	123,04 ± 14,67	

variances make it non-significant. It could be explained by sample size or coincidence. More importantly, 'afraid' and 'scared' did significantly increase, which were the targeted emotions. To generalize this to the full range of NA was not significant in the VR condition, but that was not necessary in this experiment.

Fixed Effects of Video Screen and Time on Heart Rate and Blood Pressure. The effect of Video Screen and Time on heart rate and systolic blood pressure was tested with 2 × 3 two-way ANOVA's with Video Screen (VR, 2D) and Time (before, during, after) as between Factors. Heart rate differed significantly over time, $F(2) = 10{,}513$, $p < .001$. The interaction Time x Video Screen was not significant $F(2) = 1{,}241$, *n.s.*, indicating that for both video screen conditions, the exact pattern was found. With post hoc tests, including Bonferroni correction, it was found that all means for the heart rate at time 1, 2 or 3 (before, during, after) differed significantly, before-during: $p < .001$, before-after: $p < .05$, during – after: $p < .05$. Systolic blood pressure differed significantly over time as well, $F(2) = 3.571$, $p < .05$. The interaction between Time x Video Screen was not significant, $F(2) = .235$, *n.s.*, indicating participants in both video screen conditions showed the same pattern in their increase and decrease in systolic blood pressure. With post hoc tests including Bonferroni correction, it was found that the systolic blood pressure differed significantly from during to after the video and there was a trend found for before to during, no significant contrast was found before-after, before-during: $p = 0.11$, before-after: *n.s.*, during – after: $p < .05$. The effect of Video Screen and Time on diastolic blood pressure was tested as well with 2 × 3 two-way ANOVA's as before, but then on rank transformed data, because of the violation of the normality assumption. Diastolic blood pressure did not differ significantly over time, $F(2) = .024$, *n.s.* The interaction between Time x Video Screen was not significant as well, $F(2) = .095$, *n.s.*, indicating participants in both video screen conditions did not significantly increase and decrease in systolic blood pressure and did not differ from each other in their patterns over time. These results show an interesting pattern for heart rate, which for both conditions significantly increases during watching the video and then significantly decreases afterwards but not yet to the beginning rest heart rate. The systolic blood pressure was significantly higher during watching the video than afterwards. The trend shown for the increase from before to during the video could be explained by positive 'pressure' to begin the experiment which already raised the blood pressure a bit, making the increase from before to during the movie not significant. Although this was not the case for the heart rate. In summary, the horror video did significantly increase the heart rate and systolic blood pressure, but not the diastolic blood pressure (Figs. 1, 2 and 3).

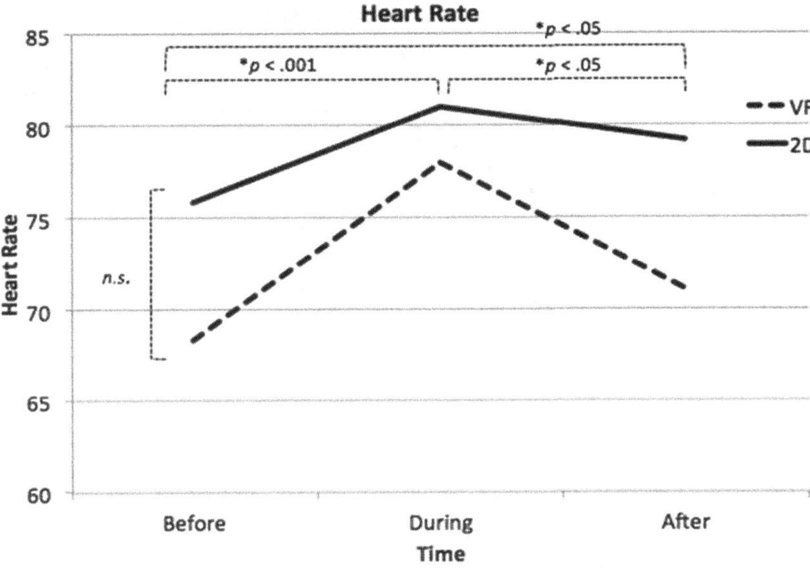

Fig. 1. Heart rate before, during and after watching a horror movie

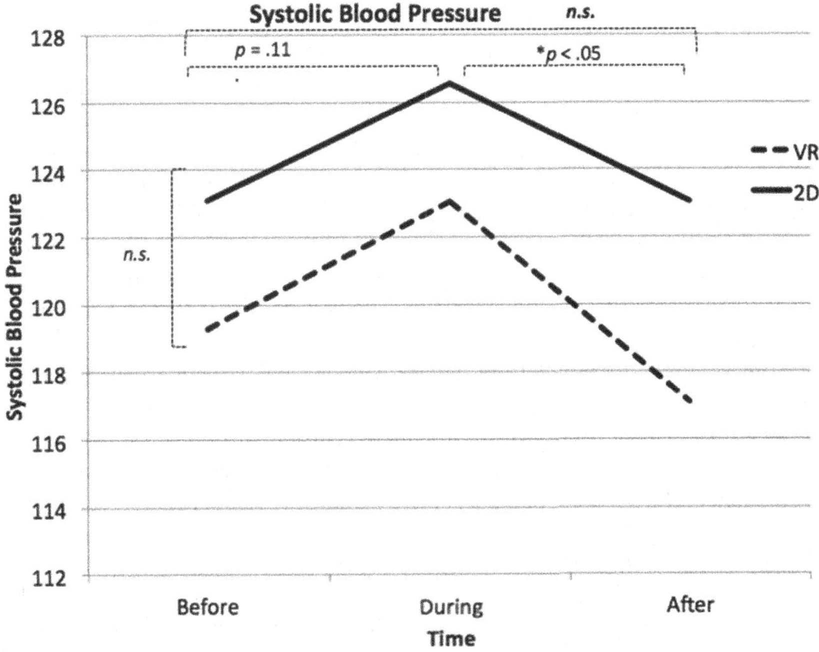

Fig. 2. Systolic blood pressure before, during and after watching a horror movie

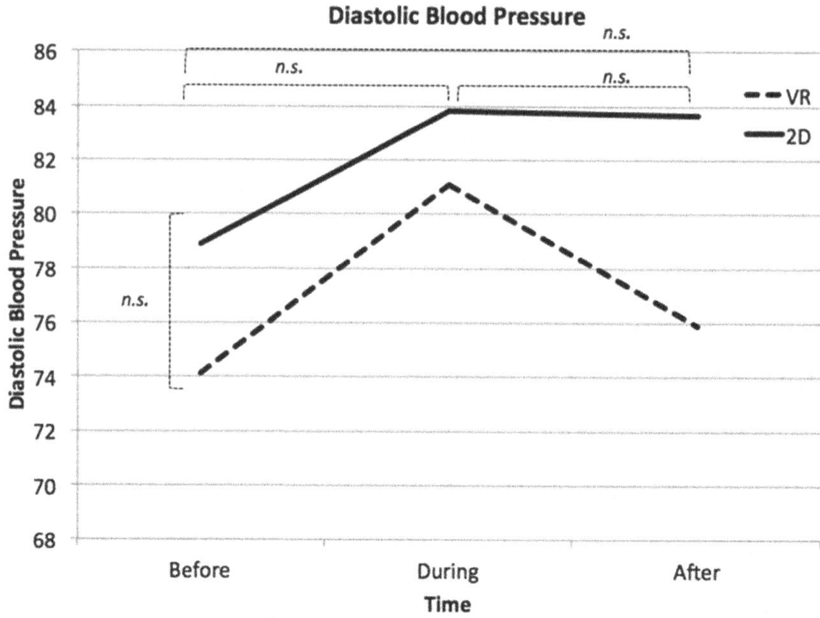

Fig. 3. Diastolic blood pressure before, during and after watching a horror movie

Random Effects of Gender. The random effects of Gender on the dependent variables heart rate and systolic blood pressure were analyzed with a mixed model ANCOVA analysis with Time as Within-Factor, Video Screen as Between-Factor and Gender as covariate. The Main effect of Time showed a trend, $F(2) = 2.996$, $p = .054$ and the Time x Gender and Time x Video Screen interactions were not significant, $F(2) = .436$, *n.s.*, $F(2) = 1.674$, *n.s.* The same mixed model ANCOVA was performed for systolic blood pressure and none of the main effect or interactions of Time x Gender and Time x Video Screen were significant, $F(2) = .687$, *n.s.*, $F(2) = .184$, *n.s.*, $F(2) = .267$, *n.s.* Indicating that there is no difference between females and males in the heart rates and systolic blood pressures in both conditions and over time. Mixed Model ANCOVA's were also performed on rank transformed 'afraid' and 'scared'. For both 'afraid' and 'scared' the main effects of Time and interactions Time x Gender and Time x Video Screen were not significant, $F(1) = .271$, *n.s.*, $F(1) = .303$, *n.s.*, $F(1) = .099$, *n.s.*, $F(1) = .354$, *n.s.*, $F(1) = .395$, *n.s.*, $F(1) = .03$, *n.s.* Indicating there is also no difference between females and males in the negative affects 'afraid' and 'scared' in both conditions and over time. Therefore, gender does not explain part of the variance in the dependent variables.

Random Effects of Personality. First it was tested if the independent variable (VR or 2D screen) has a relationship with the Personality variables (openness, conscientiousness, extraversion, agreeableness, neurotic) to decide if they can be taken as covariates. Mann Whitney tests were performed for each Personality Variable x Video Screen. Only extraversion levels differed significantly between type of video screen, $U = 307{,}5$, $z = -1{,}962$, $p = .05$, $r = -0{,}26$. All other personality variables had the same distribution and can therefore not be taken as a covariate, because they explain some of the variance in the independent variable as well as a covariate, $U = 455{,}5$, $z = 0.321$, *n.s.*, $U = 363{,}5$, $z = -1.104$, *n.s.*, $U = 386{,}5$, $z = 0.761$, *n.s.*, $U = 393$, $z = -0.652$, *n.s.* Next, the random effects of Extraversion on the dependent variables 'afraid, 'scared', heart rate and systolic blood pressure were analyzed with a mixed model ANCOVA analysis with Time as a Within-Factor, Video Screen as Between-Factor and Extraversion as covariate. The effects on diastolic blood pressure were not analyzed, because the previous analysis showed there was no effect of mood induction for diastolic blood pressure. For 'afraid' and 'scared', the ANCOVA was performed on rank transformed data, because of the violation of the normality assumption. The main effect of Time and the interactions of Time x Extraversion and Time x Video Screen were not significant for any of the dependent variables. For heart rate and 'scared', trends were found. For 'scared' the main effect Time and Time x Extraversion showed trends, $F(1) = 2{,}937$, $p = .092$, $F(1) = 3{,}136$, $p = .082$. For heart rate a trend was found for the main effect of Time and Extraversion as the covariate, $F(2) = 2.117$, $p = .13$. This indicates that when extraversion is taken as a covariate, there is a trend visible in that it could possible explain some of the variance in the dependent variables heart rate and 'scared' affect.

4 Conclusion and Discussion

This study was designed to determine whether watching a horror video with cardboard VR can induce more fear than watching the movie at a 2D smartphone screen. Results showed that both video screen conditions induced fear significantly. For both video screen conditions, the subjective measurements (PANAS-afraid, PANAS-scared) increased significantly from before to after watching the movie. For both video screen conditions, the objective measurements of fear (hear rate and systolic blood pressure) increased and/or decreased significantly. For heart rate, it increased significantly from before to during the movie and then decreased significantly, while systolic blood pressure decreased significantly from during the movie to after the movie. There was no effect of mood induction on diastolic blood pressure. The successful mood induction on the subjective ratings and the heart rate and systolic blood pressure were in line with the expectations. The finding that both video screen conditions were equally good in fear induction and showed the exact same patterns in the data was unexpected. When taking gender or extraversion as covariates, no significant part of the variance was explained by the covariates. This indicates that gender and personality do not seem to have a significant influence on the fear induction.

Strong points of this experimental design are the random assignment, the strong fear induction found in both VR and 2D video and the measurement of fear with both objective as well as subjective measurements. Improvements would be to add a third condition of inducing fear by a 'paper-based' scenario. This would allow a second comparison that would be interesting to decide how much stronger 2D and VR could induce fear than a paper-based scenario.

For the future of virtual trainings, these results show that both VR as well as 2D video can increase fear and anxiety in the user. Both in subjective as well as objective measurements. This would make virtual trainings both realistic and hopefully more effective. At the same time, there were no significant differences found between VR and 2D video screen, implying that training developers do not have to invest in (expensive) VR technology but could explore video based training. Of course, this is only based on this experiment, more research would be needed to fully investigate this perspective. A recent study for example found that 2D video can provoke anxiety in users with 'threatening stimuli' in the video, but provoke less anxiety than in real-life situations [3]. Also, besides mood induction other elements of crisis situations, such as having an overview or taking different views/perspectives in reality could also be important points for training. Perhaps that on other elements of training there is a significant difference between VR and 2D. We hope this study is a valuable contribution to current and future research in this area.

Acknowledgements. This research was conducted for the EU Horizon 2020 IMPACT project; European Commission, Grant Agreement 65338.

References

1. Amin, A., Gromala, D., Tong, X., Shaw, C.: Immersion in cardboard VR compared to a traditional head-mounted display. In: Lackey, S., Shumaker, R. (eds.) VAMR 2016. LNCS, vol. 9740, pp. 269–276. Springer, Cham (2016). doi:10.1007/978-3-319-39907-2_25
2. Ax, A.F.: The physiological differentiation between fear and anger in humans. Psychosom. Med. **15**(5), 433–442 (1953)
3. Blankendaal, R., Bosse, T., Gerritsen, C., De Jong, T., De Man, J.: Are aggressive agents as scary as aggressive humans? In: Proceedings of the 2015 International Conference on Autonomous Agents and Multiagent Systems, pp. 553–561. International Foundation for Autonomous Agents and Multiagent Systems (2015)
4. Bosse, T., Gerritsen, C., Man, J., Stam, M.: Inducing anxiety through video material. In: Stephanidis, C. (ed.) HCI 2014. CCIS, vol. 434, pp. 301–306. Springer, Cham (2014). doi: 10.1007/978-3-319-07857-1_53
5. Gosling, S.D., Rentfrow, P.J., Swann, W.B.: A very brief measure of the Big-Five personality domains. J. Res. Pers. **37**(6), 504–528 (2003)
6. Horror movie. https://www.youtube.com/watch?v=8mFFr8LBsUg
7. McLean, C.P., Anderson, E.R.: Brave men and timid women? A review of the gender differences in fear and anxiety. Clin. Psychol. Rev. **29**(6), 496–505 (2009)
8. Nieuwenhuys, A., Oudejans, R.R.: Training with anxiety: short-and long-term effects on police officers' shooting behavior under pressure. Cogn. Process. **12**(3), 277–288 (2011)
9. Rossi, V., Pourtois, G.: Transient state-dependent fluctuations in anxiety measured using STAI, POMS, PANAS or VAS: a comparative review. Anxiety Stress Coping **25**(6), 603–645 (2012)
10. Watson, D., Clark, L.A., Tellegen, A.: Development and validation of brief measures of positive and negative affect: the PANAS scales. J. Pers. Soc. Psychol. **54**(6), 1063 (1988)

Emotion Evaluation Through Body Movements Based on Silhouette Extraction

Hong Yuan[1,2], Bo Wang[1(✉)], Li Wang[1], and Muxun Xu[2]

[1] National Laboratory of Human Factors Engineering, China Astronaut Research and Training Center, Beijing 100094, China
yuanhong0624@126.com, wowbob@139.com, wanglikunyu@126.com

[2] Department of Industrial Design, Xi'an Jiaotong University, Xi'an 710049, China
xumuxun@xjtu.edu.cn

Abstract. In the modern age of technology development, the ability of computer to recognize and express emotions are expected in Human-Computer Interaction. This paper proposed a method to evaluate human emotions by extracting human explicit behaviors during interaction, which prevented interference from outside. To achieve the aim, OpenCV was used to extract silhouette features of physical behaviors and PAD scale was used to evaluate the emotions on time. And then, Emotion-Behavior Library was established based on both silhouette features and the results of PAD scale. In order to obtain positive, negative and negative emotions, Chinese folk music were used as emotional material in the experiment. Subjects were asked to express their emotions by body movements. The results verified the hypothesis: (1) behavioral features can effectively represent emotions; (2) the method for extracting the behavioral characteristics in this study is effective. Besides, we found that the front camera has a higher accuracy, for example accuracy of positive and negative was 72.5%, while the data of right camera hasn't been classified effectively.

Keywords: Emotion evaluation · Physical behavior · PAD scale · Affective computing · Emotional classification

1 Introduction

The communication between people is not only rational and logical, but also natural and emotional. In the modern age of technology development, the ability of computer to recognize and express emotions are expected in Human-Computer Interaction (HCI). As an important branch of HCI, Affective Computing is related not only to psychology of emotion, but also to computer technology and statistical analysis [1]. Human emotions are implied in explicit features which play an important role in HCI, such as verbal behaviors, facial expressions and physical behaviors [2]. With the maturity of computer vision and machine learning, the analyses of individual behaviors and emotions become more and more popular.

According to previous research, the emotional recognition of behavior was usually associated with static gestures or inflexible limited behaviors [3, 4]. This paper proposed

M. Kurosu (Ed.): HCI 2017, Part I, LNCS 10271, pp. 721–729, 2017.
DOI: 10.1007/978-3-319-58071-5_55

a method to evaluate human emotions while the interaction is in progress, which prevented interference. We focus on real-time emotional evaluation through human explicit behavior. To achieve the aim, OpenCV was used to extract silhouette features of human behaviors and (PAD) emotional scale was used to evaluate the emotions on time. We formed a model between behaviors and emotions.

2 Related Work

The research of affective computing in HCI includes facial expression, speech emotion, body movement, text emotion and so on [2, 5, 6]. And previous researchers have proposed plenty of methods to evaluate human emotions. Ekman and Friesen studied the relationship between emotional strength and posture in 1967 [7]. Camurri et al. described the features of body movements through physical parameters, such as the location and speed of the body [8], while Castellano found that emotional recognition of body movements was more effective than verbal language and facial expressions [9]. Compared with the method of subjective evaluation, extracting physical behavior was non-intrusive and less interference, which made the abstraction of data more convenient and objective [8, 9].

With the development of information technology, researchers tried to obtain human behaviors with wearable sensors and cameras, and to analyze human behaviors through computer technology [10]. The way of obtaining human behaviors with wearable sensors was more direct and accurate, but more interferential. However, the method of cameras has the advantages of non-invasive, convenient, but confined by the background and target movements [11].

Emotional recognition based on behaviors was mainly to establish an emotion-behavior library by discriminating and analyzing the characteristics of various movements, which were extracted from the movement features of the body under various emotional states [3, 4, 12]. Human movement features, such as the duration, frequency and other properties, were the basis of emotion recognition. Laban and Ullman proposed the Body Action Coding System (BACS) containing information: the part of the body (such as the left hand), direction, speed and shape (such as hand clenched into a fist), distance (curve/line), strength (weak/strong), time (continuous/fast) and fluency [13]. However, most of postures or movements do not have obvious emotional characteristics, and can't be used fully identify the resolution.

Under the condition of laboratory, emotional induction was an effective way to obtain effective emotional reaction. In the past few decades, researchers put forward lots of methods of to induce emotions including the methods of recall, imagination, image, film and music [14]. The methods of recall and imagination had instable result, while the duration was short induced by picture. The method of film had complex factors, while the music was immersive, coincident and duration long [14, 15]. In previous study, the music was mostly Western classical music, which has different effects on the Chinese people's emotion because of cultural differences [15]. In this paper, we chose "Chinese folk music emotional library" as the emotional induction material, which was established in our preliminary study. The music library can effectively induce positive, neutral and negative emotions, which are consistent in different subjects.

The PAD scale was used to evaluate the emotion in both this paper and the establishment of "Chinese folk music emotional library". The theory of discrete emotion believed that human emotion was discrete and measurable [16]. On the other hand, the 6 basic emotions, involving anger, disgust, fear, happiness, sadness and surprise [17], proposed by Ekman was applied widely. The theory of continuous emotion held that human emotion was continuous, complex and distributed in a certain range. The PAD model proposed by Mehrabian and Russell consisted of three dimensions: pleasure-displeasure, arousal-nonarousal and dominance-submissiveness [18]. Continuous emotion model was convenient for feature modeling, which can cover the typical types of discrete emotions [16].

3 Methods

3.1 Features Extraction

Silhouette features, involving the silhouette area of the target: *Area* (*Silhouette*$[t]$), the smallest external polygon area of the target: *Area* (*MinPolygon*$[t]$), and the silhouette centroid coordinate($x[t]$ and $y[t]$), were extracted through OpenCV function. And then, the extracted data was cleaned by removing the non-target data and filling the missing frame.

The features extracted from the previous step were calculated and sorted into 3 categories of parameters. There were two state parameters: relative state of silhouette area ($CI[t]$), and the barycentric coordinates of silhouette ($x[t]$ and $y[t]$). And there were four change rates of parameters: the change rate of silhouette area ($RoSC[t]$), the change rate of barycentric coordinates ($v[t]$), the change rate of silhouette area ($A[t]$), and the change rate of barycentric coordinates ($a[t]$). The time series data (the state parameters, the change rate parameters and the first derivative of change rate) were normalized by extracting the parameters of each time series data.

$$\mathrm{RoSC[t, n]} = \frac{\left(\sum_{i=t}^{t+n} Silhouette[i]\right) - \left(\sum_{i=t-n}^{t} Silhouette[i]\right)}{\sum_{i=t-n}^{t} Silhouette[i]} \tag{1}$$

$$CI[t] = \frac{Area(Silhouette[t])}{Area(MinPolygon[t])} \tag{2}$$

3.2 PAD Scale

PAD emotional scale was designed based on PAD emotional state model consisting of the dimensions of Pleasure, Arousal and Dominance. The PAD scale used in the study was simplified Chinese version revised by Researchers at the Institute of psychology Chinese Academy of Sciences based on the scale proposed by Mehrabian. Each dimension of the scale is measured by 4 items, which can be used to evaluate and classify human emotions effectively. In this study, after listening to each piece of music, subjects were asked to evaluate the scale according to their actual emotional state. More consistent the state to their emotional state more the score is close to 4, or else to −4 (see Table 1).

Table 1. Emotional scale (It was in Chinese in the experiment)

	Score	
Annoyed	−4 −3 −2 −1 0 1 2 3 4	Pleased
Sleepy	−4 −3 −2 −1 0 1 2 3 4	Awake
Powerless	−4 −3 −2 −1 0 1 2 3 4	Powerful
Scornful	−4 −3 −2 −1 0 1 2 3 4	Friendly
Calm	−4 −3 −2 −1 0 1 2 3 4	Stimulated
Submissive	−4 −3 −2 −1 0 1 2 3 4	Dominant
Sad	−4 −3 −2 −1 0 1 2 3 4	Happy
Relaxed	−4 −3 −2 −1 0 1 2 3 4	Active
Humble	−4 −3 −2 −1 0 1 2 3 4	Important
Enraged	−4 −3 −2 −1 0 1 2 3 4	Excited
Bored	−4 −3 −2 −1 0 1 2 3 4	Surprised
Influenced	−4 −3 −2 −1 0 1 2 3 4	Influential

3.3 Materials

Set-Up. The experiment was held in Beijing. The size of the experimental site was 4×4 m (Fig. 1). Two cameras were settled in front of the site and the right. Ten subjects participated in the experiment.

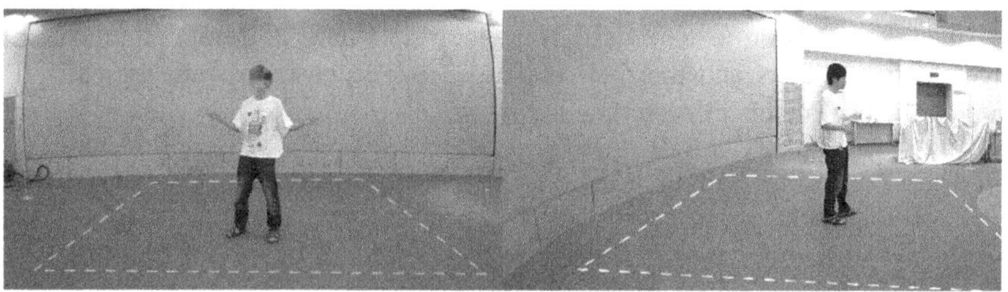

a. front camera b. right cammera

Fig. 1. Experimental stage and a subject

Emotional induction. In this study, Chinese folk music was used as the material of emotional induction, which has good immersion, persistence, and validity. A total of 21 pieces of music were chosen from "Chinese folk music emotional library", including positive, neutral and negative music each 5 pieces and from which 2 pieces were picked from each category (for test-retest reliability of the data) (see Table 2).

Table 2. Number of induction material

	Positive	Neutral	Negative
Original music	5	5	5
Repeated music	2	2	2
SUM	21		

3.4 Experimental Procedure

Firstly, emotions involving positive, medium and negative were induced by 21 periods of Chinese folk music, while 10 subjects were asked to express their emotions through body movements while listening music. Secondly, the movements of subjects were recorded by 2 cameras, the position of which were front and right of the stage. After each piece of music, the emotions of subjects were evaluated through PAD scale for a few seconds. Then, the silhouette parameters of subjects in the video were extracted through our methods. Finally, the training models were established with the parameters and PAD scales, which was used to evaluate the unknown emotions implied in body movements (see Fig. 2).

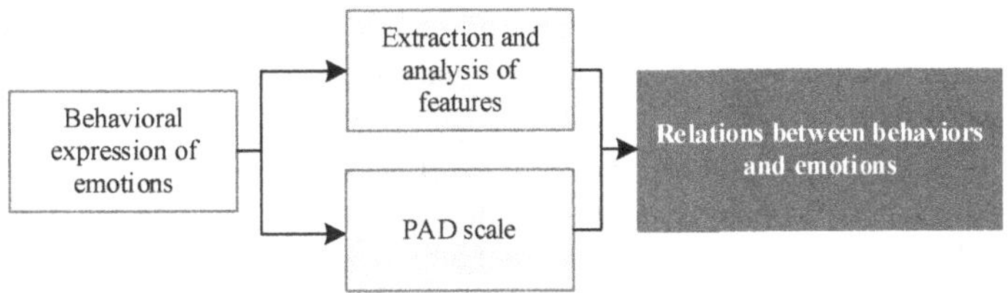

Fig. 2. Experimental procedure

4 Result Verification

4.1 Data Processing

Emotional Scale

Reliability. Software of SPSS 22 was used for data statistical analysis. Internal Consistency Coefficient of PAD emotional scale: $\alpha = 0.888$; for test-retest reliability, independent sample T of repeated induction material: $P = 0.104$. There was no significant difference between repeated induction, which indicated the consistence of perception and evaluation of subjects.

Classification. The emotions of the experimental music were divided into 2 major categories or 3 specific categories through clustering analysis (see Table 3) of PAD scale. The result of clustering analysis was consistent with the hypothesis: the first 7 pieces of music corresponded to negative emotion, the middle 7 pieces of music corresponded to neutral emotion, and the last 7 corresponded to positive emotion.

Table 3. Classification accuracy of each category

Classification	Details	Pieces of music
Type 1	Positive	15,16,17,18,19,20,21
	Negative	1,2,3,4,5,6,7,8,9,10,11,12,13,14
Type 2	Positive	15,16,17,18,19,20,21
	Neutral	8,9,10,11,12,13,14
	Negative	1,2,3,4,5,6,7

Silhouette feature data. The OpenCV was used to extract the features of the 10 subjects in each of the 21 videos, which described the body characteristics of the targets. Then the data was cleared and the missing values were processed. Finally, the normalized parameters of time series data were extracted, including the mean, median, variance, maximum, minimum and maximum of the sequence.

4.2 Emotion Recognition

Induction material was divided into 2 big categories based on the PAD scale, which could be described as negative and positive emotions; and into 3 categories, which could be described as positive, neutral, and negative emotions. The accuracy of prediction equals the correct number of recognition divided by the total number of samples and multiplied by 100%.

Table 4 lists the corresponding classification accuracy of each camera: the front camera has a high accuracy, for example accuracy of positive and negative was 72.5%; the data of right camera hasn't been classified effectively.

Table 4. Classification accuracy of each category

Camera	Classification	Accuracy
Front	Positive, neutral and negative	50.00%
Front	Positive and negative	72.50%
Right	Positive, neutral and negative	33.33%
Right	Positive and negative	52.50%

5 Conclusion and Discussion

The results verified the hypothesis: (1) behavioral characteristics can effectively represent emotion; (2) the method for extracting the behavioral characteristics in this study is effective in this study.

The internal consistency reliability and the test-retest reliability of the PAD scale was valid. Therefore, the PAD scale was a reliable and effective method for evaluating emotions. 3 categories of the classification results of PAD scale, involving positive, neutral and negative emotions, were completely consistent with the classification of the induction materials, which verified the effectiveness of the induction material.

We found that the expression of negative emotion was close to neutral. The results of classification and recognition verified the conjecture in the cluster analysis: the difference of expression between negative and neutral emotion was small, while the difference between negative and positive emotions was large.

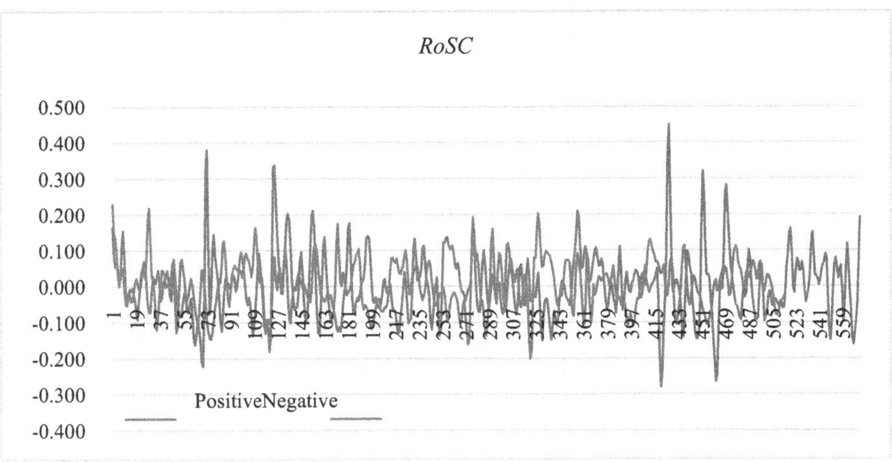

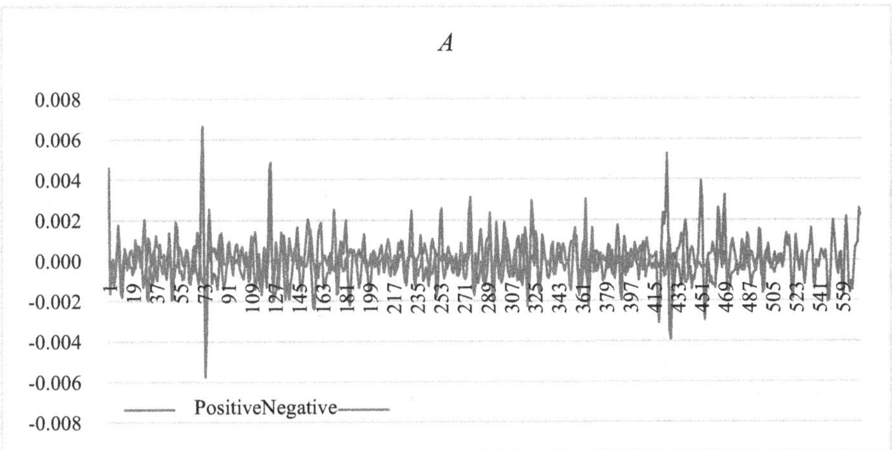

Fig. 3. *RoSC* and *A* of positive and negative emotions (The figure above is the rate of the target's movement, while the below is a derivative of the rate. Blue line represents negative emotion, while red indicates positive emotion) (Color figure online)

Table 5 presents the correlation test of correlation ($0.3 < \text{pearson} < 0.5$) between the parameters and categories. These parameters contributed greatly to the classification results, such as the variance of *A*, the variance of *RoSC* and so on.

Table 5. Correlation between parameters and categories

Parameters	Pearson	Sig.
Variance of A	.404	.000
Variance of $RoSC$	.384	.000
Mean of v	.347	.000
Median of v	.332	.000
Mean of $RoSC$	.317	.000
Number of peaks of v	.304	.000

Through analyzing the characteristics of different emotions, we found that the positive emotion was more powerful than the negative emotion. Speed and strength in BACS corresponded to $RoSC$ and A in Fig. 3. The amplitude of red line is larger than the blue, which means the positive emotion contains more energy.

Acknowledgments. This work was supported by the foundation of National Key Laboratory of Human Factors Engineering, Grant NO. SYFD18061610.

References

1. Picard, R.W.: Affective computing for HCI. Human-computer interaction: ergonomics and user interfaces. In: Proceedings of HCI International, pp. 829–833. DBLP (1999)
2. Derya, O.: Towards Social Virtual Listeners: Computational Models of Human Nonverbal Behaviors. University of Southern California (2014)
3. De Silva, P.R., Bianchi-Berthouze, N.: Modeling human affective postures: an information theoretic characterization of posture features. J. Comput. Anim. Virtual Worlds **15**(3–4), 269–276 (2004)
4. Kapur, A., Virji-Babul, N., Tzanetakis, G., et al.: Gesture-based affective computing on motion capture data. In: Proceedings of the 1st International Conference on Affective Computing and Intelligent Interaction, pp. 1–7 (2005)
5. Chunling, L., Beiji, Z., Lei, W.: Double-mode estimation of emotion intensity based on facial and action's expression. J. Syst. Simul. **21**(16), 5047–5052 (2009)
6. Ding, Y., Fu, X.: The research of affective recognition on the human motion tracking. Comput. Knowl. Technol. **7**(11), 2649–2651 (2011)
7. Ekman, P., Friesen, W.V.: Head and body cues in the judgment of emotion: a reformulation. Percept. Mot. Skills **24**(3), 711–724 (1967)
8. Camurri, A., Lagerlöf, I., Volpe, G.: Recognizing emotion from dance movement: comparison of spectator recognition and automated techniques. Int. J. Hum. Comput. Stud. **59**(1–2), 213–225 (2003)
9. Castellano, G., Kessous, L., Caridakis, G.: Emotion recognition through multiple modalities: face, body gesture, speech. In: Peter, C., Beale, R. (eds.) Affect and Emotion in Human-Computer Interaction. LNCS, vol. 4868, pp. 92–103. Springer, Heidelberg (2008). doi: 10.1007/978-3-540-85099-1_8
10. Zhang, Y., Lin, X.: Affect is computable-a survey on affective computing. Comput. Sci. **35**(5), 5–8 (2008)
11. Xiaolan, F.: Psychology of Emotion. East China Normal University Press, ShangHai (2016)

12. Shaarani, A.S., Romano, D.M.: Perception of emotions from static postures. In: Paiva, A.C.R., Prada, R., Picard, R.W. (eds.) ACII 2007. LNCS, vol. 4738, pp. 761–762. Springer, Heidelberg (2007). doi:10.1007/978-3-540-74889-2_87
13. Laban, R., Ullmann, L.: The Mastery of Movement, 4th revision edn. Princeton Book Company Publishers, Princeton (1988)
14. Jiang, J., et al.: Mood induction procedures and the recent advancement. J. Southwest China Normal Univ. (Nat. Sci. Ed.) **36**(1), 209–214 (2011)
15. Dongdong, L., Zhenbo, C., Ruina, D., et al.: Preliminary establishment and assessment of affective music system. Chin. Ment. Health J. **26**(7), 552–556 (2012)
16. Lade, P.: Probabilistic Topic Models for Human Emotion Analysis. Arizona State University (2015)
17. Scherer, K.R., Ekman, P.: Handbook of Methods in Nonverbal Behavior Research. Cambridge University Press, Cambridge (1982)
18. Mehrabian, A., Russell, J.A.: An Approach to Environmental Psychology. The MIT Press, Cambridge (1974)

Author Index